FAR EAST
MINI CHINESE-ENGLISH
DICTIONARY

遠東
迷你漢英辭典

原主編　梁實秋

遠東圖書公司印行
THE FAR EAST BOOK CO., LTD.

目　錄

部　首　表

部　首　表

序　言

本人主編的「最新實用漢英辭典」於民國六十年五月出版，因內容適合讀者需要，檢查比較方便，深受大眾推許。嗣於六十六年十二月刊行修正版，復於七十一年十月再行修正，務求改進以期完美。現在為了讀者便於取携，特重行排版，發行此一袖珍漢英辭典，由遠東圖書公司編輯部同仁精心編訂，以嶄新面貌呈獻於讀者之前。

袖珍本的漢英辭典，顧名思義，旨在縮小體積，由原有之一千三百餘頁，縮減至七百餘頁。但原收之七千三百餘單字，並未刪減，僅將原有之短詞成語之比較不大常用者酌量裁汰，故體積縮小而使用價值未受很大影響。

編輯辭典最重要事項之一便是要檢查便利，我們採用部首分列的方式是經過慎重考慮的。部首分列的方式是大眾比較最熟習的，雖然不是完全理想的。為了彌補其缺失，我們原列有四項索引，用者稱便。現在我們仍保留其中三種，僅刪略「筆畫部首索引」一種。

我們歡迎讀者指正。

梁　實　秋

一九八四年七月一日

本書出版多年，深為讀者讚許。茲為精益求精，爰再精選常用字，增加新資料，縮小版面，以利讀者隨身携帶、查閱。

遠東圖書公司編審委員會

一九九五年

體　例

一、字彙：本辭典收集之常用單字約五千餘字，短詞、成語達四萬餘條。取材範圍包括中英文各類辭典、報章雜誌及日常談話。取材標準著重現代化與實用性，常見的科學詞語，一併收羅，深信足供一般中外讀者參考之用。

二、字體：本辭典所列單字，以正體為準。俗寫與訛體則加註於本字之後，或單獨列入並加註本字正體。

三、排列：

(甲)單字的排列是根據部首(見部首表)，同一部首之單字，則依筆畫多寡排列。每一單字均編列號碼，以便檢字，如單字「一」的號碼是「1」，單字「中」的號碼是「21」。

　　一個單字如有二種或二種以上的讀音，而且意義因而變異的，則分開排列。例如「中」字在「中間」(ㄓㄨㄥ ㄐㄧㄢ) (zhōng jiān)與「中毒」(ㄓㄨㄥˋ ㄉㄨˊ) (zhòng dú)兩個詞語裡的讀音不同，解釋也不同，因此分列為「中」(ㄓㄨㄥ) (zhōng)與「中」(ㄓㄨㄥˋ) (zhòng)，但是其編號則同為一個號碼，亦即「中」(ㄓㄨㄥ) (zhōng)與「中」(ㄓㄨㄥˋ) (zhòng) 均為「21」號。

　　一個單字如果祇是讀音不同而不影響其意義時，則不分列，僅在變異的讀音後註明「又讀」字樣。

(乙)詞語的排列是按照國語注音符號的順序來決定先後。例如「打鼓」與「打草驚蛇」兩個詞語，是按「鼓」(ㄍㄨˇ) (gǔ)與「草」(ㄘㄠˇ) (cǎo)在注音符號表上的順序來決定排列的先後。

　　每一個單字下的詞語，一律以該單字開始。

例如在「文」字下的每一個詞語的第一個字，一律是「文」。讀者如果要查「以文會友」這個成語，不要查「文」字，而要查「以」字。

四、注音：本辭典計採用兩種注音符號：國語注音符號、聯合國華語注音符號(漢語拼音)。詞語後面不加注國語注音符號，以節省篇幅。

五、英解：本辭典之英文解釋，可分別爲兩大類：1.直接翻譯。2.解釋。前者適用於中英文可以直接對譯的情形(如：跑—to run，書—a book 等)，後者則在無法對譯時使用(如：旦角—a female role in Chinese opera)。本辭典英解方面之體例如下：

1. 一個詞語如有兩個或兩個以上截然不同的解釋，它的英文解釋是分開排列而冠以阿拉伯數字。例如「歲暮」的英解是① the late season of a year ② the closing years of one's life.
2. 許多中文成語、諺語的英解方式，是先直譯爲英文，然後在破折號後面再加引伸的意義。目的是使外國讀者對這些成語、諺語有較深切的瞭解。
3. 書名與拉丁文的專門名詞，一律用斜體字排印。

六、索引：本辭典共有三種索引：1.部首筆畫索引。2.國語注音符號索引。3.聯合國華語注音符號(漢語拼音)索引。

七、附錄：國語注音符號與聯合國華語注音符號對照表。

部首筆畫索引

編　法：本索引係按單字之部首編列。其屬同一部首者，再以單字筆畫多寡爲序。單字後註明單字編號。

用　法：檢查時先查出單字所屬之部首，按筆畫（除去部首筆畫數）在索引中查出單字，再根據單字編號，查出書內單字及這一單字爲首所組成的詞語。

RADICAL INDEX

In this index the characters are listed under their respective radicals. Characters with the same radical are arranged in the ascending order according to the number of strokes used in writing them. The figure to the right of each character is its identification number under which the character can be found in the body of the dictionary.

The first step in looking for a character is to find out the radical under which it is listed. The next step is to look for the character in the index according to the number of strokes (i.e. the total number of strokes used in writing the whole character minus the number of strokes used in writing the radical) which is indicated with Chinese numerals in the column to the left of the characters. With the identification number as a guide, one can locate in the dictionary the character and the entries beneath it.

戈

戶

手

火

一 部
丨 yī

1
一 丨 yī
(變調 ㄧˊ yí ; ㄧˋ yì)
1. union; uniformity; uniform 2. one; unit 3. single; alone 4. whole; all; throughout 5. a; an; the 6. to unify; to unite 7. once; as soon as 8. each; per; every time

【一巴掌】(to give someone) a slap

【一把】a handful; a bundle

【一波三折】hitting one snag after another

【一波未平，一波又起】One trouble follows another.

【一百】one hundred

【一百週年(紀念)】a centenary; a centennial

【一敗塗地】a complete failure

【一杯】a cup of; a glass of

【一輩】a generation

【一輩子】as long as one lives; a lifetime

【一包】a parcel; a package; a pack

【一般】common; general; commonly; generally

【一般見識】to hold the same kind of view

【一般性】generality

【一半】a half; half; in part

【一本】a copy; a volume

【一本正經】in a serious manner

【一本萬利】to gain enormous profit out of small capital investment

【一幫】a gang; a clique

【一鼻孔出氣】to sing the same tune

【一鼻子灰】to meet rejection, humiliation or frustration

【一筆】① one stroke ② a sum (of money); a (debt, account, etc.)

【一筆抹殺】totally negate

【一筆勾消】① all cancelled ② to settle an account once (and) for all

【一臂之力】help; assistance

【一表人材】handsome; dashing

【一邊】on one side; by the side

【一併】all; wholly; together with

【一病不起】to die of illness

【一部】a (book, motion picture, etc.)

【一部分】a part; a portion; partially

【一步登天】fast advancement in one's career, etc.

【一拍即合】to become good friends after brief contact

【一派】a school; a faction

【一派胡言】complete nonsense

【一砲而紅】to become famous all at once

【一盤散沙】utterly lacking cohesion; disunited

【一盆】a plate or tray (of food); a pot (of flower); a basin (of water)

【一旁】one side; on the sideline

【一匹】a (horse, etc.)

【一批】a batch; a shipment (of goods)

【一疋】a roll

【一瞥】a glimpse; a glance

【一篇】a literary article; a chapter

【一偏之見】a one-sided view

【一片】a denominative adjective for any object which is flat and thin

【一貧如洗】penniless; in utter destitution

【一暴十寒】to do something by fits and starts

【一脈相傳】derived from the same origin

【一枚】a (coin, medal, etc.)

【一毛不拔】very stingy; parsimonious

【一面】one side; an aspect

【一面倒】excessively dependent upon

【一面之交】a nodding acquaintance

【一面之詞】one-sided statements

【一鳴驚人】to become famous overnight; to achieve enormous success at the very first try

【一命歸陰】to die 亦作「一命歸西」

【一命嗚呼】to die

【一目了然】to understand fully at a glance

【一目十行】(said of the ability to read very fast) to read ten lines at one glance

【一髮千鈞】a critical situation

【一番好意】well-intentioned; good will

【一帆風順】to proceed smoothly without a hitch

【一反常態】to act out of one's normal behavior

【一分耕耘，一分收穫】One reaps no more than what he has sown.

【一分(價)錢，一分貨】The higher the price, the better the quality of the merchandise.

【一份(兒)】a part, portion or share

【一方】① an area or region ② a party

【一方面】① one side ② on the one hand..., on the other hand...

〔一部〕

【一封】 a (letter)「single-handedly
【一夫當關】to hold a key position
【一夫多妻】 polygamy
【一夫一妻】 monogamy
【一服】 a dose (of medicine)
【一幅】 a (painting, scroll, etc.)
【一副】 ①a pair; a set ②a (facial
【一打】 a dozen ⌊expression)
【一刀兩斷】 to sever relations by one stroke; to be through with
【一道】 ① together ② a (problem, etc.) ③ on the same path
【一旦】 ① once; whenever ② a day
【一黨專政】 one-party dictatorship
【一等】 first-class; first-rate
【一點】 ① a point ② a little bit
【一點兒】 ① a little bit ② somewhat
【一點一滴】 every drop; every bit
【一頂】 a (hat, cap, or sedan chair)
【一定】 certainly; surely; necessarily
【一度】 once; on one occasion; for a time
【一朵】 a (flower or cloud)
【一堆】 a pile or heap
【一隊】 a detachment or contingent; a (musical band)
【一對】 a pair; a couple; a brace
【一端】 ① one end ② one aspect
【一段】 ① one paragraph, passage or stanza ② a section; a length of...
【一頓】 ① a pause (in reading) ② a (meal) ③ a (dressing down)
【一動不如一靜】 Unless one is absolutely sure that he can succeed in doing something, he should not try it.
【一棟】 a (house or building)
【一塌糊塗】 in a great mess; topsy-turvy「promise; trick; flattery
【一套】 ① a suit; a set ② phony
【一頭】 ① a head (covered with gray hair, dust, skin ailments, etc.) ② (said of cattle, hogs, mules, etc.) a head ③ a jerky motion of the head
【一頭霧水】 (slang) in bewilderment or confusion; not knowing what's the matter
【一趟】 a trip; a ride
【一條】 ① a (rope, whip, snake, etc.) ② an article (of a law) ③ a carton (of cigarettes)
【一條心】 to be of one mind
【一天】 ① a whole day ② one day
【一天到晚】 from morning till night; all day long「one another
【一團和氣】 full of goodwill toward
【一團糟】 in a hopeless mess
【一通】 a (telegram, etc.)
【一同】 together with; in the company of
【一年半載】 a relatively short time
【一年到頭】 all (the) year round
【一年之計在於春】 Spring is the best time to do the year's work.
【一年四季】 all the year round
【一年一度】 once a year; annual(ly)
【一念之差】 a false step (which brings untold woes)
【一諾千金】 a solemn promise
【一來】 ① on the one hand ② as soon as (someone) arrives
【一類】 of the same class, category or species
【一勞永逸】 to make a great effort to accomplish something once (and) for all
【一覽表】 a table list, or chart
【一覽無餘】 (literally) A single glance takes in all.—a panoramic view
【一愣 or 一愣兒】 taken aback
【一了百了】 To solve the key issue will expedite the solution of the whole problem.「class
【一流】 ①first-rate ②of the same
【一溜煙】 (to get away) quickly
【一連】 ① successively ②a com-
【一連串】 a series of ⌊pany
【一輛】 a (car, truck, carriage, etc.)
【一路】 all the way「drastically
【一落千丈】 to nose-dive or decline
【一律】 without exception (or dis-
【一個】 one; a; an ⌊crimination)
【一個個】 ① one by one ② each and every one
【一個勁兒】 full of zest or enthusiasm「totally
【一概】 all; without exception;
【一概而論】 discussed or regarded in the same frame of mind or in an indiscriminating manner
【一根】 a (stick, hair or other objects which are long and slender)
【一股】 ①a streak; a strand ②one share (in stockholding) ③ a band (of bandits) ④a (strong

smell) ⑤full of (spirit, zest, etc.)
【一鼓作氣】to brace oneself (for a challenge)
【一國兩制】one country with two political systems
【一貫作風】the consistent way of doing things
【一貫作業】integrated operation
【一共】altogether; in all; all told
【一棵】a (tree); a head (of cabbage)
【一顆】a piece (of candy)
【一刻】fifteen minutes; a quarter
【一刻千金】Time is precious.
【一口】①a mouthful; a bite ②(to promise or grant a favor) without hesitation ③to insist (often falsely that somebody has done something bad)
【一口答應】to promise without hesitation
【一口氣】①in one breath; without stop ②breath
【一口咬定】to insist on saying something
【一塊兒】together; altogether
【一塊】a piece; a block
【一捆】a bundle of
【一行】a row; a line; a single file
【一夥】a group; a gang
【一會兒】①in a moment ②now... now...
【一揮而就】to finish writing an article or drawing a painting very quickly
【一回】①an occasion; a round (in boxing) ②once
【一回事】①one and the same (thing) ②one thing
【一回生二回熟】awkward at first but skillful later on
【一哄而散】(said of crowds) to disperse in a hubbub
【一己之私】one's own selfish interests
【一技之長】proficiency in a particular line (or field); professional skill
【一甲子】a cycle of sixty years
【一截】a section; a length
【一節】a section or passage
【一脚】①a kick ②to take part in something (often unsolicited)
【一…就…】no sooner...than...
【一間】a (room)
【一見鍾情】to fall in love at first sight
【一見如故】to become intimate at the first meeting
【一箭雙鵰】①to win the affection of two beauties at the same time ②to kill two birds with one stone
【一斤】one catty
【一局】①a game (of chess) ②(baseball) an inning
【一舉】with one action; at a blow; at one fell swoop
【一舉兩得】to gain two advantages by a single move; to kill two birds with one stone
【一舉一動】every movement and every action
【一絕】a special skill; a unique talent
【一蹶不振】unable to recover from a failure
【一決雌雄】to fight it out
【一齊】at the same time
【一起】①in the same place ②together
【一切】all; everything
【一竅不通】completely ignorant
【一丘之貉】people of the same ilk
【一親芳澤】to caress, kiss, or sleep with a woman
【一曲】a song
【一去不回】to leave for good
【一圈】①a circle ②one round (in a mah-jong game)
【一羣】a group; a crowd; a herd; a pack; a flock
【一息尙存】so long as one is alive (often followed by a vow to do something)
【一系列】a series of
【一下子】①at once ②at one stroke
【一些】①some; a few ②somewhat
【一笑千金】an enchanting smile
【一笑置之】to dismiss with a laugh
【一宿】one night; an overnight stay
【一線】a thread; a ray
【一線希望】a gleam of hope
【一心】①wholeheartedly ②at one
【一心一意】of one heart and mind
【一廂情願】unilateral willingness
【一向】①hitherto ②consistently
【一枝】①a (flower, pen, cigarette, etc.); a piece of (chalk) ②a branch
【一枝獨秀】to outshine others
【一知半解】incomplete comprehension
【一直】always; constantly
【一擲千金】to spend money recklessly
【一致】unanimously; one and all; consistent
【一折】①a 90 percent discount ②one fold
【一朝】①in one day ②once
【一朝千古】to die suddenly
【一朝一夕】a short period of time
【一週】①a week ②a revolution,

or circle
【一盞】a (lamp); a (cup)
【一針見血】exactly right; to the point
【一陣】a sudden gust (of wind, laughter, etc.)
【一陣子】for a while
【一章】a chapter (of a book)
【一張】a sheet (of paper); a (table, desk, painting or calligraphic work)
【一株】a (tree, weed, flower, etc.)
【一樁】an (affair); a (matter)
【一種】① one kind or type ② a species
【一剎那】in a moment
【一籌莫展】knowing not what to do; helpless
【一塵不染】immaculate; spotless
【一場】①a performance ②a (long period of association) ③ a (dream) ④a (period of happiness, grief, etc.)
【一場空】all in vain; futile
【一唱一和】One echoes the other.
【一成】10 percent
【一成不變】fixed; unchangeable; invariable; inflexible
【一齣戲】a play; a theatrical performance
【一觸卽發】(literally) One slight touch and off it goes.—imminent
【一串】a string (of coins, pearls, etc.)
【一牀】a (coverlet or comforter)
【一失足成千古恨】One pitfall leads to endless misery and regret.
【一時】①for a moment ②a period of time ③accidentally
【一時半刻】a short time; a little while
【一世】① an epoch; an age ② a lifetime ③ I (used after the name of an emperor such as Napoleon I)
【一世之雄】a great hero of his time
【一事無成】to accomplish nothing
【一視同仁】without discrimination
【一手】single-handedly
【一手包辦】① dictatorial; arbitrary ② to do something all by oneself
【一手交錢, 一手交貨】cash on delivery
【一手遮天】to hide the truth from the masses
【一扇】a (door, window, etc.)
【一身是膽】to have plenty of guts; very brave
【一身是債】(said of individuals) to be deep in debt
【一生】a lifetime
【一生受用不盡】to enjoy the benefit all one's life
【一聲不響】do not say a word
【一瞬 or 一眨眼】the twinkling of an eye; in an instant
【一雙】a couple
【一日】one day; such a day
【一日千里】to make progress or improvement at a tremendous pace
【一日之計在於晨】Morning hours are the best time of the day to work.
【一日三秋】longing for loved ones or close friends far away
【一日爲師, 終身爲父】One should respect his teacher as if the teacher were his own father, even if the teacher-student relationship has existed for only a single day.
【一任】a tour, term, or tenure (of duty)
【一如既往】as before; as always
【一則】① one item ② on the one hand
【一再】repeatedly; again and again
【一早】in the early morning
【一走了之】to evade the solution of a problem by walking away from where it exists
【一組】a set; a group
【一座】a (bridge, mountain, etc.)
【一尊】① a (Buddha statue) ② a jug (of wine)
【一次】once
【一餐】a meal
【一層】①one story or floor ②a stratum
【一蹴而幾】to succeed in doing something at the first try
【一絲不掛】stark-naked
【一絲不苟】No detail is overlooked.
【一絲一毫】a tiny bit; an iota; a trace
【一死了之】to end one's troubles or worries by death
【一掃而空】completely removed
【一所】a (school, charity institute, etc.)
【一二】a little; a few
【一一】one by one; each separately
【一意孤行】to do something against the advice of others
【一頁】one page
【一葉知秋】any sign foretelling things to come
【一言不發】to keep one's mouth shut
【一言不合】A single jarring note in

conversation (between two persons is immediately followed by a quarrel, fist fight, etc.).
【一言難盡】It is a long story.
【一言九鼎】a solemn promise or pledge
【一言興邦】A timely warning may avert a national crisis.
【一言爲定】to reach a binding agreement verbally
【一眼看去】① to take a sweeping look ②at first glance
【一飲而盡】to empty the glass at one gulp
【一氧化碳】carbon monoxide (CO)
【一樣】①alike; in the same manner ②an (object, item or article)
【一應俱全】complete with everything
【一無是處】without a single redeeming feature
【一無所得】Nothing is gained.
【一無所獲】to achieve or gain nothing (after all the efforts made)
【一無所知】to know nothing at all
【一無所長】do not have a single skill
【一無所有】to own nothing at all
【一五一十】to narrate in detail
【一窩蜂】(said of a crowd of people) to swarm
【一味】habitually; invariably
【一文不値】not worth a penny
【一問三不知】to say "I don't know" to every question
【一網打盡】to round up all (the criminals or other undesirable elements)
【一往情深】to fall deeply in love
【一望無際】to spread out far beyond the horizon
【一語道破】to hit the nail on the head
【一月】① January ② one month
【一元化】centralized; unified
【一擁而上】to rush up in a crowd

一畫

丁 2
1. ㄉㄧㄥ dīng
1. the fourth of the Ten Celestial Stems (天干) 2. population 3. attendants 4. fourth: 丁等grade D 5. small cubes of meat or vegetable
【丁香】a clove
【丁香花】lilac
【丁字街】T-shaped road junction
【丁字尺】a T-square
【丁憂】bereavement of parents

丁 2
2. ㄓㄥ zhēng
sound

七 3
ㄑㄧ qī (變調 ㄑㄧˊ qí)
the number seven
【七八成 or 七八成兒】① seventy or eighty percent ② very likely
【七拼八湊】① to cannibalize ② to piece together
【七平八穩】balanced; stable
【七零八落】scattered here and there; in confusion
【七角形】a heptagon
【七折八扣】① big discounts (in a bargain sale) ② to make allowance for exaggeration in a statement
【七尺之軀】men's average height (referring to a full-grown man)
【七長八短】of various lengths
【七上八下】an unsettled state of mind
【七嘴八舌】everybody talking at the same time
【七言詩】verses with seven characters to a line
【七月】① July ② the seventh month of the lunar year; the seventh moon

二畫

丈 4
ㄓㄤˋ zhàng
1. a unit in Chinese lineal measurement slightly longer than 10 feet 2. an elder; a senior 3. to measure; to survey
【丈母娘】a mother-in-law
【丈夫】① a husband ② a man
【丈夫氣概】manly; manliness
【丈量】to measure; to survey
【丈人】a father-in-law

三 5
ㄙㄢ sān
three; third; thrice
【三八節】Women's Day on March the 8th
【三百六十行】all trades and professions
【三胞胎】triplets
【三不管】a district not within the jurisdiction of any of the neighboring magistrates

一部

一部

【三不朽】the three imperishable—one's virtue, achievements and teachings (立德，立功，立言)
【三部曲】a trilogy
【三民主義】*The Three Principles of the People* — nationalism (民族), democracy (民權) and livelihood (民生)
【三明治】a sandwich
【三番兩次】time and again; over and over again
【三伏天】dog days
【三達德】the three virtues—wisdom, benevolence and courage (智，仁，勇)
【三代】① three generations ② the three ancient Chinese dynasties —Hsia, Shang and Chou
【三代同堂】three generations living under the same roof (under the big family system in old China)
【三等】①three grades ②the third grade
【三點裝】a bikini suit
【三讀】the third reading of a bill in a legislative session
【三度空間】three-dimensional space
【三頭六臂】a resourceful and capable man who, figuratively speaking, has three heads and six arms to use
【三頭政治】the triumvirate
【三天打魚，兩天曬網】(figuratively) to work off and on
【三年有成】Three years' hard work is crowned with success.
【三年五載】three to five years
【三輪車】a pedicab; a tricycle
【三個臭皮匠，勝過一個諸葛亮】The wisdom of the masses exceeds that of the wisest individual.
【三更半夜】late at night
【三合板】a three-ply board; plywood
【三級跳遠】hop, step, and jump
【三角】① trigonometry ② three angles
【三角板】a set square
【三角鐵】(construction) angle iron
【三角戀愛】a love triangle
【三角褲】panties; briefs
【三脚架】a tripod
【三教九流】people of all walks of life
【三緘其口】to remain silent
【三句不離本行】to talk shop frequently when conversing with people outside one's own profession
【三軍】the three armies; the armed forces
【三七二十一】Three sevens are twenty-one.
【三缺一】(mah-jong) one more player still needed
【三權分立】separation of the legislative, executive and judicial functions of a government
【三峽】the Three Gorges of the Yangtze River
【三心二意】hesitating; irresolute; vacillating
【三隻手】a pickpocket
【三振or三振出局】to strike out; a strikeout
【三叉路口】a junction where three roads meet
【三朝元老】a veteran statesman who had served under three emperors in a row
【三長兩短】unforeseen disasters or accidents
【三十六計，走爲上策】The best thing to do now is to go away.
【三十六著 or 三十六計】all the possible schemes or stratagems
【三十而立】thirty years of age when a man should stand on his own feet
【三十二開】thirty-twomo; 32mo
【三牲】three sacrificial offerings —ox, sheep and hog
【三生有幸】the greatest fortune in three incarnations (to make friends with worthy persons or to marry a virtuous and beautiful wife, etc.)
【三人行必有我師】If three of us are walking together, at least one of the other two is good enough to be my teacher.
【三餐】three meals—breakfast, lunch and supper
【三思而後行】Look before you leap.
【三三兩兩】by twos and threes
【三言兩語】a brief talk, discussion, conversation, description, etc.
【三陽開泰】a surge of good luck
【三五成羣】in groups of three or five
【三圍】the vital statistics of a woman
【三位一體】the Trinity; three-in-one
【三溫暖】sauna bath 亦作「蒸氣浴」
【三月】①March ②the third moon of the lunar calendar ③three months

上 6
1. ㄕㄤˋ shàng

1. above 2. upper; upward; up 3. better; superior 4. previous; before 5. top; summit; on 6. to ascend; to mount; to board 7. to go to court

【上報】①to be published in newspapers ②to report to a higher body; to report to one's boss

【上班】to go to office; to go on duty

【上半天】the morning; the forenoon

【上半場】the first half (of a game)

【上半身】the upper part of the body

【上半夜】before midnight

【上半月】the first half of a month

【上榜】to have one's name included in the name list of successful candidates of an examination

【上臂】the upper arm

【上邊】① the upper side ② up there

【上賓】distinguished guests

【上坡】to climb a slope

【上坡路】an ascending road

【上品】goods of superior quality

【上鋪】the upper berth

【上馬】to mount a horse

【上門】to visit

【上面】①the top; above ②the higher authorities

【上發條】to wind a watch, clock, mechanical toy, etc.

【上墳】to visit somebody's grave

【上方】①the place above ②the celestial realm

【上風】①the upper hand; advantage ②windward

【上當】to be taken in

【上等】first-class; superior quality

【上等兵】private first class (PFC)

【上帝】God

【上弔】to commit suicide by hanging; to hang oneself

【上端】the upper end

【上臺】①to go on the stage ②to assume office

【上頭】①the top; above; up ②the authorities

【上膛】(said of a gun) to be loaded

【上天】① Heaven; Providence; God ②to go up to the sky

【上(了)年紀】getting on in years

【上蠟】(textile and dyeing) waxing

【上來】Come up! 或 Come out!

【上壘】(baseball) to touch the base

【上樓】to go upstairs

【上流】① the upper part of a stream ②belonging to the upper circles

【上流社會】the upper class; the high society

【上路】①to start a journey ②(slang) good; well-behaved

【上鈎】①(fishing) to be caught by the hook ②to fall into the snare; to be tricked into doing something

【上古】prehistoric times

【上軌道】to get on the right track—to begin to work smoothly

【上工】to begin work

【上課】(said of students) to attend class; (said of teachers) to conduct class

【上口】easy to read

【上空裝】a topless suit

【上好】superior; excellent; the best

【上貨】to load (ships, trucks, etc.)

【上回】the previous occasion; last time

【上級】higher-ups; superiors

【上街】①to go into (or on) the street ②to go shopping

【上屆】the previous (election, congress, conference, tour of duty, etc.)

【上進】to make progress; to advance

【上漿】to starch (the laundry, etc.)

【上將】(army, marine, and air force) full general; (navy) full admiral

【上鏡頭】① photogenic ② to appear in a movie

【上氣不接下氣】to be out of breath

【上前】to come forward

【上去】to go up; to ascend

【上下其手】to distort facts to suit one's private ends

【上下一心】of one heart and mind

【上下文】the context

【上校】(army, marine, and air force) colonel; (navy) captain

【上限】the upper limit

【上香】to offer incense

【上行下效】The doings of superiors are imitated by inferiors.

【上行車】the up train

【上學】to go to school

【上選】the choicest

【上旬】the first ten days of a month

【上肢】the upper limbs

【上週or上禮拜or上星期】last week

【上陣】①to pitch into the work ②to go to battle

【上漲】(said of commodity prices

or flood waters) to rise
【上裝】to make up (for a theatrical performance); to dress up (as an actor or a bride)
【上車】to get on or into (a car, bus, truck or train)
【上場】①(drama) to go on stage; to enter ②(sports) to enter the court
【上船】to board a ship; to embark
【上床】to go to bed
【上士】(military rank) first sergeant
【上市】(said of new products) to go on the market
【上山】to go up a hill; to go to the mountains
【上身】①the torso; the upper part of the body ②a blouse; a jacket ③to wear ④to contract a disease
【上上下下】①up and down ②all; the whole
【上升】to soar or rise
【上乘】① a carriage drawn by a team of four horses ② (Buddhism) the Great Conveyance ③ the best in quality
【上書】to present a petition
【上述】the aforementioned
【上任】to take up an official appointment
【上座】the seat of honor
【上次】last time; the previous occasion
【上策】the best stratagem (or plan)
【上菜】① the best dishes ② to place dishes on the table
【上蒼】Heaven; God
【上層】the upper layer, level or stratum
【上司】a boss; a superior official
【上訴】① to appeal to a higher court ② to state one's case to a superior
【上鎖】to lock
【上算】a profitable deal; economical
【上顎】the palate
【上衣】upper garments; jackets
【上議院】the Upper House; the Senate
【上游】①the upper reaches (of a river) ②advanced position
【上演】to perform; to stage (a play)
【上癮】to become addicted to a certain drug or habit
【上映】to show (a movie)
【上午】forenoon; A.M.
【上尉】(navy) lieutenant; (army and air force) captain
【上文】the foregoing paragraphs or chapters
【上月 or 上個月】last month
【上元】the fifteenth of the first lunar month (which is the Lantern Festival in China)

上 6
2. ㄕㄤˇ shǎng

【上聲】falling-rising tone, one of the four tones in classical Chinese and the third tone in modern standard Chinese phonetics

下 7
ㄒㄧㄚˋ xià

1. to put down 2. to lay 3. to fall 4. to descend 5. to begin 6. below; under 7. inferior; lower 8. next
【下巴】the chin
【下擺】the lower part of a Chinese gown
【下拜】to bow
【下輩子】the next life; the next incarnation
【下班】to knock off
【下半輩子】the latter half of one's life
【下半天】the last half day; afternoon
【下半旗】to fly a flag at half-mast
【下半場】the second half (of a game)
【下半夜】the wee hours
【下筆】to start writing
【下筆成章】to write quickly and skillfully
【下邊or下邊兒】as follows; following; below; under
【下部】①the lower part ②the private parts
【下不了臺】①cannot bring to a conclusion ②to be put on the spot
【下不爲例】This does not constitute a precedent. 或 Don't do it again!
【下坡路】a descending road
【下片】to stop showing a movie
【下品】low-grade; inferior
【下聘】to present betrothal gifts
【下鋪】the lower berth
【下馬】to dismount from a horse
【下馬威】to warn against insubordination, etc. by enforcing strict disciplinary action when one first takes office
【下麵】to cook noodles
【下面】①underneath ②following ③lower levels; subordinates
【下命令】to give orders 亦作「下令」
【下飯】(said of dishes) to go along

with rice
【下方】①south and west ②below; under ③the earth
【下房】the servant's quarters
【下風】① in an inferior position
【下蛋】to lay eggs ⌊② leeward
【下等】① low-grade ② mean; depraved ⌈leave a sickbed
【下地】①to go to the fields ②to
【下地獄】to go to hell ⌈nition
【下定義】to define; to give a defi-
【下毒】to poison ⌈someone
【下毒手】to lay violent hands on
【下榻】to take up abode; to stay
【下臺】①to get off stage ②to be relieved from office
【下體】the privates; the genitals
【下帖】to sent an invitation
【下田】to work on farmland
【下女】a maid
【下來】to come down
【下樓】to descend the stairs; to go downstairs ⌈listed below
【下列】① as follows ② what are
【下流】① downstream ② to flow down ③ low; nasty; mean; scurrilous
【下流話】foul language; obscenities
【下落】whereabouts
【下崗】to come or go off sentry
【下跪】to kneel down ⌊duty
【下工】to stop working
【下工夫】to devote much time and energy to a task ⌈ish class
【下課】to get out of class; to fin-
【下海】①to turn professional (usually referring to show personalities) ②to go to sea
【下回 or 下次】next time ⌈nates
【下級】①lower levels ②subordi-
【下嫁】to marry someone beneath her station
【下屆】next (term, election, etc.)
【下酒】(said of food) to go with wine ⌈wine
【下酒菜】a dish that goes with
【下賤】low; cheap; degrading
【下降】to descend; to drop
【下決心】to make a resolution
【下棋】to play chess
【下去】①to go down ②to go on
【下弦】the last quarter of the
【下限】lower limit ⌊moon
【下鄉】to go to the country; to rusticate
【下行車】the down train
【下學】to leave for home after
【下學期】next semester ⌊school
【下雪】to snow ⌈month
【下旬】the last ten days of a
【下逐客令】to ask an unwelcome guest or visitor to leave
【下注】to put stake; to wager
【下箸】to start eating
【下墜】to fall
【下種】to sow seed ⌈cles, etc.)
【下車】to get off (trains or vehi-
【下沉】to sink; to subside
【下場】① the conclusion; the end ②to get to the playground to compete, play ball, etc. ③ an exit on the stage ⌈prepare food
【下廚】to go to the kitchen; to
【下垂】①to hang down; to droop ②(medicine) prolapse
【下船】to go ashore
【下牀】to get up
【下士】(military rank) corporal
【下手】①to start doing something ②to commit a crime ③a helper
【下山】to go down a mountain
【下身】① the lower part of the body ② the privates
【下屬】subordinates
【下水】① (ㄒㄧㄚˋ ㄕㄨㄟˇ) to launch a boat ② (ㄒㄧㄚˋ ˙ㄕㄨㄟ) internal organs of animals ⌈tem
【下水道】sewers; the sewerage sys-
【下水禮】the ceremony of launch
【下人】servants ⌊ing a ship
【下葬】to bury ⌈or policy
【下策】a bad strategy, measure
【下層】①a lower stratum, layer or deck ② low-ranking
【下顎】the lower jaw; the mandible
【下意識】subconscious
【下議院】the Lower House
【下野】to quit or resign from of-
【下游】downstream ⌊ficial posts
【下嚥】to swallow
【下午】afternoon
【下文】① the statement that follows ②further development or
【下雨】to rain ⌊information
【下獄】to put behind bars
【下月】next month

三畫

一部

〔一部〕

不 8 ㄅㄨˋ bù (變調 ㄅㄨˊ bú)
no; not; negative
【不白之冤】①a wrong that has not been righted ②falsely accused
【不敗之地】an invincible position
【不卑不亢】to conduct oneself properly
【不比】unlike
【不必】not necessary
【不便】inconvenience; inconvenient
【不怕】not afraid
【不配】①mismatch ②unequal to
【不偏不倚】①exact; just ②fair
【不平】①complaint; a grudge ②unjust
【不平等條約】an unequal treaty
【不平則鳴】Those who are discriminated against will complain.
【不毛之地】barren land
【不謀而合】to be coincident
【不滿】discontent; dissatisfaction
【不忙】to take one's time
【不妙】Something is wrong or going badly.
【不眠不休】without rest; tireless
【不免】have to; must; unavoidable
【不明飛行物體】unidentified flying object (UFO)亦作「幽浮」
【不名譽】disreputable; scandalous
【不法】unlawful; illegal
【不法之徒】lawless elements
【不費吹灰之力】do not need the slightest effort
【不凡】extraordinary; unusual; outstanding
【不分高下 or 不分軒輊 or 不分勝負】well-matched; a draw; a tie
【不分青紅皂白】indiscriminately
【不分晝夜】(to work) day and night
【不妨】no harm in (trying, doing, etc.)
【不防】by surprise; unawares
【不符】do not tally
【不服】to recalcitrate; to disobey
【不服氣】unwilling to submit
【不服輸】to refuse to concede defeat
【不孚衆望】not popular with the masses
【不負所託】to merit someone's trust
【不打自招】to make a confession without being pressed
【不得】don't; no; must not
【不得不】to have to; must
【不得了】①Good heavens! ②It's serious!
【不得人心】to be unpopular
【不得而知】do not know
【不得已】cannot help but...
【不得要領】①cannot get the gist; pointless ②don't know the right way
【不倒翁】a tumbler
【不道德】immoral; unethical
【不到黃河心不死】to refuse to give up until one reaches one's goal
【不但】not only...
【不當】unsuitable; improper; inappropriate
【不登大雅之堂】to be unpresentable
【不等】not uniform; to vary
【不敵】no match for; to be defeated
【不定】①not certain ②indefinite
【不定期】without a fixed schedule
【不對】not right; wrong
【不對勁】not in harmony; listless
【不斷】continuous; constant
【不動心】showing no interest
【不動產】real estate; immovable assets
【不動聲色】not showing any feeling or emotion; with composure
【不凍港】an ice-free port; an open port
【不透明】opaque
【不透風】stuffy
【不透氣】hermetic; airtight
【不透水】waterproof
【不停】without stop
【不妥】not the right way; improper
【不通】①(said of writings) poor; illogical ②blocked; not passable
【不同】different; distinct
【不同凡響】extraordinary; remarkable
【不同意】to disagree
【不耐煩】impatient
【不能】cannot; unable
【不能不】to have to; must; cannot but
【不念舊惡 or 不咎既往】to let bygones be bygones
【不勞而獲】to gain without effort
【不冷不熱】lukewarm
【不理】in disregard of; to ignore
【不理會】inattentive; unmindful
【不利】①not going smoothly ②bad; adverse; harmful
【不列顛】Britain
【不了了之】to conclude without concrete result or decision
【不了解】do not understand
【不料】unexpectedly; never thought

【不留情面】to be very strict; to disregard another's "face" or feelings
【不留餘地】① without leaving leeway ② to pursue to the brutal end
【不良】bad; harmful; unhealthy
【不良分子】undesirables; scums
【不良導體】a nonconductor
【不良少年】juvenile delinquents
【不靈】awkwardly; ineffectively
【不露聲色】do not show one's feelings, intentions, motives, etc.
【不倫不類】grotesque; incongruous
【不論】no matter; regardless
【不苟言笑】strictly adhere to propriety in one's behavior; serious
【不夠】not enough; insufficient
【不甘】unreconciled to
【不甘寂寞】eager to seek publicity
【不乾不淨】not clean; filthy
【不敢】dare not
【不敢當】I don't deserve it.
【不敢領教】too bad to be accepted (bought, etc.)
【不顧】in disregard of; regardless of; despite; in spite of
【不過】① only; merely ② but; nevertheless
【不過如此 or 不過爾爾】so-so
【不規則】irregular
【不軌】conspiracy, plots, etc.
【不關痛癢】irrelevant; insignificant
【不管】in disregard of; regardless of consequences
【不管三七二十一】regardless of consequences
【不公】unjust; unfair
【不攻自破】to collapse of itself
【不共戴天】absolutely irreconcilable
【不可】① no; negative ② not allowed ③ cannot
【不可磨滅】indelible
【不可多得】hard to come by; scarce
【不可理喩】unreasonable
【不可告人】not to be divulged; secret or shameful (act, etc.)
【不可救藥】incurable; beyond hope
【不可限量】limitless (opportunities); very promising
【不可捉摸】uncanny; unpredictable
【不可收拾】pandemonium; hopeless (situation, etc.); out of control
【不可勝數】countless; innumerable
【不可思議】mysterious; unimaginable
【不可一世】to be extremely arrogant
【不可逾越】impassable; insuperable
【不客氣】① impolite; rude; blunt ② You are welcome. 或 Not at all.
【不堪】cannot suffer; unendurable
【不堪回首】cannot recall without pain
【不堪設想】(said of consequences) serious or unthink
【不亢不卑】neither proud nor obsequious
【不快】① unhappy; uncomfortable ② slow
【不愧】to be worthy of; to deserve to be
【不和】at loggerheads; not on good terms
【不合】unsuitable; in disagreement with (rules, etc.)
【不合邏輯】illogical
【不合格】below standard; not qualified
【不合時宜】out of fashion; anachronistic
【不合適】not suitable; improper; inappropriate
【不合作】noncooperative
【不好】① not good ② to be spoiled; to become worse
【不好惹】not to be trifled with; not to be pushed around
【不好意思】to feel embarrassed, shy, bashful or ashamed
【不含糊】①(something) solid; very good ② to mince no words
【不寒而慄】trembling with fear
【不懷好意】with evil intention
【不會】unable; can not; will not
【不歡而散】to break up in disagreement
【不慌不忙】① leisurely; unhurried ② with full composure
【不羈】carefree; not bound by social etiquette, customs, etc.
【不及】not so (good, tall, early, etc.) as...; to be inferior to
【不及格】to fail to pass; disqualified
【不及物動詞】an intransitive verb
【不濟於事】to no avail
【不記名投票】secret ballots; secret votes
【不計其數】countless; innumerable
【不假思索】without thinking; without hesitation 亦作「不加思索」
【不假外出】absent without leave
【不結盟國家】nonaligned nations
【不解風情】do not understand implications in love affair
【不介意】do not mind

〔一部〕

【不久】within a short time; soon
【不簡單】①not simple; rather complicated ② remarkable; marvelous
【不見得】not likely; not necessarily so
【不見天日】① in total darkness ② injustice
【不見了】disappeared
【不見棺材不落淚】One refuses to be convinced until one faces the grim reality.
【不禁】cannot help...
【不僅】not only
【不盡然】not exactly so
【不近人情】unreasonable; inconsiderate
【不進則退】either to keep progressing or retrogressing
【不經事】inexperienced
【不經一事，不長一智】Wisdom comes from experience.
【不經意】inattentive(ly); careless(ly)
【不景氣】(economics) depression
【不拘】①no limit; not to be bound ② whatever
【不拘小節】to disregard trifles, niceties, etc.
【不拘一格】to follow no set pattern
【不絕如縷】(said of a situation) critical
【不期而遇】to meet by chance
【不切實際】impractical
【不巧】unfortunately
【不求甚解】to read casually
【不求聞達】to be uninterested in fame
【不遷怒】not blame others for one's own failure, mistake, etc.
【不屈】unyielding; unbending
【不屈不撓】not to be bent or cowed; unswerving
【不惜】to be ready to go to extreme lengths
【不惜工本】to spare no expense
【不下於】① as many as; no less than ② not inferior to; as good as
【不屑】do not condescend (or deign) to do something; to disdain
【不謝】Don't mention it. 或Not at all.
【不懈】untiring; indefatigable
【不曉得】do not know; ignorant of
【不肖】① a son who is not so good as his father ② good-for-nothing
【不孝】①not in accordance with filial piety ②a term referring to oneself in the obituary announcing the death of one's parent
【不修邊幅】do not care about details (especially in clothing); slovenly
【不朽】immortal; immortality
【不銹鋼】stainless steel
【不相干】irrelevant; to have nothing to do with
【不相稱】ill-matched; inharmonious
【不相識】do not know
【不相上下】equal; equally matched
【不相容】incompatible
【不祥】ominous; unlucky
【不祥之兆】a bad (or an ill) omen
【不詳】①unknown ②not detailed enough
【不想】do not want
【不像話】absurd or ludicrous (talks, acts, etc.)
【不像樣】improper (behavior); disreputable (conduct)
【不行】① not allowed; nothing doing ② unsuccessful; to no avail ③ not qualified ④ do not work
【不省人事】in a coma; unconscious
【不幸】misfortune; unfortunate
【不幸中之大幸】a lucky occurrence in the course of a disaster, such as a priceless painting saved from a fire
【不需】do not need
【不虛此行】One gains much on the trip.
【不許】not allowed; must not; prohibited
【不學無術】unlearned; ignorant
【不宣而戰】to fight without a declaration of war
【不支】unable to hang on; exhausted
【不知不覺】imperceptibly; unnoticed
【不知道】do not know; to be unconscious
【不知天高地厚】to think too much of one's abilities
【不知好歹】① unable to tell good from bad ② stubborn
【不知就裏】do not know the inside story
【不知輕重】muddled or mixed-up
【不知情】to know nothing about...; to be ignorant of...
【不知去向】to disappear without a trace
【不知自愛】to act without self-respect
【不知足】insatiable; greedy
【不知死活】muddled or mixed-up (characterized by rashness or

recklessness)
【不知所措】 stunned into inaction or stoppage of mental activity
【不知所云】 (said of statements) unintelligible
【不值得】 not worth it; unworthy of
【不值一錢】 worthless
【不值一笑】 extremely ridiculous
【不止】 ① do not stop ② not only... ③ more than...; over
【不只】 not only; not merely
【不治之症】 an incurable disease
【不置可否】 noncommittal; to make no comment
【不至於】 will not go so far as...; will not be so serious as...
【不折不扣】 ① without any discount; net cost ② absolute; out-and-out
【不戰而屈人之兵】 to subdue the enemy without fighting
【不戰而勝】 to win without fighting a battle
【不長進】 ① without improvement or progress ② good-for-nothing
【不爭氣】 to submit to defeat or failure without putting up a fight; to let someone down
【不著邊際】 far-fetched; totally beside the point
【不著痕跡】 without trace
【不准】 not allowed; forbidden
【不中聽】 (referring to unpleasant remarks or words) not worth listening
【不中意】 not quite up to one's idea
【不恥下問】 not ashamed to learn from one's inferiors
【不理不睬】 to ignore completely
【不稱意】 Things do not match one's hope.
【不成】 ① will not do ② an expression used at the end of a question
【不成體統】 (acting or talking) wildly; without regard to common practice
【不成敬意】 just a little token to show my respect to you
【不成器 or 不中用】 good-for-nothing; useless
【不成文法】 unwritten law
【不出所料】 just as expected
【不時】 ① frequently ② at any time
【不時之需】 occasional needs
【不是】 ① no; not right ② if...not ③ in the wrong
【不適】 ill; indisposed; unwell
【不識大體】 to fail to see the important points
【不識擡舉】 unappreciative; ungrateful
【不識泰山】 to fail to recognize a famous personage when meeting him face to face
【不識相】 impervious to an obvious situation
【不識時務】 ignorant of the changes of the times or failing to make use of available chances
【不識字 or 不識一丁】 illiterate
【不世之才】 a rare talent; a genius
【不受理】 ① (law) to reject (a complaint); not entertained ② (diplomacy) to refuse to entertain (a proposal)
【不上不下】 ① on a spot; in an impasse ② inappropriate
【不勝】 ① cannot bear; to be unequal to ② very; extremely; overwhelmed
【不勝枚舉】 too numerous to recount
【不勝其煩】 cannot stand the harassment, nuisance, etc.
【不聲不響】 stealthily; furtively
【不舒服】 unwell; uncomfortable
【不順眼】 incurring vexation or dislike; disagreeable
【不爽】 ① out of sorts; in a bad mood ② without discrepancy; accurate
【不然】 ① not so ② otherwise; or
【不仁】 ① not benevolent ② paralyzed; numbed
【不人道】 inhuman
【不忍 or 不忍心】 disturbed (characterized by pity); cannot bear to...
【不讓步】 to hold one's ground
【不入耳】 unpleasant to the ear; not worth listening to
【不辱使命】 to have succeeded in carrying out an assignment
【不容】 ① do not tolerate; do not allow ② do not welcome
【不貲】 immeasurable; incalculable
【不自量】 without considering one's own capability; overconfident
【不自在】 feeling uneasy or uncomfortable
【不擇手段】 by fair means or foul
【不在】 ① dead ② not in; absent

〔一部〕

【不在乎】do not care 「limits
【不在此限】not subject to the
【不在意】① to take no notice of; to pay no attention to ② inattentive; careless; negligent
【不贊一辭】to keep silent; to make no comment
【不足】① not deserving ② insufficient; not enough 「importance
【不足輕重】of little value; of little
【不足採信】①(law) unacceptable as evidence ② can not be considered as reliable
【不足爲奇】nothing strange, extraordinary or remarkable about it 「others know
【不足爲外人道】no need to let
【不作第二人想】not content with playing second fiddle 「nothing
【不作聲】to keep silence; to say
【不辭辛苦】to work with all-out effort 「ding goodbye
【不辭而別】to leave without bid-
【不測】① unpredictable ② misfortune; disaster; accident
【不才】without capability 「thing
【不曾】to have never done some-
【不錯】① to be right ② granted that; to be sure that ③ not bad
【不存芥蒂】do not harbor previous grievances
【不存在】nonexistent
【不死心】unwilling to give up
【不三不四】grotesque; incongruous
【不俗】uncommon; not hackneyed
【不速之客】an uninvited guest; an unexpected guest 「intranquil
【不安】① uneasy; disturbed ②
【不安於室】(said of women) having extramarital affairs
【不貳過】not to repeat a previous mistake 「price
【不二價】a uniform (or fixed)
【不一】to vary; to differ
【不一而足】many; numerous
【不一定】uncertain; not sure
【不宜】not suitable; inadvisable
【不遺餘力】to spare no effort; to do one's best (or utmost)
【不以爲然】to object to; to take exception to
【不亦樂乎】① What a delight it would be if.... ② extremely; awfully 「illicitly
【不義之財】loot; wealth acquired
【不翼而飛】missing inexplicably
【不雅觀】ungraceful 「than
【不亞於 or 不遜於】not worse
【不要】① don't ② don't want
【不要臉】shameless; brazen
【不要緊】① unimportant; not serious ② never mind
【不藥而癒】to recover (from illness) without medical help
【不由分說】not waiting for an explanation; unreasonable
【不由得】cannot help; cannot but
【不由自主】can't help; involuntarily
【不言而喻】self-evident; to understand without explanation
【不厭】do not mind doing something; do not tire of
【不厭其煩】to be very patient
【不無小補】It might be of some small help.
【不爲所動】to remain unmoved (by promises of reward, etc.)
【不聞不問】to care nothing about
【不穩】unsteady; unstable
【不問】① to pay no attention to; to disregard ② to let go unpunished
【不虞】①unexpected ②eventuality; contingency ③do not worry
【不育】sterility 「about
【不約而同】to accord without consulting each other
【不悅】unhappy; displeased 「not
【不用】① not necessary ② need
【不用功】do not study diligently
【不用說 or 不待說】it goes without saying; needless to say

丏 9
ㄍㄞˋ gài
1. to beg for alms 2. a beggar
3. to give

丑 10
ㄔㄡˇ chǒu
1. the second of the twelve "Terrestrial Branches" (地支) 2. the period of the day from 1 to 3 a.m. 3. a clown: 丑角 a comedian

四畫

且 11
ㄑㄧㄝˇ qiě
1. moreover; still; further 2. just; for the time being 3. both... and... 4. even

【且慢】Hold it! 或 Wait a minute.

丕 12
ㄆㄧ pī
1. great; distinguished 2. in observance of (a ruling, etc.)
【丕顯】great and distinguished; splendid

世 13
ㄕ shì
1. a generation 2. a person's life span 3. an age 4. the world
【世伯】a designation for the male friends of one's father
【世面】the various facets of human activities
【世風澆薄】There are scarcely public morals to speak of these days.
【世風日下】The moral degeneration of the world is getting worse day by day.
【世代】① a generation ② the times ③ from generation to generation
【世代交替】(biology) metagenesis; alternation of generations
【世道人心】the ways of the world and the time
【世態炎涼】snobbish; inconstancy of human relationships
【世故】① the ways of the world ② shrewd; worldly
【世紀】a century
【世家】a family holding official ranks for generations
【世界】the world
【世界末日】the end of the world; doomsday
【世界大同】universal brotherhood
【世界大戰】a world war
【世界潮流】world trends
【世交】families closely related or associated for generations
【世間 or 世上】on earth; in the world
【世襲】hereditary (title, rank, etc.)
【世系】a family tree; a pedigree
【世姪】one's close friend's son
【世仇】family feud; blood feud
【世傳】hereditary; to be handed down through generations
【世事 or 世務】affairs of the world
【世世代代】generation after generation; from generation to generation
【世人】people of the world
【世子】the crown prince
【世族】a powerful family that has great political influence for generations
【世俗】customs and traditions
【世俗之見】common views
【世外桃源】Shangri-la; a secluded paradise
【世運】the Olympiad

丘 14
ㄑㄧㄡ qiū
1. a hillock or mound 2. big; elder 3. empty 4. first name of Confucius 5. a surname
【丘陵】mounds; craggy terrains; hills
【丘壑】(literary) hills and ravines —a wooded place for retirement

丙 15
ㄅㄧㄥˇ bǐng
1. the third of the ten "Celestial Stems" (天干) 2. another name for fire 3. the tail of a fish
【丙等】roughly equivalent to the "C" grade; the third grade

五畫

丞 16
ㄔㄥˊ chéng
1. to aid; to assist 2. a deputy to an official
【丞相】the prime minister

丟 17
ㄉㄧㄡ diū
1. to throw 2. to lose 3. to put (or lay) aside
【丟掉】① to lose ② to cast away; to throw away
【丟臉 or 丟人】to lose face; to disgrace
【丟開】① to leave it off; not to mention ② to throw away
【丟棄】to cast away; to get rid of
【丟下】to throw down; to lay aside
【丟三落四】forgetful

七畫

並 18
ㄅㄧㄥˋ bìng
1. and; also; at the same time 2. on the same level with; even; equal 3. entirely; completely
【並不】really not
【並排】side by side; in the same row
【並非】by no means
【並立】① to stand together ② to exist simultaneously
【並列】to stand side by side; to juxtapose
【並駕齊驅】to keep abreast of; to

be equal 「by side; abreast
【並肩】shoulder to shoulder; side
【並且】moreover; furthermore; and
【並行不悖】to proceed together or simultaneously without interfering with each other; compatible
【並重】to lay equal stress on

丨部
ㄍㄨㄣˇ gǔn

二畫

丫 19
ㄧㄚ yā 「forks upward
something that branches or
【丫頭】① (in ancient China) a slave girl; a maid ②(in modern usage) a small girl, especially one's own daughter

三畫

中 20
1. ㄓㄨㄥ zhōng
1. the middle; among; within; between 2. China or Chinese; Sino-
【中部】the central part; the middle part
【中篇小說】a novelette
【中美】① Central America ② China and U.S.A.; Sino-American
【中美洲】Central America
【中飯】lunch; luncheon
【中鋒】the center (in basketball, soccer, military operations, etc.)
【中等】middle-class; medium
【中等教育】secondary education
【中隊】①a squadron ②a unit composed of several groups
【中斷】suspension; interruption
【中東】the Middle East (Asia)
【中提琴】a viola 「way
【中途】midway; halfway; on the
【中南半島】Indochina
【中年】middle age
【中立】neutral; neutrality
【中立國】neutral nations
【中量級】(sports) middle weight
【中落】a sudden fall of one's family fortune; to decline
【中古】the Middle Ages; medieval
【中國】① China; Cathay ② the Middle Kingdom 「dio
【中國電影製片廠】China Movie Stu-
【中國話】Chinese; the Chinese lan-
【中國城】Chinatown 」guage
【中和】① justice and peace ② (chemistry) to neutralize
【中和作用】neutralization
【中華】(originally, the region along the Yellow River where the Chinese people thrived) the Chinese nation; the Chinese people
【中級】middle rank; intermediate
【中繼站】a relay station 亦作「轉播站」
【中堅】①the main force (of an army); crack troops ②a cadre; underpinning
【中間】in the middle; in the center
【中間派】the middle-of-the-roaders
【中將】(army, marine and air force) lieutenant general; (navy) viceadmiral
【中秋節】the Mid-Autumn Festival or the Moon Festival
【中西合璧】a (good) combination or blending of Chinese and Western (fashion, style, etc.)
【中校】(army and air force) lieutenant colonel; (navy) commander
【中線】(sports) the center line; halfway line
【中心】①center ②central point
【中心人物】the central (or key) figure 「or thought
【中心思想】the gist; a central idea
【中興】revival (of a nation or family); rejuvenation; resurgence
【中型】medium-sized; middle-sized
【中性】① (chemistry) neutral(ity) ② (grammar) the neuter gender
【中學】middle school; secondary school; high school
【中旬】the middle part of a month
【中止】to suspend; to interrupt
【中指】the middle finger
【中產階級】the middle class; bourgeois
【中輟】to give up halfway
【中式】the Chinese style or fashion
【中士】a sergeant
【中沙群島】the Zhongsha Islands
【中山陵】Dr. Sun Yat-sen Mausoleum
【中樞】the central administration
【中日戰爭】the Sino-Japanese War

【中(間)人】a middleman; a mediator; an agent
【中子】neutron
【中菜】Chinese dishes
【中餐】① a midday meal ② Chinese meal
【中歐】the central part of Europe
【中醫】a Chinese herb doctor
【中亞】Central Asia
【中藥】Chinese medicine (mostly herbs)
【中央】the center; the middle
【中央集權】a centralized government
【中央情報局】Central Intelligence Agency (CIA)
【中央政府】Central Government
【中央預算】the central budget
【中午】noon; high noon; midday
【中外】Chinese and foreign
【中外野手】(baseball) a center fielder
【中尉】(army and air force) first lieutenant; (navy) lieutenant
【中文】the Chinese language
【中原】① the Central Plains — the downstream regions of the Yellow River ② the midst of a plain
【中元節】the Ghost Festival on the 15th day of the seventh lunar month
【中庸】mediocre

中 20
2. ㄓㄨㄥˋ zhòng
1. to hit (the target); to attain (a goal) 2. to be hit by; to be affected by
【中風】to suffer from a stroke of paralysis or apoplexy
【中彈】to get shot
【中的】to hit the bull's-eye
【中毒】to be poisoned; toxicosis
【中聽】pleasant to the ear
【中看】good to look at
【中肯】to the point; fair; relevant
【中計】to walk (or fall) into a trap
【中籤】to be chosen by lot
【中選】to be chosen; to be selected
【中傷】to hurt somebody insidiously
【中暑】to have a sunstroke
【中彩or中獎】to win a (lottery) prize
【中意】to suit one's fancy; agreeable
【中用】useful; serviceable

丰 21
ㄈㄥ fēng
1. good-looking; buxom 2. appearance and carriage of a person
【丰姿】appearances of a person (usually indicating grace and charm)
【丰采】good-looking
【丰韻】charming appearances or carriage

六畫

串 22
ㄔㄨㄢˋ chuàn
1. to string together 2. a string (of coins, etc.) 3. to pour into
【串門子 or 串門兒】to visit or gossip from door to door
【串通】to collude or to conspire
【串聯】series connection
【串供】collusion among witnesses or suspects for false confessions

丶部
ㄓㄨˇ zhǔ

二畫

丸 23
ㄨㄢˊ wán
1. a pellet; a small ball; a pill 2. an egg 3. used in Japanese indicating completion or completeness
【丸子】①a meat ball ②a medical pill

三畫

丹 24
ㄉㄢ dān
1. cinnabar 2. red; scarlet 3. a sophisticated decoction 4. a medical pill, ointment and powder
【丹麥】Denmark
【丹田】(Taoism) the region three inches below the navel
【丹誠】loyalty; devotion

四畫

主 25
ㄓㄨˇ zhǔ
1. a master; a leader; a chief; a host 2. Jesus Christ; God; Lord 3. to officiate at; to preside over; to take charge of 4. main; chief; primary; principal

【主辦】 to sponsor; to take charge of

【主筆】 an editorial writer of a newspaper

【主編】 an editor in chief

【主僕】 master and servant

【主謀】 the mastermind

【主犯】 the principal criminal

【主婦】 a housewife; a hostess

【主導】 leading; dominant; guiding

【主動】 to take the initiative

【主動脈】 (anatomy) the aorta

【主題】 the main theme (of an essay; the gist

【主體】 ①the subjective (as against the objective) ②the main body or the most important part of something

【主腦】 the mastermind; the chief; the leader

【主力】 the main force

【主力艦】 a battleship; a capital ship

【主力軍】 the main force

【主流】 ① the mainstream ② the essential or main aspect

【主糧】 the staple food grain

【主幹】 ① the trunk ② the main force

【主顧】 a customer; a client

【主觀】 the subjective point of view

【主管】 ① the boss; the chief ② to take charge of

【主客】 the guest of honor

【主婚】 to preside over a wedding ceremony

【主婚人】 the guardians of the marrying couple at a wedding ceremony

【主祭】 ①to officiate at a religious rite or service ②a person officiating at such a service

【主計室】 the auditing department

【主教】 a bishop

【主見】 the ideas or thoughts of one's own

【主講】 ① to lecture; to speak on a special subject ② the main speaker

【主將】 ① the commanding general ② the most important athlete in a sports team

【主角】 the leading player; the leading role

【主權】 ①sovereignty ②the right of autonomy

【主席】 a chairman; a president

【主修】 to specialize (in a subject); to major

【主旨】 the gist, substance, or purport

【主治醫師】 a physician in charge of a case

【主戰派】 the hawks

【主張】 ① an opinion ② to advocate

【主政】 ① to head the administration ② the person in charge

【主持】 to officiate at; to preside over

【主持正義】 to uphold justice

【主食】 staple food

【主使】 a mastermind; a ringleader

【主帥】 an address to the commander in chief

【主人】 ① an owner ② a host ③ a master

【主人翁】 ①a respectful term for a host ② a master

【主任】 the head of an office

【主子】 ① the emperor ② one's master

【主宰】 ① the man in charge ② a god

【主從】 ① the master and his servant ② the principal and the secondary (criminals)

【主詞】 the subject

【主隨客便】 A host respects his guest's wishes.

【主意】 an idea; a suggestion

【主義】 a principle; a doctrine

【主要】 essential; important; major

【主演】 to star; to play the leading role in a play or a motion picture

【主因】 the major (or principal) cause

五畫

乓 26 ㄆㄤ pāng

used for the sound

丿部 ㄆㄧㄝ piě

一畫

乃 27 ㄋㄞˇ nǎi

1. to be 2. but; however 3. and also; moreover 4. so; therefore 5. you; your 6. then 7. if

【乃至】 ① so that; so... as to; leading to ② hence; consequently

二畫

久 28
ㄐㄧㄡˇ jiǔ
1. long 2. for a long time 3. to detain someone long
【久別】long separation
【久病成良醫】Long illness makes the patient a good doctor.
【久留】to stay for a long time
【久候】to wait for a long time
【久久】for a long, long time
【久經風霜】to have experienced all sorts of hardships
【久居人下】to remain in a subordinate position for a long period
【久而久之】over a long period of time
【久仰】Glad to meet you.
【久仰大名】I've heard of your illustrious name for a long time.
【久違】the literary form of "Long time no see."
【久遠】a long time; forever; perpetual

三畫

之 29
ㄓ zhī
1. to go to; to leave for; to arrive at 2. zigzag; winding 3. an expletive 4. third person objective case (it; her; him; them) 5. this; that; these; those 6. (possessive particle) of
【之內】within; inside; including
【之後】after this; afterward
【之前】before this; before; prior to
【之上】above; over; on
【之字路】an S-shaped road
【之外】besides this; in addition

四畫

乍 30
ㄓㄚˋ zhà
1. at first; for the first time 2. suddenly; unexpectedly
【乍見】①to meet for the first time ②to see suddenly

乎 31
ㄏㄨ hū
1. at; in; from; than 2. an interrogative particle 3. an exclamatory particle

乏 32
ㄈㄚˊ fá
1. in want of; deficient; lack 2. exhausted; tired 3. poverty-stricken; poor
【乏善可陳】to have nothing good to report
【乏味】monotonous; dull; insipid

五畫

乒 33
ㄆㄧㄥ pīng
used for the sound: 乒乓球 table tennis

七畫

乖 34
ㄍㄨㄞ guāi
1. to oppose; to contradict; to be at variance 2. perverse; obstinate; untoward; sulky 3. obedient; well-behaved 4. cunning; artful; crafty; wily
【乖僻】unreasonable; eccentric
【乖戾】cantankerous; perverse
【乖乖】①submissive; docile; obedient ②an endearing name for children
【乖巧】clever; ingenious
【乖張】recalcitrant

九畫

乘 35
1. ㄔㄥˊ chéng
1. to ride; to mount 2. to avail oneself of; to take advantage of 3. to multiply
【乘馬】to ride a horse
【乘冪 or 乘方】(mathematics) power
【乘法】(arithmetic) multiplication
【乘風破浪】great ambition
【乘涼】to cool oneself in the shade
【乘龍快婿】an ideal son-in-law
【乘客】a passenger
【乘號】the sign of multiplication
【乘積】(arithmetic) the product
【乘機】①to avail oneself of an opportunity; to seize the right time ②to ride an airplane
【乘興】on the spur of the moment
【乘興而往，敗興而歸】to go with great enthusiasm and return disappointed
【乘虛而入】to take advantage of a weak point
【乘除】(literally) multiplication and division—wax and wane
【乘勢】to take advantage of circumstances
【乘勝追擊】to pursue enemy troops in retreat
【乘數】multiplicator or multiplier

【乘人之危】to take advantage of somebody when he is not in a position to resist

乘 35
2. ㄕㄥˋ shèng
1. historical records 2. an ancient carriage 3. Buddhist teaching—a conveyance to bring the truth to men and help them 4. a team of four horses

乙部
ㄧˇ yǐ

乙 36
ㄧˇ yǐ
1. the second of the Ten Celestial Stems 2. one 3. someone
【乙醇】ethanol; alcohol

一畫

乜 37
1. ㄇㄧㄝ miē
【乜斜】to glance sideways

乜 37
2. ㄋㄧㄝˋ niè
a very rare Chinese family name

九 38
ㄐㄧㄡˇ jiǔ
nine; ninth
【九大行星】the nine planets in the solar system—Mercury, Venus, Earth, Mars, Jupiter, Saturn, Uranus, Neptune, and Pluto
【九牛二虎】a herculean effort
【九牛一毛】an iota from a vast quantity
【九鍊成鋼】Mastery is the result of long practice or training.
【九九表】the multiplication table up to nine times nine
【九泉(地下)】Hades; the underworld
【九霄雲外】beyond the farthest limits of the sky—far, far away
【九州】①another name for ancient China ②Kyushu, an island of Japan
【九成】ninety percent
【九死一生】grave danger
【九月】① September ② the ninth month of the lunar calendar ③ nine months

二畫

乞 39
ㄑㄧˇ qǐ
to ask for alms; to beg
【乞貸 or 乞借】to beg for a loan
【乞討】to beg for food, money, etc.
【乞憐】to beg for pity and charity
【乞丐】a beggar
【乞求】to beg for; to supplicate; to implore
【乞降】to negotiate for surrender on the part of the defeated
【乞援】to ask for assistance

也 40
ㄧㄝˇ yě
1. and; also; besides; either; too 2. still 3. even 4. an expletive in Chinese writing
【也可以】① may also ② It makes no difference. 或 It's okay.
【也好】That's fine.
【也行】All right! 或That will do too.
【也許】perhaps; probably
【也是】also the same

五畫

乩 41
ㄐㄧ jī
to divine; to resolve doubts by an application to spiritual beings

七畫

乳 42
ㄖㄨˇ rǔ
1. breasts; the nipple 2. milk 3. any milk-like liquid 4. the young of animals, birds, etc. 5. to give birth 6. to triturate
【乳白】milky white; cream color
【乳名】a pet name given to a child
【乳母 or 乳娘】a wet nurse
【乳房】the udders; the breasts
【乳頭】a nipple; a teat
【乳糖】lactose; milk sugar
【乳牛】the dairy cattle; a milch cow
【乳酪】junket; curds
【乳臭未乾】very young and inexperienced like a sucking child
【乳汁】milk
【乳製品】dairy products
【乳製品工業】the dairy industry
【乳罩】a brassiere; a bra
【乳齒】milk teeth; deciduous teeth
【乳酸】lactic acid
【乳酸菌】(bacteriology) lactobacillus

【乳癌】 cancer of the breast
【乳暈】 mammary areola

十畫

乾 43
1. (乾) ㄍㄢ gān
1. clean 2. dry; dried 3. exhausted
【乾杯】 to toast 或 Bottoms up!
【乾貝 or 干貝】 a dried scallop
【乾癟】 dry and withered; shrunken
【乾冰】 dry ice
【乾麵】 dry noodles
【乾飯】 cooked rice without gravy
【乾瞪眼】 to stand by anxiously without doing anything
【乾電池】 a dry battery or cell
【乾女兒】 a nominal foster daughter
【乾酪】 cheese
【乾裂】 dry and cracked (wood, soil)
【乾糧】 dry provisions
【乾果】 dried or preserved fruit
【乾枯】 dried up; withered
【乾涸】 (said of water) to dry up
【乾旱】 drought
【乾淨 or 乾乾淨淨】 clean
【乾淨俐落】 neat and tidy; efficient
【乾洗】 dry cleaning
【乾笑】 to laugh without mirth
【乾濕表】 a psychrometer
【乾薪】 a salary for a sinecure
【乾燥】 dry
【乾燥劑】 a desiccant; a drying agent
【乾草】 hay
【乾脆】 straightforward
【乾兒(子)】 a nominal foster son

乾 43
2. ㄑㄧㄢˊ qián
1. the first of the Eight Diagrams (八卦) 2. heaven; male; a father; a sovereign

十二畫

亂 44
ㄌㄨㄢˋ luàn
1. chaos; confusion; distraction; anarchy 2. rebellion; revolt; insurrection 3. confused; perplexed; agitated; disarranged; raveled 4. out of order; out of sorts
【亂民】 rioters; mobsters
【亂罰】 to mete out unjustified punishment
【亂紛紛】 disorderly; chaotic; tumultuous
【亂黨】 a rebel party or faction
【亂來】 to act foolishly or recklessly
【亂倫】 incest
【亂喊亂叫】 to clamor; to talk wildly
【亂烘烘】 noisy and disorderly
【亂七八糟】 in confusion; topsy-turvy
【亂臣賊子】 ministers or generals who rebel against their monarch or collaborate with the enemy
【亂成一團】 topsy-turvy; in great confusion
【亂世】 times of anarchy and disorder
【亂視】 astigmatism 亦作「散光」
【亂說】 ①to say what should not be said ②to lie
【亂子】 disturbance
【亂糟糟】 ①chaotic ②confused

亅部
ㄐㄩㄝˊ jué

一畫

了 45
1. ㄌㄧㄠˇ liǎo
1. to finish; to end; to complete 2. intelligent; remarkable 3. entirely; wholly 4. to understand
【了不得】 Wonderful! 或 Excellent!
【了不起】 Wonderful!
【了當】 appropriate
【了斷】 ①to settle (a case) ②to commit suicide
【了結】 to get through with; to bring to conclusion
【了解】 to understand
【了局】 the end; the conclusion
【了事】 to finish up a matter
【了然】 to understand clearly
【了此殘生】 to end this miserable life
【了案】 to conclude a case
【了悟】 to comprehend

了 45
2. ·ㄌㄜ le
an expletive in the Chinese language

三畫

予 46
1. ㄩˊ yú
I; me

予 46
2. ㄩˇ yǔ
to give

七畫

事 47
ㄕˋ shì
1. an affair; a matter; business 2. a job; an occupation; a task 3. a service 4. duties; functions 5. a subject 6. to serve; to attend 7. to manage a business

【事倍功半】to achieve little result despite herculean effort
【事半功倍】to achieve maximum results with little effort
【事必躬親】to attend to everything personally
【事變】an incident
【事不宜遲】One must lose no time in doing something.
【事非得已】There is no other choice.
【事到如今】as things have come to such a pass
【事端】a trouble
【事態】the situation
【事例】an example; a precedent
【事故】an accident
【事過境遷】Things change with the passage of time.
【事後】after an event; afterward
【事迹】a vestige
【事蹟】the accomplishments, exploits, etc. of a person during his or her life time
【事假】private affair leave
【事件】an incident; an event
【事前 or 事先】beforehand
【事親至孝】to treat one's parents with great respect and tender affection
【事情】a matter
【事主】the victim in a criminal case
【事出有因】not entirely devoid of truth
【事實】a fact; truth; reality
【事實上】in fact; in reality
【事實勝於雄辯】Facts are more convincing than eloquent theories.
【事事】everything
【事在人爲】Human effort can achieve everything.
【事宜】① affairs; matters ② the necessary arrangements
【事已如此】things being so
【事業】① an enterprise ② a career
【事由】① the origin of a matter ② the subject (of a business letter)
【事物】things; articles; objects
【事務】business; work; general affairs
【事務所】an office
【事務員】an office clerk
【事與願違】Things do not turn out as one wishes.

二部
ㄦˋ èr

二 48
ㄦˋ èr
two; second; twice

【二八年華】(said of a girl) sixteen years of age
【二八佳人】a sixteen-year-old beauty
【二百五】(abuse) a simpleton
【二房東】a person who sublets a house rented from another
【二老】one's father and mother
【二郎腿】(to sit) cross-legged
【二愣子】a rash fellow
【二胡】a two-stringed Chinese musical instrument
【二心】disloyalty
【二重唱】(vocal) a duet
【二重奏】a duet performance on the piano
【二手貨】a used item; a second-hand commodity
【二手煙】passive smoking
【二三其德】inconsistent
【二氧化碳】carbon dioxide
【二月】① February ② the second moon of the lunar calendar ③ two months

一畫

于 49
ㄩˊ yú
1. (a particle in literary use) in; at; by; to 2. (a verb in literary use) to go or proceed; to take

【于歸】(said of a girl) to enter into matrimony
【于是】hence; consequently; thereupon

二畫

云 50
ㄩㄣˊ yún
to say; to speak

互 51
ㄏㄨˋ hù 「cally }
each other; mutually; recipro- }
【互補色】complementary colors
【互不侵犯】to refrain from invading each other
【互訪】to exchange visits 「needs }
【互通有無】to supply each other's }
【互惠】mutually beneficial
【互換】to exchange 「another }
【互相】mutually; each other; one }
【互相切磋】to improve each other by active discussion
【互爭雄長】to fight for leadership
【互助】to help each other; mutual }
【互助會】slate club ⌊help }
【互爲因果】to interact as both cause and effect

五 52
ㄨˇ wǔ
five; fifth 「asm }
【五分鐘熱度】short-lived enthusi- }
【五大洲】the five continents—Asia, Africa, Europe, the Americas, and Oceania
【五體投地】① to prostrate oneself ② to admire someone with the utmost sincerity
【五內 or 五臟】the five viscera—the heart, the lungs, the liver, the kidneys, and the spleen
【五更】the fifth watch of the night which is about 4 a.m.
【五穀】grains of all sorts
【五官】①the five organs—the ear, the eye, the mouth, the nose and the heart ② the five senses—visual, auditory, olfactory, gustatory and tactile senses
【五花八門】rich in variety
【五花肉】streaky pork
【五金】① the five metals—gold, silver, copper, iron, and tin ② metals in general ③ hardware
【五金店】a hardware store
【五經】*The Five Classics*—the Confucian canon comprising *The Book of Changes*(易經), *The Book of Odes*(詩經), *The Book of History*(書經), *The Book of Rites*(禮記), and *The Spring and Autumn Annals*(春秋)
【五權憲法】the five-power constitution of the Republic of China outlined by Dr. Sun Yat-sen
【五線譜】(music) a staff
【五行】the five primary elements—metal, wood, water, fire and earth
【五指】the five fingers—the thumb, the index finger, the middle finger, the ring finger, the little finger 「kettle black. }
【五十步笑百步】The pot calls the }
【五日京兆】office held for a short time only 「black }
【五彩】blue, yellow, red, white and }
【五一勞動節】May (or Labor) Day
【五顏六色】of variegated colors
【五味】the five flavors—sweet, sour, bitter, pungent, salty
【五月】① May ② the fifth moon of the lunar calendar ③ five months
【五月節】the Dragon Boat Festival

井 53
ㄐㄧㄥˇ jǐng
a well
【井底蛙】a person of very limited outlook and experience
【井井有條】systematic; orderly
【井水不犯河水】not to interfere with each other's affairs
【井然】orderly
【井鹽】well salt

四畫

亙 54
ㄍㄣˋ gèn
(又讀 ㄍㄥˋ gèng)
to extend (over space or time)
【亙古未有】unprecedented

六畫

些 55
ㄒㄧㄝ xiē
a small quantity or number; a little; a few; some
【些微】① very little ② slightly

亞 56
ㄧㄚˋ yà (又讀 ㄧㄚˇ yǎ)
1. second (in excellence) 2. }
【亞麻】flax ⌊Asia }
【亞馬遜河】the Amazon River in }
【亞當】Adam ⌊South America }
【亞軍】the runner-up

二部

【亞洲 or 亞細亞洲】Asia
【亞熱帶】the subtropical zone

七畫

57 **亟** ㄐㄧˊ jí
urgently; pressingly
【亟欲】very anxious to do something

亠部 ㄊㄡˊ tóu

一畫

58 **亡** ㄨㄤˊ wáng
1. to perish 2. to flee 3. lost; dead 4. the late
【亡命】to go into exile; to escape (from justice) to a place far away from home
【亡命之徒】criminals
【亡故】dead; died
【亡國】① a subjugated nation ② fall of a nation
【亡國奴】conquered (or subjugated) people
【亡魂】the spirit of the dead
【亡羊補牢】to take precaution after suffering a loss

二畫

59 **亢** ㄎㄤˋ kàng
1. proud 2. indomitable 3. excessive
【亢奮】stimulated; excited

四畫

60 **交** ㄐㄧㄠ jiāo
1. to submit; to hand in or over 2. to meet 3. to exchange 4. to intersect
【交白卷兒】to turn in a blank examination paper
【交保】to release (a suspect) on bail
【交班】to hand over to the next shift
【交臂】very close or near
【交兵】to fight (between nations)
【交迫】beleaguered; beset
【交配】①(biology) copulation ②to mate
【交鋒】to engage in battle
【交付】① to hand over ② to make payment
【交代】① to hand over responsibility ② to give an explanation
【交(叉)點】a point of intersection
【交(頭接)耳】to whisper in each other's ears
【交談】to converse
【交替】to alternate
【交通】① traffic ② communication
【交通部】Ministry of Communications
【交通警察】traffic police
【交流】to flow across each other
【交流電】an alternating current
【交割】a business transaction
【交給】to hand to; to give to
【交口稱讚】to praise somebody or something unanimously
【交互作用】interaction; interplay
【交貨】to deliver goods; delivery
【交還】to hand back; to return
【交換】to exchange
【交集】(said of different feelings) to be mixed
【交際】social intercourse
【交際費】entertainment fees
【交際舞】a social dance
【交加】to act upon (something) or to hit (someone) simultaneously by two or more forces
【交接】① to make contact with each other ② to adjoin each other ③ to hand over and to take over (duties)
【交界】a border (between two areas)
【交卷】①to hand in the examination paper ② to complete an assignment
【交情】friendship
【交心】to be frank with others
【交響樂】a symphony; symphonic music
【交響樂團】an orchestra
【交織】to interlace; to interweave
【交戰】to wage war against each other
【交戰國】a belligerent state
【交叉】to cross each other; to intersect
【交差】to report what one has done in the line of duty
【交出】to surrender; to hand over
【交涉】to negotiate; negotiation
【交手】to exchange blows (in a fight)
【交錯】to interlock
【交易】a trade; business transac-

tion
【交易所】a stock exchange; a bourse
【交易物品】a barter
【交誼】friendly relations; amity
【交遊】①to have friendly contact with ②friends
【交友】to make friends
【交惡】to be on unfriendly terms
【交尾】(said of birds) to mate
【交往】to have friendly relations

亥 61 ㄏㄞˋ hài
1. the last of the Twelve Terrestrial Branches 2. the hours between 9 and 11 p.m.

亦 62 ㄧˋ yì
also; too
【亦步亦趨】to follow the example of another person at each move
【亦即】that is; i.e.; namely; viz.
【亦然】also; too; similarly

五畫

亨 63 ㄏㄥ hēng
to go through smoothly
【亨通】to go well

六畫

享 64 ㄒㄧㄤˇ xiǎng
1. to enjoy; to receive 2. to offer 3. to entertain
【享福】to enjoy happiness and prosperity
【享年 or 享壽】the number of years lived (by one who dies old)
【享樂】to seek pleasure; to make merry
【享受】to enjoy; to indulge oneself in
【享有】to possess; to have in possession
【享用】to enjoy the use of

京 65 ㄐㄧㄥ jīng
1. the capital (of a country); a metropolis 2. great; greatness
【京畿】the capital and vicinity
【京戲 or 京劇】Peking opera
【京城 or 京師】the capital

七畫

亭 66 ㄊㄧㄥˊ tíng
1. a booth; a pavilion; a garden house or rest house 2. slim and erect 3. exactly during
【亭亭玉立】slim and graceful

亮 67 ㄌㄧㄤˋ liàng
1. bright; lustrous; brilliant; luminous; radiant; clear 2. to display; to show
【亮度】brightness; luminosity
【亮光】bright light; flash
【亮晶晶】dazzling; glistening; radiant
【亮相 or 亮像兒】to pose for the audience's admiration on the stage

人部 ㄖㄣˊ rén

人 68 ㄖㄣˊ rén
a human being; a person; people
【人本主義 or 人文主義】humanism
【人不可貌相】A man's worth cannot be measured by his looks.
【人不知鬼不覺】without the knowledge of anybody else
【人怕出名豬怕肥】Fame portends trouble for people.
【人品】character (of a person); personality
【人馬】①traffic (consisting of people and horses) ②troops (consisting of soldiers and horses)
【人滿之患】trouble of overpopulation
【人面獸心】a wolf in sheep's clothing
【人民】people
【人民團體】a civic organization
【人民陣線】the popular front
【人命關天】Human life is of utmost importance.
【人犯】a criminal; a suspect (in a criminal case)
【人道】philanthropy; humanitarianism
【人地生疏】to have trouble getting about in a strange land because of unfamiliarity with the local people and their customs
【人定勝天】Man's determination will conquer nature.
【人多嘴雜】Agreement is difficult

if there are too many people.
【人體】a human body
【人類】man; mankind; the human race
【人力】human power or strength
【人格】character; personality
【人工】① human labor ② man-made
【人工呼吸】artificial respiration
【人口】population
【人口密度】density of population
【人口統計】population statistics
【人口過剩】overpopulation
【人海浮沈】the vicissitudes of life
【人海戰術】human-sea tactics
【人際關係】human relation
【人家】a human abode
【人傑地靈】The birth (or presence) of heroes brings glory to a place.
【人間】the world of mortals
【人間地獄】pandemonium
【人見人愛】loved by all
【人盡可夫】(said of women) promiscuous
【人情】human sentiment, emotion or feeling
【人情世故】the ways of the world
【人情味】friendliness; hospitality
【人權】human rights
【人羣】a crowd, throng or multitude (of people)
【人窮志短】Poverty stifles ambition.
【人小鬼大】young but tricky
【人心】human heart, will or feeling
【人心不同，各如其面】Individual thinking is as varied as individual looks.
【人心不古】Public morality is not what it used to be.
【人心皇皇】jittery or panicky
【人像】a portrait; an image
【人行道】a sidewalk; a footpath
【人性】human nature
【人選】candidates (for certain jobs)
【人之常情】what is natural in human relationships
【人質】a hostage
【人證】witnesses
【人中】philtrum
【人種】human races
【人臣】a vassal
【人稱】①(grammar) the first, second or third person ②a nickname by which one is known
【人稱代名詞】a personal pronoun
【人師】a paragon
【人士】personages (usually plural)
【人世】the world
【人事】① human affairs ② personnel affairs ③ human endeavors
【人事關係】personal connections
【人手】①manpower ②a human hand
【人壽保險】life insurance
【人山人海】a large crowd
【人參】ginseng
【人生】human life; life
【人生觀】a view of life; an outlook on life
【人生如夢】Life is but a dream.
【人肉市場】the sex market; houses of ill fame
【人人】everybody
【人人自危】Everyone feels insecure.
【人瑞】a very old man or woman, considered a happy omen for the whole human race
【人造or人爲】man-made; artificial; imitation
【人造寶石】an imitation jewel
【人造絲】synthetic silk; rayon
【人造衛星】a satellite
【人造雨】artificial rain
【人贓並獲】(a thief or robber) caught together with the loot
【人才】a man of ability; a talent
【人才輩出】Great talents appear successively (or continuously).
【人才濟濟】There is a wealth of talents.
【人才外流】the brain drain
【人存政舉，人亡政息】The policies and regulations of an organization shift with the change of the person in charge.
【人煙】signs of a human settlement
【人言可畏】Criticisms should be feared.
【人言嘖嘖】There are plenty of criticisms.
【人仰馬翻】to suffer an utter defeat
【人影 or 人影兒】a human shadow
【人物】① a personage or figure ② people and things
【人物畫】portrait painting
【人爲萬物之靈】The human being is the most intelligent among creatures.
【人文】① humanities ② human affairs
【人文地理】human geography
【人文薈萃】(said of culture centers) gathering of talents
【人員】the personnel; the staff

【人猿】 an ape
【人緣】 relations with others
【人云亦云】 me-tooism; me-too

二畫

什 69 1. ㄕˊ shí
1. sundry; miscellaneous 2. ten 3. a squad (of ten soldiers, in former times)
【什錦】 multiple ingredients (for a dish); assorted

什 69 2. (甚) ㄕㄜˊ shé
【什麼】 what

仁 70 ㄖㄣˊ rén
1. benevolence; humanity; mercy; kindness; charity 2. kernel
【仁民愛物】 to love all people and animals
【仁厚】 benevolent and generous
【仁至義盡】 Everything to be expected in the light of benevolence and duty has been done.
【仁政】 humanitarian rule
【仁人君子】 kind-hearted gentlemen
【仁慈】 charity; kindness
【仁愛】 humanity; philanthropy
【仁義道德】 virtue and morality

仄 71 ㄗㄜˋ zè
1. oblique 2. said of the three tones other than the even tone (in ancient Chinese phonology) 3. narrow 4. uneasy

仆 72 ㄆㄨ pū (又讀 ㄈㄨˋ fù)
1. to prostrate 2. to fall

仇 73 (讎) ㄔㄡˊ chóu
1. a foe; an enemy; a rival; an adversary 2. hatred; enmity; antagonism; hostility 3. to hate
【仇恨】 ① hatred; enmity ② to hate
【仇視】 to regard with hostility
【仇殺】 a murder committed out of vendetta
【仇人】 an enemy; a foe

今 74 ㄐㄧㄣ jīn
1. present; recent; modern 2. now; currently; presently; nowadays 3. immediately; right away
【今非昔比】 Time has changed and the good old days are gone.
【今天 or 今日】 today
【今年】 this year
【今後】 hereafter; henceforward; from now on
【今朝】 today; this morning
【今世】 ① the present era ② this present life
【今生】 this present life
【今夜】 tonight

介 75 ㄐㄧㄝˋ jiè
1. a shelled aquatic animal 2. to lie between 3. (said of one's character) upright 4. great and honorable 5. to aid; to benefit 6. tiny
【介殼】 the shell
【介紹】 to introduce (a person to another)
【介紹人】 an introducer; a matchmaker
【介入】 to get involved; to interfere with
【介詞】 a preposition
【介意】 to mind; to heed
【介於】 to lie in between

仍 76 ㄖㄥˊ réng
still; yet: 仍舊 or 仍然 still; yet

三畫

仔 77 1. ㄗˇ zǐ
careful: 仔細 careful; punctilious; attentive

仔 77 2. ㄗㄞˇ zǎi
1. young animals 2. one who tends cattle

仕 78 ㄕˋ shì
1. an official 2. to enter government service
【仕途 or 仕塗】 the career in government service
【仕女】 ① young men and women ② a painting portraying beautiful women
【仕宦】 to be an official

他 79 ㄊㄚ tā
1. he; him 2. other; another 3. future
【他們】 they; them
【他方】 the other party (to a transaction, dispute, etc.)
【他鄉】 other lands or strange lands
【他鄉遇故知】 to run across an old friend in a distant land
【他殺】 homicide (as opposed to suicide)
【他山之石, 可以攻玉】 Advice from

〔人部〕

others may help one overcome one's defects. 「time in the past
【他日】① another day ② some」
【他人】other people; somebody else

〔人部〕

仗 80
ㄓㄤˋ zhàng

1. weaponry 2. to lean upon; to rely upon; to depend on 3. battle; war
【仗勢欺人】to bully the weaker on one's strength or power, or connection with powerful people
【仗義執言】to speak in accordance with justice
【仗義疏財】to think little of one's fortune in one's enthusiasm for charity, etc.

付 81
ㄈㄨˋ fù

1. to pay (money) 2. to consign; to deliver (goods)
【付託】to entrust; to commission
【付款 or 付錢】to pay (money)
【付款交單】documents against payment
【付訖 or 付清】(said of a bill, tax, etc.) paid
【付現】to pay in cash
【付之一炬 or 付丙】to burn down
【付之一笑】to laugh it away (or off)
【付賬 or 付帳】to pay a bill
【付諸實施】to put into effect
【付出】① to pay ② to give
【付郵】to post (a letter); to mail (a parcel)
【付印】①to send to (the) press for publication ②to turn over to the printing shop (after proofreading)

仙 82
ㄒㄧㄢ xiān 「2. divine

1. a god; an immortal; a fairy」
【仙風道骨】divine poise or bearing
【仙丹 or 仙藥】a panacea; a cure-all; an elixir
【仙桃】a divine peach
【仙女】a fairy
【仙境】① a fairyland ② a place of exquisite natural beauty
【仙逝 or 仙去】to die; to pass away
【仙人跳】a badger game
【仙人掌】a cactus
【仙子】a fairy; an immortal

仟 83
ㄑㄧㄢ qiān

1. leader of one thousand men 2. thousand

代 84
ㄉㄞˋ dài

1. a generation 2. a dynasty 3. an era 4. to be a substitute or an equivalent; to take the place of 「another
【代辦】to manage on behalf of」
【代筆】to write for another
【代表】①to represent; to stand for ②a representative; a delegate; a proxy
【代表團】a delegation
【代表權】representation
【代名詞】a pronoun
【代打】to pinch-hit 「substitute
【代替】to take the place of; to」
【代勞】to labor on behalf of another 「agent of; to act for
【代理】①an agent ②to serve as」
【代理商】a business agent; an agent 「tive
【代理人】an agent; a representa-」
【代溝】the generation gap
【代課】to teach on behalf of another teacher
【代號】a code name
【代換】to replace
【代價】price; cost; reward
【代簽】procuration indorsement
【代謝】① to express thanks to someone on behalf of others ② to metabolize
【代銷】to sell on consignment
【代銷商】a consignee
【代售】to be commissioned to sell something 「ments for others
【代書】one who writes legal docu-」
【代數學】algebra 「others
【代人受過】to take the blame for」
【代罪羔羊】a scapegoat
【代言】to speak in behalf of
【代言人】a spokesman; a mouthpiece 「vene for another person
【代爲說項】to intercede or inter-」
【代用】to substitute for something
【代用品】a substitute; an ersatz

令 85
1. ㄌㄧㄥˋ lìng

1. a directive; an order 2. to order 3. to cause; to make 4. nice; good; excellent
【令堂】your mother
【令郎】your son
【令出如山】Orders must be obeyed

implicitly.

【令人滿意】to make people contented

【令人髮指】to make one's blood boil

【令尊】your father

【令愛 or 令媛】your daughter

令 85
2. ㄌㄧㄥˊ líng
a ream (of paper)

以 86
ㄧˇ yǐ
by means of; because of

【以備萬一】to provide against any accidental happenings

【以暴易暴】to displace violence with violence

【以便】so as to; in order to

【以貌取人】to judge a person by his appearance or looks

【以免】in order to avoid; so as not to

【以大欺小】to bully the weak

【以德報怨】to repay injury with kindness; to return good for evil

【以毒攻毒】to fight evil with evil

【以杜後患】to forestall future trouble

【以退爲進】to make concessions in order to gain advantages

【以內】within

【以農立國】a nation based on agricultural economy

【以來】since

【以禮相待】to treat somebody with due respect

【以鄰爲壑】to profit oneself at the expense of others

【以卵投石】to fight a hopeless battle

【以寡敵衆】to fight a numerically superior enemy

【以廣招徠】in order to promote patronage or sales

【以攻爲守】to take the offensive in a basically defensive operation

【以後】after; afterward

【以及】and; including; as well as

【以假亂眞】to mix the spurious with the genuine

【以儆效尤】to warn others against making the same mistake

【以前】before

【以下】below

【以饗讀者】to offer to the reader

【以至】① up to; until ② so...that

【以致】so that; with the result that

【以身相許】(said of girls) to pledge to marry somebody

【以身殉職】to die at one's post

【以身試法】to defy the law; to dare to violate the law

【以身作則】to set examples by one's own action

【以上】above

【以柔克剛】Soft and fair goes far.

【以詞害意】to sacrifice clarity in the use of wrong words for expression

【以此類推】The rest can be done in the same manner

【以此爲戒】to take this as a lesson

【以色列】Israel

【以訛傳訛】to convey incorrectly what is already incorrect

【以一當十】to tip one against ten

【以逸待勞】to wait in comfort for an exhausted enemy

【以牙還牙】an eye for an eye, a tooth for a tooth

【以外】① other than; besides ② outside; beyond

【以爲】to regard...as; to think; to consider

【以文會友】to gather friends together for literary activities

【以往】in the past; formerly

【以怨報德】to bite the hand that feeds one

仨 87
ㄙㄚ sā
three (Peking colloquialism)

四畫

仰 88
ㄧㄤˇ yǎng
1. to look up 2. to adore, admire or revere 3. to lean or rely upon 4. to swallow

【仰慕】to adore; to admire and respect

【仰天長嘯】to make a long cry into the air

【仰賴】to look to (somebody for help); to rely upon

【仰角】an angle of elevation

【仰仗】to rely on

【仰人鼻息】to rely on others and have to watch their every expression

【仰臥】to lie on the back

【仰臥起坐】(sports) sit-up

【仰泳】(sports) backstroke

仲 89
ㄓㄨㄥˋ zhòng
1. in the middle; between two entities 2. the second in order of birth

【仲冬】midwinter

【仲秋】midautumn

【仲夏】midsummer

〔人部〕

【仲春】midspring
【仲裁】to arbitrate; arbitration

仳 90
ㄆㄧˇ pǐ
to part company 「to divorce
【仳離】to part (from one's spouse); 」

件 91
ㄐㄧㄢˋ jiàn
an auxiliary noun applied to things, clothes, etc.

任 92
ㄖㄣˋ rèn
1. a duty 2. to let (one act at will) 3. to employ (one for a job) 4. to bear (a burden) 5. an official post; office
【任憑】without restriction; (to allow someone to do something) at will
【任免】employment and discharge
【任命】to appoint; appointment
【任勞任怨】to do something without complaint despite hardships and criticisms
【任何】any; whatever
【任期】the tenure of office
【任性】doing as one pleases; unrestrained 「office
【任職】to hold a post; to be in 」
【任重道遠】The load is heavy, while the way is long.
【任人唯賢】to appoint a person according to his ability and 「virtue
【任意】arbitrary; at will 」
【任務】duty; responsibility 「gage
【任用】to employ; to hire; to en- 」

仿 93
(倣) ㄈㄤˇ fǎng
as in 仿效—to imitate; to copy
【仿製 or 仿造】to manufacture an imitation of something already in market
【仿製品】an imitation
【仿照】to pattern after

企 94
ㄑㄧˋ qì
1. to stand on tiptoe 2. to hope; to long; to expect
【企盼 or 企望】to expect or hope with eagerness 「a plan
【企圖】①to intend; to attempt ② 」
【企圖心】enterprising spirit
【企管】business management
【企劃】to design; to lay out; to plan
【企求】to desire; to hanker for
【企鵝】a penguin
【企業】an enterprise
【企業家】an entrepreneur
【企望】to hope for; to look for- 「ward to

伉 95
ㄎㄤˋ kàng
a spouse: 伉儷 a married couple

伊 96
ㄧ yī
1. he; she 2. a Chinese family 「name
【伊甸樂園】the Garden of Eden
【伊拉克】Iraq
【伊朗】Iran
【伊索寓言】*Aesop's Fables*

伍 97
ㄨˇ wǔ
1. a military unit of five soldiers (in the Chou Dynasty) 2. as in 行伍—the army 3. to associate 「4. five

伎 98
ㄐㄧˋ jì 「ty; skill; craft
talent; ability; skill: 伎倆dexteri- 」

伏 99
ㄈㄨˊ fú
1. to prostrate; to yield 2. to hide; to lie in ambush
【伏兵】an ambush 「be executed
【伏法or伏誅】to plead guilty and 」
【伏地挺身】push-up
【伏特】(electricity) a volt
【伏貼】① fitting ② to acknowledge someone's merits, etc. sincerely
【伏擊】to attack from ambush
【伏尸遍野】The battlefield is littered with the (enemy) dead.
【伏罪】①to admit guilt ②to be executed

伐 100
ㄈㄚ fā (又讀 ㄈㄚˊ fá)
1. to cut (wood) 2. to attack; to 「smite
【伐木】to fell trees 」

休 101
ㄒㄧㄡ xiū
1. rest; to rest 2. to stop; to cease 3. happiness; joy; weal
【休兵 or 休戰】① to stop fighting ② a truce; an armistice
【休克】shock
【休火山】a dormant volcano
【休會】to adjourn a meeting
【休假】a holiday; to have a holiday
【休戚相關】to share joys and sorrows with each other
【休息】to take a rest; rest

【休閒】leisure; relaxation; ease
【休閒服】casual wear; sports wear
【休想】to stop thinking
【休學】a leave of absence (for a considerable period of time) from school
【休止】to stop; to cease
【休止符】a sign of rests in staff notation
【休業】to suspend business; to close the store (for a holiday)
【休業式】a semester closing ceremony
【休養】to rest; to recuperate
【休養生息】to recuperate and multiply

伙 102 ㄏㄨㄛˇ huǒ
1. a companion; a colleague 2. household goods
【伙伴】a companion; a colleague
【伙房】a kitchen
【伙夫or伙頭軍】a cook (in military troops)
【伙同】in league with
【伙計】a shop clerk
【伙食】meals
【伙食團】a mess

五畫

伯 103 ㄅㄛˊ bó (又讀 ㄅㄞˇ bǎi)
1. one's father's elder brother; an uncle 2. a rank of the nobility—a count
【伯母】an aunt
【伯父】an uncle
【伯爵】a count
【伯爵夫人】a countess
【伯仲之間】about the same

估 104 1. ㄍㄨ gū
to estimate; to calculate; to evaluate
【估量 or 估計】to estimate; to calculate; to reckon; to conjecture
【估價】to evaluate; to appraise
【估價單】a list of cost estimate

估 104 2. ㄍㄨˋ gù
to sell (used clothing)
【估衣鋪】a secondhand clothes store

你 105 ㄋㄧˇ nǐ
you (singular)
【你們】you (plural)
【你好】How do you do? 或 How are you?
【你死我活】(to fight) until either of the combatants is killed

伴 106 ㄅㄢˋ bàn
1. a companion 2. to accompany
【伴娘】the maid of honor
【伴郎】the best man
【伴侶】a companion; a pal
【伴唱】① a vocal accompaniment ② to accompany (a singer)
【伴唱機】a karaoke 亦作「卡拉OK」
【伴奏】to accompany (a soloist)
【伴隨】to accompany; to follow
【伴舞】to be a dancing partner

伶 107 ㄌㄧㄥˊ líng
1. a drama performer; a theatrical performer; an actor; an actress 2. lonely; solitary 3. clever; intelligent
【伶仃】lonely; solitary
【伶俐】clever; intelligent; smart
【伶牙利齒】eloquent

伸 108 ㄕㄣ shēn
1. to stretch; to extend; to straighten 2. to report
【伸頭探腦】to crane, or stretch the neck in an effort to find out
【伸懶腰】to stretch and yawn
【伸開】to stretch out; to extend
【伸展】to stretch; to spread out
【伸張】to expand (power)
【伸張正義】to be a champion of justice
【伸出】to stretch outward
【伸手】to reach out one's hand
【伸訴】to present a complaint
【伸縮】to expand and contract
【伸縮性】flexibility; elasticity
【伸冤】to clear up a false charge

伺 109 1. ㄙ sì
to spy; to reconnoiter; to watch
【伺探】to investigate secretly
【伺機】to wait for one's chance
【伺機而動】to wait for a favorable moment to make a move

伺 109 2. ㄘˋ cì
to serve: 伺候to wait, or stten upon; to serve

似 110 ㄙˋ sì
1. to resemble; to seem 2. like; as if
【似乎】it seems, appears, or looks

〔人部〕

as if or as though
【似是而非】 seemingly correct but really incorrect

〔人部〕

佃 111 ㄉㄧㄢˋ diàn
1. a tenant farmer 2. to tenant a farm 3. hunting
【佃農】 a tenant farmer or share-cropper
【佃戶】 a tenant (of a farm)
【佃租】 land rent

但 112 ㄉㄢˋ dàn
as in 但是—but; however; yet
【但使】 only if; as long as
【但書】 a proviso; a condition
【但說無妨】 Just speak out what is in your mind.
【但願】 to wish; to hope

佇 113 ㄓㄨˋ zhù
1. to stand (for a long time) 2. to hope; to expect
【佇立】 to stand still; to stand motionless

佈 114 ㄅㄨˋ bù
1. to announce; to declare 2. to arrange
【佈滿】 to be covered with
【佈道】 to evangelize
【佈告】 ① a bulletin ② to make public announcement
【佈景】 scenery (for the stage)
【佈局】 the layout
【佈置】 to make arrangement
【佈施】 to make a contribution to a relief fund

位 115 ㄨㄟˋ wèi
1. position; rank 2. location
【位居津要】 to occupy a key position
【位置】 ①position (in space); location ②position (in an organization)
【位子】 a seat
【位於】 situated at; located at
【位元】 (computers) a bit

低 116 ㄉㄧ dī
1. low 2. to lower
【低迷】 (said of the sky, clouds, etc.) turbid
【低頭】 to bow one's head
【低能兒】 a mentally retarded child
【低欄】 (sports) low hurdles
【低劣】 poor in quality
【低廉】 cheap; low
【低落】 low; downcast
【低估】 to underestimate
【低級】 ①elementary; rudimentary ②vulgar; low
【低級趣味】 bad taste; vulgar interests
【低氣壓】 low atmospheric pressure
【低血糖】 (medicine) hypoglycemia
【低潮】 a low tide; a low ebb
【低沈】 low and heavy
【低垂】 to hang low
【低聲下氣】 to be meek and timid; to be submissive
【低人一等】 inferior to others
【低三下四】 lowly; mean
【低壓】 ①low pressure ②low voltage
【低窪】 low-lying (ground)
【低微】 ① mean; base; menial ② humble
【低溫】 ① low temperature ② (meteorology) microtherm
【低溫殺菌】 low temperature sterilization

住 117 ㄓㄨˋ zhù
1. to dwell; to inhabit; to live 2. to stop 3. used after verb to complement its meaning
【住口】 ①to stop talking ②Shut up!
【住戶】 a resident family
【住家】 a residence; a home
【住址】 address
【住宅】 a residence; a dwelling; a house
【住宅區】 a residential area, district or quarter
【住處】 a residence; a dwelling; lodging; a domicile
【住手】 ① Stop! ② to halt; to hold
【住宿】 to stay overnight; to lodge
【住院】 to be hospitalized
【住院醫師】 a resident (in a hospital)

佐 118 ㄗㄨㄛˇ zuǒ
to assist; to aid; to second
【佐理】 to assist
【佐證】 the evidence
【佐餐】 to be eaten together with rice

佑 119 ㄧㄡˋ yòu
to help; to protect; to aid; to bless

佔 120 ㄓㄢˋ zhàn
to seize; to usurp; to occupy; to take by force
【佔便宜】 to take advantage
【佔領】 to occupy; to capture
【佔領軍】 occupation troops

【佔據】to occupy; to take possession of
【佔線】The line's busy (or engaged).
【佔上風】to have the upper hand
【佔有】①to own; to have ②to occupy

何 121
ㄏㄜˊ hé
what; how; where; why
【何必or何須】why should; why is it necessary
【何不】why not
【何妨】There is no harm (trying, doing, etc.).
【何等】①how ②what sort of
【何樂不爲】Why not do it gladly?
【何干】What has that got to do with...?
【何故】why; for what reason
【何苦】Why take the trouble?
【何況】much less; not to mention; let alone
【何去何從】choice (of action)
【何止】far more than
【何至於】How could it have turned out (like that)? 或 How come?
【何者】which one
【何嘗】How (could it be an exception)?
【何處】where; in what place
【何時】when; at what time
【何事】What (do you want)?
【何在】①Where is (that particular thing)? ②What is (that particular reason)?
【何足掛齒】Don't mention it. (used in formal speech)
【何謂】what is meant by

余 122
ㄩˊ yú
1.(in formal speech) I; me 2. a Chinese family name

佛 123
ㄈㄛˊ fó
1.Buddha (Sakyamuni 釋迦牟尼)
2.of Buddhism
【佛門】Buddhism; the Buddhist faith
【佛法】the Buddhist doctrines
【佛堂】a Buddhist sanctuary
【佛徒】a Buddhist disciple; a Buddhist
【佛陀】Buddha
【佛家】a Buddhist
【佛教】Buddhism
【佛經】the Buddhist scriptures; the Sutras
【佛像】a statue of Buddha
【佛學】Buddhistic study
【佛手】bergamot
【佛祖】①Buddha ②Buddhist patriarchs
【佛寺】a Buddhist temple

作 124
1. ㄗㄨㄛˋ zuò
1.to do; to make 2.the works (of a writer, etc.) 3. to rise up 4. to pretend; to affect 5. to regard...as; to take...for 6. to write; to compose
【作罷】to drop; to give up
【作保】to guarantee; to vouch for
【作伴】to keep (someone) company; to serve as a companion
【作弊】to cheat (especially in examinations); to indulge in corrupt practices
【作陪】to accompany
【作品】the works
【作媒】to act as a go-between in marriage
【作夢】① to dream ② to imagine as in a dream; to have daydreams
【作法】a way of doing or handling things
【作法自斃】to get into trouble through one's own scheme
【作廢】to nullify; to cancel
【作風】one's way of doing things
【作對】to oppose; to act against
【作東】to stand treat
【作態】to strike an attitude
【作孽 or 作歹】to do evil
【作弄】to tease; to make a fool of
【作樂】to make merry; to have fun
【作亂】to rebel; to start an uprising
【作梗】to oppose secretly
【作古】to die; to pass away
【作怪】mischievous; to act mischievously
【作官】to be a government official
【作工】to labor; to work
【作客】①to be a guest ②to stay outside of one's hometown
【作活】to work (for one's living)
【作家】a writer; an author
【作假 or 作僞】to pretend; to make an imitation copy
【作嫁】to earn a living by working for others
【作姦犯科】to do evil; to break the law
【作繭自縛】to get into trouble by one's own schemes
【作曲】to compose
【作曲家】a composer
【作秀】(informal) ①to appear in a stage show ②to grandstand
【作者】a writer; an author

【作戰】to go to battle; to fight against
【作證】to act as a witness in court
【作主】to take up responsibility for making a decision
【作輟】working and stopping
【作詩】to write poems; to versify
【作勢】to put on airs; to pretend
【作壽】to celebrate a birthday
【作聲】to speak; to break silence
【作殊死戰】to fight to the bitter end
【作祟】①(said of spirits) to haunt ②(said of people) to make mischief
【作惡多端】to indulge in all sorts of evildoing
【作嘔】to nauseate
【作案】to commit a crime
【作業】students' homework
【作業系統】(computers) the operating system
【作物】crops
【作威作福】to overexert one's power and position by acting impudently
【作爲】① conduct; behavior ② to accomplish ③ to serve as; to look upon as
【作文】①to write a composition ②a composition
【作用】① functions ② effect

作 124
2. ㄗㄨㄛ zuō
【作坊】a small workshop

作 124
3. ㄗㄨㄛˊ zuó
【作踐】to abuse; to waste; to treat harshly
【作興】① allowable ② to be in good spirits ③ in vogue ④ to hold in high regard ⑤perhaps; likely

佞 125
ㄋㄧㄥˋ nìng
1. eloquent; persuasive; gifted with a glib tongue 2. obsequious; fawning 3. to believe (in superstition) 4. one given to flattery

六畫

佩 126
ㄆㄟˋ pèi
1. to wear; to carry 2. to admire; to adore 3. to be grateful 4. something worn on a girdle or clothing; a pendant
【佩服】to admire; to respect
【佩帶】to wear; to carry
【佩勳章】to wear medals

佯 127
ㄧㄤˊ yáng
1. to pretend; to feign; to sham 2. false; deceitful; feigning
【佯病】to pretend to be ill
【佯狂】to feign madness
【佯作不知】to feign ignorance; to pretend not to know
【佯死】to feign death; to pretend to be dead

佳 128
ㄐㄧㄚ jiā
1. beautiful; good; fine 2. auspicious 3. distinguished
【佳賓】distinguished or honored guests
【佳節】a festival; a carnival
【佳句】a quotable qutoe
【佳期】the wedding or nuptial day
【佳人】a beauty
【佳作】an excellent (literary) work
【佳偶】a happily married couple
【佳偶天成】an ideal couple
【佳餚】a delicacy
【佳音】good news

佼 129
ㄐㄧㄠˇ jiǎo
1. beautiful; handsome; attractive; charming 2. outstanding
【佼好】pretty; pleasant
【佼佼者】an outstanding person

使 130
1. ㄕˇ shǐ
1. to use; to employ; to apply 2. to make; to act 3. to indulge in 4. to send as diplomatic personnel; diplomatic envoys 5. if
【使命】a mission
【使得】①all right; can be done or used ②to make; to cause
【使女】a maidservant; a housemaid
【使壞】①to be up to mischief; to play a dirty trick ②to destroy
【使喚】①to run errands for ②to order others to do something
【使勁】to exert effort
【使性子】to lose one's temper
【使出】to exert
【使出渾身解數】to do one's best (in order to please or impress somebody)
【使眼色】to make eyes at
【使用】to use; to employ
【使用年限】the tenure of use

使 130
2. ㄕˋ shì
(或讀ㄕˇ shǐ)
1. to be appointed as a diplomatic envoy; to be an ambassador to 2. an envoy; an emissary; a minister
【使領館】embassies and consulates
【使館】a legation; an embassy
【使者】an envoy; an emissary

侃 131
ㄎㄢˇ kǎn
1. straightforward; frank; bold; open 2. amiable; pleasant 3. with confidence and composure
【侃侃而談】to talk with confidence and composure

來 132
ㄌㄞˊ lái
1. to come; coming; to arrive 2. to return; to come back; returning
【來賓】a guest; a visitor
【來不及】unable to make it in time
【來犯】to come to attack us
【來訪】to come to visit
【來福槍】a rifle
【來得及】there is time for...
【來到】to arrive; to come
【來頭】personal connections
【來年】the next year; the years to come
【來來往往】coming and going in great numbers
【來歷】past history; origin; background
【來歷不明】of questionable antecedents, source, origin, background, etc.
【來臨】to arrive; to approach; to come
【來路】source; (personal) background
【來路不明】of questionable origin
【來龍去脈】the beginning and subsequent development of (an incident, etc.)
【來函 or 來信】your letter
【來回】coming and going; to come and go
【來回票】a round-trip ticket
【來件】the communication received
【來信】①your letter ②to send a letter here
【來者不拒】to grant favors to whoever asks for it
【來世】①later generations ②(Buddhism) the future life
【來勢】oncoming force
【來勢洶洶】to move threateningly towards
【來生】the next life or incarnation
【來日】①tomorrow ②the future
【來日方長】There is a long time ahead.
【來人】①the person or persons who came or are coming ②the incoming envoy, messenger, etc.
【來意】the purpose of a personal call
【來由】reason; cause
【來文】incoming documents, letters, etc.
【來往】①social intercourse or connection ②coming and going
【來源】the source; the origin

侈 133
ㄔˇ chǐ
1. wasteful; luxurious; lavish; extravagant 2. to exaggerate; bragging 3. evildoing 4. excessive
【侈靡】extravagant; wasteful
【侈言】to exaggerate; to swagger

例 134
ㄌㄧˋ lì
1. a regulation; a rule; a custom 2. a precedent 3. an example; an instance 4. regular; routine
【例假】a statutory holiday; a customary holiday; a legal holiday
【例句】a sentence serving as an example
【例行公事】official routine; routine
【例證】an antecedent used to clarify or explain a point
【例如】for example; for instance; such as
【例子or例題】an example; an instance
【例外】an exception

侍 135
ㄕˋ shì
1. to serve; to wait upon 2. to accompany one's elder or superior 3. a designation for oneself when addressing an elder or a senior 4. an attendant
【侍奉】to serve; to attend on
【侍女】a maid; a maidservant
【侍候】to wait upon; to serve
【侍親】to attend one's parents
【侍者】attendants, waiters, etc.
【侍從】attendants; servants; retinue
【侍衛】bodyguards

侏 136
ㄓㄨ zhū
1. short 2. a pigmy or dwarf
【侏儒】①a dwarf ②a court jester

供 137
1. ㄍㄨㄥ gōng
to supply; to contribute to
【供不應求】The supply is unable to meet the demand.
【供電】power supply
【供過於求】The supply has outstripped the demand.
【供給】to supply; to equip; to provide
【供求】supply and demand
【供銷】supply and marketing
【供應】① to furnish ② support

供 137
2. ㄍㄨㄥˋ gòng
1. to give a statement or an account of a criminal act; to give evidence 2. to offer in worship
【供品】offerings
【供佛】to make offerings to Buddha
【供桌】the table on which sacrificial offerings are placed
【供認】to confess; a confession
【供詞】a confession to a criminal act
【供養】to offer provisions

依 138
ㄧ yī
1. to depend on; to lean to 2. to follow; to comply with; to consent; to yield to 3. to be tolerant to; to forgive 4. according to
【依憑or依靠】to rely on; to depend on
【依法】according to law
【依附】①to depend on ②to submit to
【依賴】to depend on
【依戀】to be reluctant to leave
【依舊】as usual; as before
【依據or依照】according to; in accordance with
【依稀】unclear; uncertain; not distinct
【依仗】①someone or something to fall back upon ②to rely on or count on
【依順】to be obedient
【依然】as before; as usual; still
【依此類推】The rest may be deduced by analogy.
【依次】in order (in proper sequence or position); one by one
【依存】interdependent
【依從】to comply with; to follow
【依隨】to follow (a person, a wish)
【依依不捨】unwilling to part
【依樣(畫)葫蘆】to imitate others
【依違兩可】shilly-shally
【依約】in accordance with the promise

佬 139
ㄌㄠˇ lǎo
1. a fellow; a man; a guy 2. a vulgar person; a hillbilly

七畫

侮 140
ㄨˇ wǔ
1. to bully 2. to disgrace; to insult; to humiliate 3. an insult; a bully
【侮慢】①to insult ②haughty and rude
【侮蔑】to disgrace; to slight
【侮辱】① to insult; to humiliate ② an insult

侯 141
ㄏㄡˊ hóu
1. (in ancient China) the second of the five grades of the nobility 2. the target in archery 3. a marquis; a nobleman or a high official
【侯爵】a marquis
【侯爵夫人】a marchioness

侶 142
ㄌㄩˇ lǚ
1. a companion; a mate 2. to associate with

侵 143
ㄑㄧㄣ qīn
1. to raid; to aggress 2. to encroach upon; to use force stealthily 3. to proceed gradually 4. a bad year; a year of famine or disaster
【侵犯】(law) to encroach upon other's rights; to violate; to invade
【侵奪】to seize by force
【侵呑】to misappropriate; to embezzle
【侵略】① to invade ② aggression
【侵害】to infringe or encroach upon
【侵襲】to attack stealthily
【侵佔】to take (the property, the land, etc. of another) illegally
【侵蝕】erosion; to encroach; to erode
【侵擾】to harass
【侵人犯規】(sports) a personal foul
【侵入】to intrude

侷 144
ㄐㄩˊ jú
narrow; cramped; confined
【侷處一隅】to be confined to a small place or corner
【侷促】① cramped; confined ②

fidgeting; restless
【侷促不安】 fidgeting; uneasy

便 145
1. ㄅㄧㄢˋ biàn
1. expedient; convenient; handy 2. fitting; appropriate 3. in that case; even if 4. then 5. advantageous 6. excrement and urine; to relieve oneself 7. informal; at ease; ordinary
【便帽】 a cap or hat for ordinary wear
【便祕】 constipation
【便民】 to offer greater convenience to the people
【便飯】 a meal; potluck
【便服】 ordinary clothing
【便當】 ①(ㄅㄧㄢˋ ㄉㄤ) a box lunch ②(ㄅㄧㄢˋ ˙ㄉㄤ) easy; convenient
【便條】 a note; a memo
【便溺】 to empty the bowels and to urinate
【便利】 convenience; facility
【便壺】 a chamber pot
【便捷】 easy and convenient
【便箋】 notepaper; a memo
【便鞋】 ① cloth shoes ② slippers
【便菜】 an ordinary dish
【便餐】 an informal and ordinary meal
【便所】 a toilet; a rest room
【便衣】 ① ordinary clothes; plain clothes ② a plainclothesman
【便宜行事】 to act as circumstances may require without asking for approval from superiors
【便於】 easy to; convenient to

便 145
2. ㄆㄧㄢˊ pián
cheap; inexpensive
【便佞】 a glib-tongued man
【便宜】 ①cheap; inexpensive ②to gain advantage

係 146
ㄒㄧˋ xì
1. to bind; to belong to; to attach to; to connect with 2. to be
【係數】 (mathematics) coefficient

促 147
ㄘㄨˋ cù
1. close; crowded; near 2. to urge; to hurry; to promote 3. hurried; urgent
【促進】 to urge to proceed; to promote
【促膝談心】 to sit side by side and talk intimately
【促銷】 sales promotion
【促成】 to help to materialize
【促使】 to impel; to urge; to spur

俄 148
1. ㄜˊ é
sudden; suddenly; momentarily: 「俄頃 soon」

俄 148
2. ㄜˋ è
【俄國 or 俄羅斯】 Russia
【俄語】 Russian (language)

俊 149
ㄐㄩㄣˋ jùn
1. talented; capable; superior; refined; smart; bright 2. good-looking; handsome 3. big; huge
【俊美】 good-looking; handsome
【俊傑】 a brave and superior person
【俊俏】 good-looking and smart
【俊秀】 handsome and refined
【俊偉】 superior and great

俏 150
ㄑㄧㄠˋ qiào
1. like; similar; to resemble; to be like 2. pretty and cute; good-looking 3. (commodities) enjoying brisk sale at higher prices; in great demand 4. (said of stocks) bullish
【俏皮】 ①pretty and cute ②sarcastic
【俏皮話】 a wisecrack; a jibe
【俏麗】 good-looking
【俏冤家】 (my) pretty but naughty lover

俐 151
ㄌㄧˋ lì
1. facile; easy and quick 2. sharp; clever 3. in good order; tidy; neat
【俐落】 well-executed

俑 152
ㄩㄥˇ yǒng
wooden or earthen figures of men and women buried with the dead; a tomb figure; a figurine

俗 153
ㄙㄨˊ sú
1. customs or customary 2. vulgar; unrefined 3. common; popular 4. lay (as distinguished from clerical); worldly; secular 5. tasteless; trite
【俗不可耐】 unbearably vulgar
【俗套】 social conventions
【俗念】 worldly thoughts
【俗累】 worldly troubles
【俗氣】 ① vulgarity ② hackneyed
【俗稱】 commonly called...
【俗事】 mundane affairs
【俗世】 earthly life

【俗人】①a layman as opposed to the clergy ②a vulgarian
【俗諺 or 俗話】a common saying; a proverb
【俗物】philistines; a vulgar
【俗務】chores; routines

俘 154 ㄈㄨˊ fú

1. prisoners of war 2. to capture

【俘虜】① to take prisoner ② a prisoner of war
【俘獲】to capture

俚 155 ㄌㄧˇ lǐ

1. vulgar; rustic; unpolished; unrefined 2. a small town or village; a tribe (aborigines, etc.)

【俚歌】folk songs; country songs
【俚俗】vulgar; unrefined
【俚語】slang; rustic expressions

保 156 ㄅㄠˇ bǎo

1. to guard; to shelter; to protect 2. to be responsible; to guarantee; to insure 3. to keep; to maintain

【保鑣】①a bodyguard; an armed escort ② to act as a bodyguard
【保不住】most likely; may well
【保密】to keep the secret
【保姆】a nurse who looks after small children
【保防工作】security measures
【保單】①a formal note or document of guaranty ②an insurance policy
【保留】to preserve; to reserve
【保齡球】bowling
【保齡球場】bowling alleys
【保管】to safeguard; to safekeep
【保管費】storage charges
【保護】to protect; to guard; protection
【保護(關)稅】a protective tariff
【保護人】a guardian
【保護色】protective coloration
【保皇黨】The Royalist Party
【保加利亞】Bulgaria
【保薦】to recommend (somebody for a job, etc.)
【保健】health protection; health care
【保健箱】a medical kit
【保全】to assure the safety of
【保險】①insurance ②to guarantee
【保險費】insurance premiums
【保險套】a condom; a sheath
【保險槓】a bumper
【保險公司】an insurance company
【保險箱】a safe; a strongbox
【保險人】an insurer; an underwriter
【保險絲】a fuse wire
【保值】to preserve the value (of currency)
【保障】to safeguard; to protect
【保證】to guarantee; to assure
【保證金】guaranty money
【保證書】a letter of guaranty
【保證人】a guarantor; a guarantee
【保重】Please take good care (of yourself).
【保持】to maintain; to keep
【保釋】to release on bail
【保釋金】bail
【保守】conservative
【保守主義】conservatism
【保存】①to safeguard ②to preserve
【保存期限】①the shelf life of a commodity ②the period for keeping official papers on file
【保送】to send a student to school or college without an entrance examination, usually for his high scholastic qualifications
【保安】① to ensure local security ②to ensure the workers' safety ③public security
【保安人員】security personnel
【保有】possession
【保佑】①to protect or bless ②a blessing
【保養】①maintenance ②to take care (of health) ③to maintain
【保養費】maintenance cost; upkeep
【保衛】to defend; to guard against
【保溫】① heat preservation ② to keep (water, etc.) hot; to preserve heat
【保溫杯】a thermos cup or container

俠 157 ㄒㄧㄚˊ xiá

1. a person adept in martial arts and dedicated to helping the poor and weak 2. chivalry

【俠義】chivalry; honor and gallantry

信 158 ㄒㄧㄣˋ xìn

1. honesty; truthfulness; faith; confidence; trust 2. believing; true 3. to believe or trust 4. an envoy; an emissary; a messenger 5. news; a message; information; word 6. a letter

【信筆】to write freely or aimlessly
【信步】to wander; to stroll aimlessly
【信封】an envelope
【信風】trade wind; seasonal wind
【信奉】to believe in (a religion, etc.)
【信服】to believe in; to trust
【信條】a creed or code; a dogma
【信徒】a believer (of a religion, etc.)
【信託公司】a trust company
【信念】a belief; a conviction
【信賴 or 信託】①trust ②to trust
【信鴿】a carrier pigeon
【信口開河】to talk at random; to brag
【信口胡說】to talk nonsense
【信口雌黃】to criticize wildly
【信號】a signal (with flags. lamps. etc.)
【信號燈】a semaphore; a signal lamp
【信滙】mail transfer(M/T)
【信教】to believe in a religion
【信件】mail or letters (collectively)
【信息】news; information; a message
【信心】faith; confidence
【信箱】a postbox; a letter box
【信紙 or 信箋】letter paper
【信插】a mail rack
【信差】a mailman; a postman
【信守】to abide by; to keep (a promise)
【信手拈來】to take without forethought
【信賞必罰】to give rewards or punishments strictly and impartially
【信任】①to trust; to have faith in ②trust
【信任投票】a vote of confidence
【信仰】belief; to believe in
【信譽】credit and reputation
【信用】credit
【信用卡】a credit card
【信用合作社】a credit cooperative
【信用狀 or 信用證】a letter of credit

八畫

修 159 ㄒㄧㄡ xiū

1. to repair; to mend 2. to adorn; to decorate 3. to construct; to build 4. long; slender 5. to prune; to cut; to sharpen; to trim 6. to study; to cultivate 7. to write; to compile; to edit

【修補 or 修葺】to repair; to mend
【修配】to repair and supply replacements
【修面】to shave one's face
【修復】to complete a repair job
【修道】to cultivate oneself according to a religious doctrine
【修道院】①a monastery ②a nunnery; a convent
【修訂】to revise
【修訂版 or 修訂本】a revision; the revised edition
【修女】a Catholic nun; a sister
【修理】①to repair ②to torture
【修路】①to repair roads ②to build roads
【修改 or 修正】to correct; to alter
【修剪】to trim, cut, clip, or prune
【修建】to repair and build
【修行】to practice Buddhist or Taoist rules
【修指甲】to manicure (or trim) fingernails
【修整】①to repair and maintain ②to prune; to trim
【修築】to build; to construct
【修長】tall and thin; slender
【修士】a monk
【修飾】to doll up
【修身】to cultivate oneself
【修身齊家】to cultivate oneself and put family in order
【修身自省】to look after one's conduct by self-examination
【修容】to make up one's features
【修辭】rhetoric; diction
【修辭學】rhetoric (as a subject of study)
【修業】to pursue academic studies
【修養】① to seek perfection in scholastic or ethical pursuits ② man's moral culture as the result of training

俯 160 ㄈㄨˇ fǔ

1. to face down; to come down; to bow down; to stoop 2. to condescend; to deign

【俯拜】to do obeisance to
【俯瞰 or 俯視】to look down at; to overlook
【俯就】①to adapt (usually by lowering) oneself to... ②to condescend to accept a job
【俯衝】① a dive ② to dive
【俯拾卽是】It's everywhere.
【俯視】to look down at

〔人部〕

【俯首】to bend one's head
【俯首帖耳】servile; submissive
【俯首就範】to submit; to surrender
【俯首無言】to admit one's fault or crime without protest
【俯仰無愧】to have done nothing to make one feel ashamed

俱 161 ㄐㄩˋ jù (又讀 ㄐㄩ jū)
1. altogether; all 2. to accompany
【俱備】all made ready; all complete
【俱樂部】a club
【俱全】to be available in all varieties
【俱在】all present

俸 162 ㄈㄥˋ fèng
as in 俸祿—a salary from the government; emoluments

併 163 (倂) ㄅㄧㄥˋ bìng
1.on a level with; even; equal; to go side by side 2.all; entire 3. together 4.to combine; to annex
【併發】to begin, explode, erupt, attack, occur, etc. at the same time
【併發症】(medicine) a complication
【併呑】to swallow up entirely
【併合】to unite; to integrate
【併肩】shoulder to shoulder

倆 164 1. ㄌㄧㄤˇ liǎng
craft; ability

倆 164 2. ㄌㄧㄚˇ liǎ
two; a pair; a couple
【倆口子】husband and wife

倉 165 ㄘㄤ cāng
1. a granary; a storehouse; a warehouse 2.a cabin, as in the ship 3.green
【倉廩】a granary
【倉庫】a warehouse; a storehouse
【倉皇 or 倉促】in haste; hurriedly

個 166 (箇) ㄍㄜˋ gè
1. a numerary adjunct 2. piece 3. single 4. roughly 5. an adjunct to an indefinite pronoun, as this, that
【個把月】a month or two
【個別】individual; separately
【個體】a matter, etc. having an independent and distinct quality
【個體戶】an individual business or shop
【個個】(each and) every one
【個性】personality; individuality
【個人】① the individual as contrasted with the group ② oneself ③ personal
【個人主義】individualism; egoism
【個子】physical size of a person; build
【個兒】size; height; stature
【個案】an individual case
【個位】(mathematics) a unit; a digit

倌 167 ㄍㄨㄢ guān
1. a boy or an assistant in the employ of a teahouse, tavern or restaurant 2. a euphemism for a prostitute 3. the groom

倍 168 ㄅㄟˋ bèi
1. double; to double 2. (joined to a numeral)-times; -fold 3. to rebel; to be insubordinate
【倍率】percentage
【倍加 or 倍增】to double; double
【倍數】a multiple

倏 169 ㄕㄨˋ shù
hastily; suddenly: 倏忽 all of a sudden; quickly

們 170 ㄇㄣˊ mén (語音 ·ㄇㄣ men)
an adjunct to a pronoun or noun to indicate plurality

倒 171 1. ㄉㄠˇ dǎo
to fall down; to lie down
【倒閉】to close down a shop; to go bankrupt
【倒斃】to fall dead
【倒楣】to be out of luck
【倒塌】to collapse
【倒臺】to fall from power
【倒閣】the resignation of the cabinet
【倒賬】① bad debts ② to refuse to pay loans under various excuses
【倒胃口】to spoil one's appetite

倒 171 2. ㄉㄠˋ dào
1. to inverse; to place upside down; in reverse order or the wrong direction 2. to pour out; to empty 3. on the contrary 4. after all 5. but; and yet

【倒背如流】to understand something thoroughly by heart

【倒不如】① would rather ② not better than; even worse than

【倒退】①to retreat; to fall back ② to retrospect

【倒立】① to stand upside down ②a handstand

【倒流 or 倒灌】to flow backward

【倒戈】to apostatize or tergiversate; mutiny

【倒行逆施】to go against common-sense rules

【倒敍】to narrate an incident in inverted order chronologically

【倒置】to place (things, etc.) in wrong order; to place emphasis on the wrong point

【倒轉】① to turn the other way round ② contrary to reason or one's expectation

【倒裝】① to place things in inverted order ② (rhetoric) hyperbaton

【倒車】to back up a car, locomotive, etc.

【倒數】to count from bottom to top

【倒數計時】to count down

【倒栽葱】to fall headlong

【倒彩】(Chinese opera) to applaud when a performer slips

【倒也罷了】It would have been better if....

【倒影】the reflection of something in the water

倔 172

1. ㄐㄩㄝˊ jué intransigent; hard; obstinate; stubborn

【倔強】obstinate; stubborn

【倔起】(said of a nation) to rise suddenly

倔 172

2. ㄐㄩㄝˋ juè gruff; surly; rude in manner or speech

倖 173

ㄒㄧㄥˋ xìng

1. good luck; lucky; by luck or chance; fortunate 2. to dote on; to spoil

【倖免】to escape (punishment) by luck

【倖存】to survive by good luck

倘 174

ㄊㄤˇ tǎng

if; supposing; in the event of: 倘若 if; in case

候 175

ㄏㄡˋ hòu

1. to wait; to expect 2. a period; time; a season

【候補】waiting to fill a vacancy, such as an alternate member of a committee, etc.

【候鳥】migratory birds

【候機室】a lounge or waiting room (at an airport terminal building)

【候駕】to await (your) gracious presence

【候選人】a candidate

【候診】to wait to see the doctor

【候車室】a waiting room (at a railway station or bus terminal)

【候審】(law) to await trial

倚 176

ㄧˇ yǐ

1. to rely on; to depend on 2. to lean toward; to rest on 3. biased; partial

【倚傍】to pattern after; to emulate

【倚賴 or 倚恃】to depend on; to rely on (others)

【倚老賣老】to presume on age to despise the youth

【倚靠】① to lean against ② to rely on; to depend on ③ support

【倚仗】to presume on (one's position, authority, etc.)

【倚重】to entrust a person with heavy responsibility

【倚勢凌人】to take advantage of one's position to bully people

倜 177

ㄊㄧˋ tì

1. to raise high 2. unrestrained; unoccupied

【倜儻 or 俶儻】free and easy of manner

借 178

ㄐㄧㄝˋ jiè

1. to lend 2. to borrow 3. to avail oneself of; to make use of; to resort to 4. to make a pretext of 5. if; supposing

【借貸】① to ask for a loan ② debit and credit sides

【借刀殺人】to kill one's enemy by another's hands

【借調】to transfer temporarily; loan

【借題發揮】to seize a pretext (to air one's own complaints, to attack others, etc.)

【借古諷今】to use the past to disparage the present

【借故】to find an excuse

【借故推托】to find an excuse to refuse

【借款】to borrow money; a loan

【借花獻佛】to get things from another person to entertain one's own guest

【借酒澆愁】to drown one's worries or anxieties by drinking
【借鑑 or 借鏡】to learn a lesson from another person's experience
【借據】an I.O.U.
【借主】the creditor「support from」
【借助】to have the aid of; to draw
【借重】to rely on; to seek the assistance (of)
【借書證】a library card
【借宿】to stay overnight in another's place (or hotel, etc.)
【借以】so as to; for the purpose of
【借問】Will you please tell me...?
【借用】to borrow

倡 179
1. ㄔㄤ chāng
1. a prostitute 2. wild and unre-
【倡狂】profligate 「strained」

倡 179
2. ㄔㄤˋ chàng
to lead; to introduce; to initiate; to advocate 「promote」
【倡導】to lead; to advocate; to
【倡議】to make a motion; to advo-「cate」

值 180
ㄓˊ zhí
1. prices of commodities; value; cost; to cost; to be worth 2. at the time of... 3. to meet; to hap-「pen」
【值班 or 值勤】to be on duty
【值得】to be worthy of; to deserve
【值錢】valuable; expensive
【值星】(said of army officers) to be on duty for the week 「duty」
【值日】to be one's turn to be on
【值日生】the student on duty

倦 181
ㄐㄩㄢˋ juàn
tired; weary: 倦怠 to be tired; worn out; languor
【倦鳥知還】to return home after years of wandering far away

倩 182
ㄑㄧㄢˋ qiàn
1. pretty dimples of a smiling woman 2. handsome 3. a son-in-law 4. to ask somebody to do something for oneself
【倩影】the beautiful image of a「woman」

倫 183
ㄌㄨㄣˊ lún
1. normal relationships among people 2. comparison 3. classification 4. order; logic 5. regular; ordinary 6. to choose; choice
【倫敦】London
【倫理】moral principles; ethics
【倫理學】ethics
【倫常】normal and accepted ways and relationships of people

倭 184
1. ㄨㄛ wō
name of a human race; an old name for Japan
【倭寇】(ancient usage) the dwarf pirates; the Japs

倭 184
2. ㄨㄟ wēi 「dering」
【倭遲】winding; circuitous; mean-

九畫

偃 185
ㄧㄢˇ yǎn
1. to cease; to be at rest; to stop; to suppress; to lay off 2. to lie on one's back 3. an embankment 「②to stop fighting」
【偃旗息鼓】①to stop the fanfare

假 186
1. ㄐㄧㄚˇ jiǎ
1. false; not real; phony; artificial; fake; bogus; sham 2. supposing; if 3. to borrow; to avail oneself of
【假扮】to disguise; to masquerade
【假寐】to take a nap; a catnap; a doze
【假冒】① to counterfeit ② to assume the identity of somebody else
【假面具】a mask—a false front
【假名】① a pseudonym ② kana (the Japanese syllabary)
【假髮】a wig
【假分數】an improper fraction
【假貸顏色】to tolerate; to bear
【假道】via; by way of 「late」
【假定】①if; supposing ②a postu-
【假託】a pretext; a subterfuge
【假動作】(sports) dummy play
【假公濟私】to attain private or personal ends in the name of official duties
【假話】a lie; a falsehood
【假借】to borrow
【假借名義】in the name of
【假戲眞做】to do something seriously after starting it as a joke,

ruse, etc.

【假想】① a hypothesis ② imaginary

【假想敵】a hypothetical enemy

【假象】false appearances

【假惺惺】to pretend; to shed crocodile tears

【假性近視】pseudomyopia

【假正經】hypocritical

【假裝】to pretend; to assume the appearance of

【假充】to counterfeit; to pretend

【假使 or 假如 or 假若】if; in case; supposing

【假釋】to parole; parole

【假設】a hypothesis; a supposition

【假手】to do something by means of (an agent)

【假山】a small artificial hill

【假仁假義】to be a wolf in sheep's clothing; to shed crocodile tears

【假造】①to counterfeit ②to fabricate

【假造罪名】to cook up a false charge against; to frame up

【假嗓子】falsetto

【假以時日】to give sufficient time

【假意奉承】false flattery

【假牙】a false tooth; a denture

假 186

2. ㄐㄧㄚˋ jià

a holiday

【假條】①an application for leave ②a leave permit

【假期】a vacation; a holiday

【假日】a holiday

偉 187

ㄨㄟˇ wěi

extraordinary; great; big

【偉大】great; extraordinary

【偉人】a great man

【偉業】monumental accomplishments

偌 188

ㄖㄨㄛˋ ruò

so (used as an adverb to modify an adjective)

偎 189

ㄨㄟ wēi

1. to cuddle; to embrace 2. intimate; very dear to 3. to lean on

【偎倚 or 偎依】to cuddle or curl up

偏 190

ㄆㄧㄢ piān

1. biased; not fair; prejudiced; partial 2. leaning; inclined to one side 3. an auxiliary verb indicating a sense of contrariness or determination

【偏頗】partial; biased; not fair

【偏僻】out-of-the-way; secluded

【偏偏】unfortunately it happened that...

【偏廢】① crippled ② to emphasize one thing and neglect others

【偏方】an informal recipe or prescription

【偏房】a concubine

【偏頭痛】(medicine) hemicrania

【偏袒】partiality; partial

【偏題】a catch question (in an examination)

【偏勞】① to let one person take on the work of the whole team ② "Thanks for the good work."

【偏離】to deviate; to diverge

【偏好】a hobby

【偏護】partial; to favor one side against the other

【偏激】extreme; radical

【偏見】prejudice; bias

【偏巧】it so happened; as luck would have it

【偏心】partiality; bias toward

【偏向】to lean or to be inclined

【偏執】strong inclination toward

【偏重】① to give undue emphasis to ② to have extraordinary faith in (somebody)

【偏差】errors; deviation

【偏食】to eat certain dishes only

【偏愛】to love someone or something in particular

【偏遠】remote; faraway

偕 191

ㄒㄧㄝˊ xié

(又讀 ㄐㄧㄝ jiē)

1. to accompany 2. together

【偕同】in company with; along with

做 192

ㄗㄨㄛˋ zuò

1. to work; to make; to do 2. to act as 3. to pretend to be

【做伴】to keep somebody company

【做媒】to be a matchmaker

【做夢】① to dream ② to daydream

【做法】way of doing a thing; practice

【做飯】to prepare food

【做到】to accomplish; to achieve

【做東】to play the host; to host

【做頭髮】to have one's hair done at a beauty parlor

【做禮拜】to go to church; to be at

人部

church
【做弄】to make fun of; to play jokes upon
【做官】to become an official
【做工】to work
【做客】to be a guest
【做好事】to do a good deed
【做好人】to play the role of a good guy
【做假】to cheat
【做小】to be someone's concubine
【做主】to take charge of; to be responsible for; to decide
【做莊】(gambling) to be the banker
【做事】①to handle affairs; to do a deed; to act ②to work; to have a job
【做聲】to make a sound
【做生日 or 做壽】to celebrate one's birthday
【做生意】to do business transactions
【做人】to conduct oneself; to behave
【做人情】to do something as a favor
【做賊心虛】One who has done something bad secretly cannot look others in the eye.
【做作】① affectation; pretentious ② to behave unnaturally
【做愛】to make love
【做衣服】to tailor; to have a dress made
【做樣子】to go through the motion of doing something; to pretend to do something
【做文章】① to write an essay ② to make an issue of

停 193
ㄊㄧㄥˊ tíng

1. to stop; to pause; to halt; to stay 2. to suspend; to delay 3. percentage
【停泊】to anchor; to berth; to dock
【停擺】to suspend work
【停辦】to suspend; to stop handling something
【停飛】the grounding of aircraft
【停放】to park; to place
【停電】① blackout ② to cut off power supply
【停頓】to grind to a halt
【停妥】① ready ② to have been parked in a proper place
【停留】to stay
【停工】to suspend work
【停課】to suspend class
【停刊】to stop publication
【停航】to suspend air or shipping service
【停火】to cease fire
【停機坪】an apron (at an airfield)
【停歇】to stop for a rest
【停薪】to stop or suspend payment to an employee
【停職】to suspend a person from office
【停止 or 停息】to stop; to cease
【停滯】① to be held up ② indigestion
【停戰】① to stop fighting ② a truce
【停車】to park a car
【停車場】a parking lot
【停屍間】a mortuary
【停水】to cut off the water supply
【停業】to stop doing business; to close down

健 194
ㄐㄧㄢˋ jiàn

1. healthy; strong 2. vigorous; capable 3. fond of; inclined to; liable to 4. to strengthen; to toughen
【健美】healthy and handsome
【健談】brilliant conversation
【健康】① health ② healthy
【健全】in good condition
【健行】to hike; hiking
【健壯】healthy and robust
【健身房】a gymnasium; a gym
【健身操】calisthenics
【健在】to be in good health; alive
【健忘】forgetful; liable to forget
【健忘症】(pathology) amnesia

側 195
ㄘㄜˋ cè

1. the side; sideways 2. to slant; to incline towards 3. low and narrow-minded; prejudiced
【側門】a side door
【側面】the side; the flank
【側面消息】sidelights
【側目】① a sidelong glance; to look askance ②to cause raised eyebrows
【側重】to place particular emphasis on
【側身】to sidle; on one's side; sideways
【側耳傾聽】to listen attentively
【側影】a silhouette; a profile
【側臥】to lie on the side

偵 196
ㄓㄣ zhēn

1. to detect; to spy; to scout 2. a scout; a spy; a detective
【偵破】to crack a criminal case
【偵探】①a detective ②to investi-

gate
【偵探小說】detective stories
【偵緝】to track down and arrest
【偵詢】to examine a suspect or someone concerned to gather information
【偵查】to investigate
【偵察】reconnaissance; to reconnoiter about the enemy
【偵察敵情】to gather intelligence about the enemy
【偵察機】a reconnaissance plane

偶 197 ㄡˇ ǒu
1. an idol; an image 2. coincidentally; accidentally 3. once in a while; occasionally 4. not to be taken for granted 5. an even number 6. a counterpart 7. a mate; to mate 8. one's company; fellows; buddies
【偶發】to happen accidentally
【偶犯】①a casual offense ②a casual offender
【偶像】an idol; an image
【偶數】an even number
【偶然】①by chance ②unexpectedly
【偶爾 or 偶而】occasionally

偷 198 ㄊㄡ tōu
1. to steal; to filch; to burglarize; to pilfer 2. to do something without others' knowledge; stealthily; surreptitiously
【偷渡】to stow away
【偷渡者】a stowaway
【偷偷】stealthily; secretly; covertly
【偷偷摸摸】stealthily; surreptitiously
【偷天換日】to commit a big cheat, fraud, etc.
【偷聽】to eavesdrop
【偷懶】to be lazy
【偷工減料】to jerry-build
【偷看】to steal a look
【偷空】to avail oneself of a leisure moment
【偷竊】to steal; to thieve
【偷情】to carry on a clandestine love affair
【偷襲】to attack by surprise
【偷生】to live in disgrace
【偷生怕死】cowardly; to be afraid to die or eager to save one's skin
【偷安】to seek temporary ease

十畫

傢 199 ㄐㄧㄚ jiā
1. furniture 2. a tool or tools
【傢伙】(comically) a character
【傢具 or 家具】furniture

傀 200 1. ㄎㄨㄟˇ kuǐ
as in傀儡—a puppet
【傀儡戲】a puppet show

傀 200 2. ㄍㄨㄟ guī
great; wonderful: 傀偉great and imposing

傅 201 ㄈㄨˋ fù
1.a teacher 2.to teach 3.to go together with; to add to; to be attached to

傍 202 1. (旁) ㄆㄤˊ páng
beside; by the side of
【傍邊】beside
【傍聽】to audit (at a college class)
【傍聽生】an auditor
【傍觀】to watch on the sideline
【傍偟】vacillating
【傍敲側擊】to talk in a roundabout way
【傍人】other people
【傍若無人】to act audaciously or uninhibitively as if there were no other persons around

傍 202 2. ㄅㄤ bāng
near; approaching
【傍午】near noontime; shortly before noon
【傍晚】dusk; twilight; nightfall

傍 202 3. ㄅㄤˋ bàng
1.to depend on 2.to draw near; to be close to

傑 203 ㄐㄧㄝˊ jié
1. outstanding; remarkable; extraordinary 2. a hero
【傑出】outstanding; extraordinary
【傑作】a masterpiece

傖 204 ㄘㄤ cāng
1. (said of persons) cheap; vulgar; lowly 2. confused; disorderly

傘 205 ㄙㄢˇ sǎn
1. an umbrella 2. a parachute
【傘兵】paratroopers

備 206 ㄅㄟˋ bèi
1. a sense of completeness; per-

人部

fection 2. to be equipped with 3. to get ready 4. to prepare against 5. fully; in every possible way

【備付所得稅】provision for income tax

【備馬】to saddle a horse for riding

【備胎】a spare tire

【備至】to the utmost

【備戰】①to prepare for war ②to be prepared against war

【備註】①remarks or footnotes ②space reserved for footnotes

【備案】to serve as a record

【備而不用】It's better to get ready for nothing than caught unprepared.

【備忘錄】a memorandum

【備用】reserve; spare; alternate

傚 207
ㄒㄧㄠˋ xiào
to model after; to imitate; to copy; to emulate

【傚尤 or 傚仿】emulation

十一畫

催 208
ㄘㄨㄟ cuī
to hasten; to urge; to press; to hurry

【催眠】to hypnotize; to mesmerize

【催眠術】hypnotism

【催討】to press for repayment of a debt

【催淚彈】a tear gas bomb

【催趕】①to urge someone to come or go ②to hasten to a destination

【催化劑】a catalyst

【催生劑】an axytocic

【催促】to hasten; to urge; to press

傭 209
ㄩㄥˊ yóng
(又讀 ㄩㄥ yōng)
1.to hire 2.a servant; a domestic help

【傭兵】mercenaries

【傭工】①to hire laborers ②hired laborers or servants

傲 210
ㄠˋ ào
1. proud; haughty; overbearing 2.to disdain; to despise; to look down upon 3. rash and impatient

【傲慢】haughty and overbearing; impudent

【傲氣】an air of arrogance; haughtiness

【傲視】to turn up one's nose at

傳 211
1. ㄔㄨㄢˊ chuán
1. to pass (a ball, an order, learning, etc.) on to 2. to propagate; to disseminate 3. to summon 4. to preach

【傳播】to disseminate; to spread

【傳播媒體】a mass medium

【傳播界】the media; journalistic circles

【傳布】①to disseminate ②to preach

【傳票】①a voucher ②a subpoena

【傳達】①to forward (a message) ②to inform, or notify ③a messenger

【傳導】to conduct (heat, electricity)

【傳道】①to preach a religion ②to propagate doctrines of the ancient sages

【傳單】handbills; leaflets

【傳遞】to forward; to deliver

【傳動】transmission; drive

【傳統】tradition; convention

【傳令】to deliver or give orders

【傳令兵】a soldier-messenger

【傳話】to pass on a message

【傳家寶】an heirloom

【傳教】to preach a religion (especially Christianity)

【傳教士】a missionary

【傳奇】a legend, saga, romance, etc.

【傳情】to flirt; to coquet

【傳訊】(law) to summon (someone) for interrogation

【傳眞】①a lifelike portrait by a painter ②to transmit photos, printed matter, etc.; to facsimile

【傳眞機】a fax machine

【傳授】to teach; to teach by demonstration

【傳神】a vivid portrayal

【傳聲筒】a megaphone

【傳說】hearsay; legends

【傳熱】①heat conduction ②to communicate heat

【傳染】to infect; to be contagious

【傳染病】infectious diseases

【傳宗接代】to continue the family line by producing a male heir

【傳送】to convey; to deliver

【傳誦】①to pass from mouth to mouth ②to be admired and appreciated by all

【傳衣鉢】to hand one's trade on to disciples

【傳言】①hearsay; rumor ②to

pass on a message
【傳揚】to spread (from mouth to mouth)
【傳爲佳話】to become a favorite tale
【傳聞】hearsay; unconfirmed reports
【傳閱】(said of a public notice or circular) to be passed around for perusal; to be circulated

傳 211
2. ㄓㄨㄢˋ zhuàn
as in 傳記—a biography

債 212
ㄓㄞˋ zhài
a debt; an obligation: 債款 a loan
【債臺高築】to be deep in debt
【債戶 or 債務人】a debtor
【債券】bonds issued by a government or debentures issued by a company
【債主 or 債權人】a creditor
【債務】debt or obligation

傷 213
ㄕㄤ shāng
1. a cut, wound, or injury 2. to cut or injure 3. grief; to grieve; distressed 4. to impede; an impediment 5. to hurt (feelings) 6. to make sick
【傷悲】grief; distress
【傷兵】wounded soldiers
【傷風】to catch cold; to have a cold
【傷風敗俗】to act immorally
【傷天害理】to commit crimes
【傷痛】to mourn
【傷腦筋】①to beat one's brains; to have a nut to crack ②troublesome
【傷感】to be deeply moved or touched
【傷感情】to hurt the feelings
【傷口】a wound
【傷害】to hurt; to injure; to harm
【傷害罪】(law) injury
【傷寒】typhoid fever; typhus
【傷痕 or 傷疤】a scar; a bruise
【傷懷】a distressing mood; grief
【傷患】the sick and wounded
【傷心】① to hurt one's feelings; to break one's heart ② very sad
【傷勢】the condition of an injury (or a wound)
【傷神】①to beat one's brains out ②deeply hurt
【傷殘】the wounded and disabled
【傷亡】casualties

傾 214
1. ㄑㄧㄥ qīng
1. to slant; to bend 2. to collapse; to fall flat; to upset; to subvert 3. to pour out 4. to exhaust (one's wealth, etc.); to exert oneself to do (something) 5. to admire; to be fascinated or intrigued
【傾盆大雨】to rain hard; to rain cats and dogs
【傾慕】to admire; admiration
【傾覆】① to topple ② to overturn
【傾倒】①(ㄑㄧㄥ ㄉㄠˇ) ⓐ to fall for (a woman) ⓑ to collapse ②(ㄑㄧㄥ ㄉㄠˋ) to dump
【傾談】to have a good, heart-to-heart talk
【傾聽】to listen carefully
【傾吐】to get (something) off one's chest
【傾囊相助】to exhaust (or give) all one has to help
【傾家蕩產】to go bankrupt
【傾斜】① to slant ② the angle formed by a stratum with the level; to slope
【傾銷】a cutthroat sale; dumping
【傾心】① to admire wholeheartedly ② heart-to-heart
【傾向】① to be inclined to ② a tendency; a trend
【傾訴】to pour out (one's heart, troubles, etc.)

傾 214
2. ㄎㄥ kēng
【傾人】to frame or implicate a person

僅 215
ㄐㄧㄣˇ jǐn
1. only 2. barely; scarcely; almost
【僅僅】only; hardly enough; barely
【僅容旋馬】narrow space
【僅有】to have only...; there is (or are) only...

十二畫

像 216
ㄒㄧㄤˋ xiàng
1. an image; a portrait 2. to resemble; resemblance 3. like; as
【像貌】a person's looks
【像貌非凡】a distinguished appearance
【像是】to look like; to seem
【像樣】presentable; decent

僑 217
ㄑㄧㄠˊ qiáo
to sojourn; a sojourn
【僑胞】overseas Chinese
【僑民】alien residents

【僑居】to reside in a town or country other than one's own
【僑生】children of overseas Chinese who attend schools in China
【僑務委員會】the Overseas Chinese Affairs Commission

〔人部〕

僕 218
ㄆㄨˊ pú
1. a servant 2. a modest term referring to oneself 3. (formerly) to act as a driver; to drive
【僕僕風塵】to be travel-worn and weary
【僕人】a servant
【僕從】retinue; a group of retainers
【僕役】servants

僚 219
ㄌㄧㄠˊ liáo
1. a companion; a friend 2. a colleague; subordinates 3. officials

僞 220
ㄨㄟˋ wèi (語音 ㄨㄟˇ wěi)
1. false; counterfeit 2. simulated; artificial 3. illegal; not legally constituted
【僞幣】① counterfeit money ② money issued by a puppet government
【僞君子】a hypocrite
【僞證】perjury
【僞裝】disguise; camouflage
【僞鈔】a counterfeit bank note
【僞善】hypocrisy; hypocritical
【僞造】to forge; to falsify
【僞造文書】a forgery; counterfeit documents

僥 221
ㄐㄧㄠˇ jiǎo
luck; lucky: 僥倖 by luck or chance

僧 222
ㄙㄥ sēng
a Buddhist; a priest; a monk
【僧侶】Buddhist monks
【僧多粥少】not enough (gifts, positions, etc.) to go around because there are too many people on the waiting list 亦作「粥少僧多」
【僧院】a monastery

僭 223
ㄐㄧㄢˋ jiàn
to assume; to usurp; to overstep one's authority
【僭位】to usurp the throne
【僭越】to assume (a title or powers)

僮 224
1. ㄊㄨㄥˊ tóng
1. a servant 2. a boy

僮 224
2. ㄓㄨㄤˋ zhuàng
【僮族】the name of a small tribe in southwestern China 亦作「壯族」

僱 225
ㄍㄨˋ gù
as in僱用—to hire; to engage; to employ
【僱主】an employer
【僱員 or 雇員】an employee

十三畫

僵 226
ㄐㄧㄤ jiāng
1. to lie flat 2. to be inactive; stiff; rigid; numb 3. to be at a stalemate; deadlocked
【僵立】to stand rigidly
【僵化】① heading toward a deadlock ② to become rigid; to ossify
【僵局】a deadlock; a stalemate
【僵持】to come to a deadlock
【僵屍or殭屍】①a stiff corpse ② a vampire
【僵硬】rigid; stiff

價 227
ㄐㄧㄚˋ jià
1. prices; cost; value 2. (chemistry) valence
【價碼兒】the price of a commodity
【價目】prices; quotations
【價目單】a price (or quotation) list
【價廉物美】(literally) excellent quality at low prices—a good bargain
【價格or價錢】prices
【價值】value
【價值連城】invaluable; priceless

僻 228
ㄆㄧˋ pì
1. biased 2. not easily accessible; out-of-the-way; secluded 3. not common; not ordinary; unusual
【僻靜】out-of-the-way; secluded
【僻遠】distant and out-of-the-way

儀 229
ㄧˊ yí
1. appearance; deportment; manners; looks; demeanor 2. ceremonies; rites 3. a rule, regulation, form or standard 4. customs 5. instruments; apparatus
【儀表】① appearance and deportment ② a rule; a model
【儀隊】an honor guard
【儀態】bearing; deportment; demeanor
【儀態萬方】(usually said of girls) charming poises and exquisite

bearing 「instruments; apparatus
【儀器】(laboratory, medical, etc.)
【儀式】ceremonies; rites
【儀容】looks; appearance and deportment

儂 230
ㄋㄨㄥˊ nóng
1. (in old usage) I; me 2. (Shanghai dialect) you 3. he; she

億 231
ㄧˋ yì
1. a hundred million 2. tranquility; repose 3. (according to) estimates
【億萬富翁】a billionaire

儆 232
ㄐㄧㄥˇ jǐng
1. to be on guard 2. to warn; to caution
【儆戒】to warn; to caution

儈 233
ㄎㄨㄞˋ kuài
a middleman; a go-between; a broker

儉 234
ㄐㄧㄢˇ jiǎn
(又讀 ㄐㄧㄢˋ jiàn)
1. frugal; economical; thrift 2. meager 3. a poor harvest
【儉樸】to be thrifty in daily spending
【儉省】thrift; frugal; economical
【儉以養廉】Frugality makes honesty
【儉約】thrifty and temperate

儍 235
(傻) ㄕㄚˇ shǎ
1. stupid; foolish; dumb 2. naive 3. stunned; stupefied; terrified 4. to think or work mechanically
【儍頭儍腦】① foolish-looking ② muddle-headed
【儍裏儍氣】foolish-looking or acting foolishly
【儍瓜】a fool; a silly; a blockhead
【儍呵呵】likable but stupid; silly appearance; simple-minded
【儍話】foolish talk; nonsense
【儍勁兒】①stupidity; foolishness ② sheer enthusiasm; doggedness
【儍笑】to smirk; to laugh for no conceivable reason
【儍子】an idiot; a blockhead
【儍眼】to be dumbfounded

十四畫

儐 236
ㄅㄧㄣ bīn
(語音 ㄅㄧㄣˋ bìn)
1. to entertain guests 2. to set in order; to arrange 3. to guide
【儐相】① the best man of a bridegroom ② a bridesmaid

儒 237
ㄖㄨˊ rú
1. the learned; scholars collectively 2. Confucian; Confucianism 3. weak; shrinking from hardship
【儒家】Confucianists; the Confucian school
【儒教】Confucianism
【儒學】the teachings of Confucius
【儒雅】scholarly and refined; elegant

儔 238
ㄔㄡˊ chóu
1. a companion or companions 2. a class

儕 239
ㄔㄞˊ chái
1. a class; company 2. an adjunct to show plurality 3. to match (as man and wife)

儘 240
ㄐㄧㄣˇ jǐn
1. the utmost; the extreme 2. to let (someone do it)
【儘量】as (much, soon, strong, etc.) as possible
【儘管】①even if; no matter ②not hesitate to
【儘可能】as far as possible; to the best of one's ability
【儘快】as quickly (or soon) as possible
【儘情享受】to seek pleasure to one's heart's content
【儘早】as early as possible

十五畫

償 241
ㄔㄤˊ cháng
1. to repay 2. to make restitution; to compensate 3. to fulfill (a wish) 4. to offset
【償命】a life for a life
【償付】to pay back; to pay
【償還】to repay (what one owes)
【償清】to clear off
【償債】to repay a debt

儡 242
ㄌㄟˇ lěi
1. a puppet 2. sickly and thin 3. dilapidated

優 243
ㄧㄡ yōu
1. good; excellent 2. abundant; plenty 3. players (as in an opera) 4. victory; winning 5. soft
【優美】①wonderful; graceful; fine

人部

儿部

②anything that inspires a sense of joy
【優待】favorable treatment
【優待券】①a discount ticket ②a free ticket (for a show, etc.)
【優等】an excellent grade; first-rate
【優點】merits; good qualities; advantages
【優劣】①good and bad ②bright and dull ③fit and unfit
【優良】fine; good
【優厚】munificent; liberal; favorable
【優惠】preferential; favorable
【優秀】outstanding; remarkable
【優先】priority; to take precedence
【優先權】priority
【優勢】supremacy; superiority
【優生學】eugenics
【優勝】winning; superior
【優勝劣敗】survival of the fittest
【優勝者】a winner; a champion
【優柔寡斷】to be peaceable and easygoing but lacking the strength of making quick decisions
【優哉游哉】leisurely and carefree
【優異】excellent; remarkable; brilliant
【優游】①carefree 亦作「優遊」②indecisive ③to leave one's life to fate
【優渥】munificent
【優越】superior; outstanding
【優越感】a sense of superiority

十六畫

儲 244 ㄔㄨˊ chú (又讀 ㄔㄨˇ chǔ)

1. to save; to store; saving 2. a deputy; an alternate
【儲備】savings and/or reserves
【儲戶】a depositor
【儲金】savings
【儲蓄】①to save (money) ②savings
【儲藏】①to store up; to hoard; to save and preserve ②a deposit
【儲藏室】a storeroom
【儲存】①storage; saving ②to store or stockpile

十九畫

儷 245 ㄌㄧˋ lì

1. a pair; a couple 2. husband and wife; a married couple
【儷影】the heart-warming sight of a couple in love

二十畫

儼 246 ㄧㄢˇ yǎn

1. majestic; respectable 2. (to act, talk, appear, etc.) as if; like
【儼然】dignified-looking

儿部 ㄖㄣˊ rén

一畫

兀 247 ㄨˋ wù

1. to cut off the feet 2. high and flat on the top 3. this 4. ignorant looking
【兀自】still

二畫

允 248 ㄩㄣˇ yǔn

1. to allow; to consent; to grant 2. appropriate; proper 3. sincere; loyal; faithful; truly
【允許 or 允諾】to assent; to consent; to grant; to permit etc.)
【允從】to follow (one's advice,
【允文允武】to be good at wielding both pen and weapon

元 249 ㄩㄢˊ yuán

1. the beginning; the first; original 2. the head 3. a dollar 4. the eldest; chief; big 5. (Chinese astrology) 60 years 6. the Yüan Dynasty
【元寶】a silver or gold ingot
【元配】a man's first wife
【元旦】New Year's Day
【元年】the first year of a reign, dynasty, etc.
【元老】an elder person who has held high positions for long period of time and is highly respected by the nation
【元氣】vitality and constitution

【元宵】①the Lantern Festival ②small rice-flour dumplings eaten on the Lantern Festival
【元勳】①great achievements ②a founding father
【元兇】the chief culprit; a ringleader (of a crime)
【元首】①the chief of state; the king; the president, etc. ②the beginning
【元帥】the commander in chief
【元素】(chemistry) the elements
【元月】①the first month of the lunar calendar ②January

三畫

兄 250
ㄒㄩㄥ xiōng
1. one's elder brother 2. a term used in addressing a senior of the same generation to show respect
【兄弟】①(ㄒㄩㄥ ㄉㄧˋ) brothers ②(ㄒㄩㄥ ·ㄉㄧ) ⓐ one's younger brother ⓑ a designation for juniors of the same generation among one's relatives ⓒ I (a modest term)
【兄弟鬩牆】an intramural fight
【兄長】an elder brother
【兄友弟恭】to show love and respect as good brothers should

充 251
(充)ㄔㄨㄥ chōng
1. full; sufficient 2. to fill 3. to fake; to cheat; to pretend
【充沛】brimming (with energy)
【充滿】to fill up; full of; filled with
【充分】fully; sufficient; enough
【充當】to serve as; to act as
【充電】to recharge (a battery)
【充電器】a charger
【充公】to confiscate
【充飢】to satisfy one's hunger
【充其量】at most; at best
【充斥】filled with; rife
【充實】①rich; abundant ②to fill out ③to strengthen or improve
【充數】to fill a vacancy with an incompetent person
【充足】plenty; abundant; sufficient
【充塞】full of; filled with
【充耳不聞】to turn a deaf ear to
【充裕】abundance; sufficiency; rich

四畫

兆 252
ㄓㄠˋ zhào
1. a sign (in fortune-telling) 2. to portend; to foretell 3. an omen 4. a trillion (1,000,000,000,000); a billion 5. to begin; beginning
【兆頭】a sign; an omen; a portent

兇 253
ㄒㄩㄥ xiōng
1. fierce; violent; cruel; ferocious 2. truculent; inhuman
【兇暴】cruel and violent
【兇猛】fierce; ferocious
【兇犯】a criminal; a murderer
【兇悍 or 兇狠 or 兇橫】ferocious, truculent, savage, fierce, etc.
【兇器】the murderous weapon
【兇險】cruel and mean
【兇殺】murder; homicide
【兇手】the murderer; the killer
【兇惡】evil; wicked; malignant

先 254
ㄒㄧㄢ xiān
1. first; foremost 2. before; earlier; in advance 3. the late...; the deceased... 4. one's forebears 5. the abbreviation for Mister or Sir
【先民】ancients
【先母or先慈or先妣】my late mother
【先發制人】to take the initiative
【先鋒 or 先驅】a vanguard; a forerunner; the trailblazer
【先夫】my late husband
【先父or先考or先嚴】my late father
【先導】①to lead the way ②a model; a teacher ③a guide
【先睹為快】to eagerly await a look at (something) ahead of others
【先天】①natural physical endowments ②congenital; innate; inherent
【先天不足】inborn deficiency
【先天缺陷】the birth defect
【先來後到】First come, first served.
【先禮後兵】diplomacy (or courtesy) before the use of force
【先烈】the national martyrs
【先河】a harbinger; a forerunner
【先後】①the order (of things narrated, placed, etc.) ②the ins and outs of an incident

儿部

【先見之明】the ability to discern what is coming
【先進】predecessors; seniors
【先覺】a prophet
【先前】before ; previously
【先驅】a vanguard; a forerunner; a pioneer
【先下手爲強】It's always advantageous to make the first move (or take the initiative).
【先賢or先哲】ancient saints and sages
【先知】①a prophet ②a person of foresight or forethought
【先知先覺】①a person of foresight or forethought ②having foresight
【先兆】an omen; a portent; a sign
【先斬後奏】(in a modern sense) to take action before reporting to one's superior
【先生】① an honorable title for a teacher ②a name for the elderly and learned ③ Mister; Sir ④ a husband
【先人】①previous generations② forebears
【先入爲主】One usually favors the very first idea entering his mind.
【先嚴】my deceased father
【先王】① the late king ② ancient sage sovereigns

光 255 ㄍㄨㄤ guāng

1. light; brightness; light rays 2. glossy; smooth 3. glory; glorious; honor 4. to exhaust; to use up 5. alone; only 6. bare; naked; to bare
【光波】light waves
【光芒】rays of light; brilliant rays
【光芒萬丈】radiance; radiant
【光明】① light ② bright; promising ③ open-hearted; guileless
【光明磊落】straightforward and upright
【光明正大】honest, just, and upright
【光復】to recover (a lost land)
【光頭】a baldhead; baldheaded
【光天化日】(in) broad daylight; the light of day
【光禿禿】bare; bald
【光年】a light-year
【光溜溜】①smooth and glossy ②bare; naked
【光臨】Please grace our place with your presence.
【光亮】brightness; radiant; light; shiny
【光顧】to patronize; to honor with one's presence
【光怪陸離】strange-looking; fantastic; grotesque
【光棍】a bachelor or unmarried man
【光合作用】photosynthesis
【光滑】smooth and glossy
【光輝】radiance; brightness
【光脚】bare feet; barefooted
【光景】① a situation ② around; about
【光圈】the diaphragm of a camera
【光線】a ray of light
【光纖通訊】optical fiber communication
【光學】optics
【光學儀器】optical instruments
【光榮】glory; honor; glorious
【光澤】luster
【光宗耀祖】to glorify one's forebears
【光彩】①luster; splendor; radiance ②honorable; glorious
【光彩奪目】the luster that dazzles the eyes
【光陰】time
【光陰似箭】Time passes as fast as a flying arrow.

五畫

克 256 ㄎㄜˋ kè

1. to be able to 2. to win; to overcome; to conquer 3. love of superiority 4. a gram 5. to limit
【克服】①to overcome ②to put up with
【克敵致勝】to defeat the enemy and win the battle
【克難】to overcome difficulties
【克拉】a carat
【克勤克儉】diligent and frugal
【克制】to restrain; to control

兌 257 ㄉㄨㄟˋ duì

1. to exchange; to barter 2. (said of wine, etc.) to water; to weaken by adding water
【兌換】exchange; to exchange
【兌換率】exchange rates
【兌現】① to cash ② to fulfill; to carry out

免 258 (免) ㄇㄧㄢˇ miǎn

1. to avoid; to escape; to evade 2. to forego; to spare; to excuse; to exempt 3. to dismiss (from office)
【免不了】unavoidable; to have to
【免票】①a free ticket; a free pass ②free of charge
【免費】free of charge; gratuitous

【免得】 to save (the trouble of); to avoid; so as not to
【免談】 You might just as well save your breath.
【免禮】 (usually ordered by a superior) to forego formalities
【免開尊口】 You might as well save your breath.
【免職】 to be dismissed from office
【免除】 ① to prevent ② to exempt
【免試升學】 to enter a school without taking an entrance examination
【免稅】 free of duty; duty-free
【免稅商店】 a duty-free shop
【免俗】 to forego customary routines, formalities, etc.
【免役】 exemption from military service
【免疫】 immunity
【免驗】 to be exempt from customs examination

六畫

兒 259 ㄦˊ ér
1. a child; a baby 2. a son 3. referring to oneself when addressing parents 4. As a particle after noun, pronoun, adjective, adverb, and verb, 兒 is pronounced (儿).
【兒童】 children
【兒童讀物】 juvenile publications
【兒童樂園】 an amusement park catering to children
【兒童節目】 Children's programs
【兒童心理學】 child psychology
【兒童文學】 literary writings for children
【兒女】 ① sons and daughters; children ② young men and women
【兒女情長】 Long is the love between a man and a woman.
【兒歌】 children's songs
【兒科】 pediatrics
【兒媳 or 兒媳婦】 a daughter-in-law
【兒戲】 ① child's play ② a plaything ③ to treat lightly
【兒時】 childhood
【兒子】 a son or sons
【兒孫】 ① children and grandchildren ② offspring; descendants

免 260 (兎) ㄊㄨˋ tù
1. a hare; a rabbit 2. a young boy kept for sexual perversion
【兔起鶻落】 (said of calligraphic works) bold and agile
【兔唇】 a harelip, or a cleft lip
【兔子】 a hare; a rabbit
【兔崽子】 a brat; a bastard
【兔死狐悲】 sympathy with one of its kind

九畫

兜 261 ㄉㄡ dōu
1. a head-covering; a helmet 2. overalls 3. to solicit 4. to go for a drive around; to move around 5. to surround; to wrap up 6. a small pocket in clothes
【兜風】 to go joyriding
【兜圈子】 ① to take a stroll ② to circle ③ circumlocutory; to beat about the bush
【兜售】 to peddle
【兜攬生意】 to solicit business

十二畫

兢 262 ㄐㄧㄥ jīng
to fear; to dread; apprehensive; cautious
【兢兢業業】 cautious and attentive

入部 ㄖㄨˋ rù

入 263 ㄖㄨˋ rù
1. to enter; to come into 2. to join; to come into the company of 3. to arrive at; to reach 4. to put in 5. receipts; income 6. to get out of sight; to disappear 7. to get (inside, picked, elected, etc.) 8. to agree with; to conform to 9. one of the four tones of a character 參看「入聲」
【入不敷出】 cannot make both ends meet
【入門】 to have an elementary knowledge of
【入夢】 ① to fall asleep ② to appear in one's dream
【入迷】 to be captivated or fascinated
【入木三分】 ① (said of Chinese calligraphy) a forceful style ②

〔入部〕

(comments, analyses, etc.) incisive; penetrating
【入黨】to join a political party
【入土】to bury; to be buried
【入列】to take one's place in the ranks; to fall in
【入殮】to put a corpse in a coffin; to coffin
【入港】to enter a harbor (or port)
【入股】to become a shareholder
【入骨】deep (hatred, love, etc.); to the marrow
【入口】an entrance
【入海口】an estuary
【入畫】picturesque
【入伙】① to join in an enterprise ② to join a mess
【入夥】① to join a gang ② to join in an undertaking or enterprise
【入籍】to naturalize; to be naturalized
【入境】to entry a country
【入境證】an entry permit
【入境問俗】to learn the customs of a new place when one goes there
【入侵】to invade; to intrude
【入情入理】fair and reasonable
【入席】to be properly seated at a gathering, meeting or feast
【入學】to enter school
【入學考試】an entrance examination
【入選】to be selected
【入贅】to marry into the family of one's wife
【入超】excess of import
【入場】① to enter a meeting place ② to take part in an examination
【入場券】an admission ticket
【入神】captivated; bewitched; fascinated; spellbound
【入聲】(traditional Chinese phonetics) the fourth tone
【入睡】to go to sleep; to fall asleep
【入座】properly seated
【入夜】at night; in the evening
【入眼】pleasing to the eye; agreeable to look at
【入營】to enter the barracks—to join the army
【入伍】to become a soldier (usually under the conscription system)
【入圍】① to be selected as one of the few ② to enter a trapped area
【入味】① tasty ② interesting
【入獄】to be imprisoned
【入院】to be hospitalized

二畫

內 264 ㄋㄟˋ nèi

1. inside; within; inner; interior 2. wife 3. the palace of an emperor

【內部】the interior; the internal parts
【內幕消息】inside information
【內分泌】internal secretion; endocrines
【內服藥】drugs taken orally or internally
【內弟】younger brothers of one's wife
【內地】the hinterland; the inland
【內定】to have already decided, but yet to be officially announced
【內陸】inland; interior
【內陸國】a landlocked country
【內亂】rebellion; a civil war
【內亂罪】treason
【內閣】the cabinet
【內顧之憂】worries for trouble at home
【內科】internal medicine
【內科醫生】a physician
【內河】inland rivers
【內海】inland seas; continental seas
【內涵】(logic) intension; connotation
【內行】a specialist; an expert
【內訌】an intramural fight
【內疚】deep regret; remorse
【內奸】a spy within; a traitor
【內景】indoor scenes
【內親】relatives of one's wife
【內勤】desk work
【內情】an inside story
【內銷】(said of local products) for domestic sale or market
【內線】inside contacts; a stool pigeon
【內心】heart
【內向】introversion; introverted
【內債】internal debts
【內戰】a civil war
【內政】internal (or domestic) affairs
【內出血】internal bleeding
【內傷】internal injury
【內燃機】an internal-combustion engine
【內人 or 內子】my wife
【內容】① the meaning, theme, etc. of a literary work ② content
【內在】inherent; intrinsic; internal

【內在美】inner beauty
【內臟】internal organs; viscera
【內衣】underwear; undergarments
【內憂外患】(said of countries) troubles within and without
【內應】an inside help; a planted agent
【內務】① domestic affairs; internal affairs ②(in ancient China) affairs within the palace ③ family affairs

四畫

全 265 ㄑㄩㄢˊ quán
1. perfect 2. complete; whole; total; intact; all; entire; absolute 3. to keep whole or intact
【全班】the whole class
【全部】the whole; completely; total
【全盤】total; overall
【全盤計劃】an overall program or plan
【全貌】the overall appearance
【全面】overall; comprehensive
【全面攻擊】an all-out offensive
【全民】the whole (or entire) people
【全副武裝】to be armed to the teeth
【全套】the whole set
【全體】all; everybody
【全天候】all-weather
【全能】① omnipotence ② all-round
【全年】the whole year; all the year round
【全壘打】a home run
【全力】(with) all-out effort
【全力以赴】to spare no efforts
【全國】the whole country or nation
【全國性】nationwide; countrywide
【全開】standard-sized; full-size
【全集】the complete works of (Shakespeare, etc.)
【全家】the whole family
【全家福】a family photo
【全景】a full view; a whole scene
【全局】the overall situation
【全軍】the whole (or entire) army
【全軍覆沒】The whole army was lost.
【全球】the globe; the world
【全權代表】an envoy plenipotentiary
【全休】a complete rest
【全線】all fronts; the whole line
【全心全意】wholeheartedly
【全脂奶粉】whole milk powder
【全場】the whole audience
【全程】the whole course
【全蝕】a total eclipse
【全身】the whole body
【全神貫注】to concentrate on
【全盛時代 or 全盛時期】the heyday; the zenith; the prime
【全然】completely (ignorant, etc.); totally
【全才】a versatile person
【全速】full (or maximum) speed
【全無心肝】totally heartless
【全文】a full text

六畫

兩 266 ㄌㄧㄤˇ liǎng
1. two; a pair; a couple 2. both; either 3. a tael (a unit of weight) 4. (in ancient China) a piece of cloth, etc. of about 44 feet
【兩敗俱傷】Both are hurt. 或 Nobody wins.
【兩倍】double; twice
【兩半】two halves
【兩邊or兩旁】both sides; two sides
【兩邊討好】to please both sides
【兩面】① two sides ② double; dual
【兩面夾攻】to make a pincers drive
【兩面作戰】to fight on two fronts
【兩黨制】the bipartisan system
【兩頭兒】both ends; either end
【兩難】indecisive
【兩立】to coexit; coexitence
【兩口子or兩口兒】a married couple
【兩害相權取其輕】to accept the lesser of two evils
【兩虎相鬪必有一傷】When two powers battle, one is going to get hurt.
【兩回事】two entirely different things
【兩極】the opposing poles
【兩脚書櫥】① a two-legged bookcase ② a bookworm
【兩棲部隊】amphibious force
【兩棲作戰】amphibious operations
【兩訖 or 兩清】(said of a purchase) paid and delivered; (said of an account) both sides clear
【兩情繾綣】deeply in love with each other
【兩全】to be satisfactory to both parties
【兩全其美】to profit both parties

or attain two objectives by a single act
【兩小無猜】living and playing together in childhood innocence
【兩袖清風】(usually said of an honest public servant) to attain high official ranks without money in the bank
【兩性】① both sexes ② amphoteric
【兩相好】two lovers
【兩相情願】Both parties are willing.
【兩翼】(a military term) two flanks or wings
【兩院制】the bicameral system (of a parliament)
【兩用】① serving two purposes ② (said of a coat) reversible

八部
ㄅㄚ bā

八 267 ㄅㄚ bā (變調 ㄅㄚˊ bá)
eight
【八拜之交】sworn brotherhood
【八寶飯】rice cooked with eight ingredients
【八面玲瓏】to be pleasant all round
【八面威風】having an awe-inspiring reputation everywhere
【八方 or 八區】all directions
【八哥】a mynah
【八股】corny; lacking in originality
【八開】octavo (books, paper, etc.)
【八角】Japanese star anise
【八角形】an octagon
【八九不離十】pretty close; very near
【八仙】the Eight Immortals of Taoism
【八成】nearly; almost; very likely
【八月】① August ② eight months ③ the eighth month of the lunar calendar

二畫

公 268 ㄍㄨㄥ gōng
1. unselfish; unbiased; fair 2. public 3. to make public; open to all 4. the first of old China's five grades of the nobility 5. the father of one's husband (one's husband's father) 6. one's grandfather 7. a respectful salutation 8. the male (of animals) 9. office; official duties
【公保】government insurance for public servants
【公報】an official bulletin; a gazette; a communiqué
【公報私仇】to avenge oneself on one's enemies in the name of public interests
【公布or公佈】to promulgate; to announce
【公婆】the parents of one's husband
【公平】fair; unbiased; just
【公僕】a public servant; an official
【公賣局】a government monopoly bureau
【公民】citizens
【公民投票】the referendum; the plebiscite
【公民科】civics
【公畝】an area of 100 meters square
【公墓】a public cemetery
【公法】public law
【公費】public funds; government funds
【公分】① a centimeter (cm.) ② a gram (g.)
【公憤】public indignation
【公德】social morality; social ethics
【公德心】public-mindedness
【公道】① reasonable (prices); just; fair ② justice
【公敵】a public enemy
【公噸】a metric ton
【公攤】to share (expenditures, capital investment, etc.) equally
【公堂】a court of law
【公聽會】a public hearing
【公釐】① a millimeter ② an area of one square meter
【公里】a kilometer
【公理】① right; justice ② an axiom
【公立學校】public schools
【公兩】100 grams
【公路】a highway
【公論】public opinion
【公告】① a proclamation ② to make an announcement
【公告地價】a government-assessed land price
【公幹】an official assignment or duty
【公館】① an official residence ② a residence (a polite reference to other's residence)
【公共】public (relations, health, etc.)
【公共電視】public television
【公共關係】public relations (PR)
【公共汽車】a bus; an omnibus

【公共行政】public administration
【公共秩序】public order
【公共事業】public utilities
【公共衛生】public sanitation
【公克】a gram
【公開】to make known to the public; to make public
【公款】public funds; public money
【公海】the high seas
【公害】social effects of pollution
【公毫】a centigram
【公函】an official letter
【公會】a union, league, society, federation, etc. of a certain trade
【公雞】a cock; a rooster 「mony
【公祭】a public memorial cere-
【公教人員】government employees and staffs of public schools
【公斤】a kilogram (kg)
【公爵】a duke
【公爵夫人】a duchess
【公頃】a hectare (ha)
【公權】civil rights; civic rights
【公權力】government power or authority
【公休】①an official holiday ②a holiday for a particular trade
【公信力】government credibility
【公職】government offices; official posts or ranks 「the public debt
【公債】① government bonds ②
【公正】justice; fairness; just; im-
【公證】to notarize ⌊partial
【公證結婚】a court wedding
【公證人】a notary public; a witness
【公主】a princess 「country
【公忠體國】to be loyal to one's
【公衆】the public
【公尺】a meter
【公差】official assignments (usually involving travel) 「duties
【公出】to be away on official
【公使】(diplomacy) a minister; an
【公使館】a legation ⌊envoy
【公式】a formula
【公式化】stereotyped; formulistic
【公事】official business; public affairs
【公事公辦】to discharge official duties strictly according to rules
【公審】a public trial
【公升】a liter
【公署】a government office
【公說公有理，婆說婆有理】In the presence of a superior, umpire, etc., each of two quarreling parties insists that he is right.
【公然】openly; in public
【公認】generally recognized
【公子】①(in ancient China) sons of a duke or a ranking official ②a polite designation for another's son or sons
【公子哥兒】dandies; playboys
【公廁】a public lavatory
【公寸】a decimeter
【公司】a company; a corporation
【公私分明】to be scrupulous in separating public from private interests 「ownership
【公私合營】state and private joint
【公訴】public prosecution
【公案】①a case of law ②office desks ③official business
【公而忘私】to forget oneself in the discharge of official duties
【公益】public interests or welfare
【公議】public discussion
【公有】publiclyowned; public
【公演】to stage shows for public
【公營】publicly owned ⌊viewing
【公營事業】government-owned enterprises 「erty
【公物】public or government prop-
【公務】official matters, business, duties, etc. 「civil servants
【公務員】government employees;
【公務員懲誡委員會】the Committee on the Discipline of Public Functionaries
【公文】official documents
【公寓】an apartment house
【公約】① a convention; a pact ② joint pledge 「the Christian era
【公元】in the year of our Lord...;
【公園】a park; a public garden
【公用】public (telephones, etc.)
【公用電話】a public telephone
【公用事業】public utilities

六 269
ㄌㄧㄡˋ liù (讀音 ㄌㄨˋ lù)
six 「*of Six Laws*
【六法全書】*The Complete Volume*
【六根清淨】(said of a Buddha) free from human desires and pas-
【六角形】a hexagon ⌊sions
【六神無主】shocked; stunned out of one's wits
【六月】① June ② the sixth month

〔八部〕

〔八部〕

of the lunar calendar ③ six months

兮 270 ㄒㄧ xī
a particle of pause used in ancient poetry and still used in eulogies

四畫

共 271 ㄍㄨㄥˋ gòng
1. common; same 2. all; collectively 3. to share; to work together 4. together 5. an abbreviation of the word "Communism" or "Communist"
【共謀】to collaborate; to collude
【共勉】to encourage each other
【共鳴】①(physics) resonance or sympathetic vibration ② (to inspire) the same feeling in others
【共犯】① collusion ② an accomplice
【共赴國難】to work together to save the country in time of a national crisis
【共同】common; to cooperate in (an undertaking, etc.)
【共同基金】mutual fund
【共同市場】a common market
【共和 or 共和國】a republic
【共和黨】the Republican Party
【共計】the sum total; to come to; to add up to
【共襄盛舉】Let's all work together for this worthy project.
【共享】to enjoy together; to share
【共產黨】the Communist Party
【共產主義】Communism
【共事】①to work together; to be colleagues ②(said of women) to share the same husband
【共識】common consensus
【共存】to coexist; coexistent
【共存亡】(to defend a city or place) to the last man; to live or die together
【共有】owned by all; common (traits, customs, etc.)

五畫

兵 272 ㄅㄧㄥ bīng
1. arms; weapons 2. a soldier; a serviceman 3. a piece in Chinese chess—a pawn
【兵變】mutiny; troops in mutiny
【兵不血刃】(to achieve military objective) without firing a shot in anger or without bloodshed
【兵不厭詐】Trickery is no vice in military operations.
【兵馬】troops and horses—armaments
【兵馬俑】wood or clay figures of soldiers and horses buried with the dead
【兵法】military tactics and strategy
【兵團】a large (military) unit; corps
【兵力】military strength
【兵連禍結】constantly ravaged by war
【兵臨城下】The attacking army has reached the city gates.
【兵工廠】an arsenal; an ammunition works
【兵荒馬亂】disorder caused by continuous military operations
【兵家常事】a commonplace in military operations
【兵器】weapons; arms
【兵權】authority to make military decisions
【兵凶戰危】In war everybody is a loser.
【兵制】the military system
【兵種】intraservice classification of military units according to their equipment and functions
【兵士】a soldier; a foot soldier
【兵戎】① arms; weapons ② warfare
【兵戎相見】to resort to arms
【兵蟻】a soldier ant
【兵役】(compulsory) military service
【兵役法】conscription law
【兵營 or 兵舍】barracks
【兵源】manpower as a source of conscription

六畫

其 273 ㄑㄧˊ qí
1. a pronoun—he, she, it, they; his, her, its, their 2. this; that; the 3. an interrogative used to introduce a question
【其貌不揚】ugly in appearance
【其他 or 其餘】the others; the rest
【其樂無窮】The joy is boundless.
【其來有自】It did not happen by

accident.

【其間】 in; among; in between; between

【其中】 in; among; in the midst

【其實】 in fact; as a matter of fact

【其次】 secondly; besides

具 274
ㄐㄩˋ jù

1. an appliance, implement, utensil, tool, etc. 2. talent; capability 3. to prepare; to equip 4. complete; all

【具備】 ① all complete; all ready ② to have (qualifications or advantages)

【具名】 ① to sign ② to publish a writing, letter, etc. with a byline

【具體】 concrete

【具結】 ① to submit a pledge or guarantee to a government office for fulfilling of all obligations agreed upon ② (law) to sign an affidavit

【具有】 to be provided with

【具文】 ① to prepare a document, etc. for presenting to higher authorities ② empty words

典 275
ㄉㄧㄢˇ diǎn

1. a rule; a statute; a law; a canon 2. a tale or story from the classics; an allusion 3. to pawn; to mortgage

【典範】 an example; a paragon

【典當】 ① to pawn ② a pawnshop

【典禮】 a ceremony; a rite

【典故】 an allusion; an origin

【典籍】 ancient books, statute records, etc.

【典型】 a model; a pattern

【典章】 institutions

【典試委員會】 a committee in charge of examination affairs

【典押】 to mortgage

【典雅】 refined (writing); elegant (style)

【典獄長】 the warden

八畫

兼 276
ㄐㄧㄢ jiān

1. to unite in one; to connect; to annex 2. and; also; together with; both; equally; concurrently

【兼備】 to be in possession of both

【兼併】 to annex (another country, etc.)

【兼顧】 to look after both sides

【兼課】 ① to do some teaching besides one's main occupation ② to hold two or more teaching jobs concurrently

【兼職or兼差】 to take two or more jobs concurrently; a part-time job

【兼程】 to proceed on one's trip on the double

【兼善天下】 to benefit all the people in the world

【兼任】 to serve concurrently as

【兼任教師】 a part-time teacher

【兼容並蓄】 tolerant; open-minded

【兼愛】 love without distinction

十四畫

冀 277
ㄐㄧˋ jì

1. to hope 2. another name for Hopeh Province

冂部
ㄐㄩㄥ jiōng

三畫

冉 278
ㄖㄢˇ rǎn

1. gradually 2. tender; weak 3. the outer edge of a turtle's shell

【冉冉上升】 to rise gradually

冊 279
ㄘㄜˋ cè

1. (in ancient China) a register; a book or books in general; volumes 2. a list; statistical tables; to record; records 3. an order to confer nobility titles

【冊立】 to crown an empress

【冊子】 a book; a pamphlet

四畫

再 280
ㄗㄞˋ zài

1. again; repeated 2. still; further; then

【再版】 the second printing or edition (of a book)

【再犯】 ① to repeat an offense ② a second-time offender

【再度】once more; once again
【再婚】to remarry after the annulment of a former marriage; digamy
【再嫁 or 再醮】to remarry
【再接再勵】to forge ahead in disregard of obstructions
【再教育】reeducation
【再見or再會】Good-bye. 或See you again.
【再起】① to rise again ② to assume public office again
【再娶】(said of a man) to remarry
【再現】reappearance
【再審】a retrial
【再生父母】second parents—an expression of deep gratitude to benefactors for great help rendered
【再生記憶體】(computer) regenerative
【再說】furthermore; besides
【再次】once more; once again
【再三】time and again; repeatedly
【再也不】never again

冂部

七畫

冒 281
ㄇㄠˋ mào
1. incautious; imprudent; rash 2. to risk; to brave; to be exposed to (hardships) 3. to put forth; to issue forth; to go up (as fire, smoke, etc.)
【冒牌】a fake; an imitation
【冒昧】to make bold; to presume
【冒冒失失】rash; imprudent
【冒名】to assume another's name
【冒名頂替】to assume the identity of another person
【冒犯】to offend (a superior, elder, etc.)
【冒瀆】to bother or annoy (a superior)
【冒領】to get or take something by posing as someone else for whom it is intended
【冒號】the colon
【冒火】to become angry
【冒險】to take risks
【冒險犯難】to do something despite the dangers and difficulties involved
【冒稱】to claim falsely
【冒充】to pretend to be somebody else
【冒失】hasty; reckless; rash
【冒失鬼】a rash fellow; a reckless guy
【冒然】reckless; rashly; rash
【冒死】to risk death
【冒煙】Smoke rises. 或 to belch smoke
【冒雨】to brave the rain

胄 282
ㄓㄡˋ zhòu
a helmet
【胄甲】a helmet and armor

九畫

冕 283
ㄇㄧㄢˇ miǎn
1. a ceremonial cap for high ministers in ancient China 2. a crown

冖部
ㄇㄧˋ mì

七畫

冠 284
1. ㄍㄨㄢ guān
1. a cap 2. the comb or crest of a bird
【冠冕堂皇】① elegant and stately ② high-sounding
【冠蓋雲集】(usually said of a meeting or gathering) where ranking officials congregate

冠 284
2. ㄍㄨㄢˋ guàn
1. at 20 when a young man is capped 2. first-rate 3. to wear a cap
【冠禮】(in ancient China) a capping ceremony for a young man when he reaches 20
【冠軍】a champion
【冠詞】the article

八畫

冤 285
(寃)ㄩㄢ yuān
1. oppression; injustice; a grievance; a wrong 2. feud; animosity; enmity 3. to cheat; to lie 4. to spend money recklessly 5. to make false accusations
【冤大頭】a fathead
【冤家】an enemy (but also used for lovers)
【冤家路窄】Enemies often cross

each other's path. ⌈or wrong
【冤情】 the details of a grievance⌋
【冤屈】 a grievance; a wrong
【冤仇】 feud; enmity; animus
【冤枉】 to wrong; to accuse a person with a false charge
【冤獄】 miscarriage of justice

冥 286 ㄇㄧㄥˊ míng
1. dark; obscure; dim; dusk 2. stupidity; stupid 3. far and high 4. deep 5. the unseen world; Hades 6. night
【冥冥之中】 (said of divine influence) imperceptibly but inexorably
【冥府】 the underworld; Hades
【冥想】 deep meditation
【冥思苦想】 to cudgel one's brains
【冥頑不靈】 stupid and stubborn
【冥王星】 the planet Pluto

冢 287 ㄓㄨㄥˇ zhǒng
1. a high grave 2. a peak; a summit 3. the eldest 4. great; supreme; prime

十四畫

冪 288 ㄇㄧˋ mì
1. to cover with cloth 2. a cloth cover 3. (mathematics) power

冫部 ㄅㄧㄥ bīng

三畫

冬 289 ㄉㄨㄥ dōng
1. winter 2. (the lunar calendar) the period from the 10th to the 12th month
【冬眠】 to hibernate; hibernation
【冬天 or 冬令】 winter
【冬暖夏涼】 cool in summer and warm in winter
【冬令救濟】 relief of the poor during winter months
【冬瓜】 a white gourd; a wax gourd
【冬烘】 a pedant or a pedagogue
【冬季】 the winter season
【冬至】 the winter solstice

四畫

冰 290 ㄅㄧㄥ bīng
1. ice; icicles 2. cold; frost
【冰雹】 hail; a hailstone
【冰棒】 a flavored popsicle
【冰封】 icebound
【冰刀】 the blades of ice skates
【冰點】 the freezing point
【冰凍】 to freeze
【冰凍三尺非一日之寒】 The grudge or animosity has its deep root.
【冰糖】 rock candy ⌈covered land
【冰天雪地】 frozen and snow-⌋
【冰冷】 ① icy cold; cold as ice ② cold or frosty (expressions, etc.)
【冰涼】 icy cold; very cold
【冰菓店】 a cold drink shop
【冰塊】 ice cubes; ice blocks
【冰窖】 an icehouse; a glacial vault
【冰淇淋】 ice cream
【冰橇】 a sled; a sledge; a sleigh
【冰鞋】 ice skates
【冰箱】 an icebox; a refrigerator
【冰雪聰明】 very clever; brilliant
【冰鎮】 to preserve on ice
【冰柱】 icicles
【冰川 or 冰河】 a glacier
【冰釋】 solved; to disappear with-
【冰山】 an iceberg ⌊out a trace
【冰上運動】 ice sports
【冰水】 ice water ⌈ruptible
【冰霜】 ① cold and severe ② incor-⌋
【冰原】 an ice field

五畫

冶 291 ㄧㄝˇ yě
1. to smelt; to fuse metals 2. seductive; fascinating
【冶遊】 to frequent brothels

冷 292 ㄌㄥˇ lěng
1. cold 2. (said of business, farming, etc.) off-season
【冷板凳】 ①a post which has little or no authority ② a cold reception
【冷冰冰】 icy cold; cold as ice
【冷不防】 unexpectedly
【冷盤 or 冷碟】 a dish of assorted cold meats

冫部

【冷僻】① out-of-the-way or secluded (places) ② big or hard (words)
【冷漠】indifferent; apathetic
【冷門】not popular or not in great demand
【冷鋒】a cold front
【冷淡】cold (expressions); indifferent (attitudes)
【冷凍】freezing
【冷凍庫】a freezer
【冷凍食品】frozen foods
【冷暖】the degree of cold or heat
【冷暖自知】One knows what it's like without being told.
【冷冷清清】deserted and quiet; desolate
【冷落】① cold and lonely ② cold reception; to cold-shoulder
【冷酷】merciless; heartless
【冷汗】① a cold sweat ② clammy perspiration
【冷箭】an unexpected attack or a pot shot
【冷靜】calm or composed
【冷氣】air conditioning
【冷氣團】a cold air mass
【冷氣機】an air-conditioner
【冷清】desolate; lonely; deserted
【冷却】to get cold; to cool off
【冷却劑】a coolant
【冷血動物】① cold-blooded animals ② a heartless or ruthless person
【冷笑】a sarcastic smile or grin
【冷戰】cold war
【冷嘲熱諷】sarcasm and mockery
【冷場】temporary suspension of a show, party, etc. occasioned by inefficient management
【冷水】cold water; unboiled water
【冷霜】cold cream
【冷若冰霜】as cold as an iceberg—aloof
【冷藏】to preserve by means of refrigeration
【冷颼颼】frosty; chilly
【冷言冷語】sarcastic remarks
【冷眼旁觀】① to look on coldly ② to look on with a critical eye
【冷飲】cold drinks

八畫

准 293 ㄓㄨㄣˇ zhǔn
1. to approve; to permit; to grant 2. in accordance with 3. equivalent; equal
【准將】a brigadier general
【准許】to approve; to permit; to allow

凋 294 ㄉㄧㄠ diāo
1. withered; faded 2. exhausted; emaciated
【凋零】① withered ② to pass away
【凋落or凋謝】① fallen; withered ② to pass away
【凋萎】① withered; faded ② passing away

凌 295 ㄌㄧㄥˊ líng
1. accumulated ice 2. to insult; to maltreat; to throw one's weight around 3. to rise; to ride; to soar 4. to traverse
【凌亂】in total disorder
【凌駕】to rise above others; to outstrip
【凌晨】the wee hours
【凌辱】①to insult; to maltreat ② to assault

凍 296 ㄉㄨㄥˋ dòng
1. to freeze 2. cold; icy
【凍結】to freeze (an account, etc.)
【凍僵】to be benumbed with cold
【凍瘡】frostbite; chilblains
【凍傷】to suffer injuries or illness as a result of long exposure to cold weather
【凍死】to freeze to death

十三畫

凜 297 ㄌㄧㄣˇ lǐn
1. cold; bleak 2. imposing; awe-inspiring
【凜冽】very cold; cold to the marrow
【凜然】a stern, repellent appearance arousing fear, reverence

十四畫

凝 298 ㄋㄧㄥˊ níng
1. to freeze 2. to congeal; to coagulate 3. to form; to take shape 4. to concentrate; to cohere
【凝固】(said of liquid) to congeal; to solidify
【凝結】to condense; to curdle
【凝聚】to concentrate; to curdle
【凝想】to meditate
【凝重】dignified
【凝視】to gaze (lovingly)
【凝神】to concentrate
【凝神諦聽】to listen attentively

几部 ㄐㄧˇ jǐ

299 几 ㄐㄧˇ jǐ (語音 ㄐㄧ jī)
1. a small table 2. a simplified form of the character "幾"

一畫

300 凡 ㄈㄢˊ fán
1. common; ordinary; dull 2. worldly; mortal; earthly 3. generally; every; whenever; wherever 4. altogether
【凡夫俗子】the masses; ordinary people
【凡間】the material world
【凡心】worldly desires
【凡事】everything
【凡是】all (who are present, etc. or which are black, heavy, etc.)
【凡士林】Vaseline; petrolatum
【凡人】an ordinary person
【凡爾賽】Versailles, French city and site of the Versailles Palace built by Louis XIV

九畫

301 凰 ㄏㄨㄤˊ huáng
the female phoenix, a legendary bird in Chinese mythology

十畫

302 凱 ㄎㄞˇ kǎi
1. peace; joy 2. balmy; soothing; tender 3. a victory—a triumphant return of an army
【凱歌】a song of victory
【凱旋】to return in triumph
【凱旋門】① the Arc of Triumph (in Paris, France) ② a triumphal arch

十二畫

303 凳 (櫈) ㄉㄥˋ dèng
a stool; a bench

凵部 ㄑㄩ qū

二畫

304 凶 ㄒㄩㄥ xiōng
1. evil; bad 2. famine 3. unlucky; unfortunate 4. fear; fearsome 5. very; excessive; excess
【凶暴】fierce and brutal
【凶猛】violent; ferocious
【凶多吉少】to bode ill rather than well
【凶年 or 凶歲】a year of famine
【凶悍】fierce and tough
【凶狠】fierce and malicious
【凶器】a lethal weapon
【凶險】danger; dangerous
【凶宅】a haunted house
【凶兆】a bad omen
【凶殺】homicide; murder
【凶手】a murderer; an assassin
【凶神惡煞】devils; fiends
【凶殘】bloodthirsty; merciless
【凶惡】brutish; fearful; ferocious

三畫

305 凸 ㄊㄨˊ tú
1. protuberant; convex 2. to protrude; to jut
【凸透鏡】a convex lens
【凸出】bulging out; to protrude

306 凹 ㄠ āo
1. indented; an indention 2. hollow; concave
【凹透鏡】a concave lens
【凹陷】a hollow or depression

307 出 ㄔㄨ chū
1. to go out; to come out 2. to produce; to reproduce 3. to beget 4. to happen or occur; to incur 5. to put forth; to bud 6. to divorce (a wife, etc.) 7. to chase away; to banish 8. to expend; to pay out 9. to escape; to leave (one's home, etc.) 10. to appear 11. to take office 12. to vent (one's anger, etc.)
【出版】to publish

〔凵部〕

【出版家 or 出版者】a publisher
【出版自由】freedom of publication
【出版物】publications
【出殯】to carry a coffin to the grave for burial
【出兵】to dispatch troops
【出品】products
【出馬】to go out and face something
【出沒無常】to appear and disappear at unpredictable places and times
【出賣】① to sell ② to betray
【出毛病】to be or go out of order; to go wrong
【出門】to leave one's home; to take a trip
【出面】to assume the responsibility (in mediation, negotiations, etc.)
【出名】to become famous; famous
【出發】to set out; to leave for
【出發點】① the starting point ② a basis; premises ③ a motive
【出風頭】to be in the spotlight
【出點子】to offer advice
【出動】to dispatch or send out
【出頭】to make good or to succeed
【出題】① to set a theme ② to set questions
【出庭】to appear in court
【出土】to come out of earth
【出納】a teller or treasurer
【出來】① to come out; to appear ② to make out ③ to bring to pass
【出類拔萃】outstanding; eminent
【出力】to devote one's efforts to
【出列】to leave one's place in the ranks
【出路】① the prospects (of a career, etc.) ② an outlet
【出籠】to become current
【出閣】(said of a girl) to get married
【出港】① to leave (a) port ② to send (goods) abroad
【出國】to go abroad
【出軌】to derail
【出口】①to export ② to utter; to speak ③an exit (in a theater, etc.)
【出口貨】exports
【出口成章】One's tongue is the pen of a ready writer.
【出口傷人】to make insulting remarks
【出海】to leave (a) port; to go to sea
【出海口】an estuary
【出汗】to perspire; to sweat
【出航】①to set sail ②to set out on a flight
【出乎意外】unexpectedly
【出擊】to leave (a base, camp, position, etc.) to attack or raid (the enemy)
【出家】(Buddhism) to leave home and become a monk or nun
【出嫁】to get married
【出界】(sports) out of bounds; outside
【出境】to leave a place or country
【出境證】an exit permit
【出局】(baseball) out
【出奇】① extraordinary ②(to win) by surprise
【出奇制勝】to win by surprise
【出其不意】to take by surprise; to catch (someone) off guard
【出氣】to vent one's anger
【出錢】to provide the funds
【出勤】to take a business trip
【出去】① to go out ② Get out!
【出席】to attend or to be present at
【出息】① promising ② profit
【出血】bleeding; hemorrhage
【出現】to appear; to emerge
【出巡】to go on an inspection trip
【出診】to be on house call
【出征】to go out to battle
【出主意】① to scheme; to provide an idea ② to incite or instigate
【出衆】outstanding; foremost
【出差】to go out of town on business
【出超】a favorable balance of trade 亦作「貿易順差」
【出醜】to make a scene; to lose face
【出產】to produce or grow
【出廠】(said of a product) to leave the factory
【出處】the source of an allusion or a quotation
【出師】① to move soldiers forward for attack ② to complete one's apprenticeship in a trade and make a debut as a professional
【出使】to be appointed as a diplomatic envoy
【出示】to show (something) to someone
【出事】to be in trouble; to have an accident
【出手】① to sell ② to take on a job ③an offer ④to reach out with one's hand
【出售】to sell
【出身】backgrounds; qualifications
【出神】① absorbed in ② absent-

to be close to 「self
【切膚or切己】very close to one-
【切題】to the point 「bid
【切忌】to be sure to avoid; to for-
【切記】to keep or to bear in mind
【切實】①thoroughly ②sure; cer-
【切身】personal (interests) ⌊tain
【切勿】do not by any means

刈 314 ㄧ yì
to mow; to reap: 刈草機 a mower

三畫

刊 315 ㄎㄢ kān
1. to hew; to cut 2. to engrave 3. a publication 4. to publish
【刊登 or 刊載】① to publish ② to carry (an article)
【刊物】a periodical; a publication
【刊誤表 or 勘誤表】a list of corrections attached to a publication; errata

四畫

刎 316 ㄨㄣˇ wěn
to cut the throat
【刎頸之交】profound mutual devotion between friends

刑 317 ㄒㄧㄥˊ xíng
as in 刑罰—penalty; punishment
【刑法】criminal law; the criminal code
【刑具】an instrument of torture
【刑期】a term of imprisonment
【刑求】to exact confession by means of torture
【刑場】an execution ground
【刑事】criminal; penal
【刑事犯】a criminal 「procedure
【刑事訴訟法】the code of criminal

划 318 ㄏㄨㄚˊ huá
to oar; to row
【划船】to row a boat
【划算】① to calculate; to weigh ②
⌊profitable

列 319 ㄌㄧㄝˋ liè
1. to arrange in a line; to line up 2. to enumerate 3. to display 4. a line; a series
【列島】an archipelago
【列舉】to enumerate
【列強】the various powers
【列席】to be present (at a meeting as an observer)
【列傳】collected biographies
【列車】a train
【列祖列宗】an array of ancestors

五畫

初 320 ㄔㄨ chū 「early; initial
1. first 2. original 3. junior 4.
【初版】the first edition (of a book)
【初步】① the first or initial step ② a primer, or the rudimentary knowledge of something
【初犯】① first offenses ② a first
【初冬】early winter ⌊offender
【初露鋒芒】to display one's ability for the first time
【初戀】first love
【初稿】the first draft
【初級】elementary; primary
【初級小學 or 初小】formerly, a primary school which comprises only the first four grades
【初級中學or初中】junior middle
【初交】a new friendship ⌊school
【初期】the first or initial stage
【初秋】early autumn
【初夏】early summer
【初學】① in the beginning stage of an effort to learn (a subject) ② a beginner
【初選】a primary election
【初診】①the first visit to a doctor ②to visit a patient for the first time 「tion, or intention
【初衷】the original longing, aspira-
【初出茅廬】still inexperienced
【初春】early spring
【初創】newly founded
【初試】① to try for the first time ② a preliminary examination or test
【初審】① a first hearing (of a case in court) ② a preliminary screening (of applications, entries in a contest, etc.)
【初生之犢不畏虎】Young men fresh from school are uncompromising despite difficulties or pressure from above.

刀部

【初次】the first time
【初賽】a preliminary competition
【初葉】the early years (of a century)

〔刀部〕

刪 321 ㄕㄢ shān
to delete; to take out; to erase
【刪訂】to revise (an edition)
【刪改】to remove superfluities and correct errors (in a writing)
【刪節or刪減】to abridge or condense
【刪節號】ellipsis (a punctuation mark)
【刪除】to delete; to strike out

判 322 ㄆㄢˋ pàn
to judge; to conclude
【判別】to distinguish; to tell apart
【判定】to judge; to decide
【判斷】judgment, decision or conclusion
【判例】(said of court decisions) a precedent
【判官】a fierce-looking judge in the afterlife court of law
【判決】a verdict; a sentence
【判決書】a verdict in writing
【判處】to sentence; to condemn
【判若兩人】to become a completely different person
【判罪】to declare guilty

別 323 ㄅㄧㄝˊ bié
1. to part 2. to distinguish; to differentiate 3. other; another; different 4. (in imperative expressions) do not
【別忙】Don't hurry.
【別苗頭】(informal) to rival in competition
【別名 or 別號】an alias
【別提】We needn't mention it.
【別離】parting; separation
【別管】no matter (who, what, etc.)
【別開生面】to introduce a novelty
【別具隻眼】to have an original view
【別具一格】having a unique style
【別致 or 別緻】fresh; new; novel
【別針】a safety pin; a pin; a brooch
【別出心裁】ingenious
【別生枝節】to have new complications
【別墅】a villa; a country house
【別樹一幟】to become independent
【別人】other people; others
【別字】①a word which is not correctly written or pronounced ② an alias
【別有風味】to have a unique flavor
【別有所指】to imply another thing
【別有用心】to have a hidden purpose

刨 324 ㄆㄠˊ páo
to dig; to excavate

利 325 ㄌㄧˋ lì
1. profit; benefit; advantage; gain 2. sharp 3. to benefit; to serve
【利比亞】Libya
【利弊 or 利病】advantages and disadvantages
【利尿】diuresis
【利令智昏】blinded or dulled by greed
【利祿】wealth and position
【利率】the interest rate
【利害】interest and disinterest
【利息or利錢】interest
【利市百倍】to make an enormous profit
【利潤】profit; gain; net profit
【利益】benefit; profit; advantage
【利益均霑】to let everybody have his hands on the pie
【利誘】to tempt with money or material gain
【利慾薰心】lured by profits; blinded or dulled by greed
【利用】to utilize; to make use of

六畫

刮 326 ㄍㄨㄚ guā
to pare; to shave; to scrape
【刮破】to cut or hurt (the face, etc.) in shaving
【刮目相看】to marvel at someone's progress
【刮刀】a scraper
【刮臉】to shave (the face)
【刮刮叫】wonderful; very good
【刮鬍子】① to be scolded ② to shave

券 327 ㄑㄩㄢˋ quàn
1. a ticket 2. a certificate 3. a bond

到 328 ㄉㄠˋ dào
to reach; to arrive
【到達】to reach; to arrive
【到底】① after all; at length; finally ② to reach the extremity
【到頭來】after all; in the end

【到家】① to get home ② to become proficient, or extremely well-versed

【到齊】Everybody (who is supposed to be here) has come.

【到期】to reach the deadline or date of termination; to expire

【到職】to arrive for a new assignment

【到場】to show up; to be present

【到處】everywhere; far and wide

【到處爲家】Everywhere may be one's home. ⌈or possession

【到手】to come into one's hands⌋

【到任】to assume a (high official) post

【到案】to answer a court summons

剎 329
(刹) ㄔㄚˋ chà
a (Buddhist) temple, shrine, monastery or abbey

【剎那】a moment; an instant

剁 330
ㄉㄨㄛˋ duò
to chop; to mince; to hash

制 331
ㄓˋ zhì
1. to establish; to institute; to set up 2. to prevail; to overpower; to control 3. a system 4. used before the signature in letter writing to indicate the writer is in mourning ⌈overcome

【制伏】to subdue; to subjugate; to⌋

【制服】a uniform

【制敵機先】to gain an advantage over the enemy by taking steps to forestall him

【制定】to institute; to establish

【制度】a system; an institution

【制空權】air supremacy

【制衡】to check and balance

【制限】① to restrict ② a limit

【制憲】to draw up a national constitution

【制止】to stop; to prevent

【制裁】to chastise; to sanction

【制壓】① to overwhelm ② to neutralize (enemy fire)

【制約】to restrict; to condition

刷 332
1. ㄕㄨㄚ shuā
1. to brush; to scrub; to clean; to daub 2. a brush 3. to eliminate

【刷洗】to scrub

【刷新】① to make like new; to renovate ② to make (a new ⌈sports record)⌋

【刷子】a brush

【刷牙】to brush the teeth

刷 332
2. ㄕㄨㄚˇ shuǎ

【刷選】to choose; to pick; to select

刺 333
ㄘˋ cì
1. to pierce; to stab; to prick 2. to irritate; to stimulate 3. a thorn; a splinter; small fishbones; a sting 4. to assassinate 5. a name card

【刺鼻】to irritate the nose

【刺目 or 刺眼】dazzling

【刺刀】a bayonet

【刺探】to spy; to find out secretly

【刺骨】① (said of cold) bone-chilling ② (said of hatred) bitter ⌈or deep⌋

【刺客】an assassin

【刺激】to stimulate; to irritate

【刺激品 or 刺激物】a stimulant

【刺激性】stimulativeness

【刺青】to tattoo; a tattoo

【刺繡】to embroider; embroidery

【刺殺】① to assassinate ② (baseball) to put out (a base runner)

【刺耳】screechy; grating; ear-⌈piercing⌋

【刺蝟】a hedgehog

刻 334
1. ㄎㄜˋ kè
1. to carve; to engrave; to cut 2. a quarter (of an hour) 3. cruel; heartless; unfeeling; cutting; harshly; acrimonious; biting 4. moment

【刻薄】cold-hearted; acrimonious

【刻薄寡恩】to treat harshly and to give rare generosity

【刻板】① to engrave (for printing) ② monotonous; dull; stereotyped

【刻不容緩】Not a moment is to be ⌈lost.⌋

【刻刀】a burin; a graver

【刻骨銘心】to permanently imprint (another's favor, etc.) on the mind ⌈② simple and frugal⌋

【刻苦】① assiduous; hardworking

【刻苦耐勞】to work hard without complaint

【刻畫】to depict; to portray

【刻畫入微】vivid portrayal of details

【刻己待人】self-sacrificing

【刻舟求劍】to be stubbornly un-

imaginative
【刻字】to engrave words (on stone, blocks, etc.) 「tensive attention
【刻意】to do something with in-

〔刀部〕

刻 334
2. ㄎㄜ kē
to carve; to engrave
【刻印 or 刻圖章】to make a chop by carving

七畫

則 335
ㄗㄜˊ zé
1. a law; a rule; a regulation; a standard; a norm; a criterion 2. a particle indicating consequence (usually used after a supposition) or a reason 3. a numerary particle used before news reports, advertisements, etc. 4. but; however 5. to imitate; to
follow

剃 336
ㄊㄧˋ tì 「head
to shave: 剃頭 to shave the
【剃刀】a razor
【剃度】to cut off hair and join a monastery; to tonsure

削 337
ㄒㄩㄝ xuē
(語音 ㄒㄧㄠ xiāo)
1. to cut; to pare; to shave; to whittle 2. to deprive
【削平】①to pare; to smooth ②to put down; to conquer
【削髮】to shave the head 「level
【削價】to cut price to the cost
【削減】to curtail; to cut down
【削鉛筆】to sharpen a pencil
【削趾適屨】an impractical solution of a problem 亦作「削足適履」
【削除】to take out; to omit
【削弱】to enfeeble; to weaken; to
devitalize

剋 338
ㄎㄜˋ kè
1. to overcome 2. to cut down 3. to limit 4. to engrave; to imprint 5. can; to be able to
【剋夫】to be fated to mourn one's husband's death
【剋扣】to withhold (military supplies, etc.) for personal gain
【剋妻】to be fated to mourn one's wife's death
【剋星】a person who always bars another person from success; a
jinx

剌 339
1. ㄌㄚˋ là
to go against; to contradict; perverse; disagreeable; rebellious

剌 339
2. ㄌㄚˊ lá
to slash open

前 340
ㄑㄧㄢˊ qián
1. front; forward; before 2. previous; former; preceding; past; of earlier times 3. future 4. to advance; to proceed; to progress;
【前輩】a senior 「to precede
【前邊(兒)】①the front ②ahead;
【前排】the front row 「in front
【前仆後繼】Behind the fallen is an endless column of successors.
【前門】the front door or gate
【前面】① the front; the front side ② ahead; in front
【前方】① the front (in war) ② the forward direction
【前鋒】the vanguard; the van
【前導】the guide or motorcade
【前臺】the stage; the proscenium
【前提】①a premise ②a prerequisite
【前天】the day before yesterday
【前廳】an antechamber
【前途】the prospect 「nite.
【前途茫茫】One's future is indefi-
【前途無量】to have boundless prospects
【前年】the year before last
【前例】a precedent 「ous efforts
【前功盡棄】to nullify all the previ-
【前科】a previous criminal record
【前科犯】an ex-convict
【前後】① the front and the rear; before and after ② (indicating time) around; about ③ from beginning to end; altogether
【前後矛盾】inconsistent; contradictory 「large retinue
【前呼後擁】(said of VIPs) with a
【前進】to advance; to proceed; to go forward; to progress
【前車之鑒】a lesson from the failure of one's predecessor
【前前後後】the ins and outs
【前驅】the forerunner; the vanguard
【前夕】the eve (of an event)

【前線】the front line (in war); the front
【前置詞 or 介系詞】a preposition
【前者】the former
【前兆】an omen; a premonition
【前程】① a future ② a career
【前程似錦】to have brilliant prospects
【前程萬里】to have the prospect of a very successful career
【前世】① the previous generation ② the previous life
【前事不忘，後事之師】To remember past errors insures one against repetition of the same errors.
【前哨】(military) a sentry; an outpost
【前身】the forerunner
【前生】the former life or lives
【前日】the day before yesterday
【前人種樹，後人乘凉】to profit from the labor of one's forefathers
【前任】a predecessor
【前奏】a prelude; a harbinger
【前次】the previous occasion; last time
【前思後想】to turn over (a problem) in one's mind; to ponder
【前所未有】unprecedented
【前所未聞】to have never heard of before
【前額】the forehead
【前夜】the night before last
【前言】a foreword; a preface
【前因後果】cause and effect
【前衛】① front line troops ② a forward ③ vanguard; avant-garde
【前晚】the evening before last
【前往】to go to (a place); to visit

八畫

剔 341
ㄊㄧ tī
1. to separate bones from meat; to scrape meat off bones 2. to pick out inferior materials; to scrape off 3. a rising stroke in Chinese characters
【剔除】to eliminate
【剔牙】to pick the teeth

剖 342
ㄆㄡˇ pǒu
1. to cut, rip or tear open 2. to explain; to analyze; to dissect
【剖白】to dispel suspicion by explanation
【剖腹】to cut the belly open
【剖腹自殺】(to commit) hara-kiri
【剖開】to cut or rip open
【剖解 or 剖析】① to dissect; to anatomize ② to analyze

剛 343
ㄍㄤ gāng
1. tough; unyielding; inflexible; hard; firm; strong; indomitable 2. just now 3. just; exactly 4. barely; only
【剛愎自用】stubborn; obstinate
【剛烈】tough and vehement; violent
【剛剛】① just now; just a moment ago ② just; only
【剛果】the Congo (Kinshasa)
【剛健】vigorous; energetic; robust
【剛勁】bold; vigorous; sturdy
【剛巧 or 剛好】exactly; precisely
【剛強】tough and strong; staunch
【剛直】tough and honest; upright
【剛才】just a moment ago; a very short while ago
【剛毅】tough and determined; resolute
【剛毅木訥】resolute and not eloquent

剜 344
ㄨㄢ wān
to scoop out; to gouge out; to carve out
【剜空心思】to exhaust one's wits

剝 345
1. ㄅㄛ bō
to strip; to skin; to make bare; to peel; to peel off; to shell
【剝皮】to skin; to peel off the skin
【剝得精光】stripped naked
【剝奪】to deprive or strip one of (rights, property, etc.)
【剝落】to come off; to be peeled off
【剝削】to exploit (people)

剝 345
2. ㄅㄠ bāo
to strip: 剝開to strip the covering off

九畫

副 346
ㄈㄨˋ fù
1. to assist 2. secondary; auxiliary; subsidiary 3. deputy; assistant; vice 4. a set
【副本or副張】a duplicate copy; a copy
【副標題】a subheading; a subtitle

刀部

【副官】an adjutant; an aide-de-camp
【副刊】a supplement
【副駕駛】a copilot
【副教授】an associate professor
【副校長】a provost (of a university)
【副產品】a by-product
【副作用】(medicine) side effects; by-effects
【副總統】a vice-president
【副詞】an adverb that modifies an adjective, a verb or another adverb
【副業】a side job; on the side

剪 347
(翦) ㄐㄧㄢˇ jiǎn
1. to cut or clip with scissors; to shear; to trim 2. to annihilate; to destroy completely 3. scissors; clippers; shears
【剪報】a newspaper cutting (or clipping)
【剪票】to punch a ticket
【剪髮】to cut hair
【剪刀 or 剪子】scissors; clippers
【剪貼】①to clip and paste (something out of a newspaper, etc.) in a scrapbook or on cards ② cutting out (as a schoolchildren's activity)
【剪貼簿】a scrapbook
【剪輯】①(movie) montage; film editing ② editing and rearrangement
【剪接】to edit or cut a film
【剪紙】(art and crafts) paper-cut
【剪指甲】to trim one's nails
【剪裁】to tailor clothing materials for a dress
【剪綵】to cut the ribbon

十畫

剩 348
ㄕㄥˋ shèng
to remain; to be left over; in excess; residues; remainder; surplus; remains
【剩飯】leftover rice
【剩貨】leftover goods; leftovers
【剩下】the remainder; to be left over
【剩餘】the surplus

割 349
ㄍㄜ gē
to cut; to sever; to divide
【割斷】to cut off; to sever by cutting
【割裂】to split; to slash or rip open
【割除】to cut off or out; to excise
【割捨】to part with; to give away
【割讓】to cede (land or territory)
【割草】to cut grass; to mow grass
【割愛】to give up what one treasures

創 350
1. ㄔㄨㄤˋ chuàng
1. to start; to begin; to initiate; to create; to establish; to found 2. original; unprecedented
【創辦】to start; to found
【創立】to start, found or establish
【創刊】to put out the first issue (of a periodical)
【創刊號】the first issue (of a periodical)
【創紀錄】to set a record
【創見】① an original opinion or view ② an unprecedented thing
【創舉】an unprecedented undertaking
【創新】to bring forth new ideas
【創制權】the initiative
【創始】to start; to begin; to commence
【創造】to create; to produce
【創造力】originality; creative ability
【創作】① to write (original works of literature) ② an original work of literature or art
【創意】creativity
【創業】to start a business

創 350
2. ㄔㄨㄤ chuāng
1. a wound 2. same as 瘡—a sore; a boil; an ulcer
【創口 or 創傷】a wound; a cut
【創痍滿目】nothing but ruins and debris

十一畫

剿 351
(勦) ㄐㄧㄠˇ jiǎo
to exterminate; to stamp out; to destroy; to put down
【剿滅】to exterminate
【剿匪】to launch attacks against the bandits

剷 352
ㄔㄢˇ chǎn
1. a shovel 2. to shovel; to level off; to raze to the ground
【剷平】to level to the ground; to level
【剷除】to root out; to eradicate

剽 353
ㄆㄧㄠˋ piào
1. to plunder; to rob; to steal 2.

agile; fast
【剽竊】①to purloin ②to plagiarize

十二畫

劃 354
1. ㄏㄨㄚˋ huà
1. to unify 2. to lay boundaries 3. to draw a line; to mark; to delineate 4. to plan or design 5. to set aside; to divide 6. a stroke (of a Chinese character)
【劃撥】to deposit money under the account of a seller in payment of goods purchased; to transfer funds
【劃分】to differentiate
【劃定】to delimit; to mark out
【劃清】to draw a clear line of demarcation
【劃時代】epoch-making; epochal
【劃一】to make uniform

劃 354
2. ㄏㄨㄚˊ huá
to cut

十三畫

劇 355
ㄐㄩˋ jù
1. a drama; a theatrical work; a play 2. intense; strenuous; acute; severe 3. to play
【劇本】a play; a scenario
【劇目】a repertoire
【劇坊】a theater workshop
【劇毒】deadly poison
【劇團】an opera troupe; a troupe; a theatrical company
【劇烈】strenuous; intense; hard; fierce
【劇情】the plot
【劇情簡介】a synopsis
【劇照】a stage photo; a still
【劇終】the end; a curtainfall
【劇場 or 劇院】a theater
【劇作家】a playwright; a dramatist
【劇務】①stage management ②a stage manager

劈 356
1. ㄆㄧ pī
1. to cleave; to split; to rive; to rend 2. a wedge
【劈頭】①right in the face ②at the very start
【劈哩啪啦】a descriptive sound of firecrackers, guns, etc.
【劈柴】to split or chop firewood

劈 356
2. ㄆㄧˇ pǐ
to split; to chop: 劈柴 firewood

劉 357
ㄌㄧㄡˊ liú
1. a Chinese family name 2. to kill
【劉海兒】bangs; a fringe

劊 358
ㄍㄨㄟˋ guì
(又讀 ㄎㄨㄞˋ kuài)
to amputate; to cut off
【劊子手】①an executioner ②a hatchet man

劍 359
ㄐㄧㄢˋ jiàn
a sword; a dagger; a saber
【劍拔弩張】ready to fight
【劍蘭】(botany) a gladiolus
【劍客】a swordsman
【劍及履及】to perform a task with full vigor and urgency
【劍橋】Cambridge, England
【劍術】swordsmanship; fencing

十四畫

劑 360
ㄐㄧˋ jì
1. a dose (of medicine) 2. prepared medicines or drugs 3. to prepare (medicines and drugs)

力部 ㄌㄧˋ lì

力 361
ㄌㄧˋ lì
1. strength; force; power; ability; vigor 2. vigorously; earnestly 3. to do one's best
【力不從心】to have too little power to do as much as one wishes
【力排衆議】to refute the consensus
【力大無比】without a match in physical prowess
【力圖】to try hard; to strive to
【力量】strength; force; power
【力薦】to recommend (someone) strongly
【力氣】①physical strength or power ②an effort
【力求】to do one's best to; to strive to
【力行】to practice or perform energetically

【力爭】to struggle hard
【力爭上流 or 力爭上游】to try to excel by strenuous efforts
【力挽狂瀾】(figuratively) to do one's best to reverse the course of events

〔力部〕

三畫

功 362 ㄍㄨㄥ gōng
1. a merit; an achievement; an accomplishment; an exploit 2. usefulness; effectiveness 3. a function 4.(physics) work
【功敗垂成】to fail within reach of success
【功不可沒】The contribution (to success) cannot be left unrecognized.
【功名】an official rank or an academic title (in former times)
【功夫】① time (to do something) ② efforts (devoted to a task) ③ accomplishments ④ skill
【功德】① merits and virtues ② (Buddhism) charitable and pious deeds
【功德無量】(His, your, etc.) kindness knows no bounds.
【功勞】merits; contribution
【功利主義】utilitarianism
【功課】schoolwork; homework
【功課表】a class schedule (at school)
【功虧一簣】failure to achieve success by a very narrow margin
【功效】effectiveness; efficacy
【功勳】distinctive achievements
【功臣】one who has made a significant contribution to a specific task
【功成名就 or 功成名遂】to achieve success and acquire fame
【功成身退】to retire after achieving success
【功用or功能】use; a function; effect

加 363 ㄐㄧㄚ jiā
1. plus; to add 2. to increase; to augment 3. to append
【加倍】to double; to redouble
【加班】to work overtime
【加盟】to join an alliance, a fraternity or a secret society
【加冕】to crown; to coronate
【加法】(arithmetic) addition
【加侖】a gallon
【加官晉爵】to advance in rank and position; promotion
【加工】to process (goods)
【加工出口區】an export processing zone
【加快】to speed up; to accelerate
【加寬】to broaden; to widen
【加害】to do somebody harm
【加號】the plus symbol (+)
【加護病房】an intensive care unit (ICU)
【加減乘除】addition, subtraction, multiplication and division
【加緊】to intensify; to step up
【加強】to strengthen; to reinforce
【加權指數】the weighted index number in stock trading
【加薪】to give a pay raise
【加重】to increase work loads, burdens, etc.
【加深】① to deepen ② to cause to become worse or more severe
【加熱】to heat; to warm
【加入】① to join; to accede to ② to add into
【加速】to step up; to accelerate
【加油】① to oil ② to refuel ③ to step up effort
【加油站】a gas station

四畫

劣 364 ㄌㄧㄝ liè
inferior; mean; bad; of low quality
【劣等】of inferior quality; low-grade
【劣根性】a depravity
【劣質】of poor (or low) quality; inferior
【劣勢】inferior strength or position
【劣紳】evil gentry

五畫

助 365 ㄓㄨ zhù
to help; to aid; to assist; help; assistance
【助跑】a run-up; an approach
【助動詞】an auxiliary verb
【助聽器】an audiphone
【助理】① an assistant ② to assist
【助教】a teaching assistant; a TA
【助興】to liven things up; to add to the amusement

【助學金】a stipend; a scholarship
【助陣】to cheer or root for
【助長】to encourage (a tendency); to promote the development of
【助產士】a midwife
【助手】an assistant; a helper; an aide

努 366
ㄋㄨˇ nǔ
1. to exert oneself; to make an effort 2. to protrude
【努力】to make efforts; to strive

劫 367
(刼) ㄐㄧㄝˊ jié
1. to rob; to plunder; to take by force 2. sufferings; misfortunes; disasters
【劫難】a destined calamity
【劫後餘生】life after surviving a disaster
【劫機】to skyjack; to hijack a plane
【劫持】① to threaten ② to hijack
【劫數 or 劫運】ill luck; ill fortune
【劫案】a case of robbery

劬 368
ㄑㄩˊ qú
labor; toil; diligent; to labor incessantly

劭 369
ㄕㄠˋ shào
1. to encourage; to urge 2. graceful; excellent; admirable; respectable

六畫

劾 370
ㄏㄜˊ hé
to accuse; to charge; to impeach

七畫

勁 371
1. ㄐㄧㄥˋ jìng
strong; tough; powerful; sturdy
【勁敵】a powerful enemy
【勁旅】a powerful army; crack troops

勁 371
2. ㄐㄧㄣˋ jìn
1. vigor; energy; strength 2. spirit 3. an air; manner

勃 372
ㄅㄛˊ bó
sudden(ly); quick(ly)
【勃起】to have an erection; erection
【勃然變色】to show displeasure or bewilderment all of a sudden

勅 373
(敕) ㄔˋ chì
1. an imperial decree 2. orders given to demons and spirits by Taoist priests when they exercise magic powers
【勅令】an imperial decree, edict, command, or ordinance

勇 374
ㄩㄥˇ yǒng
1. brave; courageous; bold; valiant; intrepid; fearless 2. a soldier; a conscript 3. bravery; courage
【勇猛】brave and fierce
【勇敢】brave; courageous
【勇氣】courage; bravery; valor
【勇士】a brave fighter; a warrior
【勇往直前】to march fearlessly onward
【勇於】to be brave in; to have the courage to

勉 375
ㄇㄧㄢˇ miǎn
1. to urge; to encourage 2. to strive; to make efforts; to exert oneself to
【勉勵】to encourage; to urge
【勉強】① involuntarily; reluctantly ② barely ③ to force ④ unconvincing
【勉爲其難】to take on some difficult job reluctantly

九畫

勒 376
1. ㄌㄜˋ lè
1. to force; to compel 2. to reign or rule; to control; to command 3. to engrave; to carve 4. a bridle 5. (calligraphy) a horizontal stroke
【勒令】to compel by an order or injunction
【勒令退學】suspended indefinitely
【勒戒所】a clinic where addicts are treated and made to kick the habit
【勒住】to halt by pulling in reins
【勒贖】to kidnap a person for ransom
【勒索】to blackmail; to extort

勒 376
2. ㄌㄟ lēi
to tighten
【勒死 or 勒斃】to strangle; to throttle

〔力部〕

動 377 ㄉㄨㄥˋ dòng

1. to move; to stir 2. to change; to alter 3. to act 4. to touch (one's heart); to arouse; to excite 5. to take up 6. to use 7. to eat or drink 8. movement; action

【動筆】 to start writing
【動兵】 to send out troops to fight
【動不動】 to be apt to
【動脈】 an artery
【動名詞】 (grammar) a gerund
【動蕩】 uneasy; unstable
【動態】①development ②the movement
【動彈】 to budge; to move; to stir
【動聽】 appealing to the ear
【動怒】 to lose one's temper
【動力】 ① power; dynamic force ② impetus
【動亂】 disturbance; commotion
【動工】 to start (construction) work
【動機】 motives; intentions
【動靜】 signs of action
【動氣】 to take offense; to get angry
【動情】 to have more than a fleeting interest in a woman
【動心】 ① to be perturbed mentally ② to show interest
【動向】 trends
【動刑】 to apply torture; to torture
【動產】movable property; movables
【動手】 ① to start work ② to use hands; to touch ③ to raise a hand to strike
【動手術】 ①to operate on a patient ②to have an operation
【動身】 to set out (on a trip); to depart
【動人】 ①moving ② (said of the beauty of a woman) to arouse interest
【動作】 motions; movements; actions
【動詞】 a verb
【動粗or動武】 to resort to violence
【動議】 a motion; a proposal
【動搖】 to waver; to shake
【動物】 an animal; a creature
【動物園】 a zoo
【動員】 to mobilize; mobilization
【動用】 to use or employ

勘 378 ㄎㄢ kān
(又讀 ㄎㄢ kān)

1. to investigate; to explore; to examine; to check 2. to collate; to compare critically

【勘察】 to investigate; to inspect
【勘測】 to survey
【勘誤】 to collate; to correct errors
【勘誤表】 corrigenda; errata

務 379 ㄨˋ wù

1. to attend to; to strive after; to be engaged in 2. duty; business; affairs 3. must; necessary

【務必 or 務須】 must; by all means
【務農】 to be engaged in farming
【務實】 to strive for thoroughness
【務使】 to make sure; to ensure

十畫

勝 380 1. ㄕㄥˋ shèng

1. to win; to excel; to triumph; to surpass; to get the better of 2. victory; success 3. (sports) a win 4. a scenic view; a place of natural beauty 5. excellent; distinctive; wonderful

【勝負】 victory and defeat; the outcome (of a contest); success or failure
【勝利】 ① victory ② successfully
【勝過】 to excel; to surpass
【勝仗】 a victorious battle; a victory
【勝訴】 to win a lawsuit
【勝算】 to be sure of success; odds or advantages (in a contest)

勝 380 2. ㄕㄥ shēng

to be competent enough (for a task)

【勝任】competent; qualified; equal to

勞 381 1. ㄌㄠˊ láo

1. to labor; to take the toil; to work 2. to trouble; to worry; to bother 3. meritorious deeds; services

【勞民傷財】 to tire the people and waste the resources
【勞方】 labor
【勞頓】 fatigue; exhaustion
【勞動】 ①(ㄌㄠˊ ㄉㄨㄥˋ) to toil; to labor ②(ㄌㄠˊ ·ㄉㄨㄥ) to trouble
【勞動節or勞工紀念日】 Labor Day
【勞累】 to fatigue, tire or exhaust
【勞力】 ① labor ② to labor physically
【勞力士手錶】 a Rolex watch

【勞碌】to work hard; to drudge
【勞碌命】a born laborer
【勞工】laborers; workers 「ance
【勞工保險or勞保】labor insur-
【勞苦】①to labor; to toil ②toil
【勞苦功高】meritorious service
【勞駕】to be sorry to have to trouble someone to do something
【勞心】①to labor mentally ②to be worried; to be anxious
【勞師動衆】①to waste manpower ②to involve too many people
【勞資】labor and management
【勞作】①manual work or training (at school) ②manual labor
【勞役】hard labor (as punishment)
【勞燕分飛】(said of people) to separate or part (like birds flying in different directions)

勞 381
2. ㄌㄠˋ lào 「tired)
to comfort or entertain (the
【勞軍】to cheer or entertain troops

十一畫

勢 382
ㄕˋ shì
1. power; force; influence 2. a tendency 3. the natural features 4. a situation 5. signs; gestures 6. male genitals
【勢必】certainly; to be bound to
【勢不兩立】unable to coexist; incompatible
【勢力】force; power; influence
【勢力範圍】the sphere of influence
【勢利】snobbish
【勢利眼】a snob 「matched
【勢均力敵】evenly matched; well-
【勢如破竹】to advance with irresistible force
【勢在必行】to be imperative, urgent, or essential (under the circumstances)

募 383
ㄇㄨˋ mù
1. to recruit or enlist (personnel) 2. to raise (funds); to collect
【募款】to raise funds 「lect
【募集】to recruit; to raise; to col-
【募捐】to collect contributions

勤 384
ㄑㄧㄣˊ qín
1. diligent; industrious; sedulous; hardworking 2. frequently; regularly
【勤勉】diligent; hardworking
【勤奮or勤快】diligent; assiduous; industrious 「edied by diligence.
【勤能補拙】Stupidity can be rem-
【勤勞】to toil or labor sedulously
【勤儉】diligent and frugal
【勤學】to study diligently

勠 385
ㄌㄨˋ lù
1. to unite or join (forces) 2. to kill; to slay
【勠力同心】to work together with the same objective in mind

十四畫

勳 386
ㄒㄩㄣ xūn
merits; honors; meritorious services; achievements 「ration
【勳章】a medal of honor; a deco-

十五畫

勵 387
ㄌㄧˋ lì
1. to incite; to encourage; to rouse (to action) 2. to exert oneself
【勵精圖治】(said of a government or a national leader) to pursue the task of a national buildup with determination and dedication 「determination
【勵行】to enforce or practice with
【勵志】to pursue a goal with determination

十八畫

勸 388
ㄑㄩㄢˋ quàn 「persuade
to exhort; to urge; to advise; to
【勸導】to exhort and guide
【勸告】to advise; to counsel; to exhort 「dispute
【勸和】to reconcile a quarrel or
【勸架】to mediate a quarrel
【勸解】to mediate; to exhort to peace
【勸戒】to admonish; to dissuade
【勸諫】to remonstrate (with a superior)
【勸降】to induce to surrender

【勸世】 to admonish
【勸說】 to persuade; to advise
【勸阻 or 勸止】 to dissuade
【勸慰】 to console; to soothe

勹部
ㄅㄠ bāo

一畫

勺 389
ㄕㄠ sháo 「scoop
as in勺子—a ladle; a spoon; a

二畫

匀 390
ㄩㄣ yún 「even
uniform; even: 匀稱symmetrical;

勾 391
1. ㄍㄡ gōu
1. to mark; to put a check; to mark on 2. to cancel; to cross out (or off) 3. to hook 4. to join; to connect 5. to evoke 6. to entice; to seduce 7. a hook
【勾搭】 ①to have illegitimate relations ②to conspire with
【勾畫】 to delineate; to sketch
【勾魂】 to bewitch; to enchant
【勾結】 to collude or collaborate
【勾芡】 to thicken (soup, etc.) by means of starch
【勾消】 to liquidate; to cancel
【勾心鬥角】to intrigue against each other 「tempt; to inveigle
【勾引】 to entice; to seduce; to

勾 391
2. ㄍㄡˋ gòu
1. to manage 2. business; affairs
【勾當】 a plot; an intrigue

勿 392
ㄨˋ wù
do not; not; never; a negative word used in formal speech

三畫

包 393
ㄅㄠ bāo
1. to wrap 2. to include; to contain 3. to surround 4. to guarantee 5. a parcel; a package; a bundle
【包辦】 to undertake completely
【包庇】 to harbor; to shelter
【包皮】①a wrapper; a covering ② the prepuce
【包票】 a guaranty
【包飯 or 包伙】 to board
【包袱】 ①a cloth wrapper ②a bundle in a cloth wrapper ③ a burden
【包攬】 to monopolize
【包羅萬象】 inclusive of everything
【包裹】 ① to wrap up ② a parcel
【包管】 to guarantee or assure
【包括】 to include; to comprise
【包含】 to contain; to comprise
【包涵】 to forgive or pardon
【包機】 a chartered airplane
【包心菜】 a cabbage 「dium, etc.)
【包廂】 a box (in a theater, sta-
【包裝】 to pack; packing
【包抄】 (military) to outflank
【包場】 to reserve a whole theater or cinema
【包商】 a contractor
【包容】 to tolerate; to forgive
【包子】 a steamed stuffed bun
【包紮】 to wrap; to bind up
【包藏】 to contain; to conceal
【包藏禍心】 to harbor evil intentions or malicious intent
【包圍】 to surround; to encircle

四畫

匈 394
ㄒㄩㄥ xiōng
1. the breast; the bosom; the thorax 2. to clamor
【匈奴】the Huns, an ancient nationality in China
【匈牙利】 Hungary

七畫

匍 395
ㄆㄨˊ pú
1. to crawl; to creep 2. to lie prostrate; to prostrate
【匍匐or匍伏】 ①to prostrate ②to crawl; to creep

九畫

匐 396
ㄈㄨˊ fú
1. to lie prostrate; to prostrate
2. to crawl; to creep

匕部
ㄅㄧˇ bǐ

匕 397 ㄅㄧˇ bǐ
1. a ladle; a spoon 2. an arrowhead 3. a dagger
【匕首】a dagger; a short sword

二畫

化 398 ㄏㄨㄚˋ huà
1. to change; to convert; to transform; to influence 2. short for "chemistry"
【化名】to assume a pseudonym; a pseudonym
【化糞池】a cesspool or cesspit
【化敵爲友】to convert an enemy into a friend
【化工】① Nature's work; operations of Nature ② chemical engineering
【化合】to combine (chemically)
【化合物】a (chemical) compound
【化解】to settle (disputes)
【化險爲夷】to turn peril into safety
【化學】chemistry
【化學纖維】synthetic fiber
【化學肥料】chemical fertilizer
【化妝】to make up; to apply cosmetics
【化妝品】cosmetics
【化裝】to masquerade
【化裝舞會】a masquerade
【化除】to dissolve to nothing; to dispel
【化石】a fossil
【化身】an incarnation; an embodiment
【化驗】to subject to chemical analysis
【化驗室】a laboratory
【化爲烏有】to disappear completely
【化緣】to solicit alms

三畫

北 399 ㄅㄟˇ běi (讀音 ㄅㄛˋ bò)
1. north; northern; northerly 2. northward 3. defeated
【北半球】the Northern Hemisphere
【北邊】the north; the northern part
【北極海】the Arctic Ocean
【北平】Peiping 亦作「北京」
【北美洲】North America
【北非】North Africa; North African
【北方】① the northern region ② the north
【北方人】a northerner
【北斗星 or 北斗七星】the Plough; the Big Dipper
【北海】the North Sea
【北韓】North Korea
【北回歸線】the Tropic of Cancer
【北極】①the North Pole; the Arctic Pole ② the north magnetic pole
【北極熊】a polar bear
【北極星】Polaris; the North Star
【北京】Peking
【北京狗】a pekingese
【北上】to go north
【北宋】the Northern Sung
【北歐】northern Europe
【北緯】north latitude; northern latitude

九畫

匙 400 1. ㄔˊ chí
a spoon

匙 400 2. ·ㄕ shi
a key

匚部
ㄈㄤ fāng

三畫

匝 401 ㄗㄚ zā
to make a revolution round; to encompass; to circle

四畫

匠 402 ㄐㄧㄤˋ jiàng
a craftsman; an artisan; a skilled workman
【匠心】originality; craftsmanship
【匠心經營】the original thought in any creation

匡 403 ㄎㄨㄤ kuāng
1. to rectify; to correct 2. to deliver from

【匡濟】to relieve distress
【匡正】to rectify; to correct; to reform
【匡助】to rectify; to correct

〔匚·十部〕

五畫

匣 404
ㄒㄧㄚˊ xiá
1. a case; a small box 2. a cage

八畫

匪 405
ㄈㄟˇ fěi
1.bandits; rebels; insurgents 2.「not」
【匪徒】bandits; brigands; robbers
【匪巢】a bandits' lair
【匪夷所思】unthinkable

十一畫

滙 406
ㄏㄨㄟˋ huì
1. to remit money 2. to converge 3. to flow into
【滙票】a money order; a draft; a bill of exchange
【滙費】the remitting charge or fee
【滙兌】(commerce) exchange
【滙(兌)率】the exchange rate
【滙款】①a remittance ②to remit money
【滙合】to converge; to join
【滙集 or 滙聚】to gather in one place

十二畫

匱 407
ㄎㄨㄟˋ kuì
1.to lack; deficient: 匱乏lack 2. a chest or cabinet 3. exhausted

匸部
ㄒㄧˋ xì

二畫

匹 408
1. ㄆㄧˇ pǐ
a numerary particle for horses
【匹薩 or 比薩】pizza

匹 408
2. ㄆㄧˇ pǐ
1.a bolt (of cloth) 2.to match 「3.equal」
【匹配】①to match ②matching
【匹夫之勇】foolhardiness
【匹敵】to match or equal (in a contest)

九畫

匾 409
ㄅㄧㄢˇ biǎn
as in 匾額—a (wooden) tablet

匿 410
ㄋㄧˋ nì
to hide; to conceal: 匿名信 an anonymous letter

區 411
ㄑㄩ qū
1. to distinguish; to discriminate 2.a district; an area; a zone 3. a border 4.little; few 「guish」
【區別】to discriminate; to distin-
【區分】to set apart; to consider
【區公所】a district office
【區間車】a bus traveling merely part of its normal route 「fling」
【區區】small or unimportant; tri-
【區長】a district magistrate
【區域】a district; a zone
【區域規劃】regional planning
【區域性】regional

十部
ㄕˊ shí

十 412
ㄕˊ shí
1. ten; the tenth 2. complete; completely; perfect; perfectly; extremely 「point」
【十分】①completely ②very ③10
【十拿九穩】to be very sure of
【十六開】sixteenmo
【十全十美】perfect; complete
【十項運動】decathlon 亦作「十項全能運動」
【十字路口】①the junction of crossroads ②a point of decision
【十字架】①the Cross ②a yoke one has to take
【十字軍】the Crusaders
【十足】extremely; completely

【十四行詩】(Western poetry) the sonnet
【十三點】(slang) silly
【十惡不赦】guilty of unpardonable evil
【十二指腸】a duodenum
【十二月】① December ② twelve months ③ the twelfth month of the lunar calendar
【十一月】① November ② the eleventh month of the lunar calendar ③ eleven months
【十有八九or十之八九】most probably; very likely
【十位】(arithmetic) the tens place
【十萬八千里】to be poles apart
【十萬火急】① to be in posthaste ② Most Urgent (as a mark on dispatches)
【十月】① October ② the tenth month of the lunar calendar ③ ten months

一畫

千 413
ㄑㄧㄢ qiān
1. thousand 2. many; numerous
【千變萬化】countless changes
【千篇一律】without changes; dull; monotonous
【千方百計】a thousand schemes —by hook or by crook
【千刀萬剮】to hack someone to pieces
【千叮嚀萬囑咐】to exhort repeatedly
【千頭萬緒】(said of a problem or task) very complicated or confused
【千年】a thousand years
【千里】a thousand *li*—a long distance
【千里馬】a winged steed
【千里迢迢】from afar
【千里眼】① farsightedness ② (mythology) name of a god whose eyesight that can reach the heaven ③ another name for telescope or binoculars
【千古】① a long, long time ② (used in mourning) in eternity
【千古奇聞】a forever strange tale
【千迴百折】innumerable twists and turns
【千嬌百媚】the beauty of beauties
【千斤頂】a jack
【千金】① a courteous expression referring to another's daughter ② a thousand pieces of gold
【千金小姐】a young lady of a wealthy family
【千鈞一髮】very precarious
【千軍萬馬】a large number of mounted and foot soldiers
【千奇百怪】grotesque or weird shapes
【千秋萬歲】a long, long time
【千辛萬苦】to suffer or undergo all conceivable hardships (to accomplish something)
【千眞萬確】very real; absolutely true
【千錘百鍊】① (to undergo) severe training and hammering ② (to write) with the utmost care
【千山萬水】distant (places, etc.); (a journey from) afar
【千載難逢】once in a lifetime; a very rare chance
【千言萬語】many, many words in one's heart (but one doesn't know where to begin)
【千萬】① a huge amount ② an expression used to emphasize an injunction

二畫

升 414
ㄕㄥ shēng
1. to rise; to raise; to ascend 2. to advance; to promote 3. a unit of volume measurement (especially for grain)
【升平or昇平】peace and prosperity
【升斗小民】those who live from hand to mouth
【升天】① to ascend to heaven—to die ② (Christianity) the Ascension
【升格】to promote; to upgrade
【升官發財】to attain high ranks and acquire great wealth
【升級】① (said of an official) to be promoted ② (school) to advance to a higher grade
【升降】to rise and fall
【升降機】an elevator; a lift
【升旗】to hoist a flag
【升遷】promotion
【升學】to enter a higher school
【升學考試】an entrance examination for a higher school
【升値】(economics) ① to revalue ② to appreciate

午 415
ㄨˇ wǔ

〔十部〕

1. noon; high noon 2. (in old Chinese time measurement) 11 a.m. to 1 p.m. 3. the seventh of the Twelve Terrestrial Branches (地支)

【午飯】lunch; a midday meal
【午後】afternoon
【午前】before noon; the forenoon
【午休】a noon break; a noontime rest
【午睡】an afternoon nap; a siesta
【午夜】midnight

三畫

半 416 ㄅㄢ bàn

1. half 2. very little 3. in the middle 4. partly; about half

【半百】fifty; half a hundred
【半輩子】half a lifetime
【半壁江山】half of the national territory
【半邊】half of something
【半票】a half-price ticket
【半瓶醋】a half-educated person
【半賣半送】to sell goods at rock-bottom prices
【半打】half a dozen
【半島】a peninsula
【半導體】a semiconductor
【半吊子】① a dabbler ② a rash person
【半天】① midair; in the air ② half-day; half a day ③ quite a while
【半途 or 半路】halfway; midway
【半途而廢】to stop (a task) halfway
【半推半就】to be half willing (at heart) and half unwilling (in appearance)
【半路出家】to start midway
【半官方】semiofficial
【半工半讀】part work, and part study
【半公開】semi-overt
【半空中】in midair; in the air
【半價】half-price; 50 percent discount
【半截】a half part; half (a section)
【半斤八兩】tweedledum and tweedledee
【半徑】a radius
【半球】a hemisphere
【半信半疑】half-believing and half-doubting
【半場】① a half of a game ② half-court
【半身不遂】hemiplegia—paralysis of half of one's body
【半晌】(for) quite some time; a long time
【半生不熟】① half-cooked; half-raw ② casual acquaintance
【半數】half the number; half
【半死不活】① dying ② listless; lethargic ③ more dead than alive
【半夜】① half a night ② midnight
【半夜三更】in the depth of night
【半月刊】a semimonthly; a fortnightly
【半圓】a semicircle

四畫

卉 417 (芔) ㄏㄨㄟˋ huì

1. a general term for grasses 2. myriads of

六畫

卑 418 ㄅㄟ bēi

1. low 2. debased; depraved; vile 3. inferior 4. a modest expression referring to oneself

【卑鄙】① mean ② low; inferior
【卑鄙手段】dirty tricks
【卑躬曲膝】obsequious; fawning; servile
【卑賤】low; inferior; mean; humble
【卑下】base; mean; humble
【卑職】① (self-reference) your humble servant ② a low or humble position

卒 419 1. ㄗㄨˊ zú

1. a servant; an underling; a lackey 2. a soldier 3. a unit of one hundred soldiers 4. at last; after all; at long last 5. to complete; to finish 6. dead; to die 7. a community of 300 families 8. a pawn in Chinese chess

卒 419 2. ㄘㄨˋ cù

suddenly; abruptly; hurriedly

卓 420 ㄓㄨㄛˊ zhuó

1. lofty; high 2. profound; brilliant; eminent 3. (to stand) erect; upright

【卓見】a brilliant idea or view
【卓絕】eminent; prominent; out-

standing

【卓有成效】fruitful; highly effective

【卓越】excellent; remarkable

協 421 ㄒㄧㄝˊ xié

1. to agree; an agreement 2. to be united; to bring into harmony; to coordinate 3. to assist; to aid; to help

【協定】an agreement

【協調】to coordinate; harmony

【協同】to work with (others); to join others in (accomplishing an undertaking, etc.)

【協力】to exert together

【協和】harmony; to harmonize

【協會】an association; a society

【協助】to assist; to help mutually

【協商】to negotiate; to discuss

【協奏曲】(music) a concerto

【協議】①an agreement ②to discuss

七畫

南 422 1. ㄋㄚˊ ná

【南無阿彌陀佛】(Buddhism) *Namo Amitabha*

南 422 2. ㄋㄢˊ nán

1. south; southward 2. a type of ancient music played in the south of China 3. a Chinese family name

【南北】①north and south ②from north to south ③(in ancient China) a man

【南北貨】sundry goods

【南半球】the Southern Hemisphere

【南邊】①the south; the southern side ②the southern provinces of China

【南部】southern part; south

【南美洲】South America; Latin America 亦作「拉丁美洲」

【南非】South Africa

【南方】the south; the South

【南方人】a southerner

【南瓜】a pumpkin; a cushaw

【南柯一夢】a dream

【南胡】the two-stringed Chinese viola 亦作「二胡」

【南回歸線】the Tropic of Capricorn

【南極】the South Pole; the Antarctic Pole

【南極圈】the Antarctic Circle

【南極洲】Antarctica

【南京】Nanking

【南腔北調】to speak with a mixed accent

【南下】to go down south

【南征北戰】to participate in battles everywhere

【南朝】the Southern Dynasties

【南沙羣島】Nansha Chuntao; the Spratly Islands

【南緯】latitudes south of the equator

【南轅北轍】practice diametrically opposed to preaching

十畫

博 423 ㄅㄛˊ bó

1. wide; extensive 2. abundant; ample; rich 3. broadly knowledgeable; well-read; learned; erudite 4. to exchange; to barter for 5. to gamble; to play games 6. to win; to gain

【博大精深】extensive and profound

【博得 or 博取】to win; to obtain

【博覽】to be well-read

【博覽會】a trade fair; an exhibition

【博古通今】erudite and informed

【博學】well-read; erudite

【博士】a doctorate

【博愛】indiscriminate love; fraternity

【博物館 or 博物院】a museum

卜部 ㄅㄨˇ bǔ

卜 424 ㄅㄨˇ bǔ

1. to divine; to consult the oracle 2. to foretell; to predict 3. to choose

【卜卦】to divine by the Eight Diagrams

【卜筮】divination

三畫

占 425 1. ㄓㄢ zhān

1. as in 占卜 — to divine 2. to observe

【占星術】astrology

占 425 2. (佔) ㄓㄢˋ zhàn

to occupy: 占領 to occupy by force

【占據】to occupy illegally or by

【占有】to take possession of

卡 426
1. ㄎㄚˇ kǎ
1. a card, as a visiting card; cardboard 2. an abbreviated form for "calorie" 3. a guardhouse 4. a customs barrier; a roadblock; a checkpoint 5. to block; to check

【卡賓槍】a carbine
【卡片】a card; a calling card
【卡帶】a cassette tape
【卡通】a cartoon
【卡路里】a calorie
【卡介苗】BCG (Bacillus Calmette-Guerin), a TB vaccine
【卡其布】khaki
【卡車】a truck; a lorry

卡 426
2. ㄑㄧㄚˇ qiǎ
to be squeezed in between; to be sandwiched

卡 426
3. ㄑㄧㄚˇ qiǎ
to choke; to be choked

六畫

卦 427
ㄍㄨㄚˋ guà
one of the Eight Diagrams of the *Book of Changes*

卩 部
ㄐㄧㄝˊ jié

三畫

卯 428
ㄇㄠˇ mǎo
1. the fourth of the 12 Terrestrial Branches 2. the period from 5 to 7 a.m. 3. a roll call

【卯時】the period of the day from 5 to 7 a.m.

四畫

印 429
ㄧㄣˋ yìn
1. a seal; a stamp; a chop 2. to print; to stamp; to imprint 3. an imprint

【印發】to print and distribute
【印度半島】the subcontinent of India
【印度洋】the Indian Ocean
【印台】an ink pad; a stamp pad
【印尼 or 印度尼西亞】Indonesia
【印泥】ink for imprinting of seals
【印花】a revenue stamp
【印花稅】stamp tax
【印鑑】an imprint or impression of one's chop filed with agencies concerned for checking purposes
【印象】an impression; a mental image
【印行】to publish
【印章】a general name for stamps, seals and chops
【印刷】to print
【印刷品】printed matter

危 430
ㄨㄟ wēi
1. danger; dangerous; precarious; perilous 2. restless 3. to fear; to be upset or afraid 4. lofty; high 5. just; honest; straightforward

【危難】(in) danger, peril, trouble, or distress
【危害】to endanger; to harm; to injure
【危機重重】crisis-ridden
【危急】urgent; (in) a state of emergency
【危險】danger; dangerous; unsafe
【危險份子】dangerous elements;
【危如累卵】extremely dangerous
【危在旦夕】①(said of a city under enemy attack) may fall at any moment ② may die soon; dying
【危言聳聽】to stir up others with sensational statements

五畫

卵 431
ㄌㄨㄢˇ luǎn
1. an egg; an ovum 2. roe 3. the testicles

【卵巢】ovaries
【卵生】oviparous
【卵子】① an ovum ② testes; testicles

六畫

卷 432
1. ㄐㄩㄢˇ juǎn
1. painting which can be easily folded or rolled up 2. a book 3. a division of a book; a volume 4. a test paper 5. files; filed documents

【卷子】a test paper

【卷宗】 filed documents, especially in public offices; files

卷 432
2. (捲) ㄐㄩㄢˇ juǎn
to roll up 「after defeat
【卷土重來】 to come back again

卷 432
3. ㄑㄩㄢ quān
curly; to curl: 卷曲 to curl up

卸 433
ㄒㄧㄝˋ xiè
1. to get rid of; to remove 2. to unload (cargoes, etc.) 3. to resign; to retire from office
【卸貨】 to unload (or discharge) cargoes 「ornamentes
【卸妝】 to remove make-up and
【卸任】 to quit a public office

卹 434
ㄒㄩˋ xù
1. pity; to pity; sympathy; to sympathize 2. to give relief

七畫

卻 435
(却) ㄑㄩㄝˋ què
1. still; but; yet 2. to refuse to accept 3. to retreat; to withdraw
【卻步】 to retreat or withdraw; to shrink back
【卻之不恭】 It's not polite to refuse (an offer, present, etc.).

卽 436
(即) ㄐㄧˊ jí
1. promptly; immediately; now 2. then; accordingly 3. even if—indicating supposition or sequence
【卽刻】 immediately; promptly; now
【卽將】 to be about to 「ous
【卽興】 impromptu; extemporane-
【卽興之作】 an improvisation
【卽時or卽日】 immediately; at once
【卽使】 even if
【卽速】 instantly; immediately; soon
【卽位】 to ascend the throne

十畫

卿 437
ㄑㄧㄥ qīng
1. (in ancient China) a salutation of an emperor to his ministers 2. used in addressing one's wife —Honey, Darling, Dear, etc. 3. (in ancient China) a nobleman; a high official rank 「love
【卿卿我我】 to be very much in

厂部
ㄏㄢˇ hǎn

二畫

厄 438
ㄜˋ è
1. difficulty; adversity; distress; hardship 2. impeded; cramped
【厄運】 bad luck; adversity

七畫

厚 439
ㄏㄡˋ hòu
1. thick; thickness 2. deep friendship 3. to treat kindly; generous 4. substantial 5. kind; considerate; virtuous
【厚彼薄此】 to treat with partiality
【厚道】 kind; virtuous; sincere
【厚度】 thickness
【厚禮】 lavish gifts; liberal presents
【厚葬】 an elaborate funeral
【厚愛】 to treat very kindly and generously
【厚顏無恥】 impudent; shameless
【厚望】 high hopes; high expectations

八畫

原 440
ㄩㄢˊ yuán
1. the source; the origin; the beginning 2. original; primary 3. a steppe; a vast plain; a field 4. a graveyard 5. to excuse; to pardon
【原版】 the original print or edition
【原木】 a log 「or unopened
【原封不動】 (kept or left) intact
【原動力】 ① power ② action
【原來】 originally or formerly
【原來如此】 ① I see. 或Now I understand what you mean. ② It was as it is now.
【原料】 raw materials
【原諒】 forgiveness; to forgive; to pardon
【原稿】 a manuscript

厂部

厶部

【原告】the plaintiff; the prosecutor
【原故 or 原因】a reason; a cause
【原籍】hailing from; a native of
【原先】in the beginning; originally
【原形畢露】to reveal the true nature or colors (of a person) completely
【原址】the former address
【原住民】an aborigine
【原狀】①the original condition ② the status quo
【原始】①primitive; backward ② a source
【原始分數】a raw score
【原始人】a primitive
【原任】①the predecessor ②formerly held the post of...
【原子】an atom
【原子筆】a ball-point pen
【原子彈】an atomic bomb
【原子能】atomic energy
【原則 or 原理】a principle
【原作】the original work
【原意】① original intentions ② original meaning
【原油】crude oil; crude petroleum
【原委】the reason why a thing happened; the ins and outs (of a case, story, etc.)
【原文】the original text
【原原本本】in detail; the whole (story or thing)

厝 441 ㄘㄨㄛˋ cuò
1. to place 2. to place a coffin in a temporary shelter pending burial 3. a gravestone 4. to cut or engrave

十畫

厥 442 ㄐㄩㄝˊ jué
1. to faint 2. same as 蹶—to dig 3. a personal and possessive pronoun
【厥功甚偉】to have made great contribution to the successful conclusion of a task

十二畫

厭 443 ㄧㄢˋ yàn
1. to dislike; to detest; to hate 2. to get tired of 3. satiated; surfeited
【厭煩】bored; wearied
【厭倦】to be tired of; to be weary of
【厭棄】to reject; to get rid of
【厭食】lack of appetite
【厭世】①to be disgusted with the world ②to die ③misanthropy
【厭惡 or 厭恨】to loathe; to dislike

十三畫

厲 444 ㄌㄧˋ lì
1. a coarse whetstone 2. harsh; violent; severe; stern; serious 3. to persuade; to urge; to encourage 4. bad; evil 5. an epidemic 6. to oppress; oppressive; cruel
【厲兵秣馬】to make military preparations
【厲鬼】a fierce ghost; a malicious spirit
【厲害】①fierceness; ferociousness ②very (ill, etc.); serious (damage, destruction, etc.)
【厲行】to enforce
【厲聲】to talk harshly; to shout angrily

厶部
ㄙ sī

三畫

去 445 ㄑㄩˋ qù
1. to go away; to depart 2. to get rid of; to remove 3. to be... apart 4. past; gone 5. an auxiliary verb 6. the fourth of the four tones in Chinese phonetics 7. (Peking opera) to play the part of
【去年】last year; the year past
【去留】to go or to stay
【去路】the way along which one is going
【去向】whereabouts
【去世】to die; to leave the world
【去勢】to castrate; to emasculate
【去惡從善】to shun the evil and follow the good
【去蕪存菁】to keep the good and get rid of the bad

九畫

參 446
1. ㄘㄢ cān
1. to take part in; to get involved in 2. to visit; to interview; to call on 3. to impeach; to censure 4. to recommend 5. to counsel; to consult together 6. to consider; to collate; to compare
【參半】half; half-and-half
【參謀】the staff; a counselor
【參觀】to visit, inspect or tour (a place, etc.)
【參考】①to consult; to collate ②reference
【參考書】a reference book
【參看】(please) refer to
【參加】to attend; to join
【參照】in accordance with; with reference to
【參戰】to participate in a war
【參政】to take part in politics or the government
【參政權】the right to participate in public affairs
【參雜】to mix; to add something of the different nature, quality, color, etc.
【參議員】a senator
【參議院】the upper house of a parliament
【參預】to play a part
【參與】to take part in; to participate in
【參閱】to see; to consult

參 446
2. ㄕㄣ shēn
1. name of a star 2. a ginseng

參 446
3. ㄘㄣ cēn
【參差】of irregular, different sizes; uneven

參 446
4. ㄙㄢ sān
a formal form of the Chinese character "三"—three, used in accounting to prevent fraud

又部 ㄧㄡˋ yòu

又 447
ㄧㄡˋ yòu
1. also; again; in addition to; and 2. moreover; furthermore 3. and (used in a mixed fraction such as one *and* three fourths)
【又快又好】(to do something) very fast with excellent results; efficient
【又飢又渴】both hungry and thirsty
【又驚又喜】alarmed and happy at the same time

一畫

叉 448
1. ㄔㄚ chā
1. to interlace fingers; to cross arms 2. to thrust; to pierce; to stab 3. a prong; a fork (used in catching fish, etc.) 4. to push another's neck with one's hand
【叉路】the fork of a road
【叉子】a fork
【叉腰】to stand with arms akimbo; to rest the arms on the hips

叉 448
2. ㄔㄚˇ chǎ
【叉嘮】(said of the road) divergent

二畫

及 449
ㄐㄧˊ jí
1. to reach; to attain; to come up to 2. and; as well as; with 3. just at the moment; timely; when 4. as long as; up to; until 5. to continue 6. to extend
【及第】(in ancient China) to pass the civil examinations
【及格】to pass an examination; to be qualified
【及冠之年】(said of a young man) to reach the age of 20
【及至】until; up to a given point
【及時】in time
【及早】as soon as possible; before it is too late
【及早回頭】to repent before it is too late

友 450
ㄧㄡˇ yǒu
1. a friend; friendly; friendship 2. fraternity; fraternal love 3. to befriend
【友邦】friendly nations; allies
【友好】friendly; amity (treaty, etc.)
【友軍】friendly forces
【友情 or 友誼】friendship
【友善】friendly
【友人】friends
【友愛】friendship; fraternal love

反 451
ㄈㄢˇ fǎn

〔又部〕

1. reverse; opposite; contrary 2. to return (something); to turn back; to retreat 3. to introspect; to retrospect 4. to rebel; rebellion; to revolt 5. to infer

又部

【反駁】 to refute; to retort
【反敗爲勝】 to turn defeat into victory 「one's parents
【反哺】 to show filial piety to
【反派】 a villain (in drama, etc.); a negative character
【反叛】 to rebel; to revolt; treason
【反撲】 ① to pounce on somebody again after being beaten off ②a
【反目】 to fight ⌊counterattack
【反覆】 ① not dependable ② to relapse ③ repeatedly; again and again 「again
【反覆思量】 to think over and over
【反覆無常】 capricious
【反對】 to oppose; to object
【反感】 antipathy
【反顧】 to look back; to review
【反光】 reflection; reflected light
【反躬自問】 self-examination
【反客爲主】 to exchange the positions of the host and the guest
【反抗】 to counter; to resist; to rebel; to rise up against
【反悔】 to renege (on a promise)
【反間】 to alienate the enemy coali- 「nation
【反求諸己】 to make self-exami-
【反向】 the opposite direction
【反省】 reflection; self-examination
【反正】 in any case; anyway
【反證】 the counterevidence
【反轉】 ① to turn inside out ② to return 「mal
【反常】 out-of-the-ordinary; abnor-
【反芻】 to ruminate
【反串】 ①(Peking opera) to play a role other than one's specialty② to play the role of the opposite sex 「with sarcastic remarks
【反脣相稽】 to rebut or rebuke
【反時鐘方向】 counterclockwise
【反射】 to reflect; reflection
【反作用】 ① undesirable reactions or results ② (physics) reaction
【反而】 unexpectedly; contrarily
【反義字】 an antonym
【反咬一口】 to fabricate a countercharge against one's accuser
【反顏相向】 to become hostile
【反映】 to reflect 「reaction
【反應】 ① response ② chemical
【反胃】 to upset the stomach; nau-
【反問】 to rebut ⌊seating

六畫

452
叔 ㄕㄨˊ shú
1. younger brothers of one's father; paternal uncles 2. younger brothers of one's husband 3. a general designation for members of one's father's generation who are younger than one's father 4. declining
【叔伯】 ① paternal uncles ② a relationship among cousins born of the same grandfather
【叔母】 the wife of one's father's younger brother 「father
【叔父】 a younger brother of one's
【叔姪】 uncles and nephews

453
取 ㄑㄩˇ qǔ
1. to take; to receive; to fetch; to obtain; to take hold of 2. to select; to choose 3. to summon; to recall 4. to marry; to take a
【取名】 to name; to christen ⌊wife
【取得】 to gain; to acquire; to obtain
【取代】 to replace; to substitute
【取道】 to go by way of 「violator
【取締】 to prohibit; to punish the
【取暖】 to warm oneself (by a fire,
【取樂】 to make merry ⌊etc.)
【取款】 to take money or draw money 「graph, paint, etc.)
【取景】 to find a view (to photo-
【取決】 It's up to (someone else to make the decision).
【取巧】 to take a snap course
【取消】 to cancel; to nullify
【取笑】 to laugh at; to make fun of
【取信於人】 to establish credibility among others 「haustible.
【取之不盡】 The supply is inex-
【取長補短】 to learn from others' strong points to make up for one's weaknesses
【取捨】 to accept or refuse
【取勝】 to win a victory
【取材】 to select material
【取而代之】 to usurp another's

嚷 668
1. ㄖㄤˇ rǎng
to shout; to cry; to call out loudly
【嚷叫】to bellow; to howl

嚷 668
2. ㄖㄤ rāng
【嚷嚷】① to shout; to yell ② to make widely known

十八畫

嚼 669
ㄐㄧㄠˊ jiáo
to chew; to masticate; to munch

囀 670
ㄓㄨㄢˇ zhuǎn
1. to warble; to twitter; to chirp 2. pleasing to the ear

囂 671
ㄒㄧㄠ xiāo
1. noise; clamor; hubbub 2. to be haughty or proud
【囂張】haughty; rampant; arrogant; aggressive

十九畫

囈 672
ㄧˋ yì
as in 囈語—to talk in sleep; somniloquy

囉 673
1. ㄌㄨㄛ luō
to chatter
【囉哩囉唆 or 囉唆】vexingly verbose or wordy

囉 673
2. ㄌㄨㄛˊ luó
1. noisiness 2. a band of outlaws 3. used as a slightly argumentative final particle

囊 674
ㄋㄤˊ náng
1. a bag; a sack; a purse 2. to put in a bag
【囊括】to encompass; to include; to comprise
【囊空如洗】to be dead broke; to be penniless
【囊中物】(figuratively) a thing very easy to get

二十一畫

囑 675
ㄓㄨˇ zhǔ
to ask another to do something; to instruct; to enjoin; to direct; to entrust; to charge
【囑咐】to instruct or bid (a person to do something)
【囑託】to entrust (a person with a task); to request (a person to do something)

囗部 ㄨㄟˊ wéi

二畫

囚 676
ㄑㄧㄡˊ qiú
1. a prisoner; a convict 2. to imprison
【囚犯】a prisoner; a convict; a jailbird
【囚牢or囚房】a prison; a jail; a cell
【囚禁】to imprison; to jail; to confine
【囚車】a prison cart

四 677
ㄙˋ sì
1. four; fourth 2. all around
【四壁蕭條】as poor as a church mouse
【四邊形】a quadrilateral or tetragon
【四平八穩】completely stable and safe
【四面】four sides; all sides
【四面八方】on every side; all directions; all around
【四面楚歌】facing hostility, difficulty, or frustration on all sides
【四分五裂】to fall to pieces; to be all split up
【四方】① the four directions (east, west, north, and south) ② every direction; all sides; everywhere
【四通八達】(said of a communication network) leading everywhere
【四開】quarto
【四海爲家】① (said of emperors) to make the country a big family ② to lead a wandering life
【四季】the four seasons
【四季豆】string beans; kidney beans
【四脚朝天】to fall on one's back
【四肢】the four limbs
【四周圍】all around; on all sides
【四處】everywhere; all around
【四川】Szechwan
【四重奏】(instrumental) quartet
【四散】to disperse everywhere
【四月】① April ② the fourth

口部

month of the lunar calendar ③ four months

三畫

回 678 ㄏㄨㄟˊ huí

1. to return; to go back; to bring back; to turn back 2. to reply; to answer 3. to turn round 4. the number of times 5. a kind; a sort 6. chapters in a novel 7. of Mohammedanism; Moslems

【回報】①to bring back a report ② to repay (a favor or an injury)
【回稟】 to report back (to one's superior)
【回眸】 (said of a woman) to glance back
【回府】 to return home
【回覆 or 回答】 to reply; to answer; a reply
【回電】 ① a cable or telegram sent in reply ② to wire back
【回頭】 ①to turn back ② after a while; later ③ to return ④ to repent
【回頭是岸】 Repentance is salvation.
【回條】 a receipt
【回天乏術】 Nothing can be done to revive the dead or to save the dying.
【回來】 to come back; to return
【回禮】 ① to return a salute ② to send a present in return
【回力球】 pelota; jai alai
【回祿之災】 a fire disaster
【回顧】 to look back
【回光返照】 the transient reviving of the dying
【回合】 an encounter; a round; a bout
【回航】 to sail or fly back
【回話】 ① to bring back word; to report ② a reply (usually one conveyed by a messenger)
【回擊】 to fight back; to counterattack
【回教】 Mohammedanism; Islam
【回教徒】 a Muslim
【回敬】 ① to give a gift in return ② tit for tat
【回絕】 to decline; to refuse
【回去】 ①to go back ②to return
【回心轉意】 ① to decide to return from sin to virtue ② to change one's mind
【回信】 ① a letter in reply ② to write back ③ a reply
【回鄉】 to return to one's home village
【回想】 to recollect; to recall
【回轉】 to turn round
【回程】 the return trip
【回收】 to retrieve; to recover; to reclaim
【回升】 to rise again (after a fall)
【回聲 or 回響】 an echo; reverberation
【回嘴】 to talk back; to retort
【回憶】 to recollect; to recall
【回憶錄】 memoirs; recollections
【回郵】 return mail
【回音】 ① to echo; an echo ② a response
【回味】 to ponder over

因 679 ㄧㄣ yīn

1. cause; reason 2. for; because of 3. in accordance with; according to; on the basis of; in the light of 4. to follow (a practice, convention, etc.); to carry on

【因地制宜】 to take actions that suit local circumstances
【因陋就簡】 ① to do things in the easy, simple way ② to make do with whatever is available
【因果報應】 retribution for sin
【因禍得福】 to profit from a misfortune
【因襲】 to follow conventions and traditions
【因小失大】 to try to save a little only to lose a lot
【因循】 ① to follow (old customs) ② to procrastinate
【因循苟且】 to follow routines without thinking about improvement
【因時制宜】 to do what is appropriate according to the circumstances
【因子or因數】 (mathematics) a factor
【因此】 therefore; hence; thus
【因材施教】 to teach according to the student's ability or aptitude
【因素】 factors; elements
【因而】 therefore; and so; thereupon
【因噎廢食】 to refuse making renovations for fear of a little trouble
【因爲】 inasmuch as; since; because; as

四畫

困 680 ㄎㄨㄣˋ kùn

1. difficult; hard 2. poor 3. fatigued; weary; tired 4. to trouble; to worry; to harass; to be stranded; to be hard pressed

【困頓】① tired; exhausted; fatigued ② in financial straits

【困難】difficulty; hardship

【困難重重】to be beset with difficulties

【困苦】in great distress; poverty-stricken

【困境】a predicament; straits

【困窘】embarrassment; to embarrass

【困獸之鬪】a desperate fight

【困擾or困惑】to perplex; to confuse

囤 681 ㄊㄨㄣˊ tún

to store up; to hoard; to stockpile

【囤積】to hoard commodities for speculation; to corner

囪 682 ㄘㄨㄥ cōng

a chimney; a flue

囫 683 ㄏㄨˊ hú

entire; whole

【囫圇吞棗】to read hastily without thinking

五畫

囹 684 ㄌㄧㄥˊ líng

as in 囹圄—a prison; a jail

固 685 ㄍㄨˋ gù

1. stable; firm; sturdy; secure; solid; hard; strong 2. obstinate; stubborn; insistent; steadfast 3. base; mean; ignorant 4. chronic 5. originally; certainly; as a matter of course; assuredly 6. indeed 7. admittedly; no doubt 8. to become solid; to solidify 9. to strengthen; to guard; to secure; to consolidate 10. a Chinese family name

【固定】① to fix ② fixed; regular

【固定匯率】the fixed exchange rate

【固體】solid

【固執】obstinate; stubborn

【固執己見】to stick to one's opinions

【固守成規】to stick to old rules

【固然】① of course ② no doubt; true

【固若金湯】(said of a city, military position, etc.) impregnable

【固有】intrinsic; inherent; innate

六畫

囿 686 ㄧㄡˋ yòu

1. an enclosure for keeping animals; a menagerie; a garden 2. to confine; to enclose

【囿於成見】bound by prejudice; biased

【囿於一隅】confined to a corner

七畫

圃 687 ㄆㄨˇ pǔ

1. a vegetable garden (or plot); a nursery; an orchard ; a plantation 2. a planter; a gardener

八畫

國 688 ㄍㄨㄛˊ guó

1. a country; a nation; a kingdom; a state 2. national; governmental 3. Chinese 4. a Chinese family name

【國寶】a national treasure

【國賓】a government guest

【國步艱難or國步方艱】The nation is beset by difficulties.

【國破家亡】The country is defeated and the home lost.

【國民】a citizen; the people

【國民平均所得】per capita income

【國民學校】a primary school; an elementary school

【國民中學】a junior high school

【國民身分(份)證】an ID card

【國民所得】national income

【國民外交】people-to-people diplomacy

【國防】national defense

【國父】① the father of a nation ② Father of the Republic (Dr. Sun Yat-sen)

【國定紀念日】a national commemoration or memorial day

【國定假日】a national holiday

【國都】the national capital; the capital

【國泰民安】The country is prosperous and at peace, and the people live in happiness.

【國土】territory of a nation

口部

【國內】 domestic or internal
【國難】 national crises (or calamities)
【國力】 national power (usually connoting resources and potentialities)
【國立】 (said of an institution) nationally supported or operated; national
【國曆】the national (i.e., solar) calendar
【國歌】 a national anthem
【國庫】 the national exchequer
【國號】① the name of a dynasty ② the official name of a nation
【國花】 the national flower
【國畫】 a Chinese painting
【國貨】 native goods
【國徽】 the national emblem
【國會】 Parliament, Congress, the Diet, etc.
【國籍】 nationality
【國際】 international
【國際貿易】 international trade; foreign trade
【國際地位】 international status
【國際電話】 the overseas telephone
【國際關係】 international relations
【國際化】 internationalization
【國際換日線】 International Date Line
【國際奧林匹克委員會】 International Olympic Committee (IOC)
【國際音標 or 萬國音標】 the International Phonetic Alphabet (IPA)
【國家】 a nation; a country
【國家公園】 a national park
【國家機密】 state secrets
【國境or國界】 a border; a national boundary
【國劇】Peking opera
【國君】 a sovereign; a monarch
【國軍】 the armed forces of the Republic of China
【國旗】 the national flag
【國情】 the condition of a country
【國慶(日)】the National Day (of a country)
【國產】 (said of products) native or locally manufactured
【國勢】 ① national strength② the condition of a country
【國手】 (said of athletes, etc.) national representatives, who are the national champions in any lines of activities, especially of sports and games
【國書】 ① credentials (of a diplomat) ② documents exchanged between nations
【國術】 Chinese martial arts
【國字】 Chinese characters
【國策】 national policies
【國粹】 unique cultural features of a nation; national legacies
【國色天香】 the beauty of a woman or peony
【國喪】 national mourning
【國有】 state-owned
【國宴】 state banquet
【國營事業】 a state-owned enterprise
【國務會議】 state conference
【國務卿】 Secretary of State (of the U.S. Federal Government)
【國務總理】 the premier (of the early Chinese Republican Government)
【國務院】 ① the Department of State (of the U.S. Federal Government) ② the Cabinet (of the early Chinese Republican Government) ③ State Council (in mainland China)
【國外】 outside the country; abroad
【國文】 ① the written national language ② national language and literature ③ Chinese literature (a course in Chinese schools)
【國王】 a king; a monarch
【國語】 Mandarin
【國樂】 Chinese music
【國運】 the destiny of the nation

侖 689
ㄌㄨㄣˊ lún
entire; whole

圈 690
1. ㄑㄩㄢ quān
1. a circle; a ring 2. with a return to the starting point; round 3. to circle 4. a circle—a number of persons bound together by having the same interests
【圈套】 a snare; a trap; a trick
【圈子 or 圈兒】 a circle

圈 690
2. ㄐㄩㄢˋ juàn
an enclosure or a pen for keeping livestock

九畫

圍 691 ㄨㄟˊ wéi

1. to surround; to enclose; to encircle; to hem in 2. surroundings; environment 3. the circumference of a circle formed by a person's arms

【圍脖兒 or 圍巾】a scarf; a muffler
【圍捕】to arrest (a criminal) by closing in on him from all sides
【圍爐】to sit and chat around the fireplace
【圍攻or圍困】to besiege; to beleaguer
【圍剿】to attack (bandits or rebels) from all sides
【圍棋】*go*
【圍牆】an enclosing wall; a fence
【圍裙】an apron
【圍繞】to surround; to encircle

十畫

園 692 ㄩㄢˊ yuán

1. a piece of ground used for growing flowers, fruit or vegetables; a garden; a plantation 2. a public garden, park or recreation ground

【園地】①a garden②(in a periodical) a space reserved for publishing articles or letters from readers
【園丁】a gardener
【園主】the owner of a park or a garden
【園藝】gardening; horticulture
【園遊會】a garden party

圓 693 ㄩㄢˊ yuán

1. round; circular; spherical 2. complete; to complete; to make plausible; to justify 3. satisfactory; tactful 4. a monetary unit 5. a circle

【圓盤】a disc
【圓滿】① satisfactory ② rounded out ③ complete
【圓筒】a cylinder
【圓規】a pair of compasses
【圓弧】an arc
【圓滑】tactful; slick and sly
【圓環】a rotary; a traffic circle
【圓寂】(said of Buddhist monks or nuns) to die; to pass away
【圓圈】a circle; a ring
【圓心】the center of a circle
【圓形】round; spherical; circular
【圓周】the circumference of a circle
【圓柱】a cylinder
【圓場】to mediate
【圓舞曲】waltz

十一畫

圖 694 ㄊㄨˊ tú

1. a picture; a map; a portrait; a chart; a diagram 2. to seek; to pursue 3. to plan; to scheme; to conspire 4. intention; aim; purpose 5. a Chinese family name

【圖飽私囊】to try to enrich oneself (from public services)
【圖表】charts, diagrams and tables —used in statistics
【圖片】pictures; photographs
【圖謀】to plan; to conspire
【圖謀不軌】to harbor evil intentions
【圖釘】thumbtacks; a drawing pin
【圖例】a brief explanation or key to an illustration, map, etc.
【圖利】to desire to make money or profit
【圖畫】① a drawing; a picture ② painting ③ to plot; to plan
【圖解】illustrations
【圖窮匕見】The real intention is revealed in the end.
【圖章】a seal; a chop
【圖書館】a library
【圖書管理員】a librarian
【圖書室】a reading room
【圖案】(fine arts) patterns
【圖樣】(architecture) a design

團 695 ㄊㄨㄢˊ tuán

1. a sphere; something shaped like a ball 2. a mass; a lump 3. a group; a party; a mission; an organization; a society 4. (infantry) a regiment, consisting of three battalions of foot soldiers 5. to unite

【團隊精神】team spirit
【團體】an organization; group (action, etc.)
【團體操】callisthenics done by a large group of people
【團體賽】a team competition
【團團圍住】to be completely surrounded (by rows of enemy

troops)
【團結】union; solidarity; to unite
【團聚】(said of a family, etc.) to congregate; a reunion; a gathering
【團長】a regiment commander
【團員】a member
【團圓】a union or reunion (especially of a family)

土部 ㄊㄨˇ tǔ

土 696 ㄊㄨˇ tǔ
1. earth; soil 2. land; territory; domain 3. local; native; indigenous 4. unrefined; unenlightened 5. rustic; countrified 6. opium 7. an abbreviation for Turkey
【土撥鼠】a marmot; a ground hog
【土包子】a hillbilly; a country bumpkin
【土崩瓦解】in total disorder or confusion
【土木or土木工程】civil engineering
【土匪】bandits; brigands
【土風舞】folk dance
【土豆】① peanuts ② potatoes
【土地】① land ② the God of Earth
【土地廟】the temple of the God of Earth
【土地公】the God of Earth
【土堆or土墩】a mound
【土裏土氣】rustic; countrified; hillbilly
【土豪劣紳】local ruffians and the oppressive gentry
【土星】the planet Saturn
【土質】the condition or nature of the soil
【土著or土人】a native; an aborigine
【土產】local products
【土生土長】to be born and grow up in the local community
【土壤】soil
【土葬】a burial in the ground
【土耳其】Turkey

三畫

在 697 ㄗㄞˋ zài
1. at; in; on; up to 2. to rest with; to consist in; to depend on 3. to be alive; living; to be present; to exist 4. used to indicate a progressive tense
【在逃】(said of a criminal) on the loose or still at large
【在內】① including; inclusive ② inside
【在行】to be an expert at something
【在乎】① to care; to mind ② to consist in; to depend on (whether...)
【在家】to be at home; to be in
【在劫難逃】If one is doomed, one is doomed.
【在下】my humble self; I
【在先】① before; formerly; beforehand ② in front; ahead
【在學】to be at school
【在職】to be at one's post
【在職訓練】in-service training
【在場】to be present
【在世】alive; in this world
【在座】to be present (at a gathering)
【在所難免】unavoidable; inevitable
【在所不惜】regardless of the cost or sacrifice
【在所不辭】will not hesitate to
【在意】to mind; to care about
【在押】being imprisoned
【在外】① excluding ② outside
【在位】in the position; on the throne
【在望】①to be visible ②to be in sight

圭 698 ㄍㄨㄟ guī
a jade tablet with a square base and a pointed top used in official ceremonies in ancient China
【圭臬】① ancient timepieces ② a principle for one to look up to

地 699 ㄉㄧˋ dì
1. the earth 2. land; soil; ground 3. a region; a territory; a belt; a place; a locality 4. a position; a place; a situation 5. an adjunct after a word (usually adjective) to form an adverbial phrase
【地板】a floor
【地盤】① a region under one's sphere of influence; a domain ② the foundation of a building or house
【地皮】land estate; real estate
【地痞流氓】local bullies and loafers
【地平線】the horizon

【地鋪】 a shakedown
【地面】 ① the surface of the earth ② a region; a territory
【地名】 the name of a place
【地方】 ① a locality (in contrast with the central government) ② a place ③ space; room ④ part; respect ⑤ local
【地方法院】 a district court
【地方人士】 local personalities
【地方色彩】 ① local color ② provincialism
【地帶】 a place and its vicinity
【地道】 a tunnel
【地點】 a site; a location; a place
【地段】 the locality of a piece of land (especially referring to the numbered land plots on government file)
【地洞】 a hole in the ground; a burrow
【地攤】 a stall with goods displaying on the ground for sale
【地毯】 a carpet or rug
【地圖】 a map
【地雷】 a land mine
【地牢 or 土牢】 a dungeon
【地老天荒】 (said of love) to outlast even the heaven and the earth
【地理】 ① geographical characteristics of a place ② geography
【地瓜】 sweet potatoes
【地殼】 the crust of the earth
【地基】 the foundation of a building
【地窖】 a cellar; an underground vault
【地契or地券】 a title deed for landholdings
【地球】 the earth
【地球儀】 a terrestrial globe
【地區】 an area; a region; a zone
【地下】 ① underground ② in the grave ③ on the ground
【地下道】 a tunnel; a subway
【地下鐵(道)】 the subway
【地下錢莊】 illegal banks
【地下室】 a basement
【地下舞廳】 unlicensed cabarets
【地心吸力】 gravity
【地址】 the address of a place; a location
【地震】 earthquakes; seism
【地主】 ① a host ② a landowner
【地主之誼】 the friendship or hospitality of a host
【地中海】 the Mediterranean Sea
【地勢 or 地形】 topography; terrain
【地租】 land rent
【地位】 the ranking or position (of a person)
【地域】 ① boundaries of a piece of land ② a district; a region
【地獄】 hell; Hades; the inferno

四畫

坊 700 ㄈㄤ fāng
1. a community; a subdivision of a city; a neighborhood; a city quarter; a street; a lane 2. a workshop of a trade; a mill 3. an archlike memorial building
【坊間】 city quarters; in the streets

圾 701 ㄙㄜˋ sè
garbage; refuse; waste

址 702 ㄓˇ zhǐ
1. land on which to build a house; a location; a site 2. a foundation

均 703 ㄐㄩㄣ jūn
1. equal; equally; even; level 2. to be fair 3. all; also; too 4. a potter's wheel 5. an ancient musical instrument
【均分】 to divide equally
【均等】 equality; equal; impartial; fair
【均攤】 to share equally
【均可】 all can; either will do; also can
【均衡】 equality; balance equilibrium
【均勻】 even (blending, etc.); uniform

坍 704 ㄊㄢ tān
sliding of earth (as in a landslide); to fall into ruins; to collapse; to tumble
【坍方】 a landslide; to collapse
【坍塌】 to collapse; to cave in

坎 705 ㄎㄢˇ kǎn
1. a pit; a hole; a depression 2. one of the Eight Diagrams in the *Book of Changes* 3. the sound of percussion 4. a snare; a danger; a crisis
【坎坷一生】 a lifetime of frustrations

坐 706 ㄗㄨㄛˋ zuò
1. to sit; a seat 2. to ride (on a bus, train, etc.) 3. to kneel 4.

to reach; to arrive at 5. (said of a building) to have its back towards 6. to get (profit, etc.) without work 7. to keep on; to persist in 8. (said of a building) to fall back from pressure; to sink 9. (said of guns, etc.) to recoil; to kick

〔土部〕

【坐標】(mathematics) coordinates
【坐墊】a seat cushion
【坐牢】to be jailed or imprisoned
【坐冷板凳】to hold a position with little or no power
【坐立不安】fidgety; restless
【坐落】(said of a house, building, etc.) to be located or situated at
【坐觀成敗】to look on coldly
【坐困】to be confined or walled in
【坐懷不亂】to be immune from the temptation of feminine charms
【坐騎】one's horse for riding
【坐井觀天】a very limited view, usually implying shortsightedness, ignorance, shallowness, etc.
【坐席】①to take one's seat at a banquet table ②a seat
【坐下】to sit down 或 Sit down.
【坐享其成】to enjoy the fruit without toil
【坐鎭】personally take charge of (an operation or mission)
【坐吃山空】One cannot live in security without a dependable source of income.
【坐車】by bus or train
【坐船】by boat or ship
【坐失良機】to let a golden chance slip by
【坐視】to keep hands off
【坐次】the order of seats in a meeting or feast
【坐以待斃】to do nothing to avert a crisis, peril, etc.

坑 707 ㄎㄥ kēng
1. a pit; a hole in the ground 2. to bury alive 3. to entrap
【坑騙】to cheat by tricks
【坑道】a tunnel; a pit
【坑人】to entrap, ensnare or harm someone

五畫

坡 708 ㄆㄛ pō
a slope; a bank; a hillside
【坡地】hillside fields; sloping fields
【坡度】the degree of a slope; grade

坤 709 ㄎㄨㄣ kūn
1. one of the Eight Diagrams—earth 2. compliance; obedience 3. female; feminine
【坤伶 or 坤角兒】an actress of Peking opera
【坤輿】another name of the earth

坦 710 ㄊㄢˇ tǎn
1. wide and smooth; level 2. self-possessed; composed; calm 3. frank; straightforward 4. a son-in-law
【坦白】frank; honest; to tell the truth
【坦腹東牀】①an ideal son-in-law ②to lie in bed with a bare belly
【坦蕩】① contented and composed ②(said of a road) broad and level
【坦克車or坦克】a tank
【坦率】frank; straightforward; blunt

坷 711 ㄎㄜˇ kě
1. bad luck; unfortunate 2. rugged, uneven (roads, etc.)

垂 712 ㄔㄨㄟˊ chuí
1. to hang down; to let fall 2. to hand down; to leave a name in history 3. nearly; almost; approaching 4. to condescend
【垂暮之年】in one's old age
【垂釣】to go fishing
【垂頭喪氣】to be crestfallen; to be downcast
【垂柳 or 垂楊】a weeping willow
【垂憐】to have pity on somebody
【垂靑】to bestow favors
【垂涎 or 垂涎三尺 or 垂涎欲滴】to drool; to yearn for; to covet; to crave
【垂直】perpendicular; vertical
【垂手可得】easy to obtain or get
【垂死】at the point of death; dying
【垂愛】to show gracious concern for
【垂危】(said of an illness or situation) to be in imminent danger

垃 713 ㄌㄜˋ lè
garbage; refuse; waste
【垃圾】garbage; refuse
【垃圾堆 or 垃圾場】a rubbish heap
【垃圾桶】a dustbin; a garbage can
【垃圾車】a collection truck

坪 714 ㄆㄧㄥˊ píng
1. a level piece of ground 2. (in Japanese measurement) an area of 6 feet square

六畫

垠 715 ㄧㄣˊ yín
1. the bank (of a stream) 2. a boundary; a limit

垢 716 ㄍㄡˋ gòu
1. dirt; filth; stains 2. shame; disgrace 3. (figuratively) evil-doers

型 717 ㄒㄧㄥˊ xíng
1. an earthen mold for casting 2. a model; a pattern; a standard 3. a statute; a law 4. a style; a fashion; a type

垮 718 ㄎㄨㄚˇ kuǎ
1. to topple; to collapse 2. to wear down 3. to put to rout 4. to fall (out of power)
【垮臺】the fall (of a government, project, person, etc.); collapse

七畫

埋 719 1. ㄇㄞˊ mái
1. to bury 2. to secrete; to lie in wait
【埋沒】to bury (one's talents, etc.)
【埋伏】an ambush; to ambush
【埋頭苦幹】to bury one's head (in studying); to work with all-out effort
【埋葬】to bury (a corpse)
【埋藏】to hide; to conceal

埋 719 2. ㄇㄢˊ mán
【埋怨】to grumble; to complain

城 720 ㄔㄥˊ chéng
1. a city; a town 2. the walls of a city 3. to surround a city with walls
【城堡】a fort; a castle
【城邦】a city-state
【城門】the gate of a city wall
【城府很深】(said of one's mind) shrewd and deep
【城河 or 城壕】the moat of a city
【城牆】the city wall
【城市】a city or town

埂 721 ㄍㄥˇ gěng
1. a pit; a cave 2. an irrigation ditch 3. a low bank of earth between fields

埃 722 ㄞ āi
1. fine dust 2. Egypt
【埃及】Egypt

埔 723 ㄆㄨˇ pǔ
1. a plain; an arena 2. a port; a mart

八畫

培 724 ㄆㄟˊ péi
1. to bank up with earth 2. to nourish; to strengthen; to cultivate
【培植】① to plant ② to educate
【培養】① to grow (plants) ② to raise (kids) ③ to foster
【培育】to raise; to breed

域 725 ㄩˋ yù
1. a frontier; a boundary 2. a region; a country; an area 3. to live; to stay

埠 726 ㄅㄨˋ bù
1. a harbor; a port; a pier 2. a mart on the bank of a river or seacoast

埤 727 1. ㄆㄧˊ pí
1. a low wall; a parapet 2. an increase; increasingly; to add to
【埤益】to increase

埤 727 2. ㄅㄟ bēi
low-lying

執 728 ㄓˊ zhí
1. to hold; to grasp; to seize 2. to detain; to arrest 3. to maintain or uphold (a principle, etc.); to hold on stubbornly to errors
【執筆】to write
【執迷不悟】to adhere stubbornly
【執法】to enforce (or execute) the law
【執紼(送喪)】to attend a funeral
【執行】to execute (an order); to carry out
【執照】a license; a permit
【執掌】to manage; to superintend

〔土部〕

〔土部〕

【執著】inflexible; to persist in
【執拗】persistent 「to insist on
【執意】to stick to one's own view;
【執業】① to engage in a profession or trade ② a vocation or trade
【執言】to make positive assertions

基 729
ㄐㄧ jī
1. a foundation; a base 2. an origin; a basis; a root 3. on the basis of; according to; on the strength of 4. the base of a chemical compound
【基本】① a root, foundation or base ② fundamental; basic; elementary ③ basically; on the whole; by and large
【基本工資】basic wages
【基地】a base (of operations)
【基督】Jesus Christ: 基督教 Chris-
【基金】a reserve fund ⌊tianity
【基金會】foundation 「model
【基準】a pattern; a standard; a
【基礎】①the foundation of a building ② the basis of an argument, etc. 「unit
【基層】basic level; a grass-roots
【基因】a gene
【基於】because of; in view of

堂 730
ㄊㄤˊ táng
1. a hall; an office; a reception room 2. a meeting place; a court of justice 3. a salutation for another's mother 4. an open level place on the hill 5. relatives born of the same grandfather 6. venerable; grave; imposing
【堂堂正正】dignified and imposing
【堂皇】① imposing; impressive; grand; stately ② openly and legally 「on the father's side
【堂姊妹】one's female first cousins
【堂兄弟】one's male first cousins on the father's side

堅 731
ㄐㄧㄢ jiān
1. strong and durable 2. solid; firm 3. to dedicate to; to devote to 4. calm; steady; stable; determined 5. close; intimate 6. armor, etc. 7. the strongest position or point of enemy troops 8. steadfastly; resolutely 「truth
【堅不吐實】to refuse to tell the
【堅不可摧】invulnerable; impregnable 「staunch
【堅定】determined; steadfast;
【堅定不移】unswerving; unshaka-
【堅牢】strong; durable ⌊ble
【堅固】solid; firm; stable
【堅果】nuts 「ships; firm
【堅苦卓絕】to endure all the hard-
【堅甲利兵】ready for combat
【堅決】firmly (opposed to, etc.)
【堅強】strong; staunch
【堅貞】chaste 「sist in
【堅持or堅執】to insist on; to per-
【堅持到底】to stick it out
【堅守】① to firmly stand by (one's promise, principle, etc.) ② to defend (a place) resolutely 「tion
【堅忍】fortitude; firmness; dedica-
【堅忍不拔】invincible; indomitable
【堅韌】great strength or durability
【堅毅】fortitude; dedication
【堅硬】hard and solid

堆 732
ㄉㄨㄟ duī
1. to heap up; to pile; to stack 2. a heap; a pile; a mass; a ⌊crowd
【堆肥】compost
【堆積】to store up; to heap up
【堆砌】① (composition) allusions, corny expressions, etc. senselessly heaped together ② to pile up

九畫

報 733
ㄅㄠˋ bào
1. to repay; to recompense; to requite 2. a reward; a retribution 3. to report; to announce 4. a report; a newspaper
【報備】to inform the authorities of what one plans to do
【報表】forms for reporting statistics, etc.; report forms
【報名】to enroll; to enlist 「bill
【報費】a newspaper subscription
【報廢】① to report (worn-out office equipment, etc.) as unserviceable or useless ② to scrap
【報復】① to avenge; to revenge ② to report back (after investigation) 「kindness
【報答or報恩】to repay another's
【報導】① to report (news) ② a news report

【報到】to check in; to register
【報攤】a newsstand; a news stall
【報童】a newsboy
【報告】①to report ②a report
【報國】to devote oneself to the national cause
【報關】to declare something at the customs
【報關行】a customs broker
【報館 or 報社】a newspaper office
【報考】to enter one's name in an examination
【報刊】newspapers and periodicals
【報戶口】①to apply for a residence permit ②to register
【報佳音】to carol; caroling
【報夾】a newspaper holder or clip
【報界】the press; the news circles
【報警】①to report an alarm or emergency ②to report to the police
【報喜】to announce good news
【報銷】①to give a statement on one's expenses ②to write off
【報效】①to work for; to repay another's kindness by working hard for him ②to give private means for public use
【報信】to report news; to announce
【報紙】①a newspaper ②newsprint
【報章】①newspapers ②reply letters
【報賬】to present a bill of expenses (to the employer or the accountant)
【報仇or報讎】to avenge (a grievance, etc.)
【報酬】①pay; a salary ②remuneration; reward
【報時】to give the correct time
【報稅】to report tax returns
【報載】according to newspaper reports
【報案】to report a case (such as a theft, murder, etc.) to the police
【報業】the business of the press
【報應】retribution

堡 734
ㄅㄠˇ bǎo
1. a walled village; a town 2. a petty military station; a fort; a fortress
【堡壘】a fortress; a bastion

堪 735
ㄎㄢ kān
1. to sustain; to bear; to stand 2. fit for; worthy of; adequate for
【堪當重任】to be capable of shouldering important tasks
【堪稱佳作】may be rated as an excellent piece of writing or a fine work of art

堯 736
ㄧㄠˊ yáo
1. Yao, a legendary sage king in ancient China whose reign is said to have extended from 2357 to 2255 B.C. 2. high; eminent; lofty

場 737
ㄔㄤˊ cháng
(又讀 ㄔㄤˇ chǎng)
1. an area of level ground; an open space 2. an act of a play; an act of an opera 3. the stage 4. an arena for drill; a playground 5. a farm 6. a site or place for a special purpose, as an examination, a meeting, etc. 7.(physics) a field
【場面】①pageantry ②a scene; a spectacle ③an appearance
【場地】a playground; a site
【場合】an occasion; a condition
【場所】a location; a place; an arena

堵 738
ㄉㄨˇ dǔ
1. to stop; to block up; to shut off 2. a wall
【堵住】to block up; to stop
【堵塞】to stop up; to block up; a jam

十畫

塊 739
ㄎㄨㄞˋ kuài
1. a lump (or clod) of earth 2. a lump; a piece; a cube 3. a piece of (land, bread, etc.) 4. alone; to be all by oneself
【塊頭】stature; build
【塊根】a root tuber

塌 740
ㄊㄚ tā
1. to cave in; to fall in ruins; to collapse 2. to sink; to droop
【塌鼻】a snub nose
【塌陷】to sink; to cave in; to subside

塚 741
(冢) ㄓㄨㄥˇ zhǒng
a high tomb; a mound; a grave

塑 742
ㄙㄨˋ sù

〔土部〕

〔土部〕

1. to mold (in clay, etc.); to sculpt 2. a figure; a model 3. plastics
【塑膠】plastics
【塑膠布】plastic cloth
【塑膠袋】a plastic bag
【塑像】① to make an idol, image or statue ② a statue
【塑造】to mold; to make by molding

塔 743 ㄊㄚˇ tǎ
1. a pagoda 2. a tower 3. a lighthouse
【塔頂】the top of a pagoda
【塔台】a control tower

塗 744 ㄊㄨˊ tú
1. to smear; to apply; to spread (ointment on a wound, etc.) 2. to scribble; to scrawl 3. to erase; to blot out; to efface; to obliterate 4. mud; mire
【塗抹】① to erase; to obliterate ② to scribble
【塗料】paint; coating
【塗改】to erase and change the wording of an article, etc.; to alter
【塗鴨】① to scribble ② graffiti

塘 745 ㄊㄤˊ táng
1. an embankment; a bund; a bank; a dike 2. a square pool; a pond; a tank

塞 746 1. ㄙㄜˋ sè
(語音 ㄙㄞ sāi)
1. to block; to stop up; to clog 2. to stuff; to squeeze in; to fill 3. a cork or stopper; to cork; to seal
【塞滿】to stuff full; to fill up
【塞住】to stop up; to block up
【塞子 or 塞兒】a cork; a stopper

塞 746 2. ㄙㄞˋ sài
strategic points along the frontiers
【塞翁失馬，焉知非福】A loss may turn out to be a gain.

填 747 ㄊㄧㄢˊ tián
1. to fill up; to fill in; to stuff 2. the sound of drumbeats
【填補】to fill (vacancies, etc.); to make up a deficiency
【填平】to fill up the depressions or holes on the ground
【填房】a second wife one marries after the death of the first
【填寫】to fill in (a blank, form, etc.)
【填充】① (a form of testing) filling the blanks ② to fill up; to stuff

塢 748 ㄨˋ wù
1. a low wall around a village for defense; an entrenchment; a fortified building; a castle 2. a structure which slants to a lower center on all sides

十一畫

墓 749 ㄇㄨˋ mù
a grave; a tomb; a mausoleum
【墓碑or墓表】a gravestone; a tombstone
【墓地】the site of a grave or tomb; a cemetery
【墓穴】the vault of a tomb
【墓園】a cemetery ground

塵 750 ㄔㄣˊ chén
1. dust; dirt 2. trace; trail 3. this world; ways of the world 4. vice; sensual pleasures
【塵封】to be laid idle for a long time
【塵念】worldly thoughts
【塵囂】a place filled with a hubbub and an uproar
【塵世or塵俗】this world; this mortal life
【塵埃 or 塵土】dust; dirt
【塵緣】worldly passions; mundane desires

塹 751 ㄑㄧㄢˋ qiàn
1. the moat around a city 2. a pit; a hole or cavity in the ground

塾 752 ㄕㄨˊ shú
1. an anteroom or vestibule 2. a family school; a village school; a private primary school

境 753 ㄐㄧㄥˋ jìng
1. a boundary; a frontier; a border 2. a place; an area 3. a state; a situation; circumstances
【境內】within the border; in the country
【境況】a situation; a condition
【境界】① a boundary ② a situation ③ a state (of mind); a realm

【境遇】circumstances; conditions

墅 754 ㄕㄨˋ shù
a villa; a country house

墊 755 ㄉㄧㄢˋ diàn
1. to advance (money); to pay for another and expect to be paid back 2. a cushion; a pad; a bed-mat 3. to cushion 4. to sink into 5. to dig
【墊被】a mattress
【墊補】to defray expenses not budgeted
【墊脚石】a steppingstone
【墊肩】a shoulder pad (or padding)

十二畫

墟 756 ㄒㄩ xū
1. a high mound 2. an ancient town; a ghost town 3. wild, waste land 4. a periodical marketplace where goods are bartered 5. to ruin; to destroy

墜 757 ㄓㄨㄟˋ zhuì
to fall down; to sink; the fall (of a person, a state, etc.)
【墜馬】to fall off a horse
【墜地】① to fall ② failure ③ to come to this world
【墜樓】to fall from a building
【墜落】to fall; to drop

增 758 ㄗㄥ zēng
to add to; to increase; to grow; to enlarge
【增補】to add to; to supplement
【增訂本】a revised and enlarged edition
【增光】to do credit to
【增廣】to widen (one's knowledge, etc.)
【增刊】a supplement—as of newspaper, etc.
【增加】to add to; to increase
【增減】increases and decreases
【增進】to promote (friendship, etc.); to increase (knowledge, etc.)
【增強】to strengthen; to enhance
【增值】appreciation; increment
【增值稅】VAT (value-added tax)
【增長】a rise; to grow
【增產】to increase production
【增援】to send reinforcements

墨 759 ㄇㄛˋ mò
1. black; dark 2. a black dye 3. a Chinese inkstick; ink 4. calligraphy 5. literate; letters; learning 6. statutes; institutions 7. greedy; covetous 8. to tattoo the face—one of the five punishments in ancient China
【墨寶】treasured calligraphic works
【墨綠】blackish green
【墨盒】an ink box
【墨鏡】sunglasses
【墨汁or墨水】① ink ② learning; letters
【墨守成規】to stick to old rules; conservative
【墨魚】the squid; the cuttlefish

墩 760 ㄉㄨㄣ dūn
1. a mound; a heap 2. a block of stone or wood 3. a cluster

墮 761 ㄉㄨㄛˋ duò
1. to fall; to sink; to let fall 2. to indulge in evil ways 3. lazy; idle
【墮胎】abortion; to abort
【墮落】① to indulge in evil ways; to degenerate ② the fall (of a nation, family, etc.)

十三畫

墳 762 ㄈㄣˊ fén
1. a grave; a mound 2. great; large; big 3. the banks of a river
【墳墓】a grave; a tomb
【墳地or墳場】a graveyard; a cemetery

壁 763 ㄅㄧˋ bì
1. a partition wall; the walls of a room 2. a military breastwork 3. a cliff
【壁報】a wall paper; a wall poster
【壁毯】tapestry
【壁壘分明】There is no compromise between the contending factions.
【壁爐】a fireplace
【壁虎】a house lizard or gecko
【壁畫】a mural painting; a fresco
【壁櫥】a closet; a wall chest

墾 764 ㄎㄣˇ kěn
to open new land for farming, etc.; to reclaim land
【墾丁公園】Kenting Park, Pingtung
【墾荒】to open up barren land for

〔土部〕

farming
【墾殖】to reclaim land and cultivate it

765
壅 ㄩㄥˇ yǒng
(又讀 ㄩㄥ yōng)
1. to stop; to block up 2. to bank up the roots of plants
【壅塞】to block up; to obstruct; to impede

〔土部〕

766
壇 ㄊㄢˊ tán
1. a platform for sacrificial rites; an altar 2. a hall for important meetings and ceremonies in ancient China

十四畫

767
壓 ㄧㄚ yā
1. to press 2. to control; to quell 3. to crush 4. (said of enemy troops, etc.) to close in; to press near 5. to hold (a document, etc.) without taking action; to pigeonhole 6. a way of making a stroke in Chinese calligraphy 7. to excel; to surpass others
【壓迫】①to oppress; to pressure; to force ②oppression; pressure
【壓倒】to surpass; to overwhelm
【壓倒性勝利】an overwhelming victory
【壓臺戲 or 壓軸戲】the best act of a show
【壓力】pressure
【壓根兒】totally; entirely; completely
【壓克力】(chemistry) acrylic resin
【壓壞】damaged by high pressure
【壓擠】to extrude; extrusion
【壓境】(usually said of enemy troops) to mass on, or approach the border
【壓制】①to suppress (one's anger, etc.); to restrain (usually by force) ②(military) to neutralize (enemy fire by massive bombardment)
【壓榨】①to oppress ②to extract (liquids) by applying high pressure
【壓軸好戲】the last but best one of a series of performances
【壓住】to suppress; to put down by force
【壓死】①to crush to death ②to die after being hit by a car
【壓縮】to compress; to condense
【壓碎】to crush to pieces
【壓抑】to curb; to repress

768
壑 ㄏㄨㄛˋ huò
1. a gully; a channel for water 2. a narrow ravine at the foot of a hill

769
壕 ㄏㄠˊ háo
1. the ditch around a city wall; a moat 2. a trench
【壕溝】a trench (in warfare); a ditch

十五畫

770
壘 ㄌㄟˇ lěi
1. a military wall; a rampart 2. to pile up 3. a base
【壘球】softball

十六畫

771
壟 ㄌㄨㄥˇ lǒng
1. a grave; a mound of earth 2. a high place in a field
【壟斷】a monopoly; to monopolize

772
壞 ㄏㄨㄞˋ huài
1. broken-down; decaying; rotten; out of order; useless 2. bad; poor (scores, etc.) 3. vicious; mean; evil (persons, etc.)
【壞坯子】a bad egg; a lout
【壞蛋】a bad fellow; a villain
【壞東西】a bad person or thing
【壞話】slander
【壞球】(baseball) ball
【壞血病】scurvy; scorbutus
【壞心眼兒】ill-intentioned; malicious
【壞主意】a wicked or crooked idea
【壞處】bad points; shortcomings
【壞事】①a bad thing; an evil deed ②to make things worse
【壞人】a bad guy; an evil person
【壞死】a necrosis

十七畫

773
壤 ㄖㄤˇ rǎng
1. loose soil 2. earth 3. a region; a place; a land 4. rich; abundant

二十一畫

壩 774 ㄅㄚˋ bà
1. an embankment; a dike 2. a dam

士部 ㄕˋ shì

士 775 ㄕˋ shì
1. a scholar; a man of learning; a gentleman 2. an official rank in ancient China; an officer 3. a noncommissioned officer 4. a person 5. name of a chessman in Chinese chess
【士兵or士卒】 soldiers; privates; enlisted men
【士大夫】① an official ② a general ③ a scholar
【士氣】 ① the morale of a fighting force ② the trends and temperaments of scholars in a given era
【士紳】 the gentry

一畫

壬 776 ㄖㄣˊ rén
1. the ninth of the Ten Celestial Stems 2. artful and crafty 3. great 4. pregnant

四畫

壯 777 ㄓㄨㄤˋ zhuàng
1. big; great 2. strong; robust; vigorous; sturdy 3. portly; stout 4. to strengthen 5. the prime of one's life
【壯大】 ①big and strong; vigorous ② to expand
【壯膽】 to embolden
【壯丁】① an able-bodied man ② an adult fit for military service
【壯年】 the prime of one's life
【壯麗】 splendorous
【壯烈】 courageous
【壯烈犧牲】 to die as a martyr
【壯觀】 a grand sight; a great sight
【壯闊】 magnificent; grandiose
【壯舉】 a great achievement
【壯志凌雲】 a soaring ambition
【壯志未酬】to die before the fulfillment of his ambition or aspiration
【壯士】 a brave man; a hero

九畫

壻 778 (婿) ㄒㄩˋ xù
1. one's son-in-law 2. one's husband

壹 779 ㄧ yī
an elaborate form of "一" (one) used mostly in accounting and especially in checks to prevent forgery or alterations

壺 780 ㄏㄨˊ hú
1. a pot; a jug 2. any potbellied container with a small opening

十一畫

壽 781 ㄕㄡˋ shòu
1. the life span 2. old age; a long life; longevity 3. birthday 4. to die of old age 5. to present another with gold, silk, etc. 6. to toast an elder
【壽比南山】 May your life be as lofty as the Southern Mountain Ranges.
【壽命】 the life span of a person
【壽誕】 a birthday anniversary
【壽桃】 longevity peaches
【壽禮or壽儀】 birthday gifts or presents
【壽考】 long life
【壽星】 ① a reference to a person on his birthday ② the God of Longevity ③ Canopus
【壽終正寢】 to die a natural death; to die of old age
【壽辰】 birthday

夊部 ㄙㄨㄟ suī

七畫

夏 782 1. ㄒㄧㄚˋ xià
1. summer 2. big; spacious 3. a big house; a mansion 4. Cathay, the ancient name of China 5. a dynasty in Chinese history

(2205-1782 B.C.) 「days
【夏天or夏日】summer; summer
【夏令】summer; summer time
【夏令營】summer camps
【夏季】the summer season
【夏至】the summer solstice which falls on June 21 or 22 on the Northern Hemisphere
【夏裝】a summer dress
【夏娃】(the Bible) Eve
【夏威夷】Hawaii

夏 782
2. ㄐㄧㄚˇ jiǎ 「ing pupils
【夏楚】a ferule; a rod for punish-

夕部
ㄒㄧˋ xì

夕 783
ㄒㄧˋ xì
1. dusk; sunset; evening 2. night 3. slant; oblique 4. to meet in the 「evening
【夕陽】the setting sun

二畫

外 784
ㄨㄞˋ wài
1. out; outside 2. foreign; alien 3. diplomatic 4. besides 5. to al- 「ienate
【外幣】foreign currency
【外表】an outward appearance; an exterior
【外邊】① out; outside ② faraway or distant places ③ a border region 「guests
【外賓】foreign visitors; foreign
【外部】the external of anything; outside 「grandmother
【外婆or外祖母】one's maternal
【外貌】an outward appearance
【外貿】foreign (or external) trade
【外蒙古】Outer Mongolia
【外面】① an outward appearance ② outside
【外放】① to send an official in the capital for a provincial post ② to send an official for an overseas assignment
【外帶】①a tire (cover) ②as well; besides 「than where one is
【外地】parts of the country other
【外調】to transfer (materials or personnel) to other places
【外電】dispatches from foreign news agencies
【外太空】outer space
【外套】① an overcoat ② overalls in the Ching Dynasty
【外頭】outside
【外來】outside; external; foreign
【外來語】foreign terms
【外流】to flow outward; the out- 「flow
【外國】a foreign country
【外國貨】commodities of foreign make 「an alien
【外國人or外籍人士】a foreigner;
【外國語】a foreign language
【外觀】an outward appearance
【外科】surgery
【外科醫生 or 外科大夫】a surgeon
【外殼】a shell; a case
【外快】extra income; perquisites
【外號】a nickname
【外行】① a greenhorn ② unskilled
【外行話】layman's language
【外匯】foreign exchange
【外匯交易】foreign exchange transactions 「market
【外匯市場】a foreign exchange
【外患】foreign invasion, aggression, or intrusion
【外加】plus; in addition (to)
【外界】① outsiders ② the outside ③ one's environment
【外交】diplomacy; diplomatic
【外交部】Ministry of Foreign Affairs 「Affairs
【外交部長】Minister of Foreign
【外交官】diplomatic officials; diplomats
【外交家】skillful diplomats
【外交政策】foreign policy
【外交辭令】tactful remarks; euphemisms
【外景】a location; an exterior
【外僑】foreign residents
【外勤】work done outside the 「office
【外強中乾】a paper tiger
【外銷】to export; export
【外向】extrovert; extroversion
【外星人】an E.T. (extraterrestrial)
【外形】an appearance; a contour
【外債】international loans
【外傳】①(ㄨㄞˋ ㄓㄨㄢˋ) a narrative of events not recorded in history ②(ㄨㄞˋ ㄔㄨㄢˊ) rumors are circu-

lating...
【外出】to go out
【外出血】external hemorrhage
【外商】foreign businessmen
【外傷】external injuries; bruises
【外甥】nephews
【外甥女】nieces
【外省】other provinces
【外省人】persons from another province 「foreigners
【外人】① outsiders; strangers ②
【外資】foreign capital 「husband
【外子】a reference to one's own
【外在】external; extrinsic
【外祖 or 外祖父 or 外公】one's maternal grandfather
【外宿】to stay outside (one's own home or dormitory) overnight
【外孫】sons of one's daughters
【外孫女】daughters of one's daughters 「clothing
【外衣】a coat; a jacket; outer
【外野】(baseball) outfield
【外野手】an outfielder
【外務】① foreign affairs ② affairs or work which do not really concern one or which one is not obliged to handle
【外圍】the perimeter
【外文 or 外語】a foreign language
【外遇】to have extramarital affairs
【外援】outside help; foreign aid
【外緣】① the outer rim (of an object) ② desires that come from outside temptations
【外用】external use; external application

三畫

多 785
1. ㄉㄨㄛ duō

1. many; much; too much 2. more than; much more; over 3. greatly; highly 4. to praise 5. only
【多胞胎】multiple birth 「likely
【多半】①most ②probably; most
【多邊形 or 多角形】a polygon
【多變】changeable; changeful;
【多病】constantly ill 「varied
【多謀善斷】resourceful and decisive 「ways
【多方面】many-sided; in many
【多福多壽】happiness and longevity
【多大】① How big? ② How old?
【多黨制度】the multiparty system
【多多少少】more or less
【多多益善】The more, the better.
【多退少補】to return the overcharge and demand payment of the shortage, if any
【多瑙河】the Danube River
【多難興邦】Foreign aggressions often awaken a nation from its slumbers and thus help make it strong. 「seen for many years
【多年不見】to have not met or
【多寡】number; amount
【多寡不拘】It doesn't matter how much or how little (you contribute).
【多管閑事】to poke one's nose into others' business; to be a busybody
【多虧】It is fortunate that....或 We are lucky to....或 Thanks to....
【多情】passionate; emotional
【多謝】Many thanks. 或 Thank you very much. 或 Thanks a lot.
【多心】①to be very suspicious ②
【多愁善感】sentimental 「tricky
【多重人格】multiple personality
【多時】a long time
【多事】officious; interfering; meddling 「eventful year
【多事之秋】troubled times; an
【多少】① How much? 或How many? ② more or less; somewhat
【多數】the majority; many
【多子多孫】many children and grandchildren (regarded as a blessing among old Chinese)
【多災多難】to be dogged by bad luck, misfortune, etc.
【多嘴】to have a big mouth; to shoot one's mouth off 「etc.
【多此一舉】a superfluous action,
【多次】many times; time and again
【多才多藝】versatile; very capable
【多彩多姿】colorful; many-faceted
【多疑】suspicious 「varied
【多樣化】to diversify; to make
【多餘】unnecessary; superfluous
【多雲】cloudy

多 785
2. ㄉㄨㄛ duó

how, what, etc.—in exclamatory

statements

【多麼】how (good, beautiful, etc.); what

【多美】How beautiful!

【多好】How nice! 或How wonderful!

〔夕部〕

夙 786 ㄙㄨˋ sù

1. the early morning 2. old (desires, etc.)

【夙昔】① past times; in the past ② day and night

【夙興夜寐】to rise early and sleep late—very diligent

【夙仇】an old enemy

【夙夜匪懈】to work diligently day and night

【夙願】a long-cherished wish

五畫

夜 787 ㄧㄝˋ yè

1. night; dark(ness) 2. a night trip; night traveling

【夜班】night shifts; night work

【夜不閉戶】There's no need to close doors at night.

【夜貓子】① the owl ② a person who enjoys night life

【夜盲症】night blindness; nyctalopia

【夜幕】gathering darkness

【夜大 or 夜間大學】an evening university

【夜來香】(botany) the tuberose

【夜闌人靜 or 夜深人靜】deep in the night; at the dead of night

【夜郎自大】ignorant and boastful

【夜涼如水】the chilling (autumn) night

【夜工】night work; a night job

【夜壺】a chamber pot 亦作「夜淨兒」

【夜間部】the night department (of a school, college or university)

【夜景】night scenes (of a locality)

【夜襲】to launch an attack under the cover of night

【夜校 or 夜學】a night school

【夜車】① a night train ② (figuratively) to study late at night

【夜長夢多】There'll be twists and obstacles if a problem or an issue is not settled promptly.

【夜市】business activities in night hours; markets devoted to night-time business

【夜生活】night life

【夜總會】a nightclub

【夜色】the dim light of night—moonlight

【夜色蒼茫】twilight at dusk

【夜以繼日】around the clock; night and day

【夜夜】night after night

【夜鶯】the nightingale

【夜晚or夜間】at night; in the night

八畫

夠 788 (够) ㄍㄡˋ gòu

1. enough; too much; sufficient 2. fully; quite

【夠本】enough to cover the cost

【夠不夠】Is it enough?

【夠朋友】to be true to friends; to be a friend in need

【夠面子or夠體面】to enjoy enough honor

【夠格】to be qualified

【夠勁兒】①(said of an onerous task) almost too much to cope with ② strong or hot (in taste, strength, etc.)

【夠意思】① really something; terrific ② generous; really kind

【夠味兒】enjoyable; pleasant enough

十一畫

夢 789 ㄇㄥˋ mèng

1. a dream 2. to dream 3. wishful thinking; wishful

【夢寐以求】to long for something day and night

【夢話】① an absurd and unthinkable speech ② somniloquy

【夢幻】illusion; a dream; reverie

【夢見】to dream

【夢境】dreamland

【夢鄉】asleep; dreamland; slumber

【夢想】① a daydream ② to dream of

【夢熊之喜】to give birth to a son

【夢兆】a prognostic from a dream

【夢中人】a sweetheart

【夢遺】nocturnal emission

【夢囈】① somniloquy ② nonsense

【夢遊】to somnambulate

【夢魘】nightmares; bad dreams

夤 790 ㄧㄣˊ yín

1. to hang on (power, glory, etc.) 2. to respect 3. a remote place

【夤夜】deep in the night

【另函】a separate letter
【另起爐灶】①to start a new trade or line of business ②to start all over again
【另請高明】to find someone better qualified (than myself)
【另有高就】to have found better employment elsewhere
【另眼看待】to give favored treatment
【另外】besides; in addition

叩 463
ㄎㄡˋ kòu
1.to knock; to hit 2.to ask 3. to kowtow
【叩門】to knock at a door
【叩見or叩謁】to interview or visit a superior
【叩謝】to thank politely

只 464
ㄓˇ zhǐ
1. only; merely 2. but; yet
【只不過】only; just; merely
【只怕】afraid of no one (or nothing)
【只得】to have to (do something) except...
【只管】(do anything) as you wish; please don't hesitate to...
【只好】the only alternative is to...; to have to
【只是】① but; yet ②merely; only; just
【只要】①to want only... ② all one has to do is to...
【只有】①to have...only; only; alone ②to have to (do or be)
【只因】only because; for the simple reason that...

叫 465
ㄐㄧㄠˋ jiào
1. to be called or known as 2. to cry; to shout; to scream; a shout or scream 3. to call; to summon 4. to cause
【叫罵】to scream and use foul language like a fishwife
【叫賣】to hawk
【叫苦】to complain of hardship
【叫苦連天】to be full of complaints
【叫好】to cheer; to applaud
【叫喊】to shout; to yell; to scream; to cry
【叫化子】a beggar 亦作「乞丐」
【叫貨】to order goods
【叫喚】①to call; to summon ②to shout
【叫屈】to cry out for justice; to complain of unfair treatment
【叫囂】to shout and yell; clamor
【叫醒】to waken; to wake up
【叫座(兒)】(said of plays, dramas, etc.) to have appeal to the audience
【叫做】to be called; to be known as
【叫菜】to order dishes

召 466
ㄓㄠˋ zhào
1. to summon; to call up 2. to cause; to invite
【召募or徵募】to enlist or recruit (soldiers)
【召開】to convene; to convoke
【召回】to recall (a diplomat from abroad)
【召喚】to call; to summon
【召集】①to convene (a meeting, etc.) ②to call to arms
【召見】to summon a subordinate; to be summoned by a superior

叭 467
ㄅㄚ bā
a trumpet

叮 468
ㄉㄧㄥ dīng
1. the chimes of a bell 2. to exhort or enjoin repeatedly 3. to sting, as a mosquito, etc.
【叮噹】dingdong (used for the sound of bells)
【叮嚀or丁寧】to exhort repeatedly
【叮囑】to enjoin and urge repeatedly

可 469
1. ㄎㄜˇ kě
1. may; can; to be able to 2. around; estimated at 3. an auxiliary 4. but; however 5. a Chinese family name
【可悲】sad; lamentable
【可怕】dreadful; frightening; terrible
【可否】can; may (used at the beginning of a question)
【可能】probable; possible
【可能性】possibility; probability
【可憐】pitiful; pitiable; poor; miserable
【可憐蟲】a poor creature; a poor guy
【可歌可泣】(said of bravery or fortitude in serving the nation) very moving; very touching
【可貴】valuable; praiseworthy
【可觀】① to be worth seeing ② considerable (sum of money, losses, etc.)
【可可】cocoa
【可靠】reliable (sources, etc.); dependable
【可靠性】reliability
【可口】tasty; pleasant to the palate

口部

【可口可樂】Coca Cola or Coke
【可恨】hateful; detestable; abominable
【可見】①that can be seen ②to be perceived
【可巧】by a coincidence; coincidently
【可親】kindly; friendly; amiable
【可取】worth having
【可圈可點】①(said of a writing) very good ②(said of the manner in doing something) very laudable
【可惜】It's a pity that....
【可笑】laughable; ridiculous
【可信度】(sociology) the confidence level
【可想而知】to be obvious; one can well imagine
【可行】feasible; can be carried out
【可行性】feasibility
【可恥】shameful
【可乘之機】an opportunity that can be exploited to somebody's advantage
【可是】① to be (in a more emphatic sense); will really be ② but; however
【可人】① enjoyable; lovable ② a person with many admirable qualities
【可塑性】plasticity
【可愛】lovable; likable
【可疑】① suspicious ② doubtful
【可以】①can; may ②Yes, you can. 或 Yes, you may. ③Okay. That will do.
【可有可無】dispensable; not essential
【可惡】detestable; hateful
【可謂】one may well say; it may be called
【可望而不可卽】can be looked at but not touched
【可遇而不可求】(something) considered to be uncertain
【可用】①serviceable ②employable

可 469
2. ㄎㄜˋ kè
as in 可汗—a khan

台 470
ㄊㄞˊ tái
1. a raised platform 亦作「臺」 2. a polite expression of addressing 參看「台端」
【台風】stage manners
【台端】you (an honorific in addressing one's equal)
【台階】①steps leading up to a building ②a chance to extricate oneself from an awkward position
【台鑒 or 台照】a form used after the name in the salutation of a business letter
【台柱】① an important actor in a troupe or cast ② an important person in an organization
【台詞】a stage dialogue; the actor's lines
【台灣or臺灣】Taiwan or Formosa

叱 471
ㄔˋ chì
to scold; to revile
【叱罵】to scold; to revile; to rail at
【叱喝】to yell at
【叱咤風雲】(said of a dictator, conqueror, etc.) to lord it over the world
【叱責】to scold; to blame

史 472
ㄕˇ shǐ
1. history; chronicles; annals 2. a Chinese family name
【史蹟or史跡】① historic events ② historic relics
【史家】a historian
【史前時代】the prehistoric age
【史學】history (as a science)
【史詩】an epic
【史書or史籍】a book of history; an annal
【史無前例】without precedent in history

右 473
ㄧㄡˋ yòu
1. right (as opposed to left) 2. west 3. to assist; to aid 4. to emphasize
【右邊 or 右首】the right-hand side
【右派】①the right wing ②the rightists; the conservatives
【右舷】the starboard
【右心室】the right ventricle
【右手】①the right hand ②the right-hand side
【右翼份子】a right-winger

叵 474
ㄆㄛˇ pǒ
unable; improbable

司 475
ㄙ sī
1. to have charge of; to preside over 2. a (government) department
【司法】judicature; judiciary
【司法官】a legal officer; a judge
【司法機關】judicial organs
【司令 or 司令官】a commander

【司令部】headquarters
【司令臺】a review stand
【司空見慣】something quite usual
【司機】a driver; a chauffeur
【司儀】an M.C.; an emcee

三畫

合 476
ㄏㄜˊ hé
1. to combine; to unite; to gather; to collect 2. to close; to shut 3. to suit
【合辦】to operate, or run jointly
【合併】to combine; to unite; to conjoin; to consolidate
【合不來】cannot get along with (somebody)
【合謀】to conspire together
【合法】lawful; legal; legitimate
【合得來】to get along well; to be congenial
【合訂本】a bound volume
【合同or合約】an agreement; a contract
【合理】reasonable; logical; rational
【合流】①confluence ②to flow together; to merge
【合攏】to close up
【合格】qualified; up to the standard
【合股】to pool capital; to enter into partnership
【合刊】a combined issue (of a periodical)
【合乎】to qualify; to tally with
【合夥】to enter into partnership
【合夥人】(accounting) partners
【合會】a mutual help loan association
【合婚】to be united in wedlock
【合擊】to make a joint attack on
【合計】a total; to add up to
【合家歡】a family reunion
【合金】an alloy
【合情合理】fair and reasonable
【合羣】to be gregarious
【合著】to coauthor
【合唱】to sing in chorus
【合唱團】a chorus; a choir
【合時】timely; seasonable
【合式or合適】suitable; fitting
【合身】to fit
【合奏】(music) a united performance of the full number of players
【合葬】to bury (husband and wife) in one grave
【合作or合力】to cooperate; to collaborate
【合作金庫】Cooperative Bank
【合作社】a co-op
【合算】① to reckon up ② worthwhile
【合宜】fitting; suitable; proper
【合意】(said of a thing) to suit one's fancy
【合眼】to close the eyes
【合音】(music) combination tone
【合影留念】to have a group photo taken to mark the occasion
【合胃口】to suit one's taste

吁 477
ㄒㄩ xū
a sigh

吃 478
1. (喫) ㄔ chī
1. to eat 2. to sustain
【吃不了兜着走】to land oneself in serious trouble
【吃不消】cannot stand or bear
【吃飯】to eat, take, or have a meal
【吃得消】to be able to stand (exertion, fatigue, etc.)
【吃豆腐】(slang) to make advances to a woman without serious intentions
【吃奶】to suck the breast
【吃裏扒外】to work for the interests of an opposing group at the expense of one's own
【吃力】tired; exhausted
【吃力不討好】to work laboriously only to earn criticisms
【吃零食】to eat snacks in small amounts between meals
【吃官司】to be sued (in a court of law)
【吃光】to eat up
【吃苦】to suffer hardship
【吃苦頭】to suffer
【吃苦耐勞】diligent; hardworking
【吃虧】to be at a disadvantage; to suffer a loss
【吃喝嫖賭】a dissipated or dissolute life
【吃喝玩樂】to idle away one's time in seeking pleasure
【吃角子老虎】a slot machine
【吃緊】(usually said of a military situation) hard pressed, or critical
【吃驚】surprised; frightened; startled
【吃閒飯】to live like a parasite
【吃香】to be welcome or valued everywhere; popular

〔口部〕

【吃素】to practice vegetarianism
【吃重】to play an important role
【吃吃喝喝】to be interested only in eating and drinking
【吃軟飯】to live on the earnings of a prostitute
【吃醋】to be jealous
【吃啞吧虧】to be cheated or suffer a loss but unable to talk about it for one reason or another
【吃藥】to take medicine

吃 478
2. ㄐㄧˊ jí
to stammer; to stutter

各 479
ㄍㄜˋ gè
1. each; every 2. all
【各半】half-and-half; fifty-fifty
【各別】individual; isolated (case); separate
【各得其所】Each person gets his proper position.
【各地】various places or localities
【各類】each or every sort, kind, class, species, or order
【各個擊破】to knock out one adver sary after another
【各國】each and every nation (or country)
【各行or各業】each and every trade
【各級】all or different levels
【各界】all walks of life; all circles
【各就各位】①(military) Man your posts! ② (athletics) On your marks!
【各取所需】Each takes what he wants.
【各顯神通】Each has his own way.
【各執一詞】Each (of the disputants) tells a different story.
【各種】various kinds, species, categories, etc.
【各持己見】Each sticks to his own view.
【各式各樣 or 各色各樣】all sorts, kinds, or varieties; various
【各抒己見】Each airs his own views.
【各人】everybody
【各自】each; respective
【各自爲政】Each (office) administers its affairs in its own way without coordination with others.
【各有千秋】Each shows a unique quality
【各有所好】Each has his likes and dislikes.
【各有所長】Each has a unique merit.
【各位】ladies and gentlemen

吉 480
ㄐㄧˊ jí
good; lucky; auspicious; propitious; favorable; fortunate
【吉卜賽or吉普賽】the Gipsies or the Gypsies
【吉普車】a jeep
【吉屋招租】a house for rent
【吉他】a guitar
【吉利】good luck; propitiousness
【吉祥】propitious; auspicious
【吉星高照】The lucky star shines bright.
【吉凶未卜】No one knows how it will turn out.
【吉兆 or 吉徵】a good omen
【吉人天相】Heaven helps a good man.

吋 481
ㄘㄨㄣˋ cùn
inch—a unit of length

同 482
ㄊㄨㄥˊ tóng
1. same; equal; identical; similar; common 2. to share; to agree 3. together
【同輩】of the same generation; a peer; one's equal (in seniority)
【同胞】a compatriot
【同班】a classmate
【同伴】a companion
【同病相憐】Fellow sufferers have mutual sympathy.
【同步】synchronism; to synchronize
【同袍】①comrades in arms ②to share the same robes with
【同謀】to conspire
【同門】a fellow disciple
【同盟】an alliance; a league
【同名】a namesake
【同名同姓】having the same given name and family name
【同房】to share the same room
【同父異母】having the same father but different mothers
【同等】of the same rank or class
【同等學力】(said of persons without a diploma in comparison with those who have it) with the same intellectual capacity and scholastic achievements
【同年】of the same age
【同樂晚會】an evening party
【同類】the same kind, class, or species
【同僚 or 同事】colleagues
【同流合汚】to follow the bad example of others

【同甘共苦】to share bliss and adversity together
【同感】to have the same feeling
【同歸於盡】to die together
【同好】people with the same hobby
【同行】① (ㄊㄨㄥˊ ㄏㄤˊ) in the same trade, line, occupation, or profession ②(ㄊㄨㄥˊ ㄒㄧㄥˊ) to go together
【同化】to assimilate; assimilation
【同夥】a member of the same 「group」
【同居】to cohabit
【同氣相求】People with the same ideals have an affinity for one another.
【同情】to sympathize 「pity」
【同情心】sympathies; compassion;
【同心協力】to work in cooperation
【同鄉】the people from the same province, county, town, etc.
【同姓】members of the same clan
【同性】of the same sex
【同性戀 or 同性愛】homosexuality
【同性戀者】a gay; a homosexual
【同學】a fellow student; a schoolmate
【同學會】an alumni association
【同志】a comrade
【同舟共濟】to show the mutual concern of the people in the same boat
【同儕】contemporaries
【同仇敵愾】to share the same hatred and fight against a common enemy
【同窗】a classmate or schoolmate
【同牀異夢】to have different dreams in the same bed
【同時】at the same time; simultaneously
【同室操戈】(especially said of brothers) to engage in internal strife
【同聲相應】to act in unison
【同日而語】to mention in equal 「terms」
【同仁or同人】a colleague
【同宗】of the same clan 「concur」
【同意】to agree; to consent; to
【同意書】a written consent; a letter of authorization
【同業】the people of the same trade or occupation
【同業公會】a guild; a trade union
【同樣】① in the same way, manner, or fashion; likewise ② the same 「appositive」
【同位語】(English grammar) an

吆 483
ㄧㄠ yāo
to shout; to cry 「hawk」
【吆喝】① to shout; to cry ② to

名 484
ㄇㄧㄥˊ míng
1. a name; a designation; a title; rank 2. position; honor; fame; renown; reputation 3. famous; noted; distinguished; renowned; valuable; precious; noble; rare; great 4. to name; to describe
【名不虛傳】The reputation is well supported by fact.
【名牌】① a famous brand ② a nameplate 「card」
【名片or名刺or名帖】a calling
【名滿天下】to be world-famous
【名門閨秀】a daughter of an illus- 「trious family」
【名目】a name
【名分】a role or duties proper to one's title 「name or reputation」
【名副其實】to be worthy of the
【名單】a name list; a roster; a roll
【名堂】① a dignified name or designation ② a result that is worth mentioning
【名利】fame and gain
【名利雙收】to achieve both fame and wealth
【名列前茅】to head the list of successful candidates 「table」
【名流or名人】a celebrity; a no-
【名伶】a renowned actor or actress
【名落孫山】to fail in an examination 「ated reputation」
【名過其實】to have an exagger-
【名貴】valuable; precious; rare
【名花有主】The beauty has already been won by somebody.
【名節】honor and integrity
【名氣 or 名聲 or 名望】fame; reputation; renown
【名下】① under (one's) account ② to (one's) account
【名正言順】valid in name and in reasoning; to deserve 「piece」
【名著or名作】a literary master-
【名產】a noted product or special product (of a place) 「a thing)」
【名稱】the name or designation (of
【名垂青史】to go down in history
【名師】a great teacher; a master

〔口部〕

【名勝】 a scenic spot; a resort
【名勝古跡】 places of historic interest and scenic beauty
【名人錄】 *who's who*
【名字】 the name (of a person, etc.)
【名譟一時】 (said of writers, artists, etc.) very famous at one time
【名詞】 ①a noun ②a term
【名次】 one's position or standing
【名册】 a roster; a roll
【名存實亡】 (said of established institutions) to exist in name only
【名額】 the number of openings, or quota (for employees, students, etc.)
【名醫】 a famous doctor
【名義】 ① the name ② the outward reason
【名言】 a maxim; an adage
【名揚四海】 to become famous all over the world
【名譽】 ①honor; reputation ② honorary
【名譽博士】 an honorary doctorate
【名媛】 a young lady of note

后 485 ㄏㄡˋ hòu
1. an empress 2. the god of the earth 3. after; behind 亦作「後」
【后土】 the earth; the god of the earth

吐 486 1. ㄊㄨˇ tǔ
to spit; to utter
【吐痰】 to spit phlegm; to spit
【吐露】 to confess; to disclose
【吐氣】 to give vent to pent-up feelings
【吐出】 to spit out; to utter

吐 486 2. ㄊㄨˋ tù
to vomit; to throw up; to spew
【吐血】 to vomit blood; hematemesis

向 487 ㄒㄧㄤˋ xiàng
1. to turn; to face 2. a direction; a trend 3. until now 4. a Chinese family name
【向壁虛造】 to fabricate
【向來】 hitherto; heretofore; until now
【向光性】 (biology) phototropism
【向後】 ①in the future ②to turn around
【向前】 to go forward
【向下】 downward; down
【向心力】 centripetal force
【向學】 to determine or to be inclined to study
【向上】 ① to turn upward ② to strive upward
【向日葵】 the sunflower
【向左】 towards the left
【向右】 towards the right
【向外】 ① to turn outside ② upwards of, or more (used after a number)

吏 488 ㄌㄧˋ lì
a civil officer
【吏員】 a minor official

四畫

君 489 ㄐㄩㄣ jūn
1. a sovereign; a monarch; a king; a lord 2. you (used in addressing a male in formal speech)
【君權】 sovereign power
【君主 or 君王】 a sovereign; a ruler; a monarch
【君子】 a perfect or true gentleman
【君子協定】 a gentlemen's agreement

吝 490 ㄌㄧㄣˋ lìn
stingy; niggardly; parsimonious
【吝惜】 to be stingy about
【吝嗇】 stingy; miserly; niggardly

吞 491 ㄊㄨㄣ tūn
to swallow; to engulf; to gulp
【吞併】 to annex (a foreign territory); to take possession of (another's property)
【吞沒】 ①to take possession of (another's property) ②to engulf
【吞服】 to swallow or take (medicine)
【吞吞吐吐】 to hum and haw
【吞食】 to swallow; to devour
【吞噬】 ①(said of beasts) to swallow or devour (the prey) ②(said of fire, etc.) to devour; to engulf
【吞雲吐霧】 to puff; to take puffs

吟 492 ㄧㄣˊ yín
1. to chant; to intone; to sing; to recite 2. to moan
【吟嘯】 ① to whistle or shout in freedom ② to lament
【吟誦】 to recite (a verse)
【吟遊詩人】 a troubadour; a minstrel

吠 493 ㄈㄟˋ fèi

(said of a dog) to bark

否 494
1. ㄈㄡˇ fǒu
1. no; not 2. negative
【否定】①to deny; to negate; to refute ② denial; negation
【否決】to veto; to vote down
【否認】①to deny; to reject ② denial; rejection; repudiation
【否則】otherwise; if not, then...

否 494
2. ㄆㄧˇ pǐ
evil; bad
【否極泰來】Adversity, after reaching its extremity, is followed by felicity.

吩 495
ㄈㄣ fēn
to instruct or direct
【吩咐】to instruct or direct (someone to do something)

含 496
ㄏㄢˊ hán
1. to hold in the mouth 2. to contain; to include 3. to bear
【含怒】in anger
【含淚】with tears in the eyes
【含量】content
【含恨】to cherish resentment, disappointment, etc.
【含糊 or 含混】(said of a statement, manners, etc.) vague; ambiguous
【含糊其詞】to talk ambiguously
【含情脈脈】full of tenderness (in silent communication of affection or love, especially said of young girls)
【含笑】①(botany) *Michelia figo* ② to smile; to grin
【含笑九泉 or 含笑地下】to die with satisfaction
【含羞】to blush
【含羞草】(botany) mimosa
【含辛茹苦】to undergo all sorts of hardships and deprivations
【含蓄】with concealed or implied deep meanings
【含血噴人】to bring false accusations against others
【含義】a meaning; an implication
【含冤】to be the victim of an unjust charge
【含冤莫白】unable to clear oneself of a false accusation

吮 497
ㄕㄨㄣˇ shǔn
to suck; to lick

呈 498
ㄔㄥˊ chéng
1. to submit, present, or hand in (to a superior) 2. to show, manifest, expose, display, disclose, exhibit, etc. 3. a petition or appeal
【呈報】to present or submit a report
【呈交 or 呈遞】to handle or submit (to higher authorities)
【呈請】It is requested that....
【呈現】to appear; to emerge
【呈獻 or 呈上】to present (to a superior)
【呈送】to forward or send (to a higher agency)
【呈文】a petition; an appeal
【呈閱】to submit (to a superior or higher agency) for perusal

吳 499
ㄨˊ wú
1. name of a state in the Epoch of the Three Kingdoms 2. name of a state in the Warring States period 3. a Chinese family name
【吳郭魚】a mouthbreeder

吵 500
ㄔㄠˇ chǎo
1. to quarrel; to wrangle; to dispute 2. to disturb; to annoy
【吵鬧】to quarrel noisily; to brawl
【吵架】to quarrel; to brawl; to argue
【吵嘴】to dispute

吶 501
ㄋㄚˋ nà
1. to shout 2. to speak hesitatingly
【吶喊】to give a whoop, or to shout (in a battle, etc.)

吸 502
ㄒㄧ xī
to absorb; to imbibe; to suck in; to attract; to draw; to inhale
【吸毒】to smoke opium
【吸力 or 吸引力】①(physics) gravitation ② attraction
【吸管】① a pipette ② a straw
【吸氣】to inhale
【吸取】① to absorb (knowledge) ② to suck (liquid)
【吸血鬼】a vampire
【吸塵器】a vacuum cleaner
【吸食】to suck; to take in
【吸收】① to absorb; to take in ② to recruit or enlist
【吸吮】to suck; to absorb
【吸煙】to smoke; smoking

〔口部〕

【吸煙區】a smoking area
【吸引】to attract; to draw

吹 503 ㄔㄨㄟ chuī
1. to blow; to puff 2. to brag or boast; to praise in exaggerated words 3. to break up
【吹捧】to boast (before equals or inferiors) and to flatter (superiors)
【吹毛求疵】to engage in fault-finding
【吹風機】a blower; a drier
【吹拂】(said of winds, etc.) to move or wave (grass, branches, etc.); to sway
【吹牛】to brag; to boast
【吹喇叭】to blow the trumpet
【吹口哨】to whistle
【吹灰之力】strength as little as that needed for blowing dust away
【吹噓】to recommend or praise (a person) in exaggerated words
【吹哨子】to blow the whistle
【吹奏】to play (wind instruments)

吻 504 ㄨㄣˇ wěn
1. the lip 2. the tone of one's speech 3. to kiss; a kiss
【吻別】to kiss someone good-bye
【吻合】(said of two things) to agree, correspond, match, or tally with

吼 505 ㄏㄡˇ hǒu
(said of beasts) to roar or howl

吱 506 ㄗ zī
squeaky cries of an animal
【吱喳】chatter (made by birds or animals)

吾 507 ㄨˊ wú
1. I, me, we, or us (in literary usage) 2. my; our
【吾儕or吾曹or吾輩or吾等】we; us
【吾人】we
【吾愛】my love; my darling

告 508 ㄍㄠˋ gào
1. to tell; to inform; to report 2. to accuse
【告白】a notice; an announcement
【告別】to bid farewell; to say good-bye
【告密】to tip off; to inform against somebody
【告發】to accuse or charge (someone) in a (written or verbal) report to the authorities
【告退】① to resign ② to withdraw
【告急】in urgent need of help; critical
【告假】to ask for leave of absence
【告誡】to admonish; to warn
【告知】to let know; to notify
【告狀】① to file a lawsuit ② to say something bad against a colleague, fellow student, etc. before a superior
【告吹】to fizzle out; to fail
【告示】①(ㄍㄠˋ ㄕˋ) announce; to proclaim ②(ㄍㄠˋ ˙ㄕ) an official notice, announcement, or proclamation
【告饒】to seek pardon; to apologize
【告罪】to admit a mistake
【告辭】to take leave; to say good-bye
【告訴】①(ㄍㄠˋ ㄙㄨˋ) to file a lawsuit ②(ㄍㄠˋ ˙ㄙㄨ) to tell (a person)
【告諭】to counsel; to advise

呀 509 1. ㄧㄚ yā
a creaking sound

呀 509 2. ˙ㄧㄚ ya
1. a particle used after a phrase for expressing surprise, etc. 2. to gape (as in surprise)

呃 510 ㄜˋ è
to hiccup or hiccough

呂 511 ㄌㄩˇ lǚ
a Chinese family name

呆 512 ㄉㄞ dāi (又讀 ㄞˊ ái)
1. dull; dull-witted; stupid; unintelligent 2. blank; wooden
【呆板】① boring; dull ② stiff
【呆頭呆腦】stupid; idiot-like
【呆滯】dull
【呆若木雞】very dull or stupid
【呆子 or 呆人】an idiot; a dullard

呎 513 ㄔˇ chǐ
the foot (a unit of length in English measure)

吧 514 1. ˙ㄅㄚ ba
a particle used after an imperative sentence

吧 514
2. ㄅㄚ bā
【吧孃】a bar girl

五畫

呢 515
1. ㄋㄧˊ ní
1. a woolen fabric 2. a murmur
【呢喃】①the chirps of the swallows ②to murmur; to twitter

呢 515
2. ·ㄋㄜ ne
an interrogative or emphatic particle used after a sentence

周 516
ㄓㄡ zhōu
1. the Chou Dynasty 2. a circumference; a circuit 3. complete 4. all around; everywhere 5. to aid; to provide for 6. a Chinese family name
【周報 or 周刊】a weekly
【周末】the weekend
【周密】careful and thorough
【周到】thorough; considerate
【周年】an anniversary
【周率】①(radio) a frequency ②(electricity) a cycle
【周濟 or 賙濟】to help the poor with money
【周期】a period; a cycle
【周全】①to aid; to help ②complete with all that is desired
【周詳】complete and detailed
【周旋】①to attend to guests or friends ②to deal with; to fight
【周旋到底】(said of litigation, quarrels, etc.) to fight to the end
【周折】a complicated or troublesome course of development
【周轉不靈】(said of business firms) to be in financial straits
【周遭】around
【周歲 or 周晬】one full year of life
【周圍】①surroundings; environment ②the circumference

咒 517
ㄓㄡˋ zhòu
1. to curse; to swear 2. words used as charms by Buddhist monks or Taoist priests to exorcize ghosts
【咒罵】to swear at; to curse
【咒語】①curses; imprecations ②exorcism; incantation ③hocus-pocus

咎 518
ㄐㄧㄡˋ jiù
1. a disaster; a calamity 2. a fault; a mistake 3. to blame; to punish; to censure
【咎由自取】a trouble of one's own making

呱 519
ㄍㄨ gū (語音 ㄨㄚ wā)
1. the cries of an infant 2. to wail
【呱呱墜地】(said of a baby) to come into this world
【呱呱叫】tiptop; topnotch

味 520
ㄨㄟˋ wèi
1. a taste; a flavor 2. a smell; an odor 3. a delicacy; a dainty
【味道】①a taste; a flavor ②a smell ③a feeling
【味精】monosodium glutamate
【味覺】the sense of taste; gustation

呵 521
1. ㄏㄜ hē
1. to scold in a loud voice 2. to yawn
【呵呵大笑】to roar with laughter
【呵欠】to yawn and to stretch
【呵斥 or 呵責】to scold in a loud voice

呵 521
2. ·ㄛ o
a particle used after a phrase to express surprise

咕 522
ㄍㄨ gū
1. to murmur 2. (said of hens) a cluck; (said of turtledoves, etc.) a coo
【咕噥】to murmur
【咕嚕】①a mumbled sound or an indistinct utterance ②the rumbling sound in the belly

咂 523
ㄗㄚ zā
to take in food with the tongue; to suck

咚 524
ㄉㄨㄥ dōng
1. the sound of impact caused by a falling object 2. rub-a-dub 3. rat-tat; rat-a-tat

呻 525
ㄕㄣ shēn
as in 呻吟—to groan; to moan

呼 526
ㄏㄨ hū
1. to call; to cry 2. to exhale
【呼朋引伴】to call friends and fellows together

〔口部〕

〔口部〕

【呼風喚雨】①(said of immortals with divine power) to summon wind and rain ②to stir up trouble 「loudly in excessive grief
【呼天搶地】to cry bitterly and
【呼口號】to shout slogans
【呼號】①(ㄏㄨ ㄏㄠ) to cry; to wail ②(ㄏㄨ ㄏㄠ) to call the sign (of a message sent by
【呼喊】to yell; to shout ⌊radio)
【呼喚】to call; to shout; to cry out
【呼叫】to shout; to cry out; to yell
【呼叫器】a pager; a beeper
【呼救】to cry for help; to call for
【呼氣】to expire; to exhale ⌊help
【呼吸】to breathe
【呼吸器官】the respiratory organs
【呼嘯】to roar or howl
【呼之欲出】obvious; almost certain
【呼應】to act in coordination with each other; to echo
【呼籲】to appeal; to petition

命 527 ㄇㄧㄥˋ mìng
1. life 2. a fate; destiny; a lot 3. the ordinances of Heaven 4. orders; a command
【命不該絕】not destined to die
【命脈】a lifeline 「or dub
【命名】to name, christen, baptize,
【命題】① a proposition (in logic) ②to prepare examination questions
【命令】to order; to command
【命中註定】(said of individuals) predestined
【命中】to hit the target
【命在旦夕】Death may come (to a person) any minute. 「cide
【命案】a case of murder or homi-
【命運】a fate; destiny; a lot; for- ⌊tune

咀 528 ㄐㄩˇ jǔ
as in 咀嚼—to chew; to masticate

咄 529 ㄉㄨㄛˋ duò
1. an angry cry 2. to scold in a loud voice 「bearing
【咄咄逼人】①to browbeat ②over-

咆 530 ㄆㄠˊ páo
to roar
【咆哮】①(said of a tiger, etc.) to roar ②(said of winds, etc.) to bluster ③(said of a person) to ⌊rage

咋 531 1. ㄓㄚˋ zhà
all of a sudden; suddenly

咋 531 2. ㄗㄜˊ zé
1. to bite; to gnaw 2. a loud noise 「regret
【咋舌】to show one's surprise or

和 532 1. ㄏㄜˊ hé
1. harmony; harmonious 2. peace(ful) 3. to be affable 4. the sum or aggregate 5. of Japan 6. and (語音ㄏㄢˋ) 「truth
【和盤托出】to reveal the whole
【和平】① peaceful; mild (such as the weather, etc.) ② peace
【和睦】to be on friendly terms
【和風】a gentle breeze
【和服】a (Japanese) kimono
【和談】peace talks
【和好】① to be on friendly terms ② to make up
【和會】a peace conference 「tion
【和解】to be reconciled; reconcilia-
【和局】(said of a contest) a tie or a draw 「friendly; cordial
【和氣or和和氣氣】gentle; affable
【和諧】in harmony; harmony
【和弦】(music) a chord
【和衷共濟】to be united and to work in concert 「maker
【和事老】a mediator; a peace-
【和善】kind and gentle; genial
【和尚】a Buddhist monk
【和聲】(music) harmony 「rant
【和菜】a fixed menu in a restau-
【和藹可親】amiable; benign
【和顏悅色】a peaceful and happy
【和約】a peace treaty ⌊look

和 532 2. ㄏㄜˋ hè
1. to match; to harmonize 2. to write a poem in reply

和 532 3. ㄏㄨㄛˋ huò
to knead (dough, clay, etc.); to 「mix
【和麵】to knead flour

咖 533 1. ㄎㄚ kā
a character used in transliterat- 「ing
【咖啡】coffee 「fee shop
【咖啡廳or咖啡館】a café; a cof-

咖 533
2. ㄍㄚ gā
a character used in transliterating
【咖哩】curry

咐 534
ㄈㄨˋ fù
to tell, bid, or instruct (someone to do something)

六畫

咧 535
1. ㄌㄧㄝˇ liě
to stretch (the mouth) horizontally

咧 535
2. ㄌㄧㄝˊ lié
【咧咧】to babble

咨 536
ㄗ zī
1. to inquire; to consult 2. a very formal official communication between offices of equal rank
【咨詢】to inquire; to consult
【咨政】a political advisor (to the Chinese presidency)

咪 537
ㄇㄧ mī
1.a meow (meou, miaow, miaou) 2.smiling

咫 538
ㄓˇ zhǐ
1. the foot measure of the Chou Dynasty (divided into eight inches) 2. near
【咫尺天涯】so near and yet so far

咬 539
ㄧㄠˇ yǎo
to bite; to gnaw
【咬破】to bite through
【咬緊牙關】to endure pain or hardships with determination; to persevere
【咬住】to bite into
【咬牙切齒】to gnash the teeth (in anger or hatred)
【咬文嚼字】to be overcareful or pedantic about the use of each word

咯 540
1. ㄌㄨㄛˋ luò
to cough; a cough

咯 540
2. ·ㄌㄛ lo
a phrase-final particle

咯 540
3. ㄍㄜ gē
【咯吱】to creak

咯 540
4. ㄍㄜˊ gé
【咯咯】① a low, guttural sound made by a hen when brooding or calling her chicks ②(laughter) a chuckle

咱 541
ㄗㄢˊ zán
I, me (in North China dialect)
【咱們】(inclusive) we; you and I

咳 542
1. ㄎㄜˊ ké
to cough: 咳嗽 to cough; a cough

咳 542
2. ㄎㄚˇ kǎ
to cough up: 咳痰 to cough up phlegm

咳 542
3. ㄏㄞˋ hài
an interjection of regret or remorse

咸 543
ㄒㄧㄢˊ xián
all; completely; fully; wholly

咽 544
1. ㄧㄢ yān
the throat; the larynx; the pharynx
【咽喉】① the larynx; the throat ② a narrow, throat-like passage of strategic importance

咽 544
2. ㄧㄢˋ yàn
to swallow; to gulp

咽 544
3. ㄧㄝˋ yè
to be choked; to weep or speak in a choked voice; to sob

咿 545
ㄧ yī
a form used to represent a sound
【咿啞學語】(said of a baby) to begin to babble, prattle, or lisp

哀 546
ㄞ āi
1.to grieve; to mourn; to lament 2.to pity; to sympathize; to commiserate; compassion 3. sad; sorrowful; lamentable 4. sadness; sorrow; grief
【哀鳴】to give mournful cries; to wail
【哀悼】to mourn over, or lament (someone's death)
【哀嘆】to lament; to bewail
【哀痛】to feel the anguish of sorrow
【哀樂】①(ㄞ ㄌㄜˋ) grief and joy ②

〔口部〕

(ㄞ ㄩㄝ) funeral music
【哀憐】 to pity; to commiserate
【哀歌】 a lament; an elegy; a dirge
【哀號】 to wail
【哀求】 to beg or appeal pathetically
【哀愁】 sad; sorrowful
【哀傷】 to feel sorrow or grief

品 547 ㄆㄧㄣˇ pǐn
1. personality; character 2. an article; a commodity 3. a rank or grade in the government service in former times 4. to appraise; to rate 5. to find out
【品德】 personal character
【品頭論足】 to make critical remarks about a person's physical appearance
【品格or品性】 one's moral character
【品管】 Q.C. (quality control)
【品學兼優】 to excel in morals as well as academic performances
【品質】 quality
【品種】 a species or variety
【品嘗】 to taste (food) in order to appraise, rate or grade its worth
【品味】 taste; a savor

哄 548 1. ㄏㄨㄥ hōng
(said of a group of people) to make a roaring noise
【哄堂大笑】 The whole room rocks with laughter.

哄 548 2. ㄏㄨㄥˇ hǒng
to beguile; to cheat; to defraud
【哄騙】 to defraud; to cheat; to swindle; to take in
【哄擡物價】 to rig prices
【哄孩子】 to coax a child

哆 549 ㄉㄨㄛ duō
to shiver; to tremble
【哆嗦】 to shiver with cold or tremble with fear

哇 550 1. ㄨㄚ wā
1. to vomit 2. the sound of crying by a child
【哇哇大哭】 to cry very loudly

哇 550 2. ˙ㄨㄚ wa
a phrase-final particle

哈 551 1. ㄏㄚ hā
1. a form used in transliteration 2. a sound of hearty laughter
【哈密瓜】 a honey dew melon
【哈佛大學】 Harvard University
【哈雷彗星】 Halley's Comet
【哈哈大笑】 to laugh heartily
【哈欠】 a yawn

哈 551 2. ㄏㄚˇ hǎ
【哈巴狗】 ① a Pekingese or Pekinese (dog) ② toady; sycophant

哉 552 ㄗㄞ zāi
a phrase-final particle expressing surprise, admiration, doubt, etc.

哎 553 ㄞ āi
an interjection of surprise mixed with regret

七畫

員 554 ㄩㄢˊ yuán
1. a member (of an organization, etc.) 2. a person engaged in some field of activity 3. outer limits (of land, space, etc.)
【員工】 employees (collectively)

哥 555 ㄍㄜ gē
as in 哥哥—an elder brother
【哥兒們】 ① brothers ② buddies; pals
【哥兒倆】 two brothers

哦 556 1. ㄛˊ ó
(an interjection) oh; ah

哦 556 2. ㄜˊ é
to recite (verses, etc.)

哨 557 ㄕㄠˋ shào
1. a whistle 2. to patrol 3. an outpost; a guard station
【哨兵】 a sentinel or sentry
【哨子】 a whistle

哩 558 1. ㄌㄧ lī
to speak indistinctly

哩 558 2. ㄌㄧˇ lǐ
a mile

哭 559 ㄎㄨ kū
to weep; to cry; to sob; to wail; to whimper

【哭哭啼啼】to whimper; to blubber
【哭泣】to sob; to weep
【哭笑不得】to be at a loss whether to cry or to laugh
【哭喪着臉】to look sad or mournful
【哭訴】to complain tearfully

哮 560
1. ㄒㄧㄠ xiāo
to cry out in a loud voice

哮 560
2. ㄒㄧㄠ xiào
1. to wheeze; to gasp; to breathe with difficulty 2. a roar; a howl
【哮喘】① asthma ② to wheeze

哲 561
ㄓㄜˊ zhé
1. a sage; a thinker; a philosopher 2. wise; wisdom; sagacious
【哲理】a philosophical principle
【哲學】philosophy
【哲學家】a philosopher; a thinker

哺 562
ㄅㄨˇ bǔ
1. to chew (before swallowing) 2. to feed (a baby, etc.)
【哺乳】to give suck to; to nurse
【哺乳類 or 哺乳動物】mammals
【哺育】① to feed ② to nurture

哼 563
ㄏㄥ hēng
1. to croon; to hum 2. to groan; to moan 3. the grunt of disapproval or contempt

哽 564
ㄍㄥˇ gěng
to choke; to feel a lump in one's throat
【哽塞】to choke
【哽咽】to be choked with sobs; to sob

唁 565
ㄧㄢˋ yàn
to condole with or express sympathy for
【唁電】a condolatory telegram
【唁函】a letter (or message) of condolence

唆 566
ㄙㄨㄛ suō
as in 唆使—to instigate; to incite

唉 567
ㄞ āi
(an interjection of regret or disgust) alas
【唉聲歎氣】to moan and groan

唏 568
ㄒㄧ xī
to weep or sob with sorrow; to grieve
【唏噓】to sob

唐 569
ㄊㄤˊ táng
1. the Tang Dynasty 2. a Chinese family name 3. abrupt; rude; preposterous; impertinent
【唐代 or 唐朝】the Tang Dynasty (618-907 A.D.)
【唐突】abrupt; rude; brusque; blunt
【唐人街】the Chinatown
【唐塞 or 搪塞】to do things perfunctorily

哪 570
1. (那) ㄋㄚˇ nǎ
(an interrogative particle) how; where; what; which
【哪怕】even if
【哪裏 or 哪兒】where
【哪個】① Which one? ② Who is it?
【哪些】which; who; what

哪 570
2. ·ㄋㄚ na
a phrase-final particle

咩 571
ㄇㄧㄝ miē
the cries of sheep

八畫

售 572
ㄕㄡˋ shòu
to sell
【售票】to sell tickets
【售票口】a wicket
【售票處】a ticket office; a box office
【售後服務】after service
【售貨員】a salesman; a salesgirl; a salesclerk
【售價】the (retail) price (of a commodity)

唯 573
1. (惟) ㄨㄟˊ wéi
only
【唯美主義】aestheticism
【唯命是從 or 唯命是聽】obsequious; to do whatever is told
【唯獨】only or alone; an exception
【唯利是圖】to be bent solely on profit
【唯恐】for fear that; for fear of
【唯一】the only one, the only kind, etc.
【唯有】only

唯 573
2. ㄨㄟˇ wěi
yes or no; the words one answers
【唯唯諾諾】to say yes to a supe-

〔口部〕

rior's suggestion; to be a yes man

唱 574
ㄔㄤˋ chàng

1. to sing; to chant 2. to crow; to cry 3. a song or a singing part of a Chinese opera

【唱盤】 the turntable of a phonograph
【唱票】 to count votes aloud
【唱片】 a (phonograph) record or a disc
【唱反調】 to air an opposing view
【唱歌】 to sing songs; to sing
【唱機】 a record player or phonograph
【唱戲】 to sing a Peking opera
【唱針】 a phonograph needle; a stylus
【唱遊】 a recreation class

唳 575
ㄌㄧˋ lì

the cry of a crane, wild goose, etc.

唾 576
ㄊㄨㄛˋ tuò

1. saliva 2. to spit

【唾罵】 to spit out; to revile
【唾棄】 to show contempt for
【唾手可得】 (to accomplish) with extreme ease
【唾液】 saliva

啡 577
ㄈㄟ fēi

a form used in transliterating

啄 578
ㄓㄨㄛˊ zhuó

(said of a bird) to peck

【啄木鳥】 a woodpecker
【啄食】 to eat by pecking

商 579
ㄕㄤ shāng

1. commerce; trade; business 2. a merchant; a trader; a businessman 3. to discuss; to exchange views; to confer 4. (arithmetic) the quotient

【商標】 a trademark
【商埠 or 商港】 a commercial port
【商品】 merchandise; goods
【商品展覽會 or 商展】 a trade fair
【商店】 a store; a shop
【商定】 to decide or settle through discussions
【商討】 a discussion; to discuss
【商談】 to exchange views
【商量 or 商酌】 to exchange opinions or views; to confer
【商科】 a department of commerce (in a college or university)
【商號 or 商行】 ① name of a shop or firm ② a business firm
【商界】 business circles
【商榷】 to discuss and consider
【商學院】 the college of commerce
【商場】 a market place; a bazaar
【商船】 a merchantman
【商數】 (arithmetic) the quotient
【商人】 a merchant; a businessman
【商議】 to discuss and debate
【商業】 commerce
【商務代表】 a commercial representative

問 580
ㄨㄣˋ wèn

1. to ask; to inquire 2. to interrogate; to examine 3. to ask after; to inquire after 4. to hold responsible

【問答】 questions and answers; a dialogue
【問題】 a problem; a question; an issue
【問題少年】 a juvenile delinquent
【問題兒童】 a problem child
【問卦】 to consult oracles
【問供】 to interrogate a criminal suspect
【問好 or 問候】 to ask about a person's health or welfare
【問號】 an interrogation mark
【問話】 to ask questions
【問卷】 a questionnaire
【問心無愧】 to examine oneself and find nothing to be ashamed of
【問訊】 ① to inquire after a person ② to ask; to inquire
【問斬】 to execute a prisoner by beheading him
【問世】 (said of a new book) to come out
【問罪】 to reprimand; to rebuke; to condemn
【問安】 (usually to elders) to wish somebody good health
【問案】 to try (or hear) a case

啊 581
1. ㄚ ā

an exclamatory particle

【啊唷】 "ayo" (the sound uttered when suddenly get hurt)

啊 581
2. ·ㄚ a

a phrase-final particle

啤 582
ㄆㄧˊ pí

a character used in transliterat-
【啤酒】 beer ⌊ing

啓 583
(啟) ㄑㄧˇ qǐ
1. to open 2. to begin; to start 3. to explain 4. to inform; to state 5. a letter
【啓蒙】 to enlighten「development
【啓發or啓迪】 to prompt mental
【啓動】 to start (a machine, etc.)
【啓航】 to set sail; to weigh anchor
【啓行or啓程】 to start on a journey; to set out 「something
【啓齒】 to open the mouth to say
【啓事】 a notice; an announcement
【啓示】 revelation ⌊(in writing)
【啓用】 to start using

啣 584
(銜) ㄒㄧㄢˊ xián
1. a bridle 2. to hold in the mouth 3. to harbor

啦 585
•ㄌㄚ la
a phrase-final particle
【啦啦隊】 a cheer squad

啞 586
ㄧㄚˇ yǎ
1. dumb; mute 2. hoarse; husky 3. a phrase-final particle 「son)
【啞巴or啞叭】 (a) deaf-mute (per-
【啞謎】 a riddle; an enigma
【啞鈴】 a dumbbell
【啞口無言】 to be speechless

啃 587
ㄎㄣˇ kěn
to bite; to gnaw; to nibble

唬 588
ㄏㄨˇ hǔ
1. to intimidate; to scare 2. the roar of a tiger 「bluff
【唬人】 to intimidate people; to

唸 589
(念) ㄋㄧㄢˋ niàn
to read; to chant; to recite
【唸唸有詞】 to mumble to oneself

啥 590
ㄕㄚˊ shá
what
【啥人】 (Shanghai dialect) Who are you? 或 Who is it (or there)?

啜 591
ㄔㄨㄛˋ chuò
1. to drink; to sip 2. to cry in a subdued manner; to sob
【啜泣】 to sob

九畫

啼 592
ㄊㄧˊ tí 「crow; to cry
(especially said of birds) to
【啼哭】 to cry; to weep and wail
【啼叫】 to scream; to screech
【啼笑皆非】 unable to cry or laugh

喀 593
ㄎㄚˋ kà 「ing
a character used for transliterat-
【喀嚓】 to crack; to snap

喂 594
ㄨㄟˋ wèi
hallo; please; if you please; I say

喃 595
ㄋㄢˊ nán
1. the cries of a swallow 2. to murmur; to mumble; to mutter
【喃喃自語】 to murmur to oneself

善 596
ㄕㄢˋ shàn
1. good; virtuous; goodness; virtue 2. to be good at; to be skilled in 3. to perfect; to make a success of 4. to remedy; to relieve 5. properly
【善罷甘休】 to stop quarreling, fighting, etc. with others 「cious
【善變】 changeable; fickle; capri-
【善待】 to treat (a person) well
【善男信女】 devotees of Buddha
【善良】 (said of a person) kind-hearted; well-disposed
【善後】 rehabilitation (after a disaster, a tragedy, etc.)
【善舉 or 善行】 a good deed
【善心】 a compassionate heart; kindness
【善終】 to die a natural death
【善事】 good deeds; philanthropic acts 「vice
【善惡】 good and evil; virtue and
【善惡不分】 to be unable to tell good from evil 「②well-meaning
【善意】 ①good or kindly intentions
【善有善報】 Kind deeds pay rich dividends to the doer. 「in
【善於】 to be good at; to be skilled

喇 597
1. ㄌㄚˇ lǎ
1. a horn; a trumpet; a bugle 2. a lama 3. a character used in

〔口部〕

〔口部〕

transliteration
【喇叭】① a trumpet ② a loudspeaker
【喇叭褲】bell-shaped pants
【喇叭花】(botany) morning glory
【喇嘛】a lama (a priest of Lamaism)
【喇嘛教】Lamaism

喇 597
2. ㄌㄚ lā
a character used for its sound

喉 598
ㄏㄡ hóu [gullet; guttural as in 喉嚨 —the throat; the gullet; guttural]
【喉結】Adam's apple

喊 599
ㄏㄢ hǎn
1. to shout; to scream; to cry; a loud call or cry; a shout or scream 2. to call loudly
【喊叫】to shout, scream, or cry loudly
【喊救】to call for help; to cry for help
【喊冤】to shout out one's grievance in the streets (when a high official is passing) or in court

喋 600
ㄉㄧㄝ dié
to nag; to chatter; to prattle
【喋喋不休】to keep talking; to cackle

喔 601
1. ㄨㄛ wō
the crowing of a cock; the cackling of fowls

喔 601
2. ㄛ ō
an exclamation

喘 602
ㄔㄨㄢ chuǎn
1. to pant; to gasp; to breathe hard 2. (pathology) asthma
【喘氣】① to pant; to gasp ② to take a break
【喘息】① to take breath, or a rest (after strenuous exercise) ② to pant
【喘息機會】a respite

喙 603
ㄏㄨㄟ huì
1. a beak; a bill; a snout 2. a mouth

喚 604
ㄏㄨㄢ huàn
1. to call 2. to summon 3. to arouse
【喚起】① to arouse to action ② to call; to evoke
【喚醒】to arouse; to awaken

喜 605
ㄒㄧˇ xǐ
1. a joyful thing; a happy event 2. joy 3. to like; to love; to be fond of 4. joyful; happy; delightful; pleasant; auspicious
【喜不自勝】to be delighted beyond measure
【喜馬拉雅山】the Himalayas
【喜帖】a wedding invitation
【喜怒哀樂】the feelings of joy, anger, sorrow and delight
【喜好】to be fond of; to delight in
【喜歡】to like; to be fond of; to love
【喜酒】a wedding feast
【喜劇】a comedy
【喜氣洋洋】① a joyful atmosphere ② a cheerful look or expression
【喜慶】auspicious or happy occasions
【喜鵲】the magpie
【喜新厭舊】to like the new and dislike the old
【喜訊】happy news; good news
【喜出望外】joy over unexpected good luck; unexpected joy
【喜事】an occasion for joy (especially a wedding)
【喜愛】to like; to love; to be fond of
【喜洋洋】beaming with joy; radiant
【喜悅】joy; delight; gratification

喝 606
1. ㄏㄜ hē
to drink
【喝酒】to drink (alcoholic beverages)
【喝西北風】to have nothing to eat
【喝醉】to get drunk

喝 606
2. ㄏㄜˋ hè
to shout; to call out aloud
【喝倒彩】to hoot; to hiss
【喝令】to shout an order
【喝彩】to shout "Bravo!"; to applaud

唧 607
(唧) ㄐㄧ jī
(又讀 ㄐㄧˊ jí)
1. a pump 2. the buzzing sound 3. to squirt
【唧唧喳喳】to chirp

喟 608
ㄎㄨㄟˋ kuì
to sigh heavily: 喟然長嘆 to sigh deeply

喧 609
ㄒㄩㄢ xuān
1. to talk noisily; to clamor 2. noise; hubbub; uproar; noisy
【喧賓奪主】to act like a boss where one does not belong

【喧騰】noise and excitement; hubbub
【喧鬧】hubbub; noisy
【喧嘩】uproar; turmoil
【喧囂】noise; din; uproar
【喧擾】to disturb by noisy talk
【喧嚷】clamor; hubbub; din; racket

喻 610 ㄩˋ yù

1. to use a figure of speech; an illustration; a parable 2. to know; to be acquainted with 3. to explain; to make clear; to tell the meaning of; to instruct 4. a Chinese family name

喪 611 1. ㄙㄤ sāng

1.death; dying 2.to mourn 3. funeral
【喪服】mourning dress or costume
【喪禮】funeral rites
【喪期】a mourning period
【喪事】funeral affairs
【喪葬】funeral service and burial

喪 611 2. ㄙㄤˋ sàng

1. to lose; to be deprived of 2. to be defeated 3. to decline; to go down
【喪命or喪身】to lose one's life; to die
【喪膽】to be much afraid
【喪家之狗 or 喪家之犬】an outcast
【喪盡天良】to have no conscience
【喪氣】dejected; despondent
【喪心病狂】out of one's right mind
【喪失】to lose; to be deprived of
【喪偶】to be deprived of one's spouse, especially one's wife

喬 612 ㄑㄧㄠˊ qiáo

1. tall 2. to disguise; to pretend 3. a Chinese family name
【喬遷】to move into a new and better house
【喬遷之喜】Best wishes for your new home.
【喬裝】to disguise oneself
【喬梓】father and son 亦作「橋梓」

單 613 1. ㄉㄢ dān

1. single; individual 2. alone; only 3. simple 4. of an odd number 5. a slip of paper 6. a list
【單薄】weak; feeble; flimsy
【單方面】one-sided; unilateral
【單打】(sports) singles
【單刀直入】(said of action, statement, etc.) straightforward; direct
【單調】dull; monotonous; dry; boring
【單獨】independent; alone
【單戀】one-sided love; unrequited love
【單槓】(sports) a horizontal bar
【單號】odd numbers (of seats, ticket, etc.)
【單價】a unit price
【單據】a receipt
【單槍匹馬】to take on the enemy alone
【單相思】unrequited love
【單向】one-way; unidirectional
【單行本】a separate volume
【單行道or單行線】a one-way path, or a one-way street
【單車】bicycles
【單純】① simple; plain ② unpretending
【單身】① alone; unaccompanied ② unmarried; single
【單身貴族】(colloquial) unmarried gentlemen or ladies
【單身漢】a bachelor
【單身宿舍】quarters for single men or women
【單數】①an odd number ②(grammar) singular
【單人房】a single-bed room (in a hotel)
【單人牀】a single bed
【單子】a list; a bill; a form
【單字】a single character or word
【單一】single; unitary
【單音節】monosyllabic
【單位】① a unit (in measurement) ② a military unit or organization
【單元劇】a single-episode drama

單 613 2. ㄕㄢˋ shàn

a Chinese family name

單 613 3. ㄔㄢˊ chán

the chief of the Huns (a common term during the Han Dynasty)

喳 614 ㄔㄚ chā

the sound of chattering

十畫

嗅 615 ㄒㄧㄡˋ xiù

to smell; to scent; to sniff
【嗅覺】the sense of smell

嗆 616 1. ㄑㄧㄤ qiāng

1. to peck 2. stupid; foolish

〔口部〕

嗆 616
2. ㄑㄧㄤˋ qiàng
1. to cough because of a temporary blockade of the nasal passage 2. (said of smoke, smell, etc.) to irritate the throat or nose; to suffocate

嗇 617
ㄙㄜˋ sè
stingy; parsimonious; miserly

嗩 618
ㄙㄨㄛˇ suǒ ⌈instrument
as in嗩吶—a trumpet-like wind

嗎 619
1. ㄇㄚˇ mǎ ⌈ing
a character used in transliterat-
【嗎啡】morphine

嗎 619
2. ·ㄇㄚ ma ⌈questions
a phrase-final particle used in

嗓 620
ㄙㄤˇ sǎng
1. the throat (as the source of one's voice) 2. one's voice
【嗓門兒】① one's voice ② the vocal organs
【嗓子】① the throat ② one's voice

嗔 621
ㄔㄣ chēn
1. to be angry; to take offense; to fly into a temper 2. to be ⌊annoyed with

嗚 622
ㄨ wū
1. to weep; to sob 2. to toot; to hoot; to zoom 3. Alas!
【嗚呼哀哉】(usually used in lamenting someone's death) What a tragedy!
【嗚咽】sobs; to sob; to weep

嗜 623
ㄕˋ shì ⌈relish; to like
to delight in; to be fond of; to
【嗜好】one's liking, hobby, or weakness for something

嗝 624
ㄍㄜˊ gé
to hiccup or hiccough; a belch

嗣 625
ㄙˋ sì
1. to inherit; to succeed to 2. a descendant 3. to continue; to follow ⌈pointed as heir
【嗣立】to appoint or to be ap-
【嗣後】thereafter
【嗣位】to succeed to the throne

嗤 626
ㄔ chī
to laugh or chuckle sneeringly
【嗤詆】to laugh at; to mock
【嗤之以鼻】to pooh-pooh

嗡 627
ㄨㄥ wēng
the hum or buzz of insects

嗑 628
ㄎㄜˋ kè ⌈teeth
to crack something between the

十一畫

嗷 629
(嗸) ㄠˊ áo
a cry of hunger
【嗷嗷待哺】waiting to be fed with cries of hunger

嗽 630
ㄙㄡˋ sòu
to cough; to clear the throat

嗾 631
ㄙㄡˇ sǒu ⌈2. to instigate
1. to give vocal signals to a dog
【嗾使】to instigate; to incite

嘅 632
(嘅) ㄎㄞˇ kǎi
the sound of sighing

嘈 633
ㄘㄠˊ cáo
noisy; clamorous
【嘈雜】noisy and confused

嘉 634
ㄐㄧㄚ jiā
1. to praise; to commend; to admire 2. good; fine; excellent
【嘉賓】an honored guest
【嘉勉】to praise and encourage
【嘉年華會】a carnival
【嘉惠】to benefit ⌈agement)
【嘉獎】to commend (as an encour-
【嘉耦天成】an ideal marriage ⌊divinely arranged

嘍 635
1. ㄌㄡˊ lóu ⌈follower
as in嘍囉—a bandit's lackey or

嘍 635
2. ·ㄌㄡ lou
a phrase-final particle

嘔 636
1. ㄡˇ ǒu
to vomit; to throw up
【嘔吐】to vomit; to disgorge

【嘔心瀝血】 to work one's heart out

嘔 636
2. ㄡˇ ǒu
to annoy on purpose
【嘔氣】 to be angry but refrain from showing it

嘖 637
ㄗㄜˊ zé
1. an interjection of approval or admiration 2. to argue; to dispute

嘗 638
ㄔㄤˊ cháng
1. to taste 2. to try 3. to experience
【嘗嘗 or 嘗一嘗】 to taste
【嘗試】 to try; a try

十二畫

嘩 639
1. ㄏㄨㄚ huā
an onomatopoeia, such gurgle, clang, crack, etc.

嘩 639
2. ㄏㄨㄚˊ huá
same as 譁—tumult; hubbub
【嘩衆取寵】 to try to please the public with claptrap

嘘 640
ㄒㄩ xū
1. to warm with exhaled air 2. to speak well of (another) 3. a deep sigh 4. to hiss; to boo
【嘘寒問暖】 to show a kind concern for another's comfort

嘮 641
ㄌㄠˊ láo
loquacious; garrulous; voluble
【嘮叨 or 嘮嘮叨叨】 to nag; to din

嘯 642
ㄒㄧㄠˋ xiào
1. to whistle 2. to howl; to cry or shout in a sustained voice; to roar

嘰 643
ㄐㄧ jī
1. to talk indistinctly in a low voice 2. to chirp
【嘰咕】 to grumble
【嘰嘰喳喳】 ①to chirp; to twitter ② to jabber

嘲 644
ㄔㄠˊ cháo
to ridicule; to sneer; to mock; to deride
【嘲諷】 to sneer at; to taunt
【嘲弄】 to mock; to make fun of
【嘲笑】 to laugh at; to jeer at; to sneer at; to deride

嘴 645
ㄗㄨㄟˇ zuǐ
1. the mouth; the bill or beak (of a bird); the snout (of a pig, etc.) 2. a nozzle
【嘴巴】 the mouth
【嘴甜】 honeymouthed
【嘴緊】 tight-lipped; closemouthed
【嘴饞】 gluttonous
【嘴唇】 the lips
【嘴硬】 ① to talk toughly ② to refuse to admit a mistake

嘶 646
ㄙ sī
1. the neighing of a horse 2. (said of voice) hoarse

嘷 647
ㄏㄠˊ háo
to howl; to yelp; the frantic barks or howls of dogs or wolves

嘹 648
ㄌㄧㄠˊ liáo
(said of voice) resonant
【嘹喨】 loud and clear; resonant

嘻 649
ㄒㄧ xī
1. an interjection of grief or surprise 2. laughing happily
【嘻皮笑臉】 laughing in a frolicsome manner
【嘻嘻哈哈】 laughing and talking happily
【嘻笑】 to giggle; to titter

噎 650
ㄧㄝ yē
1. to be choked with food 2. to choke off

嘿 651
ㄏㄟ hēi
an interjection

十三畫

噤 652
ㄐㄧㄣˋ jìn
to keep the mouth shut; to shut up
【噤若寒蟬】 to say or reveal nothing (especially out of fear)

器 653
ㄑㄧˋ qì
1. an instrument; an implement; a utensil; a tool; a piece of apparatus 2. magnanimity 3. talent; ability 4. to think highly of (a person)
【器皿】 food containers
【器量】 the capacity for magnanimity; tolerance
【器官】 the apparatus; the organs

〔口部〕

【器具】tools; instruments
【器重】to think highly of
【器材】implements and materials
【器宇軒昂】of dignified bearing

口部

噩 654 ㄜˋ è
1. startling; alarming; dreadful; awesome 2. grave; serious
【噩夢】a nightmare
【噩耗】shocking news (usually news of a person's death)

噪 655 ㄗㄠˋ zào
1. to be noisy 2. (said of birds, insects, etc.) to chirp
【噪音】unpleasant noise; din

噱 656 ㄐㄩㄝˊ jué
loud laughter

噸 657 ㄉㄨㄣˋ dùn
ton (a unit of weight)
【噸位】tonnage (of a ship)

噯 658 1. ㄞˋ ài
an interjection

噯 658 2. ㄞˇ ǎi
【噯氣】(medicine) belch; eructation

噹 659 ㄉㄤ dāng
a loud, resonant metallic sound

噴 660 ㄆㄣ pēn
1. to spurt; to gush 2. to spray; to sprinkle
【噴嚏】sneezing; a sneeze
【噴漆】to spray paint (or lacquer)
【噴泉 or 噴水池】a fountain
【噴射式客機】a jet airliner
【噴洒or噴灑】to spray; to sprinkle

十四畫

嚎 661 ㄏㄠˊ háo
to cry loudly; to howl; to wail
【嚎啕大哭】to cry loudly with abandon

嚀 662 ㄋㄧㄥˊ níng
to enjoin; to instruct

嚇 663 1. ㄏㄜˋ hè
1. to intimidate; to threaten 2. the sound of laughter
【嚇阻】to stop (someone) by threat

嚇 663 2. ㄒㄧㄚˋ xià
to frighten; to startle; to scare
【嚇唬】to scare; to frighten
【嚇人】① to frighten people ② horrible; terrible

嚏 664 ㄊㄧˋ tì
sneezing; a sneeze

十六畫

嚮 665 ㄒㄧㄤˋ xiàng
1. to guide; to direct; to lead 2. to lean toward; to be inclined toward
【嚮壁虛造】to fabricate out of nothing
【嚮導】a guide
【嚮往】to aspire; to long

嚥 666 ㄧㄢˋ yàn
to swallow
【嚥氣】to breathe one's last; to die

十七畫

嚴 667 ㄧㄢˊ yán
1. stern; strict; severe; grim; inclement; inexorable; relentless; rigorous; rigid; grave; solemn 2. reverence 3. tight 4. father 5. a Chinese family name
【嚴辦】to deal with severely
【嚴密】rigid; rigorous; strict; exact
【嚴防】to guard carefully
【嚴冬】severe winter; very cold winter
【嚴冷 or 嚴寒】severe cold
【嚴格or嚴厲】strict; stringent; rigid; rigorous
【嚴苛】harsh
【嚴酷】inclement; caustic
【嚴謹】careful; cautious; well-knit
【嚴禁】to prohibit or forbid strictly
【嚴刑拷打】to torture cruelly
【嚴刑峻法】severe punishments under strict laws
【嚴整】well-disciplined; in neat formation
【嚴重】serious; severe; grave
【嚴懲】to punish severely
【嚴師】a stern or strict teacher
【嚴詞譴責】to condemn sternly
【嚴慈】father (嚴) and mother (慈)
【嚴肅】serious-looking; serious

夥 791 ㄏㄨㄛˇ huǒ
1. many; much; lots of 2. a partner; a company 3. a waiter 4. a crowd
【夥伴】 a companion; a partner
【夥同】 in league with; to gang up with
【夥計】 ① a waiter; a clerk ② buddy

大 部 ㄉㄚˋ dà

大 792
1. ㄉㄚˋ dà
1. big; large 2. great 3. much 4. very; highly; extremely; greatly 5. (polite expression) your 6. the eldest; senior 7. full-grown; an adult 8. (referring to date only) before; after 9. to make large or great
【大伯】 ① one's father's elder brother; an uncle ② an uncle (a polite form of address for an elderly man) 亦作「老伯」
【大白菜】 a Chinese cabbage
【大敗】 ① to defeat utterly ② to suffer a severe defeat
【大班】 ① the manager of a foreign firm in China ② the captain (as of taxi dancers) ③ the top class in a kindergarten
【大半】 ① for the most part; mostly ② probably; likely
【大本營】 headquarters
【大便】 ① stool; shit ② to empty the bowels
【大不相同】 entirely or totally different
【大不如前】 far worse than it was before
【大不了】 ① at the worst ② serious
【大部分】 for the most part; mainly
【大牌】 (said of movie stars, etc.) leading or big-name (actors or actresses)
【大砲】 ① guns; batteries; cannons ② (slang) one who talks big
【大批】 a large batch of; a good deal of
【大麻】 ① hemp ② marijuana
【大門】 the main door or gate
【大夢初醒】 the awakening or realization (of past wrongdoings, etc.)
【大名】 ① your name (used in formal speech) ② a reputation
【大名鼎鼎】 very famous; celebrated; well-known
【大模大樣】 ① with full composure ② proudly; haughtily
【大拇指】 thumb
【大發雷霆】 to be furious
【大發利市】 to make big profits
【大發雌威】 ① (said of a woman) to get very angry ② (said of a woman athlete) to display great prowess
【大法官】 a grand justice
【大費周章】 to take great pains
【大方】 ① generous ② elegant and composed ③ experts; connoisseurs
【大放厥辭】 to boast or brag wildly
【大放異彩】 (said of sports performance, etc.) to yield unusually brilliant results
【大風大浪】 great storms
【大腹便便】 paunchy; potbellied
【大打出手】 to get into a free-for-all or a brawl
【大大小小】 the big and the small —the whole family
【大刀闊斧】 to act decisively and resolutely
【大道】 ① a wide road ② the way of virtue and justice
【大道理】 ① a persuasive argument ② a major principle
【大豆】 soybeans
【大膽】 bold; boldness
【大敵當前】 confronted with a strong opponent
【大抵】 generally speaking; for the most part
【大地】 ① the earth ② the whole territory of a nation
【大地主】 a big landowner or landlord
【大都市】 a large city; a metropolis
【大度】 magnanimity; generosity
【大肚子】 ① pregnant ② a big eater ③ a potbelly
【大多】 for the most part; mostly
【大多數】 the majority
【大隊人馬】 a large number of soldiers and horses
【大動脈】 the main artery
【大頭針】 tacks
【大提琴】 a cello
【大體】 ① generally; on the whole ② the main principle

【大廳】the main hall; the parlor
【大庭廣衆】①public places where the crowd gather ②in public
【大腿】the thigh 「reunion
【大團圓】a happy ending; a happy
【大同小異】almost the same
【大同世界】a political utopia
【大難臨頭】to be faced with great trouble 「torous actions
【大逆不道】sedition; treason; trai-
【大年初一】the first day of the lunar year 「New Year's Eve
【大年夜】on the night of the lunar
【大樓】a multistoried building
【大禮堂】an auditorium
【大理石】marble
【大力士】a hercules
【大量】①a large quantity; mass ②magnanimous
【大陸】a continent; the mainland
【大略】①brief; generally ②(a man of) great caliber ③a general outline
【大哥】①the eldest brother ②elder brother (a polite form of address for a man about one's own age) 「guy
【大個兒】a big man; a giant; a tall
【大概】most probably; generally
【大綱】a synopsis; a summary
【大姑娘】a maiden; a damsel
【大過】①a big mistake ②(said of punishment in school, etc.) a major demerit
【大規模】large-scale
【大功告成】(said of a big or difficult task) to have finally come to completion
【大公無私】all for the public without selfish considerations
【大可不必】It's unnecessary.
【大開眼界】to see something completely new or very strange
【大考】the final examination in school
【大塊頭】a tall and bulky fellow
【大快人心】(usually said of a wrong being righted, justice prevailed, etc.) to give all a lift of the heart
【大海】①a widemouthed bowl or wine cup ②the ocean
【大海撈針】to look for a needle in a haystack
【大好河山】beautiful rivers and mountains 「tuba; a bass horn
【大號】①large-size ②(music) a
【大後天】two days after tomorrow
【大喊大叫】①to shout at the top of one's voice ②to conduct vigorous propaganda 「nate
【大亨】a bigwig; a tycoon; a mag-
【大戶人家】a wealthy and influential family
【大花臉】(Peking opera) a male role of dignified type
【大話】boasts; big words
【大夥兒】①us; we ②a group of people
【大惑不解】incomprehensible
【大會】a rally; a conference
【大紅大綠】gaudy and showy
【大吉大利】very smooth going
【大家】①all of us; we ②a rich and influential family of long standing ③a famous expert; a master 「munity
【大家庭】①a big family ②a com-
【大駕】①to your gracious presence ②the carriage for a sovereign or emperor
【大街小巷】in every street and alley—all over the city
【大姊 or 大姐】the eldest sister
【大舅子】one's wife's elder brothers
【大將】①an important general; a capable commander ②a trusted lieutenant ③a senior general
【大驚小怪】to make a fuss
【大局】①the situation in general ②the fate of a nation
【大舉】①large-scale (invasions, etc.) ②a great undertaking
【大軍】a great concentration of troops
【大器晚成】A great man will take time to shape and mature.
【大千世界】the kaleidoscopic world
【大前提】a major premise
【大前天】three days ago
【大清早】very early in the morning
【大情人】a Casanova, or ladies' man
【大全】a complete collection of
【大權旁落】Power has fallen into the hands of others. 「lenged
【大權在握】to hold power unchal-
【大西洋】the Atlantic Ocean
【大喜過望】to be overjoyed

【大廈】a big building; a mansion

【大寫】① a capital letter ② the elaborate form of Chinese numerals (used especially in accounting and checks)

【大小】① adults and children ② sizes (of shoes, etc.) ③ degree of seniority

【大小便】night soil and urine

【大小不一】irregular in size, age, etc.

【大小姐】① a maiden; a Miss ② a reference to others' elder or eldest daughters

【大笑】to laugh heartily

【大顯身手】to display one's skill to the full

【大顯神通】to display one's remarkable skill or abilities to the full

【大興土木】to start a large-scale building project

【大型】(said of machines, etc.) large-sized; large-scale

【大學】① a university or college ② *The Great Learning* (one of the *Four Classics*)

【大學生】a college or university student; a collegian

【大選】①a presidential election ② general elections for congressmen

【大致】① for the most part ② about

【大智若愚】The wise man looks dumb.

【大展宏圖】to ride on the crest of success

【大張撻伐】to attack with full force

【大張旗鼓】①to make a big show ②on a grand scale

【大丈夫】a real man

【大主教】an archbishop

【大專院校】colleges and universities

【大眾】the masses; the public

【大眾化】to popularize

【大眾捷運系統】mass rapid transit (MRT)

【大眾傳播】mass communications

【大眾傳播媒體】mass (communications) media

【大眾文學】popular literature

【大吃大喝】to eat and drink extravagantly

【大吃一驚】to be greatly surprised; to be taken aback

【大徹大悟】①(usually said of oneself) a profound and complete realization ② (theology) the great revelation

【大臣】ranking officials

【大腸】the large intestine

【大出洋相】to commit a big blunder in public

【大處著眼，小處著手】to make an overall assessment but to start from details

【大吹大擂】to brag and blare

【大師】① a master ② a reverent title for a Buddhist monk

【大師傅】① a head cook; a chef ② a salutation for a Buddhist monk

【大失所望】to be greatly disappointed

【大使】an ambassador

【大使館】an embassy

【大事】important events; serious matters

【大事鋪張】to make lavish preparations

【大事化小，小事化無】to turn big problems into small problems and small problems into no problem at all

【大事宣傳】to play up; ballyhoo

【大勢所趨】general trend indicates...; according to the prevailing tendency

【大勢已去】The situation is hopeless, etc.

【大赦】an amnesty

【大少爺】①a term used by a servant to address the eldest son of the family ② a dandy; a playboy

【大手筆】the work or handwriting of a great author or calligrapher

【大聲疾呼】to urge emphatically

【大人】①(in ancient China) a respectful salutation for one's parents, seniors, etc. ② an adult

【大人物】a VIP; a big shot

【大字報】a big-character poster

【大自然】nature

【大雜燴】a hodgepodge

【大作】① your work, etc. ②(said of violence, etc.) to erupt; to upheave ③(said of music, etc.) to come out in ensemble and rather suddenly

【大宗】a large batch; lots of

【大慈大悲】the great mercy

【大才小用】to make little use of great talent

【大錯特錯】to make a gross error

【大肆咆哮】to roar with rage

【大嫂】①one's eldest sister-in-law ②a polite name for women of

〔大部〕

similar age as oneself 「cleanup
【大掃除】to make a thorough
【大蒜】garlic 「functory
【大而化之】careless; slapdash; per-
【大而無當】big but useless
【大衣】an overcoat
【大意】① the general idea; the gist ② negligent ③ high ambitions
【大搖大擺】to swagger 「different
【大有分別】poles apart or entirely
【大有可爲】very promising (projects, etc.); very hopeful
【大有人在】Such people are by no means rare. 「hind all this.
【大有文章】There's something be-
【大言不慚】to boast unabashedly or shamelessly 「ocean
【大洋】① a silver dollar ② an
【大無畏】dauntless; fearless
【大文豪】a renowned man of letters 「chief of brigands
【大王】① Your Majesty ② the
【大魚大肉】rich food (implying gluttony)
【大雨傾盆】to rain cats and dogs
【大約】about; around; probably; likely
【大元帥】a marshal; the commander in chief of the armed forces

大 792
2. ㄉㄞˋ dài
【大夫】doctor

一畫

天 793
ㄊㄧㄢ tiān
1. the sky; the heavens 2. Nature; God; Heaven 3. nature; natural 4. a day 5. seasons; weather 6. father or husband 7. something indispensable
【天崩地坼】deafening sounds—as the falling of heaven and cracking of earth 亦作「天崩地裂」
【天邊】the ends of the earth; remotest places 「and no one
【天不怕地不怕】to fear nothing
【天平 or 天秤】scales
【天馬行空】(said of calligraphic writing or works) an unrestrained and vigorous style that brims with talent
【天明】daybreak; dawn
【天命】①a heavenly mandate ② fate ③ one's life span
【天翻地覆】in total disorder or disarrangement
【天分】natural endowments; talent
【天府之國】a country with rich natural resources
【天賦】① inherent and inborn ② natural endowments
【天賦人權】inborn human rights
【天底下】in this world; under the sun
【天地】① the world; the universe ②a field of activity ③the upper and lower margins of a scroll ④ a world of difference 「heart
【天地良心】from the bottom of my
【天定】preordained; predestined
【天堂】heaven; paradise
【天體營】a nudist camp
【天天】every day
【天南地北】① poles apart ②(to chat or talk casually about) discursive
【天怒人怨】(to incur) the wrath of Heaven and opposition of man
【天籟】the sounds of nature
【天藍色】sky blue
【天理】natural law
【天理昭彰】The law of Heaven always prevails.
【天良】one's conscience
【天亮】daybreak
【天羅地網】the dragnet of justice surrounding on all sides; envelopment
【天倫之樂】family love and joy
【天高氣爽】(usually said of the crisp air in autumn) The sky is high and the weather is fine.
【天干】the Ten Celestial Stems
【天國】the Kingdom of Heaven
【天空】the sky; the firmament
【天花】(pathology) the smallpox
【天花板】the ceiling (of a room)
【天花亂墜】exaggerated description
【天昏地暗】dark above and below
【天津】Tientsin
【天經地義】a matter of course
【天氣】weather
【天氣預報】a weather forecast
【天橋】an overhead bridge or elevated passage 「and-brimstone
【天譴】God's punishment—fire-
【天下】the world

〔大部〕

【天下一家】All people under the sun are one family.
【天下烏鴉一般黑】Evil people are bad all over the world.
【天下爲公】The world is for all.
【天曉得】God knows! 或 Heaven knows!
【天險】impregnable natural barriers (for defense)
【天線】an antenna (for radio, TV, etc.)
【天性】natural disposition
【天之驕子】to be extraordinarily blessed
【天職】bounden duty
【天眞】naive; innocent
【天眞爛漫】innocent and carefree —lovely like a child
【天誅地滅】to be damned by Heaven and Earth
【天竺】the ancient name of India
【天竺鼠】a guinea pig; a cavy
【天主教】Catholicism
【天長地久】(literally) as old as heaven and earth—a very long time
【天窗】① a skylight ② as in 打開天窗說亮話—Let's be quite frank.
【天時】weather, or climates
【天使】① an angel ② an emissary from the emperor
【天生】natural; to be born with; congenital; inborn
【天然】natural
【天壤之別】vastly different; poles apart
【天資】natural endowments
【天子】the emperor
【天災】a natural disaster
【天災人禍】natural disasters and man-made calamities
【天造地設】①(said of a couple) matched by Heaven and Earth ② a natural creation; heavenly
【天作之合】a match blessed by God
【天縱英明】(said of a ruler) born with wisdom and farsightedness
【天才】a genius; natural talent
【天才兒童】a child prodigy
【天從人願】What man hoped to happen has come to pass.
【天色】the color of the sky
【天鵝】a swan
【天安門】Tien An Men (the Gate of Heavenly Peace)
【天衣無縫】without a trace; perfect (jobs); flawless (lies)
【天意】the will of Heaven; God's will
【天涯海角】faraway, remote or distant places
【天有不測風雲，人有旦夕禍福】Human fortunes are as unpredictable as the weather.
【天無絕人之路】Heaven will always leave a door open.
【天文臺】an astronomical observatory
【天文學】astronomy
【天王星】the planet Uranus
【天淵之別】vastly different

太 794
ㄊㄞˋ tài

1. very big or large 2. much; too; over; excessively; extremely; very 3. a term of respect, used in titles 4. a Chinese family name

【太保】①a very high official in ancient China ② juvenile delinquents
【太平】peace; peaceful
【太平門】(in public buildings, especially in theaters) exits, especially those leading to fire escapes
【太平間】a mortuary
【太平盛世】a reign of peace, order, and prosperity
【太平洋】the Pacific Ocean
【太妹】a girl delinquent; a tomboy
【太太】① a madame ② one's wife
【太古】prehistorical times
【太公釣魚，願者上鉤】A victim letting himself be caught of his own will.
【太空】space
【太空船】a spacecraft; a spaceship
【太空人】astronauts; cosmonauts
【太空梭】a space shuttle; a shuttle
【太后】the empress dowager
【太極拳】*taichichuan*; "shadowboxing"
【太監】a eunuch
【太虛幻境】an illusory scene
【太上皇】① the emperor's father ② (colloquial) a person who exercises supreme powers
【太子】the crown prince
【太座】one's wife (a joking expression connoting the dominating position of a wife in the family)
【太歲頭上動土】to offend or provoke the most powerful
【太陰】① the moon ② lunar
【太陽】the sun
【太陽能】solar energy
【太陽系】the solar system
【太陽穴】the temples (of a human being)
【太陽眼鏡】sunglasses

〔大部〕

夫 795
1. ㄈㄨ fū
1. a man; a male adult 2. those eligible for military service 3. a master 4. a husband 「a couple
【夫婦or夫妻】 husband and wife; 」
【夫君】 ①(in old usage) my husband ②(Tang Dynasty) a friend
【夫妻反目】 the disharmony or discord between husband and wife
【夫婿】 a reference to one's own husband
【夫唱婦隨 or 夫婦好合】 harmony between husband and wife
【夫人】 ① the wives of high officials ② Lady; Madame; Mrs.
【夫子】 ① a title of respect for the elders ② a master

夫 795
2. ㄈㄨˊ fú
1. a demonstrative pronoun—*that* in most cases 2. a final parti-
⌊cle; a particle

夭 796
1. ㄧㄠˇ yǎo
1. to die young 2. to suppress; to repress 「to a premature end
【夭折】 ①to die young ②to come 」
【夭壽】 to die young

夭 796
2. ㄧㄠ yāo
young; fresh-looking; tender

二畫

失 797
ㄕ shī
1. to let slip; to neglect; to miss 2. to lose 3. an omission; a mistake
【失敗】 to fail; a failure; a defeat
【失陪】 Please excuse me for not being able to keep you company for the moment. 「insomnia
【失眠】 to suffer from insomnia; 」
【失明】 to become blind; blind
【失當】 improper; improperly
【失掉】 to lose (a chance, confi-
【失態】 to misbehave ⌊dence, etc.)
【失調】 ① maladjustment ② to be careless about one's health, etc.
【失禮】 to be impolite; impropriety
【失利】 to suffer a defeat (or setback) 「love
【失戀】 to be jilted; to lose one's 」
【失靈】 (said of a machine, instrument, etc.) to be out of order
【失落】 to lose
【失控】 out of control; runaway
【失和】 (said of a couple) to be on bad terms; to be at loggerheads
【失怙】 to lose one's father; to be
【失火】 to catch fire ⌊orphaned
【失魂落魄】 despondent; listless
【失禁】 incontinence 「respectful.
【失敬】 Excuse me for being dis- 」
【失竊】 to be stolen
【失去】 to lose
【失效】 ①(law) to be invalidated; null and void ②(said of medicines, etc.) to lose potency or efficacy
【失笑】 cannot help laughing
【失陷】 (said of cities, territory, etc.) to fall to the enemy
【失信】 to break one's word or promise 「or education
【失學】 to lack formal schooling 」
【失血】 to lose blood
【失之毫釐，差之千里】 A slight mistake will result in a great error in the end.
【失之交臂】 to miss (a person or chance) at very close range
【失職】 to be delinquent
【失主】 (law) the owner of lost property or the victim of a robbery, burglary, etc.
【失常】 off form; to perform below one's normal capacity
【失傳】 lost (arts, skills, etc.)
【失寵】 to be in disgrace
【失事】 an accident; to meet with an accident
【失恃】 to lose one's mother
【失勢】 to lose one's position, authority, influence, etc.
【失手】 to break something or hurt somebody by accident; to slip
【失守】 ① to fail to fulfill one's duty ②(said of a city, territory, etc.) to fall into the hands of the enemy
【失身】 ①(said of women) to lose chastity ② to incur danger
【失身分 or 失身份】 (to do something) beneath one's dignity
【失聲】 to lose one's voice for crying too much
【失足】 ① to slip; to lose one's footing ② to commit a mistake

【失蹤】missing
【失策】poor tactic or strategy
【失色】to lose color; to turn pale
【失散】lost and scattered
【失算】to miscalculate
【失而復得】to be lost and found again
【失意】disappointed; frustrated
【失業】to lose one's job; jobless
【失言】to say what should not be said; an improper pronouncement, remark, etc.
【失誤】an error; an omission
【失物招領】lost items or articles (found by others) kept for claimants
【失望】disappointment
【失約】① to break one's promise ②to break a date or an appointment

央 798
ㄧㄤ yāng
1. the center; central; middle 2. the finish or conclusion; to finish 3. to request; to entreat
【央求】to beg; to entreat; to implore; to plead

三畫

夷 799
ㄧˊ yí
1. (in ancient China) barbarians in the east 2. foreign tribes or foreigners 3. at ease; peaceful 4. to level; to make level, even or smooth 5. safe 6. to eliminate; to exterminate; to kill; to execute 7. injuries; wounds 8. grades; classes 9. common; usual; ordinary 10. great; big
【夷爲平地】to level (a town, etc.) with the ground

夸 800
ㄎㄨㄚ kuā
1. big; large 2. lavish; luxurious 3. good-looking; pleasant 4. to brag
【夸誕】boastful; bragging

四畫

夾 801
1. ㄐㄧㄚˊ jiá
(又讀 ㄐㄧㄚ jiā)
1. to be wedged between; to be sandwiched 2. to squeeze; to press; to occupy both sides of 3. pincers 4. of two or more layers; lined (garments, etc.) 5. a folder to keep sheets of paper, etc. 6. to carry secretly 7. to mix; to mingle
【夾子】folders for keeping documents, papers, pictures, etc.; clips
【夾縫】a crack; a loophole (in the law)
【夾帶】① things brought in secretly such as contraband ② a crib
【夾道歡迎】to line the street to welcome
【夾攻or夾擊】to attack from both sides
【夾持】to hold in between
【夾雜】mixed-up
【夾層】a double layer; a false bottom (of a trunk, etc.)

夾 801
2. ㄐㄧㄚˋ jià
【夾竹桃】an oleander

五畫

奄 802
1. ㄧㄢˇ yǎn
1. to cover; to surround 2. suddenly

奄 802
2. ㄧㄢ yān
1. to soak; to bathe; to drown 2. to remain 3. to castrate; a castrated man
【奄奄一息】dying

奇 803
1. ㄑㄧˊ qí
1. strange; uncanny; occult; rare 2. wonderful 3. to feel strange about
【奇妙】wonderful; rare
【奇特】unique; outstanding; strange
【奇談】a strange story
【奇怪or奇異】strange; unusual; odd
【奇觀】a spectacular or wonderful sight or phenomenon
【奇貨可居】(literally) rare commodities which can be hoarded for better prices
【奇蹟】miracles; wonders
【奇景】wonderful scenes
【奇形怪狀】of strange, bizarre or grotesque shapes and sizes
【奇裝異服】strange or queer clothing
【奇恥大辱】great shame or disgrace; great insult or humiliation
【奇才】a rare talent; a genius
【奇異果】kiwi; Chinese gooseberries
【奇聞】something unheard-of
【奇遇】an unexpected encounter

奇 803
2. ㄐㄧ jī
as in 奇數—odd (numbers)

奈 804
ㄋㄞˋ nài
1. what; how; but 2. to bear; to endure
【奈何】What to do now? 或What can we do now? 或What then? 或 Why?

奉 805
ㄈㄥˋ fèng
1. to receive with respect 2. an expression of respect 3. to offer; to present 4. to admire; to love and respect 5. pay; salary 6. to serve; to wait on
【奉陪】(a polite expression) to accompany (you)
【奉命or奉令】to receive orders from above; (to do something) as ordered
【奉告】to let somebody know; to inform
【奉公守法】law-abiding
【奉還】respectfully return with thanks
【奉勸】May I venture to advise you to...?
【奉獻】(Christianity) to contribute
【奉行】to act or perform something as ordered
【奉旨】on the imperial order
【奉召】to be summoned or recalled
【奉承】① to receive respectfully ② to flatter
【奉送】① to present respectfully ② (shop language) to give away as a gift
【奉養】to support (one's parents)
【奉爲圭臬】to look up to something as a model

六畫

奔 806
1.(奔) ㄅㄣ bēn
1. to move quickly; to run; to hurry 2. to run for one's life; to flee 3. to elope
【奔波】to be on the run; to work very hard
【奔跑】to run in a great hurry
【奔放】①(said of a horse) galloping ② (said of a writing or emotional manifestation) expressive and unrestrained
【奔馳】to travel quickly; to move fast
【奔走】①to solicit help (in trying to land a job, get an appointment, etc.) ② to do a job on orders; to run errands
【奔喪】to hasten home upon the death of one's parents

奔 806
2.(奔) ㄅㄣˋ bèn
to go straight forwards; to head for

奏 807
ㄗㄡˋ zòu
1. to report to the throne 2. to play (music or musical instruments) 3. to move; to advance
【奏鳴曲】(music) a sonata
【奏捷】to win; to be victorious
【奏效】effective; efficacious
【奏樂】to play music (in solemn ceremonies)

契 808
1. ㄑㄧˋ qì
1. a contract; an agreement; a bond 2. a divining instrument in ancient China 3. to be compatible, harmonious in thought and aspiration 4. to adopt 5. to cut
【契合】to be in agreement; harmony
【契機】①(philosophy) a moment ② a turning point; a critical point of time
【契據】a contract; an agreement
【契約】a written contract or agreement

契 808
2. ㄑㄧㄝˋ qiè
1. to carve 2. to be separated from
【契闊】to be separated from one another

奕 809
ㄧˋ yì
1. great; grand; abundant 2. gorgeous; elegant; good-looking 3. worried; unsettled; anxious 4. in good order; in sequence

七畫

套 810
ㄊㄠˋ tào
1. a case; an envelope 2. a trap 3. to wear or slip on (a sweater, etc.) 4. to trap or trick a person (into telling the truth) 5. to harness 6. to pattern or model after 7. convention; a formula 8. a suit (of clothes)
【套房】a suite (of rooms)
【套牢】lockup; to lock up
【套話】to trap a person into telling the truth
【套裝】an ensemble

【畚用】to use indiscriminately

畚 811 ㄅㄣˇ běn
a bamboo or wicker scoop or a basket for earth
【畚斗】a dustpan
【畚箕】a dust basket

奚 812 ㄒㄧ xī
1. why; how; what; which 2. a servant
【奚落】to laugh at; to make a fool of

九畫

奠 813 ㄉㄧㄢˋ diàn
1. to settle; to lay (foundation, etc.) 2. to secure; to consolidate 3. to offer libations
【奠定】to lay foundation and consolidate it; to settle
【奠儀or奠敬】a money gift for a funeral

奢 814 ㄕㄜ shē
1. extravagant; wasteful; lavish 2. excess; excessive 3. to exaggerate; to brag
【奢靡】wasteful; lavish spending (of money)
【奢華】showy; to be indulgent in luxurious and expensive habits
【奢侈】luxury; wasteful; prodigal
【奢望】to entertain hopes beyond one's ability to realize; a wild hope

十畫

奧 815 ㄠˋ ào
1. mysterious; obscure; profound (learning) 2. a secret cabin or corner of a house or palace
【奧秘】deep, profound and mysterious subtle
【奧妙】① mysterious; marvelous ② the secret of doing something
【奧林匹克運動會】the Olympic Games

十一畫

奪 816 ㄉㄨㄛˊ duó
1. to take by force; to rob 2. to snatch; to grasp; to carry away (the first prize, etc.) 3. to settle; to decide in a race or contest
【奪標】to win the first prize—as in a race or contest
【奪門而出】to force one's way out
【奪魁】to win a race or tournament
【奪眶而出】(said of tears) to break out
【奪回】to recapture; to retake
【奪取】to take by force; to wrest from
【奪權】to take over power

獎 817 ㄐㄧㄤˇ jiǎng
1. to encourage; to exhort 2. to praise; to commend 3. to cite or give a prize or reward (for a merit, etc.) 4. a prize or reward
【獎杯】a cup (as a prize)
【獎牌】a gold, silver or bronze medal given as an award
【獎品】prizes or rewards
【獎勵】to encourage by rewards
【獎金】prize money; a bounty; a bonus
【獎券】a lottery ticket or raffle ticket
【獎學金】a scholarship; a fellowship
【獎章】a medal
【獎狀】a citation of meritorious services, etc.
【獎賞】①rewards in money, etc. ②to reward

十三畫

奮 818 ㄈㄣˋ fèn
1. to rise in force; to arouse; to exert with force 2. (said of a bird) to take wing 3. to advance, promote or invigorate (a cause, etc.)
【奮不顧身】to do something regardless of personal safety
【奮發圖強】to rejuvenate a nation by dedicated work
【奮發有爲】(often said of a young person) hardworking and promising
【奮鬪】to struggle; to strive
【奮力】to do one's best
【奮戰】to fight bravely
【奮勇】courageously; bravely

女部 ㄋㄩˇ nǚ

〔女部〕

女 819
ㄋㄩˇ nǚ
1. a daughter; a girl; a maiden; a lady 2. a woman; a female
【女扮男裝】a woman disguising herself as a man
【女儐相】a bridesmaid
【女朋友】a girlfriend
【女僕】a female servant; a maid
【女服務員】①an air hostess; a stewardess ②a waitress
【女郎】a maiden; a young woman; a young girl
【女伶】an actress
【女管家】a housekeeper
【女工】women labor
【女紅】needlework
【女孩】a girl
【女皇】an empress
【女強人】a successful career woman
【女權主義 or 女權運動】feminism
【女性】female; the fair sex
【女性化】feminization; to feminize
【女壻 or 女婿】a son-in-law
【女主角】a leading lady; a heroine
【女主人】a hostess
【女裝】a woman dress
【女士】Ms.; a lady
【女生】co-eds; girl students
【女生宿舍】a women's dormitory
【女人】a woman
【女子】a woman; a girl
【女厠所】a women's lavatory; a ladies' room
【女兒】①one's daughter ②a girl
【女巫】a witch 亦作「巫婆」
【女王】a queen regnant

二畫

奴 820
ㄋㄨˊ nú
1. a slave; a servant 2. a self-derogatory expression used by a girl to refer to herself in former times 3. a despicable yes-man
【奴婢】slaves; servants
【奴隸】a serf; a slave
【奴才】①a slave; a serf; a bondman ②a good-for-nothing; a useless fellow; a yes-man
【奴役】to enslave
【奴顏婢膝】fawning; obsequious

奶 821
ㄋㄞˇ nǎi
1. the breasts of a woman 2. milk 3. grandma 4. to feed with milk; to breast-feed 5. a term of respect for married women
【奶瓶】a milk bottle
【奶媽 or 奶母 or 奶娘】a wet nurse
【奶粉】milk powder
【奶奶】①a term of respect for older women ②grandma
【奶茶】tea with milk
【奶水】milk
【奶嘴】the nipple (of a nursing bottle)
【奶油】butter

三畫

奸 822
ㄐㄧㄢ jiān
1. false 2. selfish 3. disloyal 4. crafty; wicked; villainous; cunning; evil 5. adultery; fornication; licentiousness 6. a traitor; a villain
【奸計】a wicked scheme
【奸細】a spy (from the enemy side); a stool pigeon 亦作「間諜」
【奸險】crafty, mean and malicious
【奸詐】crafty; cunning
【奸臣】(formerly) a selfish, disloyal and cunning minister; a traitor
【奸商】unethical merchants; profiteers
【奸賊】a scoundrel; a traitor
【奸淫】①adultery ②lecherous ③to rape

她 823
ㄊㄚ tā
she

好 824
1. ㄏㄠˇ hǎo
1. good; nice; fine 2. pleasing (looks, taste, etc.); easy (to deal with, etc.) 3. to finish (dressing, eating, etc.) 4. very; much 5. so that 6. All right! 或 Wonderful! 或 Bravo! 7. an exclamatory expression 8. a friendly meeting 9. fit; suitable; proper
【好半天】quite a while; a long time
【好比】to be like
【好不好】①Is it all right? 或 Okay? ②Won't you...?
【好不容易】①very difficult ②after all the trouble.
【好評】favorable comment
【好歹】①emergency; an accident ②by hook or by crook ③good

and bad ④ anyhow; in any case
【好多】① How much or many? ② a good deal; so much; so many
【好聽】pleasant to hear
【好萊塢】Hollywood
【好感】a favorable impression
【好看】good-looking; beautiful; nice
【好漢不吃眼前虧】A wise man knows how to avoid being beaten.
【好極了】Excellent! 或 Wonderful!
【好傢伙】① The scoundrel! ② Fine thing indeed! ③ What a powerful blow!
【好久】① How long? ② a long time
【好景不長】Good fortune won't last forever.
【好球】Bravo! 或 well played; a good shot
【好戲】①(sarcastic) great fun ② good play
【好些】①a little better ②many (people, etc.)
【好消息】good news
【好小子】a smart guy; a wise guy
【好笑】laughable; funny; ridiculous
【好心】kind-hearted
【好像】to seem; to look like
【好轉】to take a turn for the better
【好吃】good to eat; tasty; delicious
【好處】①good points; advantages ②profit ③marriage
【好事】① good things ② charity
【好事多磨】The realization of good things is usually preceded by rough going.
【好手】an expert
【好說歹說】to try every possible way to persuade somebody
【好日子】① an auspicious day ② a wedding day ③ a happy life
【好人】① a beauty ② a person of virtue ③ a person who gets along very well with everyone
【好人難做】It's difficult to please everybody.
【好自爲之】to do one's best (to keep a job, run a business, etc.)
【好在】fortunately; luckily
【好意】goodwill; kindness
【好玩】interesting; full of fun

好 824
2. ㄏㄠˋ hào
1. to love to; to like to; to be fond of 2. to be addicted to 3. what one likes or prefers
【好大喜功】to love to brag and show off
【好賭】fond of gambling
【好動】(said of one's disposition) very active or restless
【好高騖遠】to aim high but care nothing about the fundamental; unrealistic
【好客】to be hospitable
【好奇】to be curious; curiosity
【好強】to be eager to do well in everything
【好學】to be fond of studying
【好戰】hawkish; warmongering
【好吃懶做】lazy
【好事者or好事之徒】a meddler; a busybody
【好勝】to love to win; emulative
【好色】lewd; libidinous; lustful
【好逸惡勞】to love ease and hate work; pleasure-seeking
【好勇鬥狠】combative 亦作「好鬥」
【好惡】likes and dislikes
【好問】inquisitive

如 825
ㄖㄨˊ rú
1. like; as 2. if; supposing 3. as if 4. as good as; equal to 5. to follow (advice); to listen to 6. to go to; to arrive at 7. should; ought to 8. on or in (time)
【如夢初醒】to come to a sudden realization
【如法炮製or如法泡製】to do something exactly as others have done
【如墮五里霧中】utterly being mystified
【如鳥獸散】to flee helter-skelter
【如雷貫耳】(one's famous name) has long been known to people
【如臨大敵】very careful or cautious; to take all possible precautions
【如鯁在喉】to give vent to one's pent-up feelings
【如果】if; supposing
【如何】① How (can we deal with...)? ② What do you think of it? 或 How about it? ③ What to do now? 或 How is it?
【如虎添翼】with added strength
【如花似玉】(said of a girl) young, beautiful and pure
【如火如荼】(troops) in an imposing array; luxuriant (growth, etc.)
【如獲至寶】to get what one has wished or desired for a long time
【如膠似漆】very much in love; in-

separable
【如舊】as it has always been; as usual
【如箭在弦】ready to go or start; imminent
【如今】now; nowadays
【如期】on time; punctually
【如下】as follows; as below
【如須】if (you) want to; if (you) have to
【如常】as usual
【如出一轍】(said of events) very similar; almost the same
【如釋重負】to feel greatly relieved (after discharging a duty)
【如上所述】as mentioned above
【如數家珍】to describe distinctly and in good order
【如數償還】to pay back in full
【如日中天】① to ride on the crest of success ② very influential
【如坐針氈】very anxious; in a state of agitation
【如醉如癡】to be drunk with; to be crazy about
【如此】thus; like this
【如此而已】That's what it all amounts to.
【如厠】to go to the toilet
【如意】as one wishes
【如意算盤】wishful thinking
【如影隨形】(said of two persons) inseparable; to tag after
【如魚得水】(said of friends, newlyweds, the king and the ministers, etc.) very satisfied and pleased
【如願以償】to have one's wish fulfilled

妃 826 ㄈㄟ fēi
1. a wife; a spouse 2. the concubine of a king or an emperor 3. the wife or spouse of a crown prince

妄 827 ㄨㄤˋ wàng
1. absurd; untrue; false 2. ignorant; stupid 3. reckless; rash 4. wild
【妄想】a daydream; to desire wildly
【妄自菲薄】to underestimate oneself
【妄自尊大】self-importance; conceited

四畫

妓 828 ㄐㄧˋ jì
1. a prostitute; a whore 2. a young woman who sings or dances to amuse her customers, such as 舞妓 (a female dancer), 藝妓 (a geisha)
【妓女】a prostitute; a whore

妊 829 ㄖㄣˋ rèn
pregnant; to be expecting
【妊娠】to be pregnant; pregnancy

妒 830 (妬) ㄉㄨˋ dù
jealous; envious; jealousy; envy
【妒忌 or 妒嫉】jealousy; envy

妖 831 ㄧㄠ yāo
1. weird; unaccountable; monstrous; supernatural 2. an evil; a monster; a goblin; a phantom; a ghost 3. (usually said of a woman) bewitching
【妖魔鬼怪】a general term for evil spirits
【妖媚】bewitching
【妖孽】① unlucky omens ② the monsters who cause great calamities ③ a person like a devil
【妖女】a fairy enchantress
【妖裏妖氣】seductive and bewitching
【妖怪 or 妖精】① a monster or demon ② a Circe; a siren ③ a spirit transformed from a very old animal, tree
【妖術】sorcery; witchcraft
【妖冶 or 妖艷】seductive; bewitchingly pretty
【妖言惑衆】to cheat people with sensational speeches

妞 832 ㄋㄧㄡ niū
a girl; a little girl

妙 833 ㄇㄧㄠˋ miào
1. wonderful; excellent 2. very interesting; intriguing 3. clever; subtle; ingenious
【妙不可言】ingenious beyond description
【妙年 or 妙齡】young; in one's youth
【妙計】a wonderful idea
【妙趣橫生】full of wit and humor
【妙手空空】① a wheeler-dealer ② a pickpocket
【妙手回春】the hands that cure—used to praise a good physician
【妙語如珠】sparkling discourse
【妙用】ingenious uses; (serving unexpected) subtle effects

妝 834 ㄓㄨㄤ zhuāng

1. to doll up; to adorn oneself; to apply makeup 2. jewels, etc. for adornment 3. to disguise; to pretend
【妝扮】 to doll up
【妝飾】 to adorn; to dress up

妣 835 ㄅㄧˇ bǐ
one's deceased mother

妥 836 ㄊㄨㄛˇ tuǒ
1. firm; safe; secure 2. appropriate 3. ready; set; to settle
【妥當】 ① appropriate or secure ② ready
【妥協】 ① amity ② a compromise; a reconciliation ③ appeasement (in international relations)
【妥善】 proper; appropriate
【妥善安排】 to make appropriate arrangements

妨 837 ㄈㄤˊ fáng
(又讀 ㄈㄤ fāng)
1. to hinder; to impede; to obstruct 2. to undermine; to harm; to damage
【妨害】 to impair; to be harmful to
【妨礙】 to hinder; to hamper

五畫

妯 838 ㄓㄡˊ zhóu
sisters-in-law 參看「妯娌」
【妯娌】 sisters-in-law (a reference among the wives of one's husband's brothers)

妹 839 ㄇㄟˋ mèi
as in 妹妹—a younger sister
【妹夫】 the husband of one's younger sister; a brother-in-law

妻 840 1. ㄑㄧ qī
one's formal or legal wife
【妻離子散】 The family breaks up.
【妻妾】 one's wife and concubine(s)
【妻子】 ① one's wife ② one's wife and children

妻 840 2. ㄑㄧˋ qì
to marry one's daughter to someone

妾 841 ㄑㄧㄝˋ qiè
1. a concubine 2. (in old China) a polite term used by a woman to refer to herself when speaking to her husband

姆 842 ㄇㄨˇ mǔ
1. (in old China) a governess; a woman tutor 2. a matron who looks after small children

姊 843 (姉) ㄐㄧㄝˇ jiě
(讀音 ㄗˇ zǐ)
one's elder sister or sisters
【姊妹】 sisters
【姊妹花】 beautiful sisters
【姊妹市】 sister cities
【姊夫or姊丈】 the husband of one's elder sister
【姊姊】 elder sisters

始 844 ㄕˇ shǐ
1. the beginning; the start; the first 2. to start; to begin; to be the first
【始末】 ①from beginning to end—throughout ② the ins and outs (of an incident, story, etc.)
【始亂終棄】 to desert a girl after robbing her of her chastity
【始終】 throughout; from beginning to end
【始終如一】 consistent; unremitting
【始祖】 ① the founder ② the first ancestor
【始作俑者】 the originator (usually of a bad practice, etc.)

姍 845 ㄕㄢ shān
1. to ridicule; to laugh at 2. (said of a woman) to walk slowly
【姍姍來遲】 to walk or proceed slowly (and keep others waiting)

姐 846 ㄐㄧㄝˇ jiě
1. one's elder sister or sisters 2. a general term for women, usually young
【姐妹】 sisters
【姐夫or姐丈】 the husband of one's elder sister; a brother-in-law
【姐姐】 one's elder sister

姑 847 ㄍㄨ gū
1. aunts; the sister of one's father 2. the mother of one's husband 3. the sister of one's husband 4. a general term for unmarried women 5. for the

〔女部〕

time being; meanwhile 6. a nun
【姑媽 or 姑母 or 姑姑】an aunt
【姑父 or 姑夫 or 姑丈】an uncle
【姑娘】an unmarried girl; a maiden
【姑且】for the time being
【姑且不談】to leave something aside for the moment
【姑息】to spoil (a child); to appease
【姑息養奸】To tolerate evil is to encourage evildoers.
【姑爺】a son-in-law

姓 848 ㄒㄧㄥˋ xìng

1. surname; one's family name 2. a clan; a family; people
【姓名】the full name of a person
【姓氏】the surname; the family name

委 849 1. ㄨㄟˇ wěi

1. to depute; to deputize 2. to send; to put in charge of; to commission 3. to give up; to abandon 4. to be frustrated, weakened or tired 5. really; truly; indeed 6. a grievance; a wrong 7. to stoop or lower oneself (in order to avoid an open conflict, etc.)
【委派or委任】to appoint; to commission
【委靡不振】dispirited and lethargic; in low spirits
【委託or委托】to commission; to entrust
【委內瑞拉】Venezuela
【委屈】① a grievance; complaints ② to be frustrated or wronged ③ to take an office, etc. far below one's ability ④ to put someone to inconvenience
【委曲求全】to make great concessions for the purpose of accommodating to a situation
【委實】really; indeed
【委身】① to become the wife of... ②to consign oneself to someone or something
【委罪】to impute
【委瑣】① petty; trifling ② of a wretched appearance ③ being a stickler for forms
【委以重任】to entrust someone with an important task
【委婉】tactful; unobtrusively
【委員】a member of a committee
【委員會】a committee; a council

委 849 2. ㄨㄟ wēi

【委蛇】in a carefree manner

六畫

姚 850 ㄧㄠˊ yáo

1. handsome; good-looking; elegant 2. a Chinese family name

姜 851 ㄐㄧㄤ jiāng

1. a Chinese family name 2. ginger

姣 852 ㄐㄧㄠ jiāo

1. handsome; pretty; beautiful 2. coquettish
【姣好】pretty; pleasant (looks); good-looking

姥 853 ㄌㄠˇ lǎo

1. one's maternal grandmother 2. an old woman

姦 854 ㄐㄧㄢ jiān

1. adultery; debauchery; licentiousness 2. to debauch; to ravish; to attack (a woman) sexually 3. a crook
【姦夫】① an adulterer ② a man who acts criminally
【姦婦】an adulteress
【姦淫】debauchery; adultery; to rape
【姦淫擄掠】rape and rapine

姨 855 ㄧˊ yí

1. the sisters of one's wife 2. the sisters of one's mother 3. a concubine
【姨婆】a grandaunt
【姨媽 or 姨母】the married sisters of one's mother
【姨父 or 姨丈 or 姨夫】an uncle
【姨太太】a concubine
【姨娘】a concubine of one's father

姪 856 ㄓˊ zhí

1. the children of one's brother—nephews or nieces 2. I; me (when speaking to a family friend of one's father's generation)
【姪女】nieces
【姪兒 or 姪子】nephews

姸 857 (妍) ㄧㄢˊ yán

1. beautiful; pretty; good-looking; cute; attractive; charming 2. seductive; coquettish
【姸麗】attractive; charming; beauty

姹 858
(奼) ㄔㄚˋ chà
1. young (girls) 2. charming; attractive; seductive 3. to boast; to talk big; to lie

姻 859
ㄧㄣ yīn
1. one's husband's family 2. marriage 3. relations or connections through marriage
【姻親or姻戚or姻婭】relatives by marriage
【姻緣】the invisible bond that makes a man and a woman husband and wife

姿 860
ㄗ zī
1. the manner; an air; carriage; bearing 2. looks
【姿態】① carriage; deportment; bearing ② a gesture
【姿勢】① carriage; deportment; bearing ② (in photography) a pose
【姿色】(female) beauty

威 861
ㄨㄟ wēi
1. dignity; majesty 2. authority; power; might 3. awe-inspiring; awe
【威逼利誘】to threaten and to bribe
【威名 or 威望】prestige
【威風】① power and prestige ② imposing; awe-inspiring
【威風凜凜】awe-inspiring; imposing
【威尼斯】Venice, a city in Italy
【威力】① the force that inspires awe ② military force ③ the destructive force (of a typhoon, earthquake, nuclear device, etc.)
【威脅】to threaten; intimidation; a threat; intimidation
【威士忌】whisky
【威嚴】① sternness; severity ② an awe-inspiring air
【威武】an awe-inspiring display of military force, etc.

娃 862
ㄨㄚˊ wá
1. a beautiful woman 2. a baby; a child 3. exquisite; fine
【娃娃】a baby; a young child
【娃娃臉】a baby face; baby-faced
【娃娃車】a baby car or carriage

七畫

娓 863
ㄨㄟˇ wěi
1. complying; subservient 2. attractive; beautiful
【娓娓】(to talk) tirelessly
【娓娓動聽】persuasive (accounts, narration, etc.)

娉 864
ㄆㄧㄥ pīng
good-looking; elegant; charming; graceful
【娉婷】graceful and charming

姬 865
ㄐㄧ jī
1. a beautiful lady; a charming girl 2. a concubine 3. a Chinese family name

娑 866
ㄙㄨㄛ suō
to dance

娘 867
(孃) ㄋㄧㄤˊ niáng
1. mother 2. girls or women
【娘娘腔】sissy; womanish
【娘家】one's wife's family

娛 868
ㄩˊ yú
to amuse; to give pleasure to; to entertain; amusement; entertainment; pleasure
【娛樂】amusement; entertainment; to amuse; to entertain
【娛樂活動】recreational activities
【娛樂場所】entertainment establishments

娜 869
1. ㄋㄨㄛˇ nuǒ
tender, slender and graceful

娜 869
2. ㄋㄨㄛˊ nuó
the word used in a female name

娜 869
3. ㄋㄚˋ nà
a word used in the transliteration of a western female name

娟 870
ㄐㄩㄢ juān
pretty; good-looking; graceful; attractive

娥 871
ㄜˊ é
1. good; beautiful 2. a common name for a girl 3. a Chinese family name

娩 872
1. ㄨㄢˇ wǎn
complaisant

〔女部〕

娩 872
2. ㄇㄧㄢˇ miǎn
to give birth to a child

八畫

婆 873
ㄆㄛˊ pó
1. an old woman 2. the mother of one's husband 3. one's grandmother
【婆婆】①the mother of one's husband ②a term of respect for an old lady
【婆婆媽媽的】①sissy ②mawkish; oversentimental ③nagging
【婆家】one's husband's family
【婆媳】a woman and her daughter-in-law
【婆娑起舞】to start dancing

婀 874
ㄜ ē
1. graceful; elegant 2. a Chinese family name
【婀娜多姿】graceful; well-poised

娶 875
ㄑㄩˇ qǔ
to take a wife
【娶親 or 娶妻】(said of a man) to take a wife

姘 876
(姘) ㄆㄧㄣ pīn
to make love without a formal wedding; illicit intercourse
【姘夫】a man one cohabits with

婉 877
ㄨㄢˇ wǎn
1. amiable; genial; agreeable; pleasant 2. good-looking; beautiful
【婉謝】to decline (an invitation, a present, etc.) with great gentleness and courtesy
【婉轉】(to persuade or state something) mildly; gently; suavely—without hurting another's feelings
【婉言相勸】to persuade gently
【婉約】①(said of speech) gentle, smooth and courteous ②(style of poetry) restrained; soft; plaintive

婚 878
ㄏㄨㄣ hūn
1. to wed; to marry 2. marriage
【婚禮】a wedding (ceremony)
【婚假】a wedding leave
【婚嫁】to wed; marriage
【婚期】the date of a wedding
【婚事】marriage
【婚姻】marriage
【婚約】a marriage contract; betrothal

婢 879
ㄅㄧˋ bì
1. a maidservant; a female slave 2. (in old China) a humble term used by a girl to refer to herself

婦 880
ㄈㄨˋ fù
1. a woman; a female 2. the wife of one's son 3. a wife 4. a married woman; a matron
【婦道】①(ㄈㄨˋ ㄉㄠˋ) female virtues, especially chastity ②(ㄈㄨˋ ·ㄉㄠ) womanhood
【婦女】women; females; womenfolk
【婦女會】a women's association
【婦女節】Women's Day, on March 8
【婦產科】the department of gynecology and obstetrics
【婦人】①a woman; a female ②a married woman
【婦人之仁】womanly kindness

婪 881
ㄌㄢˊ lán
covetous; greedy; avarice

娼 882
(倡) ㄔㄤ chāng
a prostitute; a whore
【娼妓】a streetwalker; a prostitute

婊 883
ㄅㄧㄠˇ biǎo
a prostitute

婟 884
(嫵) ㄨˇ wǔ
attractive; lovely

九畫

婷 885
ㄊㄧㄥˊ tíng
pretty; attractive; graceful

媒 886
ㄇㄟˊ méi
1. a marriage go-between; a matchmaker 2. a medium
【媒體】a medium
【媒介】①a go-between ②a medium
【媒妁 or 媒人】a matchmaker

媚 887
ㄇㄟˋ mèi
1. to flatter 2. to please 3. to love 4. attractive;

fascinating; seductive 5. to coax
【媚外】to fawn on a foreign power

十畫

嫁 888 ㄐㄧㄚˋ jià
1. (said of a woman) to get married; to marry a man 2. to marry off a daughter 3. to impute (blame, a crime, etc.) to another
【嫁禍】to impute blame, a crime, punishment, etc. (to another person)
【嫁娶】marriage
【嫁妝】a bride's trousseau; a dowry

嫂 889 ㄙㄠˇ sǎo
the wife of one's elder brother
【嫂子 or 嫂嫂】a sister-in-law

媳 890 ㄒㄧˊ xí
as in 媳婦—a daughter-in-law

媽 891 ㄇㄚ mā
1. one's mother 2. a woman servant
【媽媽】mama; mother
【媽祖】Matsu, Goddess of the Sea

媾 892 ㄍㄡˋ gòu
1. to marry; to wed 2. to negotiate peace; amity 3. to couple; to copulate
【媾和】to make peace

嫉 893 ㄐㄧˊ jí
1. jealous; envious; jealousy 2. to hate; to detest
【嫉妒】jealous; envy; jealousy
【嫉恨】to hate out of jealousy
【嫉惡如仇】not to compromise with evil deeds or evil persons

嫌 894 ㄒㄧㄢˊ xián
1. to detest; to dislike 2. ill will; a grudge 3. to suspect; suspicion 4. to complain; to reject; to object
【嫌棄】to reject; to give up in disgust
【嫌隙】the suspicion born out of dislike; an old grudge
【嫌疑】suspicion; to suspect
【嫌疑犯】a suspect (of a crime, etc.)

十一畫

嫖 895 ㄆㄧㄠˊ piáo
to patronize whorehouses; to visit prostitutes; to go whoring
【嫖賭】to patronize whorehouses and gambling houses—to lead a life of debauchery

嫡 896 ㄉㄧˊ dí
1. the legal wife as opposed to a concubine 2. the sons born of the legal wife
【嫡妻】a legal wife
【嫡親】blood relatives
【嫡嗣】the eldest son born of the official wife of a man

嫣 897 ㄧㄢ yān
captivating; charming; lovely; fascinating
【嫣紅】bright red; rich crimson

嫦 898 ㄔㄤˊ cháng
【嫦娥】(Chinese legend) Chang-o, who ascended the moon after secretly eating her husband's elixir of life

嫩 899 ㄋㄣˋ nèn
1. tender; delicate 2. young; immature 3. (of color) light
【嫩芽】a tender shoot
【嫩葉】a young leaf; a tender leaf

十二畫

嬉 900 ㄒㄧ xī
to have fun; to sport; to play; to frolic
【嬉皮】hippies
【嬉皮笑臉】grinning cheekily; smiling and grimacing
【嬉鬧】to romp
【嬉戲】to frolic; to play; to sport
【嬉笑】to be laughing and playing

嫺 901 (嫻) ㄒㄧㄢˊ xián
1. refined; gracious 2. skillful; skilled
【嫺靜】quiet and refined (women)
【嫺熟】expert; adept in; skilled in
【嫺雅】polished; cultured; refined

嬋 902 ㄔㄢˊ chán
graceful; ladylike; attractive; beautiful; pretty
【嬋娟】① graceful ② the moon; moonlight

〔女部〕

嬌 903
ㄐㄧㄠ jiāo
1. tender; delicate; beautiful; lovely 2. spoiled; pampered; coddled
【嬌美】beautiful and graceful
【嬌媚】beautiful; handsome
【嬌滴滴】fascinatingly beautiful
【嬌嫩】delicate and soft; tender
【嬌妻】a beloved wife
【嬌小】dainty and little
【嬌小玲瓏】delicate and refined
【嬌羞】bashful; modest and retiring
【嬌嗔】(said of women) to get angry
【嬌生慣養】to live a sheltered life
【嬌柔】beautiful and frail
【嬌縱】to pamper
【嬌娃】a beauty

十三畫

嬡 904
ㄞˋ ài
the daughter (a complimentary term referring to the daughter of the person one is speaking to)

嬴 905
ㄧㄥˊ yíng
1. to win 2. to have a surplus

嬝 906
(嫋) ㄋㄧㄠˇ niǎo
delicate; graceful
【嬝嬝】①(said of a willow) waving gracefully ② (said of a young woman) appealingly slender and delicate

十四畫

嬰 907
ㄧㄥ yīng
an infant; a baby; a suckling
【嬰孩 or 嬰兒】a baby; an infant
【嬰兒奶粉】soft curd milk

十五畫

嬸 908
ㄕㄣˇ shěn
1. an aunt (the wife of one's father's younger brother) 2. a sister-in-law (the wife of one's husband's younger brother)

十七畫

孀 909
ㄕㄨㄤ shuāng
a widow
【孀居】to remain in widowhood; to live as a widow

孅 910
ㄒㄧㄢ xiān
slender; thin; small; fine; delicate
【孅弱】frail; weak; delicate

子部
ㄗˇ zǐ

子 911
ㄗˇ zǐ
1. a child; a son; an offspring 2. a seed; an egg 3. the first of the twelve Terrestrial Branches (地支) 4. a rank of the nobility equivalent to a viscount 5. a designation used in speaking of or to a man in former times (somewhat similar to 'mister')
【子民】the people
【子彈】a bullet
【子弟】young dependents; children
【子女】sons and daughters; children
【子宮】the womb; the uterus
【子宮癌】uterine cancer
【子句】(grammar) a clause
【子爵】a viscount
【子虛烏有】pure imagination
【子時】the period of the day from 11 p.m. to 1 a.m.
【子子孫孫】generation after generation of descendants
【子嗣】a son; a male offspring
【子孫】descendants; posterity
【子音】a consonant
【子午線】a meridian

孑 912
ㄐㄧㄝˊ jié
1. the larvae of mosquitoes 2. solitary; unaccompanied; lonely
【孑孓】the larvae of mosquitoes
【孑然一身】alone

孓 913
ㄐㄩㄝˊ jué
the larvae of mosquitoes

一畫

孔 914 ㄎㄨㄥˇ kǒng

1. a hole; an orifice; an opening; an aperture 2. very; exceedingly 3. of or pertaining to Confucius or Confucianism 4. urgent; badly 5. a Chinese family name

【孔孟】Confucius and Mencius
【孔廟】a Confucian temple
【孔夫子 or 孔子】Confucius
【孔急】urgent; urgently
【孔雀】a peacock
【孔武有力】(said of a man) very strong and brave; herculean

二畫

孕 915 ㄩㄣˋ yùn

to be pregnant; to conceive

【孕婦】a pregnant woman
【孕育】to nourish; to foster

三畫

字 916 ㄗˋ zì

1. a word; a character; a letter; a logograph 2. to betroth a girl 3. (formerly) a name or style taken at the age of 20, by which one was sometimes called

【字母】an alphabet; a letter (of an alphabet)
【字典】a dictionary; a lexicon; a thesaurus
【字體】(printing) a style of letter or character; a type
【字帖】a copybook
【字條】a brief note
【字裏行間】between the lines; the overtone (of a piece of writing)
【字號】① a mark made with letters or characters ② the name of a shop
【字畫】① the strokes in a character ② calligraphy and painting
【字彙】① vocabulary ② a glossary
【字跡】one's handwriting
【字跡工整】neat writing
【字據】a receipt; a certificate
【字紙簍兒】a wastebasket
【字首】a prefix
【字義】the definition, connotation, or meaning of a word
【字眼】a word; a character
【字尾】a suffix

存 917 ㄘㄨㄣˊ cún

1. to live; to exist; to survive; to remain 2. to keep; to deposit

【存歿】a question of remaining in existence or not
【存放】to deposit (money); to leave (something somewhere) for safekeeping
【存放處】a depository
【存檔】to place on file; to file
【存底】to keep a file copy
【存糧】to store up grain
【存根】a counterfoil; a stub
【存款】① a deposit ② to make a deposit
【存款簿】a deposit book
【存貨】remaining (still unsold) goods
【存心】intentional; on purpose
【存摺】a bankbook; a passbook
【存在】to exist; to be present
【存案】to put (a legal document, etc.) on public record; to file
【存疑】① a remaining doubt ② to leave a doubtful point unquestioned
【存有】being
【存亡】life-and-death; survival and downfall
【存亡關頭】at a most critical moment

四畫

孜 918 ㄗ zī

never weary; unwearied and diligent

【孜孜不倦】to work with diligence and without fatigue

孝 919 ㄒㄧㄠˋ xiào

filial piety; of or having to do with filial piety

【孝服】mourning dress
【孝道】the principle of filial piety
【孝悌 or 孝弟】to be a dutiful son and to be respectful to one's elder brothers
【孝敬】to show filial piety and respect for one's parents
【孝心】filial piety
【孝行】filial conduct
【孝順】to show filial obedience or devotion for (one's parents)
【孝子】① a devoted child ② a bereaved son
【孝思】the heart of filial piety

〔子部〕

五畫

孟 920 ㄇㄥˋ mèng
1. a Chinese family name 2. the eldest of children 3. rude; rough 4. of or having to do with Mencius 5. the first month of a season
【孟浪】rude; rough; rash
【孟加拉】Bengal
【孟子】Mencius

季 921 ㄐㄧˋ jì
1. a season; a quarter of a year 2. the last (month of a season) 3. the youngest (of brothers) 4. a Chinese family name
【季風】(meteorology) the monsoon
【季節】a season
【季軍】the second runner-up in a contest

孤 922 ㄍㄨ gū
1. solitary; lone; lonely; friendless; helpless; unaided 2. fatherless; orphaned 3. (said of disposition) eccentric 4. negligent in an obligation
【孤僻】(said of a person's disposition) eccentric; idiosyncratic
【孤負 or 辜負】to let down
【孤島】an isolated island
【孤單 or 孤獨】solitary; alone
【孤陋寡聞】ignorant
【孤立】isolation; isolated; unaided
【孤零零 or 孤寂】lonely; friendless
【孤苦伶仃】lonely and helpless
【孤魂】a wandering soul
【孤家寡人】① alone ② a bachelor
【孤掌難鳴】to be unable to cope with a situation or accomplish something without help
【孤兒】an orphan
【孤兒院】an orphanage

六畫

孩 923 ㄏㄞˊ hái
1. a child; an infant; a baby 2. young; small
【孩提 or 孩抱】an infant; childhood
【孩子 or 孩兒 or 孩童】a child
【孩子氣】childish; childishness

七畫

孫 924 ㄙㄨㄣ sūn
1. a grandchild; a descendant 2. a Chinese family name
【孫女】a granddaughter
【孫中山or孫逸仙or孫文】Dr. Sun Yat-sen
【孫子or孫兒】①a grandchild ②a grandson

八畫

孰 925 ㄕㄨˊ shú
1. (in literary texts) what; which 2. who; whom
【孰是孰非】Which is right and which is wrong?

九畫

孱 926 ㄔㄢˊ chán
as in 孱弱—weak; feeble; frail

孳 927 ㄗ zī
1. to bear or beget in large numbers 2. to work with sustained diligence
【孳息】①to grow ②interest (from money)
【孳生or孳衍】to grow and multiply

十一畫

孵 928 ㄈㄨ fū
1. to hatch (eggs); to incubate 2. to emerge from eggs or spawn
【孵卵】to hatch eggs; to incubate
【孵化】to emerge from eggs; to spawn

十三畫

學 929 ㄒㄩㄝˊ xué
(語音 ㄒㄧㄠˊ xiáo)
1. to learn; to study; to imitate 2. of or having to do with learning; academic
【學步】(said of a child) to learn to walk
【學派】a school (of thought)
【學費】tuition
【學分】units, credits, or semester hours
【學風】school traditions
【學府】an institute of higher learn-

ing
【學徒】①an apprentice ②a student
【學童】school children
【學年】an academic (or a school) year
【學歷】educational background
【學齡】school age
【學科】a subject; a course
【學會】① a learned society; an institute ②to succeed in learning (a skill)
【學籍】one's status as a student of a particular school
【學究】a pedagogue; a pedant
【學期】a (school) term; a semester
【學習】to learn; to study
【學校 or 學堂】a school
【學制】an educational system
【學者】a scholar; a learned person
【學長】one's senior at school
【學潮】a student strike
【學士】a holder of the bachelor's degree
【學識】erudition; learning; scholarship
【學舍】a school building
【學生 or 學子】a student; a pupil
【學生證】a student's identity card
【學生時代】school days
【學術】learning; science
【學術界】academic circles
【學說】a theory
【學人】a scholar
【學以致用】to make use of what one has learned
【學藝】① sciences and arts ② to learn a trade
【學業】schoolwork
【學業成績】scholastic attainments (or achievements)
【學有專長】to have acquired a specialty from study
【學無止境】There is no limit to knowledge.
【學位】an academic degree
【學問】learning; scholarship; erudition
【學院】① a college (in a university) ②an academy

十四畫

孺 930 ㄖㄨˊ rú
a young child; an infant
【孺子】a child; a boy

十七畫

孽 931 (孼) ㄋㄧㄝˋ niè
1. the son of a concubine 2. a monster 3. sin; evil
【孽子】① a son born of a concubine ② a sinner

十九畫

孿 932 ㄌㄩㄢˊ luán
twin
【孿生】born as twins; to bear twins

宀部 ㄇㄧㄢˊ mián

二畫

它 933 ㄊㄚ tā (讀音 ㄊㄨㄛ tuō)
it; that; this
【它們】they

宂 934 ㄖㄨㄥˇ rǒng
1. redundant; superfluous 2. disorderly
【宂長】① superfluous ② (said of writing) verbose ③ tediously long
【宂員】a supernumerary

三畫

宅 935 ㄓㄞˊ zhái (讀音 ㄓㄜˊ zhé)
a dwelling; a residence; a house
【宅第】a mansion
【宅心仁厚】a benevolent and generous nature
【宅子】a residence; a house
【宅院】a house with a courtyard

宇 936 ㄩˇ yǔ
1. a house; a roof 2. look; appearance; countenance 3. space
【宇宙】the universe

守 937 ㄕㄡˇ shǒu
1. to guard; to protect; to defend; to watch 2. to wait 3. to keep (a secret, etc.) 4. to stick to; to

maintain 5. to abide by
【守備】to be on garrison duty
【守秘密】to keep a secret
【守法】to abide by the law
【守分】to stick to what one is suited for
【守寡】to remain in widowhood
【守口如瓶】to keep one's mouth shut
【守候】to wait; to bide one's time
【守護】to guard; to protect
【守紀律】to observe the rules
【守節】① to remain a widow forever although one is still young ② to stick to principle
【守舊】sticking to old ways; conservative
【守更】to keep watch during the night
【守孝】to be in mourning for one's parent
【守信 or 守信用】to keep promises; to honor one's words
【守株待兔】stupid and unimaginative in doing things
【守成不變】holding to existing custom
【守時】punctual
【守身如玉】to keep one's integrity intact in adversity
【守則】rules; regulations
【守財奴】a miser
【守喪】to remain in mourning for one's parent
【守歲】to see the old year out and the new year in by staying up on the Lunar New Year's Eve
【守夜】to keep night watch
【守衛】① to guard ② a guard
【守望相助】(said of neighbors in a community) to help each other in guarding against enemies
【守約】to keep a promise; to honor a pledge

安 938 ㄢ ān

1. peaceful; quiet; calm; tranquil 2. to quiet; to stabilize; to pacify; to console 3. to put; to place; to arrange 4. to be content with 5. how; why 6. safe; secure; stable 7. a Chinese family name
【安步當車】① to be content to go on foot instead of riding in a vehicle ② to be content with a simple life
【安排】arrangements; to arrange
【安貧樂道】happy to lead a simple, virtuous life
【安眠藥】hypnotics; soporifics
【安非他命】amphetamine
【安分】to be law-abiding
【安分守己】content or happy to be what one is; law-abiding
【安撫】to pacify
【安定】stable; steadfast; to stabilize
【安定人心】to reassure the public
【安頓】to put in order; to help settle down
【安泰】in good health
【安內攘外】to maintain internal security and to expel foreign invasion
【安寧】peace; repose; tranquility
【安樂】comfort
【安樂死】euthanasia
【安康】in a state of peace and good health
【安好】well; safe and sound
【安靜】quiet; tranquil; still; peaceful
【安居樂業or安家樂業】to live and work in peace and content
【安琪兒】an angel
【安全】① safe; secure ② safety; security
【安全帽】a safety helmet
【安全門】an exit
【安全帶】a safety belt (or strap)
【安全島】a traffic island
【安全第一】safety first
【安全感】a sense of security
【安全設施】safety devices (or equipment, installations)
【安息】to rest
【安歇】to rest; to sleep
【安心】to have peace of mind; to be relieved
【安詳】(said of one's manner) undisturbed; composed
【安置】① to put in a proper place ② to settle (people in need of employment, refugees, etc.)
【安裝】to install (a device)
【安插】to plant; to get a position (for a person) in an organization
【安適】peaceful and comfortable
【安身】to find settled place for life
【安身立命】to enjoy peace and stability both physically and spiritually
【安睡】to sleep soundly
【安然無恙】completely uninjured; safe and sound
【安如泰山】not in the slightest danger

【安葬】 to bury (the dead); to inter
【安安靜靜】 peaceful and serene
【安安穩穩】 secure and stable
【安逸】 ease and comfort
【安危】 security and danger
【安慰】 to console; to soothe
【安穩】 ① smoothly ② peacefully
【安於】 to be content with

四畫

宋 939 ㄙㄨㄥˋ sòng
1. the Sung Dynasty (960-1279 A.D.); of, or having to do with, the Sung Dynasty 2. a state in the Warring States period 3. a Chinese family name

完 940 ㄨㄢˊ wán
1. to finish; to complete; to bring to a conclusion 2. to run out; to use up 3. whole; complete; perfect; intact
【完備】 complete with everything
【完畢】 finished; completed
【完璧歸趙】 to return something intact to its owner
【完美】 perfect
【完美主義】 perfectionism
【完滿】 (said of meetings, negotiations, etc.) satisfactory; successful
【完蛋】 (colloquial) ruined; busted
【完了】 ① finished; over ② hopeless
【完工 or 完竣】 finished or completed
【完好】 flawless; faultless; perfect
【完好無缺】 intact; undamaged
【完婚 or 完姻】 to get married
【完結】 to come to an end; to end
【完全 or 完完全全】 complete; entire
【完整】 complete; whole
【完成】 to accomplish; to complete
【完成任務】 to complete one's mission
【完善】 immaculate perfect

宏 941 ㄏㄨㄥˊ hóng
great; vast; wide; ample
【宏大】 great; grand; vast; immense
【宏都拉斯】 Honduras
【宏圖】 an ambitious plan
【宏亮】 (said of a voice) loud and clear
【宏旨】 the main theme
【宏揚】 to disseminate
【宏偉】 magnificent; grand
【宏願】 an ambition

五畫

宗 942 ㄗㄨㄥ zōng
1. an ancestor; a clan 2. a sect; a religion 3. to believe in 4. a Chinese family name
【宗廟】 the imperial ancestral temple
【宗教】 religion
【宗教信仰】 religious belief
【宗教儀式】 religious rites; ritual
【宗親】 members of the same clan
【宗旨】 a purpose; an objective
【宗師】 one whose virtue and learning command the respect of others
【宗室】 ① the imperial family ② the ancestral shrine of a large clan
【宗族】 a clan; a paternal clan

官 943 ㄍㄨㄢ guān
1. a government official 2. of, or having to do with, the government or the state 3. (biology) an organ 4. a Chinese family name
【官辦】 run or operated by the government
【官兵】 officers and men
【官派】 to be appointed by the government
【官方】 the government (as opposed to private citizens); official (information, sources, etc.)
【官俸】 the salary drawn from the government
【官府】 ①the local authorities ②a feudal official
【官邸】 an official residence
【官吏】 a government official
【官僚】 bureaucrats
【官僚政治】 officialism; bureaucracy
【官架子】 the airs of an official; bureaucratic airs
【官階】 the rank
【官腔】 a bureaucratic tone; official jargon
【官銜】 the formal title (of a government official)
【官職】 a government post or position
【官制】 the system of civil service
【官差】 ① official business ② a government messenger

宀部

【官場 or 官界】 officialdom
【官事】 ① public affairs ② a lawsuit
【官署】 a government agency
【官司】 a lawsuit
【官印】 an official seal of a government agency
【官員】 an official
【官運】 a person's opportunity of official promotion
【官運亨通】 to have a successful official career

宀部

宙 944 ㄓㄡˋ zhòu

infinite time; time without beginning or end; eternity

定 945 ㄉㄧㄥˋ dìng

1. to decide; to fix; to settle 2. definite; sure 3. stable 4. to remain

【定名】 to give a name; to christen
【定命 or 定數】 predestination
【定單】 an order (for goods)
【定奪】 to decide; to settle
【定理】 (mathematics) a theorem
【定力】 (Buddhism) strength of concentration
【定量】 fixed amount
【定論】 an accepted argument (not questioned any more)
【定律】 (science) a law
【定稿】 ① to finalize a manuscript, text, etc. ② a final version or text
【定購】 to order (goods, etc.)
【定冠詞】 definite article "the"
【定貨】 to order goods; to place an order for goods
【定婚】 to be betrothed
【定價】 ① to fix a price ② a list price
【定金 or 定錢】 down payment; earnest money
【定居】 to settle down
【定局】 an irreversible situation
【定期】 periodic; regular
【定親】 to betroth
【定情】 ①to get married ②to fall in love
【定心丸】 something capable of setting someone's mind at ease
【定型】 to finalize the design
【定時】 ① to set time ② at fixed time
【定時炸彈】 a time bomb
【定神】 ① to compose oneself ② to concentrate one's attention
【定則】 (science) a rule
【定罪】 to declare someone guilty
【定做or定製】 to be made to order; to custom-tailor
【定案】 ① to decide on a verdict ② a verdict
【定義】 a definition
【定位】 ① a location; orientation ② to position

宛 946 ㄨㄢˇ wǎn

1. as if; as though 2. crooked; roundabout 3. a Chinese family name

【宛轉】 (to persuade, explain, etc.) mildly and indirectly; tactfully
【宛如or宛若】 as if; as though; like
【宛延】 long and winding

宜 947 ㄧˊ yí

1. right; fitting; proper; good 2. should; ought to; had better 3. a matter 4. to fit; to suit; to put in order 5. a Chinese family name

【宜室宜家】 to make a harmonious and orderly home (used as a congratulatory message on wedding)
【宜人】 pleasant; agreeable; delightful

六畫

客 948 ㄎㄜˋ kè

1. a guest 2. a stranger; an alien; a foreigner 3. a customer 4. a spectator; an audience 5. foreign; strange; alien 6. an adventurer 7. a Chinese family name

【客滿】 (said of theater tickets, etc.) sold out; a full house
【客房】 a guest room
【客店 or 客館】 an inn; a hotel
【客套】 civilities
【客廳】 a parlor; a living room
【客觀】 objective
【客戶】 a client
【客機】 a passenger plane; an airliner
【客家話】 Hakka
【客氣】 polite; courteous; sticking to the proprieties
【客氣話】 polite remarks
【客棧】 an inn
【客串】 (said of an amateur actor or actress, etc.) to be a guest

performer; (said of an established actor or actress) to play unimportant roles for a promotional purpose

【客人】a guest

【客座教授】a visiting professor

【客運】passenger transportation

宣 949 ㄒㄩㄢ xuān

1. to announce; to declare 2. to propagate; to circulate 3. a Chinese family name

【宣佈 or 宣布】to announce

【宣判】to announce the verdict

【宣導】to guide (the people) by creating a better understanding

【宣讀】to read out (a declaration, an announcement, etc.) in public

【宣勞】①(ㄒㄩㄢ ㄌㄠˊ) to comfort (people in distress) by an official message ②(ㄒㄩㄢ ㄌㄠˋ) to contribute one's labor, time and energy, to a public cause

【宣告】to announce; to declare

【宣泄】① to reveal, disclose, or divulge (a secret) ② to drain (liquid)

【宣戰】to declare war

【宣稱】to claim; to assert

【宣傳】to publicize; (sales) propaganda

【宣傳品】propaganda material

【宣傳車】a propaganda car

【宣示】to make publicly known

【宣誓】to take an oath

【宣誓就職】(said of government officials) to be sworn in

【宣言】a declaration; a manifesto

【宣揚】to publicize and exalt

室 950 ㄕˋ shì

1. a room; an apartment; a home 2. wife

【室內】indoor

【室內裝璜 or 室內裝潢】interior decoration

【室內設計】interior design

【室內運動】indoor sports

【室外】outdoor (as opposed to indoor)

【室外運動】outdoor activities

【室溫or室內溫度】room temperature

宦 951 ㄏㄨㄢˋ huàn

1. a government official; the government service 2. castrated

【宦官】a eunuch 亦作「太監」

【宦海浮沉】the ups and downs in officialdom

七畫

宮 952 ㄍㄨㄥ gōng

1. a palace 2. castration

【宮殿】a palace

【宮廷】the living quarters of a monarch in his palace

【宮女】a court lady; a lady-in-waiting

【宮闕】a palace (as seen from outside)

宰 953 ㄗㄞˇ zǎi

1. to preside; to govern 2. to slaughter 3. a Chinese family name

【宰割】① to cut up (meat) ② to partition or dismember (a country) ③ to kill; to destroy

【宰相or宰執】a prime minister (in former times)

【宰殺】to slaughter; to butcher; to kill

害 954 ㄏㄞˋ hài

1. to injure; to hurt; to damage; to destroy 2. to kill 3. damage; injury; harm; detriment 4. a vital point

【害病】to get sick; to fall ill

【害怕】to be afraid of; to fear

【害羣之馬】a black sheep; a public nuisance

【害喜】pregnant

【害羞 or 害臊】shy; bashful

【害處】shortcomings; harm disadvantages

【害蟲】injurious or noxious insects

【害人】to harm or injure others

【害人精】a mischief-maker

宴 955 ㄧㄢˋ yàn

1. to entertain; to feast 2. leisurely; comfort; ease

【宴客】to entertain guests at a banquet

【宴會 or 宴席】a banquet; a feast

【宴請】to entertain (to dinner)

【宴饗】(said of the emperor) to give a great dinner

【宴爾新婚】the bliss of the newlyweds

【宴飲】to feast; to dine and wine

宵 956 ㄒㄧㄠ xiāo

night; dark; evening

【宵禁】a curfew

【宵小】thieves; evildoers

【宵衣旰食】diligent in discharging official duties
【宵夜】a snack before going to bed

宀部

家 957
ㄐㄧㄚ jiā

1. home; house; household; family; of a household; domestic 2. a specialist

【家破人亡】with one's home in ruins and family members dead or scattered
【家貧如洗】to be in extreme poverty
【家僕or家丁】a servant (in a family)
【家譜】a family pedigree
【家母】my mother
【家法】domestic discipline
【家訪or家庭訪問】a visit to the parents of schoolchildren or young workers
【家父】my father (used in a polite conversation)
【家道中落】to suffer a fall in one's family fortune
【家當】the belongings of a family
【家電用品】home appliances
【家庭】a home; a household
【家庭背景】family background
【家庭計劃】family planning—birth control
【家庭教育】home education
【家庭主婦】a housewife
【家庭生活】home life; family life
【家庭作業】homework
【家徒壁立or家徒四壁】extremely poor
【家累】a family burden
【家和萬事興】Harmony in the family is the basis for success in any undertaking.
【家伙or傢伙】(colloquial) ①a tool; a utensil; a weapon ②a fellow; a guy
【家計】a family livelihood
【家家戶戶】every family and household
【家教】① family education ② a tutor
【家境】the financial condition of a family
【家具 or 傢俱】furniture
【家眷】one's family; one's dependents
【家禽】domestic fowls; poultry
【家信 or 家書】a letter from home or addressed to a member of the family
【家鄉】one's hometown
【家學淵源】(from) a family of scholars
【家訓】family precepts
【家長】the head of a family or household
【家政】① housekeeping ② home economics
【家醜不可外揚】Don't wash your dirty linen in public.
【家產or家財or家業】family property
【家常便飯】① an ordinary plain meal (such as one normally gets at home); potluck ② routine
【家常話】an ordinary conversation
【家畜】livestock; domestic animals
【家傳秘方】a secret recipe handed down in the family
【家世】one's family background
【家事】housekeeping; housework
【家屬】one's family or dependents
【家人】the members of one's family
【家族】a family; a clan
【家務】household affairs; housework
【家喻戶曉】well-known; widely known
【家園】hometown; native heath
【家用】domestic expenses

容 958
ㄖㄨㄥˊ róng

1. a face; an expression; a countenance 2. to contain; to hold 3. to allow; to permit 4. to forgive; to pardon 5. to forbear; forbearance
【容貌】looks; a countenance; features
【容納】① to contain ② to tolerate
【容量】the capacity
【容光煥發】to have a face radiant with well-being
【容器】a container
【容許】to allow; to permit
【容身】to find living space
【容忍】to endure; to bear; to tolerate
【容易】① easy ② apt to; liable to
【容顏】a facial appearance

八畫

密 959
ㄇㄧˋ mì

1. dense; tight; thick 2. close; intimate 3. secret; confidential; hidden
【密報】to send a secret message (or report)
【密閉】airtight; hermetic
【密不透風】tightly shut; hermetically sealed

【密佈 or 密布】closely or densely spread over; (with secret agents, guards, etc.) everywhere
【密碼】a secret code
【密謀】① to plot ② a secret scheme
【密密麻麻】very dense
【密訪】① to pay a secret visit ② to make investigation by traveling incognito
【密封】to seal tightly or securely
【密度】density
【密談】to have a secret or close conversation
【密探】a secret detective; a spy
【密告】to tip off
【密函】a secret letter; a confidential letter
【密集】concentrated; crowded together
【密件】confidential or secret documents
【密切】(said of relations, contact, etc.) close or intimate
【密切注意】to pay close attention to
【密使】a secret emissary
【密室】a secret chamber
【密商】to hold private counsel (or secret talks)
【密醫】an unlicensed doctor; a quack
【密友】a close friend; an intimate
【密約】a secret engagement or appointment

宿 960 1. ㄙㄨˋ sù
1. to stay overnight; to lodge; to sojourn 2. long-harbored; long-cherished 3. of the former life; inborn; innate; destined 4. veteran; old
【宿命】predestination
【宿命論】fatalism
【宿疾】a chronic disease
【宿昔】① the past ② long-standing
【宿舍】a dormitory
【宿儒】a learned scholar
【宿醉】hangover
【宿怨】an old grudge; an old feud
【宿願】a cherished hope

宿 960 2. ㄒㄧㄡˇ xiǔ
an ancient term for a constellation; an asterism

宿 960 3. ㄒㄧㄡˋ xiù
night

寂 961 ㄐㄧˊ jí
1. the death of a Buddhist monk or nun 2. quiet; still; serene; peaceful; desolate
【寂寞】lonely; lonesome
【寂寥】lonely; deserted; desolate; still
【寂靜】quiet; still

寄 962 ㄐㄧˋ jì
1. to send; to transmit; to mail 2. to entrust; to consign; to commit; to deposit
【寄賣 or 寄售】to consign (goods, etc.) for sale
【寄放 or 寄存】to place or leave (a thing) in (another's) custody
【寄託 or 寄托】to consign or commit (one's soul to God, emotions to writing, etc.)
【寄件人】a sender
【寄居】to live temporarily (with a family, in a place, etc.)
【寄情】to give expression to one's feelings (through writing, etc.)
【寄信】to send or mail a letter
【寄生蟲】a parasite
【寄人籬下】to live in another's house
【寄宿】to lodge (at another's house)
【寄養】to send a child to another family for temporary care

寅 963 ㄧㄣˊ yín
1. the third of the Twelve Terrestrial Branches (地支) 2. a fellow officer; a colleague 3. a horary sign (for the period from 3 to 5 a.m.)
【寅支卯糧 or 寅吃卯糧】unable to make both ends meet
【寅時 or 寅刻】the period of the day from 3 a.m. to 5 a.m.

寇 964 ㄎㄡˋ kòu
1. bandits; enemies; robbers 2. to invade; to pillage; to plunder 3. a Chinese family name
【寇盜 or 寇匪】insurgents

九畫

富 965 ㄈㄨˋ fù
1. rich; wealthy; affluent; abundant; plentiful 2. a Chinese family name
【富麗堂皇】splendid; gorgeous
【富貴】wealth and high position
【富豪】a man of wealth and influ-

〔宀部〕

ence

【富家子】children of a wealthy family

【富甲天下】the richest in the world

【富強】(said of a state) wealthy and powerful

【富商】a wealthy merchant

【富庶】(said of land) plentiful and populous

【富饒】plentiful; abundant; rich

【富足】well-off; well-to-do

【富有】① to abound in; to teem with ② rich; wealthy

【富翁】a rich man

【富於】rich in (imagination, creative capacity, etc.)

【富裕】rich; wealthy; prosperous

寐 966 ㄇㄟˋ mèi

a sound sleep; a deep sleep; to doze; to sleep

寒 967 ㄏㄢˊ hán

1. cold; chilly; wintry 2. poor

【寒毛】downy hair (on human body)

【寒風】a cold wind

【寒風刺骨】The cold wind chilled one to the bone.

【寒帶】the Frigid Zone

【寒冷】cold; chilly; chilling

【寒流】① a cold current; polar currents ② a scholar of little means

【寒假】the winter vacation

【寒氣】chilly air; cold air

【寒心】afraid; fearful

【寒暄 or 寒溫】to talk about the weather (in a conversation)

【寒顫】to tremble with cold or fear

【寒舍】(a self-depreciatory term) my poor house

【寒傖】①ugly; unsightly ②shabby; disgraceful

【寒酸】① poverty ② unpresentable (dress, gifts, etc.)

寓 968 ㄩˋ yù

1. to live temporarily; to sojourn; to dwell 2. to consign

【寓所】one's residence or dwelling

【寓意】a moral (of a fable)

【寓意深刻】to be pregnant with meaning

【寓言】a fable; an allegory

十一畫

寞 969 ㄇㄛˋ mò

still; silent; quiet; lonely

察 970 ㄔㄚˊ chá

to examine; to observe; to investigate; to survey; to study; to scrutinize

【察辦】to investigate a case and determine how to handle it

【察訪】to investigate by visiting the sources of information

【察看】to observe; to watch

【察勘】to survey; to examine

【察核】to investigate a case and then decide what to do

【察覺】to be conscious of; to perceive

寧 971 ㄋㄧㄥˊ níng

1. peace; repose; serenity; tranquility 2. would rather; had rather; would sooner 3. could there be

【寧靜】quiet; tranquil; serene; placid; calm

【寧缺毋濫】It is better to leave a deficiency uncovered than to have it covered without discretion.

【寧死不屈】would rather die than submit (or surrender)

【寧爲玉碎，不爲瓦全】would rather die for justice than live in disgrace

【寧願or寧可or寧肯】would rather; would sooner

寡 972 ㄍㄨㄚˇ guǎ

1. widowed; surviving the spouse 2. lonely; alone; solitary 3. little; few; scant; rare

【寡不敵衆】to be overpowered by the enemy's larger number

【寡婦】a widow

【寡廉鮮恥】shameless; unabashed

【寡人】(the royal) we

【寡言】taciturn; not given to talk

【寡慾】having few desires; ascetic

寢 973 ㄑㄧㄣˇ qǐn

1. to sleep; to rest 2. a tomb 3. a residence 4. stop; end

【寢寐難安】a restless sleep (from worries)

【寢具】bedding

【寢室】a bedroom

寥 974 ㄌㄧㄠˊ liáo

1. as in寥寥無幾—few; not many

2. deserted; desolate; empty

實 975 ㄕ shí

1. real; true 2. practically 3. honest; faithful 4. concrete; substantial 5. fact; reality 6. fruit; seed

【實地調查】an on-the-spot investigation
【實力】strength
【實力相當】to be well-matched in strength
【實例】a living example; an example
【實況】factual conditions
【實況轉播】a live broadcast; a live telecast
【實話】the truth
【實惠】a real benefit; substantial
【實話實說】to tell the truth (without adding or withholding anything)
【實際】① actual; real ② practical; realistic ③ reality; practice
【實際情況】the actual situation
【實踐】to practice (a principle); to put in practice
【實情】the real picture or real story (of a case)
【實習】to practice what one has been taught
【實習生】a trainee
【實習醫生】an intern(e)
【實效】real effect; effect
【實現】to realize (a plan, etc.); (said of a dream, etc.) to come true
【實行】to practice (a principle)
【實值】net value; intrinsic value
【實質】essence; substance
【實至名歸】Where there is real ability, there is fame.
【實施】to put (regulations, plans, etc.) into effect; to implement
【實在 or 實實在在】① really; truly ② real; concrete ③ well-done
【實業】industry; business
【實業界】the business world or circles; industry
【實驗】① to experiment; to test ② an experiment; a test
【實驗劇場】an experimental theater
【實驗室】a laboratory
【實物】goods or produce (as opposed to money)
【實用】① practical use ② useful

寨 976 ㄓㄞˋ zhài

a stockade: 寨子 a stockaded village

十二畫

審 977 ㄕㄣˇ shěn

1. to examine; to review; to investigate 2. to know; to discern; to appreciate 3. cautious 4. really; indeed

【審判】① to try (a case or person in a law court) ② a trial
【審美觀念】esthetic sense (or notions)
【審定】to authorize (a publication, etc.)
【審訂】to examine and revise
【審理】to try; to hear
【審核】to examine and consider
【審計】① an audit ② to audit
【審計部】Ministry of Audit
【審查 or 審察】to examine; to review
【審慎】cautious; careful
【審案】to hold court trial
【審議】consideration; deliberation
【審問 or 審訊】to hold a hearing (on a legal case); to interrogate a prisoner
【審閱】to examine; to review

寫 978 ㄒㄧㄝˇ xiě

to write; to sketch; to draw; to represent

【寫稿】to write for (or contribute to) a magazine, etc.
【寫照】an image; portrayal; a description
【寫眞】to draw or paint a portrait
【寫實】realistic (as distinct from romantic)
【寫生】to draw, or paint, from nature; to sketch
【寫字】to write
【寫作】writing
【寫意】(said of painting) to make an impressionistic portrayal

寬 979 ㄎㄨㄢ kuān

1. broad; wide; spacious; vast 2. magnanimous; lenient; tolerant; liberal; forgiving; indulgent 3. to loosen; to widen 4. well-off

【寬大】lenient; magnanimous
【寬大爲懷】magnanimous; benignant; liberal; open-hearted
【寬度 or 寬窄】width; breadth
【寬廣】vast; broad; spacious; wide
【寬闊】roomy; wide; spacious
【寬厚】tolerant and generous

【寬宏大量】 magnanimous; benignant; broad-minded
【寬限】 ①to extend a time limit ② a moratorium
【寬心】 to feel at rest; to set one's mind at ease
【寬敞】 spacious; roomy
【寬恕or寬容】 to forgive; to pardon
【寬鬆】 loose and comfortable
【寬衣】 ① a loose garment ② to remove the upper coat (for relaxation)
【寬衣解帶】 to undress
【寬裕】 well-to-do; well-off; ample

十三畫

寰 980 ㄏㄨㄢˊ huán
a large domain; a vast space
【寰宇 or 寰球】the world; the earth

十六畫

寵 981 ㄔㄨㄥˇ chǒng
1. a concubine 2. to favor; to dote on; to patronize 3. favor or love
【寵壞】 to spoil (a child)
【寵幸】 to show speial favor to a lady or minister
【寵辱】 in favor or out of favor
【寵愛】 to favor or patronize
【寵兒】 a favored person; a favorite

十七畫

寶 982 (寳) ㄅㄠˇ bǎo
1. treasure 2. precious; valuable 3. respectable; honorable
【寶貝】 ①a cherished thing ②darling
【寶寶】 baby
【寶刀未老】 old but still vigorous in mind and body
【寶島】 a treasure island
【寶典】 a valuable book
【寶塔】 a pagoda
【寶貴】 valuable; precious
【寶庫】 a treasury; a treasure house
【寶劍】 a treasured sword
【寶石】 a precious stone; a gem; a jewel
【寶山空回】 to gain nothing from a rare opportunity
【寶座】 the throne
【寶物or寶藏】 a treasure; a treasury
【寶玉】 a precious stone

寸部
ㄘㄨㄣˋ cùn

寸 983 ㄘㄨㄣˋ cùn
1. a measure of length (equal to about 1/10 foot) 2. as small as an inch; small; tiny; little
【寸步不離】 to tag; to follow closely
【寸步難行】 hard to walk even an inch
【寸土必爭】 Even an inch of land has to be fought for.

三畫

寺 984 ㄙˋ sì
a temple; a mosque; a shrine; a monastery

六畫

封 985 ㄈㄥ fēng
1. a numerary adjunct for letters 2. to install as a feudal lord or a nobleman 3. to seal; to block 4. a wrapper; an envelope
【封閉】 to seal; to close completely
【封面】 the cover (of a book)
【封面女郎】 a cover girl
【封地】 a fief; a feud; a manor
【封套】 an envelope; a wrapper
【封條】 a sealing tape
【封口】 ①to seal (a letter) ②to block the entrance (to a passage) ③to heal
【封建制度】 the feudal system
【封殺】 (baseball) to shut out; force play
【封鎖】 to blockade (a place)
【封鎖新聞】 to suppress news
【封印】 (postal service) a seal

七畫

射 986 ㄕㄜˋ shè
(動詞語音 ㄕˊ shí)
(音律名 ㄧˋ yì)
(於"僕射"等 ㄧㄝˋ yè)
1. to shoot 2. to send out (light, heat, etc.) 3. archery
【射門】 (in soccer, etc.) to shoot or

kick the ball toward the goal
【射獵】hunting
【射擊】to shoot; shooting: 射擊場 a shooting range
【射箭】to shoot an arrow; archery
【射線】(physics) a ray 「target }
【射中】to hit (with a shot) the }
【射程】a range (of the projectile)
【射手】an archer; a shooter

八畫

專 987
ㄓㄨㄢ zhuān

1. to concentrate; to focus 2. to monopolize 3. to specialize 4. exclusive; special
【專賣】a monopoly
【專美】to attain distinction alone
【專門】① a specialty; a special field ② exclusively
【專門人材】the people with professional skill
【專訪】a report produced by a journalist after having paid a special visit to the person or persons concerned
【專斷】arbitrary
【專題】a special subject 「topic }
【專題報導】a report on a special }
【專題演講】a lecture on a special topic
【專欄】a special column (in a newspaper or magazine)
【專欄作家】a columnist
【專利】a monopoly; a patent
【專利品】a patent; a patent article
【專利連鎖店】a franchise chain
【專攻】to specialize in
【專科學校】a junior college
【專款】the fund designated for a specific use 「cific purpose }
【專函】a letter written for a spe- }
【專橫】dictatorial; arbitrary; despotic; tyrannical 「special use }
【專機】a plane designated for a }
【專家】a specialist; an expert
【專權】to be dictatorial
【專線】① a special railway line ② a special telephone line
【專職】① sole duty; specific duty ② full-time 「cratic }
【專制】tyrannical; despotic; auto- }
【專政】dictatorship
【專注】to concentrate one's attention on 「particular purpose }
【專車】a train or bus run for a }
【專長】a special skill; a specialty
【專程】a special trip
【專誠】with the exclusive purpose }
【專使】a special envoy 「of }
【專人】a person specially assigned }
【專才】a specialist 「for a task }
【專案】a special case (to be dealt with separately)
【專一】to concentrate one's attention on; single-minded
【專業】① a special field of study; a specialty ② a specialized trade
【專業化】specialization 「cialty }
【專業訓練】training in a spe- }
【專業知識】professional knowledge
【專業人員】the personnel in a specific field
【專有名詞】a proper noun
【專員】a specialist in the govern- }
【專用】to use exclusively 「ment }

將 988
1. ㄐㄧㄤ jiāng

1. (used with a verb expressing future action) going to; about to 2. used with a noun functioning as a direct object 3. to nourish
【將來】the future; the days to come
【將功贖罪】to atone for mistakes by meritorious service
【將計就計】to deal with an opponent by taking advantage of his scheme
【將就】to manage with something unsatisfactory 「nearly }
【將近】approximately; close to; }
【將軍】① a general or admiral ② a call to indicate a checkmate (in Chinese chess) ③ to challenge
【將信將疑】half in doubt; skeptical
【將錯就錯】to accept the consequences of a mistake and try to adapt oneself thereto

將 988
2. ㄐㄧㄤˋ jiàng

1. a general; an admiral; a military leader of high rank 2. to lead (soldiers)
【將門虎子】a capable young man from a distinguished family
【將士】officers and men
【將帥】a general 「mander }
【將才】the talent as a field com- }

〔寸部〕

〔寸部〕

尉 989 ㄨㄟˋ wèi

1. a company-grade military officer 2. (in former times) a grade of military official

【尉官】 a junior officer

九畫

尊 990 ㄗㄨㄣ zūn

1. to honor; to respect; to venerate; to revere; to esteem 2. honored; honorable; noble; esteemed; respectable

【尊卑】①seniors and juniors ②superiors and inferiors

【尊夫人】(courteously) your wife

【尊貴】noble; honorable; respectable

【尊駕】(courteously) you; your esteemed self

【尊敬】to respect; to revere; respect; reverence

【尊親】(courteously) your parents

【尊姓大名】(courteously) your name

【尊長】an elder; a senior

【尊稱】an honorific term; a title of respect

【尊師重道】to respect the teacher and his teachings

【尊嚴】dignity; honor; respectability

尋 991 1. ㄒㄩㄣˊ xún

1. a measure of length in former times (roughly equivalent to eight feet) 2. to seek; to search

【尋寶】to hunt for treasure

【尋覓】to search for; to look for

【尋訪】to look for (somebody whose whereabouts is unknown)

【尋短見】to end one's own life; to commit suicide

【尋樂or尋歡作樂】to seek amusement

【尋根問底or尋根究底】to probe deeply

【尋開心】(dialect) to make fun of; to joke

【尋花問柳】①to enjoy natural beauty in springtime ②to seek carnal pleasure

【尋找】to look for; to seek for

【尋常】usual; ordinary; common

【尋人啓事】a notice in a missing person column

【尋幽探勝】to visit scenic spots

尋 991 2. ㄒㄧㄣˊ xín

to beg; to entreat

十一畫

對 992 ㄉㄨㄟˋ duì

1. right; correct; proper 2. parallel; opposing 3. a pair; a couple 4. to check; ascertain 5. to; as to; with regard to 6. to be directed at

【對白】dialogue

【對保】to confirm or verify a guaranty

【對半】a half; one half

【對比】contrast; correlation

【對簿公庭】to face or confront each other in court at a trial

【對不起 or 對不住】①to let a person down ②I am sorry.

【對罵】to call each other names

【對面】on the opposite side

【對方】the other side (or party)

【對付】to deal with; to cope with

【對答】to answer questions

【對答如流】to give answers fluently

【對待】to treat (a person kindly, cruelly, etc.)

【對等】equal

【對調】to exchange positions

【對頭】an opponent; an adversary

【對內】for domestic or internal (consumption, use, etc.)

【對牛彈琴】to speak to someone about something completely incomprehensible to him

【對壘】to confront each other

【對立】to be opposed to each other

【對流】(physics) convection

【對聯】a Chinese couplet

【對路】①to satisfy the need ②to be to one's liking; to suit one

【對開】folio

【對口】to speak or sing alternately

【對抗】to be opposed to each other

【對抗賽】a duel meet

【對號】①to check the number ②to fit; to tally ③a check mark

【對話】a dialogue; a conversation

【對換】to exchange; to barter; to swap

【對勁or對勁兒】in the right or agreeable condition

【對獎】to check the results of a lottery or raffle to see if one holds the winning ticket

【對講機】an interphone; an intercom

【對象】the object (of an action); the subject (of consideration)
【對質】to face each other and exchange questions (in order to find out the truth)
【對峙】to face (or confront) each other
【對折】a 50% discount
【對照】to compare; to contrast
【對照表】a contrastive or comparative table
【對證】to establish evidence through personal confrontation or signed statement
【對症下藥】(figuratively) to take the right remedial steps to correct a shortcoming
【對準】① to adjust (a machine part needing adjustment) to the right or proper position ② to aim at
【對稱】symmetry; symmetrical
【對唱】a musical dialogue in antiphonal style; antiphonal singing
【對手】an opponent; a match
【對策】a measure (to deal with a problem, etc.); a countermeasure
【對偶】① to match; to pair ② verbal parallelism (in poetry)
【對岸】the opposite shore
【對應】corresponding; homologous
【對味兒】① to one's taste ② to seem all right
【對外】for foreign or overseas (consumption, use, etc.)
【對外貿易】foreign trade
【對於】to; as to; with regard to

十三畫

993
導 ㄉㄠˋ dào
(語音 ㄉㄠˇ dǎo)

to guide; to lead; to instruct; to conduct; to direct
【導體】an electric conductor
【導論 or 導言】an introduction
【導航】to navigate; navigation
【導火線】① a fuse (for setting off explosives) ② the direct cause (of a development or event)
【導致】to lead to; to cause something to happen
【導師】① a spiritual guide ② a tutor
【導遊】a tourist guide
【導演】the director

小部
ㄒㄧㄠˇ xiǎo

994
小 ㄒㄧㄠˇ xiǎo

1. small; little; tiny 2. minor 3. young; junior 4. humble; mean 5. slight; unimportant; trivial
【小白臉】a handsome young man with effeminate features
【小班】① the lowest of the three grades of kindergarten children ② a first-rate brothel (in Peking)
【小本經營】(business) to run or operate with a small capital
【小癟三】(dialect) a bum; a trash
【小標題】a subheading; a subhead
【小便 or 小解】① to urinate; to make water ② urine; urination
【小部份 or 小部分】a small part; the minority
【小不點兒】a very small or tiny thing or person
【小便宜】a small advantage
【小品文】an essay
【小舖子 or 小鋪子】a small store
【小買賣 or 小生意】small business
【小麥】wheat
【小妹】① a little sister ② a little girl ③ a young female servant
【小貓】a kitten
【小米】millet
【小費】a tip (given to a waiter, porter, etc.)
【小販】stall holders; peddlers
【小腹】the lower abdomen
【小刀】① a small sword ② a pocket knife
【小島】an islet
【小道消息】hearsay; the grapevine
【小旦】(Chinese opera) a female role
【小弟】① a little brother ② a little boy ③ a young male servant
【小調】folk songs; ballads
【小店】① an inn; a lodging house ② a small store ③ my or our store (a self-depreciatory term)
【小電影】(slang) a porno film
【小動作】petty action; little tricks
【小偷】a thief; a burglar
【小題大做】to make much of a trifle; a storm in a teacup
【小提琴】violin

〔小部〕

【小艇】a small boat; a skiff
【小腿】the calf (of the leg)
【小鳥依人】(said of a child or young girl) lovely and pliant like a little bird
【小妞兒】a small girl; a young girl
【小年夜】the night before Lunar New Year's Eve
【小女】(a self-depreciatory term) my daughter
【小喇叭】a trumpet
【小老婆】a concubine
【小老頭兒】a man who ages prematurely
【小嘍囉】lackeys; underlings
【小兩口子】a young couple
【小路】a path; a trail
【小個子】a little chap; a small fellow
【小狗】a young dog; a puppy
【小姑】one's husband's younger sister
【小姑獨處】to remain a spinster
【小姑娘】a missy; a young girl
【小過】①a minor mistake ②a minor demerit
【小鬼】① the spirits serving the ruler of the lower world ②an imp; a mischievous child
【小開】a businessman's son
【小考】a quiz or test conducted for students by the teacher
【小看】to think little of; to slight
【小康】①(said of a family) well-to-do ②(said of a nation) fairly prosperous and secure
【小河】a rivulet
【小孩】a child
【小號】small size (as distinct from medium and large sizes)
【小戶人家】a poor, humble family
【小花樣】a little stunt
【小夥子 or 小夥兒】a young fellow
【小鷄】a chick
【小家碧玉】a daughter of a humble family
【小家庭】a small family
【小姐】a young (unmarried) lady
【小舅子】a brother-in-law (one's wife's younger brother)
【小器or小氣】① narrow-minded② niggardly
【小氣鬼】a niggard
【小巧玲瓏】① (said of a woman) petite ②(said of a decorative item) small and exquisite
【小曲 or 小曲兒】a ditty
【小犬】① (a self-depreciatory term) my son ②a puppy
【小寫】a lowercase letter (of the Roman alphabet)
【小心】careful; cautious
【小心翼翼】very timidly; very gingerly
【小心眼兒】narrow-minded
【小型】small-sized; miniature
【小學】a primary school; an elementary school
【小學生】a (primary school) pupil
【小指 or 小拇指】the little finger
【小住】to sojourn
【小酌or小飲】a little drink or a few drinks (of some alcoholic beverage)
【小吃】a snack
【小吃館】a small restaurant; an eatery
【小丑】a clown
【小醜跳梁】petty thieves going on the rampage
【小產】a miscarriage
【小腸】the small intestine
【小時】an hour
【小時了了】very intelligent when young
【小時候】as a child; in childhood
【小事】a trifle; a trivial matter
【小市民】the urban petty bourgeois
【小嬸】a sister-in-law
【小聲】to lower one's voice; to speak low
【小生】the young man's role (especially in Chinese opera)
【小叔】a brother-in-law
【小樹】a sapling
【小數】a decimal fraction; a decimal
【小數點】the decimal point
【小說】a novel; fiction: 小說家 a novelist
【小人】a mean person
【小子】a young fellow (usually with slight contempt)
【小組】a group formed for a specific purpose
【小組討論】a group discussion
【小册子】a pamphlet or brochure
【小菜】plain dishes (as distinct from expensive courses)
【小聰明】clever or smart in a small way
【小廝】a servant (especially a mean one); a subaltern; an underling
【小兒痲痺症】poliomyelitis; polio
【小兒科】① pediatrics ② (slang) parsimonious
【小耳朵】①(slang) DBS (Direct Broadcasting Satellite) ②a spy

【小二】(formerly) a waiter at a tavern
【小姨子】a sister-in-law (one's wife's younger sister)
【小意思】① a trifle; a triviality ② a small token of regard (such as a gift)
【小鴨】a duckling
【小丫頭】a little girl (expressing contempt or endearment)
【小夜曲】(music) a serenade
【小羊】a lamb
【小娃娃】a small child
【小我】the individual; the ego; the self
【小玩藝兒】a small toy or plaything

一畫

少 995
1. ㄕㄠˇ shǎo
1. small or little (in number, quantity, or duration) 2. missing; lost 3. to stop; to quit
【少不了】① indispensable; cannot do without ② unlikely to be lost
【少來這一套】Let's have no more of this.
【少量】a small amount (or quantity); a little; a few
【少管閒事】Mind your own business.
【少見】seldom seen; unique; rare
【少見多怪】to wonder much because one has seen little
【少頃】a little while; a short while; a short time
【少許】a little bit; a little; a sprinkling of
【少數】①a few; a small number (of) ② minority
【少有】rare; scarce

少 995
2. ㄕㄠˋ shào
young; youthful; junior; juvenile
【少不更事】young and inexperienced
【少婦】a young woman
【少奶奶】the wife of the young lord or master
【少年】①a boy; a juvenile; a youth ② young
【少年犯罪】juvenile delinquency
【少年老成】young but competent
【少女】a young girl; a damsel
【少將】major general (in the army, air force and marine corps); rear admiral (in the navy)
【少校】major (in the army, air force and marine corps); lieutenant commander (in the navy)
【少壯】young and energetic
【少壯派】the stalwarts
【少爺】a young master (of a rich family); a young lord
【少尉】second lieutenant (in the army, air force or marine corps); ensign (in the navy)

三畫

尖 996
ㄐㄧㄢ jiān
sharp; acute; pointed; keen
【尖兵】(military) a point
【尖端科學】the frontiers of science
【尖銳】① sharp-pointed ② sharp; keen ③shrill; piercing ④intense; acute
【尖酸】(said of words, speech, etc.) sarcastic; petty; mean
【尖酸刻薄】unsympathetic; merciless; pitiless

五畫

尙 997
ㄕㄤˋ shàng
1. yet; still 2. to uphold; to honor; to esteem
【尙可】① passable; acceptable ② still permissible; still possible
【尙佳】passable; not too bad
【尙祈or尙希】I hope.... 或 I pray....
【尙且】① yet; still ② even
【尙有可爲】still retrievable

尢部
ㄨㄤ wāng

一畫

尤 998
ㄧㄡˊ yóu
1. to feel bitter against; to reproach; to blame 2. a mistake; an error 3. especially or particularly 4. special or outstanding 5. a Chinese family name
【尤其】above all; in particular; particularly; especially
【尤甚】① more than; worse than ② especially so; particularly so
【尤物】①an uncommon person ② a woman of extraordinary beauty

九畫

就 999 ㄐㄧㄡˋ jiù

1.to receive 2.to undergo 3.to assume 4.to follow 5.to come or go to 6.to suit; to fit 7.forthwith; right away 8.exactly; precisely 9.namely 10.even if

【就範】to give up; to be subdued; to yield

【就地】on the spot

【就地取材】①to acquire necessary material locally ②to employ local talents

【就地正法】to execute an offender summarily right on the spot

【就近】at the nearest convenient place

【就寢】to go to bed

【就緒】to be complete; to be all set; ready

【就學】to go to school

【就職】to be sworn in; to be inaugurated

【就是】①exactly ②namely; that is ③even if; even though ④only; but

【就事論事】to confine the discussion to the matter at issue

【就任】to take office

【就座】to take one's seat

【就此】then; thereupon; thereafter

【就算】(colloquial) even though; even if; granted that

【就醫】to receive or undergo medical treatment

【就義】to become a martyr to a worthy cause or principle

【就業】to get employment; to get a job

【就業輔導】placement or appointment service

【就要】to be about to; to be going to

十四畫

尷 1000 ㄍㄢ gān

embarrassed; ill at ease

【尷尬】embarrassing; embarrassed

尸部 ㄕ shī

尸 1001 ㄕ shī

1.a corpse 2.to preside; to direct

【尸位素餐】to neglect the duties of an office while taking the pay

一畫

尺 1002 1. ㄔˇ chǐ

1.a unit in Chinese linear measurement, equivalent to $\frac{1}{3}$ meter 2.a ruler; a rule

【尺碼】①dimensions (of an object) ②measure; size

【尺牘or尺翰】letters; correspondence

【尺度】measure; a scale

【尺寸】a small quantity

尺 1002 2. ㄔˊ chí

as in 尺寸—measurements; dimensions; size

二畫

尼 1003 ㄋㄧˊ ní

as in 尼姑—a nun

【尼泊爾】Nepal

【尼羅河】the Nile River; the Nile

【尼龍】(textile) nylon

【尼古丁】nicotine

【尼加拉大瀑布】Niagara Falls

【尼庵 or 尼姑庵】a nunnery

四畫

尾 1004 ㄨㄟˇ wěi

1.the tail; the rear; the stern (of a ship); rear; back 2.last; final 3.remaining 4.a Chinese family name

【尾巴】a tail

【尾大不掉】to have subordinates too powerful to control

【尾追】to chase after

【尾聲】①a coda ②an epilog ③an end

【尾數】①an odd sum; odd change ②the balance of an account

【尾隨】to follow close behind; to tail

尿 1005 ㄋㄧㄠˋ niào

1.urine 2.to urinate

【尿布】a diaper; a napkin; a nappy

【尿盆】a chamber pot; a urinal

【尿道】 a urethra; a urinary canal
【尿壺】 a bedpan; a chamber pot
【尿牀】(said of a child) to wet the bed

局 1006
ㄐㄩ jú
1. an office; a bureau 2. a situation; a state of affairs 3. an inning 4. a game
【局部】 having to do only with a part; partial; local
【局面or局勢】 an aspect; a situation
【局內人】 an insider
【局限】 to limit; to confine
【局促】 ① narrow-minded ② nervous; ill at ease ③ narrow; cramped
【局外人】 an outsider

屁 1007
ㄆㄧˋ pì
1. a fart 2. the hip
【屁股】 the hip; the buttocks; the rump; the bottom
【屁滾尿流】to be frightened out of one's wits
【屁話】 Baloney!

五畫

居 1008
ㄐㄩ jū
1. to dwell; to reside; to inhabit; to occupy 2. an abode; a dwelling 3. to stay put; to be at a standstill
【居民】 residents or inhabitants
【居多】 to be the majority; mostly
【居留權】 the right of permanent residence (in a foreign country)
【居高臨下】①to overlook ②to enjoy a strategic advantage by holding a high ground overlooking the enemy position
【居功】 to take credit (for a success, achievement, etc.)
【居家】 to lead one's life at home
【居心】 to harbor (evil) intentions
【居心叵測】 There is no way of telling his (or her) real intentions.
【居住】 to dwell; to inhabit; to live
【居中】 situated in the middle
【居中調停 or 居中斡旋】 to mediate (between two quarreling parties)
【居士】 ①a retired scholar ②a secular Buddhist devotee
【居首】 to be at the head
【居然】 incredibly; to my surprise
【居所】a residence (usually a temporary one)

屆 1009
ㄐㄧㄝˋ jiè
a numerary adjunct for periodic terms or events
【屆滿】 (said of a term) to expire
【屆期】(said of an appointed time) to arrive
【屆時】 at the appointed time

屈 1010
ㄑㄩ qū
1. to bend; to flex; to bow; to crook 2. to humiliate; to humble 3. wrong; injustice 4. in the wrong 5. to be in an inferior or uncomfortable position 6. a Chinese family name
【屈服】to succumb, yield, or submit to (power, a threat, etc.); to give in
【屈打成招】 to confess under torture to a crime one hasn't committed
【屈就】 to accept a job too humble for one's position or ability
【屈膝】 to kneel down
【屈指可數】 can be counted on one's fingers—very few
【屈指一算】 to count on one's fingers
【屈辱】 humiliation; disgrace
【屈從】 to submit to; to yield to

六畫

屋 1011
ㄨ wū
a house; a room; a shelter
【屋頂】 a roof
【屋脊】 the ridge of a roof
【屋主】 the owner of a house
【屋簷】 the eaves

屍 1012
ㄕ shī
a corpse; a carcass
【屍體or屍首or屍身】 a corpse; remains
【屍骨】 the skeleton of a corpse

屎 1013
ㄕˇ shǐ
excrement

七畫

展 1014
ㄓㄢˇ zhǎn

1. to open 2. to stretch; to extend 3. to unfold; to unroll 4. to expand; to dilate 5. to prolong 6. to visit

尸部

【展覽】 to exhibit; to display
【展覽會】 an exhibition or exposition
【展開】 ①to spread out; to unfold ② to start (an activity, task, etc.)
【展現】to present before one's eyes; to develop
【展轉】① to turn round and round ② indirectly
【展翅】 to spread the wings; to fly
【展示】 to show; to display; to exhibit
【展示會】 an exhibition; a trade show
【展望】 the prospects of an undertaking

屑 1015 ㄒㄧㄝ xiè
1. chips; crumbs; bits; odds and ends; trifles 2. to care; to mind

八畫

屏 1016 1. ㄆㄧㄥ píng
1. a shield; a screen 2. to shield; to guard
【屏風 or 屏幕】 a screen
【屏東】 Pingtung county in Taiwan
【屏障】① a barrier② to shield; to guard

屏 1016 2. ㄅㄧㄥ bǐng
to reject; to discard; to dismiss; to get rid of; to abandon
【屏絕】 to stop having contact or intercourse with
【屏氣 or 屏息】to hold one's breath
【屏棄】 to discard; to throw away
【屏斥】 to reproach; to rebuke
【屏除】 to get rid of; to banish

屜 1017 (屉) ㄊㄧˋ tì
a drawer

九畫

屠 1018 ㄊㄨˊ tú
to slaughter; to butcher; to massacre
【屠夫】 a butcher
【屠刀】 a butcher's knife
【屠殺 or 屠戮】 to massacre
【屠宰】 to slaughter (livestock)
【屠宰場】 a slaughterhouse; an abattoir

十一畫

屢 1019 ㄌㄩˇ lǚ
frequently; repeatedly; again and again
【屢屢】 frequently; again and again
【屢見不鮮】 not rare; nothing new
【屢試不爽】to have the same result or reaction (usually positive result or reaction) after each try
【屢次】 repeatedly; frequently

十二畫

層 1020 ㄘㄥˊ céng
a layer; a stratum; a story (of a building)
【層巒疊嶂】 peaks rising one upon another
【層出不窮】 to happen again and again
【層次】 ①order (of importance or priority) ②the arrangement of ideas (in writing or speech)

履 1021 ㄌㄩˇ lǚ
1. shoes 2. to step on; to tread on; to follow
【履歷】 one's personal history
【履歷表】 a biographic sketch
【履險如夷】 to go through danger as if there were no danger at all
【履新 or 履任】 to take or assume one's new office or post
【履行】 to fulfill or carry out
【履約】 to keep or fulfill an agreement

十八畫

屬 1022 1. ㄕㄨˇ shǔ
1. a category; a class; a kind 2. to belong to; to be subordinate to
【屬地】 a territory; a colony
【屬下】 one's subordinate
【屬實】 true
【屬於】 to belong to

屬 1022 2. ㄓㄨˇ zhǔ
1. to compose (a piece of writing) 2. to instruct
【屬目】 to gaze; to look at eagerly
【屬託】to ask or instruct somebody to do something
【屬意】 to have a preference for

屮 部
ㄔㄜˋ chè

一畫

屯 1023 ㄊㄨㄣˊ tún
1. to station (an army) 2. to stockpile
【屯糧】 to hoard up or stockpile grains
【屯積】 to hoard up
【屯聚】 to assemble; to gather together
【屯紮】 to encamp

山 部
ㄕㄢ shān

山 1024 ㄕㄢ shān
a mountain; a hill
【山撥鼠】 a marmot
【山崩】 a landslide; a landslip
【山坡】 a mountainside; a hillside
【山脈】 a mountain range; mountains
【山貓】 a wildcat; a lynx
【山盟海誓】 a vow between lovers that their mutual love will last as long as the mountain and the sea
【山明水秀or山清水秀】 The mountains are bright and the waters are fair. (descriptive of scenic beauty)
【山峯】 a mountaintop
【山地】 a mountainous region
【山巔 or 山頂】 a mountaintop; a hilltop
【山東】 Shantung Province
【山洞】 a cave; a tunnel; a grotto
【山林】 ① a mountain forest ② the place where a hermit lives
【山陵】① a plateau ② an imperial tomb
【山路】 a mountain path
【山麓】 the foot of a mountain
【山巒】the chain of mountains with pointed peaks
【山歌】 a mountaineers' song
【山高水長】 (descriptive of the virtues of a great man) to be like lofty mountains and mighty streams
【山溝】 a gully; a ravine; a valley
【山岡】 a ridge; a mountain ridge
【山谷】 a dale; a ravine; a gorge
【山河】 mountains and rivers—(figuratively) the territory of a nation
【山海關】 Shanhai Pass
【山洪】 mountain torrents
【山洪暴發】 A flood is unleashed from the mountains all of a sudden.
【山雞】 a pheasant
【山脊】 a mountain ridge; a ridge
【山脚】 the foot of a mountain
【山澗】 mountain creeks
【山丘】 mountains and hills
【山區】 a mountain area
【山泉】 a mountain spring
【山窮水盡】in a desperate situation
【山西】 Shansi Province
【山楂】 a hawthorn
【山寨】 a mountain fortress
【山珍海味】 a sumptuous repast
【山莊】 a country house, or villa, built in the mountains
【山中】 in the mountains
【山川】 mountains and rivers
【山水】 ① mountains and rivers ② natural scenery; a landscape
【山水畫】 a landscape painting
【山人】 a hermit; a recluse
【山隘】 a mountain pass
【山野】 mountain villages and the remote wilderness
【山崖】 a cliff
【山腰or山腹】 the mid-slope of a mountain
【山羊】 a goat
【山岳 or 山嶽】 mountains

三畫

屹 1025 ㄧˋ yì
to rise high; to stand erect
【屹立】 to stand erect; to stand magnificent (like a mountain)
【屹然】 firm and erect (like a mountain)

四畫

岔 1026 ㄔㄚˋ chà
1. to branch; to fork 2. a fork; a branching point
【岔道 or 岔路】 a diverging road
【岔開】 ① to branch off ② to change (the subject of conversa-

〔山部〕

tion) ③ to stagger
【岔口】a fork (in a road)
【岔子or岔兒】a trouble; an accident

岌 1027 ㄐㄧˊ jí
1. (said of a peak) rising high above others 2. perilous; hazardous
【岌岌可危】in a very critical situation

五畫

岡 1028 (崗) ㄍㄤ gāng (又讀 ㄍㄤˇ gǎng)
the ridge (of a hill or mountain)
【岡陵】a mound

岬 1029 ㄐㄧㄚˇ jiǎ
a cape; a promontory; a headland; a point
【岬角】a cape; a promontory

岳 1030 ㄩㄝˋ yuè
1. a great mountain; a high mountain 2. the parents of one's wife
【岳母】one's mother-in-law
【岳父 or 岳丈】one's father-in-law

岸 1031 ㄢˋ àn
1. a shore; a bank; a beach; a coast 2. majestic 3. proud
【岸然】a solemn and dignified look

岩 1032 ㄧㄢˊ yán
1. a large rock 2. a mountain
【岩壁】①(geology) a dyke ②a cliff
【岩洞 or 岩穴】a cavern; a grotto
【岩漿】(geology) magma; lava
【岩石】a rock; a crag
【岩層】a rock stratum; a rock formation
【岩岸】(geography) a rocky coast
【岩鹽】rock salt

七畫

峭 1033 ㄑㄧㄠˋ qiào
1. steep; precipitous 2. harsh; unkind; sharp; severe
【峭拔】① high and steep ②(said of penmanship or calligraphic style) vigorous
【峭壁】a precipice; a cliff
【峭直】stern; strict

峯 1034 ㄈㄥ fēng
1. a peak; a summit 2. a hump
【峯巒】peaks and ridges

島 1035 ㄉㄠˇ dǎo
an island; an isle
【島民】an islander
【島國】an island nation
【島嶼】islands; islets and islands

峻 1036 ㄐㄩㄣˋ jùn
1. high; lofty 2. steep 3. severe; harsh; rigorous
【峻嶺】a lofty range (of mountains)
【峻峭】① precipitous ② strict; severe
【峻刑】severe punishment or penalty

峽 1037 ㄒㄧㄚˊ xiá
1. a gorge 2. an isthmus 3. straits
【峽谷】(geography) a dale; a gorge
【峽灣】(geography) a fjord

八畫

崇 1038 ㄔㄨㄥˊ chóng
1. to honor; to respect; to revere; to adore; to worship 2. high; lofty; noble; dignified; exalted
【崇拜】to worship; to idolize; to adore
【崇高】lofty; sublime; high
【崇敬】to honor; to revere
【崇山峻嶺】lofty and precipitous peaks
【崇尚】①to uphold; to advocate ②fashion; a trend
【崇洋】to admire everything of foreign (especially western) origin

崎 1039 1. ㄑㄧ qī
rugged; uneven; rough
【崎嶇】(said of terrain) uneven; rough; rugged

崎 1039 2. ㄑㄧˊ qí
the banks of a winding river

崔 1040 ㄘㄨㄟ cuī
1. a Chinese family name 2. high and steep

崖 1041 ㄧㄞˊ yái
1. a cliff; a precipice 2. the brink; the verge 3. precipitous;

project—(figuratively) a job or task
【工程師】 an engineer
【工時】 a man-hour
【工商界】 the industrial and business circles
【工商業】 industry and commerce
【工人】 a laborer; a workman
【工人階級】 the working class; labor class
【工資】 wages
【工作】 ① to work ② one's job or duty
【工作天】 a man-day
【工作人員】 workers
【工蟻】 a worker (ant)
【工藝】 technology; a craft
【工藝品】 handicrafts; handmade products
【工業】 industry; industrial
【工業革命】 Industrial Revolution
【工業國家】 industrial nations or powers
【工業化】 industrialization
【工業區】 an industrial park
【工業學校】 technical schools
【工業用水】 industrial water
【工友】 an office boy; an office errand man
【工於心計】 scheming; crafty
【工欲善其事，必先利其器】 Good tools are prerequisite to the successful execution of a job.

二畫

左 1065 ㄗㄨㄛˇ zuǒ

1. the left side 2. the east side 3. improper 4. supporting (documents, etc.); to assist 5. to be demoted; to descend 6. inconvenience 7. erroneous; mistaken 8. unduly stubborn 9. to disregard

【左臂】 the left arm
【左邊】 the left side; the left-hand side
【左派】 ① a radical; a leftist ② a leftist faction
【左撇子】 a left-handed person; a southpaw; a portsider
【左方】 on the left; to the left
【左鄰右舍】 neighbors
【左輪槍】 a revolver; a six-shooter
【左顧右盼】 inattentive
【左傾】 left-leaning
【左支右絀】 not have enough money to cover the expenses
【左轉】 to turn left
【左手】 the left hand
【左側】 on the left side
【左思右想】 to think over and over; to ponder
【左翼】 ① (politics) the left wing or leftist ②(ball games) the left wing ③(military operations) the left flank
【左右】 ①left and right—nearby; at hand ② servants; aides ③ to sway
【左右逢源】 to get help from all sides
【左右開弓】 to slap someone's face with both hands
【左右手】 ①left and right hands ②top aides
【左右爲難】 to be in a dilemma

巧 1066 ㄑㄧㄠˇ qiǎo

1. clever; witty 2. ingenious; artful 3. a clever feat; a stunt 4. pretty; cute 5. coincidence; coincidental

【巧辯】 an ingenious argument
【巧妙】 ingenuity; ingenious; skillful
【巧得很】 quite by coincidence
【巧奪天工】 ingenuity that rivals the work of God
【巧立名目】 to fabricate various excuses
【巧克力糖】 chocolate
【巧合】 a coincidence
【巧取豪奪】 to rob others by hook or by crook
【巧手】 a skillful person; a dab
【巧遇】 a chance encounter

巨 1067 (鉅) ㄐㄩˋ jù

1. great; big 2. very

【巨擘】 ① the thumb ② the foremost figure (in a field)
【巨富】 a multimillionaire
【巨大】 giant (size); mammoth
【巨頭】 a national leader; a big chief
【巨流】 a mighty current
【巨款】 a huge sum of money
【巨細靡遺】 not to leave out any detail
【巨星】 ① a giant star ② a superstar
【巨型】 a large model (of cars, etc.)
【巨著】 a great book; a monumental literary work
【巨人】 a giant
【巨子】 ① a business tycoon ② a master; a maestro
【巨額】 a great deal of
【巨毋霸or巨無霸】 (figuratively) a giant

〔工部〕

〔己部〕

四畫

巫 1068 ㄨ wū (語音 ㄨ wǔ)
1. a wizard or witch 2. witchcraft; sorcery
【巫婆】a witch
【巫師】a sorcerer; a wizard
【巫山雲雨】a rendezvous between two lovers—coitus
【巫術】black magic; witchery; sorcery
【巫醫】a witch doctor

七畫

差 1069 1. ㄔㄚ chā
1. errors; mistakes 2. difference; discrepancy 3. (mathematics) difference
【差別】discrepancy; distinction
【差價】price differences
【差距】gap; disparity; difference
【差強人意】barely satisfactory
【差錯】① errors; mistakes ② accidents
【差額】the difference between two amounts or figures
【差以毫釐，謬以千里】A slight error in the beginning results in a big mistake in the end.
【差異】① discrepancy; difference ② to differ

差 1069 2. ㄔㄚ chā
1. to differ 2. wrong 3. to want; to fall short of 4. not up to standard
【差不多】① almost the same ② almost; nearly ③ just about enough
【差點兒】① almost; nearly ② nearly the same ③ not good enough
【差勁】disappointing; poor (work, etc.)

差 1069 3. ㄔㄞ chāi
1. a messenger; an errand man 2. to dispatch; to send (a person) 3. one's duty or job 4. an errand
【差遣or差使】to dispatch or send (a person on an errand, etc.)
【差事】a job
【差人or差役】an official messenger

差 1069 4. ㄘ cī
uneven; irregular

己部 ㄐㄧˇ jǐ

己 1070 ㄐㄧˇ jǐ
1. self; one's own; oneself 2. the sixth of the Ten Celestial Stems (天干)
【己任】one's duty or obligation
【己所不欲，勿施於人】Do not do to others what you don't want to be done to you.

已 1071 ㄧˇ yǐ
1. to cease 2. to come to an end; to finish 3. already 4. used to indicate the past 5. excessive; very; much 6. a final particle to add emphasis
【已故】the deceased; the late...
【已開發國家】a developed country
【已經】already
【已去】already gone
【已然】to be already so
【已死】already dead
【已往】before; in the past

巳 1072 ㄙˋ sì
1. the sixth of the Twelve Terrestrial Branches (地支) 2. 9 to 11 a.m.
【巳時 or 巳牌】the period of the day from 9 a.m. to 11 a.m.

一畫

巴 1073 ㄅㄚ bā
1. name of an ancient state which occupied today's eastern Szechwan 2. a crust formed as a result of heat or dryness 3. to expect; to hope for anxiously 4. used with parts of human body (such as hands, cheeks, chin, etc.) 5. a final particle implying closeness or adhesion 6. to be close to 7. (physics) a bar
【巴不得】can't wait to...; would that
【巴拿馬運河】the Panama Canal
【巴勒斯坦】Palestine
【巴黎】Paris
【巴結】①to curry favor; to toady;

to flatter ② to exert oneself for advancement
【巴西】Brazil
【巴掌】①the palm of the hand ② a slap
【巴士】a bus
【巴望】to hope for anxiously

六畫

巷 1074
ㄒㄧㄤˋ xiàng
as in 巷道 or 巷子—a lane; an alley
【巷口】an entrance to a lane
【巷議】local rumors or gossips

巾 部
ㄐㄧㄣ jīn

巾 1075
ㄐㄧㄣ jīn
1.a napkin or towel 2.a headgear
【巾帕】①a napkin or kerchief ② a headwrapper
【巾幗英雄】a heroine

二畫

市 1076
ㄕˋ shì
1.a market (place) 2.a city 3.to buy or sell
【市面】①market conditions ② the sights and splendors in big cities
【市民】citizens
【市內】in the city
【市立】municipal
【市公所】a city or town office
【市儈】① a broker ② a crafty businessman
【市集 or 市場】a market (place)
【市價】market prices; the current price (of a commodity)
【市郊】suburbia
【市井之徒】vulgar people who place money before anything else in life
【市井無賴】the scoundrels of the marketplace
【市區】①the area within the city limits ②the downtown area
【市鎮】small towns; towns
【市長】the mayor of a city
【市政】municipal administration
【市政府】a city government
【市場調查】a market survey
【市容】the appearance of a city
【市議會】a city council

布 1077
ㄅㄨˋ bù
1. cloth; textiles 2. to declare, announce or proclaim 3. to display; to distribute or disseminate; to spread out
【布帛】(collectively) cloth or textiles
【布匹 or 布疋】piece goods; dry goods
【布防】to organize the defense
【布袋】a calico sack (for grains, etc.)
【布道】(religion) to evangelize
【布店】a drapery store
【布丁】a pudding
【布雷】to lay mines; to mine
【布告】①a public notice ② to make a public announcement
【布告欄】a notice board; a bulletin board
【布穀鳥】a cuckoo
【布景】sets; a setting
【布局】① overall arrangement ② the composition (of a picture, a piece of writing, etc.) ③ the position (of pieces on a chessboard)
【布置】to fix up; to decorate
【布施】(Buddhism) almsgiving; donation
【布商】dry goods dealers; clothiers
【布衣】① dresses made of common cloth ② commoners

三畫

帆 1078
1. (帆) ㄈㄢ fān
1. a sail (of a boat) 2. a boat
【帆船】a sailboat

帆 1078
2. (帆) ㄈㄢ fān
canvas; sailcloth: 帆布 canvas

四畫

希 1079
ㄒㄧ xī
1. rare; strange 2. to hope; to wish; to desire 3. to come to a stop gradually 4. to become silent 5. very; much
【希慕】to long for; to be desirous of
【希圖】to hope and scheme for
【希臘】Greece; Greek
【希臘人】a Greek

【希罕】①rare; uncommon ②to care; to value
【希冀】to desire; to wish for
【希奇】strange; rare; uncommon
【希企 or 希求】to hope for
【希世之珍】a very rare treasure
【希有】very rare
【希有之事】a rarity; an uncommon occurrence
【希微】extremely little (amount); very little
【希望】a hope; a wish; expectations; to hope; to wish; to desire

巾部

五畫

帕 1080
ㄆㄚˋ pà
1. a turban 2. to wrap and bind 3. a handkerchief 4. a veil 5. a curtain made of cloth

帖 1081
1. ㄊㄧㄝ tiē
1. submissive or obedient 2. proper
【帖耳】(literally) to droop one's ears like a dog—submissive

帖 1081
2. ㄊㄧㄝˇ tiě
1. an invitation card 2. a label; a document 3. a copybook (of calligraphy) 4. a medical prescription
【帖子or帖兒】①an invitation letter or card ②a money order

帘 1082
ㄌㄧㄢˊ lián
1. a flag sign of a winehouse or tavern 2. a door or window screen
【帘子or帘兒】a screen for a door or a window

帚 1083
ㄓㄡˇ zhǒu
a broom; a besom

帛 1084
ㄅㄛˊ bó
(collectively) silk fabrics

六畫

帥 1085
ㄕㄨㄞˋ shuài
(又讀 ㄕㄨㄛˋ shuò)
1. commander-in-chief 2. to lead; to command 3. to follow (with orders) 4. (slang) dashing; smart looking
【帥領】to command

帝 1086
ㄉㄧˋ dì
1. the emperor 2. a god 3. Heaven (as a divine being) 4. imperial
【帝國】an empire; a monarchy
【帝國主義】imperialism
【帝號】the appellation of an emperor
【帝制】monarchy
【帝祚】the imperial throne
【帝業】the reign of an emperor
【帝位】the emperor's throne
【帝王】the emperor; the throne; the king

七畫

師 1087
ㄕ shī
1. a divison in the Chinese army 2. an army 3. a model; an example 4. a teacher; a tutor 5. to teach 6. to pattern or model after another 7. a specialist (of painting, music, etc.) 8. a local administrative chief
【師表】a model worthy of emulation
【師門】a school or sect founded by a master
【師母 or 師娘】the wife of one's tutor, teacher or master
【師法】①to pattern after; to imitate ②methods taught by one's teacher
【師範大學】a normal university
【師範教育】normal education
【師範學院】a normal college
【師傅】①(collectively) teachers; masters; tutors ②the tutors of a king ③a polite term of address for an artisan as a carpenter, cook, etc.
【師父】①tutors; masters; teachers ②a respectful term of address for monks, nuns, etc.
【師徒】the master and his student(s)
【師其故智】to copy an old method
【師心自用】conceited; opinionated
【師長】①one's teachers; faculty members ②a division commander
【師丈】the husband of one's teacher
【師承】to have learned under (especially referring to a particular school of learning)
【師出無名】to fight a war without a just cause

【師事】to serve and respect (another) as one's teacher
【師生】teachers and students
【師資】① teachers ② the qualifications of a teacher

席 1088
ㄒㄧˊ xí

1. a mat 2. a feast 3. a seat 4. to take a seat 5. to rely on
【席不暇暖】very busy
【席地而坐】to sit on the ground
【席捲】① to take away everything ② to sweep across
【席卷天下 or 席捲天下】to conquer the world
【席捲而去】to take everything away
【席次】the order of seats
【席位】a seat (at a conference, etc.)

八畫

帳 1089
ㄓㄤˋ zhàng

1. a canopy above the bed 2. a tent 3. a curtain; a mosquito net 4. a scroll (sent as a gift for a wedding, funeral, etc.) 5. same as賬—accounts
【帳簿】an account book
【帳篷】a tent; a mat-shed
【帳目】accounts; itemized bills
【帳房】① a cashier ② a cashier's office
【帳單】a bill; a check
【帳款】funds on account; credit
【帳戶】a bank account
【帳子】a mosquito net

帶 1090
ㄉㄞˋ dài

1. a girdle; a sash; a belt; a band 2. to wear (a smile, sword, etc.) 3. to bear; to bring along 4. to lead (the way, troops, etc.); to head (an army, etc.) 5. a climatic zone
【帶兵】①to lead troops ②to carry arms
【帶隊】①to lead a group ② the leader of a group, party or mission
【帶動】to drive; to spur on
【帶頭】to pioneer; to initiate; to lead
【帶來】to bring here
【帶領】to lead (an army, a party, etc.)
【帶路 or 帶道】to lead the way
【帶壞】to lead astray
【帶回】to bring back
【帶勁】① energetic ② interesting; exciting
【帶去】to bring away; to take along
【帶孝】to wear mourning
【帶笑】smilingly; wearing a smile
【帶信(兒)】to take a message
【帶傷】to get wounded or injured
【帶上】① to present to you ② to bring out (the prisoner, etc.) ③ in addition to
【帶子】a ribbon; laces (of shoes, boots, etc.)
【帶魚】ribbonfish; hairtail

帷 1091
ㄨㄟˊ wéi

a curtain; a screen; a tent
【帷幔】screens; cloth partitions
【帷幕】① a tent ② a military tent
【帷幄】a military tent

常 1092
ㄔㄤˊ cháng

1. common; normal 2. long; lasting; eternal 3. regular; frequent; often 4. ordinarily; usually 5. a rule; a principle 6. a Chinese family name
【常備軍】the standing army
【常典】usual rites; regular ceremony
【常態】a normal carriage or manner
【常年】all the year round
【常禮】common or everyday courtesy
【常理】convention; general consent
【常例】regular order or procedures
【常規】ordinary rules or practices
【常客】a frequenter
【常會】① regular meetings or conventions ② to be apt to; to happen often
【常久】for a long time
【常見】to see or to be seen frequently
【常青 or 常綠】evergreen
【常情】man's natural action or reaction under certain circumstances
【常去】to go often
【常駐】① standing (members, etc.) ②(said of policeman, etc.) to be stationed (at a locality, etc.) ③ durable (beauty or youthfulness)
【常常】often; frequently
【常春藤】ivy; bindwood
【常識】① general knowledge (as distinct from expertise) ② common sense
【常設】standing; permanent

〔巾部〕

【常人】ordinary people
【常任】standing (members of a committee, government organ, etc.)
【常有】usually; often
【常言】a popular saying; a proverb
【常務委員 or 常委】the standing members of a committee
【常用】to use often; used often

九畫

幅 1093 ㄈㄨˊ fú
1. the breadth of cloth; a width (of cloth) 2. a border 3. a numerary adjunct for pictures, scrolls, etc.
【幅度】①(said of stocks, commodity prices, etc.) the rate of rise or fall ②a range; an extent
【幅員】the territory (of a country)

帽 1094 ㄇㄠˋ mào
1. a hat; a headwear 2. a cap (of a fountain pen, screw, etc.)
【帽帶】hat strings
【帽徽】insignia on a cap
【帽架】a hatrack; a hat tree
【帽舌】a visor
【帽子】①a hat; a cap ②a label; a tag
【帽簷】the brim of a hat

幀 1095 ㄓㄥˋ zhèng
1. a numerary adjunct (for paintings, pictures, photos, etc.) 2. one of a pair—as of scrolls

十畫

幌 1096 ㄏㄨㄤˇ huǎng
a curtain; a cloth screen; a strip of cloth
【幌子】something to dazzle or cheat another with, as boasts or swashbuckling ways; a facade

十一畫

幕 1097 ㄇㄨˋ mù
1. a screen; a curtain 2. a tent 3. an advisor; staffs 4. an act 5. to cover
【幕僚】staffs; secretaries; advisors
【幕後】behind the scenes; backstage
【幕後新聞】behind-the-scenes news
【幕後人物】behind-the-scenes personalities; string-pullers
【幕後操縱】to pull strings behind the scenes

幛 1098 ㄓㄤˋ zhàng
a scroll of silk or cloth embroidered with appropriate wording sent as a gift for a wedding, funeral, etc.

十二畫

幟 1099 ㄓˋ zhì
1. a flag; a pennant; a pennon 2. a mark; a sign

幣 1100 ㄅㄧˋ bì
1. currency; money 2. a present; an offering
【幣帛】gifts (in money and silks)
【幣值】the purchasing power of a currency
【幣制】a currency system

十四畫

幫 1101 (帮) ㄅㄤ bāng
1. to help; to assist 2. a gang; a group; a class; a fleet 3. the sides of a shoe or gutter
【幫派】a faction
【幫浦】a pump
【幫忙or幫助】help; assistance; to help or assist
【幫倒忙】to cause trouble while trying to help
【幫工】an assistant of a skilled worker
【幫會】① secret societies ② an underworld gang
【幫腔】to give verbal support to a person
【幫兇】an accomplice in a crime
【幫襯】help; aid; assistance
【幫手】a helper; an assistant

干部
ㄍㄢ gān

干 1102 ㄍㄢ gān
1. to offend; to oppose; to invade 2. to interfere; to intervene 3. to concern; to involve 4. to seek; to beseech 5. the bank (of a river, etc.) 6. a shield 7. (how)

many or much; a group 8. a stem
【干貝】a dried scallop
【干名采譽】to seek publicity
【干犯】①to offend ②to invade
【干你屁事】None of your business.
【干連】to involve; to implicate
【干祿】① to seek an official post ②official emolument
【干戈】warfare; armed conflicts
【干係】involvement; implication
【干休】to give up; to bring to an end
【干政】to interfere in politics
【干涉】to interfere; interference
【干擾】①to disturb; to interfere ②(physics) interference; to jam
【干預】to intervene; to interfere; intervention

二畫

平 1103
ㄆㄧㄥˊ pìng
1. level; even 2. equal 3. peaceful 4. to conquer; to quell (a revolt); to calm down 5. to control; to regulate 6. (said of prices) to go back to normal after sharp rises 7. (sports) to make the same score 8. to pacify; to bring peace to 9. short for Peiping
【平白(無故)】without reason or cause; without provocation
【平輩】of the same generation
【平步青雲】(said of a career or social position) a meteoric rise
【平平】average; common; so-so
【平平安安】without any accident
【平鋪直敍】straight reporting; factual description
【平面】a plane, or plane surface
【平民】a commoner; a civilian
【平民政治】popular government; democracy
【平反】to reverse or redress a miscarriage of justice
【平凡】common; ordinary; usual
【平分】to divide equally
【平分秋色】(said of two sides) to share (fame, etc.); to equal each other in (achievements, etc.)
【平方】(mathematics) a square
【平房】a one-storied house; a bungalow
【平復】①(said of situations, social order, etc.) to calm down; to subside ②to recover from an illness, etc.
【平淡】commonplace; insipid; ordinary
【平等】equality; equal
【平等互利】equality and mutual benefit
【平地】①a piece of level ground; the plain ②suddenly
【平定】①(said of situations, etc.) settled ②to quell (rebellions, etc.)
【平臺】①a flat-top building ②a stadium-like building ③balcony, open porch or portico
【平坦】level, even and smooth (going, roads, etc.)
【平添】to add something unexpectedly
【平亂】to suppress a rebellion or revolt
【平空】to occur without any reason or cause; to fabricate or invent
【平衡】equilibrium; balance
【平衡力】equilibrant
【平滑】even and smooth
【平緩】①gently ②mild; gentle
【平價】①a fair price ②to lower prices
【平交道】a level crossing
【平靜】quiet; calm
【平局】a draw; a tie
【平劇】Peiping opera; Peking opera
【平均】the average
【平均年齡】composite life
【平均壽命】mean life
【平起平坐】①to treat another as one's equal ②to show no deference
【平息】to come to an end; to subside
【平心靜氣】to be calm and fair (in resolving a dispute, etc.)
【平心而論】to discuss something fairly; to be fair
【平信】ordinary mail
【平行】①parallel ②of equal rank
【平直】fair and frank
【平整】①to level ②neat; smooth
【平裝】paperback; paperbound
【平常】①normal; natural ②usual(ly) ③ordinary; so-so
【平常心】the absence of excitement, expectation, etc; composure
【平時】ordinarily; in normal times
【平時不燒香，臨時抱佛脚】Last-

〔干部〕

minute efforts are useless if no preparatory work has been done beforehand.

【平手】(in a competition, etc.) to draw; to tie another

【平生】in all one's life; throughout one's life

【平聲】level tone—the first tone in classical Chinese phonetics

【平日】on usual days; ordinarily

【平素】usually; ordinarily

【平安】safe and sound; peace

【平安無事】All is well. 或 safe and without any mishaps; safe and sound

【平易近人】(said of one's personality) easy to approach; easy to get along with

【平野】an open field

【平穩】steady and smooth; stable

【平原】a plain; a steppe

【平庸】commonplace; dull

三畫

年 1104 ㄋㄧㄢˊ nián

1. a year 2. one's age 3. a Chinese family name

【年表】a chronicle

【年譜】a biography arranged in chronological order

【年邁 or 年老】to get old; aged

【年(夜)飯】the dinner for the whole family on the eve of the Lunar New Year

【年分 or 年份】age; time

【年俸 or 年薪】an annual salary

【年富力強】the prime of one's life

【年代】① an age, era, generation, etc. ② years in a decade

【年底 or 年終 or 年尾】the end of a year

【年度】a year fixed arbitrarily for convenience, a better administrative purpose, etc., as a fiscal year, a school year, etc.

【年度決算】(accounting) annual closing

【年年】every year; year after year

【年禮】New Year's presents

【年利or年息】annual interest (rate)

【年曆】a calendar with the whole year printed on one sheet

【年齡】age

【年輪】annual rings (indicating the age of a tree)

【年糕】New Year's cake

【年高德劭】advanced in years and virtue

【年關】the end of a year when all accounts and debts must be settled

【年號】the title of an emperor's reign

【年華】time; years; age

【年華虛度】to have spent one's best years without any achievements

【年會】an annual meeting or convention

【年級】(in school) a grade

【年紀】years; age

【年假】New Year's holidays or vacation

【年節】the three major festivals of the year—the Dragon Boat, the Mid-Autumn and the Lunar New Year festivals

【年久失修】worn down by the years without repair

【年鑑】an almanac; a yearbook

【年金】an annuity

【年前】before the turn of the year

【年輕】young; youthful; youth

【年輕貌美】young and pretty

【年限】a service life

【年長】old or aged; older

【年初】the beginning of the year

【年事】the age of a person

【年少】young

【年深日久】after a long lapse of time

【年資】① the years one spends in an endeavor or job ② seniority

【年菜】food and dishes prepared for the Lunar New Year

【年歲】① the age of a person ② years; an age ③ harvests

【年夜】New Year's Eve

【年幼無知】ignorance for being young of age

【年逾不惑】to have passed 40

五畫

幷 1105 (併) ㄅㄧㄥˋ bìng

1. on a level with; even; equal 2. and; also; or; at the same time

幸 1106 ㄒㄧㄥˋ xìng

1. well-being and happiness 2. fortunately; luckily; thanks to 3. to feel happy about; to favor 4. an imperial tour

【幸免於難】to have luckily sur-

vived an accident or incident
【幸福】happiness and well-being; bliss
【幸虧or幸好or幸喜】luckily; fortunately
【幸災樂禍】to take pleasure in others' misfortune
【幸而】luckily; fortunately; thanks to
【幸運】① good luck ② lucky
【幸運之神】the goddess of fortune

十畫

幹 1107
ㄍㄢˋ gàn
1. the trunk (of a tree, etc.) 2. the main part of anything 3. talents; capable; skillful 4. to do; to attend to business; to manage 5. (slang) to kill
【幹部】a cadre
【幹麼】① Why? 或 Why (are you) doing this? ② What (do you do)?
【幹道or幹線】a trunk (or main) line
【幹掉】to kill or eliminate (a person)
【幹練】capable and experienced
【幹活兒】to work; to do a job
【幹勁兒】enthusiasm; drive; vigor
【幹事】① to manage business or affairs ② a clerk; a member of an executive committee
【幹員】a very capable officer or official

幺部
ㄧㄠ yāo

幺 1108
(么) ㄧㄠ yāo
1. tiny; small; insignificant 2. the youngest son or daughter of a family 3. one on dice; one 4. lone; alone
【幺麼】tiny; diminutive; minute
【幺麼小醜】a despicable wretch
【幺兒】the youngest son

一畫

幻 1109
ㄏㄨㄢˋ huàn
1. illusion; hallucination; magic; fantasy 2. illusory; changeable; unreal
【幻夢】a daydream; a fantasy; a fantasm
【幻滅】disillusionment
【幻燈片】a slide
【幻燈機】a slide projector
【幻景】a mirage; Fata Morgana
【幻境】a dreamland
【幻覺】hallucination; a phantasm; a fantasy
【幻想】to daydream; reverie; a vision
【幻想曲】a fantasia or fantasy
【幻象】a vision; an illusion; a phantasm or fantasm
【幻影】an unreal and visionary image

二畫

幼 1110
ㄧㄡˋ yòu
1. young; delicate 2. to take care of the young
【幼苗】a tender seedling
【幼童】a young child
【幼童軍】a cub scout
【幼嫩】young and tender; delicate
【幼年】childhood
【幼女童軍】a brownie
【幼小】young and small
【幼稚 or 幼穉】immature; naive
【幼稚園】a kindergarten
【幼蟲】a larva
【幼子】a young son
【幼兒】an infant; a baby
【幼芽】young buds; plumules

六畫

幽 1111
ㄧㄡ yōu
1. dark; gloomy 2. lonely; solitary 3. quiet; tranquil 4. deep; profound 5. hidden; secret 6. to imprison; to confine
【幽默】humorous; humor
【幽美】pathetically beautiful
【幽冥】① dark; obscure ② (Buddhism) hell
【幽明異路】The dead and the living do not mix.
【幽憤】resentment; to sulk
【幽浮】UFO (unidentified flying object)
【幽靈】the disembodied spirit of a dead person; a ghost
【幽谷】a deep valley
【幽會】a tryst, or secret meeting (between a couple in love)
【幽魂】the spirit of a dead person;

a ghost
【幽禁】 to confine; to imprison
【幽靜】 tranquil; placid; serene
【幽閑】 ①(said of a woman) gentle and graceful ② leisurely and carefree
【幽暗】 dim; gloomy
【幽雅】 chaste and elegant
【幽幽】 ① deep; profound; unfathomable ② dim
【幽怨】 hidden bitterness (of a lady frustrated in love)

广部

九畫

幾 1112 1. ㄐㄧˇ jǐ
1. how many (or much) 2. a few; some 3. which; when
【幾分】 a bit; somewhat; rather
【幾度】 ① several times ② how many times ③ how many degrees ④ several degrees
【幾天】 ① several days ② how many days
【幾年】 ① several years ② how many years
【幾何】 ① how much ② geometry
【幾何學】 geometry
【幾回 or 幾次】 ① several times ② how many times
【幾許】 how many; how much
【幾時】 what time; when
【幾曾】 Was it ever so? 或 Has it ever happened?

幾 1112 2. ㄐㄧ jī
1. small; tiny; slight 2. nearly 3. an omen; a portent
【幾殆】 in great danger
【幾乎】 almost; nearly
【幾微】 an omen; a portent

广部 ㄧㄢˇ yǎn

三畫

庄 1113 (莊) ㄓㄨㄤ zhuāng
1. a farmhouse 2. a marketplace 3. a banker (in gambling games) 4. a cottage

四畫

庇 1114 ㄅㄧˋ bì
to hide; to conceal; to harbor; to protect
【庇護】 to give protection to; to harbor
【庇護所】 a sanctuary or asylum
【庇祐】 (said of a god) to give divine assistance to a mortal
【庇蔭】 to shelter; to harbor

序 1115 ㄒㄩˋ xù
1. a preface; a foreword 2. order
【序幕】 the prologue; the prelude
【序論】 an introduction (in a piece of writing)
【序曲】 a prelude
【序數】 an ordinal number
【序言 or 序文】 a preface; a foreword

五畫

底 1116 ㄉㄧˇ dǐ
1. underside; base; foundation 2. the end
【底本】 the master copy
【底邊】 the base (of a triangle, etc.)
【底牌】 cards in one's hand
【底片】 (photography) a negative
【底定】 ① to establish peace in a region after an insurgence is put down ② to settle (disturbed waters)
【底稿】 a manuscript; MS. or ms.
【底價】 the floor or minimum price
【底細】 ① the unapparent details (of a matter); ins and outs ② the unknown background (of a person)
【底下】 the underside; the downward position
【底下人】 servants; underlings
【底線】 the base line; the bottom line
【底薪】 base pay
【底子 or 底兒】 ① basis ② a manuscript ③ a shoe sole
【底座】 a support; a base; a stand
【底層】 ① the bottom layer ② the ground floor

庖 1117 ㄆㄠˊ páo
the kitchen; the cuisine
【庖代】 to act for another
【庖丁】 a cook
【庖廚】 a kitchen

店 1118
ㄉㄧㄢˋ diàn
1. a shop; a store 2. an inn; a hotel
【店鋪】a store; a shop
【店面】a shop front
【店東or店主】a proprietor (of a store)
【店家】a manager (of an inn, shop, etc.)
【店小二】a waiter (in an inn or tavern)
【店員】a shop clerk; a shopman

庚 1119
ㄍㄥ gēng
1. the seventh of the Ten Celestial Stems (天干) 2. the age (of a person)

府 1120
ㄈㄨˇ fǔ
1. a mansion 2. a government office (or agency) 3. an administrative district in former times; a prefecture 4. your home 5. a treasury; archives
【府邸 or 府第】a mansion
【府庫】a treasury for public funds
【府綢】poplin
【府上】① your native place ② your home ③ your family

六畫

度 1121
1. ㄉㄨˋ dù
1. an instrument for measuring length 2. a kilowatt-hour 3. a unit of measurement for angles, etc.; a degree 4. (number of) times 5. a system 6. a manner; bearing 7. to pass 8. consideration; careful thought
【度量】① an instrument for measuring ② the capacity for forgiveness
【度量衡】weights and measures
【度假】to spend one's holidays (or vacation)
【度數】a reading (of a barometer, thermometer, etc.)
【度日】to make a living
【度日如年】to pass days as if they were years (because of deep anxiety, worries, or misery)

度 1121
2. ㄉㄨㄛˋ duò
to consider; to measure; to infer
【度德量力】to act with due consideration of one's own abilities

七畫

座 1122
ㄗㄨㄛˋ zuò
a seat; a stand
【座標or坐標】(mathematics) co-ordinates
【座談會】a discussion meeting; a symposium
【座落or坐落】to be situated or located at
【座上客】a guest of honor
【座次】seating order
【座右銘】a motto
【座無虛席】There is standing room only.
【座位】a seat

庫 1123
ㄎㄨˋ kù
1. a storeroom; a granary 2. a treasury
【庫房】a storeroom; a warehouse
【庫藏】the contents of a storeroom
【庫存】a stock; reserve

庭 1124
ㄊㄧㄥˊ tíng
1. a hall 2. a yard 3. the imperial court 4. a court of justice
【庭訓】exhortation or admonition from one's father
【庭長】a chief justice; a presiding judge
【庭上】①in court (of justice) ② at (imperial) court
【庭闈】① parents' abode ② parents
【庭園】a garden
【庭院】a courtyard; a garden

八畫

庵 1125
ㄢ ān
1. a hut; a cottage 2. a nunnery
【庵寺】① a nunnery ② a temple

庶 1126
ㄕㄨˋ shù
1. born of a concubine 2. numerous 3. general; common 4. the common people; the commoners 5. almost
【庶民 or 庶衆 or 庶人】the commoners; the multitude; the populace
【庶幾】① almost; nearly ② probably ③the capable and the virtuous
【庶羞】the various kinds of delicacies
【庶政】the numerous affairs of the state
【庶子】① the son of a concubine ② an ancient official title

广部

【庶務】general affairs

康 1127 ㄎㄤ kāng
1. healthy 2. peaceful 3. abundant 4. level, even and smooth (road, etc.)
【康復】recovery (from illness)
【康泰】healthy and free from trouble
【康寧】healthy and undisturbed
【康樂】① (wholesome) recreation ② peace and happiness
【康健】in good health; healthy
【康莊大道】a level and easy thoroughfare leading to many places

庸 1128 ㄩㄥ yōng (又讀 ㄩㄥˊ yóng)
1. mediocre; common 2. stupid 3. a hired laborer 4. to require 5. to reward 6. an interrogative (as how, etc.)
【庸民】the common people; the masses
【庸夫愚婦】simple, ignorant people
【庸碌 or 庸庸碌碌】mediocre; common
【庸人】a mediocre person
【庸人自擾】(literally) Stupid people create trouble for themselves.
【庸才】a man of mediocre ability
【庸俗】vulgar; unrefined
【庸醫】a quack doctor; a quack
【庸言】a commonplace; a platitude

九畫

廁 1129 ㄘㄜˋ cè
as in廁所—a toilet, lavatory or latrine

廂 1130 ㄒㄧㄤ xiāng
1. a side room 2. a box in the theater 3. the vicinity or outskirts of a city
【廂房 or 廂屋】a side room

十畫

廈 1131 ㄒㄧㄚˋ xià (語音 ㄕㄚˋ shà)
a tall building; an edifice

廉 1132 ㄌㄧㄢˊ lián
1. incorrupt; upright 2. inexpensive; cheap 3. to examine; to inspect
【廉明】incorruptible and intelligent
【廉吏】an incorrupt official
【廉價】a low price
【廉價品or廉價貨物】a bargain; cheap goods
【廉節】frugal; thrifty
【廉潔】incorrupt; incorruptible
【廉恥】the integrity of character and a sense of honor
【廉察】to inspect; to investigate
【廉售】to sell at a low price
【廉讓】to sell (property) at a low price

廊 1133 ㄌㄤˊ láng
a portico; a corridor; a hallway
【廊廟】the court (of a monarch)
【廊廟之志】political aspiration
【廊子】a corridor; a portico; a hallway

十一畫

廄 1134 ㄐㄧㄡˋ jiù
a stable

廖 1135 ㄌㄧㄠˋ liào
a Chinese family name

廓 1136 ㄎㄨㄛˋ kuò
1. open; wide 2. empty
【廓土】an open ground
【廓清】to liquidate; to clean up; to wipe out
【廓然】① spacious ② vast; boundless ③ unprejudiced; unbiased

廕 1137 ㄧㄣˋ yìn
to shelter; to harbor; to protect

十二畫

廚 1138 ㄔㄨˊ chú
1.a kitchen 2.a closet; a chest; a cupboard
【廚房】a kitchen
【廚夫or廚子or廚師】a chef; a cook
【廚櫃】a closet; a chest; a cupboard
【廚具】kitchen utensils

廝 1139 ㄙ sī
1. a servant 2. a fellow; a guy 3. each other; together
【廝打】to have a mêlée; to fight

【廝鬧】to have a spree
【廝混】① to mingle ② to fool around together ③ to make trouble
【廝殺】to slaughter one another (as in a battle); to fight at close quarters
【廝守】to take care of each other

廟 1140
ㄇㄧㄠˋ miào

as in 廟宇—a temple; a shrine
【廟堂】① the ancestral temple of the royal family ②the court (of a monarch)
【廟號】the posthumous title of an emperor
【廟會】a fair held at the site of a temple when the faithful converge to worship the deity
【廟祝】a temple attendant

廠 1141
ㄔㄤˇ chǎng

a factory; a plant; a workshop
【廠房】a factory building
【廠址】a factory site or location
【廠長】a factory manager
【廠主】a factory owner; a mill owner
【廠商】manufacturers

廢 1142
ㄈㄟˋ fèi

1. to give up; to abandon 2. to reject 3. useless; disused 4. disabled
【廢票】①an invalidated ballot ② a used ticket
【廢掉】to abolish; to abrogate
【廢鐵】scrap iron
【廢料】useless materials; waste materials
【廢話】rubbish; nonsense; a meaningless remark
【廢氣】waste gas; exhaust
【廢棄】to abandon as useless; to discard
【廢寢忘餐】so absorbed (in a pursuit) as to neglect sleep and meals
【廢墟】ruins (of a city, castle, etc.)
【廢止or廢除】to abolish; to annul; to repeal
【廢紙】wastepaper
【廢置不用】to shelve or put aside as useless
【廢弛】to neglect
【廢水】wastewater; liquid waste
【廢人】a disabled person
【廢物】① waste material; rubbish ② a good-for-nothing
【廢物利用】the utilization of waste material

廣 1143
ㄍㄨㄤˇ guǎng

1. wide; broad; spacious 2. to extend 3. Kwangtung or Kwangsi
【廣播】①to broadcast; to telecast ② a broadcast
【廣播電臺】a broadcasting station; a radio station
【廣播節目】① a radio program; a broadcast ② a television program; a telecast
【廣播劇】a radio drama; a radio play
【廣播員】a broadcaster; a radio announcer
【廣博】wide; extensive
【廣被】far-reaching (love or benefit)
【廣漠】boundless; vast
【廣泛】extensive; widespread
【廣大】vast
【廣大無邊】boundless
【廣東】Kwangtung Province
【廣土衆民】(said of a country) having a large territory and a large population
【廣告】advertisement
【廣告片】an advertising film
【廣告欄】the ad column
【廣告公司】an advertising agency
【廣告客戶】an advertiser
【廣告業】advertising
【廣開才路】to open all avenues for people of talent
【廣開言路】to encourage freedom of speech
【廣闊】wide; extensive; vast; spacious
【廣結善緣】to make friends all around
【廣交】to make friends extensively
【廣西】Kwangsi Province
【廣州】Canton or Kwangchow
【廣場】a square (in a city); a plaza
【廣而言之】generally speaking
【廣義】the broad definition

十六畫

廬 1144
ㄌㄨˊ lú

1. a thatched cottage 2. Mt. Lu (in Kiangsi)
【廬舍】a cottage; a hut
【廬山眞面目】the real appearance (of a thing or person in disguise)

龐 1145
ㄆㄤˊ páng

1. disorderly; confused 2. enor-

mous 3. a face
【龐大】immense; huge; enormous
【龐然大物】①a huge object ②a mammoth animal
【龐雜】disorderly; confused

二十二畫

廳 1146 ㄊㄧㄥ tīng
1. a central or main room of a house 2. a hall 3. a government agency
【廳房】a central room open to a number of other rooms; a hall
【廳堂】the central room of a house; a hall
【廳長】the director of a department under a provincial government

廴部 ㄧㄣ yǐn

四畫

延 1147 ㄧㄢ yán
1. to lengthen; to spread; to extend 2. to delay; to defer 3. to prolong 4. to invite 5. to procrastinate
【延聘】to invite the service of
【延宕 or 延擱】to procrastinate
【延年益壽】to lengthen one's life
【延攬】to recruit the service of (talented men)
【延緩】to postpone; to put off; to defer
【延頸舉踵 or 延頸企足 or 延企】to expect or look forward anxiously
【延期】to be postponed; to be put off
【延請】to invite (talented people to provide assistance)
【延展性】(physics) ductility
【延續】to continue; to be continued
【延遲】to delay; to be delayed
【延長】to lengthen; to extend; to prolong
【延長線】an extension
【延燒】(said of fire) to spread
【延壽】to prolong one's life
【延伸】to extend; to stretch
【延髓 or 延腦】medulla oblongata; the afterbrain
【延誤】to fail because of procrastination

廷 1148 ㄊㄧㄥ tíng
the imperial court; the court
【廷議】a discussion at imperial court

六畫

建 1149 ㄐㄧㄢ jiàn
1. to establish; to build 2. to propose; to suggest
【建坪】the floor space of a building in *ping* (equivalent to 36 square feet)
【建黨】to found a political party
【建都】to select a city as the capital (of the empire)
【建立】to establish; to build; to set up; to found
【建國】①to found (or establish) a state ②to build up a country
【建交】to establish diplomatic relations
【建築】①to build; to construct ②a building or structure
【建築師】an architect
【建築物】a building; a structure
【建設】to construct; to build; construction
【建設性的】constructive
【建樹】an achievement; contribution
【建造】to build; to construct; to frame
【建議】to propose; to suggest
【建議案】a proposal

廾部 ㄍㄨㄥˇ gǒng

二畫

弁 1150 ㄅㄧㄢ biàn
1. a conical cap worn on ceremonious occasions in ancient times 2. in the Ching Dynasty low-ranking military officers
【弁言】a preface

四畫

弄 1151 ㄋㄨㄥˋ nòng
(讀音 ㄌㄨㄥˋ lòng)
1. to play with 2. to make fun of; to mock 3. to handle; to do
【弄飯】 to prepare a meal
【弄通】 to get a good grasp of
【弄好】 ① to get or put into (good) shape ② to finish doing something ③ to do well
【弄糊塗】 to puzzle; to confuse
【弄壞】 to bungle; to spoil
【弄假成眞】 to turn simulation into reality unintentionally
【弄僵】 to bring to a deadlock
【弄巧成拙】 to bungle an ingenious scheme
【弄淸】 to make clear; to clarify; to understand fully
【弄權】 to abuse one's power
【弄璋】 to give birth to a son
【弄潮兒】 ① a seaman ② a beach swimmer
【弄姿】 (said of women) to act coquettishly
【弄糟】 to mess up; to bungle; to spoil
【弄髒】 to stain; to soil; to smear
【弄錯】 to make a mistake
【弄瓦】 to give birth to a daughter

六畫

弈 1152 ㄧˋ yì
as in 弈棋—the "*go*" game

十二畫

弊 1153 ㄅㄧˋ bì
1. bad; undesirable 2. dishonesty; fraud 3. exhausted; tired 4. disadvantages
【弊病 or 弊端】 corrupt practices
【弊害】 harm; damage
【弊帚自珍 or 弊帚千金】 One loves something of little value simply because it is his own.

弋 部
ㄧˋ yì

弋 1154 ㄧˋ yì
1. to catch; to take 2. to shoot with arrow and bow
【弋獲】 to catch (game in hunting, a thief, etc.)

三畫

式 1155 ㄕˋ shì
1. fashion; style 2. a pattern; a type 3. a system 4. a ceremony
【式樣】 ① a type; a model ② a mode; a style
【式微】 the decline (of a nation, etc.)

十畫

弒 1156 ㄕˋ shì
to kill or murder one's superior, senior, etc.
【弒母】 matricide; to commit matricide
【弒父】 patricide; to commit patricide
【弒君】 regicide; to commit regicide

弓 部
ㄍㄨㄥ gōng

弓 1157 ㄍㄨㄥ gōng
1. a bow 2. bent; arching; arched 3. a measure of length (equal to five Chinese feet)
【弓弩手or弓箭手or弓手】 an archer
【弓箭 or 弓矢】 bow and arrow
【弓匠】 a bowyer
【弓弦】 a bowstring
【弓形】 (mathematics) a segment of a circle

一畫

引 1158 ㄧㄣˇ yǐn
1. to pull 2. to guide 3. to introduce 4. to quote 5. to retire 6. a unit of length (=33⅓ meters) 7. to cause
【引避】 to avoid
【引爆】 to ignite; to detonate
【引發】 (chemistry) initiation
【引導】 to guide; to lead
【引渡】 to extradite; extradition
【引退】 to retire; to resign

弓部

【引狼入室】to bring in a troublemaker
【引力】gravitation
【引領而望】to long for; to expect eagerly
【引路】to lead the way
【引號】a quotation mark; a quote
【引吭高歌】to sing aloud
【引火】to ignite; to light; to kindle a fire
【引咎】to take the blame on oneself
【引咎辭職】to resign from office as a gesture to show self-reproach
【引見】to present a person to the emperor, etc.
【引薦】to recommend
【引進】① to recommend ② to introduce from elsewhere
【引經據典】① to quote from classics ② pedantic
【引起】to cause; to give rise to
【引擎】an engine
【引線】① a sewing needle ② a go-between ③ a fuse
【引證】to cite supporting evidence
【引出】to draw forth; to lead
【引伸 or 引申】to expound
【引人注目】noticeable; conspicuous
【引人入勝】① to lead one into wonderland ② (said of books) absorbing
【引入歧途】to lead (somebody) astray
【引以爲戒】to learn a lesson (from a previous error)
【引誘】to induce; to lure; to entice; to tempt
【引文】a quoted passage; a quotation
【引用】to quote

弔 1159 (吊) ㄉㄧㄠˋ diào
1. to condole; to console 2. to mourn 3. to hang; to suspend; suspended
【弔帶】suspenders; garters
【弔燈】a low-hanging ceiling lamp, such as a chandelier
【弔環】flying rings
【弔祭】to mourn over (somebody's death)
【弔起】① to hang ② to lift by crane
【弔橋】① a suspension bridge ② a drawbridge over the moat
【弔銷】to revoke; to withdraw
【弔銷執照】to withdraw a license
【弔車】① a wrecker (or a truck crane) ② a cable car
【弔扇】a ceiling fan
【弔死】to die by hanging
【弔喪】to attend a memorial service
【弔嗓子】(Chinese opera) to sing aloud off stage as a vocal training and practice
【弔索】a sling
【弔兒郎當】to act or behave irreverently; to do things perfunctorily
【弔唁】to condole
【弔慰】to condole with
【弔胃口】to tantalize
【弔文】a message of condolence; a funeral oration

二畫

弗 1160 ㄈㄨˊ fú
not: 弗如 not as good as

弘 1161 ㄏㄨㄥˊ hóng
1. great; capacious 2. to enlarge; to broaden
【弘大】great; immense
【弘揚】to propagate; to promote; to develop
【弘遠】far and wide
【弘願】great ambition

三畫

弛 1162 ㄕˇ shǐ (又讀 ㄔˊ chí)
to unstring; to relax; to neglect
【弛緩】to relax

四畫

弟 1163 1. ㄉㄧˋ dì
1. a younger brother 2. a junior
【弟婦 or 弟媳】a sister-in-law
【弟弟】a younger brother
【弟兄】① brothers ② soldiers
【弟子】① a disciple; a pupil ② a youth

弟 1163 2. (悌) ㄊㄧˋ tì
to show brotherly love

五畫

弦 1164 ㄒㄧㄢˊ xián
1. strings (of bows, etc.) 2. the chord of an arc 3. the first or last quarter of a lunar month
【弦外之音】overtones; connotations

【弦月】 a crescent moon
【弦樂隊】 a string orchestra (or band)
【弦樂器】 a stringed instrument

弧 1165
ㄏㄨˊ hú
1. a wooden bow 2. a segment of a circle
【弧度】 circular measure
【弧形】 an arc; a curve

六畫

弭 1166
ㄇㄧˇ mǐ
1. to stop; to end 2. the ends of a bow
【弭兵】 to stop war
【弭亂】 to stop disturbance of a civil war

七畫

弱 1167
ㄖㄨㄛˋ ruò
1. weak; fragile; feeble; tender 2. inferior 3. young 4. a little less than
【弱不禁風】 so weak as to have inadequate strength to withstand the wind
【弱點】 a weak point; a weakness
【弱冠】 a twenty-year-old man; a youth
【弱小】 small and weak
【弱小民族】 a small nation
【弱者】 the weak and the timid
【弱視】 amblyopia
【弱肉強食】 the weak falling victim to the strong—the law of the jungle

八畫

張 1168
ㄓㄤ zhāng
1. to open; to stretch; to extend 2. to display 3. a sheet (of paper); a leaf (of a book)
【張燈結彩】 decorated with lanterns and colored hangings (for a joyous occasion)
【張貼】 to paste up
【張力】 tensile strength; tension
【張羅】 ①to raise funds ②to set a snare for birds ③to serve guests ④to take care of; to get busy about
【張冠李戴】 wrong attribution; misappropriation
【張開】 to stretch open; to open
【張口結舌】 agape and tongue-tied
【張狂】 to dissipate without inhibition
【張皇失措】 to lose composure; panicky
【張手】 to open one's hands
【張嘴】 ① to open the mouth ② to ask for a loan or a favor
【張三李四】 anybody; every Tom, Dick, and Harry
【張牙舞爪】 (said of wild beasts) to frighten people by showing the fangs and flourishing the paws
【張揚】 to publicize; to make widely known
【張望】 to look around; to look about

強 1169
1. (强、彊) ㄑㄧㄤˊ qiáng
1. strong; powerful; vigorous 2. better 3. violent
【強暴】 ① violent; fierce; ferocious; atrocious ② rape
【強風】 (meteorology) strong breeze
【強大】 powerful and strong
【強盜】 a robber; a bandit
【強敵】 a powerful foe or enemy
【強調】 to emphasize; to stress
【強度】 intensity (of light, etc.)
【強力膠】 glue
【強烈】 violent; strong; intense; severe; acute; keen
【強國】 a powerful country; a power
【強悍】 fierce; truculent
【強橫】 tyrannical; despotic; dictatorial
【強化】 to strengthen; to intensify
【強加】 to impose; to force
【強姦】 to rape; to violate
【強勁】 powerful; forceful
【強權】 brute force; might
【強心劑】 a heart stimulant
【強行】 to force
【強壯】 strong; vigorous; virile; energetic; robust
【強身】 to strengthen the body
【強盛】 strong and prosperous
【強人】 ① robbers ② a strongman
【強韌】 strong; tough; tenacious
【強硬】 ① hard; strong ② defiant

強 1169
2. (强、彊) ㄑㄧㄤˇ qiǎng
1. to force 2. to make an effort; to strive
【強逼or強迫】 to force (one to do something)
【強辯】 to obstinately stick to false reasoning or a lame excuse
【強求】 to demand; to extort; to exact; to impose

【強取】to take by force
【強制】compulsory; to compel; to force
【強制執行】forcible execution; to execute forcibly
【強佔】to occupy forcibly; to take (property, one's wife, etc.) by force
【強人所難】to force someone to do something against his will
【強詞奪理】to argue irrationally
【強顏歡笑】to assume a joyous mood reluctantly

強 1169
3. (强、彊) ㄐㄧㄤˋ jiàng
inflexible; obstinate; stubborn
【強脾氣】an obstinate disposition

十二畫

彈 1170
1. ㄉㄢˋ dàn
a pellet; a bullet; a bomb
【彈道飛彈】a ballistic missile
【彈頭】a projectile nose; a warhead
【彈弓】a slingshot; a catapult
【彈殼】an empty cartridge case
【彈盡援絕】The ammunition is gone, and reinforcements are nowhere in sight.
【彈匣】(military) a magazine
【彈子房】a billiard room; a poolroom
【彈藥】ammunition
【彈藥庫】an ammunition depot; a magazine
【彈丸之地】a very small piece of land

彈 1170
2. ㄊㄢˊ tán
1. to rebound 2. to play 3. to impeach
【彈力】elasticity; elastic force
【彈劾】to impeach
【彈劾權】impeachment power
【彈簧】a spring: 彈簧刀 a switchblade
【彈簧墊】a trampoline
【彈琴】to play (stringed instruments)
【彈性】elasticity; resilience
【彈性疲乏】elastic fatigue
【彈指之間】a very brief space of time
【彈奏】to play

彆 1171
ㄅㄧㄝˋ biè
awkward
【彆扭】① awkward; refractory ② an awkward situation
【彆氣】silently resentful

十四畫

彌 1172
ㄇㄧˊ mí
1. to fill 2. more
【彌補】to stop or fill up (a gap); to supplement
【彌漫】to be present all over; to fill the air
【彌封】to seal examinee's name on an examination paper
【彌留】on the point of death from a serious disease
【彌撒】(Catholic) a Mass
【彌月】the completion of the first month after birth of a child

十九畫

彎 1173
ㄨㄢ wān
to bend; to curve
【彎路】① a tortuous path ② a detour
【彎曲】bent; curved
【彎彎曲曲】having many bends or curves

⺕部
ㄐㄧˋ jì

八畫

彗 1174
ㄏㄨㄟˋ huì
1. a broom 2. a comet 3. to expose to sunlight
【彗星】a comet

十畫

彙 1175
ㄏㄨㄟˋ huì
1. a category; a class; a series 2. to categorize 3. to collect
【彙報】to collect (all information) and report
【彙編】to edit (data, etc.)
【彙集】to collect (materials, etc.)
【彙注】a collection of footnotes, etc., for expounding a book, etc.

彡部
ㄕㄢ shān

四畫

形 1176
(形) ㄒㄧㄥˊ xíng
1. a form; a shape 2. a complexion 3. a terrain; a contour 4. expression; to describe 5. in comparison 6. to show
【形貌】a countenance
【形單影隻】to be all alone
【形態】an appearance; a form; a state 「a form or shape
【形體】the human body which has
【形同虛設】to exist in name only
【形骸】one's body or skeleton
【形跡or形迹】①one's behavior or conduct ②one's appearance and manner 「that arouses suspicion
【形跡可疑】behavior or a manner
【形象】① a form; an image ②(fine arts) form as contrasted to substance
【形形色色】of all shapes and colors; a great variety and diversity
【形狀】the appearance, or shape of a thing
【形成】to form; to take shape
【形式】①form②formality③style
【形式上】nominally 「or contour
【形勢】① a situation ② a terrain
【形容】① to describe ② shape; form 「ated appearance
【形容枯槁】a thin, bony, or emaci-
【形容詞】an adjective
【形蹤】① the whereabouts of a person ② the behavior or conduct of a person
【形蹤不定】to wander here and there unpredictably
【形似】to resemble; to look like
【形色倉皇】to look anxious and tense
【形影不離】(usually said of lovers and devoted couples) inseparable, like a person and his shad-
【形影相弔】solitary; lonely ⌊ow
【形影相隨】inseparable; very intimate

六畫

彥 1177
ㄧㄢˋ yàn
a man of ability and virtue; an erudite scholar

八畫

彩 1178
ㄘㄞˇ cǎi
1. colors; variegated colors 2. makeup in various Chinese operas 3. special feats or stunts in Chinese operas 4. ornamental; brilliant; gay 5. prize money; stakes in a gambling game
【彩筆】① the pen that produces masterpieces ② color crayons
【彩排】a dress rehearsal
【彩票】a lottery ticket; a raffle ticket 「ribbon)
【彩帶】a colored streamer (or
【彩頭】good luck; lucky 「tern
【彩繪】a colored drawing or pat-
【彩虹】a rainbow 「or evening
【彩霞】rosy clouds in the morning
【彩飾】to adorn; to ornament;
【彩色】color ⌊adornments
【彩色版】chromolithograph printing
【彩色電視】color television
【彩色軟片】color film
【彩雲】clouds of many hues

彬 1179
ㄅㄧㄣ bīn
intelligent, refined and gentle
【彬彬有禮】refined and courteous

彪 1180
ㄅㄧㄠ biāo
1. a tiger cub 2. stripes or streaks on the skin of a tiger 3. tall and big; shining and brilliant; outstanding
【彪炳】brilliant and shining; splendid (achievements, examples, etc.)
【彪形大漢】a whale of a man

九畫

彭 1181
ㄆㄥˊ péng
1. big 2. longevity 3. proud

十一畫

彰 1182
ㄓㄤ zhāng
1. ornamental 2. evident; obvious; clear 3. to manifest; to make known
【彰明】to manifest; to clarify

【彰明較著】extremely obvious and ostensible
【彰顯】to manifest

十二畫

彳部

影 1183
ㄧㄥˇ yǐng
1. a shadow; an image 2. a trace; a vague impression 3. to copy and imitate 4. to hide 5. a sundial
【影本】a facsimile edition; a rubbing
【影片】a motion picture; movies
【影評】brief comments on motion pictures
【影評人】a movie critic
【影迷】a movie fan
【影碟片】a videodisk
【影壇】the movie circles; moviedom
【影集】a miniseries (or a mini series)
【影劇界】movie and drama circles
【影響】to affect; to influence
【影像】an image; a portrait
【影星】a movie star
【影展】a photographic exhibition; a film festival
【影射】① to counterfeit (trademarks, etc.); to delude; to humbug ② to hint by suggestive remarks
【影子】①a shadow ②(figuratively) a trace
【影印】①photogravure ②xerography
【影印本】a photostatic copy

彳部
彳 chì

四畫

彷 1184
1. ㄆㄤˊ páng
hesitating; unsettled
【彷徨】to hesitate; undecided

彷 1184
2. ㄈㄤˇ fǎng
like; similar to; to resemble
【彷彿】① to seem; as if ② to be more or less the same; to be alike

役 1185
ㄧˋ yì
1. military service 2. to guard the frontier 3. to dispatch 4. to employ as a servant 5. to serve 6. to do
【役使】to make (someone) work

五畫

彼 1186
ㄅㄧˇ bǐ
1. that; those 2. another; the other 3. there
【彼此】both parties; each other
【彼此彼此】We are alike. 或 We are in similar position.
【彼此之間】between you and me; between two parties

往 1187
1. ㄨㄤˇ wǎng
1. to go toward; to depart; to be bound for 2. formerly; past; bygone
【往返】to come and go; to and fro
【往年】in the years past
【往來】①to go and return ②personal contact between two parties, etc.
【往後】① backward ② hereafter
【往還】① coming and going ② contact between two people or parties
【往昔】in the past; in ancient times
【往常】usually; heretofore; in the past
【往事】things that have come to pass
【往日】in the past
【往往】usually; often; frequently
【往往如此】It happens frequently that.... 或 usually like that

往 1187
2. ㄨㄤˋ wàng
an adverb indicating time or direction
【往好處想】to think of the better possibilities of a situation, etc.
【往前看】to look forward
【往下說】to talk on 或 Go ahead.
【往右轉】to turn right

征 1188
ㄓㄥ zhēng
1. to journey far away 2. to attack; to conquer; to tame 3. to levy taxes; to collect taxes 4. to take; to snatch
【征伐】to battle; to be on the warpath
【征服】to conquer; conquest
【征討】to quell; to subjugate
【征戰】to fight in battle

【征收】to levy and collect (taxes); to impose
【征衣】① traveling clothes ② warrior's costume

徂 1189
ㄘㄨˊ cú
1. to go to; to go ahead; to advance 2. the preposition "to" 3. to die 4. past
【徂謝】① to wither ② to die

彿 1190
ㄈㄨˊ fú
like; similar to; as if

六畫

待 1191
1. ㄉㄞˋ dài
1. to treat; to entertain 2. to await; to wait for 3. need 4. until
【待聘】to wait for employment
【待命】to await orders
【待發】ready to depart
【待領】(said of money, articles) to wait for a claimant
【待客】to receive (or entertain) guests
【待機】to await the opportune moment (for action)
【待價而沽】to wait for the right (favorable) price to sell
【待續】to be continued
【待查】yet to be investigated
【待人接物】the way one treats people
【待如己出】to treat a child as if he were one's own
【待字閨中】(said of a young woman) not betrothed yet
【待要】to be about to
【待遇】①pay, salary, or remuneration ② the manner of treating people

待 1191
2. ㄉㄞ dāi
1. to stay 2. later
【待不住】can't or won't stay long
【待一會兒】just a little while

徇 1192
1. (殉) ㄒㄩㄣˋ xùn
1. to show 2. to issue orders in the army 3. to follow; to comply with 4. quick 5. to die for a cause
【徇難】to die for a just cause

徇 1192
2. ㄒㄩㄣˊ xún
1. pervading 2. to profit

【徇私】to profit oneself; favoritism; nepotism
【徇私舞弊】to play favoritism and commit irregularities

很 1193
ㄏㄣˇ hěn
1. very; quite 2. fierce; cruel 3. disobedient; quarrelsome 4. dispute; quarrel

徊 1194
ㄏㄨㄞˊ huái
(又讀 ㄏㄨㄟˊ huí)
1. hesitating; irresolute; indecisive 2. to move to and fro; to walk around

律 1195
ㄌㄩˋ lǜ
1. a law; a rule; a regulation; a statute 2. to bind by law; to control or restrain; to discipline 3. a series of standard bamboo tuning pitch pipes used in ancient music 4. a form in Chinese poetry — a stanza of eight lines
【律令】①laws and regulations ② a Taoist incantation
【律師】① a lawyer; a barrister ② a polite expression for Buddhist monks
【律師事務所】a lawyer's office

後 1196
ㄏㄡˋ hòu
1. behind; at the back of 2. afterwards; to come after 3. descendants; posterity 4. an auxiliary to indicate "then" or "afterwards"
【後輩】① juniors; inferiors ② descendants
【後備軍人】military reservists
【後備人員】backup personnel
【後半部】the latter portion of a book
【後半生】the latter half of one's life
【後補】① to make amends ② to replenish
【後部】behind; the back of
【後排】a back row
【後門】the back door
【後面】① behind ② afterwards
【後母 or 繼母】one's stepmother
【後方】the rear (as contrasted to the war front)
【後福】the blessings to follow; the good days to come
【後代or後嗣】descendants or posterity
【後盾】a support; a backing
【後臺】①a backstage ② (usually

彳部

in politics) one's backing or backers

【後頭】①behind ② in the future

【後天】①the day after tomorrow ②acquired; postnatal

【後天性免疫不全症候群】AIDS (Acquired Immune Deficiency Syndrome)

【後退】to retreat; to withdraw; retreat

【後年】the year after next

【後來】then; afterwards

【後來居上】The latecomer (or new-comer) ends up in front.

【後力不繼】to lack the strength to continue

【後路】① the route of retreat ② room for a maneuver; a road for retreat

【後輪】a rear wheel

【後跟 or 後跟兒】the heel

【後顧之憂】the worries behind

【後果】consequences

【後悔】to regret; remorse

【後悔不已】to be overcome with regret

【後悔莫及】It will be too late to regret.

【後會有期】See you again.

【後患】the lurking dangers which will become manifest afterward

【後患無窮】an endless flow of disastrous aftermath

【後繼無人】There is no successor (capable of continuing the task).

【後進】juniors; the rising generation

【後期】① to be behind schedule ② the latter part of an era

【後起之秀】a remarkable young person

【後勤】logistic service in the rear

【後序 or 後敍】an epilog(ue)

【後知後覺】to know afterwards

【後者】the latter

【後事】matters calling for immediate attention after a person's death—as funerals, etc.

【後生可畏】The young hold potentials for greatness.

【後生小子】naive youths; young greenhorns

【後人】① one's descendants or posterity ② to be behind others (in doing good things, charity work, etc.)

【後任】the successor to an office after the incumbent quits

【後坐力】recoil

【後遺症】(pathology) aftereffect; sequela

【後裔】descendants

【後衛】① the rear guard (in military operations) ② the fullback (in football); the guard (in basketball)

【後援】reinforcement from the rear; support

【後院】a backyard

七畫

1197 **徐** ㄒㄩˊ xú

slow; calm; composed; gently

【徐步】to walk slowly

【徐娘半老】a flirtatious middle-aged woman who still retains traces of her erstwhile beauty

【徐緩】slowly; unhurriedly

【徐徐】①steady; relaxed and dignified ②slow

【徐徐而來】to come with relaxed and dignified steps

1198 **徑** ㄐㄧㄥˋ jìng

1. a narrow path; a byway; a shortcut 2. a diameter 3. direct; straight 4. already — implying a sense of surprise

【徑直】straight; directly

【徑自】without consulting anyone

【徑賽】(sports) track events

1199 **徒** ㄊㄨˊ tú

1. disciples; followers; pupils; apprentices 2. a crowd; a gang; a group of people 3. to go on foot 4. a punishment 5. only; merely; in vain 6. empty, as empty-handed 7. foot soldiers; infantry

【徒步】to go on foot

【徒費口舌】to waste one's breath

【徒弟】an apprentice; a disciple; a pupil

【徒勞】futile effort

【徒勞無功】to labor in vain

【徒行】to go on foot; to walk; to hike

【徒刑】a prison term; imprisonment

【徒衆】a gang; a group of followers

【徒手】barehanded

【徒手致富】from rags to riches

【徒然】in vain; useless; meaningless

【徒子徒孫】followers

【徒增】to increase (cost, trouble, age, etc.) without gaining advan-

tage of any kind 「reputation
【徒擁虛名】to have an undeserved

八畫

得 1200
1. ㄉㄜˊ dé
1. to get; to obtain; to acquire 2. complacent 3. agreement 4. can; may 5. All right! 或 That's enough!
【得標】 to win the contract 「sick
【得病】 to get sick or ill; to fall
【得不到 or 得不着】 cannot get
【得不償失】 not worth the effort
【得票】 to gain votes; the votes one obtained in an election
【得分】 to score; a score
【得到】 to succeed in getting or obtaining
【得道多助】 Those who uphold justice shall not be alone.
【得當】 proper; appropriate (ways, arrangements, measures, etc.)
【得體】 proper (deportment, behavior, conduct, etc.)
【得天獨厚】 to be particularly favored by nature
【得力】 ① capable (assistants, etc.) ② thanks to ③ to get help from
【得隴望蜀】 greedy; avarice; cupidity
【得過且過】 to harbor no ambition of achievement; easygoing; to muddle on
【得空兒】 to have spare time
【得救】 to obtain salvation; to be
【得獎】 to win a prize 「saved
【得悉】 to have learned; to hear of
【得心應手】 very smooth operation
【得知】 to have learned; to have become acquainted with 「filled
【得志】 to have one's ambition ful-
【得逞】 to succeed 「favor of
【得寵】 to be favored; to win the
【得失】 gain and loss; success and failure; merits and faults
【得失參半】 to have both merits and demerits, advantages and disadvantages, gain and loss, etc.
【得勢】 to be in a powerful position; to become influential; to be at the helm
【得手】 to succeed (in performing a task, usually a criminal act)
【得勝】 to win
【得人心】 to be popular 「the law
【得罪】 ① to offend ② to violate
【得寸進尺】 The more one gets, the more one wants. 「able
【得宜】 proper; appropriate; suit-
【得意】 to be complacent; to be very satisfied
【得意揚揚】 an appearance of extreme satisfaction; proudly
【得意忘形】 to have one's head turned by success; to get dizzy
得 1200 ⌊with success
2. ㄉㄟˇ děi
1. must; should; ought to 2. to
得 1200 ⌊need; to take
3. •ㄉㄜ de
an adverbial expletive

徘 1201
ㄆㄞˊ pái
1. hesitating; irresolute; indecisive 2. to walk to and fro; to move around
【徘徊】 ① to linger; to walk to and fro ② hesitating ③ to fluctuate
【徘徊流連】 to walk to and fro hesitatingly with reluctance to
徜 1202 ⌊leave
ㄔㄤˊ cháng 「loitering
going to and fro; lingering;
【徜徉】 lingering or loitering

徙 1203
ㄒㄧˇ xǐ
1. to move one's abode; to migrate 2. to be exiled
【徙居 or 徙移】to move; to migrate
【徙善】 to change for the better

從 1204
1. (从) ㄘㄨㄥˊ cóng
1. from; by; whence; through 2. to undertake; to manage; to engage in 3. to follow; to yield to; to listen to; to obey 4. a follower; an attendant
【從不】 never 「from the side
【從旁】(to help, to encourage, etc.)
【從豐 or 從優】 liberally (as of payment); (to pay) according to a higher scale 「throughout
【從頭至尾】from beginning to end;
【從天而降】 (literally) to descend from heaven—very unexpectedly
【從來】 from the beginning
【從良】 (said of a prostitute) to get married, or to become a decent woman again

彳部

【從寬】to be lenient
【從緩】to bide one's time; to postpone
【從簡】(said of ceremonies) to be simple; to forgo pageantry
【從今以後】from now on
【從軍】to enlist oneself in military service
【從前】once upon a time; a long time ago
【從輕發落】to use leniency in meting out punishment
【從小】from one's childhood
【從新做人】to start one's life anew
【從政】to enter politics; to become a government official
【從中】① in the process (of doing something) ② from the inside (of something) ③ in the middle
【從長計議】to take time to make careful deliberations
【從事】to be engaged in (a task); to devote oneself to
【從善如流】to forge ahead in doing what is right
【從屬】subordinate
【從戎】to join the armed service
【從早到晚】from morning till night
【從此以後】from now on; henceforth
【從一而終】to be faithful to one husband all her life
【從未】to have never (happened, etc.)

從 1204
2. (从) ㄗㄨㄥˋ zòng
1. an attendant; a servant 2. secondary; the relation other than one's direct blood relatives 3. an accessory 4. vice
【從犯】an accessory

從 1204
3. ㄘㄨㄥ cōng
1. lax; easy 2. plentiful; abundant 3. to urge
【從容】① unhurried; calm; composed ② plentiful; plenty of
【從容不迫】in an unhurried or leisurely manner

從 1204
4. (縱) ㄗㄨㄥ zōng
from north to south

御 1205
ㄩˋ yù
1. to drive a chariot or carriage 2. a driver; an attendant 3. to resist; to keep out 4. to control; to manage; to superintend; to tame (a shrew); to harness 5. imperial 6. to wait on; to set before, as food; to present to
【御林軍】imperial guards
【御花園】an imperial garden
【御駕】① the imperial carriage ② the emperor
【御駕親征】The emperor personally led his soldiers in a military operation.
【御前】in the presence of the emperor
【御旨】an imperial decree
【御膳】the imperial cuisine
【御膳房】the imperial kitchen
【御賜】bestowed by the emperor
【御醫】the emperor's physician
【御用】(said of articles, etc.) used by the emperor

九畫

徧 1206
ㄅㄧㄢˋ biàn
(語音 ㄆㄧㄢˋ piàn)
1. all over; everywhere 2. the whole (world, etc.)
【徧佈 or 徧布】everywhere; all over
【徧地】everywhere; all places
【徧體鱗傷】to suffer injuries all over one's body
【徧及】all over

徨 1207
ㄏㄨㄤˊ huáng
1. agitated; alarmed 2. irresolute
【徨徨】agitated and indecisive; alarmed and anxious

復 1208
ㄈㄨˋ fù
1. to return; to come back 2. to answer; to reply 3. to repeat; again; repeatedly 4. to recover; a recovery 5. to return to a normal state
【復命】to report to a superior or elder after completing an assigned mission
【復發】(said of illness) a relapse; to relapse
【復返】to return
【復電】a cable reply; to cable a reply
【復古】to revive old customs, etc.
【復工】(said of workers on strike, etc.) to go back to work; (said of a plant after work stoppage) to start operations again
【復刊】to resume publication
【復合】to reunite
【復函】① to write a letter in reply

②a letter in reply
【復活】 resurrection; to revive
【復活節】 the Easter holiday
【復交】 to reestablish diplomatic relations; to resume friendship
【復健】 rehabilitation
【復健中心】 a rehabilitation center
【復習】 to review lessons learned
【復新】 to make new
【復興】 to revive; to restore
【復學】 to go back to school (after a prolonged absence)
【復職】 to reinstate an official to his former position; reinstatement
【復診】 visits to a doctor, hospital, etc. after the first visit for the treatment of the same disease
【復查】 to check; to reexamine
【復仇】 to avenge; (to) revenge
【復出】 to come out again
【復審】① toreexamine ② (law) to review a case
【復任】 to return to one's former office
【復甦 or 復蘇】 to come to life again; to revive; recovery
【復議】 to discuss a project which had been rejected or discarded previously
【復業】 to resume to business again
【復位】 to be restored to the throne
【復元】 to have recovered
【復原】 to restore
【復員】 to demobilize; demobilization

循 1209
ㄒㄩㄣˊ xún
1. to follow; to comply with 2. to postpone 3. in orderly fashion 4. (obsolete) to touch 5. to inspect
【循例】 according to rules
【循規蹈矩】 law-abiding; to obey the rules and regulations
【循環】 circulation
【循環系統】 the circulatory system
【循環小數】 recurring decimals
【循環賽】 a round robin
【循序漸進】 to follow in proper sequence and make gradual progress
【循循善誘】 to lead students gradually and patiently on the right path

十畫

徬 1210
ㄆㄤˊ páng
anxious, agitated and indecisive
【徬徨】 to be anxious, agitated and not knowing what to do

傜 1211
ㄧㄠˊ yáo
compulsory labor service; conscript labor
【傜役】 compulsory labor service; corvée

微 1212
ㄨㄟˊ wéi
(又讀 ㄨㄟ wēi)
1. small; minute; little; slight 2. low; mean; humble 3. a polite expression for "I, my, me" 4. weak; sickly; feeble 5. subtle 6. obscure 7. hidden; concealed 8. to spy 9. if not; but for
【微波爐】 a microwave oven
【微薄】 low; mean; trifling; thin; little
【微不足道】 insignificant
【微妙】 subtle (positions); delicate (relations); obscure and mysterious (meanings, etc.)
【微風】 a breeze
【微服出遊】 to make a tour in disguise
【微電腦】 a microcomputer
【微量】 trace; micro
【微觀】 microscopic
【微乎其微】 extremely trifling or minute; an iota
【微積分】 calculus
【微血管】 (anatomy) capillaries
【微小】 ① very small; minute ② very low (voices, sounds, etc.)
【微笑】 to smile; a smile
【微醺】 slightly drunk
【微生物】 microbes; microorganisms
【微弱】 weak or feeble
【微詞】 a hint or circumlocution (to point out another's mistake, etc.)
【微恙】 a slight indisposition
【微微】 small; minute; diminutive
【微雨】 a light rain; a drizzle

十二畫

徵 1213
1. ㄓㄥ zhēng
1. to summon 2. to levy or raise (taxes) 3. to call to arms 4. to ask; to inquire 5. to request; to seek for 6. to prove; to evidence 7. signs

【徵兵】 to draft able-bodied male citizens for military service
【徵兵制】 the conscription system
【徵聘】 to solicit a competent person for a vacancy
【徵調】 to issue orders to conscript men and make military deployment
【徵購】 requisition by purchase
【徵候】 symptoms, or indications
【徵候群】 a symptom group
【徵集】 to collect or requisition; to levy
【徵求】 to seek; to solicit (answers, etc.); to want (an office clerk, etc.)
【徵求會員】 to recruit members
【徵求意見】 to solicit others' views
【徵信所】 a credit information office
【徵詢】 to solicit opinions, consent, etc.
【徵召】 to draft the capable and virtuous for public service
【徵兆】 a symptom; an omen
【徵收】 to collect (taxes, duty, etc.)
【徵稅】 to levy and collect taxes
【徵文】 to solicit writings publicly
【徵用】 to requisition; to conscript

徵 1213
2. ㄓˇ zhǐ
one of the five musical notes in Chinese scale

徹 1214
ㄔㄜˋ chè
1. penetrating 2. to remove 3. a tax in tithe 4. to manage; to cultivate (farms) 5. to destroy 6. to deprive
【徹底】①(said of a stream, etc.) to be able to see the bottom ②to get to the bottom of; thorough
【徹底澄清】 to clarify a matter thoroughly
【徹頭徹尾】thoroughly; from beginning to end
【徹骨】penetrating the bone; to the bone
【徹夜】 all through the night
【徹悟】 to understand thoroughly

德 1215
ㄉㄜˊ dé
1. morality; decency; virtues 2. favor; kindness 3. behavior; conduct 4. to feel grateful 5. Germany; German
【德高望重】 (said of a person) of virtue and prestige
【德國or德意志】Germany; Deutschland
【德國麻疹】 German measles
【德行】 ① morality and conduct ② (colloquial) manners or appearances
【德政】 benevolent administration or government
【德澤】 the kindness and charity extended to the people
【德文】 the German language; German
【德望】 virtuous conduct and high prestige
【德育】 moral education

十三畫

徼 1216
1. ㄐㄧㄠˋ jiào
1. frontiers 2. to take an inspection trip

徼 1216
2. (儌) ㄐㄧㄠˇ jiǎo
to be lucky; fortunate
【徼幸】lucky; (said of happy events) beyond one's expectations

十四畫

徽 1217
ㄏㄨㄟ huī
1. honorable 2. stops on a lute 3. a streamer, flag, pennant, etc.; a flag-sign 4. an emblem; a badge 5. Anhwei or Huichow
【徽章】 a badge

心部
ㄒㄧㄣ xīn

心 1218
ㄒㄧㄣ xīn
1. the heart 2. the mind 3. conscience; moral nature 4. intention; idea; ambition 5. the core; the inside 6. one of the 28 constellations
【心病】 ① mental disorder ② worries which one cannot share with another
【心不在焉】 absent-minded
【心平氣和】① calmly ② to be very fair, without involving one's personal feelings
【心滿意足】 to be fully contented; complacent
【心目中】 ①in one's heart or mind ② in one's memory
【心扉】 (figuratively) the door of one's heart

【心煩】 piqued; annoyed; fretful
【心煩意亂】 fretful and confused
【心房】 ① (anatomy) auricles ② soul; mind
【心浮氣躁】 to be unsettled and short-tempered
【心服口服】 to admit somebody's superiority, etc. with sincerity
【心腹】 ① loyalty ② a region of great strategic importance ③ a confidant
【心腹之患】 the threat from within
【心得】 what one gains from intense study, meditation or long practice
【心膽俱裂】 to be terror-stricken
【心蕩神馳】 to be infatuated (with a stunning beauty, etc.); rapt
【心地】 conscience; intentions
【心地光明】 clear conscience; upright
【心地善良】 good-natured; kind-hearted
【心電圖】 an electrocardiogram
【心電感應】 telepathy
【心毒手辣】 callous and cruel; cold-blooded
【心動】 ① palpitation or fluttering of the heart ② to become interested in something
【心態】 mentality
【心頭】 ① the heart; the mind ② the heart of an animal
【心疼】 ① (literally) heartache ② to love dearly
【心跳】 ① heartbeat ② palpitation of the heart caused by fear
【心田】 ① one's heart ② one's disposition
【心痛】 to feel the pangs of heart
【心理】 ① mentality; psychology ② thought and ideas ③ mental
【心理輔導】 psychological counseling
【心理建設】 mental readjustment
【心理學】 psychology
【心理作用】 mental reaction
【心理測驗】 a mental test
【心力交瘁】 to feel exhausted both mentally and physically
【心裏話】 one's innermost thoughts and feelings
【心裏有數】 aware of something without speaking out
【心連心】 heart linked to heart
【心靈】 mind; spirit; spiritual
【心領】 ① to understand without verbal exchange ② to appreciate
【心領神會】 to know or understand without being told
【心亂如麻】 extremely confused and disturbed
【心高氣傲】 proud and arrogant
【心肝】 ① a darling; a honey; a sweetheart ② conscience
【心甘情願】 to be totally willing; willingly
【心廣體胖】 A clear conscience contributes to physical well-being.
【心口】 ① the bosom ② one's utterance and what he really thinks
【心口如一】 to speak one's mind frankly
【心坎(兒)】 ① the heart's chord ② bosom ③ the center of the heart
【心曠神怡】 to feel way above par; to feel on top of the world
【心狠】 hardhearted; flinty; heartless
【心花怒放】 to be brimming with joy
【心懷】 to cherish; to harbor
【心灰意懶】 to be downcast and disappointed
【心灰意冷】 to feel discouraged and hopeless
【心慌】 to be greatly shaken and perturbed; panicky
【心慌意亂】 to lose one's wits totally
【心機】 schemes; designs; craftiness
【心跡 or 心迹】 real intentions
【心急】 impatient
【心悸】 palpitation of the heart
【心焦】 anxious; worried; vexed
【心驚膽戰】 shuddering and terrified; to tremble with fear
【心驚肉跳】 trembling with fear trepidation
【心境 or 心情】 a mood; a humor
【心淨 or 心靜】 calm
【心細】 cautious; careful(ness)
【心弦】 the heart's chord
【心心相印】 a complete meeting of minds
【心性】 temperament; tempers
【心虛】 a guilty conscience
【心緒】 a mood; the state of mind
【心血】 energy; painstaking care
【心血來潮】 to hit upon a sudden idea
【心懸兩地】 divided attention; to have worries at two places at the same time
【心胸】 ① will; ambition ② capacity for tolerance
【心直口快】 honest and outspoken

〔心部〕

【心智】mentality
【心照不宣】a tacit understanding or agreement
【心中】in one's heart or mind
【心中有數】to know fairly well
【心腸】① heart ② affections; sympathies ③ conscience ④ a natural bent of the mind
【心室】ventricles
【心事】secrets in one's mind
【心神不定】a confused state of mind
【心上人】a sweetheart; a lover
【心聲】① spoken language ② the heart's desire; intentions
【心術】designs; schemes; intentions
【心如刀割】heartbroken
【心如止水】a mind without worries, cares, ambitions or worldly desires
【心軟】soft-hearted; tender-hearted
【心臟】the heart (as an organ)
【心臟病】(a) heart disease
【心臟病發作】a heart attack
【心醉】① to admire without reserve ② to be captivated or held spellbound
【心思】① ideas ② intentions ③ a mood
【心碎】heartbreak; heartbroken
【心酸】heartsore; grief-stricken; to sadden
【心算】mental arithmetic
【心愛】(things or persons) dear to one's heart
【心安理得】to feel at ease and justified
【心儀】to look upon someone as a model due to admiration
【心意】① ideas; intentions; opinions ② regard
【心有餘悸】one's heart still fluttering with fear
【心有餘而力不足】resources or ability at one's command inadequate to achieve what is desired, or to do what one wishes
【心眼(兒)】① one's intention; conscience ② mind ③ cleverness or wits
【心無旁騖】single-minded
【心窩】① in one's heart ② the region between the ribs
【心悅誠服】to concede or submit willingly
【心猿意馬】cannot make up one's mind; indecision
【心願】① a wish aspiration ② a promise to a god

一畫

必 1219 ㄅㄧˋ bì
1. must; necessarily 2. an emphatic particle
【必備條件】the requisitions (for)
【必得】①(ㄅㄧˋ ㄉㄟˇ) to have to ②(ㄅㄧˋ ㄉㄜˊ) determined to possess something
【必定】most certainly; to be sure to
【必讀】a must for reading
【必恭必敬】displaying full courtesy; showing great respect
【必修科】a required course in the college curriculum; an obligatory course
【必須】must; to have to
【必需】what is essential or indispensable
【必需品】daily necessities
【必勝】will most certainly win
【必然】to have to be (like this)
【必然之勢】a natural trend
【必死之心】with one's back to the wall
【必要】necessary; need

三畫

忌 1220 ㄐㄧˋ jì
1. jealous; to envy 2. to fear; a fear 3. to shun 4. to prohibit; (to) taboo 5. death anniversaries of one's parents, etc.
【忌憚】to dread; (to) scruple
【忌妒】to be jealous of; to envy
【忌口 or 忌嘴】to be on a diet
【忌恨 or 忌心】jealousy; to envy and hate
【忌諱】① a taboo ② to avoid as taboo ③ to avoid as harmful ④ vinegar
【忌辰or忌日】death anniversaries of one's parents, etc.

忍 1221 ㄖㄣˇ rěn
1. to endure; to bear; to tolerate; to put up with; to suffer 2. merciless; truculence 3. to forbear; to repress
【忍不住】① cannot stand it any more ② can not help (laughing, etc.)
【忍痛】① to bear pain with dignity ② (to give up or sell something) reluctantly
【忍耐】patience; forbearance; patient
【忍飢挨餓】to suffer hunger

【忍俊不禁】cannot help smiling or laughing
【忍氣吞聲】to keep quiet and swallow the insults
【忍心】hardhearted; to steel one's heart
【忍住】to hold back the manifestation of feelings by the force of will
【忍受】to endure; to bear; to suffer
【忍讓】to be forbearing and conciliatory
【忍辱負重】to suffer all disgrace and insults in order to accomplish a task
【忍無可忍】beyond one's endurance; can not stand (insults or provocation) any longer

忐 1222 ㄊㄢˇ tǎn

1. timid; apprehensive 2. indecisive; vacillating
【忐忑】① indecisive ② apprehensive ③ a fidget; to fidget ④ honesty

志 1223 ㄓˋ zhì

1. to make up one's mind to pursue some object; to be bent on doing something 2. will; purpose 3. an ideal; ambition; wish 4. annals; records
【志不在此】to have an ambition for things beyond what is presently available or obtainable
【志得意滿】fully satisfied or contented; complacent
【志同道合】to share the same ambition and purpose; of one mind
【志氣】ambition; will
【志趣】purpose and interest; inclination; a bent
【志趣相投】of similar purpose and interest
【志向】purpose; ambition
【志士】① a man of purpose and virtue ② a man of high ambitions
【志士仁人】people of purpose and virtues
【志在必得】to get it at any cost
【志在千里】cherishing a great ambition
【志願】①voluntary ②aspiration; ambition

忘 1224 1. ㄨㄤˋ wàng

1. to forget 2. to omit; to miss (a line, etc.) 3. to neglect; to overlook
【忘本】ungrateful
【忘不了】will not or cannot forget
【忘掉 or 忘卻】to forget
【忘了】to forget; to have forgotten
【忘懷】unmindful; to forget; forgetful
【忘記】①to fail to remember; to forget ② to neglect
【忘其所以】to be beside oneself with enthusiasm, etc.
【忘情】to be unmindful of all emotions and the ups and downs of life; to be unmoved
【忘形】to get carried away
【忘恩負義】ungrateful
【忘憂草】day lily
【忘我】oblivious of self-existence

忘 1224 2. 讀音 ㄨㄤˊ wáng

【忘八】① a tortoise ② a cuckold

忙 1225 ㄇㄤˊ máng

1. busy; short of time; fully occupied 2. hurried; in haste; to make haste
【忙忙碌碌 or 忙碌】①busy; fully occupied ② hurriedly; in great haste
【忙得不可開交】as busy as one can possibly be
【忙得很】very busy
【忙裏偷閒】to steal a moment of leisure under the pressure of heavy workload
【忙亂】busy and flurried
【忙中有錯】Errors are likely to occur in haste.
【忙甚麼】What (are you) busy about? 或 Why the rush?
【忙於】busy doing something

忖 1226 ㄘㄨㄣˇ cǔn

to surmise; to consider; to presume; to suppose
【忖度】to suppose; to consider
【忖思】to imagine 亦作「忖想」

四畫

忡 1227 ㄔㄨㄥ chōng

worried; anxious; uneasy; sad
【忡忡】worried and sad

忤 1228 ㄨˇ wǔ

1. recalcitrant; disobedient 2. a blunder; a mistake; wrong
【忤逆】①recalcitrant; stubborn de-

fiance ② disobedient to one's parents

快 1229 ㄎㄨㄞˋ kuài

1. quickly; fast; hasty; soon 2. nearly; near 3. to hurry up; to make haste 4. quick-witted; ingenious 5. sharp (blades, etc.); keen 6. pleasant; happy 7. honest; straightforward

〔心部〕

【快報】a dispatch; a bulletin
【快板】quick tempo
【快步】a half step; a trot
【快跑】to run fast; Go quick! 或 On the double!
【快馬加鞭】to proceed as quickly as possible; posthaste
【快慢】speed
【快門】a camera shutter
【快刀斬亂麻】to straighten up a complicated or messy situation by taking drastic steps and with dispatch
【快遞】express delivery
【快點兒】Make it snappy. 或 Be quick!
【快電】an urgent cable
【快艇】a speedboat; a motorboat
【快樂 or 快活】happy; joy
【快乾漆】quick-drying paint
【快感】a pleasant feeling
【快鍋】a pressure cooker
【快攻】a quick attack (in ball games)
【快捷】speedy; fast; nimble
【快些】Hurry! 或 faster than
【快照】a snapshot
【快車】an express train
【快車道】a speedway
【快說】Speak up! 或 Be quick!
【快人快語】the straight talk of a straightforward person
【快走】Hurry, let's go. 或 Beat it!
【快嘴快舌】quick of tongue
【快餐】a quick meal; a snack
【快速】fast; quick; prompt
【快慰】happy; satisfying; to be pleased

忱 1230 ㄔㄣˊ chén

1. sincere; sincerity 2. to rely on
【忱悃】sincere sentiments

忸 1231 ㄋㄧㄡˇ niǔ
(讀音 ㄋㄩˇ nǚ)

1. to be accustomed to; to be inclined to (evils, etc.) 2. bashful; ashamed
【忸怩】blush; ashamed; bashful; coyly

忪 1232 1. ㄓㄨㄥ zhōng

1. agitated 2. frightened

忪 1232 2. ㄙㄨㄥ sōng

參看「惺忪」

忠 1233 ㄓㄨㄥ zhōng

1. faithful; loyal; sincere; patriotic 2. devoted; honest
【忠烈】to be loyal till death; martyrdom
【忠烈祠】a martyrs' shrine
【忠良】① faithful and honest ② virtuous persons
【忠告】honest or sincere advice; sincere counsel
【忠肝義膽】having good faith, virtue and patriotism
【忠厚】honest and tolerant; kind and big-hearted
【忠孝兩全】both loyal to one's country and filial to one's parents
【忠心】loyalty; faithfulness; sincerity
【忠心耿耿】loyal, faithful and true
【忠信】faithful and honest
【忠貞】loyal (subjects, etc.); patriotic
【忠貞不貳】the loyalty that can stand all tests and trials
【忠誠】loyal; faithful; staunch
【忠實】① loyal and faithful ② reliable or truthful (reports, etc.)
【忠義】① faithful and virtuous ② people of loyalty and virtue
【忠言逆耳】Truth seldom sounds pleasant.
【忠勇】loyal and courageous

念 1234 ㄋㄧㄢˋ niàn

1. to think of; to miss; to remember 2. to read out aloud; to chant 3. to study; to attend school 4. twenty
【念佛】to call out Buddha's name aloud as an expression of devotion
【念頭】an idea; a thought
【念念不忘】to have (somebody or something) always in one's mind
【念念有詞】to mumble; to mutter
【念舊】to remember old friends
【念經】to chant or intone scriptures
【念咒】to chant or intone charms
【念珠】a Buddhist rosary

【念書】① to read a book aloud ② to study ③ to receive an education

忽 1235 ㄏㄨ hū

1. suddenly; abruptly 2. to disregard; to be indifferent; to neglect 3. to forget 4. one millionth of a tael

【忽地】abruptly; unexpectedly
【忽冷忽熱】① now hot, now cold —abrupt changes of temperature ② sudden changes in one's affection, attitude, enthusiasm, etc.
【忽略】to overlook; to neglect
【忽起忽落】① sudden rise and sudden fall ② the erratic fluctuation of market prices, etc. ③ sudden changes (of mood); now..., now...
【忽視】to disregard; to overlook; to neglect
【忽然(間)】suddenly; unexpectedly

忿 1236 ㄈㄣˋ fèn

1. anger; indignation; fury 2. complaining; hatred

【忿懣】anger; a grudge
【忿忿不平】resentful and complaining angry
【忿怒】indignation; wrath; fury;
【忿恨】animosity; resentment

忝 1237 ㄊㄧㄢˇ tiǎn

1. ashamed; to disgrace 2. a depreciatory expression referring to oneself 3. to be unworthy of the honor

【忝不知恥】shameless
【忝辱家門】to disgrace one's family
【忝爲知己】As an intimate friend of yours, I.... 或(I'm sure you'll forgive me) since we have been good friends.

五畫

怏 1238 ㄧㄤˋ yàng

discontented; disheartened; dispirited

怖 1239 ㄅㄨˋ bù

1. terrified; frightened 2. to frighten; to threaten

怕 1240 ㄆㄚˋ pà

1. to fear; to dread; afraid; scared apprehensive 2. maybe; perhaps; I am afraid....; I suppose....

【怕不怕】Are you afraid?
【怕老婆 or 怕太太】henpecked
【怕冷】to dread cold (weather, etc.)
【怕羞】shy; bashful
【怕甚麽】What are you afraid of?
【怕事】to be timid and overcautious
【怕生】to be shy with strangers
【怕熱】to dislike heat
【怕人】① frightening; horrible ② (said of wild beasts and birds) to shun human beings
【怕死】to be afraid of death
【怕癢】to be afraid of tickling

怙 1241 ㄏㄨˋ hù

1. to rely on 2. one's father 3. things or persons that one relies on

【怙恃】① those one relies on (as troops, gangsters, etc.) ② one's parents—father (怙) and mother (恃)
【怙惡不悛】incorrigible; obdurate and irreclaimable
【怙惡凌人】to intimidate and oppress others

怦 1242 ㄆㄥ pēng

eager; anxious; impulsive

【怦怦】① eager and anxious (to do something) ② faithful and upright ③ with quick beating; pit-a-pat
【怦然】with a sudden shock

怡 1243 ㄧˊ yí

1. harmony; on good terms 2. pleasure; joy; jubilation

【怡情養性】(said of things or environs) to contribute to one's peace of mind or inner tranquility
【怡神】to inspire peace and harmony in one's mind
【怡然自得】happy and contented
【怡養】to enjoy good health and live a happy life

性 1244 ㄒㄧㄥˋ xìng

1. nature; natural property; temper 2. a quality or property 3. sex

【性別】the sex of a person—male or female
【性變態】sexual perversion
【性病】venereal diseases—VD
【性命】a person's life

〔心部〕

【性能】① natural ability ② qualities and capabilities of machinery
【性格】disposition; personality; character
【性感】sex appeal; sexy
【性急】impetuous; impulsive; impatient
【性交】sexual intercourse
【性教育】sex education
【性器 or 性器官】sexual organs; genitals
【性情 or 性向】disposition
【性向測驗】aptitude test
【性行爲】sexual behavior
【性質】property; characteristics; nature
【性子】① a temper; a disposition ② strength; potency
【性騷擾】sexual harassment
【性慾】sexual desire or urge

怯 1245 ㄑㄧㄝˋ qiè (語音 ㄑㄩㄝˋ què)
1. lacking in courage; cowardly 2. nervous; socially timid; fright; fear; afraid
【怯懦】cowardice
【怯場】stage fright
【怯弱】timid, weak and cowardly; cowardice

怪 1246 ㄍㄨㄞˋ guài
1. strange; queer; monstrous; odd; peculiar 2. to be surprised at 3. a ghost; a goblin; an apparition; a monster; an evil spirit 4. uncanny; weird 5. rather; very (interesting, tired, etc.) 6. to blame
【怪不得】① No wonder! ② cannot put the blame on
【怪癖】strange hobbies; eccentricities
【怪僻】peculiar; eccentric; queer
【怪模怪樣】queer appearance and manner
【怪談】weird talks
【怪裡怪氣】strange; queer; eccentric
【怪傑】an extraordinary person
【怪事】How strange! 或 strange happenings or things
【怪手】an excavator
【怪獸】a rare animal; a monster
【怪人】a peculiar person
【怪物】① a monster; a strange creature ② an eccentric fellow

怔 1247 ㄓㄥ zhēng
terrified; stunned; scared
【怔忪】scared and nervous; fearful
【怔忡】severe palpitation

怜 1248 1. (伶) ㄌㄧㄥˊ líng
(often said of a child, young girl, etc.) agile, nimble, or bright; cute and pleasing
【怜俐 or 伶俐】agile; nimble
【怜牙俐齒】to have a glib tongue

怜 1248 2. ㄌㄧㄢˊ lián
an abbreviated form of 憐 — to pity; pity

怵 1249 ㄔㄨˋ chù
1. scared; afraid; frightened; timorous 2. to entice; to induce
【怵目驚心】frightening; shocking

怎 1250 1. ㄗㄣˇ zěn
why; how; what
【怎奈】but alas; except that
【怎能】how can (he do this to me?) 或 how could (you...?)
【怎敢】How can one dare? 或 don't dare
【怎樣】How? 或 In what way?

怎 1250 2. ㄗㄜˇ zě
Why? 或 How? 或 What?
【怎麼 or 怎樣】Why? 或 How? 或 What?
【怎麼辦】How (or what) to do now? 或 What should (I, etc.) do?
【怎麼得了】There is no telling the serious consequences.
【怎麼搞的】How did it happen? 或 Look at what you've done!
【怎麼會】How could this be possible?
【怎麼行】How could it be possible?
【怎麼說】What (did he, etc.) say?

怒 1251 ㄋㄨˋ nù
1. temper; anger; rage; angry; furious 2. to put forth with vigor (as plants, etc.); to sprout; to spring up 3. forceful and vigorous
【怒罵】to curse in rage
【怒目相視】to look black at each other
【怒髮衝冠】intense anger; to bristle with anger
【怒放】① in full bloom ② (figuratively) wild with joy
【怒號】(said of winds) howling; roaring
【怒吼】to roar; roars
【怒火】flames of fury; fury
【怒氣】anger; wrath; rage; fury
【怒氣沖沖】furious; angry; in a

great rage 「shouts
【怒叱】to shout in rage; angry
【怒視】to look at someone angrily

思 1252 ㄙ sī

1. to think; to contemplate; to consider 2. memory; remembrance; to remember; to recall; to think of 3. to mourn; to grieve 4. to admire 5. to pine for 6. a final particle to sound off an expression
【思慕】① to admire (a girl, etc.) ② to remember (old days, etc.)
【思念】to remember (old days, friends, etc.); to recall
【思路】(usually said of writing) the clarity of thinking, or the lack of it
【思慮】consideration; contemplation; to think carefully
【思考】to ponder; to think; contemplation
【思考力】the power to think, analyze and speculate
【思鄉病】homesickness; nostalgia
【思想】① thought; ideas; mentality ② to think of; to recall
【思想落伍】old-fashioned in thinking; outdated ideas
【思想家】a thinker
【思緒】a train of thought
【思潮】① the prevailing trend of thought ② the changing tides of one's thought
【思春】(usually said of girls) to pine for the opposite sex
【思忖 or 思量】to think; to consider; to ponder
【思索】to study; to ponder over
【思維 or 思惟】thought; thinking

怠 1253 ㄉㄞ dài

1. idle; remiss; lax; negligent 2. to treat coldly
【怠慢】① to neglect a visitor or guest (often used as a polite expression) ② lax and crude; idle and remiss
【怠惰】idle and lazy
【怠忽】to be remiss; to neglect

急 1254 ㄐㄧ jí

1. quick; quickly; with expedition 2. urgent; hurried; hasty 3. anxious; very eager; worried
【急病】a sudden illness
【急迫】urgent; pressing
【急忙】urgently; hastily; hurriedly; quickly; in a hurry
【急電】① an urgent cable ② to call urgently 「angry torrents
【急湍】a swift flow of water;
【急難】① a crisis; an emergency ② to offer help in an emergency
【急流】swift currents; rapids
【急流勇退】to retire when one has ridden the crest of success
【急公好義】to be enthusiastic about charity work
【急功近利】so eager to be successful that one sees only the immediate advantages
【急口令or繞口令】a tongue twister 「great hurry
【急急忙忙】in great haste; in a
【急救】first-aid; first aid
【急救箱】a first-aid kit 「patch
【急件】an urgent document; a dis-
【急遽】quick (falls, rises, etc.)
【急起直追】to rise and make a hot chase; to make amends as quickly as possible
【急切】① urgent; anxiously (awaiting, etc.) ② in a hurry; in haste
【急性闌尾炎】acute appendicitis 亦作「急性盲腸炎」
【急性子or急性兒】impatient; rash; quick-tempered
【急需】to need urgently
【急智】quick-witted 「treatment
【急診】(medicine) emergency
【急中生智】suddenly hit upon a way out of a predicament
【急事】an urgent matter
【急躁】rash and impatient
【急促】① urgently; hastily; hurriedly ② (said of time) short
【急速】hurriedly; hastily
【急於】to be in a hurry or anxious to (finish the task, conclude the war, etc.); eager
【急用】(for) urgent use or need

怨 1255 ㄩㄢ yuàn

1. ill will; hatred; enmity; animus; resentment 2. to resent; to complain; to blame (others); to impute
【怨忿】animus; bitterness; a grudge
【怨懟】ill will; hatred; a grudge
【怨歎】to sigh with bitterness
【怨天尤人】(figuratively) to impute

〔心部〕

all faults and wrongs to others; to be neurotically dissatisfied
【怨恨】ill will; enmity; animus
【怨氣】spite; complaints; resentment
【怨聲載道】(said of bad administration, etc.) Complaints can be heard everywhere.
【怨偶 or 怨耦】an unharmonious couple
【怨尤】complaining; a grudge; a grumble
【怨言】complaints; grumbles

怱 1256 (悤、匆) ㄘㄨㄥ cōng
hasty; hastily; hurriedly
【怱忙】haste; in haste; hastily; hurriedly
【怱促 or 怱遽】haste; hastily
【怱怱】hurriedly

六畫

恆 1257 (恒) ㄏㄥˊ héng
1. constant; regular; persevering 2. lasting; continual; continually
【恆河沙數】innumerable; countless
【恆久】constancy; lasting; forever
【恆心】perseverance
【恆星】fixed stars
【恆齒】(anatomy) permanent teeth
【恆產】immovable property—real estate
【恆常】① permanent; constant ② regular; common (practices, etc.)

恃 1258 ㄕˋ shì
to rely on; to depend on; to presume upon
【恃強凌弱】to use one's strength (or power) to bully the weak
【恃寵】to presume on being a favorite (of a high-placed personality)
【恃才傲物】to be arrogant because of one's talents or ability

恍 1259 ㄏㄨㄤˇ huǎng
1. absent-minded; unconscious 2. all of a sudden; suddenly 3. seem; as if
【恍惚 or 恍恍惚惚】① in a trance; absent-minded ② dimly; faintly
【恍然大悟】to come to understand suddenly
【恍如隔世】so different that it is as if a generation had passed
【恍若 or 恍如】as if; as though

恢 1260 ㄏㄨㄟ huī
1. great; immense; enormous; vast; extensive 2. to recover; to restore; to regain
【恢復】to restore; to regain; to recover
【恢復原狀】to restore the original condition
【恢宏 or 恢弘】extensive; magnanimous

恨 1261 ㄏㄣˋ hèn
1. to resent; to hate; hatred; hate 2. to regret
【恨不得】to wish that one could (do something which is not proper to do)
【恨透了】to hate to the utmost degree

恤 1262 (卹) ㄒㄩˋ xù
1. to relieve; to help 2. to sympathize; to be considerate
【恤貧】to give relief to the poor
【恤孤】to relieve orphans

恪 1263 ㄎㄜˋ kè
(又讀 ㄑㄩㄝˋ què)
respectful; reverent; to respect; respectfully
【恪守】to observe (rules) strictly
【恪遵】to obey or follow (orders, rules, etc.) with respect

恫 1264 1. ㄊㄨㄥ tōng
pain
【恫瘝在抱】to show intimate concern over the people's hardships

恫 1264 2. ㄉㄨㄥˋ dòng
to threaten, intimidate, or scare loudly
【恫嚇】to threaten; to intimidate

恬 1265 ㄊㄧㄢˊ tián
quiet; peaceful; undisturbed
【恬澹 or 恬淡】contented; indifferent to worldly gain
【恬靜】undisturbed; having peace of mind; tranquil

恰 1266 ㄑㄧㄚˋ qià
proper; appropriate; suitable
【恰到好處】neither too much nor too little; just right
【恰當】appropriate; fitting; apt; apposite
【恰好】①just; exactly ②by coincidence
【恰巧】by coincidence; by chance

【恰值】just at the time of
【恰如 or 恰似】just like; just as if; just as though
【恰如其分】just suited or becoming to one's importance

恐 1267
ㄎㄨㄥˇ kǒng
1. to fear; to dread 2. I am afraid....
【恐怖】terror; horror; fear
【恐怖分子】terrorists
【恐怕】perhaps; I think; maybe 或 I'm afraid that....
【恐龍】a dinosaur
【恐嚇 or 恐喝】to intimidate; to threaten; to menace; to blackmail
【恐嚇信】a blackmailing letter
【恐慌】① panic; panicky ② (economic) depression or crises
【恐懼】fear; dread; fright

恕 1268
ㄕㄨˋ shù
1. to forgive; to excuse 2. Excuse me. 3. benevolence
【恕不奉陪】I am sorry but I cannot keep you company.
【恕不遠送】I am sorry I connot escort you farther.
【恕罪】to forgive a fault; to pardon an offense

恙 1269
ㄧㄤˋ yàng
1. disease 2. worry

恣 1270
1. ㄗˋ zì
to throw off restraint; to dissipate; to debauch
【恣肆】licentious; willful
【恣意】unscrupulous; willful; unbridled
【恣意妄爲】to act willfully

恣 1270
2. ㄘ cī
【恣睢】① carefree; unbridled ② extremely conceited

恩 1271
ㄣ ēn
favor; grace; gratitude; kindness; benevolence; mercy; charity
【恩德】benevolence; benignity; generosity; bounty
【恩典】①(in old China) an imperial favor ② a favor
【恩惠】kindness; charity
【恩將仇報】to return evil for good; ungrateful
【恩情】loving-kindness; devotion (between friends, teacher and student, husband and wife, etc.)
【恩准】to grant graciously
【恩寵】the emperor's affection or favor
【恩師】a teacher to whom one is greatly indebted
【恩人 or 恩主 or 恩公】a benefactor (of the ruler)
【恩澤】the pervading benevolence
【恩賜】① a gift of grace from the emperor ② to bestow (favors)
【恩愛】(said of a married couple) mutual affection
【恩愛夫妻】an affectionate couple
【恩怨】① gratitude and grudges ② resentment; grievance

息 1272
ㄒㄧˊ xí
1. a breath 2. news; tidings 3. to stop; to end 4. interest (on money) 5. a son 6. to rest
【息怒】to let one's anger cool off
【息款 or 息金 or 息錢】interest (on money)
【息跡 or 息影】to live in retirement
【息息相關】related as closely as each breath is to the next
【息事寧人】to settle disputes and bring about peace

恭 1273
ㄍㄨㄥ gōng
respectful; reverent; deferential
【恭讀】to read respectfully
【恭賀】to congratulate
【恭賀新禧】Happy New Year.
【恭候】to await respectfully
【恭謹】respectfully serious
【恭敬 or 恭恭敬敬】respectful; reverent
【恭請】to invite respectfully; to invite with respect
【恭喜】Congratulations!
【恭喜發財】(a familiar Lunar New Year's greeting) Congratulations and be prosperous.
【恭祝】I, or we, congratulate you upon....
【恭迎】to welcome respectfully
【恭維 or 恭惟】to praise; to flatter

恥 1274
(耻) ㄔˇ chǐ
shame; disgrace; humiliation; to feel ashamed
【恥笑】to laugh at; to ridicule

七畫

悄 1275 ㄑㄧㄠˇ qiǎo
quiet
【悄悄地】 stealthily; secretly; in a clandestine way
【悄然】 ① quietly ② sorrowfully

悅 1276 ㄩㄝˋ yuè
to delight; to gratify; to please; contented; pleased; gratified
【悅目】 pleasant to the eye
【悅耳】 pleasant to the ear; musical

悌 1277 ㄊㄧˋ tì
to show brotherly love; love and respect for one's elder brother

悔 1278 ㄏㄨㄟˇ huǐ
to regret; to repent; remorse
【悔不當初】 to regret a previous mistake
【悔改】 to repent of (a sin); to be repentant of
【悔過】 to show penitence; to be repentant
【悔過書】 a written statement of repentance pledging not to commit the same offense again (a form of punishment)
【悔恨】 to feel remorse for; to regret; remorse
【悔之已晚】 It is too late to repent or regret.
【悔悟】 to awake from sin; to repent

悍 1279 ㄏㄢˋ hàn
1. violent; fierce; cruel 2. audacious; brave 3. stubborn
【悍婦】 a shrew; a virago; a termagant
【悍將】 ① a brave general ② a recalcitrant general
【悍妻】 a shrewish wife
【悍然】 outrageously; rudely; unreasonably
【悍然不顧】 to ignore (advice) stubbornly

悚 1280 ㄙㄨㄥˇ sǒng
fearful; terrified; frightened
【悚慄 or 悚惶 or 悚懼】 to tremble with fear; frightened; terrified
【悚然】 in terror; terror-stricken

悖 1281 ㄅㄟˋ bèi
to go against; to go counter to; to revolt against; contrary to
【悖逆】 to revolt; to rebel
【悖理】 absurd; unreasonable; irrational
【悖禮】 uncivil; impolite
【悖棄】 to turn away from something in revolt

悟 1282 ㄨˋ wù
to become aware of; to realize; to awake to; to comprehend
【悟道】 (Buddhism) to awake to Truth
【悟性】 understanding; the capacity for understanding

悠 1283 ㄧㄡ yōu
1. far; long; vast; extensive 2. sad; pensive; meditative 3. gentle; slow; soft 4. to swing
【悠久 or 悠長】 long in time
【悠閒】 leisurely; unrestrained; unhurried
【悠然】 unhurriedly; in a leisurely manner; naturally
【悠哉悠哉】 ① anxiously ② free from restraint; carefree
【悠揚】 ① flowing gently sometimes high, sometimes low (as sound); ② extending far (as scenery)
【悠遠】 distant; far (in time or space)

悉 1284 ㄒㄧ xī
1. to know 2. all; whole; total; entire
【悉心】 with one's whole heart
【悉數】 all; the entire sum (of money)

患 1285 ㄏㄨㄢˋ huàn
1. suffering; adversity; disaster; peril 2. trouble; worry 3. to be troubled by; to be worried about
【患部】 (said of wounds or skin diseases) the infected part
【患得患失】 to worry about worldly gain and loss
【患難】 suffering; distress; adversity; trouble
【患難之交】 the friendship cemented in adversity
【患者】 a patient (at a hospital)
【患處】 the wounded part

悤 1286 (匆、怱) ㄘㄨㄥ cōng
excited; hurried; agitated
【悤忙or悤卒or悤遽】 hasty; hurried

您 1287 ㄋㄧㄣˊ nín
a deferential form of "你"

八畫

悱 1288 ㄈㄟˇ fěi
1. inarticulate; unable to give

vent to one's emotion 2. sorrowful

【悱惻】affected by sorrow; sad at heart; sorrowful

悵 1289 ㄔㄤˋ chàng
disappointed; frustrated; dissatisfied; sorry

【悵然】disappointed

【悵惘】depressed; in low spirits

悸 1290 ㄐㄧˋ jì
1. palpitation of the heart 2. fear

【悸動】to palpitate with terror

悻 1291 ㄒㄧㄥˋ xìng
angry; indignant; enraged

【悻悻然or悻悻】angry; huff; enraged

悴 1292 ㄘㄨㄟˋ cuì
1. haggard; worn-out; tired out 2. worried; sad

悼 1293 ㄉㄠˋ dào
to mourn (for or over); to lament; to regret; to grieve

【悼念】to mourn; to grieve over

【悼傷】to remember (the deceased) with sorrow

【悼亡】to be bereaved of one's wife

悽 1294 ㄑㄧ qī
1. grieved; sorrowful; afflicted 2. tragic; pathetic; pitiful; grievous

【悽涼】dreary; desolate

【悽苦】suffering tragically

【悽悽】pathetic; pitiful; grievous

【悽悽惶惶】hurriedly; hastily

【悽切 or 悽楚】pathetic; pitiful

【悽愴】① pathetic; pitiful ② cold; dreary; desolate

【悽然 or 悽惻】sad; sorrowful

【悽慘】tragic; heartrending

惆 1295 ㄔㄡˊ chóu
1. regretful; rueful; disconsolate; melancholy 2. frustrated; disappointed

【惆悵】rueful; regretful

情 1296 ㄑㄧㄥˊ qíng
1. feelings; emotions; sentiments 2. fact; detail; situation; condition 3. love; affection; passion 4. nature; reason

【情報】information; intelligence reports

【情報員】a secret agent; an intelligence agent

【情不自禁】to feel an irresistible impulse

【情面】① friendship; regard for others ② face (self-respect, reputation)

【情分】① friendship ② good intentions; good will; solicitude

【情夫】the paramour of a married woman

【情婦】a mistress; the other woman

【情竇初開】(said of girls) to reach puberty; first awaking of love

【情敵】a rival in a love affair

【情調】① a mood; taste ② (psychology) affective feeling tone

【情投意合】to be congenial

【情同手足】to be attached to each other like brothers

【情郎】a girl's lover

【情理】reason; common sense

【情侶】lovers

【情歌】a love song

【情感】emotions; feelings; affection

【情況】a situation; circumstances

【情話】whispers of love; lovers' prattle

【情話綿綿】occupied with endless whispers of love

【情懷】a mood; feelings

【情節】① a plot (of a play, novel, etc.) ② details (of an affair or event); circumstances

【情景】a scene; a sight

【情境】circumstances; a situation

【情趣】sentiment; interest

【情形】a situation; circumstances; conditions

【情緒】① emotions; a mood ② depression; the sulks

【情勢】a situation; the state of affairs

【情深似海】(usually said of parental love) Love is as deep as the sea.

【情商】to ask for a favor as a friend

【情書】a love letter; a billet-doux

【情人】a paramour, sweetheart or lover

【情人節】St. Valentine's Day

【情操】① sentiment (connoting highbrow and complicated sentiment) ② noble thoughts and feelings

【情愫 or 情素】innermost feelings

【情誼 or 情義】friendship; amity

【情意】feeling; sentiment; affection

【情由】reason; cause

心部

【情有可原】pardonable; excusable
【情文並茂】(said of a composition) rich in feelings and eloquent in expression
【情網】the cobweb of love
【情願】① to be willing ② would rather

惋 1297 ㄨㄢ wàn
1. to regret 2. to be alarmed
【惋惜】to feel sorry for (a loss, etc.); to regret

惕 1298 ㄊㄧ tì
1. cautious; watchout; prudent; careful; to be on the alert 2. afraid 3. anxious
【惕厲】to exercise caution and discipline

惘 1299 ㄨㄤ wǎng
dejected; frustrated; discouraged
【惘然】in a daze; stupefied; at a loss

惦 1300 ㄉㄧㄢ diàn
to remember; to bear in mind; to miss; to be concerned about; to keep thinking about
【惦念】to worry about; to miss (a friend or beloved one)
【惦記or惦掛】to feel concern about someone far away

惜 1301 ㄒㄧ xí
1. to pity; to sympathize; to regret; to feel sorry for somebody 2. to value highly; to have a high opinion of (something); to show love or fondness for 3. to spare; to grudge
【惜別】to say good-bye
【惜福】to refrain from leading an excessively comfortable life

惟 1302 (唯) ㄨㄟ wéi
1. to think; to meditate 2. only; alone 3. but; however
【惟妙惟肖】so skillfully imitated as to be indistinguishable from the original
【惟命是聽or惟命是從】always do as one is told; to be slavishly obedient
【惟獨】only; alone
【惟利是圖】interested only in material gain
【惟恐】for fear that; lest; afraid of
【惟我獨尊】egoistic; arrogant
【惟一】the only one

悶 1303 1. ㄇㄣ mèn
low spirits melancholy; depressed; bored; in
【悶悶不樂】depressed; sulky; unhappy
【悶氣】the sulks; pent-up sorrow or resentment

悶 1303 2. ㄇㄣ mēn
1. (said of weather, rooms, etc.) oppressive or suffocating; stuffy 2. (said of a sound) muffled 3. to shut oneself or somebody indoors 4. to cover the tea pot for a while when one makes tea with boiling water
【悶聲不響】to keep one's mouth shut; to remain silent; to remain quiet
【悶熱】sticky; sultry; sweltering
【悶死】to die of suffocation

惑 1304 ㄏㄨㄛ huò
1. to confuse; to perplex; to delude; to beguile; to mislead; to misguide; to puzzle 2. to doubt; to suspect

悲 1305 ㄅㄟ bēi
1. sad; sorrowful; mournful; woeful; rueful; doleful 2. to lament; to deplore; to mourn; to pity; to sympathize
【悲憫】to pity; to have sympathy for
【悲憤】① to lament and resent (an injustice) ② grief and indignation
【悲悼】to mourn (for or over)
【悲歎】to lament; to deplore; to sigh over
【悲天憫人】to be concerned over the destiny of mankind
【悲痛】grieved; deep sorrow
【悲慟】to weep loudly for sorrow
【悲憐】to take pity on (a person)
【悲涼】sad and dreary; somber; dismal
【悲觀】pessimistic
【悲歡離合】the sorrow of parting and the joy of union in life
【悲劇】a tragedy
【悲戚】rueful; doleful; mournful
【悲泣】to sob, or weep, sorrowfully
【悲喜交集】intermingling of sorrow and joy
【悲壯】tragically heroic
【悲傷】sad; sorrowful
【悲慘】tragic(al); pathetic; miserable

【悲從中來】to feel sadness welling up

惠 1306
ㄏㄨㄟˋ huì
1. to benefit; benefit; to profit; profit; to favor; a favor 2. kind; benevolent; gracious 3. gentle and yielding
【惠臨】(honorific expression) to favor with one's presence
【惠顧】① to patronize (my business establishment) ② your kindness, favor or patronage
【惠澤】benevolence; favor
【惠存】to be so kind as to keep (my gift)
【惠賜】to be kind enough to give (me something)

惡 1307
1. ㄜˋ è
1. bad; evil; wickedness; vice; wicked 2. fierce; ferocious
【惡霸】a powerful bully; a local tyrant
【惡報】retribution; evil recompense
【惡魔or惡鬼】a demon; a fiend; the devil
【惡夢】a nightmare
【惡名】a bad reputation; ill fame; notoriety
【惡模惡樣】a fierce or ferocious appearance
【惡毒】venomous; vicious; malicious
【惡徒or惡棍】a scoundrel; a rascal; a villain
【惡劣】① of very poor quality, very inferior ② rude; distasteful ③ vile; satanic
【惡果】undesirable consequences; disastrous effect
【惡貫滿盈】to reach the limit of crimes (tolerated by Heaven)
【惡耗】news of death or disaster
【惡化】to get worse; to degenerate
【惡習】a bad habit
【惡行】an evil deed; a wicked act
【惡性】malignant; virulent; vicious
【惡性倒閉】fraudulent insolvency
【惡性循環】a vicious circle
【惡兆】an ill omen
【惡臭】an offensive odor; a bad smell
【惡勢力】vicious power
【惡人】a bad man; a scoundrel
【惡作劇】mischief; a practical joke
【惡意】① malicious; spiteful ② malice; evil intentions
【惡有惡報】Evil will be recompensed with evil.
【惡運】bad luck; ill luck

惡 1307
2. ㄜˇ ě
to disgust; to sicken; to scorn
【惡心】① nauseated ② disgust

惡 1307
3. ㄨˋ wù
to hate; to detest; to dislike; to abhor; to loathe

九畫

惰 1308
ㄉㄨㄛˋ duò
lazy; idle; indolent
【惰性】inertia; sloth; laziness

惱 1309
ㄋㄠˇ nǎo
1. to anger; to exasperate; to trouble; to irritate; to vex; to annoy 2. angered; offended; annoyed; vexed
【惱怒】angry; indignant; anger; rage; indignation
【惱恨】to be angry at; to be vexed at
【惱火】to become irritated; annoyed
【惱羞成怒】to be moved to anger by the feeling of shame
【惱人】irritating

惶 1310
ㄏㄨㄤˊ huáng
1. afraid; fearful; apprehensive 2. anxious; uneasy 3. flurried; hurried
【惶恐】apprehensive; fearful; afraid
【惶惶】① anxious; uneasy ② hurried; hasty

愐 1311
ㄇㄧㄢˇ miǎn
1. to remember; to give thought to 2. shy
【愐愧】bashful; shy; modest
【愐懷】to think of; to remember

愕 1312
ㄜˋ è
startled; astonished; amazed
【愕然】stunned; dumbfounded; astonished

愣 1313
ㄌㄥˋ lèng
1. dumbfounded 2. reckless; rash; irresponsible; rude 3. outspoken
【愣頭愣腦】① rash; reckless ② stupid; in a stupor
【愣小子】a little fool; a rash young fellow
【愣住了】to be taken aback

惺 1314
1. ㄒㄧㄥ xīng

〔心部〕

1. clever; intelligent; wise 2. wavering; indecisive
【惺惺作態】to be affected; to simulate (friendship, innocence, etc.)
【惺忪】① indecisive ② (said of eyes) not yet fully open on waking up

〔心部〕

惺 1314
2. ㄒㄧㄥˇ xǐng
to become aware of; to awake from ignorance

愀 1315
ㄑㄧㄠˇ qiǎo
1. anxious-looking 2. to show a sudden change of expression
【愀愴】rueful; doleful; sad; sorrowful
【愀然】① turning pale or red suddenly ② anxious; sorrowful

惻 1316
ㄘㄜˋ cè
to feel anguish
【惻隱之心】innate mercy; natural compassion

愉 1317
ㄩˊ yú
happy; contented; pleased
【愉快】cheerful; happy; pleased; delighted
【愉悅】joyful; glad; happy

愜 1318
ㄑㄧㄝˋ qiè
cheerful; satisfied; contented
【愜意】satisfied; contented

想 1319
ㄒㄧㄤˇ xiǎng
1. to think; to consider; to suppose 2. to hope; to expect 3. to plan 4. to remember with longing; to miss 5. to want; would like to
【想必(是)】presumably; probably
【想不到】to one's surprise; unexpectedly
【想不通】can't figure it out
【想不開】to take some misfortune too seriously
【想法子】to devise means; to think of a scheme
【想法】an idea; an opinion; a view
【想到or想起】to think of; to remember
【想通】to straighten out one's thinking
【想念】to miss (something or someone)
【想家】homesick; nostalgic
【想見】to infer; to gather
【想想看】to think about it
【想像】to imagine; to fancy
【想像力】imagination
【想入非非】to indulge in wishful thinking

惹 1320
ㄖㄜˇ rě
to provoke; to rouse; to induce; to attract; to cause; to bring upon oneself; to offend; to incur
【惹麻煩】to excite trouble; to invite trouble
【惹火燒身】to ask for trouble
【惹禍】to bring disaster or misfortune
【惹起】to incite; to provoke; to incur
【惹事】to create trouble
【惹是非 or 惹是生非】to incur unnecessary trouble; to stir up ill will
【惹人注目】to attract attention

愁 1321
ㄔㄡˊ chóu
1. distressed; worried; unhappy; sad; melancholy 2. depressing; saddening; gloomy 3. to worry about; to be anxious about 4. sorrow; woe
【愁眉不展】to wear a sad or distressed expression
【愁眉苦臉】a distressed expression
【愁苦】distress; misery
【愁緒】a sad mood; a gloomy mood
【愁容滿面】to wear a sad look; to look distressed

愍 1322
ㄇㄧㄣˇ mǐn
to pity; to commiserate
【愍恤】to feel pity; to show kindness (toward people)

愆 1323
ㄑㄧㄢ qiān
1. a fault; a mistake; a misdemeanor 2. to lose 3. a malignant disease
【愆過】a fault; a mistake
【愆期】to fail to meet a deadline

愈 1324
ㄩˋ yù
1. to recover (from illness); to heal 亦作「癒」 2. to a greater degree; even more and more
【愈加or愈益】increasingly; more
【愈甚】intenser; to become intense

意 1325
ㄧˋ yì

1. a thought; an idea; sentiments 2. intention; inclination 3. expectations 4. meaning 5. a hint; a suggestion
【意大利】Italy
【意圖】to intend to do something; intention
【意念】an idea
【意料】expectations
【意會】to sense; to perceive spontaneously (not through explanations)
【意見】an opinion; a suggestion; a view
【意見箱】a suggestion box
【意境】a frame of mind; conception
【意氣】spirits; heart; emotion
【意氣風發】high-spirited and vigorous
【意氣相投】congenial; to share the same aspirations and have the same temperament
【意氣用事】to act on impulse
【意下如何】How about it? 或What do you think?
【意想不到】never thought of; unexpectedly
【意向】intentions; inclinations
【意興闌珊】to feel dispirited
【意旨】intention; meaning; will
【意志】volition; will; will power
【意志消沉】dejected; low-spirited
【意中人】the person with whom one is in love
【意識】consciousness
【意思】①meaning ②intention; desire ③ interest
【意思意思】to serve as a token
【意義】meaning; significance
【意有未盡】to wish to continue doing something one has done for a long time
【意外】①unexpected; accidental ② a surprise; an accident
【意外事件】an accident
【意謂】It seems to say....
【意味】①an impression ② to portend
【意味深長】meaningful; profound in meaning
【意欲】volition; desire; to want to do something
【意願】inclination; wish; volition

愚 1326
ㄩˊ yú

1. stupid; foolish; silly; unwise; unintelligent 2. to fool; to cheat; to deceive 3. (courteous self-reference) I; me
【愚笨】stupid; foolish
【愚昧】benighted; stupid; ignorant
【愚鈍】dull-witted; stupid
【愚弄】to make a fool of somebody
【愚見】my humble opinion
【愚蠢】stupid; dull
【愚人】a fool; a simpleton
【愚人節】All Fools' Day

感 1327
ㄍㄢˇ gǎn

1. to find; to feel; to sense; to perceive; to respond to 2. to affect, move, or touch 3. feeling; sensation; emotion 4. to be grateful
【感冒】①a cold ② to catch a cold
【感到】to feel; to sense
【感動】(mentally) to move, affect, or touch
【感歎】to exclaim
【感歎號】the exclamation mark
【感同身受】to feel deeply moved by a kindness (shown to somebody else) as if one were actually the object thereof
【感念】to remember with gratitude
【感官】① the senses ② a sensory organ
【感慨】emotional excitement; regrets
【感化】to reform (a person); to influence (a person) by personal examples of moral uprightness
【感化院】a reformatory
【感懷】①stirred or aroused emotions (often used in titles of old-style poems) ② to recall with emotion
【感激】to feel grateful
【感覺】① sense; feeling ② to feel; to sense
【感覺神經】sensory nerves
【感情】feelings; emotions; devotion (between friends, relatives, etc.)
【感情用事】to appeal to emotions
【感謝】to thank; gratitude
【感想】mental reaction; an impression
【感性】perceptual
【感召】the inspiration (to do a noble or brave deed) given by religious teachings, great leaders, etc.
【感觸】feeling; mental reaction
【感受】to perceive; to feel
【感傷】sentimental; sentimentality
【感染】to be infected with; to affect
【感恩圖報】to feel grateful for a kind act and plan to repay it
【感恩節】Thanksgiving Day
【感應】① to feel and respond ②

(physics) induction

愛 1328 ㄞˋ ài

1. to love; to like; to be fond of; to be kind to 2. love; affection; kindness; benevolence; likes 3. to be apt to

【愛不忍釋or愛不釋手】loving something too much to part with it
【愛莫能助】desirous but unable to help
【愛慕】to adore; adoration
【愛撫】to caress
【愛戴】to love and support
【愛女】a beloved daughter
【愛憐】to show love or fondness for
【愛戀】to be in love with
【愛國】patriotic
【愛國心】patriotism
【愛克司光】X rays; Roentgen rays
【愛好】to be interested in, or to love (sport, art, etc.)
【愛好者】a lover (of art, sports, etc.); a fan
【愛護】to give kind protection to; to take kind care of
【愛妾】a beloved concubine
【愛情】love
【愛惜】to prize; to cherish; to value
【愛虛榮】vainglorious
【愛心】compassion; kindness
【愛神】Cupid
【愛人】①a sweetheart; a lover ②to love others
【愛滋病毒】AIDS virus
【愛斯基摩人】the Eskimos
【愛死症or愛死病or愛滋病】AIDS (Acquired Immune Deficiency Syndrome)
【愛爾蘭】Ireland
【愛屋及烏】to extend love to someone who is close or dear to one's direct object of love

十畫

愧 1329 (媿) ㄎㄨㄟˋ kuì

ashamed; conscience-stricken; shameful; abashed

【愧不敢當】(an expression used to show humbleness and politeness) ashamed to accept (an honor); do not deserve (a gift, compliment, etc.)
【愧赧】to redden from shame
【愧疚】to feel the discomfort of shame
【愧怍】to feel shame; ashamed

愴 1330 ㄔㄨㄤˋ chuàng

broken-hearted; sad; sorrowful

【愴然】broken-hearted; in anguish of sorrow

慍 1331 ㄩㄣˋ yùn

angry; indignant; displeased; irritated; vexed

【慍懟】to resent
【慍怒】angry; irritated; displeased
【慍色】a displeased look

愼 1332 ㄕㄣˋ shèn

cautious; careful; scrupulous; prudent

【愼密】meticulous
【愼重】cautious; careful; prudent; discreet
【愼重其事】to do something in a serious manner

慊 1333 1. ㄑㄧㄢˋ qiàn

to resent

慊 1333 2. ㄑㄧㄝˋ qiè

contented; gratified; pleased; satisfied

慌 1334 ㄏㄨㄤ huāng

to lose self-possession; to lose one's head; panic; confused

【慌忙】hurried and flustered; hurry-scurry
【慌亂】in a hurry and confusion
【慌張or慌慌張張】flustered; nervous and confused

慈 1335 ㄘˊ cí

1. kind; benevolent; benignant; charitable; merciful; loving; fond 2. of one's mother; maternal

【慈悲】benevolence; pity; mercy
【慈眉善目】a benign face
【慈祥】(said of elderly persons) benevolent; kind; benign
【慈善】benevolence; charity; philanthropy
【慈善機構】a charity organization
【慈善家】a philanthropist
【慈善事業】a charitable enterprise
【慈愛】(said of elderly persons) benevolence; affection; love; kindness

態 1336 ㄊㄞˋ tài

1. an attitude; a position 2. a manner; carriage; deportment; bearing 3. a situation; a condition; circumstances 4. (physics) state of matter

【態度】① an attitude ② a manner

慇 1337
ㄧㄣ yīn
1. mournful; sorrowful 2. regardful; respectful
【慇懃】polite; courteous; civil
【慇慇】mournful; sad; melancholy

十一畫

慘 1338
ㄘㄢˇ cǎn
1. sorrowful; tragic; miserable; sad 2. cruel; merciless; brutal 3. dark; gloomy; dull 4. disastrous-ly
【慘白】dreadfully pale; pale
【慘敗】to suffer a crushing or ignominious defeat; crushing defeat
【慘不忍睹】so tragic that one cannot bear to look at it
【慘澹 or 慘淡】① laborious; arduous ② gloomy; dismal; dim
【慘澹經營 or 慘淡經營】to manage with great pains
【慘痛】bitter; very painful; agonizing
【慘叫】to give a bloodcurdling scream or shriek
【慘劇】a tragic event; a calamity
【慘絕人寰】a rare tragedy on earth; bloodcurdling (atrocities)
【慘兮兮的】sad-looking
【慘狀】a tragic sight; a miserable condition
【慘重】heavy; grievous; disastrous
【慘遭橫禍】to meet a tragic accident
【慘死】to meet a violent or tragic death
【慘案】a cruel murder case
【慘無人道】inhuman; brutal

慢 1339
ㄇㄢˋ màn
1. slow; sluggish 2. negligent 3. haughty; rude; disrespectful; arrogant; supercilious 4. to postpone; to defer
【慢跑】to jog; jogging
【慢慢 or 慢慢兒】① slowly; unhurriedly ② gradually; little by little
【慢慢來 or 慢來】① to come or occur slowly ② Don't rush! Take your time.
【慢動作】slow motion
【慢條斯理】unhurried; leisurely
【慢吞吞】irritatingly slow
【慢工出細活】Fine products come from slow work.
【慢些 or 慢點兒】to slow down a bit
【慢性】① chronic (disease, etc.) ② slow (in taking effect)
【慢性病】a chronic disease
【慢著】Go slow! 或 Wait a minute!
【慢車】a local train; a slow train
【慢車道】slow-traffic lanes
【慢走】① Don't go yet! 或 Halt! ② (polite formula) Good-bye!

慣 1340
ㄍㄨㄢˋ guàn
1. habitual; customary; usual; accustomed 2. to spoil (a child) 3. to be accustomed to; to be used to
【慣例】custom; usual (or established) practice
【慣壞】to spoil (a child)
【慣竊 or 慣賊】a habitual thief; an incorrigible thief
【慣常】customary; usual
【慣於】accustomed to; used to
【慣用】commonly used
【慣用伎倆】customary tactics; old tricks

慟 1341
ㄊㄨㄥˋ tòng
extreme grief
【慟哭】to weep bitterly

慨 1342
ㄎㄞˇ kǎi (又讀 ㄎㄞˋ kài)
1. to sigh emotionally 2. generous; magnanimous
【慨歎】to deplore or lament with sighs

慷 1343
ㄎㄤ kāng
(又讀 ㄎㄤˇ kǎng)
1. ardent; impassioned 2. generous; liberal; magnanimous; unselfish
【慷慨】① generous ②(usually said of a hero) vehement; fervent
【慷慨激昂】(said of speech or conduct) impassioned; arousing
【慷慨解囊】to make generous contributions (of funds)

慳 1344
ㄑㄧㄢ qiān
1. stingy; niggardly; parsimonious; close 2. deficient
【慳吝】stingy; niggardly; miserly

慵 1345
ㄩㄥ yōng
(又讀 ㄩㄥˇ yǒng)
indolent; lazy; idle

〔心部〕

【慵惰 or 慵懶】lazy; indolent; idle

慪 1346 ㄡ ōu
1. same as 嘔—to irritate; to exasperate 2. to be stingy about something
【慪氣】to become exasperated; to be difficult and sulky

慫 1347 ㄙㄨㄥˇ sǒng
to instigate; to incite
【慫慂or慫恿】to instigate; to incite

慚 1348 (慙) ㄘㄢˊ cán
ashamed; mortified; humiliated
【慚愧】ashamed

慧 1349 ㄏㄨㄟˋ huì
intelligent; bright; wise
【慧根】(Buddhism) the root of wisdom that can lead one to truth
【慧黠】(literary language) clever and artful; astute
【慧星】a comet
【慧眼】① insight ② (Buddhism) the eye of religious insight
【慧眼識英雄】Discerning eyes can tell greatness from mediocrity.

慰 1350 ㄨㄟˋ wèi
to console; to comfort; to soothe; to assuage; to relieve
【慰勞】to entertain and cheer (sometimes by means of material gifts)
【慰留】to try to retain (a person intending to resign) in office
【慰藉】to console
【慰問】to show sympathy by making inquiries
【慰問金】money sent to express one's gratitude or sympathy

慼 1351 (慽) ㄑㄧ qī
1. mournful; woeful 2. ashamed
【慼容】a sad look; a sorrowful expression
【慼慼】sorrowful; sad; rueful

慾 1352 ㄩˋ yù
desire; appetite; passion; lust; greed
【慾念】desire; a longing; a craving
【慾令智昏】Greed can benumb reason.
【慾火焚身】The fire of lust is so hot that it consumes the body.
【慾望】desire; a longing; aspirations

慕 1353 ㄇㄨˋ mù
1. to yearn for; to long for 2. to adore; to admire
【慕名】① eager for fame ② to admire another's reputation
【慕名而來】①to be attracted to a place by its reputation as a scenic spot, etc. ②to visit a stranger far away because of his or her reputation as a hero, great beauty, etc.

憂 1354 ㄧㄡ yōu
1. pensive; mournful; grieved; sad 2. anxiety; to worry about; concerned about; anxious; apprehensive
【憂憤】grieved and indignant
【憂勞成疾】to lose one's health because of care
【憂慮】worried; anxious
【憂患】suffering; hardship; misery
【憂懼】anxious and fearful
【憂慼】sad and worried
【憂心忡忡】care-ridden; to have a heart loaded with worry
【憂愁】melancholy; grief; sad
【憂傷】worried and grieved
【憂鬱】melancholy; depressed; dejected

慮 1355 ㄌㄩˋ lǜ
1. to consider; to take into account 2. to worry about; anxious about

慶 1356 ㄑㄧㄥˋ qìng
1. festivity; blessing; felicity; joy 2. to celebrate; to congratulate; to rejoice
【慶典】national festivities and celebration ceremonies
【慶功宴】a celebration party
【慶賀】to celebrate; to rejoice; to offer congratulations
【慶幸】to congratulate or rejoice oneself
【慶祝】to celebrate; celebration
【慶生會】a birthday party

十二畫

憐 1357 ㄌㄧㄢˊ lián
1. to sympathize; to pity 2. as in 憐惜—to feel tender regard for 3. touching

【憐憫or憐閔or憐愍】to pity; to take compassion on; to commiserate
【憐香惜玉】to have a tender heart for the fair sex
【憐愛】to feel pity and love for

憎 1358 ㄗㄥ zēng
to hate; to loathe; to abhor; to abominate; to detest
【憎恨】to hate
【憎惡】to abominate; to detest; to abhor

憔 1359 ㄑㄧㄠˊ qiáo
emaciated; haggard; worn
【憔悴】①to look haggard ②to suffer distress, worries, etc. ③(said of plants) withered

憧 1360 ㄔㄨㄥ chōng
1. indecisive; irresolute 2. to aspire; to yearn
【憧憬】to imagine something or a place with yearning or longing

憒 1361 ㄎㄨㄟˋ kuì
muddleheaded; confused in one's mind
【憒亂】confused in one's mind; at a loss

憫 1362 ㄇㄧㄣˇ mǐn
1. to pity; to commiserate; to feel concerned over 2. to sorrow; to grieve

憑 1363 ㄆㄧㄥˊ píng
1. to rely upon 2. to lean on 3. to be based on; to go by; to base on; to take as a basis 4. a basis; proof; evidence 5. no matter (what, how, etc.)
【憑本事】by virtue of sheer competence or talent (as distinct from pure luck or chance)
【憑單】a certificate; a receipt
【憑弔】①to pay homage to (the deceased) ②to contemplate (a ruin, relics, etc.) with emotion
【憑眺】to look far from an eminence
【憑良心】as one's conscience dictates
【憑空】without substantial support or proof
【憑藉】①by means of ②to rely on ③something on which one relies
【憑據】a basis (for belief or supposition); grounds; reasons; proof
【憑仗 or 憑恃】to rely upon; to depend upon
【憑證】a voucher; proof; evidence
【憑甚麼】why; on what ground (or basis)

憋 1364 ㄅㄧㄝ biē
1. to suppress inner feelings with efforts 2. to feel oppressed
【憋不住】cannot suppress (feelings, emotions, etc.); cannot help (speaking out something)
【憋扭】to be of contrary opinion
【憋氣】to suffer breathing obstruction

憊 1365 ㄅㄟˋ bèi
tired; exhausted; weary

憩 1366 (憇) ㄑㄧˋ qì
to rest; to repose
【憩息or憩歇】to rest; to take a rest

憨 1367 ㄏㄢ hān
1. silly; stupid; foolish 2. naive; straightforward
【憨厚】simple and honest
【憨笑】to giggle; to titter; to smile foolishly
【憨直】honest and straightforward

憲 1368 ㄒㄧㄢˋ xiàn
1. law; a code; a statute; an ordinance; a constitution 2. intelligent 3. a reference to superiors
【憲兵】military police; gendarmes
【憲法】constitution (of a national government)
【憲令】laws and ordinances
【憲章】a charter (or rule)
【憲政】constitutional government

十三畫

憤 1369 ㄈㄣˋ fèn
to resent; indignant; indignation; angry
【憤憤不平】resentful or indignant because of injustice
【憤怒】anger; wrath; indignation; rage
【憤慨】anger (especially at injustice); indignation
【憤恨】resentment
【憤世嫉俗or憤嫉】resentful of the world; misanthropic; cynical
【憤然】angrily

〔心部〕

憶 1370
ㄧ yì to remember; to bear in mind; to recall; to recollect
【憶起】to call to mind; to recall

憾 1371
ㄏㄢ hàn
regret; remorse; dissatisfaction
【憾事】a regrettable thing

懂 1372
ㄉㄨㄥˇ dǒng
to understand; to comprehend; to know
【懂不懂】Do you understand?
【懂得】to understand; to comprehend
【懂道理】to be reasonable
【懂事】(said of the young) familiar with human affairs

懈 1373
ㄒㄧㄝˋ xiè
negligent; remiss; relaxed; inattentive
【懈慢】neglectful; negligent
【懈怠】to neglect; slack; negligent

懊 1374
ㄠˋ ào
to regret; to resent; regretful
【懊惱】to feel remorseful and angry
【懊悔】to regret; remorseful; regretful

應 1375
1. ㄧㄥ yīng
as in 應該—should; ought to; need
【應否】should or should not
【應得】that one deserves to receive; deserved
【應當】duty-bound; should; ought to
【應屆畢業生】graduating students or pupils
【應有】due; proper; deserved
【應有盡有】Nothing is wanting.

應 1375
2. ㄧㄥˋ yìng
1. to respond to; to answer; to echo; to react to 2. to comply with; to grant 3. to deal with; to cope with 4. to assent to
【應變】① to prepare oneself for change ② to adapt oneself to changes
【應變措施】an emergency measure
【應聘】to accept an offer of employment
【應門】① to keep the gate ② to answer the door
【應付】to deal with; to cope with; to handle
【應答】to reply; to answer
【應對】① to answer questions ② repartee
【應對如流】to answer questions fluently
【應考】to participate in an examination
【應急】to meet an emergency
【應接不暇】too busy to make proper response to
【應景兒】to do something appropriate on the occasion
【應召女郎】a call girl
【應召入伍】to be drafted (for military service)
【應戰】to accept a challenge; to meet the enemy on the battlefield
【應診】(said of a doctor) to see patients
【應徵】① to respond to a want ad ② to be recruited
【應酬】① social appointments ② to treat with courtesy
【應時】① seasonable ② to adapt oneself to the times
【應試】to take examinations
【應聲蟲】a servile sycophant
【應邀】at somebody's invitation
【應驗】to come true; to be fulfilled
【應允】to assent; to consent
【應運而生】to come with the tide of fashion
【應用】① to utilize; to make use of ② for practical application
【應用文】practical writing

懇 1376
ㄎㄣˇ kěn
cordial; sincere; earnest
【懇談】to talk in a sincere manner
【懇切】very sincere; earnest
【懇求】to implore; to plead
【懇親會】PTA (parent-teacher association or meeting)
【懇請】to ask earnestly; to implore; to entreat

十四畫

懦 1377
ㄋㄨㄛˋ nuò
timid; cowardly; weak
【懦夫】a coward
【懦弱】weak; cowardly

十五畫

懲 1378 ㄔㄥˊ chéng
(又讀 ㄔㄥˇ chěng)
1. to punish; to chastise; to reprimand; to reprove; to warn 2. to stop
【懲辦】 to take disciplinary action against
【懲罰】 to punish; to penalize; a penalty
【懲戒】 to reprimand; to punish
【懲治】 to remedy by punishment
【懲惡勸善】 to punish wickedness and encourage virtue

十六畫

懷 1379 ㄏㄨㄞˊ huái
1. bosom; breast 2. to hold; to harbor 3. to think of; to recollect 4. to conceive (a child)
【懷抱】 an embrace; a hug; to embrace; to hug
【懷錶】 a pocket watch
【懷胎 or 懷孕 or 懷妊】 to become pregnant; to conceive
【懷念】 to have a sweet memory of
【懷鬼胎】 to harbor an evil scheme
【懷恨 or 懷仇】 to bear a grudge
【懷舊】 ① to yearn for the past ② to think of old friends
【懷鄉】 homesick
【懷想】 to remember with fondness; to yearn for
【懷中】 ① in the arms ② in the mind
【懷春】 (usually said of young girls) to begin to think of love, or become sexually awakened
【懷才不遇】 to have talent but no opportunity to use it
【懷疑】 to doubt; to suspect

懶 1380 ㄌㄢˇ lǎn
lazy; indolent; idle; inactive; listless
【懶怠 or 懶惰】 lazy; idle; indolent
【懶骨頭or懶蟲】 lazybones; a lazy person
【懶散】 indolent; inactive
【懶洋洋】 indolent; sluggish

懵 1381 1. (懞) ㄇㄥˊ méng
ignorant: 懵懵無知 quite ignorant

懵 1381 2. ㄇㄥˇ měng
muddleheaded; confused
【懵懂】 ① muddleheaded ② ignorant

懸 1382 ㄒㄩㄢˊ xuán
1. to hang or be hanged or hung; to suspend or be suspended 2. to be in suspension; to be in suspense; unsettled; unsolved 3. unfounded; without a basis; unsupported 4. far apart 5. to be concerned for
【懸念】 worry and concern for a friend or close family member far away
【懸梁自盡】 to hang oneself
【懸掛】 to hang (decorations)
【懸空】 to be suspended (or hung) in the air
【懸壺濟世】 to practice medicine or pharmacy
【懸旗】 to hoist a flag; to hang a flag
【懸賞】 to offer a prize, or reward (for the capture of a criminal, etc.)
【懸殊】 very different
【懸案】 an unsettled case
【懸而未決】 suspense; in suspense
【懸疑】 suspense
【懸崖】 a precipice
【懸崖勒馬】 to stop just before committing a serious blunder
【懸崖峭壁】 overhanging precipices and steep cliffs

十七畫

懺 1383 ㄔㄢˋ chàn
to confess one's sin; to repent
【懺悔】 to repent of one's sin; to feel repentance
【懺悔錄】 confessions

十八畫

懼 1384 ㄐㄩˋ jù
1. to fear; to dread; to be afraid of 2. to frighten
【懼怕】 to fear; to dread; to be afraid of
【懼內】 henpecked
【懼高症】 acrophobia

懾 1385 ㄓㄜˊ zhé
fearful; awe-struck
【懾服】 to yield from fear

懿 1386 (懿) ㄧˋ yì
1. virtuous; fine; good; exem-

plary 2. having to do with womanly virtue; modest; chaste
【懿德】fine virtue
【懿行】a virtuous deed
【懿言】fine words

〔戈部〕

十九畫

戀 1387
ㄌㄧㄢˋ liàn
1. to love (one of the other sex); to be in love 2. to feel a persistent attachment (for a thing)
【戀母情結】Oedipus complex
【戀父情結】Electra complex
【戀家】to be reluctant to leave home
【戀舊】to yearn for the past
【戀情】love between man and woman
【戀棧】reluctant to give up a position (particularly a public post) one is holding
【戀人】a sweetheart
【戀愛】tender passions

戈部
ㄍㄜ gē

戈 1388
ㄍㄜ gē 「family name}
1. a spear; a lance 2. a Chinese
【戈壁】Mongolian for "desert"
【戈壁大沙漠】the Gobi Desert

一畫

戊 1389
ㄨˋ wù 「Stems}
the fifth of the Ten Celestial

二畫

戌 1390
ㄒㄩ xū
the eleventh of the Twelve Terrestrial Branches
【戌時】7-9 p.m.

戍 1391
ㄕㄨˋ shù
to guard; to defend 「frontier}
【戍邊】to guard the border or the
【戍守or戍衛】to be stationed as garrison troops at (a fortified place, the border, etc.)
【戍人 or 戍卒】garrison soldiers; a frontier guard

戎 1392
ㄖㄨㄥˊ róng
1. war; fighting 2. arms; the apparatus of war 3. military affairs; army 4. barbarians to the west 「tary career}
【戎馬生涯】an army life; a mili-
【戎裝 or 戎衣】military dress
【戎伍】the ranks; the army

三畫

成 1393
ㄔㄥˊ chéng
1. completed; accomplished; finished; fixed; settled; to accomplish; to succeed; to complete 2. to achieve 3. to become 4. acceptable; all right 5. able; capable 6. one tenth 7. a Chinese family name
【成敗】success or failure
【成本】(commerce) cost
【成品】finished products
【成名】to become famous
【成佛】to become a Buddha
【成分】①an ingredient; a component ②a factor ③personal background
【成堆】to pile up 「a pair}
【成對or成雙】to match; to form
【成套】to form a complete set
【成天】all day long; the whole day
【成年】to reach adulthood; to come of age 「month after month}
【成年累月】year after year and
【成立】①to establish; to found; to set up ②(said of a relation, theory, etc.) to hold good or to be recognized as irrefutable
【成果】achievements; the fruits (of efforts)
【成規】an established practice, rule or regulation; a rut
【成功】success
【成何體統】What a scandal!
【成婚 or 成親】to get married
【成績】records established or set
【成績單】a report card
【成家】(said of men reaching adulthood) to get married
【成交】to get accepted by both parties, or to go through a busi-

ness deal; to strike
【成就】an achievement; an accomplishment
【成就感】a sense of fulfillment
【成見】a prejudice; a bias
【成千累萬or成千成萬】countless; numerous
【成全】to help (others) accomplish something
【成羣】in groups; in large numbers
【成羣結隊】to band together
【成效】result; effect
【成效卓著】The achievement is outstanding.
【成行】to embark on a journey
【成形】to take shape
【成長】to grow up; growth
【成熟】to mature; to ripen
【成日】the whole day; all day
【成人】an adult; a grownup
【成災】to cause disaster
【成材or成器】to become a useful person
【成衣】ready-made clothes; garments
【成藥】patent medicine
【成因】the cause of formation
【成樣】an established model (of manufactured goods)
【成爲】to become; to turn into
【成爲泡影】to come to nothing
【成文】existing writings
【成語】an idiom; a phrase
【成員】a member

戒 1394
ㄐㄧㄝˋ jiè
1. to warn; to admonish; to caution 2. to abstain from; to refrain from; to give up 3. to guard against; to avoid 4. a commandment; Buddhist monastic discipline
【戒備】on guard (against enemy attacks, natural disasters, etc.)
【戒備森嚴】to be heavily guarded
【戒掉】to abstain or give up (a bad habit)
【戒賭】to abstain from gambling
【戒條 or 戒律】don'ts; (Buddhism) the rules; commandments
【戒懼】to be afraid and watchful
【戒心】watchfulness; on one's guard
【戒指】a ring (on a finger)
【戒尺】a ferule
【戒除】to abstain from; to give up
【戒煙】to give up smoking
【戒嚴】to impose a curfew
【戒嚴令】martial law

我 1395
ㄨㄛˇ wǒ (讀音 ㄜˇ ě)
1. I; me; my 2. we; our; us 3. self
【我們】we; us
【我方】our side; we
【我國】our country
【我家】my home; my house
【我行我素】to act according to one's will regardless of others' opinions

〔戈部〕

四畫

或 1396
ㄏㄨㄛˋ huò
1. a certain; some 2. perhaps; probably 3. or
【或多或少】more or less
【或許】perhaps; probably; maybe
【或者 or 或是】① or ② perhaps
【或早或晚】sooner or later
【或謂 or 或曰 or 或云】some people say that...

戕 1397
ㄑㄧㄤˊ qiáng
1. to slay; to kill; to destroy 2. to be injurious
【戕害】to slay

戔 1398
ㄐㄧㄢ jiān
small; little; tiny
【戔戔之數】an insignificant amount (of money)

七畫

戚 1399
ㄑㄧ qī
1. relatives by marriage 2. sad; woeful; mournful 3. a battle-ax 4. a Chinese family name
【戚戚】① mournful ② touched

九畫

戡 1400
ㄎㄢ kān
1. to subdue; to suppress; to put down 2. to kill
【戡亂】to suppress a rebellion

十畫

截 1401
ㄐㄧㄝˊ jié
1. to cut; to section; to truncate 2. a slice; a division; a section

〔戈部〕

3. to detain; to withhold 4. to keep; to set in order 5. to stop; to close; to end

【截斷】 to disrupt; to cut off
【截獲】 to capture by interception
【截擊】 to intercept
【截角】 to cut off or tear off a corner (of an envelope, a ticket, etc.); to truncate
【截肢】 amputation
【截止】 to close (application, registration, etc.) upon reaching the deadline
【截長補短】 to even up scarcity and superabundance
【截然】 distinctly

十一畫

戮 1402 ㄌㄨˋ lù

1. to slay; to massacre; to slaughter 2. to unite or join
【戮力】 to join forces; to cooperate
【戮力同心】 to join forces and work for a common cause

十二畫

戰 1403 ㄓㄢˋ zhàn

1. war; warfare; fighting; battle 2. to contest; to fight; to contend 3. to shudder 4. a Chinese family name
【戰敗】 to suffer (a) defeat; to be defeated
【戰備】 war preparations
【戰馬】 a war-horse; a battle steed
【戰犯】 a war criminal
【戰俘】 prisoners of war
【戰鬥】 ① to fight; to combat; to engage in a battle ②(military) action
【戰鬥機】 a fighter plane; a fighter
【戰鬥員】 a combatant
【戰慄】 to tremble; to shudder; to shiver
【戰利品】 a trophy; booty; a prize; loot
【戰亂】 chaos and social upheavals brought about by war
【戰略】 strategy
【戰鼓】 battle drums
【戰國時代】 the Epoch of Warring States (403-221B.C.)
【戰果】 military achievements; war results
【戰況 or 戰局】 the war situation
【戰壕】 a trench
【戰火】 flames of war
【戰績】 military successes (or exploits)
【戰績輝煌】 brilliant combat performances
【戰機】 ①an opportunity for combat ② a fighter
【戰艦】 a warship; a battleship
【戰區】 a war zone or area
【戰戰兢兢】 trembling with fear; very cautious
【戰爭】 war
【戰車】 ① a tank (an armored vehicle) ② a chariot
【戰場 or 戰地】 a battlefield
【戰時】 wartime
【戰士】 a warrior; a fighting man
【戰事】 war; hostilities
【戰勝】 to conquer; to win a victory
【戰書】 a written declaration of war
【戰術】 tactics; the art of war
【戰死】 to die in battle
【戰役】 a (military) campaign; a battle
【戰友】 a comrade in arms

十三畫

戲 1404 1. (戱) ㄒㄧˋ xì

1. to play; to toy; to sport 2. to jest; to have fun; to make fun 3. a drama; a play; a show 4. a game
【戲班】 a dramatic troupe
【戲票】 an admission ticket for a play
【戲碼】 a repertoire
【戲迷】 a drama fan
【戲法(兒)】 jugglery; a trick; magic
【戲臺】 a stage (for plays)
【戲弄 or 戲耍】 to play a trick on; to tease
【戲謔】 a joke; a witticism; a jest; fun
【戲劇】 drama; the theater
【戲劇化】 to dramatize; dramatic
【戲劇家】 a playwright; a dramatist
【戲曲】 a drama; a play
【戲裝】 theatrical (or stage) costume
【戲水】 to play in water
【戲子】 a dramatic player
【戲詞】 an actor's lines 亦作「臺詞」
【戲言】 a joke; a witticism
【戲園子 or 戲場 or 戲樓】 a playhouse; a theater
【戲院】 a theater; a movie house

戲 1404 2. ㄏㄨ hū

alas; oh; o; ah

十四畫

戴 1405 ㄉㄞˋ dài
1. to wear on the head, the nose, the ear, or the hand; to put on 2. to support; to sustain; to bear 3. a Chinese family name 4. to respect; to honor 「old
【戴綠帽or戴綠頭巾】to be a cuck-
【戴高帽】to receive a compliment or flattery; to flatter
【戴孝】to go into mourning
【戴罪立功】to atone for a mistake or failure by meritorious services
【戴眼鏡】to wear glasses or spec-
⌊tacles

戳 1406 ㄔㄨㄛ chuō
1. to jab; to poke; to pierce 2. a chop; a stamp; a seal
【戳記】a stamp; a seal
【戳印】① to stamp ② a stamp

戶 部
ㄏㄨˋ hù

戶 1407 ㄏㄨˋ hù
1. a door 2. a household; a family 「banking)
【戶頭or戶名】a depositor (in
【戶內】indoor; indoors
【戶內運動】indoor games
【戶口】households
【戶口普查】census taking; a census
【戶口名簿】a household identifi-
【戶籍】a domicile ⌊cation book
【戶長】the household head
【戶政】the administration with regard to residents and residence
【戶外】outdoor; outdoors
【戶外運動】cutdoor games

四畫

戽 1408 ㄏㄨˋ hù
a pail; a bucket

房 1409 ㄈㄤˊ fáng
1. a house; a building 2. a room; a chamber 3. a compartmentalized structure 4. a wife; a concubine 5. a Chinese family name
【房門】a door to a room
【房地產】real estates
【房東】the landlord (of a house)
【房東太太】a landlady
【房客】the tenant (of a house); a guest (at a hotel, etc.)
【房間】a room; a chamber
【房契】a house ownership certificate 「house or houses
【房產】property in the form of a
【房租】a house rental
【房屋 or 房子】a house; a building

所 1410 ㄙㄨㄛˇ suǒ
1. a place; a location; a position 2. a building; an office 3. that which
【所費不貲】to have spent a fortune
【所得】①income ②what one gets
【所得稅】income tax ⌊or receives
【所到之處】wherever one goes
【所好】one's hobbies or likes
【所向披靡】(said of an invincible army) victorious wherever it goes
【所向無敵】undefeatable; invincible
【所需】needs or requirements (in doing something)
【所學】one's specialty; what one has majored in 「acquaintance
【所知】① what one knows ② an
【所致】as a result of
【所長】① (ㄙㄨㄛˇ ㄓㄤˇ) the head or director of an office ② (ㄙㄨㄛˇ ㄔㄤˊ) one's specialty
【所屬】subordinates; subordinate agencies 「place; a location
【所在】① where one dwells ② a
【所在地】a seat 「duct
【所作所爲】actions; behavior; con-
【所以】therefore; so; consequently
【所有】①belongings ②to own ③
【所有權】ownership ⌊all; every
【所有者or所有人】an owner; a
【所謂】so-called ⌊proprietor
【所願】one's wishes

五畫

扁 1411 1. ㄅㄧㄢˇ biǎn
1. flat 2. a tablet

【扁平】thin and flat
【扁擔】a flat carrying pole or shouldering pole
【扁蹋鼻】a snub nose
【扁桃腺】the tonsils

〔手部〕

扁 1411
2. ㄆㄧㄢ piān
small
【扁舟】a small boat; a skiff

六畫

扇 1412
1. ㄕㄢ shàn
1. a fan 2. a numerary auxiliary for door or gate leaves
【扇形】fan-shaped; a sector (of a circle)
【扇子】a fan

扇 1412
2. (搧) ㄕㄢ shān
to fan; to instigate; to incite
【扇動】to incite; to instigate
【扇惑】to instigate and mislead; to agitate

八畫

扉 1413
ㄈㄟ fēi
a door leaf
【扉葉 or 扉頁】a flyleaf; a title page

手部
ㄕㄡˇ shǒu

手 1414
ㄕㄡˇ shǒu
1. hand; of the hand; having to do with the hand 2. to have in one's hand; to hold 3. a skilled person; a person 4. action 5. personally
【手把】a handle
【手背】① the back of the hand ② (gambling) having bad luck
【手臂】the arm from the wrist up
【手筆】① a literary work or handwriting ② the courage of spending money on a grand scale
【手錶】a wrist watch
【手邊】at hand; handy
【手帕 or 手絹兒】a handkerchief
【手忙脚亂】to be in a flurry
【手面闊綽】extravagantly generous or liberal; lavish
【手法】workmanship; artistry; skill; technique
【手風琴】an accordion
【手到擒來】to capture an enemy easily
【手電筒】a flashlight; an electric torch
【手段】① the means (as opposed to the end) ② a devious way of dealing with people
【手套】gloves; gauntlets; mittens
【手頭】① on hand; at hand; in hand ② financial conditions
【手頭緊】① short of cash (or money) ② closefisted
【手提袋】a valise; a Boston bag
【手提箱】an attaché case; a suitcase
【手推車】a handcart; a wheelbarrow
【手拿】to hold in hand; to take by hand
【手拉手】hand in hand
【手榴彈】a hand grenade
【手稿】manuscript
【手工】handwork; handiwork
【手工藝】handicrafts; handiwork
【手工藝品】fancy works; handicraft articles
【手工業】a manual trade
【手銬】handcuffs
【手脚】① hand and foot ② motion; action ③ tricks; juggles
【手脚俐落】nimble; agile
【手巾】a towel
【手氣】(gambling) luck
【手巧】dexterous; skillful
【手球】(sports) handball
【手鎗】a pistol; a revolver; a gun
【手下】① subordinates ② under the leadership of
【手下敗將】one who has suffered defeat at (my, your, etc.) hands
【手下留情】to show leniency or mercy
【手心】① the center of the palm ② (figuratively) control
【手相】the lines of the palm by which fortunetellers tell one's fortune
【手續】procedures; red tape
【手指頭】① fingertips ② fingers
【手指】① a finger ② to point at something with the index finger
【手札】a personally handwritten letter
【手掌】the palm (of the hand)
【手杖】a cane; a walking stick

【手鐲】 a bracelet
【手抄本】 a hand-copied book
【手勢】 a gesture; a sign; to sign
【手上】 in one's hands
【手術】 a surgical operation; surgery
【手刃】 to kill someone personally with a sword
【手足】 brothers
【手足情深】 The love between brothers is deep.
【手足無措】 to be at a loss what to do
【手册】 a handbook; a manual
【手藝】 handicrafts; a trade
【手印】 an impression of the thumb as a signature
【手癢】 ① an itch on one's hands ② to have an itch to do something
【手無寸鐵】 totally unarmed
【手舞足蹈】 to caper beyond oneself with joy
【手腕】 ① the wrist ② skill; tact; tricks; ability
【手紋】 the lines on the palm
【手語】 dactylology; sign language

才 1415 ㄘㄞˊ cái

1. natural abilities; a gift; talent; a mental faculty 2. a gifted person; a talented person; a brilliant man; a talent 3. people of a certain type 4. certainly; indeed 5. just; just now

【才貌雙全】 (said of women) talented and good-looking
【才德全備or才德兼備】 to have both talent and virtue
【才能or才力】 talent; abilities; a gift
【才女】 a talented woman
【才略】 talent for scheming
【才幹】 talent or ability to get things done; competence
【才華】 brilliance (of mind); a gift; talent
【才華出衆】 of uncommon brilliance
【才氣】 talent; brilliance
【才氣洋溢】 brilliant intelligence
【才情】 brilliant expression of emotions (in a writing)
【才學】 intelligence and scholarship
【才智】 intelligence; brilliance
【才識】 ability and insight
【才疏學淺】 untalented and unlearned (a polite expression referring to oneself)
【才子】 a talented person; a genius
【才子佳人】 an ideal couple
【才思敏捷】 to have an agile imagination and skill
【才藝卓絕】 to stand out in talent

一畫

扎 1416 1. ㄓㄚ zhā

to pierce; to prick

【扎根】 to take root
【扎實】 solid; firm
【扎手】 ① to prick the hand ② difficult to handle
【扎眼】 dazzling; garish

扎 1416 2. ㄓㄚˊ zhá

to struggle; to strive

【扎營】 to pitch a tent; to encamp

二畫

扑 1417 ㄆㄨ pū

to beat; to strike

【扑撻】 to whip; to lash; to flog
【扑擊】 to hit; to strike

扒 1418 1. ㄅㄚ bā

1. to claw; to strip 2. to rake 3. to climb; to scale

【扒皮】 to peel off the skin

扒 1418 2. ㄆㄚˊ pá

1. to gather up; to rake up 2. to stew; to braise 3. to scratch; to claw

【扒竊】 to pick pockets and steal
【扒手】 a pickpocket

打 1419 1. ㄉㄚˇ dǎ

1. to strike; to beat 2. to attack; to fight 3. to smash 4. to do, make, get, fetch, play, buy, etc. (depending on the object) 5. to; from; toward

【打靶】 target practice
【打敗】 ① to defeat ② to suffer a defeat
【打敗仗】 to suffer a defeat
【打包】 to pack
【打包票】 to vouch for; to guarantee
【打飽嗝兒】 to belch after a solid meal
【打抱不平】 to help the victims of injustice
【打扮】 to make up
【打邊鼓】 to incite; to instigate
【打不破】 unbreakable

【打不倒】 unconquerable 「for
【打不過】 to be no fighting match
【打破】 to smash to pieces; to break
【打破紀錄】 to break the record
【打破砂鍋問到底】 to interrogate persistently
【打拍子】 to beat time 「jong, etc.
【打牌】 to play a card game, mah-
【打屁股】 spanking
【打麻將】 to play mah-jong
【打馬虎眼】 to act dumb
【打罵】 to beat and scold
【打毛線衣】 to knit a woolen sweater
【打發】① to dispatch; to send away ② to fire; to dismiss ③ to spend (time)
【打翻】 to overturn; to tip over
【打分數】 to grade (students' papers); to grade (a performance)
【打打鬧鬧】 to fight in jest or for fun
【打得火熱】 ①to be in the middle of a white-hot battle ② to be passionately in love with each other 「throw
【打倒】 to knock down; to over-
【打鬥】 a fight; a skirmish; to fight
【打蛋】 to beat, stir or whip eggs
【打地鋪】 to make a bed on the floor or the ground
【打掉】 to destroy; to knock out; to wipe out 「order ② to bribe
【打點】 ① to examine and put in
【打點滴】 to administer intravenous drip
【打電報】 to telegraph; to cable
【打電話】 to make a telephone call; to telephone
【打賭】 to make a bet
【打哆嗦】 to tremble; to shiver
【打斷】 ① to break ② to interrupt
【打斷念頭】 to give up an idea
【打動】 to move (a person mentally)
【打頭陣】 to lead the attack
【打探】 to find out
【打嚏噴 or 打噴嚏】 to sneeze
【打鐵趁熱】 Strike while the iron is hot. 「through inquiries
【打聽】 to inquire; to find out
【打退堂鼓】 to give up halfway; to back out
【打通】 to establish a connection
【打鬧】 to quarrel and fight noisily
【打蠟】 to wax
【打雷】 to thunder 「of water
【打撈】 to drag sunken things out
【打獵】 to go hunting
【打量】 to size up; to look someone up and down
【打領帶】 to tie a necktie
【打落水狗】 to attack someone already down in his luck
【打歌】 to promote a new song by singing it frequently in public appearance
【打嗝兒】 to hiccough
【打個照面】 to meet face to face
【打鼓】 ① to beat a drum ② to feel uncertain or nervous
【打穀】 to thresh grain
【打滾兒】 to roll about
【打官腔】 bureaucratic jargon
【打官司】 to have a lawsuit
【打光棍】 (said of a man) to remain a bachelor
【打工】 to do odd jobs as distinct from a regular employment
【打拱作揖 or 打躬作揖】 to salute with folded hands again and again
【打卡】 to record the time of one's presence or departure by punching a time clock 「a nap
【打瞌睡or打盹兒】to doze; to take
【打開】 ① to open ② to turn on
【打開天窗說亮話】 to speak frankly
【打開僵局】 to break the impasse
【打垮】 to strike down
【打孔】 to drill a hole; to punch a hole; to perforate
【打哈哈】 ①to roar with laughter ② to have fun; to frolic; to make merry ③ to talk irrelevantly in an apparent effort to avoid touching the real issue
【打哈欠】 to yawn
【打鼾 or 打呼嚕】 to snore
【打火機】 a (cigarette) lighter
【打火印 or 打烙印】 to brand (cattle)
【打基礎】 to lay the foundations
【打擊】 to give a blow to 「ment
【打擊樂器】 a percussion instru-
【打家劫舍】 to raid homes and plunder houses; to rob
【打架】 to have a brawl, a blow, a row or a fight

【打劫】to plunder; to loot
【打結】to tie a knot; to make a knot
【打交道】to associate with; to have dealings with
【打攪】to bother; to disturb; to trouble
【打尖】to lodge temporarily
【打更】to beat the night watches
【打起精神】to cheer up
【打氣】①to inflate ②(figuratively) to pep up
【打氣筒】an air pump
【打球】to play a ball game
【打情罵俏】to tease one's lover by showing false displeasure
【打趣】to make fun of another; to tease
【打拳】to practice boxing
【打消】to give up (an intention, etc.)
【打小報告】to inform secretly on a colleague, etc.
【打信號】to signal
【打響】①to start shooting ②to win initial success
【打知名度】to seek publicity
【打折扣】①at a discount ②to detract (from some desirable quality)
【打招呼】①to say hello ②to use one's influence in other's behalf
【打顫 or 打冷顫】to shudder
【打針】to give or receive an injection
【打仗】to engage in a battle; to fight
【打主意】①to decide what to do ②to scheme for something to which one has no claim
【打住】Hold! 或Stop it!
【打轉兒】①to revolve ②to go round
【打腫臉充胖子】to try to satisfy one's own vanity at any cost
【打中】to hit the mark
【打赤膊】to bare the upper body
【打赤脚】to go barefoot (barefooted)
【打岔】to interrupt another's speech
【打成平手】to fight to a draw
【打成一片】to combine into a whole
【打手勢】to gesticulate
【打手】thugs hired by men of wealth or power
【打傷】to wound or injure by beating
【打水】to draw water (from a well, a spring, etc.)
【打水漂兒】to make ducks and drakes
【打擾】to disturb; to bother; to trouble
【打如意算盤】to expect things to turn out as one wishes
【打字】to do typing work; to typewrite; to type
【打字機】a typewriter
【打字員】a typist
【打雜兒】to drudge to do odds and ends
【打坐】(said of a Buddhist) to sit in meditation
【打草稿】to prepare a draft
【打草驚蛇】to cause undesired agitation
【打從】from; since
【打死】to beat to death; to shoot to death
【打掃】to clean (a room, house, etc.)
【打傘】to use an umbrella
【打散】to break up; to scatter
【打碎】to smash to pieces; to break to pieces
【打算】①to plan; to intend; to prepare ②a plan; intention
【打算盤】①to use an abacus ②to reckon ③calculating; shrewd
【打暗號】to hint; to give a cue
【打耳光】to box somebody's ears
【打牙祭】to have a rare sumptuous meal
【打噎】to belch; to hiccup
【打游擊】①to engage in guerrilla warfare ②(humorously) to use, borrow or take another's belongings without permission
【打烊】to close the store for the night
【打魚】to catch fish with nets
【打圓場】to mediate a dispute

打 1419
2. ㄉㄚˊ dá

a dozen

扔 1420
ㄖㄥ rēng

1. to throw; to hurl 2. to abandon; to discard

【扔掉】to throw away
【扔下】to throw down; to put aside

三畫

扣 1421
ㄎㄡˋ kòu

1. to tap; to strike; to rap; to pull 2. to fasten; to button; to buckle 3. to detain; to confine 4. to deduct 5. a button; a hook; a buckle 6. to impound; to withhold 7. to cover on top

【扣扳機】to pull the trigger

手部

〔手部〕

【扣帽子】to put a label on some-
【扣門】to knock at a door ⌊one
【扣留】to keep in custody
【扣緊】to button (or fasten) tightly
【扣起來】①to button up (one's coat, etc.) ②to take (a person) into custody
【扣薪】to deduct a certain amount from an employee's pay
【扣住】held or fastened (by a button, hook, etc.); to hook
【扣除】to deduct
【扣人心絃】(said of music, writing, etc.) very touching
【扣子】a button; a buckle; a hook
【扣押】to detain; to keep in cus-
【扣問】to stop and ask ⌊tody

扛 1422
ㄎㄤ kāng
to lift (especially when only a single person is involved)
【扛在肩上】to carry on the shoulder; to shoulder

托 1423
ㄊㄨㄛ tuō
1. to hold, or lift, on the palm 2. to entrust; to charge 3. a tray; a pad
【托鉢】(Buddhism) to beg for alms
【托病】on the pretext of sickness
【托盤】a tray
【托夢】(said of a spirit or deity) to convey a message to a mortal through his dream
【托福】Thanks. (used in reply to others' congratulations on a success, a narrow escape, etc.)
【托福(測驗)】Test of English as a Foreign Language (TOEFL)
【托付】to entrust; to charge; to consign
【托管】trusteeship; mandate
【托辭】①to make excuses ②a pretext; an excuse
【托兒所】a nursery school
【托運】to consign for shipment; to check

四畫

扭 1424
ㄋㄧㄡˇ niǔ
1. to wrench; to twist; to turn; to wring 2. to seize; to grasp
【扭打】to have a grapple or to grapple with somebody
【扭斷】to dislocate (the bones) by twisting or wrenching
【扭揑】①to mince ②to do things in an unmanly way
【扭乾】to wring (a towel, clothes,
【扭曲】to twist ⌊etc.) dry
【扭曲作直】to distort the fact
【扭轉】①to wring; to wrench; to twist ②to turn (the tide of a war or contest) for the better ③to turn round ⌈situation
【扭轉乾坤】to retrieve a hopeless
【扭傷】a sprain; to wrench
【扭腰】①to twist the hip or the waist ②to sprain one's back

扮 1425
ㄅㄢˋ bàn
to dress up; to disguise; to play
【扮鬼臉】to make faces
【扮作】to dress up as ⌈role)
【扮演】to play or act (a part or

扶 1426
ㄈㄨˊ fú
1. to support; to prop up; to aid; to help; to shield; to shelter; to harbor; to protect 2. to lean upon ⌈handrail or balustrade
【扶梯】a flight of stairs with a
【扶靈 or 扶柩 or 扶櫬】to escort a casket or coffin
【扶植】to help grow or develop
【扶助】to aid; to help; to assist
【扶持】to back up; to support
【扶手】a handrail (of a staircase) or any support to be held by the hand
【扶疏】(said of a plant) luxuriant
【扶桑】①(botany) hibiscus ②Japan ③where the sun rises
【扶搖直上】to rise (in a career) very fast as if to be lifted by a cyclone ⌈livelihood
【扶養】to provide with means of

扯 1427
ㄔㄜˇ chě
1. to tear 2. to pull; to drag; to haul; to strain 3. to lump 4. to talk nonsense; to lie; to prevaricate; to digress
【扯破】to tear to pieces or shreds
【扯後腿】to hinder someone from
【扯住】to grasp firmly ⌊action

扳 1428
ㄅㄢ bān ⌈fingers)
1. to pull 2. to count (on one's

【扳倒】 to pull down
【扳開】 to pull open
【扳機】 a trigger
【扳手】 ① a spanner; a wrench ② a lever (on a machine)

批 1429 ㄆㄧ pī

1. to comment; to judge; to criticize 2. a whole batch (of things or people); a large quantity or number 3. to slap
【批判or批斷】 to appraise; to judge
【批評】 to criticize; criticism; comment
【批評家】 a critic
【批發】 wholesale
【批發價】 a wholesale price
【批發商】 a wholesale dealer; a wholesaler
【批鬥】 to criticize and denounce someone
【批改】 to correct (students' papers)
【批註】 to write commentaries
【批准】 to approve; to ratify
【批示】 to instruct or direct (usually by writing on the paper carrying a message from a subordinate)
【批閱】 to read (a message from a subordinate) and write down comments or instructions

找 1430 ㄓㄠˇ zhǎo

1. to seek; to look for; to search for; to find 2. to return (change)
【找徧or找遍】 to have searched or looked everywhere
【找麻煩】 ① to ask for trouble ② to pick on somebody; to find fault
【找門路】 to look for employment by seeking help from the right connections
【找對象】 to look for a partner in marriage
【找齊】 ① to make equal; to even up ② to make up a deficiency
【找錢】 to give change
【找尋】 to search for; to look for
【找碴兒or找錯兒】 to pick (up) quarrels
【找事】 ① to look for jobs ② to look for trouble
【找人】 to look for someone
【找死】 to invite death; to seek death

技 1431 ㄐㄧˋ jì

skill; ingenuity; dexterity; special ability; tricks
【技能】 skill; technical ability
【技工】 a skilled worker
【技巧】 ingenuity; dexterity; adroitness; skill
【技師】 an engineer or a technician
【技術】 techniques; technology; skill
【技術高超】 in possession of superb skills or superb techniques
【技術學校】 a technical school
【技術水準】 technological standards
【技術(人)員】 technicians; technical personnel
【技藝】 skill; art; craft
【技癢】 anxious or itching to demonstrate some skill

抄 1432 ㄔㄠ chāo

1. to copy; to transcribe; transcription; to plagiarize 2. to confiscate 3. to seize; to take
【抄本】 a handwritten copy; a transcript
【抄謄 or 抄錄 or 抄寫 or 抄繕】 to make a copy of; to transcribe
【抄稿】 to make a neat copy (of a draft)
【抄家滅門】 to confiscate the property and exterminate the family (of an offender)
【抄近路】 to take a shortcut
【抄襲】 ① to plagiarize; to copy off ② to attack the flank of
【抄下來】 to take down (words from the blackboard, a book, etc.)
【抄寫員】 a copyist

抉 1433 ㄐㄩㄝˊ jué

1. to choose; to pick; to select 2. to gouge; to dig
【抉擇】 choice; to choose

抒 1434 ㄕㄨ shū

1. to give expression to; to express 2. to relieve; to ease; to lighten; to unburden
【抒發】 to express; to voice; to give expression to
【抒懷】 to relieve the heart of emotions
【抒情】 to express one's feelings
【抒情詩】 a lyric; a lyric poem; lyric poetry
【抒情文】 lyrical writing

抓 1435 ㄓㄨㄚ zhuā

1. to scratch 2. to grasp; to

seize; to take; to snatch; to make a snatch at; to catch 3. to arrest
【抓辮子】to seize on someone's mistake
【抓破】to injure skin by scratching
【抓破臉】① to hurt the face by scratching ② to break off friendly relations
【抓空】to use leisure moments
【抓緊】to grasp firmly
【抓取】to take by grasping
【抓住】① to grasp; to grip; to clutch ② to keep from going away; to hold ③ to grip somebody's attention
【抓人】to arrest
【抓賊】to catch a thief
【抓耳撓腮】① to tweak one's ears and scratch one's cheeks ② impatient ③ agitated ④ depressed
【抓藥】to buy (Chinese herbal) medicine according to a doctor's prescription
【抓癢】to scratch an itchy part

〔手部〕

把 1436
1. ㄅㄚˇ bǎ

1. a handle; a hold 2. to take 3. to hold 4. to guard; to watch over; to keep under surveillance 5. a bundle; a grasp; a handful 6. around; about; approximately; more or less 7. sworn
【把柄】a hold (on somebody); a handle
【把風】a person posted as a lookout, especially, in a robbery or other criminal acts
【把舵】① to steer the rudder ② a helmsman
【把牢】strong; dependable
【把關】① to guard a pass ② to check on
【把戲】① acrobatic performances as juggling, etc. ② a trick or scheme ③ a child; a toddler
【把兄弟】sworn brothers
【把持】to monopolize; to dominate or control
【把持不定】vacillating; undecided
【把式】① movements in Chinese boxing ② a skilled laborer ③ a skill
【把守】to guard or defend
【把手】① to hold hands ② a handle
【把握】① something one holds in hand ② confident ③ to have a firm grasp of the situation
【把玩】to fondle

把 1436
2. ㄅㄚˋ bà

as in 把兒 or 把手 or 把子—a handle

投 1437
ㄊㄡˊ tóu

1. to throw; to pitch; to toss 2. to present as a gift 3. to lodge; to stay 4. to head (west, etc.) 5. agreeable; congenial; harmonious; to fit in with; to cater to 6. to join; to submit to 7. to project; to cast 8. to deliver (mail, etc.); to send (letters, etc.)
【投保】to take out an insurance policy
【投奔】① to flee (to freedom) ② to seek employment or protection from somebody
【投筆從戎】(said of a student or intellectual) to join the army voluntarily
【投票】to cast a vote
【投票權】the ballot; the right to vote
【投票所】a polling place; polls
【投放】① to throw in ② to put (money) into circulation; to put (goods) on the market
【投遞】to send or deliver (letters, etc.); delivery
【投胎】to get into the cycle of reincarnation
【投桃報李】to return a favor with a favor
【投籃】(basketball) to shoot
【投稿】① a contributed article ② to contribute an article
【投考】to go in for an examination
【投靠】to go and seek refuge with somebody
【投合】to see eye to eye; to agree with
【投懷送抱】(said of a woman) overtly aggressive in love affairs; acting like a man-chaser
【投機】① to speculate ② to see eye to eye
【投機分子】an opportunist; a speculator
【投機取巧】to speculate and take advantage of an opportunity
【投機事業】speculative business
【投井】to drown oneself in a well
【投其所好】to cater to another's pleasure
【投契】meeting of minds (between friends)
【投親】(said of an orphan, etc.) to go and live with one's relatives
【投下】① to throw down; to drop

② to invest (capital)
【投效】to offer one's services to
【投閒置散】to stay idle
【投降】to surrender; to capitulate
【投擲】to throw (a discus, etc.)
【投炸彈】to throw bombs
【投誠】(said of enemy troops, bandits, etc.) to voluntarily surrender to the government forces
【投石問路】(said of burglars) to throw a stone into a house to find out if the occupants are awake
【投射】①to project; to shoot ②to harvest profit from speculation
【投手】(baseball) a pitcher
【投身】①to give oneself to (the revolutionary cause, a military career, etc.) ② to find employment or shelter
【投書 or 投函】to send a letter to (a newspaper editor, etc.)
【投入】①to throw in ②to join (the army, revolutionaries, etc.)
【投資】to invest; investment
【投資公司】an investment company
【投宿】to stay or check in (at a hotel, etc.) for the night
【投案】to surrender oneself to justice or the police
【投影】①(mathematics) projection ②(art) cast shadow ③to project
【投緣】to be on intimate terms at once

抗 1438
ㄎㄤˋ kàng

1. to resist; to oppose 2. to reject; to refute; to rebuke; to defy 3. high and virtuous 4. to raise; to set up 5. to hide; to conceal; to screen; to secrete
【抗暴】to oppose tyranny
【抗命】to disobey orders
【抗敵】① to resist or fight enemy troops ②to equal or match
【抗體】an antibody
【抗力】(physics) resistance or resistance strength
【抗衡】to compete; to match
【抗拒】to resist; to oppose
【抗戰】① to fight the invading army ②the War of Resistance against Japan (1937-1945)
【抗爭】to contend; to oppose; to resist
【抗生素】antibiotics
【抗議】to protest
【抗議遊行】a protest march

抖 1439
ㄉㄡˇ dǒu

1. to shiver; to tremble 2. to shake; to jerk 3. to rouse 4. (colloquial) to make good; to become well-to-do
【抖動】to shake; to tremble
【抖摟】①to waste; to squander ②to expose another's secrets ③to catch cold ④to shake off
【抖擻精神】to pull oneself together or to muster one's energies (for an important task ahead)

折 1440
1. ㄓㄜˊ zhé

1. to break; to snap 2. to bend; to humble; to bow 3. to judge; to decide a course 4. to sell, barter or exchange 5. a discount in the price 6. to fold 7. to tear into halves; to destroy 8. to submit to; to be willing
【折半】to reduce by half
【折磨】to submit to an ordeal; trials and afflictions
【折服】①to acknowledge the superiority of others ②to submit
【折斷】to snap; to break
【折扣】abatement; a discount in the price
【折合】(said of two currencies, etc.) equivalent to
【折回】to turn back (half way)
【折價】(said of an article used in repaying a debt, etc.) equivalent to
【折舊】depreciation (especially said of machinery in use)
【折現】to convert into cash
【折中 or 折衷】to compromise; a compromise
【折煞 or 折殺】to break one's luck
【折射】refraction; to refract
【折壽】(said of excessive happiness, blessings, etc.) that will cut one's natural allotment of life expectancy
【折扇】a folding fan
【折算】calculated at; equivalent to
【折損】to damage

折 1440
2. ㄕㄜˊ shé

1. to lose money; to fail in business 2. to break; to snap

折 1440
3. ㄓㄜ zhē

1. to turn upside down; to fall head over heels 2. to pour all

手部

out

【折騰】①to turn upside down ②to toss about ③to waste

【折跟頭】to somersault; to fall head over heels

(手部)

抑 1441
ㄧˋ yì

1. to press down; to repress 2. to restrain; to force to (do, perform, etc.) 3. to bend or lower (one's head) 4. or; or if; still; else; either; then 5. but; an opening particle of an expression 6. an exclamatory, roughly equivalent to "oh," or "alas" 7. to stop

【抑且or抑或】besides; moreover; or

【抑止or抑制or抑遏】to restrain; to suppress; to repress

【抑揚頓挫】melodious; cadence

【抑鬱】sad and melancholy

扼 1442
(搤) ㄜˋ è

1. to repress; to restrain; to control 2. to clutch; to grasp; to grip 3. to hold and defend (a city, etc.)

【扼制】to repress

【扼殺】to strangle; to throttle

【扼守】to hold and defend

【扼要】①to hold a strategic position ② in summary

【扼腕】(literally) to seize one's wrist—① disappointment; regret ② anger ③ excitement

承 1443
ㄔㄥˊ chéng

1. to receive; to inherit; to succeed 2. to undertake; to make it one's responsibility 3. by (order of) 4. to continue; to carry on 5. to hold; to contain; to support; to bear 6. to confess 7. with thanks; obliged 8. to please

【承包】to contract

【承包商】a contractor

【承辦】to handle (a case); to be responsible for (a task); to undertake

【承平】successive peaceful reigns

【承蒙】to be obliged to

【承奉】by order of; in compliance with an order

【承擔or承當】to take or to shoulder (the responsibility, task, etc.)

【承諾】a promise; to promise

【承攬】to take full charge or responsibility (usually under contract)

【承購】to act as a purchasing agent

【承管】to take full charge and responsibility (of)

【承歡膝下】to please one's parents by living with them

【承接】to receive and carry on; to continue; to succeed to

【承襲】to inherit (a title, etc.)

【承先啓後】to be heir to ancient sages and the teacher of posterity (usually said of a person of profound learning)

【承受】to take; to receive; to accept; to bear

【承認】① to confess; to admit ② to recognize (a nation, etc.)

【承載】to bear the weight of

【承租】to rent

五畫

抱 1444
ㄅㄠˋ bào

1. to embrace; to enfold; to hold in the arms 2. to harbor; to cherish; to bosom 3. to adopt 4. ambition

【抱病or抱恙】indisposed; sick or ill

【抱不平】indignant at injustice

【抱佛脚】(literally) to clasp Buddha's feet—a last-minute rush

【抱負】aspirations; ambition

【抱定決心】determined

【抱頭痛哭】to bury one's head in one's arms and cry bitterly

【抱頭鼠竄】to run helter-skelter

【抱憾】to deplore; to regret

【抱恨終身】to regret something to the end of one's days

【抱緊】to hold tightly in one's arms

【抱歉】to feel sorry about; to regret

【抱薪救火】to add fuel to the fire — to make the situation even worse

【抱着】to hold in one's arms; to embrace

【抱殘守缺】sticking to old ways

【抱怨】to complain; to grumble

抨 1445
ㄆㄥ pēng

to impeach; to censure

【抨擊】to criticize; to lash

披 1446
ㄆㄧ pī (又讀 ㄆㄟ pēi)

1. to open (a book, scroll, etc.);

to unroll 2. to spread out; to disperse 3. to thumb through or read casually 4. to throw on (a garment, etc.); to wear untidily

【披麻帶孝】to put on mourning apparel (especially said of sons or daughters of the deceased)

【披靡】① (said of grass, etc.) blown about by the wind ②(said of an army) beaten and scattered; routed

【披風】a cape

【披頭散髮】disheveled hair (often referring to an untidy woman)

【披瀝 or 披肝瀝膽】to talk without reserve; to have a heart-to-heart talk

【披掛上陣】to wear full battle dress and go into battle

【披肩】a shawl

【披荊斬棘】①to cultivate land as a pioneer ②to travel through thick bushes and dense jungles

【披星戴月】①to travel by night ② to toil night and day

【披閱】to read

抵 1447 ㄉㄧˇ dǐ

1. to resist; to oppose 2. to prop; to sustain 3. to offset; to balance 4. to substitute; to give as an equivalent 5. to offer as collateral 6. to arrive at; to reach (a place) 7. to go against; to offend against (the law and regulations)

【抵命】a life for a life

【抵達】to arrive at or reach (a place)

【抵擋】to resist; to sustain

【抵賴】to deny mistakes or crimes one has committed, or to renege a promise one has given

【抵抗or抵禦】to resist; to oppose; to withstand

【抵抗力】the force or power of resistance

【抵換】to substitute (one thing for another)

【抵銷】to offset; to counteract

【抵制】①to resist ②to boycott

【抵償】to pay a debt with goods or by labor

【抵賬or抵帳】to repay a debt with goods or articles of equivalent value

【抵觸】in contravention of (the law or regulations)

【抵罪】to mete out appropriate punishment for a crime committed

【抵死】①to persist ②excessive

【抵押】to mortgage; to collateralize

抹 1448 1. ㄇㄛˇ mǒ

1. to wipe; to rub; to mop 2. to smear; to apply to 3. to obliterate; to blot out

【抹布】a dish cloth; a mopper; a cleaning rag

【抹片】a smear (for microscopic examination)

【抹去 or 抹掉】to wipe out

【抹殺 or 抹煞】to withhold recognition for; do not give credit to

抹 1448 2. ㄇㄛˋ mò

1. to plaster 2. a tight undergarment 3. to turn

抽 1449 ㄔㄡ chōu

1. to draw out; to pull out; to take out 2. to sprout; to put forth shoots; to bud 3. to rid; to take away 4. to whip; to lash 5. to smoke (cigarettes, etc.) 6. to shrink

【抽風機】an exhaust fan

【抽打】to lash; to whip

【抽調】to transfer (personnel or material)

【抽屜】a drawer

【抽考】① to select at random a few students from a class for a test ② an unannounced quiz or test

【抽空兒or抽閒】to find time (to do something)

【抽筋】to be seized by spasms or cramps

【抽獎】to draw a lottery or raffle

【抽泣 or 抽噎】to sob

【抽籤】to draw (or cast) lots

【抽取】①to charge or collect a certain percentage of a sum ② to take at random from a batch of samples, etc.

【抽薪止沸】to stop or prevent trouble by removing the cause

【抽象】abstract

【抽象畫】abstract painting

【抽選】to select from a lot

【抽查】to investigate, survey or test a part of a group

【抽出】to draw out; to pull out

【抽身】to get away (while one is fully occupied)

【抽水】to pump water

【抽水馬桶】a flush toilet

〔手部〕

【抽稅】to levy taxes
【抽絲剝繭】to make a painstaking investigation or examination
【抽烟 or 抽煙】to smoke (a pipe, cigars, cigarets, etc.)
【抽樣or抽樣調查】a sample; sampling

押 1450
ㄧㄚ yā
1. to mortgage; to pawn; to pledge 2. to detain or imprison (temporarily) 3. to escort 4. a signature
【押當】①to pawn ②a pawnshop
【押滙】documentary draft negotiation
【押解】to transfer or deport (suspects, prisoners, goods, etc.) from one place to another under escort or guard
【押金】a cash pledge; a deposit
【押歲錢】money given to children by elders on the Lunar New Year's Eve
【押送】to send (goods or criminals) to another place under escort or guard
【押韻】to rhyme

拂 1451
1. ㄈㄨˊ fú
1. to brush; to shake; to whisk 2. to dust 3. a duster 4. to oppose; to disobey 5. to expel; to drive away
【拂面】(said of breezes, leaves, etc.) to brush or caress the face lightly or gently
【拂逆or拂戾】①disagreeable ②disastrous
【拂曉 or 拂曙】daybreak; dawn
【拂袖而去】to leave in displeasure or anger
【拂塵】①to shake off dust ②a duster made of long animal hairs
【拂拭】to wipe and clean (a piece of furniture, etc.)

拂 1451
2. (弼) ㄅㄧˋ bì
1. to aid; to assist 2. to make correct or right
【拂士】a straightforward adviser; a wise counselor

拇 1452
ㄇㄨˇ mǔ
1. the thumb 2. the big toe
【拇指】the thumb

拈 1453
ㄋㄧㄢˊ nián
1. to take or hold with fingers 2. to draw (lots)
【拈花惹草】to fool around with women; lewd and prurient
【拈香】to offer incense; to burn joss sticks

拆 1454
ㄔㄞ chāi
(讀音 ㄔㄜˋ chè)
1. to split; to break; to rip open 2. to take down; to tear down (a house, etc.); to destroy; to dismantle 3. to analyze; to scrutinize
【拆封】to break up a seal; to open a sealed envelope
【拆臺】(literally) to pull down the stage—to split up; to pull away a prop
【拆開】to take apart; to dismantle (a machine, etc.)
【拆夥】to break up partnership
【拆毀】to damage; to destroy
【拆洗】to unpick (a bedspread, etc.) and wash; to take apart (a machine, etc.) for cleaning
【拆卸】to take apart a large cargo
【拆信】to open a letter
【拆除】to dismantle and get rid of
【拆穿】to expose (a secret, etc.)
【拆散】to break up or split apart (a family, a married couple, etc.); to dismantle
【拆閱】to open (a letter, document, etc.) and read

拉 1455
1. ㄌㄚ lā
1. to pull; to drag; to hold; to draw 2. to discharge (especially stool, urine, etc.) 3. to lengthen; to elongate 4. to play
【拉拔】to help (a protégé) advance
【拉票】to solicit votes; to canvass
【拉平】to even up; to end up in a draw
【拉倒】① Never mind. ② to pull down
【拉丁美洲】Latin America
【拉丁文】Latin (language)
【拉肚子】to suffer from diarrhea
【拉尿】to urinate
【拉鍊】a zipper
【拉攏】①to befriend another person with a view to winning him over ②to make two persons or parties become friends
【拉關係】to seek special favor or help from somebody by elaborating on one's relationship with him
【拉開】① to pull open; to draw aside ② to increase the distance

between 「to hang on firmly
【拉緊】①to draw or pull tight ②
【拉近】to draw close or near
【拉鋸】①to cut with a saw ②to be locked in a seesaw struggle
【拉鋸戰】a seesaw battle; stalemate
【拉住】to hold on firmly
【拉車】to pull or haul a cart (or ricksha)
【拉扯】①to pull and drag ②to implicate or involve ③to talk a lot outside of one's topic
【拉長】①to prolong (business, voice, etc.) ②to draw
【拉出去】to pull out; to drag out
【拉屎】to go to stool; to empty the bowels; to move one's bowels
【拉手】①to hold another's hands ②to pull by the hand
【拉生意】to solicit business; to tout
【拉雜】①rambling; jumbled ②(said of a room, etc.) untidy
【拉斯維加斯】Las Vegas, a gambling resort in New Mexico, U.S.A.

拉 1455
2. ㄌㄚˊ lá
【拉遢】dirty; untidy

抛 1456
(拋) ㄆㄠ pāo
1. to throw; to cast; to hurl 2. to abandon; to reject; to give up 3. to cast aside; to leave behind
【抛錨】①to cast anchor ②to break down
【抛頭露面】(said of women in old China) to go out and be seen in public; to hold a job which involves a lot of exposure to the public (considered unbecoming to a decent woman)
【抛戈棄甲】to throw away weapons and armor—to be routed
【抛棄】to abandon; to throw away; to give up
【抛繡球 or 抛綵球】to throw an embroidered ball—to choose a husband
【抛擲】①to cast; to throw; to hurl ②to throw away; to abandon
【抛磚引玉】(literally) to throw a brick and to get a piece of jade in return
【抛出】①to throw out; to cast away ②(especially in the stock market) to sell
【抛物線】a parabola

拌 1457
1. ㄅㄢˋ bàn
to mix
【拌嘴】to wrangle; to quarrel
【拌勻】to mix evenly or properly

拌 1457
2. ㄆㄢˋ pàn
to throw away; to abandon

拐 1458
ㄍㄨㄞˇ guǎi
1. to kidnap; to abduct 2. to turn or change direction 3. to swindle 4. same as 柺—a staff for an old person; a cane
【拐騙 or 拐誘】①to abduct; to kidnap ②to swindle
【拐杖】a staff; a stick
【拐彎兒 or 拐角(兒)】①to turn the corner ②at the corner
【拐彎抹角兒】①to proceed along a zigzag road ②a roundabout way of talking; circumlocution

拍 1459
ㄆㄞ pāi (讀音 ㄆㄛ pò)
1. to strike with the hand; to slap; to clap; to pat; to swat 2. the time or beat of a piece of music 3. to fawn; to flatter
【拍馬屁】to flatter; to soft-soap; to claw (or curry) favor
【拍賣】to auction off; an auction
【拍打】to pat; to slap or tap lightly
【拍電 or 拍發電報】to cable
【拍電影 or 拍片】to shoot a film
【拍照】to take a picture or photo
【拍攝】to take (a picture)
【拍手 or 拍掌】to clap hands
【拍子】(music) time; rhythm
【拍案叫絕】to show extreme surprise or admiration by pounding the table

拎 1460
ㄌㄧㄥ līng
to haul; to take; to carry; to lift

拒 1461
ㄐㄩˋ jù
1. to defend; to ward off; to resist 2. to refuse; to reject
【拒捕】to resist arrest
【拒馬】an abatis
【拒付】to refuse to pay; to dishonor (a check)
【拒繳】to refuse to pay (taxes or money one is obliged to pay)
【拒絕】to refuse
【拒絕來往】to sever communica-

tions, intercourse or relations

【拒人於千里之外】(literally) to keep people a thousand miles away—extremely indifferent and cool

〔手部〕

拓 1462
1. ㄊㄨㄛˋ tuò

1. to expand; to aggrandize; to open up (new frontiers, etc.); to develop 2. to push with hands

【拓荒】to open up virgin soil

【拓展】to expand (business, etc.); to realize (great ambitions, etc.)

拓 1462
2. (搨) ㄊㄚˋ tà

to copy characters from an ancient tablet or tomb by rubbing over a paper placed on its surface

拔 1463
ㄅㄚˊ bá

1. to pull out; to uproot 2. to promote (another to a higher position, etc.) 3. to stand out; outstanding; remarkable 4. to attack and take (a city); to capture

【拔得頭籌】to become the first to do something

【拔刀相助】to help another (usually a stranger) for the sake of justice

【拔腿】to take to one's heels

【拔河】a tug of war

【拔取】to take or capture

【拔去眼中釘】(figuratively) to remove a person one hates most

【拔羣 or 拔萃】(said of persons) to stand out; outstanding

【拔擢】to promote; to raise

【拔除】to uproot; to eradicate

【拔草】to weed

【拔牙】to extract a tooth

【拔營】to strike camp

拗 1464
1. ㄠˇ ǎo

to bend or twist so as to break

拗 1464
2. ㄠˋ ào
(又讀 ㄧㄠˋ yào)
(語音 ㄋㄧㄡˋ niù)

1. obstinate; stubborn; unmanageable; recalcitrant 2. hard to pronounce

【拗不過】to be unable to dissuade

【拗口】to twist the tongue

拗 1464
3. ㄩˋ yù

to restrain; to repress; to curb; to suppress

拖 1465
(拕) ㄊㄨㄛ tuō

1. to drag along, after or out 2. to procrastinate; to drag out; to delay 3. to involve; to implicate

【拖把】a mop

【拖帶】①to drag along ②to involve

【拖泥帶水】confused, sloppy and muddled (style of writing or acting); unable to make a decision

【拖累】① to involve or implicate ② a drag

【拖垮】to be worn down

【拖家帶眷】to have a family burden

【拖欠】to owe and delay payment for a long time; arrears

【拖鞋】slippers

【拖車】a trailer

【拖長】① to lengthen ② to drag on (or out)

【拖船】a tugboat

【拖時間】to stall for time; to delay

【拖曳】to drag; to pull; to tow

【拖油瓶】a woman's children by previous marriage

【拖延】to procrastinate; to delay

拙 1466
ㄓㄨㄛˊ zhuó

1. stupid; crude; poor (works, etc.); slow and clumsy 2. a conventional term referring to oneself

【拙劣】clumsy and inferior

【拙見】(used in polite conversation) my humble idea or view

【拙荊 or 拙妻】(used in polite conversation) my stupid wife

【拙著 or 拙作】(used in polite conversation) my (poor) writing

拘 1467
ㄐㄩ jū

1. to apprehend; to detain; to arrest 2. inflexible; to adhere rigidly to (conventions, etc.) 3. confined

【拘捕】to detain or arrest (a suspect)

【拘拿】to arrest

【拘泥or拘板】to be tied down by conventions

【拘泥小節】to be punctilious

【拘禮】strict adherence to social etiquette

【拘留 or 拘繫】to detain; detention

【拘留所】a detention house to keep criminal suspects pending a court decision

【拘謹】restrained and cautious—

implying social timidity
【拘禁or拘囚】to detain; to imprison
【拘束】①to tie (someone) down; to restrain ②timid and awkward
【拘押】to take into custody

拚 1468
ㄆㄢ pàn
1.to go all out 2.at the risk of 3.to reject
【拚命 or 拚死】to risk one's life

抿 1469
ㄇㄧㄣˇ mǐn
1. to smooth (hair); to stroke; to caress 2. to purse up (lips); to contract; to tuck 3. to sip; a sip
【抿嘴笑】to smile with mouth closed

招 1470
ㄓㄠ zhāo
1. to beckon with one's hand; to summon 2. to raise (an army, capital, etc.); to recruit 3. to confess; to admit 4. a poster; a notice; a signboard 5. to cause; to effect; to incite; to incur; to invite 6. to entice; to induce 7. to welcome; to receive 8. to infect; to be infectious 9. (now rarely) a target; a bull's-eye 10. a move; a trick; a device
【招標】invitation to bid at a tender
【招兵買馬】to raise an army (usually in preparation for an insurrection)
【招牌】①the signboard of a store or any other business concern ②the reputation of a large business firm or a quality product
【招聘】to advertise for office vacancies
【招募】①to enlist troops (usually mercenaries) ②to solicit (investment, capital, etc.)
【招蜂引蝶】(said of a woman) to act like a habitual flirt
【招撫】to call to surrender; to pacify
【招待】①to serve; to entertain ②a reception ③a receptionist
【招待會】a reception
【招待券】a free ticket
【招待所】a guest house; a hostel
【招徠】to solicit customers
【招攬】①to collect; to gather together ②to canvass; to solicit customers
【招領】to advertise for the claimant or legal owner of a lost article
【招供】①to confess (to a crime, etc.) ②a confession (by a criminal)
【招考】to advertise for employees or students through competitive examinations
【招呼】①to beckon; to call ②to take care of ③to engage in a fight ④to watch out; to mind
【招呼站】a designated bus or taxi stop
【招集】to gather together
【招架】to resist; to defend; to ward off blows
【招架不住】to be unable to hold on (or off)
【招親】to take a husband
【招降】to call for surrender (of the enemy, etc.)
【招致】to bring about; to incur
【招式】a stance or posture in Chinese martial art
【招收】to advertise for students, apprentices, etc.
【招手兒】to wave a hand
【招生】to enroll students
【招數】①a scheme; a trick; a device ②one move in Chinese martial art
【招惹】to incur; to bring upon oneself
【招認】①confession ②to confess (to a certain crime, etc.)
【招租】(said of a house) for rent
【招財進寶】to bring in wealth and riches
【招安】to grant amnesty and enlistment to bandits, etc.
【招搖】to act ostentatiously
【招怨】to inspire hatred; to incur animosity or grudges
【招怨樹敵】to inspire animosity and make enemy

拜 1471
ㄅㄞ bài
1. to do obeisance; to salute; to pay respects to 2. to appoint (as a government official); an appointment 3. to visit; to pay a visit to; to call on (or at)
【拜拜】①to bring hands together and take a bow ②a worshipping festival in Taiwan
【拜別】to say good-bye or farewell
【拜佛】to worship Buddha
【拜訪】to pay a visit to; to visit
【拜服】to admire (another's erudi-

tion, courage, moral strength, etc.) 「heels for a woman

【拜倒石榴裙下】to fall head over

【拜讀】(a polite expression) to read with respect

【拜託】a polite expression in asking another to do something for oneself

【拜年】to call on another and offer New Year's greetings

【拜官】to be appointed to a public

【拜賀】to congratulate ⌊office

【拜候 or 拜會 or 拜望】to visit; to call on 「or superior)

【拜見】to visit, or call on (an elder

【拜金主義】mammonism

【拜謝】to express one's thanks

【拜壽】to congratulate one on his

【拜神】to worship gods ⌊birthday

【拜謁】to pay a courtesy call

六畫

拭 1472

ㄕˋ shì 「to dust; to clean

1. to wipe; to rub (eyes, etc.) 2.

【拭目以待】to wait for the result anxiously; to wait and see

【拭淚】to wipe tears

拮 1473

ㄐㄧㄝˊ jié

laboring hard; occupied

【拮据】① troubles or difficulties ② in financial straits

拯 1474

ㄓㄥˇ zhěng 「to lift up

1. to save; to deliver 2. to raise;

【拯救】① deliverance ② to save; to rescue; to deliver

【拯恤】to save and help (the refugees, the poor, etc.)

括 1475

ㄎㄨㄛˋ kuò

(又讀 ㄍㄨㄚ guā)

1. to include; to embrace 2. to seek; to search for 3. to come; to arrive 4. to bound; to tie 5. to restrain 「aggregation

【括號】(mathematics) the sign of

【括弧】brackets; braces; parentheses—〔 〕; { }; ( )

拱 1476

ㄍㄨㄥˇ gǒng

1. to fold hands before the breast when making a bow; to salute 2. to encircle with the hands 3. to surround 4. (architecture) arched (doors, windows, etc.) 5. to raise up (in the middle); to hump up; to arch

【拱門】an arched door or doorway

【拱廊】a cloister

【拱橋】an arched bridge

【拱手讓人】to give up something to others without putting up a ⌊fight

拴 1477

ㄕㄨㄢ shuān

1. to tie up; to fasten 2. to drive a wedge between two parties

【拴著】tied up; fastened

【拴上】to fasten (the door, win- ⌊dow, etc.)

拾 1478

1. ㄕˊ shí

1. to pick up; to collect 2. to put away 3. a formal form of the figure "ten" used to prevent fraud in a document or check 4. an armlet used by archers

【拾掇】① to tidy up ② (colloquial) to punish ③ to repair

【拾荒】to glean and collect scraps (to eke out an existence)

【拾起】to pick up

【拾取】to collect; to pick up

【拾人牙慧】to plagiarize

【拾穗】to glean

拾 1478

2. ㄕㄜˋ shè

to go up; to ascend

持 1479

ㄔˊ chí

1. to hold; to grasp 2. to maintain; to support; to keep 3. to manage 4. a tie or stalemate

【持平】fair and unbiased

【持刀】to hold a knife

【持家】① to run one's home ② to keep the family estates

【持久】to hold out; to last for a long time; lasting; durable

【持槍】① to hold a gun ② (military) to port arms 「interrupted

【持續】continuous; incessant; un-

【持之以恆】to persevere

【持有】to hold

按 1480

ㄢˋ àn

1. to place the hand on; to press, control, etc. with one's hand 2. to examine 3. to stop; to halt;

to repress 4. to impeach; to censure 5. according to; in (good order); as 6. to follow (a map, river, etc.) 7. a note; a comment
【按兵不動】to refuse to send troops to relieve friendly forces in distress
【按部就班】(to do things) in good order or according to logical order
【按摩】① massage ② to massage
【按捺】to restrain, repress or hold back (one's anger, etc.)
【按鈕】① a push button ② to push the button
【按理】according to common practice or simple reasoning; normally
【按例】according to precedents
【按鈴】to ring the bell
【按期】according to the dates, periods, etc. agreed upon or specified
【按照】in accordance with; according to
【按住】to repress or restrain
【按時】① according to the time specified or agreed upon ② on time ③ regularly
【按日】daily; every day
【按月】monthly; by the month

指 1481
1. ㄓˇ zhǐ
1. the finger 2. to point; to direct 3. to indicate; to refer to; to mean 4. the number of people 5. intentions 6. the main theme 7. to hope 8. to depend on
【指標】① (mathematics) characteristic ② an index sign
【指派】to appoint; to assign
【指明】to indicate clearly; to point out
【指名】to mention by name
【指名道姓】to mention someone's name
【指腹爲婚】a prenatal betrothal
【指導】① direction or guidance ② to instruct; to direct; to guide
【指點】to teach; to advise
【指定】① to appoint ② to indicate clearly and with certainty ③ to allot
【指南】a directory; a guidebook; a primer
【指南針】a compass
【指令】a directive
【指鹿爲馬】to confound right and wrong
【指控】to accuse; to charge
【指揮 or 指麾】to conduct or direct (an orchestra, etc.); to command (an army, etc.)
【指揮官】the commander
【指揮若定】to retain full composure even in command of a big operation
【指教】① direction and guidance ② (a polite expression) your advice or counsel
【指向】to point to; to direct to
【指指點點】① gesticulating ② to point; to indicate
【指針】① a guide; a manual ② an index
【指正】① to correct ② (a polite expression) to present herewith for your correction
【指證】to produce evidence (in court, etc.); to prove
【指使】to hire or entice another to do a task for oneself
【指示】① instruction; indication ② to direct; to instruct
【指數】index; exponent
【指日可待】can be expected very shortly or soon
【指認】to identify (a suspect, a lost item, etc.) from a group
【指責】to accuse; to censure
【指桑罵槐】to scold somebody indirectly
【指引】to direct; to guide; guidance
【指紋 or 指印】a fingerprint
【指望】to hope for; to expect

指 1481
2. ㄓˊ zhí
【指頭】fingers

指 1481
3. ㄓ zhī
【指甲】a fingernail

挑 1482
1. ㄊㄧㄠ tiāo
1. to carry things with a pole on one's shoulder; to shoulder 2. to select; to choose; to pick 3. to pick by pitchfork
【挑夫】a coolie; a bearer; a porter
【挑大樑】to play the leading role; to shoulder the main responsibility
【挑擔】to carry a load with a carrying pole
【挑剔】① to be very particular in making selection ② to nitpick
【挑開】to brush aside with a poker

〔手部〕

or stick 「to select
【挑揀or挑取】 to pick; to choose;」
【挑選】 to select; to choose
【挑錯】 to find fault; to pick flaws
【挑三揀四】 to be choosy

挑 1482
2. ㄊㄧㄠˇ tiǎo

1. to stir; to provoke; to arouse 2. to dally; to make a pass at; to seduce 「putes
【挑撥】 to instigate; to cause dis-」
【挑撥離間】 to stir up ill will or bad feelings; to sow discord
【挑逗or挑鬥】 to seduce; to arouse amorous desires 「by lamplight
【挑燈夜戰】 to continue working」
【挑動】 ① to arouse; to seduce ② to instigate; to incite
【挑弄是非】 to stir up one side against the other
【挑釁】 to provoke 「challenge
【挑戰】 to challenge to a duel; a」
【挑唆】 to stir up something with mischievous intentions

挖 1483
ㄨㄚ wā

1. to scoop out; to dig out 2. to engrave with a knife; to cut or
【挖煤】 to mine for coal 」gouge
【挖洞】 to make a hole or cave
【挖苦】 ① to ridicule ② a dig
【挖空心思】 to cudgel (or rack) one's brains
【挖角】 to lure away the employees of another company or organization by making attractive offers
【挖掘】 to dig; to excavate
【挖肉補瘡】 to make up for a deficit by raising loans
【挖耳朵】 to pick ears

拷 1484
ㄎㄠˇ kǎo

to flog, whip or torture (in order to get a confession, etc.)
【拷貝】 a copy
【拷打】 to flog; to whip; to torture
【拷問or拷訊】 to extort information or confessions by means
」of torture

拳 1485
ㄑㄩㄢˊ quán

1. a fist 2. sparring feats; various forms of boxing 3. strength
【拳打腳踢】 to beat up; to strike
【拳頭】 a fist 」and kick
【拳擊】 boxing; the boxing art
【拳擊手】 a boxer; a pugilist
【拳拳服膺】 to adhere to faithfully
【拳賽】 a boxing match
【拳王】 a boxing champion

拿 1486
(拏) ㄋㄚˊ ná

1. to hold in one's hand; to grasp; to take 2. to arrest; to apprehend; to capture 3. to use; to employ (a method, device, etc.) 4. with; in 5. (now rarely) to be confined or restrained
【拿不定主意】 cannot make up one's mind
【拿得起，放得下】 able to advance or retreat, to attack or withdraw, etc. as the occasion demands; flexible
【拿定主意】 to make up one's mind
【拿揑】 ① deliberately make things difficult for others ② to pretend to observe rules of propriety
【拿緝】 to search and arrest
【拿去】 Take it away. 或to take
【拿出】 to take out 」away
【拿手】 to be particularly good or dexterous at
【拿手好戲】 one's specialty
【拿穩】 ① to hold steadily ② to predict with confidence

挈 1487
ㄑㄧㄝˋ qiè

「raise
1. to lead 2. to rise above; to」
【挈領】 to make a summary

七畫

挨 1488
ㄞ āi (又讀 ㄞ ái)

1. (to stay) near, next to, close to; to lean to 2. to suffer (from cold, hunger, etc.) 3. to wait; to delay; to put off 4. according to order 5. (now rarely) to rub
【挨罵】 to be blamed; to be scolded
【挨門挨戶】 to go from door to
【挨打】 to suffer a beating 」door
【挨冷受凍】 to suffer from cold
【挨近】 near to; to be close to
【挨著】 ① next to ② one by one
【挨揍】 to take a beating
【挨餓】 to suffer from hunger or
」starvation

挪 1489
ㄋㄨㄛˊ nuó

to move; to shift; to transfer

【挪動】 to move
【挪借】 to borrow from the public funds 「from the public funds
【挪移】 ① to move ② to borrow
【挪威】 Norway
【挪用】 to use money for a purpose not originally intended
【挪用公款】 to embezzle public money

挫 1490 ㄘㄨㄛˋ cuò
1. to defeat; to frustrate 2. to damp 3. to humiliate; to treat harshly
【挫敗】 a setback
【挫敵】 to defeat the enemy
【挫折】 a setback; defeat; failure

振 1491 1. ㄓㄣˋ zhèn
1. to arouse to action; to raise; to rise 2. to pull up; to save; to relieve 3. to shake; to flap as wings 4. to restore order
【振筆直書】 to write rapidly; to wield the pen furiously
【振臂一呼】 to arouse to action
【振奮】 ① to arouse; to stimulate ② encouraging; exciting
【振盪】 ① (physics) vibration ② (electricity) oscillation 「brate
【振動】 (physics) vibration; to vi-
【振起】 to stir up; to get aroused
【振興】 to promote or develop (industrial endeavor, etc.); to prosper
【振振有詞】 to talk fluently and loudly (as if one has all the reasons on his side)
【振作】 to arouse (oneself)

振 1491 2. ㄓㄣ zhēn
benevolent and generous

挽 1492 ㄨㄢˇ wǎn
1. to draw (a bow, etc.); to pull 2. to restore 3. to seize 4. to roll up (sleeves, etc.) 「to stay
【挽留】 to request to stay; to urge
【挽回】 to try with effort to turn back an adverse tide; to retrieve
【挽救】 to save (a situation, a failing concern, etc.)
【挽手】 to hold hands; arm in arm

挺 1493 ㄊㄧㄥˇ tǐng
1. to stand straight (or upright); to square; to straighten; rigid 2. to pull up 3. unyielding; tough 4. outstanding; remarkable 5. to thrust forward (as one's breast) 6. to sustain; to endure; to stand; to hold out 7. very 8. the number of machine guns
【挺拔】 independent, eminent and outstanding 「erect
【挺立】 to stand upright; to stand
【挺好】 very good; quite good
【挺胸】 to thrust out one's chest
【挺直】 straight and upright; erect
【挺身】 to straighten one's back
【挺身而出】 to thrust oneself out to face a challenge
【挺而走險】 ① to risk danger in desperation ② to be forced to break the law 亦作「鋌而走險」

捆 1494 ㄎㄨㄣˇ kǔn
1. to bind; to tie up 2. a bundle
【捆綁】 to bind 「etc.)
【捆起來】 to tie up (a prisoner,
【捆押】 to tie up and escort

捋 1495 1. ㄌㄜˋ lè
to pluck; to gather in the fingers
【捋虎鬚】 to offend the powerful

捋 1495 2. ㄌㄩˇ lǚ
to stroke (one's beard, etc.)
【捋鬍鬚】 to stroke one's beard

捋 1495 3. ㄌㄨㄛ luō
1. to rub one's palm along (something long) 2. to squeeze with hands

捉 1496 ㄓㄨㄛ zhuō
1. to seize; to grasp; to catch; to hold 2. to apprehend; to arrest
【捉摸不定】 unpredictable
【捉迷藏】 ① to play hide-and-seek; hide-and-seek ② to beat about the bush
【捉刀】 to ghostwrite
【捉拿】 to apprehend; to arrest
【捉弄】 to play a joke (or trick) on (somebody); to make fun of
【捉姦】 to catch a person in the act of adultery (usually by the wronged husband or wife)
【捉襟見肘】 hard-pressed for money; in financial straits
【捉住】 to catch; to seize
【捉賊】 to catch thieves
【捉妖】 (Taoism) to exorcise

〔手部〕

1497
挾 ㄒㄧㄝˊ xié
(又讀 ㄒㄧㄚˊ xiá)
1. to clasp or hold under the arm 2. to embrace; to bosom 3. to presume upon (one's influence, advantage, etc.) 4. to extort
【挾帶】①(ㄒㄧㄝˊ ㄉㄞˋ) to carry under arms ②(ㄐㄧㄚˊ ㄉㄞˋ) ⓐ to smuggle ⓑ things smuggled (into a country or an examination room, etc.)
【挾貴自重】to be proud of one's high position
【挾持】①to grasp someone on both sides by the arms ②to hold someone under duress

1498
捍 ㄏㄢˋ hàn
to defend; to guard; to ward off
【捍衛】to defend (a nation's territory, etc.); to protect
【捍禦】to ward off

1499
捕 ㄅㄨˇ bǔ
1. to arrest; to catch; to seize 2. (formerly) a policeman
【捕風捉影】talks that are not substantiated by any evidence or proof
【捕撈】to fish for (aquatic animals and plants); to catch
【捕獲】to arrest; to catch
【捕捉】to chase or hunt down
【捕食】to catch and feed on; to prey on
【捕殺】to catch and kill (wild or unlicensed dogs, etc.)
【捕手】(baseball) a catcher
【捕魚】to catch fish; to fish

1500
捐 ㄐㄩㄢ juān
1. tax; duty; charge; dues 2. to donate; to contribute; to subscribe 3. to buy or purchase (an official rank) 4. to give up (one's life for a cause, etc.) 5. to remove
【捐款】① to donate money ② donations
【捐棄】to renounce; to reject
【捐錢】to donate money; donations
【捐軀】to die for one's country or duty
【捐血】①to donate blood ②blood donation
【捐獻】to contribute; contributions
【捐助】to contribute; to donate (to help the poor, relief work, etc.)
【捐贈】to donate or contribute

1501
捎 ㄕㄠ shāo
1. to carry; to take or bring along at one's convenience 2. to brush over lightly 3. to wipe out

1502
揑 (捏) ㄋㄧㄝ niē
1. to knead; to pinch; to squeeze or press with fingers 2. to mold (mud, etc.) 3. to fabricate; to trump up; to make up
【揑報or揑告】to fabricate a report or charge
【揑手揑脚】stealthily; to pussyfoot
【揑造】to fabricate (evidence, etc.); to trump up (charges, etc.)
【揑造罪名】to fabricate an accusation
【揑造謠言】to fabricate and spread rumors
【揑塑】to mold (mud) into a statue, etc.

八畫

1503
捨 (舍) ㄕㄜˇ shě
1. to reject; to give up; to abandon; to relinquish; to renounce; to part with; to forsake; to let go 2. to give alms
【捨本逐末】to concentrate on details but forget the main purpose or objective
【捨不得or捨不了】reluctant to give up, let go, etc.
【捨命】in disregard of one's safety or life
【捨得】to be willing to part with (a person, thing, etc.)
【捨己爲人】to give up one's own interests for the sake of others
【捨近求遠】to reject what is near at hand and seek for what is far away
【捨棄】to give up or renounce
【捨身】to give up one's life
【捨生取義】to sacrifice oneself for righteousness

1504
捧 ㄆㄥˇ pěng
1. to hold something in both hands 2. to boost; to flatter; to treat as a VIP 3. to support, cheer or render assistance by one's presence
【捧腹 or 捧腹大笑】to hold one's sides with laughter
【捧場】to render support or assis-

tance, by one's presence, endorsement, etc.

捫 1505 ㄇㄣˊ mén

to feel or touch with hands; to hold

【捫心自問】to examine oneself; introspection

【捫心無愧】to examine oneself and find nothing to be ashamed of

据 1506 1. ㄐㄩ jū

as in 拮据—stiff joints in the hand, used most often to describe financial stringency or short of money

据 1506 2. ㄐㄩˋ jù

1. same as 據—according to 2. same as 倨—arrogant; haughty

捱 1507 ㄞˊ ái

1. to suffer; to endure 2. to procrastinate; to put off 3. to rub (shoulders) 4. to draw near; to come close to

【捱過】to weather, or to survive (a crisis, an ordeal, etc.)

捲 1508 ㄐㄩㄢˇ juǎn

1. to roll up 2. a roll 3. to curl (hair, etc.); curly (hair) 4. to sweep off

【捲髮】①to curl hair (at a hairdresser's, etc.) ②curly hair

【捲逃】to clear up everything and run away; to abscond

【捲土重來】to stage a comeback; resurgence

【捲筒】a reel

【捲尺】a tape measure or tapeline

【捲繞】to wind

【捲入】to be drawn into

捻 1509 1. ㄋㄧㄢˇ niǎn

1. to nip with fingers 2. the "Nien Bandits" 3. to twist 4. something made by twisting

【捻燈】to turn up the wick of a lamp

捻 1509 2. ㄋㄧㄝ niē

to pinch or knead with the fingers

捷 1510 (㨗) ㄐㄧㄝˊ jié

1. to win; to triumph; the prizes of a victory 2. swift; quick; rapid; agile

【捷報】a report of success in an examination; a war bulletin announcing a victory

【捷克人】a Czechoslovak

【捷克斯拉夫or捷克】Czechoslovakia

【捷徑】a shortcut; a snap course

【捷足先得 or 捷足先登】The first prize will go to the nimblest.

【捷運】rapid transit

【捷運系統】a rapid transit system

掀 1511 ㄒㄧㄢ xiān

1.to lift with the hands; to raise 2.to stir; to stir up; to cause; to rise

【掀動】to raise; to stir up; to instigate

【掀開】to open; to uncover or unveil (a secret, etc.)

【掀起】to stir up (a movement, etc.)

掃 1512 1. (埽) ㄙㄠˇ sǎo

1. to sweep with a broom; to clear away; to clean 2. to wipe out; to weed out; to exterminate; to mop up 3. sweepingly; totally 4. to paint (the eyebrows, etc.)

【掃平 or 掃清】to quell an uprising, etc.; to put down

【掃描】(electricity) scanning

【掃墓 or 掃墳】(literally) to sweep the tomb—to pay respects to one's ancestor at his grave

【掃蕩】to make a clean sweep of (enemy troops, rebels, etc.); a mop-up operation

【掃地】①to sweep the floor ②(said of reputation) to soil

【掃黑】to crack down on crime

【掃黃】to crack down on pornography

【掃興】①to throw cold water on; to spoil pleasure ②to feel disappointed or discouraged

【掃除】①to sweep up; to clean ②to eliminate

【掃射】①to strafe (with machine gun fire) ②to look around

掃 1512 2. (埽) ㄙㄠˋ sào

a broom

【掃帚 or 掃把】a broom

【掃帚星】①(astronomy) a comet ②a jinx

授 1513 ㄕㄡˋ shòu

1. to give; to hand over to; to confer (a degree, prize, etc.) 2.

to teach; to tutor 3. to give up (one's life, etc.)
【授命】 to sacrifice one's life
【授徒】 to teach students or pupils
【授課】 to teach; to tutor
【授獎】 to award a prize
【授精】 to inseminate; insemination
【授權】 ①to authorize; ②to license
【授職】 to give an official job to
【授意】 to intimate; to inspire
【授業】 to teach; to tutor
【授與】 to confer; to give

掄 1514
1. ㄌㄨㄣˊ lún
to select; to choose
【掄選or掄擇】 to select (competent persons, adequate materials, etc.)
【掄元】 to come out first in examinations

掄 1514
2. ㄌㄨㄣ lūn
1. to turn or spin with hands or arms 2. to brandish 3. to squander
【掄刀】 to swing a knife

掏 1515
ㄊㄠ tāo
1. to take out; to pull out 2. to dig; to scoop out
【掏錢】 to take out money; to spend money
【掏耳朵】 to pick or clean ears
【掏腰包】 (colloquial) to shell out; to spend one's own money

掐 1516
ㄑㄧㄚ qiā
1. to dig the nail into 2. to cut with fingernails; to nip; to pinch; to give a pinch 3. to hold; to grasp; to clutch; to gather with the hand
【掐斷】 to break; to nip
【掐住】 to seize; to grasp; to hold
【掐死】 to choke to death by strangling with hands

掉 1517
ㄉㄧㄠˋ diào
1. to turn 2. to fall; to drop; to shed 3. to lose 4. to fall behind; to lag behind 5. to change; to substitute 6. to move; to shake; to wag 7. used as an adverbial particle after verbs expressing conditions of fulfillment
【掉包兒】 to substitute stealthily one thing for another
【掉隊】 to drop out; to fall behind
【掉動】 ①to move; to stir ②to change
【掉頭】 ①to turn one's head (and walk away) ②to shake one's head ③to turn back ④to get beheaded
【掉頭就走 or 掉頭不顧】 to turn one's head and walk away
【掉淚】 to come to tears; tears falling
【掉過來】 ①to turn around ②on the other hand
【掉換】 to change; to exchange; to invert; to substitute
【掉下來】 to fall down
【掉轉】 to turn back; to turn round
【掉色(兒)】 to discolor; to fade
【掉以輕心】 to lower one's guard; to treat something lightly

排 1518
ㄆㄞ pái
1. a row; a line; a rank 2. to arrange; to put in order 3. (military) a platoon 4. to clear out 5. to expel; to exclude 6. to rehearse 7. a raft 8. to push
【排版】 (printing) to set type
【排便】 defecation; the evacuation of the bowels
【排名】 to list names according to the order of seniority or position
【排檔】 a gear (in an automobile engine)
【排隊】 to line up; to stand in a queue
【排頭】 to stand first in the line
【排尿】 to urinate; to micturate
【排列】 to arrange in series, rows, etc.
【排練or排演】 to rehearse for a show
【排卵】 (biology) to ovulate
【排骨】① ribs of animals; spareribs ②(slang) a skinny person
【排開】 to spread out
【排行】one's seniority among brothers and sisters
【排擠】① to expel somebody out of an inner circle or clique, etc. ② to push aside; to elbow out
【排解】 to resolve (disputes); to mediate
【排氣管】 an exhaust pipe
【排球】 volleyball
【排遣】 (said of a disappointed person) to find comfort in
【排戲】 to rehearse for a show

【排泄】to excrete; to discharge; excretion
【排泄物】excreta; excrement
【排長】a platoon leader
【排斥】to discriminate against; to expel
【排場】① ostentation and extravagance ② a person's social position
【排除】to get rid of; to remove
【排山倒海】overwhelming or sweeping
【排水】to drain water; drainage
【排水量】① the volume of water displacement ② displacement (of a ship)
【排水溝】a discharge ditch; a drainage ditch
【排水管】a drainpipe
【排水系統】a drainage system
【排印】to set type and print
【排外】antiforeign; chauvinistic

掘 1519
ㄐㄩㄝˊ jué
to dig; to excavate; to make a hole or cave
【掘井】to dig a well
【掘穿】to dig through
【掘鑿】excavation

掖 1520
1. ㄧˋ yì (語音 ㄧㄝˋ yè)
1. to support another; to extend a helping hand; to promote 2. armpits 3. side; by the side

掖 1520
2. ㄧㄝ yē
1. to conceal; to tuck away; to hide 2. to fold; to roll up (part of one's clothing)

拼 1521
(拚) ㄆㄧㄣ pīn
1. to join together; to incorporate; to put together; to make a whole 2. to spell (a word) 3. to risk
【拼盤】assorted cold dishes
【拼命】① to risk one's life ② with all one's might
【拼法】spelling
【拼湊】① to put bits together to make a whole ② (machinery) to cannibalize ③ to raise money here and there
【拼音】to spell phonetically

掙 1522
1. ㄓㄥ zhēng
1. to make efforts; to strive 2. to get free from
【掙脫】to break away with force; to shake off
【掙開】to get free with effort
【掙扎】to struggle; a struggle; to strive

掙 1522
2. ㄓㄥˋ zhèng
1. to struggle (for one's life, etc.) 2. to earn (money, etc.)
【掙錢】to earn money

掠 1523
ㄌㄩㄝˋ lüè
1. to take by force; to rob; to plunder; to pillage 2. to brush; to pass lightly on the side; to sweep past 3. to whip; to flog 4. a long stroke to the left in Chinese calligraphy
【掠奪】to seize or rob by force
【掠過】to skim over
【掠取】to take by force; to rob
【掠食】to hunt for food

掛 1524
(挂) ㄍㄨㄚˋ guà
1. to hang up; to suspend 2. to ring off 3. to worry; to think of; anxious 4. with one's name registered or listed; recorded 5. to hitch; to get caught
【掛牌】(said of lawyers, doctors, etc.) to go into practice
【掛名】in name only; nominally; titular
【掛念 or 掛懷 or 掛心】to be anxious about; to worry about
【掛慮】to be worried or anxious about
【掛鉤】a hook for hanging clothes, etc. (usually nailed to the wall)
【掛號】① registered (mail, etc.); to register a mail ② to register (at the outpatient department of a hospital)
【掛號信】a registered letter
【掛號處】a register office (of a hospital)
【掛欠 or 掛賬】(to buy) on credit; to owe
【掛鐘】a wall clock
【掛帥】to be appointed commander-in-chief
【掛彩】① to hang colored silk in celebration of happy occasions ② to get wounded in action
【掛礙】to meet many obstacles and obstructions
【掛一漏萬 or 掛漏】totally incomplete or inadequate
【掛意】to mind

〔手部〕

〔手部〕

採 1525
ㄘㄞˇ cǎi

1. to pluck (flowers, etc.); to gather; to collect 2. to select; to adopt 3. (now rarely) to drag 4. (now rarely) to beckon; to take notice of

【採買】 to pick and buy; to purchase
【採伐】 to fell (trees); to open up (a mine)
【採訪】 to cover (a news item or story); to interview
【採訪記者】 a news reporter
【採訪新聞】 to cover a news item
【採納】 to accept or adopt (an idea, opinion, proposal, etc.)
【採購】 to purchase
【採購團】 a purchase mission
【採光】 ① lighting ② to pick or pluck until none is left
【採鑛】 to mine (for minerals)
【採花賊】 a rapist
【採集】 to gather (samples, etc.); to collect (materials, etc.)
【採取】 to take or adopt (an attitude, a measure, etc.)
【採信】 to believe; to accept as true
【採茶】 to pick tea leaves
【採用】 to adopt (a suggestion, new technique, etc.)

探 1526
1. ㄊㄢˋ tàn

1. to find; to search; to prospect; to feel (in a pocket or bag) 2. to spy; to investigate 3. a spy; a detective; a secret agent 4. to try; to venture; to tempt 5. to explore 6. to visit; to inquire about

【探訪】 to investigate; to make inquiries
【探討】 to investigate; to study; to explore (possibilities, etc.); to approach (a problem, etc.); to discuss (causes or effects, etc.)
【探頭探腦】 to act stealthily
【探聽】 to investigate secretly
【探聽虛實】to try to find out about an opponent or adversary
【探囊取物】 as easy as taking things out of one's own pocket
【探戈】 (dancing) tango
【探勘】 to prospect
【探究】 to investigate; to probe
【探監】 to visit a prisoner
【探求】 to seek; to search for; to find out
【探親】 to visit one's relatives
【探險】 to undertake an exploratory trip; exploration
【探險隊】 an expedition team; an exploration party
【探險家】 an explorer
【探信 or 探詢】 to make inquiries
【探照燈】 a searchlight
【探視】 to visit (a patient, etc.)
【探測】 to survey; to sound
【探索】 to probe; to search for; to look into
【探問】 to inquire about or after
【探望】 ① to visit ② to look about

探 1526
2. ㄊㄢ tān

to try; to tempt; to test

控 1527
ㄎㄨㄥˋ kòng

1. to accuse; to charge; to sue 2. to control; control 3. to draw (a bow)

【控告】 to accuse
【控告人】 an accusant; an accuser
【控制】 to control; control; to dominate
【控詞】 a charge; a complaint
【控訴】 ① to appeal to a higher court ② to accuse before an authority
【控訴狀】 a written appeal
【控訴人】 the appellant

接 1528
ㄐㄧㄝ jiē

1. to receive; to accept 2. to welcome; to meet 3. to join; to connect 4. to graft 5. to come close to; to make contact with 6. to succeed to

【接班】 to relieve another in work
【接辦】 to succeed another in managing a task
【接待】to receive (a guest); reception
【接待人員】 reception personnel
【接頭】 ① to have a firm grasp of the situation so that one can manage a matter by oneself ② to make contact with (the responsible person) ③ a joint
【接替】 to relieve; to succeed (a predecessor)
【接通】 to put through
【接納】 to accept (a proposal, advice, etc.)
【接力賽跑】 a relay race

【接連】repeatedly; to continue
【接連不斷】continuously; incessantly
【接骨】to set broken bones
【接管】to take over (the management of)
【接客】①(said of a hotel, etc.) to receive lodgers or guests ②(said of prostitutes) to receive patrons in boudoirs
【接合】to connect; to assemble
【接濟】to give financial or material assistance to
【接見】to receive (a visitor, etc.)
【接近】to come close; to approach
【接戲】(said of an actor) to sign a contract for a role in a new movie
【接洽】to contact, discuss or negotiate
【接線生】a switchboard operator
【接續】to continue; to connect
【接枝】(botany) to graft; a graft
【接著】① then; shortly afterwards ② to follow; to add ③ to catch
【接住】to catch (a flying object)
【接踵而至】to follow at the heels of
【接觸】①(said of nations) to wage war against each other ② to make contact with
【接收】to take over; to receive
【接收天線】a receiving antenna
【接手】① to carry on the task of the predecessor ② assistants or aides
【接受】to accept (an invitation, an assignment, etc.)
【接生】to practice midwifery
【接生婆】a midwife
【接任】to take over an office; to succeed
【接壤】adjoining boundary; adjacent to
【接送】① to receive and send off (guests or visitors) ② transportation to and from a certain place
【接二連三】one after another; continuously
【接應】to stand ready for assistance; to come to somebody's aid
【接吻】to kiss; a kiss

推 1529
ㄊㄨㄟ tuī

1. to push; to shove 2. to look into; to find out; to ponder; to infer; to deduce 3. to shirk; to shift (responsibility, etc.); to refuse 4. to elect; to recommend; to praise; to esteem 5. to move along; to change in succession (as seasons) 6. to extend; to enlarge

【推波助瀾】to add fuel to the fire; to incite
【推本溯源】to trace the origins
【推翻】① to overthrow (a government, etc.); to topple ② to stultify (a theory, principle, etc.)
【推倒】① to overturn ② to shove
【推斷 or 推論】to infer; inference
【推動】to push (a sales project, etc.)
【推土機】a bulldozer
【推託】to make excuses
【推拏 or 推拿】① to massage ② to fix a dislocated bone by massage
【推理】to reason (out); to infer
【推理小說】detective stories
【推廣】to propagate; to popularize
【推己及人】to put oneself in another's position
【推究】to study; to investigate
【推薦】to recommend (somebody for a job, etc.)
【推薦書or推薦信】a letter of recommendation
【推進】to push forward; to advance
【推進機 or 推進器】a propeller
【推舉】① to recommend for a post ②(weightlifting) to press
【推敲】① to weigh or consider words in writing ② to investigate or examine carefully
【推求】to ascertain; to analyze and study (for a solution, an answer, etc.)
【推卻】to decline (an invitation, offer, etc.)
【推卸】to be irresponsible
【推銷】to promote sales; to sell
【推銷員】a salesman or saleswoman
【推心置腹】to treat others with the utmost sincerity
【推想】to infer; to deduce
【推行】to promote (a cause, movement, etc.)
【推許】to praise; to approve (a performance)
【推選】to elect
【推陳出新】to find new ways of doing things from old theories
【推出】① to push out ② to present (a picture, a show, etc.)
【推崇】to respect; to praise highly
【推事】(court) a judge
【推讓】to yield to someone as a token of deference to the other

party ⌈tation, etc.); to reject
【推辭】to decline (an offer, invi-
【推測】to infer; to deduce; to predict; to conjecture ⌈excuses
【推三阻四】to make numerous
【推算】to calculate; to reckon
【推諉】to make excuses; to shirk (responsibility, etc.)

〔手部〕

措 1530 ㄘㄨㄛˋ cuò
1. to place 2. to collect; to arrange; to manage; to handle 3. to abandon; to renounce 4. to make plans
【措施】a (political, financial, etc.) measure; a step ⌈or unprepared
【措手不及】to be caught unawares
【措辭】wording (of a letter, diplomatic note, etc.); diction

掩 1531 ㄧㄢˇ yǎn
1. to cover; to hide; to conceal; to cover up 2. to shut; to close 3. to mount a surprise attack; to take or catch by surprise
【掩蔽】to cover; to conceal; to
【掩埋】to bury ⌊shelter
【掩面而泣 or 掩泣】to cover one's face and weep
【掩蓋】to cover up; to conceal
【掩口而笑】to laugh in secret
【掩護】① to cover (friendly troops on a special assignment) ② camouflage
【掩飾】to cover; to conceal
【掩人耳目】to hoodwink people
【掩藏】to hide; to conceal
【掩耳盜鈴】to deceive oneself
【掩映】① the mingling, or contrast, of light and shadow (usually said of enchanting scenery) ② to set off (one another)

掮 1532 ㄑㄧㄢˊ qián
to bear a load on the shoulder
【掮客】a broker

捶 1533 ㄔㄨㄟˊ chuí
1. to beat; to thrash; to pound 2. a stick for beating
【捶打】to beat; to thump
【捶胸頓足】to beat one's breast and stamp one's feet—in deep ⌊grief

掌 1534 ㄓㄤˇ zhǎng
1. the palm of the hand; the sole of the foot; paws of an animal 2. to slap with one's hand; to smack 3. to have charge of; to supervise; to control
【掌舵】① to steer a ship ② the steersman ③ the man in charge
【掌櫃】a shopkeeper
【掌管 or 掌理】to take charge of; to supervise
【掌權】to be in power or authority
【掌心】the center of the palm
【掌政】to head a government
【掌上明珠or掌珠】a beloved daughter; the apple of one's eye
【掌聲】clapping; applause
【掌聲如雷】thunderous applause
【掌握】in one's grasp; within one's ⌊power

掣 1535 ㄔㄜˋ chè
1. to pull; to drag; to draw 2. to hinder 3. to snatch away
【掣後腿】to hinder

掰 1536 ㄅㄞ bāi
as in 掰開—to pull apart with ⌈hands

九畫

揀 1537 ㄐㄧㄢˇ jiǎn
1. to select; to choose; to pick 2. to pick up (something another has left behind, etc.)
【揀破爛的】a ragpicker; a ragman
【揀選】to choose; to select; to pick

揉 1538 ㄖㄡˊ róu
1. to rub; to knead 2. to crumple by hand 3. to massage 4. to subdue; to make smooth or peaceful 5. mixed-up; confused
【揉合】to combine; to blend
【揉搓】① to rub; to massage ② to tease or play jokes on
【揉眼睛】to rub eyes

描 1539 ㄇㄧㄠˊ miáo
1. to trace; to draw; to sketch 2. to describe; to depict
【描摹】to imitate (an old painting, etc.); to copy ⌈describe
【描繪】to paint; to sketch; to
【描寫】to describe; to portray
【描述】to describe

揍 1540 ㄗㄡˋ zòu

1. to beat; to slug (somebody); to hit hard 2. to smash

【揍人】 to slug a person

提 1541 1. ㄊㄧˊ tí

1. to lift by hand; to pull up 2. to cause to rise or happen 3. to mention; to bring forward; to suggest 4. to obtain; to make delivery; to draw out 5. a rising stroke (in Chinese calligraphy)

【提拔】 to promote (a person); to elevate

【提包】 a handbag; a valise

【提筆】 to lift one's pen—to write

【提名】 to nominate 「against

【提防】 to be on the alert; to guard

【提到 or 提及】 to mention

【提籃】 a handbasket

【提鍊】 to refine (crude oil, etc.); to extract 「raise (prices, etc.)

【提高】 to lift (morale, etc.); to

【提高警覺】 to be on the ball

【提綱】 an outline

【提供】 ① to offer (proposals, opinions, etc.); to provide (assistance, etc.) ② to sponsor (a TV or radio program, etc.) 「bank

【提款】 to draw money from a

【提款單】 a withdrawal slip

【提貨】 to make delivery of goods or cargo

【提交】 ① to hand over to the custody of ② to submit to another body for discussion

【提起】 ① to lift up; to arouse (oneself to action, etc.) ② to mention

【提起精神】 to cheer up

【提挈】 to help; assistance

【提前】 ① to give precedence or priority to ② (to complete a task, etc.) ahead of schedule

【提親】 a matchmaking

【提琴】 a violin 「approval, etc.)

【提請】 to submit something (for

【提取】 ① to draw (deposits from the bank) ② to pick up 「aid

【提攜】 help; assistance; to help; to

【提心弔膽】 cautious and anxious; jittery

【提箱】 a suitcase

【提醒】 to remind

【提訊】 to arraign

【提倡】 to promote (a cause, etc.); to advocate 「to put forth

【提出】 to raise (a question, etc.);

【提示】 ① to hint; a hint ② (drama) to prompt; to give a cue 「ulate; to elate; to refresh

【提神】 ① to watch out ② to stim-

【提審】 to bring forward for trial

【提升】 to promote (an officer, etc.); to elevate 「advance

【提早】 ahead of schedule; in

【提案】 a motion; a proposal

【提議】 to propose a proposal, suggestion, etc.

【提要】 ① to bring forth the main points ② a synopsis; a summary

提 1541 2. ㄉㄧ dī

to hold or take in hand

揖 1542 ㄧ yī

1. to bow with hands folding in front 2. to yield politely; to defer to

【揖讓】 ① courtesy between the host and his guests ② to abdicate

插 1543 (揷) ㄔㄚ chā

1. to insert; to put in; to stick into 2. to interpose; to get a word in edgeways 3. to plant 4. to take part in

【插播新聞】 spot news

【插隊】 to cut in; to push in

【插頭】 a plug

【插圖】 illustrations or plates

【插科打諢】 (said of clowns in a show) to ad-lib; buffooneries; jesting

【插花】 to arrange flowers

【插話】 ① to break into a conversation ② digression

【插畫】 illustrations (in a book, magazine, etc.)

【插(入)句】 a parenthesis

【插曲】 ① a musical interlude ② songs and tunes used in motion picture dubbing ③ an episode

【插翅難飛】 completely surrounded

【插手】 to take part in; to meddle

【插入】 to stick into; to insert

【插座】 a receptacle; a socket; an outlet

【插嘴 or 插口】 to interrupt a narration, conversation, etc.; to chip in

【插秧】to transplant rice seedlings

揚 1544
ㄧㄤˊ yáng
1. to raise 2. (said of flames) blazing 3. to wave; to flutter 4. to praise; to acclaim 5. to display; to expose; to make evident; to make known 6. high or raised (voice, cry, etc.) 7. to scatter; to spread 8. to stir; to get excited 9. a Chinese family name
【揚眉吐氣】to feel proud and elated after one suddenly comes to fame, wealth or good luck
【揚名天下】to have one's name spread far and wide; to become worldfamous
【揚帆】to set sail
【揚棄】to discard; to renounce
【揚長而去】to stride away without looking back; to stalk off
【揚言】to exaggerate; to declare in public
【揚揚自得】to be complacent
【揚揚得意】to be smug and complacent
【揚威】to show one's great authority, superiority, power, etc. to attain eminence (in a certain field, etc.)

揠 1545
ㄧㄚˋ yà
to pull up or out
【揠苗助長】to spoil things by excessive enthusiasm

換 1546
ㄏㄨㄢˋ huàn
to exchange; to change; to alter; to substitute
【換班】(said of factory workers) to change a shift; to relieve (guard or sentry duties)
【換邊】(sports) to change sides
【換擋】to shift gears
【換湯不換藥】a change in form but not in content
【換崗】to relieve a guard or sentry
【換季】① the change of seasons ② to change clothing or uniforms according to the season
【換氣】to breathe; to take breath (in swimming)
【換錢】① to change money (into small change) ② to convert one currency to another ③ to barter goods for money
【換取】to change; to exchange
【換新】to change something for a new one
【換人】substitution (of players)
【換算】to convert (one system of measurement into another)
【換算表】a conversion table
【換衣 or 換衣服】to change a dress
【換言之 or 換句話說】in other words

握 1547
ㄨㄛˋ wò
1. to hold fast; to grasp 2. a handful
【握別】to part; to shake hands at parting
【握力】a grip
【握緊】to hold fast; to grasp firmly
【握拳】to clench one's fist
【握手】to shake hands
【握手言歡】to hold hands and converse cheerfully

揣 1548
ㄔㄨㄞˇ chuǎi
1. to measure; to weigh; to estimate; to calculate; to reckon 2. to try; to probe (for possibilities); to put out a feeler
【揣摩】① to learn; to examine ② to assume; to speculate
【揣度】to speculate; to conjecture
【揣測】to conjecture; to fathom; to speculate

揩 1549
ㄎㄞ kāi
to wipe; to scrub; to rub; to dust; to clean
【揩油】to make some (usually small) outside gains not included in a deal

揪 1550
(揫) ㄐㄧㄡ jiū
1. to clutch; to grasp with one's hand 2. to pull; to drag 3. to pick on
【揪心】① anxious ② heartrending
【揪出】to uncover; to ferret out
【揪耳朵】to hold (another) by the ear

揮 1551
ㄏㄨㄟ huī
1. to wield (a sword, pen, etc.); to move; to shake; to wave; to brandish; to make a light or rapid stroke 2. to conduct; to direct (troop movements, a concert, a course of action, etc.) 3. to wipe away (sweat, tears, etc.) 4. to scatter; to sprinkle 5. to squander (money, etc.) 6. to swing (fists)

搭 1567
ㄉㄚ dā
1. to attach to; to join together; to add to 2. to hang over 3. to raise; to build (a shed, etc.); to put up; to pitch (a tent, etc.) 4. to travel by; to take (a passage on a bus, train, boat, etc.) 5. to help; to rescue 6. a short garment 7. a cover; to cover
【搭配】①to match (colors, etc.) ② to select (items as a present to a person, or dishes for a feast)
【搭擋】① a partner ② to cooperate
【搭夥】to go into partnership; to join
【搭機】to board an airplane
【搭救】to rescue; to help
【搭腔】①to answer; to respond ② to talk to each other
【搭車】to take a car, bus or train
【搭乘】to travel by (air, ship, bus, etc.)
【搭船】to board a ship
【搭訕】to converse heedlessly or absent-mindedly
【搭載】to carry (passengers)

搶 1568
1. ㄑㄧㄤˇ qiǎng
1. to take by force; to snatch; to rob; to loot 2. to do something in haste, as in an emergency; to rush 3. to oppose 4. to try to beat others in a performance
【搶奪】to rob; to loot; to plunder
【搶灘】to make a forced beach landing
【搶購】to try to beat others in making purchases (as in time of war, etc.)
【搶劫】to rob; robbery
【搶救】to make emergency rescue
【搶鏡頭】① to outshine others ② (said of cameramen) to fight for a vantage point in taking news pictures
【搶修】to race against time in making a repair job
【搶先】to rush ahead; to try to be the first
【搶收】to get the harvest in quickly
【搶手貨】a commodity in great demand
【搶案】(law) a case of robbery

搶 1568
2. ㄑㄧㄤ qiāng
1. head (winds); adverse 2. to strike; to hit; to knock

搧 1569
(扇) ㄕㄢ shān
1. to fan 2. to stir up; to incite 3. to slap on the face
【搧風】to fan
【搧動】to stir up; to incite; to agitate

搬 1570
ㄅㄢ bān
1. to move; to transport 2. to present
【搬動】to move; to shift
【搬弄是非】to stir up or incite trouble between people
【搬家】to move from one dwelling to another
【搬救兵】to ask for help
【搬移or搬遷】to move
【搬運】to move; to transport; to carry
【搬運費】carriage; freight
【搬運工人】a porter; a docker

搪 1571
ㄊㄤˊ táng
1. to ward off; to keep out 2. to parry
【搪塞】to stall somebody off; to parry something

摀 1572
ㄨˇ wǔ
1. to cover; to conceal; to hide 2. to put into an airtight container (in cooking)
【摀蓋】to cover up; to hide
【摀著耳朵】to cover one's ears

搴 1573
ㄑㄧㄢ qiān
to pull or pluck up
【搴旗斬將】to defeat the enemy decisively

搞 1574
ㄍㄠˇ gǎo
1. to stir up; to cause trouble 2. to do; to carry on; to be engaged in 3. to get; to secure 4. to set up; to start; to organize
【搞鬼】(said of a person) to cause trouble or pull legs in secret
【搞垮】to overthrow; to cause to fail
【搞花樣or搞把戲】to play tricks; to cheat
【搞清楚】to make clear

十一畫

摘 1575
ㄓㄞ zhāi
(讀音 ㄓㄜˊ zhé)
1. to take off (one's hat, etc.); to pluck; to pick 2. to choose; to select 3. to jot down (notes) 4.

〔手部〕

〔手部〕

to expose; to unveil (a conspir-
【摘錄】an excerpt ⌊acy, etc.)
【摘花】to pluck flowers
【摘記】notes or observations (by an author)
【摘取】to select; to pick; to take
【摘下】to pick off (flowers, etc.);
【摘除】to excise ⌊to take off
【摘要】①to summarize ②an ab-
⌊stract

摑 1576
ㄍㄨㄛˊ guó
to slap another on his face; to smack; to box

摟 1577
1. ㄌㄡ lōu
1. to hold up; to tuck up 2. to squeeze or extort (money, etc.) 3. to gather up; to collect; to rake together

摟 1577
2. ㄌㄡˇ lǒu
to hold in the arms; to embrace; to hug ⌈embrace
【摟抱】to hold in the arms; to

摒 1578
ㄅㄧㄥˋ bìng
1. to get rid of; to expel 2. to arrange in order
【摒棄】to abandon; to get rid of
【摒除】to get rid of; to remove

摔 1579
ㄕㄨㄞ shuāi
1. to throw to the ground; to fling; to break 2. to get rid of; to shake off (a tail, etc.) 3. to fall down; to tumble; to lose one's balance
【摔破】① to suffer bruises or injuries in a fall ②to break something by dashing it on the ground
【摔跤】to fall down; to suffer a fall
【摔角】to wrestle; wrestling
【摔傷】to get hurt in a fall
【摔死】to fall to death

摧 1580
ㄘㄨㄟ cuī
1. to break; to smash; to destroy; to injure; to harm 2. to damp 3. to cause to cease; to extinguish 4. to be sad and sorrowful; to grieve
【摧毀】to destroy (enemy positions, heavy weapons, etc.)
【摧折】to break; to destroy; to smash ⌈humiliate
【摧殘】① to destroy; to ruin ② to

摺 1581
ㄓㄜˊ zhé
1. to fold (paper, etc.); to plait 2. a folder; a folded brochure 3. curved and winding 4. to pull and break
【摺疊】to fold up (clothing, etc.)
【摺痕】a crease; a fold
【摺角】to make a dog-ear; to dog-
【摺尺】a folding ruler ⌊ear
【摺床】a folding bed
【摺扇】a folding fan

摸 1582
ㄇㄛ mō
(又讀 ㄇㄠ māo)
1. to feel or touch lightly with fingers; to caress 2. to grope 3. to try to find out; to feel out 4. to seek after; to try to get at
【摸不著頭腦】to be at a loss
【摸黑兒】to do something in the dark
【摸彩】to draw lots to determine the prize winners in a raffle or lottery
【摸索】① to do things slowly② to grope (in the dark, the meaning of, etc.); to feel (in one's pocket, etc.) ⌈job
【摸魚or摸灰】to idle; to loaf on a

摩 1583
ㄇㄛˊ mó
1. to chafe; to scour; to rub; to scrape 2. friction 3. to feel with the hand 4. (now rarely) to work and encourage each other (especially in study) 5. to learn from long and constant study
【摩登】modern; fashionable
【摩天大樓 or 摩天樓】skyscrapers
【摩托車】a motorcycle
【摩納哥】Monaco
【摩羯座】(astronomy) Capricornus
【摩拳擦掌】①to get ready for a fight ②to be eager to start on a task ⌈tion
【摩擦】①to chafe; to scour②fric-
【摩抄 or 摩挲】① (ㄇㄛˊ ㄙㄨㄛ) to caress, touch, rub, etc. with the hand ②(ㄇㄚ ·ㄙㄚ) to smooth out creases with the hand

摹 1584
ㄇㄛˊ mó

1. to copy; to make an exact copy 2. to model or pattern after; to imitate
【摹本】a facsimile
【摹仿】to copy; to model or pattern after; to imitate; to ape
【摹擬】to model or pattern after

摯 1585
ㄓˋ zhì
1. sincere; cordial 2. a Chinese family name
【摯友】a bosom friend

十二畫

撅 1586
ㄐㄩㄝ juē
1. to break; to snap 2. to stick up; to protrude
【撅嘴】to pout

撐 1587
(撑) ㄔㄥ chēng
1. to prop; to support 2. to stretch tight; to burst 3. to pole or punt (a raft or a boat) 4. to maintain; to keep up; to go on with 5. to open
【撐破】to burst
【撐竿跳】the pole vault
【撐開】to prop open
【撐住】to prop with a pole; to prop from under
【撐持】to prop up; to sustain
【撐腸拄腹】to fill the stomach
【撐場面】to maintain an outward show of prosperity
【撐船or撐舟】to pole (or punt) a boat
【撐傘】to prop open an umbrella
【撐腰】to support, or to give backing to someone

撈 1588
ㄌㄠ lāo (讀音 ㄌㄠˊ láo)
1. to pull or drag out of the water 2. to fish up; to get by improper means
【撈本兒】① to win back money (lost in gambling) ②to recover invested capital
【撈起】to recover from water, the riverbed, etc.
【撈取】to fish for; to gain
【撈一票】to make money, legally or otherwise
【撈一把】to reap some profit; to profiteer
【撈什子】an eyesore

撒 1589
1. ㄙㄚ sā
1. to relax; to ease 2. to loosen; to unleash 3. to exhibit; to display; to show
【撒旦】Satan
【撒溺 or 撒尿】to urinate; to piss; to pee; to pass urine
【撒哈拉沙漠】the Sahara Desert
【撒謊】to tell a lie; to lie
【撒嬌】①to show pettishness, as a spoilt child ②(said of a woman) to pretend to be angry or displeased
【撒手鐧】the climaxing act; one's specialty
【撒手塵寰】to pass away
【撒野】to act boorishly

撒 1589
2. ㄙㄚˇ sǎ
to scatter; to sprinkle; to disperse
【撒水】to sprinkle or spray water
【撒散】to spread; to scatter about

撤 1590
ㄔㄜˋ chè
to remove; to withdraw; to take back
【撤辦】to fire a delinquent official and subject him to disciplinary action
【撤退】(said of troops) to move back or withdraw
【撤離】(said of troops) to move away or withdraw
【撤回】to take back or withdraw
【撤換】to replace
【撤去or撤走】to withdraw; to remove
【撤銷】to abolish; to do away with
【撤職】to remove from office
【撤出】(said of troops) to withdraw or pull out
【撤除】to abolish; to do away with; to remove; to dismantle

撥 1591
ㄅㄛ bō
1. to dispel; to remove 2. to poke 3. to move; to transfer 4. to distribute; to issue 5. to set aside; to set apart; to appropriate
【撥付】to make payment; to appropriate
【撥動】① to move (the minute hand, etc.) by finger ② to turn (a switch)
【撥浪鼓】a rattle drum
【撥弄】① to toy with ② to move to and fro ③ to stir up (disputes)
【撥開】to push aside
【撥款】to issue or appropriate funds; an appropriation
【撥冗】to set aside a little time (for a special purpose) out of a

〔手部〕

tight schedule
【撥雲見日】to give up sin in favor of virtue
【撥用】to appropriate

撇 1592
1. ㄆㄧㄝ piē
1. to cast away; to throw away; to abandon 2. to skim
【撇開】to dismiss or exclude (from discussion or consideration); to set aside
【撇淸】to pretend innocence

撇 1592
2. ㄆㄧㄝˇ piě
1. (calligraphy) a stroke made in the lower left direction 2. to purse the mouth (in contempt or to resist an impulse to cry)
【撇嘴】to purse the mouth

撓 1593
ㄋㄠˊ náo
1. to bend; to daunt; to subjugate 2. to hinder; to obstruct 3. to scratch; to rub

撚 1594
ㄋㄧㄢˇ niǎn
to twist with fingers; to toy with
【撚香】to burn joss sticks in worship

撕 1595
ㄙ sī
to tear; to rip
【撕破 or 撕毀】to tear; to rip
【撕票】to kill a hostage
【撕掉】to tear up; to tear off
【撕開】to tear open; to rip open
【撕碎】to tear or rip to pieces

撞 1596
ㄓㄨㄤˋ zhuàng
1. to bump; to run into; to collide; to dash 2. to meet by chance
【撞騙】to swindle
【撞倒】to knock down by bumping
【撞鬼】to encounter a ghost
【撞開】to burst open
【撞壞】to damage by bumping
【撞擊】to ram; to dash
【撞見】to meet unexpectedly; to run into
【撞球】① billiards ② billiard balls
【撞球場】a billiard room; a billiard saloon
【撞傷】to injure by bumping (as in car accidents)
【撞入 or 撞進】to thrust into

撫 1597
ㄈㄨˇ fǔ
1. to stroke; to touch 2. to soothe; to comfort; to console; to relieve 3. to bring up; to rear; to nurture; to foster
【撫摸 or 撫摩】to pass one's hand over; to stroke
【撫弄】to stroke; to fondle
【撫恤】to relieve
【撫恤金】a pension
【撫養or撫育】to bring up; to rear
【撫慰】to soothe; to comfort; to console

播 1598
ㄅㄛˋ bò (語音 ㄅㄛ bō)
1. to sow; to seed 2. to spread; to propagate 3. to move 4. to cast away; to abandon
【播報】to broadcast on the air
【播放】to broadcast (news, etc.)
【播弄】① to stir up disputes on purpose ② to make a mess (of something)
【播種】to sow seed; to sow; to seed
【播散】to disseminate
【播送】to broadcast (messages, programs, etc.)
【播音】to make broadcasts; to transmit
【播音員】a broadcaster; an announcer

撩 1599
1. ㄌㄧㄠˊ liáo
1. to provoke; to excite; to stir up; to tease; to tantalize 2. disorderly; confused
【撩撥】to provoke; to entice
【撩動肝火】to stir up anger
【撩亂】confused; disorderly
【撩人】to make one excited

撩 1599
2. ㄌㄧㄠ liāo
1. to raise; to hold up 2. to sprinkle

撬 1600
1. ㄑㄧㄠˋ qiào
to pry; to prize
【撬開】to open by prying

撬 1600
2. ㄑㄧㄠ qiāo
to raise; to lift

撲 1601
ㄆㄨ pū
1. to beat; to strike; to pound 2. to dash; to smash 3. to throw oneself on; to spring at 4. to flap; to flutter
【撲滿】a savings box; a piggy bank
【撲滅】to exterminate (vermins); to extinguish (a fire)

【撲粉】① to powder (one's face) ② face powder
【撲打】to beat; to pat; to swat
【撲通】a plop; a splash; a thump
【撲過來】to come in a dash
【撲克】poker (a gambling game)
【撲克牌】playing cards
【撲空】① to fail to meet a person one intended to meet ② to do a thing in vain
【撲救】to fight (a fire)
【撲食】to seize for prey
【撲殺】to kill
【撲朔迷離】①(said of a person) to look both like a man and a woman ② vague or ambiguous

撰 1602 ㄓㄨㄢˋ zhuàn
to write; to compose
【撰稿】to prepare manuscripts; to write
【撰稿人】a copywriter; a writer
【撰寫】to write or compose (usually light works)
【撰述】to write an account of (facts, happenings, etc.); to narrate
【撰文】to compose; to write

撮 1603 ㄘㄨㄛ cuō
(又讀 ㄘㄨㄛˋ cuò)
1. to take with fingers 2. to gather 3. to extract; to summarize 4. a pinch of
【撮弄】① to juggle ② to incite ③ to make fun of; to kid
【撮合】to bring (two persons or parties) together; to make a match

撣 1604 (撢) ㄉㄢˇ dǎn
1. to dust; to brush lightly; to whisk 2. as in 撢子—a duster

十三畫

撼 1605 ㄏㄢˋ hàn
to shake; to rock; to jolt; to joggle
【撼動】to shake; to rock
【撼天動地】to shake both the heaven and the earth—to cause a great sensation

擂 1606 1. ㄌㄟˊ léi
1. to grind; to pestle 2. to beat; to hit
【擂鼓】to beat a drum

擂 1606 2. ㄌㄟˋ lèi
參看「擂臺」
【擂臺】a platform for contests in martial arts; an arena

擄 1607 ㄌㄨˇ lǔ
(又讀 ㄌㄨㄛˇ luǒ)
to capture; to take captive
【擄掠】to plunder; to rob; to pillage
【擄獲】to capture; to take captive
【擄人勒贖】to kidnap a person for ransom

擁 1608 ㄩㄥˇ yǒng
(又讀 ㄩㄥ yōng)
1. to hug; to embrace; to hold 2. to have; to possess 3. to crowd; to throng; to swarm 4. to follow; to support
【擁抱】to embrace; to hug; to hold in one's arms
【擁戴】to support a leader or ruler; (to) support
【擁護】to advocate; to support; to back
【擁擠】crowded; packed
【擁上心來】(said of memories, emotions, etc.) to well up
【擁塞】to block up; a jam
【擁有】to have; to possess; to own

擅 1609 ㄕㄢˋ shàn
1. unauthorized; arbitrary 2. to monopolize; to take exclusive possession 3. to be good at; to be expert in
【擅改】to change or revise without authorization
【擅長】to excel in; to be good at
【擅自】to do something without authorization
【擅自行動】to act presumptuously
【擅自作主】to take an unauthorized action
【擅用】to use without permission

操 1610 ㄘㄠ cāo
1. to handle; to manage 2. to hold; to grasp 3. to exercise; to drill 4. to speak
【操勞】①to work hard ②to look after
【操練】to drill; to practice
【操戈】to take up arms
【操槍】rifle drill
【操心】① to worry about ② to rack one's brains

〔手部〕

〔手部〕

【操行】conduct (in the moral sense); behavior or conduct of a student
【操之過急】to be too eager for success
【操持】to manage; to handle
【操場】an athletic ground; a playground
【操守】moral fortitude; integrity
【操神】to worry
【操作】to manipulate or operate (a machine)
【操縱】to manage, control, manipulate or operate
【操演】to drill; to exercise

擔 1611
1. (担) ㄉㄢ dān
to shoulder; to take upon oneself
【擔保】to guarantee; to pledge
【擔負】① a burden; responsibility ② to assume a responsibility; to undertake
【擔待】to be lenient
【擔當】to take (responsibility) upon oneself, or undertake (a task)
【擔擱】to delay; delay
【擔架】a stretcher
【擔心】to worry; to feel anxious
【擔任】to take charge of (a task); to hold the post of
【擔憂】to be anxious; to worry; to apprehensive

擔 1611
2. ㄉㄢ dàn
1. a load; a burden 2. as in 扁擔—a carrying pole 3. a unit of weight or capacity

擇 1612
ㄗㄜ zé (又讀 ㄓㄞ zhái)
to select; to choose; to pick out
【擇期】to select a good time or day (for an undertaking, a wedding, etc.)
【擇善固執】to choose what is good and stick to it
【擇偶】to select a spouse or a mate
【擇友】to choose friends

擋 1613
1. ㄉㄤ dàng
used in the combination of 摒擋—to arrange in order; to pack up for traveling

擋 1613
2. ㄉㄤ dǎng
1. to obstruct; to impede; to stop; to resist; to ward off 2. a fender; a blind 3. a gear
【擋風玻璃】a windshield
【擋泥板】a mudguard, or a fender
【擋路】to be in the way
【擋駕】to decline to receive visitors
【擋箭牌】① a shield ② an excuse; a pretext
【擋住】to block; to impede; to hinder; to obstruct

擒 1614
ㄑㄧㄣ qín
to arrest; to capture
【擒拿 or 擒捉 or 擒獲】to arrest; to capture

據 1615
(据) ㄐㄩ jù
1. according to; on the basis of; on the grounds of 2. to depend on 3. to occupy; to take possession of; to seize 4. proof; evidence 5. a Chinese family name
【據點】a base (for operations or activities)
【據理力爭】to argue vigorously on the basis of sound reason or justice
【據悉】It is reported that....
【據稱】according to reports, assertions, or claims
【據實】according to the fact
【據守】to hold a position against attack; to make a stand
【據說】It is said that.... 或 according to hearsay
【據此】(a conventional phrase in official correspondence) on these grounds
【據我看(來)】as I see it; in my opinion
【據我所知】as far as I know
【據爲己有】to take possession (of what does not belong to oneself)

擀 1616
ㄍㄢ gǎn
1. to stretch out with a rolling pin 2. to polish; to shine
【擀麪】to roll dough

撿 1617
ㄐㄧㄢ jiǎn
to pick up; to collect
【撿破爛的】a rag picker; a junk collector
【撿柴】to collect firewood

擊 1618
ㄐㄧ jí
to beat; to strike; to attack
【擊敗】to defeat; to beat; to conquer
【擊倒】to knock down
【擊退】to beat back; to drive back
【擊落】to shoot down (aircraft)

【擊毀】to wreck; to destory
【擊潰】①to knock to pieces ②to rout (the enemy troops)
【擊中目標】to hit the target
【擊中要害】to hit somebody's vital point
【擊沉】to sink (vessels by torpedoing, bombing, or bombarding)
【擊碎】to knock (or smash) to pieces

擎 1619 ㄑㄧㄥˊ qíng
to lift; to support

十四畫

擠 1620 ㄐㄧˇ jǐ
1. to push; to jostle 2. to wring; to squeeze; to twist; to press 3. to crowd; to throng; to pack
【擠眉弄眼】to make eyes; to wink
【擠滿】to pack (a place, car, etc.) to capacity
【擠兌】a run on a bank
【擠奶or擠乳】to draw or press milk
【擠來擠去】to push about; to jostle
【擠壓】extruding

擡 1621 (抬) ㄊㄞˊ tái
to lift; to raise; to carry
【擡頭】①to raise one's head ②(said of the price) an upsurge; (said of fortune) a turn for the better ③a bank's salutation for a client
【擡頭挺胸】(literally) chin up and chest out—full of confidence or pride
【擡槓】to argue for the sake of arguing
【擡舉】to do a good turn or favor

擢 1622 ㄓㄨㄛˊ zhuó
1. to take out; to pull out; to extract; to pick out; to select 2. to promote; to raise (in rank)
【擢升 or 擢昇】to advance; to promote (to a higher position or rank)
【擢用】to pick and promote (promising employees or subordinates)

擣 1623 (搗) ㄉㄠˇ dǎo
1. to pound; to beat 2. to attack 3. to harass; to disturb
【擣米】to hull rice in a mortar

擬 1624 ㄋㄧˇ nǐ
1. to plan; to intend; to decide; to determine 2. to draft; to draw up; to design 3. to imitate
【擬定】to draw up or map out (a plan); to draft
【擬稿】to prepare manuscripts or write copies (for publication)
【擬請】to intend to ask or request
【擬人法】(rhetoric) personification

擯 1625 ㄅㄧㄣˋ bìn
1. to expel; to reject; to oust; to get rid of; to discard 2. same as 儐—an usher
【擯棄】to cast away; to set aside; to discard; to desert
【擯斥】to reject; to expel; to repudiate
【擯除】to expel; to oust; to eliminate

擦 1626 ㄘㄚ cā
1. to wipe; to mop; to scrub; to polish 2. to spread on; to put on 3. to rub; to graze; to scratch 4. to brush; to shave
【擦玻璃】to wipe glass; to wipe windowpanes
【擦皮鞋】to shine shoes
【擦地板】to mop the floor
【擦亮】to shine (shoes, utensils, etc.)
【擦乾】to swab up; to wipe dry
【擦乾淨】to wipe clean
【擦汗】to wipe off sweat or perspiration
【擦去】to wipe off
【擦洗】to scrub
【擦鞋童】a shoeshine boy; a shoeblack
【擦鞋油】shoe polish
【擦拭】to clean; to cleanse
【擦身而過or擦肩而過】to pass each other so close that they almost rub each other
【擦傷】a scratch; to suffer a scratch
【擦子】a rubber; an eraser

擱 1627 ㄍㄜ gē
1. to lay; to leave; to put 2. to file 3. to delay; to put aside
【擱淺】①to run aground; to get stranded ②(said of negotiations) to come to a deadlock
【擱下】to put aside or lay down (work)
【擱置】to shelve or pigeonhole (a plan, proposal, etc.)

〔手部〕

擤 1628 ㄒㄧㄥˇ xǐng
to blow (the nose)
【擤鼻涕】 to blow the nose

擰 1629 1. ㄋㄧㄥˊ níng
to twist; to pinch; to wring

擰 1629 2. ㄋㄧㄥˋ nìng
1. to wrench; to twist; to screw 2. wrong; mistaken 3. to differ; to disagree
【擰開】 to wrench apart

十五畫

擲 1630 ㄓˊ zhí
to throw; to cast
【擲標槍】 (sports) ① javelin throw ② to throw the javelin
【擲鐵餅】 (sports) discus throw
【擲鉛球】 (sports) shot put
【擲骰子 or 擲色子】 to cast dice

擷 1631 ㄒㄧㄝˊ xié (又讀 ㄐㄧㄝˊ jié)
to pick; to collect; to gather
【擷取精華】 to pick the best

擴 1632 ㄎㄨㄛˋ kuò
to enlarge; to magnify; to expand; to extend
【擴大】 ① to enlarge; to expand ② to swell; to distend
【擴建】 to extend (a factory, mine, etc.)
【擴展】 to stretch; to extend; to spread
【擴張】 ① to extend; to spread; to expand ② to dilate; dilation
【擴充】 to expand; to enlarge
【擴散】 ① (physics) to diffuse; diffusion ② to scatter about
【擴音器】 a megaphone; a microphone

擺 1633 ㄅㄞˇ bǎi
1. to arrange; to display; to place; to put 2. to wave; to swing; to oscillate; to wag 3. a pendulum 4. to assume; to put on
【擺佈】 ① to manage or handle (a person) ② to arrange
【擺平】 ① (slang) to make satisfied ② to put down something securely
【擺渡】 to ferry
【擺動】 to sway; to swing
【擺脫】 to free oneself from; to cast off; to shake off (a tailer)
【擺弄】 ① to toy with; to play with ② to make fun of; to trick
【擺闊】 to show off one's wealth
【擺架子】 to be snobbish; to put on airs
【擺設】 to furnish and decorate (a room)
【擺手】 to swing one's arms
【擺烏龍】 to talk irresponsibly

擾 1634 ㄖㄠˇ rǎo
1. to disturb; to agitate; to harass 2. to trespass on somebody's hospitality 3. disorder
【擾亂】 to disturb; to agitate
【擾攘】 tumult; hustle and bustle

攆 1635 ㄋㄧㄢˇ niǎn
1. to expel; to oust; to drive 2. to catch up
【攆出去】 to throw (someone) out; to drive away
【攆走】 to drive (someone) away; to dismiss

攀 1636 ㄆㄢ pān
1. to hold to; to climb; to hang on; to clamber 2. to involve
【攀附】 to hang on or to attach oneself to (power, glory, etc.)
【攀登】 to climb; to scale
【攀談】 to drag another into conversation
【攀龍附鳳】 to establish oneself by riding on the coattails of a brilliant master
【攀折】 to injure (a plant) by picking or breaking
【攀岩】 rock climbing
【攀緣】 ① (Buddhism) to be affected by one's environment ② to climb

十七畫

攔 1637 ㄌㄢˊ lán
to impede; to obstruct; to hinder; to block
【攔擊】 to intercept and attack; to volley
【攔劫】 to intercept and rob
【攔截】 to intercept; to attack or stop on the way
【攔住】 to obstruct; to block; to hinder
【攔車】 to stop a vehicle

【攔阻】 to impede; to obstruct

攘 1638 1. ㄖㄤˇ rǎng
confused; disorderly
【攘攘】 in a state of confusion

攘 1638 2. ㄖㄤˊ ráng
1. to take by force 2. to eliminate; to repel; to resist 3. to shake
【攘奪】 to take by force
【攘除】 to rid; to eliminate; to dispel

攙 1639 ㄔㄢ chān
1. to lead (a person) by the hand 2. to mix; to blend
【攙扶】 to lead (a person) by the hand
【攙合 or 攙和】 to mix; to blend
【攙雜】 to make impure; to add imitation goods or inferior products to a shipment of merchandise in violation of business ethics

十八畫

攜 1640 (携、擕、攜) ㄒㄧㄝˊ xié (讀音 ㄒㄧ xī)
1. to take; to carry 2. to help; to lead
【攜帶】 to carry with oneself; to take along
【攜手】 ① to hold each other's hand ② to cooperate

攝 1641 ㄕㄜˋ shè
1. to take in; to absorb; to attract 2. to take a photograph (or a shot) of 3. to regulate 4. to represent
【攝取】 to take in; to absorb
【攝氏寒暑表or攝氏溫度計】a centigrade thermometer
【攝影】 photography; to take a photograph of
【攝影棚】 a sound stage; a (movie) studio
【攝影機】 a camera

十九畫

攤 1642 ㄊㄢ tān
1. to spread; to open 2. to divide equally; to apportion 3. a booth; a stand; a stall 4. a collection of liquid; a pool of (water, mud, blood, etc.)
【攤牌】 a showdown; to have a showdown
【攤派】 to apportion
【攤販】 a vender or stallkeeper
【攤開】 to spread out; to unfold
【攤還】 to amortize
【攤子or攤兒】 a stand; a booth; a stall
【攤位】 a stall or booth (especially a fixed one in a market)

二十畫

攪 1643 1. ㄐㄧㄠˇ jiǎo
1. to stir; to mix 2. to agitate; to disturb; to annoy
【攪拌or攪動】 to stir or churn; to mix
【攪拌器】 a mixer; an agitator
【攪亂】 to disturb; to ruffle; to disarrange
【攪和】 ① to mingle ② to confuse
【攪局】 to spoil; to disturb

攪 1643 2. (搞) ㄍㄠˇ gǎo
to do; to manage; to handle

攫 1644 ㄐㄩㄝˊ jué
to seize; to take hold of; to snatch; to catch
【攫奪】 to seize; to snatch; to grab
【攫取】 to take by force; to seize

二十一畫

攬 1645 (擥) ㄌㄢˇ lǎn
1. to be in full possession of 2. to take into one's arms 3. to make a selective collection of 4. to take on; to undertake 5. to grasp; to monopolize 6. to round up
【攬鏡自照】 to hold a mirror to watch one's own reflection
【攬權】 to grasp full authority
【攬勝】 to enjoy scenery

支 部 ㄓ zhī

支 1646 ㄓ zhī
1. to pay; to disburse; to defray 2. to support; to sustain 3. to prop up; to put up 4. to prick

up; to raise 5. to send away; to put somebody off 6. a branch; a subdivision 7. a term for indicating amount or number 8. (textile) count 9. as in 地支, the Terrestrial Branches used in calculation with the Celestial Stems (天干)

【支派】① a subdivision; a branch (of a school of thought) ② to appoint

【支配】①to dominate ②to manage

【支票】a cheque or check

【支票簿】a checkbook

【支付】to pay (what is owed); to defray

【支離】① to disintegrate ② incoherent; fragmented; broken

【支離破碎】completely disintegrated

【支流】① a tributary (of a river) ② nonessentials

【支領 or 支取】to draw money

【支節】a joint (of bones, etc.)

【支解】to dismember

【支氣管】bronchi

【支線】a branch line

【支柱】a prop; a support; a stay

【支持】to support; to sustain

【支撐】to prop up; to support

【支出】expense; expenditure

【支使】① to order about ② to send away

【支應】① to take charge of cash receipts and payments ② to look after; to take care of

【支吾其詞】to speak haltingly or ambiguously

【支援】to aid; to support; to assist

【支用】to disburse

八畫

支 部
ㄆㄨ pū

二畫

收 1647
ㄕㄡ shōu

1. to draw together; to gather; to collect 2. to contain 3. to receive; to accept; to take 4. to end; to come to a close 5. to retrieve; to take back

【收報機】a telegraph receiver

【收盤】the closing quotation (of a stock or commodity) for the day

【收票員】a ticket collector

【收買】① to bribe ② to buy up ③ to win (support, people's hearts, etc. by less than honorable means)

【收發】to receive and send out (official papers, documents, etc.)

【收費】to collect fees; to charge

【收費站】a toll station

【收復】to recover (lost territory)

【收到】to receive; to obtain

【收攤】to pack up the stall or booth (after a day's business is over)

【收聽】to tune in; to listen to (the radio)

【收攬】① to collect extensively ② to win (the people's hearts)

【收留】to take somebody in

【收斂】① to collect (taxes, grains, etc.) ② to contract ③ to weaken or disappear ④ to pull in one's horns

【收錄】① to employ; to recruit ② to include (in a list, etc.)

【收攏】to draw something in

【收割 or 收刈】to reap; to harvest

【收購】to buy up; to purchase

【收工】to end the day's work

【收看】to watch (television)

【收款人】a recipient (of remittance); a payee

【收穫】① harvest; fruits (of efforts) ② to reap

【收回】to recover; to recall; to retrieve

【收賄】to accept bribes; bribery

【收集】collection; to collect; to gather

【收件人】an addressee; a consignee

【收據】a receipt

【收起】to pack up

【收訖】received

【收錢】to collect payments

【收下】to accept; to receive

【收效】to get the desired result or effect

【收心】to concentrate attention

【收支】income and expenditure

【收場】①conclusion ②to wind up; to end up

【收成】harvest

【收拾】① to clear away; to tidy ② to manage ③ to punish

【收受】 to receive; to accept
【收稅】 to collect taxes
【收入】 ①to take in; to include ② income; earnings; revenue; receipts 「commodate
【收容】 to give shelter to; to ac-
【收藏】 to collect and keep
【收藏家】 a collector 「systole
【收縮】 ①to shrink; to contract ②
【收縮壓】 systolic pressure
【收益】 to get benefit; to benefit
【收押】 to take (a criminal suspect) into custody; to detain
【收音】 (radio) reception 「radio
【收音機】 a radio receiving set; a
【收銀機】 a cash register
【收養】 to adopt (a child)

三畫

改 1648
ㄍㄞˇ gǎi

1. to change; to transform; to convert; to alter 2. to correct 3. to revise 4. to switch over to

【改編】 ① to make a revision (of a book) ②to reorganize (a military unit, etc.) ③ (said of a movie, stage play, etc.) adapted from or based on (a book, novel,
【改變】 to change; to alter ⌊etc.)
【改變主意】 to change one's mind
【改道】 ① to change the course (of a river) ②to change one's route 「appearance
【改頭換面】 to change only the
【改天】 some other day
【改良or改善】 to ameliorate; to
【改革】 to reform ⌊improve
【改過】 to mend one's ways; to correct one's mistakes
【改過遷善】 to repent and be good
【改過自新】 to turn over a new leaf
【改觀】 to assume a new look
【改口or改嘴】 to say something different from what one is expected to say or has been saying 「fession or career
【改行】 to change one's trade, pro-
【改換】 to replace; to change
【改嫁or改醮】 (said of a woman) to remarry 「build
【改建or改造】 to remodel; to re-
【改進】 to improve; to better
【改期】 to postpone a scheduled event 「return to virtue
【改邪歸正】 to give up evil and
【改寫】 to rewrite; to adapt
【改弦易轍】 to change rules and systems
【改選】 to hold a new election
【改制】 to change a system
【改正】 to correct; to amend
【改裝】① to change dress ② to convert (a machine, vehicle, etc.) for a new use; to refit; to reequip
【改朝換代】 the change of regime
【改日】 some other time; later on
【改組】 to reshuffle (an organization); to reorganize
【改作文】 to correct compositions (for students)
【改錯】 to correct mistakes

攻 1649
ㄍㄨㄥ gōng

1. to attack; to raid; to assault 2. to accuse; to charge; to assail; to criticize; to rebuke 3. to work at; to apply oneself to; to study 「quer
【攻破or攻克】 to attack and con-
【攻打】 to attack; to raid; to invade
【攻讀or攻書】 to apply oneself diligently to study
【攻擊】 ① to attack ② to accuse
【攻取】 to attack and capture
【攻下】 ① to succeed in capturing (a city, a fort, etc.) by attack ② to overcome
【攻陷】 to succeed in capturing (a city, a fort, etc.) by attack
【攻佔】 to attack and occupy
【攻勢】 the offensive
【攻守】 offense and defense

四畫

放 1650
ㄈㄤˋ fàng

1. to let go; to release; to free; to liberate; to loosen; to relax 2. to put; to place 3. to put in; to add 4. to dissipate; to debauch; to indulge
【放榜】 to announce or publish the result of a competitive examination 「sense!
【放屁】 ① to let out gas ② Non-
【放馬後砲】 to criticize or make comments on something after it is already over; to second-guess

〔攴部〕

〔攴部〕

【放風箏】to fly a kite
【放大】to magnify; to enlarge
【放大鏡】a magnifying glass
【放蕩】dissolute; debauched; dissipated
【放牛】to pasture cattle
【放浪形骸】to abandon oneself to Bohemianism
【放領】to lease (public land)
【放過】to let go
【放開】to relax or loosen (a grasp, etc.); to let go
【放寬】to ease or relax (restrictions, etc.); to liberalize
【放款】a loan; loaning; to loan
【放火】to set fire; to commit arson
【放假】to have or give a holiday or vacation
【放棄】① to give up; to abandon ②(law) to waive
【放晴】(said of the weather) to clear up
【放下】to put (or lay) down
【放心】to be free from anxiety
【放心不下】to be kept in suspense
【放學】to return home from school at the end of the day's classes
【放置】to place; to put down
【放逐】to exile; to banish
【放唱片】to play a phonograph
【放射】to emit; to radiate; to send out
【放手】①to let go ②to give up ③to have a free hand
【放手去做】to act without considering consequences or difficulties
【放生】to free or release a captured animal (out of pity)
【放聲大哭】to cry loudly
【放水】① to let water out ② to let the other side win (a game, contest, etc.) purposely
【放任】to let (a person) do as he pleases; to let (a matter) take its own course
【放縱】①to debauch; to dissipate; to indulge ②to break rules of conduct
【放肆】to take liberties
【放鬆】to relax; to ease; to loosen; to slacken
【放焰火】to set off fireworks
【放映】to project (on the screen); to show
【放映機】a projector

五畫

政 1651 ㄓㄥˋ zhèng

1. government 2. politics; political affairs 3. administration; management
【政變】a coup d'état; a coup
【政府】a government
【政府機關】a government agency
【政黨】a political party
【政體】a political system; a polity
【政令】a government order (or decree)
【政論】articles, statements or comments about politics
【政略】a government policy
【政綱】the platform (of a political party)
【政客】a politician who places personal gain above public interests
【政界】political circles; officialdom
【政見】political views; politics
【政見發表會】a show and tell
【政局】the political situation or scene
【政權】regime; political power
【政治】① politics ② government administration
【政治庇護】political asylum
【政治犯】a political prisoner
【政治活動】political activities
【政治家】a statesman
【政事or政務】affairs of the government
【政策】a policy
【政要】government VIPs
【政務委員】a minister without portfolio

故 1652 ㄍㄨˋ gù

1. former; past; earlier; previous; old; ancient 2. intentional; willful; on purpose 3. cause; reason 4. to die 5. an incident; an event; a matter 6. consequently; hence; therefore 7. a friend; an acquaintance
【故步自封】to confine oneself to the old method or traditional way
【故都】a former capital
【故態復萌】The old (bad) attitude is back.
【故弄玄虛】to puzzle people intentionally
【故里】one's hometown
【故國】①one's fatherland②an old country ③one's hometown
【故宮博物院】National Palace Museum
【故交or故知or故友】an old friend
【故居】one's former residence

【故鄉】one's homeland
【故障】a bug or breakdown (of a machine)
【故主】the former king or master
【故事】a story; a narrative; a tale
【故人】①an old friend ②one's former wife
【故意】intentional; on purpose

六畫

效 1653 (効) ㄒㄧㄠˋ xiào
1. to imitate; to mimic; to follow 2. effect; effectiveness; efficacy 3. to devote 4. to offer
【效命】①to obey orders ②to pursue an end at the cost of one's life
【效法】to take as a model; to imitate
【效能】effect
【效勞】to render service; to work for
【效力】①effect; efficacy ②to render service
【效率】efficiency
【效果】effect; result
【效忠】to be loyal to; allegiance
【效益】beneficial result; benefit
【效用】usefulness; use; utility

七畫

敍 1654 (敘、叙) ㄒㄩˋ xù
1. to tell; to narrate; to describe; to express 2. to talk about; to chat 3. to arrange in order 4. to rate or evaluate (as a basis for reward, appointment, etc.); to assess
【敍別】to get together for talk before a separation
【敍舊】to talk about the old days
【敍說or敍述】to tell; to narrate
【敍言or敍文】a preface; a foreword

教 1655 1. ㄐㄧㄠˋ jiào
1. a religion 2. an order; a directive 3. to educate 4. to urge; to incite; to bid; to instigate 5. to instruct; instruction(s); to advise; advice 6. to have; to let; to make
【教派】religious sects
【教名】one's Christian name or forename
【教父】godfather
【教導】①to instruct ②guidance
【教導有方】skillful in teaching and providing guidance
【教堂】a church; a mosque
【教條】a doctrine
【教廷】the Holy See; the Vatican
【教徒】a (religious) believer or follower
【教練】①a coach (of athletes); an instructor ②to train
【教官】a military instructor; a drillmaster
【教科書】the textbook
【教化】① culture ② to bring enlightenment to the people by education
【教會】the church
【教會學校】a church school
【教誨】to teach and admonish
【教皇or教宗】the Pope; the Pontiff
【教學】①instruction; teaching ②to teach and to learn
【教訓】①a lesson ②to admonish; teachings
【教職】the occupation of teaching
【教職員】the teaching and administrative staff of a school
【教主】a religious leader
【教師】a teacher
【教師節】Teacher's Day
【教士】an evangelist; a priest; a clergyman
【教室】a classroom
【教授】a professor
【教材】teaching materials
【教唆】to instigate; to incite; to abet
【教義】a creed
【教友】a fellow believer (of a religion)
【教養】to bring up; to rear
【教務主任】the dean of studies (of a primary or secondary school)
【教務處】the office of the dean of studies
【教育】①to educate ②education
【教育部】Ministry of Education
【教育部長】a minister of education
【教育費】the cost of education
【教育家】an educator or educationist
【教育界】educational circles
【教育制度】the educational system
【教育程度】the level of education
【教員】a member of the teaching profession; a teacher

教 1655 2. ㄐㄧㄠ jiāo
to teach; to guide
【教壞】to misguide; to lead astray
【教書】to teach (usually for a living)

敏 1656 ㄇㄧㄣˇ mǐn
1. quick; agile; speedy; clever;

〔攴部〕

smart; nimble; sensitive 2. diligent; industrious; earnest; eager
【敏感】① sensitive ② (medicine) allergic
【敏捷】agile; adroit; quick; nimble
【敏銳】keen; sharp; sharp-witted; acute

救 1657
ㄐㄧㄡˋ jiù 「aid; to help
to save; to relieve; to rescue; to
【救兵】relieving troops; reinforcements 「Help!
【救命】① to save one's life ②
【救命恩人】the savior of one's life
【救護】to relieve and nurse (the wounded, etc.); to rescue
【救護車】an ambulance
【救活】to resuscitate; to revive
【救火】① to try to extinguish a fire ② firefighting
【救急】① to give help in emergency ② to apply first aid
【救濟】to relieve (the suffering, the poor, etc.)
【救濟金】relief funds
【救濟院】a poorhouse; a workhouse
【救星】a savior
【救治】to treat and cure (the sick); to remedy 「siah
【救(世)主】the Savior; the Messiah
【救助】to relieve or help (persons)
【救生艇 or 救生船】a lifeboat
【救生圈】a life ring; a life buoy
【救生衣】a life jacket
【救生員】a lifeguard; a lifesaver
【救災】to relieve victims of a disaster 「tressed)
【救援】to help or aid (the distressed)
【救援投手】(baseball) a relief pitcher

敕 1658
(勅) ㄔˋ chì
1. an imperial order or decree 2. cautious 3. to warn; to caution
【敕令】a rescript

敗 1659
ㄅㄞˋ bài
1. to defeat or be defeated; to fail; to go down 2. to decline; to decay; to wither 3. to spoil or be spoiled; to corrupt or be corrupted
【敗北】to suffer defeat; a defeat
【敗筆】① a worn-out writing brush ② poor calligraphy
【敗類】① to ruin or corrupt one's fellows ② corrupt people
【敗露】(said of a crime, plot, etc.) to fail and be exposed
【敗壞】to ruin or be ruined
【敗壞門楣】to disgrace one's family
【敗績】a defeat
【敗(家)子】a wastrel; a prodigal; a spendthrift
【敗將】① a defeated enemy general ② one who is defeated in a contest
【敗血病 or 敗血症】septicemia
【敗興而歸】to come back disappointed
【敗陣or敗仗】a defeat
【敗訴】to lose a lawsuit 「thrown
【敗亡】to be defeated and overthrown

八畫

敝 1660
ㄅㄧˋ bì
1. worn-out; broken; tattered 2. exhausted; tired 3. (a self-depreciatory term) my or our
【敝國】my or our country
【敝屣】worn-out shoes—useless things
【敝姓】my family name
【敝帚自珍】Everyone values things of his own.

敞 1661
ㄔㄤˇ chǎng
1. open; uncovered 2. spacious; broad 「open car
【敞篷(兒)車】an open coach; an open car
【敞開】to open; to unfold
【敞快】straightforward and broad-minded 「breast; décolleté
【敞胸露懷or敞胸】to bare the breast; décolleté
【敞著】open

敢 1662
ㄍㄢˇ gǎn
1. to dare 2. to have the confidence to; to be sure; to be certain 3. bold; courageous; daring 4. to make bold; to venture
【敢請】I venture to request....
【敢情】① naturally; of course ② originally ③ perhaps; maybe
【敢作敢當】to have the courage to accept the consequences of one's doing
【敢作敢為】to have the courage to do what one believes should be done 「to-die corps
【敢死隊】a suicide squad; a dare-to-die corps
【敢問】I venture to ask....
【敢於】to dare to; to be bold in

散 1663
1. ㄙㄢˋ sàn

1. to scatter; to disperse 2. to end; to be over; to stop 3. to disseminate; to give out

【散播】 to disseminate; to spread
【散佈or散布】 ① to scatter; to sprinkle ② to spread
【散步】 to take a walk, a stroll, or a ramble
【散發】 ① to send out; to emit ② to distribute; to issue; to give out
【散落】 to be strewn or scattered
【散亂】 confused; in disorder
【散光】 astigmatism; astigmatic
【散夥】 (said of a group) to disband
【散會】 to dissolve a meeting
【散心】 to have some recreation
【散場】 (said of a show, a meeting, etc.) to be over
【散失】 to get scattered and lost; missing
【散熱】 to dissipate heat

散 1663
2. ㄙㄢˇ sǎn

1. loose; loosened 2. idle; leisurely 3. powdered medicine

【散兵】 ① skirmishers ② stragglers
【散彈】 a grapeshot; a pellet
【散記】 random notes
【散居】 to live in scattered places
【散裝】 not in a package; bulk
【散文】 prose

敦 1664
1. ㄉㄨㄣ dūn

1. honest; sincere; candid 2. to deepen or strengthen (relations, etc.) 3. to urge; to press

【敦品力學】 upright in character and diligent in the pursuit of knowledge
【敦聘 or 敦請】 to cordially invite
【敦睦】 to have cordial and friendly ties
【敦厚 or 敦篤】 honest; sincere
【敦煌】 Tunhwang, Kansu Province
【敦促】 to urge or press earnestly

敦 1664
2. ㄉㄨㄟˋ duì

a sort of container

九畫

敬 1665
ㄐㄧㄥˋ jìng

1. to respect; to revere; to honor; to esteem 2. to present; to offer

【敬陪末座】 to sit below the salt
【敬奉】 ① to receive respectfully ② to present (or offer) respectfully
【敬老尊賢】 to revere the aged and honor the wise
【敬禮】 to salute
【敬告】 to tell respectfully
【敬賀】 to congratulate with respect
【敬候】 ① to inquire after respectfully ② to await respectfully
【敬酒】 to drink a toast; to toast
【敬啓】 to state with respect (a conventional phrase in correspondence)
【敬請】 to invite respectfully
【敬請指教】 I humbly request your advice.
【敬謝】 to thank respectfully
【敬香】 to offer incense
【敬祝】 to wish respectfully (a conventional phrase used at the end of a letter)
【敬重】 to respect; to esteem
【敬稱】 an honorific appellation
【敬呈】 to present with respect
【敬贈】 to present respectfully
【敬愛】 to respect and love
【敬意】 respects; regards
【敬仰or敬佩】 to admire; to esteem; to respect
【敬畏】 to hold in awe; to venerate

十畫

敲 1666
ㄑㄧㄠ qiāo

1. to rap; to strike; to tap; to beat; to knock 2. as in 敲扑——a truncheon 3. to extort; to blackmail; to overcharge

【敲邊鼓】 to speak for someone in order to help him
【敲破】 to smash; to shatter
【敲門】 to knock at (or on) the door
【敲打or敲擊】 to rap; to knock; to beat
【敲鑼】 to beat a gong
【敲詐】 to blackmail
【敲竹槓】 to extort money; to fleece
【敲鐘】 to toll a bell

十一畫

敵 1667
ㄉㄧˊ dí

1. an enemy; a foe; a rival 2. to

〔攴部〕

攴部

oppose; to resist 3. to match; to rival; to equal
【敵對】to be hostile to; to oppose
【敵機】an enemy plane; a hostile plane
【敵軍】enemy troops; hostile forces
【敵情】the enemy's situation
【敵衆我寡】We are outnumbered by the enemy.
【敵視】to regard with hostility
【敵手】an opponent; a match; a rival
【敵人】an enemy; a foe
【敵意】enmity; hostility; antagonism

敷 1668
ㄈㄨ fū
1. to apply or spread over (a surface); to paint 2. to suffice; to be enough 3. to state; to explain; to expound
【敷設】to install; to arrange; to lay
【敷藥】to salve; to apply a salve
【敷衍】①to act in a perfunctory manner ②to deal with a person insincerely
【敷衍了事】to carry out a task in a perfunctory manner

數 1669
1. ㄕㄨˋ shù
1. number; quantity; amount; sum 2. (mathematics) numbers 3. several; a few 4. a plan; an idea 5. fate; destiny 6. art
【數倍】several times; manifold
【數目 or 數額】number; sum
【數天】several days; a few days
【數年】several years; a few years
【數年如一日】with perseverance and consistency
【數量】quantity; amount
【數據】data
【數學】mathematics
【數值】numerical value
【數字】a numeral; a figure; a digit
【數以萬計】by tens of thousands; numerous

數 1669
2. ㄕㄨˇ shǔ
1. to count; to enumerate 2. to count (as best, etc.); to be reckoned as exceptionally (good, bad, etc.)
【數不清】innumerable; countless
【數典忘祖】to forget one's origin; ungrateful
【數落】to blame; to reprove
【數數兒】to name numbers; to count
【數一數二】either the best or second only to the best

數 1669
3. ㄕㄨㄛˋ shuò
often; frequently
【數見不鮮】not uncommon; nothing new

十二畫

整 1670
ㄓㄥˇ zhěng
1. orderly; systematic; neat; tidy 2. sharp 3. whole; complete; entire; intact 4. to tidy; to set in order; to adjust; to arrange; to repair; to make ready
【整編】to reorganize troops
【整批】batch
【整隊】①(said of troops, etc.) to form neat lines; to file ②the whole unit, band, column, etc.
【整頓】to put in order, or to put to right a poorly managed organization, firm, etc.
【整套】the whole set
【整體】the whole
【整體規劃】corporate planning
【整天or整日】the whole day; all day long
【整年】the whole year
【整理】to arrange; to put in order; to adjust
【整流器】(physics) ①a rectifier ②a commutator
【整合】(geology) conformity
【整潔】neat and clean
【整齊】① neat; tidy ② even
【整齊劃一】neat and uniform
【整修】to rebuild; to renovate
【整形】orthopedics
【整形手術】plastic operation
【整治】①to set in order; to adjust and repair ②to dredge (a river)
【整裝】to dress up
【整裝待發】(usually said of troops on an expedition) to pack up and be ready to go
【整飭】①orderly; systematic ②to set to order
【整除】to divide exactly
【整數】a whole number; an integer; a round sum
【整人】(slang) to give someone a hard time; to fix somebody
【整容】① to improve one's looks by plastic surgery ② to tidy one's appearance (by shaving, a

haircut, etc.); face-lifting
【整肅】① strict; rigid; stern ② to purge (a government or political leader) ③ to rectify
【整夜】all night; the whole night

十三畫

斂 1671 ㄌㄧㄢˇ liǎn
1. to draw together; to contract 2. to hold back; to restrain 3. to collect; to gather
【斂財】to collect wealth illegally or immorally

十四畫

斃 1672 ㄅㄧˋ bì
1. to come to a bad end; decline; destruction 2. to fall; to prostrate 3. dead; to come to the end of life 4. (colloquial) to kill or execute by shooting; to shoot
【斃命】to meet violent death; to get killed

文部 ㄨㄣˊ wén

文 1673 1. ㄨㄣˊ wén
1. a composition; an article 2. language 3. literature; education; culture 4. elegant; civil; polite; polished; mild; suave; cultured; urbane 5. civilian or civil (as opposed to military) 6. a former monetary unit
【文筆】the pen; literary talent
【文不對題】The content of the writing is inconsistent with the title.
【文憑】a diploma
【文盲】an illiterate
【文明】civilized; civilization
【文法】grammar
【文風】① literary style ② popular interest in learning
【文風不動】① no change from origin ② calm; quiet
【文旦】a shaddock; a pomelo
【文定】to become betrothed
【文壇】the literary circles, world, or arena
【文體】literary style
【文稿】a manuscript
【文告】a public notice; a manifesto
【文官】a civil servant
【文科】the liberal arts
【文豪】a literary lion; a great writer
【文化】culture; civilization
【文化交流】cultural exchange
【文化事業】cultural enterprises
【文化水準】the cultural standing or level
【文件】documents; legal papers
【文具】writing tools; stationery
【文情並茂】Both the language and the content are excellent.
【文獻】records; documents
【文學】literature
【文學家】a literary man; a litterateur
【文學界】the literary world, circles, or arena
【文學作品】literary works
【文學院】a college of liberal arts
【文選】a selection of literary works; an anthology
【文職】a civil post
【文質彬彬】elegant and refined in manner
【文摘】an abstract; a digest
【文縐縐】pedantic
【文章】an article; a composition
【文書】① documents; records ② an archivist
【文人】① a man of letters ② a man with a civilian background
【文弱書生】an effeminate scholar
【文字】① a letter; a character; written language ② writing
【文辭】diction; phraseology; language
【文采】① elegant appearances ② beautiful or gorgeous color
【文義】the meaning of a written article
【文藝】literature (as one of the fine arts); belles-lettres
【文藝復興】the Renaissance
【文藝界】the literary circles
【文雅】graceful; refined; polished
【文武百官】all the civil and military officials
【文武全才】a master of both the pen and the sword
【文物】cultural artifacts

文 1673 2. ㄨㄣˋ wèn
to cover up; to conceal; to gloss over
【文過飾非】to cover up one's fault

by clever use of words in writing

八畫

〔斗・斤部〕

斌 1674 ㄅㄧㄣ bīn
equally fine in external accomplishments and internal qualities

斐 1675 ㄈㄟˇ fěi
1. elegant; beautiful 2. a Chinese family name
【斐然成章】beautifully composed

斑 1676 ㄅㄢ bān
1. speckles; spots; mottles 2. mottled; variegated; motley
【斑白】(said of hair) gray
【斑駁】motley (in color)
【斑馬】a zebra
【斑馬線】a zebra crossing
【斑點】specks; spots; mottles
【斑斕】gorgeous; resplendent
【斑鳩】the ringdove; the cushat
【斑紋】stripes; striped

斗部 ㄉㄡˇ dǒu

斗 1677 ㄉㄡˇ dǒu
1. Chinese peck (a unite of dry measure for grain) 2. a large container for wine 3. one of the 28 constellations
【斗篷】a mantle; a cape
【斗膽】great intrepidity or boldness
【斗笠】a broad-brimmed rain hat (usually worn by farmers)
【斗室】a little room; a small room
【斗筲之人】shallow common men (Confucius' description of officials of his times)

六畫

料 1678 ㄌㄧㄠˋ liào
1. to conjecture; to reckon; to estimate 2. to infer; to anticipate; to foresee 3. to consider; to calculate 4. to manage; to handle; to care 5. material; stuff; makings
【料到】to foresee; to expect
【料理】① to manage; to dispose of ② a Japanese dish
【料想】to reckon; to imagine; to expect; to presume
【料中】to guess correctly
【料事如神】to foresee with divine accuracy
【料子】cloth; fabric; material

七畫

斜 1679 ㄒㄧㄝˊ xié
inclined; sloping; slanting; leaning; oblique; diagonal
【斜坡】a slope
【斜面】① (mathematics) an inclined plane ②(machinery) a bevel (face); an oblique plane
【斜對面】diagonally opposite
【斜體字】italics
【斜線】an oblique line
【斜視】① to look askance ② squint
【斜陽】the setting sun

九畫

斟 1680 ㄓㄣ zhēn
1. to fill a cup with (tea or wine) 2. to consider
【斟酒】to pour wine or liquor into a cup or glass
【斟酌】① to fill a cup, or glass, with wine or liquor ② to consider

十畫

斡 1681 ㄨㄛˋ wò
to revolve; to turn; to rotate
【斡旋】to mediate; mediation

斤部 ㄐㄧㄣ jīn

斤 1682 ㄐㄧㄣ jīn
1. catty 2. an ax 3. discerning; keen in observation
【斤兩】weight
【斤斤計較】to be particular about

every point, detail, or trifle

一畫

斥 1683
ㄔˋ chì
1. to accuse; to blame; to reproach; to reprove; to censure 2. to expel; to drive off; to banish; to eject 3. to survey; to observe; to reconnoiter
【斥罵or叱罵】 to denounce; to scold
【斥責 or 叱責】 to reprimand; to rebuke; to censure; to denounce

四畫

斧 1684
ㄈㄨˇ fǔ
1. a hatchet; an ax 2. to chop; to cut; to trim
【斧子 or 斧頭】an ax(e); a hatchet
【斧鉞】the executioner's ax—(figuratively) capital punishment

七畫

斬 1685
ㄓㄢˇ zhǎn
1. to cut 2. to kill; to behead
【斬釘截鐵】 to speak, or act, with determination and courage
【斬新 or 嶄新】 brand-new
【斬首】 to guillotine; to behead
【斬首示衆】 to behead a criminal and exhibit the severed head to the public as a warning to would-be offenders
【斬草除根】 to eliminate the cause of trouble completely

八畫

斯 1686
ㄙ sī
1. this; these; such; here 2. a connecting particle—then; thus
【斯里蘭卡】 Sri Lanka
【斯文】 cultured; gentle; elegant; refined

九畫

新 1687
ㄒㄧㄣ xīn
1. new; fresh; novel 2. modern; recent 3. beginning; starting 4. the prefix "neo"
【新版】the new edition (of a book)
【新編】 ① a new version ② newly organized
【新兵】 recruits
【新名詞】 new terms; new terminology
【新發明】a new invention
【新房】 ① a bridal chamber ② a new house
【新臺幣】 New Taiwan Dollar (NT$)
【新年】 New Year
【新娘 or 新娘子】 a bride
【新郎】 a bridegroom
【新曆】 the solar calendar; the Gregorian calendar
【新婚】 newly married
【新婚夫婦】 newlyweds
【新紀元 or 新時代】 a new era
【新加坡】 Singapore
【新舊交替】 the transition from the old to the new
【新近】 recently; newly; lately
【新進(人員)】① new employees of an organization ② a novice
【新居】 a new residence
【新奇】 novel; new
【新氣象】 a prevailing new atmosphere
【新秀】 a person who has begun to distinguish himself in a given field
【新鮮】 ① fresh ② new; original; novel
【新興】 newly risen; burgeoning
【新竹】 Hsinchu, Taiwan Province
【新裝】 ① a new dress ② newly installed
【新潮流】 a new trend
【新陳代謝】 ① (biology) metabolism ② the new superseding the old
【新出爐】① freshly baked ② newly produced or manufactured
【新春】 ① the early spring ② the Lunar New Year
【新創】 newly devised; newly started; newly founded
【新式】 of a new style; modern
【新手】 a new hand (at a job); a greenhorn; a novice
【新生】 ① newborn ② a new student ③ a new life; rebirth
【新生地】reclaimed land; tidal land
【新人】① new employees ② a bride ③ a new love ④ a man with modern thoughts
【新任】 newly appointed
【新英格蘭】 New England
【新穎】 novel; new; original
【新聞】 news

斤部

【新聞媒體】news media
【新聞封鎖】a news blackout
【新聞稿】a press release
【新聞廣播】a news broadcast; a newscast
【新聞記者】a journalist; a reporter; a correspondent
【新聞界】the circle of journalists; the press circle
【新聞人物】people in the news
【新聞自由】freedom of the press
【新約全書】the New Testament
【新月】① (astronomy) a new moon ② a crescent

十四畫

斷 1688 ㄉㄨㄢˋ duàn

1. to cut apart; to sever 2. to give up; to abstain from 3. to judge; to decide; to conclude 4. to break; broken 5. absolutely; decidedly; certainly

【斷編殘簡】fragmentary works (of a writer)
【斷電】power failure; a blackout
【斷定】to determine; to conclude
【斷斷續續】intermittent; off and on
【斷頭臺】a guillotine
【斷奶】to wean or be weaned
【斷糧】to run out of food supply
【斷根】to be cured completely (as a disease or addiction)
【斷後】① to cover a retreat ② to have no offspring
【斷交】① to break off relations with someone ② to sever diplomatic relations
【斷絕】to break off (relations); to sever
【斷絕邦交】to sever diplomatic ties
【斷絕關係】to sever relations; to disown (a prodigal son)
【斷氣】to breathe one's last
【斷袖之癖】male homosexuality
【斷章取義】to interpret a thing out of context
【斷腸】heartbroken
【斷水】to cut off water supply
【斷然】① absolutely; definitely ② resolute; drastic
【斷層】(geology) a fault
【斷送】to lose for good
【斷崖絕壁】broken ridges and steep cliffs
【斷言】to be absolutely sure; to say with certainty
【斷垣殘壁】the broken fences and walls

方部
ㄈㄤ fāng

方 1689 ㄈㄤ fāng

1. square; rectangular 2. honest; morally upright 3. a region; an area; a place 4. a prescription; a recipe 5. a direction 6. occultism 7. just now; just then 8. (mathematics) power 9. (classifier) short for square meter or cubic meter 10. side; party 11. a method; a way 12. an aspect 13. one side 14. a Chinese family name

【方便】① convenient; handy ② to do somebody a favor ③ (colloquial) to go to the lavatory
【方帽】square caps worn by college graduates
【方面】① a direction; a quarter; a district; a sphere; a field ② (in this or that) respect; (on the one, or other) hand; (on this or that) topic, subject, etc.
【方法】a method; a way
【方糖】cube sugar; sugar cubes
【方略】a general plan
【方格】a square (in a checkerboard pattern)
【方括號】square brackets ([ ])
【方今】now; at present; currently
【方向】orientation; a direction; a course
【方向盤】a steering wheel
【方興未艾】to be still growing
【方形】a rectangle
【方針】a principle; a policy
【方正】irreproachable (conduct)
【方城之戰】mah-jong game
【方程式】an equation
【方式】a mode; a manner; a way
【方子】a medical prescription
【方才 or 方纔】just a moment ago
【方案】a plan; a project; a design; a scheme; a program
【方言】a dialect
【方外之人】Buddhist or Taoist priests
【方位】the points of the compass; a direction
【方圓or方員】① neighborhood ② squares and circles

四畫

於 1690
1. ㄩ yú
1. in; on; at; by; from 2. than; then; to; with reference to 3. compared with 4. a Chinese family name
【於是】then; so; thus; thereafter
【於是乎】then; thereupon; so; thus
【於事無補】It doesn't help the situation.

於 1690
2. ㄨ wū
an interjection roughly equivalent to hurrah, bravo, alas, etc.
【於乎 or 於戲】Ah!

五畫

施 1691
ㄕ shī
1. to act; to do; to make 2. to bestow; to grant; to give (alms, etc.) 3. to apply 4. a Chinese family name
【施肥】to apply fertilizers
【施放】to discharge; to fire
【施工】to start construction or building
【施工中】abuilding; under construction
【施加】to exert; to bring to bear on
【施救】to rescue and resuscitate
【施洗】to baptize
【施行】①(law) to enforce; to execute ②to perform
【施行細則】bylaws
【施展】to display (one's feat, talent, skill, etc.)
【施政】(government) to administer; to govern
【施捨】to give to charity
【施恩】to give favors to others
【施與】to give to the poor; to give to charity
【施用】to use; to employ

六畫

旁 1692
1. (㫄) ㄆㄤˊ páng
1. side 2. by the side of; nearby 3. other; else
【旁白】(drama) aside
【旁邊 or 旁邊兒】①the side; by the side of ②nearby; in the vicinity of
【旁門左道】heresy; unorthodox ways
【旁聽】to audit
【旁聽生】an auditor (at a class)
【旁觀】to look on
【旁觀者】an onlooker; a bystander; a spectator
【旁觀者淸】The onlooker is clearheaded (because he can see what's going on with detachment).
【旁敲側擊】to ask seemingly irrelevant questions or speak aimlessly with a hidden purpose
【旁系親屬】collateral relatives
【旁徵博引】to quote widely or extensively
【旁人】① bystanders; onlookers; outsiders ② the others
【旁若無人】to act as if there weren't any bystanders

旁 1692
2. ㄅㄤˋ bàng
【旁午】① busy; complicated ② crisscross

旅 1693
ㄌㄩˇ lǚ
1. to travel; to lodge 2. a traveler; a passenger 3. a multitude; people 4. (military) a brigade; troops 5. to proceed together; to do things together
【旅費】traveling expenses
【旅店】a tavern; an inn
【旅途】on one's way (to a destination); during one's trip
【旅館 or 旅社】a hotel; a hostel; an inn
【旅客】a traveler; a passenger
【旅居】to stay in a place for a while
【旅行】to travel
【旅行袋】a traveling bag
【旅行團】a traveling party; a tourist group
【旅行支票】a traveler's check
【旅行車】a station wagon
【旅行社】a travel agency; a travel bureau
【旅程】the route a traveler takes from one place to another
【旅遊】a tour; tourism

七畫

旋 1694
1. ㄒㄩㄢˊ xuán
1. to return; to turn back 2. to revolve; to circle; to spin; to move in an orbit 3. a very short

while: 旋踵a very short time 4. to urinate

【旋律】 melody

【旋即】 forthwith; immediately afterwards

【旋乾轉坤】 immense power to reverse a situation

【旋轉】 to turn round and round

【旋轉門】 a revolving door

旋 1694
2. ㄒㄩㄢˋ xuàn
1. to whirl; a whirl 2. at the time; at the last moment; as soon as 3. to heat wine

【旋風】 a whirlwind

旌 1695
ㄐㄧㄥ jīng
1. a kind of flag, banner, standard, etc. ornamented with feathers 2. to cite (one's merits, virtues, etc.); to make manifest

【旌旗】 a general name for flags and banners

【旌旗蔽空or旌旗蔽日】 (literally) There are so many flags that they cover the whole sky (or darken the sun).—a very large army

族 1696
ㄗㄨˊ zú
1. a tribe; a family 2. a race (of people) 3. a class or group of things with common features

【族譜】 the pedigree of a clan

【族人】 fellow clansmen

十畫

旗 1697
ㄑㄧˊ qí
1. a flag; a pennant; a banner; a streamer 2. a sign; an insignia; an emblem 3. an administrative division of Mongolia (蒙古) and Tsinghai (青海) 4. the Manchus

【旗袍】 chi-pao

【旗杆 or 旗竿】 a flagstaff

【旗鼓相當】 of approximately equal strength, ability, etc.

【旗開得勝】 to win in the first battle, game or match

【旗幟】 flags, pennants, streamers, etc.

【旗魚】 spearfish

旖 1698
ㄧˇ yǐ
1. romantic; tender 2. charming; lovely; attractive; graceful 3. the fluttering of flags

【旖旎】 ① (said of flags) fluttering ② (said of scenery) enchanting

【旖旎風光】 a romantic or charming sight

无部
ㄨˊ wú

无 1699
ㄨˊ wú
the ancient form of 無—not; no; negative; without

【无妄之災】 an unexpected trouble or bad break

七畫

既 1700
(旣) ㄐㄧˋ jì
1. since; as 2. already 3. to finish 4. all

【既得利益】 vested interests

【既定】 already decided or fixed

【既來之則安之】 Since we (or you) are already here, let's make ourselves (or yourself) at home.

【既成事實】 a fact already accomplished

【既是 or 既然】 since (it is so, etc.); this being the case

【既然如此】 this being the case; since it is so

【既往不咎】 Let bygones be bygones.

日部
ㄖˋ rì

日 1701
ㄖˋ rì
1. the sun 2. a day 3. every day; daily 4. Japan; Japanese 5. time 6. day; daytime

【日薄西山】 declining rapidly; old age; approaching one's grave; one's day are numbered

【日報】 a daily newspaper

【日班】 the day shift (in factories, etc.)

【日本】 Japan

【日不暇給】 too many things to do in a day

【日暮途窮】 at the end of one's rope

【日復一日】 day after day

【日內瓦】 Geneva, Switzerland

【日理萬機】 (literally) to manage 10,000 things in a day—very busy

【日利or日息】 daily interest (rate)
【日曆】 a calendar
【日晷or日表】 a sundial
【日光】 sunshine; the light of the sun
【日光燈】 a fluorescent lamp
【日光浴】 a sunbath
【日後】 in the days to come; in future
【日積月累】 gradual accumulation over a long time
【日記】 a diary
【日久見人心】 Time reveals a person's heart.
【日久情生】 Having been together for a long time, people come to have a tender feeling for each other.
【日見or日漸】 with each passing day
【日期】 date
【日前】 a few days ago; recently
【日趨】 gradually; day by day
【日新月異】 continuous improvement; ever newer
【日薪】 day wages
【日行一善】 to do one good deed a day
【日誌】 a daily record
【日常】 common; usually; ordinarily; daily
【日常生活】 daily life
【日程】 ①an itinerary ②the agenda on a specific day (of a conference)
【日出】 sunrise
【日蝕 or 日食】 solar eclipse
【日上三竿】 rather late in the morning—about 9 a.m. (often used to describe someone who gets up late)
【日子】 ① time; duration ② life; living
【日坐愁城】 to be in deep worry every day
【日以繼夜】 day and night; continuously
【日夜】 day and night
【日有進步】 to show improvements or progress day by day
【日有所思，夜有所夢】 One dreams at night what one thinks in the day.
【日文or日語】 the Japanese (language)
【日月潭】 Sun Moon Lake
【日月如梭】 How fast time flies!
【日用品】 daily necessities

一畫

旦 1702 ㄉㄢˋ dàn

1. daybreak; dawn 2. day; morning 3. a female role in Chinese opera

【旦不保夕】 not knowing how the day will end
【旦角 or 旦脚】 a female role in Chinese opera
【旦夕之間】 within a single day; between morning and evening—a very short time

二畫

旨 1703 ㄓˇ zhǐ

1. a purpose; will; intention; objective 2. an imperial decree 3. good; excellent; beautiful 4. tasty; pleasant to the palate; delicious

【旨趣】 purposes and intentions
【旨意】 ①will; intention ②an imperial decree; God's will

早 1704 ㄗㄠˇ zǎo

1. early; earlier; soon; beforehand; previous; premature; in advance 2. morning 3. ago; before 4. Good morning!

【早班】 the morning shift
【早到】 to arrive early
【早點兒】 earlier; sooner
【早年】 years ago; in bygone years
【早婚】 to marry young; early marriage
【早期】 the early stage
【早起】 to get up early; to rise early
【早先】 some time ago; before
【早知如此】 If it had been known that things would turn out this way....
【早產】 premature birth
【早晨】 daybreak; (early) morning; dawn
【早場】 a morning show (at a cinema, theater, etc.)
【早出晚歸】 to go out early and return late
【早春】 ① early spring ② early spring tea
【早市】 a morning market
【早熟】 ①(said of plants, etc.) to ripen early ②(said of a person) to reach puberty early ③ precocious
【早上】 early in the morning
【早日】 at an earlier date; soon
【早操】 morning calisthenics
【早餐 or 早點 or 早飯】 breakfast
【早安】 Good morning!
【早已 or 早就】 to have already...

(日部)

【早晚】① morning and evening ② sooner or later

旬 1705
ㄒㄩㄣˊ xún

1. a period of ten days 2. a period of ten years (usually used to indicate a person's age) 3. widespread; throughout 4. to tour; to inspect

【旬年】① a full year ② ten years
【旬日】ten days 「months
【旬月】① a whole month ② ten

旭 1706
ㄒㄩˋ xù

1. brightness or radiance of daybreak 2. the rising sun 3. smug, proud or complacent

【旭日】the rising sun

三畫

旱 1707
ㄏㄢˋ hàn

1. drought; dry 2. (by) land route (as opposed to waterway)

【旱潦】droughts and floods
【旱季】a dry season
【旱象】the signs of drought
【旱災】a drought

四畫

旺 1708
ㄨㄤˋ wàng

1. prosperous; to prosper; to flourish 2. vigorous; prolific; productive 3. (said of light, fires, etc.) brilliant; bright or brightly 「season; a busy season

【旺季】(said of business) a boom
【旺盛】①prosperous; vigorous ②

昂 1709 ⌊high (morale)
ㄤˊ áng

1. to raise 2. lofty and proud; bold and not easily bent; straightforward 3. high 4. expensive;

【昂貴】expensive; costly ⌊costly
【昂首】to raise one's head high
【昂首闊步】to stride proudly ahead
【昂然】proud and bold; haughtily
【昂揚】high-spirited

昆 1710
ㄎㄨㄣ kūn

1. an elder brother 2. descendants; posterity 3. multitudes 4. together; in unison

【昆明】Kunmin 「for Kun opera
【昆曲】① Kun opera ② melodies
【昆仲】brothers
【昆蟲】insects 「brothers
【昆玉】(a polite expression) your

昇 1711
ㄕㄥ shēng

1. to ascend 2. peace; peaceful

【昇平】time of peace 「of status
【昇格】to elevate status; elevation
【昇華】①(chemistry) to sublime ② the rising of things to a higher
【昇級】to promote ⌊level
【昇降】promotion and demotion
【昇降機】an elevator

昊 1712
ㄏㄠˋ hào 「heavens

1. summer time 2. the sky; the

【昊天罔極】(said of parental love) as vast as the boundless heavens

昌 1713
ㄔㄤ chāng

1. proper; good; straight (talk) 2. prosperous; robust; vigorous; to make prosperous; to glorify 3. light; brightness 4. a Chinese family name

【昌明】① to expound and elaborate ② flourishing; developing ③ glorious
【昌盛】① prosperous ② glory

明 1714
ㄇㄧㄥˊ míng

1. light; bright; brilliant 2. clear; understandable; to clarify; to understand; obvious; evident 3. intelligent; clever 4. eyesight; the seeing faculty 5. day; daybreak; dawn 6. to state; to assert; to show 7. next (day or year) 8. the Ming Dynasty (1368-1644 A.D.) 9. aboveboard; honest 10. a Chinese family name

【明白】① to understand; to know (a trick, secret, etc.) ② clever and bright; smart ③ obvious
【明白了當】straightforward; clear-cut
【明辨是非】to know distinctly what is right and what is wrong
【明媚】fair and enchanting, or bright and charming
【明眸皓齒】(said of a woman) with bright eyes and sparkling
【明明】obviously; plainly ⌊teeth

【明明白白】clear; clearly; obviously; evidently
【明目張膽】(to do some shameful or unlawful acts) openly or shamelessly
【明礬】alum
【明天】tomorrow
【明年】next year; the coming year
【明朗】① open-minded; straightforward ② to become clear; to clarify
【明理】understanding; reasonable
【明瞭】① to understand ② clear and evident
【明亮】bright (eyes, etc.); well-illuminated (rooms, etc.)
【明令】a written order; a government order or decree
【明快】① lucid and lively (style, etc.) ② straightforward
【明鑑】① a clear mirror ② (your) penetrating judgment
【明鏡高懸】transcending or perspicuousness intelligence in judgment
【明槍暗箭】overt and covert attack
【明槍易躲，暗箭難防】It's easy to dodge an open attack but difficult to escape from a clandestine one.
【明確】clear and definite; unequivocal
【明蝦】a prawn
【明修棧道，暗度陳倉】to feign action in one place and to make the real move in another
【明顯】evident; obvious; clear
【明信片】a postcard; a postal card
【明星】①a bright star ②a movie star ③Venus
【明知】to know perfectly well; to be fully aware
【明知故問】to ask about something one already knows
【明智】sensible; sagacious; wise
【明智之舉】a wise move; an intelligent or sensible act
【明哲保身】(often said of people living under tyranny) A wise person who knows what's best for himself can safeguard his personal security.
【明爭暗鬬】(often said of intramural fights) to fight overtly and covertly
【明察】to be sharp and perspicacious
【明察秋毫】able to examine the tiniest things (as the tip of a hair) — sharp discerning intelligence
【明查暗訪】to investigate openly and secretly
【明示】to express clearly
【明說】to speak frankly; to speak up
【明日 or 明兒】① tomorrow ② one of these days; some day
【明日黃花】① outmoded; obsolete ② what has already taken place
【明暗】brightness and darkness
【明眼人】a man of clear mind and high intelligence
【明文規定】clearly stipulated in regulations, laws, agreements, contracts, etc.

昏 1715
ㄏㄨㄣ hūn

1. dusk; dark 2. confused; muddled; mixed-up; demented 3. unclear of sight; dizzy 4. (now rarely) same as 婚—to marry

【昏昧】stupid; stupidity
【昏迷】in a coma; delirious; stupor
【昏倒 or 昏厥】to faint; to swoon
【昏頭昏腦】to feel dizzy, confused, and mixed-up
【昏天黑地】① very dark (as before a storm) ② stupid or ignorant ③ dizzy
【昏亂】stupid and confused
【昏聵】muddled, confused and stupid
【昏花】poor of vision
【昏昏沉沉】dizzy and sleepy; slumberous
【昏昏欲睡】drowsy; sleepy
【昏黃】twilight; dim
【昏眩】dizzy; faint; giddy
【昏睡】deep slumber; lethargic sleep
【昏暗】dim; dusky
【昏庸 or 昏愚】muddle-headed; stupid; imbecile

易 1716
ㄧˋ yì

1. to exchange; to barter 2. easy 3. to change (places, jobs, owners, etc.) 4. amiable; lenient 5. the *Book of Changes* 6. a Chinese family name

【易地而處】to look at a matter from the other fellow's viewpoint
【易開罐】a ring-pull can
【易主】to change owners or masters
【易手】to change hands
【易燃物】combustibles; inflammables
【易如反掌】as easy as turning over the palm of one's hand
【易言之】in other words

【易位】①to change places or positions; to transpose ②to dethrone

昔 1717 ㄒㄧˊ xí

1. bygone; of old; formerly; ancient 2. a night; an evening 3. the end

【昔日】in former days (or times)
【昔人】the ancient people

五畫

星 1718 ㄒㄧㄥ xīng

1. any heavenly body that shines; stars, planets, satellites, etc. 2. a spark or sparks 3. droplets; small particles of anything; very tiny 4. name of one of the 28 constellations 5. a movie star 6. by night; nocturnal

【星斗】stars; heavenly bodies
【星團】(astronomy) a constellation
【星羅棋布】numerous and arrayed like stars in heaven or pieces on a chessboard (usually said of archipelagos, etc.)
【星光】starlight
【星光燦爛】a star-studded gathering
【星河】(astronomy) the Milky Way
【星號】an asterisk(☆)
【星期】week
【星期六】Saturday
【星期日 or 星期天】Sunday
【星期四】Thursday
【星期三】Wednesday
【星期二】Tuesday
【星期一】Monday
【星期五】Friday
【星球】planets; stars
【星系】(astronomy) a galaxy
【星宿】①(ㄒㄧㄥ ㄒㄧㄡˋ) planets or stars in heaven ②(ㄒㄧㄥ ˙ㄙㄨ) a person who is considered an incarnation of a star
【星象學】astrometry
【星星】stars, planets and satellites
【星星之火，可以燎原】Small things may cause big trouble.
【星形】a star-polygon
【星辰】stars; heavenly bodies
【星子 or 星兒】tiny bits, droplets or particles
【星座】(astronomy) a constellation
【星散】to scatter and spread like stars
【星夜】①night; a starlit night ②(to travel, escape, etc.) by night
【星月交輝】any gathering or congregation of famous or august personalities
【星雲】(astronomy) a nebula

映 1719 ㄧㄥˋ yìng

1. to mirror; to reflect; a reflection 2. to project (slides, pictures, etc.) 3. to shine; shining; to blind; blinding (glare, light, etc.)

【映象】image
【映照】to shine and reflect
【映射】to shine upon; to cast light upon

春 1720 ㄔㄨㄣ chūn

1. spring, the first of the four seasons 2. sensuality; lustful; lewd; pornographic 3. alive; vitality; living 4. joyful and transient 5. youth

【春夢】something that is illusory and transient
【春風】①spring breezes ②good education ③sexual intercourse ④favor; grace ⑤happy smiles
【春風滿面】to smile broadly; a cheerful look
【春風得意】to attain a high official rank; to ride on the crest of success
【春風化雨】salutary influence of education
【春天】spring; springtime
【春暖花開】During the warmth of spring all the flowers bloom.
【春雷】spring thunder
【春聯】New Year's couplets written on strips of red paper and pasted on doors
【春光】①lustful scenes—as a sexual act ②spring scenes (natural charms in spring)
【春光明媚】a sunlit and enchanting scene of spring
【春宮圖】pornographic drawings
【春寒料峭】the chill of early spring
【春花秋月】①the best things at the best time ②flight of time
【春暉】the light of the spring sun —parental love and care
【春回大地】Spring returns to the good earth.
【春假】spring holidays; the spring vacation

【春節】the Lunar New Year's holidays
【春捲】spring rolls
【春秋】① a year ② spring and autumn ③ age ④ annals of any state during the period of Warring States ⑤ *Spring and Autumn Annals* ⑥ annals; history
【春秋鼎盛】in the prime of one's life
【春秋時代】the Epoch of Spring and Autumn, approximately from 770 to 403 B.C.
【春宵】① spring nights ② a wedding night
【春宵苦短】The wedding night is always too short (to the newlyweds).
【春心蕩漾】the surging of lustful desire
【春裝】spring clothes
【春色】① spring scenery ② a joyful appearance or expression ③ sensual or carnal scenes
【春意】① spring in the air ② thoughts of love
【春藥】aphrodisiac
【春雨】spring rains or showers

昧 1721
ㄇㄟˋ mèi
1. obscure; dark 2. to hide; to pocket 3. to ignore (one's conscience, etc.) 4. blind; ignorant 5. to faint; fainting
【昧良心】to ignore one's conscience
【昧於事理】to be ignorant of good reason, judgment, common practice, etc.

昨 1722
ㄗㄨㄛˊ zuó
yesterday; lately; past
【昨天 or 昨日】yesterday
【昨死今生】to be reborn; to lead a new life from now on
【昨晚】last night

昭 1723
ㄓㄠ zhāo
1. bright; luminous 2. prominent; eminent; evident; obvious 3. to make open; to show; to display
【昭告】to declare or announce to the public
【昭顯】prominent; eminent; evident
【昭雪】to redress (a miscarriage of justice)
【昭彰】prominent; eminent; obvious; evident
【昭著】famous; eminent
【昭示】to decree, declare, etc. officially
【昭然若揭】very obvious

是 1724
ㄕˋ shì
1. yes; right; positive (as contrasted to negative) 2. the verb to be (for all persons and numbers) 3. this, that, or which
【是不是】Is it true or not? 或 Are you...? 或 Is he...?
【是非】① right and wrong; yes and no ② gossip; scandal ③ discord
【是非顛倒】to confound right and wrong
【是非題】a true-or-false problem
【是非曲直】right and wrong, proper and improper
【是非之地】a place where one is apt to get into trouble
【是否】Is it...? 或 Are you...? 或 Is he...?
【是的】yes; right 或 That's it.
【是故】therefore
【是何居心】What evil intention is this!
【是是非非】gossip(s); scandal(s)

六畫

晏 1725
ㄧㄢˋ yàn
1. clear (sky, sea, water, etc.) 2. late 3. peaceful; quiet 4. a Chinese family name
【晏起】to get up late
【晏寢】to sit up late
【晏然】peaceful and easy; quiet and comfortable
【晏如】peaceful and easy

時 1726
(旹) ㄕˊ shí
1. a season 2. an era; an epoch; an age; a period 3. time; fixed time 4. hours 5. often; frequently 6. fashionable 7. proper and adequate 8. opportune (moments); opportunity 9. timely; seasonable 10. now... now...; sometimes... sometimes...
【時髦】fashionable; modern; up-to-date
【時分】① seasons; periods ② time
【時代】an era; an epoch; a period
【時態】(grammar) tense
【時來運轉】to get a break (after a long period of bad luck)
【時令】time of year; seasons
【時過境遷】Things have changed

with the passage of time.

【時光】time

【時刻】① time; hour ② always; constantly; continually

【時刻表or時間表】a timetable; a schedule

【時候】time; hour; juncture; moment

【時機】opportunity

【時機成熟】The right time has come. 或The opportune moment is here.

【時價】current prices; prevailing prices

【時節】a period of the year; season

【時間】① time; the hour ② time —as opposed to space

【時局】the national situation; the world situation

【時期】①times; a period ② duration

【時下】nowadays; in these days

【時效】(law) prescription; the duration of validity

【時限】a time limit; a deadline

【時興】fashionable or seasonable

【時值】the time being...

【時至今日】up to now

【時針】the hour hand of a clock or watch

【時裝】① fashionable dresses ② (in show biz) modern dresses

【時裝展覽】a fashion show

【時鐘】a clock

【時差】①(astronomy) the equation of time ② the time difference of two places located on different longitudes or time zones

【時辰】① the 12 divisions of a day named after the 12 Terrestrial Branches ② the time for...

【時常 or 時時】often; frequently

【時時刻刻】constantly; always

【時事】current events

【時勢】the time and circumstances

【時尙 or 時好】a fad

【時速】speed per hour

【時日】① time ② an auspicious time ③ this day

【時而】from time to time; sometimes

【時宜】proper at the time

【時遇不濟】to be out of luck

【時運亨通】to be lucky

晉 1727 (晋) ㄐㄧㄣˋ jìn

1. to advance; to flourish; to increase 2. Tsin (a state during the Epoch of Spring and Autumn, occupying parts of today's Shansi and Hopeh provinces) 3. another name for Shansi Province 4. the Tsin Dynasty (265 - 420 A.D.) 5. a Chinese family name

【晉級】promotion; to promote

【晉見】to have an audience with

【晉升】to rise in rank; to promote

【晉謁】to visit or call on (a superior)

晃 1728 1. ㄏㄨㄤˇ huǎng

1. brightness 2. dazzling; glaring 3. a flash; to flash past; to appear and disappear very quickly

晃 1728 2. ㄏㄨㄤˋ huàng

to rock; to sway; to shake

【晃蕩】to sway; to oscillate

【晃動】to rock; to sway

晌 1729 ㄕㄤˇ shǎng

1. high noon 2. a certain duration or interval of time 3. (Northeast China dialect) a day's work

【晌午】midday; (colloquial) high noon

七畫

晚 1730 ㄨㄢˇ wǎn

1. sunset; evening; night 2. late 3. drawing toward the end 4. younger; junior

【晚輩】the younger generation; one's juniors

【晚報】an evening (or an afternoon) paper

【晚班】the night shift

【晚飯 or 晚餐】dinner; supper

【晚點】(said of a train, ship, etc.) late behind schedule

【晚年】old age; one's later (or remaining) years

【晚娘】a stepmother

【晚娘面孔】an unsmiling face

【晚禮服】formal evening dress

【晚會】an evening gathering or meeting

【晚婚】late marriage

【晚間】evening; night

【晚近】lately; recently; modern

【晚景】① scenes at sunset ② circumstances in one's old age

【晚期】the later period

【晚起】to rise or get up late

【晚霞】sunset clouds

【晚場】an evening show
【晚上】in the evening or night
【晚安】Good evening! 或 Good night!
【晚宴】a dinner party

晝 1731
ㄓㄡˋ zhòu
day; daytime; daylight
【晝寢】to take a nap; a siesta
【晝夜】day and night

晤 1732
ㄨˋ wù
1. to meet; to see face to face 2. enlightened; wise
【晤談】to meet and talk; to converse
【晤商】a face-to-face negotiation; to discuss in an interview

晦 1733
ㄏㄨㄟˋ huì
1. the last day of every month in the lunar calendar 2. night; evening; dark 3. obscure; indistinguishable 4. as in 晦氣—unlucky; bad luck
【晦澀】hard to understand
【晦暗】dark; gloomy

晨 1734
ㄔㄣˊ chén
morning; daybreak
【晨光】daylight; daybreak
【晨昏or晨夕】morning and evening
【晨昏顚倒】to mistake morning for evening and evening for morning
【晨曦】morning light; daybreak

八畫

普 1735
ㄆㄨˇ pǔ
universal; all; widespread; everywhere; general
【普徧or普遍】widespread; universal
【普徧性 or 普遍性】universality
【普渡衆生】(Buddhism) to deliver or save all beings
【普天同慶】The whole world joins in the rejoicing, celebration or congratulations.
【普天之下】all over the world
【普通】ordinary; common; plain
【普通考試】the junior-grade civil service examination (in modern China)
【普及】① universal; available to all ② to popularize; to disseminate
【普及本】a paperback edition
【普降甘霖】timely rain for all drought areas
【普選】universal suffrage; general elections
【普照】(said of sunshine, God's grace, etc.) to shine upon all
【普查】a general survey

景 1736
1. ㄐㄧㄥˇ jǐng
1. scenery; views 2. prospects; circumstances; situations 3. (in motion pictures, stage shows, etc.) settings; background scenes 4. big and strong 5. great 6. high 7. bright and luminous 8. to admire; to respect 9. a Chinese family name
【景觀】(geography) landscape
【景氣】(economics) booming; prosperity
【景象】appearances; scenes; conditions; outlooks; sights
【景致or景緻】scenes; views; vista
【景色 or 景物】scenery; landscapes
【景仰】to admire and respect

景 1736
2. (影) ㄧㄥˇ yǐng
shadow; reflection; image

晰 1737
ㄒㄧ xī
clear; clearly; distinct

晳 1738
ㄒㄧ xī
1. (said of one's skin) fair; white 2. to discriminate; to distinguish

晴 1739
ㄑㄧㄥˊ qíng
1. (said of the weather) fine; fair; bright; clear 2. when the rain stops
【晴天】a fine day; a cloudless day
【晴天霹靂】a bolt from the blue
【晴朗】(said of the sky) fine and cloudless sky
【晴空萬里】a clear and boundless sky
【晴雨表 or 晴雨計】a barometer

晶 1740
ㄐㄧㄥ jīng
1. crystal 2. bright; clear; brilliant; radiant
【晶片】a chip
【晶體】(radio) crystal
【晶瑩】sparkling

智 1741
ㄓˋ zhì
1. talented; capable; intelligent; clever; wisdom; wit 2. prudence

〔日部〕

3. a Chinese family name
【智謀】tactics; strategy
【智囊】a wise person; a wise advisor
【智囊團】a brain trust; a think tank
【智能】intelligence and capability
【智能不足】mental retardation
【智力】intelligence
【智力商數or智商】intelligence quotient (I.Q.)
【智力測驗】an intelligence test; an IQ test
【智利】Chile, or Chili
【智慧】wisdom; intelligence
【智慧財產權】intellectual property rights
【智識份子or知識份子】intellectuals
【智勇兼備 or 智勇雙全】both intelligent and brave

晾 1742
ㄌㄧㄤˋ liàng
1. to dry in the air; to air; to hang in the wind to dry 2. to dry in the sun
【晾乾】to dry in the air
【晾衣服】to hang clothes in the wind to dry
【晾衣繩】a clothesline

九畫

暄 1743
ㄒㄩㄢ xuān
1. comfortable and genial (climates); warm 2. (dialect) fluffy
【暄暖】warm and comfortable

暇 1744
ㄒㄧㄚˋ xià
(又讀 ㄒㄧㄚˊ xiá)
leisure; free time; spare time

暉 1745
ㄏㄨㄟ huī
1. the sunshine 2. bright; radiant
【暉映】bright and brilliant

暈 1746
1. ㄩㄣ yūn
1. to faint; to swoon 2. giddy and dizzy 3. (usually used sarcastically) to do things without a purpose
【暈倒】to faint and fall; to swoon
【暈頭轉向】①to feel dizzy and giddy ②so confused that one doesn't know what to do, say, etc.
【暈過去】to pass out; to faint
【暈厥】(medicine) syncope; to faint

暈 1746
2. ㄩㄣˋ yùn
1. (meteorology) a halo; vapors; a mist 2. dazzled; to feel faint or dizzy
【暈機】airsick
【暈車】to be bussick, trainsick or carsick
【暈船】to be seasick

暑 1747
ㄕㄨˇ shǔ
1. hot; heat; the heat of summer 2. midsummer; summer
【暑假】summer vacation
【暑期】①summer ②the summer vacation
【暑期班】a summer class or school
【暑氣迫人】The summer heat is very oppressive.
【暑熱 or 暑氣】the scorching heat; the heat of summer
【暑溽】hot and humid

暗 1748
ㄢˋ àn
1. dim; dark; obscure 2. stupid; ignorant 3. secret; clandestine; stealthy 4. hidden
【暗盤】a price or quotation which is kept from public knowledge but made known to selected few
【暗房】(photography) a darkroom
【暗訪】to investigate in secret
【暗淡 or 暗澹】①(said of colors, etc.) faded, dull and not fresh ②(said of business, etc.) dim
【暗地裏】secretly; stealthily; clandestinely
【暗度陳倉】illicit affairs; adultery
【暗流】a subterranean flow
【暗溝】a sewer
【暗號】a secret mark, sign, signal or password
【暗計】①to calculate or count in one's heart ②a conspiracy
【暗礁】①a submerged (or hidden) reef ②an unseen obstacle
【暗箭傷人】to stab somebody in the back
【暗泣】to weep behind others' backs
【暗喜】to feel happy secretly
【暗笑】to laugh in one's heart
【暗想】to muse; to ponder
【暗中】①in secret ②(to do something) in the dark or without light
【暗中摸索】to grope in the dark
【暗處】an obscure corner; a secret

place
【暗示】①to hint; to suggest ②a hint; a suggestion
【暗殺】assassination; to assassinate
【暗自】inwardly; to oneself; secretly
【暗藏】to hide; to conceal
【暗色】dark colors; deep colors
【暗算】a secret plot; to plot in secret
【暗無天日】① (said of a place, room, etc.) very dark ②(said of a nation, locality, etc.) lawlessness
【暗語】a code word
【暗喩】a metaphor; a concealed analogy

暖 1749 (煖) ㄋㄨㄢˇ nuǎn
warm or genial (weather)
【暖房】a hothouse; a greenhouse
【暖流】①(geography) warm ocean currents ②(meteorology) warm air currents
【暖爐】a brazier
【暖和】① warm ② to warm up
【暖氣】warm vapor; warm air
【暖氣爐】a gas heater
【暖氣裝置or暖氣設備】central heating installation; a heater

暌 1750 ㄎㄨㄟˊ kuí
1. in opposition 2. to separate; to part
【暌違】(said of friends) separated; parted; separation

十畫

暢 1751 ㄔㄤˋ chàng
1. smoothly; fluently 2. easily accessible 3. with gusto; to one's heart's content 4. long; expanding 5. luxuriant; luxuriance 6. (to state or elaborate) freely; without restraint; clear 7. very
【暢達】clearly and smoothly
【暢談】to talk to one's heart's content
【暢通】unimpeded; unblocked
【暢快】cheerful and exuberant
【暢懷】to one's heart's content
【暢銷】a booming sale; to sell well
【暢銷書】a best seller
【暢行無阻】to meet no obstacle wherever one goes
【暢所欲言】to speak one's mind freely
【暢遊】to enjoy a sightseeing tour
【暢飲】to drink to one's heart's content

十一畫

暮 1752 ㄇㄨˋ mù
1. sunset; evening; dusk 2. closing (years); late
【暮年or暮齡】closing years of one's life
【暮鼓晨鐘】① (literally) evening drums and morning bells—used in Buddhist temples to tell time ② ringing statements or remarks which arouse the public from degeneracy or warn against lurking danger, etc.
【暮氣沉沉】① (said of a person) despondent and dejected; lethargy ②(said of atmosphere) dead and dull; gloomy
【暮春】late spring
【暮色】dusk; twilight; the gloaming

暫 1753 ㄓㄢˋ zhàn
(讀音 ㄗㄢˋ zàn)
1. temporarily; for a short time; not lasting 2. suddenly; abruptly
【暫別】to part for a short time
【暫定】①(said of time) tentatively set on, at, etc. ②(said of a number, price, place, etc.) tentatively fix at
【暫停】① to stop, halt or suspend temporarily ② a time-out
【暫候】to wait for a short time
【暫緩】to postpone or delay for a while; to put off; to defer
【暫濟燃眉】to temporarily relieve an emergency or an urgent need
【暫借】to borrow for a short time
【暫且】for the time being
【暫行】temporary; provisional
【暫時】for the time being; temporarily

暴 1754 1. ㄅㄠˋ bào
1. cruel; savage; fierce; violent 2. sudden 3. short-tempered
【暴斃】to meet a sudden death
【暴民】mobs or mobsters
【暴發】① a violent eruption ② to break out ③ to become rich or to attain a high position all of a sudden
【暴發戶】an upstart; a parvenu
【暴風 or 暴風雨】a storm; a tempest
【暴風雪】a snowstorm; a blizzard

【暴跌】(said of prices) to slump
【暴投】(baseball) a wild pitch
【暴跳如雷】to be infuriated; to be enraged; furious
【暴殄天物】a reckless waste of grains, etc.
【暴怒】furious; to blow one's top
【暴力】violence; brute force
【暴戾】despotic and tyrannical
【暴亂 or 暴動】a riot; a rebellion
【暴君】a tyrant; a despot
【暴行】violence; atrocities
【暴漲】(said of a water level or a commodity price) to rise sharply or quickly
【暴政】tyrannical rule
【暴躁】irritable; fretful; irascible
【暴飲暴食】to eat and drink excessively

(日部)

暴 1754
2. (曝) ㄆㄨˋ pù
to expose

暱 1755
(昵) ㄋㄧˋ nì
intimate; close
【暱愛】love or affection (between opposite sexes)

十二畫

曇 1756
ㄊㄢˊ tán
clouds
【曇花】the epiphyllum
【曇花一現】to appear and then quickly disappear

暨 1757
ㄐㄧˋ jì
1. and 2. to reach; to attain; to overtake 3. up to; till

曆 1758
ㄌㄧˋ lì
1. a calendar 2. an era; an age 3. to calculate; to count
【曆書】an almanac

曉 1759
ㄒㄧㄠˇ xiǎo
1. daybreak; dawn 2. to explain 3. to know; to understand
【曉風殘月】(literally) the morning breeze and the lingering moon —nature at daybreak
【曉得】to know; to be aware of
【曉以大義】(to persuade someone to follow the right path) by telling him what is right
【曉諭or曉示】to explain; to tell; to give explicit instructions

十三畫

曖 1760
ㄞˋ ài
1. dim; indistinct 2. vague; ambiguous
【曖昧】① ambiguous; obscure ② a secret impropriety

十四畫

曙 1761
ㄕㄨˋ shù
dawn; daybreak: 曙色 light at daybreak
【曙光】the first light of morning; light at dawn

十五畫

曠 1762
ㄎㄨㄤˋ kuàng
1. open; wide; broad; vast; spacious 2. free from worries and petty ideas 3. to neglect
【曠廢】to neglect
【曠工】to neglect work
【曠課】to cut school; to truant
【曠職】① to be absent from the office without leave ② to neglect official duties
【曠世之才】a man of brilliance unequaled by his contemporaries
【曠野】wild plains; a prairie

曝 1763
ㄆㄨˋ pù
to expose to sunlight; to sun
【曝露】to expose oneself to the weather 亦作「暴露」
【曝光】(photography) exposure
【曝曬】to expose to sunlight; to sun

十六畫

曦 1764
ㄒㄧ xī
sunshine; sunlight

十七畫

曩 1765
ㄋㄤˇ nǎng
past; former
【曩昔or曩時】in the past; in former times

十九畫

曬 1766
(晒) ㄕㄞˋ shài to expose to sunlight; to dry in the sun
【曬太陽】 to be exposed to the sun
【曬圖】 to make a blueprint; a blueprint
【曬乾】 to dry in the sun
【曬黑】 (said of skin) darkened by overexposure to the sun

曰部
ㄩㄝ yuē

曰 1767
ㄩㄝ yuē
1. (an archaic usage) to say 2. to call; to name

二畫

曲 1768
1. ㄑㄩ qū
1. bent; crooked; twisted; winding 2. little known; obscure 3. wrong; unjustifiable
【曲流】 a meander
【曲棍球】 ① hockey ② a hockey ball
【曲解】 to misinterpret; to distort
【曲線】 curved line; curve
【曲直】 right and wrong
【曲折】 ①bends; curves; ②complicated
【曲尺】 a (carpenter's) square
【曲意逢迎】 to try in every way to flatter someone

曲 1768
2. ㄑㄩˇ qǔ
1. a type of verse for singing, which emerged in the Southern Sung (南宋) and Kin (金) dynasties and became popular in the Yüan Dynasty 2. a piece of music; a song
【曲調】 tunes; melodies
【曲高和寡】 caviare to the general
【曲終人散】 The music is over and the people are gone.—the sadness one feels after a fanfare

曳 1769
ㄧˋ yì (語音 ㄧㄝˋ yè)
to haul; to tug; to drag; to trail
【曳引機】 a tractor

三畫

更 1770
1. ㄍㄥ gēng
1. (formerly) the watches of the night 2. a night watchman 3. to change; to alter; to shift 4. to experience 5. to alternate
【更夫 or 更卒】 a night watchman
【更動】 to shift; to switch; to change
【更替】 to alternate; to take turns
【更年期】 (physiology) the menopause
【更漏】 an hourglass; a sandglass
【更改】 to change (over); to alter
【更換 or 更易】 to change; to alter
【更新】 to renew; to renovate
【更正】 to correct; to put right
【更衣】 to change clothes
【更衣室】 a changeroom; a dressing room

更 1770
2. ㄍㄥˋ gèng
more; further; to a greater degree
【更妙】 still better; more interesting
【更多】 more; still more
【更好】 better或So much the better.
【更壞】 worse; even worse; worse still
【更加】 even more
【更勝一籌】 even better

五畫

曷 1771
ㄏㄜˊ hé
1. what 2. why not 3. how
【曷故】 why; what for

六畫

書 1772
ㄕㄨ shū
1. writings; a book 2. to write 3. a letter 4. a document; a certificate 5. the style of the calligraphy; script
【書包】 a satchel; a schoolbag
【書報】 books and newspapers
【書評】 a book review
【書眉】 the upper margin of a book page
【書面答覆】 a written reply
【書名】 the title of a book
【書目】 a book catalogue
【書法】 calligraphy
【書房 or 書齋】 a study
【書獃子 or 書呆子 or 書癡】 a pedant; a bookworm

〔曰部〕

【書單】a booklist
【書店 or 書局】a bookstore
【書蠹】a bookworm
【書套】a book jacket; a slipcase
【書攤】a bookstand; a bookstall
【書櫃 or 書櫥】a bookcase
【書刊】books and magazines
【書畫】works of calligraphy and painting
【書畫家】a master in calligraphy and painting
【書籍】books
【書記官】a clerk of a law court
【書家 or 書法家】a calligrapher
【書夾】bookends
【書架】a bookshelf; a bookrack
【書柬 or 書簡】letters
【書卷氣】bookishness
【書簽】① a book label pasted on the cover ② a bookmark 亦作「書籤」
【書寫】to write
【書信or書函】letters; correspondence
【書香門第】a literary family
【書桌 or 書案】a desk
【書生】a student; a scholar
【書頁】a page

七畫

曹 1773 ㄘㄠˊ cáo
1. a plural particle 2. a Chinese family name

曼 1774 ㄇㄢˋ màn (又讀 ㄨㄢˋ wàn)
1. delicately beautiful; graceful
2. long; vast; prolonged
【曼陀林】(music) a mandolin
【曼谷】Bangkok, capital of Thailand

八畫

曾 1775 1. ㄗㄥ zēng
1. older or younger by three generations 2. a Chinese family name
【曾祖母】one's great-grandmother
【曾祖父】one's great-grandfather
【曾孫】one's great-grandchildren
【曾孫女】one's great-granddaughter

曾 1775 2. ㄘㄥˊ céng
ever; once
【曾幾何時】only a short time ago
【曾經】to have had the experience of

替 1776 ㄊㄧˋ tì
1. to take the place of; to replace; to substitute 2. to decay; to decline 3. to neglect 4. for; on behalf of
【替換or替代】to replace; to substitute
【替身】a double; an understudy
【替身演員】a stunt man
【替死鬼】a scapegoat

最 1777 ㄗㄨㄟˋ zuì
extreme; superlative
【最大】the biggest; the largest; the greatest; the maximum
【最低】the lowest; the minimum; the least; at least
【最低限度】①the lowest limit ② at least
【最多】the most; at most
【最短】the shortest
【最高】the highest; the superlative; the supreme
【最高法院】the Supreme Court
【最高峯】the summit; the climax
【最高當局】the highest authorities
【最高統帥】the supreme commander
【最高級】① the highest; the summit ② (linguistics) the superlative degree
【最高潮】the climax; the culmination
【最好】① the best ② had better
【最後】the last; the ultimate; the final
【最後通牒】an ultimatum
【最壞】the worst; the meanest
【最惠國】the most favored nation
【最佳 or 最優】the best
【最近】① the nearest; the closest ② recently; lately
【最小】the least; the smallest; the minimum
【最先】① the first; the earliest; the foremost ② at first; in the beginning
【最新】the newest; the latest
【最終】the final; the last; the ultimate
【最長】the longest
【最初】① the first; the earliest ② at first; in the beginning
【最少】the least; the minimum
【最矮】(said of stature) the shortest; (said of houses) the lowest

九畫

【有始有終】to carry out an undertaking from start to finish—not to give up halfway
【有事】①to be busy ②to meet with an accident
【有識之士】knowledgeable people; farsighted people; thinking people
【有勢力】powerful; influential
【有恃無恐】There is no fear when one has something to fall back upon.
【有傷和氣】detrimental to friendship
【有聲有色】(said of a description or performance) vivid; impressive
【有生之年】for the rest of one's life
【有生以來】since one's birth
【有說有笑】to talk and laugh
【有染】to have an affair with
【有人】some people; anyone; somebody
【有人緣兒】(said of people) popular
【有如】just like; as if; as though
【有增無減】①to increase steadily ②to get steadily worse or serious
【有罪】guilty; sinful
【有所不知】to be unaware of something
【有礙or有害】detrimental; harmful
【有礙觀瞻】to be an eyesore
【有案可查】to be on record
【有一次】on one occasion; once
【有益】advantageous; useful; profitable; beneficial
【有意】①to intend; purposeful ②to be interested
【有意見】to have something to say
【有意識】conscious
【有意思】interesting; exciting; enjoyable; amusing
【有言在先】to have agreed before
【有眼不識泰山】to fail to recognize a great person
【有眼無珠】to lack discerning power
【有為】capable of great achievements
【有問必答】to answer all questions asked
【有問題】questionable; doubtful; unreliable
【有望】hopeful; promising
【有緣】linked by ties of fate
【有勇無謀】to be foolhardy
【有用】useful; practical; beneficial

四畫

朋 1781
ㄆㄥˊ péng
1. a friend; a companion 2. a group; a clique
【朋比為奸】to gang up for evil doings
【朋黨】a faction; a clique
【朋友】a friend

服 1782
1. ㄈㄨˊ fú
1. clothes; dress; garments; costume 2. to wear (clothes) 3. to obey; to be convinced; to yield; to concede
【服服帖帖】obedient; docile
【服毒】to take poison
【服氣】to yield or submit willingly
【服刑】to serve a prison term
【服裝】costumes; dress; clothes
【服飾】costume and accessories
【服侍】to wait upon; to attend on
【服輸】to concede defeat
【服罪】to admit one's crime
【服從】to obey; to follow; to submit to
【服喪】to remain in mourning
【服役】①to undergo hard labor ②to undergo military service
【服膺】to keep (a teaching, principle, etc.) in mind and stick to (it)
【服務】①service ②to work as an employee
【服務臺】a service desk
【服務員】an attendant; a steward
【服用】to take (medicine, etc.)

服 1782
2. ㄈㄨˋ fù
(Chinese medicine) a dose

六畫

朔 1783
ㄕㄨㄛˋ shuò
1. to begin 2. north 3. the first day of the month of the lunar calendar
【朔望】the first and the 15th days of the lunar month

朕 1784
ㄓㄣˋ zhèn
1. the royal "we" (used exclusively by the emperor or king to mean "I") 2. omens; auguries; portents; signs
【朕兆】omens; portents; auguries; signs

七畫

〔月部〕

〔木部〕

朗 1785 ㄌㄤˇ lǎng
1. bright; clear 2. resonant; sonorous
【朗讀 or 朗誦】 to read aloud

望 1786 ㄨㄤˋ wàng
1. to view; to watch; to gaze into the distance 2. to hope; to expect 3. the 15th day of each month of the lunar calendar 4. reputation; prestige 5. to call on; to visit
【望梅止渴】 to console oneself with false hopes
【望風披靡】 to flee helter-skelter at the mere sight of the oncoming force
【望塵莫及】 to be left far behind
【望穿秋水】 to aspire earnestly
【望子成龍】 to hope one's children will have a bright future
【望族】 a family of renown
【望眼欲穿】 to aspire earnestly
【望遠鏡】 a telescope

八畫

朝 1787 1. ㄓㄠ zhāo
1. morning 2. a day
【朝不保夕】 precarious
【朝令夕改】 to change rules very frequently
【朝露】 morning dew—a symbol of transience
【朝會】 a morning rally (in schools)
【朝氣】 fresh spirit
【朝氣蓬勃】 full of vigor and vitality
【朝秦暮楚】 to be fickle or capricious
【朝夕】 ①day and night ②a very brief period of time
【朝朝暮暮】 every day; always; day and night
【朝思暮想】 to yearn day and night
【朝三暮四】 to be inconsistent
【朝陽】 the morning sun

朝 1787 2. ㄔㄠˊ cháo
1. an imperial court 2. a dynasty 3. to go to imperial court 4. to face
【朝拜】 ① to worship; to pay respects to (a sovereign) ②to pilgrimage
【朝代】 a dynasty
【朝廷】 the court (of a sovereign); an imperial court
【朝綱】 ① rules of an imperial court ② the imperial court
【朝後】 to face backward
【朝見 or 朝覲】 to be received in audience by a sovereign
【朝政】 the affairs of the state
【朝山 or 朝聖】 to go on a pilgrimage
【朝野】 the government and the people

期 1788 1. ㄑㄧˊ qí (又讀 ㄑㄧ qī)
1. periods; times 2. a designated time; a time limit 3. to expect; to hope; to wait
【期末考試 or 期考 or 期終考試】 the final examination of a school term; the final
【期滿】 The term (or period) has expired.
【期待 or 期望】 to expect; to hope
【期刊】 a periodical
【期間】 a period; a term
【期期艾艾】 stammering
【期限】 a time limit; a deadline
【期許】 to expect to; expectation
【期中考試】 a midterm examination

期 1788 2. (讀) ㄐㄧ jī
one year
【期服】 one-year mourning
【期年】 the first anniversary

十四畫

朦 1789 ㄇㄥˊ méng
1. the state of the moon just before setting 2. dim; vague; hazy 3. to deceive; to swindle
【朦朧】 ① the appearance of the moon just before setting ② dim; vague

木部 ㄇㄨˋ mù

木 1790 ㄇㄨˋ mù
1. a tree 2. wood; timber 3. made of wood; wooden 4. simple; honest 5. senseless; benumbed 6. a coffin
【木板】 planks; boards
【木筏】 a wooden raft
【木棉】 silk cotton

【木頭】①wood ②a stupid fellow
【木頭人兒】a stupid fellow; an idiot
【木炭】charcoal
【木訥】honest and slow-witted
【木乃伊】a mummy
【木瓜】a papaya
【木棍 or 木棒】a wooden club
【木工】①a carpenter; a woodworker ②carpentry
【木屐】clogs; pattens
【木匠】a carpenter; a woodworker
【木箱】a wooden box; a wooden trunk
【木柵】a stockade
【木樁】a wooden post or pile
【木柴】firewood
【木材】lumber; timber
【木偶】a puppet
【木偶戲】a puppet show
【木已成舟】(literally) The timber has been turned into a boat already.—It is irrevocable.
【木屋】a log cabin

一畫

未 1791 ㄨㄟˋ wèi

1. not yet 2. not 3. the eighth of the Twelve Terrestrial Branches 4. 1:00-3:00 p.m.

【未必】not always; not necessarily
【未必盡然】not always so
【未卜先知】to foresee accurately
【未免】①It must be admitted that.... ②necessarily; unavoidably
【未定】uncertain; unfixed; undefined
【未能】to fail to; cannot
【未能免俗】incapable of being exempted from usual custom
【未來】future; in the future
【未老先衰】to become senile before one's time
【未了】unsettled; unfixed; unfinished
【未敢苟同】(literary language) can not agree
【未開發】(said of land, resources, etc.) undeveloped
【未婚】unmarried; single
【未婚夫】one's fiancé
【未婚男子】a bachelor
【未婚妻】one's fiancée
【未及】not enough time left to do it
【未經】to have not yet (gone through)
【未竟之志】an unfulfilled ambition
【未決】undecided; uncertain; unsettled
【未知數】①(mathematics) an unknown number ②unknown; uncertain
【未嘗】①not necessarily ②never
【未嘗不可】It is not necessarily impermissible or impossible.
【未成年】not yet come of age; minor
【未成熟】unripe; immature
【未曾】never before
【未遂】attempted without success
【未完】unfinished; not completed
【未亡人】a widow
【未雨綢繆】to take precautions before it is too late

末 1792 ㄇㄛˋ mò

1. last; final 2. late; recent 3. unimportant; insignificant 4. the end; the tip 5. the four limbs

【末班】the last scheduled train, bus, ship, or airplane in a day
【末代】the last reign (of a dynasty)
【末奈何 or 沒奈何】There is no way out.
【末年】the declining years of one's life, a dynasty, etc.
【末了】in the end; finally
【末世】the last years (of a dynasty)
【末梢】the tip; the end
【末日】①the last day; doom ②(Christianity) Doomsday; Judgment Day
【末葉】①posterity; descendants ②the last part of a dynasty ③the latter part of a century
【末尾】the end

本 1793 ㄅㄣˇ běn

1. the root of a plant 2. the root; the origin; the source; the basis; the foundation 3. original 4. a book; a copy 5. capital (in business) 6. our; this; the present 7. according to; based on 8. the beginning; the starting point

【本班】this (or our) class, squad, team, section, etc.
【本部】①headquarters ②this ministry; our ministry
【本埠】this city; the local area
【本末倒置】to mistake the means

for the end
【本名】 one's formal name
【本分】 one's part; one's role; one's duty
【本俸or本薪】 the basic salary (exclusive of various additional allowances)
【本當】 should have, or ought to have
【本黨】 our party; this party
【本地】 the local area
【本地風光】 local scenery
【本地人】 a native
【本土】 the mainland; a country proper
【本能】 instinct
【本來】 ① originally ② of course
【本來面目】 true looks; true colors
【本利or本息】 principal and interest
【本領】 ability; skill; talent
【本國】 one's home country
【本行】 ① one's trade; one's specialty ② this bank; our bank
【本屆】 current; this year's
【本金】 principal as distinct from interest
【本期】 ① this term ② the present class (of students or cadets)
【本錢】 capital (in business)
【本校】 our (or this) school
【本縣】 our (or this) county, prefecture, etc.
【本鄉】 our (or this) village
【本性】 the real nature
【本性難移】 One's nature cannot be altered.
【本質】 essence; the intrinsic nature
【本旨】 the real intention or meaning
【本着】 in the light of; in accordance with
【本週】 this week
【本初子午線】 the prime meridian
【本市】 this city; our city
【本事】 ①(ㄅㄣˇ ㄕˋ) a story (or a plot) of a play, movie, etc. ② (ㄅㄣˇ ·ㄕ) ability; skill; talent
【本身】 oneself; personally; itself
【本省】 this province; our province
【本省人】 a native of this province
【本日】 today
【本人】 ① I; me ② himself; herself; yourself ③ personally
【本子 or 本兒】 a book; a notebook
【本色】 ① the original color ② the real look
【本案】 the present case; this case
【本意】 the original intention
【本義】 the original meaning
【本應】 should have; ought to have
【本文】 the main body of a writing
【本月】 this month

札 1794
ㄓㄚˊ zhá
1. (in ancient China) a thin wooden tablet for writing 2. correspondence; a letter 3. (in ancient China) documents or instructions to a subordinate 4. (now rarely) to die before one comes of age
【札記】 a notebook in which one records his comments on the book he is reading

二畫

朱 1795
ㄓㄨ zhū
1. red; vermilion 2. a Chinese family name
【朱批】 writing comments or remarks in red with a brush
【朱門】 rich and influential families
【朱紅】 bright red; vermilion
【朱砂 or 硃砂】 cinnabar
【朱儒or侏儒】 a dwarf; a pygmy or pigmy

朴 1796
1. ㄆㄛˋ pò
saltpeter

朴 1796
2. (樸) ㄆㄨˇ pǔ
1. (said of clothing, manner, etc.) plain; simple 2. a kind of oak (*Quercus dentata*)

朽 1797
ㄒㄧㄡˇ xiǔ
1. to rot; to decay 2. old and useless
【朽敗】 decayed and rotten
【朽木】 ① rotten wood; decayed trees ② a good-for-nothing
【朽木不可雕】 A congenital defeatist cannot be taught to succeed.
【朽木糞土】 decayed wood and filthy soil—a hopeless person
【朽壞】 to decay; to rot; decayed

朵 1798
(朶) ㄉㄨㄛˇ duǒ
1. a flower; a cluster of flowers; a bud 2. a lobe of the ear
【朵頤】 the movement of the jaw in eating—the palate

三畫

李 1799
ㄌㄧˇ lǐ
1. as in 李子 — plums 2. (now rarely) a judge; a justice 3. a Chinese family name
【李代桃僵】to substitute this for that
【李下之嫌】a position that invites suspicion
【李樹】the plum tree

杉 1800
ㄕㄢ shān
the various species of fir and pine; a China fir

杏 1801
ㄒㄧㄥˋ xìng
1. an apricot 2. almonds—apricot kernels 3. apricot flowers
【杏壇】(in a broad sense) the teaching profession
【杏臉生春】to have a cheerful look
【杏林】a term used in praising a good and kind physician or referring to the medical profession in general
【杏花】apricot blossoms
【杏仁兒】almonds; apricot kernels
【杏眼】apricot-like eyes—a woman's large eyes
【杏眼桃腮】large eyes and rosy cheeks (of a beauty)

杓 1802
1. ㄅㄧㄠ biāo
name of a constellation—the handle of the Dipper

杓 1802
2. (勺) ㄕㄠˊ sháo
a receptacle or container, as a cup, ladle, spoon, etc.; the handle of such
【杓子】a wooden ladle

材 1803
ㄘㄞˊ cái
1. materials—especially timber—for building houses, furniture, etc. 2. material in its broadest sense 3. properties of a substance 4. ability; aptitude 5. a coffin
【材能 or 才能】ability; capability
【材料】①raw materials ②materials (such as data, statistics, figure, information for writing an article, story, novel, etc.) ③ ingredients of a preparation (of food, medicine, etc.) ④makings; stuff
【材幹】①gifts; talent; ability ②timber

村 1804
(邨) ㄘㄨㄣ cūn
1. a village; the countryside; a hamlet 2. vulgar; coarse 3. simple-minded; naive
【村夫】①a villager ②a vulgar and naive person
【村婦】a village woman
【村女 or 村姑】a country girl
【村落 or 村子】a village; a hamlet
【村長】the village chief
【村莊】a village; a farmstead

杖 1805
ㄓㄤˋ zhàng
1. a stick; a staff; a cane 2. (an old punishment) to beat with a cane; flogging with a stick 3. (now rarely) a mourning staff 4. to presume on (one's connections, influence, etc.)
【杖擊】to hit or beat with a cane

杜 1806
ㄉㄨˋ dù
1. to plug (a hole, leak, etc.); to stop; to prevent; to put an end to something 2. to shut out; to restrict; to impede 3. the russet pear (*Pyrusbetulaefolia*) 4. to fabricate; to practice forgery 5. a Chinese family name
【杜弊】to prevent corrupt practices
【杜門謝客】to refuse to see visitors
【杜口】to shut one's mouth and say nothing
【杜絕】①to stop (a bad practice, etc.) for good; to eradicate ②to cut off (relations with) ③irrevocable (contracts, title deeds, etc.)
【杜絕後患】to prevent and eliminate possible harmful consequences
【杜鵑】a cuckoo 亦作「子規」
【杜鵑花】azaleas
【杜撰】to fabricate (a story, etc.); to trump up

杞 1807
ㄑㄧˇ qǐ
1. a species of willow 2. a medlar 3. Chi, name of a state in the Chou Dynasty in today's Honan Province
【杞人憂天】A man entertains imaginary or groundless fears.

束 1808
ㄕㄨˋ shù

〔木部〕

1. to bind 2. a bunch; a bundle 3. to control; to restrain; restraint

【束縛】restrictions; to restrain; to bind up

【束脩】(literally) ten pieces of dried meat—tuition

【束之高閣】(literally) to place (something) high in the attic—to shelve it and forget about it

【束手待斃】(literally) to wait for one's death with hands tied—to be a sitting duck

【束手就擒】to put up no fight and allow oneself to be caught

【束手無策】no way out; at the end of the rope

四畫

杭 1809 ㄏㄤˊ háng

1. Hangchow 2. same as 航—to sail; to cross a stream; to navigate

杯 1810 ㄅㄟ bēi

a cup; a tumbler; a glass; a goblet

【杯盤狼藉】(literally) Empty glasses and plates are scattered all over.—The feast is over.

【杯葛】①a boycott ②to boycott

【杯弓蛇影】extremely suspicious

【杯中物】wine; alcoholic drinks

【杯水車薪】too inadequate and useless

杳 1811 ㄧㄠˇ yǎo

1. deep and expansive 2. quiet; silent

【杳然】quiet and silent; lonely

【杳杳無蹤】gone without leaving a trace

【杳無音信】without any news of someone for a long time

東 1812 ㄉㄨㄥ dōng

1. the east; eastern 2. to travel eastward 3. the host; the master

【東北】①northeast ②Manchuria

【東半球】the Eastern Hemisphere

【東奔西走】to run about busily

【東邊】the east side; on the east

【東拼西湊】to scrape (money, etc.) for a purchase, project, etc.; to patch up from bits

【東方】①the east ②Oriental ③a Chinese family name

【東風】an east wind

【東倒西歪】①(said of drunkards) to walk unsteadily ②(said of a scene, room, village, etc.) dilapidated

【東道主】the host at a dinner party

【東南】southeast

【東南西北】(literally) east, south, west and north—all directions

【東南亞】Southeast Asia

【東挪西借】to borrow all around

【東拉西扯】to talk aimlessly or without much thought; to ramble

【東海】the East China Sea

【東漢】the Eastern Han (25-220 A.D.)

【東家】①the host ②the owner of a company or shop

【東經】longitude east of Greenwich

【東京】①Tokyo ②(in the Han Dynasty) Loyang ③(in the Sung Dynasty) Kaifeng

【東西】①(ㄉㄨㄥ ㄒㄧ) ⓐ east and west ⓑ from east to west ②(ㄉㄨㄥ ·ㄒㄧ) ⓐ things; objects; matters ⓑ a contemptible fellow

【東張西望】to look around; to gaze around

【東窗事發】to come to light或The game is up.

【東床快婿】a son-in-law

【東施效顰】to imitate awkwardly

【東山再起】(said of a retired person, etc.) to take up official duties again

【東印度羣島】the East Indies

【東洋 or 東瀛】Japan

杵 1813 ㄔㄨˇ chǔ

1. a pestle; a baton used to pound the laundry 2. to poke

【杵臼之交】true friendship which disregards discrepancy in wealth, influence, fame, etc.

枇 1814 ㄆㄧˊ pí

as in 枇杷—loquats

【枇杷膏】condensed loquat extract

板 1815 ㄅㄢˇ bǎn

1. a board; a plank 2. a plate (of tin, aluminum, etc.); a slab 3. printing blocks 4. rigid; stern; stiff

【板凳】a wooden stool

【板畫】a woodcut

【板起面孔or板著臉】to make a long face

【板球】(sports) cricket

【板子】①a flogging board ②a

printing block
【板擦兒】a wiper or an eraser (for a blackboard, etc.)

松 1816
ㄙㄨㄥ sōng
pines; firs ②the conifers
【松柏】① the pine and the cypress
【松柏節操】honest and virtuous conduct; fortitude
【松柏長青 or 松柏長春】(a congratulatory expression on someone's birthday) May you live long and remain strong like the evergreen pine and cypress!
【松濤】the soughing of the wind in the pines which sounds like roaring waves
【松林】a pinery
【松果】a strobile
【松鶴遐齡】longevity
【松花江】the Sungari River
【松節油】turpentine
【松鼠】the squirrel
【松樹】a pine

枉 1817
ㄨㄤˇ wǎng
1. crooked 2. to waste; useless; in vain 3. to wrong; to do or suffer wrong; aggrieved; oppression 4. (in polite language) to request another to deign or condescend to
【枉法】to abuse law
【枉費】to waste; to be of no avail
【枉費工夫】to spend time and work in vain
【枉費心機】to scheme, plan or cudgel one's brains to no purpose or in vain
【枉駕】I'm honored by your visit.
【枉曲】bent; crooked; warped
【枉然】useless; to no purpose; in vain
【枉死】to die through injustice

析 1818
ㄒㄧ xī
1. to split; to divide; to separate 2. to interpret; to explain; to analyze
【析疑】to explain a doubt; to clarify a doubt
【析義】interpretation and elaboration of the meaning of something

枕 1819
1. ㄓㄣˇ zhěn
a pillow
【枕邊人】wife (who shares the same pillow with her husband)
【枕畔】beside the pillow
【枕木】railway sleepers; railroad ties
【枕套】a pillowcase; a pillowslip
【枕頭】a pillow
【枕巾】a pillow cover
【枕席難安】cannot sleep—very worried and anxious

枕 1819
2. ㄓㄣˋ zhèn
to use something as a pillow; to pillow
【枕戈待旦】to be on the alert
【枕藉】to lie in complete disarray or to lie about on each other
【枕經籍史or枕經籍書】to be excessively fond of ancient books

林 1820
ㄌㄧㄣˊ lín
1. a forest; a grove; a copse 2. a collection of books, works, literary extracts, etc. 3. circles; numerous; many; a great body of (capable persons, etc.) 4. a Chinese family name
【林木】a forest; woods
【林地】forest land; woodland
【林立】(literally) to stand up like a forest—a great many; a forest of (stacks, derricks, etc.)
【林林總總】numerous; multitudinous
【林區】a forest zone; a forest region; a forest
【林場】① wooded land; a forest ② a logging station
【林子】a grove; a forest
【林業】the forestry industry
【林蔭大道】an avenue; a boulevard

枝 1821
1. ㄓ zhī
1. the branches of a tree; a branch 2. limbs 3. to branch off
【枝頭】on the branch
【枝條】a twig
【枝幹】the trunk and the branches
【枝節】① branches and knots—minor matters ② obstacles; complications
【枝子 or 枝兒】a branch; a bough
【枝椏】branches; twigs 亦作「枝丫」
【枝葉】① branches and leaves ② complications and diversities ③ children; offspring
【枝葉扶疏】(said of trees) luxuriant

枝 1821
2. ㄑㄧˊ qí

〔木部〕

【枝指】 a forked finger; an additional finger

果 1822 ㄍㄨㄛˇ guǒ

1. the fruit of a plant 2. effect (in cause and effect); result; a consequence 3. surely; really; exactly 4. to stuff; to fill 5. to succeed

【果皮】 peel; peelings
【果木 or 果樹】 fruit trees
【果腹】 to fill one's stomach (usually with poor food); to feed on
【果斷】 (said of a person) resolute
【果糖】 fructose, or fruit sugar; levulose
【果嶺】 (golf) green
【果敢】 having the determination and courage to do something
【果核】 a kernel; a fruit stone; a pit
【果決】 daring and determined
【果汁】 fruit juice
【果汁機】 ① a juicer ② a blender
【果眞】 really; if really
【果實】 fruit
【果肉】 pulp
【果然】 ① exactly as one expected ② having eaten enough
【果仁】 a kernel
【果園兒 or 果園子】 an orchard

枚 1823 ㄇㄟˊ méi

1. the stalk; the trunk as opposed to branches 2. a numerary auxiliary (used in connection with coins, fruits, stamps, bombs, etc.) 3. a gag for troops marching at night when silence means a lot

【枚舉】 to enumerate; to recount one by one

杰 1824 (傑) ㄐㄧㄝˊ jié

a hero; an outstanding person

五畫

枯 1825 ㄎㄨ kū

1. withered; dry 2. dried wood 3. ill health; emaciated

【枯槁】 ① (said of a person's appearance) pale, dry and emaciated; haggard ② withered and dry
【枯乾】 dry (branches, or fruit)
【枯黃】 withered and yellow
【枯竭】 (said of source of supply) exhausted; dried up
【枯井】 a dried-up well; a dry well
【枯朽】 dry and decayed; rotten
【枯燥】 ① dry ② uninteresting; dull
【枯燥無味】 dry and tasteless—uninteresting; monotonous
【枯死】 to wither; to dry up and die
【枯葉】 dried leaves
【枯萎】 withered

柺 1826 (枴、拐) ㄍㄨㄞˇ guǎi

a staff for an old person; a cane

【柺杖】 an old person's staff; a cane

枵 1827 ㄒㄧㄠ xiāo

empty

【枵腹從公】 to do one's duty even with an empty stomach

架 1828 ㄐㄧㄚˋ jià

1. a prop; a stand; a rack; a frame 2. to prop up; to set up; to support 3. a framework or scaffold 4. to frame up (a charge, etc.); to fabricate 5. to lay something on 6. a quarrel

【架起】 to set up; to prop up
【架橋】 to build a bridge
【架式】 a style; a manner; a pose
【架勢】 (colloquial) a posture; a stance
【架設】 to build over something
【架子】 ① a rack; a stand; a frame; a scaffold ② a skeleton; an outline

枷 1829 ㄐㄧㄚ jiā

a cangue; a pillory—worn by prisoners in former times

【枷鎖】 ① the cangue and lock ② (figuratively) bondage; shackles

柿 1830 ㄕˋ shì

the persimmon: 柿子the persimmon fruit

枸 1831 1. ㄍㄡˇ gǒu

a medlar

【枸杞】 *Lycium chinense*, a Chinese wolfberry

枸 1831 2. ㄍㄡ gōu

【枸橘】 a large acid orange

柒 1832 ㄑㄧ qī

another form of 七 (seven), used in writing checks, etc. to prevent fraud

柄 1833
ㄅㄧㄥˇ bǐng
(又讀 ㄅㄧㄥˋ bìng)
1. the handle of something 2. authority; power 3. to operate; to handle; to control 4. a handle
【柄國】to reign over a state

柏 1834
讀音 ㄅㄛˊ bó
(語音 ㄅㄞˇ bǎi)
as in 柏樹—a cypress
【柏油】asphalt

某 1835
ㄇㄡˇ mǒu
1. a certain person or thing 2. formerly used in place of "I"
【某某】so-and-so; a certain person
【某年】a certain year
【某些】certain (things, people, etc.)
【某種】certain (reasons, results, etc.)
【某處】a certain place; somewhere
【某時or某時候】sometime; a certain time
【某日】a certain day
【某人】① a certain person ② a pronoun used in place of one's own name

染 1836
ㄖㄢˇ rǎn
1. to dye 2. to soil; to pollute 3. to get infected; to catch a disease; infectious 4. to have an affair with 5. (in Chinese painting and calligraphy) to make strokes
【染病】to get infected; to catch a disease; to fall ill
【染坊】a dyeing mill
【染毒】① to be infected with venereal disease ② to use narcotics
【染料】dyestuff; dye
【染指甲】to paint fingernails
【染指】to encroach on
【染色】to dye
【染色體】(genetics) a chromosome

柔 1837
ㄖㄡˊ róu
1. as in 柔嫩—soft and tender 2. amiable; pliant; yielding; submissive; gentle; supple 3. the new grass budding in spring
【柔媚】amiable, pliant and yielding
【柔道】judo
【柔能克剛】Soft and subtle approach can disarm a man of hot temper.
【柔和】soft; gentle; amiable; tender
【柔情似水】tender and soft as water
【柔腸寸斷】brokenhearted
【柔順】gentle and yielding
【柔弱】weak (physique); low and gentle (voice, etc.)
【柔軟】soft; yielding; lithe
【柔軟體操】calisthenics

柑 1838
ㄍㄢ gān
a mandarin orange
【柑橘】① oranges and tangerines ② citruses

柳 1839
ㄌㄧㄡˇ liǔ
1. a willow tree 2. name of one of the 28 Constellations 3. (figuratively) a singsong house; the red-light district 4. a tumor; a swelling; a lump 5. a Chinese family name
【柳眉】the eyebrows of a beautiful woman
【柳條】a withe; a willow branch
【柳巷花街】the red-light district
【柳絮】willow catkins
【柳橙】an orange
【柳暗花明】an enchanting sight in springtime
【柳葉兒】willow leaves
【柳腰】a willowy waist; a slender waist

柚 1840
ㄧㄡˋ yòu
1. a pumelo or pomelo; a shaddock 2. a teak; a teak tree
【柚木】① a teak (tree) ② teak; teakwood

柩 1841
ㄐㄧㄡˋ jiù
a coffin with a corpse in it

柯 1842
ㄎㄜ kē
1. *Pasania cuspidata*, a tall evergreen tree 2. the handle of an ax 3. the stalk or the trunk of a plant 4. a Chinese family name
【柯達】Kodak, a brand name

柱 1843
ㄓㄨˋ zhù
1. a pillar; a post 2. a cylinder 3. to support 4. to stab; to pierce
【柱廊】a colonnade
【柱子】a pillar; a post

柬 1844
ㄐㄧㄢˇ jiǎn
1. a letter; an invitation or visiting card 2. to select; to pick
【柬帖】① an invitation card ② (in old China) a red visiting card

〔木部〕

查 1845 1. ㄔㄚˊ chá

1. to investigate; to check; to seek out; to look into 2. (used at the beginning of the official correspondence) It appears....或 It seems....或 It is known....或 It is found that.... 3. a wooden raft

【查辦】to investigate into the irregularities (of an official, etc.) and mete out due punishment
【查票】to examine or check tickets
【查明】to investigate and clarify
【查訪】to go around and make inquiries
【查封】the execution of a court order by which all property of a debtor would be placed under legal custody until further action
【查點】to check (the number of prisoners, students, a list of goods, etc.)
【查對】to check or examine one by one; to verify
【查看】to investigate; to look into (a matter)
【查勘】to survey and examine
【查核】to check and examine
【查號台】directory information
【查獲】to hunt down and seize
【查勤】to make the rounds and check officers, etc. to see if they are doing their duties during office hours
【查詢】to inquire about; to inquire
【查賬 or 查帳】to audit (accounts)
【查賬員 or 查帳員】an auditor
【查證】to investigate and verify
【查出】to find out; to discover
【查收】to check the goods delivered and take them over
【查字典】to look it up in a dictionary
【查案】to investigate into a case
【查驗】to investigate; to inspect

查 1845 2. ㄓㄚ zhā

a Chinese family name

柴 1846 ㄔㄞˊ chái

1. firewood; brushwood; fagots 2. thin; emaciated 3. (now rarely) a fence 4. a Chinese family name

【柴米夫妻】a couple who live from hand to mouth
【柴米油鹽】daily necessities
【柴火 or 柴薪】firewood; fuel
【柴油】diesel oil
【柴魚】dried bonito

柵 1847 ㄓㄚˋ zhà

a fence of bamboos or wood; a palisade; a railing of posts

【柵欄兒】a fence; a palisade; a railing

枱 1848 ㄊㄞˊ tái

1. same as 檯—a desk or table 2. an ancient unit of measurement

六畫

栓 1849 ㄕㄨㄢ shuān

1. a wooden pin; a peg 2. a bolt; a plug 3. a stopper; a cork

栖 1850 (棲) ㄑㄧ qī (又讀 ㄒㄧ xī)

1. (said of birds) to roost; to perch 2. to settle; to live

【栖栖皇皇】vexed; rushing about

栩 1851 ㄒㄩˇ xǔ

1. a species of oak 2. glad; pleased

【栩栩如生】(said of a portrait, etc.) true to life; lifelike; to the life

栗 1852 ㄌㄧˋ lì

1. a chestnut tree 2. strong and firm; tough; durable 3. respectful; fearful; awe-inspiring 4. to tremble 5. majestic; dignified; 6. a Chinese family name

【栗鼠】a squirrel
【栗子】chestnuts
【栗色】chestnut color; maroon

株 1853 ㄓㄨ zhū

1. a tree; a numerary auxiliary for counting trees or similar things 2. roots that grow above the ground

【株連】to involve others in a crime one committed

核 1854 ㄏㄜˊ hé

1. a kernel; a fruit stone; a walnut; a pit 2. to investigate; to examine; to verify; to check 3. a nucleus; nuclear 4. a hard lump

【核辦】to study and examine (a case, etc.) and act accordingly
【核覆】to make a reply after thorough investigation
【核定】①to decide after examination ②to check and ratify
【核對】to verify; to check (the facts)
【核桃】a walnut
【核能】nuclear energy
【核能電廠】a nuclear power station
【核計】to examine and calculate
【核心】①the core (of a matter, etc.) ②the inner circle (of a political party, government, etc.)
【核准】to approve; approval
【核仁】①a nucleolus ②the kernel (of a fruit stone)
【核子】a nucleus; a nucleon
【核子戰爭】nuclear war
【核子武器】nuclear weapons
【核算】to examine and calculate
【核議】to decide after consideration

校 1855 1. ㄒㄧㄠˋ xiào
1. a school 2. field-grade (officers)
【校門】a gate of a school or college
【校服】school uniform
【校隊】the school team
【校歌】a school song; a college song
【校規】school regulations
【校刊】a school magazine
【校花】a campus queen; a school belle
【校徽】a school emblem; a badge
【校警】the police guards of a school
【校旗】a school flag
【校慶】anniversary celebrations of a school
【校訓】a school motto
【校長】a principal; a schoolmaster
【校車】a school bus
【校舍】school premises
【校醫】a school doctor or physician
【校友】an alumnus or alumna
【校務】school administration
【校譽】the reputation or prestige of a school or college
【校園】the school ground; the campus

校 1855 2. ㄐㄧㄠˋ jiào
1. to compare 2. to proofread; proofs 3. to revise (books, etc.); to collate
【校訂】to revise
【校對】①to proofread ②a proofreader ③to calibrate
【校正】to correct; to correct proofs
【校閱】①to collate ②to inspect troops, honor guards, etc.

根 1856 ㄍㄣ gēn
1. the root of a plant 2. a base; a foundation 3. the beginning, cause, or source of something 4. (mathematics) the root of a number 5. (chemistry) radical 6. a piece (of string, rope, etc.); a (stick, spear or thing of slender shape)
【根本】①a root; a base; a foundation ②basically
【根本辦法】basic methods or measures
【根本觀念】a radical conception
【根部】the root of a plant
【根號】(mathematics) the radical sign
【根基】foundation (in learning)
【根莖】a rhizome; a rootstock
【根據】① a basis; grounds ② in accordance with (the regulation, etc.)
【根據地】a base (of operations); a home base
【根絕】to root out (a problem, vice, etc.)
【根治】a radical treatment (for a disease, etc.); to cure (a disease) for good
【根除】thoroughly to do away with
【根深蒂固】time-honored; deep-rooted
【根由 or 根源】the source, origin or cause of something

格 1857 ㄍㄜˊ gé
1. to correct; to adjust or regulate 2. to reach; to come or go to 3. to influence 4. to resist; to attack; to fight 5. to obstruct; to block 6. to study thoroughly; to search to the very source; to investigate 7. a standard; a form; a rule; a pattern 8. a frame; a trellis 9. squares formed by crossed lines
【格鬥】a brawl; a hand-to-hand fight
【格調】① literary or artistic style; form; pattern ② personality
【格林威治時間】Greenwich Mean Time (GMT)
【格律】① standard; form; pattern ② the meter of poetry, etc.
【格格不入】totally incompatible

〔木部〕

〔木部〕

with

【格局】structure and form; style; setup
【格式】form; patterns
【格殺勿論】to kill on sight; to shoot on sight
【格子】a trellis; a lattice
【格言】a proverb; a motto; a maxim
【格外】extraordinary; exceptional; especially

桀 1858
ㄐㄧㄝˊ jié
1. ferocious and cruel 2. name of the last ruler of the Hsia Dynasty 3. same as 傑, outstanding and brave
【桀驁不馴】obstinate and unruly

案 1859
ㄢˋ àn
1. a narrow, long table 2. according to; on the strength of; following this precedent 3. a legal case; legal records; a legal offense 4. to press 亦作「按」
【案發】a crime or conspiracy coming to the open
【案頭】on the desk
【案件or案子】a legal case; a crime
【案情】the ins and outs of a crime
【案情大白】The riddle of a puzzling case has been completely unraveled.
【案由】a brief; a summary

桌 1860
(棹) ㄓㄨㄛ zhuō
1. a table; a desk 2. dishes for guests around the table—usually consisting of 20 courses 3. a tableful of guests (10 to 12 persons at a round table)
【桌布】a tablecloth
【桌面】the top of a table
【桌燈】a desk lamp
【桌球】table tennis; ping-pong

桑 1861
ㄙㄤ sāng
the mulberry tree
【桑田】a plantation of mulberry trees
【桑間濮上】a place notorious for profligacy
【桑葚】a mulberry; mulberry fruit
【桑蠶】a silkworm
【桑葉】mulberry leaves
【桑榆】① the west ② the closing years of one's life
【桑園】mulberry fields

栽 1862
ㄗㄞ zāi
1. to plant 2. to care; to assist 3. to fall; to fail 4. young trees, saplings, cuttings for planting
【栽培】① to plant and cultivate ② to educate people ③ to give special favor
【栽跟頭】① to stumble (both literally and figuratively) ② to be greatly embarrassed
【栽植or栽種】to plant; to raise; to grow
【栽贓】to place stolen goods in somebody's place with the intention of incriminating him

桂 1863
ㄍㄨㄟˋ guì
1. a short name of Kwangsi Province 2. cassia or cinnamon
【桂林】Kweilin, capital of Kwangsi Province
【桂冠詩人】a poet laureate, or a laureate
【桂花】sweet osmanthus
【桂圓】① a longan ② dried longan

桃 1864
ㄊㄠˊ táo
a peach
【桃李滿門】to have many pupils
【桃李滿天下】(said of a master or teacher) His students have spread throughout the world.
【桃花】the peach blossom
【桃花臉】the peachblossom face of a beauty; rosy cheeks
【桃花心木】mahogany
【桃花運】luck in love; a romance
【桃紅】pink; light red
【桃紅柳綠】a description of the beautiful scenes of spring
【桃樹】a peach tree
【桃色新聞】news of illicit love

桅 1865
ㄨㄟˊ wéi
the mast of a ship
【桅竿】the mast of a boat
【桅檣】a mast

框 1866
ㄎㄨㄤˇ kuǎng
(又讀 ㄎㄨㄤ kuāng)
1. a frame 2. to frame 3. the skeleton (of a lantern, etc.)

桎 1867
ㄓˋ zhì
1. as in 桎梏—fetters; shackles 2. to fetter 3. to suffocate

桐 1868
ㄊㄨㄥˊ tóng
a paulownia
【桐樹】a tung tree
【桐油】tung oil

桔 1869
1. ㄐㄧㄝˊ jié
a well sweep
【桔梗】a Chinese bellflower

桔 1869
2. ㄐㄩˊ jú
an abbreviated form of 橘, a mandarin orange or tangerine
【桔子】a small mandarin orange

七畫

梧 1870
ㄨˊ wú
1. a firmiana 2. a support; a prop 3. to support; to prop up
【梧桐】a firmiana
【梧鼠技窮】at one's wits' end

桶 1871
ㄊㄨㄥˇ tǒng
a bucket; a tub; a pail; a barrel

梁 1872
ㄌㄧㄤˊ liáng
1. a bridge 2. beams of a house 3. a ridge; a swelling 4. Liang, name of a dynasty (502 to 557 A.D.) 5. a state during the Epoch of Warring States, also known as Wei(魏) 6. a Chinese family name
【梁上君子or樑上君子】(literally) gentlemen up on the beams—burglars

梅 1873
ㄇㄟˊ méi
1. prunes; 梅子 plums 2. a Chinese family name
【梅毒】syphilis
【梅花】① plum blossoms ② a wintersweet
【梅花鹿】sika; a spotted deer
【梅妻鶴子】the life of a hermit
【梅雨】the rainy season in early summer when plums are ripening

梓 1874
ㄗˇ zǐ
1. *Catalpa ovata*, a tall, stately tree with palm-shaped leaves and yellow flowers in summer 2. one's native place or hometown 3. to carve words on a woodboard; printing blocks

梔 1875
(栀) ㄓ zhī
a gardenia
【梔子花】Cape jasmine

梗 1876
ㄍㄥˇ gěng
1. the branch or stem of a plant 2. to prick or pierce with a thorn; thorny 3. an outline; a synopsis; a summary 4. to block; to obstruct 5. stubborn; stiff 6. fierce and fearless 7. an ailment; bane; distress 8. to straighten 9. honest; straight
【梗概】an outline; a summary; a synopsis
【梗直】straight and honest; outspoken
【梗塞】to obstruct; to block

條 1877
ㄊㄧㄠˊ tiáo
1. an article, section, clause, etc. of an agreement, pact, treaty, law, etc. 2. in good order; (to present) one by one 3. a numerary adjunct for something narrow and long, as roads, fish, ropes, dogs, snakes, etc. 4. stripes (calligraphy or painting)
【條幅】a vertical hanging scroll of calligraphy or painting
【條條大道通羅馬】Every road leads to Rome.
【條理】① reasonable; logical ② orderly; in good order
【條理井然】in good order and with good reasoning
【條例】rules, regulations, or laws
【條列】to list item by item
【條規】rules and regulations
【條款】an article of laws; a section, chapter, or clause of agreements, regulations, etc.
【條件】① terms; conditions ② articles, clauses, etc. in an agreement, etc.
【條文】the text of a treaty, regulation, law, etc.
【條紋】stripes; streaks; the grain (of wood)
【條約】a treaty (between nations)

梟 1878
ㄒㄧㄠ xiāo
1. an owl; a legendary bird said to eat its own mother 2. a smuggler of contraband, narcotics, etc. 3. brave and unscrupulous
【梟雄】an unscrupulous, brave and capable person

〔木部〕

梵 1879
ㄈㄢˋ fàn
1. clean and pure 2. Sanskrit 3. a Brahman 4. anything pertaining to Buddhism
【梵諦岡】the Vatican
【梵文】the written Sanskrit
【梵語】the spoken Sanskrit

梯 1880
ㄊㄧ tī
1. a ladder; steps; stairs 2. something to lean or depend on 3. terraced 4. private; intimate 5. a phase
【梯田】terraced paddies on a slope
【梯階】① steps of a ladder ② keys to accomplish something
【梯形】①(geometry) trapezoid ② a flat raised piece of land in gardens
【梯次】phases (in the induction of military draftees)

械 1881
ㄒㄧㄝˋ xiè
(又讀 ㄐㄧㄝˋ jiè)
1. weapons 2. implements; machinery; machines 3. shackles; fetters 4. to arrest and put in prison

梢 1882
ㄕㄠ shāo
1. the tip of a branch or things of similar shape 2. the end of something—the result, etc. 3. the rudder

梭 1883
ㄙㄨㄛ suō
1. a weaver's shuttle 2. to move to and fro 3. swift
【梭巡】to patrol to and fro

梆 1884
ㄅㄤ bāng
a watchman's rattle made of wood or bamboo

梳 1885
(梳) ㄕㄨ shū
1. a comb; a coarse comb 2. to comb
【梳理】① combing ② (textile) carding
【梳洗】to comb one's hair and wash up
【梳粧】(said of a woman) to doll up; to dress and make up
【梳粧打扮】to dress smartly; to be dressed up
【梳粧臺】a dressing table where cosmetics, toilet requisites, etc. are laid out for use
【梳子 or 梳兒】a comb

桿 1886
ㄍㄢˇ gǎn
a wooden pole, cane, stick, or club
【桿菌】a bacillus; bacilli

八畫

棃 1887
(梨) ㄌㄧˊ lí
1. a pear 2. Chinese opera
【棃樹】the pear tree
【棃渦】dimples
【棃園】the operatic circle
【棃園子弟】operatic players

棄 1888
(弃) ㄑㄧˋ qì
1. to discard; to cast aside 2. to reject; to abandon; to desert 3. to forget 4. to throw away one's own life
【棄官】to give up one's office
【棄甲曳兵】(said of military troops) to throw away their armor and trail their weapons behind them—to be totally defeated
【棄舊迎新】to reject the old and welcome the new—as in the case of taking a second wife
【棄捐】to reject; to abandon
【棄權】(in voting) to abstain; a waiver
【棄邪歸正】to reject evil ways and start on the right track
【棄置】to cast aside
【棄世】to die
【棄暗投明】to renounce a bad cause and join the camp of justice
【棄養】the death of one's parents
【棄嬰】a foundling
【棄物】trash; discarded useless things

棉 1889
ㄇㄧㄢˊ mián
cotton
【棉被】a cotton quilt
【棉布】a cotton cloth
【棉袍】a cotton-wadded long gown
【棉線】cotton thread; cotton
【棉絮】fluffed cotton; cotton batting
【棉織物or棉織品】cotton (piece) goods
【棉紗】cotton yarn
【棉繩】cotton cord
【棉襖】a cotton-padded Chinese jacket

棋 1890
(碁、碁) ㄑㄧˊ qí
1. any piece used in the game of chess 2. chess or other similar games
【棋盤】a chessboard
【棋逢敵手】a good match; to be well-matched in a contest
【棋高一著】to be superior in intelligence, stratagem, skill, etc. than one's opponent
【棋局】① the chessboard with the pieces arranged ② a game of chess
【棋手】a high-graded chess player
【棋子】chess pieces
【棋王】a chess champion

棍 1891
ㄍㄨㄣˋ gùn
1. a club; a stick; a cudgel; a truncheon 2. a rascal; a villain; a ruffian
【棍棒 or 棍子】clubs; sticks
【棍騙】to swindle; to cheat

棒 1892
ㄅㄤˋ bàng
1. a club; a stick; a truncheon 2. to hit with a club 3. good; strong; wonderful
【棒棒糖】a lollipop
【棒喝】① to bang and bawl in rebuke of a student ② to arouse a person from his evil ways—as if by using a club
【棒球】baseball
【棒球場】a diamond; a baseball stadium

棗 1893
ㄗㄠˇ zǎo
jujube (*Zizyphus vulgaris*), commonly called date
【棗泥】jujube paste, used as stuffing for pastry or dumplings
【棗紅】purplish red
【棗樹】a jujube tree

棘 1894
ㄐㄧˊ jí
1. buckthorns; thorny brambles 2. urgent
【棘手】difficult to handle

棧 1895
ㄓㄢˋ zhàn
1. a storehouse; a warehouse 2. a tavern; an inn 3. a road made along a cliff
【棧房】① a storehouse; a warehouse ② a tavern; an inn
【棧道】a log-formed road along a steep cliff

棟 1896
ㄉㄨㄥˋ dòng
the main beam of a house
【棟梁 or 棟樑】① the ridgepole and beams ② (figuratively) a man of great ability
【棟梁之才 or 棟樑之才】a man of tremendous promise

棚 1897
ㄆㄥˊ péng
a tent; a shed; a (mat) awning

棠 1898
ㄊㄤˊ táng
the sweet pear tree; the wild plum

森 1899
ㄙㄣ sēn
1. luxuriant vegetation or luxuriant growth of trees 2. dark and obscure; severe 3. serene; majestic
【森巴舞】samba, originated in Brazil
【森林】forest
【森林浴】a green shower
【森羅萬象】the phenomena of the universe
【森然】awe-inspiring; trembling
【森嚴】stern and severe

椒 1900
ㄐㄧㄠ jiāo
1. pepper 2. mountaintops

棲 1901
ㄑㄧ qī (又讀 ㄒㄧ xī)
1. to rest; to stay; to perch; to settle 2. the place one stays 3. (now rarely) a bed
【棲居】to dwell; to live
【棲棲遑遑】anxious; nervous
【棲息】to rest; to stay; to perch
【棲處】①(ㄑㄧ ㄔㄨˇ) to stay (at a place) ②(ㄑㄧ ㄔㄨˋ) an abode (usually temporarily)
【棲身】to live; to stay; to dwell

棺 1902
ㄍㄨㄢ guān
a coffin (usually made of wood in China)
【棺木 or 棺材】a coffin
【棺殮】① coffin and graveclothes ② to put a shrouded corpse into a coffin
【棺槨】inner and outer coffins in ancient times

棵 1903
ㄎㄜ kē
a numerary adjunct for trees

〔木部〕

植 1904
ㄓˊ zhí
1. to plant; to set up; to erect 2. (now rarely) to lean on 3. plants; vegetation
【植黨營私】 to form a faction for selfish ends
【植樹】 to plant trees
【植樹節】 Arbor Day on March 12, death anniversary of Dr. Sun Yat-sen
【植物】 vegetables; plants; flora
【植物界】 the vegetable kingdom
【植物學】 botany
【植物學家】 a botanist
【植物人】 a vegetable
【植物油】 vegetable oil
【植物園】 a botanical garden; an arboretum

椎 1905
ㄓㄨㄟ zhuī
(又讀 ㄔㄨㄟˊ chuí)
1. a hammer; a mallet; a bludgeon; a mace 2. to beat; to hammer; to hit; to strike 3. as in 椎骨—a vertebra
【椎擊】 to strike with a hammer
【椎心泣血】 deep sorrow; extreme grief

椅 1906
ㄧˇ yǐ
as in 椅子—a chair; a bench
【椅背】 the back of a chair
【椅墊子】 a chair cushion
【椅套】 chair covers

椏 1907
ㄧㄚ yā
the forking branch of a tree

棕 1908
(椶) ㄗㄨㄥ zōng
as in 棕櫚(樹)—the palm tree
【棕色】 brown, the color of palm fibers
【棕簑】 a coir rain cape; a coir raincoat

九畫

椹 1909
ㄓㄣ zhēn
a block: 椹板 a chopping board

椰 1910
ㄧㄝ yē
a coconut; a coconut palm; a coconut tree
【椰子】 a coconut

椿 1911
ㄔㄨㄣ chūn
as in 椿庭—one's father
【椿齡or椿壽】 venerable age; long life
【椿萱】 one's parents

楓 1912
ㄈㄥ fēng
as in 楓樹—a maple

楊 1913
ㄧㄤˊ yáng
1. a poplar 2. a willow 3. a Chinese family name
【楊桃】 a carambola or star fruit
【楊柳】 a willow
【楊花】 poplar blossoms; poplar filaments

楔 1914
ㄒㄧㄝˋ xiè
1. to wedge 2. a gatepost 3. a wedge
【楔形文字】 cuneiform; sphenogram
【楔子】 ① a wedge ② a preface; a foreword; a prologue

楞 1915
1. ㄌㄥˊ léng
1. angular 2. an edge 3. Ceylon

楞 1915
2. (愣) ㄌㄥˋ lèng
stupid; imbecile; rude

榆 1916
ㄩˊ yú
an elm

楚 1917
ㄔㄨˇ chǔ
1. name of a powerful feudal state which existed 740-330 B.C. 2. a Chinese family name 3. clear; neat 4. distress; suffering
【楚囚對泣】 to lament a common misery
【楚館秦樓】 brothels
【楚楚動人】 (said of a young woman) delicate and attractive
【楚楚可憐】 tender and pathetic
【楚材晉用】 Talents of one country are employed by other countries.

業 1918
ㄧㄝˋ yè
1. work; occupations; professions; vocations; callings; trades 2. estate; property 3. already
【業績】 the track record
【業經or業已】 to have already been
【業主】 the proprietor; the owner
【業務】 business activities
【業餘】 ① amateur ② spare time

楣 1919
ㄇㄟˊ méi
the lintel (over a door)

極 1920
ㄐㄧˊ jí
1. to exhaust 2. extreme (ly); utmost; highest; topmost; farthest 3. poles 4. to reach; to arrive at
【極品】a thing of the highest grade
【極大】maximum
【極地】the polar regions
【極點or極頂】the zenith; the apex; the climax
【極度】extremely; exceedingly
【極端】an extreme; extremely
【極樂世界】(Buddhism) Paradise
【極力】to make the utmost effort
【極口稱讚】to praise lavishly
【極好】very good; superb; excellent
【極壞】the worst
【極盡】to use to the utmost
【極其】very; exceedingly; highly
【極圈】the polar circles
【極權國家】a dictatorial nation
【極限】(mathematics) limit
【極刑】death penalty; capital punishment
【極致】the ultimate attainment; the acme
【極盛】the heyday; the prime; the zenith; the acme

楷 1921
ㄎㄞˇ kǎi
1. regular; standard 2. a model; a norm 3. (calligraphy) standard script
【楷模】a model (for imitation)
【楷書】standard script of handwriting

楹 1922
ㄧㄥˊ yíng
a pillar; a column
【楹聯】the scrolls hung on a pillar

十畫

榕 1923
ㄖㄨㄥˊ róng
a banyan tree

榔 1924
ㄌㄤˊ láng
1. a betel palm 2. a betel nut
【榔頭】a hammer

榛 1925
ㄓㄣ zhēn
a hazel: 榛子 a hazelnut
【榛莽】thickets; bushes

榭 1926
ㄒㄧㄝˋ xiè
a pavilion; an arbor; a kiosk

榫 1927
ㄙㄨㄣˇ sǔn
tenon and mortise
【榫頭】a tenon

榨 1928
ㄓㄚˋ zhà
to squeeze or press (for juice)
【榨取】to exploit; to squeeze; to extort
【榨菜】preserved mustard seasoned with salt and hot pepper
【榨油】to extract oil
【榨油水】to extort money from people

榜 1929
1. ㄅㄤˇ bǎng
a publicly posted roll of successful examinees
【榜示】to post for public attention
【榜首】the top candidate of an examination
【榜上無名】to fail in an examination
【榜樣】an example; a model

榜 1929
2. ㄅㄥˋ bèng
1. to oar 2. a whip; a rod
【榜楚】to beat; to flog; to whip

榻 1930
ㄊㄚˋ tà
a couch; a bed
【榻榻米】(Japanese) tatami

榴 1931
ㄌㄧㄡˊ liú
a pomegranate
【榴槤】(botany) a durian

榮 1932
ㄖㄨㄥˊ róng
1. glory; honor 2. luxuriant; lush; teeming
【榮民】retired servicemen; veterans
【榮歸】①(said of a high official) to retire in glory ②to return home in triumph
【榮華富貴】honor and wealth
【榮獲】to get or win the honor
【榮幸】honored; to have the honor of
【榮辱】honor and dishonor
【榮宗耀祖】to bring glory to one's family and ancestors
【榮耀】glory; honor; splendor
【榮膺 or 榮任】to have the honor of being appointed (to a post)
【榮譽】honor

槃 1933
(盤) ㄆㄢˊ pán

〔木部〕

1. a wooden tray 2. great
【槃根錯節】① very complicated; difficult to solve or explain ② (said of old social forces) deep-rooted

槁 1934 (稾) ㄍㄠˇ gǎo
withered; dead; rotten
【槁木死灰】a person utterly without vitality or ambition

構 1935 ㄍㄡˋ gòu
to frame; to form; to build; to establish; to constitute; to scheme
【構圖】composition (in drawing)
【構亂】to stir up disorder
【構禍】to bring disaster
【構陷】to frame a charge against someone
【構想】an idea; a plan; a scheme
【構成】to constitute; to form
【構造】structure; construction
【構思】① to weigh something mentally ② to plot; a plot

槌 1936 ㄔㄨㄟˊ chuí
a hammer

槍 1937 ㄑㄧㄤ qiāng
1. a spear; a lance; a javelin 2. a rifle; a pistol; a gun
【槍斃 or 槍決】to execute by shooting
【槍炮】firearms; guns
【槍法】① marksmanship ② art of using spears
【槍彈】a cartridge; a shell; a bullet
【槍托】the rifle butt; the gun stock
【槍林彈雨】a fierce battle (in which one faces a rain of bullets and artillery shells)
【槍桿】① the shaft of a spear ②a rifle; arms
【槍口】a muzzle (of a rifle, pistol, etc.)
【槍械】weapons
【槍枝】rifles
【槍戰】a gun battle; a shoot-out
【槍殺】to shoot
【槍手】①(ㄑㄧㄤ ㄕㄡˇ) a rifleman; a gunman ②(ㄑㄧㄤ ·ㄕㄡ) ⓐa substitute examinee ⓑ a ghost writer
【槍傷】bullet (or gunshot) wounds
【槍聲】the report or crack of a gun; a shot

槓 1938 ㄍㄤˋ gàng
1. a lever; a carrying pole 2. (sports) a bar 3. to sharpen (a knife) 4. to argue; to dispute 5. to cross out
【槓鈴】(sports) a barbell
【槓桿】a lever; a pry

榷 1939 ㄑㄩㄝˋ què
1. to monopolize 2. to levy taxes

十一畫

概 1940 (槩) ㄍㄞˋ gài
1. general; overall; roughly 2. without exception; categorically 3. the manner of carrying oneself; deportment
【概念】a concept; a conception
【概論】a general discussion; an outline
【概略】an outline; a summary
【概觀】a general view; a conspectus
【概括】to summarize; to sum up
【概況】a general situation
【概要】a summary; an outline; a synopsis; a résumé

槳 1941 ㄐㄧㄤˇ jiǎng
an oar

樂 1942 1. ㄩㄝˋ yuè
1. music 2. a Chinese family name
【樂譜】a score (of music); musical notes
【樂隊】a band; an orchestra
【樂團】① a philharmonic society ② a philharmonic orchestra
【樂器】a musical instrument
【樂曲】a piece of music; a musical composition
【樂章】a movement (of a symphony, sonata, etc.)
【樂師】musicians

樂 1942 2. ㄌㄜˋ lè
1. happy; glad; joyful; joyous; cheerful; elated; content; pleased; delighted; willing 2. pleasant; agreeable; enjoyable; pleasing; comfortable
【樂不可支】to be overwhelmed with joy
【樂不思蜀】too happy to think of home
【樂得】to be very glad to

【樂陶陶】 cheerful; happy; joyful
【樂天知命】 to be content with what one is; happy-go-lucky
【樂土】 a land of comfort; a paradise
【樂觀】 optimistic
【樂極生悲】 Happiness is followed by sorrow when it reaches an extreme.
【樂捐】 to donate voluntarily
【樂趣】 delight; pleasure; joy; fun
【樂事】 a pleasant thing or matter
【樂善好施】 willing to do good and give help to the poor; charitable
【樂子】 joy; fun
【樂此不疲】 to delight in a thing and never get tired of it
【樂而忘返】 to be a slave of pleasure
【樂以忘憂】 to seek pleasure in order to free oneself from care
【樂意】 ① willing ② pleased
【樂業】 to like one's job or trade
【樂於】 to like or love (doing something)
【樂園】 a paradise; Elysium

1942 **樂**
3. ㄧㄠˋ yào
to love; to be fond of; to delight in
【樂羣】 fond of company and learning from one's friends

1943 **槽**
ㄘㄠˊ cáo
1. a manger 2. a trough; a flume; a chute

1944 **樁**
ㄓㄨㄤ zhuāng
1. a stake; a post; a pile 2. a numerary auxiliary for affairs or matters

1945 **樟**
ㄓㄤ zhāng
a camphor tree: 樟腦油 camphor oil
【樟木】 ① a camphor tree ② the wood of a camphor tree
【樟腦】 camphor
【樟腦丸】 a camphor ball; a moth-ball

1946 **樊**
ㄈㄢˊ fán
1. a bird cage 2. disorderly; confused; messy 3. a Chinese family name
【樊籠】 ① a cage to confine birds or wild beasts ② (figuratively) the place or condition of confinement

1947 **樓**
ㄌㄡˊ lóu
as in 樓房—a building of two stories or more; a tower
【樓頂】 the top of a tall building
【樓梯】 a staircase
【樓閣 or 樓臺】 a tower
【樓下】 downstairs
【樓上】 upstairs

1948 **標**
ㄅㄧㄠ biāo
1. to show; to indicate; to mark; to symbolize 2. a mark; a sign; a symbol; an indication; a label 3. a model; a paragon 4. to bid; to tender
【標本】 ① a specimen ② appearance and substance
【標榜】 ① to glorify ② to profess ③ to boost
【標名】 a label; a title
【標明】 to label; to indicate; to mark clearly
【標的】 a target; an objective; a purpose; an aim
【標點】 punctuation
【標點符號】 a punctuation mark
【標題】 a heading; a title; a headline
【標高】 elevation
【標購】 to buy at public bidding
【標竿】 a guidepost
【標記】 a mark; an indication
【標價】 ①the tag price; the listed price ②to indicate the price of a commodity on a tag
【標籤】 a label; a tag
【標槍】 a javelin; a spear; a lance
【標新立異】 to try to be fanciful
【標致 or 標緻】 (said of females) good-looking
【標識 or 標誌】 a mark; a sign; a symbol
【標準】 ① a standard; a criterion ② typical
【標準桿】 (golf) par
【標準國語 or 標準語】 Mandarin Chinese; Mandarin
【標準化】 to standardize
【標售】 to sell by tender
【標語】 a slogan; a motto

1949 **樞**
ㄕㄨ shū
a hinge; a pivot
【樞紐】 the vital point; the key; the pivot
【樞機主教】 a cardinal of the Catholic Church

1950 **模**
1. ㄇㄛˊ mó
1. a model; a norm 2. to imitate; to copy
【模範】 an example; a model
【模範生】 a model student

【模仿】to imitate; to copy
【模特兒】①a model (for artists, photographers, etc.); ②a manikin
〔木部〕
【模擬】to simulate; to imitate
【模稜兩可】equivocal; ambiguous
【模糊】①dim; vague; ambiguous ②to obscure
【模式 or 模型】a model; a formula; a miniature; a pattern

模 1950
2. ㄇㄨˊ mú
a mold; a form; a matrix
【模樣】appearances; looks

樣 1951
ㄧㄤˋ yàng
1. appearances; looks 2. a style; a pattern; a mode; a form 3. a sort; a kind; a variety 4. a sample
【樣板】①a sample plate ②a templet ③a model; a prototype; an example
【樣本】a sample
【樣品】a specimen; a sample (of a commodity)
【樣張】a specimen sheet
【樣式】style; modes; patterns
【樣樣】each and every; all; every kind

十二畫

樸 1952
ㄆㄨˇ pǔ
1. (said of dress, clothing, literary style, etc.) plain; simple 2. the substance of things; things in the rough 3. honest; sincere; simple
【樸樸實實or樸實】①simple; plain (said of dresses, style, etc.) ② honest; sincere
【樸拙】simple and naive
【樸素】(said of dresses, etc.) simple and plain

樵 1953
ㄑㄧㄠˊ qiáo
1. firewood; fuel 2. to gather fuel or firewood 3. a woodcutter 4. to burn 5. a tower; a lookout
【樵夫 or 樵客 or 樵子】a woodcutter
【樵薪】to gather fuel or firewood
【樵叟】an old woodcutter

樺 1954
ㄏㄨㄚˋ huà
a birch

橄 1955
ㄍㄢˇ gǎn
as in 橄欖 —an olive: 橄欖油 olive oil
【橄欖球】American football; rugby

樽 1956
ㄗㄨㄣ zūn
1. a wine vessel; a goblet; a bottle; a wine jar 2. (said of vegetation) luxuriant

樹 1957
ㄕㄨˋ shù
1. trees 2. to plant 3. to erect; to establish
【樹碑】to erect a memorial tablet
【樹皮】bark
【樹末 or 樹梢】the tip of a tree
【樹苗】a seedling; a sapling
【樹木】trees
【樹大招風】Famous persons attract criticisms easily.
【樹德】to exemplify one's integrity
【樹黨】to form a clique, gang, faction, party, etc.
【樹敵or樹怨】to make an enemy of; to make enemy; to antagonize
【樹立】to establish (a reputation, etc.)
【樹林】a forest; woods
【樹幹】the trunk of a tree
【樹根】the root of a tree
【樹膠】resin; gum
【樹下】under the tree
【樹枝】boughs or branches of a tree
【樹脂】resin
【樹上】on the tree; above the tree
【樹叢】a grove of trees
【樹葉】the leaves of a tree; foliage
【樹陰 or 樹蔭】the shade of a tree
【樹影】the shadow of a tree

橇 1958
ㄘㄨㄟˋ cuì
(又讀 ㄑㄧㄠ qiāo)
a sledge for transportation over mud or snow; a sleigh

橋 1959
ㄑㄧㄠˊ qiáo
1. a bridge; any bridgelike structure 2. beams of a structure 3. tall; high; elevated
【橋牌】(card games) bridge
【橋墩】the buttresses of a bridge
【橋頭】either end of a bridge
【橋梁】any material which forms the span of a bridge
【橋拱】a bridge arch
【橋下】below the bridge
【橋上】on the bridge

1960 **橙** ㄔㄥˊ chéng (語音 ㄔㄣˊ chén)
the orange: 橙汁 orange juice
【橙黃色】orange (color)

1961 **橘** ㄐㄩˊ jú
the mandarin (or the Chinese) orange; a tangerine
【橘黃】an orange color
【橘紅】tangerine (color)
【橘子汁】orange juice

1962 **橡** ㄒㄧㄤˋ xiàng
an acorn
【橡皮】① an eraser ② rubber
【橡皮筋】rubber bands
【橡膠】rubber
【橡膠樹】a rubber tree
【橡樹】an oak

1963 **橢** ㄊㄨㄛˇ tuǒ
as in 橢圓形的 — oval; oblong; elliptical
【橢圓】(mathematics) an ellipse

1964 **機** ㄐㄧ jī
1. mechanics; machinery 2. opportune; opportunity 3. a crucial point; a pivot 4. tricky; cunning 5. an aircraft; a plane; an airplane
【機密】secret; confidential; classified
【機密文件】secret or confidential documents
【機房】①a storage for textile machinery ② an engine room
【機動性】(military) mobility
【機能】functions; functional
【機靈】clever; smart; sharp; intelligent
【機伶鬼兒】a quick-witted or clever fellow
【機率】the probability
【機構】an organization
【機關】① an organization; an institution ② a machine ③ a stratagem; an intrigue
【機關槍】a machine gun
【機會】opportunity
【機件】component parts of a machine
【機警】alert
【機器】machinery; a machine
【機器人】a robot
【機羣】an air armada; a fleet of airplanes
【機械】①a machine ②mechanical ③(said of persons) cunning or shrewd
【機械化】mechanization
【機型】① the type (of an aircraft) ② the model (of a machine)
【機智】alertness; quick wit; tact
【機長】an aircraft (or crew) commander
【機車】①motorcycles ②a locomotive
【機場】an airport; an airfield
【機身】the fuselage
【機座】machine base; machine foundation
【機艙】the cockpit of a small airplane; the cabin of an airliner
【機宜】a matter and its arrangements; a line of action; guidelines; a policy
【機翼】wings of an airplane
【機要】confidential and important
【機要秘書】a confidential secretary
【機油】lubricating oil; lubricant
【機務人員】① maintenance personnel ② ground crew
【機遇】chance; opportunity; luck
【機員】a member of an aircraft crew
【機緣】chance and opportunity
【機運】luck; fate

1965 **橫** 1. ㄏㄥˊ héng
1. horizontal; crosswise; lateral 2. east to west or vice versa 3. by the side of; sideways 4. to move crosswise; to traverse 5. unrestrainedly; turbulently
【橫刀奪愛】to take away another's woman by force
【橫渡】to cross (a river, ocean, etc.)
【橫隊】a rank; a row
【橫了心】to steel one's heart (as a result of anger; an indication of determination, etc.); in desperation
【橫列】to arrange in a horizontal line
【橫流】(said of a river) to overflow
【橫膈膜】the diaphragm
【橫亙】① crosswise; horizontal ② to span; to traverse
【橫貫公路】① any highway that runs from east to west ② the Cross-Island or East-West Highway in Taiwan
【橫跨】to stretch over or across
【橫七豎八】in total disorder or disarray

〔木部〕

【橫寫】to write horizontally
【橫行】①to run wild ②to move sideways—as crabs
【橫行霸道】to bully; to terrorize; to act tyrannically
【橫陳】to lie down with limbs fully stretched
【橫衝直撞】(said of a bull, car, truck, etc.) to bump; to jostle and elbow one's way right and left
【橫生枝節】①side issues or new problems that come or appear unexpectedly ②to raise obstacles; to complicate an issue deliberately
【橫豎】①(ㄏㄥˊ ㄕㄨˋ) in any case; anyway ②(ㄏㄥˊ ·ㄕㄨ) horizontal and perpendicular; in every direction
【橫坐標】(mathematics) an abscissa
【橫財】a windfall; illegal gains
【橫掃】to sweep away; to roll back
【橫溢】① brimming; overflowing ② to brim; to overflow

橫 1965
2. ㄏㄥˋ hèng
1. cross-grained; perverse 2. presumptuous and unreasonable 3. unexpected; uncalled for 4. violent; cross
【橫禍】unexpected misfortune or disaster
【橫死】a violent death; to meet with a sudden death

十三畫

檀 1966
ㄊㄢˊ tán
sandalwood
【檀島】the Hawaiian Islands
【檀香】①incense made of sandalwood ② *Santalum album*

檄 1967
ㄒㄧˊ xí
a summons to arms in ancient times
【檄文】a written summons to arms for a cause

檐 1968
(簷) ㄧㄢˊ yán
1. eaves of a house 2. the brim

檔 1969
ㄉㄤˇ dǎng
(又讀 ㄉㄤˋ dàng)
1. an abbreviation for 檔案 (files) 2. shelves; pigeonholes 3. a wooden crosspiece, as the rung of a ladder, etc.
【檔期】a schedule for showing motion pictures in a theater
【檔案】archives; official files (of government offices)
【檔案管理】file management

檜 1970
ㄎㄨㄞˋ kuài
(又讀 ㄍㄨㄟˋ guì)
the Chinese juniper or cypress
【檜木】timber of a Chinese cypress or juniper

檢 1971
ㄐㄧㄢˇ jiǎn
1. a book label 2. to sort; to gather 3. to inspect; to check up; to collate 4. to discuss thoroughly 5. a form; a pattern 6. to restrict; to regulate
【檢點】①to behave (oneself) ②to inspect and arrange; to check
【檢定】①to inspect and approve (or sanction) ②inspection
【檢討】to review and discuss (past performances, etc.); to make self-examination
【檢舉】to inform the authorities of an unlawful act, plot, etc.
【檢修】to examine and repair; to overhaul
【檢查】to inspect; to examine; to test
【檢查人員】an inspector (as a customs officer, etc.)
【檢察官】a court prosecutor; a procurator
【檢束】to discipline; to restrain
【檢疫】quarantine
【檢疫所】the quarantine office
【檢驗】to inspect and examine
【檢閱】to inspect or review (troops)

十四畫

檸 1972
ㄋㄧㄥˊ níng
as in 檸檬—lemon
【檸檬水】lemonade
【檸檬色】citrine
【檸檬酸】citric acid

檬 1973
ㄇㄥˊ méng
1. a kind of locust or acacia 2. lemon

檻 1974
1. ㄐㄧㄢˋ jiàn
railings; bars, as window or door bars

檻 1974
2. ㄎㄢˇ kǎn
a doorsill; a threshold

櫃 1975
ㄍㄨㄟˋ guì
1. a cabinet; a wardrobe; a cupboard 2. a shop counter
【櫃臺】the counter in a store

檯 1976
(枱) ㄊㄞˊ tái ⌈table lamp
a table: 檯布 a tablecloth 檯燈 a

檳 1977
ㄅㄧㄣ bīn ⌈betel (nut)
as in 檳榔—the areca (nut); the

十五畫

櫓 1978
(樐) ㄌㄨˇ lǔ
1. an oar; a scull; a sweep 2. (in ancient warfare) a big shield; a
【櫓夫】an oarsman ⌊long spear

櫛 1979
ㄐㄧㄝˊ jié
1. a comb; a comb of many fine teeth 2. to comb the hair 3. to weed out; to eliminate; to delete
【櫛比】(said of houses) joined closely together ⌈trious
【櫛風沐雨】hardworking; indus-

櫥 1980
(橱) ㄔㄨˊ chú
as in 櫥櫃—a closet; a sideboard; a cupboard; a cabinet, etc.
【櫥窗】a show window; a showcase

十七畫

欄 1981
ㄌㄢˊ lán
1. a railing; a balustrade; a fence 2. a pen for domesticated animals
【欄杆】① a railing; a balustrade ② silk trimming for girls

櫻 1982
ㄧㄥ yīng
the cherry; the cherry blossoms
【櫻桃】cherries ⌈of a woman
【櫻脣】the small, beautiful mouth

十八畫

權 1983
ㄑㄩㄢˊ quán
1. to weigh (the significance, etc.); to assess 2. power; authority; inherent rights; jurisdiction; influence 3. an expedient way; expediency; alternative 4. temporarily; for the time being
【權柄】authority; power
【權謀】schemes and power; the use of schemes and power
【權代】to act in another's place temporarily
【權能】① authority; powers and functions ② (law) the exercise
【權利】rights ⌊of one's rights
【權力】power; authority ⌈figures
【權貴】ranking officials; influential
【權衡】to weigh, consider or assess
【權限】limitation of power or authority
【權臣】powerful courtiers
【權勢】power and influence
【權宜】expedient; temporary (measures, etc.) ⌈shift
【權宜之計】an expedient; a make-
【權益】rights and interests
【權要】① bigwigs; powerful persons ② confidential matter
【權威】① an authority (in certain sphere of knowledge) ② power and prestige

二十一畫

欖 1984
ㄌㄢˇ lǎn
the olive

欠部
ㄑㄧㄢˋ qiàn

欠 1985
ㄑㄧㄢˋ qiàn
1. to owe; to owe money 2. deficient; lacking 3. to raise slightly (a part of the body) 4. to yawn
【欠款】① to owe money ② debts
【欠佳】not satisfactory
【欠繳】to have not paid (one's due, tax, etc.) ⌈short of money
【欠錢】① to owe money ② to be
【欠缺】① to lack; deficient; short of ② shortcomings
【欠債】to be in debt; to owe money
【欠賬】① to owe money; to buy on credit ② overdue bills

〔欠部〕

【欠身】to get ready to stand up as a gesture of courtesy
【欠稅】tax arrears
【欠資郵票】a postage due stamp

二畫

次 1986 ㄘˋ cì

1. the next in order; secondary 2. inferior; lower 3. vice or deputy (ministers, etc.) 4. by; at (the feast, table, etc.); in the midst 5. a grade; grading; order; sequence 6. time (each occasion of a recurring action or event)

【次等 or 次一等】a lower or inferior class or category; of the second grade or quality
【次(等)貨】seconds; inferior goods; substandard goods
【次第】① order; grade; sequence ② in order; one by one
【次年】the next year
【次序】order, sequence, succession, etc.
【次長】a vice minister; a deputy minister
【次數】the number of times
【次日】the next day; the following day
【次子】the second son
【次要】secondary; not very important
【次於】next to...; inferior to...

四畫

欣 1987 ㄒㄧㄣ xīn

glad; gladly; joyful; joyfully; delighted; happy

【欣逢】happy to be present (on a joyful occasion)
【欣悉】delighted to learn; to have happily learned that
【欣喜】joyful; happy; delight
【欣喜欲狂or欣喜若狂】to be beside oneself with joy
【欣羨】to admire or envy
【欣欣向榮】①(said of flowers in spring) blossoming ②(said of business, financial situations, etc.) flourishing; thriving; prospering
【欣賞】to appreciate, enjoy or admire
【欣然】gladly; with pleasure
【欣慰】comforted; contented; satisfaction

七畫

欲 1988 ㄩˋ yù

1. to desire; to intend; to long for; to want; wish; desire; expectation; longing 2. about to; on the point of

【欲罷不能】unable to stop even if one wants to
【欲蓋彌彰】The more one tries to cover up (a secret, etc.), the better-known it will become.
【欲擒故縱】to try to get something by feigning uninterestedness or making concessions
【欲速不達】Haste makes waste.
【欲言又止】to wish to speak but keep silent on second thought
【欲望】desires; to long for; longings

欷 1989 ㄒㄧ xī

as in 欷歔—to sob

八畫

款 1990 (欵) ㄎㄨㄢˇ kuǎn

1. sincerity; sincere; sincerely 2. an article, an item, etc. (in a contract, treaty, etc.) 3. to entertain; to treat well 4. slowly; slow 5. to knock (at a door) 6. a fund; a sum of money; money 7. empty (words, etc.)

【款待】to entertain with courtesy and warmth; hospitality
【款款】① sincerely ② slowly
【款曲】① heartfelt feelings ② to conduct oneself with great tact in social gatherings
【款項】a sum of money; a fund; money
【款式】fashions; styles; patterns
【款額】the amount of money involved

欽 1991 ㄑㄧㄣ qīn

1. to respect; respectful; to admire 2. a term used to address a monarch in ancient China — Your Majesty

【欽佩】to admire; to respect
【欽慕or欽遲】to admire; to look up to
【欽差大臣】imperial inspector generals
【欽賜】granted or bestowed by the

emperor
【欽仰】to admire and respect; to look up to

欺 1992
ㄑㄧ qī

1. to cheat; to deceive; to swindle; to impose on; to take advantage of 2. to disregard the dictates of one's own conscience 3. to insult; to bully

【欺騙】to cheat; to deceive; to swindle
【欺瞞】to deceive; to cheat
【欺負】to insult; to oppress; to bully
【欺凌】to mistreat; to insult; to bully
【欺詐】to swindle; to defraud; to cheat
【欺世盜名】to win fame by cheating the world
【欺善怕惡】to oppress the good and timid and fear the wicked
【欺人太甚】You have insulted me beyond the limit.
【欺壓】to cheat and oppress
【欺侮】to insult or ridicule; to bully

九畫

歇 1993
ㄒㄧㄝ xiē

1. to rest 2. to sleep 3. to come to an end; to stop 4. to lodge

【歇店】to stay or lodge at an inn
【歇腿兒】① to rest one's feet after a long walk ② to rest at a place; to stay at an inn
【歇後語】a common expression whose last part is omitted
【歇脚】to rest the feet after walking
【歇息】to take a rest
【歇手】to stop doing something
【歇斯底里】hysteria
【歇宿】to spend the night; to stay for the night
【歇業】to close shop

歆 1994
ㄒㄧㄣ xīn

1. (said of gods, etc.) to accept offerings, etc. 2. to admire; to submit to willingly 3. to move

【歆羨】to admire; to envy (another's beauty or luck)

十畫

歉 1995
ㄑㄧㄢ qiàn

1. deficient; insufficient; deficiency 2. a poor crop or harvest 3. to regret; sorry 4. an apology; apologetic

【歉收】a bad harvest
【歉意】regrets; apologies

歌 1996
ㄍㄜ gē

1. to sing; to chant 2. to praise 3. a song 4. poems with rhythms and rhymes suitable for use as lyrics in songs

【歌譜】music scores
【歌臺舞榭】the stage—where songs and dances are performed
【歌功頌德】① to praise another (usually one's superior) for his achievements and virtues ② to flatter
【歌后】a very accomplished female vocalist
【歌集or歌本】a collection of songs; a songbook
【歌妓】(formerly) female entertainers somewhat like the geisha girls in Japan
【歌劇】operas
【歌曲】a song; a tune; a ballad
【歌星】a singing star; an accomplished vocalist
【歌唱】to sing; to chant
【歌手】a songster; a vocalist
【歌聲】the singing voice
【歌詞】lyrics or words of a song
【歌頌】to sing praises
【歌謠】a ballad; a folk song
【歌舞劇】a musical; an operetta; a light opera
【歌舞昇平】reign of peace and prosperity (when people can rejoice with singing and dancing)
【歌詠】to sing praises; to sing; to eulogize

十一畫

歎 1997
(嘆) ㄊㄢ tàn

to sigh in wonderment or lamentation; to exclaim

【歎氣】to sigh
【歎息】① to sigh in lamentation; to lament ② to exclaim ③ a sigh
【歎賞】to praise and admire
【歎爲觀止】the most magnificent sight of all; an unrivaled sight

歐 1998
ㄡ ōu

1. Europe; European 2. same as 嘔—to vomit 3. same as 毆—to beat 4. same as 謳—to sing 5. (electricity) ohm, the SI unit of electrical resistance 6. a Chinese family name

【歐美】Europe and America
【歐化】Europeanization
【歐洲】Europe
【歐洲共同市場】European Common Market (ECM)
【歐亞】Europe and Asia; Eurasia

十三畫

歛 1999 ㄌㄧㄢˇ liǎn

1. to collect; to gather 2. to hold together 3. to deduct; to subtract 4. to desire; to ask for something

十四畫

歟 2000 ㄩˊ yú

a final particle indicating doubt, surprise, exclamation, etc.

十八畫

歡 2001 ㄏㄨㄢ huān

1. pleased; glad; jubilant 2. pleasures; joys 3. a lover 4. in full swing; active and energetic; quick

【歡度佳節】to celebrate a festival with jubilation
【歡天喜地】overjoyed
【歡樂】joy; happiness; gaiety
【歡呼】to cheer with jubilation; to hurrah
【歡聚】①a happy reunion; a joyful meeting ②to gather together happily
【歡喜】joyful; happy
【歡笑】cheer and laughter—great joy; jubilation
【歡心】(to win another's) favor or heart; love
【歡欣鼓舞】to be overjoyed; to be filled with exultation
【歡聲雷動】to cheer thunderously; roaring applause
【歡送】to send off; to give a farewell party
【歡顏】happy looks or appearances
【歡迎】to welcome; a welcome

止部 ㄓˇ zhǐ

止 2002 ㄓˇ zhǐ

1. to stop; to desist; to still 2. to rest in; to stay 3. deportment 4. to detain 5. to prohibit 6. to come to; to arrive at 7. still; calm; stagnant 8. only

【止步】to stop; to go no further
【止付】to stop payment
【止痛】to stop pain; to kill pain
【止痛藥】the painkiller; the anodyne
【止咳】to stop coughing
【止渴】to quench thirst
【止血】to stop bleeding or hemorrhage
【止瀉】to stop diarrhea
【止住】to stop; to halt; to desist
【止癢】to stop or alleviate itching

一畫

正 2003 1. ㄓㄥˋ zhèng

1. the obverse side; the right side 2. appropriate; proper 3. formal 4. to rectify; to correct 5. pure; not contaminated 6. straightforward and unbending; honest and virtuous 7. the person in charge; the person in command; the principal (as against the secondary) 8. to mete out punishment for a criminal 9. original (texts, etc.) 10. exactly; just; right 11. positively 12. main; principal 13. sharp; punctually 14. just; unbiased

【正本】the original copy
【正本清源】to overhaul thoroughly
【正比 or 正比例】direct proportion
【正步】the goose step; the parade step
【正派】honest, proper and straightforward; virtuous
【正門】the front door; the main entrance
【正面】the right side; the obverse side; the head (of a coin)
【正法】①the proper law or rule ②to execute (a death convict); execution
【正方形】(geometry) a square
【正負】positive and negative

1. to pass; to elapse 2. to undergo; to go through; to experience 3. things or duration that had come to pass 4. all previous (occasions, sessions); what has taken place 5. through; throughout; successive 6. to last (a certain period of time)

【歷代】successive generations; the dynasties in their successive order

【歷年】in the years past

【歷來】hitherto; till now; heretofore

【歷覽】to travel and see; to visit

【歷歷如繪】vividly; distinctly

【歷歷在目】as if it were taking place right before one's eyes; vividly

【歷練】to practice and experience

【歷劫】to experience many mishaps and misfortunes

【歷屆】successive (or all) previous

【歷久不衰】long-lasting

【歷久彌堅】to remain unshakable and become even firmer as time goes by

【歷盡艱難】to have gone through all kinds of hardships and difficulties

【歷經】to have experienced, undergone or encountered many times

【歷險】to undergo or experience adventures and dangers

【歷程】process; course

【歷時】to last (a certain period of time)

【歷史】history

【歷史家】a historian

【歷任】to have held the following posts

十四畫

歸 2011 ㄍㄨㄟ guī

1. to come back; to return 2. to return (something to its owner) 3. (said of a woman) to marry 4. to pledge allegiance to 5. to belong; to attribute 6. to turn over to; to put in somebody's charge 7. a Chinese family name

【歸併】to merge into; to unite with; to put together

【歸附】to pledge allegiance to

【歸檔】to return (a document, materials, etc.) back to file; to file away

【歸隊】to return to the ranks

【歸天 or 歸西】to pass away

【歸途】on the way home

【歸納】to induct (a theory, natural law, etc.); to sum up

【歸寧】(said of a woman) to visit her parents after marriage

【歸類】to categorize; to classify

【歸根結底】fundamentally; basically

【歸功於】to attribute the success to

【歸化】① to be naturalized as a citizen ②(said of a protectorate state, etc.) to pledge allegiance to

【歸還】to return (something to its owner)

【歸結】to sum up

【歸咎】to lay the blame on...; to impute

【歸期】the date of one's return

【歸僑】returned overseas Chinese

【歸心似箭】to be anxious or eager to return home

【歸向】① the direction of movement ② to turn toward; to incline to

【歸程】the homeward journey

【歸屬】① ownership ② to belong

【歸順】to yield; to submit; to surrender

【歸入】to classify; to include

【歸葬】to bring back one's remains home for burial

【歸罪】to lay the blame on another

【歸宿】① a home to return to ② (said of a woman) marriage ③ conclusions

【歸案】to arrest a criminal and bring him to court for prosecution

【歸隱】to retire; retirement

【歸於】to belong to; to be attributed to

歹 部
ㄉㄞˇ dǎi

歹 2012

1. ㄉㄞˇ dǎi evil; vicious; bad; wicked; depraved; crooked

【歹毒】vicious; malicious; malice

【歹徒】hoodlums; ruffians; scoundrels

【歹念】evil thoughts

【歹意】malicious intent; bad intentions

歹 2012
2. (歹) ㄜ è (now rarely) the remains of a person

二畫

死 2013
ㄙˇ sǐ
1. to die; to die for; dead; death 2. used as an intensive or superlative; very; extremely 3. condemned (persons whose lives are numbered, as criminals on the death row) 4. inanimate; dull and stupid; inert; insensible; lifeless 5. obstinate or stubborn; persevering; resolute; resolutely 6. rigid, fixed or unchangeable (regulations, etc.); immovable (drawers, etc.) 7. impassable; closed

【死板】wooden (persons); rigid (regulations); fixed and unchangeable (methods, etc.)
【死別】to be parted by death; death-partings
【死不瞑目】to be unwilling to die (because of some unfinished tasks, unfulfilled wishes, intensive grudges, etc.)
【死不認錯】stubbornly refuse to admit one's guilt or mistake
【死不足惜】Death is not to be regretted (if it serves a purpose).
【死皮賴臉 or 死不要臉】brazen-faced and unreasonable
【死得其所】to die a worthy death
【死黨】sworn confederates; sworn followers
【死讀書】to read (a book) without thinking
【死對頭】arch enemies or rivals
【死腦筋】a one-track mind
【死裏逃生】to escape death by a narrow margin
【死路】①a blind alley; a dead end ②a fatal route
【死路一條】no way out; doomed
【死後】after death; postmortem
【死活】dead or alive
【死火山】an extinct volcano
【死灰復燃】(said of emotion, especially love, crushed rebellious force, dormant ideas, etc.) rekindled; rejuvenated
【死寂】deathly stillness
【死記】to memorize by rote
【死勁兒】all one's strength
【死結】① a fast knot (as opposed to slip knots) ② an impasse
【死角】a dead angle; the defiladed space
【死期】the time of death; the hour of doom
【死氣沉沉】hopeless and gloomy; a dead atmosphere
【死囚】a death convict
【死去活來】half dead
【死心】to think no more of something
【死心塌地】wholeheartedly; unreservedly
【死心眼兒】obstinate and simple-minded
【死巷 or 死胡同】a dead-end alley
【死刑】a death penalty
【死訊】news of someone's death
【死者】the dead; the deceased
【死屍】a corpse
【死守】to defend (a position, city, etc.) to the last
【死傷】the dead and wounded
【死水】stagnant (or stagnating) water
【死人】a dead person
【死罪】the capital punishment
【死要面子】to try to preserve one's face at all costs
【死有餘辜】Death will not expiate all his crimes.
【死因】the cause of death
【死硬派】diehards
【死無對證】to lack evidence because of the death of a principal witness
【死無葬身之地】to die without a place for burial (a phrase usually used as a warning to somebody)
【死亡】to die; death
【死亡率】death rate; mortality
【死亡證書】a death certificate
【死於非命】to die an unnatural death

四畫

歿 2014
(殁) ㄇㄛˋ mò
to die; death
【歿世不忘】shall never forget

殀 2015
ㄧㄠˇ yǎo
1. to die young or untimely 2. to be wronged or aggrieved

五畫

殆 2016 ㄉㄞˋ dài
1. precarious; dangerous; danger; perilous 2. tired 3. afraid 4. nearly; almost 5. only; merely; even
【殆已無望】nearly hopeless

殄 2017 ㄊㄧㄢˇ tiǎn
1. to end; to terminate 2. to exterminate; to extirpate; to weed out; to wipe out 3. to waste
【殄滅】to exterminate thoroughly; to extirpate

殃 2018 ㄧㄤ yāng
1. disaster; misfortune; calamities 2. the return of the spirit of the deceased
【殃及池魚】to cause trouble or bring disaster to innocent people
【殃及無辜】Trouble involves the innocent people.

殂 2019 ㄘㄨˊ cú
to die; dead; death
【殂沒】to die; to perish; death
【殂落 or 殂謝】to pass away; to demise

六畫

殉 2020 ㄒㄩㄣˋ xùn
1. to die for a cause 2. (originally) to be buried with the dead (usually said of slaves, loyal servants, concubines, etc.)
【殉道】to die for the right cause; to die a marty's death
【殉道者】a martyr
【殉國】to die for one's country
【殉情】to die for love
【殉職】to die while performing one's work

殊 2021 ㄕㄨ shū
1. different; special; strange 2. distinguished; outstanding 3. extremely; very 4. really; indeed 5. still; yet 6. exceed; over
【殊途同歸】to reach the same destination (or goal) by different routes
【殊寵】special favor
【殊榮】special honors
【殊死戰】a life-or-death battle
【殊異】special; extraordinary

八畫

殖 2022 ㄓˊ zhí
1. to grow in abundance; to prosper 2. to plant 3. to become wealthy 4. to colonize; colonization
【殖民】to colonize
【殖民地】a colony

殘 2023 ㄘㄢˊ cán
1. to destroy; to injure; to damage; to spoil 2. to wither 3. cruel and fierce; heartless and relentless 4. crippled; disfigured 5. remnants or residues; the little amount of something left 6. incomplete 7. to kill
【殘暴】cruel and heartless
【殘兵敗將】the remnants of a defeated army
【殘破】①damaged; dilapidated ② not complete; deficient
【殘廢】crippled, maimed, or disabled
【殘留】to remain; to be left over
【殘羹剩飯】the remains of a meal; leftovers
【殘酷】cruelty; heartlessness; cold-bloodedness; savagery
【殘骸】① incomplete remains ② the wreckage (of an airplane, ship or truck)
【殘害】to oppress cruelly; to injure heartlessly; to slaughter
【殘花敗柳】fallen angels; prostitutes
【殘疾】physical deformity
【殘局】① the aftermath of war, revolution or great upheaval ② an unfinished chess game
【殘缺 or 殘闕】incomplete; fragmentary
【殘殺】to massacre; to slaughter
【殘生】one's remaining years
【殘忍】cruel; heartless; brutal; savage
【殘存】surviving
【殘而不廢】disabled but useful
【殘餘】remnants; survivals; remains

十畫

殞 2024 ㄩㄣˇ yǔn
1. to die; to perish 2. same as 隕—to fall
【殞沒 or 殞命】to perish; to die

【殞落 or 殞墜】 to fall
【殞石】 a meteorite

十一畫

〔歹部〕

殤 2025
ㄕㄤ shāng
1. to die young; to die prematurely 2. national mourning

十二畫

殫 2026
ㄉㄢ dān
to use up; to exhaust
【殫精竭慮】 to devote one's entire energy and thought

十三畫

殭 2027
ㄐㄧㄤ jiāng
dead and stiff
【殭尸or殭屍】 a vampire; a reanimated corpse
【殭硬】 stiff

殮 2028
ㄌㄧㄢˋ liàn
to prepare a body for the coffin; to encoffin
【殮埋 or 殮葬】 to shroud and bury

十四畫

殯 2029
ㄅㄧㄣˋ bìn
1. to lay a coffin in a memorial hall 2. to carry to the grave
【殯殮】 a funeral
【殯車】 a hearse
【殯儀館】 a funeral parlor

十七畫

殲 2030
ㄐㄧㄢ jiān
to annihilate; to exterminate; to destroy
【殲滅】 to annihilate; to wipe out
【殲敵】 to destroy the enemy

殳部
ㄕㄨ shū

五畫

段 2031
ㄉㄨㄢˋ duàn
1. a section; a division; a part; a paragraph 2. a stage
【段落】 ① end (of a paragraph, stage, etc.) ② a paragraph

六畫

殷 2032
1. ㄧㄣ yīn
1. flourishing; prosperous 2. polite; courteous 3. sad; sorrowful 4. eager; eagerly 5. an alternative name for the latter half of the Shang (商) Dynasty
【殷富】 wealthy; prosperous; well-off
【殷切】 ardent; eager
【殷勤 or 慇懃】 courteous; polite; civil
【殷盛】 thriving; flourishing; prosperous; abundant

殷 2032
2. ㄧㄢ yān
as in 殷紅—dark red

七畫

殺 2033
1. ㄕㄚ shā
1. to kill; to put to death; to slaughter 2. extremely; exceedingly 3. to weaken; to deflate 4. to fight
【殺風景】 to spoil or ruin happiness
【殺敵】 to fight the enemy
【殺頭】 to behead
【殺退】 to put to flight; to rout
【殺戮】 to kill; to slay
【殺掠】 to kill and plunder
【殺害】 to murder; to kill
【殺雞警猴】 to punish somebody as a warning to others
【殺雞取卵】 to kill the hen to get eggs—a very foolish act
【殺價】 to reduce prices; to cut price down
【殺氣】 ① (said of a sight or scene) a very severe or chilling appearance ② a murderous atmosphere
【殺蟲劑】 the insecticide
【殺手】 a hit man; a killer
【殺身之禍】 a fatal disaster
【殺身成仁】 to sacrifice one's own life for justice
【殺傷】 to kill and wound
【殺生】 killing

【殺人】 to kill a person; to murder
【殺人不眨眼】 cold-blooded, hard-hearted, or very cruel
【殺人犯】 a murderer; a homicide
【殺人如麻】 to have killed many people
【殺人罪】 homicide; murder
【殺人未遂】 an attempted murder
【殺人越貨】 to kill and rob

殺 2033
2. ㄕㄞˋ shài
to degrade; to decline; to diminish; to abate

八畫

殼 2034
(殻、壳) ㄑㄩㄝˋ què
(又讀 ㄎㄜˊ ké)
(語音 ㄑㄧㄠˋ qiào)
shells; husks; coverings

殽 2035
ㄧㄠˊ yáo
1. confusion; disorder; mess 2. dishes
【殽亂】 disorderly; confused; messy

九畫

殿 2036
ㄉㄧㄢˋ diàn
1. a palace; a palace hall; a temple; a sanctuary 2. the rear; the rear guard
【殿堂or殿宇】 a palace; a sanctuary
【殿後】 the rear, or rear guard (of marching troops)
【殿軍】 ①the rear guard (of marching troops) ② the last-placed winner in a contest
【殿下】 Your, His, or Her Highness

毀 2037
ㄏㄨㄟˇ huǐ
1. to destroy; to ruin; to damage; to injure 2. to libel; to slander; to abuse; to revile; to defame
【毀謗or毀詆】 to libel; to slander; to malign
【毀滅】 to demolish; to ruin; to destroy
【毀壞】 to destroy; to injure; to damage
【毀棄】 to abrogate; to repeal; to dissolve; to annul; to rescind
【毀容】 to disfigure
【毀損】 to damage; to injure; to disfigure
【毀於一旦】 to be ruined or destroyed in one day
【毀譽參半】 to draw both praises and criticisms
【毀約】 to break one's promise

十一畫

毅 2038
ㄧˋ yì
firm; resolute; endurance; fortitude
【毅力】 perseverance; indomitability
【毅然】 firmly; courageously

毆 2039
ㄡ ōu
to beat; to hit; a blow
【毆打】 to fisticuff
【毆傷】 to injure by beating

毋部
ㄨˊ wú

毋 2040
ㄨˊ wú
(imperative) do not; no
【毋寧】 rather... (than); (not so much...) as
【毋需】 do not need
【毋庸】 need not
【毋庸諱言】 There's no need for reticence.

一畫

母 2041
ㄇㄨˇ mǔ
1. one's mother 2. mother—(figuratively) the origin 3. female
【母馬】 a mare
【母牛】 a cow
【母老虎】 ① a shrew; a termagant ② a tigress
【母鹿】 a roe deer; a roe
【母狗】 a bitch
【母雞】 a hen
【母姊會】 a mother-sister conference
【母親】 mother
【母親節】 Mother's Day
【母校】 one's alma mater; Alma Mater
【母豬】 a sow
【母獅】 a lioness
【母子】 ① mother and son ② principal and interest
【母愛】 maternal love
【母夜叉】 ① an ugly female devil ② an ugly and fierce woman
【母音】 a vowel

毋部

【母語】① one's native language ② a parent language

三畫

每 2042 ㄇㄟˇ měi

every; each; per

【每每】 repeatedly; often
【每逢】 every time or whenever
【每當】 whenever; every time
【每天 or 每日】 every day; daily
【每年】 every year; annually; yearly
【每隔】 every (three hours, five days, two feet, etc.)
【每下愈況 or 每況愈下】 getting worse and worse
【每處】 everywhere
【每人】 everybody; everyone; each one
【每次】 every time; each time
【每月】 every month; monthly

四畫

毒 2043 ㄉㄨˊ dú

1. poison; toxins 2. poisonous; noxious 3. to poison

【毒品】 narcotic drugs; narcotics
【毒罵】 to scold ferociouly and maliciously; to revil
【毒打】 to beat cruelly or savagely
【毒辣】 cruel; malicious; spiteful
【毒瘤】 cancer growth
【毒害】 to injure atrociously; to murder
【毒計】 a malicious scheme
【毒氣】 poisonous gas; noxious gas
【毒刑】 cruel punishment; brutal torture
【毒性】 toxicity; poisonousness
【毒蟲】 a poisonous insect
【毒殺 or 毒死 or 毒斃】 to poison to death
【毒蛇 or 毒虺】 a venomous snake
【毒手】 a murderous scheme (or hand)
【毒刺】 a poisonous prick
【毒餌】 poison bait
【毒牙】 a poison fang
【毒藥】 poisonous drugs; poison

比部 ㄅㄧˇ bǐ

比 2044 1. ㄅㄧˇ bǐ

1. to compare with 2. to liken; to compare to 3. to compete 4. than 5. to

【比不上】 to be inferior to
【比目魚】 a flatfish; a sole
【比方說】 for example; for instance
【比對】 to collate
【比擬】 ① to liken; to compare to ②a parallel
【比例】 ratio; proportion
【比例尺】 scale (of a map, model, etc.)
【比率】 ratio; proportion
【比畫】 ①to gesticulate; to gesture 亦作「比手畫脚」 ②to come to blows
【比基尼泳裝】 bikini
【比價】 to compare prices or bids
【比較】 ① comparative; relatively ②to compare
【比較級】(grammar) the comparative degree
【比値】 specific value; ratio
【比照】 according to; in the light of
【比重】 specific gravity
【比試】 ① have a competition ② to measure with one's hand or arm
【比如】 such as; like
【比賽】 a contest; a match; a tournament
【比翼雙飛】 to fly side by side
【比喻】 ①a metaphor; a simile ② to compare to; to liken

比 2044 2. ㄅㄧˋ bì

1. close; near; neighboring 2. to stand side by side

【比比皆是】 to be found or seen everywhere—very common
【比鄰】 close neighbors
【比肩作戰】 to fight shoulder to shoulder

五畫

毗 2045 ㄆㄧˊ pí

1. to assist 2. to adjoin

【毗連】 (said of lands) adjacent to

毛部 ㄇㄠˊ máo

毛 2046 ㄇㄠˊ máo

1. hair; fur; feathers; down 2.

vegetation 3. ten cents; a dime 4. gross; untouched; unpolished 5. flurried; panicstricken; scared 6. very young; little 7. a Chinese family name
【毛筆】a writing brush; a hair pencil
【毛病】① fault; defects; shortcoming; blemish ② trouble; disorder ③ disease; illness
【毛皮】fur; pelt
【毛毛蟲】a caterpillar 亦作「毛蟲」
【毛毛雨】drizzle
【毛毯】a woolen blanket
【毛料】woolen material
【毛骨悚然】to shudder with fear; to be horror-stricken
【毛孔】pores (of the skin)
【毛巾】a towel
【毛細管】a capillary tube; a capillary
【毛線】woolen yarn; knitting wool
【毛線衣】a sweater; wool
【毛織物 or 毛織品】woolen textiles
【毛氈】① a woolen carpet ② felt
【毛手毛脚】① restless; uneasy ② to take liberties with a woman by the actions of one's hands
【毛茸茸】hairy; downy
【毛躁】①irritable ②rash and restless
【毛遂自薦】to recommend oneself
【毛衣】woolen sweaters; sweaters
【毛襪】woolen stockings

七畫

毫 2047 ㄏㄠˊ háo
1. fine hair 2. a measure of length 3. a writing brush 4. a dime 5. a measure of weight
【毫不 or 毫無】not at all; not in the least
【毫不相干】totally unrelated
【毫不在乎】do not mind or care at all
【毫米】millimeter (mm.)
【毫髮】extremely little
【毫釐】extremely small space; an iota
【毫克】milligram (mg.)
【毫升】milliliter (ml.)
【毫無價值】good for nothing
【毫無疑問】There is no doubt.

八畫

毯 2048 ㄊㄢˇ tǎn
a rug; a carpet; a blanket

九畫

毽 2049 ㄐㄧㄢˋ jiàn
as in 毽子 or 毽兒—a shuttlecock

十三畫

氈 2050 (毡、氊) ㄓㄢ zhān
1. felt 2. a blanket
【氈帽】a felt cap or hat

氏 部
ㄕˋ shì

氏 2051 1. ㄕˋ shì
1. family name; surname 2. a character placed after a married woman's maiden name; née 3. the title of a government position in former times
【氏族】a family; a clan

氏 2051 2. ㄓ zhī
name of an ancient barbarian tribe

一畫

氐 2052 1. ㄉㄧ dī
1. name of an ancient barbarian tribe to the west 2. same as 低—low

氐 2052 2. ㄉㄧˇ dǐ
1. foundation 2. same as 抵—on the whole

民 2053 ㄇㄧㄣˊ mín
1. the people; the subject; the populace; the public 2. civilians 3. a Chinese family name
【民胞物與】to be kind to people and animals
【民兵】① a militiaman ② a militia force
【民不聊生】The people cannot live in peace.
【民法】the civil law; the civil code
【民房】a civilian house
【民風】popular customs
【民歌】a folk song; a ballad
【民航機】an airliner; a civil air-

plane (or aircraft)
【民航局】Civil Aeronautics Administration (CAA)
【民間】among the people
【民情】the condition of the people
【民權】civil rights; people's rights
【民窮財盡】The means of the people have been used up
【民心】popular sentiments; popular support
【民選】popularly elected
【民脂民膏】the hard-own possessions of the people
【民治】government by the people
【民主】democratic; democracy
【民主黨】Democratic Party (of the United States)
【民主政治】democracy
【民主主義】democratism
【民主潮流】the tide of democracy
【民衆】the people; the multitude; the masses; the populace
【民衆團體】a civic organization
【民生】the people's livelihood
【民生物資】daily necessities
【民生問題】problems of the people's livelihood
【民族】a nation; a people
【民族性】national character
【民族意識】national consciousness
【民族英雄】a national hero
【民族舞蹈】race dance
【民俗】folkways
【民意】public opinion; popular sentiments
【民意代表】people's representatives
【民意機關】the people's representative body
【民意測驗】a poll; polltaking
【民謠】a folk song
【民營】privately owned
【民怨沸騰】Discontent among the people is boiling.
【民運】①civil transport ②democratic movement

〔气部〕

四畫

氓 2054
1.（甿）ㄇㄥˊ méng
the people; the populace
【氓隸】people who are engaged in laborious work

氓 2054
2. ㄇㄤˊ máng
a rascal; a vagabond

气部
ㄑㄧˋ qì

四畫

氛 2055
ㄈㄣ fēn
air; atmosphere; prevailing mood

五畫

氟 2056
ㄈㄨˊ fú
fluorine
【氟化物】(chemistry) fluoride

六畫

氣 2057
ㄑㄧˋ qì
1. air; gas; vapor; the atmosphere 2. breath 3. spirit; morale 4. influence 5. bearing; manner 6. smells; odors 7. to be angry; to be indignant; rage; anger 8. to provoke; to goad; to make angry; to annoy 9. weather
【氣魄】spirit; vigor; moral strength
【氣派】a dignified air
【氣泡】air bubbles
【氣氛】atmosphere; mood
【氣忿 or 氣憤】to be angry, furious, enraged or indignant
【氣度】① spirit; air; bearing ② capacity for tolerance
【氣頭兒上】right in the middle of one's fit of rage
【氣體】gas; the gaseous body; vapor
【氣團】a mass of cold or hot air
【氣筒】an air pump; an inflator
【氣餒】despondent; crestfallen
【氣惱】to be sulky; to be sullen
【氣流】an airflow; an air current
【氣量大】magnanimous; generous
【氣量小】narrow-minded
【氣概】spirit; air; bearing; manner
【氣管】trachea; windpipe
【氣管炎】tracheitis
【氣功】(Chinese boxing) a system of deep breathing exercises
【氣孔】pores (on the skin); stomas

(on a leaf); the spiracle or blowhole (of a whale); vesicles (of the igneous rock)
【氣候】① climate; weather ② situations
【氣化】to evaporate; to vaporize
【氣昏了】to be driven mad by anger
【氣急敗壞】desperate and low-spirited
【氣絕】to breathe one's last
【氣球】a balloon
【氣息】breath
【氣象】① weather; climates ② atmosphere
【氣象報告 or 氣象預報】a weather forecast
【氣象臺】a weather station
【氣象局】a weather bureau
【氣象萬千】Nature abounds in changes.
【氣質】dispositions; temperament
【氣喘】① to pant; to gasp ② asthma
【氣喘如牛】to pant like an ox
【氣冲冲】furious; to fly into a rage
【氣勢】vehemence; fervor
【氣勢磅礴】of great momentum
【氣數 or 氣運】destiny; fate; fortune
【氣死人】infuriating; exasperating
【氣色】complexion; color
【氣壓】air pressure
【氣味】smacks; smells; odors
【氣味相投】having the same tastes and temperament; congenial
【氣溫】the temperature
【氣宇軒昂】dignified; exalted

氤 2058 ㄧㄣ yin
the spirit of harmony (between heaven and earth)
【氤氳】① the spirit of harmony (between heaven and earth) ② misty; dense ③ the spirit of vigor or prosperity

氧 2059 ㄧㄤˇ yǎng
oxygen
【氧化】to oxidize or be oxidized; oxidation
【氧化物】the oxide

七畫

氫 2060 ㄑㄧㄥ qing
hydrogen: 氫化物 the hydride
【氫彈】hydrogen bombs

八畫

氯 2061 ㄌㄩˋ lù
chlorine
【氯化鈉】sodium chloride

氮 2062 ㄉㄢˋ dàn
nitrogen

水部 ㄕㄨㄟˇ shuǐ

水 2063 ㄕㄨㄟˇ shuǐ
1. water 2. a general term for seas, lakes, rivers, etc. 3. liquid; juice 4. flood disaster; flood 5. a Chinese family name
【水壩】a dam
【水濱 or 水邊 or 水畔】the shore
【水波】ripples of water
【水泡 or 水皰】① a bubble ② a blister
【水盆】a basin
【水平】horizontal
【水瓶座】(astrology) Aquarius (or Water Carrier)
【水門 or 水閘】a sluice gate; a floodgate
【水蜜桃】a honey peach
【水面】the water surface; the water level
【水母】*Aurelia aurita*, a jellyfish
【水分】moisture; water content
【水道 or 水路】① a watercourse; a waterway ② (by) water
【水稻】aquatic rice (as opposed to hill rice)
【水到渠成】The thing takes care of itself.
【水痘】chicken pox; varicella
【水滴】water drops
【水底】at the bottom of water
【水電】water and electricity
【水電費】charges for water and electricity
【水塔】a water tower
【水獺】an otter (*Lutra lutra*)
【水潭 or 水塘】a pool; a pond
【水土保持】soil conservation
【水土不服】one's system disagreeing with a new natural environment
【水桶】a bucket; a pail
【水泥】cement

水部

【水鳥】 water birds; waterfowls
【水牛】 a water buffalo
【水來土掩】 to attempt to stop any onslaught
【水雷】 a mine (against the ship)
【水力】 water power
【水力發電】 hydraulic power generation
【水力發電廠】 a hydraulic power plant
【水利】 water conservancy
【水利工程】 hydraulic engineering
【水流】 water current; water flow
【水量】 water volume; amount of water
【水陸】 land and water
【水落石出】 The truth comes into light eventually.
【水龍頭】 a faucet; a cock; a tap
【水溝】 a ditch; a drain; a gutter
【水缸】 a large pottery jug for holding water
【水果】 fruit
【水鬼】① a water goblin ② (slang) a frogman
【水管】 a water pipe
【水坑】 a water hole; a pool
【水庫】 a reservoir
【水壺】 a canteen
【水花】 foam; froth; spray
【水火不相容】 Water and fire can not coexist. —(figuratively) incompatible
【水患】 floods; flood disaster
【水餃兒】 Chinese ravioli; boiled dumplings
【水酒】 diluted wine
【水晶】 crystal; crystallized quartz
【水晶體】 ①(anatomy) the lens (of eyes) ② the crystalline lens
【水晶球】 a crystal ball
【水井】 a well
【水軍】 (formerly) the navy; naval units
【水汽】 water vapor; moisture; steam
【水球】 (sports) water polo
【水槍】 a squirt gun
【水泄不通】 so crowded
【水仙花】 a narcissus; a daffodil
【水箱】 a water tank
【水星】 the planet Mercury
【水性楊花】(said of women) fickle and lascivious
【水質】 properties of particular specimens of water
【水蛭】 a leech
【水蒸氣】 water vapor; steam; vapor
【水準】 a standard; a level
【水中撈月】 to make obviously futile efforts
【水腫】 dropsy; hydrophilic swelling
【水池 or 水池子】 a pool; a pond
【水車】 ① a water wheel ② a water cart
【水產】 marine products
【水勢】 ① the flow of the water ② the direction of flowing water
【水手】 a sailor; a mariner
【水深】 the depth of water
【水深火熱】 an abyss of suffering
【水上人家】 boat dwellers
【水上運動】 water sports; aquatic sports
【水溶性】 solubility
【水災】 flood disaster; floods
【水族館】 an aquarium
【水彩】 watercolor
【水彩畫】 a watercolor painting; a watercolor
【水槽】 a water trough; a water tank
【水草】 ① waterweeds ② water and grass
【水鴨】 a teal
【水壓】 water pressure
【水銀】 mercury (an element)
【水銀燈】 a mercury lamp
【水汚染】 water pollution
【水位】 the water stage; the water level
【水汪汪的】(said of women's eyes) bright and attractive
【水域】 waters; a water area
【水源】 ① the riverhead; the waterhead ② a source of water
【水運】 transportation by water

一畫

永 2064 ㄩㄥˇ yǒng

long in time; everlasting; eternal; permanent
【永別】 to part for good; to die
【永不】 will never
【永不分離】 never to be separated
【永恒】 eternity; eternal; everlasting; perpetual
【永久】permanent; perpetual; eternal; lasting
【永訣】 to be gone forever—to die
【永誌不忘】 to remember forever
【永垂不朽】 immortal (accomplishment, fame, etc.)
【永世】 forever; eternity
【永生】 ① for ever ② eternal life
【永存】 to remain forever; to live for ever and ever

【永無寧日】Never will there be days of peace.
【永遠】forever; eternally; perpetually

二畫

氾 2065
ㄈㄢˋ fàn
1. to spread; to fill everywhere 2. extensive; vast; boundless 3. floating
【氾濫】① to overflow; in flood ② to spread far and wide
【氾論 or 汎論】general discussion

汁 2066
ㄓ zhī
juice; the natural fluid; sap

汀 2067
ㄊㄧㄥ tīng
1. a low, level land along a river 2. a shoal
【汀洲】an islet in a stream; a shoal

求 2068
ㄑㄧㄡˊ qiú
1. to ask for; to pray for; to beg 2. demand 3. to seek 4. to covet; to desire
【求貸】to ask for loan
【求和】to seek peace with an enemy
【求婚】to propose (to a woman)
【求解】① to seek help in distress ② to seek the solution to a mathematical problem
【求教】to seek instruction; to seek advice
【求救】to seek relief; to ask for rescue
【求見】to seek an interview
【求籤】to seek divine guidance by drawing lots
【求親】① to seek a marriage alliance ② to ask for help from relatives
【求情】to ask for mercy; to plead
【求全】① to seek a satisfactory result ② to try to preserve oneself
【求全責備】to criticize so that everything will become perfect
【求賢若渴】to seek talent with eagerness
【求學】to receive education; to study
【求知】to seek knowledge
【求知慾】a thirst (or craving) for knowledge
【求之不得】to be exactly what has been sought eagerly
【求職】positions wanted
【求證】to seek verification or confirmation
【求助】to resort to; to seek help
【求神問卜】to seek divine advice
【求生】to try to remain alive
【求勝】to strive for victory
【求饒】to ask for forgiveness; to seek pardon
【求人】① to ask for help ② to look for talents
【求仁得仁】to seek for virtue and get virtue—to want something and succeed in getting it
【求才】positions vacant
【求愛】to woo; to court
【求偶】to seek a spouse
【求援】to seek relief; to ask for help

三畫

汎 2069
ㄈㄢˋ fàn
1. afloat; to float 2. extensive; widespread
【汎舟】to row a boat; boating
【汎稱】generally called

汕 2070
ㄕㄢˋ shàn
a basket for catching fish

汐 2071
ㄒㄧˋ xì
the flow of the tide at night

汗 2072
1. ㄏㄢˋ hàn
sweat; perspiration
【汗馬功勞】distinguished services in war
【汗毛】down
【汗牛充棟】(said of books, etc.) overabundant; numerous
【汗流滿面】to perspire all over one's face
【汗流浹背】to perspire all over
【汗垢】sweat mixed with dirt
【汗巾】a girdle; a sash
【汗腺】a sweat gland
【汗衫】a T-shirt
【汗如雨下】to sweat profusely
【汗顏】to perspire from shame

汗 2072
2. ㄏㄢˊ hán
as in 可汗—a khan

池 2073
ㄔˊ chí
1. a pond; a pool; a moat 2. an

〔水部〕

enclosed space with raised sides
【池塘】 a pond
【池沼】 ponds and swamps
【池水】 pond water
【池子】 ① a pond ② orchestra stalls in a theater
【池鹽】 lake salt 「others
【池魚之殃】disasters brought on by

汝 2074
ㄖㄨˇ rǔ 「ral) ye; you
you; thou; thee; thy: 汝輩 (plu-

江 2075
ㄐㄧㄤ jiāng 「River
1. a large river 2. the Yangtze
【江畔】 the riverbank; beside the river 「literary talent or energy
【江郎才盡】 to have used up one's
【江輪】 a river steamship 「worse
【江河日下】 to go from bad to
【江湖】 ① rivers and lakes ② wandering; vagrant ③ sophisticated and shrewd ④ practicing quackery; a quack
【江西】 Kiangsi Province
【江心補漏】 to try to prevent a disaster when it is too late
【江山】 the mountains and rivers of a country—the land; the throne
【江山美人】 the throne and the beauty
【江山易改，本性難移】 Changing one's nature is harder than changing mountains and rivers.
【江蘇】 Kiangsu Province
【江洋大盜】 a notorious bandit ⌊leader

汛 2076
ㄒㄩㄣˋ xùn
1. to sprinkle 2. abundant water; a flood 3. menses; menstruation 「son
【汛期】 (irrigation) the flood sea-

汞 2077
ㄍㄨㄥˇ gǒng
(又讀 ㄏㄨㄥˋ hòng)
mercury (an element)

汚 2078
(汙、污) ㄨ wū
1. dirty; filthy 2. to stain; to mar 3. corrupt
【汚衊】 to libel; to slander
【汚點】 a blot; a stain; a smear; a
【汚泥】 mud ⌊defect; a flaw
【汚吏】 a corrupt official
【汚垢】 dirt; filth
【汚穢】 dirty; filthy 「filthy
【汚穢不堪】 intolerably dirty or
【汚濁】 muddy; dirty; foul; filthy
【汚水】 sewage; filthy water
【汚染】 to contaminate; to pollute
【汚辱】 ① to humiliate ② to rape
【汚損】 to stain and damage

四畫

汨 2079
ㄇㄧˋ mì 「ince
name of a river in Hunan Prov-

汩 2080
1. ㄍㄨˇ gǔ
1. to dredge (a channel, etc.) 2. confused; disorderly 3. the sound of waves
【汩沒】 to sink; to decline
【汩亂】 to cause disorder

汩 2080
2. ㄩˋ yù
rapid; fleeting: 汩流 rapids

汰 2081
ㄊㄞˋ tài 「nate; to remove
1. excessive 2. to sift; to elimi-
【汰揀】 to wash and polish

汪 2082
ㄨㄤ wāng
1. (said of water) deep and extensive 2. a puddle 3. (said of liquid) to soak; to collect; to accumulate 「the sea
【汪洋大海】 the vast expanse of
【汪汪】 ① (said of water) deep and extensive ② the barking of dogs; a bowwow ③ brimming with ⌊tears

汲 2083
ㄐㄧˊ jí
to draw water or liquid
【汲汲】 anxious; avid; restless(ly); to crave
【汲取】 to draw; to derive
【汲水】 to draw water
【汲引】 to employ people of talent

決 2084
(决) ㄐㄩㄝˊ jué
1. to decide; to conclude; to judge 2. (said of a dike) to burst; to break 3. certain; definite 4. to execute a person
【決不】 never 「ise
【決不食言】 never to break a prom-
【決非】 by no means; in no way
【決鬥 or 決鬪】 a duel; to fight a

duel

【決定】to determine; to decide

【決定權】the say; the power to make decisions

【決斷】to decide; to conclude; to make a decision

【決堤】the collapse of a dike

【決裂】① to burst open ② a rupture

【決口】a rupture; an opening

【決心】to make up one's mind; to resolve

【決選】a runoff (election)

【決戰】a decisive battle; to fight a decisive battle

【決勝】① certain to bring victory ② to decide a contest

【決然】resolutely; firmly

【決策】an adopted policy; a decision

【決死】life-and-death

【決賽】the final (of a contest, race, etc.)

【決算】a final financial statement

【決議】① a resolution (reached at a meeting) ② to decide; to resolve

【決無】never; by no means; impossible

沁 2085
ㄑㄧㄣˋ qìn

to soak; to seep; to percolate; to ooze; to exude

【沁人心脾】to affect people deeply

【沁入】to soak into; to permeate

沃 2086
ㄨㄛˋ wò

1. to irrigate 2. (said of land) fertile

【沃土】fertile land

【沃壤】fertile soil

【沃野千里】an endless expanse of fertile land

汽 2087
ㄑㄧˋ qì

gas; steam; vapor

【汽門】a steam valve

【汽笛】a steam whistle; a siren

【汽艇】a motorboat; a steam launch

【汽缸】cylinders (in automobiles, etc.)

【汽鍋】a (steam) boiler

【汽化】vaporization; to vaporize

【汽車】an automobile

【汽車電影院】a drive-in theater

【汽車旅館】a motel

【汽車工業】the auto industry

【汽車間】a garage

【汽船】a steamship; a steamboat; a steamer

【汽水(兒)】soda water; soft drinks or soda pop

【汽油】gasoline; gas

【汽油彈】① a napalm bomb ② a fire bomb or Molotov cocktail

沆 2088
1. ㄏㄤˊ háng

to ferry; a ferry

沆 2088
2. ㄏㄤˋ hàng

1. a vast expanse of water 2. mist 3. flowing

【沆瀣一氣】(to talk, think, etc.) in the same vein; the meeting of minds

沌 2089
ㄉㄨㄣˋ dùn

turbid; unclear; chaotic

沈 2090
1. (沉) ㄔㄣˊ chén

1. to sink; to submerge 2. to indulge in; to be addicted to 3. (said of sleep) deep; sound; fast 4. for a long time 5. delaying; postponement 6. heavy (in weight) 7. latent; hidden 8. to straighten (one's face); to put on a grave expression 9. to retain (one's composure); to restrain; to contain

【沈沒】to sink

【沈默】silence; silent; reticent

【沈默寡言】taciturn; reticent

【沈默是金】Silence is golden.

【沈悶】① depressed ② dull and heavy (atmosphere); hot and humid

【沈迷】to indulge in; to wallow in

【沈湎】to wallow in; to be abandoned (or given) to

【沈浮】① ups and downs in a person's life ② to follow or change with prevailing customs, practices, etc. ③(now rarely) very many

【沈甸甸的】①(said of swords, etc.) heavy and not easy to wield ② heavy ③ heavy (at heart); serious (looks)

【沈澱】to precipitate; to settle

【沈澱物】sediment

【沈痛】to be deeply grieved

【沈溺】to be imbibed or to indulge in

【沈落】to sink; to fall down

【沈淪】to drown and perish (in water, sins, etc.)

【沈寂】① newsless; traceless ②

quiet; silent ③ to lie low
【沈浸】① to permeate; to submerge; to be steeped in ② very erudite
【沈靜】calm; quiet; placid
【沈香(木)】aloeswood; eaglewood
【沈住氣】Steady (on)!
【沈著】calm and steady; composed
【沈重】① heavy (in weight) ② heavy (at heart); serious (looks) ③ calm, steady and graceful
【沈船】① a shipwreck ② to scuttle a ship
【沈睡】deep slumber; sound sleep
【沈醉】① dead-drunk ② to become intoxicated
【沈思】to ponder; to contemplate; to meditate
【沈吟】① to hesitate ② to ponder
【沈魚落雁】(said of women) extremely beautiful
【沈冤】an unredressed grievance or wrong of long standing

沈 2090 2. ㄕㄣˇ shěn
a Chinese family name

沐 2091 ㄇㄨˋ mù
1. to shampoo; to wash; to bathe; to cleanse 2. a holiday; a leave; to take a leave 3. to receive favor
【沐猴而冠】Clothes do not make the man.
【沐雨櫛風】to work and toil
【沐浴or沐洗】① to bathe ② to steep in or receive favor ③ to soak in

沖 2092 (冲) ㄔㄨㄥ chōng
1. to wash away; to rinse; to flush 2. to soar; to rise rapidly or shoot up 3. to pour water (to powder, etc.); to infuse 4. empty; void 5. to dash against; to clash with 6. childhood 7. to neutralize; to make void
【沖淡】① to dilute ② to play down ③ to make few demands on life
【沖天 or 沖霄】to shoot up to the sky
【沖開水】to pour boiled water on
【沖口而出】to blurt out
【沖昏頭腦】to turn someone's head; dizzy
【沖積】alluviation
【沖積扇】(geology) alluvial fan
【沖積物】sediment; deposit
【沖擊】to lash or pound against
【沖洗】① to flush ② (photography) to develop or process negatives
【沖撞】to offend (especially a superior, etc.)
【沖茶】to make tea
【沖刷】erosion; to scour; to wash out
【沖散】to disperse by the use of force

沙 2093 ㄕㄚ shā
1. sand; tiny gravel or pebbles 2. the land around water; a beach; a sandbank; a desert 3. to pick, select or sift 4. (said of fruit, especially melons) overripe 5. hoarse 6. sandy—not glossy or smooth; granular 7. a kind of clay for making utensils, etc.
【沙包】① sandbags ② a porcelain vessel shaped like a small jug
【沙漠】a desert
【沙漠之舟】the ship of the desert —the camel
【沙彌 or 沙僧】a Buddhist novice
【沙發】a sofa
【沙袋】sandbags
【沙丁魚】a sardine
【沙堆or沙丘】a sand dune; a sand hill
【沙灘】a sandbank; a sandy beach
【沙糖】crystal sugar; granular sugar
【沙土】sandy soil
【沙拉】salad
【沙拉醬】salad dressing
【沙拉油】salad oil
【沙漏】① an hourglass ② a sand filter
【沙礫】pebbles; gravel; grit
【沙龍】a salon
【沙鍋】① an earthenware cooking pot ② food cooked and served in such a pot
【沙坑】a sand pit
【沙皇】a czar or a tsar (of Russia)
【沙金】alluvial gold
【沙紙】sandpaper; emery paper
【沙洲】a shoal; a sand bar; a sandbank
【沙場】a battlefield
【沙石】① gravel ② sandstone
【沙士】sarsaparilla
【沙沙聲響】a rustle
【沙鷗】a sea gull
【沙啞】(said of the voice) hoarse; husky
【沙眼】trachoma
【沙烏地阿拉伯】Saudi Arabia
【沙文主義】chauvinism

沒 2094 1. ㄇㄛˋ mò
1. to sink; to submerge 2. to

overflow; to rise beyond 3. to disappear 4. to go into oblivion 5. none; exhausted 6. eliminated 7. completed finished 8. to take property away from another; to confiscate 9. to die

【沒沒無聞】unknown; nameless

【沒奈何】to have no alternative; cannot but (do)

【沒落】①to sink ②the decline (of an empire, etc.)

【沒齒難忘】to remember (a favor) as long as one lives

【沒收】to confiscate; confiscation

沒 2094 2. ㄇㄟˊ méi

1. none; nothing; no 2. not yet; negative

【沒把握】not sure; uncertain

【沒命】① with one's all-out effort ②to die; dead

【沒法兒 or 沒法子】no way out; no alternative (but...)

【沒大沒小】ill-mannered or rude to one's elders

【沒道理】unreasonable; not justified

【沒多少】not much; not many

【沒頭沒腦】(to utter, do, etc. something) all of a sudden; illogical

【沒了】①to disappear ② without

【沒來】to have not come

【沒來由】without any cause or reason; uncalled-for

【沒良心】without conscience

【沒骨氣】chicken-hearted

【沒規矩】inappropriate; impudent

【沒關係】It does not matter. 或 Never mind.

【沒勁兒】①to have no interest in, or desire for anything ② listless

【沒見過世面】unsophisticated; inexperienced and green

【沒見識】inexperienced and ignorant

【沒精打彩】listless; dispirited

【沒趣兒】① uninteresting ② rebuke; snub; rebuff

【沒心腸】no heart for

【沒心眼兒】①careless ②frank

【沒想到】unexpectedly; to have not thought about

【沒指望】hopeless

【沒志氣】without ambition

【沒轍】Nothing can be done about it.

【沒主意】to lose one's head; cannot make up one's mind

【沒種】cowardly

【沒出息】(said of persons) useless; good-for-nothing

【沒事(兒)】①all right; O.K. ② without anything to do

【沒事找事】① to ask for trouble ② to cavil

【沒甚麼】① Nothing! 或Never mind! ②not difficult, bad, etc.

【沒造化】unlucky; out of luck

【沒錯兒】① I'm quite sure. ② can't go wrong

【沒意思】weary; bored

【沒有】no; not; without

【沒胃口】① to have lost one's appetite ②to have no interest in something

【沒完】① continuous; without end ② There will be no end to this.

【沒王法】lawless; without justice

【沒用】useless; of no use

沚 2095 ㄓˇ zhǐ

a sandy islet in a stream; a small sandbank

沏 2096 1. ㄑㄧ qī

1. to infuse 2. (said of the flowing water) rapidly; turbulently

【沏茶】to infuse tea; to make tea

沏 2096 2. ㄑㄩ qū

to drench with water

沓 2097 ㄊㄚˋ tà

1. repeated; reiterated 2. joined or connected; piled up 3. lax 4. talkative

【沓沓】① lax ② chattering and talkative ③ running quickly

【沓雜】crowded and mixed; confused

沛 2098 ㄆㄟˋ pèi

1. copious; abundance; full of 2. quickly; rapidly; sudden 3. to fall prostrate 4. to reserve water for irrigation 5. tall; high; great

五畫

沫 2099 ㄇㄛˋ mò

1. tiny bubbles on the surface of water; froth; suds; lather 2. saliva

沮 2100 1. ㄐㄩ jū

name of a river in Shantung

水部

Province; name of a river in Shansi Province

〔水部〕

沮 2100
2. ㄐㄩˇ jǔ

1. to stop; to abate 2. to lose; to be defeated 3. to spoil; to injure; to destroy or damage

【沮喪】despondent; crestfallen; downcast

沮 2100
3. ㄐㄩˋ jù

as in 沮洳—damp, lowlying land

沸 2101
ㄈㄟˋ fèi

1. boiling (water, etc.) 2. to gush; bubbling up

【沸點】the boiling point

【沸騰】① boiling—when liquid turn to steam ② bubbling and boiling—unrest; seething

【沸水】boiling water

油 2102
ㄧㄡˊ yóu

1. a general name for oil, fat, grease, either animal or vegetable 2. anything in liquid form which is inflammable, as gasoline, etc. 3. to oil 4. to varnish; to paint 5. greasy 6. sly; polished and over-experienced 7. luxuriant; prospering; flourishing

【油布】oilcloth (used as a waterproof covering)

【油墨】printing ink

【油門】① a throttle ② an accelerator

【油豆腐】fried bean curd

【油燈】an oil lamp

【油頭粉面】pomaded hair and powdered face — descriptive of a frivolous youngster

【油條】① fritters of twisted dough—a Chinese specialty usually for breakfast ② a suave, well-oiled person, long on experience but short on sincerity

【油田】an oil field

【油桶】an oil drum

【油膩】(said of food) greasy; oily

【油料】petroleum, oil and lubricant (POL)

【油亮】glossy; shiny

【油輪】an oil tanker; a tanker; an oiler

【油膏】ointment

【油管】oil pipes; oil pipelines

【油礦】an oil field; oil deposit

【油畫】oil paintings

【油煎】to fry in oil or fat

【油井】an oil well

【油漆】① paint; varnish ② to paint

【油漆匠】an oil painter

【油腔滑調】suave and sly; glib

【油箱】a fuel tank

【油脂】① (chemistry) olein ② oil and grease; fats

【油紙】oilpaper

【油廠】① an oil refinery ② an oil extracting mill

【油船】a tanker

【油商】an oil dealer; an oilman

【油水兒】① the cream or essence of something ② side profit or outside gains in a deal—as kickbacks, etc.

【油然】① copious; luxuriant; flourishing ②(rarely) halting

【油然而生】(said of love, etc.) to well up

【油嘴滑舌】sweet and smooth words which are not backed by sincerity

【油菜】rape

【油層】an oil reservoir; an oil layer

【油煙】soot; lampblack

【油印】to mimeograph

【油印機】a mimeograph

【油污】greasy dirt

河 2103
ㄏㄜˊ hé

1. a general name for rivers, streams, and waterways 2. Ho, the Yellow River in northern China, 2,700 miles long

【河壩or河隄or河堤】embankments; levees; dikes

【河北】① north of the river ② Hopeh Province

【河邊】the riverside

【河濱 or 河畔 or 河岸】the riverbanks; the riverside; the waterfront

【河馬】a hippopotamus, or a hippo

【河道】the course of a river; a waterway

【河東獅吼】the display of shrewishness

【河豚】the globefish; a blowfish; a Puffer

【河南】Honan Province

【河流】streams, rivers or channels of water

【河溝】a brook

【河谷】a river valley

【河口】a river mouth; a stream outlet

【河漢】the Milky Way

【河清海晏】halcyon days; time of peace and prosperity

【河渠】 a reservoir; waterways
【河心】 the middle of a river
【河洲】 a sand bar or islet in a river
【河牀】 the riverbed; the floor of a river
【河山】 rivers and mountains—the territory of a country
【河山變色】 The situation of the land is greatly changed.
【河水不犯井水】 Everyone minds his own business.

沼 2104 ㄓㄠˇ zhǎo
a lake; a pond; a pool; a marsh
【沼氣】 marsh gas; methane
【沼澤】 a marsh; a swamp

沽 2105 ㄍㄨ gū
1. to buy 2. to sell 3. crude; inferior (quality) 4. (now rarely) negligent
【沽名釣譽】 to do something, not for the sake of achievement, but for the sake of fishing for a good reputation or fame
【沽酒】 ① to buy wine ② spirits or wine bought from stores

治 2106 ㄓˋ zhì (動詞讀音 ㄔˊ chí)
1. to administer; to control; to govern; to manage; to rule 2. to regulate; to harness (a river) 3. the seat of the local government 4. to treat (a disease); to cure 5. to study 6. to punish 7. peaceful and orderly
【治本】 to deal with (or cure) a trouble, etc. at the source
【治標】 to cope with the symptoms only
【治病】 to treat a disease or ailment
【治理】 ①to administer; to manage; to govern ②to harness; to regulate
【治療】 to treat or cure (a disease); therapy
【治亂】 order and disorder; peace and upheaval
【治亂興亡】 the rise and fall of a nation
【治國】 to govern a nation
【治績】 the merits or achievements of an administration
【治家】 to manage a household
【治學】 to devote oneself to learning
【治裝】 to pack or arrange one's baggage before taking a trip
【治產】 to manage property
【治世】 a time of peace and order as a result of enlightened government
【治事】 to transact business
【治罪】 to punish a criminal according to law
【治喪】 to manage a funeral
【治安】 public security
【治愈 or 治癒】 to succeed in curing a disease; to heal

沾 2107 ㄓㄢ zhān
1. to moisten; to wet 2. to tinge; to stain; to contaminate 3. to be imbued with; to be infected with 4. to benefit from 5. to touch
【沾邊】 ① to touch on (or upon) only lightly ② to be relevant
【沾光】 to benefit from the support or influence of someone
【沾襟】 to moisten sleeves with tears
【沾親帶故】 ① having personal connections, close or remote ② to rub off some glory on friends and relatives
【沾沾自喜】 smug and complacent
【沾濕】 ① to moisten; damp or wet ② steeped in; imbued with
【沾水】 to soak in water
【沾染】 to become addicted to (bad habits, practices, etc.)
【沾漬】 imbued with; to soak in

況 2108 (况) ㄎㄨㄤˋ kuàng
1. moreover; in addition; not to mention... 2. to compare; comparative 3. situations; conditions 4. to visit; to call on 5. a Chinese family name
【況且】 moreover; besides; furthermore

沿 2109 1. ㄧㄢˊ yán
1. to follow; to go along; along 2. to hand down; to continue 3. successive; continuous
【沿邊兒】 along the edge
【沿途】 along the way
【沿路】 along the road; along the way
【沿革】 vicissitudes or history (of a system, institution, etc.)
【沿河】 along the river
【沿海】 ①along the coast ②offshore
【沿海一帶】 in the seaboard region
【沿襲】 to follow the old or tradi-

〔水部〕

〔水部〕

tional (practices, customs, precedents, etc.)
【沿線】along a railway or highway
【沿著】to follow or go along...
【沿岸】along the coast of...; littoral
【沿用】to continue following the old practices, customs, etc.

沿 2109
2. ㄧㄢˋ yàn
the edge of something; the brim

泄 2110
1. ㄒㄧㄝˋ xiè
1. to leak out; to reveal 2. to vent 3. to scatter; to disperse
【泄憤】to vent one's anger
【泄漏or泄露】to leak out (secrets, etc.)
【泄恨】to vent one's hatred or anger
【泄水道】sluiceway

泄 2110
2. ㄧˋ yì
1. mild and easy 2. many; crowded
【泄沓】①garrulous and disorderly ②easygoing; lax in moral attitude

泊 2111
ㄅㄛˊ bó (又讀 ㄆㄛˋ pò)
1. to stay; to anchor a ship; to moor 2. to drift 3. tranquil and quiet 4. a lake; a body of water
【泊船】to moor a boat

泅 2112
ㄑㄧㄡˊ qiú
to swim: 泅渡 to swim across

泌 2113
1. ㄅㄧˋ bì
1. swift and easy gushing of water 2. name of a river in Honan Province

泌 2113
2. ㄇㄧˋ mì
to seep out; to excrete; to secrete
【泌尿科】the urological department
【泌尿器官】urinary organs

泓 2114
ㄏㄨㄥˊ hóng
1. clear, deep water; limpid water 2. the ancient name of a stream in Honan Province

法 2115
1. (灋) ㄈㄚˇ fǎ
1. an institution 2. law; regulations; rules; the statutes; legal 3. methods; ways of doing things 4. to pattern or model after; to emulate 5. (Buddhism) the "way"—doctrines, etc. 6. tricks; magic arts 7. expert or standard (calligraphy, painting, etc.) 8. penalty; punishment
【法部 or 法務部】the Ministry of Justice
【法碼】standard weights
【法門】the way, or method of learning something
【法典】①a code of laws; a statute book ② the scriptures of Buddhism
【法定】legal
【法定代理人】a legal representative
【法條】items or articles of law
【法庭】a law court; a tribunal
【法統】the system of justice
【法老】Pharaoh, title of an ancient Egyptian king
【法理】① the principle or theory of law ② the doctrines of Buddhism
【法令】a general term for laws and regulations
【法律】laws
【法律顧問】a legal advisor
【法律制裁】legal sanctions
【法律程序】legal procedure
【法規】laws and regulations
【法官】a judge (at court); a justice
【法號】the religious name of a Buddhist monk or nun
【法紀】law and discipline
【法警】① the judicial police ② a bailiff
【法學】the science of law
【法學博士】a Doctor of Laws (LL.D.)
【法學家】a jurist
【法治】rule of law
【法場】① an execution ground ② any place set aside for religious practices
【法師】① a salutation for a Buddhist monk ② a Taoist high priest
【法事】Buddhist rituals performed on special occasions
【法則】①a way or method; a pattern or model considered as a standard ②a formula in mathematics ③ an agreement which has the same binding force as law
【法案】a law; a statute
【法醫】an expert in forensic medicine employed by a court of law, such as a coroner
【法外施恩】to be lenient within the

limits of the law
【法網】 the dragnet or the arms of law
【法院】 a court of justice; a court of law

法 2115
2. ㄈㄚˊ fá
【法子】 a method; a way

法 2115
3. ㄈㄚ fǎ
a way, especially used in 沒法兒 "No way out."

法 2115
4. ㄈㄚˋ fà
1. the Frank 2. France; French
【法蘭西 or 法國】 France
【法蘭絨】 flannel
【法郎】 franc (a monetary unit of France)
【法文】 the French language
【法語】 the spoken French; French

泝 2116
ㄙㄨˋ sù
same as 溯—to go upstream or to trace up to the source
【泝流】to go against the current; to go upstream
【泝源】 to trace up to the source

泠 2117
ㄌㄧㄥˊ líng
1. clear sounds 2. mild and comfortable 3. same as 伶—a drama performer; an actor; an actress
【泠冽】 clear
【泠泠】 ① gurgling sound ② cool ③ clear and crisp sound

泛 2118
ㄈㄢˋ fàn
1. to float; to drift 2. not exact or precise; not practical 3. not sincere; not intimate 4. generally (speaking); as a whole; pan 5. to be suffused with
【泛泛之交】 a casual acquaintance
【泛濫成災】 a disaster caused by flooding waters
【泛指】 to generally indicate
【泛舟】 to row a boat; boating
【泛稱】 generally called...

波 2119
ㄅㄛ bō (又讀 ㄆㄛ pō)
1. waves; breakers 2. to undulate; undulation; to fluctuate; fluctuations 3. to affect; to involve; to implicate; to entangle
【波多黎各】 Puerto Rico
【波段】 a wave band
【波動】 ① undulation ② (said of prices) fluctuations
【波濤洶湧】 to billow—a term used figuratively to describe tumultuous situations
【波蘭】 Poland
【波瀾壯闊】 surging forward with great momentum
【波浪】 billows; breakers; waves
【波羅的海】 the Baltic Sea
【波及】 ① to affect; to involve ② (said of a fire) to engulf; to spread to
【波折】 twists and turns of a matter; obstructions or obstacles
【波斯貓】 a Persian cat
【波斯菊】 coreopsis
【波斯灣】 the Persian Gulf

泣 2120
ㄑㄧˋ qì
to weep; to come to tears without crying
【泣血】 to weep blood (an expression used especially after one's name in a mourning notice for one's parents)
【泣訴】 to tell one's sorrows or grievances in tears

泡 2121
1. ㄆㄠˋ pào
1. bubbles; suds; froth; foam 2. a blister 3. to steep; to soak; to dip; to infuse (tea, etc.) 4. (slang) to dawdle; to fool around (especially with women)
【泡泡糖】 bubble gum
【泡沫】 suds; foam; froth
【泡湯】 ① to make soup by infusing in hot water ②(said of a dream) busted; (said of money) wasted; (said of hope) dashed
【泡茶】 to infuse tea; to make tea
【泡水】 to soak in water
【泡菜】 vegetables preserved in salted water
【泡影】 the shadow of bubbles—unreality

泡 2121
2. ㄆㄠ pāo
1. loose and soft; spongy 2. an amount of excrement or urine

泥 2122
1. ㄋㄧˊ ní
1. mud; mire; earth; soil; clay 2. to paste; to plaster 3. mashed vegetables or fruit; paste
【泥巴 or 泥土】 mud; clay; earth; soil
【泥淖】 mud; quagmires

〔水部〕

〔水部〕

【泥濘】 muddy
【泥漿】 mire
【泥鰍 or 泥鰌】 a loach; a mudfish
【泥沼】 mire; swamp; morasses
【泥磚】 sun-dried mud bricks
【泥沙】 ① mud and sand; silt ② something worthless
【泥水匠】 a bricklayer; a plasterer
【泥塑】 a clay sculpture
【泥娃娃】 a clay doll

泥 2122
2. ㄋㄧˋ nì
1. to be tied down by conventions, old practices; very conservative 2. to request with sweet words 3. inapplicable
【泥古】 to stick to ancient ways 「and thoughts」

泯 2123
ㄇㄧㄣˇ mǐn
to destroy; to eliminate; to put an end to; to vanish 「a trace」
【泯滅 or 泯沒】 to vanish without
【泯絕】 to be lost for ever; extin- 「guished」

注 2124
ㄓㄨˋ zhù
1. to pour (liquid) 2. to concentrate; to engross; preoccupation 3. same as 註—to annotate 4. stakes (in gambling)
【注目】 to gaze at; to stare at
【注目禮】 (military) parade salute
【注定】 to be doomed; to be destined 「annul」
【注銷】 to nullify; to cancel; to
【注重】 to lay stress on; to emphasize 「footnotes; annotations」
【注釋 or 注解】 ① to annotate ②
【注視】 to look attentively
【注射】 to inject; to get a shot
【注疏】 notes and commentaries
【注入】 to pour into; to empty into
【注意】 to pay attention to; to 「watch」
【注意力】 attention
【注音】 to make phonetic transcriptions 「Symbols (for Mandarin)」
【注音符號】 the National Phonetic

泱 2125
ㄧㄤ yāng
1. great; profound 2. (said of clouds) turbulent
【泱泱大國】 a great country

泳 2126
ㄩㄥˇ yǒng 「of swimming」
1. to swim 2. types or methods

泉 2127
ㄑㄩㄢˊ quán
1. a spring; a fountain 2. money (archaic) 3. a Chinese family name 「abode of a recluse」
【泉林】 ① natural scenery ② the
【泉水】 spring water
【泉源】 a fountainhead; a springhead; a source; a wellspring

泰 2128
ㄊㄞˋ tài
1. great; big 2. quiet; calm; peace; ease 3. Thailand 4. good luck 5. same as 太—very; much; too; excessive
【泰半】 more than half; the greater part; the majority
【泰斗】 ① Mountain Tai and the Dipper ② a leading authority (in certain field or discipline)
【泰國】 Thailand
【泰山】 ①Mountain Tai (in Shantung) ②(figuratively) great importance ③one's wife's father; father-in-law ④Tarzan
【泰山壓卵 or 泰山壓頂】 (literally) It is like Mountain Tai crushing an egg.—overwhelming force
【泰然 or 泰然自若】 unperturbed
【泰晤士河】 the Thames River

六畫

洄 2129
ㄏㄨㄟˊ huí 「eddies」
(said of water) whirling: 洄瀾

洋 2130
ㄧㄤˊ yáng
1. an ocean 2. foreign; Western; Occidental 3. imported
【洋房】 a Western-style house
【洋服】 Western clothes; Occidental dress
【洋鐵】 tin plate; galvanized iron
【洋流】 the marine current
【洋行】 a foreign business firm
【洋化】 to be westernized
【洋貨】 foreign goods
【洋酒】 imported wine and spirits
【洋相】 to make an exhibition of oneself
【洋裝】 ① Western dress ② Western binding (for books)
【洋人】 a Westerner; a foreigner
【洋菜】 agar 亦作「石花菜」

【派遣】 to dispatch
【派系】 ① factions (within a political party, etc.) ② affiliation with (a school or party)
【派出所】 a police station

流 2143
ㄌㄧㄡˊ liú
1. to flow; to discharge 2. to wander; to stray 3. a branch; a division 4. a class; a rank 5. unsettled; unfixed; mobile
【流弊】 long accumulated evil effect; abuses 「villain; a rascal}
【流氓】 a hoodlum; a hooligan; a}
【流民】 refugees
【流芳百世】 to hand down a fine reputation through generations
【流放 or 流徙】 to exile; to banish
【流彈】 a stray bullet
【流動】 ① to be in flowing motion ②on the move ③mobile; itinerant 「rary domicile}
【流動戶口】 the registered tempo-}
【流動性】 mobility; fluidity
【流體】 fluid
【流涕】 to shed tears「to ventilate}
【流通】 in circulation; to circulate;}
【流年】 ①years that flow by one after another ②the change of one's fortune in a given year
【流年不利】 to have a year of ill}
【流淚】 to shed tears ⌊luck}
【流覽】 ①to take a comprehensive look ②to skim over
【流浪】 to wander about; to rove
【流浪漢】 a vagabond; a bum; a drifter「ing from place to place}
【流離失所】homeless and wander-}
【流理台】 a set of kitchen units including such items as a kitchen}
【流利】 fluent ⌊sink, a range, etc.}
【流里流氣】 rascally「to linger on}
【流連】reluctant to leave; to tarry;}
【流連忘返】 to forget to go home because of pleasures elsewhere
【流露】 to reveal unknowingly; to manifest 「strange land}
【流落】 to become an outcast in a}
【流寇】 wandering bandits
【流汗】 to perspire; to sweat
【流血】 to shed blood; to bleed
【流線型】 streamlined
【流星】 (astronomy) a meteor
【流行】 ①to be in vogue; fashionable; prevalent ②(said of a contagious disease) to spread, rage, or be rampant
【流行性感冒】 influenza; flu
【流質】 liquid
【流產】 ① abortion ② to prove abortive; to fail to materialize
【流暢】 (usually said of the style of writing) fluent; smooth
【流程】 ① technological process ② (mining) circuits
【流傳】 to transmit, or be transmitted, from person to person, or from generation to generation; to spread 「away}
【流失】 to run off; to be washed}
【流逝】 (said of time) to elapse; to pass; passage 「the quicksand}
【流沙】 ① sediment (in rivers) ②}
【流水】 flowing water; current
【流水賬】 running account; journal account「troops) to roam about}
【流竄】 (said of bandits or rebel}
【流蘇】 tassels (of flags)
【流速】 current velocity
【流言】 idle talk; rumor; hearsay
【流鶯】 a streetwalker
【流螢】 a firefly
【流亡】 to be exiled; to wander in a strange land 「area}
【流域】 drainage basin; drainage}

七畫

浙 2144
ㄓㄜˋ zhè
1. Chekiang 2. name of a river

浚 2145
ㄐㄩㄣˋ jùn
1. to dredge 2. deep
【浚泥船】 a dredger

浡 2146
ㄅㄛˊ bó
to rise; excited
【浡然】 ①rising ②flourishingly

浣 2147
ㄏㄨㄢˇ huǎn
(又讀 ㄨㄢˇ wǎn)
1. to wash; to rinse 2. ten days; any of the three ten-day divisions of a month
【浣滌 or 浣濯】 to wash; to rinse
【浣熊】 a racoon

浩 2148
ㄏㄠˋ hào 「many}
1. massive; great; vast 2. much;}

〔水部〕

水部

【浩渺 or 浩淼】(said of a body of water) vast or extensive
【浩歎】to heave a deep sigh
【浩浩蕩蕩】(said of an army in march) moving in an imposing manner
【浩瀚】vast
【浩劫】a catastrophe; a calamity
【浩然】great; overwhelming

浦 2149
ㄆㄨˇ pǔ
1. the shore; the beach; the riverside 2. a Chinese family name

浬 2150
ㄌㄧˇ lǐ
(a unit of distance used chiefly in navigation) a nautical mile; a geographic mile; a sea mile

浪 2151
1. ㄌㄤˋ làng
1. waves; billows; breakers 2. dissolute; debauched; rash; unrestrained
【浪漫】① debauched ② romantic
【浪費】to waste; to lavish; waste
【浪蕩】to debauch; to dissipate
【浪頭】the crest of a wave
【浪花】spray of breaking waves
【浪迹天涯】to wander about far away from home
【浪潮】①tide; waves②(figuratively) tide; tendency
【浪人】① a vagrant ② a dismissed courtier ③ a jobless person
【浪子】a prodigal; a debauchee; a loafer

浪 2151
2. ㄌㄤˊ láng
flowing; fluent

浴 2152
ㄩˋ yù
1. to bathe; to wash 2. a bath
【浴盆】a bath; a bathtub
【浴巾】a bath towel
【浴血苦戰】to fight a bloody battle
【浴室】a bathroom
【浴衣】a bathrobe; a bathing gown

浮 2153
ㄈㄨˊ fú (又讀 ㄈㄡˊ fóu)
1. to float; to waft 2. to overflow; to exceed 3. empty; superficial; unsubstantial; unfounded; groundless
【浮標】a buoy
【浮冰】floating ice; (ice) floes
【浮萍】duckweed
【浮名】an empty name or honor
【浮雕】(sculpture) relief
【浮動】① to waft; to float; to drift ② to be unsteady; to fluctuate
【浮屠or浮圖】① Buddha ② a pagoda; a stupa
【浮筒】a float; a buoy
【浮力】(physics) buoyancy
【浮光掠影】superficial opinions, descriptions, sketches, etc.
【浮華】vanity; superficial beauty
【浮橋 or 浮梁】a pontoon bridge
【浮現】(said of memories, etc.) to rise before one's mind
【浮腫】① (medicine) dropsy; edema ② bloated; swollen
【浮沈】① rise and fall ② to follow the trend
【浮屍】a floating corpse
【浮世繪】a (Japanese) woodcut
【浮生若夢】Life is like a dream.
【浮水】(dialect) to float; to waft
【浮躁】restless; impatient; rash
【浮辭】untruthful remarks; unfounded statements
【浮雲】floating clouds

海 2154
ㄏㄞˇ hǎi
1. the sea; the ocean 2. a great number of people, etc. coming together—(figuratively) a huge gathering 3. an area; a field 4. great; unlimited
【海拔】the elevation or height above sea level
【海豹】a seal
【海報】a poster
【海邊】the seashore; the seaside; the beach
【海盤車or海星】an asteroid; a starfish
【海平面】sea level
【海埔新生地】the tidal land
【海馬】a hippocampus; a sea horse
【海鰻】a conger pike; a sea eel
【海綿】sponge
【海綿墊】a foam-rubber cushion
【海面】the sea surface
【海防】coastal defense
【海防部隊】coastal defense forces
【海風】a sea wind; a sea breeze
【海帶】kelp; a sea tangle
【海島】an island (in the sea)
【海盜】a pirate; a sea rover
【海膽】a sea urchin
【海底】the bed or bottom of the sea
【海底撈針】to make a futile search

【海底撈月】 to strive in vain
【海釣】 offshore angling 「ver
【海獺or海狸】 a sea otter; a bea-
【海濤】 sea waves; billows
【海灘 or 海濱】 the seashore; the beach
【海塘 or 海堤】 a sea embankment
【海豚】 a dolphin 「the country
【海內】within the four seas; within
【海南島】 Hainan (an island off
【海難】 a wreck ⌊South China)
【海鳥】 a seafowl; a seabird
【海浪】 seas; sea waves 「tance
【海里】nautical mile, a unit of dis-
【海流】 the ocean current
【海量】 ① magnanimous ② great capacity for alcoholic drinks
【海路】 a sea route; a seaway
【海螺】 a sea univalve; a conch
【海洛因】 heroin 「ship
【海輪】a seagoing (or oceangoing)
【海狗】 a seal
【海港】 a seaport; a harbor
【海龜】 a green turtle 「house
【海關】 the customs; a custom
【海關人員】 customs officers
【海口】 ① a seaport ② bragging
【海枯石爛】 (I will remain faithful to you) even if the sea dries and stones rot. 「less
【海闊天空】endlessly vast; bound-
【海涵】broad-mindedness; forgive-
【海岬】 a cape ⌊ness
【海角天涯】the farthest end of the
【海景】 the seascape ⌊earth
【海軍】 the navy; naval
【海軍陸戰隊】 the Marine Corps
【海軍官校】 a naval academy
【海軍中將】 a vice-admiral
【海軍中校】a commander (above a lieutenant commander) 「grade
【海軍中尉】 a lieutenant junior
【海軍少將】 a rear admiral
【海軍少校】 a lieutenant com-
【海軍少尉】 an ensign ⌊mander
【海軍上將】an admiral
【海軍上校】a captain (just below a rear admiral)
【海軍上尉】 a lieutenant (just below a lieutenant commander)
【海軍總司令】 the commander in chief of the navy; (in the U.S.) the chief of naval operations
【海峽】 straits; a channel
【海嘯】 a tsunami 「cacies
【海鮮】fresh seafood; marine deli-
【海蜇】 a sea blubber; a jellyfish
【海潮】 ocean tides
【海產】 marine products; seafood
【海獅】 a sea lion
【海誓山盟】 to vow eternal love
【海市蜃樓】 a mirage
【海扇】 a scallop 「a sea slug
【海參】a trepang; a sea cucumber;
【海水汚染】 seawater pollution
【海水浴】 sea bathing
【海藻】 seaweed
【海葬】 burial at sea
【海鷗】 a sea gull 「seashore
【海岸】 the coast; the seaside; the
【海岸線】 the coastal line
【海牙】 The Hague
【海燕】 a petrel
【海晏河清】time of peace and calm
【海洋】 seas and oceans; the ocean
【海洋資源】 marine resources
【海外】 overseas; abroad
【海外僑胞】 overseas Chinese
【海灣】 a bay; a gulf
【海王星】 the planet Neptune
【海隅】 remote regions by the sea
【海域】 a sea area; a marine area
【海員】 a sailor; a seaman; a mariner
【海運】 marine transportation

浸 2155 ㄐㄧㄣˋ jìn
1. to dip; to immerse; to soak; to permeate; to percolate 2. gradual; gradually
【浸泡】 to soak; to immerse
【浸濕】 to soak
【浸蝕】 erosion; to erode 「deluged
【浸水】to immerse or dip in water;
【浸染】 to be contaminated gradually 「soak
【浸潤】 to pass in gradually; to
【浸漬】 to soak or be soaked

浼 2156 ㄇㄟˇ měi
1. to stain; to soil; to contaminate; to defile 2. full of water 3. to entrust
【浼汚】 to soil; to besmirch

涇 2157 ㄐㄧㄥ jīng
name of a river in Shensi (陝西)
【涇渭分明】 to be entirely different

〔水部〕

涅 2158 (湼) ㄋㄧㄝ niè
1. to blacken; to dye black 2. to block up
【涅槃】 Nirvana

涉 2159 ㄕㄜˋ shè
1. to wade 2. to cross 3. to experience 4. to involve; to entangle
【涉獵】 to dabble in; to browse
【涉及】 to involve; to relate to
【涉嫌】 to be involved (in a crime)
【涉險】 to adventure
【涉世未深】 inexperienced in affairs of the world
【涉足】 to set foot in
【涉足其間】 to set foot there

消 2160 ㄒㄧㄠ xiāo
1. to vanish; to disappear; to die out 2. to disperse; to eliminate; to remove; to alleviate; to allay; to extinguish; to quench 3. to need; to take
【消磨】 to while away (time)
【消磨時間】 to kill time; to pass the time
【消弭】 to put an end to; to terminate; to bring to an end
【消滅】 ① to annihilate ② to die out
【消費】 consumption; to consume
【消費品】 consumer goods
【消費合作社】 a consumers' cooperative
【消費者】 a consumer
【消防】 fire fighting
【消防隊】 a fire brigade
【消防隊員】 a fire fighter; a fireman
【消防車】 a fire engine
【消防栓】 a fireplug; a hydrant
【消毒】 to disinfect; to sterilize
【消毒水】 antiseptic solution
【消耗】 to consume (or expend)
【消耗戰】 a war of attrition
【消化】 ① to digest (food); digestion ② to absorb mentally
【消化不良】 indigestion; dyspepsia
【消化器官】 the digestive organs
【消化系統】 the digestive apparatus
【消魂 or 銷魂】 to be held spellbound (by a beautiful woman)
【消極】 negative; pessimistic; passive
【消減】 to decrease; to lessen; to diminish
【消氣】 to allay one's anger
【消遣】 pastimes; diversions; recreation
【消息】 news; tidings; information
【消息靈通】 well-informed
【消長】 rise and fall; vicissitudes
【消腫】 to remove or reduce a swelling
【消愁解悶】 to quench sorrow and dissipate worry
【消沈】 depressed; dejected; low-spirited
【消除】 to eliminate; to get rid of
【消失】 to vanish; to disappear
【消逝】 to die away; to vanish
【消受】 ① to endure ② to enjoy
【消瘦】 skinny; emaciated; wasted
【消暑】 to relieve summer heat
【消暑止渴】 (said of a drink) to relieve summer heat and quench thirst
【消融】 to melt
【消災】 to prevent calamities
【消散】 to scatter and disappear
【消夜 or 宵夜】 a midnight snack
【消炎】 to eliminate inflammation
【消炎片】 sulfaguanidine tablets
【消音器】 a silencer; a muffler

涓 2161 ㄐㄩㄢ juān
a small stream; a rivulet; a brook
【涓滴歸公】 (said of an honest official) to hand over every cent of public money to the government treasury
【涓涓】 trickles; a small stream

涎 2162 ㄒㄧㄢˊ xián
as in 涎沫—saliva
【涎皮賴臉or(涎皮)涎臉】 shameless; brazen

涔 2163 ㄘㄣˊ cén
1. a puddle 2. tearful

涕 2164 ㄊㄧˋ tì
1. tears 2. snivel
【涕零】 to shed tears
【涕泣】 to weep; to cry
【涕泣沾襟】 to wet the front part of one's garment with tears

涖 2165 ㄌㄧˋ lì
1. to arrive 2. the murmur of flowing water
【涖臨】 to be present; to arrive

涌 2166 ㄩㄥˇ yǒng
to rise; to spring; to gush out; to

pour out; to surge
【湧出】 to gush out

八畫

涯 2167
ㄧㄚˊ yá
1. the water's edge; a bank 2. a limit 3. faraway places
【涯際 or 涯岸】 the edge; the limit

液 2168
ㄧㄝˋ yè (讀音ㄧˋ yì)
liquid; juices; secretions; sap
【液體】 liquid
【液化】 to liquefy or be liquefied; liquefaction
【液化天然氣】 liquefied natural gas
【液汁】 liquid; fluid; juices; sap

涵 2169
ㄏㄢˊ hán
1. wet, damp and marshy 2. to contain 3. lenient and broad-minded
【涵蓄】 (said of manners, etc.) reserved
【涵養】 ① capability to be kind, lenient, patient, or broad-minded under all circumstances ② to cherish and nourish

涸 2170
ㄏㄜˊ hé (語音ㄏㄠˋ hào)
drying up; dried-up; exhausted

涼 2171
ㄌㄧㄤˊ liáng
1. cool; chilly 2. thin 3. discouraged; disappointed 4. name of one of the 16 states during the Eastern Tsin
【涼拌】 (said of food) cold and dressed with sauce
【涼風】 a cool breeze
【涼臺】 a balcony; a veranda
【涼亭】 a shed along a highway to provide a place of rest for travelers
【涼了半截兒】 to be greatly disappointed
【涼開水】 cold boiled water
【涼快】 ① cool and comfortable ② to cool oneself
【涼蓆】 a sleeping mat (usually made of straw or bamboo) used in summer
【涼鞋】 sandals; summer shoes; slippers
【涼爽】 cool and comfortable
【涼颼颼的】 chilly

淅 2172
ㄒㄧ xī
1. water for washing rice; to wash rice 2. name of a river in Honan Province
【淅米】 to wash rice
【淅瀝】 ①the sound of raindrops ② the sound of falling leaves in the wind

淆 2173
ㄧㄠˊ yáo
confused and disorderly; mixed
【淆亂視聽】 to confuse and muddle the truth
【淆雜】 mixed; miscellaneous

淌 2174
ㄊㄤˇ tǎng
to flow down; to trickle; to drip
【淌汗】 to perspire
【淌眼淚】 to shed tears; to be in tears

淖 2175
ㄋㄠˋ nào
slush; mud: 淖濘 slushy mud

淑 2176
ㄕㄨˊ shú
1. good; pure; virtuous 2. (said of women) beautiful or charming 3. clear
【淑女】 gentlewomen; ladies
【淑愼】 (said of women) gentle and respectful
【淑媛】 ① a rank of court ladies in ancient China ②ladies; gentlewomen

淒 2177
ㄑㄧ qī
1. cloudy and rainy 2. cold and chilly 3. sorrow; sorrowful; miserable; desolate
【淒迷】 ① (said of sights) desolate ②(said of the mood) despondent
【淒風苦雨】 chilly winds and cold rains that inspire sadness in a person's mind
【淒冷】 desolate; bleak
【淒厲】 ① sad and sorrowful ② bleak and harsh
【淒涼】 desolate and sorrowful; lonely; lonesome
【淒愴or淒慘】heartrending; heartbreaking
【淒然】 very sorrowful

淋 2178
1. ㄌㄧㄣˊ lín
1. to soak with water; to drip 2. gonorrhea
【淋巴腺】 lymphatic glands
【淋病 or 淋症】 gonorrhea
【淋漓盡致】 (to narrate, describe, argue, etc.) thoroughly; com-

〔水部〕

pletely
【淋濕】 to be soaked, splashed wet
【淋雨】 to get wet in the rain
【淋浴】 a shower; a shower bath

〔水部〕

淋 2178
2. ㄌㄧㄣˊ lín
to filter; to strain

淘 2179
ㄊㄠˊ táo
1. to wash (especially rice); to wash in a sieve 2. to dredge; to scour 3. to eliminate the inferior (by exams, contests, etc.)
【淘米】 to wash rice
【淘汰】 ① to eliminate inferior contestants, goods, etc. ② elimination
【淘汰賽】 elimination series
【淘金】 ① to pan gold ② to make quick bucks or high profits
【淘金者】 a gold digger
【淘氣】 naughty, or annoying (children)
【淘氣鬼】 a mischievous imp

淚 2180
(泪) ㄌㄟˋ lèi
tears
【淚滴 or 淚珠】 teardrops
【淚痕】 traces of tears
【淚如泉湧】 tears welling up like a fountain
【淚如雨下】 The tears come down like rain.
【淚眼】 teary eyes
【淚汪汪的】 tearful; brimming with tears

淙 2181
ㄘㄨㄥˊ cóng
1. the sound of flowing water 2. water flowing
【淙淙】 ① the gurgling sound of flowing water — especially a creek ② the tinkling sound of metals or gems

淡 2182
ㄉㄢˋ dàn
1. weak or thin (tea, etc.) 2. tasteless; insipid 3. off-season; slack 4. light (in color); slight 5. without worldly desires 6. same as 氮—nitrogen
【淡泊】 to lead a tranquil life without worldly desires
【淡泊名利】 to be indifferent to fame and wealth
【淡薄】 ① thin; weak; light ② to become indifferent ③ dim; faint
【淡漠】 indifference; aloofness
【淡化】 ① desalination ② to play down
【淡季】 slack seasons (for business)
【淡水】 ① fresh water ② Tamsui
【淡水湖】 freshwater lakes
【淡水魚】 fishes grown in fresh water
【淡然置之】 to take it easy
【淡色】 a light color; light-colored
【淡掃蛾眉】 (said of a woman) to apply a light make-up
【淡雅】 (said of attire, decoration, etc.) light, simple but graceful or elegant
【淡忘】 to fade from one's memory
【淡月】 a slack month (for business, etc.)

淤 2183
ㄩ yū
1. muddy sediment; mud; sediment 2. stalemated; blocked; to silt up
【淤泥】 sediment at the bottom of a river, ditch, etc.; silt
【淤積】 to silt up; to clog up
【淤血】 blood clot
【淤塞】 to silt up; to block

淩 2184
(凌) ㄌㄧㄥˊ líng
1. to pass; to traverse; to cross 2. to intrude; to insult or bully

淪 2185
ㄌㄨㄣˊ lún
1. to sink into ruin, etc.; to fall; submerged 2. ripples; eddying water
【淪落】 to get lost (in a strange land, etc.)
【淪迴】 an eddy
【淪陷】 occupied by or lost to the enemy
【淪喪】 to be lost or ruined
【淪亡】 lost or ruined

淨 2186
ㄐㄧㄥˋ jìng
1. clean; pure; to cleanse; to purify 2. empty; vain 3. a role in Chinese opera with a heavily painted face 4. completely; totally 5. only; merely; nothing but 6. net (income, etc.)
【淨土】 *sukhavati*; the land of the pure
【淨利】 net profit
【淨化】 to purify
【淨價】 a net price
【淨値】 net value
【淨賺】 net earnings
【淨重】 net weight
【淨身】 to castrate; castration
【淨水】 clean water

淬 2187 ㄘㄨㄟˋ cuì

1. to temper iron or steel for making swords, etc. (also used figuratively) 2. to dip into water; to soak; to dye

【淬勉】to persuade; to urge and advise

【淬勵】to encourage

淮 2188 ㄏㄨㄞˊ huái

name of a river flowing from West China into the Gulf of Pohai

【淮南】the region south of the Huai River

【淮水 or 淮河】the Huai River

淫 2189 ㄧㄣˊ yín

1. licentious; lewd; lascivious; libidinous; dissolute 2. obscene; pornographic 3. to seduce; to debauch; to tempt; temptation 4. things related to sexual desire and behavior

【淫蕩】(said of women) wanton and lascivious

【淫亂】debauchery

【淫穢】dirty (books, etc.); obscene

【淫書】obscene books

【淫辭】obscene expressions; wanton language

【淫泆】debauchery; wantonness

【淫威】① awe-inspiring power ② excessive use of powers and punishments

【淫慾】wanton desires; sexual desire

淳 2190 ㄔㄨㄣˊ chún

1. pure; clean; simple; sincere; honest 2. a couple or pair (of chariots) 3. big; great

【淳樸】sincere and simple (villagers, etc.); unsophisticated

【淳良】pure, simple and honest

【淳厚】simple and sincere

淵 2191 ㄩㄢ yuān

1. deep waters; a gulf; an abyss 2. profound; depth; erudition; extensive

【淵博】(said of learning) erudite

【淵藪】the place where things or persons flock together—a hotbed

【淵源】① the source ② relationship

深 2192 ㄕㄣ shēn

1. deep; depth 2. profound; mysterious; difficult 3. close; intimate 4. very

【深表同情】to express deep sympathy

【深不可測】extremely abstruse; unfathomable

【深謀遠慮】to think and plan far ahead; foresight

【深明大義】to forget self-interest in the face of an event of great significance

【深得民心】to win strong popular support; well-received

【深度】① depth (of a river, box, tank, etc.) ② profundity (of learning, etc.) ③ understanding (of the ways of the world); sophistication

【深藍】dark blue

【深感】to feel keenly or deeply

【深更半夜】deep in the night; midnight

【深宮】the forbidden palace; the harem

【深刻】① profound significance ② penetrating (views, comments, etc.)

【深厚】① long and close (friendship, relationship, etc.) ② profound (learning, training, etc.) ③ deep-seated; solid

【深呼吸】to breathe deeply

【深紅】dark red

【深交or深情厚誼】long, intimate friendship

【深究】to study, deliberate, search or delve into something deeply

【深居簡出】to lead a secluded life

【深切】deeply; sincerely; intensely

【深秋】late fall; late autumn

【深淺】① deep or shallow; depth ② (said of colors) deep or light ③ (good or evil) intentions

【深情】deep affection or love

【深信】to believe strongly; firmly convinced

【深信不疑】to believe without a shadow of doubt

【深省】to make a thorough self-examination

【深知】to know thoroughly; to realize fully

【深摯】close or intimate (friendship, etc.); deep (affection); sincere

【深讎or深仇】deep animosity or hatred

【深仇大恨】a deep-seated hatred

【深沈】① dark ② (said of a person) impenetrable; unfathomable; calm

【深長】profound meaning, (significance, etc.)

【深處】the deep, inner or obscure

part (of woods, heart, etc.)
【深山】 deep in the mountain
【深入】 (to research, study, delve, etc.) deeply or thoroughly into something; to reach or penetrate deep (into enemy territory)
【深入淺出】 to explain in everyday language the results of a profound study, etc.
【深入人心】 to impress deeply upon everyone's mind
【深造】 to pursue advanced study
【深藏不露】 Real knowledge is not showy.
【深思】 deep thought; contemplation; to think deeply
【深思熟慮】 to think and contemplate thoroughly; to ponder
【深邃】 deep and far; profound and abstruse
【深奧】 deep; abstruse; profound
【深黯】 dark; dark and obscure
【深意】 deep or abstruse meaning
【深夜】 deep in the night
【深淵】 an abyss
【深遠】 deep and far (in meaning, significance, etc.)

混 2193
1. ㄏㄨㄣˋ hùn

1. disorderly; confused 2. to mix; mixed; to mingle or blend 3. to fool around; just to get along 4. to do things at random or without purpose
【混飯吃】 just to make ends meet
【混(混沌)沌】 ① the chaotic world in prehistoric times ② ignorant and dumb
【混沌初開】at the dawn of civilization
【混同】 to merge; to combine
【混凝土】 concrete
【混亂】 confusion; chaos
【混合】 to mix, mingle or blend together
【混合雙打】 mixed doubles
【混合物】 a mixture; a blend
【混號 or 混名】 a nickname
【混混】 ① dark; opaque ② to drift through (life) ③ a hoodlum; a rascal
【混進】 to infiltrate; to sneak into
【混血兒】a human hybrid; a mixed-blood
【混戰】 a melee; a wild battle
【混帳 or 混賬】 Scoundrel! 或 Rascal!
【混世魔王】 a fiendish person who causes an upheaval in the world
【混日子】 just to make a living
【混入】 to mix oneself inside a body of people, an organization
【混雜】 ① to mix ② motley; heterogeneous ③ disorderly; confused
【混爲一談】 to lump together

混 2193
2. (渾) ㄏㄨㄣˊ hún

turbid; muddy; not clear
【混蛋】 Bloody fool!
【混濁】 turbid; not clean or pure
【混水】 ① turbid water ② troubled waters ③ illegal activities
【混水摸魚】 to fish in troubled waters

混 2193
3. ㄏㄨㄣˇ hǔn

confused and not distinguishable
【混亂】 confusion; disorder; chaos
【混淆】 mixed, confused and indistinguishable
【混淆是非】 to confound right and wrong
【混淆視聽】to confuse public opinion

清 2194
ㄑㄧㄥ qīng

1. pure; clean; clear 2. brief; scarce 3. virtuous; honest 4. to arrange; to place in order 5. to conclude; to terminate; to settle 6. clear, simple and easily understandable 7. Ching Dynasty (1644-1911) 8. to clean
【淸白】 (said of a person's character, etc.) clean; innocent
【清平】① peace and justice ②(said of a disposition) pure, honest and peace-loving
【淸名】 an unimpeachable reputation
【淸明】 ① clean and just (administration) ② one of the 24 solar periods in a year which falls on April 5 or 6 when people visit their ancestral tombs, also known as Tomb-Sweeping Day
【淸風明月】 (literally) the soothing wind and the bright moon — aloof
【淸福】 an easy and carefree life
【淸道夫】 a scavenger
【淸單】 a detailed list of items which serves as a receipt, statement, etc.
【淸淡】 ① not enthusiastic; calm ② slack ③(said of food) simple; without grease or heavy seasoning

【清點】to check; to make an inventory
【清燉】to stew or steam meat without seasoning
【清湯】consommé; clear soup
【清朗】① clear and loud (sound, voice, etc.) ② clear and crisp (weather)
【清理】① to settle (accounts, etc.); clearance (of sales, etc.) ② to arrange; to tidy up
【清冽】clear and cold (water)
【清流】① a clear stream ② virtuous scholars
【清廉】clean, honest and capable (officials, etc.)
【清涼】refreshing (weather, water, etc.); nice and cool
【清涼飲料】a cold drink; a cooler
【清高】morally lofty or upright
【清稿】a fair copy
【清規】Buddhist rules
【清規戒律】restrictions and fetters
【清官】honest officials
【清苦】poor but clean and honest
【清寒】①poor but clean and honest ②(said of weather, etc.) cold and crisp ③(said of moonlight) cold and bright
【清華大學】National Tsing Hua University
【清潔】clean; sanitary
【清潔隊】a cleaning squad
【清潔工人】street cleaners; sanitation workers
【清潔劑】a detergent
【清教徒】the Puritans
【清淨】clean and pure
【清靜】quiet (houses, surroundings, etc.)
【清癯】thin but healthy
【清泉】a crystal-clear fountain
【清晰】① loud and clear (in radio reception, talking, listening, etc.) ② clearly
【清洗】to wash; to clean
【清秀】good-looking; well-shaped
【清閒】at leisure
【清新】refreshing (style, fashion, etc.); fresh
【清心寡慾】to purge one's mind of desires and ambitions
【清香撲鼻】A sweet scent assails one's nostrils.
【清醒】①to come to; wide awake ②clear-minded; sober
【清眞寺】a mosque
【清蒸】(cooking) steamed; to steam
【清查】to check, investigate, survey thoroughly
【清澈】limpid (water); crystal-clear
【清朝】the Ching or Manchu Dynasty (1644-1911)
【清晨 or 清早】early in the morning; dawn
【清償】to pay off all one's debts
【清場】(said of movie theaters) to have every moviegoer out before the next show starts
【清唱】to sing Chinese opera without wearing costume or makeup
【清除】①to eliminate, rid of, clear away, liquidate, or remove ② to clean or tidy up (a house)
【清楚 or 清清楚楚】① clear; without ambiguity ② to understand
【清瘦】thin and lean
【清水】clear (or fresh) water
【清爽】① sober ② quiet and comfortable ③ clear and easy to understand ④ to have everything (debts, etc.) settled; relieved
【清脆】clear and crisp (note, sound, etc.); sharp and loud
【清算】① to liquidate; liquidation ② to purge
【清一色】uniformly; homogeneous
【清雅】neat and refined (taste, adornment, etc.); graceful
【清幽】quiet and secluded
【清樣】final proofs

淺 2195
ㄑㄧㄢˇ qiǎn

1. shallow; superficial 2. easy; simple 3. (color) light 4. (said of land) narrow and small
【淺薄】superficial; shallow; meager
【淺灘】a shoal
【淺陋】vulgar; crude; shallow
【淺海】a shallow sea; an epeiric sea
【淺交】not on intimate terms
【淺見】① a shortsighted view ②(a polite expression) my shallow view
【淺近 or 淺易】simple; easy to understand
【淺笑】a smile; to smile
【淺嘗輒止】do not study further or deeper
【淺色】light colors
【淺而易見 or 淺顯】apparent; obvious; easily understood

淹 2196
ㄧㄢ yān

1. to submerge; to drown; to soak; to steep in; to flood 2. to

〔水部〕

delay; to procrastinate 3. to stay; to be stranded
【淹沒】① drowned ② to waste a talent as if by submerging it
〔水部〕
【淹通古今】to be thoroughly acquainted with the old and modern
【淹死】drowned

添 2197 ㄊㄧㄢ tiān
1. to add to; to increase; to replenish (stock, etc.) 2. to have a baby
【添補】to make complete; to complete what is lacking
【添飯】to have another helping (or bowl) of rice
【添福添壽】(a well-wishing expression) to add to your happiness and your longevity
【添附】to enclose; to supplement; to add to; additional
【添丁】to beget a son
【添購 or 添置】to purchase; to make additional purchase of
【添貨】(said of a store) to replenish stock
【添加】to add to; to increase
【添加劑】(chemistry) an additive
【添設】to set up additionally
【添上】① to add to ② besides; in addition to
【添造】to expand; to construct; to build more
【添油加醋or添油加醬】to embellish or blow up a story or report with something which is usually not true

涮 2198 ㄕㄨㄢ shuàn
1. to rinse (a container, etc.) 2. to boil in a chafing pot 3. to cheat with lies
【涮洗】to rinse
【涮羊肉 or 涮鍋子】mutton cooked in a chafing pot

淼 2199 ㄇㄧㄠ miǎo
(said of water) extensive or overwhelming

九畫

渙 2200 ㄏㄨㄢ huàn
1. as in 渙然—scattered; dispersed 2. name of a river
【渙發】high-spirited
【渙然冰釋】(said of a grudge, misunderstanding, etc.) to vanish
【渙散】① lacking concentration or organization ②(said of morale) to collapse

渚 2201 ㄓㄨ zhǔ
a sand bar in a river

渝 2202 ㄩ yú
1. to change one's mind 2. another name of Chungking 3. another name of the Chialing River in Szechwan

減 2203 ㄐㄧㄢ jiǎn
to decrease; to reduce; to lessen; to diminish; to subtract; to cut
【減半】to reduce to a half
【減免】①to mitigate or annul (a punishment) ②to reduce or remit (taxation, etc.)
【減法】(arithmetic) subtraction
【減肥】to reduce (weight)
【減俸 or 減薪】a pay cut
【減退】to fall; to abate; to decrease
【減號】the minus sign (−)
【減緩】to retard; to slow down
【減價】to cut down prices; to mark down; to reduce prices
【減輕】to lighten; to lessen; to mitigate
【減刑】① to commute a sentence ② a commutation of sentence
【減產】to cut production or output
【減少or減低】to decrease; to diminish; to lessen; to reduce
【減弱】to weaken; to subside
【減資】the reduction of captial
【減速】to slow down; to decelerate

渡 2204 ㄉㄨ dù
1. to cross (a river or ocean) 2. a ferry
【渡輪】a ferry steamer
【渡過難關】to tide over a difficulty
【渡口】a ferry
【渡河】to cross a river
【渡假】to spend one's holidays
【渡船】a ferryboat

渣 2205 ㄓㄚ zhā
dregs; lees; grounds; sediment
【渣滓or渣子】grounds; sediment; dregs; lees

渠 2206 ㄑㄩ qú
1. a drain; a channel; a ditch 2. great; deep 3. he; she

【渠道】① an irrigation ditch ② a channel

渤 2207
ㄅㄛˊ bó
(said of water) swelling or rising
【渤海】Pohai, a gulf of the Yellow Sea

渥 2208
ㄨㄛˋ wò
1. to dye 2. great (kindness)
【渥澤】profound benefaction

渦 2209
1. ㄨㄛ wō
a whirlpool; an eddy
【渦輪機】a turbine

渦 2209
2. ㄍㄨㄛ guō
name of a river

港 2210
ㄍㄤˇ gǎng
1. a harbor; a seaport 2. a bay; a gulf 3. short for Hongkong
【港幣】Hongkong currency
【港口】a harbor; a seaport; a port
【港九】Hongkong and Kowloon
【港警】the harbor police
【港澳】Hongkong and Macao
【港灣】① a harbor ② a bay; a gulf

渲 2211
ㄒㄩㄢˋ xuàn
to color with paint
【渲染】① to color with paint ② to make exaggerated additions in a story or report; to play up

測 2212
ㄘㄜˋ cè
to measure; to survey
【測定】to determine
【測度】to speculate; to conjecture; to guess
【測量】① survey ② to survey
【測量員】a surveyor
【測謊器】a lie detector; a polygraph
【測驗】① to test; to examine ② a quiz or test

渴 2213
ㄎㄜˇ kě
1. thirsty 2. to long; to crave; to pine
【渴求】to crave for; to search for earnestly
【渴死】extremely thirsty
【渴望】to long for; to crave for; to aspire after

湃 2214
ㄆㄞˋ pài
billowy; turbulent

渺 2215
ㄇㄧㄠˇ miǎo
1. endlessly long or vast 2. tiny; infinitesimal 3. indistinct; blurred
【渺茫】① boundless ② indistinct
【渺渺】blurred; indistinct
【渺小】very small; tiny; infinitesimal
【渺無人跡】remote and uninhabited

游 2216
ㄧㄡˊ yóu
1. to swim; to float; to waft; to drift 2. same as 遊—to wander about 3. part of a river 4. a Chinese family name
【游牧民族】nomadic people; nomads
【游動】to move about
【游廊】a covered corridor; a veranda
【游離】(said of a radical, valence, nucleus, etc., in chemistry) free; ionization; liberation
【游擊】a hit-and-run attack
【游擊隊】a guerrilla band; guerrillas
【游擊手】(baseball) a shortstop
【游手好閒 or 游蕩】loitering about and doing nothing; loafing
【游說】to lobby; to canvass (for a cause, project, etc.)
【游資】idle capital; idle money
【游絲】gossamer
【游移不定】undecided; hesitating
【游泳 or 游水】swimming
【游泳池】a swimming pool
【游泳衣】a swimming suit

渾 2217
1. ㄏㄨㄣˊ hún
1. entire; complete 2. to blend; to merge 3. muddy; turbid
【渾蛋】"rotten egg"—(abusive language) a blackguard
【渾天儀】(astronomy) an armillary sphere
【渾厚】①(said of one's character) simple and honest ② (said of writing, painting, etc.) simple and vigorous
【渾渾噩噩or渾噩】muddle-headed; ignorant
【渾球】a zany
【渾濁】turbid; muddy
【渾身】one's entire body; from head to toe
【渾身解數】every means of solution
【渾身是膽】very daring; fearless
【渾水】muddy water
【渾然】completely
【渾然一體】a unified entity
【渾圓】①tactful; sophisticated ②a

sphere ③ perfectly round

渾 2217 2. ㄏㄨㄣˋ hùn

chaotic; confused; messy

【渾沌】chaos; confusion; mess

【渾沌初開】when the universe was taking shape

湄 2218 ㄇㄟˊ méi

shore; bank; the margin (of the water)

湊 2219 (凑) ㄘㄡˋ còu

1. to put together 2. to raise (fund) 3. to happen by chance 4. to move close to; to press near

【湊合】① to manage to collect or gather together ② to make do with what is available ③ to improvise ④ not too bad; passable

【湊近】to get near; to approach

【湊齊】① to manage to line up enough people for a game ② to manage to collect all the parts to form the whole

【湊巧】by chance; by coincidence

【湊數】① to make up the proper number ② to play an unimportant role

【湊熱鬧】① to take part in merriment ② to add trouble to

【湊在一起】① to put together ② (said of people) to gang up; to team up

【湊足】to manage to raise enough money for a purpose

湎 2220 ㄇㄧㄢˇ miǎn

1. drunk 2. unaware 3. changing

湍 2221 ㄊㄨㄢ tuān

rapidly flowing

【湍流】rapids; torrent; swift current

【湍急】(said of water) swift; rapid

湔 2222 ㄐㄧㄢ jiān

to wash

【湔雪】to wipe away (disgrace, etc.)

湧 2223 ㄩㄥˇ yǒng

1. to gush; to pour 2. to rise

【湧進】to swarm (or sweep) into

【湧泉】a fountain; a spring

【湧現】to crop up (in one's mind)

【湧出】to well out; to spring out

【湧上來】① to well up ② to come in a sweep

湖 2224 ㄏㄨˊ hú

1. a lake 2. a Chinese family name

【湖泊 or 湖澤 or 湖沼】lakes

【湖邊 or 湖濱 or 湖畔】the shore of a lake; beside the lake

【湖光山色】the natural beauty of lakes and mountains

【湖心】the middle of a lake

【湖沼】lakes and marshes

【湖水】lake water

湘 2225 ㄒㄧㄤ xiāng

1. name of a river flowing through Hunan 2. an alternative name of Hunan

【湘江 or 湘水】the Hsiang River, flowing through Hunan

【湘繡】Hunan-style embroideries

湛 2226 ㄓㄢˋ zhàn

1. dewy 2. deep; profound 3. same as 沈—to sink 4. a Chinese family name

【湛藍】dark blue; azure

【湛新】brand-new

【湛然】① (said of water) transparent ② quiet; calm

湮 2227 ㄧㄣ yīn

1. to bury 2. to block 3. long (in time)

【湮沒】to bury or be buried

【湮沒不彰】to fall into the shade

【湮滅】to bury; to destroy (evidence)

湯 2228 1. ㄊㄤ tāng

1. hot water 2. soup; broth 3. a Chinese family name

【湯麪】noodles with soup

【湯頭】a prescription of herbal medicines

【湯匙】a spoon

【湯勺】a soup ladle

【湯水】① name of a river in Honan ② soup

【湯藥】decoction of Chinese medicine

【湯碗】a large bowl for holding soup

【湯圓 or 湯糰】balls of glutinous rice

湯 2228 2. ㄕㄤ shāng

(said of water) flowing

十畫

溫 2229
(温) ㄨㄣ wēn
1. warm; lukewarm; to warm 2. to review; to revise 3. temperature 4. a Chinese family name
【溫飽】 adequately fed and clothed
【溫帶】 the Temperate Zone
【溫帶氣候】 temperate climate
【溫度】 temperature
【溫度計 or 溫度表】 a thermometer
【溫暖】 warm; warmth
【溫故知新】 to learn new things by reviewing old things
【溫開水】 lukewarm boiled water
【溫酒】 to heat wine; lukewarm wine
【溫情】 kindness; warm-heartedness
【溫泉】 a hot spring; a spa
【溫習】 to review (what has been learned)
【溫馨】 warm and fragrant
【溫煦 or 溫和】 gentle; mild; temperate; warm
【溫馴】 meek; docile; tame
【溫差】 difference in temperature
【溫牀】 a hotbed
【溫室】 a greenhouse
【溫順】 gentle; good-natured; docile; obedient
【溫柔】 warm and tender; sweet-natured
【溫柔鄉】 (literally) land of the tender—①a brothel ②the enthralling experience of enjoying female charms in an intimate manner
【溫潤】 ① mild and smooth ② beautiful and tender
【溫存】 tender; loving; caressing
【溫文爾雅】 gentle and graceful

源 2230
ㄩㄢ yuán
a source; a head (of a stream)
【源頭】 a head or a source (of a stream)
【源流 or 源委 or 原委】 full particulars; all the details; the whole story
【源源不絕】 to continue without end
【源遠流長】 to have a long history

溘 2231
ㄎㄜ kè
sudden; abrupt; unexpected
【溘逝】 to die suddenly

溟 2232
ㄇㄧㄥ míng
1. drizzle 2. vast; boundless 3. the sea; the ocean

溝 2233
ㄍㄡ gōu
1. a ditch; a waterway; a moat 2. a groove; a rut
【溝通】 to bring about an unobstructed interflow of (feelings, ideas, etc.)
【溝壑】 a valley, gorge, or canyon
【溝渠】 a ditch; a drain; a gutter; a channel

溜 2234
1. ㄌㄧㄡ liù
1. rapids 2. a row; a column 3. surroundings; neighborhood
【溜溜 or 遛遛】 to stroll; to ramble

溜 2234
2. ㄌㄧㄡ liū
1. to go secretly and quietly 2. to slip; to slide
【溜冰】 to skate; skating
【溜冰鞋】 a pair of skates
【溜冰場】 a skating rink
【溜達】 to stroll; to ramble
【溜之大吉】 to leave stealthily; to slip out

準 2235
ㄓㄨㄣˇ zhǔn
1. level; even 2. a rule; a criterion; a standard; accurate; accuracy 3. to aim; to sight 4. would-be (son-in-law, bride, etc.); to-be 5. (law) quasi- 6. certainly
【準備】 ①to prepare; to get ready ② to plan
【準頭】 accuracy; a standard
【準確】 correct; accurate; precise
【準新娘】 a would-be bride
【準新郎】 a would-be bridegroom
【準時】 punctual; punctuality
【準繩】 ① a criterion; a standard ②(carpenter's) marking line
【準則】 a rule; a standard; a criterion

溢 2236
ㄧˋ yì
1. to flow over; to brim over 2. excessive
【溢出】 to brim over; to flow over
【溢於言表】 (said of emotions or inner feelings) to show clearly in one's utterances and manners

溥 2237
ㄆㄨˇ pǔ
1. great; wide; vast 2. universal

〔水部〕

（水部）

【溥天同慶】universally celebrated
【溥天之下】everywhere under the sun

溯 2238 ㄙㄨˋ sù
1. to go upstream; to go against a stream 2. to trace; to recall
【溯江而上】to go upstream in a boat
【溯自】ever since
【溯游】to go upstream
【溯源】to trace back to the source

溪 2239 ㄒㄧ xī (又讀 ㄑㄧ qī)
a mountain stream: 溪流 a brook
【溪谷】a valley; a canyon; a gorge
【溪澗 or 溪水】a mountain stream

溲 2240 ㄙㄡ sōu
1. to urinate 2. to immerse; to soak; to drench

溷 2241 ㄏㄨㄣˋ hùn
1. dirty 2. messy
【溷跡】to conceal
【溷濁】dirty; muddy

溺 2242 1. ㄋㄧˋ nì
1. to drown 2. to indulge
【溺死 or 溺斃】to be drowned
【溺愛】to lavish one's love upon (a child)

溺 2242 2. ㄋㄧㄠˋ niào
to urinate
【溺器】a urinal; a bedpan
【溺牀】to wet the bed

溶 2243 ㄖㄨㄥˊ róng
1. to dissolve; to melt 2. (said of rivers) having much water
【溶點】the melting point
【溶化 or 溶解】to dissolve; to melt
【溶劑】a dissolvent; a solvent
【溶解度】solubility
【溶入】to dissolve into

溽 2244 ㄖㄨˋ rù
moist; humid
【溽暑】sweltering summer weather

滂 2245 ㄆㄤ pāng
torrential; overwhelming
【滂湃】surging; overwhelming; torrential
【滂沱】① (said of rain) torrential ②(said of tears) streaming

滄 2246 ㄘㄤ cāng
blue; azure; green
【滄茫】endlessly vast; boundless
【滄溟 or 滄海】the blue sea
【滄海桑田 or 滄桑】the vicissitudes of life
【滄海一粟】a grain in the boundless sea—infinitely small

滅 2247 ㄇㄧㄝˋ miè
1. to destroy; to ruin; to wipe out; to exterminate 2. to put out; to extinguish; to go out
【滅門】to put a whole family to death
【滅頂】to be drowned
【滅口】to kill a person to prevent him from disclosing a secret
【滅火器】a fire extinguisher
【滅跡】to destroy evidence
【滅盡天良】to destroy utterly one's conscience
【滅絕】to exterminate; to annihilate; to wipe out
【滅種】to commit genocide
【滅亡】to perish

滇 2248 ㄉㄧㄢ diān (又讀 ㄊㄧㄢˊ tián)
an alternative name of Yünnan

滋 2249 ㄗ zī
1. to grow 2. to increase; to multiply 3. to nourish 4. to give rise to 5. to spurt out 6. juice; sap
【滋補】to nourish; nutritious; tonic
【滋長】to grow; to thrive
【滋事】to create trouble
【滋生】to reproduce in large numbers
【滋擾】to disturb peace and order; to harass
【滋潤】①to freshen; to enrich ②to moisten; moist
【滋養品】nutrient; nutritive food; nourishment
【滋味】taste; flavor

滑 2250 ㄏㄨㄚˊ huá
1. to slip; to slide; to glide 2. smooth; slippery 3. insincere; dishonest; cunning
【滑板】①(machinery) a slide ②(table tennis) feint play ③a skateboard
【滑倒】to slip and fall
【滑動】(physics) to slide

【滑頭】a crafty person; a cunning person
【滑頭滑腦】sly; crafty; guile
【滑梯】a slideway (for children's amusement)
【滑壘】(baseball) base sliding
【滑輪】①a roller ②a pulley
【滑稽】funny; comical; ridiculous
【滑跤】to slip and fall down
【滑翔】to glide
【滑翔機】a glider
【滑翔翼】a hang glider
【滑行】to slide; to coast; to taxi
【滑雪】to ski; to slide or travel on skis
【滑水】water skiing
【滑草運動】grass skiing

滔 2251
ㄊㄠ tāo
1. fluent 2. to fill; to prevail
【滔滔】flowing smoothly; fluent
【滔滔不絕】talking fluently and endlessly
【滔滔雄辯】a torrent of eloquence
【滔天大罪】heinous crimes

滓 2252
ㄗˇ zǐ
dregs; lees; sediment

十一畫

滌 2253
ㄉㄧˊ dí
1. to wash; to cleanse 2. to sweep
【滌去】to wash off; to wash away
【滌除】①to do away with ②to sweep away ③to wash away

滯 2254
ㄓˋ zhì
at a standstill; stagnant; impeded; blocked; stationary
【滯悶】to have pent-up feeling
【滯留】①to remain at a standstill ②to loiter; to detain
【滯銷】sales slump
【滯塞不通】obstructed and impeded
【滯礙】to obstruct; to impede

滲 2255
ㄕㄣˋ shèn
to permeate; to percolate; to infiltrate; to seep; to ooze
【滲透】to seep through; to permeate
【滲出】to seep out; to ooze out
【滲入】①to permeate; to seep into ②(said of influence, etc.) to penetrate

滴 2256
ㄉㄧ dī
1. water drops 2. to drip
【滴答】to ticktack; ticktack
【滴管】a medicine dropper; a pipette
【滴下】to drip
【滴水穿石】Persistent efforts can overcome any difficulty.

滸 2257
ㄏㄨˇ hǔ
waterside; shore

滾 2258
(滚) ㄍㄨㄣˇ gǔn
1. to turn round and round; to roll; to rotate 2. boiling
【滾邊】①an embroidered hem ②to stitch a hem around a border
【滾蛋】Get out! 或 Go to hell! 或 Beat it!
【滾地球】(baseball) ground ball
【滾動】to roll; to trundle
【滾燙】boiling; steaming hot
【滾瓜爛熟】learned very thoroughly
【滾滾】(said of flowing waters) rolling; torrential; billowing
【滾滾而來】to come in torrents
【滾出去】①to roll out ②Get out!
【滾石不生苔】A rolling stone gathers no moss.
【滾水】boiling water
【滾熱】piping hot

滿 2259
ㄇㄢˇ mǎn
1. full; filled 2. plentiful; abundant 3. proud; haughty 4. to expire 5. completely; entirely; perfectly 6. Manchu
【滿杯】a full cup
【滿不在乎】do not care at all
【滿滿的】full to the brim; brimful
【滿門】the whole family
【滿門桃李】a lot of students
【滿面笑容 or 滿面春風】looking happy and cheerful; all smiles
【滿目瘡痍】Misery and suffering greets the eye everywhere.
【滿分】a perfect score; full marks
【滿腹牢騷】to have a heart full of discontents, grievances, complaints, etc.
【滿腹狐疑】to be filled with suspicion
【滿腹經綸】very erudite
【滿頭大汗】with one's brow bead-

〔水部〕

ed with perspiration
【滿天下 or 滿地】everywhere; all over the world
【滿天星】①(botany) *Serissa foetida* ② the sky filled with stars
【滿腦子】to have one's mind stuffed with
【滿壘】full base
【滿臉通紅】The face reddens all over.
【滿口胡說】to talk nonsense 或 Nonsense! 或Rubbish!
【滿口稱讚】to praise unreservedly
【滿口應承 or 滿口答應】to promise with great readiness
【滿懷】a heart full of (enthusiasm, sorrow, etc.)
【滿街】all over the street
【滿腔熱血】full of patriotic fervor
【滿清】the Ching Dynasty (1644-1911)
【滿心歡喜】to be filled with joy
【滿招損，謙受益】Haughtiness invites losses while modesty brings profits.
【滿洲】Manchuria
【滿場】① the whole assembly ② Tickets sold out!
【滿城風雨】widespread excitement over a scandal, an incident, etc.
【滿身】the whole body
【滿身是汗】to sweat all over
【滿載】fully laden
【滿載而歸】to return home fully laden with riches, gifts, etc.
【滿足】to satisfy or be satisfied; content
【滿座】① all the audience; all the attendants ② a capacity audience
【滿嘴】to have a mouthful of (food, honeyed words, etc.)
【滿以爲】to have counted on or expected something to happen (but it did not)
【滿意】satisfied; content
【滿月】① a full moon 亦作「望月」 ②(of a baby) to be one month old

漁 2260
ㄩˊ yú
1. to fish 2. to seek; to pursue 3. to seize; to acquire forcibly
【漁民】fishermen
【漁夫 or 漁郎 or 漁人】a fisherman
【漁利】to seek profits or gains by unethical means
【漁獵】①fishing and hunting ②to seek (illegal gains)
【漁港】a fishing harbor
【漁獲量】a catch
【漁會】a fishermen's association
【漁舟 or 漁船】a fishing boat
【漁人得利 or 漁翁得利】The fisherman catches both (while the snipe and the clam are locked in a fight).
【漁村】a fishing village
【漁業】fishery
【漁網】a fishing net
【漁翁 or 漁父】an old fisherman

漂 2261
1. ㄆㄧㄠ piāo
to drift; to float; to be tossed about
【漂泊】to drift; to wander
【漂浮】to drift; to float
【漂蕩】① to drift about; to be tossed (by waves) ② to wander; to ramble about
【漂流】to drift
【漂零】①(said of leaves) to be scattered about ② to live a lone wandering life
【漂搖】to wave; to flutter

漂 2261
2. ㄆㄧㄠˇ piǎo
to bleach
【漂白】to bleach
【漂白劑】a decolorant

漂 2261
3. ㄆㄧㄠˋ piào
pretty; nice; sleek
【漂亮】①pretty; handsome ②wise in worldly ways ③ brilliant; beautiful

漆 2262
1. ㄑㄧ qī
1. a varnish tree; a lacquer tree 2. varnish; lacquer 3. to varnish; to lacquer; to paint
【漆工or漆匠】a varnisher; a painter
【漆器】lacquer wares

漆 2262
2. ㄑㄩˋ qù
pitch-black
【漆黑】pitch-black; coal black; raven

漏 2263
ㄌㄡˋ lòu
1. to divulge; to disclose 2. leak; to leak 3. to slip or omit unintentionally; to neglect 4. a water clock; an hourglass
【漏風】not airtight

【漏風聲】to disclose a secret
【漏斗】a funnel
【漏掉】to be missing or left out
【漏電】electric leakage
【漏洞】a shortcoming; a loophole
【漏接】(baseball) passed ball
【漏氣】(said of air) to leak out
【漏水】(said of containers, holds, etc.) leaking
【漏稅】to evade tax payment
【漏夜】in the dead of night
【漏網之魚】a fish that has escaped the net—a criminal who has escaped punishment

溉 2264
ㄍㄞˋ gài
1. to water; to irrigate 2. to wash

演 2265
ㄧㄢˇ yǎn
1. to perform for entertainment; to act; to play 2. to expound 3. to exercise; to practice 4. to evolve; to develop
【演變】to develop and change; to evolve
【演練】drill
【演技】acting
【演進】to evolve; to develop
【演講】to deliver a speech; to orate
【演講比賽】an oratorical contest
【演習】military exercises; maneuvers
【演戲】① to act in a play ② to playact
【演唱】to sing onstage
【演出】(said of entertainers) to perform; to present (a play)
【演說】to deliver a speech
【演說家】an orator
【演奏】(said of musicians) to perform
【演奏會】a concert; a recital
【演算】to do mathematical problems
【演員】an actor or actress

漕 2266
ㄘㄠˊ cáo
to transport grain by water

漠 2267
ㄇㄛˋ mò
1. a desert 2. unconcerned; indifferent 3. quiet; silent
【漠不關心】to pay no attention at all; do not care at all
【漠視】① to despise ② to ignore ③ to underestimate
【漠然】①indifferent; unmoved ② completely ignorant

漣 2268
ㄌㄧㄢˊ lián
1. ripples 2. weeping
【漣漪】ripples

漪 2269
ㄧ yī
ripples

漩 2270
ㄒㄩㄢˊ xuán
(又讀 ㄒㄩㄢˋ xuàn)
a whirlpool
【漩渦】①a whirlpool ②a dispute; a quarrel

漢 2271
ㄏㄢˋ hàn
1. of the Han Dynasty (206 B.C.-220 A.D.) 2. of the Chinese people or language 3. a man; a fellow 4. name of a tributary of the Yangtze River
【漢堡】① Hamburg, Germany ② a hamburger
【漢化】sinicized; assimilated by the Chinese
【漢奸】a traitor (to China)
【漢朝】the Han Dynasty (206 B.C.-220 A.D.)
【漢城】Seoul, capital of South Korea
【漢子】① a man ② a husband
【漢英詞典】a Chinese-English dictionary

漫 2272
1. ㄇㄢˋ màn
1. overflowing 2. uncontrolled; uninhibited 3. reckless; wild 4. unsystematic; aimless 5. to spread or extend over 6. all over the place; everywhere
【漫步】to ramble; to stroll
【漫不經心】heedless; unmindful; inattentive; unconcerned
【漫罵】to abuse or slander with abandon
【漫條斯理 or 慢條斯理】leisurely
【漫畫】a cartoon; a caricature
【漫畫家】a cartoonist; a caricaturist
【漫長】endless; infinite
【漫山遍野】so numerous as to cover the mountains and the plains
【漫遊】to travel about for pleasure
【漫無邊際】① boundless ② rambling
【漫無目標】aimless; at random

漫 2272
2. ㄇㄢˊ mán
(said of an expanse of water)

〔水部〕

vast or endless
【漫漫長夜】a long, long night which seems to have no end
【漫天大謊】a monstrous lie
【漫天討價or漫天要價】to quote an exorbitant price in anticipation of haggling

漬 2273 ㄗˋ zì
1. to soak 2. to dye 3. to be caked with
【漬痕】a stain; a spot; a smear

漱 2274 ㄕㄨˋ shù (讀音 ㄙㄡˋ sòu)
1. to rinse; to gargle 2. to wash
【漱口】to gargle the throat
【漱口水】a gargle; a mouthwash
【漱口盂 or 漱口杯】a mouth washing cup; a mug

漲 2275 1. ㄓㄤˋ zhàng
to swell; to expand
【漲潮】(said of the tide) to flow

漲 2275 2. ㄓㄤˇ zhǎng
to go up or rise (as prices, water, etc.)
【漲幅】(said of commodity prices, stocks, etc.) the rate of increase or rise
【漲跌】price fluctuation
【漲價】to raise prices; appreciation

漸 2276 1. ㄐㄧㄢˋ jiàn
gradually; little by little; by degrees
【漸漸 or 漸次】gradually
【漸進】to advance little by little
【漸入佳境】to get better and better

漸 2276 2. ㄐㄧㄢ jiān
1. to soak; to permeate 2. (said of the territory) to reach
【漸染】to soak; to imbue

滷 2277 ㄌㄨˇ lǔ
1. gravy; broth; sauce 2. salty; salted
【滷蛋】a marinated egg
【滷味】pot-stewed fowl, meat, etc. served cold

漿 2278 ㄐㄧㄤ jiāng
1. thick fluid; starch 2. to starch
【漿果】a berry
【漿糊】paste

十二畫

潔 2279 ㄐㄧㄝˊ jié
1. clean; spotless; pure; stainless; immaculate 2. to clean; to keep clean
【潔白】clean and white; immaculate
【潔癖】mysophobia
【潔淨】clean; untainted; stainless
【潔身自好or潔身自愛】to exercise self-control so as to protect oneself from immorality

潑 2280 ㄆㄛ pō
1. to pour; to sprinkle; to spill 2. ferocious; fierce; spiteful; villainous
【潑婦】a virago; a shrew; a termagant
【潑辣】① ferocious; spiteful ② pungent
【潑冷水】(figuratively) to dampen the enthusiasm of 亦作「澆冷水」

潛 2281 ㄑㄧㄢˊ qián
1. to hide; to conceal 2. to dive 3. hidden; secret; latent
【潛伏】① to lie hidden ② latent; hidden
【潛伏期】a latent period
【潛逃】to flee secretly; to slip away
【潛力】potential; hidden force
【潛心研究】to study diligently with a quiet mind
【潛水】to dive
【潛水艇 or 潛艇】a submarine
【潛入】① to enter secretly; to slip in ② to dive into (water)
【潛在】latent
【潛在意識or潛意識】subconsciousness
【潛藏】to be in hiding
【潛移默化】to change and influence unobtrusively and imperceptibly

潘 2282 ㄆㄢ pān
1. a Chinese family name 2. water in which rice has been washed

潢 2283 ㄏㄨㄤˊ huáng
a lake or a pond
【潢池弄兵】to disregard a disaster

澗 2284 ㄐㄧㄢˋ jiàn
a mountain stream
【澗壑】a valley; a ravine
【澗溪】a stream in a valley

潦 2285
1. (涝) ㄌㄠˋ lào
to flood; floods

潦 2285
2. ㄌㄠˇ lǎo
a puddle

潦 2285
3. ㄌㄧㄠˊ liáo
1. disheartened; disappointed 2. without care
【潦倒】disappointed; down in luck
【潦草】① perfunctory ② (said of handwriting) hasty and careless; illegible

潤 2286
ㄖㄨㄣˋ rùn
1. moist; glossy; fresh 2. to moisten; to freshen 3. to enrich; to benefit 4. to embellish
【潤筆】remuneration (or fee) for writing or painting
【潤滑】① to lubricate ② smooth
【潤滑劑】a lubricant
【潤滑油】lubricating oil
【潤飾 or 潤色】to embellish or polish a writing
【潤澤】① moist and glossy ② to invigorate; to moisten

潭 2287
ㄊㄢˊ tán
1. deep water; a deep pool 2. deep; profound

潮 2288
ㄔㄠˊ cháo
1. the tide 2. damp; moist; wet 3. (now rarely, said of gold, silver, etc.) inferior in skill or fineness
【潮流】① tides ② a current; a trend
【潮汐】morning tide and evening tide; tides
【潮濕】humid; damp
【潮水】the tide

潺 2289
ㄔㄢˊ chán
the sound of water flowing
【潺潺】the murmuring of flowing water

潸 2290
ㄕㄢ shān
tears flowing; to weep
【潸然】tears falling

潰 2291
ㄎㄨㄟˋ kuì
1. a river overflowing its banks 2. broken up; scattered 3. (military) defeated 4. (said of a dike or dam) to burst
【潰敗】(military) defeated and scattered; a rout
【潰不成軍】completely routed
【潰逃】to escape in disorder; to flee pell-mell
【潰爛】bursting of an abscess; inflamed
【潰散】defeated and dispersed
【潰瘍】an ulcer

澄 2292
ㄔㄥˊ chéng
(語音 ㄉㄥˋ dèng)
1. clear and still (water) 2. to purify water by letting the impurities settle down to the bottom 3. to pacify
【澄清】① to purify water by letting the impurities settle down to the bottom ② to set right ③ to clarify ④ clear
【澄澈】crystal clear

澈 2293
ㄔㄜˋ chè
1. thoroughly; completely 2. to understand 3. clear water
【澈底】thoroughly; completely
【澈頭澈尾】out and out; thoroughly
【澈查】to investigate thoroughly

澎 2294
1. ㄆㄥ pēng
the roaring of colliding billows
【澎湃】the roaring of billows; to surge

澎 2294
2. ㄆㄥˊ péng
the Pescadores
【澎湖】the Penghus, or the Pescadores, in the Taiwan Straits

澆 2295
ㄐㄧㄠ jiāo
1. to water (plants, flowers, etc.) 2. to sprinkle water on 3. perfidious; faithless; ungrateful
【澆灌】to water (plants, etc.)
【澆花】to water flowers

十三畫

澡 2296
ㄗㄠˇ zǎo
to wash; to bathe
【澡盆】a bathtub
【澡堂 or 澡塘】a public bath; a bathhouse

澤 2297
ㄗㄜˊ zé

〔水部〕

〔水部〕

1. the place where water gathers; a marsh 2. grace; favors; kindness 3. brilliance; radiance; luster; bright; glossy; smooth 4. to benefit; to enrich
【澤被天下】Benefits spread to all people.

澱 2298 ㄉㄧㄢˋ diàn
1. sediment; dregs; precipitate 2. indigo
【澱粉】starch

澳 2299 ㄠˋ ào
1. deep waters—where seagoing vessels can moor 2. name of various places (see below)
【澳門】Macao
【澳大利亞 or 澳洲】Australia

澹 2300 ㄉㄢˋ dàn
quiet and tranquil
【澹泊】having no worldly desires or ambitions
【澹泊名利】to be indifferent toward fame and wealth

激 2301 ㄐㄧ jī
1. to stir up; to rouse; to arouse; to urge; to excite 2. sudden; great; very 3. heated (debate, battle, etc.); fierce; angry; vexed 4. abnormal; unusual; drastic 5. to turn back the current—as a dike
【激發】to stir up; to arouse
【激憤】wrathful; indignant
【激盪】to surge; turmoil; stirring
【激動】aroused; excited; agitated
【激怒】to irritate; to infuriate; to provoke; to enrage
【激勵】to arouse and encourage; to impel
【激烈】heated (debates, battles, etc.)
【激流】rapids
【激進分子or激烈分子】radicals; extremists
【激將法】urging or prodding somebody by derision, sarcasm, etc.
【激起】to arouse; to excite; to stir up
【激情】fervor; ardor; passion
【激戰】a fierce combat
【激賞】to heap high praise on (a work, person, etc.)
【激昂 or 激昂慷慨】high-spirited; tremendously excited

濁 2302 ㄓㄨㄛˊ zhuó
1. (said of water) turbid or muddy 2. (said of the world) evil, corrupt, tumultuous 3. (said of a person) stupid and idiotic 4. name of a constellation
【濁流】a turbid stream
【濁水】turbid or muddy water
【濁音】a voiced sound

濃 2303 ㄋㄨㄥˊ nóng
1. (said of drinks, liquids, etc.) thick; strong; heavy; concentrated 2. (said of colors) deep; dark 3. dense 4. (said of a smell) strong; heavy
【濃密】(said of the growth of vegetation, beard, hair, etc.) dense; thick
【濃淡】①(said of color) deep or light ②(said of drinks) strong or weak ③(said of make-up) heavy or light ④(said of liquid generally) concentrated or diluted
【濃度】①(chemistry) concentration ② density
【濃湯】thick soup
【濃厚】①(said of material things) thick and dense ②(said of feelings, interest, etc.) deep; great
【濃情蜜意】strong affection and deep love
【濃妝 or 濃粧】heavy make-up
【濃妝艷抹】to wear heavy make-up
【濃茶】strong tea
【濃縮】① to enrich ② to condense; to concentrate
【濃煙】thick smoke; heavy smoke
【濃霧】heavy fog; dense mist
【濃郁】strong; heavy; rich
【濃雲密佈】Dark clouds stretch all over the sky.—a sign of an impending storm

凜 2304 ㄌㄧㄣˇ lǐn
1. desolate; deserted 2. cold; chilly
【凜冽】ice-cold; bone-chilling
【凜然】awe-inspiring

十四畫

濘 2305 1. ㄋㄧㄥˋ nìng
muddy; miry

濘 2305 2. ㄋㄥˋ nèng
pasty; soft and mashy
【濘泥】mire; mud

濛 2306
ㄇㄥˊ méng
misty; drizzly
【濛濛細雨】drizzle; to drizzle

澀 2307
(澁) ㄙㄜˋ sè
1. rough; harsh; not smooth 2. a slightly bitter taste that numbs the tongue—as some unripened fruits; puckery 3. (said of writing, reading, etc.) difficult or jolting 4. slow of tongue
【澀味】astringent taste

濠 2308
ㄏㄠˊ háo
a moat; a trench or ditch
【濠溝】a trench

濟 2309
1. ㄐㄧˋ jì
1. to relieve; to aid 2. to cross a stream 3. to succeed; to be up to standard 4. to benefit; benefits 5. a ford
【濟困扶危】(literally) to relieve the less privileged and help the endangered—compassionate
【濟世】to benefit the world
【濟燃眉之急】to help meet an urgent need
【濟弱扶傾】to help the weak and aid the needy

濟 2309
2. ㄐㄧˇ jǐ
1. various; varied; numerous 2. elegant and dignified 3. name of various counties and a river
【濟濟一堂】to gather together or congregate in this hall

濤 2310
ㄊㄠˊ táo
(又讀 ㄊㄠ tāo)
a big wave; a billow; a heavy swell

濡 2311
ㄖㄨˊ rú
1. to moisten; to immerse; to wet 2. to linger; to procrastinate 3. glossy; smooth 4. to tolerate; to endure

濫 2312
ㄌㄢˋ làn
1. to overflow; to flood; to inundate; inundation 2. to do things without plans; reckless 3. to practice no self-restraint; to give way to unbridled license 4. to abuse (one's power, influence, etc.) 5. false; not true 6. superfluous words or expressions
【濫伐】excessive felling of trees
【濫墾】to cultivate farms in areas where soil conservation should be maintained
【濫交】to befriend at random
【濫殺】to kill at random
【濫觴】the very origin or source (of a practice, tradition, etc.)
【濫竽充數】to hold a post without the necessary qualifications just to make up the number
【濫用】①to spend excessively ② to abuse

濯 2313
ㄓㄨㄛˊ zhuó
1. to wash 2. to eliminate vices 3. grand; magnificent 4. a Chinese family name
【濯濯】① bright and brilliant ② (said of mountains) bare; bald ③ to be fat and sleek

濬 2314
ㄐㄩㄣˋ jùn
1. to dredge a waterway; to dig or wash (a well, etc.) 2. deep; profound
【濬哲】profound wisdom

濱 2315
ㄅㄧㄣ bīn
1. water's edge; to border on 2. same as 瀕—near at hand 3. (military) a low, level seacoast
【濱海地區】the coastal region; the coast
【濱近】close to; near to

濕 2316
(溼) ㄕ shī
damp; moist; wet; humid; to get wet
【濕度】humidity
【濕淋淋】dripping wet; drenched
【濕氣】humidity; dampness; moisture
【濕疹】eczema
【濕潤】damp; to moisten

十五畫

濺 2317
ㄐㄧㄢˋ jiàn
to splash; to sprinkle; to spray; to spill
【濺落】to splash down

瀆 2318
ㄉㄨˊ dú
1. a ditch 2. a river 3. to desecrate; to profane; to blaspheme; to be rude and disrespectful 4. to annoy
【瀆職】malfeasance

〔水部〕

〔水部〕

濾 2319 ㄌㄩˋ lǜ
to filter; to strain out
【濾過性病毒】virus
【濾水池】a depositing reservoir

瀑 2320 1. ㄆㄨˋ pù
a waterfall; a cascade; a cataract
【瀑布】a waterfall; a cataract

瀑 2320 2. ㄅㄠˋ bào
a pouring rain which comes all of a sudden; a sudden shower
【瀑布】a waterfall; a cascade

瀉 2321 ㄒㄧㄝˋ xiè
1. to drain; water flowing down 2. diarrhea; to have loose bowels
【瀉肚(子)】diarrhea
【瀉出】to leak out; to spurt out
【瀉藥or瀉劑】laxatives; purgatives

瀋 2322 ㄕㄣˇ shěn
1. juice; fluid; liquid; water 2. short for Shenyang (Mukden), capital of Liaoning Province
【瀋陽】Mukden (Shenyang), capital of Liaoning Province

瀏 2323 ㄌㄧㄡˊ liú
1. (said of water) clear; bright and clear; the appearance of a clear stream 2. a fast-blowing wind; a cool wind 3. to get away secretly; to take French leave
【瀏覽】to glance over; to skim through

十六畫

瀕 2324 ㄅㄧㄣ bīn
1. near; close to; to border 2. water's edge
【瀕臨】near; on the brink of
【瀕死or瀕於死亡】on the brink of death

瀚 2325 ㄏㄢˋ hàn
vast; expansive

瀝 2326 ㄌㄧˋ lì
1. to fall down by drops; to drip; to trickle 2. remaining drops of wine 3. to strain water or liquids
【瀝青】①asphalt; pitch ②another name of resin

瀟 2327 ㄒㄧㄠ xiāo
1. the sound of beating rain and whistling wind; the roar of a strong wind 2. name of a stream in Hunan
【瀟瀟】a whistling wind and rushing rain
【瀟灑 or 瀟洒】(usually said of a man's manner) dashing and refined

十七畫

瀰 2328 ㄇㄧˊ mí
(said of water) brimming; overflowing
【瀰漫】① brimming or overflowing water ② to permeate

瀾 2329 1. ㄌㄢˊ lán
a great wave; a huge billow

瀾 2329 2. ㄌㄢˋ làn
1. overflowing; dripping wet; a vast expanse of water 2. thin rice paste
【瀾漫】① overflowing; inundating ② wet through ③ sprightly

十八畫

灌 2330 ㄍㄨㄢˋ guàn
1. to water; to fill; to pour (on, into, at); to irrigate 2. to offer a libation 3. shrubs; bushy clumps
【灌迷湯】to flatter; (said of a woman) to utter sweet words to a man for ulterior purposes
【灌木】shrubs
【灌溉】to irrigate; irrigation
【灌救】to save life by forcing medicine down the throat of a dying person
【灌注】① to pour into ② to teach ③ to concentrate (attention) on
【灌腸】to give an enema or clyster
【灌唱片 or 灌音】to cut a record
【灌輸】to instill; to teach; to impart (knowledge to someone); to inculcate
【灌水】to pour water into something
【灌醉】to force someone to drink until he is drunk

十九畫

灑 2331
(洒) ㄙㄚˇ sǎ
1. to splash; to sprinkle (liquids) 2. to wash
【灑脫】casual and carefree
【灑水】to spill water; to sprinkle water
【灑掃】to sprinkle water and sweep

灘 2332
ㄊㄢ tān
a beach; a sandbank; a shoal
【灘頭陣地 or 灘頭堡】a beachhead

二十一畫

灞 2333
ㄅㄚˋ bà
name of a river in Shensi
【灞橋折柳】to part from friends; to bid farewell

二十二畫

灣 2334
ㄨㄢ wān
1.a bay; a gulf; a cove 2.the bend of a stream 3. to anchor; to moor

火部
ㄏㄨㄛˇ huǒ

火 2335
ㄏㄨㄛˇ huǒ
1. fire; flames; to burn with fire 2. fury; anger; temper 3. urgency; urgent; imminent; pressing 4. (Chinese herbal medicine) the latent "heat" in human body
【火把 or 火炬】a torch
【火爆】(dialect) fiery; irritable
【火併】an intramural fight
【火苗子 or 火苗兒】flames
【火夫 or 火伕】a kitchen assistant; (military) a cook
【火腿】Chinese ham
【火腿三明治】a ham sandwich
【火辣辣】burning
【火力】① firepower ② thermal
【火力發電廠】a thermoelectric plant
【火爐子】a stove
【火鍋】a chafing pot; a chafing dish
【火光】the light or glow of fire
【火坑】① a situation of extreme hardship or difficulty ② prostitution
【火海】a great fire; a conflagration
【火候】① the time used in cooking a certain food ② scholastic achievement ③ Taoist alchemy
【火花】sparks
【火化】to cremate; cremation
【火紅】red as fire; fiery; flaming
【火雞】a turkey
【火急】very urgent; imminent
【火箭】a rocket
【火警 or 火警警報】a fire alarm
【火氣】①(Chinese medicine) internal heat ②temper
【火星】① the planet Mars ② sparks
【火燭】① candlelight ② an inflammable substance
【火種】① tinder; embers kept for starting a new fire ② any burning object which causes a fire disaster
【火車】a train
【火車票】train tickets
【火車站】a railway station
【火車時間表】a train schedule
【火柴】a match
【火柴盒】a matchbox
【火場】the scene of a fire
【火勢】the intensity and scope of a fire
【火舌】tongues of flame
【火燒眉毛】very urgent or imminent
【火首】one whose house is the first to catch fire
【火山】a volcano
【火傷】a burn
【火上加油】(literally) to pour oil on the flame — to make things worse
【火熱】passionate; enthusiastic; intimate
【火災】a fire disaster
【火災保險 or 火險】fire insurance
【火葬】to cremate; cremation
【火葬場】a crematory; a crematorium
【火傘高張】the scorching sunshine in summer—like a fully spread umbrella of fire
【火速】urgently; imminent; urgent
【火藥】gunpowder
【火藥庫】a powder magazine; an ammunition depot
【火藥味or火藥氣息】the smell of gunpowder — a tense situation

which can easily erupt into open hostilities
【火燄】flames

二畫

火部

灰 2336
ㄏㄨㄟ huī
1. ashes; dust 2. lime 3. gray (color) 4. disheartened; disappointed or discouraged 5. (now rarely) to break into tiny pieces or particles
【灰白】pale; ashen
【灰蒙蒙】dusky; overcast
【灰姑娘】Cinderella
【灰燼】ashes; ember
【灰心】disappointed; discouraged; disheartened
【灰塵】dust
【灰色】gray color
【灰暗】murky gray; gloomy

三畫

灸 2337
ㄐㄧㄡˇ jiǔ
(Chinese medicine) to cauterize by burning moxa; moxa cautery; moxibustion

灼 2338
ㄓㄨㄛˊ zhuó
1. to burn; to cauterize 2. bright; clear; luminous; brilliant 3. flowers in full bloom
【灼傷】burn
【灼熱】intense heat; red-hot

災 2339
(灾、菑、烖) ㄗㄞ zāi
a disaster; a calamity; a catastrophe
【災民】refugees created by disasters
【災難or災變】disasters; calamities
【災害or災患】disasters; calamities
【災荒】famine caused by floods or droughts
【災情】the extent of a disaster or calamity
【災情慘重】①The situation in the afflicted area is serious. ②(now often used comically) heavy losses
【災區】the afflicted area; the disaster area

四畫

炎 2340
ㄧㄢˊ yán
1. burning; hot; sultry 2. to blaze; to flame; to flare up 3. inflammation
【炎涼】①(said of weather) hot and cold ② snobbishness
【炎夏】hot summer
【炎熱】(said of weather) very hot
【炎炎】① awe-inspiring ② very hot

炊 2341
ㄔㄨㄟ chuī
to cook
【炊具】cooking utensils
【炊事】cooking
【炊烟】the smoke from a kitchen fire
【炊烟裊裊】smoke spiraling from kitchens
【炊烟四起】cooking smoke all around—It's about mealtime.

炕 2342
ㄎㄤˋ kàng
1. dry; to dry 2. hot 3. *kang*, a brick bed warmed by a fire underneath (in North China)

炙 2343
ㄓˋ zhì
to burn; to cauterize; to roast; to broil; to heat
【炙手可熱】very influential and powerful

炒 2344
ㄔㄠˇ chǎo
to fry; to stir-fry
【炒米粉】to fry rice noodles; fried rice noodles
【炒麵】to fry noodles; fried noodles
【炒飯】to fry rice; fried rice
【炒蛋】scrambled eggs
【炒地皮】to engage in land speculation
【炒股票】to manipulate stock trading
【炒熱】① to jack up the price of stocks by manipulation ② to make an ordinary news event a top story by sensational reporting
【炒菜】to fry vegetables or meat; fried dishes
【炒魷魚】(slang) to be fired

五畫

炫 2345
ㄒㄩㄢˋ xuàn
1. to show off; to display; to flaunt 2. dazzling; bright; shining
【炫惑】to dazzle and confuse
【炫耀】① to flaunt; to show off ② bright and brilliant

炬 2346 ㄐㄩˋ jù
1. a torch 2. fire

炮 2347 1. ㄆㄠˊ páo
as in 炮製—to refine medicinal herbs

炮 2347 2. (砲) ㄆㄠˋ pào
a big gun, cannon, etc.

炮 2347 3. (炰) ㄅㄠ bāo
1. to roast or bake 2. to dry by heat

炯 2348 (烱) ㄐㄩㄥˇ jiǒng
bright; brightness; clear: 炯戒 a clear warning

炳 2349 ㄅㄧㄥˇ bǐng
bright; luminous

炸 2350 1. ㄓㄚˋ zhà
1. to explode; to burst; to bomb 2. to get mad 3. to disperse boisterously; to flee in terror
【炸彈】bombs
【炸燬】to blow up; to blast
【炸傷】to be injured in bombing or explosion
【炸死】to kill by bombing
【炸藥】dynamite; explosives

炸 2350 2. ㄓㄚˊ zhá
to fry in oil or fat; to deep-fry
【炸雞】① to fry chicken ② fried chicken
【炸醬麵】a kind of noodles served with fried bean sauce and minced meat

炭 2351 ㄊㄢˋ tàn
1. charcoal 2. coal 3. (chemistry) C—carbon
【炭筆】charcoal for drawing
【炭水化合物】carbohydrate

為 2352 1. ㄨㄟˊ wéi
simplified form of 爲—to be; to do; to make

為 2352 2. ㄨㄟˋ wèi
simplified form of 爲—for

六畫

烏 2353 ㄨ wū
1. a crow, raven or rook 2. dark color 3. how; what; when 4. Alas! 5. (now rarely) the sun 6. a Chinese family name
【烏梅】dried plums
【烏木】ebony
【烏托邦】①utopia—an ideal place or state ②*Utopia*
【烏溜溜】(said of eyes) dark and liquid
【烏龍茶】oolong tea
【烏龜】①a turtle; a tortoise ②a cuckold
【烏合之衆】a mob; a rabble
【烏黑】pitch-dark (night); raven black (hair)
【烏雞 or 烏骨雞】dark-skinned and dark-boned chicken
【烏賊】the cuttlefish; the inkfish
【烏鴉】a crow; a raven
【烏有】nothingness
【烏烟瘴氣】(said of air) heavily polluted; now also used figuratively to indicate corruption, confusion, etc.
【烏魚】black mullet
【烏魚子】mullet's roe
【烏雲】① dark clouds ②(figuratively) a woman's black hair
【烏雲密佈】as dark clouds mass up—A heavy downpour is in the making or the situation is getting dangerous or imminent.

烈 2354 ㄌㄧㄝˋ liè
1. fiery; acute; vehement; fierce; strong; violent 2. honest and virtuous; just and straightforward; chaste 3. merits; achievements
【烈女】a girl of virtuous upbringing
【烈火】a blazing fire; a fierce fire
【烈酒】strong drink; a stiff drink
【烈士 or 烈漢】martyrs
【烈日】the scorching sun
【烈日當空】the scorching sun high up in the sky
【烈焰】blazing flames; a violent or fierce fire

烝 2355 ㄓㄥ zhēng
1. to rise—as steam 2. many; numerous 3. lewdness, incest, etc. among the older generation 4. to steam 亦作「蒸」
【烝民】the people; the masses

烘 2356 ㄏㄨㄥ hōng
1. as in 烘烤—to bake; to roast

火部

2. to dry or warm near a fire
【烘焙】to dry (herbal medicine) over a fire
【烘托】to make conspicuous by contrast
【烘乾】to dry beside or over a fire
【烘乾機】a clothing dryer

〔火部〕

烤 2357 ㄎㄠˇ kǎo
1. to roast; to bake; to toast 2. to warm by a fire 3. scorching
【烤麵包】to toast bread
【烤麵包機】a toaster
【烤箱】an oven for baking
【烤肉】① to barbecue ② barbecue
【烤鴨】①to roast duck ②roasted duck

烟 2358 ㄧㄢ yān
simplified form of 煙

烙 2359 ㄌㄠˋ lào
(讀音 ㄌㄨㄛˋ luò)
1. to burn 2. to brand; to iron 3. to bake in a pan
【烙鐵】an iron; a branding iron
【烙印】to brand; a brand

七畫

烽 2360 ㄈㄥ fēng
(in ancient China) a tall structure (on a city wall, etc.) where fire was made to signal enemy invasion or presence of bandits
【烽火】signal fires; beacon fires
【烽火連年】continuous wars
【烽烟四起】a land or country beset by war

烹 2361 ㄆㄥ pēng
1. to cook; to boil; to decoct 2. (cooking) to add bean sauce and dressing after frying 3. (slang) to frighten (away)
【烹調 or 烹飪】to cook or prepare (food); cooking
【烹煮】to cook; to boil

焉 2362 ㄧㄢ yān
1. an interrogative—how, why, when, etc. 2. a pronoun—it 3. an adverb—there; here 4. a conjunctive—and so; so that 5. a final particle indicating numerous senses
【焉能】How can (one do it, succeed, etc.)?
【焉敢】How dare...?
【焉知非福】How could you know it is not a blessing?

八畫

焙 2363 ㄅㄟˋ bèi
to dry or heat near a fire; to toast; to bake

焚 2364 ㄈㄣˊ fén
to burn; to set fire to
【焚膏繼晷】(figuratively) to be very diligent in study
【焚化】①to cremate ②to burn (offerings, etc.) for the dead ③ to put to fire
【焚化爐】an incinerator
【焚毀】to burn up; to destroy by fire
【焚香】to burn incense
【焚燒】to burn; to destroy by burning

焦 2365 ㄐㄧㄠ jiāo
1. scorched or burned; charred 2. the smell or stench of things burned 3. worried and anxious 4. a Chinese family name
【焦煤 or 焦炭】coke
【焦點】① focus ② a burning point; a focal point
【焦慮】deeply worried and anxious
【焦慮不安】to be on pins and needles
【焦黃】pale yellow
【焦急】very anxious; in deep anxiety
【焦距】(physics) focus
【焦躁】worried, anxious and getting impatient

無 2366 ㄨˊ wú
1. negative; not; no; none 2. without; destitute of; wanting; to lack; to have not 3. no matter what (or how); not yet
【無比】incomparable; peerless
【無病呻吟】① to groan for no reason ②(said of writing) affected sentimentality
【無不】all without exception
【無明火】fury; wrath; anger
【無名小卒】a nobody; an unimportant person
【無名指】the ring finger
【無名英雄】an unsung hero
【無法】unable; incapable
【無法形容】beyond description

【無法無天】lawless and godless

【無非】no other than; nothing but

【無分軒輊】well-matched; a draw

【無妨】① doesn't matter ② there's no harm

【無風不起浪】There must be a cause or reason for this.

【無敵】matchless; invincible

【無的放矢】(literally) to shoot without a target—indiscriminate; to attack without a cause

【無地自容】extremely embarrassed or ashamed

【無毒】poisonless; harmless

【無獨有偶】It happens that there is a similar case.

【無端】without cause or reason

【無動於衷】① unmoved; flinty-hearted ② to remain firm

【無奈】can't help it

【無能】incompetent; incapable

【無能爲力】unable to help; can't do anything about it; powerless

【無賴】a villain; a rascal

【無理】unreasonable

【無理取鬧】to make trouble without a cause

【無力】①feeble; weak ②cannot afford

【無利可圖】profitless

【無立錐之地】very poor; stark poverty

【無聊】①ennui; boredom ②nonsensical; silly

【無路可走】at the end of one's rope; no way out

【無論】① no matter; whatever ② let alone; to say nothing of

【無論如何】anyway; in any case

【無辜】innocent; guiltless

【無故】uncalled-for; without cause or reason

【無關】irrelevant; to have nothing to do with

【無關緊要】not important; of no consequence or significance

【無可奈何】having no alternative; to have to

【無可厚非】shouldn't be blamed too much for that—no serious mistakes committed

【無可救藥】incorrigible; incurable

【無孔不入】to let no opportunity slip by (in the pursuit of one's selfish ends)

【無害】harmless; not injurious

【無後】heirless; without posterity

【無話不談】to keep no secrets from each other

【無稽之談 or 無稽之言】groundless utterances; wild talks; rumors

【無疾而終】to die without any apparent ailment or disease

【無幾】① not much; not many; little ② not long afterwards; shortly

【無際】(said of space) boundless

【無計可施】helpless; at one's wit's end

【無濟於事】won't help the matter; to no avail

【無家可歸】homeless

【無價之寶】a priceless treasure

【無堅不摧】to overrun all fortifications

【無精打采】listless; dejected; despondent; low-spirited

【無拘無束 or 無拘束】freely; unconstrained; carefree

【無期】no definite term or date

【無期徒刑】life imprisonment

【無奇不有】Nothing is too strange (in the world, this school, etc.).

【無牽無掛】to have no cares

【無情】callous; heartless; ruthless

【無窮】endless; boundless; limitless

【無窮無盡】endless; infinite; boundless; limitless

【無隙可乘】to have no loophole to exploit

【無瑕】without blemish, defect or fault—perfect

【無懈可擊】flawless; invulnerable

【無效】① ineffective; useless; to no avail ② invalid; null and void

【無限】limitless; boundless; infinite

【無線電】radio; wireless

【無線電話】radiophone

【無心】① unintentional ② in no mood

【無形中】insidiously; unknowingly

【無須】unnecessary; no need to

【無知】ignorant; (said of a child) innocent

【無中生有】(literally) to make something out of nothing—to fabricate; to invent; to frame up

【無恥】shameless; brazen; impudent

【無產階級】the proletariat

【無出其右】Nobody can better him. 或 second to none

【無師自通】to acquire a skill without being taught

【無時無刻】always; all the time

【無視】to pay no attention to

【無傷大雅】It doesn't matter.
【無上光榮】the highest honor
【無聲】noiseless; silent
【無數】① countless; numerous ② an uncertain number of
【無雙】peerless; matchless; unique; unrivaled
【無人過問】(literally) Nobody asks about it. 或 Nobody cares about it.
【無足輕重】of little significance
【無罪】innocent; guiltless; not guilty
【無私】selfless; unselfish
【無所不在】omnipresent; ubiquitous
【無所不能】omnipotent
【無所不知】to know everything; omniscient
【無所不爲】ready to do anything, however bad it may be
【無所事事】to do nothing; to idle away one's time
【無所適從】don't know where to turn to; indecisive
【無所謂】do not care
【無惡不作】to stop at nothing in doing evil
【無礙】① no harm; all right ② (Buddhism) *apratihata*
【無一不精】to be an expert in everything
【無依無靠】with no one to turn to or rely on
【無益】useless; without benefit
【無異】not different from; tantamount to
【無意】to have no interest in; to have no intention (of doing something)
【無意中or無意間】unexpectedly; accidentally
【無意識】① (psychology) unconsciousness ② unintentional
【無業遊民】a vagrant
【無憂無慮】carefree
【無垠】(said of space) boundless, limitless
【無恙】to feel well; all right
【無影無踪】(to vanish or disappear) without a trace
【無誤】correct; right
【無微不至】very thoughtful; to considerate in every way
【無味】① tasteless; dull (offers, etc.) ② unpalatable
【無往不利】successful in whatever one does
【無望】① hopeless; to despair of ② do not expect that...
【無妄之災】unexpected misfortunes
【無虞匱乏】no fear of deficiency
【無與倫比】beyond comparison; peerless; unique; unparalleled
【無緣】① no opportunity or chance ② unable to ③ an inexplicable animosity toward somebody
【無緣無故】without cause or reason
【無庸置疑】unquestionable
【無用】useless; of no use

然 2367
ㄖㄢˊ rán
1. yes; most certainly; permission; right; correct 2. however; but; still; nevertheless; on the other hand 3. really; if so 4. same as 燃— to burn
【然後】then; afterward; later
【然而】however; but; nevertheless

焰 2368
(燄) ㄧㄢˋ yàn
(又讀 ㄧㄢˊ yán)
1. flames; blazes 2. glowing; brilliant

九畫

煉 2369
ㄌㄧㄢˋ liàn
1. to smelt; to refine; to condense (milk); to temper (a metal) with fire 2. (Chinese medicine) to keep herbs, etc. boiling for a long time 3. to train; to form character by hardship
【煉鋼】to refine steel; steelmaking
【煉鋼廠】a steel refinery; a steel mill
【煉製】to refine
【煉乳】condensed milk
【煉油】① oil refining ② to extract oil by heat ③ to heat edible oil
【煉油廠】an oil refinery
【煉獄】the purgatory

煙 2370
(烟) ㄧㄢ yān
1. smoke; fumes 2. tobacco; a smoke; a cigarette 3. mist; vapor 4. opium
【煙幕】a smoke screen
【煙斗】a pipe (for smoking)
【煙蒂 or 煙頭】a cigarette butt
【煙毒】the poisoning effect of opium-smoking
【煙鬼】an opium smoker or addict;

a heavy smoker
【煙花巷or煙花柳巷】a red-light district
【煙火】① kitchen smoke which suggests presence of humans ② cooked food (as distinct from herbs and fruits which are supposed to be the food of immortals) ③ a signal fire or beacon ④ fireworks ⑤ smoke and fire
【煙灰】cigarette ashes; cigar ashes
【煙灰缸】an ashtray
【煙禁】prohibition of opium smoking
【煙消雲散】to vanish completely; to disappear
【煙嘴兒】a cigarette holder
【煙草 or 菸草】tobacco
【煙囱】a chimney; a stovepipe
【煙絲】cut-tobacco for pipe smoking
【煙癮】① opium or tobacco addiction ② a craving for tobacco
【煙霧】smoke; mist; vapor; smog

煤 2371
ㄇㄟˊ méi
1. coal; charcoal; coke 2. carbon; soot
【煤炭】coal; anthracite
【煤礦】① a coal mine ② a coal shaft
【煤礦工人】a coal miner
【煤氣】gas (for lighting or heating)
【煤氣中毒】gas poisoning
【煤油】kerosene

煥 2372
ㄏㄨㄢˋ huàn
1. bright; brilliant; lustrous; luminous 2. (said of an appearance) shining; vigorous and elegant
【煥發】scintillating; shining; radiant
【煥然一新】brand-new

煩 2373
ㄈㄢˊ fán
1. to vex; to annoy; to worry 2. annoying 3. to trouble 4. superfluous and confusing
【煩悶or煩懣】annoyed; downcast; bored; depressed; vexed; worried
【煩惱】worries; cares; worried
【煩亂】confusing
【煩請】Would you mind...?
【煩囂】① the hubbub of a noisy place ② cares and worries of this world
【煩心】vexation
【煩雜】petty and varied; confusing and disorderly
【煩躁】vexed; short-tempered
【煩瑣】petty and multitudinous; tedious
【煩文縟節】petty formalities; red tape

煮 2374
(煑) ㄓㄨˇ zhǔ
to cook; to boil; to stew; to decoct
【煮沸】to boil
【煮飯】to cook rice; to cook meals
【煮豆燃萁】fraternal persecution
【煮爛】to stew something until it's tender
【煮鶴焚琴】to destroy something fine by behaving rudely
【煮熟】to cook thoroughly
【煮菜】to prepare food or dishes

煎 2375
ㄐㄧㄢ jiān
1. to fry in fat or oil 2. to decoct 3. (figuratively) to torment; to kill
【煎餅】pancakes
【煎蛋】① to fry eggs ② fried eggs
【煎炒】to fry; to stir-fry
【煎熬】① to decoct until almost dry ② to torture; to torment
【煎藥】to make a decoction of herbal medicines
【煎魚】to fry fish

煞 2376
1. ㄕㄚˋ shà
1. a fierce god; a malignant deity; an evil spirit; a goblin 2. very; much; extremely 3. to bring to an end; to conclude
【煞費苦心】to have made painstaking effort
【煞風景】to spoil pleasure
【煞星】a malignant star—(usually said of a person) that brings wars, deaths, calamities, disasters, etc.
【煞是】very (interesting, encouraging, etc.)

煞 2376
2. ㄕㄚ shā
1. to tighten; to bind 2. to offset; to reduce; to mitigate 3. an auxiliary particle in old usage 4. to brake; to stop; to bring to a close
【煞車】① to fasten goods on a truck or cart with ropes ② to brake

煦 2377
ㄒㄩˇ xǔ
1. warm and cozy 2. kindness; favors; good graces; kind and gracious
【煦煦】① kind; gracious; benevo-

lent ②(said of weather) warm and fine

照 2378 ㄓㄠˋ zhào
〔火部〕
1. to shine upon; to light or illumine 2. a certificate or license 3. according to; in accordance with; to pattern on or after 4. to compare, collate, survey, etc. 5. to photograph; to take a picture; to shoot 6. to look after; to take care of 7. to notify or proclaim 8. sunshine 9. a picture

【照辦】to act upon; to comply with; to manage, or handle something according to instructions, orders, etc.
【照本宣科】to repeat what the book says
【照片】a photograph; a snapshot
【照面】to meet; to come face to face
【照明設備】illuminating equipment
【照發】to issue as before
【照例】to follow precedents or usual practices; as a rule
【照料】to take care of; to look after
【照錄 or 照抄】to record or copy exactly as what is said or written
【照顧】①to look after; to take care of ②to patronize ③to consider
【照舊】as usual; as before
【照相】to take a picture or photograph
【照相館】a photostudio
【照相機】a camera
【照相師】a photographer
【照准】to approve (a request); to grant
【照常】as usual
【照射】to shine or light upon; to radiate
【照收】①to duly receive ②to accept accordingly
【照說】as a rule
【照算】① to calaulate or charge (the listed items) accordingly ② to charge without deduction, discount, etc.
【照耀】to radiate; to light up; to shine
【照樣】① to pattern after; to copy ② as usual; in the old manner
【照應】① to take care of; to look after ② to correlate

十畫

熙 2379 ㄒㄧ xī
1. bright and brilliant; glorious 2. expansive; spacious 3. flourishing; prosperous; booming 4. peaceful and happy
【熙來壤往 or 熙來攘往】the hustle and bustle of large crowds
【熙熙壤壤 or 熙熙攘攘】crowded and noisy; hustle and bustle

熊 2380 ㄒㄩㄥˊ xióng
1. a bear 2. shining bright 3. a Chinese family name
【熊貓】a panda
【熊心豹膽】tremendous bravery or courage
【熊熊】flaming and glorious; shining
【熊熊大火】a blazing fire

熏 2381 (燻) ㄒㄩㄣ xūn
1. smoke; to smoke; to burn; smoked (meat, fish, etc.) 2. (said of smell) to assail nostrils 3. warm; mild 4. to move or touch 5. same as 曛 or 薰 6. to scent; to fumigate
【熏陶】to influence; to educate; to train
【熏天】overwhelming
【熏黑】to blacken by smoke
【熏炙】to cauterize
【熏肉】to smoke meat; smoked meat; bacon
【熏染】to influence
【熏死】suffocated to death (by fumes, stench, etc.)
【熏魚】①to smoke fish② smoked fish

熄 2382 ㄒㄧˊ xí
1. to extinguish (a fire); to put out (a light) 2. to quash; to destroy; to obliterate
【熄滅】to extinguish (a fire); to put out (a light); to die out
【熄燈】to turn or switch off the light
【熄火】① to stop the fire (in the boiler)—to stop operation ② to turn off the lamp or light

煽 2383 ㄕㄢ shān
1. to stir up; to instigate; to incite; to fan 2. flaming; blazing; to flame
【煽動】to incite; to stir up (a strike, uprising, etc.)

【煽火】to fan the fire

熔 2384 (鎔) ㄖㄨㄥˊ róng
to smelt; to weld or fuse metals
【熔爐】a smelting furnace; a melting pot
【熔化】to smelt; to melt
【熔解】to smelt; to melt; to fuse
【熔鑄】founding; casting
【熔岩】lava

熒 2385 ㄧㄥˊ yíng
1. bright; shining; luminous 2. dazzling; glittering; sparkling; glimmering 3. to doubt; to suspect

十一畫

熟 2386 ㄕㄨˊ shú (讀音 ㄕㄡˊ shóu)
1. cooked or well-done (as opposed to raw); prepared or processed 2. ripe (fruit); to ripen 3. very familiar; well versed; experienced; conversant 4. careful or painstaking (survey, study, inspection, etc.) 5. deep or sound (sleep)
【熟讀】to read thoroughly; to memorize by rote
【熟能生巧】Practice makes perfect.
【熟面孔】a familiar face
【熟練】experienced, skilled or dexterous
【熟路】a familiar route
【熟客 or 熟主顧】an old customer or patron; a frequent visitor
【熟記】to learn by heart; to memorize
【熟悉】very familiar with
【熟習】to be skilled in
【熟知】well acquainted or familiar with; to know well
【熟視】to look carefully and for a long time
【熟識】very familiar with
【熟手】an experienced or skilled hand
【熟睡】a sound sleep; to sleep soundly
【熟人】an old acquaintance
【熟諳】to be well versed in; to be an expert in

熬 2387 1. ㄠ āo
1. to extract (oil, etc.) by applying heat 2. to cook; to stew or simmer 3. to endure with perseverance; to suffer with patience (an ordeal, etc.); to sustain
【熬粥】to cook congee or gruel by simmering
【熬出來 or 熬出頭】to have gone through all sorts of ordeal
【熬夜】to burn the midnight oil
【熬藥】to decoct medicinal herbs

熬 2387 2. ㄠ āo
1. to cook; to stew 2. to be worn down by worries, cares; discouraged or despondent; dejected

熱 2388 ㄖㄜˋ rè
1. hot; heated; burning; to heat 2. fever 3. earnest; ardent; zealous; enthusiastic; passionate
【熱病】fever
【熱門】something very much in vogue or fashion; a craze
【熱帶】the tropics: 熱帶魚 tropical fish
【熱度】① heat; temperature ② enthusiasm
【熱湯】hot soup
【熱騰騰】piping hot; steaming hot
【熱鬧】①bustling; populous; noisy ②prosperous; thriving ③lively; merry
【熱淚盈眶】tearful; eyes moistening
【熱浪】a heat wave; a hot wave
【熱烈】fervent; passionate; vehement
【熱戀】to be passionately in love
【熱量】the quantity of heat; calories
【熱絡】on friendly terms; very intimate
【熱狗】a hot dog
【熱烘烘的】red-hot; white-hot
【熱氣】hot vapor; hot gas; hot air; heat
【熱切】fervent; earnest; sincerely
【熱情】passion; ardor; fervor
【熱血】hot-blooded; fiery-spirited; fervent; zealous
【熱血沸騰】to seethe with fervor
【熱心】zealous; warm-hearted
【熱忱】enthusiasm; sincerity; earnest
【熱誠】earnestness; sincerity
【熱身運動】warm-up exercise
【熱水瓶】a thermos (bottle)
【熱水器】a water heater
【熱愛】to love passionately
【熱飲】hot drinks

熨 2389
1. ㄩㄣˋ yùn
to iron (clothes or cloth)
【熨斗】an iron (for pressing clothes)
【熨衣服】to iron clothes

熨 2389
2. ㄩˋ yù
to settle (matters)

十二畫

熾 2390
ㄔˋ chì
1. intense; vigorous; energetic 2. burning hot; flaming
【熾熱】intense heat; intensely hot

燈 2391
ㄉㄥ dēng
1. a lamp; a lantern; a burner 2. Buddhadharma; the Buddhist doctrine 3. a valve; a tube
【燈泡兒】an electric bulb; a light bulb
【燈謎】lantern riddles
【燈塔】a lighthouse
【燈籠】a lantern: 燈籠褲knickerbockers
【燈光】lamplight; lights; illumination
【燈火】lamplight; lights; illumination
【燈紅酒綠】a scene of debauchery
【燈心 or 燈蕊】lampwick; wick
【燈蛾撲火】a suicidal act; an act of self-destruction
【燈油】lamp oil

燃 2392
ㄖㄢˊ rán
to burn; to ignite; to light
【燃眉之急】a matter as urgent as if the eyebrows had caught fire
【燃放】to set off (fireworks, etc.)
【燃料】fuel
【燃燒】to burn; to be on fire; to be in flames; combustion

燎 2393
1. ㄌㄧㄠˊ liáo
1. to burn over a wider and wider area; to set fire to 2. to be brilliant
【燎原】to set the prairie ablaze

燎 2393
2. ㄌㄧㄠˇ liǎo
to singe

燉 2394
1. ㄉㄨㄣˋ dùn
1. to stew; to simmer 2. to warm

燉 2394
2. ㄉㄨㄣ dūn
Tunhwang, Kansu

燒 2395
ㄕㄠ shāo
1. to burn 2. to roast; to stew 3. to boil; to heat 4. to run a fever; to have a temperature 5. a fever
【燒杯】a beaker
【燒餅】a sesame seed cake
【燒烤】to roast
【燒燬】to burn down; to destroy in fire
【燒焦】to scorch; to sear; to singe
【燒酒】white spirits
【燒香】to burn joss sticks in worship
【燒殺】burning and killing; atrocities committed by enemy troops, bandits, etc.
【燒傷】burns
【燒水】to boil water; to heat water
【燒死】to burn to death

熹 2396
(㶿) ㄒㄧ xī
1. faint sunlight; dawn 2. giving out faint light
【熹微】① faint light at dawn ② (said of morning sunlight) dim; pale

燕 2397
1. ㄧㄢˋ yàn
1. a swallow 2. comfort; ease 3. to feast; to enjoy
【燕麥】oats
【燕麥片】oatmeal
【燕好】(said of husband and wife) very fond of each other
【燕瘦環肥】beautiful women, each of whom is attractive in her own way
【燕子or燕兒】a swallow
【燕安】comfort; ease; peace
【燕爾新婚】marital happiness
【燕尾服】a swallowtail; a tailcoat
【燕語(呢喃)】the soft chirping of swallows

燕 2397
2. ㄧㄢ yān
a state in what is Hopeh (河北) today during the Epoch of Warring States

燙 2398
ㄊㄤˋ tàng
1. to scald; to burn 2. to heat; to warm 3. very hot 4. to iron
【燙髮】to have a permanent wave
【燙金】gilding; bronzing
【燙手】① to scald one's hand ② difficult to handle or manage
【燙傷】a burn; a scald

【燙衣服】 to iron clothes

2399
燜 ㄇㄣ mèn
(又讀 ㄇㄣ mēn)
to cook with mild heat in a closed vessel; to cook in a casserole

十三畫

營 2400 ㄧㄥ yíng
1. military barracks; a camp; a battalion 2. to manage; to administer; to handle; to operate; to run
【營房】 barracks
【營利】 to engage in making profit
【營火】 a campfire
【營救】 to rescue or deliver
【營建】 to manage or handle the construction of; to construct
【營長】 a battalion commander
【營生】 to make a living
【營造or營建】 to build; to construct; to
【營造商】 a (building) contractor
【營私舞弊】 to seek personal gain illicitly while holding a public post; to practice graft
【營業】 to engage in business; business operation
【營業執照】 a business license
【營業時間】 business hours
【營養】 nutrition; nourishment
【營養不良】 malnutrition

燧 2401 ㄙㄨㄟ suì
1. as in 燧石—flint 2. a beacon

燠 2402 1. ㄩ yù
warm

燠 2402 2. ㄠ ào
as in 燠熱—very hot; sweltering

燦 2403 ㄘㄢ càn
as in 燦爛—bright; brilliant; resplendent

燬 2404 ㄏㄨㄟ huǐ
1. fire; a blaze 2. to destroy by fire; to burn away; to burn down

燥 2405 ㄗㄠ zào
1. arid; dry; parched 2. impatient; restless
【燥熱】 dry and hot

燴 2406 ㄏㄨㄟ huì
1. to put (a variety of materials) together and cook; to braise 2. to serve (noodles, rice, etc.) with a topping of meat, vegetables, etc., in gravy

燭 2407 ㄓㄨ zhú
1. a candle 2. to illuminate; to shine upon
【燭臺】 a candlestick; a candlestand
【燭光】 ① (physics) candle power ② candlelight
【燭心 or 燭芯】 candlewick

十四畫

燼 2408 ㄐㄧㄣ jìn
1. embers; ashes; cinders 2. victims of disasters

十五畫

爆 2409 ㄅㄠ bào
1. to explode; to burst; to crack 2. to quick-boil; to quick-fry
【爆破】 to demolish by explosives; demolition
【爆米花】 popcorn
【爆發】 ① to explode; to blow up ② to break out; to erupt; to flare up
【爆裂】 to burst; to erupt; to crack
【爆炸】 to explode; to blow up
【爆炸力】 explosive force; the impact of explosion
【爆竹】 firecrackers

爍 2410 ㄕㄨㄛ shuò
1. to glitter; to glisten; to sparkle 2. to melt

十六畫

爐 2411 ㄌㄨ lú
a stove; an oven; a fireplace; a hearth
【爐臺兒】 a mantel
【爐火純青】 The skill is mature.
【爐子】 a stove; a furnace; a kiln
【爐竈】 ① a cooking stove ② (figuratively) a start; an enterprise

十七畫

爛 2412 ㄌㄢˋ làn
1. overripe; rotten; to rot; to fester 2. cooked soft; well cooked 3. bright; brilliant 4. to scald; to burn; to scorch 5. worn-out 6. dissolute
【爛漫】① resplendent ② dissipated; debauched ③ fast asleep ④ naive
【爛攤子】a shambles
【爛泥】soft mud; mire
【爛好人】one who cannot say no to requests for help or favor
【爛貨】① (abusive language) a woman of easy virtue ② worthless goods
【爛賬】uncollectable debts
【爛熟】① very ripe ② thoroughly familiar
【爛醉如泥】dead drunk

爪 部
ㄓㄠˇ zhǎo

爪 2413 1. ㄓㄠˇ zhǎo
1. a nail 2. a claw; a talon
【爪牙】lackeys; cat's-paws
【爪牙鷹犬】lackeys and hired ruffians
【爪印】a trace; a print; a nail mark

爪 2413 2. ㄓㄨㄚˇ zhuǎ
as in 爪子—a claw; a paw; a talon

四畫

爬 2414 ㄆㄚˊ pá
1. to creep; to crawl 2. to climb; to clamber 3. to scratch 4. to lie face downwards
【爬起來】to get up
【爬牆】to climb a fence
【爬行】① to crawl; to creep ② a crawl
【爬蟲】a reptile
【爬山】to climb mountains
【爬山者】an alpinist; a mountaineer

爭 2415 ㄓㄥ zhēng
1. to contend; to struggle; to strive 2. to fight; to dispute; to argue; to quarrel 3. short of; to lack; to be deficient in
【爭霸】to contend (or struggle) for hegemony
【爭霸戰】a fight for hegemony; a power struggle
【爭辯】to argue; to debate; to dispute
【爭面子】to try to win or excel for the sake of face
【爭風吃醋】to fight for the affection of a man or woman
【爭鬥or爭鬪】to struggle; to conflict
【爭奪】to struggle for; to contend for
【爭端】the cause of dispute, or quarrel
【爭光】to win glory
【爭功】to contend for credit
【爭氣】don't let down; to try to win credit for
【爭強鬥勝】to desire to excel over others
【爭取】to win over; to compete for
【爭權奪利】to fight for selfish gains
【爭先恐後】anxious to be ahead of others
【爭雄】to struggle or contend for supremacy
【爭執 or 爭持】to argue or dispute obstinately
【爭吵】to quarrel; to wrangle
【爭議 or 爭論】to dispute; to argue
【爭妍鬥艷】to contend in beauty and fascination

八畫

爲 2416 1. (為) ㄨㄟˊ wéi
1. to do; to act 2. to manage; to handle; to exercise; to administer; to govern 3. to serve as 4. to become 5. to be
【爲憑 or 爲據】to use as proof; to use as evidence
【爲非作歹】to do evil
【爲富不仁】wealthy but unkind
【爲頭 or 爲首】① to be the head or leader ② headed by; led by
【爲難】① troubled; in difficulties or a dilemma ② to make things difficult (for another)
【爲患 or 爲害】to bring trouble
【爲期不遠】in the near future; soon
【爲學】to engage in studies
【爲止】① until; till; up to ② no further
【爲證】to serve as proof; to serve as evidence
【爲主】mainly; to be the most important

【爲時過早】premature; too early
【爲生】to make a living
【爲人】one's personality, character or temperament
【爲人師表】to be a model of virtue for others
【爲所欲爲】to do as one pleases
【爲業】as a means of livelihood
【爲伍】to associate or mix (with)

爲 2416
2. (為) ㄨㄟˋ wèi
for; for the good of; for the sake of
【爲民除害】to remove the evils from the people
【爲國捐軀】to sacrifice one's life for the fatherland
【爲國爭光】to struggle for the glory of one's country
【爲何】Why? 或 for what reason
【爲虎作倀】to help an evil person do evil
【爲…起見】in order to...; for the purpose of...
【爲甚麼】What for? 或 Why?
【爲人說項】to say a good word for someone
【爲人作嫁】to work for others without profiting oneself
【爲此】because of this; for this reason

十四畫

爵 2417
ㄐㄩㄝˊ jué
1. a degree or a title of nobility; peerage; the rank or dignity of a peer 2. an ancient wine pitcher with three legs and a loop handle
【爵士】Sir (a title of nobility)
【爵士音樂】jazz; jazz music
【爵位】a degree of nobility

父部
ㄈㄨˋ fù

父 2418
1. ㄈㄨˋ fù
1. father 2. a male relative of an elder generation 3. to do father's duties
【父母】parents; father and mother
【父母官】a local official; a magistrate
【父老】elders
【父親】father
【父親節】Father's Day (falling on August 8)
【父兄】male seniors in a family
【父子】father and son

父 2418
2. ㄈㄨˇ fǔ
a respectful term for an elderly man in ancient times

四畫

爸 2419
ㄅㄚˋ bà
as in 爸爸—father; papa

六畫

爹 2420
ㄉㄧㄝ diē
father
【爹娘 or 爹孃】father and mother; parents

九畫

爺 2421
ㄧㄝˊ yé
1. father 2. master; sir 3. god
【爺兒們】men and boys
【爺兒倆】father and son; father and daughter
【爺爺】①grandfather; grandpa② sir

爻部
ㄧㄠˊ yáo

七畫

爽 2422
ㄕㄨㄤˇ shuǎng
1. refreshing; bracing; pleasant; crisp; agreeable; brisk 2. to feel well 3. frank; straightforward; open-hearted 4. to fail; to miss; to lose 5. to be in error
【爽朗】① (said of weather, etc.) refreshing ② straightforward; open-minded
【爽口】palatable; tasty
【爽快】① straightforward; open-hearted ② readily and briskly ③ comfortable; pleasant
【爽直】outspoken; straightforward
【爽身粉】talcum powder

〔父·爻部〕

【爽約】to fail to keep a promise

十畫

〔爿・片・牙部〕

爾 2423 ㄦˇ ěr
1. you; thou 2. that; this; those; these; such; so 3. a particle used after adjectives 4. only
【爾後】thereafter; afterwards
【爾爾】so-so; not so outstanding
【爾虞我詐】each trying to cheat or outwit the other

爿部 ㄑㄧㄤˊ qiáng

四畫

牀 2424 (床) ㄔㄨㄤˊ chuáng
1. a bed; a couch 2. the ground under a body of water
【牀鋪】a bed and bedding
【牀單】bed linen; a bedsheet; sheets
【牀墊】a mattress
【牀罩】a bedspread
【牀蓐】bedding; bedclothes
【牀位】berths or bunks (in a ship or on a train)

十三畫

牆 2425 (墻) ㄑㄧㄤˊ qiáng
a wall; a fence
【牆壁】a wall (of a building)
【牆角】a corner between two walls

片部 ㄆㄧㄢˋ piàn

片 2426 1. ㄆㄧㄢˋ piàn
a piece; a slice; a fragment; a chip
【片片】in pieces; in fragments
【片面】① unilateral ② unfair
【片面之詞】one-sided remarks
【片名】title of a motion picture
【片段】① passages or fragments of a writing ② parts; fragments
【片刻】a little while; a moment
【片甲不留】to wipe out the enemy to a man
【片假名】katakana
【片酬】remuneration for a movie actor or actress for starring in a film
【片長】the length of a motion picture in terms of showing time

片 2426 2. ㄆㄧㄢ piān
1. a photograph 2. a phonograph record

四畫

版 2427 ㄅㄢˇ bǎn
1. household registers 2. printing plate 3. edition 4. supporting boards used in building walls
【版本】an edition
【版面】① space of a whole page ② layout of a printed sheet
【版圖】① population and territory ② territory; dominion
【版畫】a print
【版權】copyright
【版權所有】All rights reserved.
【版稅】royalties (on books)

八畫

牌 2428 ㄆㄞˊ pái
1. a bulletin board 2. a tablet; a signboard; a plate 3. a card; a tag; a label 4. a trademark; a brand
【牌坊】an honorific arch or portal
【牌九】Chinese dominoes
【牌局】a gambling game
【牌照】a license plate; a license
【牌子】① a bulletin board ② a card; a label ③ a brand ④ a signboard; a plate
【牌位】an ancestral tablet

牙部 ㄧㄚˊ yá

牙 2429 ㄧㄚˊ yá
1. teeth 2. to bite 3. ivory articles 4. a broker
【牙縫兒】space between the teeth

【牙疼 or 牙痛】 toothache
【牙膏】 toothpaste
【牙垢】 tartar on the teeth
【牙科】 dentistry
【牙科醫生 or 牙醫】 a dentist
【牙籤(兒)】 a toothpick
【牙線】 dental floss
【牙周病】 periodontosis
【牙刷】 a toothbrush
【牙牙學語】 (said of an infant) to begin to babble, prattle, or lisp
【牙齦】 gums

牛部
ㄋㄧㄡˊ niú

牛 2430 ㄋㄧㄡˊ niú
1. an ox; cattle; a cow; a bull 2. a Chinese family name 3. (said of a person) stubborn; headstrong
【牛排】 steak; beefsteak
【牛脾氣】 stubbornness; obstinacy
【牛皮紙】 kraft paper; brown paper
【牛糞】 cow dung
【牛刀小試】 ① to try to kill a fly with a long spear ② the first small display of a master hand
【牛痘】 cowpox; vaccinia
【牛頭不對馬嘴】 irrelevant; unconnected
【牛奶 or 牛乳】 (cow's) milk
【牛奶糖】 butter candy; toffee; taffy
【牛腩】 sirloin; tenderloin
【牛仔】 a cowboy
【牛郎織女】 the Cowherd and the Weaving Maid
【牛鬼蛇神】 ① absurdities ② forces of evil
【牛角】 horns of cattle
【牛群】 a herd of cattle
【牛車】 an oxcart; an ox-drawn cart
【牛舍or牛棚or牛欄】 a cattle pen, shed, or yard
【牛肉】 beef
【牛肉麪】 noodles served with stewed beef
【牛肉乾】 dried roast beef
【牛仔褲】 blue jeans; jeans
【牛油】 butter
【牛飲】 to drink heavily; to drink like a fish
【牛蛙】 a bullfrog

二畫

牝 2431 ㄆㄧㄣˋ pìn
female of an animal
【牝雞司晨】 a woman usurping man's power

牟 2432 ㄇㄡˊ móu
1. to seek 2. to bellow (or low)
【牟利】 to seek profits

三畫

牡 2433 ㄇㄨˇ mǔ (又讀 ㄇㄡˇ mǒu)
a male animal
【牡馬】 a stallion
【牡丹】 a peony
【牡蠣】 an oyster
【牡鹿】 a stag

牠 2434 ㄊㄚ tā (讀音 ㄊㄨㄛ tuō) (又讀 ㄊㄜ tē)
it

牢 2435 ㄌㄠˊ láo
1. a pen; a stable; a cage 2. a jail; a prison 3. secure; stable; firm; fast 4. worried; concerned 5. sacrifice
【牢不可破】 unbreakable; invulnerable
【牢籠】 ① to cover; to include ② a cage; a prison
【牢固】 secure; firm
【牢靠】 ① sturdy; stable; secure; firm ② reliable; trustworthy; dependable
【牢記】 to keep firmly in mind
【牢騷】 grumbling; complaint
【牢獄】 a jail; a prison

四畫

牧 2436 ㄇㄨˋ mù
1. to pasture; to shepherd 2. a pasture 3. to govern 4. a magistrate
【牧馬】 to pasture horses
【牧笛】 a shepherd's pipe
【牧童】 a cowboy; a shepherd boy
【牧牛】 to pasture cattle; to herd cows
【牧場】 a pasture; a ranch
【牧師】 a preacher; a clergyman

【牧草】herbage; pasture
【牧羊】to pasture sheep; to tend sheep
【牧羊犬】a shepherd dog; a collie
【牧羊人】a shepherd

牛部

物 2437
ㄨˋ wù
1. a thing; matter; a being 2. content; substance 3. the physical world; nature 4. other people
【物品】things; articles
【物美價廉】(said of merchandise) excellent quality and reasonable price
【物體】(physics) a body; an object
【物理學】physics
【物歸原主】Things return to their proper owners.
【物換星移】vicissitudes of human affairs with the elapse of time
【物極必反】As soon as a thing reaches its extremity, it reverses its course.
【物價】commodity prices
【物價指數】a price index
【物質】(physics) matter
【物證】material evidence
【物主】the owner (of a thing)
【物資】materials; supplies; goods
【物色】to seek (talent); to scout for (talent)
【物以類聚】Birds of a feather flock together.
【物以稀爲貴】A thing is valued if it is rare.

五畫

牲 2438
ㄕㄥ shēng
as in 牲口 or 牲畜—livestock

牴 2439
ㄉㄧˇ dǐ
to gore
【牴觸】to contradict; to conflict

六畫

特 2440
ㄊㄜˋ tè
1. special; unique; peculiar; particular; extraordinary; unusual; outstanding; distinguished; exclusive 2. just; merely; only
【特別】special; peculiar; particular
【特快車】a special express
【特派】specially dispatched or appointed
【特派記者】an accredited journalist
【特派員】a correspondent (of a news agency, newspaper, etc.)
【特大】exceptionally big; the most
【特大號】king-size; extra large size
【特地】on purpose; specially
【特定】① specially designated ② specific; given
【特例】a special case; an exceptional case
【特立獨行】to be self-reliant
【特刊】the extra edition, special edition or special supplement (of a newspaper or magazine)
【特級】superfine
【特技】special skills; stunts; aerobatics
【特價】a specially reduced price
【特獎】a special prize; a grand prize
【特權】privileges
【特寫】① a feature story (in a news paper or magazine) ② a close-up (in a movie)
【特效藥】a specific; a wonder drug
【特性 or 特點】characteristics; peculiarities
【特選】carefully chosen; handpicked
【特質】special qualities; characteristics; peculiarities
【特製】manufactured for a specific purpose
【特徵】distinctive features; characteristics
【特准】to permit as a special case
【特種部隊】special forces
【特種營業】special business operations (such as cabarets, bars, winehouses, etc.)
【特產】unique or special products (of a place)
【特長】special merits; a specialty
【特使】a special envoy
【特赦】special pardon; an amnesty
【特殊】special; unusual; unique
【特色】special features; characteristics
【特務】a secret agent
【特約】① a special agreement or contract ② specially or exclusively engaged
【特約診所】a clinic exclusively engaged by an organization

七畫

牽 2441
ㄑㄧㄢ qiān
1. to lead along; to drag; to pull; to tug; to haul 2. to involve; to

affect 3. to control; to restrain
【牽動】 to influence
【牽牛花】 morning glory
【牽念】 to feel anxious about
【牽累or牽連】 to drag (into trouble); to involve; to implicate
【牽掛】 to be concerned for; to worry about
【牽強】 forced; farfetched; unnatural
【牽強附會】 to give a forced interpretation; to distort the meaning
【牽制】 ①to restrain; to curb ②to divert (enemy attention)
【牽扯】 complication (of a matter); to involve; to implicate
【牽腸掛肚】 to be very worried about
【牽涉】 to involve; to implicate
【牽手】 ①to lead by the hand ②one's wife
【牽引】 ①to involve (in trouble) ②to draw

八畫

犂 2442 (犁) ㄌㄧˊ lí
1. to till; to plough 2. a plough
【犂田】 to plough (or plow) a field

犀 2443 ㄒㄧ xī
1. (said of armor, weapons, etc.) sharp-edged and hard 2. a rhinoceros
【犀牛】 the rhinoceros
【犀利】 ①hard and sharp ②trenchant; sharp
【犀角】 ① a rhinoceros horn ② bone of the forehead

犄 2444 ㄐㄧ jī
a horn
【犄角】 ①a horn ②a corner

九畫

犍 2445 ㄐㄧㄢ jiān
a castrated bull

十畫

犒 2446 ㄎㄠˋ kào
to reward (soldiers, laborers, etc.) with material gifts
【犒師or犒軍】 to cheer troops
【犒賞】 to reward (one for contributions) with money or gifts

十一畫

犛 2447 ㄌㄧˊ lí
1. a black ox 2. as in 犛牛—a yak

十五畫

犢 2448 ㄉㄨˊ dú
a calf

十六畫

犧 2449 ㄒㄧ xī
1. sacrifice (as homage to a deity); a beast of a uniform color for sacrifice 2. to give up (for the sake of something of greater value); to sacrifice
【犧牲】 ①sacrifice (offered to a deity) ②to sacrifice
【犧牲品】 ①a loss leader—a popular article sold for a fraction of its normal price ②a sacrificial lamb

犬部 ㄑㄩㄢˇ quǎn

犬 2450 ㄑㄩㄢˇ quǎn
a dog; a canine
【犬馬之勞】 one's own service (a self-depreciatory term)
【犬齒or犬牙】 a cuspid; a canine tooth
【犬子】 my son (a self-depreciatory term)
【犬牙相錯or犬牙交錯】 interlocking

二畫

犯 2451 ㄈㄢˋ fàn
1. to violate; to offend; to break (regulations or laws) 2. to commit (crimes, etc.) 3. to invade; to attack 4. a criminal 5. to have a recurrence of
【犯病】 to fall back into an old illness or a bad habit
【犯法】 to violate the law

【犯規】(sports) to commit a foul
【犯規者】an offender
【犯忌諱】to violate a taboo
【犯上作亂】to rebel against authority
【犯人】a criminal; a prisoner
【犯罪】(to commit) a crime, an offense or a sin 「take
【犯錯or犯錯誤】to make a mis-

四畫

狀 2452
ㄓㄨㄤˋ zhuàng
1. appearance; look; shape; form 2. condition; state; situation 3. written appeal 4. a certificate 5. to describe; to narrate; description
【狀態】situation; state; condition
【狀況】situation; circumstances; 「condition
【狀子】a plaint
【狀元 or 狀頭】① the top successful candidate in the imperial examination ② the very best

狂 2453
ㄎㄨㄤˊ kuáng
1. crazy; mad; mentally deranged 2. violent 3. unrestrained; uninhibited; wild 4. haughty
【狂暴】wild; fierce; ferocious; brutal 「about madly
【狂奔】to run about wildly; to run
【狂飆】a hurricane
【狂風暴雨】a violent storm
【狂瀾】① violent waves ② violent disturbances
【狂亂】wild; frenzied; frantic; mad
【狂歡】to revel; to rejoice with wild excitement
【狂犬病】rabies; hydrophobia
【狂想曲】(music) a rhapsody
【狂熱】fanatical; feverish
【狂人】① a lunatic ② an extremely conceited fellow
【狂傲】unreasonably haughty
【狂妄】① wild; irrational; crazy ② extremely conceited

狄 2454
ㄉㄧˊ dí
1. name of a barbarian tribe to the north of ancient China 2. a Chinese family name
【狄斯耐樂園】Disneyland, U.S.A.
【狄斯可】disco 亦作「迪斯可」

五畫

狎 2455
ㄒㄧㄚˊ xiá
to show familiarity, intimacy, or disrespect 「with disrespect
【狎侮】to be impolite to; to treat

狗 2456
ㄍㄡˇ gǒu
1. a dog 2. (figuratively) a lackey; a footman; a servile person; a follower 3. damned; cursed
【狗屁 or 狗屁不通】Nonsense! 或 Rubbish! 「viser
【狗頭軍師】a good-for-nothing ad-
【狗腿子】(figuratively) a hired thug; a henchman
【狗拿耗子,多管閒事】to poke one's nose into others' business
【狗急跳牆】A person takes desperate measures in a critical situation. 「humiliating fashion
【狗血噴頭】to be scolded in a very
【狗屎】(literally) dog's droppings —utterly worthless
【狗肉】dog meat
【狗嘴吐不出象牙來】A mean fellow never speaks nice things.
【狗咬呂洞賓】to mistake a good man for a bad one
【狗眼看人低】to act like a snob
【狗窩】a kennel; a doghouse

狐 2457
ㄏㄨˊ hú
as in 狐狸—the fox
【狐媚】to charm by flattery; to be 「sycophantic
【狐狸狗】a spitz
【狐狸精】an enchantress
【狐狸尾巴】a fox's tail—something that reveals one's true form or evil intentions
【狐假虎威】to bully the weak because of one's association with the powerful
【狐羣狗黨】a gang of scoundrels
【狐臭】an armpit odor 「kind.
【狐死兔悲】One grieves for one's
【狐疑】suspicious; doubt; suspicion

狒 2458
ㄈㄟˋ fèi
the baboon

狙 2459
ㄐㄩ jū 「ambush
1. a monkey; an ape 2. to lie in

【狙擊】 to attack by surprise; to snipe
【狙擊手】 a sniper

六畫

狠 2460
ㄏㄣˇ hěn
1. vicious; cruel; atrocious 2. severe(ly); extreme(ly)
【狠命】 to make a desperate effort
【狠毒】 atrocious; malicious
【狠心】 heartless; pitiless

狡 2461
ㄐㄧㄠˇ jiǎo
1. cunning; crafty; sly; wily; artful; shrewd 2. suspicion; to suspect
【狡辯】to defend oneself in a devious way; to quibble
【狡賴】 to prevaricate
【狡猾or狡黠】 cunning; crafty; sly; wily; artful
【狡詐】deceitful; cunning; swindling
【狡飾】 to deceive; to lie

狩 2462
ㄕㄡˋ shòu
1. to hunt in winter 2. an imperial tour
【狩獵】 hunting; to hunt or trap game

七畫

狼 2463
ㄌㄤˊ láng
1. the wolf 2. a heartless, cruel person; cruel and heartless; cunning and crafty 3. name of a constellation
【狼狽】 ①desperate②in a difficult position ③ embarrassed ④ heartless and cruel persons
【狼狽不堪】 to be in utter disorder
【狼狽爲奸】 to work hand in glove
【狼呑虎嚥】 to gobble up; to wolf down
【狼狗or狼犬】 ①a German shepherd ②a wolfhound
【狼心狗肺】 heartless and cruel
【狼人】 a wolf man

狸 2464
(貍) ㄌㄧˊ lí
1. a fox 2. a racoon dog
【狸貓】 a kind of wild cat

狹 2465
ㄒㄧㄚˊ xiá
narrow; narrow-minded
【狹路相逢】 enemies or rivals coming face to face
【狹小】 (said of rooms, etc.) narrow and small
【狹窄】 narrow; cramped
【狹長】 long and narrow
【狹隘】 narrow-minded; parochial;
【狹義】 the narrow sense narrow

八畫

猖 2466
ㄔㄤ chāng
wild; mad; impudent; unruly; reckless
【猖狂】 wild; unrestrained; unbridled
【猖獗】 rampant; on the rampage

猙 2467
ㄓㄥ zhēng
as in 猙獰—fierce-looking; hideous; repulsive

猛 2468
ㄇㄥˇ měng
1. bold; brave; fierce; violent 2. sudden and quick (strikes, thrusts, etc.) 3. severe; strict; stringent 4. a Chinese family name
【猛烈】 fierce; violent and savage
【猛攻】 to attack in full force or savagely; a furious assault
【猛虎】 a ferocious tiger
【猛火】 a raging fire
【猛將】 a brave or courageous general
【猛追】 to be in hot pursuit of
【猛撞】 to ram or bump suddenly and with force
【猛獸】 fierce wild beasts
【猛然】 suddenly; abruptly

猜 2469
ㄘㄞ cāi
1. to guess; to suspect; to doubt 2. cruel and suspicious
【猜不透】 unable to guess (what's on his mind, etc.)
【猜謎】 ① to solve riddles ② to guess
【猜忌】 to be jealous and suspicious
【猜拳】 to play the finger-guessing game (usually in drinking)
【猜著 or 猜中】 to guess correctly; to make out
【猜測 or 猜想】 to guess; to speculate; to conjecture
【猜疑】 suspicion; to suspect; to doubt

猝 2470
ㄘㄨˋ cù
sudden; abrupt; hurried; unex-

pected 「pared
【猝不及防】to be caught unpre-

九畫

〔犬部〕

猥 2471 ㄨㄟˇ wěi

1. vulgar; wanton; low; lewd and licentious 2. varied; numerous; many; multitudinous 3. the bark of a dog

【猥褻】obscene; obscenity; lewd

猶 2472 ㄧㄡˊ yóu

1. like; similar to; tantamount to; as if 2. still; yet; even; especially; while 3. a kind of monkey 4. a Chinese family name 5. strategy; scheme; plot

【猶太教】Judaism

【猶太人】the Jewish people; Jews

【猶如】just like 「tate

【猶疑or猶豫】undecided; to hesi-

猩 2473 ㄒㄧㄥ xīng

1.scarlet; red 2.a yellow-haired

【猩紅熱】scarlet fever ⌊ape

【猩猩】a chimpanzee; an orangutan

猴 2474 ㄏㄡˊ hóu 「impish (child)

1. the monkey 2. naughty or

【猴急】very impatient

十畫

猿 2475 (猨) ㄩㄢˊ yuán

an ape; a gibbon

【猿類】anthropoid

【猿猴】apes and monkeys

獅 2476 ㄕ shī

the lion

【獅子鼻】a snub nose

【獅子頭】stewed meatballs

【獅子狗】a poodle

【獅子會】International Association of Lions Clubs 亦作「國際獅子會」

【獅子座】(astronomy) Leo

猾 2477 ㄏㄨㄚˊ huá

cunning; shrewd; crafty

獃 2478 (呆) ㄉㄞ dāi (又讀 ㄞˊ ái)

1. stupid; silly; follish; idiotic; a fool 2. maladroit; awkward; clumsy; bungling 3. to stay

【獃板】dull and mechanical; without flexibility 「appearance

【獃頭獃腦】a silly or clumsy

【獃住了】dumbfounded

【獃若木鷄】very dull or stupid

【獃子】an idiot; a stupid person

獄 2479 ㄩˋ yù

1. jail; prison 2. a lawsuit

【獄吏】a jailer; a warden

【獄卒 or 獄丁】jailers; gaolers

十一畫

獒 2480 ㄠˊ áo

a large fierce dog; a mastiff

獐 2481 ㄓㄤ zhāng 「deer

the roe deer; the hornless river

【獐頭鼠目】facial features suggesting cunning and meanness

十二畫

獠 2482 ㄌㄧㄠˊ liáo

1. also known as 夷, a primitive tribe in Southwest China 2. (said of one's looks) fierce 3. nocturnal hunting 4. a monster; a wicked person

十三畫

獨 2483 ㄉㄨˊ dú

1. alone; solitary; single 2. only 3.to monopolize 4.to be old and without a son 5.how 或 Is it possible? 「soliloquy

【獨白】(dramatics) monologue;

【獨排衆議】to hold one's own opinion against that of the majority

【獨木橋】a single-plank bridge

【獨木舟】a canoe

【獨到】original 「special merits

【獨到之處】originality (of ideas);

【獨當一面】to handle a major task or assignment unaided

【獨斷獨行】to act arbitrarily

【獨特 or 獨一無二】unique

【獨吞】to pocket (profit) without

sharing (it) with anyone else
【獨立】independence; independent
【獨立國協】Commonwealth of Independent States (reformed after the disintegration of U.S.S.R. in 1992)
【獨立自主】①the independence of sovereignty ②to act independently and with the initiative in one's own hands
【獨家新聞】a scoop; an exclusive news report
【獨脚戲】a one-man show
【獨角獸】a unicorn (a legendary animal)
【獨居】to live alone
【獨具匠心】to have originality
【獨具隻眼 or 獨具慧眼】to have a remarkable view
【獨行】①to walk alone ②to insist on one's ways in doing things
【獨占 or 獨佔】to monopolize
【獨占鼇頭】①to emerge first in the civil service examination in former times ②to come out first
【獨唱】singing solo; a vocal recital
【獨處】to stay alone
【獨創】(literally) to create all by oneself—unique; original
【獨善其身】to conduct oneself virtuously
【獨生女】the only daughter
【獨生子 or 獨子】the only son
【獨樹一幟】to take a distinctive course or attitude of one's own
【獨自】alone; personally
【獨奏】(music) a solo performance
【獨裁】dictatorship; dictatorial
【獨往獨來】(literally) to come and go alone—to act independently without seeking company

十四畫

獲 2484 ㄏㄨㄛˋ huò
1. to get; to obtain; to incur; to capture; to catch; to reap 2. can; able 3. a slave-girl
【獲得】to get or obtain; to acquire
【獲救】to be rescued or saved
【獲獎】to win a prize
【獲勝】to triumph; to obtain victory
【獲益】to get profit; to win

獰 2485 ㄋㄧㄥˊ níng
an awe-inspiring look; a fierce appearance

十五畫

獵 2486 ㄌㄧㄝˋ liè
to hunt; to chase; field sports
【獵槍】a hunting gun; a shotgun
【獵取】to chase after; to hunt
【獵犬or獵狗】a hunting dog; a hound
【獵裝】hunting dress
【獵食】to hunt for food
【獵人】a hunter; a huntsman
【獵艷】to chase after pretty women
【獵鷹】a falcon
【獵物】game; a quarry

獸 2487 ㄕㄡˋ shòu
1. a general name for quadruped; a beast or animal 2. bestial; beastly
【獸皮】animal skin or hide
【獸檻】a pen or cage for animals
【獸性】① bestiality ② animal passions or desires
【獸性大發】to raise one's animal disposition
【獸醫】a veterinarian
【獸慾】carnal desire; lust (especially referring to rape)

十六畫

獺 2488 ㄊㄚˇ tǎ
an otter

獻 2489 ㄒㄧㄢˋ xiàn
1. to present; to forward; to offer; to dedicate; to donate 2. to display; to show; to stage 3. to curry (favor, etc.); to flatter or cater to
【獻寶】①to present a treasure ②to offer a scheme or one's valuable experience ③to show off what one treasures
【獻媚】to curry favor; to toady
【獻禮】①the ceremony of offering presents ②to present a gift
【獻花】to present flowers or bouquets; to lay a wreath
【獻技 or 獻藝】to display one's feat
【獻計】to present or offer advice or a scheme for adoption
【獻醜 or 獻拙】to show my poor skill or talent (a polite expression)

【獻身】 to offer or dedicate oneself (to a cause, one's nation, etc.)
【獻詞】 a dedication; a dedication speech
【獻殷勤】 to flatter; to ingratiate

〔玄·玉部〕

十七畫

獼 2490
ㄇㄧˊ mí
as in 獼猴—a rhesus monkey

玄 部
ㄒㄩㄢˊ xuán

玄 2491
ㄒㄩㄢˊ xuán
1. far and obscure; occult or mystic 2. dark or black 3. deep and profound; abstruse and subtle 4. silent and meditative 5. pretending 6. a Chinese family name
【玄妙】 profound, abstruse and subtle
【玄關】 ① the entrance to Buddhism ② the door of a house ③ a vestibule
【玄機】 (Taoism) the profound and mysterious truth
【玄孫】 great-great-grandson
【玄奧】 ① abstruse and subtle ② mysteries; profundities

六畫

率 2492
1. ㄕㄨㄞˋ shuài
1. to lead (troops, a team, etc.); to command 2. to follow; to act in accordance with 3. rash and hasty 4. generally; in general; usually 5. simple and candid; frank; straightforward; to the point 6. (said of men) dashing
【率同】 accompanied by; to lead all the others in (visiting, inspecting, etc.)
【率領】 to lead (troops, a team, etc.); to head (a mission, etc.)
【率先】 to be the first; to take the lead
【率性】 ① one's natural disposition ② to act according to the dictates of one's conscience
【率直 or 率眞】 candid; frank; honest; straight
【率衆】 to lead a crowd
【率師】 to lead troops
【率由舊章】 to follow old practices or precedents

率 2492
2. ㄌㄩˋ lǜ
1. (mathematics) ratio 2. a suffix used to indicate a measure or rate 3. to calculate

玉 部
ㄩˋ yù

玉 2493
ㄩˋ yù
1. a precious stone—especially jade; a gem 2. a polite expression for "your" 3. a designation of things belonging to a girl or young woman 4. (said of a person, especially a woman) pure; fair; beautiful 5. a Chinese family name
【玉佩】 jade pendants on a girdle
【玉米or玉蜀黍】 maize; Indian corn
【玉女】 ① a young and beautiful girl ② your daughter ③ an angel in the fairyland
【玉蘭花】 magnolia blossoms
【玉皇大帝or玉帝】 the Jade Emperor, the supreme deity in Taoism
【玉器】 jade articles
【玉璽】 the imperial seal
【玉簫】 a jade flute
【玉照】 your photograph or picture
【玉鐲】 a jade bracelet
【玉成其事】 to assist another in accomplishing a task or attaining a goal
【玉石俱焚】 to destroy indiscriminately, be it jade or rock
【玉手】 fair hands; hands of a pretty lady
【玉液(瓊漿)】 top-quality wine
【玉殞香消】 the death of a woman

王 2494
1. ㄨㄤˊ wáng
1. a king; a ruler 2. a prince, the highest rank of nobility 3. great; of a tremendous size 4. the strongest or most powerful 5. a salutation of respect 6. an audience with the ruler or emperor 7. a Chinese family name

【王八 or 忘八】① a turtle; a tortoise ② a cuckold ③ a man who works in a brothel ④ an s.o.b.
【王八蛋】a term of revilement similar to "s.o.b."
【王牌】a trump card
【王妃】a prince's concubine
【王國】a kingdom
【王冠】a crown
【王宮】a royal palace
【王后】the queen
【王朝】a dynasty
【王儲】a crown prince
【王室】① the royal family ② the imperial or royal court
【王子】a prince
【王孫公子】blue-blooded young men; aristocrats
【王爺】① a nobleman ② Your Imperial Highness
【王位】the throne; the crown

王 2494
2. ㄨㄤˋ wàng
to rule; to govern

二畫

玎 2495
ㄉㄧㄥ dīng
the jingling or tinkling sound
【玎璫】ding-dong; the jingling or tinkling sound

三畫

玖 2496
ㄐㄧㄡˇ jiǔ
1. a black jade stone 2. an elaborate form of 九, nine, used in checks, etc. to prevent fraud

四畫

玫 2497
ㄇㄟˊ méi
1. the rose 2. another name of black mica—a sparkling red gem
【玫瑰】① the rose (blossoms) ② black mica—a sparkling red gem
【玫瑰紅】① rose red ② rose-red

玩 2498
1. ㄨㄢˊ wán
1. to play (with); to toy with 2. to find pleasure in; to amuse oneself with
【玩票】to do a payless job
【玩兒命】to play with one's life at stake; to do daredevil tricks
【玩把戲】to play little tricks; to juggle
【玩弄】to toy with
【玩花樣】to play tricks; to cheat
【玩火自焚】Whoever plays with fire will get burnt.
【玩具】toys
【玩笑】① jokes; jesting ② to take something less seriously than it deserves
【玩耍】to play
【玩偶】dolls
【玩意兒or玩藝兒】① toys ② activities for entertainment or relaxation ③ a thing ④ (slang) a louse
【玩物】a plaything; a toy

玩 2498
2. ㄨㄢˋ wàn
1. to joke; to take things lightly; to toy with 2. something to amuse oneself—as antiques, etc. 3. (now rarely) to learn
【玩弄】① to juggle with ② to fool; to play jokes on
【玩世不恭】to be a cynic, beatnik or hippie; to take everything lightly
【玩味】to ponder

玨 2499
(珏) ㄐㄩㄝˊ jué
two pieces of jade fastened together

五畫

玲 2500
ㄌㄧㄥˊ líng
the tinkling of jade pendants
【玲瓏】① pleasing; delicate; cute; fine; regular ② bright ③ tinkling of jades
【玲瓏剔透】① exquisitely carved ② (said of a person) very bright

玷 2501
ㄉㄧㄢˋ diàn
1. a flaw or blemish in a piece of jade; a stain; a defect; a spot 2. to stain; to blemish; to disgrace
【玷辱】to disgrace (one's family name, etc.)
【玷汙or玷污】a stain (in one's reputation, etc.)

玳 2502
ㄉㄞˋ dài
the tortoise shell
【玳瑁】a hawksbill turtle

珊 2503
ㄕㄢ shān

〔玉部〕

玉部

1. coral 2. the tinkling of pendants
【珊瑚礁】 coral reefs

珍 2504 ㄓㄣ zhēn
1. precious; rare; very valuable 2. valuables; treasures 3. delicacies
【珍品】 delicacies; treasures
【珍貴】 valuable; treasurable; precious
【珍奇】 rare and precious
【珍禽異獸】 rare birds and animals
【珍惜】 to treasure
【珍羞or珍饈】 dainties; rare delicacies
【珍珠】 pearls
【珍重】 ① to value highly ② to take good care of (yourself)
【珍視】 to value highly
【珍藏】 to treasure
【珍愛】 to value; to love dearly
【珍玩】 curios of great value

玻 2505 ㄅㄛ bō
as in 玻璃—glass
【玻璃杯】 a glass; a tumbler
【玻璃瓶】 a glass bottle
【玻璃圈】 (slang) the gay circle
【玻璃窗】 a glass window
【玻利維亞】 Bolivia

珀 2506 ㄆㄛˋ pò
as in 琥珀—amber

六畫

珠 2507 ㄓㄨ zhū
1. a pearl 2. a bead; a drop 3. the pupil of the eye
【珠寶】 jewelry; pearls and valuables
【珠胎暗結】 to be pregnant (as a result of a love affair)
【珠聯璧合】 an excellent match
【珠光寶氣】 to be richly bejeweled
【珠璣】 exquisite or excellent wording of a piece of writing
【珠算】 calculation with an abacus
【珠圓玉潤】 ① smooth and sweet (voice) ② smooth and easy (style in writing)

班 2508 ㄅㄢ bān
1. a grade; a seat or position 2. a class or company; a set; a group 3. a squad (of soldiers) 4. to distribute 5. to return 6. same as斑—variegated; of different colors 7. of equal rank, same generation, etc. 8. a shift; duty 9. scheduled runs (of the bus, etc.)
【班駁 or 班駁陸離】 variegated
【班白 or 斑白】 gray-headed; graying
【班門弄斧】 to show off one's talent or skill before an expert
【班底】 ① ordinary members of a theatrical troupe ② (in politics, etc.) hard-core followers
【班機】 an airliner on the scheduled flight
【班級】 ① a grade ② a class
【班長】 ① (military) a squad leader ② (in school) the leader of a class
【班車】 a regular bus
【班師】 to withdraw troops after a victorious campaign
【班次】 ① the flight number of an airliner ② the designated number of a scheduled train ③ the grade or class (of a student) ④ sequence

珮 2509 (佩) ㄆㄟˋ pèi
jade pendants

琉 2510 ㄌㄧㄡˊ liú
1. a glossy and bright stone 2. glazed
【琉璃】 ① glass ② porcelain ③ colored glaze ④ glossy gems
【琉璃瓦】 encaustic tiles; glazed tiles
【琉球】 Ryukyu

七畫

現 2511 ㄒㄧㄢˋ xiàn
1. to emerge; to appear 2. current; now 3. in time of need; extempore 4. cash 5. ready; available 6. actual
【現代】 modern; the present world
【現代化】 to modernize; modernization
【現款 or 現金】 cash; ready money
【現貨】 stock goods; goods on hand
【現階段】 the present stage
【現今】 nowadays; at present; now
【現金買賣 or 現金交易】 business transactions in cash; cash transactions
【現象】 phenomena; appearances
【現形】 to reveal one's true form
【現行】 existing; presently valid

【現行犯】(law) *flagrante delicto*
【現狀】things as they are; the *status quo*
【現場】the scene (of an incident); a site
【現成】ready; ready-made
【現實】① reality ② pragmatic; real
【現世】① the world nowadays; present ② to bring shame on oneself
【現身說法】to act as an example to others
【現任】present (job, or employment)
【現在】now; at present
【現役軍人】military personnel on active service
【現有】to have on hand; existing

球 2512 ㄑㄧㄡˊ qiú

1. a ball or anything shaped like a ball 2. the globe; the earth
【球拍】rackets (for tennis, etc.)
【球門】the goal (in football, etc.)
【球迷】fans of ball games
【球隊】teams for playing ball games
【球僮】a caddy
【球鞋】tennis shoes; sneakers
【球形】spherical; globular; bulbous
【球場】a playground for ball games
【球賽】a ball game
【球衣】the jacket for a ballplayer
【球網】a net (for ball games)
【球員】a ballplayer

理 2513 ㄌㄧˇ lǐ

1. reason; logic; cause; truth; right 2. law; principles; doctrine; theory; science 3. to arrange 4. to govern; to operate; to regulate; to manage; to run 5. to reply or answer; to respond 6. texture; grain (in wood, skin, etc.) 7. name of a religious sect
【理賠】(insurance) adjustment
【理髮】to cut the hair; to have a haircut
【理髮店 or 理髮廳】a barbershop
【理髮小姐】a woman barber
【理髮師】a barber; a hairdresser
【理當】ought to; to be obliged to
【理念】a rational concept; an idea
【理論】① theory ② to argue
【理工科】departments of natural sciences and engineering in a college
【理虧】to be on the wrong side
【理會】①to understand; to comprehend ②to heed; to pay attention to
【理解】to comprehend; to understand
【理解力】understanding; perception
【理屈】to be on the wrong side
【理想】① ideal ② ideas; thought
【理性】(philosophy) reason; rationality
【理直氣壯】with confidence for one knows that he is in the right
【理智】intellect; reason
【理事會】the board of directors
【理事長】the board chairman
【理財】to manage finances
【理睬】to pay attention to; to heed
【理所當然】as a matter of course; naturally
【理由】reasons; grounds
【理應】duty-bound to; ought to
【理喻】to appeal with reason

琅 2514 ㄌㄤˊ láng

1. a kind of stone resembling jade 2. clean and white; pure; spotless
【琅璫入獄】to be put in jail clanking with manacles

八畫

琢 2515 ㄓㄨㄛˊ zhuó

1. to cut, chisel or polish jade, gems 2. to improve; to polish; to refine
【琢磨】① to cut and polish ② to study and improve ③to ponder over; to consider

琨 2516 ㄎㄨㄣ kūn

fine rocks next to jade in quality

琪 2517 ㄑㄧˊ qí

a piece of jade; a white gem

琥 2518 ㄏㄨˇ hǔ

1. a jade ornament in the shape of a tiger 2. amber
【琥珀】amber

琺 2519 ㄈㄚˇ fǎ

as in琺瑯(質)—enamel; enamelware

琬 2520 ㄨㄢˇ wǎn

1. a kind of jade tablet slightly tapering at the top 2. the virtue of a gentleman
【琬琰之章】an esteemed letter

〔玉部〕

琴 2521 ㄑㄧㄣˊ qín
1. *chin,* a Chinese fretted instrument with seven or five strings somewhat similar to the zither 2. a musical instrument
【琴鍵】a key
【琴弦】the string of a stringed instrument
【琴師】a player of the stringed instrument; a pianist
【琴瑟和鳴】marital harmony

琵 2522 ㄆㄧˊ pí
the four-stringed guitar or the balloon-guitar
【琵琶】*pi-pa*—a short-necked fretted lute of Chinese origin
【琵琶別抱】to marry another husband

琶 2523 ㄆㄚˊ pá
(語音 ·ㄆㄚ pa)
a four-stringed guitar or balloon-guitar

琳 2524 ㄌㄧㄣˊ lín
a fine piece of jade; a gem
【琳琅滿目】(literally) Good gems fill the eyes.—a vast array of beautiful and fine things

九畫

瑟 2525 ㄙㄜˋ sè
1. *se,* a large horizontal musical instrument 2. varied and many 3. elegant and stately; majestic 4. bright and clear; pure and clean 5. same as 索—alone; lonely; solitary
【瑟瑟】the heaving sound of wind
【瑟縮】① stiff and numb—as from cold ② timid and trembling ③ the heaving sound of wind

瑁 2526 ㄇㄟˋ mèi
a tortoise shell

瑋 2527 ㄨㄟˇ wěi
1. a kind of jade 2. rare; precious; splendorous

瑄 2528 ㄒㄩㄢ xuān
an ornamental piece of jade about 6.5 inches in diameter

瑕 2529 ㄒㄧㄚˊ xiá
1. a flaw, spot, or blemish in a piece of jade 2. a fault, error, blemish or flaw
【瑕不掩瑜】The defects do not outweigh the merits.
【瑕疵】defects; flaws; blemishes
【瑕瑜互見】(said of a single person) to have both good and bad qualities

瑙 2530 ㄋㄠˇ nǎo
agate; cornelian

瑛 2531 ㄧㄥ yīng
1. the glitter or sheen of jade 2. a transparent piece of jade; a crystal

瑜 2532 ㄩˊ yú
1. a fine and flawless piece of jade; a perfect gem 2. the brilliancy of jade; the luster of gems 3. excellences; virtues 4. as in 瑜珈—yoga, a mystic and ascetic practice in Hindu philosophy

瑞 2533 ㄖㄨㄟˋ ruì
1. something portending good luck or fortune; good omen: 吉瑞 signs of good luck 2. lucky; auspicious 3. a jade tablet given to feudal princes on their investiture, as a sign of authority and rank
【瑞典】Sweden
【瑞士】Switzerland

瑚 2534 ㄏㄨˊ hú
coral

十畫

瑩 2535 ㄧㄥˊ yíng
1. the luster of jade 2. a jade-like pebble 3. smooth and glossy; clean and shining 4. transparent; pure 5. (said of a person) bright and clever
【瑩潤】clear and lustrous

瑤 2536 ㄧㄠˊ yáo
1. a precious jade or stone 2. clean, pure and white 3. treasurable; valuable; precious
【瑤箋 or 瑤函】(a polite expression) your letter
【瑤池】a fairyland

瑣 2537 ㄙㄨㄛˇ suǒ

1. trifles; petty; frivolous; trifling 2. troublesome; annoying 3. a jade chain 4. a palace gate

【瑣屑】petty; unimportant; insignificant; small

【瑣事】trifles; trivial matters

【瑣碎】①trifling; petty and varied ②a slight indisposition or ailment

瑰 2538 ㄍㄨㄟ guī

1. fabulous; great; extraordinary 2. a stone which is a little less valuable than jade; a kind of jasper

【瑰寶】a treasure; a gem

【瑰麗】fabulously beautiful

【瑰瑋】rare and precious; treasurable

瑪 2539 ㄇㄚˇ mǎ

as in 瑪瑙—agate; cornelian

【瑪賽克】mosaic 亦作「馬賽克」

十一畫

瑾 2540 ㄐㄧㄣˇ jǐn

fine jade: 瑾瑜 a fine piece of jade

璀 2541 ㄘㄨㄟˇ cuǐ

the luster or glitter of jade and gems

【璀璨】the brilliancy and luster of pearls and precious stones

璇 2542 ㄒㄩㄢˊ xuán

1. fine jade 2. name of a constellation

【璇宮】an exquisite room ornamented with fine gems; a swanky palace

璃 2543 ㄌㄧˊ lí

glass; a glassy substance

璋 2544 ㄓㄤ zhāng

an ancient jade ornament used in state ceremonies; a jade tablet

十二畫

璞 2545 ㄆㄨˊ pú

1. an uncarved or unpolished jade 2. (figuratively) natural; unadorned

十三畫

璧 2546 ㄅㄧˋ bì

1. a round and flat piece of jade with a circular hole in it 2. a general name of all kinds of jade, jade-wares and ornaments

【璧合】a perfect match

【璧人】a fine-looking person

【璧玉】a round and flat piece of jade with a circular hole in it

環 2547 ㄏㄨㄢˊ huán

1. a jade ring or bracelet; a ring; a bracelet 2. earrings for women; ear-ornaments 3. around; round; to surround 4. a link 5. (sports) a ring

【環保署】the Environmental Protection Agency (EPA) in the Central Government

【環抱】to surround; to encircle

【環島】around-the-island

【環列】to surround on all sides

【環流】①to flow or travel around in circles ②circulation; circumfluence

【環顧】① to look around ② to review

【環顧四週】to look around

【環節】a segment; a link

【環境】surroundings; environment

【環境保護】environmental protection

【環境汚染】environmental pollution

【環境衛生】environmental sanitation

【環球】around the globe

【環繞】to surround; to move round; to circle

【環遊世界】to take a round-the-world tour

璨 2548 ㄘㄢˋ càn

bright and brilliant; lustrous and luminous

璫 2549 ㄉㄤ dāng

1. richly ornamented 2. pearls for filling up ear punctures to prevent the holes from closing 3. ancient headgear

十四畫

璽 2550 ㄒㄧˇ xǐ

1. the seal of an emperor or a king 2. the formal seal of a state; the national emblem

十五畫

瓊 2551
ㄑㄩㄥˊ qióng
1. fine jade or agate 2. excellent; beautiful
【瓊麻】sisal
【瓊樓玉宇】① the Palace of the Moon ② a magnificent or splendid building
【瓊漿】good wine
【瓊枝玉葉】lineal imperial descendants
【瓊瑤】① fine jade ② your letter ③ a literary piece written for others

十六畫

瓌 2552
ㄍㄨㄟ guī
1. same as 瑰—a kind of jasper 2. extraordinary; fabulous or admirable
【瓌寶】an extraordinary treasure

瓜部
ㄍㄨㄚ guā

瓜 2553
ㄍㄨㄚ guā
melons, gourds, cucumbers, etc.
【瓜棚】the framework for melon vines
【瓜分】to apportion; to partition
【瓜代】to relieve or replace (an official) upon the expiration of his term of office
【瓜田李下】a position that invites suspicion
【瓜葛】melon vines—a multitude of relatives
【瓜子兒】melon seeds
【瓜子臉】an oval face

十一畫

瓢 2554
ㄆㄧㄠˊ piáo
a ladle (often made of a dried calabash): 瓢蟲 a ladybug; a ladybird

十四畫

瓣 2555
ㄅㄢˋ bàn
1. petals 2. sections (as of oranges) 3. a valve; a lamella 4. fragments

瓦部
ㄨㄚˇ wǎ

瓦 2556
1. ㄨㄚˇ wǎ
1. earthenware; pottery 2. a tile 3. watt
【瓦房】a tiled house
【瓦釜雷鳴】an unworthy man creating sensations and enjoying popularity
【瓦楞紙】corrugated paper
【瓦礫】①rubble; ruin ②worthless things
【瓦罐】an earthen jar
【瓦解】to fall apart; to collapse; to disintegrate
【瓦斯】gas; poisonous gas used in war
【瓦解冰銷】to disintegrate like tiles and to dissolve like ice
【瓦斯筒】a gas cylinder

瓦 2556
2. ㄨㄚˋ wà
to cover a roof with tiles; to tile

六畫

瓷 2557
ㄘˊ cí
porcelain; chinaware
【瓷土】kaolin(e); porcelain clay
【瓷器】porcelain; porcelain ware; chinaware; china
【瓷磚】small porcelain tiles used for wall paneling or floor pavement

八畫

瓶 2558
(甁、缾) ㄆㄧㄥˊ píng
a bottle; a pitcher; a jug; a vase
【瓶頸】a bottleneck
【瓶裝】bottled
【瓶塞兒】a bottle stopper or plug; a cork

九畫

甄 2559
ㄓㄣ zhēn
1. a potter's wheel 2. to make pottery ware 3. to examine; to discern 4. to grade (competence, etc.) by examinations 5. to make clear
【甄選】to select (talented people,

etc.)
【甄用】to employ by an examination

十一畫

甎 2560
(磚、塼) ㄓㄨㄢ zhuān
brick: 甎瓦 bricks and tiles
【甎廠】a brickfield; a brickyard
【甎窰】a brickkiln

十三畫

甕 2561
ㄨㄥˋ wèng
a jar; a jug; a pot
【甕中之鼈】something that can be caught easily

甘部
ㄍㄢ gān

甘 2562
ㄍㄢ gān
1. tasty; delicious 2. luscious; sweet 3. willing 4. to enjoy 5. pleasant; pleasing 6. a Chinese family name
【甘拜下風】to admit defeat willingly
【甘美】delicious; tasty; palatable
【甘藍菜】a kale; a cabbage
【甘霖】a seasonable rain; a timely rain
【甘霖普降】Seasonable rain has fallen everywhere.
【甘露】sweet dew
【甘苦】① happiness and suffering ② hardships and difficulties experienced in work
【甘苦備嘗】to have tasted both sweetness and bitterness
【甘休】willing to stop or halt
【甘心】① willingly; willing ② joyous; happy
【甘心情願】perfectly willing
【甘之如飴】to be quite content even in adversity
【甘蔗】sugarcane
【甘蔗板】a bagasse board
【甘薯 or 甘藷】sweet potatoes
【甘草】licorice
【甘肅】Kansu Province
【甘油】glycerin(e)
【甘於】to be willing to; to be happy to
【甘願】willing; willingly; readily

四畫

甚 2563
1. ㄕㄣˋ shèn
1. to a great extent; to a high degree; very; exceedingly 2. more than
【甚囂塵上】widely reported or speculated
【甚至】even to the extent that...; even; to go so far as...
【甚而】so much so that...
【甚殷】very sincerely; very badly
【甚爲不解】much perplexed; completely at a loss
【甚於】(to be worse, harder, better, etc.) than...

甚 2563
2. (什) ㄕㄜˊ shé
as in 甚麼—what
【甚麼話】What nonsense! 或 Bosh!
【甚麼事】① What's the matter? ② no matter what; whatever it is
【甚麼樣】What kind? 或 What sort?

六畫

甜 2564
ㄊㄧㄢˊ tián
1. sweet; luscious 2. agreeable; pleasant
【甜美】① sweet; luscious ② pleasant; refreshing
【甜蜜】sweet as honey; honeyed; affectionate; fond; happy
【甜點】sweet; dessert
【甜頭】①sweet taste ②good; benefit
【甜心】a sweetheart
【甜食】sweet food; sweetmeats
【甜言蜜語】honeyed words; cajolery
【甜玉米】sweet corn; sugar corn
【甜味】sweet taste

生部
ㄕㄥ shēng

生 2565
ㄕㄥ shēng
1. to live; life; living; alive 2. to be born; to come into being or existence 3. to breed; to bear; to beget; to produce 4. unripe; raw; uncooked 5. unfamiliar; strange 6. savage; untamed; bar-

〔生部〕

barian 7. a pupil; a student 8. the male character type in Chinese opera 9. creatures
【生病】to get sick; to fall ill
【生不逢辰】to be born at a wrong time; unlucky
【生怕】very anxious; very apprehensive
【生啤酒】draught beer
【生平】①one's brief biographical sketch ②in the course of life
【生米煮成熟飯】What is done cannot be undone.
【生命】life
【生命力】vitality
【生命線】a lifeline (in a figurative sense)
【生髮油】hair tonic
【生動】vivid; lively; lifelike
【生態】the relations and interactions between organisms and their environment, including other organisms
【生鐵】pig iron; crude iron
【生吞活剝】to use someone's ideas without fully understanding them
【生來】by nature; inborn
【生冷】(said of food) uncooked and cold
【生離死別】separation in life and parting at death—the bitterest sorrows to man
【生理】physiological functions and processes; physiology
【生力軍】a vital new force
【生靈塗炭】The people are suffering from extreme privation (during wartime).
【生路】①a way to make a living; a way to survive ②a strange road
【生龍活虎】(like) a live dragon or a live tiger — full of vigor and vitality
【生花妙筆】ability for exquisite writing
【生活】①life ②to live
【生活必需品】necessities of life
【生活費】living expenses
【生活方式】the ways of living
【生活水準】the standard of living
【生火】to make a fire; to build a fire
【生還】to come back alive; to survive
【生還者】a survivor
【生機】①liveliness ②the chance of survival
【生計】livelihood; living
【生薑】green ginger
【生氣】①vitality; liveliness ②to get angry; to get mad
【生氣蓬勃】vigorous; active; lively
【生前】before one's death
【生趣】the pleasure of life
【生效】to go into effect
【生銹】to rust
【生性】natural disposition; nature
【生殖】(biology) reproduction
【生殖器】reproductive organs; genitals
【生長】to grow; to develop; growth
【生吃】to eat (something) raw
【生產】①to produce ②to give birth to
【生產力】productivity
【生產率】the production rate
【生產過剩】overproduction
【生產技術】production technique
【生產線】production line
【生辰】birthday
【生手】a beginner; a novice
【生身父母】real parents (as distinct from foster parents)
【生生不息or生生不已】to breed in endless succession
【生疎or生疏】unfamiliar; unskilled
【生水】unboiled water
【生日】birthday
【生字】a new word; an unfamiliar word
【生財有道】to be expert in making money
【生菜】raw vegetables; salad
【生存】to survive; survival; existence
【生存空間】living space; lebensraum
【生絲】raw silk
【生死關頭】a life-and-death crisis
【生死之交】deep friendship
【生澀】(said of a piece of writing) difficult to read or understand
【生兒育女】to give birth to children and rear them
【生疑】to become suspicious
【生意】①business; trade ②vitality
【生涯】①a career; a life ②livelihood
【生硬】awkward; stiff
【生物】①a living thing ②biology
【生物界】the biological world
【生物學】biology

六畫

產 2566 ㄔㄢˇ chǎn

1. to bear (offspring); to lay

(eggs) 2. to produce; to bring about
【產品】 products
【產品說明會】 a show and tell
【產房】 a lying-in room; a maternity room
【產婦】 a lying-in woman
【產地】 a producing center
【產量】 production; output; yield
【產卵】 to lay eggs; to spawn
【產後】 after childbirth; postnatal
【產假】 maternity leave
【產期】 time of childbirth
【產前】 before childbirth; prenatal
【產權】 ownership (of real estate)
【產銷】 production and marketing
【產生】 to produce
【產額】 the amount of production; output
【產業】 ①property; estate ②industry
【產業革命】 the Industrial Revolution
【產物】 products; outcomes

七畫

甥 2567 ㄕㄥ shēng
1. a nephew (son of a sister) 2. a son-in-law who assumes one's own name and lives under one's own roof
【甥女】 a niece (daughter of a sister)

甦 2568 ㄙㄨ sū
to come back to life; to rise from the dead; to revive; to resurrect; to regain consciousness
【甦醒】 to come back to life; to revive; to come to

用部
ㄩㄥˋ yòng

用 2569 ㄩㄥˋ yòng
1. to use; to employ 2. to exert 3. use 4. effect 5. finance 6. to need; need 7. to eat; to drink
【用兵】 to manipulate troops
【用不慣】 unaccustomed to the use of
【用不著】 there is no need to
【用不完】 too many or too much for use
【用品】 articles for use
【用法】 directions for using or operating something
【用得着】 ① to need ② it is necessary to
【用地】 land for a specific use
【用途 or 用處】 a purpose
【用力】 to exert oneself; to make an effort; to put forth one's strength
【用光or用完】 to use up; to run out of; to exhaust
【用功】 to study diligently; to study hard
【用戶】 a customer (of a utility); a user; a consumer
【用盡心機】 to have tried every means
【用具】 a tool; an appliance; an implement
【用錢】 ① to spend money ② commission
【用情不專】 to be frivolous in affairs of the heart
【用心】 to take care; to pay attention
【用心良苦】 well-intentioned but little understood
【用刑】 to torture
【用之不竭】 It cannot be used up.
【用水】 ① to use water ② water for a specific use
【用人】 ① to employ people ② a servant
【用意】 an intention; a purpose; an idea
【用語】 terminology; phraseology

甩 2570 ㄕㄨㄞˇ shuǎi
1. to throw away; to discard; to cast away 2. to leave (somebody) behind 3. to swing
【甩不掉】 cannot get rid of
【甩了】 to have thrown away

二畫

甫 2571 ㄈㄨˇ fǔ
1. (euphemism) a man 2. (euphemism) father 3. then and only then 4. just; immediately after; a short while ago 5. barely

甬 2572 ㄩㄥˇ yǒng
1. a measure of capacity (equal to 10斗) 2. alternative name of Ningpo, Chekiang
【甬道or甬路】 the central path in a hall

四畫

甭 2573 ㄅㄥˊ béng
unnecessary; do not have to

田部
ㄊㄧㄢ tián

〔田部〕

田 2574
ㄊㄧㄢ tián
1. agricultural land; cultivated land; a field; a rice field; farmland; cropland 2. to hunt game 3. a Chinese family name
【田地】① agricultural land ② position; condition; a plight
【田螺】 a mud snail; a pond snail
【田埂】 ridges between plots of farmland
【田鷄】 a frog
【田間】 in the field
【田徑賽】 track and field events
【田契】 a title deed for agricultural land
【田主】 a landlord (of agricultural land)
【田莊】 a farmhouse; a farmstead
【田產】 real estate
【田舍】 a farmhouse
【田租】 the land rental paid by a tenant farmer
【田野】 fields; cultivated lands
【田園】 fields and gardens
【田園詩人】 a pastoral poet; an idyllist

由 2575
ㄧㄡˊ yóu
1. reason; cause; a source; derivation 2. from 3. up to (someone to make a decision) 4. by; through
【由不得】 involuntarily; unable to do as one pleases
【由來】 ①derivation; a source ②so far; up to now
【由來已久】 It has been so for quite some time.
【由衷】 from the depth of one's heart; heartfelt
【由衷之言】 words uttered in sincerity
【由此】 hence; from this; therefore
【由此可見】 thus it can be seen; this shows; that proves
【由於】 because of; owing to; due to; as a result of

甲 2576
ㄐㄧㄚˇ jiǎ
1. the first of the Ten Celestial Stems 2. armor; shell; crust 3. most outstanding 4. a measure of land in Taiwan (equal to 0.97 hectare)
【甲板】 the deck (of a ship)
【甲等】 grade A
【甲骨文】 oracle-bone scriptures
【甲殼類】 the crustacean
【甲冑】 armor; a panoply
【甲狀腺】 thyroid
【甲蟲】 a beetle
【甲魚】 a green turtle (*Trionyx sinensis*)

申 2577
ㄕㄣ shēn
1. the ninth of the Twelve Terrestrial Branches 2. to appeal; to plead 3. to state; to set forth; to explain; to explicate 4. to extend; to expand 5. to inculcate (especially repeatedly) 6. a brief name of Shanghai
【申報】 to declare; to file (tax returns)
【申報戶口】 to report one's address for the domiciliary register
【申辯】 to argue; to contend
【申明】 to explain; to expound
【申覆】 to reply to a superior
【申告】 to appeal to a court of law
【申誡】 a reprimand; a rebuke
【申請】 application
【申請書】 an application form; a written request
【申請人】 an applicant
【申斥】 to reprimand; to rebuke
【申時】 3-5 p.m.
【申述】 to state; to explain in detail
【申訴】 to appeal; to lodge a complaint
【申冤】 to appeal for justice regarding a false charge

二畫

男 2578
ㄋㄢˊ nán
1. a human male; a man; a boy; a son 2. a baron
【男扮女裝】 disguised as a woman
【男儐相】 a best man (at a wedding)
【男朋友】 a boyfriend
【男僕】 a male servant
【男低音】 (music) bass
【男女平等】 equal rights for both sexes
【男女同校】 coeducation
【男女關係】 relations between the two sexes
【男女有別】 Males and females should be distinguished.
【男高音】 (music) tenor

【男歡女愛】The couple are enraptured with love.
【男爵】a baron
【男爵夫人】a baroness
【男性】①the male sex ②the masculine gender
【男裝】male costume; men's clothing
【男中音】(music) baritone, or barytone
【男生】a boy student
【男子 or 男人】a man
【男子漢】a manly man
【男廁所】men's room
【男才女貌】The man is able and the woman is beautiful. — an ideal couple

甸 2579
ㄉㄧㄢˋ diàn
1. suburbs or outskirts of the capital 2. to govern; to rule 3. farm crops

町 2580
1. ㄊㄧㄥˇ tǐng
the boundary between agricultural land
【町畽】waste land; a paddock

町 2580
2. ㄉㄧㄥ dīng
(in Japan) a street; a city block

四畫

界 2581
ㄐㄧㄝˋ jiè
1. a boundary 2. to limit; to demarcate; to define; to delimit 3. world
【界碑】a landmark; a boundary stone
【界限】①a border ②to limit; to restrict
【界線】a boundary; a borderline
【界外球】(sports) out-of-bounds

畏 2582
ㄨㄟˋ wèi
1. to stand in awe of; to fear; to dread; to be afraid of 2. to revere; to respect
【畏避】to evade because of fear
【畏途】a dangerous path
【畏懼】to dread; to be scared of; to fear
【畏怯】to fear; to be scared of
【畏首畏尾】to harbor fear fore and aft
【畏罪】to be afraid of punishment
【畏罪自殺】to kill oneself from fear of punishment
【畏縮】to shrink; to recoil; to cringe; to flinch

畋 2583
ㄊㄧㄢˊ tián
1. to cultivate land 2. to hunt game

五畫

畔 2584
ㄆㄢˋ pàn
1. a boundary between fields 2. a side; a bank 3. same as 叛—to rebel; to betray

畚 2585
ㄅㄣˇ běn
a bamboo basket for carrying earth
【畚箕】a bamboo basket for carrying earth or dirt

畜 2586
1. ㄔㄨˋ chù
1. a dumb creature; an animal 2. livestock
【畜生】dumb creatures; animals

畜 2586
2. ㄒㄩˋ xù
to rear or raise (livestock or children)
【畜牧】animal husbandry
【畜牧場】a livestock farm; a range; a grazing ground

畝 2587
ㄇㄨˇ mǔ
mu, a Chinese land measure (equal to 733 ½ square yards)

留 2588
(畱) ㄌㄧㄡˊ liú
1. to remain; to stay; to be at a standstill 2. to ask somebody to stay 3. to detain; to obstruct; to keep; to delay 4. to leave 5. to preserve; to reserve
【留步】(Please) do not trouble yourself by accompanying me to the door
【留不住】unable to detain; unable to make someone stay
【留名】to leave behind a good reputation
【留得青山在，不愁沒柴燒】As long as there is life, there is hope.
【留待】to wait until
【留連 or 留戀】reluctant to leave; unwilling to part with
【留連忘返】so enchanted as to forget about home
【留客】to detain a guest
【留後路】to leave a way out
【留級】to fail to get promoted to the next grade at school

(田部)

【留情】 to show mercy; to relent
【留下】 ① to leave ② to detain; to stop ③ to remain; to stay ④ to preserve 「heed
【留心】 to pay attention; to take
【留學】 to study abroad 「abroad
【留學生】 a student studying
【留職停薪】 leave without pay
【留置】 to detain; to put aside
【留滯】 to remain at a standstill; to stay 「one stay
【留住】 to succeed in making some-
【留守】 (said of troops) to remain stationed at a camp in the rear
【留神】 to pay attention; to be
【留聲機】 a phonograph 「careful
【留任】 to stay in a position for another term
【留宿】 to keep (a quest) overnight
【留意】 to pay attention; to be careful; to be cautious
【留一手 or 留後手】 to hold back a trick or two
【留言】 to leave a message
【留影】 to take a photo as a memento 「extremes
【留餘地】 to refrain from going to

六畫

畦 2589 ㄒㄧ xī (語音 ㄑㄧˊ qí)
1. land of 50 *mu* (畝) 2. a plot, piece, or parcel of land 3. a
「farmer; a laborer

畤 2590 ㄓˋ zhì
a place for worshipping Heaven, Earth, and the five sage kings in ancient times

略 2591 (畧) ㄌㄩㄝˋ lüè
1. approximate; rough; brief 2. slight; small in extent 3. to scheme; to plan 4. strategy 5. to invade; to seize 6. to omit; to leave out 7. to survey the boundaries
【略同】 about the same; similar
【略可】 acceptable in general
【略去】 to omit; to leave out; to delete 「just a little
【略知一二】 to know or understand
【略識之無】 only slightly literate
【略勝一籌】 slightly better
【略述】 to describe briefly; to outline 「briefly refer to
【略說】 to say a few words about;
【略有所聞】 to have heard something (about it)
【略微】 slightly; a little; somewhat

畢 2592 ㄅㄧˋ bì
1. to complete; to finish; to end 2. whole; total; complete
【畢竟】 after all; in the long run; ultimately
【畢生】 in one's whole life; throughout one's lifetime; lifelong
【畢業】 to be graduated; to graduate; graduation
【畢業班】 the graduating class
【畢業典禮】 a commencement
【畢業論文】 a thesis 「tion
【畢業考試】 a graduation examina-
【畢業證書 or 畢業文憑】 a diploma
【畢業生】 a graduate

異 2593 (異) ㄧˋ yì
1. different; difference 2. peculiar; extraordinary; uncommon; strange; unusual 3. foreign; unfamiliar; unknown 4. to marvel; to wonder 5. to separate
【異邦】 a foreign country
【異母兄弟】 brothers born of different mothers
【異地 or 異鄉 or 異域】 a strange land; a foreign land
【異端邪說】 heretical beliefs; heresy
【異類】 those of a different class or kind 「mood on a foreign land
【異國情調】 an exotic touch or
【異客】 a stranger
【異口同聲】 People are unanimous in their opinion.
【異己】 a dissident
【異教徒】 a heathen; a pagan
【異曲同工】 The writings are different, but the excellence is the same.
【異趣】 different tastes or interests
【異想天開】 to have fantastic notions
【異常】 extraordinary; different; unusual; strange 「days
【異日】 ① another day ② bygone
【異議】 dissent; objections
【異樣】 unusual; extraordinary
【異味】 uncommon smell 「story
【異聞】 unusual news; a strange

七畫

番 2594
1. ㄈㄢ fān
1. to take turns 2. order in series 3. a time 4. a kind of; a sort of 5. barbarians
【番號】a numerical designation of a military unit
【番茄】a tomato
【番茄醬】tomato ketchup
【番茄汁】tomato juice
【番石榴】a guava
【番薯】a sweet potato

番 2594
2. ㄆㄢ pān
a county in Kwangtung

番 2594
3. ㄅㄛ bō
martial-like

畫 2595
ㄏㄨㄚˋ huà
1. to paint or draw (a picture); a painting; a drawing 2. to mark off; to delimit 3. to plan; to design; a plan 4. a stroke in a Chinese character
【畫板】a drawing board
【畫筆】a painting brush
【畫餅充飢】(literally) to try to satisfy hunger by drawing cakes —to value empty names
【畫布】a canvas (for painting)
【畫眉鳥】the thrush
【畫面】the full length and breadth of a picture
【畫法】a method of painting or drawing
【畫分 or 劃分】to mark off; to divide; to demarcate
【畫圖】to draw pictures
【畫廊】a gallery (for paintings)
【畫龍點睛】to add the punch line; to add the finishing touch
【畫稿】drafts for paintings or drawings
【畫刊】a pictorial magazine
【畫框】a picture frame
【畫虎類狗】to fail because of undue ambition
【畫家】a painter; an artist
【畫架】an easel
【畫界】to delimit; to mark boundaries; to demarcate
【畫具】articles used for painting; painting tools
【畫像】①to paint a portrait ②a portrait
【畫展】an art exhibition
【畫師】a painter; an artist
【畫室】an artist's studio
【畫蛇添足】to make undesirable additions; superfluous
【畫册】a picture or painting album
【畫一 or 劃一】to make uniform
【畫意】the mood of a painting

畯 2596
ㄐㄩㄣˋ jùn
1. the official in charge of farmland in ancient times 2. rustic; crude

八畫

畸 2597
ㄐㄧ jī
1. fields with irregular boundaries 2. malformed; misshapen; deformity 3. fractional remainders
【畸角子 or 畸角兒】a corner
【畸形】malformation; abnormality; deformity

當 2598
1. ㄉㄤ dāng
1. to undertake or assume (responsibilities, etc.); to accept 2. to face 3. equal; well-matched 4. the very same (place, year, day, etc.) 5. ought to; should; must 6. just at (a time or a place) 7. to work as; to serve as
【當班】to be on duty by turns
【當兵】to serve in the army; to be a soldier
【當面】right in one's face; face to face
【當面言明】to state clearly in one's presence
【當代】in the present age
【當道】①to be in power ②to block one's way
【當地】this place; local
【當頭棒喝】to arouse a person from stupidity by drastic means
【當天】on the same day; on that very day
【當年】that year
【當機立斷】to make quick decisions in the face of problems
【當即】immediately; right away
【當家】to housekeep; to be the master of a family, an organization, etc.
【當街】in the street

【當今】① the present time; today ② the reigning emperor
【當局】 the authorities
【當局者迷，旁觀者清】 The onlooker sees the game more clearly than the players.
【當前】 present; current
【當權】 to be in power
【當心】 to be careful; to be cautious
【當心扒手】 Beware of pickpockets!
【當選】 to get elected; to be elected; to win an election
【當之無愧】 fully deserve (a title, an honor, etc.); to be worthy of
【當政】 to be in power (or office)
【當中】 right in the middle
【當衆】 in the presence of all
【當衆宣佈】 to announce publicly
【當差】 to do a duty; to be on duty
【當場】 on the spot; then and there
【當場出醜】 to suffer embarrassment right before a crowd
【當初】 at first; in the beginning
【當時】 ① at that time; then ② at the very moment; immediately
【當事者 or 當事人】 those directly involved
【當日】 on the same day; on that very day
【當然】 ① of course; naturally ② as it should be; only natural
【當仁不讓】 do not refuse to accept a reward or position which one deserves
【當務之急】 a business or task of the greatest urgency at present
【當晚】 on the same night; on that very night

當 2598
2. ㄉㄤˋ dàng
1. proper; appropriate 2. to pawn; to mortgage; to pledge 3. to take as; to regard as; to consider as
【當票】 a pawn ticket
【當鋪】 a pawnshop
【當眞】 to be serious; no joking
【當作 or 當做】 to regard as; to treat as
【當耳邊風】 to take no serious heed to (advice, etc.)

當 2598
3. ㄉㄤˇ dǎng
to mistake something for another
【當是】 to mistake something for another; to think that...

十畫

畿 2599
ㄐㄧ jī (又讀 ㄑㄧˊ qí)
areas near the capital; the royal domain

十四畫

疆 2600
ㄐㄧㄤ jiāng
1. the boundary; the border; the frontier 2. a limit
【疆界】 borders; frontiers
【疆域 or 疆土】 territory

疇 2601
ㄔㄡˊ chóu
1. agricultural land; fields 2. who 3. formerly; previously 4. a class; a category; a rank

十七畫

疊 2602
(叠) ㄉㄧㄝˊ dié
1. to fold up 2. to pile up 3. to repeat; to duplicate 4. a stack of (bank notes)
【疊羅漢】 (sports) pyramid
【疊起】 ① to fold up ② to pile up
【疊韻】 two words of the same rhyme

疋 部
ㄆㄧˇ pǐ

疋 2603
ㄆㄧˇ pǐ
a roll (of cloth); a bolt (of cloth)

六畫

疏 2604
(疎或疏，七畫)
1. ㄕㄨ shū
1. thin; sparse; few 2. unfamiliar; distant; unfriendly 3. careless; neglectful 4. to channel; to remove obstructions 5. coarse
【疏密】 ① looseness and density ② neglect and watchfulness
【疏於防範】 to fail to take precautions
【疏導】 ① to channel ② to enlighten
【疏通】 to clean or dredge (a waterway)
【疏漏】 careless omissions; slips; oversights

【疏忽】careless; remiss; negligent; oversight; to neglect
【疏濬】to clean or dredge (waterways)
【疏失】remiss; at fault; negligent
【疏財仗義】to give generously and be a champion of justice
【疏散】to disperse; dispersion
【疏鬆】① loose ② puffy
【疏於職守】to neglect one's duty
【疏遠】(said of relations) not close

疏 2604
2. ㄕㄨˋ shù
1. to present point by point 2. to explicate; to annotate

九畫

疑 2605
ㄧˊ yí
1. doubtful; dubious; skeptical; doubt; to doubt; to question 2. suspicious; to suspect 3. strange; incomprehensible; mysterious; questionable 4. sham; dummy; false
【疑犯】a criminal suspect
【疑點】① a doubtful or questionable point ② a suspicious point
【疑難】a question; a problem; a puzzle
【疑慮】anxiety; misgivings
【疑惑】to doubt; to suspect
【疑心】① to doubt ② suspicion
【疑心病】① hypochondria ② skepticism
【疑信參半】do not believe entirely
【疑神疑鬼】to have unnecessary suspicions
【疑似】could be; suspected to be
【疑案】an unsettled case; an uncertain case
【疑義】dubious interpretation
【疑問】a question; doubt; uncertainty
【疑問代名詞】interrogative pronouns
【疑問句】an interrogative sentence
【疑雲】clouds of suspicion or misgivings (darkening one's mind)

疒部
ㄔㄨㄤˊ chuáng

二畫

疔 2606
ㄉㄧㄥ dīng
a boil; a carbuncle

三畫

疙 2607
ㄍㄜ gē
a wart; a pustule; a pimple
【疙瘩】① a wart; a pustule; a pimple ② a knot in one's heart; a hang-up

疚 2608
ㄐㄧㄡˋ jiù
1. prolonged illness 2. mental discomfort 3. a guilty conscience

疝 2609
ㄕㄢˋ shàn
as in 疝氣—hernia

四畫

疤 2610
ㄅㄚ bā
1. as in 疤痕—a scar 2. a birthmark

疥 2611
ㄐㄧㄝˋ jiè
scabies: 疥瘡 sores from scabies
【疥癬】scabies; the itch; mange; ringworm

疫 2612
ㄧˋ yì
an epidemic; a plague; a pestilence: 疫苗 vaccine

五畫

疲 2613
ㄆㄧˊ pí
weary; tired; fatigued; exhausted
【疲憊】fatigued; tired; weary
【疲憊不堪】extremely tired
【疲乏 or 疲倦】tired; exhausted; weary
【疲勞】fatigue; exhaustion; weariness
【疲勞過度】excessive fatigue
【疲勞轟炸】① harassing air raids ② a long and tedious harangue
【疲軟】① tired and feeble ② (said of commodities) to decrease in demand ③ (said of finance) to weaken
【疲於奔命】tired from running around

疹 2614
ㄓㄣˇ zhěn
rashes: 疹子 measles; carbuncles

疒部

疼 2615
ㄊㄥˊ téng
1. to ache; to hurt; pain; sore 2. to dote on; to be fond of (a child)
【疼愛】to be fond of (a child)

疾 2616
ㄐㄧˊ jí
1. disease; suffering 2. to hate; to detest 3. swift; rapid; quick; fast
【疾病】diseases
【疾風知勁草】Adversity tests the character of a man.
【疾苦】suffering (especially under an oppressive government)
【疾駛 or 疾馳】to move swiftly; to dart; to fleet
【疾走】to walk quickly; to run
【疾惡如仇】to hate evil as much as one hates an enemy
【疾言厲色】(literally) to speak fast with a harsh look—to lecture severely

病 2617
ㄅㄧㄥˋ bìng
1. illness; disease; ailment 2. to be ill 3. blemish; fault 4. to injure; to harm 5. to worry 6. to hate 7. to insult
【病變】pathological changes
【病魔】the curse of disease
【病沒 or 病歿】to die of illness
【病發】to fall ill
【病房】a sickroom; a ward
【病倒】to fall ill; to be confined in bed due to illness
【病毒】viruses
【病態】morbid (or abnormal) state
【病痛】slight illness; indisposition
【病例】number of cases of a particular disease
【病歷】medical history (of a patient)
【病假】sick leave
【病菌】germs; bacteria; viruses
【病情 or 病狀】the condition of a patient
【病徵】symptoms of a disease
【病症】a disease; an ailment
【病牀】a sickbed
【病蟲害】blight
【病人】a sick man; a patient
【病入膏肓】so advanced in one's disease as to be past remedy
【病容】a sickly look; an emaciated look
【病從口入】Diseases enter by the mouth.
【病死】to die of an illness
【病因or病原】the cause of a disease
【病危】about to die of an illness
【病愈 or 病癒】to recover from illness; to get well

症 2618
ㄓㄥˋ zhèng
1. disease; an ailment 2. symptoms or manifestations of a disease
【症候or症狀】symptoms or manifestations of a disease

痂 2619
ㄐㄧㄚ jiā
scab over a sore

疱 2620
(皰) ㄆㄠˋ pào
acne: 疱疹 ① a bleb ② herpes

疵 2621
ㄘ cī (又讀 ㄘˊ cí)
a defect; a flaw; a mistake

六畫

痌 2622
ㄊㄨㄥ tōng
aching; painful: 痌瘝在抱 to have a constant concern for the suffering of the people

痊 2623
ㄑㄩㄢˊ quán
healed; cured; recovery
【痊愈 or 痊癒】to have been cured; to have recovered from illness

痕 2624
ㄏㄣˊ hén
a mark; a scar; a trace: 痕跡 a trace

痔 2625
ㄓˋ zhì
as in 痔瘡—piles; hemorrhoids

七畫

痛 2626
ㄊㄨㄥˋ tòng
1. painful; aching 2. sorrowful; sad; bitter; poignant; bitterly 3. heartily; to one's heart's content
【痛不欲生】to grieve to the extent of wishing to die
【痛罵】to berate; to revile; to vituperate
【痛風】gout (a disease)
【痛打】to beat soundly; to give a severe thrashing
【痛定思痛】to feel pangs over a past defeat, failure, mistake, etc.

【痛改前非】to repent past mistakes
【痛哭】to weep bitterly「anguish
【痛哭流涕】to shed tears of
【痛苦】painful; suffering; pain; anguish
【痛快】very happy; delighted
【痛快淋漓】satisfying in every respect
【痛恨】to detest; to hate deeply
【痛擊】to give a hard blow
【痛惜】to regret deeply
【痛心】heartbroken; very sorry
【痛心疾首】to hate deeply; to feel bitter about...「denounce
【痛斥】to scold severely; scathingly
【痛責】to scold severely
【痛毆】to beat savagely
【痛飲】to drink to one's heart's content「to abhor; disgusting
【痛惡】to hate bitterly; to detest;

痘 2627
ㄉㄡˋ dòu
smallpox 亦作「天花」: 痘苗 vaccine

痙 2628
ㄐㄧㄥˋ jìng
spasm; convulsions「a jerk
【痙攣】convulsions; spasm; cramp;

痢 2629
ㄌㄧˋ lì
as in 痢疾—dysentery; diarrhea

痣 2630
ㄓˋ zhì
moles; nevus

痠 2631
ㄙㄨㄢ suān
muscular pains
【痠疼 or 痠痛】(said of bones, muscles, etc.) to ache

痞 2632
ㄆㄧˇ pǐ
1. dyspepsia; a spleen infection 2. a ruffian; a scoundrel「drel
【痞棍or痞子】a rascal; a scoun-

八畫

痰 2633
ㄊㄢˊ tán
phlegm; expectoration; sputum
【痰盂 or 痰罐】a spittoon

痱 2634
(痱) ㄈㄟˋ fèi「heat
heat rashes; heat spots; prickly
【痱子】heat rashes; heat spots
【痱子粉】talcum powder; baby powder

痲 2635
ㄇㄚˊ má
1. measles 2. leprosy 3. to stupefy; to benumb; to anesthetize; to paralyze 4. a pockmark
【痲痹】paralysis; palsy; numbness
【痲瘋】leprosy
【痲疹】measles
【痲子】① pockmarks ② a person with a pockmarked face

痼 2636
ㄍㄨˋ gù
a chronic disease: 痼疾 an incurable chronic disease

瘀 2637
ㄩ yū
as in 瘀血—a hematoma
【瘀膿】pus
【瘀傷】a contusion; a bruise

瘁 2638
ㄘㄨㄟˋ cuì
1. disease; illness 2. overfatigued; toil

痴 2639
ㄔ chī
the simplified form of "癡", 參看「癡」

九畫

瘍 2640
ㄧㄤˊ yáng「an ulcer
skin diseases or infections; sores;

瘋 2641
ㄈㄥ fēng
insane; crazy; mad; mentally deranged; lunatic; wild
【瘋癲 or 瘋瘋癲癲】insane; mentally deranged
【瘋狗】a mad dog; a rabid dog
【瘋狂】crazy; mad; insane; wild; irrational
【瘋話】gibberish; jargon
【瘋人 or 瘋子】a lunatic; a madman; a maniac

瘌 2642
ㄌㄚˋ là「by favus
favus: 瘌痢頭a head made bald

瘧 2643
ㄋㄩㄝˋ nüè
as in 瘧疾—malaria
【瘧蚊】an anopheles

十畫

疒部

瘟 2644 ㄨㄣ wēn
as in 瘟疫—an epidemic; a plague; a pestilence

瘡 2645 ㄔㄨㄤ chuāng
1. an ulcer; a sore; a boil 2. a wound
【瘡疤】the scar of an ulcer
【瘡痍滿目】One sees suffering everywhere.

瘦 2646 ㄕㄡ shòu
thin; lean; slim; meager; scrawny; emaciated
【瘦骨嶙峋】very skinny
【瘦小】thin and small
【瘦長】skinny and tall; tall and lean
【瘦肉】lean meat
【瘦弱】thin and weak; emaciated and frail

瘠 2647 ㄐㄧ jí
1. thin; lean; meager 2. (said of land) sterile, infertile, or unproductive
【瘠土】sterile soil; infertile soil
【瘠瘦】emaciated; lean and weak

瘤 2648 (瘤) ㄌㄧㄡ liú
a tumor; a swelling; a lump

十一畫

瘴 2649 ㄓㄤ zhàng
as in 瘴氣—miasma; swamp vapor
【瘴癘】disease or epidemic attributed to miasma; poisonous vapor

瘸 2650 ㄑㄩㄝ qué
1. a cripple; a lame man 2. to be lame
【瘸腿】crippled; lame

十二畫

療 2651 ㄌㄧㄠ liáo
to treat (a disease); to relieve; to heal
【療法】a cure; a therapy
【療效】curative effect
【療治】to treat (a disease)
【療養】to recuperate; to convalesce
【療養院】a sanatorium; a sanitarium

癌 2652 ㄧㄢ yán (又讀 ㄞ ái)
cancer: 癌細胞 cancer cells

癆 2653 ㄌㄠ láo
as in 癆病 or 癆症—tuberculosis; consumption

十三畫

癖 2654 ㄆㄧ pǐ
1. chronic swelling of the spleen 2. addiction; a habitual inclination

癒 2655 (瘉) ㄩ yù
healed; cured

十四畫

癟 2656 (癟) ㄅㄧㄝ biě
flat; sunken; not full
【癟嘴子】a person who has lost all teeth
【癟三】a bum; a tramp

癡 2657 (痴) ㄔ chī
1. idiotic; silly; foolish; stupid 2. to besot
【癡迷】infatuated; besotted
【癡情】blind love; blind passion; infatuation
【癡笑】to giggle; to titter
【癡心】①blind love; infatuation ② a silly wish; daydreaming
【癡心妄想】silly and fantastic notions
【癡人說夢】an idiot's gibberish; nonsense
【癡騃 or 癡呆】stupid; foolish; imbecile; idiotic; dull; silly

十五畫

癢 2658 (痒) ㄧㄤ yǎng
to itch; to tickle

癥 2659 ㄓㄥ zhēng
obstruction of the bowels
【癥結】① obstruction of the bowels ② a difficult point (of a problem); a bottleneck; a crux

十六畫

癩 2660 ㄌㄞ lài
1. leprosy 2. favus; scabies 3. bad
【癩皮狗】①a mangy dog ②a disgusting creature
【癩蝦蟆】the toad

【癩瘡】scabies

十七畫

癮 2661
ㄧㄣˇ yǐn
1. addiction; a habitual craving 2. strong interest (in a sport or pastime)
【癮頭】addiction
【癮君子】an opium eater; a heavy smoker

癬 2662
ㄒㄩㄢˇ xuǎn
(讀音 ㄒㄧㄢˇ xiǎn)
ringworm; tetter

十九畫

癲 2663
ㄉㄧㄢ diān
mentally deranged; insane; mad; crazy; lunatic
【癲癇】epilepsy

癱 2664
ㄊㄢ tān
paralysis
【癱瘓】paralyzed; standstill
【癱軟】(said of arms, legs, etc.) weak and limp

癶 部
ㄅㄛ bō

四畫

癸 2665
ㄍㄨㄟˇ guǐ
the last of the Ten Celestial Stems

七畫

登 2666
ㄉㄥ dēng
1. to ascend; to climb; to rise 2. to record; to register; to enter 3. to take; to employ 4. to board 5. to step on; to tread
【登報】to make an announcement in the newspaper
【登門拜訪】to make a special call on another at his house; to visit
【登峯造極】to reach the summit of achievement; to reach the acme
【登堂入室】to ascend to the hall and reach the inner room—to master learning or skill
【登徒子】a lecher; a debauchee
【登陸or登岸】to go ashore; to land
【登陸艇】landing craft; landing ship tank (LST)
【登陸戰】landing operations
【登龍門】to enter a successful career with the help of an influential person
【登革熱】dengue fever
【登基】to ascend the throne
【登機】to board a plane
【登記or登錄】to check in; to register
【登記簿】a register
【登記處】a registry; a registration office
【登場】①(said of actors, entertainers, etc.) to appear on the stage ②(said of products) to appear in the market ③to be gathered and taken to the threshing ground
【登船】to take a boat
【登時】immediately; at once
【登山】to climb a mountain; to mountaineer
【登山隊】a mountaineering party
【登山協會】an alpine association
【登載】(said of a periodical or newspaper) to carry (an article); to publish (a news story)

發 2667
ㄈㄚ fā
1. to shoot; to launch 2. to issue; to publish 3. to begin; to start 4. to reveal; to disclose; to uncover 5. to become; to come to be 6. to utter; to express; to speak 7. to set off; to set out 8. to illuminate; to help out
【發白】to turn white; to turn pale
【發包】to contract with a contractor for a construction program
【發報】to transmit messages
【發報機】a telegraph transmitter
【發榜】to publish the result of a competitive examination
【發表】to make public; to publish; to announce
【發布or發佈】to announce; to promulgate
【發排】to send (manuscripts) to the composing room
【發牌】to deal cards
【發配】to banish (a criminal) to a

癶部

frontier garrison 「to get fat }
【發胖】to put on (or gain) weight; }
【發脾氣 or 發怒】to lose one's temper; to get angry; to get mad
【發麻】numb; benumbed
【發霉】to get mildewed; to mildew
【發毛】to feel a shudder
【發悶】①(ㄈㄚ ㄇㄣ) (said of the weather) to become oppressive ②(ㄈㄚ ㄇㄣˊ) to become low-spirited, depressed, or dejected
【發明】①to invent; to devise ②an }
【發明家】an inventor ⌊invention }
【發粉 or 發酵粉】baking powder
【發憤圖強】(said of a nation) to strive for progress with determination 亦作「發奮圖強」
【發放】①to issue; to distribute; to provide; to extend ②to dispose of 「sane }
【發瘋】to go mad; to become in- }
【發福】① to become rich and happy ②(jocularly) to become fat 「perous; thriving }
【發達】to evolve; developed; pros- }
【發抖】to tremble; to shiver
【發單 or 發票】an invoice; a bill of sale
【發電】① to generate electric power ② to send a telegram
【發電機】a generator; a dynamo
【發電廠】a power plant 「ate }
【發動】to start; to launch; to initi- }
【發動機】a motor; an engine
【發條】a spring (of a mechanical device)
【發難】① to spearhead a rebellion or revolution ② to ask difficult questions
【發牢騷】to grumble; to complain
【發亮 or 發光】to shine; to glitter
【發落】to deal with (an offender)
【發稿】(journalism) to send out a story or report for publication
【發刊】to start or launch (a magazine, newspaper, etc.)
【發號施令】to issue orders
【發汗】① to perspire or sweat ② diaphoresis 「show anger }
【發狠】① to exert oneself ② to }
【發火】① to become angry ② to burst into flames ③ to go off
【發揮】to bring (skill, talent, etc.) into full play 「effect) to tell }
【發揮作用】to be effective; (said of }

【發昏】① to faint ② to lose one's head 「feel nervous }
【發慌】to lose one's composure; to }
【發迹】to rise (in business, career, etc.) 「irrationally }
【發酒瘋】to get drunk and behave }
【發掘】to unearth; to dig out; to excavate
【發噱 or 發笑】to laugh
【發覺】① to discover; to find ② (said of crimes, plots, etc.) to be uncovered
【發起人】an originator; an initiator
【發球】to serve a ball (in tennis, handball, etc.) 「vent; to let out }
【發泄or發洩】to give vent to; to }
【發酵】to ferment; fermentation
【發酵乳】ferment milk; yogurt
【發現or發見】to discover; to find; discovery 「to employees }
【發薪水】to hand out paychecks }
【發信】to send or post a letter
【發祥地】the cradle; a birthplace
【發行】①(ㄈㄚ ㄒㄧㄥˊ) (said of currency, bonds, books, etc.) to issue; to publish ②(ㄈㄚ ㄏㄤˊ) ⓐ to sell wholesale ⓑ a wholesaler
【發行量】the volume of circulation
【發行人 or 發行者】a publisher
【發展】to develop; to grow; to }
【發愁】to worry ⌊expand }
【發出】to send forth; to generate
【發誓】to swear; to take an oath
【發射】to launch; to shoot; to catapult
【發射臺】a launching pad
【發燒 or 發熱】to have a temperature; to have a fever
【發售】to go on sale 「ity }
【發神經】to go crazy; to lose san- }
【發生】to happen; to occur; to arise
【發生關係】① to have something to do with ② to have an affair with
【發生衝突】to have a conflict
【發人深省】to stimulate deep thought
【發作】① to show effect ② to have a fit (of anger) ③(said of illness) to have a relapse
【發慈悲】to show mercy or pity
【發財】to acquire wealth; to become rich 「scatter }
【發散】to disperse; to dissipate; to }
【發酸】to become sour; to sour

【發送】① to send ② to hold a funeral service
【發呆or發獃】to look absent-minded
【發芽】to sprout
【發炎】to become inflamed; to become infected
【發言】to speak; to voice one's views
【發言人】a spokesman
【發音】to pronounce; pronunciation
【發揚】to exalt; to enhance
【發揚光大】to enhance and glorify
【發癢】to itch
【發問】to ask questions; to raise questions
【發育】① to grow up; to develop ② to send forth and nourish
【發育不良】maldevelopment
【發源】①an origin; a source ②to originate
【發源地】(said of rivers, etc.) the place of origin

九畫

凳 2668
(櫈) ㄉㄥˋ dèng
as in 凳子 or 凳兒—a stool

白部
ㄅㄛˊ bó

白 2669
ㄅㄞˊ bái (讀音 ㄅㄛˊ bó)
1. white; clear; bright; clean; pure; plain 2. empty; blank 3. in vain; for nothing 4. free of charge; gratis 5. the spoken part in an opera, etc. 6. to state; to explain 7. a Chinese family name
【白璧微瑕】a small defect
【白布】plain white cloth; calico
【白跑一趟】to make a futile trip
【白葡萄酒】sherry
【白螞蟻 or 白蟻】a termite
【白忙】to busy oneself to no purpose
【白茫茫】showing a vast expanse of whiteness
【白米】white polished rice
【白面書生】①an inexperienced young scholar ②a fair-complexioned young scholar
【白髮蒼蒼】hoary-headed
【白搭】futile; in vain; to no avail
【白帶】(medicine) leucorrhea
【白頭偕老】(said of a married couple)to stick to each other to the end of their lives
【白糖】white sugar; refined sugar
【白天】daytime
【白蘭地】brandy
【白領階級】the white-collar class
【白鷺】an egret
【白宮】the White House, Washington D.C.
【白開水】boiled water
【白話】spoken Chinese; vernacular Chinese
【白話文】writings in vernacular Chinese
【白金】①platinum ②silver
【白金漢宮】Buckingham Palace, England
【白淨】perfectly clean; immaculate
【白駒過隙】the swiftness of the lapse of time
【白皙】white-skinned
【白血病】leukemia
【白血球】white blood cells; leucocytes
【白癬】favus; honeycomb ringworm
【白熊】a polar bear
【白晝】broad daylight
【白賺】to earn with little or no effort
【白種人】the white people; the Caucasians
【白癡】an idiot
【白首】a hoary head—the old age
【白手成家or白手起家】to rise in life by one's own efforts
【白日】① daytime;daylight② the sun
【白日夢】a daydream; reverie
【白熱化】(said of a contest, movement, etc.) to reach the climax
【白菜】① *Brassica pekinensis*, Chinese cabbage ② white rape
【白醋】plain vinegar
【白色人種】the white race
【白送】to give away; to give gratis
【白皚皚】(usually said of snow) white and clean
【白衣天使】angels in white—nurses
【白眼】①the whites of the eyes ② disdain; contempt
【白銀】silver
【白雲】white clouds
【白用心機or白費心機】to scheme in vain

一畫

百 2670
ㄅㄞˇ bǎi (讀音 ㄅㄛˊ bó)
1. hundred 2. many; numerous 3. all
【百倍】one hundred times

【百寶箱】a jewel case; a jewel box
【百般】all sorts; every kind
【百弊叢生】All the ill effects appear.
【百步穿楊】(archery) superior marksmanship
【百米賽跑】the 100-meter dash
【百發百中】to hit the target at every shot
【百廢待興】All neglected matters are yet to be dealt with.
【百分比 or 百分率】a percentage
【百分之百】absolutely
【百讀不厭】(said of a book) not boring even after repeated reading; very interesting
【百聽不厭】worth hearing a hundred times
【百年】① a hundred years; a century ② a lifetime
【百年大計】a project of vital and lasting importance
【百年好合】a harmonious union lasting a hundred years (a conventional congratulatory message on a wedding)
【百年樹人】It takes one hundred years to cultivate a man.
【百鍊成鋼】Mastery comes from long training.
【百感交集】Lots of emotions crowd into the heart.
【百工】① all sorts of officers ② all sorts of handicraftsmen
【百科全書】an encyclopedia
【百口莫辯】unable to give a convincing explanation for self-defense
【百孔千瘡】in a state of ruin or extreme distress
【百合花】the lily
【百花齊放】All flowers are in bloom.
【百貨公司】a department store
【百貨商場】an emporium
【百家爭鳴】All schools of thoughts contend for attention.
【百姓】①the common people; the people ② all existing family names
【百折不撓】indomitable; unswerving
【百褶裙 or 百襉裙】a pleated skirt
【百戰百勝】victorious in every battle
【百尺竿頭，更進一步】to make still further progress
【百事通】an expert in everything; an all-rounder
【百事俱廢】Everything is neglected.

白部

【百獸之王】the king of all animals—the lion
【百日咳】whooping cough
【百思莫解】incomprehensible
【百依百順】to yield to all the wishes (of a child, etc.) 亦作「百縱千隨」
【百葉窗】Venetian blinds
【百無禁忌】There are no taboos or restrictions at all.
【百無一失】sure to succeed if certain rules are followed
【百萬】a million
【百萬富翁】a millionaire
【百聞不如一見】Seeing is believing.

二畫

皁 2671
(皂) ㄗㄠˋ zào
1. black 2. menial labor 3. a menial; a lictor 4. soap
【皁白不分】to fail to distinguish between right and wrong

皀 2672
ㄗㄠˋ zào
soap

三畫

的 2673
1. ㄉㄧˋ dì
1.clear; manifest 2.a target; a goal

的 2673
2. ㄉㄧˊ dí
accurate; exact; proper
【的確】certainly; surely

的 2673
3. ˙ㄉㄜ de
1. a bound subordinate particle translatable by "'s" or with terms interchanged by "of" 2. by "-ly" 3. by an adjectival ending, a prepositional phrase, or a relative

四畫

皆 2674
ㄐㄧㄝ jiē
all; every; entire
【皆大歡喜】Everybody is satisfied.
【皆可】all acceptable

皇 2675
ㄏㄨㄤˊ huáng
1. imperial; royal 2. an emperor

3. beautiful; brilliant 4. uneasy; anxious 5. a term of respect for an ancestor
【皇帝】an emperor
【皇太后】the empress dowager
【皇太子 or 皇儲】the crown prince
【皇天后土】Heaven and Earth
【皇陵】an imperial mausoleum
【皇冠】an imperial crown
【皇宮】an imperial palace
【皇后】an empress
【皇家】the imperial family (or house)
【皇親國戚】relatives of the emperor
【皇室】the imperial household; the royal household
【皇上】His Majesty
【皇恩】imperial favor or kindness

皈 2676 ㄍㄨㄟ guī
to follow
【皈依】to be converted to (Buddhism)

五畫

皋 2677 (臯) ㄍㄠ gāo
1. a marsh; a swamp 2. a shore

六畫

皎 2678 ㄐㄧㄠˇ jiǎo
1. white; clean 2. bright; lustrous; brilliant
【皎潔】brightly clean
【皎如日星】as bright as the heavenly bodies

七畫

皓 2679 ㄏㄠˋ hào
white and bright
【皓皓】gleaming; brilliant; glistening; bright
【皓齒】white teeth; sparkling teeth
【皓月當空】The bright moon hangs in the sky.

皖 2680 ㄨㄢˇ wǎn
1. name of an ancient state in what is today's Anhwei 2. an alternative name of Anhwei

十畫

皚 2681 ㄞ ái
pure white; white and clean; brightly white

皮部 ㄆㄧˊ pí

〔皮部〕

皮 2682 ㄆㄧˊ pí
1. skin; fur; hide; leather; rind; peltry; bark 2. a thin sheet 3. naughty 4. a Chinese family name
【皮包】a handbag or purse
【皮包骨】skinny
【皮毛之見】a superficial view or opinion
【皮筏】a kayak
【皮膚病】skin disease
【皮膚科】dermatology
【皮帶】a leather belt
【皮蛋】duck's eggs preserved in lime
【皮條客】a pimp
【皮艇】a skin boat
【皮囊】a leather bag
【皮革】leather
【皮貨】furs
【皮夾子】a wallet
【皮夾克】a leather jacket; Windbreaker
【皮球】a rubber ball
【皮鞋】leather shoes
【皮笑肉不笑】treacherous; crafty; putting on a false smile
【皮箱】a suitcase or valise (especially of leather)
【皮靴】leather boots
【皮尺】a tape measure; a tape
【皮襖】a fur coat; a leather coat
【皮衣】fur clothing
【皮影戲】the shadow show

五畫

皰 2683 (疱) ㄆㄠˋ pào
pimples

十畫

皺 2684 ㄓㄡˋ zhòu
1. wrinkles; creases; folds; rumples 2. to wrinkle; to fold; to contract; to crease; to crumple
【皺眉or皺眉頭】to frown; to knit

the brows 「rumples
【皺紋】wrinkles; creases; folds; }
【皺紋紙】crepe paper

皿部
ㄇㄧㄣˇ mǐn

2685
皿 ㄇㄧㄣˇ mǐn
(又讀 ㄇㄧㄥˇ mǐng)
a shallow container (such as a dish, plate, saucer, etc.)

三畫

2686
盂 ㄩˊ yú
1. a basin; a broad-mouthed receptacle for holding liquid; a jar 2. a party for hunting

四畫

2687
盅 ㄓㄨㄥ zhōng
a small cup

2688
盆 ㄆㄣˊ pén
a bowl; a basin; a tub
【盆地】(geology) a basin
【盆栽】① a potted plant; a bonsai 亦作「盆景」② to plant in a pot

2689
盈 ㄧㄥˊ yíng
to fill; to become full 「pluses
【盈利or盈餘】profit; gains; sur- }
【盈虧】①(said of the moon) waxing and waning ② profits and losses
【盈盈】①(said of water) clear and abundant ②(said of a woman's bearing) easy and graceful

2690
盃 (杯) ㄅㄟ bēi
a cup; a tumbler

五畫

2691
益 ㄧˋ yì
1. to increase; to add to; to augment 2. in a higher degree; to a greater extent; more 3. benefit; profit; advantage
【益發 or 益加】increasingly; more and more; all the more
【益智】① to grow in intelligence or wisdom ② the longan
【益處】advantages; benefit; profit

2692
盍 ㄏㄜˊ hé
1. what 2. why not 3. to get to- 「gether }

2693
盎 ㄤˋ àng
1. a basin; a pot; a bowl 2. abundant; plentiful; rich
【盎然】abundant; full; exuberant
【盎斯】an ounce 亦作「盎司」

六畫

2694
盒 ㄏㄜˊ hé
a small box; a case

2695
盔 ㄎㄨㄟ kuī
1. a helmet 2. a basin; a pot
【盔甲】helmets and mail; armor

七畫

2696
盛 1. ㄕㄥˋ shèng
1. abundant; rich; exuberant; flourishing; prosperous 2. (said of fire, storm, etc.) to rage
【盛名】a glorious name; great reputation 「famous personality
【盛名之累】the trouble of being a }
【盛大】grand; magnificent; majestic
【盛典】a grand occasion; a big ceremony
【盛怒】in great anger; wrath
【盛開】in full bloom
【盛況空前】unprecedented in grandeur, festivity, etc.
【盛會】a grand gathering; a magnificent assembly
【盛極一時】to be in vogue for a time 「through arrogance
【盛氣凌人】to treat others rudely }
【盛情】warm thoughtfulness; utmost sincerity
【盛情難卻】It is hard to turn down the offer made with such warmheartedness.
【盛夏】midsummer
【盛行】to be popular or in vogue
【盛裝】in full dress; in rich attire

【盛產】 to abound in; to be rich in
【盛世】 a prosperous age or period
【盛宴】 a grand banquet

盛 2696
2. ㄔㄥˊ chéng
1. to take (loose material) into a bowl or basin 2. to hold; to contain

盜 2697
ㄉㄠˋ dào
to steal; to rob; to misappropriate
【盜版】 a pirated edition
【盜賣】 to misappropriate and sell
【盜墓】 to steal from graves
【盜伐】 to fell trees unlawfully
【盜匪】 robbers; bandits; brigands
【盜壘】 base stealing (as of baseball)
【盜錄】 to pirate (records, etc.)
【盜汗】 (pathology) night sweats
【盜竊】 theft; larceny to pilfer
【盜取】 to steal
【盜賊】 a thief; a robber; a bandit
【盜印】 to pirate; piracy
【盜用】 to embezzle; to usurp

八畫

盞 2698
ㄓㄢˇ zhǎn
1. a small shallow container; a small cup 2. a numerical adjunct denoting lamps

盟 2699
ㄇㄥˊ méng
1. a covenant; an oath; a vow; to covenant; to ally 2. a Mongol league
【盟邦】 an allied country; allies
【盟國】 allied powers; allies
【盟軍】 allied troops; allied forces
【盟約】 a treaty of alliance

九畫

盡 2700
ㄐㄧㄣˋ jìn
1. to exhaust; to use up 2. to put to the best use 3. to complete; to finish; to accomplish 4. all; entirely; totally; completely; wholly 5. the utmost
【盡本分】 to do what one is supposed to do, no more and no less
【盡付東流】 all in vain
【盡頭】 the extremity; the end
【盡力】 to make efforts; to exert oneself; to do one's best
【盡力而爲or盡力爲之】 to do one's best
【盡量】 as much as possible
【盡歡而散】 to leave only after each has enjoyed himself to the utmost
【盡情】 to one's heart's content
【盡孝】 to do one's filial duty
【盡心】 to devote all one's energies
【盡興】 to enjoy to one's heart's content
【盡職】 to do one's duty
【盡忠報國】 to devote oneself to one's country
【盡是】 all are; without exception; to be full of
【盡善盡美】 flawless; perfect
【盡人事以聽天命】 One does one's best and leaves the rest to Heaven.

監 2701
1. ㄐㄧㄢ jiān
1. to supervise; to superintend; to oversee; to direct; to inspect 2. to confine; to keep in custody; to imprison
【監票】 (in elections) to scrutinize a ballot
【監票人or監票員】 a ballot supervisor; a scrutineer
【監督】 to supervise; to superintend; to oversee
【監聽】 to monitor
【監考】 to proctor or invigilate an examination
【監考員】 a proctor; an invigilator
【監護】 custody; to act as the guardian
【監護人】 a guardian (of a minor)
【監禁】 ① to confine; to imprison ② custody; confinement
【監製】 to direct or supervise the manufacture of
【監察】 to supervise; to control; control
【監察委員】 a member of the Control Yüan
【監察院】 Control Yüan (one of the five major branches of the government of the Republic of China)
【監視】 ① to keep a watchful eye on ② to monitor
【監視器】 a watchdog; a monitor
【監押】 to keep (a person) in custody
【監獄 or 監牢】 a prison; a jail

監 2701
2. ㄐㄧㄢˋ jiàn

1. an official position in former times 2. a government establishment (such as a school) in former times 3. a eunuch

十畫

盤 2702 ㄆㄢˊ pán

1. a tray; a plate; a dish 2. twisted; entangled; entwined; intricate; winding; to entangle; to entwine 3. to investigate; to interrogate 4. (said of a chess match, etc.) a round

【盤點】to check; to make an inventory of
【盤尼西林】penicillin
【盤弄】①to tamper with ②to provoke
【盤根錯節】very complicated
【盤貨】to make an inventory of stock
【盤詰or盤問】to interrogate closely
【盤踞】①to occupy ②to squat with the legs crossed
【盤據】(usually said of enemy troops, rebels or bandits) to occupy and hold a place
【盤旋】to circle; to hover around
【盤查】to question; to cross-examine
【盤纏】traveling expenses
【盤繞】to twine; to wind round
【盤算】to make a mental calculation

十一畫

盥 2703 ㄍㄨㄢˋ guàn

1. to wash one's hands 2. to wash

【盥洗】to wash oneself
【盥洗室】a washroom; a restroom; a lavatory

盧 2704 ㄌㄨˊ lú

1. black 2. a Chinese family name

【盧森堡】Luxemburg, Europe

十二畫

盪 2705 ㄉㄤˋ dàng

1. to toss about; to swing 2. to wash

【盪秋千】to swing (in a swing)
【盪漾】①to be gently tossed about ②to ripple

目部 ㄇㄨˋ mù

目 2706 ㄇㄨˋ mù

1. the eye 2. to look; to regard; to see 3. a table of contents; a category

【目標】①an objective; a target; to target ②an aim; a goal
【目不暇給 or 目不暇接】So many things come into sight that the eyes are kept fully occupied.
【目不斜視】to look straight ahead
【目不轉睛】to look attentively
【目不識丁】completely illiterate
【目瞪口呆】dumbfounded; stupefied
【目的】a purpose; an objective; an end; an aim
【目的地】a destination
【目睹or目覩】to see directly; to witness
【目錄】①contents②a list; a catalogue
【目光】insight; vision; sight
【目光炯炯】to have eyes with a piercing gleam
【目光銳利】sharp-sighted; sharp-eyed
【目空一切】to look down on everyone or everything
【目擊】to witness
【目今 or 目前】now; the present
【目眩】dazzled
【目中無人】to be supercilious; to be overweening with the eyes
【目送】to gaze after; to follow with the eyes
【目無法紀】to disregard all laws and regulations; lawless
【目無尊長】to show no respect to elders and superiors

二畫

盯 2707 ㄉㄧㄥ dīng

to stare at; to gaze at; to fix one's eyes on; to keep a close watch

三畫

盲 2708 ㄇㄤˊ máng

1. blind; to blind 2. deluded
【盲目】①blind ②lacking insight or understanding ③reckless; aimless
【盲腸】the cecum, or caecum
【盲腸炎】appendicitis
【盲人】a blind person
【盲從】to follow blindly
【盲啞學校】a school for the blind and the mute

直 2709
ㄓˊ zhí
1. straight; to straighten 2. upright and honest; fair; unbiased 3. vertical; longitudinal; from top to bottom 4. outspoken; frank; straightforward 5. directly; firsthand 6. continuous; uninterrupted 7. stiff; numb 8. just; simply; only; merely 9. a vertical stroke (in Chinese characters)
【直達】to go nonstop to; through
【直達車】a through train, bus, etc.
【直到】①till; until ②up to
【直立】to stand erect
【直接】direct; firsthand; directly
【直截了當】straightforward; flatly
【直徑】①a straight path ②a diameter
【直覺】intuition
【直轄市】a special municipality
【直銷】to sell directly or direct sale by a manufacturer instead of through an agent
【直線】①a straight line ②steep; sharp
【直性子】frank; straightforward
【直尺】a straightedge
【直陳】to describe truthfully; to state frankly
【直腸】the rectum
【直上青雲】to hit the highest literary honors
【直昇機】a helicopter
【直屬】to be under the direct control or jurisdiction of
【直率or直爽】straight-forward; candid; frank
【直譯】word-for-word translation
【直言】① to speak out ② outspoken remarks
【直言不諱】to speak plainly and frankly

四畫

相 2710
1. ㄒㄧㄤ xiāng
1. each other; one another; mutually; reciprocal 2. substance

【相伴】to accompany somebody
【相比】to compare with each other
【相配】to match well
【相反】contrary; opposed to each other
【相逢】to come across
【相符】to tally; to correspond
【相輔相成】to complement each other; to reciprocate and complement
【相得益彰】Each gains in appearance from the presence of the other.
【相當】①equivalent; to correspond to ②considerable ③appropriate; fit
【相等】equal; equivalent
【相對】① corresponding ② relative ③ opposite; face to face
【相提並論】to mention (two things or persons of different worth) in the same breath
【相同】① the same ② similar
【相連】connected; joined; linked
【相隔】to be separated by; to be apart
【相告】to tell; to pass information
【相干or相關】related; connected; to have to do with
【相顧失色】to look at each other in dismay
【相剋】mutually destructive
【相互】one another; mutually; reciprocally
【相會】to meet together
【相繼】in succession
【相救】to rescue; to help out of difficulty
【相見恨晚】to regret having not met earlier
【相近】close (in amount, quality, degree, etc.); approximate
【相距】away from
【相聚】to meet together; to assemble
【相求】to ask for a favor; to beg; to entreat
【相親相愛】to be kind to each other and love each other
【相去無幾】The difference is insignificant.
【相勸】to persuade; to offer advice
【相信】to believe; to have faith in
【相像】to resemble; to be similar
【相形見絀】to be outshone
【相形之下】in comparison with
【相知】① bosom friends; great friends ② to know each other well
【相助】to help; to help each other
【相撞】to collide with each other

【相持不下】 persistently opposing each other with neither giving way
【相差】 to differ
【相稱】 to fit each other; to match each other; to be symmetrical
【相處】 to spend time together; to live together
【相傳】 ①(said of a report) to be transmitted from person to person ②to be passed or handed down from generation to generation
【相識】 ① to know each other ② an acquaintance
【相贈】 to present a gift; to give a present
【相左】 to disagree; to differ; to conflict with each other
【相思】 to miss each other
【相思病】 lovesickness
【相似 or 相若】 alike; similar
【相愛】 to love each other
【相安無事】 at peace with each other
【相依為命】 to rely upon each other for life
【相應不理】 to disregard another's request
【相映成趣】to form an interesting or delightful contrast
【相遇】 to meet each other
【相約】 to make an appointment

相 2710
2. ㄒㄧㄤˋ xiàng
1. to examine; to study; to read 2. a countenance; facial features 3. the prime minister (in feudal times) 4. to assist; to help
【相片】 a photograph; a photo
【相貌】 a countenance; a physiognomy; a face; facial features
【相貌堂堂】 to have a dignified appearance
【相機】 a camera
【相機行事】to act as circumstances dictate
【相親】 an interview prior to marriage
【相紙】 (photography) printing paper; photographic paper
【相士】 ①a fortuneteller ②to appraise a person's latent ability
【相聲】 a Chinese comic dialogue; a cross talk
【相册】 a photo album

盼 2711
ㄆㄢˋ pàn
1. to look 2. (descriptive of the black and white of the eyes) well defined 3. to hope; to expect
【盼望】 to hope; to wish

眇 2712
ㄇㄧㄠˇ miǎo
1. tiny; fine; small 2. blind in one eye
【眇眇忽忽】 indistinct; too small to identify
【眇小】 very small; tiny; insignificant

盾 2713
ㄕㄨㄣˇ shǔn
(又讀 ㄉㄨㄣˋ dùn)
1. a shield; a buckler 2. a guilder, a monetary unit in Holland
【盾牌】 ① a shield ②(figuratively) a pretext; an excuse

省 2714
1. ㄕㄥˇ shěng
1. a province; provincial 2. economical; frugal; to economize 3. to save; to omit; to reduce; to abridge
【省分】 a province
【省得】 ① lest ② to avoid; to save (trouble, etc.)
【省道】 a provincial highway
【省力】 to save energy or labor
【省立學校】 a provincial school
【省略】 to omit; to abridge; omission
【省會】 a provincial capital
【省界】 provincial boundaries
【省錢】 to save money; economical
【省卻】 to avoid (trouble, etc.); to save (time, etc.)
【省下】 to save (money)
【省政府】 the provincial government
【省主席】 the governor of a province
【省吃儉用】 frugal and thrifty
【省時】 to save time; timesaving
【省事】 ① to save trouble ② easy
【省議會】 the provincial assembly
【省議員】 a provincial assemblyman

省 2714
2. ㄒㄧㄥˇ xǐng
1. to examine (oneself, etc.); to reflect; to introspect 2. to understand; to know 3. to visit (one's seniors, etc.) 4. to test; an examination 5. memory
【省察】 ①to examine ②to introspect
【省視】 to survey; to inspect
【省悟】 to realize; awakening; realization; to awaken to (truth, etc.)

眉 2715
ㄇㄟˊ méi
1. eyebrows 2. the side 3. the top margin of a printed page in

a book 4.a rare Chinese family name
【眉筆】an eyebrow pencil
【眉毛】the eyebrows
【眉目】①a general facial appearance ②a general sketch or idea of things
【眉目傳情】to make sheep's eyes (at someone)
【眉飛色舞】to be overjoyed; to be exultant
【眉來眼去】(between a man and a woman) to converse with eyes
【眉開眼笑】very happy, joyful or jubilant
【眉睫】①very close, imminent or urgent ②eyebrows and eyelashes
【眉清目秀】good-looking; pleasant facial features
【眉梢】the ends of the eyebrows
【眉宇】①a facial appearance ②the forehead

看 2716
1. ㄎㄢˋ kàn
1. to see; to look at; to observe; to watch; to read 2. to examine; to consider; to think 3. to visit; to call on 4. to present (tea, wine, etc.) 5. to depend on
【看病】①to see a doctor ②to examine the patient
【看不慣】to detest; to disdain
【看不起】to look down upon
【看不上眼】①to detest; to disdain ②not up to one's standard
【看破】①to see through a thing ②to be resigned to what is inevitable
【看破紅塵】to see through the vanity of life (and to become a Buddhist monk or nun)
【看法】an opinion; a viewpoint
【看得起】to think highly of
【看待】to treat (another, a child, friend, etc.); treatment
【看臺】(sports) bleachers
【看透】①to see through (a trick, conspiracy, etc.) ②to be resigned to what is inevitable
【看頭】that which is worth seeing or reading
【看來】it looks as if; evidently
【看過】①to take a look at ②to make a perusal of ③to have seen or read
【看看】①to take a look at ②to examine and survey ③to visit or call on ④to see the sights ⑤to thumb through (a book, etc.)
【看見 or 看到】to see; to catch sight of
【看齊】①(military) to dress ②to emulate (someone)
【看輕】to despise; to underestimate
【看情形】depending on circumstances
【看戲】to watch a show
【看著辦】to see what happens and act accordingly
【看中】to feel satisfied with; to prefer; to like
【看重】to esteem; to regard as important; to value
【看成】to look upon as; to regard as
【看出】to make out; to see
【看穿】to see through (a trick)
【看書】to read a book
【看作】to regard as; to consider to be
【看錯】①to mistake someone or something for another ②to misjudge someone's ability, character, etc.
【看醫生】to consult a doctor or physician
【看一看】to take a look; to have a look
【看樣子】it seems; it looks as if

看 2716
2. ㄎㄢ kān
1. to watch; to mind; to look after 2. to guard; to keep under surveillance
【看門】①a doorkeeper or gatekeeper ②to watch or guard the door
【看管】①to take into custody; to guard; to safeguard ②a custodian
【看護】①to nurse; to take care ②a nurse (in hospital)
【看家】①to stay at home and look after the house ②a houseguard ③(money, etc.) saved for a rainy day
【看家本領】one's specialty or special skill
【看家狗】a watchdog
【看守】①to watch or guard ②to detain
【看守所】a detention house for prisoners awaiting trials

五畫

眛 2717
ㄇㄟˋ mèi
dim-sighted; poor-visioned
【眛於】blind to

眠 2718
ㄇㄧㄢˊ mián
1. to sleep; sleep 2. to hibernate; hibernation

眩 2719 ㄒㄩㄢˋ xuàn

1. to confuse; to dazzle 2. dizzy; giddy; confused vision

【眩惑】to confuse and cheat (the people); to mislead
【眩耀】dazzling; to dazzle

眨 2720 ㄓㄚˇ zhǎ

to wink; to blink

眞 2721 (真) ㄓㄣ zhēn

1. true; real; factual; substantial; actual; truly 2. the highest sincerity one is capable of

【眞皮】① dermis ② genuine leather
【眞憑實據】indisputable proof
【眞面目】(literally) the real face —true colors; true character; the actual thing behind a false front
【眞諦】the real meaning; the essence
【眞理】① truth ② righteousness
【眞工夫】a true skill or accom-}
【眞空】vacuum ⌊plishment}
【眞空吸塵器】a vacuum cleaner
【眞話】the truth 「and fake}
【眞假or眞僞】true and false; real}
【眞金不怕火煉】Truth is ultimately louder than lies or slanders.
【眞切】① true and concise; vivid ② (to see or hear) clearly
【眞槍實彈】real guns and bullets
【眞情】① actual happenings (of an incident, etc.) ② real affections
【眞確】authentic; true; accurate
【眞心】from the bottom of one's heart; sincere; wholehearted
【眞心話】words from the bottom of one's heart 「ing, etc.)}
【眞相】the truth (about a happen-}
【眞相大白】The truth is out.
【眞摯】sincere; sincerity; faithful; true
【眞正】① actually; real ② genuine
【眞珠】natural pearls
【眞誠】sincere; genuine; true
【眞實】actual; true; real; factual
【眞實性】reliability; truthfulness
【眞材實料】genuine material and solid substance
【眞才實學】①solid learning; genuine talent ②truly learned; high-}
【眞愛】true love ⌊ly competent}

六畫

眸 2722 ㄇㄡˊ móu

the pupil of the eye—the eyes

眼 2723 ㄧㄢˇ yǎn

1. the eye 2. a look; a glance 3. a tiny hole; an opening; an orifice; an aperture 4. a key point

【眼巴巴】① expectantly; eagerly; anxiously ②helplessly (watching something unpleasant happen)
【眼皮 or 眼瞼】eyelids
【眼明手快】to see things clearly and act speedily
【眼淚】tears 「cerning ability}
【眼力】① eyesight; vision ② dis-}
【眼高手低】to have great aims but poor abilities
【眼光】sight; insight; vision; eye — discerning ability; power of judgment 「sight}
【眼花】eyesight blurred; dim of}
【眼花撩亂】(scenes so varied and confusing as) to dazzle the eyes
【眼紅】① red-eyed ② covetous; envious ③ angry
【眼睫毛】eyelashes 「outlook}
【眼界】one's field of vision; an}
【眼鏡】glasses; spectacles
【眼鏡蛇】a cobra
【眼睛】the eyes
【眼球 or 眼珠】eyeballs
【眼前】① right before one's eyes ② at this moment; now; at present
【眼線】(said of crime investigation) a contact, a stool pigeon, or an informer 「(for a horse)}
【眼罩】①an eyeshade ②blinkers}
【眼睜睜】① right before one's eyes; publicly ② attentively ③ to watch helplessly
【眼中釘】an eyesore 「eyes}
【眼神or眼色】expression of the}
【眼熟】seemingly familiar by sight
【眼藥水】eyewash; eyewater; eyedrops 「socket}
【眼窩 or 眼眶】an orbit; an eye}

眺 2724 ㄊㄧㄠˋ tiào

to look far away; to take a look at faraway things; to look far into the distance

【眺望】to look far away

眾 2725 (衆) ㄓㄨㄥˋ zhòng

1. many; numerous 2. a crowd; a multitude; all; the masses 3. public or popular (opinion, views, etc.)
【眾叛親離】(said of a dictator at his downfall) opposed by the masses and deserted by followers —to be utterly isolated
【眾目睽睽】the glare of the public; the public gaze
【眾多】numerous
【眾矢之的】the target of public censure (or attacks)
【眾生】①all living creatures ② beasts or animals
【眾說紛紜】Opinions vary.
【眾人】all people; the multitude
【眾所週知】universally known; as everyone knows
【眾議紛紜】Public opinions or views are divergent.
【眾望所歸】to command public respect and support

眷 2726 ㄐㄩㄢˋ juàn
1. to look back — to regard; to care for; to concern 2. to admire; to love 3. relatives; dependents
【眷念】to think of or remember with affection
【眷戀】to be attached to someone
【眷顧】to care for; to concern
【眷屬】dependents; family
【眷村】a military dependents' village

七畫

睏 2727 ㄎㄨㄣˋ kùn
drowsy; sleepy

八畫

睛 2728 ㄐㄧㄥ jīng
1. the pupil of the eye 2. eyes

睡 2729 ㄕㄨㄟˋ shuì
to sleep; to rest with eyes closed
【睡帽】a nightcap
【睡眠】sleep
【睡袋】a sleeping bag
【睡蓮】a water lily
【睡覺】to sleep; to go to bed
【睡醒】to wake up from sleep
【睡著】to have fallen asleep
【睡衣 or 睡袍】a sleeping gown; pajamas
【睡意】sleepiness; drowsiness
【睡眼惺忪】to have a drowsy look
【睡午覺】to take a siesta or afternoon nap

睜 2730 ㄓㄥ zhēng
to open the eyes
【睜開眼睛說瞎話】to tell a barefaced lie
【睜一隻眼，閉一隻眼】to pretend not to see — to overlook purposely

睦 2731 ㄇㄨˋ mù
friendly; amiable; to befriend; to be on friendly terms

睫 2732 ㄐㄧㄝˊ jié
1. as in 睫毛—eyelashes 2. to blink; to wink

睬 2733 ㄘㄞˇ cǎi
1. to look; to watch 2. to notice; to pay attention to

督 2734 ㄉㄨ dū
1. to oversee; to superintend; to supervise 2. to reprove; to censure 3. a marshal; a general 4. a viceroy or governor-general 5. a Chinese family name
【督導】to direct and supervise
【督工】①to oversee working ②an overseer
【督學】an inspector of educational establishments
【督察】① to superintend and oversee; to act as a watchdog ② an inspector
【督促】to urge; to press

睪 2735 (睾) ㄍㄠ gāo
1. the marsh 亦作「皋」 2. high; lofty 3. the testicle, or testis

九畫

睹 2736 (覩) ㄉㄨˇ dǔ
to witness; to see; to look at; to observe; to gaze at
【睹物思人】to see the things one is reminded of the owner

睽 2737 ㄎㄨㄟˊ kuí
1. separated 亦作「暌」 2. in opposition 3. to squint 4. to stare at 5. unusual; strange

【睽違】to separate; separation

瞄 2738
ㄇㄧㄠˊ miáo
to aim at; to take aim; to look at attentively

〔目部〕

睿 2739
ㄖㄨㄟˋ ruì
1. to understand thoroughly 2. wise and clever 3. the profoundest (learning)
【睿智】superior intelligence

十畫

瞎 2740
ㄒㄧㄚ xiā
1. blind; blindly 2. rash; reckless; heedless; (to do things, etc.) without purpose or reason; at random; groundlessly 3. (dialect) to become tangled (said of thread, etc.)
【瞎掰】to make a futile effort
【瞎忙】to be busy for nothing
【瞎鬧】to make nonsense; to fool around
【瞎了眼睛】Blind fool!
【瞎攪or瞎搞】to do a thing without any plan or method
【瞎扯】to talk recklessly; to tell lies
【瞎說】to talk nonsense; wild talks
【瞎子】a blind man

瞑 2741
1. ㄇㄧㄥˊ míng
(又讀 ㄇㄧㄥˇ mǐng)
to close the eyes
【瞑目】①to close the eyes ②to die without regret or in peace

瞑 2741
2. ㄇㄧㄢˋ miàn
to throw into a state of confusion

瞌 2742
ㄎㄜ kē
to be tired and to doze off: 瞌睡 to doze off while sitting

十一畫

瞞 2743
ㄇㄢˊ mán
1. to hide the truth; to fool others by lying; to deceive 2. dim-sighted; poor vision
【瞞騙】to deceive and lie
【瞞天過海】very clever and daring in deceiving others
【瞞哄】to hide (the truth) and cheat

瞠 2744
ㄔㄥ chēng
to look straight at; to stare at
【瞠目結舌】amazed and speechless
【瞠乎其後】far behind, without any hope of catching up

十二畫

瞬 2745
ㄕㄨㄣˋ shùn
1. to blink, wink or twinkle 2. a very short time; in the twinkling of an eye
【瞬間】in an instant
【瞬息萬變】many changes within a short time

瞳 2746
ㄊㄨㄥˊ tóng
1. as in 瞳孔—the pupil of the eye 2. ignorant

瞪 2747
ㄉㄥˋ dèng
to stare at; to open (one's eyes) wide; to glare at
【瞪眼】to stare at angrily

瞭 2748
1. ㄌㄧㄠˇ liǎo
1. to understand 2. clear and bright
【瞭解】to comprehend; to understand
【瞭然】clear and evident; plain and fully understandable
【瞭如指掌】to know thoroughly

瞭 2748
2. ㄌㄧㄠˋ liào
as in 瞭望—to look down from a higher place
【瞭望臺】a watchtower; a lookout (post)

瞧 2749
ㄑㄧㄠˊ qiáo
1. to see; to look at 2. to steal a glance; to glance quickly
【瞧不起】to look down upon; to despise
【瞧不上眼】not worth seeing
【瞧得起】to think much of somebody
【瞧見】to see; to catch sight of
【瞧一瞧】to take a look

瞥 2750
ㄆㄧㄝ piē
to have a casual and short glance; to catch a glimpse of
【瞥見】to catch sight of; to catch a glimpse of

十三畫

瞻 2751
ㄓㄢ zhān
1. to look; to look up 2. to regard respectfully; to reverence
【瞻前顧後】(literally) to look forward and backward—very cautious
【瞻仰】①to pay respects to ②to look up to
【瞻望】to look forward to a faraway place

十四畫

矇 2752
1. ㄇㄥˊ méng
1. blind 2. (figuratively) ignorant; stupid and obstinate
【矇蔽】to hide the truth from a superior
【矇矓】① hazy; sight-blurred ② half-asleep; drowsy; somnolent

矇 2752
2. ㄇㄥ mēng
1. as in 矇騙—to deceive; to cheat 2. lucky
【矇混】to fake and cheat

十九畫

矗 2753
ㄔㄨˋ chù
1. rising sharply; steep 2. lofty; upright; straight 3. luxuriant growth
【矗立】rising up steeply

二十一畫

矚 2754
ㄓㄨˇ zhǔ
to watch; to observe or gaze at carefully; to pay attention to
【矚目】to be the focus of attention

矛部
ㄇㄠˊ máo

矛 2755
ㄇㄠˊ máo
a lance; a spear: 矛頭a spear-head
【矛盾】to contradict; contradiction; inconsistency

四畫

矜 2756
1. ㄐㄧㄣ jīn
1. to feel sorry for; to pity; to be sympathetic with; to compassionate 2. to brag; to boast 3. self-esteem; self-control; dignified; selfdiscipline 4. to emulate
【矜持】to carry oneself with dignity and reserve
【矜飾】to brag and pretend

矜 2756
2. ㄍㄨㄢ guān
a widower 亦作「鰥」

矢部
ㄕˇ shǐ

矢 2757
ㄕˇ shǐ
1. an arrow; a dart 2. to vow; to take an oath; to pledge 3. to display
【矢口否認】to deny flatly
【矢志不移】to take an oath not to change one's mind

二畫

矣 2758
ㄧˇ yǐ
1. a final particle denoting the perfect tense 2. an auxiliary denoting determination 3. (in usage) both particles or auxiliaries indicating exclamations or questions

三畫

知 2759
1. ㄓ zhī
1. knowledge 2. to know; to understand; to recognize; to be aware of 3. to acquaint; to be familiar with; to befriend 4. to control; to operate; to direct 5. to wait on
【知名】well-known
【知名度】name recognition; name familiarity
【知道】to know; to realize; to understand
【知難而退】to withdraw or quit after learning of the difficulties, hardships, etc. involved
【知了】the cicada, or broad locust
【知己】①a close or intimate friend

② intimate ③ to know oneself
【知覺】① consciousness ② perception
【知趣】knowing what to do in a delicate situation
【知曉 or 知悉】to know; to be aware of
【知心話】secrets from the bottom of one's heart
【知識】knowledge; learning; information
【知識分子】intellectuals; the intelligentsia
【知足】to be content with what one has had
【知足常樂】Contentment brings happiness.
【知音】a close or intimate friend

知 2759
2. (智) ㄓˋ zhì
the learned; the wise; brains

五畫

矩 2760
ㄐㄩˇ jǔ
1. a carpenter's square 2. a rule; a regulation; a pattern 3. to carve
【矩形】a rectangle; rectangular
【矩陣】(mathematics) a matrix

七畫

短 2761
ㄉㄨㄢˇ duǎn
1. short; brief 2. to be deficient; to want; to lack; to owe 3. shortcomings; faults; mistakes
【短兵相接】(military) hand-to-hand combat
【短跑】a sprint; a dash
【短跑健將】a sprinter
【短篇小說】short stories
【短片】a short (film)
【短評】a short comment or critique
【短命】to die early; to die young
【短打】(baseball) to bunt; a bunt
【短路】(electricity) short circuit
【短褲】knee pants; shorts; short pants
【短見】① shortsightedness ② suicide
【短劍】a dagger
【短期】short-term; a short period
【短缺or短少】to fall short; deficient
【短小】short and small
【短小精悍】short but energetic
【短程】short distance; short-range
【短處】shortcomings; faults; defects
【短促or短暫】(said of time) brief; short; transient
【短襪】socks

八畫

矮 2762
ㄞˇ ǎi
1. a short person; a dwarf 2. short; low; low-ranking
【矮胖】short and fat
【矮櫈子】a low bench or stool
【矮個兒】a person of short stature
【矮小】short-statured

十二畫

矯 2763
ㄐㄧㄠˇ jiǎo
1. to straighten; to correct; to rectify 2. to falsify; to forge 3. strong and powerful; vigorous 4. to raise (one's head) high
【矯捷】agile; vigorous and nimble
【矯健】strong and vigorous
【矯情】to be affectedly unconventional
【矯正】to correct or rectify
【矯揉造作】to behave in an affected manner
【矯枉過正】to be overstrict in correcting mistakes, faults, etc.

石部
ㄕˊ shí

石 2764
1. ㄕˊ shí
1. rocks; stones; minerals, etc. 2. a calculus, as a kidney calculus (commonly known as a kidney stone) 3. stone tablets 4. medicines 5. barren, as a barren woman 6. name of an ancient musical instrument 7. a Chinese family name
【石碑】a stone tablet; a stele
【石版畫】a lithograph
【石壁】a stone wall; a precipice
【石破天驚】world-shaking; sensational
【石墨】graphite; plumbago
【石磨】a millstone; a grindstone
【石門水庫】the Shih-men Reservoir in northern Taiwan
【石綿瓦】an asbestos tile

【石雕】①stone carving ②carved stone
【石頭】stones; rocks
【石礫】gravel
【石榴】a pomegranate
【石膏】gypsum; plaster
【石膏像】a plaster bust; a plaster statue
【石窟】a grotto
【石塊】a piece of stone or rock; a pebble; a boulder
【石灰】lime
【石階】stone steps
【石匠】a stonemason
【石器】stoneware; stone implements
【石器時代】the Stone Age
【石像】a statue or bust of stone
【石柱】a stone pillar
【石沈大海】no news at all; to disappear forever
【石子】pieces of stone; pebbles
【石子路】a graveled path; a macadam road
【石油】crude oil; petroleum
【石油公司】a petroleum company
【石油工業】petroleum industry
【石英】quartz

石 2764
2. ㄉㄢˋ dàn
1. a dry measure for grains roughly equivalent to 120-160 pounds; picul 2. a weight measure equivalent to about 110 pounds

四畫

砂 2765
ㄕㄚ shā
1. sand; coarse sand; gravel 2. coarse—not smooth 3. infinitesimal
【砂布】emery cloth; abrasive cloth
【砂糖】crude sugar; brown sugar
【砂土】a sandy soil
【砂礫】gravel; pebbles
【砂金】gold dust; placer gold; alluvial gold
【砂紙】sandpaper; emery paper
【砂眼】(medicine) trachoma

砌 2766
ㄑㄧˋ qì
1. to lay (bricks, etc.); to pave; to raise in layers; to build 2. steps
【砌牆】to build a wall

砍 2767
ㄎㄢˇ kǎn
1. to chop; to hack; to fell (trees, etc.); to cut down 2. to throw at
【砍伐】to fell (trees, etc.)
【砍斷】to break apart by chopping
【砍頭】to behead; to decapitate
【砍柴】to chop or cut firewood
【砍傷】to wound by hacking or cutting
【砍死】to hack to death

砒 2768
ㄆㄧ pī
arsenic: 砒霜 arsenic trioxide (As_2O_3)

五畫

砥 2769
ㄉㄧˇ dǐ (又讀 ㄓˇ zhǐ)
1. a whetstone; a grindstone 2. to discipline; to polish
【砥礪】to discipline and polish; to encourage
【砥柱】an indomitable person

砧 2770
ㄓㄣ zhēn
1. a rock with a flat top on which the laundry is beaten and washed; an anvil 2. an ancient instrument for torture
【砧板】a chopping block

砰 2771
ㄆㄥ pēng
1. the sound of crashing stones 2. Bang!
【砰然】loud; deafening; roaring

砝 2772
ㄈㄚˇ fǎ
standard weights used in scales; steelyard weights
【砝碼(兒)】steelyard weights

破 2773
ㄆㄛˋ pò
1. to break 2. dilapidated; destroyed; ruined 3. to defeat; to beat (the enemy); to capture (enemy territory) 4. to expose; exposed; (to see) through; to lay bare 5. to spend (money, etc.) 6. to solve or break (a murder case, etc.); to analyze 7. to come to an end 8. paltry
【破布】rags
【破破爛爛】tattered; tumble-down; dilapidated
【破門而入】to break into a house
【破滅】to come to nil
【破廟】a dilapidated temple
【破費】to spend money
【破釜沈舟】to cut off all means of retreat
【破天荒】never before—for the first time; unprecedented
【破土典禮】a ground-breaking ceremony

〔石部〕

【破爛兒】 wastes or refuse; junk
【破例】 to make an exception
【破裂】 ① to break off; rupture; severance ② broken; cracked
【破口大罵】 to abuse freely and loudly
【破獲】 to break (into a secret hideout) and capture (criminals, loots, etc.) 「late
【破壞】 to ruin; to destroy; to vio-
【破紀錄】 to break a record
【破戒】 ① (usually said of monks, nuns, etc.) to break the rules ② to make an exception 「dated
【破舊】 shabby; worn-out; dilapi-
【破鏡重圓】 (said of a divorced or separated couple) reunion and reconciliation
【破曉】 daybreak; dawn
【破折號】 a dash 「a loophole
【破綻】 a slip, flaw or weak point;
【破竹之勢】 overwhelming force;
【破產】 bankruptcy ⌊irresistible
【破除】 to eliminate; to get rid of
【破傷風】 tetanus
【破財】 to lose money
【破財消災】 to suffer unexpected financial losses and forestall calamities
【破碎】 ① to come to pieces ② broken (heart, hope, etc.)
【破損】 broken or damaged; ruined
【破案】 to break a criminal case;
⌊ to solve a case

砸 2774
ㄗㄚˊ zá

1. to crash and break; to squash; to smash; to knock; to pound 2. to ruin; to fail; to be bungled 3. to mash; to beat to a pulp
【砸爛】 to crush to a mash
【砸傷】 to be injured by a crashing object
【砸碎】to break to pieces; to smash

砲 2775
ㄆㄠˋ pào

a simplified form of 礮—artillery
【砲艦】 a gunboat

六畫

硃 2776
ㄓㄨ zhū

1. vermilion 2. imperial (the signature and instructions of an emperor were written in red)
【硃批】 an imperial rescript
【硃砂】 cinnabar
【硃砂痣】 a red mole

硫 2777
ㄌㄧㄡˊ liú

as in 硫磺—sulphur, or sulfur
【硫酸】 sulfuric acid

研 2778
(硏) ㄧㄢˊ yán

1. to go to the very source; to study; to investigate; to research; to examine 2. to grind; to powder 「abrade; to polish
【研磨】 ①to grind; to pestle ②to
【研討】 to study and discuss; to investigate and research
【研討會】 a seminar; a symposium
【研究】 to study and research
【研究室】 a research laboratory
【研究生】 a graduate student
【研究所】 a research laboratory; a research institute; a graduate
【研究員】 a researcher ⌊school
【研究院】 a research institute
【研習】 to research and study
【研習會】 a study meeting or conference
【研製】 ① to manufacture; to develop ② (Chinese medicine) to prepare medicinal powder by grinding

七畫

硬 2779
ㄧㄥˋ yìng

1. hard; stiff; solid; firm 2. rigid; inflexible; obstinate; very insistent; unyielding 3. to solidify; to harden; to stiffen 4. by force; to manage to do something in a forced manner 5. (said of quality) good 6. able (person)
【硬幫幫】 ① hard and firm ② stiff
【硬逼】 to compel or force
【硬幣】 hard money (as opposed to paper money); coins; specie
【硬拚】 to fight recklessly
【硬度】 hardness
【硬體】 (computers) hardware
【硬朗】 (said of the aged) sturdy and strong 「gard of obstacles
【硬幹】 to do something in disre-
【硬漢】 a man of fortitude
【硬化】 ① to stiffen; to solidify ② sclerosis
【硬性規定】 rigid and inflexible ruling

【硬紙板】 cardboard
【硬著頭皮】to do something against one's will
【硬撐】 to hold on firmly despite extreme adversity, pain, etc.
【硬說】to insist on saying; to assert
【硬要】 to want or demand insistently

硯 2780
ㄧㄢˋ yàn
an inkstone: 硯臺—an ink-slab; an inkstone

八畫

硼 2781
ㄆㄥˊ péng
1. as in 硼砂—borax 2. (chemistry) boron
【硼酸】 boric acid

碌 2782
ㄌㄨˋ lù
1. mediocre; common 2. busy; occupied 3. a kind of stone roller
【碌碌】 ①mediocre; commonplace ②busy

碑 2783
ㄅㄟ bēi
as in 碑碣—a stone tablet
【碑銘】 a part of an inscription on a tablet, usually in rhyme
【碑誌or碑文】 an inscription on a tablet

碎 2784
ㄙㄨㄟˋ suì
1. broken; smashed; torn; to break to pieces; to smash 2. trivial; unimportant; trifling 3. garrulous; gabby
【碎步兒】 short quick steps
【碎片】 fragments; splinters; shreds; chips
【碎裂】 torn or broken to pieces
【碎屍萬段】 to inflict severe punishment
【碎石子】 gravel; macadam

碉 2785
ㄉㄧㄠ diāo
a stone chamber
【碉堡】 a fort; a pillbox; a blockhouse

碰 2786
(掽) ㄆㄥˋ pèng
1. to collide; to hit; to touch; to bump 2. to meet unexpectedly; to run into 3. to take one's chance
【碰壁】 ①to meet rejection ②to encounter difficulties
【碰面 or 碰頭】 to meet
【碰倒】 to tumble down after being hit by something
【碰到】 ① to meet someone unexpectedly ② to touch something
【碰釘子】 to be rebuked
【碰見】 to meet or encounter someone unexpectedly; to run into
【碰巧】 by coincidence; accidentally
【碰撞】 to hit; to run into
【碰運氣】 ①to try one's luck ②sheer luck

碘 2787
ㄉㄧㄢˇ diǎn
iodine: 碘酒 iodine tincture

碍 2788
ㄞˋ ài
a simplified form of 礙—to obstruct; to hinder

碗 2789
(盌、椀) ㄨㄢˇ wǎn
a bowl (especially a small one)
【碗碟】 bowls and dishes
【碗櫃】 a cupboard
【碗筷】 bowls and chopsticks

九畫

碧 2790
ㄅㄧˋ bì
1. green; blue; verdant; emerald green 2. as in 碧玉—jasper; emerald
【碧綠】 verdant; emerald green
【碧草如茵】a carpet of green grass

碩 2791
ㄕˊ shí
(語音 ㄕㄨㄛˋ shuò)
great; large
【碩果僅存】the only one of its kind to have survived
【碩士】 a holder of the master's degree

碳 2792
ㄊㄢˋ tàn
carbon 亦作「炭」: 碳水化合物carbohydrate

碟 2793
ㄉㄧㄝˊ dié
a dish or plate (especially a small one)
【碟影片】 a videodisc
【碟影機】 a videodisc player

十畫

確 2794
ㄑㄩㄝˋ què
1. sure; certain; secure; real; true; valid 2. firm; firmly
【確定】 ①to decide; to fix; to settle; to determine ②certain; sure
【確立】 to establish firmly
【確切】 accurate; exact; precise

〔石部〕

【確信】to be convinced; to believe firmly
【確知】to know for sure
【確實】real; true; certain
【確認】to certify; to affirm; to confirm
【確鑿】accurate; precise

碾 2795
ㄋㄧㄢˇ niǎn
1. a stone roller 2. to mill; to roll; to crush
【碾米廠】a rice-husking mill
【碾碎】to pulverize

碼 2796
ㄇㄚˇ mǎ
1. yard (a measure of length) 2. a symbol; a code; a sign or thing indicating number
【碼頭】a dock; a quay; a wharf; a pier
【碼頭工人】a stevedore

磁 2797
ㄘˊ cí
1. magnetic; magnetism 2. porcelain; china
【磁片 or 磁碟片】(computers) a diskette; a floppy disc
【磁帶】a magnetic tape
【磁碟】a magnetic disk
【磁頭】a magnetic head
【磁鐵】a magnet; magnetic iron
【磁器】porcelain
【磁性】magnetism
【磁場】the magnetic field

磋 2798
ㄘㄨㄛ cuō
to file; to polish (jade, stone, horn, etc.)
【磋商】to exchange views; to hold a discussion or consultation

磅 2799
1. ㄅㄤˋ bàng
1. a pound 2. scales 3. to weigh
【磅秤】scales giving the weight in avoirdupois

磅 2799
2. ㄆㄤ pāng
the noise of stone crashing
【磅礴】boundless; majestic; extensive

磕 2800
ㄎㄜ kē
to strike; to bump; to knock; to collide
【磕頭】to kowtow

磊 2801
ㄌㄟˇ lěi
1. a heap of stones 2. great; massive
【磊落】①a lot of ②open-hearted; candid

磒 2802
ㄩㄣˇ yǔn
to fall down: 磒石 a meteor; a meteorite

磐 2803
ㄆㄢˊ pán
1. as in 磐石—a massive rock 2. to linger around 3. to league together

十一畫

磨 2804
1. ㄇㄛˊ mó
1. to dawdle; to waste time; to while away 2. to rub; to grind; to polish; to wear 3. sufferings; obstacles; setbacks
【磨墨】to rub down an ink stick
【磨滅】①to wear out ②to obliterate
【磨刀】to sharpen a knife
【磨難】sufferings; obstacles; difficulties
【磨鍊】to train; to harden; to discipline
【磨光】to polish; to burnish
【磨拳擦掌】ready for fight
【磨杵成針】Persistent efforts can achieve difficult things.
【磨石子地】terrazzo floor
【磨擦】① to rub ② friction
【磨蹭】to be tardy; to be slow; to dawdle away
【磨損】wear and tear; to wear away

磨 2804
2. ㄇㄛˋ mò
1. a mill 2. to turn around 3. to grind (grain, etc.)
【磨坊】a mill (referring to the building)

磧 2805
ㄑㄧˋ qì
1. gravel and sand in shallow waters 2. a desert

磚 2806
ㄓㄨㄢ zhuān
bricks 亦作「甎」

十二畫

磷 2807
ㄌㄧㄣˊ lín
1. phosphorus 亦作「燐」 2. water flowing between stones

磺 2808
ㄏㄨㄤˊ huáng
sulfur; brimstone

礁 2809
ㄐㄧㄠ jiāo
a reef

十三畫

礎 2810 ㄔㄨˇ chǔ
a plinth

十四畫

礙 2811 (碍) ㄞˋ ài
1. to obstruct; to hinder; to be in the way 2. harmful; detrimental
【礙事】to be in the way
【礙手礙脚】to be very much in the way
【礙眼】to be an eyesore
【礙於情面】for fear of hurting somebody's feelings

十五畫

礫 2812 ㄌㄧˋ lì
as in 礫石—gravel; a pebble; shingle

礪 2813 ㄌㄧˋ lì
1. a whetstone 2. to sharpen (a knife)

礦 2814 (鑛) ㄎㄨㄤˋ kuàng
1. a mineral; ore 2. mining 3. a mine: 礦工—a miner
【礦坑】a mining shaft; a pit
【礦區】a mining district; an ore field
【礦泉水】mineral water
【礦石】a mineral; ore
【礦物】a mineral

十六畫

礮 2815 (砲) ㄆㄠˋ pào
1. a catapult 2. an artillery piece; a cannon; a gun
【礮兵】①an artilleryman; a gunner ②artillery
【礮彈】a cannon ball or shot; a shell
【礮臺】a gun emplacement; a battery; a fort
【礮艇】a gunboat
【礮火】artillery fire; gunfire
【礮灰】cannon fodder
【礮轟】to cannonade
【礮擊】to bombard; to shell
【礮聲】the thunder of cannonade

示部 ㄕˋ shì

示 2816 ㄕˋ shì
1. to show; to indicate 2. to make known; to notify; a notice 3. to instruct 4. to demonstrate
【示範】to set an example
【示範表演】demonstration (of a skill)
【示警】to give a warning
【示衆】to exhibit to the public
【示愛】to show one's tender feeling to one of the opposite sex
【示意】to drop a hint; to motion
【示威】to demonstrate (by a mass meeting or parade)
【示威遊行】demonstration

三畫

社 2817 ㄕㄜˋ shè
1. the god of land 2. an association; an organization; a corporation; an agency 3. society; a community
【社評or社論】an editorial
【社團】an association; a corporation
【社會】society; a community
【社會福利】social welfare
【社會地位】social status; social position
【社會新聞】human interest stories or crime stories
【社稷】the god of land and the god of grain—a country
【社交】social intercourse; sociality
【社交舞】social dancing; ballroom dancing
【社區】a community
【社長】the president or director (of an association, newspaper, etc.)
【社員】a member

祀 2818 ㄙˋ sì
as in祀奉—to worship; to offer sacrifices to
【祀典】religious rites or services

四畫

祇 2819 1. ㄑㄧˊ qí
1. the god of the earth 2. peace; serenity; to be at rest

祇 2819 2. (只、祗) ㄓˇ zhǐ
(原讀ㄓ zhī)
only; merely
【祇得 or 祇好】to have to
【祇要】only if

〔示部〕

祈 2820 ㄑㄧˊ qí
1. to pray 2. to beg; to entreat; to beseech; to supplicate; to request respectfully
【祈禱】to pray; to offer a prayer
【祈求】to pray for; to appeal for

五畫

祐 2821 ㄧㄡˋ yòu
divine help
【祐助】(said of a deity) to help (a mortal)

祕 2822 (秘) ㄇㄧˋ mì (又讀 ㄅㄧˋ bì)
secret; confidential; hidden; unknown mysterious
【祕密】secret; confidential; hidden; clandestine
【祕密文件】a classified document
【祕方】a secret recipe
【祕訣】a knack; secrets (of success, etc.); the key (to the solution of a problem)
【祕書】a secretary

祖 2823 ㄗㄨˇ zǔ
1. one's grandfather or grandmother 2. ancestors; forebears 3. a founder; an originator 4. to follow the example of; to imitate 5. a Chinese family name
【祖母】one's grandmother
【祖墳】an ancestral grave
【祖父】one's grandfather
【祖國】one's homeland; one's fatherland
【祖籍】one's ancestral home
【祖先 or 祖宗】forefathers; ancestors; forebears
【祖產】ancestral estate
【祖傳】inherited from one's ancestors; hereditary
【祖孫】ancestors and descendants

祛 2824 ㄑㄩ qū
to dispel; to expel; to remove
【祛災】to dispel disasters

祝 2825 ㄓㄨˋ zhù
1. to wish someone happiness; to pray for happiness 2. to congratulate; to felicitate 3. to celebrate 4. a Chinese family name
【祝福】①to bless ②to wish happiness to
【祝賀】to congratulate; to felicitate
【祝壽】to celebrate someone's birthday
【祝融】the god of fire

神 2826 ㄕㄣˊ shén
1. gods; deities; immortals; spiritual beings 2. soul; mind; spirit 3. appearances; looks; expressions; airs 4. supernatural; marvelous; wondrous; miraculous; mysterious; mystical 5. smart; clever
【神不知鬼不覺】extremely stealthy
【神不守舍】out of one's wits; delirious
【神秘】mysterious; mystical; mystery
【神妙】marvelous; wondrous
【神廟】a temple of the gods
【神明】the gods; deities; divinities
【神父】a Catholic father
【神態】looks; appearances; facial expressions
【神通廣大】possessing marvelous abilities
【神童】a child prodigy
【神龕 or 神殿】a sanctuary
【神化】to deify
【神話】a myth; mythology
【神魂顛倒】to be held spell-bound; to be infatuated
【神機妙算】①stratagems so wonderful that they seem to be conceived by divine beings ②wonderful foresight
【神經】nerve
【神經病】① neurosis; mental disorder ② a neurotic
【神經過敏】① excessively sensitive ②(medicine) hyperaesthesia
【神經質】nervosity
【神經錯亂】mental disorder
【神奇】marvelous; miraculous
【神祇】the gods; the spirits
【神氣】①(ㄕㄣˊ ㄑㄧˋ) divine atmosphere② (ㄕㄣˊ ·ㄑㄧ) ⓐ dignified; imposing ⓑ to put on airs
【神氣活現】as proud as a peacock
【神槍手】a sharpshooter; a marksman
【神情】an appearance; an air
【神效】marvelous effect
【神仙】an immortal; a celestial being
【神像】①an image of a dead person ②an idol
【神學院】a seminary (for training priests or ministers)

【神職人員】 the clergy
【神志不清】 unconscious; in a state of a coma
【神智不清】 muddleheaded
【神出鬼沒】 to appear and disappear quite unpredictably like gods and demons
【神聖】 holy; sacred; divine
【神彩 or 神色】 a countenance; a look; an expression
【神采奕奕】 ①in high spirits ② glowing with health and radiating vigor
【神似】 lifelike; to be alike in spirit
【神色自若】 to look unperturbed
【神速】 marvelously fast
【神髓】 essence; quintessence
【神醫】 a marvelous physician
【神遊】 to tour (a place) by imagination
【神往】 to have one's thoughts or imagination absorbed in some wonderful thing or place
【神韻】 ①(said of a person) an appearance and a carriage; an air ②(said of paintings or calligraphic works) poetic quality
【神勇】 extraordinarily brave

祠 2827
ㄘ cí
1. a temple; a shrine 2. the spring worship

祟 2828
ㄙㄨㄟˋ suì
1. the evil influence of gods or demons 2. (said of ghosts or evil spirits) to haunt

六畫

祥 2829
ㄒㄧㄤˊ xiáng
auspicious; propitious; favorable
【祥瑞or祥兆】 a good (or an auspicious) omen

票 2830
ㄆㄧㄠˋ piào
1. a bill; a note 2. a ticket 3. a ballot 4. a hostage 5. amateur performance
【票房】 ①a box office; a ticket window ②a club of amateur Peking opera actors ③box office—(figuratively) the power of a show or performer to attract an audience
【票亭】 ticket stands
【票根】 a ticket stub; a counterfoil
【票價】 the price of a ticket
【票據】 bills; notes; receipts
【票箱】 a ballot box
【票選】 to elect by casting ballots
【票數】 the number of votes or ballots
【票額】 face value

祭 2831
ㄐㄧˋ jì
1. to worship; to offer sacrifices to; to honor by a rite or service 2. to wield
【祭品】 offerings; sacrificial articles; sacrifices
【祭典】 services or ceremonies of offering sacrifices
【祭壇】 an altar
【祭祖】 to perform rites in honor of ancestors
【祭祀】 to worship; to offer sacrifices to; to honor by a service or rite

八畫

祿 2832
ㄌㄨˋ lù
1. happiness; prosperity 2. official pay; salary
【祿位】 official salary and rank

禁 2833
1. ㄐㄧㄣˋ jìn
1. to prohibit; to forbid; to ban 2. to confine; to imprison; to detain 3. secret 4. a royal residence
【禁閉 or 禁錮】 ① to prohibit entry into government services ② to imprison; to confine
【禁品】 contraband
【禁地】 a forbidden ground
【禁令】 a prohibition; a ban
【禁臠】 ① a forbidden thing; one's exclusive domain ②a precious thing
【禁菓】 the forbidden fruit
【禁忌】 ① a taboo; to taboo ② to avoid; to abstain from
【禁區】 ①a forbidden region; a restricted zone ② a preserve
【禁止】 to forbid; to prohibit; to ban
【禁止停車】 No parking.
【禁止吸煙】 No smoking.
【禁止入內】 No admittance.
【禁食】 fast; to fast
【禁書】 banned books
【禁足】 to forbid a soldier to leave the barracks on holidays as a form of punishment

禁 2833
2. ㄐㄧㄣ jīn
to stand; to endure; to bear; to withstand;

示部

【禁不起】unable to endure
【禁不住】① unable to endure; unable to withstand ② can not help
【禁得起 or 禁得住】able to withstand; able to stand

示部

九畫

禍 2834 ㄏㄨㄛˋ huò
1. calamity; disaster; misfortune; evil 2. to bring disaster upon; to harm; to injure; to do evil to 3. to punish
【禍不單行】Misfortunes never come singly (or single).
【禍端or禍根】the cause of a misfortune or disaster
【禍亂】disturbances; disastrous disorder
【禍國殃民】to bring disaster upon the state and the people
【禍害】harm; injury; evil
【禍患】misfortune; disaster; harm; evil
【禍水】a woman who is often the source of troubles
【禍從口出】Careless talks may land one in trouble.

福 2835 ㄈㄨˊ fú
happiness; good fortune; good luck; a blessing; bliss
【福庇or福蔭】(a complimentary phrase) your fortunate protection
【福利】welfare
【福利社】a store doing business on the premises of a school, factory, government agency, etc.
【福建】Fukien Province
【福氣】good luck
【福相】a countenance of good luck
【福星高照】to ride the high tide of good luck
【福澤】blessedness; good fortune; happiness
【福音】① good news ② the gospel

十一畫

禦 2836 ㄩˋ yù
to guard against; to take precautions against
【禦敵】to guard against the enemy
【禦寒】to protect oneself from cold

十二畫

禧 2837 ㄒㄧ xī (又讀 ㄒㄧˇ xǐ)
happiness; blessings; auspiciousness

禪 2838 1. ㄔㄢˊ chán
1. Zen Buddhism 2. meditation; intense contemplation
【禪房】a hermitage; a monastery
【禪寺】a Buddhist temple

禪 2838 2. ㄕㄢˋ shàn
as in 禪讓—to abdicate (the throne)

十三畫

禮 2839 ㄌㄧˇ lǐ
1. courtesy; propriety; decorum; politeness; civility; etiquette 2. rites; ceremony 3. a gift; a present
【禮拜】① church service; worship ② a week
【禮拜堂】a chapel; a church
【禮拜天or禮拜日】Sunday 亦作「星期天」
【禮砲】a gun salute; a salvo
【禮品 or 禮物】a gift; a present
【禮聘】to cordially invite the service of
【禮帽】a ceremonial hat or cap
【禮貌】etiquette; politeness; civility
【禮服】ceremonial dress
【禮單】a list of presents
【禮堂】① an auditorium ② a hall decorated for a wedding ceremony or funeral service
【禮節】etiquette
【禮教】ethical education
【禮金】a cash gift
【禮券】gift coupons sold by a shop, which the recipient may convert into goods (or cash) at the shop in question
【禮成】Ceremony is over.
【禮尚往來】Courtesy emphasizes reciprocity.
【禮讓】to make way humbly or modestly
【禮讚】to adore; to glorify
【禮俗】manners and custom
【禮儀】etiquette; protocol; decorum
【禮遇】to treat with courtesy

十四畫

禱 2840 ㄉㄠˇ dǎo
to pray; to beseech; to plead; to entreat
【禱告】a prayer; to pray

内部 ㄖㄡˊ róu

四畫

禹 2841 ㄩˇ yǔ
1. Yü, the legendary founder of the Hsia (夏) Dynasty (21st-16th century B.C.) 2. a Chinese family name

八畫

禽 2842 ㄑㄧㄣˊ qín
1. birds; fowls 2. same as 擒—to catch; to capture
【禽獸】①dumb creatures ②birds and beasts

禾部 ㄏㄜˊ hé

禾 2843 ㄏㄜˊ hé
1. grains still on the stalk 2. the rice crop
【禾苗】rice seedlings
【禾稈】the stalk of a rice plant

二畫

禿 2844 (禿) ㄊㄨ tū
bald; bare
【禿頭】baldheaded; bald; a bald head
【禿子】a baldhead; a baldpate

秀 2845 ㄒㄧㄡˋ xiù
1. brilliant; excellent; competent; outstanding 2. beautiful; elegant; graceful; delicate; fine 3. (said of grain crops) to put forth new flowers or ears
【秀麗 or 秀氣 or 秀雅】beautiful; elegant; graceful; fine
【秀色可餐】(said of a woman) very attractive
【秀外慧中】beautiful and intelligent

私 2846 ㄙ sī
1. private; personal; person-to-person 2. secret; clandestine 3. to have illicit relations or an affair with 4. contraband 5. prejudice; biased; to favor 6. selfish; selfishly 7. reproductive organs of both sexes
【私奔】to elope; elopement
【私房錢】private savings
【私底下or私下】privately; secretly
【私定終身】(in old China) to pledge to marry without the permission of parents
【私通】① to collaborate with enemy forces or a foreign country ② to have an illicit affair with parties other than one's spouse; adultery
【私立】(usually said of schools, hospitals, etc.) established and operated by private funds
【私家偵探】a private detective
【私交】personal friendship
【私酒】bootleg; moonshine
【私心】selfishness; favoritism
【私章】a personal seal; a private chop
【私產】private property
【私處】private parts; reproductive organs of both sexes
【私事】personal affairs; private affairs
【私生活】one's private life
【私生子】an illegitimate child; a bastard
【私人】individual; personal; private
【私自】personally; privately
【私藏】① private collection ② to keep something against the law
【私有】privately-owned
【私營】privately-operated
【私欲 or 私慾】① personal or selfish desires ② greediness

三畫

秉 2847 ㄅㄧㄥˇ bǐng
1. to hold in hand 2. to take charge of; to rule 3. authority 4. an ancient grain measure; a measure for liquid
【秉性 or 稟性】nature; a natural disposition or temperament
【秉持】① to adhere to (one's principles, etc.) ② to hold in hand (a spear, etc.)

四畫

〔禾部〕

秋 2848
(秌) ㄑㄧㄡ qiū
1. autumn; fall 2. time; a period 3. a season 4. a year 5. a harvest; ripening of grains
【秋天】autumn; fall
【秋老虎】scorching heat in early autumn
【秋高氣爽】the clear and crisp autumn climate
【秋海棠】(botany) a begonia
【秋毫】① trifles ② a writing brush
【秋季】autumn (season)
【秋千 or 鞦韆】a swing
【秋收】the autumn harvest
【秋霜】① autumn frost—(figuratively) snowy hair ② severity; sternness

科 2849
ㄎㄜ kē
1. a department 2. a section 3. a class; a variety; a family (of plants or animals) 4. rules; laws 5. the action in Chinese opera 6. a subject in the civil service examination of former times 7. a branch of academic or vocational studies 8. to mete out (prison terms, etc.); to levy (taxes, etc.); to fine someone
【科班】① a Chinese operatic company which operates a class to train young pupils ② very formal or orthodox training one received when young
【科目】① subjects, courses, classifications of academic studies ② the civil examination system in former times
【科幻小說】science fiction
【科技】science and technology
【科學】science
【科學家】scientists
【科學界】① the world of science ② the community of scientists
【科威特】Kuwait
【科員】a junior government employee

秒 2850
ㄇㄧㄠˇ miǎo
1. (said of time or a degree) a second 2. the beard of grain
【秒針】the second hand

五畫

秦 2851
ㄑㄧㄣˊ qín
1. the feudal state of Chin (879-221 B.C.) in the Chou Dynasty, which later unified the whole country under the Chin Dynasty (221-206 B.C.) 2. another name of Shensi Province 3. the ancient name of China as known to the people of the Western Region (西域) 4. a Chinese family name
【秦樓楚館】brothels
【秦始皇】Chin Shih Huang, or the First Emperor of Chin, 259-210 B.C.

租 2852
ㄗㄨ zū
1. to rent; to lease; to let; to hire; to charter 2. rent; rental 3. taxes; to tax
【租費】royalties
【租賃】to rent (a house, etc.); to lease
【租戶】a tenant
【租界】a foreign settlement or concession
【租借】lend-lease; to rent
【租金】rent or rental
【租售】for rent or sale
【租約】a lease
【租用】to rent for use; to be tenanted

秧 2853
ㄧㄤ yāng
1. rice seedlings 2. tree saplings; very young plants for transplanting 3. fry 4. (now rarely) to cultivate; to grow
【秧苗】rice seedlings

秤 2854
1. ㄔㄥˋ chèng
1. a weighing scale; a balance; a steelyard 2. to weigh with a scale, etc.
【秤錘】the weight used with a steelyard

秤 2854
2. ㄆㄧㄥˊ píng
scales for measuring weight

秩 2855
ㄓˋ zhì
1. order; orderly 2. official ranks 3. official salaries 4. a decade
【秩序】① order ② arrangement
【秩序井然】in perfect order

六畫

移 2856
ㄧˊ yí
1. to change; to alter; to influence; to affect 2. to shift; to move 3. to forward; to transmit;

to transfer; to transplant; to convey 4. to give; to endow
【移民】① to immigrate; immigration ② to emigrate; to settle people (in a new region, etc.); to colonize ③ an immigrant ④ an emigrant
【移動】to move; to shift; to change
【移開】to move away
【移花接木】① to cheat by sleight of hand ② to graft
【移交】to turn over
【移居】to move to another town, country, etc. for settlement
【移情別戀】to shift one's love to another person
【移植】① to transplant ② grafting; transplanting
【移轉】to transfer (certain rights, holdings, etc.)

七畫

稍 2857
ㄕㄠ shāo
1. slightly; a little; slight 2. somewhat; rather 3. gradually
【稍後】shortly (or soon) afterward
【稍候or稍等】to wait for a while (or moment)
【稍息】At ease!
【稍縱即逝】transient; fleeting
【稍微or稍許】slightly; a little; a bit

稀 2858
ㄒㄧ xī
1. thin (liquids, etc.); watery; diluted 2. rare; scarce; uncommon 3. scattered; sparse
【稀薄】(said of air) thin or rare
【稀飯】congee; gruel; porridge
【稀客】a guest who seldom comes to visit
【稀罕】① rare; rarity; scarce ② to care
【稀奇】① strange; rare ② to care
【稀釋】to dilute (liquids)
【稀少】few; little; scarce; rare; sparse
【稀疏】scattered or dispersed; sparse

稅 2859
ㄕㄨㄟˋ shuì
taxes; duties on commodities
【稅單】① a tax invoice ② a tax form
【稅率】tax rates; duty rates
【稅款 or 稅金】tax money
【稅捐】taxes and surtaxes
【稅收】tax revenue
【稅務機關】tax offices

稈 2860
ㄍㄢˇ gǎn
the stalk of grain; straw

程 2861
ㄔㄥˊ chéng
1. a form; a pattern 2. degree; extent 3. a schedule; an agenda; order 4. a journey; a road 5. distance 6. a Chinese family name
【程度】① degree; extent ② standard ③ general achievement in academic studies
【程序】procedures; processes
【程式】① standard procedures ② (computers) a program
【程式設計】programing

八畫

稟 2862
ㄅㄧㄥˇ bǐng
1. to report to a superior or one's seniors; to petition; to appeal 2. one's natural endowments or gifts
【稟報or稟告】to report to a superior superior or elder
【稟明】to clarify a matter to a superior or elder
【稟賦】a natural endowment, gift or disposition
【稟性】a natural disposition or temperament

稔 2863
ㄖㄣˇ rěn
1. the ripening of paddy or rice; a harvest 2. a year 3. to accumulate; to hoard 4. to be familiar with somebody

稚 2864
(穉) ㄓˋ zhì
young and tender; small; delicate; immature; childish
【稚嫩】① tender and delicate ② young and tender
【稚氣】innocence of a child; childishness
【稚子】young children

稜 2865
ㄌㄥˊ léng
1. a corner; an angle; an edge 2. a square piece of wood 3. an awe-inspiring air
【稜角】① an angle; a corner ② pointedness

稗 2866
ㄅㄞˋ bài
1. barnyard grass 2. small; little 3. novels, legends, etc.

〔禾部〕

【稗官野史】 unofficial historical writings

稠 2867
ㄔㄡ chōu

1. dense; closely crowded together 2. (said of liquids) thick; viscous

【稠密】 crowded; dense

九畫

種 2868
1. ㄓㄨㄥˇ zhǒng

1. seeds of grain 2. races (of human beings) 3. descendants; posterity 4. a species; a genus; a kind or sort

【種類】 a sort, kind, variety or class

【種種】 ① various kinds ② short-cropped hair ③ simple and sincere (as rural people)

【種子】 a seed

【種族】 (said of people) a race or tribe

【種族歧視】 racial discrimination

種 2868
2. ㄓㄨㄥˋ zhòng

1. to plant; to sow; to cultivate 2. to vaccinate

【種痘】 vaccination (against smallpox); to vaccinate

【種田】 to farm; to till the land

【種瓜得瓜，種豆得豆】 One reaps what he sows.

【種植】 to plant

稱 2869
1. ㄔㄥ chēng

1. to weigh; to measure weight 2. to claim; to report; to declare 3. to call; to name; a name; an appellation 4. to offer as an excuse (as illness) 5. to say; to tell; to state 6. to speak laudatory words; to praise 7. to take up (arms, etc.)

【稱霸】 to become the most powerful nation in the world or part of the world; to hold an undisputed position of strength

【稱道】 to praise or acclaim

【稱號】 a title; a designation

【稱呼】 a name by which one addresses another; to address; to name

【稱許】 to approve and praise; approval and praise

【稱兄道弟】 on first-name terms; very intimate

【稱臣】 to be subjugated; to submit to the victor

【稱讚】 to praise; to acclaim

【稱譽】 to praise; to acclaim; to extol

稱 2869
2. ㄔㄥˋ chèng

1. a steelyard; a weighing machine 2. fit; proper; suitable; well-matched 3. symmetrical; to be equal to; corresponding to

【稱職】 well qualified; competent

稱 2869
3. ㄔㄣˋ chèn

fit; suitable; in accordance with

【稱心】 to have something as one's wish

【稱心如意】 very gratifying and satisfactory; happy and contented

十畫

穀 2870
ㄍㄨˇ gǔ

1. grain; corn; cereals 2. lucky; happy; favorable; good 3. to live; while alive

【穀類】 grain and corn; cereals

【穀子】 millet

【穀倉】 a barn for storing grain; a granary

稿 2871
(稾) ㄍㄠˇ gǎo

1. a manuscript; a sketch; a rough draft or copy 2. a pattern or copy book for drawing 3. straw; a stalk of grain

【稿費 or 稿酬】 payment to a writer on a piecework basis

【稿件】 ① contribution to a publication; writings ② manuscripts; a sketch

【稿紙】 manuscript or draft paper

稷 2872
ㄐㄧˋ jì

panicled millet

稼 2873
ㄐㄧㄚˋ jià

1. to farm, plant, sow or cultivate 2. grain; crops

稻 2874
ㄉㄠˋ dào

paddy or rice

【稻米】 rice or paddy

【稻田】 a paddy field; a rice field

【稻子】 unhulled rice

【稻草】 rice straw

【稻草人】 a scarecrow

【稻秧】 rice seedlings; rice shoots

稽 2875
1. ㄐㄧ jī
1. to investigate; to examine; to inspect; to verify 2. to stay; to delay or procrastinate
【稽考】to examine; to verify
【稽核】to examine and audit
【稽查or稽察】to examine and investigate

稽 2875
2. ㄑㄧˇ qǐ
to kowtow; to bow to the ground

十一畫

穌 2876
ㄙㄨ sū
1. to mow grass 2. to revive; to come to; to rise again

穎 2877
(頴) ㄧㄥˇ yǐng
outstanding; remarkable; talented; distinguished
【穎慧】clever; bright; intelligent
【穎秀】outstandingly talented

穆 2878
ㄇㄨˋ mù
1. peaceful; serene 2. respectful; reverent 3. profound 4. majestic; solemn 5. the right side of an ancestral shrine 6. a Chinese family name
【穆然】peaceful and respectful

積 2879
ㄐㄧ jī
1. to accumulate; to store up; to amass 2. long (time); old; deep-rooted; longstanding 3. (mathematics) product
【積分】① accumulated points ② integral calculus
【積年累月】for years and months—a long time
【積勞成疾】to fall sick from persistent overwork
【積極】active(ly); positive(ly); persistent(ly)
【積欠】accumulated debts; outstanding debts; arrears
【積習】a deep-rooted practice; an old habit
【積蓄】savings
【積少成多】Economy in trifles will ensure abundance.
【積水】to accumulate water; accumulated water (in low-lying areas after a shower)
【積壓】to neglect handling official papers, legal cases, etc.

十二畫

穗 2880
ㄙㄨㄟˋ suì
1. fruits or grains in a cluster grown at the tip of a stem or stalk 2. the ear of grain 3. another name of Canton 4. a candle snuff; a candlewick

十三畫

穢 2881
ㄏㄨㄟˋ huì
1. vile; wicked 2. dirty; filthy 3. obscene; wanton (ways or conduct) 4. ugly and abominable 5. weeds on a farm
【穢物】filth

穠 2882
ㄋㄨㄥˊ nóng
luxuriant growth of plants
【穠纖合度】(said of a girl's figure) well-proportioned

十四畫

穩 2883
ㄨㄣˇ wěn
1. stable; stability; steady; firm 2. sure; certain 3. secure; security
【穩當】proper and secure
【穩定】① to stabilize ② stable; steady
【穩固】stable and firm; secure
【穩健】firm and steady
【穩紮穩打】to proceed steadily and step by step
【穩重】steady, calm, and dignified

穫 2884
ㄏㄨㄛˋ huò
to reap or harvest; to cut grain

穴部
ㄒㄩㄝˋ xuè

穴 2885
ㄒㄩㄝˋ xuè
1. a cave; a den; a hole 2. points in the human body where acupuncture can be applied 3. (Chinese boxing) points in the human body where nerve centers are supposed to be located, a

strike at which may cause paralysis or even death
【穴道】① see 穴 2. and 3. ② an underground channel

〔穴部〕

二畫

究 2886
ㄐㄧㄡˋ jiù
(又讀 ㄐㄧㄡ jiū)
1. to examine; to study; to investigate exhaustively; to dig into 2. finally; in the end; after all 3. actually; really
【究竟】① the very source; the outcome ② after all; finally; actually; exactly

三畫

穹 2887
ㄑㄩㄥ qiōng
(又讀 ㄑㄩㄥˊ qióng)
1. high and vast 2. the sky
【穹蒼】the sky; the firmament

空 2888
1. ㄎㄨㄥ kōng
1. empty; hollow; void 2. to empty; to exhaust; to reduce to extremity 3. fictitious; unreal; impractical 4. vain and useless (efforts, etc.); ineffective; fruitless 5. high and vast 6. the sky; space 7. (Buddhism) sunyata; empty; void; vacant; nonexistent 8. merely; only
【空門】Buddhism
【空防】air defense
【空腹】on an empty stomach
【空蕩蕩】empty; deserted
【空洞】① vast and empty ② (said of writings, thought, etc.) shallow
【空頭支票】① a dishonored check; a check that bounces ② an empty promise
【空談】empty talks; idle chatter
【空難】a plane crash or collision
【空口無憑】(said of a promise or pledge) Mere verbal statement has no binding force.
【空曠】expansive; vast and boundless
【空歡喜】joy that ends in disappointment
【空間】space
【空軍】the air force
【空氣】air or atmosphere (also used figuratively)
【空氣汚染】air pollution
【空前絕後】(said of a remarkable achievement, masterpiece, etc.) not equaled before or after
【空襲】an air raid; an air attack
【空心菜】a water convolvulus
【空虛】empty; void; emptiness
【空穴來風】(said of news, or information) groundless or baseless
【空中巴士】an air bus
【空中飛人】a trapeze artist; trapezist
【空中大學】an open university
【空中小姐】a stewardess (of a passenger plane); an air hostess
【空中少爺】(informal) a male flight attendant
【空城計】① a bluff ② nobody left behind to guard the house
【空手】empty-handed; unarmed
【空手道】karate, a type of Oriental boxing
【空運】air freight; to transport by air

空 2888
2. ㄎㄨㄥˋ kòng
1. leisure; free time; spare time 2. blank (space); vacant; vacancy; to leave blank or vacant 3. spacious—implying a sense of awe 4. a chance; an opportunity 5. wanting; deficient; impoverished
【空白】a blank in a paper or form
【空白支票】a blank check
【空房】an unoccupied house or room
【空檔】① vacant space in a movie theater schedule ② free time
【空地】a vacant area; a vacant lot; a vacancy
【空缺】① a vacant position; a vacancy ② scarcity
【空隙】a crevice; a gap; a loophole
【空閒 or 空暇】leisure; spare time
【空位】a vacant or unoccupied seat

四畫

穿 2889
ㄔㄨㄢ chuān
1. to wear (clothes, shoes, etc.) 2. to pierce through; to penetrate or bore through; to thread 3. to cross (a street, etc.)
【穿戴】to wear (clothes, ornaments, etc.)
【穿透】to penetrate; to pierce through

【穿鞋】to put on shoes 「between
【穿針引線】to serve as a go-
【穿著】① attire; dress ② dressed in
【穿揷】①to serve as a go-between ②the insertion of an episode or interlude 「dubious explanations
【穿鑿附會】to offer far-fetched or
【穿梭】① busy comings and goings of people ② to shuttle back and forth
【穿越】to pass through; to cross (a bridge, street, tunnel, etc.)

突 2890
ㄊㄨ tú
1. abrupt; sudden; unexpected; suddenly; unexpectedly 2. to offend; to go against 3. to break through (enemy encirclement) 4. to project or jut out 5. a chimney
【突變】① an unexpected change ② mutation
【突破】①to break or smash (old records, etc.) ②to break through
【突飛猛進】to progress rapidly
【突擊】to attack (or assault) suddenly; to raid
【突起】① to rise up all of a sudden ② to break out; suddenly appear
【突襲】surprise attack
【突出】① outstanding; remarkable ② to jut out
【突然】suddenly; unexpectedly
【突如其來】suddenly; abruptly
【突圍】to break through enemy encirclement or siege

五畫

窈 2891
ㄧㄠˇ yǎo 「tranquil
1. deep; obscure; secluded 2.
【窈窕】①(said of young women) attractive and charming ②far
窄 2892 └ and deep
ㄓㄞˇ zhǎi (又讀 ㄗㄜˊ zé)
1. narrow; contracted; tight 2. mean; narrow-minded
【窄小】①(said of a dress) tight and small ②(said of a room, etc.) narrow and small

六畫

窒 2893
ㄓˋ zhì 「to stuff up
to block; to stop up; to obstruct;
【窒息】to suffocate; to smother

窕 2894
ㄊㄧㄠˇ tiǎo
1. slender 2. quiet and modest; charming and attractive 3. good; beautiful; wonderful

七畫

窖 2895
ㄐㄧㄠˋ jiào
1. a cellar; a vault; a pit 2. to store things in a cellar, etc.

窗 2896
(窓、牕、牎) ㄔㄨㄤ chuāng
a window; a skylight
【窗明几淨】(said of rooms) neat and bright 「window curtain
【窗簾or窗帘】a screen, blind or
【窗戶】a window

窘 2897
ㄐㄩㄥˇ jiǒng
1. hard-pressed; poverty-stricken 2. to embarrass 3. afflicted; distressed
【窘態】an embarrassed look
【窘境】a predicament; a plight

八畫

窟 2898
ㄎㄨ kū
1. a hole; a cave; a pit 2. to dig the ground and build underground living quarters
【窟窿 or 窟穴】holes

窠 2899
ㄎㄜ kē
1. a den; a burrow 2. a nest 3. a hole 4. a dwelling for people
【窠臼】a set pattern or rule; a stereotype

九畫

窩 2900
ㄨㄛ wō
1. a cave; a den; a nest 2. an apartment; living quarters; a house 3. to hide; to harbor (a criminal, etc.) 4. to bend; to crease 5. a hollow part of the human body; a pit
【窩囊】① stupid, cowardly and timid; good-for-nothing ②to feel

〔穴部〕

vexed
【窩藏】to harbor (outlaws); to keep (stolen goods)
【窩兒裏反】an intramural fight

窪 2901 ㄨㄚ wā
1. deep; hollow; low-lying 2. a pit; a hole; a hollow; a depression
【窪地】marsh land; low-lying land

十畫

窮 2902 ㄑㄩㄥˊ qióng
1. poor; impoverished; destitute 2. distress; affliction 3. the extreme; the farthest; an end 4. thoroughly
【窮途 or 窮途末路】extremely distressed or difficult state; in straits
【窮鬼】a poverty-stricken fellow
【窮光蛋】a destitute fellow; a pauper
【窮開心】to enjoy moments of happiness even in poverty
【窮苦】destitute; poverty; poverty-stricken
【窮困潦倒】to be penniless and frustrated
【窮極無聊】① to do very foolish things in desperation ② to be utterly bored ③absolutely senseless
【窮小子】a poor bum (a contemptuous expression)
【窮鄉僻壤】out-of-the-way regions
【窮凶極惡】extremely violent and wicked; atrocious
【窮追不捨】to pursue relentlessly
【窮人】destitute people; the poor
【窮酸】(said of a scholar) poor, jealous and pedantic

窖 2903 (窯) ㄧㄠˊ yáo
1. a kiln; a brick furnace 2. pottery 3. a pit in a coal mine; a coal shaft 4. a cave—for human dwelling 5. a brothel: 窰子 a brothel; a prostitute

十一畫

窺 2904 ㄎㄨㄟ kuī
to watch or see in secret; to spy; to peep; to pry into
【窺探】to spy on; to peep; to pry into
【窺視】to peep at; to spy on
【窺測】to watch and assess (a situation, development, etc.)
【窺伺】to watch and wait (for a chance to attack, etc.)

十二畫

窿 2905 ㄌㄨㄥˊ lóng
a hole; a cavity

十三畫

竄 2906 ㄘㄨㄢˋ cuàn
1. to escape; to run away; to flee 2. to change or alter (the wording) 3. to banish; to execute
【竄逃】to flee in disorder
【竄改】to interpolate; to tamper

竅 2907 ㄑㄧㄠˋ qiào
1. a hole; a cavity 2. apertures 3. the crux, key points, gist of a matter; a knack
【竅門】the key to something; a knack

十六畫

竈 2908 (灶) ㄗㄠˋ zào
1. a place for cooking; a kitchen 2. a cooking stove or furnace
【竈君 or 竈神 or 竈王爺】the god of the kitchen

十七畫

竊 2909 ㄑㄧㄝˋ qiè
1. to steal; to burglarize 2. a thief; a burglar 3. to usurp 4. stealthy
【竊聽】to eavesdrop; eavesdropping
【竊聽器】a listening-in device; a bug
【竊據】the occupation of an area, or a city by rebels
【竊竊私語】to talk stealthily or in a very low voice; to whisper
【竊取】to steal
【竊笑】to laugh in secret
【竊賊】a thief; a burglar
【竊案】a theft or larceny case

立部 ㄌㄧˋ

立 2910 ㄌㄧˋ lì
1. to stand 2. to establish; to found; to build; to erect; to create; to start 3. to stand on one's own feet; to live 4. immediately; at once
【立碑】to erect a monument
【立法】to legislate; to make laws
【立法委員】a legislator; a lawmaker
【立法院】Legislative Yuan
【立方】(mathematics) cube
【立定】(word of command) Halt!
【立體】① three-dimensional ② a solid
【立竿見影】The outcome may be known immediately.
【立刻 or 立即】at once; immediately; promptly; right away
【立脚點 or 立足點】a footing; a foothold
【立志】to make up one's mind to pursue some object; to resolve
【立正】to stand at attention 或 Attention!
【立錐之地】space just enough for the point of a drill—very small space
【立場】a position; a stand; an attitude
【立誓】to take an oath; to vow; to swear
【立身處世】to establish oneself and manage to get along in the world
【立足】① to have a foothold somewhere ② to base oneself upon
【立嗣】to adopt an heir
【立案】to accredit (a school, etc.)
【立遺囑】to make one's will
【立業】to establish a business

五畫

站 2911 ㄓㄢˋ zhàn
1. to stand 2. a station; a stop; a center for rendering certain services
【站票】a ticket for standing room; an SRO (standing room only) ticket
【站立】to stand
【站崗】to stand guard; to stand sentry
【站起來】to stand up; to rise
【站長】the head of a station; stationmaster
【站住】(word of command) Halt! 或 to stop; to stand
【站穩】to stand firm

竚 2912 (佇) ㄓㄨˋ zhù
to stand for a long time
【竚候】to stand and wait

六畫

竟 2913 ㄐㄧㄥˋ jìng
1. to come to an end; to terminate; to go through the whole course; to finish; to complete 2. rather unexpectedly; somewhat to one's surprise; in a way thought to be rather unlikely
【竟敢】to dare (somewhat to one's surprise); to have the audacity
【竟然】somewhat unexpectedly; somewhat to one's surprise
【竟夜】all night; the whole night

章 2914 ㄓㄤ zhāng
1. a piece of writing; a chapter 2. a system; a statute; an organized body 3. an emblem; a seal; a stamp 4. to make clear; to make known 5. a pattern; an example 6. a Chinese family name
【章回小說】a serial novel
【章節】chapters and sections (of a piece of writing)
【章程】① a set of regulation; constitution ② a solution; a way
【章魚】an octopus

七畫

童 2915 ㄊㄨㄥˊ tóng
1. a child; a minor; a virgin 2. (said of land, etc.) bare; barren 3. a Chinese family name
【童僕】a boy servant
【童年】childhood; youth
【童工】child labor; a child laborer
【童話】nursery stories; fairy tales
【童心未泯】to retain a childish heart
【童貞】virginity; chastity
【童裝】children's garments
【童山濯濯】①an unforested mountain ② baldheaded
【童子 or 童孺】a minor; a child; a boy; a lad
【童子軍 or 童軍】a boy scout

【童謠】nursery rhymes; nursery songs

竣 2916
ㄐㄩㄣˋ jùn
accomplished; completed
【竣工】(said of a construction project) to be completed

竦 2917
ㄙㄨㄥˇ sǒng
1. respectful 2. awed
【竦然】fearful; scared

九畫

竭 2918
ㄐㄧㄝˊ jié
1. to exhaust; to use up 2. to devote, or put forth (efforts, etc.)
【竭力】to do one's best
【竭盡】to exhaust; to use up
【竭誠】wholeheartedly; with all sincerity

端 2919
ㄉㄨㄢ duān
1. an extreme; an end 2. a beginning 3. correct; proper; upright 4. leads; a clue 5. to carry carefully 6. cause
【端倪】an outline; a clue; signs
【端賴】to rely entirely upon
【端詳】① to study or examine in detail; to scrutinize ② details; the whole story ③ dignified and serene
【端正】① correct; proper ② to correct; to rectify ③ regular; well-formed; symmetric
【端莊】sober; dignified
【端視】to look steadily
【端坐】to sit properly or straight
【端陽節 or 端午節】the Dragon-Boat Festival

十五畫

競 2920
ㄐㄧㄥˋ jìng
to compete; to vie: 競爭to compete; to vie; competition
【競技】a race; a contest; a tournament
【競選】to campaign; to run for
【競爭者】a competitor
【競賽】a race; a contest

竹部
ㄓㄨˊ zhú

竹 2921
ㄓㄨˊ zhú
1. bamboo 2. slips of bamboo for writing
【竹筏】a bamboo raft
【竹筒】a bamboo tube
【竹籃】a bamboo basket
【竹林】a bamboo grove
【竹竿】a bamboo pole or cane
【竹筍 or 竹荀】bamboo shoots
【竹椅】a bamboo chair

三畫

竿 2922
ㄍㄢ gān
a bamboo pole; a bamboo rod

四畫

笆 2923
ㄅㄚ bā
a bamboo fence

笑 2924
ㄒㄧㄠˋ xiào
1. to laugh; to smile; to grin; to giggle; to titter; to chuckle; to snicker 2. to ridicule; to deride; to jeer
【笑柄】a laughingstock; a joke
【笑談】① a laughingstock ② laughing conversation ③ to laugh over
【笑裏藏刀】(literally) to conceal a dagger behind a smile—very treacherous
【笑臉】a smiling face
【笑口常開】grinning all the time
【笑話百出】to make many ridiculous mistakes
【笑話】① a joke ② a ridiculous error ③ Nonsense! ④ to ridicule
【笑逐顏開】to beam with smiles
【笑聲】sound of laughter
【笑容】a smile
【笑容可掬】to be radiant with smiles
【笑靨 or 笑渦】dimples appearing with a smile

五畫

笙 2925
ㄕㄥ shēng
a kind of panpipe with 13 reeds
【笙歌】music and songs

笠 2926
ㄌㄧˋ lì
1. a bamboo hat 2. a bamboo

shade or covering

笛 2927 ㄉ丨ˊ dí
as in 笛子—a flute

笨 2928 ㄅㄣˋ bèn
1. stupid; dull 2. clumsy; awkward
【笨頭笨腦】stupid; muddleheaded; dull; blockheaded
【笨瓜】a fool
【笨拙】unskilled; clumsy; awkward
【笨重】① cumbersome; too heavy for convenient handling ②clumsy
【笨手笨脚】all thumbs
【笨人】a fool; a simpleton; a dullard; an idiot

符 2929 ㄈㄨˊ fú
1. a tally carried for identification, as a warrant, etc.; an identification tag or label 2. an auspicious omen 3. a charm; a talisman; a spell 4. to tally; to correspond; to match; to accord 5. a symbol; a sign
【符合】to correspond; to match; to tally
【符號】a symbol; a sign
【符咒】a charm; a spell; an amulet

第 2930 ㄉ丨ˋ dì
1. sequence; order 2. rank; grade; degree 3. a mansion; a residence
【第六感】the sixth sense; extrasensory perception (ESP)
【第三】third; tertiary
【第二】second; secondary
【第一】first; primary
【第一流】first-rate; first-class
【第一線】the first line; the front
【第一次】the first time

六畫

筆 2931 ㄅ丨ˇ bǐ
1. a writing brush; a pen; a pencil 2. writer's skill or style 3. to write 4. a stroke; a touch 5. a unit of amount 6. (formerly) prose
【筆名】a pen name; *nom de plume*; a pseudonym
【筆法】①a calligraphic style ② a writing style
【筆鋒】① a penpoint ② forcefulness of writing
【筆挺】(said of dress) smooth ironed; spick-and-span; trim
【筆筒or筆架】a tubular penrack or penholder
【筆畫】the number of strokes (in a character)
【筆跡】one's handwriting
【筆記】notes taken (of lectures, speeches, etc.)
【筆記簿】a notebook
【筆直】perfectly straight
【筆試】a written examination
【筆友】pen pals

筍 2932 (笋) ㄙㄨㄣˇ sǔn
bamboo shoots or sprouts

等 2933 ㄉㄥˇ děng
1. rank; grade 2. same; equal 3. to wait 4. when; till 5. and so on; etc.; and the like 6. common
【等待】to wait for; to await
【等等】and so forth; et cetera; etc.
【等號】the equal mark or sign(=)
【等候】to wait; to await; to expect
【等級】grade; rank
【等距離】equal distance; equidistance
【等閒視之】to regard it as of no importance
【等人】to wait for someone
【等一會兒 or 等一等 or 等一下】to wait a little while
【等於】①to be equal to ②tantamount to; the same as

筏 2934 ㄈㄚˊ fá
a raft

筐 2935 ㄎㄨㄤ kuāng
a rectangular chest or box woven from bamboo strips (or wicker); a shallow basket

筒 2936 ㄊㄨㄥˇ tǒng
(又讀 ㄊㄨㄥˊ tóng)
a tube; a pipe; a cylinder

筋 2937 ㄐ丨ㄣ jīn
1. tendons; sinews; muscles 2. veins that stand out under the skin 3. plant fibers resembling a tendon
【筋疲力竭】to be completely exhausted
【筋斗】a somersault 亦作「跟頭」
【筋骨】①bones and muscles—physique; build (of one's body) ② strength

答 2938 1. ㄉㄚˊ dá
1. to answer; to reply 2. to reciprocate; to return

〔竹部〕

【答辯】to reply (to a verbal attack); to speak in self-defense
【答非所問】to give an irrelevant answer
【答覆】to reply to, or answer (an inquiry, etc.); an answer; a reply
【答禮】to return a salute
【答錄機】an answering machine
【答話】to reply orally
【答謝】to convey one's thanks (for a favor, etc.)
【答案】solution, answers (to examination questions, puzzles, etc.)

答 2938
2. ㄉㄚ dā
a variant of 答(ㄉㄚˊ)used only in some phrases
【答理】to answer a person; to respond
【答應】①to assent or agree to (a request); to promise (to do something) ②an answer

策 2939
ㄘㄜˋ cè
1. a whip (for goading horses) 2. expository writings on government affairs 3. orders of appointment 4. a plan; a scheme; a stratagem 5. to whip; to spur; to urge; to impel
【策動】to machinate; to maneuver; to instigate
【策勵】to urge; to impel; to spur
【策略】a stratagem; a scheme; tactics
【策畫】to plan; to make plans

七畫

筵 2940
ㄧㄢˊ yán
1. a bamboo mat 2. a feast; a banquet
【筵席】①a mat for sitting on ②a feast; a banquet

筷 2941
ㄎㄨㄞˋ kuài
chopsticks

八畫

箋 2942
(牋) ㄐㄧㄢ jiān
1. a commentary; a note 2. fancy note paper, letter paper, or stationery

箏 2943
ㄓㄥ zhēng
a kite

箔 2944
ㄅㄛˊ bó
1. foil; gilt 2. a curtain 3. paper tinsel burnt as offerings to the dead

箕 2945
ㄐㄧ jī
1. a winnowing basket; a sieve 2. a dust basket; a garbage basket; a dustpan 3. nonspiral lines on a fingertip
【箕踞】(said of a person) to sit with legs sprawled out

算 2946
ㄙㄨㄢˋ suàn
1. to count; to figure; to reckon; to compute; to calculate 2. to plan; to scheme 3. to infer; to guess; to foretell
【算盤】an abacus
【算命 or 算卦】to tell one's fortune
【算命的 or 算命先生】a fortune-teller
【算了】①Forget about it. ②settled; (said of a case) concluded
【算計】①to consider; to plan ②to plot against someone
【算起來】in total; all told
【算清】to find out the sum, ratio, etc. of
【算賬】①to settle an account ②to get even (with a person)
【算數】to count; to stand; to mean what one says
【算術】arithmetic

箝 2947
ㄑㄧㄢˊ qián
1. tongs; pincers; tweezers 2. to tweezer
【箝緊】to clasp tightly
【箝制】to use pressure upon; to force; to pin down
【箝子】tongs; tweezers; pincers

管 2948
ㄍㄨㄢˇ guǎn
1. a tube; a pipe; a duct 2. a wind instrument 3. to control; to manage; to take care of; to keep 4. to heed; to pay attention to 5. to provide 6. to guarantee 7. to meddle in; to interfere in; to bother about 8. a key 9. a Chinese family name
【管道】①a pipeline; a conduit ②a channel (for communication, etc.)
【管理】to manage; to administer; to handle; to take care of
【管理員】a keeper; an administrator; a custodian; a janitor
【管窺蠡測】restricted in vision and shallow in understanding

【管家】①(ㄍㄨㄢˇ ㄐㄧㄚ) to housekeep ②(ㄍㄨㄢˇ ・ㄐㄧㄚ) a housekeeper
【管家婆】a housekeeper
【管教】to direct and teach (children, students, etc.)
【管轄】to have jurisdiction over
【管絃樂】orchestral music
【管制】to control; control
【管束】to control; to restrain
【管樂隊】a wind band; a band
【管樂器】wind instruments; the wind
【管用】useful; effective; to work

箚 2949 ㄓㄚˊ zhá
1. correspondence; letters 2. (in former times) written directives or instructions to a lower government agency
【箚記】① a notebook ② to put down by items

箇 2950 ㄍㄜˋ gè
same as 個—a numerary adjunct for practically everything
【箇中秘密】the inside story

九畫

箱 2951 ㄒㄧㄤ xiāng
1. a box; a chest; a trunk 2. the box or body of a carriage
【箱籠】boxes; chests; trunks

箭 2952 ㄐㄧㄢˋ jiàn
1. an arrow 2. a sign which is like an arrow 3. *Sinarundinaria nitida*, a variety of bamboo
【箭靶】a target for archery
【箭筒】a quiver
【箭在絃上】① imminent action expected ② There can be no turning back.
【箭鏃】an arrowhead

箸 2953 ㄓㄨˋ zhù
chopsticks

箴 2954 ㄓㄣ zhēn
1. a probe; a needle 2. to warn; to admonish
【箴言】a maxim; warning words; admonitions

節 2955 ㄐㄧㄝˊ jié
1. a node; a knot; a joint 2. a passage; a paragraph; a section 3. principles; integrity; fidelity; constancy; uprightness 4. a festival; a holiday 5. seasons 6. (music) beats; rhythm; time 7. to restrain; to control; to restrict 8. to curtail; to economize
【節拍】(music) beats, rhythm or time
【節目】a program; items on a program
【節目單】a program (of a concert, show, etc.)
【節令】festivals
【節錄】① to excerpt ② an excerpt
【節骨眼】a critical moment
【節儉】to be frugal; to practice austerity; to economize
【節制】to restrict; to hold down; to limit; to control
【節制生育】birth control亦作「節育」
【節省 or 節約】to economize; to save
【節日】a festival; a holiday
【節操】constancy; fidelity; integrity
【節哀順變】to restrain grief and accept the change (common advice to the bereaved)
【節外生枝】to bring about extra complications; to hit a snag

範 2956 ㄈㄢˋ fàn
1. a model; a form; an example; a pattern 2. range; scope; limits 3. to observe the proper rules
【範本】① a copy or copybook (for penmanship, calligraphy, painting, etc.) ② a model; an example
【範例】an example; a model
【範疇】category
【範圍】range; scope; a sphere

篇 2957 ㄆㄧㄢ piān
1. a numerary adjunct for compositions, poems, etc. 2. a chapter; a section; a part 3. a page 4. books; volumes
【篇目】titles; headings
【篇幅】① the length (of a piece of writing) ② space (of a periodical or newspaper)

篆 2958 ㄓㄨㄢˋ zhuàn
1. as in 篆書—the seal type, an ancient calligraphic style 2. a seal
【篆刻】to cut a seal in the seal type

十畫

築 2959 ㄓㄨˊ zhú
to build (out of earth, rock, etc.)

〔竹部〕

【築堤】to build a dike or embankment
【築路】to build roads
【築巢】to build a nest

篡 2960
ㄘㄨㄢˋ cuàn
to usurp; to seize (power, the throne, etc.)
【篡改】to alter a piece of writing with an evil intent; to tamper (with a document, etc.)
【篡位】to seize the throne

篤 2961
ㄉㄨˇ dǔ
1. deep; much; great; profound 2. dangerous; serious 3. generous 4. to consolidate; to make solid 5. to limit
【篤定】(informally) very confident; assured
【篤信】① to have sincere faith in ② honest; trustworthy
【篤實】① sincere; honest; candid; faithful ② solid; sound

篙 2962
ㄍㄠ gāo
the pole for punting a boat; a boat pole

篩 2963
ㄕㄞ shāi
1. a sieve; a screen; a sifter; a strainer 2. to sieve; to screen; to sift; to strain
【篩選】screening; sieving; sifting
【篩子】a sieve; a sifter

十一畫

篷 2964
ㄆㄥˊ péng
1. a covering; an awning; a tent 2. a sail; a boat
【篷車】a wagon

簇 2965
ㄘㄨˋ cù
1. a cluster; a crowd; crowded 2. an arrowhead 3. to crowd together; to cluster together
【簇新】brand-new
【簇擁】attended by a crowd

簍 2966
ㄌㄡˇ lǒu
a basket made by weaving bamboo slats, wickers or twigs

十二畫

簡 2967
(简) ㄐㄧㄢˇ jiǎn
1. brief; succinct; terse; simple 2. (in ancient China) a slip or tablet of bamboo for writing 3. a letter; a note 4. to designate or appoint (an official) 5. a Chinese family name
【簡報】a briefing
【簡便】simple and convenient
【簡明】brief and clear; concise
【簡單】① simple; brief ② ordinary
【簡陋】simple and crude
【簡歷】biographical notes; a resume
【簡略】brief; sketchy
【簡化】to simplify; simplification
【簡潔】(said of a piece of writing) brief and to the point; succinct
【簡介】a brief introduction; a synopsis
【簡直】①simply; outright; at all ② honest; unaffected
【簡章】a brief and concise statement of regulations, procedures, etc.
【簡稱】to be called or known as... for short
【簡而言之】in short; briefly; in a word
【簡易】simple; easy
【簡要】brief and concise
【簡約 or 簡短】brief; terse; succinct; short

簪 2968
ㄗㄢ zān
(又讀 ㄗㄣ zēn)
1. a clasp for clipping the cap and hair together 2. a hairpin for women 3. to stick (in the hair, etc.); to wear

簧 2969
ㄏㄨㄤˊ huáng
1. a reed; the metal tongue in a reed organ 2. a reed organ 3. a spring or catch in a machine

簫 2970
ㄒㄧㄠ xiāo
a vertical flute of bamboo

十三畫

簷 2971
ㄧㄢˊ yán
1. the eaves of a house 2. the edge or brim of anything sloping downward — as that of a hat, umbrella, etc.

簽 2972
ㄑㄧㄢ qiān
1. to sign one's name; to put down one's signature; to subscribe; to endorse 2. bamboo slips used for drawing lots or divination 3. a label
【簽名】to sign; a signature
【簽到】to sign on an attendance

book of an office, firm or factory
【簽訂】to conclude and sign (a treaty, etc.)
【簽條】①a label ②an office note; a memo
【簽證】a visa; to visa
【簽收】to sign after receiving something
【簽署】to sign or initial (a document)
【簽字筆】a felt pen; a felt-tip pen
【簽約】to sign a contract, treaty, etc.

簾 2973
ㄌㄧㄢˊ lián
1. a loose hanging screen for a door or window, usually made of stringed beads, bamboo slabs, etc.; blinds; a curtain 2. a flag as a shop sign

簿 2974
ㄅㄨˋ bù
1. books 2. to record; to register
【簿記】bookkeeping

十四畫

籃 2975
ㄌㄢˊ lán
a basket
【籃球】basketball
【籃球賽】a basketball game

籌 2976
ㄔㄡˊ chóu
1. chips, tallies, etc. for calculating purposes 2. to plan; to prepare 3. to raise (money) 4. to assess or estimate
【籌備】to prepare and plan; to arrange
【籌辦】to plan and sponsor (a show, sports event, school, etc.)
【籌碼】chips (in gambling, etc.); a counter
【籌募】to raise; to collect (funds)
【籌款】to raise funds
【籌劃】to deliberate and plan; a layout
【籌建】to prepare the construction of

籍 2977
ㄐㄧˊ jí
1. books; volumes; reading materials 2. one's hometown or native place
【籍貫】one's native place or home town

十五畫

籐 2978
ㄊㄥˊ téng
same as 藤—vines; canes; climbing plants; rattans
【籐椅】a rattan armchair

十六畫

籠 2979
ㄌㄨㄥˊ lóng
(又讀 ㄌㄨㄥˇ lǒng)
1. a cage; a coop 2. to include; to encompass
【籠統】general; indiscriminate
【籠絡】①to entice, tempt, ensnare or cajole ②to befriend another with a view to winning him over
【籠罩】to cover completely; to permeate; to shroud
【籠中鳥】restricted and confined
【籠子】a cage; a coop

十七畫

籤 2980
(籖) ㄑㄧㄢ qiān
1. a slip of bamboo engraved with signs to be used in gambling or divination; a lot 2. a label 3. a small sharp-pointed stick

十九畫

籬 2981
ㄌㄧˊ lí
a bamboo fence; a hedge: 籬笆a bamboo fence

籮 2982
ㄌㄨㄛˊ luó
1. a bamboo basket with a square or rectangular bottom and a round top 2. a piece of sievelike ware with a broad edge
【籮筐】a large basket made of bamboo

二十六畫

籲 2983
ㄩˋ yù
to appeal; to request; to urge; to ask; to implore; to beseech

米部
ㄇㄧˇ mǐ

米 2984
ㄇㄧˇ mǐ
1. hulled or husked rice; uncooked rice 2. a shelled or a husked seed 3. meter (the fundamen-

〔米部〕

tal unit of length in the metric system)
【米飯】cooked rice
【米粉】① rice flour ② thin noodles made of rice flour
【米糠】rice bran; paddy chaff
【米酒】rice wine; rice beer
【米食】a rice diet

四畫

粉 2985 ㄈㄣˇ fěn
1. flour 2. powder 3. white (color) 4. to whitewash; to plaster 5. to make up; to doll up; to powder
【粉筆】chalk
【粉撲兒】a powder puff
【粉盒】a powder box; a vanity case
【粉紅】pink
【粉飾】① to whitewash; to embellish; to touch up ② to make up
【粉身碎骨】(even) at the cost of one's life; great danger or very risky
【粉刷】to plaster or whitewash (a wall, etc.)
【粉刺】pimples; acne
【粉碎】① to shatter; to crush up; to smash ② broken into pieces

五畫

粗 2986 ㄘㄨ cū
1. thick; bulky; big 2. coarse; rough; crude 3. gruff; husky 4. rude; vulgar 5. brief; sketchy
【粗暴】rude; violent; rough
【粗鄙】vulgar; crude
【粗大】thick and big
【粗魯or粗鹵】rude; impolite; rough
【粗略】cursory; rough; sketchy
【粗獷】① rough; rude; boorish ② bold and unconstrained; rugged
【粗話】obscene language
【粗活】work of a laborer or coolie; work which demands little brains but lots of brawn
【粗心】careless (in work)
【粗心大意】rash and careless; inadvertency
【粗枝大葉】careless; sketchy (description)
【粗製濫造】to turn out (products) in large quantities without any regard for quality
【粗壯】stout; sturdy; brawny; muscular
【粗重】① bulky (products, etc.) of low value ② work that needs more muscles than brains
【粗茶淡飯】simple food; plain fare
【粗率】① crude and coarse ② careless
【粗人】① a person of little education ② a boor; an unrefined person
【粗糙】(said of a surface, etc.) coarse; rough; unpolished
【粗俗】coarse; vulgar; unrefined
【粗野】rude; boorish

粒 2987 ㄌㄧˋ lì
1. a grain (of rice, etc.) 2. to get grain to eat 3. a pill; a bead

粘 2988 (黏) ㄋㄧㄢˊ nián
to paste up; to attach to; to stick up; to glue
【粘貼】to paste; to stick

六畫

粟 2989 ㄙㄨˋ sù
1. grain; paddy 2. millet 3. goose flesh; goose pimples; goose bumps; goose skin
【粟米】millet; grain

粥 2990 ㄓㄨˋ zhù
(語音 ㄓㄡ zhōu)
congee; rice gruel
【粥少僧多】(literally) The congee is not enough for the many monks.—not enough for circulation or distribution

粵 2991 ㄩㄝˋ yuè
1. Kwangtung Province 2. Kwangtung and Kwangsi Provinces
【粵劇】Canton opera

粧 2992 (妝) ㄓㄨㄤ zhuāng
1. toilet; to adorn; to doll up 2. woman's personal adornments 3. a bride's trousseau 4. to disguise or pretend
【粧扮】to doll up
【粧奩】a bride's trousseau; a dowry

七畫

粲 2993 ㄘㄢˋ càn
1. bright and clear; radiant 2. beautiful; splendid; excellent 3. smiling; laughing 4. well-

polished rice
【粲爛】brilliant; sparkling; radiant

粱 2994 ㄌㄧㄤˊ liáng
maize; grain; sorghums

八畫

精 2995 ㄐㄧㄥ jīng
1. polished rice; unmixed rice 2. the essence; the essentials 3. energy; spirits 4. the male sperm; semen 5. fine and delicate; exquisite 6. dedicated; intensive 7. very; completely; extremely 8. keen; smart; sharp; clever 9. skilled; to specialize in 10. a goblin; a spirit; a demon
【精疲力竭】exhausted; worn-out
【精品】an exquisite article
【精美】exquisite; delicate and beautiful
【精密】minute or detailed; precise
【精明】keen or sharp; clever
【精打細算】calculate carefully and budget strictly
【精挑細選】very choosy
【精通】well versed in; good at; expert at
【精力】stamina; vitality; energy
【精力旺盛】to be full of vitality
【精煉】to rectify; to refine; refined
【精良】exquisite; fine; excellent
【精靈】an elf; a fairy
【精華】the essence; the essentials
【精簡】to simplify
【精進】to devote oneself to improvement
【精巧】exquisite; fine and delicate (workmanship, etc.)
【精確】precise; accurate; precision; accuracy
【精細】① fine (materials, etc.); delicate and painstaking (workmanship, handicraft, etc.); exquisite ② very careful and attentive
【精心傑作】a masterpiece; a brainchild
【精選】to pick the best; to handpick; to select
【精緻】fine; exquisite; delicate
【精製】specially picked and baked (tea, etc.); highly finished; refined
【精湛】consummate; exquisite; perfect
【精裝本】a deluxe edition
【精忠報國】to serve one's fatherland with unreserved loyalty
【精誠團結】to unite together with utmost sincerity; esprit de corps
【精純】① pure ② to refine
【精深】profound; profundity
【精神】① one's spirit ② lively; vigorous ③ mental
【精神飽滿】in high spirits; vigorous and energetic
【精神病】mental illness
【精神病院】an asylum
【精神分裂症】schizophrenia
【精神抖擻】high-spirited; sprightly
【精神恍惚】absent-minded
【精神失常】mental disorder
【精銳】crack; picked
【精子】spermatozoa 亦作「精蟲」
【精彩】① the highlight or climax (of a play, etc.); the most attractive or wonderful part (of something) ② Wonderful! 或 Bravo! 或Excellent!
【精萃】cream; pick
【精粹】the essence or essentials; refined and pure
【精髓】the marrow; the essence; the pith
【精義】the essential significance
【精益求精】Second best is not good enough.—to try for the best
【精鹽】refined salt; purified salt

粹 2996 ㄘㄨㄟˋ cuì
1. pure; unmixed; perfect; unadulterated 2. the essence; the best

九畫

糊 2997 ㄏㄨˊ hú
1. paste 2. to paste 3. scorched 4. not clear; blurred; confused; ambiguous; unintelligible
【糊塗】① mixed-up; confused ② stupid; foolish
【糊塗蟲】a blunderer; a bungler
【糊裏糊塗】(to do something) without thinking; confused or mixed-up
【糊口】to make a living; to live from hand to mouth 亦作「餬口」

糉 2998 (粽) ㄗㄨㄥˋ zòng
glutinous rice tamale—made by wrapping the rice in broad leaves of reeds and boiled for a few hours—usually with other ingredients, such as dates, meat, oysters, beans, etc.
【糉子 or 粽子】glutinous rice dumplings; rice tamale

粈 2999 ㄖㄡˇ rǒu
to mix; mixed
【粈合】to mix together; to blend

十畫

糗 3000 ㄑㄧㄡˇ qiǔ
parched grain, rice, etc.; dry food; dry rations

糕 3001 (餻) ㄍㄠ gāo
cakes; pastries; steamed dumplings
【糕餅】cakes and biscuits
【糕餅店】a pastry shop

糖 3002 ㄊㄤˊ táng
sugar: 糖果 candy; sweets
【糖尿病】diabetes
【糖果店】a candy shop
【糖漿】syrup; molasses
【糖廠】a sugar mill; a sugar refinery
【糖水】sweetened water; sugar solution

十一畫

糜 3003 ㄇㄧˊ mí
1. congee; porridge; rice gruel 2. rotten; mashed; corrupted 3. to waste
【糜爛】① rotten; corrupt debauchery ② to oppress and destroy the people (through devious means)

糞 3004 ㄈㄣˋ fèn
1. night soil; manure; dung 2. to fertilize the land 3. to sweep
【糞便】excrement; night soil
【糞堆】a dunghill
【糞坑】a manure pit; a cesspool

糙 3005 ㄘㄠ cāo
1. coarse or unpolished; rough 2. rude; rough; rash; desultory; careless
【糙米】unpolished rice

糟 3006 ㄗㄠ zāo
1. sediment or dregs of wine 2. to soak food items (as fish, meat, etc.) in wine or wine sediment 3. (said of a plan, arrangement, etc.) to become a mess, or in bad shape 4. decayed; rotten; spoiled 5. not sturdy or strong 6. lousy; a louse
【糟蹋】① to waste (talent, great ability, etc. on trifles); to degrade or debase ② to insult
【糟糕】What a mess! 或 Too bad!

糠 3007 ㄎㄤ kāng
1. husks of rice; rice bran or chaff 2. of inferior quality; not sturdy; empty inside; things of no value 3. spongy

糢 3008 (模) ㄇㄛˊ mó
blurred; indistinct
【糢糊】blurred; indistinct; unclear; confused

糨 3009 (糡) ㄐㄧㄤˋ jiàng
1. paste; to paste together; to starch; starched 2. thick
【糨糊】paste; glue

十二畫

糧 3010 (粮) ㄌㄧㄤˊ liáng
1. grain; food; provisions; rations 2. farm or land taxes
【糧行】a store selling grain and provisions
【糧餉】army provisions and payroll
【糧食】foodstuffs; provisions
【糧倉】a granary

十四畫

糯 3011 (穤、稬) ㄋㄨㄛˋ nuò
glutinous rice
【糯米】polished glutinous rice

糸部 ㄇㄧˋ mì

一畫

系 3012 ㄒㄧˋ xì
1. a system; a line; a connecting link; a connection 2. lineage; a genealogy 3. (politics) a clique; a theoretic or party line 4. (in a college or a university) a department or school 5. to relate to; to bear on 6. to be
【系統】a system; systematic
【系列】① a line or lineage ② a

row; a series
【系主任】the head or chairman of a department (in a college)

二畫

糾 3013 ㄐㄧㄡ jiū
(又讀ㄐㄧㄡˇ jiǔ)
1. to supervise; to inspect; to investigate 2. to correct; to censure; to impeach; to discipline 3. to collaborate; to band together; to entangle; to bind together; to involve; involved
【糾紛】disputes; quarrels; entanglements
【糾葛】an endless involvement; a dispute
【糾合】to band together
【糾劾】to censure and impeach
【糾結】to band together; to collaborate
【糾正】to correct; to check; to discipline; to rectify
【糾察】① to discipline; to investigate; to picket ② a disciplinary officer
【糾纏】① to tangle; to involve; entanglement ② to pester

三畫

紀 3014 ㄐㄧˋ jì
1. a historical record; annals; chronicles 2. a period of 12 years 3. a century 4. to arrange; to put in order 5. institutions; laws and regulations; discipline 6. the age of a person 7. a geological period 8. a Chinese family name
【紀念】to remember; to commemorate
【紀念碑】a monument; a memorial
【紀念品】a souvenir; a memento
【紀念日】a commemoration day; a memorial day; an anniversary
【紀念冊】an autograph book
【紀錄】① a record; to take notes ② a recorder
【紀錄片】a documentary film
【紀律】discipline; laws and regulations
【紀元後】A.D. (anno Domini)
【紀元前】B.C. (before Christ)

紂 3015 ㄓㄡˋ zhòu
1. the last emperor of the Yin Dynasty, whose name stands for tyranny 2. the crupper of a saddle

紆 3016 ㄩ yū
1. to wind; to spiral; to bend; to twist; to distort; to meander 2. a knot in one's heart; melancholy
【紆廻or迂迴】circuitous; winding (roads)
【紆緩】slow; dilatory

約 3017 ㄩㄝ yuē
1. an agreement; a covenant; a contract; a treaty 2. brief(ly); simply 3. about; around; approximately; estimated 4. a date; an appointment or engagement; a rendezvous; to make an appointment; to date 5. poor; poverty; hardship; straitened 6. (mathematics) to reduce 7. to bind; to restrain 8. vague(ly)
【約莫】or so; about; approximately
【約定】to agree upon; to agree to
【約略】① brief(ly); sketchy ② approximate
【約會】an appointment or engagement; a date
【約期】an appointment or engagement; to make an appointment
【約請】to invite
【約束】to bind or restrain; restraint; restriction

紅 3018 1. ㄏㄨㄥˊ hóng
1. red; vermilion; rosy 2. to blush; to redden 3. eminent; influential; (said of players) very popular 4. specially favored; a favorite
【紅包】①a red paper bag containing money as a gift ② a bribe or kickback
【紅寶石】a ruby
【紅粉佳人】a young beauty
【紅粉知己】a girlfriend; a mistress
【紅豆】① *Abrus precatorius*, the red bean—a love pea亦作「相思子」② *Ormosia*
【紅糖】brown sugar
【紅通通】glowing; aglow; bright red
【紅娘】a nonprofit-making woman go-between for lovers
【紅利】a net profit; a bonus
【紅蘿蔔】a radish
【紅鸞星動】a wedding being imminent
【紅綠燈】red and green lights; traffic lights
【紅光滿面】a healthy and hearty look
【紅血球】red blood cells; erythrocyte
【紅心】the bull's-eye (of a target)

〔糸部〕

【紅杏出牆】(said of a married woman) to have a lover; to commit adultery
【紅磚】red bricks
【紅腫】a red swelling of the skin
【紅茶】black tea
【紅塵】the mundane world; the world of mortals
【紅十字會】Red Cross Society
【紅人】① the trusted lieutenant of the boss ② Red Indians
【紅潤】(said of the skin, cheeks, etc.) glowing, tender and rosy
【紅色】red color
【紅藥水】mercurochrome
【紅顏】① young beauties ② youths ③ rosy cheeks
【紅顏薄命】(a popular Chinese saying) Beauties are often ill-fated.
【紅外線】infrared rays
【紅暈】a blush; a flush

紅 3018
2. ㄍㄨㄥ gōng
work; working

紈 3019
ㄨㄢˊ wán
processed fine and light silk
【紈袴子弟】a good-for-nothing young man from a wealthy family

紉 3020
ㄖㄣˋ rèn
1. to sew; to stitch 2. to tie; to wear 3. to feel deeply 4. to thread a needle

四畫

紋 3021
ㄨㄣˊ wén
1. stripes; lines; streaks; veins 2. ripples (of water) 3. (finger) prints 4. wrinkles (on the face) 5. to tattoo
【紋理】lines; stripes; veins; grain
【紋身】tattoo; to tattoo the body

納 3022
ㄋㄚˋ nà
1. to receive; to take; to accept; to admit; to adopt 2. to offer as tribute 3. to enjoy; to feel 4. to repress; to restrain 5. to patch old clothes 6. a Chinese family name
【納悶】① to feel depressed ② to feel curious
【納涼】to enjoy the cool air
【納賄】① to offer bribes ② to receive bribes
【納諫】to accept an admonition
【納稅】to pay duties or taxes
【納稅人】the taxpayer
【納入】to bring into

紐 3023
ㄋㄧㄡˇ niǔ
1. a knot; a tie; a cord 2. a hold (of a vessel) or handle 3. a button
【紐扣】a button

純 3024
ㄔㄨㄣˊ chún
1. pure; net (profits, etc.); unalloyed 2. sincere; honest; simple; faithful 3. completely; purely; entirely 4. (now rare) great; large
【純白】pure white
【純樸】simple and sincere
【純毛】all-wool; 100% wool
【純度】purity
【純良】kind; honest
【純潔】innocent; pure and clean
【純金】pure gold; unalloyed gold
【純淨】pure and clean
【純眞】pure, sincere and faithful
【純正】① pure and genuine ② honest; sincere
【純種】thoroughbred; purebred
【純熟】proficient; very skillful; adroit
【純屬虛構】The matter is an out-and-out fabrication.
【純粹】① pure; genuine ② completely

紓 3025
ㄕㄨ shū
1. to relax; to slacken; to slow down; to mitigate 2. to extricate from; to remove (causes of difficulties, poverty, etc.); to free from
【紓難】to extricate from trouble or danger

紕 3026
ㄆㄧ pī
1. errors; mistakes; blunders 2. (said of cloth, thread, etc.) to become unwoven or untwisted
【紕漏】errors or mistakes; something going wrong

紗 3027
ㄕㄚ shā
1. gauze; thin silk or cloth 2. yarn, as cotton yarn
【紗布】① gauze ② a bandage
【紗窗】a window screen

紙 3028
ㄓˇ zhǐ
paper
【紙板】cardboard
【紙幣】paper money; bank notes
【紙牌】playing cards

【紙條】 a slip of paper
【紙盒】 a carton; a paper box
【紙漿】 paper pulp
【紙錢兒】 paper money burnt as offerings to the dead
【紙張】 paper; sheets of paper
【紙上談兵】 impractical schemes; empty talks
【紙醉金迷】 to indulge in a wanton life
【紙業】 the paper industry or enterprise

級 3029
ㄐㄧˊ jí
1. a grade; a class (at school) 2. a level; a degree; a mark of merit; a rank 3. a step (of a flight of steps) 4. a decapitated head
【級別】 ranks; levels; grades; scales
【級俸】 a scale of salaries
【級會】 a class meeting (at school)
【級長】 a class leader; a monitor
【級任導師】 a homeroom teacher

紛 3030
ㄈㄣ fēn
1. confused; disorderly 2. numerous; many; varied
【紛飛】 to whirl around in confusion; to fly all over
【紛紛】 ① numerous and disorderly ②(said of people moving) in droves; numerous and in great confusion
【紛亂】 confusion; chaotic
【紛爭】 a dispute; to dispute; to wrangle; to quarrel
【紛擾】 to confuse; turmoil; disturbance

紡 3031
ㄈㄤˇ fǎng
1. to reel; to spin 2. reeled pongee (a kind of thin silk)
【紡織】 to spin and weave; spinning and weaving
【紡織機】 looms
【紡織廠】 a textile mill
【紡織業】 the textile industry
【紡紗】 to spin cotton, etc. into yarn
【紡紗機】 a jenny; a spinning jenny

紊 3032
ㄨㄣˋ wèn
confused; tangled; involved; disorderly
【紊亂】 confused; tangled; chaotic

素 3033
ㄙㄨˋ sù
1. pure white silk 2. white (color) 3. plain; simple 4. mourning 5. vegetable food; a vegetarian diet 6. heretofore; up to the present 7. usually; generally 8. the original constitution of things; matter; elements
【素不相識】 to have never met or seen before
【素昧平生】 to have never known, met or seen before; to be a total stranger
【素描】 (said of writing or painting) a sketch
【素來】 heretofore; always; up to the present
【素淨】 ① simple, or plain (clothes) ② simple, or not greasy (food)
【素行】 daily conduct or behavior
【素質】 ① one's natural talent ② white
【素稱】 usually called; reputed to be
【素食】 vegetarian food
【素日】 usually; commonly; daily; regularly; frequently
【素稔】 to have known or been familiar with
【素雅】 simple but elegant
【素養】 one's general capacity and disposition as a result of long and regular self-discipline; accomplishments

索 3034
1. ㄙㄨㄛˇ suǒ
1. a thick rope; a cable 2. solitary; alone; lonely 3. to search or inquire into 4. laws and regulations; rules 5. to demand; to ask; to exact 6. to need
【索賠】 to demand compensation; to claim
【索命】 (usually referring to a ghost, a victim of injustice) to demand one's life
【索價】 to demand a price; to quote a price
【索求】 to seek (persons, jobs, etc.)
【索取】 ① to ask for ② to extort
【索然無味】 not interesting; tasteless
【索引】 ① the index (of a book) ② to bring together

索 3034
2. ㄙㄨㄛˊ suó
to decide to go ahead and do something without any more consideration; may as well; simply
【索性】 directly; to go all the way

五畫

紮 3035
1. (紥) ㄓㄚˊ zhá

〔糸部〕

1. to bind, tie or fasten; to make a bundle; a bundle 2. to stop; to station; to post

【紮營】to bivouac; to station troops; to encamp

糸部

紮 3035
2. (紥) ㄗㄚ zā
to bind; to tie; to fasten

【紮緊】to tighten; to fasten securely

紫 3036
ㄗˇ zǐ
purple; violet

【紫丁香花】a lilac
【紫羅蘭】(botany) the violet
【紫菜】(botany) laver
【紫色】purple; violet
【紫藥水】gentian violet solution
【紫外線】ultraviolet rays

累 3037
1. ㄌㄟˇ lěi
1. to accumulate through a length of time 2. to pile up 3. to repeat; repeatedly; successively

【累犯】①to offend or violate the law repeatedly ②a recidivist
【累代】generation after generation
【累累】① repeatedly; successively ②piling up ③countless
【累積】to accumulate; to pile up
【累計】to include previous figures in the calculation
【累加】to acculate; to increase
【累次】repeatedly; many times

累 3037
2. ㄌㄟˋ lèi
1. to involve; involvement; to implicate 2. to owe; to be in debt 3. tired; weary; fatigue 4. (said of eyes) to strain 5. a family burden

【累病了 or 累倒了】to become sick owing to hard work
【累壞了】to become ill as a result of backbreaking toil
【累及他人】to involve or implicate others
【累及無辜】to involve the innocent
【累人】to wear down; to be tiring

累 3037
3. ㄌㄟˊ léi
1. a nuisance 2. to fasten; to bind

【累贅】①a nuisance; a burden; a troublesome thing ②wordy; verbose

細 3038
ㄒㄧˋ xì
1. tiny; small; little 2. thin; slender; tall but lean; slim 3. fine 4. petty; trifling; detailed 5. precise; exquisite; delicate (workmanship, etc.)

【細胞】a cell
【細部】details (of a drawing); minute parts
【細密】①(said of materials) fine and delicate ② careful; cautious
【細目】detailed items
【細微】tiny; minute
【細雨】a misty rain; drizzle
【細語】low and tender talk; pillow talk

紳 3039
ㄕㄣ shēn
1. the middle class as a group or individuals; the gentry; a gentleman 2. a sash; a girdle 3. to tie

【紳士】a gentleman; an esquire
【紳商】the gentry and merchant class

紹 3040
ㄕㄠˋ shào
1. to bring together; to connect 2. to hand down; to continue

【紹興酒】the Shaohsing wine

絃 3041
ㄒㄧㄢˊ xián
1. the string of a musical instrument; a cord 2. first and last quarters of the moon

【絃外之音】overtones; connotations; suggestion
【絃樂】string music
【絃樂隊】a string band

終 3042
ㄓㄨㄥ zhōng
1. the end; to come to the end; the conclusion 2. death; to die 3. finally; at last; in the end; after all 4. whole; all

【終點】①the terminus; the final point; the end; a destination ② (sports) finish
【終端機】a terminal
【終年】① the whole year; throughout the year ② the age at which one dies
【終老】throughout one's life; until death
【終了】to end; to complete; to conclude; to terminate
【終歸】① the conclusion; to end or conclude ②finally; after all; at last
【終極】the finality or end
【終結】the end, conclusion, termination, etc.
【終其一生】throughout one's life

【終須】to have to...in the end
【終止】to stop; to end
【終站】the terminal stop or station
【終身伴侶】a life company—wife or husband
【終身事業】a lifelong career
【終生】the whole life
【終日】throughout the day
【終於】in the end; finally; at last

組 3043 ㄗㄨˇ zǔ
1. a group; a team; a section; a department; an organization; a union 2. to organize; to arrange; to unite; to form 3. tassels; a fringe; a girdle; a tape
【組閣】(government) to form a cabinet
【組合】① (mathematics) combinations ② to unite; to make up ③ a company; a union
【組曲】(music) a suite
【組織】① to organize; to constitute ② an organization; a formation ③ (biology) tissue; texture
【組長】the chief of a department or section in a government agency
【組成】to form; to constitute

絆 3044 ㄅㄢˋ bàn
1. shackles; fetters 2. to stumble; to trip over; to trip
【絆倒】to trip over; to trip
【絆脚石】a stumbling block
【絆住】to be detained, hindered or held back; to be bogged down

六畫

結 3045 1. ㄐㄧㄝˊ jié
1. to tie; to knot; to weave 2. a knot 3. to unite; to join; to connect 4. to congeal; coagulation 5. to form; to found; to constitute 6. to bear fruit; a result; an outcome 7. to pay, or settle (as an account, etc.) 8. a node
【結疤】to heal up; to scar
【結拜】sworn (brothers, or sisters); to pledge in a sworn brotherhood
【結伴】to accompany
【結冰】to freeze; to form ice
【結盟】to ally with; alignment
【結褵】to be married
【結論】the conclusion (of a meeting, argument, etc.)
【結構】① structure ② (said of a piece of writing) the arrangement of ideas; presentation
【結果】① (said of plants) to bear fruit ② the result, outcome or consequence ③ in the end; finally
【結合】① to get united; to combine with ② to get married; to marry
【結核病】tuberculosis
【結夥】to gang up; to collude
【結滙】to sell foreign exchange to (or to buy it from) banks; foreign exchange settlement
【結婚】marriage; to get married
【結婚證書】a marriage certificate
【結集】to concentrate (troops, etc.); concentration (of troops, etc.)
【結交】to associate with; to befriend; to make friends with
【結晶】to crystallize; crystallization; crystal
【結局】the outcome; the result; the end
【結帳or結賬】to settle accounts; to pay up
【結仇 or 結讎 or 結寃】to contract ill will or animus of
【結石】(pathology) stone; calculus
【結識】to know or associate with
【結束】to conclude; to end; to wind up
【結紮】(medicine) ligation; to ligature
【結綵】to festoon (for celebration)
【結存】the credit balance; (said of government finance) foreign exchange reserves
【結算】to settle accounts; settlement of accounts
【結業】to graduate; to conclude or complete a training course
【結尾】the conclusion; the end
【結網】to make a net
【結餘】a cash surplus; a surplus
【結緣】to associate on good terms
【結怨】to arouse ill will or dislike; to incur hatred

結 3045 2. ㄐㄧㄝ jiē
1. to stutter; to stammer 2. tough; strong; durable 3. to bear (fruit); to form (seed)
【結巴】to stutter; to stammer
【結實】① strong; sturdy ② tough; durable; solid

〔糸部〕

絕 3046 ㄐㄩㄝˊ jué

1. to sever; to break off; to cut 2. to renounce; to decline 3. to run out of; exhausted; used up 4. without match; peerless 5. isolated; to separate 6. to discontinue; to stop; to cease 7. without posterity 8. extremely; utmost; absolutely 9. to destroy 10. leaving no leeway 11. a poem of four lines

【絕版】out-of-print (books)
【絕筆】① one's last writing (before death) ② to discontinue writing
【絕壁】cliffs
【絕不】never
【絕妙】extremely good or wonderful
【絕妙好辭】quotable quotes; the last say in (wisecracks, quotes, etc.)
【絕命】to die; death
【絕代佳人】a matchless beauty
【絕頂聰明】extremely bright, intelligent or clever
【絕對】absolute(ly); definite(ly)
【絕斷】to sever or cut off (relationship, etc.)
【絕糧】to run out of food supplies
【絕路】a dead end; an impasse
【絕倫】without match; peerless
【絕口】① never to mention again ② to stop talking about
【絕後】① heirless ② (said of extremely good writings, paintings, etc.) probably cannot be repeated again
【絕迹】to vanish completely
【絕技】a feat or stunt
【絕佳】extremely good; excellent
【絕交】to cut off or sever friendship, diplomatic relations, etc.
【絕境】the end of one's rope; an impasse
【絕響】① lost arts ② (said of a great musician) cannot be heard again
【絕招】① unique skill ② an unexpected tricky move (as the last resort) ③ a masterstroke
【絕症】an incurable disease; a fatal illness
【絕種】(said of species of animals, etc.) extinction; extinct
【絕食】to fast
【絕嗣】without heir or posterity
【絕色】an incomparably beautiful girl
【絕藝】a unique feat, stunt or performance
【絕無僅有】very rare; unique
【絕望】hopeless; desperate; despair
【絕緣體】an insulator

絞 3047 ㄐㄧㄠˇ jiǎo

1. to twist; to twine; to wring 2. to hang (a criminal) 3. rudeness 4. to mix up

【絞痛】an acute or gripping pain caused by cholera, appendicitis, etc.
【絞架】gallows
【絞盡腦汁】to cudgel one's brains
【絞肉機】meat mincer

絡 3048 1. ㄌㄨㄛˋ luò

1. to wrap around; to encompass 2. a net; a web 3. a cellulose structure in fruits, as melons 4. to associate; to unite; connected 5. a halter 6. (said of blood vessels) capillaries 7. to unreel silk 8. cotton fiber 9. hemp

【絡腮鬍子】whiskers
【絡繹不絕】(said of people) to come one after another; continuous

絡 3048 2. ㄌㄠˋ lào

a web or net

絢 3049 ㄒㄩㄢˋ xuàn

bright and brilliant; adorned and stylish

【絢爛】bright and brilliant
【絢麗】gorgeous; magnificent

給 3050 1. ㄐㄧˇ jǐ

1. to provide; provisions; to supply; supplies 2. to award; to approve; to grant 3. sufficiency; affluence 4. glib; eloquent

【給假】to grant a leave of absence
【給獎】to award prizes
【給水】a water supply
【給與】to give

給 3050 2. ㄍㄟˇ gěi

1. to give 2. for; for the benefit of 3. to let; to allow

【給付】to pay

絨 3051 ㄖㄨㄥˊ róng

1. fine wool; woolen; velvety; velvet 2. any kind of woolen

goods or fabric with a feltlike surface 3. fine; furry; flossy
【絨布】flannel; felt
【絨毛】down
【絨褲】sweat pants

統 3052
ㄊㄨㄥˇ tǒng
1. to govern; to rule; to control 2. to unify; to unite 3. wholly; totally; all; completely; generally 4. succession; from generation to generation
【統領】a commanding officer
【統計】① statistics ② to count
【統計學】statistics (as a science)
【統治】to reign; to rule; to govern
【統治者】the ruler
【統籌】to plan as a whole
【統稱】known together as
【統帥】the commander in chief
【統率】to lead (troops, a mission, etc.); to rule; to govern
【統一】to unify; uniform; unitary
【統一發票】a uniform invoice
【統御 or 統馭】to reign; to rule

絲 3053
ㄙ sī
1. silk 2. very fine thread, fiber, etc. as those making a spider's web 3. a general name of silk fabrics or goods 4. strings of musical instruments 5. infinitesimal; a trace; a thread; a tiny bit
【絲帶】silk ribbons
【絲瓜】the sponge gourd (the fruit of a loofah); towel gourds
【絲毫】the tiniest, slightest, or least bit
【絲毫不爽】very reliable or accurate
【絲織品】silk fabrics; silk goods
【絲綢】silk cloth; silk
【絲絨】velvet
【絲絲入扣】ingenious and touching; right on the beat
【絲襪】silk stockings; silk socks

絮 3054
ㄒㄩˋ xù
1. raw, coarse, old, waste cotton or silk 2. wooly; fluffy 3. catkins and similar blossoms 4. padding; cushioning 5. (said of chatter, writing, etc.) windy 6. to wad with cotton
【絮叨】tiresomely talkative; to nag
【絮絮不休】to din; to chatter

七畫

絹 3055
ㄐㄩㄢˋ juàn
1. a kind of thick, loosely-woven raw silk fabric 2. a handkerchief
【絹扇】a fan made with silk

綁 3056
ㄅㄤˇ bǎng
to tie; to bind; to fasten
【綁票 or 綁架】to kidnap for ransoms
【綁匪】a kidnaper
【綁緊】to bind or fasten tight

綏 3057
ㄙㄨㄟ suī
(又讀 ㄙㄨㄟˊ suí)
1. to repose; to pacify; to appease; to soothe; to tranquilize 2. to retreat
【綏靖】to pacify; pacification

經 3058
ㄐㄧㄥ jīng
1. classic books; religious scriptures; books of significant value 2. the warp of a fabric; things running lengthwise 3. common or customary ways, rules, regulations, etc. 4. to plan; to arrange; to regulate; to rule; to manage; to deal in; to engage in 5. menses 6. human arteries, etc. 7. as a result; after 8. to pass through or by 9. longitude
【經脈】blood vessels
【經費】a budget; funds
【經典】① religious scriptures ② Chinese classics
【經度】degrees of longitude
【經年累月】for months and years
【經理】① a manager (of a company) ② to manage, direct, regulate, etc.
【經歷】① one's past experiences ② to undergo; to go through
【經過】to pass by or through
【經紀人】① a manager (of entertainers, boxers, etc.) ② a broker; an agent
【經濟】① economy; economic ② economical; to economize
【經濟命脈】the economic lifeline
【經濟基礎】an economic base
【經濟蕭條】economic stagnation
【經濟學】economics

【經濟學家】 an economist
【經久耐用】 (said of goods) durable
【經銷】 to sell as a consignee
【經線】 longitude; the meridian
【經常】 frequently; often; constantly
【經世濟民】 to govern and benefit the people
【經手】 to handle; to deal with
【經商】 to go into business
【經書】 classic books
【經由】 by (a person); through or via (a place)
【經驗】 experience; empirical
【經營】 to operate or manage (a shop, a business, etc.)
【經緯】 ① longitude and latitude ② the warp and the woof
【經文】 classical text

綑 3059
(捆) ㄎㄨㄣˇ kǔn
1. a bundle; to make a bundle; to tie up; to bundle up 2. to weave
【綑綁】 to bind; to tie up
【綑緊】 to bind tight; to tighten the rope

八畫

綜 3060
ㄗㄨㄥˋ zòng
1. to sum up 2. in view of; to take account of 3. to arrange 4. synthesis 5. to examine into
【綜覽】 to view generally
【綜理】 to be in overall charge
【綜括】 to sum up; to encompass all
【綜合】 synthesis; to synthesize
【綜合報導】 a comprehensive dispatch
【綜合所得稅】 consolidated income tax
【綜藝節目】 a variety show

綠 3061
1. ㄌㄩˋ lǜ
green (color)
【綠寶石】 emerald; beryl
【綠豆】 the green beans; green lentils
【綠燈】 ① (transportation) the green light ② permission to go ahead with some project; the green light
【綠卡】 a green card, permanent residence permit issued by the U.S. government
【綠化】 to plant trees, build parks, or lay out lawns in deserts or urban areas
【綠洲】 an oasis
【綠茶】 green tea
【綠藻】 algae; chlorophyceae; chlorella
【綠油油】 bright green
【綠蔭】 a green shade; the shade of trees

綠 3061
2. 讀音 ㄌㄨˋ lù
【綠林好漢 or 綠林豪傑】 ① heros of the greenwood ② brigands

綢 3062
ㄔㄡˊ chóu
1. a general name of all silk fabrics 2. fine and delicate 3. (now rarely) to twine and tangle
【綢緞】 a general name of silk goods
【綢緞莊】 a mercery

維 3063
ㄨㄟˊ wéi
1. to tie; to hold fast; to secure 2. to maintain; to safeguard 3. to unite; to hold together 4. long and slender—as fibers 5. an initial particle—only, but, etc. 6. a pattern or rule
【維妙維肖】 so skillfully imitated as to be indistinguishable from the original; remarkably true to life
【維他命 or 維生素】 vitamins
【維那斯 or 維納斯】 Venus
【維護】 to safeguard; to preserve; to uphold
【維繫】 to maintain; to keep
【維修】 to keep in (good) repair; to service; to maintain
【維持】 to maintain; to keep; to guard and support; to sustain; to preserve
【維持秩序】 to keep order
【維持治安】 to maintain public order
【維也納】 Vienna

綱 3064
ㄍㄤ gāng
1. the large rope of a net, round which it is netted, and by which it is drawn 2. main points; an outline 3. a principle; discipline
【綱領】 an outline
【綱紀】 ① a principle; discipline; law; order ② a manager; a magistrate
【綱要】 main points; an outline

網 3065
ㄨㄤˇ wǎng
1. a net; a network; a web 2. (figuratively) the dragnet; the

arms of law 3. to bring together; to collect
【網膜】a retina
【網路】a network
【網羅】to bring together; to collect
【網開一面】to leave one side of the net open—to give a wrongdoer a way out
【網球】tennis
【網球拍】a racket (for playing tennis)
【網球場】a tennis court
【網子】a net

綴 3066
ㄓㄨㄟˋ zhuì
1. to put together; to combine; to compose 2. to mend clothes; to patch up; to sew; to stitch 3. to decorate; to stud
【綴補】to patch up (clothes)

綵 3067
ㄘㄞˇ cǎi
1. varicolored silk; a silk festoon 2. motley; varicolored
【綵轎】a gaily decorated sedan chair
【綵球】a ball wound up from varicolored silk

綺 3068
ㄑㄧˇ qǐ
1. beautiful; magnificent; fine; fair; gorgeous; resplendent; elegant 2. twilled silk cloth
【綺年玉貌】(said of a girl) young and beautiful enchanting
【綺麗】beautiful; fair; resplendent;

綽 3069
ㄔㄨㄛˋ chuò
1. spacious; roomy 2. delicate
【綽號or綽名】a nickname; a sobriquet
【綽綽有餘】① There is enough room to spare. ② generous feeling
【綽約多姿】charmingly delicate

綾 3070
ㄌㄧㄥˊ líng
very fine silk cloth; damask silk
【綾羅】silk gauze

綿 3071
(緜) ㄇㄧㄢˊ mián
1. cotton 2. everlasting; endless 3. weak
【綿薄】(a polite expression) my feeble strength, limited power, or poor abilities
【綿綿不絕】to last forever
【綿亙】to stretch in an unbroken chain
【綿延】to stretch over a long distance
【綿羊】sheep

緊 3072
ㄐㄧㄣˇ jǐn
1. tight; firm; fast; secure; taut; tense; close 2. urgent; critical; pressing
【緊繃】to stretch taut
【緊逼】① to press hard; to close in on ② (basketball) press
【緊迫】urgent; pressing
【緊密】① rigidly precise; rigorous ② compact and orderly ③ to close together ④ rapid and intense
【緊鄰】a close neighbor
【緊急】urgent; critical
【緊接著】to follow close behind
【緊緊】tightly; firmly; closely
【緊張】nervous; taut; tight; tension
【緊湊】① compact ② (said of an entertainment program, a show, a composition, etc.) one climax after another
【緊縮】to retrench; to curtail
【緊要關頭】a critical moment
【緊握】to grasp firmly

緋 3073
ㄈㄟ fēi
as in 緋紅—scarlet; crimson
【緋聞】sexy news 亦作「桃色新聞」

綫 3074
(線) ㄒㄧㄢˋ xiàn
1. a line 2. threads
【綫索】a clue

九畫

緒 3075
ㄒㄩˋ xù
1. the end of a thread or string 2. a clue 3. a beginning 4. a task; an enterprise 5. mood 6. remnants; remains; leftovers
【緒論】a preface; a foreword; an introduction

緘 3076
ㄐㄧㄢ jiān
1. to seal; to close 2. a letter
【緘默】to keep silence

線 3077
(綫) ㄒㄧㄢˋ xiàn
1. a line 2. threads 3. wires
【線民】a stool pigeon; an informer
【線條】lines; streaks

【線路】① (electricity) a circuit ② a narrow path
【線圈】a coil
【線裝本 or 線裝書】a book bound in the traditional Chinese style
【線索】a clue; a lead

〔糸部〕

緞 3078
ㄉㄨㄢˋ duàn
satin
【緞帶】a satin ribbon

緝 3079
1. ㄑㄧˋ qì
1. to arrest; to capture 2. to twist and join (cords) 3. to continue 4. to hem clothing
【緝捕】to search and arrest; to capture
【緝獲】to arrest; to capture; to seize
【緝私】to arrest smugglers

緝 3079
2. ㄑㄧ qī
to sew in close and straight stitches

締 3080
ㄉㄧˋ dì
to connect; to join; to unite
【締盟】to form an alliance
【締結】to conclude (treaties, agreements, etc.)
【締交】to establish diplomatic ties or friendship
【締造】to construct; to compose; to build; to found; to create

緣 3081
ㄩㄢˊ yuán
1. a cause; a reason 2. to go along; to follow 3. a hem; a margin; an edge; a fringe 4. relationship by fate; predestined relationship
【緣分】predestined relationship
【緣故 or 緣由】a cause; a reason
【緣起】① origins ② a preface

編 3082
ㄅㄧㄢ biān
1. to knit; to weave 2. to put together; to organize; to form; to arrange 3. to fabricate; to make up; to invent 4. to compile; to edit 5. a volume
【編排】① to arrange in order ② to write and present (a play, etc.)
【編派】to libel; to vilify
【編隊】formation (of aircrafts, etc.)
【編年史】chronicles; annals
【編列】to list (the expenses for a project in the budget); to compile
【編號】① to arrange under numbers; to number ② a serial number
【編輯】① to edit; to compile ② an editor
【編輯部】an editorial department; the editorial office
【編劇】① to write a play ② a playwright
【編寫】① to compile ② to compose
【編織】to knit
【編制】① organization ② to work out; to draw up
【編者】an editor
【編著 or 編撰】to edit; to compile
【編審】① to edit and screen (textbooks, etc.) ② a member of the editing and screening committee
【編入】① to include (in a budget) ② to enlist; to recruit
【編造】① to fabricate ② to prepare (a budget)
【編纂】to compile
【編譯】① to translate and compile ② a translator; an interpreter
【編舞】to choreograph

緩 3083
ㄏㄨㄢˇ huǎn
1. slow; gradual; tardy; leisurely; unhurried 2. to delay; to slacken; to put off; to postpone; to defer 3. to revive; to refresh
【緩兵之計】delaying tactics
【緩慢】slow
【緩和】① to subside; to relax; to alleviate ② calm; mild
【緩刑】① to suspend a sentence; to reprieve ② a reprieve; probation
【緩衝】to serve as a buffer; to buff
【緩議】to defer the discussion

緬 3084
ㄇㄧㄢˇ miǎn
1. distant; far; remote 2. to think of something or somebody in the past
【緬甸】Burma
【緬靦】shy; bashful
【緬懷】to think of; to remember

緯 3085
ㄨㄟˇ wěi
1. the woof 2. parallels showing latitude on a map
【緯度】degrees of latitude (in geography)

練 3086
ㄌㄧㄢˋ liàn
1. to practice; to train; to exercise 2. skilled; experienced 3. to soften and whiten raw silk by boiling
【練達】experienced; sophisticated
【練習】① to train; to practice (so as to gain skill) ② exercises
【練習生】a trainee; an apprentice

繞 3106
ㄖㄠˋ rào
1. to go around; to make a detour 2. to march round; to circle
【繞道or繞路】 to make a detour; to detour
【繞過】 to pass over a point by a detour
【繞口令兒】 a tongue twister
【繞圈子or繞圈兒】 ①to go round and round ②to talk in a roundabout way
【繞行】 ①to detour ②to orbit; to revolve around
【繞彎兒】 to take a stroll

繡 3107
(綉) ㄒㄧㄡˋ xiù
1. to embroider 2. embroidery
【繡花】① embroidery ② to embroider
【繡花鞋】 embroidered shoes
【繡球】 a ball of rolled silk

十三畫

繩 3108
ㄕㄥˊ shéng
1. a rope; a cord; a line 2. to restrain 3. to rectify; to correct
【繩梯】 a rope ladder
【繩之以法】 to prosecute according to the law
【繩子or繩索】 a rope; a line; a cord

繪 3109
ㄏㄨㄟˋ huì
to draw (pictures): 繪畫painting; drawing
【繪圖】 ① to draw pictures ② to prepare (engineering) drawings
【繪影繪聲 or 繪聲繪影】 to give a very vivid description

繮 3110
(韁) ㄐㄧㄤ jiāng
(又讀 ㄍㄤ gāng)
as in繮繩—reins; a bridle; a halter

繳 3111
ㄐㄧㄠˇ jiǎo
1. to surrender (articles); to submit 2. to pay (taxes, tuition, etc.)
【繳費】 to pay fees
【繳納】 to pay (taxes, tuition, etc.)
【繳款】 to make payments
【繳卷】 to hand in examination papers
【繳械or繳槍】 to disarm; to hand over weapons
【繳稅】 to pay taxes

繫 3112
1. ㄒㄧˋ xì
to connect; to link; to join
【繫念】 to feel concerned about

繫 3112
2. ㄐㄧˋ jì
to bind; to tie; to hang up

繭 3113
ㄐㄧㄢˇ jiǎn
1. cocoons; a chrysalis 2. a callus

十四畫

辮 3114
ㄅㄧㄢˋ biàn
a braid; a plait; a pigtail; a queue

纂 3115
ㄗㄨㄢˇ zuǎn
1. a kind of red cloth 2. to compile; to collect
【纂修】 to compile; to edit

繽 3116
ㄅㄧㄣ bīn
1. abundant; plentiful; thriving 2. disorderly; confused
【繽紛】 ①flourishing; thriving ②chaotic

繼 3117
ㄐㄧˋ jì
1. to continue; to carry on 2. then; afterwards 3. to follow; to inherit; to succeed to
【繼母】 a stepmother
【繼父】 a stepfather
【繼續】 to continue; to last; to go on
【繼承】 to inherit; to succeed to
【繼承人】 a successor; an heir
【繼任】 to succeed to an office
【繼則 or 繼而】 and then; next
【繼位】 to succeed to the throne

繾 3118
ㄑㄧㄢˇ qiǎn
as in 繾綣—entangled

十五畫

續 3119
ㄒㄩˋ xù
1. to continue; to extend; to renew 2. to add; to supply more
【續聘】 to continue to employ (a person)
【續訂】 to renew one's subscription
【續集】 the sequel (of a movie, etc.)
【續借】 to renew (a library book)
【續絃】 (said of a man) to remarry
【續約】 to renew a contract

纏 3120
ㄔㄢˊ chán

1. to wind round; to twine round; to bind; to wrap; to tangle 2. to bother persistently 3. to pester; to worry 4. to deal with
【纏綿】 affectionate; inseparable
【纏住】 entangled; to wrap tightly
【纏身】 to be delayed; to be held up by or burdened with something
【纏繞】 ① to wind round; to twine around ② to bother persistently

纍 3121 ㄌㄟˊ léi
1. strung together 2. a heavy rope 3. to tie; to bind; to twine around; to wind round
【纍纍】 ① strung together ② tired; exhausted ③ despondent

十七畫

纔 3122 ㄘㄞˊ cái
1. just now; just then 2. only 3. not until; for the first time; then and only then
【纔來】 to have just come or arrived

纖 3123 ㄒㄧㄢ xiān
tiny; minute; fine; delicate; slender
【纖細 or 纖小】 fine; tiny; minute
【纖瘦】 delicate and slender
【纖弱】 fragile; delicate
【纖腰】 a slender waist (of a woman)
【纖維】 fiber

二十一畫

纜 3124 ㄌㄢˇ lǎn (又讀 ㄌㄢˋ làn)
a hawser; a cable: 纜車 a cable car
【纜繩】 cordage; a thick rope

缶部 ㄈㄡˇ fǒu

三畫

缸 3125 ㄍㄤ gāng
a cistern; a crock

四畫

缺 3126 ㄑㄩㄝ quē
1. deficient; lacking; short; incomplete; defective 2. a vacancy; an opening
【缺乏 or 缺少】 to lack; to be short of
【缺德】 deficient in the sense of morality; mischievous
【缺德鬼】 a mean fellow
【缺點 or 缺憾】 a defect; a shortcoming; a flaw
【缺課】 to be absent from class
【缺貨】 (merchandise) to run out of stock
【缺席】 to be absent (from a meeting, etc.)
【缺陷】 a defect; a shortcoming; a handicap; inadequacy
【缺額】 vacancies waiting to be filled
【缺氧】 oxygen deficit

十一畫

罄 3127 ㄑㄧㄥˋ qìng
to exhaust; to use up; to empty

十二畫

罈 3128 (罎) ㄊㄢˊ tán
an earthenware jar or jug for wine

十四畫

罌 3129 ㄧㄥ yīng
a jar with a small mouth
【罌粟】 an opium poppy

十八畫

罐 3130 ㄍㄨㄢˋ guàn
a vessel; a container; a jar; a jug; a can
【罐頭】 canned goods

网部 ㄨㄤˇ wǎng

三畫

罔 3131 ㄨㄤˇ wǎng
1. to libel; to slander; to deceive 2. not

罕 3132
ㄏㄢˇ hǎn ⌈found; rare
rare; few; seldom: 罕見 rarely⌋
【罕事】a rare thing or event

六畫

罣 3133
ㄍㄨㄚˋ guà
1. hindrance; obstruction 2. a sieve 3. to be concerned; to be worried
【罣礙】hindrance; to block
【罣誤】to be remiss; to be at fault

八畫

罩 3134
ㄓㄠˋ zhào
1. a bamboo basket for catching fish 2. to coop; to cover; to wrap 3. a cover; a shade 4. a mantle; a cloak
【罩不住】(informal) unable to control a situation ⌈an overall
【罩袍】a dust-robe; a dust-gown;⌋

罪 3135
ㄗㄨㄟˋ zuì
1. sin; crime; fault; vice; evil; guilt 2. suffering; pain
【罪犯】a criminal; an offender
【罪大惡極】a heinous crime; a cap-
【罪孽】sin ⌊ital offense
【罪該萬死】The crime deserves death for ten thousand times.
【罪魁or罪魁禍首】a ringleader; a chief offender ⌈offenses
【罪行】criminal acts; atrocities;⌋
【罪證】proof of a crime; evidence of one's guilt ⌈blame others
【罪人】①a criminal; a sinner ②to⌋
【罪惡】sin; crime; vice; evil; guilt
【罪有應得】The punishment is well ⌊deserved.

置 3136
ㄓˋ zhì
1. to put; to place 2. to establish; to set 3. to procure; to purchase
【置信】to believe ⌈to ignore
【置之不理】to disregard it totally;⌋
【置之度外】to give no thought to
【置產】to buy an estate
【置身事外】to stay away from an
【置疑】doubt ⌊affair

九畫

罰 3137
ㄈㄚˊ fá
to punish; to penalize; to fine
【罰款】① a fine ② to fine
【罰金】to impose a fine; a fine

署 3138
1. ㄕㄨˇ shǔ
a public office

署 3138
2. ㄕㄨˋ shù
1. to arrange 2. to write down; to put down 3. to be a deputy
【署名】to sign one's name

十畫

罵 3139
ㄇㄚˋ mà ⌈to revile
to call names; to swear; to curse;⌋
【罵人】to call names; to scold

罷 3140
1. ㄅㄚˋ bà
to cease; to stop; to finish; to be done with ⌈people)
【罷免】to recall (officials by the⌋
【罷了】(as a sentence-final phrase) merely; only; that's all ⌈office
【罷官or罷職】to remove from⌋
【罷工】(said of workers) to strike
【罷課】to boycott classes
【罷休】to cease; to stop ⌈fire
【罷黜】to remove from office; to⌋
【罷手】to stop; to pause; to give up

罷 3140
2. ˙ㄅㄚ ba ⌈ticle
same as吧—a sentence-final par-⌋

罷 3140
3. ㄆㄧˊ pí ⌈weary
as in 罷弊 — tired; exhausted;⌋

十一畫

罹 3141
ㄌㄧˊ lí
1. sorrow; grief 2. to meet (disaster, misfortune, etc.); to be stricken by
【罹難】to fall victim to a disaster

十四畫

羅 3142
ㄌㄨㄛˊ luó
1. thin, light silk 2. a net; a snare 3. to arrange over a wide space 4. a Chinese family name

网部

【羅盤】a compass
【羅馬尼亞】Romania
【羅曼蒂克】romantic
【羅曼史】a romance; a love affair
【羅列】to arrange for display; to ⎱
【羅網】a net; a snare ⎣spread out ⎰

十九畫

羈 3143
ㄐㄧ jī
1. a bridle 2. to confine; to restrain; to bind 3. to lodge at another's house
【羈絆】to restrain; to confine
【羈留】① to detain (an offender) ② to stop over
【羈押】to take into custody

羊 部
ㄧㄤˊ yáng

羊 3144
ㄧㄤˊ yáng
a sheep; a goat
【羊毛】wool
【羊羣】a flock of sheep or goats
【羊腸小徑 or 羊腸小道】a narrow, winding path
【羊水】amniotic fluid
【羊肉】mutton
【羊入虎口】(literally) a sheep in a tiger's mouth—a hopelessly perilous situation

三畫

美 3145
ㄇㄟˇ měi
1. beautiful; pretty; fine; fair 2. good; excellent; exquisite; nice 3. to be pleased with oneself 4. to praise
【美不勝收】(said of landscape, etc.) too many beautiful or excellent things to be fully appreciated ⌈woman); beauty ⎱
【美貌】a beautiful face (of a ⎰
【美滿】(said of a life, home, etc.) happy; sweet ⌈dream ⎱
【美夢】a fond dream; a beautiful ⎰
【美妙】exquisite; very pleasant
【美名】high prestige; a good repu- ⎱
【美德】virtue ⎣tation ⎰
【美男子】a handsome man; an Adonis ⌈beauty ⎱
【美女】a beautiful woman; a ⎰
【美麗】beautiful; pretty; fair
【美輪美奐】splendid and magnifi- ⎱
【美感】the esthetic sense ⎣cent ⎰
【美國or美利堅or美利堅合衆國】the United States; the United States of America; America
【美觀】pleasant to the eye
【美觀大方】beautiful and dignified
【美工】① art designing ② an art ⎱
【美好】exquisite; fine ⎣designer ⎰
【美化】①to beautify ②Americanized ⌈dollar ⎱
【美金or美元】the (American) ⎰
【美洲】the Americas
【美中不足】a flaw that mars per- ⎱
【美術】the fine arts ⎣fection ⎰
【美術館】an art museum (or gal- ⎱
【美人】a beauty; a belle ⎣lery) ⎰
【美人魚】a mermaid
【美容】to apply make-up or undergo plastic surgery
【美容師】a beautician
【美容院】a beauty parlor
【美意】a kind intention; goodwill
【美言】① a fine saying ② commending remarks
【美味】delicious; tasty

四畫

羔 3146
ㄍㄠ gāo
as in 羔羊—a lamb

五畫

羚 3147
ㄌㄧㄥˊ líng
an antelope

羞 3148
ㄒㄧㄡ xiū
1. ashamed; abashed 2. shy; bashful 3. to disgrace; to insult; ⎱
【羞答答】shy; bashful ⎣to shame ⎰
【羞愧】mortified; disgraced
【羞怯】shy and nervous
【羞恥】a sense of shame ⌈grace ⎱
【羞辱】to shame; to insult; to dis- ⎰
【羞澀】①to act awkwardly because of shame ②to be short of
【羞於啓齒】too shy to speak out one's mind

七畫

羣 3149
(群) ㄑㄩㄣˊ qún
a group; a multitude; a host; a crowd; a swarm; a large number
【羣島】an archipelago
【羣龍無首】a multitude without a leader; leaderless
【羣居】to live as a group; gregarious
【羣衆】a crowd; a mob

羨 3150
ㄒㄧㄢˋ xiàn
as in 羨慕—to envy; to covet

義 3151
ㄧˋ yì
1. justice; righteousness 2. generosity; charity; philanthropy; chivalry 3. meaning; connotations 4. artificial; unreal; false 5. a Chinese family name
【義不容辭】Moral obligation prohibits declination of the call.
【義賣】a charity sale; a bazaar
【義母】a foster mother
【義父】a foster father
【義大利 or 意大利】Italy
【義大利脆餅】a pizza
【義女】a foster daughter
【義工】a volunteer worker
【義舉】an act of charity; a chivalrous deed
【義氣】① spirit of justice or righteousness ② loyalty to friends
【義肢】artificial limbs
【義士】a patriot; a freedom-seeker
【義子】a foster son
【義演】a charity performance (by entertainers); a charity show
【義無反顧】to pursue justice without ever turning back
【義務】duty; obligation
【義務教育】compulsory education

十畫

羲 3152
ㄒㄧ xī
Fu Hsi (伏羲), a legendary ruler who introduced houses

十三畫

羶 3153
(羴) ㄕㄢ shān
the odor of a sheep or goat

羹 3154
ㄍㄥ gēng
thick soup; broth

羸 3155
ㄌㄟˊ léi
1. lean; emaciated 2. weak; feeble 3. to entangle; to bind
【羸弱】emaciated and weak

羽部
ㄩˇ yǔ

羽 3156
ㄩˇ yǔ
1. feathers; plumes 2. wings of a bird 3. one of the five notes in the Chinese musical scale
【羽毛】feathers; plumes; down
【羽毛球】badminton
【羽翼】assistants; helpers

四畫

翁 3157
ㄨㄥ wēng
1. the father 2. the father-in-law 3. an old man 4. a title of respect 5. a Chinese family name
【翁姑】a woman's parents-in-law

翅 3158
ㄔˋ chì
1. as in 翅膀—wings 2. fins

五畫

翌 3159
ㄧˋ yì
as in 翌日—tomorrow

習 3160
ㄒㄧˊ xí
1. to learn; to familiarize oneself with; to receive training in 2. habit; custom; practice 3. to follow; to repeat
【習是成非】Through usage the wrong becomes the right.
【習題】problems to be worked out in the course of study; exercises
【習慣】habit; to be accustomed to
【習性】temperament; dispositions
【習作】to learn to do
【習俗】custom; practice
【習以爲常】having been accustomed to it

六畫

羽部

翔 3161
ㄒㄧㄤˊ xiáng
1. to soar 2. same as 詳—[detailed]

八畫

翠 3162
ㄘㄨㄟˋ cuì
1.bluish green 2.green jade 3. [a kingfisher]
【翠玉】emerald; blue jade

翡 3163
ㄈㄟˇ fěi
1. a kingfisher 2. emerald
【翡翠】①a kingfisher or halcyon ②emerald

九畫

翦 3164
ㄐㄧㄢˇ jiǎn
same as 剪—to trim; to clip; to cut with scissors

翩 3165
ㄆㄧㄢ piān
to fly swiftly
【翩翩】①to fly swiftly; to flutter ②(descriptive of movement) lightly and swiftly ③complacent ④elegant

翫 3166
ㄨㄢˋ wàn
1. careless or casual due to familiarity 2. to play
【翫味】appreciation

十畫

翰 3167
ㄏㄢˋ hàn
1. a white horse 2. a long and hard feather 3. a piece of writing

十一畫

翳 3168
ㄧˋ yì (又讀 ㄧ yī)
1. to screen; to conceal 2. the haziness of objects due to weakened vision 3. the chariot cover made of feathers 4. the film over a diseased eye

翼 3169
ㄧˋ yì
1. wings 2. fins 3. to assist; to help 4. to protect; to patronize

十二畫

翹 3170
1. ㄑㄧㄠˊ qiáo
1. long tail feathers 2. to raise 3. outstanding
【翹企 or 翹首】to long eagerly

翹 3170
2. ㄑㄧㄠˋ qiào
to project upward; to stick up; to turn upward
【翹辮子】to die

翻 3171
ㄈㄢ fān
1. to fly; to flutter 2. to turn; to upset; to capsize 3. to rummage 4. to translate 5. to fall out
【翻版】a reprint of a book (with or without proper permission)
【翻臉】to show displeasure; to get angry; to turn hostile
【翻臉無情】to turn against a friend and show him no mercy
【翻跟頭 or 翻筋斗 or 翻跟斗】① to turn a somersault ② (aeronautic) to loop the loop
【翻滾】to roll; to toss; to tumble
【翻供】to withdraw a confession; to retract a testimony (at a law court)
【翻開】to turn open
【翻修】to rebuild; to overhaul
【翻船】(said of a boat) to capsize
【翻山越嶺】to travel over mountains and valleys
【翻身】①to turn the body over ② to rise from poverty to affluence; to have a break of fortune
【翻然悔悟】quickly wake up to one's mistakes
【翻案】to reverse a previous verdict
【翻譯】to translate; to interpret
【翻印】to reprint (a book with or without proper permission)
【翻閱】to browse; to look over

翺 3172
(翱) ㄠˊ áo
1.to soar; to fly 2.to roam; to wander
【翺翔】① to soar; to fly ② to roam

十四畫

耀 3173
ㄧㄠˋ yào (又讀 ㄩㄝˋ yuè)
1.to shine; to dazzle 2.to show off
【耀眼】dazzling; to dazzle
【耀武揚威】①bluff and bluster; to show off one's strength or power ②to parade military prowess

老部
ㄌㄠˇ lǎo

老 3174 ㄌㄠˇ lǎo

1. old; aged 2. always 3. the youngest 4. very 5. a particle indicating ordinal numbers to designate order of birth 6. parents 7. a particle used before a man's family name to indicate familiarity and friendship 8. (said of meat, etc.) tough; overcooked 9. to treat with the reverence to the aged 10. (said of color) dark

【老百姓】the people; the common people
【老鴇】a procuress
【老板 or 老闆】① a boss; a master ② a keeper; a proprietor
【老板娘】①a proprietress; proprietor's wife ②boss's wife; a mistress
【老半天】quite a while
【老本】①a principal; a capital; the original investment ②an old edition
【老蚌生珠】a son born in one's old age
【老兵】an old soldier
【老不修】an old lecher
【老婆】(vulgar usage) wife
【老牌 or 老牌子 or 老牌兒】① an old brand ② a veteran (actor or actress)
【老鋪 or 老店】an old store
【老馬識途】experienced and capable of leading others wisely
【老毛病】① an old ailment ② an old weakness
【老謀深算】experienced and astute
【老命】① the life of an old person ② one's dear life
【老夫】①(used by an old man) I; me ② an old husband
【老夫老妻】an old couple
【老婦(人) or 老太婆】an old woman
【老搭檔】an old partner
【老大】① old ② the eldest child ③ the leader of a gang ④ extremely; exceedingly
【老大不小】to have come of age
【老當益壯】to gain vigor with age
【老爹】① one's father ② respectful address for an aged man
【老調重彈】to play the same old tune
【老掉牙】old-fashioned; outdated; obsolete
【老態龍鍾】the appearance of senility and dotage of the aged
【老太太】an old lady
【老太爺 or 老先生】①(in addressing an aged man) venerable sir ② an old gentleman
【老饕】a glutton
【老頭子】① an old chap; an old fellow ② one's husband
【老天爺】Heaven
【老年】old age; old life; late years
【老年(性)痴呆症】(pathology) senile dementia
【老娘】① one's old mother ② self-reference of a virago in a quarrel
【老淚縱橫】(said of an aged person) tearful
【老老or姥姥】① a midwife ② one's maternal grandmother
【老練】experienced; skilled; expert
【老哥or老兄】my dear friend (used among males)
【老古董】① antiques; curios ② an ultraconservative
【老規矩】old rules; old practices
【老公】① an old man ② one's husband
【老好人】a soft-hearted person
【老糊塗】a dotard
【老狐狸】①an old fox ②a cunning old man
【老虎】a tiger
【老花眼】presbyopia 亦作「老光」
【老家】①one's original home ② hell
【老交情】old friendship
【老舊】old-style; old-fashioned
【老奸巨猾】shrewd and crafty
【老氣】① an experienced air or style ② old-fashioned ③(said of colors) plain or dark
【老千】a swindler
【老前輩】a term used to address one's senior or an aged person
【老羞成怒】to be angry as a result of embarrassment
【老學究】an old pedant
【老帳】① old debts ② old scores
【老主顧】an old customer
【老成】sophisticated; experienced
【老處女】an old maid; a spinster
【老師】a teacher
【老實】honest; truthful
【老少咸宜】suitable for both the old and the young
【老手】an old hand

【老生常談】a cliché
【老鼠】a rat; a mouse
【老人】an old person
【老弱殘兵】①old and weak surviving soldiers ②incompetent workers
【老早】①very early ②long ago
【老祖宗】ancestors; forefathers
【老粗】a rude fellow; a boor
【老一輩】the older generation
【老爺】①sir ②an old man
【老么】①the youngest child of a family ②the youngest one in a group
【老油條】a sleeky fellow
【老友 or 老朋友】an old friend
【老眼昏花】the blurred vision of an old person
【老樣子】the way a thing or person used to look
【老鷹】the eagle
【老外】(slang) a foreigner
【老頑固】a stubborn person
【老遠】a very long way; very far

考 3175 (攷) ㄎㄠˇ kǎo

1. one's deceased father 2. to test; to examine 3. to check; to investigate; to study
【考妣】one's deceased father and mother
【考慮】to consider; to weigh; to think over
【考古】to study the life and culture of ancient people
【考覈or考核】to review or assess (a plan, proposal, etc.); to evaluate
【考績】to grade the service
【考究】①to examine and consider ②elaborate; beautiful ③tasteful; elegant; choosy; particular
【考據】to search for proofs (in textual research)
【考卷】an examination paper
【考區】an examination district
【考取 or 考中 or 考上】to pass an examination (for admission to employment, a school, etc.)
【考察】to inspect; to examine
【考場】an examination hall or site
【考試】an examination; a test; a quiz
【考生】an examinee
【考驗】①to test; to try ②a test; a trial
【考問】to examine and question; to examine orally

四畫

耆 3176 ㄑㄧˊ qí

to be in one's sixties; old
【耆年碩德】aged and virtuous
【耆碩or耆宿】a respected old person

五畫

耇 3177 ㄓㄜˇ zhě

1. those who; he who 2. a particle combining with some words to form adverbials

而部 ㄦˊ ér

而 3178 ㄦˊ ér

1. accordingly; otherwise 2. and yet; but; nevertheless 3. you 4. on the condition that; supposing that; if 5. and; also
【而後】then; afterwards; later; thenceforward; thereafter
【而今】now
【而且】①and ②moreover; furthermore; besides
【而已】merely; only; and that is all

三畫

耐 3179 ㄋㄞˋ nài

to bear; to endure; to stand; to resist
【耐磨】(said of metals) wearproof
【耐力】endurance; staying power; stamina
【耐久】lasting a long time; durable
【耐心 or 耐性】patience; perseverance
【耐熱】heat-proof
【耐人尋味】intriguing; perplexing
【耐用】durable; sturdy

耍 3180 ㄕㄨㄚˇ shuǎ

to play; to sport
【耍把戲】to juggle; to play tricks
【耍脾氣】to lose one's temper
【耍大牌】to act like a prima donna
【耍流氓】to behave like a hooligan; to act rudely
【耍弄】to make a fool of; to deceive
【耍花招兒】①to show off some

special skill ② to play tricks
【耍嘴皮子】to brag; to talk big
【耍(無)賴】to be perverse
【耍威風】to throw one's weight about; to be overbearing

耒部
ㄌㄟ lei

四畫

耙 3181
ㄆㄚˊ pá（又讀 ㄅㄚˋ bà）
1. a harrow; a drag 2. to rake

耕 3182
ㄍㄥ gēng
（語音 ㄐㄧㄥ jīng）
to till; to plough; to cultivate
【耕地】①cultivated land ②to till land
【耕田】to till land
【耕種】① to plough and sow; to cultivate ②cultivation
【耕作】to cultivate land and grow crops
【耕耘】to till and weed; to cultivate
【耕耘機】a power tiller

耘 3183
ㄩㄣˊ yún
to weed

耗 3184
ㄏㄠˋ hào
1. to expend; to use up; to waste; to squander; to consume 2. news; a report
【耗費】to expend; to squander
【耗盡】to exhaust; to use up
【耗子】a mouse; a rat
【耗損】to diminish by expending

耳部
ㄦˇ er

耳 3185
ㄦˇ ěr
1. ears 2. (a phrase-final particle) only; merely
【耳鬢廝磨】(usually said of childhood lovers) very intimate
【耳鳴】buzzing in the ears; tinnitus aurium
【耳目】① ears and eyes ② one's attention or notice ③ an informer
【耳目衆多】There are many spies.
【耳目一新】to have a completely new impression
【耳朵】ears
【耳提面命】to give instructions earnestly
【耳聾】deaf
【耳光】a box on the ear
【耳環】earrings
【耳機】an earphone
【耳垂】an ear lobe; a lobule
【耳熟】much heard of
【耳熟能詳】so frequently heard about that it can be told (in detail or word by word)
【耳濡目染】thoroughly imbued with what one frequently hears and sees
【耳塞】an earplug
【耳挖子】an ear pick
【耳聞】① to hear ② what one hears about; hearsay
【耳語】to whisper into another's ear

三畫

耶 3186
1. ㄧㄝˊ yé
a phrase-final particle for a question

耶 3186
2. ㄧㄝ yē
transliteration of English names
【耶誕卡(片)】a Christmas card
【耶誕節】Christmas
【耶誕樹】a Christmas tree
【耶穌(基督)】Jesus (Christ)

四畫

耽 3187
ㄉㄢ dān
1. to indulge in; to be addicted to 2. delightful and enduring 3. (said of ears) large and drooping 4. negligent
【耽溺】to indulge in (evil ways)
【耽擱】① to stay; to stop over; a stopover ② to delay
【耽憂】to worry
【耽誤】to delay; to hold up

耿 3188
ㄍㄥˇ gěng
1. bright 2. upright; incorruptible 3. a Chinese family name
【耿耿於懷】to keep something anxiously in one's mind

〔耳部〕

【耿介】① magnificent ② upright; just; righteous
【耿直】 honest; upright

恥 3189
ㄔˇ chǐ
same as 恥—shame

五畫

聆 3190
ㄌㄧㄥˊ líng
to listen; to hear: 聆聽 to listen to

聊 3191
ㄌㄧㄠˊ liáo
1. somehow; somewhat; a little 2. to rely; to depend 3. as in 聊天—to chat; a chat 4. interest 5. for the time being
【聊勝一籌】 to surpass only a little bit
【聊勝於無】 It's better than nothing.
【聊以自慰】 just to console oneself

六畫

聒 3192
ㄍㄨㄚ guā
clamorous; uproarious
【聒聒叫】 very good; wonderful; excellent
【聒噪】 to be uproarious; to be noisy

七畫

聖 3193
ㄕㄥˋ shèng
1. a sage 2. sacred; holy
【聖誕老人】 Santa Claus
【聖誕卡】 a Christmas card
【聖誕紅】 a poinsettia
【聖誕節】 Christmastide; Christmastime
【聖誕樹】 a Christmas tree
【聖地】 a holy ground
【聖徒】 an apostle; a saint
【聖潔】 holy and immaculate
【聖經】 the Bible
【聖賢】 sages and virtuous men; saints
【聖旨】 an imperial decree
【聖上】 His Majesty
【聖人】 a sage; a saint

聘 3194
ㄆㄧㄣˋ pìn
1. to invite for service; to employ; to engage 2. to be betrothed; to be engaged 3. to pay respect by sending an envoy 4. to ask; to inquire
【聘金】 money paid at a betrothal
【聘請】 to engage; to appoint
【聘書】 the letter of appointment
【聘用】 to employ; to engage

八畫

聚 3195
ㄐㄩˋ jù
to come or put together; to gather; to assemble; to collect
【聚賭】 to assemble for gambling
【聚落】 a village; a town
【聚會】 to assemble; to gather
【聚積】 to accumulate
【聚集or聚攏】 to gather; to assemble
【聚精會神】 to concentrate oneself
【聚居】 to live together
【聚沙成塔】 Accumulation of small amounts results in a huge quantity.
【聚首】 to get together; to meet
【聚餐】 to get together for luncheon or dinner

聞 3196
1. ㄨㄣˊ wén
1. to hear; to have heard 2. to learn; learning; to understand 3. to convey, forward or transmit (a message, etc.) 4. to smell 5. to make known 6. a Chinese family name
【聞名】 ① famous; distinguished ② to hear of someone's name
【聞名天下】 world-famous; known far and wide
【聞風響應】 to hear the news and rise up in response
【聞風喪膽】 to become terror-stricken at the news
【聞風而起】 to rise up on hearing the news
【聞訊】 to hear of the message

聞 3196
2. ㄨㄣˋ wèn
reputation
【聞達】 eminent; famous and influential

十一畫

聯 3197
ㄌㄧㄢˊ lián
1. to unite; to ally; to connect; to join; to make an alliance with

2. allied (forces, etc.); joint (effort, etc.); mutual (guaranties, etc.) 3. a couplet
【聯播】a radio hookup
【聯邦】a federal union; a federal state
【聯盟】an alliance; a union; to form an alliance, etc.
【聯名】to sign together
【聯絡】to communicate with; to contact
【聯貫】to link or string together; connection
【聯合】to unite; to form an alliance of some kind; joint (effort, etc.)
【聯合國】United Nations
【聯合聲明】a joint statement or declaration
【聯歡會】a get-together; a social gathering; a gay party
【聯結】to join together or gang up
【聯軍】allied forces
【聯繫】①to unite; to link; to relate ②to get in touch with
【聯想】association of ideas; to associate
【聯手】to join hands (with someone); to gang up
【聯署】to sign jointly
【聯誼(活動)】activities for promoting fellowship
【聯姻】connections through marriage
【聯營】(said of two or more business setups) joint operation; a pool

聰 3198 ㄘㄨㄥ cōng
1. clever; astute; bright; quick of apprehension 2. with a good faculty of hearing
【聰明】①clever; bright; intelligent ②sharp hearing and seeing faculties
【聰明絕頂】extremely clever or intelligent
【聰穎】clever and bright

聲 3199 ㄕㄥ shēng
1. sound; voice; a tone 2. music 3. language; a tongue 4. reputation; fame 5. to make known
【聲名狼藉】a notorious reputation
【聲明】to announce; to declare
【聲東擊西】(literally) to make noise in the east while striking in the west—feigning tactics
【聲討】to condemn or attack (a rebel, traitor, etc.) by words
【聲淚俱下】to cry while speaking
【聲響】① sound; noise ② reputation
【聲張】to make known; to announce
【聲稱】to assert; to declare
【聲勢浩大】an impressive display of power or influence
【聲嘶力竭】The voice gets husky as a result of exhaustion.
【聲音】a sound; a voice
【聲望】fame; reputation; prestige
【聲樂】vocal music
【聲樂家】a vocalist
【聲援】to give moral support

聳 3200 ㄙㄨㄥˇ sǒng
1. to alarm; to alert; to warn; to be sensational 2. to rise up; to stretch up erect or at full length 3. to be born deaf 4. to urge; to egg on
【聳動】①to urge; to egg on②to be moved or alarmed
【聳立】to tower aloft; to rise up steeply
【聳肩】to shrug shoulders
【聳然】cliffy; rising in sharp elevation
【聳恿】to urge; to egg on

十二畫

職 3201 ㄓˊ zhí
1. a profession or a vocation; a career 2. a post; a position 3. an office; official duties 4. to govern; to direct; to manage 5. used in place of "I" in documents to a superior 6. only; particularly
【職等】official rank; grade of position
【職守】one's official duties, charge, etc.
【職責】one's position and responsibility; charge
【職業】a profession; a vocation; an occupation
【職業婦女】career women
【職業介紹所】an employment agency
【職業學校】a vocational school
【職業訓練】vocational training
【職業專科學校】a vocational junior college
【職務】one's official duties or obligations
【職位】one's office; one's position in an office
【職員】staff members or employees of a company, office, etc.

〔聿・肉部〕

十六畫

聽 3202
1. ㄊㄧㄥ tīng

1. to hear; to listen 2. to obey; to follow 3. to wait for 4. a hall
【聽命】 to follow orders
【聽筒】 a telephone receiver
【聽課】 to attend class teaching or lectures
【聽候】 to wait for
【聽話】 ① to obey; obedient ② to wait for word or a reply
【聽見】 to hear
【聽覺】 hearing; the sense of hearing
【聽取】 to listen (with due attention); to hear (a report)
【聽戲】 to see an operatic show
【聽信】 ① to listen to and believe (what others said) ② to wait for news, messages, information, etc.
【聽診器】 a stethoscope
【聽衆】 an audience; listeners
【聽說】 ① It is reported that.... 或 It is said that.... ② to obey
【聽從】 to listen to (another's advice, etc.); to listen and follow

聽 3202
2. ㄊㄧˋ tìng

1. to let 2. to comply with; to submit to 3. to manage; to govern; to rule 4. to judge and decide
【聽憑or聽任】 to let someone do whatever he likes
【聽天由命】 to resign oneself to fate
【聽其自然】 to let things take their course

聾 3203
ㄌㄨㄥˊ lóng

1. deaf; hard of hearing 2. deaf—stupid and ignorant
【聾子】 a deaf person
【聾啞學校】 a deaf-and-dumb school

聿 部
ㄩˋ yù

七畫

肄 3204
ㄧˋ yì

1. to study; to learn; to practice 2. to toil; to work hard 3. remnants; leftovers 4. fresh twigs
【肄業】 to learn; to study (at a certain school)

肆 3205
ㄙˋ sì

1. to let loose; to indulge in; to behave without restraint 2. a shop; a marketplace; a place to display goods 3. to exhibit; to display 4. to execute a criminal and expose his corpse in the market 5. to extend; to expand 6. to assault; to attack suddenly 7. to use to the utmost; to exhaust 8. an elaborate form of 四 (four) to prevent forgery
【肆虐】 ① to do damage unhinderedly ② reckless and oppressive rampant
【肆無忌憚】 indulgent and reckless

肅 3206
ㄙㄨˋ sù

1. respectful; reverential; to pay respects; to salute 2. solemn; serious; majestic; awe-inspiring 3. to usher in 4. neat and quiet 5. to withdraw; to shrink (as in cold weather, etc.) 6. a Chinese family name
【肅穆】 ① solemn ② peaceful
【肅立】 to stand upright as a mark of respect
【肅敬】 respectful
【肅靜】 ① a solemn silence ② peaceful
【肅清】 to wipe out or eliminate (rebels, etc.)
【肅然起敬】 great respect rising in one's heart

八畫

肇 3207
ㄓㄠˋ zhào

1. to begin; to start; to commence 2. to found; to devise 3. to incur (misfortune, etc.) 4. to adjust; to make right
【肇端】 the beginning; the start; to originate or initiate
【肇禍】 to incur or court misfortune
【肇始】 to begin
【肇事】 to stir up trouble or disturbances

肉 部
ㄖㄨˋ ròu

肉 3208 ㄖㄡ ròu (讀音 ㄖㄨ rù)
1. flesh 2. physical; carnal 3. meat of animals; meat or pulp of fruits, etc. 4. flesh and blood —dearest, as one's children 5. slow-motion
【肉搏】 hand-to-hand combat
【肉包子】 steamed dumplings stuffed with meat 「ransom
【肉票】 a hostage kidnapped for a }
【肉舖】 a butcher's shop
【肉麻】 a creepy feeling; disgusting
【肉體】 flesh and blood; physical
【肉塊】 chopped meat; meat chops
【肉醬】 meat pulp
【肉食】 to eat meat; meat-eating; carnivorous
【肉絲兒】 shredded meat 「pink }
【肉色】 flesh-colored; yellowish }
【肉鬆】 fried shredded meat; meat fluff 「naked eye }
【肉眼】 ①a layman's eyes ②the }
【肉丸子】 meatballs

二畫

肋 3209 ㄌㄟ lèi (讀音 ㄌㄜ lè)
the ribs; the sides
【肋骨】 the ribs

肌 3210 ㄐㄧ jī 「skin }
1. tissue; muscles; flesh 2. the }
【肌膚】 ①the skin and flesh ②the intimate relation between man }
【肌肉】 muscles ⌊and woman }

三畫

肖 3211 ㄒㄧㄠ xiào
to resemble; to be like; alike; }
【肖像】 a portrait ⌊similar }

肘 3212 ㄓㄡ zhǒu 「the elbow }
1. the elbow 2. to catch one by }
【肘子】 ① the upper part of a leg of pork ② the elbow

肚 3213 1. ㄉㄨ dù 「bowels }
the belly; the abdomen; the }
【肚皮 or 肚子】 the abdomen; the }
【肚皮舞】 a belly dance ⌊belly }
【肚量】 capacity for tolerance and forgiveness 「button }
【肚臍(眼)】 the navel; the belly }

肚 3213 2. ㄉㄨ dǔ
the stomach

肛 3214 ㄍㄤ gāng
the anus

肝 3215 ㄍㄢ gān
as in 肝臟—the liver
【肝病】 a liver ailment 「sincerity }
【肝膽相照】 to show the deepest }
【肝腸寸斷】 heartbroken; deep sorrow
【肝炎】 hepatitis
【肝癌】 cancer of the liver

四畫

股 3216 ㄍㄨ gǔ
1. the thigh; the haunches; the hips 2. a department; a section 3. shares; stock 4. a puff; a blast (of hot air) 5. a bunch or }
【股票】 stocks ⌊band (of bandits) }
【股票市場 or 股市】 the stock market
【股份 or 股分】 shares or stock
【股份有限公司】 a limited liability company 「holder }
【股東】 a shareholder or stock- }
【股權】 the ownership of a share or stock
【股長】 the head of a subdivision

肢 3217 ㄓ zhī
1. the four limbs of a person 2. the legs of an animal 3. the wings or feet of a bird
【肢體】 the body 「ment }
【肢解】 to dismember; dismember- }

肥 3218 ㄈㄟ féi
1. fat; plump; portly; obese; corpulent 2. fat (of meat) 3. sufficiency; affluence; plenty 4. fertile 5. to fertilize (land) 6. fertilizers 7. baggy
【肥胖】 fat; obese
【肥料】 fertilizers; manure
【肥缺】 a lucrative post
【肥壯】 husky
【肥碩】 big and corpulent (persons)

〔肉部〕

【肥肉】fat meat
【肥皂】soap
【肥皂粉】detergent powder
【肥皂水】suds; soapsuds
【肥沃】fertile (land)

肩 3219 ㄐㄧㄢ jiān
1. shoulders 2. to shoulder (responsibility, etc.); to sustain 3. to employ; to appoint
【肩膀】① the shoulder ② a sense of responsibility
【肩負】to take on; to undertake; to shoulder; to bear
【肩胛骨】the scapula

肪 3220 ㄈㄤˊ fáng (又讀 ㄈㄤ fāng)
fat

肯 3221 (同、肎) ㄎㄣˇ kěn (又讀 ㄎㄥˇ kěng)
to be willing; to approve of; to consent to; to permit; to agree
【肯定】affirmative; positive; sure; definite

育 3222 ㄩˋ yù
1. to produce; to give birth to; to breed 2. to raise; to bring up; to nourish; to nurse 3. to educate
【育種】breeding
【育幼院】a nursery school

肴 3223 ㄧㄠˊ yáo
cooked food, especially meat and fish; dishes
【肴饌】rich food; sumptuous dishes

五畫

肺 3224 ㄈㄟˋ fèi
as in 肺臟—the lungs
【肺部】lungs
【肺腑之言】words from the bottom of one's heart
【肺活量】vital capacity; lung capacity
【肺結核or肺癆】tuberculosis; consumption
【肺炎】pneumonia
【肺癌】lung cancer

胃 3225 ㄨㄟˋ wèi
the stomach; the gizzard (of birds and fowls)
【胃病】a stomach ailment
【胃痛】a stomach pain or ache
【胃口】appetite
【胃潰瘍】a gastric ulcer
【胃鏡】a gastroscope
【胃腸】the stomach and intestines
【胃液】gastric juice
【胃炎】gastritis
【胃癌】a gastric carcinoma

胄 3226 ㄓㄡˋ zhòu
1. descendants; posterity; offspring 2. the eldest (son, etc.)

背 3227 1. ㄅㄟˋ bèi
1. the back 2. the reverse side; the back side 3. to cast away; to turn one's back on; to give up 4. to go against; to rebel 5. to remember by rote; to commit to memory in detail 6. (now rarely) to faint; to lapse into a coma
【背包】a knapsack
【背部】the back (of a man or an animal, etc.)
【背叛】to rebel; to betray
【背面】the reverse side; the back side
【背風】on the lee side; leeward
【背負】to carry on the back
【背道而馳】to proceed in opposite directions
【背地裏】behind one's back; secretly
【背離】to deviate from; to depart from
【背後】behind one's back
【背景】background
【背棄】to renounce; to betray
【背心】a vest; a waistcoat
【背信】to break one's word or promise
【背書】① to recite a lesson ② to endorse a check ③ endorsement
【背誦】to recite
【背影】the sight of one's back
【背約】to break one's promise

背 3227 2. ㄅㄟ bēi
to bear or shoulder (a load, burden, etc.); to carry on the back
【背帶】suspenders
【背黑鍋】to take the blame for another person

胎 3228 ㄊㄞ tāi
1. a fetus; an embryo 2. an unpolished, semiprocessed molding of something

【胎盤】 the placenta
【胎記】 a birthmark
【胎死腹中】 (literally) death in the womb—(said of a plan, or operation) to fail or be discarded before it gets started; abortive
【胎兒】 a fetus; an unborn baby; an embryo
【胎位】 the position of a fetus

胖 3229
1. ㄆㄤˋ pàng
obese; fat; corpulent
【胖子】 a fat or corpulent person; a fatty

胖 3229
2. ㄆㄢˊ pán
comfortable

胚 3230
ㄆㄟ pēi
1. a three-month-old fetus; three months of pregnancy 2. things in the embryonic stage; unfinished moldings 3. the tender sprouts of plants
【胚胎】 ① the origination or beginning of things ② an embryo
【胚芽】 a sprout; to germinate

胞 3231
ㄅㄠ bāo
1. the placenta 2. children of the same parents

胡 3232
ㄏㄨˊ hú
1. to blunder; reckless; wildly; disorderly 2. stupidly; blindly; confusedly 3. (in ancient China) a general name of the northern tribes (北狄) 4. (an interrogative particle) How? 或Why? 或When? 5. (now rarely) long and lasting 6. a Chinese family name
【胡桃】 walnuts
【胡塗】 confused; muddleheaded; stupid
【胡同兒】 a lane 亦作「衚衕兒」
【胡鬧】 reckless, irresponsible words or actions
【胡來】 to proceed (with a matter, etc.) recklessly and without thought
【胡蘿蔔】 the carrot
【胡亂】 ① at random ② not choosy
【胡攪】 to cause confusion or a disturbance recklessly
【胡瓜】 a cucumber
【胡混】 to fool around
【胡椒】 pepper
【胡扯】 ①random talk ②wild talk; lies
【胡說】 Nonsense! 或wild talk; to talk nonsense
【胡說八道】 to talk nonsense; wild talk; lies
【胡謅】 wild talk; nonsensical talk; to invent (something false); to lie
【胡作非爲】 to bully others as if the law were nonexistent; to do as one pleases
【胡思亂想】 to daydream; to give one's thoughts free rein
【胡言亂語】 to talk nonsense; to gibber; lies or wild talk

胤 3233
ㄧㄣˋ yìn
long successions of descendants; posterity

六畫

胭 3234
(臙) ㄧㄢ yān
1. cosmetics, especially referring to rouge and face powder 2. the throat 亦作「咽」
【胭脂】 rouge

胯 3235
ㄎㄨㄚˋ kuà
space between the legs; the groin
【胯部】 the crotch

胰 3236
ㄧˊ yí
as in 胰臟: the pancreas

胱 3237
ㄍㄨㄤ guāng
the bladder

胴 3238
ㄉㄨㄥˋ dòng
1. the large intestine 2. as in 胴體: the trunk; the body

胸 3239
(胷) ㄒㄩㄥ xiōng
1. the chest; the breast; the bosom; the bust; the thorax 2. one's ambition or aspiration 3. the mind (as narrow-minded, etc.); one's capacity
【胸部】 the chest; the thorax
【胸膛】 the breast or bosom; the mind
【胸口】 the middle of the chest
【胸花】 a corsage
【胸懷】 ambition or aspiration; mind
【胸襟開闊】 broad-minded; large-minded
【胸針】 a brooch
【胸衣】 corsets
【胸有成竹】 to have had ready or well-thought-out plans or designs in one's mind (in coping with a

matter, situation, etc.)

能 3240 ㄋㄥˊ néng

1. can; to be able to 2. capability; talent; competence 3. energy, as atomic energy

【能不能 or 能否】can or can't; may or may not
【能耐】skill; ability; capability
【能力】① power, as the power of the Almighty, etc. ② a faculty; ability; capability
【能量】①(physics) energy ②capabilities
【能夠】able to; capable of; can; may
【能幹】capable; able; very competent and efficient
【能見度】visibility
【能屈能伸】adaptable; flexible
【能者多勞】The capable are usually the busy ones.
【能手】a capable or competent person; an expert
【能言善辯】eloquent and glib in argument
【能源】the sources of energy
【能源危機】the energy crisis

脂 3241 ㄓ zhī

1. the fat of animals; grease; lard; tallow 2. the gum or sap of trees; resin 3. to anoint; to grease; to lubricate 4. cosmetics

【脂粉】rouge and face powder—cosmetics
【脂粉氣】feminine; sissy
【脂肪】the fat of animals or plants

脆 3242 (脃) ㄘㄨㄟˋ cuì

1. brittle; fragile; hard but easily broken (as glass, porcelain, etc.) 2. crisp 3. light; shallow; thin 4. (said of the operation, etc. of something) easy, quick and convenient; neat

【脆弱】weak; fragile; delicate

脅 3243 ㄒㄧㄝˊ xié

1. the sides of the trunk from armpits to ribs; the flank 2. to threaten with force; to force 3. to shrug (shoulders); to shrink

【脅迫】to threaten with force; to coerce; coercion
【脅持】① to take somebody on both sides by the arms ② to hold somebody by violence
【脅從】to be forced to join (rebellion, banditry, etc.)

脈 3244 (衇、脉) ㄇㄛˋ mò (又讀 ㄇㄞˋ mài)

1. the blood vessels; the veins or arteries; the circulation system 2. the pulse 3. a mountain range 4. things that are related and form a system of some kind 5. stipules or stems of a leaf

【脈搏 or 脈息】the pulse; pulsation
【脈脈含情】(said of eyes) quietly sending the message of love
【脈絡】things that are related and form a system of their own

脊 3245 ㄐㄧˇ jǐ (又讀 ㄐㄧˊ jí)

1. the spine; the spinal column 2. the ridge

【脊梁】① the back 亦作「脊背」② (construction) a ridgepole
【脊椎】the vertebrae
【脊椎骨】a vertebra; the spine
【脊髓】the spinal cord

胳 3246 ㄍㄜ gē

the arms; the armpits 亦作「肐」

【胳臂】the upper arm
【胳肢窩】the armpit

七畫

脣 3247 (唇) ㄔㄨㄣˊ chún

the lips; the labia

【脣膏】lipstick
【脣紅齒白】red lips and white teeth—very handsome or beautiful
【脣槍舌劍】a heated verbal exchange or debate
【脣舌】① eloquence ② explanation

脫 3248 ㄊㄨㄛ tuō

1. to strip; to undress; to take off 2. to abandon; to renounce; to cast off 3. to leave; to escape from; to get out of 4. to omit; omission; to miss out 5. to slip off 6. if; in case; perhaps

【脫皮】①(said of some kinds of reptiles or insects) ecdyses; to molt ② to cast off the skin; to peel
【脫胎換骨】① to disembody (and become immortal) ② to change

〔肉部〕

oneself in side out

【脫逃】to escape from; to withdraw or run away

【脫離】① to break away ② away from; out of

【脫落】to drop; to fall off

【脫軌】to derail

【脫光】to strip nude

【脫口而出】to speak without thinking of the consequence

【脫節】① disconnected; irrelevant or incoherent ② luxation; to dislocate

【脫臼】dislocation (of the joints)

【脫韁野馬 or 脫韁之馬】(literally) an unbridled wild horse—forceful and unrestrained

【脫下】to take off

【脫鞋】to take off shoes

【脫卸】to relinquish or shirk (one's responsibility)

【脫險】to be out of danger

【脫手】①(said of goods or stock at hand) to sell out ②to slip off one's hands

【脫售】to sell out

【脫身】to get away from; to escape

【脫水】to dehydrate; dehydration

【脫水機】a hydroextractor; a whizzer

【脫罪】to exonerate someone from a charge

【脫衣舞】a striptease

【脫穎而出】(in a race, competition, etc.) to overtake others or outscore rival teams

脯 3249
1. ㄈㄨˇ fǔ

1. dried and seasoned meat 2. preserved fruits

脯 3249
2. ㄆㄨˊ pú

flesh or meat in the general area of the chest or breast

脖 3250
ㄅㄛˊ bó

the neck

脚 3251
(腳) ㄐㄧㄠˇ jiǎo

1. the foot or feet 2. the base or foundation of anything

八畫

脹 3252
ㄓㄤˋ zhàng

1. full-stomached; glutted 2. swelling of the skin, etc. 3. to expand; expansion

【脹氣】① inflated with air ② (medicine) flatulence

胼 3253
(胼) ㄆㄧㄢˊ pián

calluses

【胼胝or胼手胝足】calluses on the hands and feet—to toil or work hard

腋 3254
ㄧㄝˋ yè (讀音 ㄧˋ yì)

the armpits; the part under the forelegs of animals

【腋毛】armpit hair

【腋窩】the armpits

腌 3255
1. ㄤ āng (又讀 ㄚ ā)

as in 腌臢: unclean; dirty; filthy

腌 3255
2. (醃) ㄧㄢ yān

to salt; to pickle

腎 3256
ㄕㄣˋ shèn

1. the kidneys 2. the testicles

【腎臟】the kidneys

【腎臟病】a kidney ailment or disease

【腎臟結石 or 腎結石】(pathology) kidney stone; nephrolithiasis

腐 3257
ㄈㄨˇ fǔ

1. to decay; to rot; rotten; putrid; to disintegrate; stale 2. corrupt; evil 3. old; worn-out; useless or worthless 4. to castrate; castration (as a punishment in ancient China) 5. short for 豆腐—bean curd

【腐敗】①corrupt and rotten (practice, administration, etc.) ② putrid; decayed; to decay; to decompose

【腐爛】to rot or decay

【腐朽】decayed; rotten

【腐臭】decaying and with a bad odor or stench

【腐蝕】① to erode; erosion; to corrode; corrosion ②(chemistry) to etch; etching

【腐蝕劑】a corrodent

腑 3258
ㄈㄨˇ fǔ

the bowels; the entrails; the viscera

腔 3259
ㄑㄧㄤ qiāng

1. the cavity—especially referring to the chest and belly 2. a cavity in any vessel 3. a tune 4. an accent of one's pronuncia-

tion; a tone of one's voice 5. a manner

【腔調】①a tune; the melody of a tune ②an accent ③a manner or style of behavior

腕 3260 ㄨㄢˇ wǎn

the wrist

脾 3261 ㄆㄧˊ pí

1. the spleen 2. a temper; a disposition

【脾臟】the spleen

【脾胃】① the stomach ② appetite ③one's temperament or natural inclination

腊 3262 1. ㄒㄧˊ xí

1. dried meat 2. very; extremely

腊 3262 2. ㄌㄚˋ là

an abbreviated form of 臘

【腊梅】plum flowers

九畫

腥 3263 ㄒㄧㄥ xīng

1. raw, undressed meat 2. an offensive smell, especially of fish or blood

【腥風血雨】(literally) winds carrying an offensive smell of flesh and rain of blood—the carnage of war

【腥味兒】an offensive smell of fish, etc.

腦 3264 ㄋㄠˇ nǎo

the brain

【腦袋】the head

【腦海】the mind

【腦筋】brains; mentality; mental capacity

【腦震盪】brain concussion

【腦中風】(pathology) stroke

【腦神經】cranial nerves

【腦子】①the brain ②mental capability

【腦溢血】a stroke; apoplexy

【腦炎】encephalitis

腫 3265 ㄓㄨㄥˇ zhǒng

to swell; a swelling; a boil

【腫瘤】(medicine) a tumor

【腫脹】to swell; swelling

腰 3266 ㄧㄠ yāo

1. the midriff; the waist 2. the kidneys 3. the middle of something; the waist portion of a region

【腰包】① a purse; a billfold; a wallet ②one's money

【腰部】the waist

【腰帶】① a girdle; a waistband ② (anatomy) a pelvic girdle

【腰果】a cashew nut

【腰纏萬貫】very rich; loaded

【腰酸背疼】a sore waist and an aching back

【腰圍】①the waist; the waistline ②a girdle

腳 3267 (脚) ㄐㄧㄠˇ jiǎo (讀音 ㄐㄩㄝˊ jué)

1. the feet 2. the leg or base of something

【腳本】the script of a play, an opera, etc.

【腳步】steps; paces; strides; footsteps

【腳夫】a porter or coolie

【腳踏板】① a footboard ② a pedal

【腳踏車】a bicycle

【腳踏實地】to do a job honestly and with dedication

【腳後跟 or 腳跟】① the heel of the foot ②(figuratively) foothold

【腳指頭】toes

【腳指甲】toenails

【腳掌】the sole (of the foot)

【腳色】① a character; a role ② personal background of examinees under the old civil service examination system ③ a talented or resourceful person

【腳印兒】footprints; footmarks; footsteps

腴 3268 ㄩˊ yú

1. fat 2. plump and soft 3. fertile 4. intestines of dogs and hogs 5. rich

腸 3269 ㄔㄤˊ cháng

the intestines; the bowels

【腸子】the intestines

【腸炎】intestinal or bowel catarrh; enteritis

【腸癌】bowel cancer

【腸胃】intestines and the stomach

腹 3270 ㄈㄨˋ fù

1. the belly; under the chest; the abdomen 2. the front part 3. the inside; inner

【腹背受敵】to be attacked from front and rear

【腹部】the abdomen; the belly

【腹地】a hinterland; the interior

【腹痛】bellyache

【腹稿】(literally) a manuscript in the mind — a rough plan or sketch not yet put down in black and white
【腹瀉】diarrhea
【腹議】to criticize in one's mind
【腹語】ventriloquy, or ventriloquism

腺 3271
ㄒㄧㄢˋ xiàn
as in 腺體: a gland

腼 3272
(覥)ㄇㄧㄢˇ miǎn
1. shy; bashful 2. (said of girls) quiet and graceful
【腼腆】bashful; shy

腮 3273
(顋) ㄙㄞ sāi
the cheeks
【腮幫子】(colloquial) the cheek

十畫

腿 3274
ㄊㄨㄟˇ tuǐ
the legs and the thighs

膀 3275
1. ㄅㄤˇ bǎng
the upper arms
【膀臂】① the arms ② capable aides

膀 3275
2. ㄆㄤˊ páng
the bladder
【膀胱】the bladder
【膀胱結石】a calculus of the bladder
【膀胱炎】cystitis

膀 3275
3. ㄅㄤ bāng
to make passes at (used in the phrase 弔膀子)

膏 3276
1. ㄍㄠ gāo
1. fat; grease 2. ointment 3. fertile 4. the region just below the heart 5. grace; favors 6. sweet 7. (Chinese medicine) a paste-like preparation for external use 8. plaster 9. (food and fruit) cooked to a very thick or pasty form
【膏藥】① medicated plaster attached to pieces of cloth or paper ② propaganda
【膏腴之地】fertile land

膏 3276
2. ㄍㄠˋ gào
1. to lubricate; to grease; to make smooth or glossy 2. to enrich; to freshen

膊 3277
ㄅㄛˊ bó
the shoulders; the upper arms

十一畫

膚 3278
ㄈㄨ fū
1. the skin; the surface 2. skin-deep; shallow; superficial 3. (now rarely) great, as achievements or merit
【膚淺】shallow or superficial (views, etc.)
【膚色】color of the skin

膜 3279
1. ㄇㄛˋ mò
(又讀 ㄇㄛˊ mó)
1. membrane 2. a film; a thin coating

膜 3279
2. ㄇㄛˊ mó
as in 膜拜: to kneel and worship

膝 3280
ㄒㄧ xī
the knee
【膝蓋】the knee
【膝下承歡】to please one's parents by living with them

膠 3281
ㄐㄧㄠ jiāo
1. glue; gum 2. resin; sap 3. anything sticky 4. rubber; plastics 5. to stick on or together; to adhere 6. stubborn; obstinate
【膠布】rubber cloth; plastic cloth
【膠片】film
【膠帶】an adhesive tape
【膠囊】a medical capsule
【膠捲兒】unexposed film
【膠鞋】rubber shoes; galoshes
【膠著】stalemated; at a stalemate; at a standstill
【膠水】glue; size

膛 3282
ㄊㄤˊ táng
1. the breast; the chest 2. a cavity 3. the chamber of a firearm

十二畫

膨 3283
ㄆㄥˊ péng
to expand; to swell; to inflate
【膨脹】inflation; bloated; to swell

膩 3284
ㄋㄧˋ nì
1. fatty or greasy (food) 2.

〔肉部〕

smooth 3. dirty 4. bored; tired; weary 5. intimate (friends)
【膩人】① boring; tiresome ② too greasy
【膩友】bosom friends

〔肉部〕

膳 3285
(饍) ㄕㄢˋ shàn
meals; food; provisions
【膳食】meat; victuals
【膳宿】food and lodging
【膳宿費】boarding charges

十三畫

膿 3286
ㄋㄨㄥˊ nóng
pus or purulent matter
【膿包】①a pustule; an abscess②a good-for-nothing; a useless person
【膿腫】purulent swellings
【膿瘡】an abscess; a boil

膽 3287
(胆) ㄉㄢˇ dǎn
1. the gall 2. courage; bravery; audacity 3. the internal parts, etc. of a vessel 4. the tube of a tire, basketball, etc.
【膽大包天】recklessly bold; extremely audacious
【膽大妄爲】audacious and reckless
【膽量】courage; bravery; guts
【膽敢】so audacious as to; to dare
【膽固醇】cholesterol; cholesterin
【膽怯】frightened; afraid; fainthearted
【膽小】timid; cowardly
【膽小鬼】a coward
【膽小如鼠】as scared as a mouse
【膽汁】bile
【膽戰心驚】to tremble with fear
【膽石】a gallstone
【膽識】courage and wisdom
【膽子】courage; bravery; audacity; nerve

膾 3288
ㄎㄨㄞˋ kuài
minced meat
【膾炙人口】(said of interesting things, good writings, etc.) to be talked about by everyone

膺 3289
ㄧㄥ yīng
1. the breast of a person 2. (now rarely) a belt across the breast of a horse 3. to receive; to be given (a responsibility, etc.); to undertake; to shoulder; to bear; to sustain 4. (now rarely) to punish (the enemy, etc.) by war
【膺選】to be elected
【膺任】to be appointed to or given (an office, etc.)

臀 3290
ㄊㄨㄣˊ tún
1. the buttocks; the behind; the bottom; the rump 2. (now rarely) the bottom of a ware or vessel
【臀部】the buttocks; the bottom; the rump

臂 3291
ㄅㄧˋ bì (又讀 ㄅㄟˋ bèi)
the arms (of a human being or a tool, machine, etc.)
【臂膀】the arm
【臂章】an arm badge; a brassard

臃 3292
ㄩㄥˇ yǒng
(又讀 ㄩㄥ yōng)
1. to swell; a swelling 2. fat and clumsy
【臃腫】fat and clumsy

臆 3293
ㄧˋ yì
1. one's breast, heart, thoughts, etc. 2. one's personal views or feelings
【臆度or臆測】to guess or conjecture; speculation
【臆斷】an arbitrary judgment

臉 3294
ㄌㄧㄢˇ liǎn
the face (used both in its physical and figurative senses)
【臉盆】a washing basin
【臉皮厚】shameless; brazen
【臉蛋兒】the shape of a woman's face
【臉孔】the face
【臉紅】a blush; to blush
【臉頰】cheeks
【臉色】① facial expression ② a complexion

臊 3295
1. ㄙㄠ sāo
a bad odor or smell, as that of decaying fish, meat, fox, sheep, etc.

臊 3295
2. ㄙㄠˋ sào
1. ashamed; bashful 2. minced meat

臌 3296
ㄍㄨˇ gǔ
to expand; to swell; swollen
【臌脹】① expansion; to swell ② dropsy

十四畫

臍 3297 ㄑㄧˊ qí
1. the navel; the umbilicus 2. the underside of a crab
【臍帶】the umbilical cord

十五畫

臘 3298 ㄌㄚˋ là
1. sacrifice at the end of the lunar year 2. the end of the lunar year 3. salted and smoked meat, fish, chicken, etc. 4. the age of a Buddhist monk
【臘梅】plum flowers
【臘腸狗】a dachshund
【臘肉】salted and dried meat
【臘味】preserved meat
【臘月】the 12th moon of the lunar year

十八畫

臟 3299 ㄗㄤˋ zàng
a general name of all the internal organs in the chest and abdomen; the viscera
【臟腑】① viscera; entrails ② one's integrity, aspirations, etc.

臣部 ㄔㄣˊ chén

臣 3300 ㄔㄣˊ chén
1. a subject; a vassal 2. to subjugate; to conquer 3. a term for "I" used by officials when addressing the king or emperor 4. (in ancient China) a polite term for "I" 5. a minister; an official; a statesman
【臣民】subjects of a kingdom
【臣服】① to be conquered or subjugated ② to serve a king or emperor as his minister
【臣僚】officials in a monarchy
【臣妾】concubines; female attendants in ancient China
【臣子】a minister of state; officials

二畫

臥 3301 ㄨㄛˋ wò
1. to lie down; to rest; to sleep 2. to lay or place across; to lie across
【臥病】bedridden on account of illness
【臥鋪】a sleeping berth on a train or ship
【臥房】a bedroom
【臥倒】to lie down (on the ground to escape enemy fire or detection)
【臥底】(said of thieves, etc.) to act as a stool pigeon

十一畫

臨 3302 ㄌㄧㄣˊ lín
1. to look down from above—preside over 2. to approach; to descend; to come to; to reach; to visit 3. on the point of; near to; during; at; whilst; while 4. to copy; to imitate 5. temporary; provisional 6. a Chinese family name
【臨別】at the time of parting; on departure
【臨盆】parturition; childbirth
【臨摹】to copy or imitate (paintings or calligraphy)
【臨機應變】to make changes or adjustments as the situation demands
【臨近】close by; close to; close on
【臨行or臨走】on the point of departure
【臨陣磨鎗】to make preparations at the last moment
【臨陣脫逃】to absent oneself when one's presence counts
【臨終or臨死】at one's deathbed; just before dying
【臨牀】clinical
【臨時】for the time being; temporary; provisional
【臨時抱佛脚】to do something too late and without preparation
【臨時工】a short-term worker
【臨時演員】an extra
【臨危授命】to give a very important assignment in time of a national emergency

自部 ㄗˋ zì

〔自部〕

自 3303 ㄗˋ zì

1. self; personal; private; in person; personally 2. from 3. natural; naturally 4. a Chinese family name

【自白】confession
【自白書】an affidavit
【自卑】to underestimate oneself
【自卑感】a sense of inferiority
【自備】self-provided
【自暴自棄】to abandon oneself to a dissipated life
【自閉症】(psychiatry) autism
【自不量力】to do something beyond one's ability
【自滿】complacency; to be satisfied with oneself
【自鳴得意】smug
【自鳴清高】to consider oneself morally superior to others
【自命不凡 or 自負】conceited
【自費】to pay one's own expenses
【自焚】to burn oneself to death—self-immolation
【自大】conceited; egomaniacal; egotistic
【自得其樂】to find joy in one's own way (no matter what others may think)
【自動】① voluntary; of one's own free will ② automatic
【自動販賣機】a vending machine
【自動提款機】a cashomat
【自動化】automation; to automate
【自討沒趣】"You ask for it!"—to get an insult unnecessarily
【自討苦吃】to ask for trouble
【自投羅網】to walk right into a trap
【自歎不如】to admit with regret that one is not as good
【自來水】running water; tap water
【自來水廠】a waterworks
【自立】independent; self-supporting
【自立門戶】to establish one's own school of thought or clique
【自力更生】to achieve self-renewal with one's own effort; self-reliance
【自戀】narcissism
【自告奮勇】to volunteer
【自甘墮落】to abandon oneself to wanton ways
【自耕農】owner-farmers
【自古以來】since ancient times
【自顧不暇】to have trouble even in taking care of oneself
【自誇】to brag; to boast
【自豪】to feel proud of; to take pride in
【自後 or 自今】from now on
【自畫像】a self-portrait
【自己】self; oneself; one's person
【自己人 or 自家人】persons closely related with each other
【自給自足】self-sufficient
【自盡】to commit suicide; to kill oneself
【自居】to consider oneself to be (a genius, VIP, famous figure, etc.)
【自覺】① to feel something concerning oneself; aware ② self-consciousness
【自欺欺人】to deceive oneself and others as well
【自取滅亡】to take the road to one's doom
【自取其辱】to ask for an insult
【自習 or 自修】to learn and practice by oneself
【自新】to make a new person out of oneself; self-renewal
【自信】self-confidence
【自相矛盾】inconsistent
【自相殘殺】to engage in an intramural fight
【自行車】a bicycle; a bike
【自省】self-examination; introspection
【自詡 or 自吹自擂】to brag; to boast
【自許】to regard oneself as; conceited
【自尋煩惱】to look for trouble
【自制】self-restraint; self-discipline
【自治】① self-discipline ② autonomy
【自找麻煩】to look for trouble
【自主】independent; autonomy
【自主權】sovereignty (of a state)
【自助洗衣店】a launderette
【自助餐】a buffet lunch or supper
【自助餐廳】a cafeteria
【自轉】(astronomy) rotation
【自傳】an autobiography
【自重】self-respect; self-discipline; self-esteem
【自稱】to call oneself; to claim
【自食其力】to live by one's own exertion
【自食其果 or 自作自受】to reap the fruit of what one has sown
【自始至終】from beginning to end
【自視】to consider, to think or to imagine oneself
【自殺】to commit suicide; suicide

【自首】 to give oneself up to the law
【自身】 oneself
【自身難保】 unable even to protect oneself
【自生自滅】 to grow and die without outside interference
【自述】 to narrate one's own story or experience
【自然】 ①nature ②at ease; natural ③certainly; surely; of course ④(in primary school) a subject or course of study concerning natural sciences
【自然而然】 a matter of course
【自認】 ①to believe ②to accept adversity with resignation
【自責】 to blame oneself; self-reproach
【自在】 ①at ease (with oneself and the world) ②freely
【自作多情】 to imagine oneself as the favorite of one of the opposite sex
【自作主張】 to take liberties; to decide for oneself
【自作聰明】 presumptuous; pretentious
【自尊】 ① self-respect; self-esteem ②egotistic
【自尊心】 a sense of self-respect; self-esteem
【自慚形穢】 to feel inferior to others
【自從】 since then; ever since
【自私(自利)】 selfish; selfishness
【自愛】 self-respect
【自以爲是】 self-approbation
【自縊】 to hang oneself
【自由】 ①freedom; liberty ②at ease ③of one's own free will
【自由戀愛】 free love
【自由行動】 free action
【自由式】 (swimming) freestyle
【自由自在】 carefree
【自幼】 since childhood
【自言自語】 to talk to oneself
【自我】 self; ego
【自我陶醉】 to indulge in daydreaming
【自慰】 ① self-consolation ② onanism
【自衛】self-defense; to defend oneself
【自衛隊】 militia corps
【自問】 to ask oneself
【自娛】 to amuse oneself
【自圓其說】 to explain oneself away
【自願】 voluntary
【自怨自艾】 to blame and censure oneself

四畫

臭 3304 1. ㄔㄡˋ chòu

1. stinking; smelly 2. notorious; flagrant; disreputable 3. very; much; soundly; sternly 4. (said of friendship, love, etc.) to cool off 5. foul and petty; worthless 6. an odor; a stench
【臭皮囊】 the human body
【臭罵】 a stern scolding; to scold soundly
【臭美】 presumptuous; smug
【臭豆腐】 the fermented bean curd (a popular Chinese food item)
【臭氣冲天】 a stinking smell assaulting one's nostrils
【臭小子】 a bum; a tramp
【臭蟲】 the bedbug
【臭味相投】 birds of the same feather

臭 3304 2. (嗅)ㄒㄧㄡˋ xiù

1. scent; smells; odors 2. to smell

十畫

至部 ㄓˋ zhì

至 3305 ㄓˋ zhì

1. to arrive at; to reach (a destination) 2. very; extremely; to indicate the superlative degree —the most
【至多】 at (the) most
【至理名言】 a proverb of lasting value
【至高無上】 the highest; the most exalted; the supreme
【至關緊要】 of utmost importance
【至交】 one's closest friend
【至今】 until now; so far; up to the present time
【至親好友】 close relatives and dear friends
【至誠】sincere; the greatest sincerity
【至少】 at least; the least
【至此】 ①to come here ②to have developed to this point
【至死不變】 consistent or unswerving (love, faith, etc.)
【至死不渝】to remain faithful until death

【至友】the closest friend; a close friend
【至於】①as to; with regard to ②to the extent of

〔臼部〕

三畫

致 3306 (致) ㄓˋ zhì
1. to send; to present; to convey; to transmit; to extend (thanks, etc.) 2. to cause to come; to cause (injury, death, etc.) 3. to achieve; to attain; to amass (fortune) 4. one's principle, interest, hobby, etc. 5. to bring about; to occasion or result in 6. to retire; to resign
【致命】①to sacrifice one's life ②fatal; fatality
【致命傷】① a mortal wound ② vulnerability; the weak point
【致富】to become rich
【致電】to send a telegram or cable
【致力】to devote or dedicate oneself to
【致賀】to extend or offer congratulations
【致敬】to salute
【致謝】to offer thanks; to thank
【致仕】to resign from office
【致辭】to address; to deliver a speech
【致死】to cause death; to result in death
【致意】to convey one's best wishes or regards
【致癌物質】(medicine) carcinogen

八畫

臺 3307 (台) ㄊㄞˊ tái
1. a lookout; an observatory; a tower 2. a terrace; an elevated platform; a stage; a stand 3. a title of respect 4. short for Taiwan 5. a Chinese family name
【臺幣】Taiwan currency
【臺風】the deportment of an actor or actress on stage
【臺地】a tableland; a plateau
【臺階】①brick or stone steps ②a means to save face or resolve a dispute
【臺柱子】a mainstay
【臺詞】actor's lines
【臺灣】Taiwan (Formosa)
【臺灣海峽】Taiwan Strait
【臺灣省】the Province of Taiwan

臼部
ㄐㄧㄡˋ jiù

臼 3308 ㄐㄧㄡˋ jiù
1. a mortar for unhusking rice 2. a socket at a bone joint

四畫

舀 3309 ㄧㄠˇ yǎo (讀音 ㄎㄨㄞˇ kuǎi)
to ladle out (water)

五畫

舂 3310 ㄔㄨㄥ chōng
1. to thresh (grain in order to remove the husk) 2. to pound

七畫

舅 3311 ㄐㄧㄡˋ jiù
1. a maternal uncle (one's mother's brother) 2. a brother-in-law (one's wife's brother) 3. a woman's father-in-law 4. a man's father-in-law
【舅媽】a maternal aunt (one's mother's brother's wife)
【舅父】a maternal uncle (one's mother's brother)

與 3312 1. ㄩˇ yǔ
1. and; with; together with 2. to give; to impart
【與虎謀皮 or 與狐謀皮】to try to persuade someone to do what is against his interest
【與其…不如】It's better to...than...; 或 rather...than...; ...rather than...
【與衆不同】extraordinary; uncommon
【與世長辭】to pass away
【與世無爭】to stand aloof from worldly success
【與日俱增】to be on the increase

與 3312 2. ㄩˋ yù
to take part in; to participate in
【與會】to participate in a confer-

ence

與 3312
3. ㄩˊ yú
same as歟—one of the interrogative particles

九畫

興 3313
1. ㄒㄧㄥ xīng
1. to rise; to thrive; to prosper; to flourish 2. to happen; to take place; to occur 3. to start; to begin; to launch; to initiate; to establish; to found; to open
【興奮】excited; stimulated; excitement
【興奮劑】a stimulant
【興風作浪】to cause unrest
【興隆】prosperous; thriving; vigorous
【興建】to establish; to build; to construct
【興起】to gain power; to rise
【興師問罪】to mobilize troops to chastise rebels
【興盛】prosperous; thriving; vigorous
【興衰】rise and fall; vicissitudes
【興亡】rise and fall; prosperity and adversity
【興旺】prosperous; thriving

興 3313
2. ㄒㄧㄥˋ xìng
1. cheerful; happy; gay; merry 2. interest; enthusiasm
【興高采烈】cheerful; elated; in high spirits; jubilant
【興趣】interest
【興致】interest; eagerness; enthusiasm
【興沖沖】cheerful; sprightly; gay

十畫

舉 3314
(擧) ㄐㄩˇ jǔ
1. to lift; to raise 2. to recommend; to commend; to praise 3. entire; all; whole 4. manner; deportment 5. to give birth to a child
【舉辦】to sponsor, organize, or initiate
【舉目無親】There is not a single friend or relative around.—to have no one to turn to (for help)
【舉發】to expose (a secret or conspiracy)
【舉動】① manner; behavior ② movement
【舉例】to give examples
【舉例說明】to illustrate
【舉國上下】the entire nation regardless of classes
【舉家】the whole family
【舉薦】to recommend (a person)
【舉棋不定】indecisive; irresolute
【舉起】to lift; to raise
【舉行】to hold (examinations, rallies, parties, etc.); to take place
【舉止】deportment; conduct
【舉證】to give proof or evidence
【舉重】weightlifting
【舉出】to enumerate; to itemize
【舉世無匹 or 舉世無雙】without a match in the world—unique
【舉世聞名】to be known to the whole world; world-renowned
【舉手】to raise one's hand
【舉手之勞】(literally) the trouble involved in raising a hand—little effort
【舉足輕重】so important is the role one plays in a matter that each step one takes may affect it in a significant way
【舉一反三】to infer the rest from what is already known

十二畫

舊 3315
ㄐㄧㄡˋ jiù
1. old; past; former 2. ancient; antique 3. longstanding
【舊病復發】to have a relapse of an old ailment
【舊地重遊】to revisit a place
【舊曆年】the Lunar New Year
【舊觀】the former appearance
【舊觀念】old ideas
【舊貨】secondhand goods; junk
【舊貨攤】a junk store
【舊交】an old friend
【舊金山】San Francisco
【舊址】a former site; a former address
【舊賬】old debts; old bills
【舊主】one's former master
【舊式】out-of-date; old-style; old-fashioned
【舊書】① a used book ② ancient books
【舊書店】a secondhand bookstore
【舊書攤】a secondhand bookstand
【舊日】bygone days; former times
【舊雨新知】old friends and new acquaintances

〔臼部〕

〔舌・舛部〕

舌部
ㄕㄜˊ shé

舌 3316 ㄕㄜˊ shé
the tongue
【舌頭】the tongue
【舌戰】to debate with verbal confrontation

二畫

舍 3317 1. ㄕㄜˋ shè
1. a house 2. an inn 3. to halt; to stop; to rest 4. a self-depreciatory possessive pronoun for the first person singular in formal speech
【舍間 or 舍下】my humble house
【舍監】a dormitory superintendent

舍 3317 2. ㄕㄜˇ shě
same as 捨—to throw away

四畫

舐 3318 ㄕˋ shì
to lick
【舐犢情深】very affectionate toward one's children (like a cow caressing her calves with the tongue)

六畫

舒 3319 ㄕㄨ shū
1. to unfold; to stretch; to open; to relax 2. slow; unhurried; leisurely 3. a Chinese family name
【舒眉】to show pleasure
【舒服】comfortable; cosy; comfort
【舒坦】happy; comfortable
【舒緩】leisurely; relaxed; to relax
【舒展】to limber up; to unfold; to relax; to stretch
【舒暢】① pleasant; comfortable ② leisurely and harmonious
【舒適】comfortable; cosy; snug

八畫

舔 3320 ㄊㄧㄢˇ tiǎn
to lick; to taste

九畫

舖 3321 (鋪) ㄆㄨˋ pù
a shop; a store

十畫

舘 3322 (館) ㄍㄨㄢˇ guǎn
a mansion; a building

舛部
ㄔㄨㄢˇ chuǎn

舛 3323 ㄔㄨㄢˇ chuǎn
1. chaotic; disorderly; messy; confused; mixed up 2. to run counter to; to disobey; to oppose; to deviate from 3. mishap

六畫

舜 3324 ㄕㄨㄣˋ shùn
Shun, a legendary ruler said to have ruled ancient China around 2200 B.C.

八畫

舞 3325 ㄨˇ wǔ
1. to dance; to prance 2. to brandish; to wave 3. to stir up
【舞弊】misconduct, malpractice or irregularities (of an official); to bribe
【舞蹈】① dancing ② a dance
【舞動】① to dance ② to brandish
【舞臺】a stage (in a theater)
【舞廳】a dance hall
【舞女】a taxi dancer; a dancing girl
【舞龍】a dragon dance
【舞文弄墨】① to amuse oneself with writing ② to tamper with documents (for fraudulent purposes)
【舞會】a dancing party; a dance; a ball

【舞曲】 dance music; a dance tune
【舞池】 a dance floor
【舞獅】 a lion dance

舟 部
ㄓㄡ zhōu

舟 3326 ㄓㄡ zhōu
a boat; a ship; a vessel
【舟楫】 ① ships; vessels ② a capable assistant

三畫

舢 3327 ㄕㄢ shān
as in 舢板 or 舢舨—a sampan

四畫

航 3328 ㄏㄤ háng
1. a ship; a boat; a vessel 2. to navigate
【航空】 aviation; aeronautics
【航空母艦】 an aircraft carrier; a flattop
【航空公司】 an airline
【航空信】 airmail
【航海】 maritime navigation; a voyage; to sail on the seas
【航線】 routes (of an airline or shipping company)
【航行】 ① to sail ② to fly
【航程】 the distance of an air or a sea trip; sail

般 3329 1. ㄅㄢ bān
1. kind; sort; class 2. same as 搬—to carry; to move 3. same as 班—to return; to call back

般 3329 2. ㄅㄛ bō
(Buddhism) intelligence: 般若 *prajna*, wisdom

五畫

舵 3330 ㄉㄨㄛˋ duò
a rudder; a helm
【舵手】 a helmsman; a steersman

舶 3331 ㄅㄛˊ bó
an ocean-going ship
【舶來品】 imported goods; foreign goods

船 3332 ㄔㄨㄢˊ chuán
a ship; a boat; a vessel; a craft
【船板】 the deck (of a ship)
【船夫 or 船家】 a sailor; a boatman
【船到橋頭自然直】 It will take care of itself when the time comes.
【船隻】 ships; boats; crafts; vessels
【船長】 the captain or skipper (of a boat)
【船主】 the owner (of a boat)
【船艙】 the hold or cabin (of a boat)
【船隖or船塢】 a dock (in a shipyard)
【船桅】 the mast (of a ship)
【船員】 the crew (of a ship)
【船運】 to transport by ship

七畫

艇 3333 ㄊㄧㄥˇ tǐng
a long, narrow boat

十畫

艘 3334 ㄙㄠ sāo
a numerary adjunct for ships

艙 3335 ㄘㄤ cāng
the hold or cabin (of a ship): 艙房cabins

十四畫

艦 3336 ㄐㄧㄢˋ jiàn
a warship; a man-of-war; a naval vessel
【艦隊】 a fleet; a naval task force
【艦艇】 naval vessels
【艦長】 the captain or skipper of a naval vessel

艮 部
ㄍㄣˋ gèn

艮 3337 1. ㄍㄣˋ gèn
one of the Eight Diagrams for divination

艮 3337 2. ㄍㄣˇ gěn

1. (said of food) tough; leathery 2. (said of clothing) simple 3. (said of one's personality) honest; upright

一畫

良 3338 ㄌㄧㄤˊ liáng
1. good; fine; desirable 2. very 3. instinctive; inborn; innate
【良伴】a good companion
【良方】① a good remedy; a good prescription ② a good course of action
【良機】a good chance
【良家子女】children of good parentage
【良久】for a very long time
【良心】conscience
【良辰美景】a pleasant day coupled with a fine landscape
【良師益友】good teachers and helpful friends
【良人】① a good person ② one's husband
【良藥苦口】Good advice is never pleasant to the ear.
【良莠不齊】some good, some bad
【良緣】a harmonious union

十一畫

艱 3339 ㄐㄧㄢ jiān
1. difficult; hard 2. mourning for one's parents
【艱難】difficulty; distress; hardship
【艱苦】trying; hard; privation
【艱困】difficult
【艱鉅or艱辛】hard; arduous; laborious
【艱險】difficult and dangerous
【艱深 or 艱澀】abstruse; difficult

色部 ㄙㄜˋ sè

色 3340 ㄙㄜˋ sè (語音 ㄕㄞˇ shǎi)
1. a color; a tinge; a tint; a hue 2. facial expression; a look; an appearance 3. sensuality; lust; lewdness; carnal pleasure 4. worldly things 5. a kind; a sort
【色盲】color-blind; achromatopsy
【色膽包天】extremely daring in lewdness
【色狼or色鬼】(slang) a lecherous person
【色情】sexual passion; lust
【色紙】colored paper
【色澤or色彩】a tinge; a color; a hue; a tint
【色素】pigment

十八畫

艷 3341 (豔) ㄧㄢˋ yàn
beautiful

艸部 ㄘㄠˇ cǎo

艸 3342 ㄘㄠˇ cǎo
grass; straw; weeds

二畫

艾 3343 ㄞˋ ài
1. moxa 2. fine; fair; beautiful; good 3. old 4. to cease; to stop; to discontinue

三畫

芋 3344 ㄩˋ yù
a taro

芍 3345 ㄕㄠˊ sháo (讀音 ㄕㄨㄛˋ shuò)
Paeonia, a peony
【芍藥】a Chinese herbaceous peony

芒 3346 ㄇㄤˊ máng
1. *Miscanthus sinensis*, a kind of grass whose leaves can be used to make sandals 2. a sharp point 3. (botany) beards of wheat 4. rays (of stars)
【芒果】a mango
【芒刺在背】ill at ease

四畫

芙 3347 ㄈㄨˊ fú
as in 芙蓉—a hibiscus

芝 3348 ㄓ zhī
1. a kind of purplish fungus symbolizing nobility 2. a kind of fragrant herb 3. a Chinese family name
【芝麻】a sesame

芥 3349 ㄐㄧㄝˋ jiè
1. as in 芥菜—a mustard plant 2. tiny
【芥末】ground mustard
【芥蒂】① remorse; a grudge ② a barrier which mars friendship

芬 3350 ㄈㄣ fēn
fragrance; aroma; a sweet smell; perfume
【芬芳】fragrant; aromatic

芭 3351 ㄅㄚ bā
1. a fragrant plant 2. a palmetto: 芭蕉 a plantain
【芭樂】guava
【芭蕾舞】ballet
【芭蕉】a plantain

花 3352 ㄏㄨㄚ huā
1. a flower 2. a flowering plant 3. a prostitute 4. as in 天花—smallpox 5. varicolored 6. fireworks 7. to spend
【花苞】a bud
【花瓣】the petal (of a flower or blossom)
【花邊】① lace; an embroidered hem (of a garment) ② fancy borders (in printing)
【花邊新聞】a sidebar
【花盆】a flower pot
【花瓶】a vase
【花圃】a flower bed
【花費】to spend; to expend
【花粉】pollen
【花燈】a fancy lantern (made for the Lantern Festival on the 15th of the first moon)
【花彫 or 花雕】rice wine of the best quality from Shaohsing (紹興)
【花團錦簇】① a conglomeration of splendid and beautiful things ② a group of richly attired women
【花童】a bridal page
【花籃】a flower basket
【花柳病】a venereal disease; V.D.
【花岡岩】granite
【花好月圓】perfect conjugal bliss
【花花綠綠】varicolored; colorful
【花花公子】a beau; a fop; a playboy
【花花世界】the gay and material world
【花卉】flowering plants
【花甲】(said of a person) 60 years old
【花錢】to spend money
【花圈】a garland; a wreath; a lei
【花香】fragrance of a flower
【花枝招展】(said of beautifully dressed women) like a flowering branch attracting people's attention
【花招兒】a sly trick
【花車】a float; a decorated vehicle in parade
【花市】a flower market
【花生米】a peanut
【花生醬】peanut butter
【花束】a bouquet; a bunch of flowers
【花容月貌】(said of a woman) fair as a flower and the moon
【花草】flowers and grass
【花色】varieties; kinds; sorts
【花言巧語】honeyed words
【花樣】a pattern; a style; a model
【花紋】a decorative design or pattern
【花園】a flower garden; a garden

芳 3353 ㄈㄤ fāng
1. sweet-smelling; fragrant; aromatic 2. your (used commonly in addressing a young lady) 3. virtuous; honorable; good
【芳名】① your name (used especially in speaking to a woman) ② a good reputation
【芳鄰】one's neighbor (a polite expression)
【芳齡】age (of a young lady)
【芳心】the affection, or heart (of a young lady)
【芳香】fragrance; aroma
【芳踪】your whereabouts

芸 3354 ㄩㄣˊ yún
1. a strong-scented herb; rue 2. same as 耘 — to weed
【芸芸衆生】① people of the world ② all living things

芹 3355 ㄑㄧㄣˊ qín
as in 芹菜—celery

芽 3356 ㄧㄚˊ yá

a sprout; a shoot; a bud

芻 3357
ㄔㄨˊ chú
1. to cut grass; to mow 2. hay; fodder 3. to feed (livestock) 4. animals that feed on grass
【芻糧】fodder for horses and food for men

〔艸部〕

五畫

苑 3358
ㄩㄢˋ yuàn
1. a garden; a park 2. a gathering place

苒 3359
ㄖㄢˇ rǎn
(said of flowers and grass) lush or delicate
【苒荏】time passing gradually

苔 3360
1. ㄊㄞ tāi
moss; lichen
【苔蘚】moss and lichen

苔 3360
2. ㄊㄞ tāi
as in 舌苔—fur (on the tongue)

苗 3361
ㄇㄧㄠˊ miáo
1. a sprout 2. descendants; posterity 3. (said of children) peevish or disobedient 4. the Miao tribe in southwestern China 5. summer hunting 6. a Chinese family name 7. a beginning or omen
【苗圃】a seedbed; a nursery
【苗頭】the first sign of success
【苗條】(said of a woman) slim

苛 3362
ㄎㄜ kē
harsh; severe; rigorous; caustic
【苛刻】harsh; pitiless; relentless; merciless; unkind; cold-hearted
【苛求】to be very exacting
【苛政】despotic rule; despotism; tyranny
【苛責】to criticize severely; to rebuke; to excoriate

苞 3363
ㄅㄠ bāo
1. a variety of rush 2. a bract 3. to wrap 4. profuse; thick 5. seeds with the germ ready to burst; seeds bursting up

若 3364
1. ㄖㄨㄛˋ ruò
1. if; suppose; supposing; assuming; provided that 2. you 3. similar to; like
【若非】unless; if not
【若干】some; a few; several
【若即若離】to keep at arm's length
【若是】if; suppose
【若要】if...has (have) to...
【若隱若現】half-hidden; discernible at one moment and gone the next (like a will-o'-the-wisp)
【若無其事】as if nothing had happened; to remain calm

若 3364
2. ㄖㄜˇ rě
as in 般若(ㄅㄛ ㄖㄜˇ)—(Buddism) *prajna*, wisdom

苦 3365
ㄎㄨˇ kǔ
1. bitter 2. painful; hard; difficult; laborious; miserable 3. strenuous; earnest; diligent 4. to abhor 5. to feel miserable about
【苦不堪言】painful or miserable beyond description
【苦悶】boredom; bored; distressed; low-spirited; depressed; dejected
【苦命】a hard lot
【苦頭兒】hardship(s)
【苦惱】misery; distress; trouble
【苦難】privation; suffering; hardship
【苦力】① strenuous efforts; hard work ② a coolie; a laborer
【苦幹】① to make a strenuous effort ② to do something against great odds
【苦瓜】a bitter gourd (*Momordica charantia*)
【苦工】toil; hard labor
【苦口婆心】to exhort or remonstrate with earnest words prompted by a kind heart
【苦盡甘來】The happy sunny days are coming after all the hardships endured.
【苦勸】earnest exhortation; to exhort or advise earnestly
【苦笑】to force a smile; a forced smile
【苦心】great pains taken for something
【苦行者】an ascetic
【苦學】to study or learn under adversity
【苦戰】to fight against heavy odds
【苦衷】a reason for doing something not easily understood by others

【苦中作樂】to find joy amid hardship; to enjoy in adversity
【苦楚 or 苦痛】pain; suffering
【苦處】the cause of pain; difficulty
【苦肉計】a trick of securing another's faith by intentionally injuring oneself; acting the underdog to win sympathy
【苦澀】①bitter and astringent ② agonized; pained; anguished
【苦味】a bitter taste

英 3366
ㄧㄥ yīng
1. a flower; a leaf; a petal 2. surpassing; outstanding; prominent; distinguished 3. fine; handsome 4. English; British 5. a hero; an outstanding person 6. a Chinese family name
【英鎊】the pound sterling 亦作「英磅」
【英美】Britain and America
【英明】(said of leaders) intelligent; sagacious; perspicacious
【英名】fame; glory; renown
【英畝】(square measure) acre
【英挺】outstanding; prominent
【英里】(linear measure) mile
【英格蘭】England
【英國】Great Britain; Britain; the United Kingdom; England
【英漢辭典】an English-Chinese dictionary
【英俊】(said of a man) handsome
【英雄】a hero; a great man
【英尺】foot
【英姿】a dashing appearance
【英才】a person of outstanding ability or talent
【英寸】(linear measure) inch
【英文】the (written) English language; English
【英語】the (spoken) English language; English
【英勇】brave; courageous

茁 3367
ㄓㄨㄛˊ zhuó
1. sprouting; growing 2. strong; sturdy; vigorous
【茁壯】vigorous; strong

茂 3368
ㄇㄠˋ mào
(又讀 ㄇㄡˋ mòu)
1. exuberant; lush; luxuriant; flourishing; healthy; vigorous; strong 2. fine; fair; excellent
【茂盛】luxuriant; flourishing; lush; exuberant

范 3369
ㄈㄢˋ fàn
1. the bee 2. a Chinese family name

茄 3370
ㄑㄧㄝˊ qié
an eggplant; an aubergine

茅 3371
ㄇㄠˊ máo
1. couch grass 2. a Chinese family name
【茅房】① a thatched house ② a latrine
【茅舍】①a straw hut; a thatched house ② my humble cottage
【茅廁】a latrine; a lavatory; a water closet
【茅塞頓開】to come to an understanding all of a sudden
【茅屋】a thatched house; a straw hut

茉 3372
ㄇㄛˋ mò
as in 茉莉—white jasmine

苟 3373
ㄍㄡˇ gǒu
1. against principle; illicit; improper 2. careless 3. if
【苟同】to agree without giving serious thought
【苟合】① to join or associate against one's principle ②an illicit sexual act
【苟且】①against one's principle ② perfunctory ③ illicit (sexual relations)
【苟且偷生】to drag out an ignominious existence
【苟延殘喘】to prolong one's life only temporarily; to be on one's last legs; to linger on in a steadily deteriorating condition

六畫

茗 3374
ㄇㄧㄥˊ míng
(又讀 ㄇㄧㄥˇ mǐng)
tea; a tea plant: 茗具 a tea set

荔 3375
ㄌㄧˋ lì
as in 荔枝—a lichee

茫 3376
ㄇㄤˊ máng
1. vast; boundless 2. vague; uncertain
【茫茫大海】the boundless ocean
【茫然】vague; blank; uncertain
【茫無頭緒】①(said of things) to

艸部

be all in a jumble ② not knowing where or how to start

〔艸部〕

茲 3377
ㄗ zī
1. this 2. now; here; at present 3. year
【茲事體大】This is a big problem. 或 This is a serious matter.

茶 3378
ㄔㄚˊ chá
tea: 茶杯 a teacup
【茶房】a waiter; an attendant
【茶點】refreshments
【茶樓 or 茶館 or 茶肆】a tearoom; a teahouse
【茶壺】a teapot
【茶話會 or 茶會】a tea party; a tea reception
【茶几】① a teapoy ② a small table
【茶具】tea utensils; tea-things
【茶室】① a tearoom ② a brothel
【茶水】tea or boiled water
【茶葉】tea leaves
【茶園】① a tea plantation ② (formerly) an opera theater

茹 3379
ㄖㄨˊ rú (又讀 ㄖㄨˇ rǔ)
1. entangled roots 2. to eat; to taste; to mouth 3. (figuratively) to experience 4. stinking
【茹毛飲血】(said of primitive people) to eat birds and beasts uncooked

荀 3380
ㄒㄩㄣˊ xún
1. name of an ancient state 2. a kind of herb 3. a Chinese family name

草 3381
ㄘㄠˇ cǎo
1. grass; straw; a herb; a weed 2. coarse; crude 3. a draft (of writing); to draft 4. the script type of Chinese calligraphy
【草包】a grass bag—a crude fellow
【草本】① a manuscript ② herbaceous
【草皮】a young grass cover
【草坪 or 草地】a lawn; meadow; pasture
【草莓】a strawberry
【草帽】a straw hat
【草料】fodder; hay
【草稿 or 草藁】a rough draft
【草菅人命】to attach no importance to human life
【草裙舞】a Hawaiian dance; a hulahula
【草蓆】astraw mat
【草鞋】straw sandals
【草創】① the beginning or initial period (of a project) ② to make the rough copy
【草繩】a straw rope; a grass rope
【草書】the script type of calligraphy
【草率】careless; perfunctory
【草草了事】to dispose of a thing carelessly or hastily
【草叢】a thick growth of grass
【草案】a draft plan; a proposed plan
【草藥】herb medicine
【草原】a prairie; grassland; a steppe

荏 3382
ㄖㄣˇ rěn
1. *Perilla frutescens*, whose seeds are birds' feed 2. soft; weak; fragile
【荏苒】(said of time) to elapse imperceptibly; to slip by

荒 3383
ㄏㄨㄤ huāng
1. uncultivated; desolate; wild; waste; deserted; barren 2. absurd; ridiculous 3. famine; scarcity; deficiency 4. to neglect
【荒謬】grossly absurd; ridiculous; preposterous
【荒廢】to neglect; to leave completely unattended to
【荒島】an uninhabited island; a barren island
【荒唐 or 荒誕】absurd; nonsensical
【荒土 or 荒地】uncultivated land; waste land; the wilderness
【荒年】a year of bad crops; a year of famine
【荒涼】desolate; deserted; wild
【荒腔走調】out of tune
【荒蕪】deserted and desolate; desolation

荐 3384
(薦) ㄐㄧㄢˋ jiàn
1. repeatedly; again and again 2. to offer; to recommend 3. a straw mattress

七畫

荷 3385
1. ㄏㄜˊ hé
a lotus; a water lily
【荷包】a purse; a pouch (carried with oneself)
【荷包蛋】fried eggs
【荷蘭】Holland; the Netherlands
【荷花】a lotus flower

【荷爾蒙】hormone

荷 3385
2. ㄏㄜˋ hè
1. a load; a burden 2. to bear; to carry; to shoulder 3. to receive

荻 3386
ㄉㄧˊ dí
1. *Anaphalis yedoensis* 2. *Miscanthus sacchariflorus*, a kind of reed

荼 3387
ㄊㄨˊ tú
1. *Sonchus oleraceus*, a kind of bitter-tasting vegetable; sow thistle 亦作「苦荼」 2. to harm; to poison
【荼毒生靈】to injure the people
【荼炭】suffering of the common people 亦作「塗炭」

莊 3388
ㄓㄨㄤ zhuāng
1. solemn; dignified; stately; august; sober; gravity 2. a large farmhouse; a manor house 3. a village; a hamlet 4. a market; a shop; a store; a bank 5. a Chinese family name
【莊家】① a farmhouse ② the banker (in gambling games)
【莊稼】① farming ② crops; harvests
【莊稼地】a farm; a field
【莊稼漢 or 莊稼人】a farmer
【莊重】dignified; solemn
【莊嚴】①dignified; solemn; stately; august ②to adorn; to make solemn
【莊園】a manor

莒 3389
ㄐㄩˇ jǔ
1. taros 2. name of an ancient state 3. name of a county in Shantung

莓 3390
ㄇㄟˊ méi
1. berries 2. moss; lichen

莖 3391
ㄐㄧㄥ jīng
a stalk; a stem

莘 3392
ㄕㄣ shēn
(又讀 ㄒㄧㄣ xīn)
1. long 2. numerous 3. *Asarum sieboldi*
【莘莘學子】students in large numbers

莞 3393
ㄨㄢˇ wǎn
as in 莞爾—smiling

莠 3394
ㄧㄡˇ yǒu
(又讀 ㄧㄡˋ yòu)
1. foxtail (a kind of weed) 亦作「狗尾草」 2. bad; ugly; undesirable

莢 3395
ㄐㄧㄚˊ jiá
as in 莢果—a pod

莫 3396
ㄇㄛˋ mò
1. not 2. a Chinese family name
【莫名其妙】① incomprehensible; mysterious; baffling ② impossible (as in "an impossible person")
【莫非】① certainly; surely ② all; all-inclusive; the whole amount of ③ Can it be that...?
【莫大】greatest; utmost
【莫逆之交】close friendship; bosom friends
【莫須有】a trumped-up charge; false accusation
【莫測高深】unfathomable; inscrutable
【莫斯科】Moscow

莉 3397
ㄌㄧˋ lì
as in 茉莉—white jasmine

莽 3398
(莾) ㄇㄤˇ mǎng
1. bushy; weedy 2. *Illicium anisatum*, a poisonous bushy plant 3. rude; uncultured; impolite; reckless
【莽夫or莽漢】a rude fellow; a rough
【莽撞】rude; rough; uncultured

莎 3399
ㄕㄚ shā
a kind of insect
【莎士比亞】William Shakespeare

荳 3400
(豆) ㄉㄡˋ dòu
beans, peas, etc.; legumes

八畫

菅 3401
ㄐㄧㄢ jiān
Themeda triandra, a coarse grass (used for making brushes, brooms, etc.)

菊 3402
ㄐㄩˊ jú
as in 菊花—a chrysanthemum

菌 3403
ㄐㄩㄣˋ jùn
1. fungi; mushrooms 2. bacteria

〔艸部〕

菖 3404 ㄔㄤ chāng
as in 菖蒲—a sweet flag; a calamus

菜 3405 ㄘㄞ cài
1. vegetables; greens 2. as in 菜肴—food eaten with rice or alcoholic drinks 3. a dish; a course
【菜圃or菜園】a vegetable garden or field
【菜刀】a kitchen knife
【菜單兒】a bill of fare; a menu
【菜攤兒】a vegetable vendor's stall
【菜農】a vegetable grower
【菜瓜】cucumber
【菜市場】a grocery market; a vegetable market

菠 3406 ㄅㄛ bō
spinach
【菠薐菜 or 菠菜】spinach

華 3407 1. ㄏㄨㄚˊ huá
1. Cathay; China 2. splendid; majestic; gorgeous; colorful; brilliant; bright; fine; beautiful; luxurious 3. prosperous; thriving
【華府】Washington D.C.
【華燈初上】(descriptive of urban scenes at dusk) Colorful lamps are beginning to light up.
【華麗】magnificent; resplendent; gorgeous
【華僑】overseas Chinese
【華夏】Cathay
【華爾茲舞】waltz
【華裔】foreign citizens of Chinese origin
【華語】the Chinese language; Chinese

華 3407 2. ㄏㄨㄚˋ huà
1. luster; brilliancy; glory; splendor 2. a Chinese family name
【華山】Mountain Hua, a sacred mountain in Shensi Province

菇 3408 ㄍㄨ gū
mushrooms; a fungus

菁 3409 ㄐㄧㄥ jīng
1. the flower of the leek 2. the rape turnip 3. luxuriant; lush
【菁華】essence 亦作「精華」

菲 3410 1. ㄈㄟˇ fěi
1. a kind of radish 2. thin; trifling; meager 3. frugal; sparing
【菲薄】①to slight; to belittle ②thin; humble; poor ③frugal; thrifty

菲 3410 2. ㄈㄟ fēi
1. fragrant 2. the Philippines 3. luxuriant

菸 3411 ㄧㄢ yān
a tobacco leaf
【菸酒】tobacco and alcoholic drinks
【菸草】tobacco

萃 3412 ㄘㄨㄟˋ cuì
1. a thick or dense growth of grass 2. a group; a set 3. to gather; to meet; to congregate
【萃取】(chemistry) extraction

萄 3413 ㄊㄠˊ táo
as in 葡萄—grapes

萊 3414 ㄌㄞˊ lái
1. fields lying fallow 2. wild weeds 3. to weed
【萊因河】the Rhine River

萋 3415 ㄑㄧ qī
1. luxuriant foliage; a dense growth of grass 2. many; crowded

萌 3416 ㄇㄥˊ méng
1. to bud; to sprout; to germinate; to shoot forth 2. to harbor (a thought) 3. the beginning; initiation; initial
【萌芽】①the initial stage of something ②to sprout; to be in bud

萍 3417 ㄆㄧㄥˊ píng
1. duckweed 2. moving about rootlessly; traveling or wandering
【萍水相逢】to meet by accident

萎 3418 ㄨㄟˇ wěi
1. to wither 2. ill; sick 3. to fall; to decline; to weaken
【萎靡不振】unable to pick oneself up; despondent; lethargic
【萎謝】(said of flowers) to wither; to fade
【萎縮】①to dry up and shrink; to shrink back ②to atrophy

菡 3419 ㄏㄢˋ hàn
another name of water lily or lotus flower

萏 3420
ㄉㄢˋ dàn
as in 菡萏 — another name of 「water lily」

菩 3421
ㄆㄨˊ pú
1. a fragrant herb 2. the sacred tree of the Buddhists
【菩提樹】①a peepul tree ②(Buddhism) a bo tree
【菩薩】① Bodhisattva ② Buddha
【菩薩心腸】kind-hearted; compassionate

菱 3422
ㄌㄧㄥˊ líng
a water chestnut
【菱角】a water chestnut
【菱形】a rhomb or rhombus; rhombic

荊 3423
(荆) ㄐㄧㄥ jīng
1. a kind of bramble; a thorn 2. a cane for punishment used in ancient China 3. (a polite expression) my wife 4. (in ancient China) name of one of the nine political regions 5. a Chinese family name
【荊棘】①thorns; thorny②a difficult situation

菓 3424
ㄍㄨㄛˇ guǒ
fruits and nuts

九畫

萬 3425
(万) ㄨㄢˋ wàn
1. ten thousand 2. all; omni- 3. a very great number; myriad 4. very; extremely; absolutely 5. name of an ancient dance 6. a Chinese family name
【萬不得已】① if the worst comes to happen ②to have no alternative; to have to do it; very reluctantly
【萬民】all the people
【萬分】very; extremely
【萬能】omnipotent; almighty
【萬年青】a Chinese evergreen
【萬念俱灰】completely discouraged; extremely pessimistic
【萬籟俱寂】All is still. 或All sounds are hushed (in the dead of the night).
【萬里長城】the Great Wall (of China)
【萬靈藥】a panacea; a cure-all
【萬古流芳】a good name that will last forever
【萬國音標】International Phonetic Alphabet (IPA) 亦作「國際音標」
【萬貫 or 萬貫家私】very wealthy; very rich
【萬花筒】a kaleidoscope
【萬千】numerous; myriads
【萬全之計】an absolutely safe measure, plan, device, etc.
【萬象更新】a new year—as all things change from old to new
【萬幸】extremely lucky; very fortunate indeed
【萬丈深淵】an abyss of 100,000 feet—a bottomless abyss
【萬衆一心】all for one and one for all; with one aspiration in their hearts; solidarity
【萬世師表】(literally) a paragon for all generations—Confucius
【萬壽無疆】May you attain boundless longevity!
【萬聖節】All Saints' Day
【萬人空巷】Everyone (in a city) turns out (to watch a spectacle, to welcome a hero, etc.)
【萬紫千紅】(said of flowers) a vast display of dazzling colors
【萬歲】(a slogan) Long live the....
【萬一】①one ten thousandth—a very tiny fraction ②just in case that; if by any chance ③something not anticipated or happening accidentally
【萬無一失】not the least mishap or mistake; absolutely safe or sure; certain to succeed
【萬物】all things under the sun; all God's creation

萱 3426
ㄒㄩㄢ xuān
a daylily (*Hemerocallis fulva*) whose edible dried flowers are known as 金針菜
【萱堂】one's mother

落 3427
1. ㄌㄨㄛˋ luò
1. to fall; to decline; to wither; weakened; fallen 2. to lose 3. few and far-spaced; to stand apart; loose and scattered 4. a village; a hamlet 5. to put (pen to paper) 6. to settle down 7. a pile; a heap
【落泊 or 落魄】jobless and listless; down in one's luck; out of luck
【落榜or落第】to flunk (or fail in)

a competitive examination for a job or school admission

【落寞】desolate and scattered; lonely

【落地】①to be born ②to fall to the ground

【落地窗】a French window

【落點】① (in tennis, badminton, handball, etc.) placement ②(military) the point of a fall

【落湯雞】dripping wet; drenched and bedraggled

【落難】to encounter difficulty, disaster, calamity, etc.; to be out of luck

【落淚】to cry or weep; to shed tears

【落落大方】natural; unaffected; easy

【落空】to come to nothing

【落後】to fall behind; to lag behind

【落花生】a groundnut, or peanut

【落荒而逃】to be defeated and run away the battlefield

【落脚】to stay at; to stop at

【落井下石】to beat a person when he's already down

【落下】to fall down; to drop

【落選】to fail in an election

【落差】the drop in elevation

【落成】completion (of a new building, etc.)

【落實】① practicable ② to carry out

【落水】to fall into water

【落日】the setting sun

【落英繽紛】fallen flowers scattering and flying around like snow flakes

【落伍】anachronistic; to outdate

【落網】(said of a criminal) to be caught; to be captured

落 3427
2. ㄌㄠˋ lào

1. to fall or drop (in prices, etc.) 2. (said of a bird, etc.) to land; to perch 3. to get 4. a net income; a surplus

【落價】to come down in prices

葉 3428
1. ㄧㄝˋ yè

1. a leaf; a petal (of a flower) 2. a leaf or two pages (of a book) 3. a period; an era or epoch 4. something light and tiny—as a small boat in a lake 5. a Chinese family name

【葉落歸根】When a person gets old, he thinks of going back home.

【葉落知秋】Revealing signs foretell things to come.

【葉綠素】(biochemistry) chlorophyll

葉 3428
2. ㄕㄜˋ shè

used in names of places

著 3429
1. ㄓㄨˋ zhù

1. apparent; obvious; famous 2. to write; to author 3. writings; a literary work; books 4. to set forth; to manifest; to make known

【著名or著稱】famous; renowned; celebrated

【著述or著作】①to write ②a literary work

【著作權】copyright

著 3429
2. (着) ㄓㄨㄛˊ zhuó

1. to wear (garments, etc.) 2. a move (on the chessboard, in action, plans, etc.) 3. to apply (color, etc.); to start

【著筆】to begin to write or paint

【著力】to apply force; to exert

【著陸】(said of an airplane) to land; to alight; to descend to the ground

【著落】whereabouts; results

【著想】for the sake of

【著重】to emphasize; emphasis

【著手】to start doing something

【著色】to apply coloring; to color

著 3429
3. (着) ㄓㄠˊ zháo

1. to hit the bull's-eye; right to the point; very worthwhile 2. to catch (fire, cold, etc.) 3. to make a move or take action; to use

【著魔】to be bewitched; to be possessed

【著迷】to be fascinated

【著眼】to watch; to eye with attention

著 3429
4. (着) ㄓㄠ zhāo

1. to bear; to take 2. a plan; a method

【著涼】to catch cold

【著慌 or 著急】anxious or worried

著 3429
5. (着) ·ㄓㄜ zhe

an adverbial particle

葛 3430
ㄍㄜˊ gé

dolichos (*Pueraria thunbergiana*), a creeping, edible bean whose fibers can be made into linen-like cloth and whose roots are used in herbal medicine

葡 3431
ㄆㄨˊ pú
1. a grape; a vine 2. short for Portugal
【葡萄】grapes
【葡萄糖】glucose
【葡萄乾】raisins
【葡萄酒】grape wine; port wine; a vintage; wine
【葡萄柚】a grapefruit

董 3432
ㄉㄨㄥˇ dǒng
1. to supervise; to oversee; to rectify; to correct 2. short for directors 3. a Chinese family name
【董事會】a board of directors
【董事長】a board director; the chairman of the board of directors

葫 3433
ㄏㄨˊ hú
as in葫蘆—a bottle gourd or a calabash

葬 3434
ㄗㄤˋ zàng
to bury, inter or consign to a grave
【葬禮】a funeral or burial service
【葬身之地】a burial ground
【葬送】to bury or waste (one's talent, future, hopes, etc.)
【葬儀】burial or funeral rites

葵 3435
ㄎㄨㄟˊ kuí
as in 葵花—a sunflower
【葵花油】sunflower oil

葷 3436
ㄏㄨㄣ hūn
1. a meat and fish diet; meat-eating (as opposed to what vegetarians are practicing) 2. strong smelling foods or spices—such as onions, leeks, garlic, etc. 3. obscene or dirty language, narration, films, etc.

葺 3437
ㄑㄧˋ qì
1. to repair 2. thatched 3. to pile up; to heap together
【葺補】to repair and mend

葱 3438
(蔥) ㄘㄨㄥ cōng
1. scallions; onions 2. bright green

蒂 3439
(蔕) ㄉㄧˋ dì
1. a peduncle or footstalk of a flower or fruit; a stem; a base 2. a (cigaret) butt

葯 3440
ㄧㄠˋ yào
(讀音 ㄩㄝ yuè)
1. angelica 2. a simplified form as 藥

韮 3441
(韭) ㄐㄧㄡˇ jiǔ
as in 韮菜 — fragrant-flowered garlic; (Chinese) chives

十畫

蒐 3442
ㄙㄡ sōu
1. to gather; to collect 2. to hunt or search for; hunting
【蒐羅】to search and collect
【蒐集】to collect or gather

蒙 3443
ㄇㄥˊ méng
1. to cover (up); to wrap 2. naive; childish 3. ignorant; gullible; stupid 4. to cheat; to deceive; to fool 5. to bear; to take 6. short for Mongolia
【蒙蔽】to deceive; to swindle; to fool
【蒙騙】to fool with the intention to cheat
【蒙難】to suffer disaster; to be in distress
【蒙古】Mongolia; Mongolian
【蒙古大夫】a medical quack
【蒙混】to hoodwink; to deceive and swindle
【蒙羞】to suffer shame or insult
【蒙在鼓裡】to be deceived

蒜 3444
ㄙㄨㄢˋ suàn
garlic
【蒜頭兒】the garlic head
【蒜泥】mashed garlic

蒲 3445
ㄆㄨˊ pú
1. various kinds of rush from which mats, bags, etc. are made; vines of the rushes 2. a Chinese family name
【蒲公英】the dandelion
【蒲扇】a rush-leaf fan

蒸 3446
ㄓㄥ zhēng
1. steam; to steam; to cook by steaming 2. to evaporate 3. twigs or slender branches as fuel 4. crowded; crowds; the masses
【蒸發】evaporation; to evaporate

〔艸部〕

【蒸餾】distillation; to distill
【蒸餾水】distilled water
【蒸籠】a tight basket and sieve of bamboo for steaming food
【蒸餃】steamed ravioli
【蒸汽 or 蒸氣】steam; vapor
【蒸汽機】a steam engine
【蒸蒸日上】(usually said of business, etc.) getting more and more prosperous

蒼 3447 ㄘㄤ cāng
1. green; deep green or blue 2. gray (hair); hoary 3. old 4. the masses
【蒼白】pale; pallid
【蒼茫】a vast expanse without a boundary
【蒼天】① the heavens; the sky ② springtime
【蒼老】(said of people) hoary and old
【蒼涼 or 蒼凉】desolate; bleak
【蒼生】the ordinary people; the masses
【蒼蠅】the fly
【蒼蠅拍】a flyswatter; a flyflap

蓄 3448 ㄒㄩ xù
1. to collect; to store; to save up; to reserve 2. to cultivate (long hair or a beard); to grow 3. to raise; to rear; to breed 4. to wait; to expect
【蓄髮】to grow or cultivate long hair
【蓄洪】to store floodwater
【蓄積】to store or save up; storage or savings
【蓄水池】a reservoir
【蓄意】to harbor certain intentions or ideas; premeditated (murder, etc.)

蓆 3449 ㄒㄧ xí
a mat, especially a straw mat

蓉 3450 ㄖㄨㄥ róng
as in 芙蓉—the hibiscus

蓋 3451 (盖、葢) ㄍㄞ gài
1. to cover; to hide 2. a lid; a covering 3. to build; to construct; to erect 4. to affix (a seal) 5. (an initial particle) now; then; but; because 6. (a particle indicating doubt) for; perhaps; possibly; about 7. to surpass; to excel 8. to brag; to boast
【蓋圖章 or 蓋印】to affix the seal
【蓋棺論定】When one's coffin is covered, one's deserts can be properly judged.
【蓋仙】a brag
【蓋世】surpassing one's generation; without a match
【蓋世無雙】unrivaled; matchless; peerless
【蓋子】① a lid; a cover ② a shell (of a tortoise, etc.)

蓑 3452 ㄙㄨㄛ suō
a raincoat or cloak of straw, rushes, coir, etc.
【蓑衣】a coir raincoat

蓓 3453 ㄅㄟ bèi
as in 蓓蕾—a flower bud; a bud

蓊 3454 ㄨㄥ wěng
(said of vegetation) luxuriant; flourishing; lush
【蓊鬱】the lush or luxuriant growth of vegetation

蒞 3455 (莅) ㄌㄧ lì
to arrive

十一畫

蓬 3456 ㄆㄥ péng
1. *Erigeron acer*, a species of raspberry 2. tangled 3. disheveled (hair) 4. flourishing; prospering
【蓬勃】booming; vigorously
【蓬蓽生輝】(Your gracious presence) has added glitter to my humble house.
【蓬頭垢面】disheveled hair and a dirty face—very untidy in appearance
【蓬萊仙境】a fairyland; a paradise
【蓬鬆】disheveled; very loose

蓮 3457 ㄌㄧㄢ lián
1. the lotus, or water lily 2. the "clean" land—Buddhist Paradise
【蓮蓬】the cupule of a lotus
【蓮蓬頭】a finely perforated nozzle for a shower bath
【蓮花】lotus blossoms or water lilies
【蓮藕】the lotus root
【蓮霧】the wax apple

蔻 3458 ㄎㄡ kòu
cardamon seeds
【蔻丹】red nail polish (a transliter-

ation of the trade name "Cutex")

蔑 3459 (衊) ㄇㄧㄝˋ miè
1. to disdain; to slight; to despise; to neglect; to disregard; to feel contempt for 2. without; none; no 3. to cast away 4. tiny; small
【蔑視】to disdain; to slight; to flout or disregard (rules, etc.); to defy (orders, etc.)

蔓 3460 ㄇㄢˋ màn
plants with creeping tendrils or vines
【蔓延】to spread; to creep

蔗 3461 ㄓㄜˋ zhè
sugarcane
【蔗糖】sugar from sugarcane; cane sugar

蔚 3462 ㄨㄟˋ wèi
1. (said of vegetation) luxuriant; ornamental and colorful 2. *Artemisia japonica*
【蔚藍】sky-blue
【蔚爲奇觀】to present a magnificent sight; to offer a thrilling view

蔡 3463 ㄘㄞˋ cài
1. a large turtle 2. name of an ancient state in the Epoch of Spring and Autumn 3. a Chinese family name

蔣 3464 ㄐㄧㄤˇ jiǎng
a Chinese family name

蔬 3465 ㄕㄨ shū
1. vegetables; greens 2. a vegetarian diet; vegetable food

蔔 3466 ㄅㄛˊ bó
(語音 ·ㄅㄛ bo)
as in 蘿蔔 — a common name for such edible roots as turnips, carrots, radishes

蔭 3467 ㄧㄣˋ yìn
1. the shade of trees; shade 2. to shelter; to protect 3. (with) the support or blessing of

十二畫

蔽 3468 ㄅㄧˋ bì
1. to cover 2. to hide; to conceal; to shelter 3. to screen; to separate
【蔽風雨】to shelter from the wind and rain
【蔽護】to shelter; to protect
【蔽塞】① to block up ② ignorance

蕃 3469 1. ㄈㄢˊ fán
1. (said of vegetation) flourishing; luxuriant 2. to increase; to multiply; to propagate 3. numerous; plentiful
【蕃衍】to propagate rapidly

蕃 3469 2. (番) ㄈㄢ fān
barbarians (as opposed to native Chinese); foreign; uncivilized
【蕃茄】a tomato
【蕃茄醬】tomato catsup; tomato paste
【蕃薯】a sweet potato

蕉 3470 ㄐㄧㄠ jiāo
1. the banana 2. the plantain

蕊 3471 ㄖㄨㄟˇ ruǐ
1. a flower bud; an unopened flower 2. the stamens or pistils of a flower

蕙 3472 ㄏㄨㄟˋ huì
1. a species of fragrant grass with red flowers and black seeds in early fall 2. a species of fragrant orchid
【蕙質蘭心】(said of a lady) beautiful and intelligent

蕞 3473 ㄗㄨㄟˋ zuì
very small; tiny
【蕞爾小國】a very small state

蕨 3474 ㄐㄩㄝˊ jué
the bracken

蕭 3475 ㄒㄧㄠ xiāo
1. a common variety of artemisia; oxtail-southernwood 2. reverent; respectful 3. quiet; lonely; desolate 4. a Chinese family name
【蕭條】①(said of a place or situation) deserted; desolate ②(said of business) sluggish; depressed; slack
【蕭然】① desolate; deserted ② in commotion; disorderly
【蕭灑】elegant; stately and easy (in one's appearance and man-

〔艸部〕

ner) 「autumn
【蕭颯】cool and soothing winds of
【蕭瑟】① chilly, desolate, deserted, lonely, etc. ② to rustle; to sough

〔艸部〕

蕩 3476
ㄉㄤˋ dàng
1. a pond; a pool 2. to cleanse; to wash away 3. to shake; to oscillate; to move to and fro; to loaf about; unsettled; vagrant 4. dissipated; wanton; debauched; licentious; of loose morals 5. agitated; disturbed 6. vast; large; magnificent
【蕩婦】a woman of loose morals
【蕩氣迴腸】(said of music or writing) very touching; pathetic
【蕩鞦韆】to swing on a swing
【蕩然無存】to have nothing left
【蕩漾】① moving, as in ripples ② agitated or excited ③ to rise and fall like waves; to ripple

蕪 3477
ㄨˊ wú
1. a luxuriant growth of weeds 2. decayed or rotten vegetation 3. confused; mixed-up; in disorder 4. waste; neglected, as
【蕪菁】the turnip ⌊land
【蕪雜】disorderly and confusing

十三畫

3478
薄 1. ㄅㄛˊ bó
(語音 ㄅㄠˊ báo)
1. thin; light; slight 2. to despise; to slight; to disdain 3. barren; not fertile 4. to cover; to hide or conceal; to shut 5. a screen 6. a patch of grass 7. to close in; to press near 8. frivolous
【薄片】a thin slice 「short-lived
【薄命】①star-crossed; ill-fated ②
【薄暮】around sunset; dusk
【薄利多銷】to cut down the profit margin in order to sell more —commercial tactics
【薄海騰歡】cheers from all over the country
【薄情】heartless; ungrateful
【薄弱】weak; fragile

薄 3478
2. ㄅㄛˋ bò
as in 薄荷—peppermint

蕾 3479
ㄌㄟˇ lěi 「opened flower
as in 蓓蕾—a flower bud; an un-

薇 3480
ㄨㄟˊ wéi 「thorn-ferns
Osmunda regalis, a kind of fern;

薈 3481
ㄏㄨㄟˋ huì
1. a luxuriant growth of vegetation 2. to cover or conceal
【薈萃】① flourishing or thriving ② (said of distinguished people) to gather; to assemble

薑 3482
ㄐㄧㄤ jiāng
ginger

薔 3483
ㄑㄧㄤˊ qiáng
as in 薔薇—the roses

薛 3484
ㄒㄩㄝ xuē
1. a kind of marsh grass 2. name of an ancient state in today's Shantung Province 3. a Chinese family name

薦 3485
ㄐㄧㄢˋ jiàn
1. to recommend; to offer; to present 2. fodder for animals; grass 3. a straw mat 4. food and dishes 5. to repeat; repeatedly 「duce
【薦舉or薦引】to propose; to intro-

薪 3486
ㄒㄧㄣ xīn 「ary; pay
1. firewood; fuel; fagots 2. sal-

十四畫

薩 3487
ㄙㄚˋ sà
a general name of Buddhist gods or immortals; Buddha

薯 3488
ㄕㄨˇ shǔ
a yam; a potato
【薯條】French fries

薰 3489
ㄒㄩㄣ xūn
1. to cauterize 2. to perfume; to embalm 3. to smoke; to fumi-
【薰陶】to edify ⌊gate 4. warm
【薰心】to becloud the mind

藉 3490
1. ㄐㄧㄝˋ jiè

1. a mat, pad, or cushion of grass (or straw) 2. to rely on; to lean on; on the strength of; to avail oneself of; by means of
【藉故】to avail oneself of a certain excuse or pretext
【藉口】an excuse; a pretext

藉 3490 2. ㄐㄧˊ jí
disorder; confusion

藍 3491 ㄌㄢˊ lán
1. blue; indigo 2. an indigo plant 3. a Chinese family name
【藍寶石】sapphire
【藍本】the original; a blueprint
【藍圖】a blueprint; an outline of a project
【藍領階級】blue-collar

藏 3492 1. ㄘㄤˊ cáng
1. to hide; to conceal 2. to store; to save; to hoard
【藏匿】to hide; to harbor (criminals)
【藏拙】to hide one's weak points
【藏身】to hide oneself; to conceal
【藏書】① to collect books ② a book collection

藏 3492 2. ㄗㄤˋ zàng
1. Tibet; Tibetans 2. a storage; a warehouse; a depository 3. a collective name for the Buddhist and Taoist scriptures
【藏青】indigo blue
【藏文】the Tibetan language

藐 3493 ㄇㄧㄠˇ miǎo
1. to slight; to despise; to belittle; to treat with disdain 2. small; petite
【藐小】small; petty; insignificant
【藐視】to disdain; to slight; to despise

十五畫

藕 3494 ㄡˇ ǒu
rhizomes, or rootstocks of the lotus
【藕斷絲連】The ties are severed but not completely.

藝 3495 ㄧˋ yì
art; skill; talent; craft; dexterity
【藝名】a stage name, or a screen name (of an entertainer)
【藝妓】a geisha girl; a geisha
【藝術】art: 藝術家 an artist
【藝術品】a work of art; an objet d'art
【藝人】an entertainer

藤 3496 ㄊㄥˊ téng
a rattan; a vine
【藤條】a rattan
【藤椅】a rattan chair; a cane chair

藥 3497 ㄧㄠˋ yào
(讀音 ㄩㄝˋ yuè)
1. medicine; remedy; a drug; pharmaceuticals 2. to kill with poison; to poison
【藥片】a tablet of medicine
【藥品】pharmaceutical products; drugs
【藥粉】medicinal powder
【藥單or藥方】a (medicinal) prescription
【藥力】the potency or effect of a drug
【藥量】dosage
【藥膏】ointment; salve
【藥罐子】① a drug boiler ② one who is perennially ill
【藥劑師】a pharmacist; a druggist
【藥局 or 藥房】a druggist's store; a dispensary; a pharmacy
【藥箱】a medicine chest; a medical kit
【藥水】liquid medicine
【藥材】medicinal substance
【藥草】medicinal herbs
【藥丸】a pill medicine; a pill

藩 3498 ㄈㄢˊ fán
a fence; a hedge; a boundary; a frontier; a barrier
【藩籬】① a fence; a hedge ② anything acting as a hedge ③ a barrier
【藩屬】a vassal state; a protectorate

十六畫

藹 3499 ㄞˇ ǎi
1. exuberant; luxuriant; lush 2. gentle; kind; amiable 3. gloomy; dim

藻 3500 ㄗㄠˇ zǎo
1. algae; pondweeds 2. diction; wording; language
【藻飾】① embellishment in writing ② to polish writings

艸部

蘆 3501 ㄌㄨˊ lú
1. reeds; rushes 2. gourds
【蘆薈】 aloes
【蘆筍】 (botany) asparagus
【蘆葦】 reeds

蘗 3502 (孽) ㄋㄧㄝˋ niè
1. the son of a concubine 2. sin; evil 3. calamity
【蘗子】 the son of a concubine

蘇 3503 ㄙㄨ sū
1. purple perilla 亦作「紫蘇」 2. to revive; to come back to life; to resurrect 3. to awake 4. to rest 5. short for Kiangsu Province or Soochow 6. a Chinese family name
【蘇打】 soda
【蘇醒】 to come to; to awaken; to revive

蘊 3504 (藴) ㄩㄣˋ yùn
1. to collect; to gather 2. to store; to have in store 3. deep; profound 4. sweltering; sultry
【蘊釀】 (said of a storm, trouble, etc.) to brew; to foment
【蘊藉】 refined and cultivated
【蘊藏】 to have in store; to be rich in

蘋 3505 ㄆㄧㄥˊ píng
as in 蘋果—an apple

十七畫

蘚 3506 ㄒㄧㄢˇ xiǎn
as in 蘚苔—(botany) moss; lichen

蘭 3507 ㄌㄢˊ lán
as in 蘭花—an orchid; a cymbidium

十九畫

蘸 3508 ㄓㄢˋ zhàn
to dip
【蘸筆】 to dip a writing brush in ink

蘿 3509 ㄌㄨㄛˊ luó
1. a kind of creeping plant; a wistaria 2. as in 蘿蔔 — a radish; a turnip
【蘿蔔乾】 a dried radish or turnip
【蘿蔔糕】 turnip pudding

虍 部
ㄏㄨ hū

二畫

虎 3510 ㄏㄨˇ hǔ
1. a tiger 2. fierce; savage; vigorous; brave
【虎背熊腰】 heavy and muscular build of the body
【虎皮】 ①a tiger skin ②seeming bravery
【虎父無犬子】 There will be no laggard among the children of a brave or talented man.
【虎頭蛇尾】 to start doing something with vigor but fail to see it through
【虎口】 ①a tiger's mouth—a dangerous place ② the part of a hand between the thumb and the index finger
【虎口餘生】 to have a narrow escape
【虎視眈眈】 to gaze with the cruel greed of a tiger

三畫

虐 3511 ㄋㄩㄝˋ nüè
1. cruel; ferocious; atrocious 2. to tyrannize over; to oppress
【虐待】 to maltreat; to torture

四畫

虔 3512 ㄑㄧㄢˊ qián
reverence; reverent; respectful; pious
【虔誠】 devout; piety; sincerity; pious
【虔敬】 reverent; reverently

五畫

處 3513 1. ㄔㄨˇ chǔ
1. a place; a spot; a location; a locality 2. a department in a government agency 3. a special quality
【處處】 ① everywhere ② in all respects
【處所】 a place; a locality

處 3513
2. ㄔㄨˇ chǔ
1. to place oneself in; to be faced with; to live in 2. to get along 3. to dispose of; to handle 4. to sentence; to punish 5. to dwell; to live
【處罰】 to punish
【處分】 ① to take action against; to punish ② to deal with (a matter)
【處方】 to prescribe
【處女】 a virgin
【處女膜】 the hymen; the maiden-head
【處女作】 a maiden work
【處理】 ① to handle; to deal with ② to treat by a special process
【處境】 the position or situation one is in
【處決】 ① to decide; to resolve ② to execute (an offender)
【處心積慮】 to have in mind for a long time
【處刑】 to punish; to execute; to mete out a sentence
【處之泰然】 to maintain composure
【處世】 to conduct oneself in life
【處死】 to punish with death

六畫

虛 3514
ㄒㄩ xū
1. empty; hollow; void; unoccupied 2. unreal; false; deceptive; unfounded; groundless 3. weak; feeble 4. abstract; shapeless
【虛名】 an empty reputation
【虛度】 to fritter away; to dream away
【虛脫】 (medicine) collapse; prostration
【虛構】 made-up; to trump up; to frame
【虛懷若谷】 to be open-minded
【虛幻】 illusory; visionary; unreal
【虛假】 false; unreal; dishonest
【虛驚】 a false alarm
【虛情假意】 hypocrisy; insincerity
【虛線】 ① a dotted line ② an imaginary line
【虛心】 open-minded
【虛張聲勢】 to bluff
【虛實】 ① true or false ② the actual situation
【虛弱】 debility; weak; feeble
【虛榮】 vanity; empty glory; vainglorious
【虛榮心】 vainglory; vanity
【虛歲】 age according to Chinese calculation
【虛有其表】 to appear better than it is
【虛無】 nothingness; emptiness; nil; void
【虛僞】 spurious; insincere; hypocrisy

七畫

虜 3515
ㄌㄨˇ lǔ
(又讀 ㄌㄨㄛˇ luǒ)
1. a captive; a prisoner 2. to take prisoner; to capture alive
【虜獲】 ① to capture ② men and arms captured

號 3516
1. ㄏㄠˋ hào
1. a designation; a title 2. sizes 3. a call 4. a number 5. a mark; a sign 6. a store; a shop 7. a bugle 8. date
【號令】 a command; an order
【號角】 a bugle; a horn
【號誌】 a signal; a sign
【號召】 a call; to summon
【號稱】 ① to claim; to profess ② to be known as
【號子】 (slang) a stock exchange
【號外】 an extra

號 3516
2. ㄏㄠˊ háo
to cry; to shout; to howl; to wail
【號咷 or 號啕】 to burst out crying; to weep aloud; to wail

十一畫

虧 3517
ㄎㄨㄟ kuī
1. to lose; to damage; to have a deficit 2. to lack; to want; short; deficient 3. to treat unfairly; to be unfair to 4. fortunately; luckily 5. used in a mocking sense 6. the waning; to wane
【虧待】 to maltreat
【虧空】 ① to spend more than one makes ② a loss; a deficit
【虧欠】 ① a deficit ② insufficiency ③ to owe
【虧心事】 something which gives one a guilty conscience
【虧損】 ① a deficit; a loss; to deplete ② enfeebled or weakened by illness

〔虫部〕

虫部
ㄏㄨㄟˇ huǐ

二畫

3518 虱 (蝨) ㄕ shī
a louse
【虱目魚】milkfish

三畫

3519 虹 ㄏㄨㄥˊ hóng
(語音 ㄍㄤˋ gàng)
a rainbow
【虹霓】a rainbow and its reflection

四畫

3520 蚌 ㄅㄤˋ bàng
an oyster

3521 蚊 (螡) ㄨㄣˊ wén
a mosquito; a gnat
【蚊香】a mosquito coil; mosquito incense
【蚊帳】a mosquito net

3522 蚤 ㄗㄠˇ zǎo
a flea

五畫

3523 蚯 ㄑㄧㄡ qiū
as in 蚯蚓—an earthworm

3524 蚱 ㄓㄚˋ zhà
as in 蚱蜢—a locust; a grasshopper

3525 蛀 ㄓㄨˋ zhù
1. worms that eat into wood or books 2. (said of worms) to eat into; to bore
【蛀齒 or 蛀牙】decayed teeth; dental caries
【蛀蟲】a moth

3526 蛇 (虵) ㄕㄜˊ shé
a snake; a serpent
【蛇蠍】snakes and scorpions—things to be dreaded
【蛇行】①to take a zigzag course ②to creep along; to crawl

3527 蛋 ㄉㄢˋ dàn
1. an egg 2. a fellow
【蛋白 or 蛋清】egg white; albumen
【蛋白質】protein; albumen
【蛋糕】cake
【蛋殼】the eggshell
【蛋黃】yolk

六畫

3528 蛙 ㄨㄚ wā
a frog
【蛙人】a frogman
【蛙泳】(swimming) the breaststroke

3529 蛔 ㄏㄨㄟˊ huí
an ascarid; a roundworm

3530 蛛 ㄓㄨ zhū
a spider
【蛛絲馬跡】clues; leads
【蛛網】a spider's web; a cobweb

3531 蛤 1. ㄍㄜˊ gé
a clam

3531 蛤 2. ㄏㄚˊ há
as in 蛤蟆 or 蝦蟆—a toad

七畫

3532 蛹 ㄩㄥˇ yǒng
a chrysalis; a pupa

3533 蛻 ㄕㄨㄟˋ shuì
(又讀 ㄊㄨㄟˋ tuì)
1. to slough; to exuviate 2. exuviae; a slough
【蛻變】①to undergo transformation ②decay
【蛻皮】to exuviate; to slough

3534 蛾 ㄜˊ é
a moth
【蛾眉】long, slender eyebrows arched like the antennae of a moth

3535 蜀 ㄕㄨˇ shǔ
1. Shu, an ancient kingdom in

what is Szechwan today 2. an alternative name of Szechwan(四川)

蜂 3536 ㄈㄥ fēng
a bee; a wasp
【蜂蜜】 honey
【蜂房 or 蜂窩 or 蜂巢】 a honeycomb; a beehive;

蜈 3537 ㄨˊ wú
as in 蜈蚣—a centipede

八畫

蜥 3538 ㄒㄧ xī
as in 蜥蜴—a lizard

蜘 3539 ㄓ zhī
as in 蜘蛛—a spider

蜚 3540 (飛) ㄈㄟ fēi
to fly
【蜚短流長】 to spread rumors; to gossip; rumors; gossips

蜜 3541 ㄇㄧˋ mì
1. honey; nectar (in a flower) 2. sweet; syrupy; honeyed
【蜜蜂】 a honeybee; a bee
【蜜月】 a honeymoon

蜷 3542 ㄑㄩㄢˊ quán
to wriggle; to be coiled; to be curled up
【蜷伏】 to curl up; to huddle up; to lie with the knees drawn up

蜻 3543 ㄑㄧㄥ qīng
a dragonfly

蜿 3544 ㄨㄢ wān
to creep; to wriggle; to wind up
【蜿蜒】 creeping; snaky

九畫

蝙 3545 ㄅㄧㄢ biān (又讀 ㄅㄧㄢˇ biǎn)
as in 蝙蝠—a bat

蝌 3546 ㄎㄜ kē
as in 蝌蚪—a tadpole

蝕 3547 ㄕˊ shí
1. to eclipse; an eclipse 2. to erode; to eat up slowly

蝗 3548 ㄏㄨㄤˊ huáng
as in 蝗蟲—a locust

蝦 3549 ㄒㄧㄚ xiā
a shrimp: 蝦米 dried shrimps

蝴 3550 ㄏㄨˊ hú
as in 蝴蝶—a butterfly

蝶 3551 (蜨) ㄉㄧㄝˊ dié
a butterfly

蝸 3552 ㄍㄨㄚ guā
as in 蝸牛—a snail

十畫

螃 3553 ㄆㄤˊ páng
as in 螃蟹—a crab

融 3554 ㄖㄨㄥˊ róng
1. very bright; glowing; burning 2. to melt 3. to melt into; to blend; to harmonize 4. cheerful; happy; joyful
【融合 or 融和】 to blend; to fuse
【融化】 to melt; to fuse; to thaw
【融會貫通】 well digested and completely understood
【融解】 to melt; to thaw
【融洽】 (said especially of human relations) harmonious

螞 3555 ㄇㄚˇ mǎ
1. an ant 2. a kind of leech

螢 3556 ㄧㄥˊ yíng
a luminous insect; a firefly; a glowworm
【螢火蟲】 a firefly; a glowworm

十一畫

螫 3557 ㄓㄜ zhē (又讀 ㄕˋ shì)
1. a poisonous insect; a scorpion 2. to sting

螳 3558 ㄊㄤˊ táng
as in 螳螂—a mantis

螺 3559 ㄌㄨㄛˊ luó
1. a spiral shell; a conch 2. an

〔虫部〕

alias of wine cups 3. a spiral
【螺旋】 a screw; a spiral
【螺絲 or 螺絲釘】 a male screw; an external screw; a screw

〔虫部〕

蟄 3560 ㄓ zhí (語音 ㄓㄜˊ zhé)
as in 蟄伏—to hibernate; hibernation

蟋 3561 ㄒㄧ xī
as in 蟋蟀—a cricket (insect)

蟑 3562 ㄓㄤ zhāng
as in 蟑螂—a cockroach; a roach

十二畫

蟒 3563 ㄇㄤˇ mǎng
as in 蟒蛇—a python; a boa

蟠 3564 ㄆㄢˊ pán
1. to coil; to curl up 2. to occupy
【蟠踞】 to occupy

蟬 3565 ㄔㄢˊ chán
1. a cicada 2. continuous; uninterrupted
【蟬聯】 to keep on without interruption

蟲 3566 ㄔㄨㄥˊ chóng
insects; worms
【蟲害】 damage to farm crops caused by pests; insect pest

十三畫

蟹 3567 (蠏) ㄒㄧㄝˋ xiè
a crab

蟻 3568 ㄧˇ yǐ
an ant
【蟻附】 to swarm over (as ants swarm over their prey)

蟾 3569 ㄔㄢˊ chán
a toad

蠅 3570 ㄧㄥˊ yíng
a fly
【蠅頭微利】 petty profits

蠍 3571 ㄒㄧㄝ xiē
a scorpion

十四畫

蠔 3572 ㄏㄠˊ háo
an oyster 亦作「牡蠣」
【蠔油】 oyster sauce

十五畫

蠟 3573 ㄌㄚˋ là
1. wax 2. as in 蠟燭—a candle
【蠟筆】 a crayon
【蠟淚】 wax guttering; drips from a burning candle
【蠟像】 a wax figure; a waxwork

蠡 3574 ㄌㄧˊ lí
1. a calabash 2. a calabash shell serving as a dipper; a dipper
【蠡測】 to be very naive (like one trying to measure the ocean with a calabash)

蠢 3575 (惷) ㄔㄨㄣˇ chǔn
1. to wriggle; to squirm 2. stupid; foolish; dull; silly
【蠢才 or 蠢材】 a simpleton; a fool; an idiot

十七畫

蠱 3576 ㄍㄨˇ gǔ
1. poison; venom; harm 2. to bewitch; to enchant
【蠱惑】 to confuse by magic or witchcraft; to put under a spell; to enchant

十八畫

蠶 3577 ㄘㄢˊ cán
a silkworm: 蠶繭 the cocoon of the silkworm
【蠶豆】 a horse bean; a fava bean
【蠶絲】 natural silk; silk

蠹 3578 (蠧) ㄉㄨˋ dù
1. a moth 2. moth-eaten; worm-eaten 3. an insect that eats up the resources—(figuratively) an embezzler
【蠹國害民】 to rob the state and hurt the people

十九畫

蠻 3579
ㄇㄢˊ mán
1. barbarous; savage; barbarians in the south 2. quite; pretty; very; fairly
【蠻橫】barbarous; savage
【蠻族】barbarian tribes; savage tribes; primitive people

血 部
ㄒㄩㄝˋ xuè

血 3580
ㄒㄩㄝˋ xuè
(語音 ㄒㄧㄝˇ xiě)
1. blood; blood relationship 2. the menses 「earned capital
【血本無歸】no return of hard-}
【血糖】blood sugar; blood glucose
【血統】blood relationship; a strain; lineage; consanguinity; pedigree
【血濃於水】Blood is thicker than water.
【血淚】tears and blood—extreme sorrow 「sanguinary
【血淋淋】blood-dripping; bloody;}
【血管】blood vessels
【血口噴人】to curse and slander; to make false accusations against others
【血庫】a blood bank
【血海深仇】a blood feud; intense and deep-seated hatred
【血汗】blood and sweat—hard toil
【血汗錢】money earned by very hard work or toil; hard-earned money
【血紅】as red as blood; scarlet
【血跡】bloodstained; bloodstains
【血氣方剛】(said of youths) hot-tempered; easily excited; full of vigor
【血球】blood corpuscles; blood cells 「sanguinary
【血腥】reeking of blood; bloody;}
【血型】a blood type; a blood group
【血屬 or 血親】blood relatives
【血肉模糊】(said of human bodies) badly mutilated; mutilated beyond recognition
【血壓】blood pressure
【血液】the blood 「strain
【血緣】blood; blood relationship; a}

行 部
ㄒㄧㄥˊ xíng

行 3581
1. ㄒㄧㄥˊ xíng
1. to walk; to go on foot 2. to move; to go; to travel 3. to act; to do; to work 4. to publish 5. to be current; to prevail 6. able; capable 7. all right; O.K.; enough 8. baggage for travel 9. a road; a path
【行不行】(a term used in requesting permission) can; may
【行騙】to cheat; to deceive; to swindle 「move
【行動】to act; to move; to make a}
【行動電話】the cellular telephone
【行動自如】to move freely or without impairment 「for travel
【行囊】one's baggage and money}
【行禮】① to salute; to bow curtsey or kowtow to show respect ② to undergo a ceremony
【行李 or 行裝】baggage; luggage
【行賄】to bribe; to offer a bribe
【行進】(military) to move forward; to march
【行將就木】dying; nearing death
【行徑】① one's conduct or behavior; actions ② a path; a trail
【行軍】① the movement of an army; a march ② the deployment of military forces
【行乞】to beg; to be a beggar
【行竊】to steal 「be on sale
【行銷】to sell; to effect sales; to}
【行星】the planets
【行刑】①to execute (criminals); execution ②to torture (prisoners)
【行兇】to commit killing or murder
【行政】① government; administration of public affairs ② the executive branch of a government
【行政機關】administrative organizations
【行政院】Executive Yuan
【行車】① the movement of vehicles ② to drive a vehicle
【行程】① a traveler's route or itinerary ② to embark on a journey ③ a march; a journey

【行尸走肉】a walking corpse—an absolutely useless person
【行駛】to drive (cars); to sail or steer (boats)
【行事曆】a calendar
【行善】to do good deeds; to do charitable work
【行人】pedestrians; passers-by
【行人道】sidewalks of a street
【行走】to walk
【行蹤or行踪】tracks or whereabouts of a person
【行蹤不明】whereabouts unknown
【行刺】to assassinate
【行色匆匆】in a hurry to leave
【行醫】to practice medicine
【行有餘力】to have extra resources
【行爲】① behavior; conduct ② (law) acts
【行雲流水】(literally) moving clouds and flowing water—a natural and flowing style of writing, etc.

行 3581
2. ㄒㄧㄥˋ xìng
one's conduct or behavior
【行狀】a brief biography of the deceased
【行誼】conduct and virtues

行 3581
3. ㄏㄤˊ háng
1. a row; a line; a series 2. a business firm; a company 3. a trade; a line; a profession 4. order of brothers (and sisters) according to seniority 5. a generation
【行列】the rank and file; rows and columns
【行號】shops; stores; business establishments
【行行出狀元】Every trade has its master. 或 One may distinguish himself in any trade.
【行家】a professional; an expert
【行情】① market prices of certain commodities; a quotation; market ② general standing of a person in terms of finance, influence, popularity, etc.
【行業】a trade; an occupation

三畫

衍 3582
ㄧㄢˇ yǎn
1. to overflow; to spread out 2. ample; plenty and abundant 3. (said of fields or plains) level; plane and even 4. a lake; a marsh 5. a slope 6. superfluous
【衍生】to derive from

五畫

衒 3583
ㄒㄩㄢˋ xuàn
1. to brag; to boast; to show off 2. to recommend oneself

術 3584
ㄕㄨˋ shù
1. a skill; a feat 2. a way or method to do something
【術語】professional jargon; terminology; technical terms

六畫

街 3585
ㄐㄧㄝ jiē
a street; a road in a city; a thoroughfare
【街道】streets; roads in a city or town
【街頭巷尾】throughout the city; in every nook and corner of the city

七畫

衙 3586
ㄧㄚˊ yá
1. a government office 2. to meet; to gather; to congregate 3. (Tang Dynasty) a front hall of the palace
【衙門】"*yamen*"—a government office in feudal China

九畫

衝 3587
1. ㄔㄨㄥ chōng
1. to rush; to thrust; to forge ahead; to dash 2. to charge forward; to hit with force 3. a thoroughfare; a hub; a strategic place 4. to offend
【衝鋒陷陣】to charge ahead and take enemy positions
【衝動】① an impulse; a sudden urge ② to be excited
【衝突】a conflict; a fight; a clash
【衝浪】to surf
【衝力】impulsive forces; momentum

【衝擊】to strike against; to pound against; to charge
【衝勁】aggressiveness; enterprising spirit; drive
【衝撞】①to collide; to ram ②to offend; to treat impolitely
【衝出】to rush out; to dash out
【衝刺】a spurt; a sprint

衝 3587
2. ㄔㄨㄥˋ chòng
1. to head or go (south, north, etc.) 2. strong (smell) 3. brave and fierce 4. for (your, his, etc.) sake 5. to direct (one's attack, etc.) toward
【衝著】for (your, his, etc.) sake

十畫

衞 3588
(衛) ㄨㄟˋ wèi
1. to guard; to protect; to defend 2. a keeper; a bodyguard; a guard
【衞兵】(military) guard; sentry
【衞冕】to defend a title
【衞星】satellites
【衞生】sanitation; sanitary; public health
【衞生棉】a sanitary napkin
【衞生紙】tissue paper; toilet paper
【衞生設備】sanitary facilities
【衞生所】a public health clinic
【衞生衣】a kind of tight cotton underwear

衡 3589
ㄏㄥˊ héng
1. to weigh; to measure; to assess; to consider 2. horizontal 3. railings 4. a beam 5. the beam of a steelyard
【衡量】to weigh; to measure; to consider

十八畫

衢 3590
ㄑㄩˊ qú
a thoroughfare; a highway junction
【衢道】a side street; crossroads

衣部
ㄧ yī

衣 3591
1. ㄧ yī
1. clothing; dress; apparel; garments; attire 2. a coating; a covering 3. skin or peel of fruits
【衣鉢】teaching, skill, etc. handed down from a master to his pupil
【衣帽間】a cloakroom (in restaurants, etc.); a checkroom
【衣服】clothes; clothing; dress
【衣料】clothing material
【衣領】a collar
【衣櫃】a wardrobe; a chest of drawers for clothing
【衣冠不整】sloppily dressed
【衣冠禽獸】a gentleman in appearance but a beast in conduct
【衣冠楚楚】in immaculate attire; dressed like a gentleman
【衣架】a rack for clothes; a clotheshorse; a coat hanger
【衣襟】lapels of a garment
【衣箱】a box or chest for storing clothes
【衣著】clothing; attire; apparel; dress
【衣櫥】a wardrobe; a clothespress
【衣衫襤褸】ragged clothing
【衣裳】clothes; garments; clothing
【衣索比亞】Ethiopia
【衣物】clothing and other articles of daily use

衣 3591
2. ㄧˋ yì
to clothe; to wear; to dress
【衣錦還鄉】to return home in glory

三畫

表 3592
ㄅㄧㄠˇ biǎo
1. outside; external; apparent; appearance; exteriors; superficial 2. to announce; to manifest; to show 3. as in表親—relatives on the side of one's mother's sisters or brothers; relatives on the side of one's father's sisters 4. a report to the emperor 5. a table; a schedule; a chart; a form
【表白】to express or state clearly
【表皮】①the epidermis ②the cuticle (of plants)
【表面】on the surface; externally; outwardly
【表明】to indicate or state clearly or plainly
【表達】to convey or transmit (one's feelings, meaning, etc.); to present; to express; to make known

〔衣部〕

【表態】to make known one's position towards an issue
【表裏不一】to think in one way and behave in another
【表裏一致】honest and sincere
【表露】to make plain; to express or expose; to voice
【表格】a form or blank (for filling); a table or chart
【表姊妹】female first cousins
【表決】to vote; to put to the vote
【表情】facial expression
【表現】① to appear ② to behave ③ to distinguish oneself
【表兄弟】male first cousins
【表彰】to honor; to cite; citation
【表示】to express; to show; to indicate; expression; reaction
【表率】an example; a paragon
【表層】a surface layer
【表演】to perform; to demonstrate; a performance; demonstration; a show
【表揚】to praise in public; to cite for all to know

衫 3593 ㄕㄢ shān
a shirt; a garment; a gown

四畫

衰 3594 ㄕㄨㄞ shuāi
1. to decline; weakening; failing (health, etc.) 2. declining or falling (nations, etc.)
【衰敗】to decline and disintegrate
【衰退】failing (energy, strength, etc.)
【衰老】senile; senility
【衰落 or 衰亡】the decline and fall
【衰竭】exhaustion; prostration
【衰弱】to debilitate; weak; sickly; not healthy
【衰微】to decline; to wane; declining

衷 3595 ㄓㄨㄥ zhōng
1. the bottom of one's heart; honest; sincere 2. good and virtuous; goodness 3. proper; appropriate; befitting; propriety 4. undergarments
【衷曲】the voice of one's heart; inner feelings; words from the bottom of one's heart
【衷心】cordial; heartfelt; wholehearted
【衷心感謝】to thank sincerely
【衷腸 or 衷懷】innermost feelings; sincere words

衾 3596 ㄑㄧㄣ qīn
(又讀 ㄑㄧㄣˊ qín)
1. a large coverlet or quilt 2. garments or dress for the deceased
【衾枕】quilts and pillows

袁 3597 ㄩㄢˊ yuán
1. the graceful look of a flowing robe 2. a Chinese family name

五畫

袈 3598 ㄐㄧㄚ jiā
as in 袈裟—the cassock or robe of a Buddhist monk

袖 3599 ㄒㄧㄡˋ xiù
1. the sleeve 2. to hide or put things in sleeves
【袖口】the cuff (of a sleeve); the far ends of sleeves; a wristband
【袖扣】cuff links
【袖珍】pocket-size; pocket
【袖珍本】a pocket book; a pocket edition
【袖手旁觀】to look on without even lifting a finger (to help, etc.)

袋 3600 ㄉㄞˋ dài
a bag; a sack; a pocket; a pouch
【袋鼠】the kangaroo

袍 3601 ㄆㄠˊ páo
a long gown; a robe: 袍澤comrades in arms

袒 3602 ㄊㄢˇ tǎn
1. to bare; to strip; bared 2. to protect or screen (with an implication of prejudice)
【袒露】to expose
【袒護】to shield; to protect; to screen; to side with; to be partial

被 3603 1. ㄅㄟˋ bèi
1. bedding; a coverlet; a quilt 2. to cover; to shroud 3. to spread; to reach 4. placed before verbs to show a passive voice 5. because of; due to
【被迫or被逼】to be compelled or forced to
【被單兒】a bedsheet; a bedspread

【被動】passive; to act on order
【被套】ticking
【被告】the accused; the defendant
【被害】to be killed or murdered
【被搶】to be robbed
【被褥】coverlets and mattresses; bedding
【被子】a quilt
【被窩兒】a quilt folded like a sleeve for sleeping

被 3603
2. (披) ㄆㄧ pī
1. to put on or throw on (garments, etc.) without buttoning up 2. to disperse or spread out
【被髮左衽】hair unbound and coats buttoned on the left side—to become a barbarian

六畫

袴 3604
(絝、褲) ㄎㄨˋ kù
trousers; drawers; breeches; pants; panties

裁 3605
ㄘㄞˊ cái
1. to cut paper, cloth, etc. with a knife or scissors 2. to diminish; to reduce 3. to delete 4. to consider; to decide; to judge 5. a form; a style 6. sanctions 7. to weight; to measure 8. to kill
【裁判】①a judge; a referee; an umpire ②a verdict or judgment by law
【裁縫】①(ㄘㄞˊ ㄈㄥˊ) to tailor; to make dress ②(ㄘㄞˊ ·ㄈㄥ) a tailor; a dressmaker 亦作「裁縫師」
【裁開】to cut apart with a knife or scissors
【裁剪】to tailor; to cut out (a dress)
【裁減】①to reduce (personnel, the staff, etc.) ②reduction
【裁決】①to judge and decide ②a ruling; a judgment; a decision
【裁軍】disarmament
【裁員】to eliminate unnecessary personnel; to lay off workers

裂 3606
ㄌㄧㄝˋ liè
1. to crack; to break; a crack 2. to split or divide up (profits, etc.); to rend; to sever
【裂縫】a crack; a breach; a crevice
【裂開】to split, rip or break apart
【裂口】a crack; a chink
【裂痕】①a chasm (in friendship, etc.) ②a fissure; a split

七畫

裊 3607
ㄋㄧㄠˇ niǎo
1. curling up (as smoke, etc.); wavering gently 2. around; all around, as sound of music or voices of spring
【裊裊】①curling up ②continuous (sound of music, etc.)

裙 3608
ㄑㄩㄣˊ qún
a skirt; a petticoat; an apron

裏 3609
1. (裡) ㄌㄧˇ lǐ
1. within; inside 2. used to indicate time of day, night, a season, etc. 3. the lining of a dress or clothes
【裏面兒】inside; within
【裏頭】inside
【裏裏外外】inside and out
【裏子】the lining of a garment, a hat or shoes
【裏應外合】the joining of forces within and without

裏 3609
2. ·ㄌㄧ li
used after 這 and 那 to mean "here" and "there" respectively

裔 3610
ㄧˋ yì
1. descendants; posterity 2. the hem of a garment, robe, etc. 3. remote or border regions

裕 3611
ㄩˋ yù
1. abundance; affluent; plenty; to be abundant 2. tolerant (administration, etc.); lenient (punishment, etc.) 3. generous; magnanimous 4. slowly; to take time

裘 3612
ㄑㄧㄡˊ qiú
furs; any garments, robes, etc. of fur

補 3613
ㄅㄨˇ bǔ
1. to repair; to patch; to mend; to fill 2. to add to; to supplement; to supply 3. addenda; supplements; complements 4. nutritious; nutrient 5. rich foods; tonics 6. to nourish 7. to make up; to help (finance, etc.); to sub-

sidize 8. to appoint to or fill a post 9. to be of help; benefit
【補票】to buy one's ticket after one gets on a bus, a train, etc.
【補品】foods or medicines of highly nutritious value; tonics
【補發】to issue or distribute behind schedule
【補釘or補釘】patches (of a garment, etc.)
【補貼】to subsidize; a subsidy; an allowance
【補考】a make-up test
【補給】(military) provisions; supplies; to supply
【補救】to save the situation
【補習】private tutoring to supplement regular schooling; to tutor
【補習班】a class for supplementary schooling
【補鞋匠】a cobbler
【補助】to subsidize; to help (finance, etc.)
【補助金】a grant
【補注or補註】supplementary notes; to make supplementary notes
【補償】to compensate; to make up
【補充】to add; to supplement
【補足】to make up a deficit; to make complete or whole
【補牙】to fill a tooth cavity; to have a tooth stopped
【補藥】tonics

裝 3614
ㄓㄨㄤ zhuāng
1. to fill in or up; to pack; to load 2. to pretend; to feign 3. to adorn; to dress or make up; ornamental dressing; to decorate (a room, etc.) 4. to disguise 5. to store; to keep 6. to install (machines, equipment, etc.) 7. clothes and personal effects
【裝備】equipment or an outfit
【裝扮】① adornment; make-up; to dress or doll up; attire ②to disguise
【裝病】to pretend illness; to malinger
【裝配】to assemble (a machine)
【裝滿】to fill up
【裝模作樣】to act affectedly; to be pretentious; to strike a pose
【裝瘋賣傻】to pretend to be crazy and stupid; to play the fool
【裝訂】to bind pages into a volume or book; binding
【裝聾作啞】to pretend to hear and know nothing
【裝糊塗】to pretend not to know; to feign ignorance 亦作「裝憨兒」
【裝貨】to load or pack goods
【裝潢】to decorate (a room, shop, etc.); decoration
【裝甲部隊】armored troops or units
【裝甲車】an armored vehicle; a tank
【裝腔作勢】affected; pretentious; to strike an attitude
【裝箱】to pack in a box or chest; to box
【裝飾】①to doll up; to deck; to make up ②to adorn; to embellish
【裝設】to install; to equip
【裝睡】to feign sleep; to pretend to be asleep
【裝載】loaded with; to pack; to stow
【裝死】to play dead; to feign death
【裝運】to pack and transport; to load and ship

裟 3615
ㄕㄚ shā
a cassock or robe of a Buddhist monk

八畫

裸 3616
ㄌㄨㄛˇ luǒ
as in 裸裎—bare; nude; naked
【裸體】nude; naked; without a stitch on
【裸露】uncovered; exposed
【裸裎】naked; undressed

裨 3617
ㄅㄧˋ bì
1. to aid; to supplement 2. to benefit; to help
【裨益】to benefit; benefit

裱 3618
ㄅㄧㄠˇ biǎo
1. to mount (paintings, calligraphy, etc.) 2. a scarf
【裱褙】to mount (paintings, etc.)

裳 3619
ㄔㄤˊ cháng
(語音 ·ㄕㄤ shang as in 衣裳)
dress; garments; clothing

裴 3620
ㄆㄟˊ péi
the look of a flowing gown

裹 3621
ㄍㄨㄛˇ guǒ
1. to tie up; to wrap or bind 2. things wrapped, as a parcel 3. to surround; to encompass 4. to

close in and force obedience
【裹腿】leggings; puttees
【裹足不前】to be afraid to move ahead

製 3622
ㄓˋ zhì
1. as in 製造—to produce; to manufacture; to make; to create 2. to compose (writings, literature, etc.); literary works 3. to cut out garments and make them 4. a form; a model; a pattern
【製版】to make a printing plate
【製品】products; manufactures
【製圖】to make (or draw) maps, charts, etc.
【製作】to make; to produce; to manufacture
【製作人】a producer

褂 3623
ㄍㄨㄚˋ guà
an overcoat; a robe or gown; a jacket

九畫

複 3624
ㄈㄨˋ fù
1. double; overlapping 2. complex (concepts, etc.); compound (interest, etc.) 3. to repeat; to reiterate
【複本】a duplicate
【複合】compound; complex; composite
【複句】a complex sentence
【複寫】to duplicate or produce copies of a piece of writing, etc. with carbon paper, etc.
【複選】a run-off (election)
【複製】to make a reproduction; to reproduce; to duplicate
【複查】to reinvestigate; to check again
【複雜】complex; complicated
【複賽】(sports) a semifinal; a play-off
【複印】duplication

褊 3625
ㄅㄧㄢˇ biǎn
1. narrow; small; petty 2. small size clothes 3. narrow minded
【褊急】short-tempered; lacking patience

褐 3626
ㄏㄜˊ hé
1. coarse woolen cloth; coarse cloth; haircloth; rough cloth 2. the poor or destitute 3. as in 褐色—brown

褓 3627
ㄅㄠˇ bǎo
1. swaddling bands; swaddling clothes 2. as in 襁褓—infancy
【褓母】a nurse; a baby-sitter

褙 3628
ㄅㄟˋ bèi
to mount (paintings, or calligraphic works)

十畫

褥 3629
ㄖㄨˋ rù
bedding; quilts or coverlets; a mattress; cushion; bedclothes

褪 3630
ㄊㄨㄣˋ tùn
1. to take off one's clothing; to strip 2. to fall off; to fade, as color 3. to retreat; to move backward
【褪色】color fading

褫 3631
ㄔˇ chǐ
1. to strip off; to deprive of 2. to undress forcibly
【褫奪公權】to strip or deprive one of one's civil rights

褲 3632
(袴) ㄎㄨˋ kù
drawers; trousers; pants: 褲襪 pantyhose

十一畫

褶 3633
ㄓㄜˊ zhé
to fold; pleated: 褶裙 a pleated skirt

褸 3634
ㄌㄩˇ lǚ
1. the collar or lapel of a garment 2. (said of clothes) tattered; in rags

褒 3635
(襃) ㄅㄠ bāo
1. to praise; to cite; to commend; a citation 2. big; great
【褒貶】to praise and disparage; criticisms
【褒獎】to praise and cite; to commend and award

襁 3636
(繦) ㄑㄧㄤˇ qiǎng
swaddling clothes for an infant; a broad bandage for carrying an infant on the back
【襁褓】①swaddling clothes or carrying band for an infant ②infancy

襄 3637
ㄒㄧㄤ xiāng
1. to help; to assist 2. to

〔衣部〕

achieve; to accomplish; to complete 3. to rise; to raise 4. high [a bank) 5. to remove
【襄理】an assistant manager (of
【襄助】to help; to assist

〔西部〕

褻 3638
(褻) ㄒㄧㄝˋ xiè
1. underwear; clothes worn in one's bedroom or house 2. dirty; filthy 3. intimate (sometimes denoting a degree of indecency) 4. to slight; to look down upon
【褻瀆】①to slight; to abuse; to insult; to blaspheme; to desecrate ②(a polite expression) to bother others with trifles, etc.

十三畫

襟 3639
ㄐㄧㄣ jīn
1. the lapel or collar of a garment or robe 2. aspiration; ambition; the mental outlook 3. (said of waters) to converge
【襟懷】one's feelings, ambitions, aspirations, bosom, (breadth of) mind, etc.

襖 3640
ㄠˇ ǎo
a coat; a jacket or top garment padded with cotton or lined with fur

十四畫

襤 3641
ㄌㄢˊ lán
1. ragged garments; clothes without a hem 2. shabbily dressed
【襤褸】(said of clothes) tattered

十五畫

襪 3642
(袜) ㄨㄚˋ wà
stockings; socks: 襪帶 garters

十六畫

襯 3643
ㄔㄣˋ chèn
1. inner garments; underwear 2. to provide a background 3. a lining; a liner 4. to line
【襯布】lining cloth
【襯托】to bring into relief; to set off; to supplement; to embellish; to provide a contrast; a foil
【襯裙】a petticoat; an underskirt
【襯衫】a shirt

襲 3644
ㄒㄧˊ xí
1. to put on; to clothe in; to wear 2. a suit (of clothes); a set (of dress) 3. repeated; double 4. hereditary; to inherit 5. to raid; to assail 6. to plagiarize; to appropriate
【襲擊】①a surprise attack ②to raid

襾部
ㄧㄚˋ yà

西 3645
ㄒㄧ xī
1. west; the west; western 2. Western; the West; European; American; Occidental; foreign
【西伯利亞】Siberia
【西北】northwest
【西班牙】Spain
【西半球】the Western Hemisphere
【西部】the western part (of a territory); the West
【西方】① west; the West or Western ② a Buddhist paradise
【西風】a west wind; a westerly; a wester
【西風東漸】the spread of Western influences to the East
【西點】①western-style dessert ② West Point
【西南】southwest
【西曆】the Gregorian calendar
【西瓜】watermelons
【西行】to go west; to travel westward
【西學】Western learning
【西裝】Western-style clothes; a Western suit
【西式】Western-style; Occidental style; European or American style
【西藏】① Tibet ② Tibetan
【西餐】Western food; European or American meals
【西藥】Western medicines or pharmaceuticals
【西諺】a Western proverb; European or American aphorisms
【西洋史】history of Europe and America
【西洋人】Westerners
【西元】the Gregorian calendar, which begins with the year in

which Christ was supposedly born; A.D. 亦作「公元」

三畫

要 3646
1. ㄧㄠˋ yào

1. necessary; important; essential; necessity 2. must; should; ought to 3. to want; to demand; to need; to require; to desire; to take 4. to summarize; a summary; a generalization; a synopsis 5. will; shall—to indicate the future tense 6. brief 7. if; in case

【要不然】otherwise; or

【要不得】extremely bad; inappropriate; condemnable

【要不是】If it were not for....或But for....

【要面子】to be keen on face-saving

【要命】① very; extremely; awfully ② too much to endure

【要犯】an important or dangerous criminal; a most-wanted criminal

【要飯的】a beggar

【要得】① good; well done; bravo ② acceptable; okay

【要道】① an important road or passage ② the essential points of what is good and appropriate

【要點】the important or main points; the gist; the essential points

【要領】essential points; essentials

【要害】① fatal points; a vital part; a crucial point ② strategic locations or points

【要好】① to desire to excel ② to be friend ③ to be in love with

【要緊】important and urgent

【要訣】the secret of doing something; the key to doing something successfully

【要職】an important post

【要旨】key points; themes; epitomes

【要衝】a strategic position; a key place; a communication hub

【要事】an important matter; an urgent business

【要是】if; in case

【要人】a VIP; a prominent figure

【要塞】a fortress; a strategic point

【要素】essentials; chief ingredients or elements or factors

要 3646
2. ㄧㄠ yāo

1. to invite 2. to engage; to make an agreement 3. to ask for; to demand 4. to coerce; to threaten

【要求】① to demand; to request ② a demand; a request

【要挾】to blackmail; to put pressure on; to coerce; to threaten

六畫

覃 3647
ㄊㄢˊ tán

1. to spread to; to involve 2. deep and vast; profound

十二畫

覆 3648
ㄈㄨˋ fù

1. to pour out 2. to overturn; to topple 3. a reply; to reply; to respond 4. to defeat; to destroy 5. to cover; to screen 6. to repeat; a second time; again

【覆電】a telegram in reply

【覆蓋】to cover

【覆信】① a letter in reply ② to reply a letter

【覆選】① an election by delegates; an indirect election ② a run-off (election)

【覆巢之下無完卵】If a country is beaten, all its people will suffer.

【覆試】① to test again ② a second test or examination

【覆審】a retrial of a case

【覆水難收】There is no use crying over spilt milk.

【覆議】① to discuss again ② a renewed discussion

【覆文】an official reply in written form

十三畫

覈 3649
(核) ㄏㄜˊ hé

1. to test; to examine; to investigate 2. deep; deeply 3. the stone (of a fruit)

【覈實】to examine or investigate the fact or truth

十七畫

覊 3650
(羇) ㄐㄧ jī

to travel; to be on a tour or trip

【覊旅】a traveler 亦作「羇旅」

〔襾部〕

〔見部〕

見部
ㄐㄧㄢˋ jiàn

見 3651 ㄐㄧㄢˋ jiàn
1. to see; to perceive; to understand; to observe or examine 2. to visit; to see; to call on or at; to meet 3. to receive (visitors, etc.); to come face to face with 4. *vide*; see

【見報】to appear in the newspapers
【見不得人】too ashamed to show up in public
【見面】to come face to face; to see; to meet
【見面禮】gift(s) given at one's first meeting, especially with a relative of a junior generation
【見方】square, as a foot square
【見風轉舵】to go with the tide
【見到】①to meet; to see ②to perceive or think of
【見多識廣】experienced and knowledgeable
【見利忘義】to forget one's integrity under the temptation of personal gain
【見諒】to pardon me; to forgive me; to excuse me
【見過世面】to have seen much of the world; experienced; sophisticated
【見怪】to take offense; to blame; to mind
【見客】to receive guests
【見機行事】to act as the circumstances dictate; to do as one sees fit
【見解】one's views, ideas or observations or opinions about something
【見棄】to be cast away or rejected
【見習】apprenticeship; probation
【見效】effective; efficacious
【見笑】①to be laughed at ②to incur ridicule (by one's poor performance)
【見賢思齊】to see the virtuous and think of equaling or emulating them
【見證】to bear witness
【見識】①knowledge and experience; scope; sense ②to experience (something new)
【見世面】to see the world; to enrich one's experience
【見死不救】to see someone in mortal danger without lifting a finger to save him
【見異思遷】easily moved by what one sees or hears
【見義勇爲】to have the courage to do what is right regardless of consequences; to act heroically
【見外】to treat as an outsider
【見聞】what one has seen and heard—experience; knowledge

四畫

規 3652 ㄍㄨㄟ guī
1. regulations; laws; rules; customs or usages 2. a pair of compasses 3. to plan; to scheme 4. to advise so as to correct

【規避】to evade; to shun or avoid
【規模】① patterns; formulas ② scale; magnitude; scope; extent
【規範】a norm; a standard
【規定】①to rule; to specify; to stipulate; to regulate ② rules or regulations
【規律】① laws, rules or regulations; discipline ② regular; regularity
【規格】specifications
【規畫】①to map out or draw up (a plan) ②a plan or scheme
【規誡】to admonish
【規諫】to advise or admonish
【規矩】① rules; practices ② well-behaved; well-disciplined ③ the compass and square
【規勸】to admonish; to give friendly advice
【規則】①a rule or regulation ② regular; fixed; inflexible

覓 3653 (覔) ㄇㄧˋ mì
to seek; to search or look for

【覓保】to find a guarantor

五畫

視 3654 ㄕˋ shì
1. to look at; to observe; to inspect; to see; to watch 2. to consider or regard as; to take it for 3. to compare; to be equivalent to

【視聽】①what one saw and heard

② public opinion ③ audio-visual
【視同兒戲】to take it lightly; to regard it as unimportant
【視力】the visual faculty; eyesight
【視覺】the sense of sight
【視察】to inspect
【視事】① to administer; to govern or rule ② to be installed or inaugurated; to be sworn in
【視如敝屣】to regard as worn-out shoes 「what one has seen }
【視若無睹】to be undisturbed by }
【視死如歸】to look upon death as going home—fearless and dauntless
【視而不見】(literally) to look but see nothing—absent-minded; to ignore

九畫

覩 3655 (睹) ㄉㄨˇ dǔ 「witness }
to see; to gaze at; to observe; to }
【覩物思人】to think of someone who is dead or far away upon seeing something he left behind

親 3656 1. ㄑㄧㄣ qīn
1. parents 2. relatives 3. to love; intimate; near to; dear 4. personally; personal; in person; self 5. to kiss
【親筆】one's own handwriting; to write personally
【親朋】relatives and friends
【親密】intimate; intimacy; close
【親痛仇快】(said of a mistake, blunder, etc.) to pain one's friends and please one's enemies
【親暱】intimate; very dear to
【親歷其境】to be on the spot or scene in person; to experience personally
【親臨】to arrive personally
【親骨肉】one's own flesh and blood
【親口】(said of words, etc.) right from one's own mouth; to state or tell personally
【親和力】① (chemistry) affinity ② affability; amiability
【親近】to be near to or intimate }
【親戚】relatives ⌊with; to be close to }
【親切】intimately; cordially; kind
【親信】a confidant
【親兄弟明算賬】Financial matters should be settled clearly even between brothers.
【親事】marriage 「hands }
【親手】personally; with one's own }
【親身】personally; in person
【親屬】relatives; family members
【親屬關係】kinship
【親人】close relatives—as one's parents, brothers, spouse, children, etc.
【親子關係】parent-child relations
【親自 or 親身】personally; in person
【親自出馬】to go out and take care of something in person; to confront (the enemy, etc.) personally 「the same clan }
【親族】one's kinsmen; members of }
【親嘴 or 親吻】to kiss
【親愛】love; affection; dear
【親友】friends and relatives
【親眼看見】to witness; to see with }
【親王】a prince ⌊one's own eyes }

親 3656 2. ㄑㄧㄥˋ qìng
relatives by marriage
【親家】① relatives as a result of marriage ② parents of the married couple

十畫

覬 3657 ㄐㄧˋ jì
as in 覬覦—to covet; to desire something belonging to others

十三畫

覺 3658 1. ㄐㄩㄝˊ jué
1. to wake up from sleep 2. senses 3. to be conscious of; to sense 4. to awaken; to realize; to discover 5. to tell; to feel
【覺得】① to be conscious of; to realize; to sense ② to feel ③ to think; to be of the opinion
【覺醒】to wake up
【覺悟】to become aware; to realize

覺 3658 2. ㄐㄧㄠˋ jiào
a sleep; a nap

十四畫

〔見部〕

〔角部〕

覽 3659
ㄌㄢˇ lǎn
1. to look at; to sightsee 2. to read
【覽勝】to tour a resort; to see or visit a scenic spot

十八畫

觀 3660
ㄍㄨㄢ guān
1. to see; to observe; to behold; to view; to take a view of; to look; to inspect 2. sights; views 3. to display 4. a point of view; a conception
【觀摩】to emulate the good points of others; to compare notes
【觀點】a point of view; one's view on a certain matter
【觀念】a conception; an idea; a view
【觀禮】to attend a ceremony
【觀感】one's feelings or emotional reactions after seeing or reading something
【觀光】sightseeing; to see the sights
【觀光團】a tour group; a tourist group
【觀光客】a tourist
【觀光事業】tourism; the tourist industry
【觀看】to look at; to see
【觀護所】a probation office
【觀瞻】① the appearance or outward look of something ② to look at; to see; to view
【觀戰】to witness a battle; to observe a military operation
【觀衆】the audience or spectators
【觀察】to observe; to watch; to inspect
【觀賞】to see and enjoy
【觀測】to observe and survey
【觀(世)音】the Goddess of Mercy
【觀望】a wait-and-see attitude; to wait and see; to hesitate

角部
ㄐㄩㄝˊ jué

角 3661
1. ㄐㄧㄠˇ jiǎo
1. the horn of an animal 2. a direction; a corner 3. an angle 4. a tenth of a dollar; a 10-cent piece 5. something in the shape of a horn 6. a cape; a promontory
【角膜】(anatomy) cornea
【角度】①an angle ②angular measure

角 3661
2. (讀音) ㄐㄩㄝˊ jué
1. to compete; to contest; to wrestle 2. a corner 3. a dramatic role; a character 4. one of the five musical notes in ancient Chinese music
【角逐】to contest (for a post, etc.)
【角色】a role; a character

六畫

解 3662
ㄐㄧㄝˇ jiě
1. to unfasten; to untie; to loosen 2. to solve (difficult problems, etc.) 3. to explain; to clarify 4. to understand 5. ideas; views 6. to break up, separate or disperse 7. to take off; to strip 8. to relieve; to alleviate (pain, etc.) 9. to cut apart; to dissect 10. to dissolve 11. to discharge (water, etc.); to defecate
【解剖】①anatomization; to dissect; dissection ② to analyze; analysis
【解聘】to relieve one of his duties; to dismiss or discharge a person from his post
【解悶兒】to kill time; to dispel loneliness
【解放】to untie or set free; to liberate
【解答】① explanations or answers to certain questions ② to answer or explain
【解毒】to detoxify; to antidote
【解凍】① to thaw ② to unfreeze (funds, assets, etc.)
【解體】disintegration; dissolution
【解脫】to extricate
【解雇】to get fired; to fire; to dismiss; to discharge
【解渴】to quench thirst; to allay thirst
【解開】to untie; to unbind; to loosen; to undo
【解惑】to remove doubts
【解甲歸田】to be demobilized
【解酒】to neutralize the effect of alcoholic drinks; to alleviate a hangover
【解救】to deliver (the people from tyranny, etc.); to rescue
【解決】①to settle (a dispute, fight,

etc.); to solve (a problem) ② to dispose of; to finish off
【解饞】 to satisfy a desire for delicious food
【解除】 ① to annul or cancel (a contract, agreement, etc.) ② (law) to restore to the original status ③ to relieve (a person of his duties, etc.) ④ to remove; to get rid of
【解釋】 to explain; explanation
【解散】 to dismiss; to disband
【解憂】 to alleviate sorrow; to relieve worries
【解危】 to head off danger
【解圍】 ① to resolve difficulties for others; to save others from embarrassment, etc. ② to raise a siege
【解約】 to annul a contract or agreement

十一畫

觴 3663
ㄕㄤ shāng
1. a general name of all sorts of wine vessels 2. to offer drinks to others

十三畫

觸 3664
ㄔㄨˋ chù
1. to touch; to contact 2. (said of an animal) to ram with the horn; to ram; to butt 3. to move or touch emotionally 4. to offend; to infuriate
【觸目驚心】 frightening; blood-curdling
【觸發】 ① to touch off (a war, dispute, etc.) ② to move or touch (one's feelings)
【觸犯】 ① to offend; to incur the displeasure of ② to violate or infringe (regulations, rules, etc.)
【觸電】 to get an electric shock
【觸動】 ① to touch something, and move it slightly ② to move one's heart
【觸痛】 to touch a tender spot
【觸怒】 to infuriate; to offend
【觸類旁通】 to draw an analogy; to understand by means of inference processes
【觸擊】 (baseball) a bunt
【觸礁】 ① to strike a submerged reef; to run aground ② to hit a snag; to meet unexpected difficulty
【觸覺】 the sense of touch

言部
ㄧㄢˊ yán

〔言部〕

言 3665
ㄧㄢˊ yán
1. speech; words 2. to say; to talk; to speak; to mean; to express 3. a language; a dialect
【言必信，行必果】 Promises must be kept and action must be resolute.
【言不及義】 to make idle talks; to talk frivolously
【言不由衷】 not speaking one's mind; not to talk from the bottom of one's heart
【言明】 to state clearly; to make a statement; to declare
【言談】 words and speech; conversation
【言聽計從】 to have full confidence in someone
【言論】 speech
【言論自由】 freedom of speech
【言過其實】 to exaggerate; to boast or brag; to overstate
【言歸正傳】 Let's go back to the main topic.
【言歸於好】 to resume friendship; to be on good terms again; to reconcile
【言和】 to make peace; to reconcile
【言教】 to give verbal directions
【言簡意賅】 Few words were spoken, but none of the major points was missing.
【言行】 words and deeds
【言行一致】 to practice what one preaches
【言之過早】 still too early to say; premature to say
【言之成理】 to present in a reasonable way; to talk sense
【言之有物】 (said of a speech or writing) having substance; convincing
【言出如山】 A promise is a promise.
【言詞 or 言辭】 words or expressions; statements; wording; diction
【言而有信】 to be as good as one's word
【言猶在耳】 The words are still ringing in the ear.
【言外之意】 overtones

【言語】 spoken language; speech; words

言部

二畫

計 3666
ㄐㄧˋ jì

1. a scheme; a plot; a trick 2. a plan; a program; to discuss or plan 3. to calculate; to count 4. a mechanical measuring device

【計謀】 a scheme; to scheme
【計分】 ①to count scores or points ②divided or classified as follows
【計量】 to calculate; to weigh; to estimate
【計略】 to scheme; to deliberate; a scheme
【計畫or計劃】 a plan; a program; to plan; to devise
【計畫書】 a prospectus
【計較】 ①to haggle; to fuss about ②to negotiate ③to care ④to plan
【計件】 to reckon by the piece
【計程車】 a taxi
【計時】 to count time to see how long something lasts
【計策】 a scheme; a device
【計算】 ①to calculate; to count ②to consider
【計算機】 a calculating machine; a computer

訂 3667
ㄉㄧㄥˋ dìng

1. to draw up or conclude (a contract, etc.) 2. to subscribe to (a magazine, etc.) 3. to edit; to collate; to revise 4. to arrange; to settle; to fix 5. to make reservations

【訂報】 to subscribe to a newspaper
【訂房間】 to make room reservations
【訂定】 ①to fix or arrange beforehand ②specified in a contract between the two parties concerned
【訂立】 to conclude (a contract, etc.)
【訂購】 to order (a product) in advance
【訂戶】 ①a subscriber (to a newspaper, etc.) ②a person with a standing order for milk, etc.
【訂貨】 to place an order for goods
【訂貨單 or 訂單】 an order form
【訂婚】 to engage or betroth; an engagement
【訂金】 deposit
【訂正】 to revise; to correct
【訂座】 to make reservations for seats in theaters, restaurants, etc.
【訂閱】 to subscribe to (a publication)

訃 3668
ㄈㄨˋ fù

an obituary; 訃聞 an obituary notice

三畫

討 3669
ㄊㄠˇ tǎo

1. to quell; to put down; to suppress 2. to denounce; to condemn 3. to marry (a wife or concubine) 4. to demand; to beg for; to get 5. to study; to examine into; to research 6. (rarely) to govern; to administer

【討伐】 to quell (an uprising, etc.)
【討飯】 to beg for food; to be a beggar
【討論】 to discuss; discussion
【討論會】 a forum; a symposium
【討好】 ①to curry favor; to please; to fawn on ②to be rewarded with a fruitful result
【討價還價】 to haggle over prices; to bargain
【討教】 May I ask for your advice?
【討救兵】 to seek help
【討媳婦】 to get a wife for one's son
【討債】 to demand repayment of a loan
【討生活】 to make a living
【討饒】 to ask for mercy
【討人喜歡】 likable; delightful
【討厭】 troublesome; nasty; to dislike

訊 3670
ㄒㄩㄣˋ xùn

1. to ask; to inquire; to question 2. information; news 3. to put on trial; to question in court; to interrogate

【訊息】 news; information; tidings

訓 3671
ㄒㄩㄣˋ xùn

1. to lecture; to teach; to exhort 2. (to serve as) a lesson 3. an old proverb, etc.

【訓勉】 to exhort and encourage
【訓導】 to teach and guide
【訓練】 to drill; to train; training
【訓練班】 a training class
【訓話】 to lecture; to exhort

【訓誡】 to admonish
【訓斥】 to reprimand; to rebuke
【訓示】 instructions; to admonish

訕 3672 ㄕㄢ shàn
1. to sneer at 2. to abuse 3. embarrassed; shamefaced
【訕笑】 to laugh or sneer at; to ridicule; to mock; to deride

訖 3673 ㄑㄧˋ qì
1. to come to an end; to conclude; cleared or settled 2. until 亦作「迄」

託 3674 ㄊㄨㄛ tuō
1. to commission; to entrust to 2. to ask; to request 3. to consign 4. to use as an excuse or pretext 5. to send (messages, etc.) indirectly
【託夢】 (said of a dead person) to appear in one's dream
【託福考試】 TOEFL (Test of English as a Foreign Language)
【託付】 to entrust to; to commission
【託故】 to make an excuse
【託管】 to trust; to mandate
【託人】 to ask somebody to do something for oneself
【託辭】 to make excuses; pretexts or excuses
【託兒所】 a public nursery
【託運】 to consign for shipment; to check

記 3675 ㄐㄧˋ jì
1. to remember; to call to mind; to keep in mind 2. to record; to register 3. a book recording anecdotes, etc. 4. seals or chops; a sign; a mark
【記分】 ① to record scores or points ② to register a student's mark
【記分員】 a scorer; a marker
【記得】 to remember
【記牢】 to commit to memory firmly
【記錄】 ① to record; to note down ② a note-taker ③ a record 亦作「紀錄」
【記錄片】 a documentary film
【記掛】 to remember and be anxious about
【記過】 to record a demerit
【記功】 to record a merit
【記號】 a mark; a sign; a symbol
【記恨 or 記仇】 to bear a grudge
【記下來】 to take down (dictation, etc.)
【記性】 memory
【記敍文】 narrative writing
【記者】 a reporter; a journalist
【記賬】 ① to buy or sell on credit ② to record buying, selling, etc. in books
【記述】 to record and narrate
【記入】 to enter... in; to make an entry
【記載】 to record; an account
【記憶】 memory or recollection
【記憶力】 a retentive faculty
【記憶猶新】 The memory is still fresh.

四畫

訟 3676 ㄙㄨㄥˋ sòng
1. a lawsuit; litigation 2. to argue over the right and wrong of something; to dispute; to demand justice 3. publicly; in public
【訟案】 a case at law

訛 3677 ㄜˊ é
1. rumors 2. errors; erroneous; wrong 3. to extort; to swindle; to deceive; to bluff 4. to move about 5. to change
【訛傳】 false rumors; wrong information
【訛誤】 errors; mistakes

訝 3678 ㄧㄚˋ yà
to wonder; surprised or to express surprise;

訣 3679 ㄐㄩㄝˊ jué
1. to part; to separate 2. sorcery; an occult art 3. a formula of doing something; the secret of doing things
【訣別】 ① to say good-bye; to bid farewell ② to part forever
【訣竅】 the secret or knack of doing something

訪 3680 ㄈㄤˇ fǎng
1. to visit; to call on 2. to look for; to find out
【訪客】 a visitor; a caller
【訪查】 to inquire about and investigate

〔言部〕

〔言部〕

【訪問】 to visit; to call upon
【訪問團】 a visiting mission

設 3681 ㄕㄜˋ shè

1. to lay out; to display 2. to establish; to set up; to found 3. to furnish; to provide 4. to arrange; to plan or devise 5. supposing that; in case of

【設備】 ① equipment ② defense works
【設法】 to think up a method; a way
【設防】 to fortify; to garrison
【設立】 to establish; to set up
【設計】 ①to map out a scheme ② to design
【設計者】 the designer
【設下圈套】 to set a snare
【設想】 ① an idea ② to imagine; to think
【設置】 ①to establish; to set up; to found ② establishment; installations
【設施】 ① to plan and execute ② installations; facilities
【設身處地】 to put oneself in another's position
【設宴】 to throw a banquet

許 3682 ㄒㄩˇ xǔ

1. to promise; to approve; to permit 2. to praise; to commend 3. (said of a young girl) to be betrothed 4. to expect 5. perhaps; maybe 6. about

【許配or許聘】 to betroth; to affiance
【許多】 many; numerous; much
【許諾】 to promise; a promise
【許可】 to approve; to permit or allow
【許可證】 a permit; a license
【許婚】 (said of a girl) to betroth
【許久】 for a long time
【許願】 ① to make a vow (to a god) ② to promise somebody a reward

五畫

訴 3683 ㄙㄨˋ sù

1. to tell; to inform 2. to accuse; to charge 3. to appeal 4. to resort to

【訴苦】 to complain about one's grievances
【訴諸武力】 to resort to force
【訴狀】 a plaint; a petition
【訴訟】 a lawsuit; to go to law; litigation

訶 3684 ㄏㄜ hē

to scold in a loud voice: 訶護 divine protection

診 3685 ㄓㄣˇ zhěn (又讀 ㄓㄣ zhēn)

1. to examine (diseases, ailments, etc.); to diagnose 2. to tell; to report

【診脈】 to feel the pulse
【診斷】 to diagnose (a disease); a diagnosis
【診斷書】 a written diagnosis
【診療 or 診治】 to diagnose and treat
【診所】 a clinic; a dispensary

註 3686 ㄓㄨˋ zhù

1. an explanatory note; a footnote; a commentary or remark 2. to register; to record or list

【註明】 to explain or state clearly in writing
【註定】 destined; predestined; doomed
【註解】 explanatory notes; to explain
【註脚】 explanatory notes; footnotes
【註銷】 to cancel; to nullify; to annul
【註釋】 explanatory notes
【註册】 to register; registration
【註册商標】 a registered trademark

詆 3687 ㄉㄧˇ dǐ

as in 詆毀—to censure; to slander; to defame

詠 3688 (咏) ㄩㄥˇ yǒng

1. to sing; to hum 2. the chirping of birds

【詠歎】 to sigh (usually in admiration)

詎 3689 ㄐㄩˋ jù

an interjection indicating surprise

【詎料】 unexpectedly

詐 3690 ㄓㄚˋ zhà

1. deceitful; false; fake; crafty 2. to deceive; to cheat; to lie; to swindle; to pretend; to feign 3. to trick into; to bluff somebody into giving information

【詐騙】 to swindle

【詐欺】fraud; imposture; cheating
【詐稱】to tell a lie; to state falsely
【詐術】fraud; cheating; guile; chicanery
【詐財】to cheat for money
【詐死】to fake death; to play dead

詔 3691 ㄓㄠˋ zhào
1. to proclaim; to announce 2. to instruct; to teach and direct; to coach 3. an imperial decree or mandate
【詔令】an imperial decree or edict

評 3692 ㄆㄧㄥˊ píng
1. to comment; to criticize; to review 2. comments; reviews 3. to judge
【評判】to criticize; to judge or decide, as in a beauty contest, etc.
【評分】marks or points given by a judge
【評定】to examine, judge and decide
【評斷】to decide; to arbitrate
【評理】to ask a third party to judge which side is right
【評量】to weigh; to evaluate
【評論】to comment; to review
【評價】① to appraise ② an objective assessment of the worth or merit of a person, a piece of writing, etc.
【評選】to choose through public appraisal
【評語】comments; criticism

詛 3693 ㄗㄨˇ zǔ
1. to curse; to imprecate 2. to vow; to pledge
【詛咒】to curse; to imprecate

詞 3694 ㄘˊ cí
1. words; phrases; statements; speech; expressions 2. a part of speech in grammar 3. to talk, speak or tell 4. (Chinese literature) *tzu*, a form of poetry
【詞不達意】The language cannot convey the ideas intended.
【詞典】a dictionary 亦作「辭典」
【詞彙】①a dictionary ②a vocabulary
【詞句】expressions; words and phrases
【詞曲】poems and songs
【詞藻】ornate terms or expressions
【詞語】words and expressions; terms

証 3695 (證) ㄓㄥˋ zhèng
evidence; proof; a certificate; to certify

六畫

詣 3696 ㄧˋ yì
1. to go (to a place); to arrive 2. to visit; to call on 3. achievements

詢 3697 ㄒㄩㄣˊ xún
1. to inquire 2. to deliberate and plan 3. truely
【詢察】to investigate and inquire
【詢問】to inquire; to ask
【詢問處】an information desk

試 3698 ㄕˋ shì
1. to try; to test; to experiment 2. to use 3. to examine 4. to sound out; to put up a trial balloon 5. to compare
【試辦】to do something on an experimental basis
【試飛】to test a new airplane in flight; a trial flight
【試探】to test; to sound out; to probe
【試題】questions in a test or examination
【試圖】to attempt; to try
【試管】a test tube
【試管嬰兒】a test-tube baby
【試卷】a test paper; an examination paper
【試想】to think it over; just think
【試行】to try out something
【試場】an examination place
【試穿】to try on (a garment, etc.)
【試演】a dress rehearsal; a preview
【試驗】an experiment; to experiment
【試映】to give a preview; a preview (of a movie)
【試問】May we ask...?
【試用】to use on a trial basis
【試用人員】probational personnel

詩 3699 ㄕ shī
1. poetry; poems; poetic 2. anything or quality as an offspring of pure imagination 3. short for *The Book of Odes* edited by Confucius
【詩篇】poems

〔言部〕

【詩歌】① poems and songs collectively ② poetry
【詩集】a collection of poems
【詩句】a stanza or line in a poem
【詩情畫意】(said of a landscape) idyllic
【詩選】a selection of poems
【詩人】a poet
【詩意】the poetic quality; the romantic atmosphere
【詩韻】① rhyme of verses ② a rhyme book

詫 3700 ㄔㄚˋ chà
1. surprised; to wonder 2. to brag; to boast 3. to cheat; to deceive 4. to inform
【詫異】to be surprised

詬 3701 ㄍㄡˋ gòu
1. to insult; to shame 2. to berate; to abuse
【詬病】to insult; to criticize; to blame

詭 3702 ㄍㄨㄟˇ guǐ
1. to cheat; to deceive; to feign; to defraud 2. strange; rare; odd; peculiar; uncanny; weird 3. cunning; shrewd; stealthy 4. to urge oneself 5. to go against; to defy; to contradict
【詭計】a trick; an artful device or trap
【詭計多端】very tricky or crafty
【詭異】strange; odd; abnormal; weird

詮 3703 ㄑㄩㄢˊ quán
1. to explain; to expound 2. the truth or core of something 3. to weigh; to assess; to rate; to appraise
【詮釋】to interpret; to explain

詰 3704 ㄐㄧㄝˊ jié
1. to question; to ask 2. to punish 3. to prohibit
【詰屈聱牙】(said of writings) hard and difficult to read
【詰問】to demand an explanation angrily

話 3705 ㄏㄨㄚˋ huà
1. words; sayings 2. to speak; to talk; to converse; to say 3. language
【話別】to bid farewell; to say goodbye
【話柄】words or behavior as material for others' gossip
【話不投機】not seeing eye to eye in conversation or talk
【話題】the topic of conversation or discussion
【話筒】① a microphone ② a telephone transmitter ③ a megaphone
【話家常】to chitchat
【話劇】a play or drama (as distinct from opera)
【話匣子】① a phonograph ② a chatterbox
【話中有話 or 話裏有話】overtones in conversation

該 3706 ㄍㄞ gāi
1. should; ought to 2. fated to 3. to owe 4. that; the said (person, etc.) 5. to be somebody's turn to do something 6. to deserve 7. inclusive
【該當】① ought to; should ② to deserve
【該地】that place; the said place
【該項】that item; that matter
【該處】① that place ② that department
【該死】to deserve death 或 Go to hell! 或Confounded!

詳 3707 ㄒㄧㄤˊ xiáng
1. complete; detailed; details 2. to know the details 3. please see... for details 4. to explain; to interpret
【詳密】detailed and comprehensive
【詳談】to speak in detail
【詳略】detailed or brief
【詳解】to explain in detail
【詳盡】detailed and complete
【詳情】details of an event, etc.
【詳細】in every detail and particular
【詳述】to narrate in complete detail

詹 3708 ㄓㄢ zhān
1. to talk too much; verbosity 2. to reach

詼 3709 ㄏㄨㄟ huī
1. funny; humorous 2. to ridicule; to joke
【詼諧】funny; humorous; comical

誅 3710 ㄓㄨ zhū
1. to kill; to execute; execution 2. to punish 3. to weed out; to exterminate
【誅滅】to eliminate; to eradicate

誇 3711 ㄎㄨㄚ kuā

1. to exaggerate; to boast; to brag 2. big; great 3. to show off 4. to praise
【誇大】① to exaggerate ② arrogant
【誇大其詞】to exaggerate
【誇口】to boast; to brag; to talk big
【誇獎】to praise; to acclaim; to extol
【誇張】to exaggerate; to overstate
【誇讚】to praise; to extol
【誇耀】to flaunt; to show off

七畫

認 3712 ㄖㄣˋ rèn
1. to recognize; to know; to make out 2. to admit; to acknowledge 3. to accept; to resign oneself to 4. to adopt 5. to promise to do something
【認明】to see clearly; to recognize
【認命】to resign oneself to destiny
【認定】① to conclude or decide; to believe firmly ② to set one's mind on
【認同】to identify; identification
【認領】① to identify and claim (a child, etc.) ②(said of a man) to adopt a child born out of wedlock
【認可】to sanction; to approve
【認清】to see or know clearly (which is which)
【認知】cognition
【認眞】to be serious; to be earnest
【認賬 or 認帳】① to acknowledge a debt ② to admit a mistake
【認屍】to identify (dead) bodies
【認識】① to know ② to understand
【認輸】to concede defeat; to give up
【認罪】to plead guilty
【認錯】①to admit a fault or mistake ②to make identification incorrectly
【認爲】to think that...; to consider that...

誌 3713 ㄓˋ zhì
1. to write down; to put down; to record 2. a record
【誌慶or誌喜】to offer congratulations
【誌哀】to condole

誓 3714 ㄕˋ shì
1. to pledge; to vow; to swear 2. to take an oath (of allegiance, office, etc.)
【誓不兩立】to vow to fight till oneself or the other party falls
【誓不甘休】to vow never to let the offender get away with it
【誓詞】an oath; a pledge
【誓言 or 誓約】a vow; an oath

誕 3715 ㄉㄢˋ dàn
1. birth 2. preposterous; absurd 3. an initial particle
【誕辰】birthday
【誕生】birth

誘 3716 ㄧㄡˋ yòu
1. to guide; to lead 2. to decoy; to tempt; to allure; to lure; to captivate
【誘騙】to induce by deceit; to beguile
【誘導】to guide; to induce; induction
【誘敵】to induce the enemy (to make a wrong move)
【誘拐】to seduce; to entice; to abduct; to kidnap
【誘惑】① to entice; to lure; to allure; to tempt; to beguile ② to attract; attractive
【誘餌】① a bait ② a shill
【誘因】an inducement

誡 3717 ㄐㄧㄝˋ jiè
1. to warn; to admonish 2. a commandment

語 3718 1. ㄩˇ yǔ
1. language; speech 2. a word; a sentence 3. a saying; a proverb 4. a sign; a signal 5. to speak; to say; to talk
【語病】illogical use of words
【語法】wording; grammar; syntax
【語調】the tone of one's speech; intonation
【語態】(grammar) voice
【語錄】quotations
【語彙】vocabulary
【語驚四座】The statement was received with raised eyebrows.
【語句】sentences; phrases
【語氣】①(grammar) mood ②the tone (of one's speech); the manner of speaking
【語助詞】a grammatical particle; an auxiliary
【語重心長】One's words are seri-

言部

〔言部〕

ous and (one's) heart is thought- ⌊ful.
【語詞】words; phrases
【語塞】unable to utter a word in self-defense
【語意】the meaning (of a word, etc.) 「brief to be clear.
【語焉不詳】The statement is too
【語言】a language; speech
【語音】① a phone ② pronunciation
【語無倫次】to talk incoherently
【語文】language and literature

語 3718
2. ㄩˋ yù
to tell; to inform; to admonish

誠 3719
ㄔㄥˊ chéng
1. sincere; honest; cordial; sincerity 2. true; real; truly; indeed; actually
【誠非所料】It is really unexpected.
【誠服】to obey (or submit) willingly 「ed; cordial
【誠懇 or 誠摯】sincere; trueheart-
【誠心】sincerity; wholeheartedness
【誠心誠意】earnestly and sincerely
【誠實】honest; upright; trustworthy; honesty
【誠意】sincerity; good faith

誣 3720
ㄨˋ wù (語音 ㄨ wū)
to accuse falsely; to bring a false charge against 「fy; to smear
【誣衊】to slander; to libel; to vili-
【誣賴】to slander; to accuse falsely; to incriminate falsely
【誣告 or 誣控】to accuse falsely; to bring a false charge against

誤 3721
ㄨˋ wù
1. an error; a mistake 2. to harm; to suffer 3. to delay 4. to miss 5. by accident
【誤謬】a mistake; an error
【誤導】to mislead
【誤點】(said of trains, etc.) to be behind time 「affairs
【誤國】to mismanage national
【誤會 or 誤解】to misunderstand; to misinterpret; to misconstrue; a misunderstanding 「able
【誤信】to believe what is unreli-
【誤差】(mathematics) an error
【誤傳】to transmit (facts) incorrectly
【誤食】to eat (something poisonous or inedible) by mistake
【誤事】to ruin a plan through mismanagement, etc.; to bungle matters
【誤殺】① unintentional homicide; manslaughter ② to kill or murder a person mistaken for the intended victim 「of others
【誤人子弟】to mislead the children
【誤認】to identify incorrectly
【誤入歧途】to go astray (morally)

誥 3722
ㄍㄠˋ gào
1. to grant; to confer 2. to admonish 3. a written admonition 「ferment of titles
【誥命】a monarch's orders of con-

誦 3723
ㄙㄨㄥˋ sòng
1. to recite; to intone; to chant 2. poetry; poems; songs
【誦經】to recite passages from ⌊scriptures

誨 3724
ㄏㄨㄟˋ huì
(又讀 ㄏㄨㄟˇ huǐ)
1. to teach; to instruct 2. instructions 3. to admonish 4. to induce 「ness
【誨人不倦】to teach without weari-

說 3725
1. ㄕㄨㄛ shuō
1. to speak; to talk; to say 2. to explain; to clarify 3. a description; a narration; a statement 4. a theory 5. to scold
【說不得】① unspeakable; indescribable ② unfit for mention ③ unavoidable
【說不定】maybe; perhaps; probably
【說不過去】unacceptable to one's sense of propriety or justice
【說不出口】unutterable
【說媒 or 說親】to propose a marriage as a matchmaker
【說夢話】① to talk in one's sleep ② to talk nonsense
【說明】① to explain; to clarify; to expound ② expository writing
【說明書】a written explanation
【說法】① to preach Buddhism ② the way of reasoning; an argument 「cerned person
【說風涼話】to talk like an uncon-
【說大話】to brag 「excusable
【說得過去】acceptable; passable;

【說得好】well said
【說得好聽】to make an unpleasant fact sound attractive
【說得有理】to sound reasonable
【說到】to speak of; to mention
【說到做到】to do what one says
【說來話長】It is a long story....
【說來說去】to say the same thing over and over again
【說理】①to give a sermon; to preach ②to be reasonable; to argue
【說溜了嘴】to have a slip of the tongue; to blurt out something
【說過】to have said or mentioned
【說合】to help arrange a union
【說和】to act as a mediator
【說好說歹】to speak both well and ill in an attempt to influence or induce
【說話】①to speak; to talk; to say ②to tell stories ③a chat; a talk ④gossip; talk
【說謊】to tell a lie; to lie
【說教】to preach; to deliver a sermon
【說起】①to start talking about; to bring up (a subject) ②with reference to; as for
【說情】to solicit a favor or to ask for mercy on behalf of others
【說笑 or 說說笑笑】to joke; to talk and laugh
【說笑話】to tell jokes
【說閒話】to gossip; to criticize
【說項】to speak favorably of another
【說長道短】to criticize others
【說出】to speak out; to reveal; to utter
【說穿 or 穿破】to unravel or expose by some remarks; to tell what something really is
【說書】to tell stories
【說走就走】to announce the intention to leave and really mean it
【說辭】excuses; pretexts
【說曹操，曹操就到】Talk of the devil and the devil appears.
【說錯了話】to speak what should not have been uttered
【說一不二 or 說一是一】to be a man of his word; to keep one's promise; to stand by one's word

說 3725 2. ㄕㄨㄟˋ shuì

to persuade; to influence
【說服】to persuade; to convince
【說客】a professional commissary in ancient times sent by one monarch to another with a view to convincing him 亦作「說士」

八畫

課 3726 ㄎㄜˋ kè

1. a class meeting 2. a course (of study) 3. a lesson 4. to impose; to levy; to tax 5. a session at divination 6. a suboffice or bureau 7. to supervise
【課本】a textbook
【課表】a school timetable
【課堂】a classroom
【課題】①a task or problem (for students) ②a theme; a question for study
【課長】a section chief
【課程】a curriculum
【課程表】a school schedule; a class schedule
【課稅】to levy taxes; to impose taxes
【課業】schoolwork; lessons
【課外】outside class; extracurricular
【課外活動】extracurricular activities
【課文】the text or contents of a lesson
【課餘or課後】after school or class

誰 3727 ㄕㄟˊ shéi (讀音 ㄕㄨㄟˊ shuí)

1. who 2. anyone; someone
【誰知道or誰知】①Who knows? ②Who would have thought?
【誰是誰非】Who is right and who is wrong?

誹 3728 ㄈㄟˇ fěi

to attack; to condemn; to slander
【誹謗】to libel; to slander

誼 3729 ㄧˋ yì (又讀 ㄧˊ yí)

1. friendship 2. same as 義—justice; righteousness

調 3730 1. ㄊㄧㄠˊ tiáo

1. to mix; to blend 2. to regulate; to adjust 3. balance; regular 4. to make fun of; to tease 5. to mediate

〔言部〕

〔言部〕

【調配】①to mix; to blend ②to coordinate; to arrange
【調皮】①naughty ②sly; treacherous; unruly; tricky
【調皮搗蛋】making troubles; mischievous; ungovernable
【調頻】(electricity) frequency modulation (FM)
【調幅】(radio) amplitude modulation (AM)
【調停 or 調解】to mediate
【調理】①to train; to teach ②to nurse impaired health ③to take care of
【調侃】to scoff; to mock; to jeer
【調和】①to mix; to blend ②to harmonize ③to adjust; to tune ④to mediate; to reconcile
【調劑】①to prepare drugs ②to adjust; to make adjustments
【調節】①to regulate; to adjust ②to moderate
【調情】to flirt; to play at love
【調戲】to flirt with (women)
【調笑】to tease; to make fun of
【調製】to prepare or concoct
【調整】to adjust; to tune up
【調色】to mix colors; to mix paints
【調音】tuning
【調養】to nurse one's health; to take care of oneself
【調味】to season foods; to mix flavors
【調味品】seasoning; spice; dressing; condiment material

調 3730
2. ㄉㄧㄠˋ diào

1. to transfer; to move 2. to collect; to mobilize 3. a tune; a melody; an accent
【調包】to substitute an inferior thing in secret
【調兵遣將】(literally) to move troops and despatch generals—to prepare for war
【調派】to assign
【調度】①to move (available equipment or manpower) about according to needs ②a dispatcher
【調動】to transfer; to shift; to move (troops)
【調頭寸】to scrape up enough cash
【調虎離山】(literally) to induce the tiger out of the mountain—to use the stratagem of luring the opponent out of his citadel
【調換】to exchange; to replace; to swap
【調職or調任】to transfer to a new post
【調查】to investigate; to study; to probe; to survey; investigation
【調走】to send away; to banish

諂 3731
ㄔㄢˇ chǎn

as in諂媚—to flatter; to fawn; to toady

諄 3732
ㄓㄨㄣ zhūn

patient or earnest (in explaining, teaching, etc.)
【諄諄教誨 or 諄諄教導】to teach and admonish with patience

談 3733
ㄊㄢˊ tán

1. to talk; to converse; to chat 2. what is said or talked about; a talk
【談判】negotiation; to negotiate
【談天】to chat idly
【談天說地】to chat about all sorts of subjects
【談吐】the way a person talks; the manner of speaking
【談論】to discuss; to talk about
【談何容易】How easy it is just to talk about it! (But it is easier said than done.)
【談虎色變】(literally) to turn pale at the mention of a tiger—to turn pale when something horrible is mentioned
【談話】a statement; a talk; a chat; to talk
【談情說愛】(said of a couple in love) to chat intimately
【談笑風生】to talk cheerfully and humorously
【談心】to have a tête-à-tête

請 3734
ㄑㄧㄥˇ qǐng

1. to request; to ask; to beg 2. please 3. to hire; to seek the service of; to engage
【請便】as you please
【請帖 or 請柬】an invitation card
【請託】to ask for a favor
【請客】to invite guests; to give a party
【請假】to ask for leave of absence
【請教】to request advice; to consult
【請求】to request; to ask; to beg
【請示】to ask for instructions
【請坐】Please have a seat.
【請罪】①to ask for punishment ②to appeal for leniency
【請辭】to request permission to re-

sign 「after (an elder)
【請安】to pay respects; to inquire
【請勿】please don't
【請問】May I ask you...? 或Please
【請願】to petition ⌊tell me....
【請願書】a written petition

諍 3735
ㄓㄥ zhēng
1. to expostulate; to remonstrate; to admonish 2. to dispute; to compete
【諍言】a remonstrance; an expostulation; forthright admonition

諒 3736
ㄌㄧㄤˋ liàng
1. honest; sincere 2. to forgive; to excuse 3. to guess; to infer 4. stubborn 「standing
【諒解】to forgive; to be under-

論 3737
1. ㄌㄨㄣˋ lùn
1. to discuss; to comment on; to talk about 2. to debate; to dispute 3. a theory; a dissertation; an essay 4. to regard; to consider 5. in terms of; by
【論辨】argumentation
【論調】the tone or argument (of a speech, etc.) 「a thesis
【論點】the point at issue; an issue;
【論斷】to discuss and judge
【論功行賞】to evaluate services and grant rewards accordingly
【論及】to touch upon
【論據】grounds or bases (of an argument) 「argument
【論戰or論爭】controversy; debate;
【論政】to discuss politics; to make comments on politics
【論證】demonstration; to expound and prove 「work
【論著】a treatise; a discourse; a
【論述】to discuss; to expound
【論說】a theory, or thoughts (advanced in a treatise)
【論說文】an argumentative treatise
【論文】a treatise; a thesis; an essay

論 3737
2. ㄌㄨㄣˊ lún
an alternative of 論(ㄌㄨㄣˋ) for some phrases
【論語】*The Analects of Confucius,* one of the *Four Books*

九畫

諡 3738
(謚) ㄕˋ shì
a posthumous title

諭 3739
ㄩˋ yù
1. to notify by a directive, etc.; to instruct; to tell 2. a decree; an edict 「an edict
【諭示】to notify or announce by

諛 3740
ㄩˊ yú
to flatter; to toady: 諛辭 flattery

諜 3741
ㄉㄧㄝˊ dié
1. glib; garrulous; voluble 2. spying; espionage
【諜報】a spy's report; information obtained through espionage

諠 3742
(喧) ㄒㄩㄢ xuān
to bawl; to shout 「an uproar
【諠譁】turmoil; a hubbub; tumult;

諢 3743
ㄏㄨㄣˋ hùn
ridicule; derision; a joke; a jest
【諢名】a nickname; a sobriquet

諧 3744
ㄒㄧㄝˊ xié
1. harmonious; congruous 2. to come to an agreement; to settle 3. to joke; to jest
【諧和】harmony; harmonious; accord; agreement; concordant
【諧星】a comedian
【諧音】①(said of characters) representing sound ②(physics) harmonics

諫 3745
ㄐㄧㄢˋ jiàn
to admonish; to remonstrate: 諫言 admonition

諮 3746
ㄗ zī
1. to inquire; to confer; to consult 2. an official communication between offices of the same level 「seek advice
【諮詢】to inquire and consult; to
【諮商】(psychology) counseling

諱 3747
ㄏㄨㄟˋ huì
1. to conceal; to hide 2. to shun; to avoid; taboo 3. name of a deceased elder member of the

family
【諱莫如深】kept as a top secret; to avoid mentioning something completely
【諱疾忌醫】to conceal one's ailment and refuse to consult the doctor—to refuse to face a harsh reality
【諱言】to avoid mentioning something

〔言部〕

諳 3748 ㄢ ān
as in 諳練—skilled in; versed in; familiar with

諷 3749 ㄈㄥˋ fèng
1. to recite; to chant 2. to satirize 3. to admonish in a roundabout way
【諷刺】①to satirize; to mock ②irony
【諷喻】a parable; an allegory

諸 3750 ㄓㄨ zhū
1. all; various 2. a contraction of 之乎 or 之於 (as prepositions —in, to, from, etc.)
【諸多】many; numerous
【諸公 or 諸君】all the gentlemen; you gentlemen
【諸侯】the feudal princes; dukes or princes under an emperor
【諸如】such as
【諸如此類】various things like this
【諸子百家】the numerous schools of thinkers, or their works in the late Chou Dynasty
【諸位】Ladies and Gentlemen

諺 3751 ㄧㄢˋ yàn
as in 諺語—a proverb; a saying; a saw; an adage

諾 3752 ㄋㄨㄛˋ nuò
1. to assent 2. to promise; to pledge
【諾貝爾獎】Nobel prizes
【諾言】a promise; a pledge

謀 3753 ㄇㄡˊ móu
1. to scheme; to plan; to plot; to design 2. a scheme; a stratagem; a conspiracy 3. astute; resourceful 4. to consult 5. to seek; to try to get
【謀面】to meet each other; to see each other
【謀反】to plot a revolt; to conspire against the state
【謀利】to seek profit
【謀略or謀策】① a strategy; a plot; a scheme ② (said of a person) resourceful; astute
【謀害】① to plot against someone ② to murder
【謀畫】to scheme; to plot; to plan; to design; to devise
【謀求】to try to get; to seek
【謀職】to try to find employment; to hunt for a job
【謀士】a strategist; a resourceful man; an adviser; a counselor
【謀事在人, 成事在天】Man proposes, but God disposes.
【謀殺】to murder
【謀生】to make a living; to get a livelihood
【謀財害命】to commit murder out of greed; to murder somebody for his money

謁 3754 ㄧㄝˋ yè
to have an audience with; to see a superior
【謁陵】to pay homage to a great leader by visiting his tomb or mausoleum
【謁見】to have an audience with; to see a superior

謂 3755 ㄨㄟˋ wèi
1. to tell; to say 2. to name; to call; to designate 3. to think; to be of the opinion; to assume 4. meaning; sense

謔 3756 ㄋㄩㄝˋ nüè
1. to jest; to joke; to banter; to tease 2. to ridicule; to satirize
【謔而不虐】to joke without hurting anyone

十畫

謎 3757 ㄇㄧˊ mí
(又讀 ㄇㄟˋ mèi)
a riddle; a puzzle; a conundrum; an enigma
【謎底】an answer to a riddle; a truth
【謎語】a riddle; a conundrum

謄 3758 ㄊㄥˊ téng
to transcribe; to copy
【謄本】a transcript; a copy
【謄寫】to copy; to transcribe

謊 3759
ㄏㄨㄤˇ huǎng
1. a lie 2. to lie
【謊報】to report a falsehood
【謊話 or 謊言】a lie

謐 3760
ㄇㄧˋ mì
silent; quiet; serene; still
【謐靜】quiet; calm; tranquil; serene; silent

謗 3761
ㄅㄤˋ bàng
to slander; to libel; to condemn
【謗言】a libel; a slander; defamatory remarks

謙 3762
ㄑㄧㄢ qiān
modest; humble; retiring; self-effacing
【謙卑】humble; self-depreciating
【謙恭】respectful; unassuming
【謙謙君子】a modest gentleman
【謙虛】①modest; unassuming; self-effacing ② to make modest remarks
【謙遜】humble; modest; unassuming
【謙讓】to yield from modesty
【謙辭】①modest speech; a humble remark ②to decline out of humbleness

講 3763
ㄐㄧㄤˇ jiǎng
1. to speak; to talk 2. to pay particular attention to; to be particular about 3. to explain; to explicate 4. as to; when it comes to 5. to have recourse to
【講評】to review (a literary work, a game, etc., especially in speech)
【講道】to preach; to give sermons
【講臺】a platform; a dais; a podium
【講堂】a lecture hall; a lecture room
【講題】the topic (of a speech)
【講理】①to have regard for reason ②to argue with someone in order to convince him that he is wrong
【講稿】the manuscript of a prepared speech; lecture notes
【講故事】to tell stories
【講課】to teach; to lecture
【講和】to make peace; to conclude peace
【講話】to talk; to speak; to address
【講價】to haggle over prices; to bargain
【講解】to discuss and explain
【講究】①to be particular or elaborate (about something); to have regard for ②(said of dress, etc.) tasteful
【講求】① to investigate; to study ②to strive for; to be elaborate about
【講習】short-term training or instruction
【講學】to lecture; to discourse on an academic subject
【講師】a lecturer; an instructor
【講授】to teach; to lecture; to instruct
【講述】to explain and discuss (subjects, problems, etc.)
【講座】a lectureship; a professorship; a chair
【講義】① teacher's handouts at school; (mimeographed or printed) teaching materials ② commentaries on classics
【講演】to speak or lecture; a speech

謝 3764
ㄒㄧㄝˋ xiè
1. to thank 2. to decline 3. to fade; to wither
【謝幕】a curtain call; to bow to the audience on stage at the end of the show
【謝帖or謝函】a letter of thanks; a thank-you note; a thank-you letter
【謝天謝地】Thank Heaven! (or God!)
【謝禮】① a gift sent as a token of gratitude ② an honorarium
【謝絕】to decline (an offer, etc.)
【謝絕參觀】No visitors allowed.
【謝謝】Thank you. 或 Thanks.
【謝師宴】a dinner party given by graduating students in honor of their teachers
【謝罪】to apologize
【謝詞】a thank-you speech
【謝恩】to express thanks for great favors

謠 3765
ㄧㄠˊ yáo
1. rumor 2. a ballad; a folk song; a song
【謠傳】① unfounded report; hearsay ② according to rumor; it is rumored
【謠言】unfounded report; rumor

十一畫

〔言部〕

謾 3766
ㄇㄢˋ màn
1. to scorn; to disdain 2. disrespectful; rude
【謾罵】to revile scornfully; to rail

謫 3767
ㄓㄜˊ zhé
1. to censure; to reproach 2. to punish; to penalize 3. one's fault 4. to exile; to banish (an official) to a distant place
【謫居】to live in exile
【謫仙】an immortal living among mortals—a genius; a prodigy

謬 3768
ㄇㄧㄡˋ miù
(又讀 ㄋㄧㄡˋ niù)
1. incorrect; wrong; mistaken 2. absurd; unreasonable
【謬論】an absurd statement; a fallacious argument
【謬誤】an error; inaccuracy; fallacy

謳 3769
ㄡ ōu
to sing; to chant: 謳歌to eulogize; to glorify;

謹 3770
ㄐㄧㄣˇ jǐn
1. cautious; prudent; careful; attentive 2. sincerely; reverent; deferential
【謹防】to guard carefully against; to take precautions against
【謹防扒手】Beware of pickpockets!
【謹防假冒】Beware of imitations!
【謹記】to remember with reverence
【謹慎】prudent; cautious
【謹嚴】strict; rigorous
【謹言慎行】to be prudent in making statements and careful in personal conduct

十二畫

譏 3771
ㄐㄧ jī
1. to ridicule; to jeer; to sneer 2. to inspect
【譏諷】to ridicule; to deride; to satirize
【譏笑】to laugh at; taunts; sneers

譁 3772
ㄏㄨㄚˊ huá
noise; tumult; hubbub; clamor; uproar
【譁衆取寵】to practice demagogy; to make seditious speeches
【譁然】uproarious; boisterous; tumultuous

證 3773
ㄓㄥˋ zhèng
1. to give evidence; to bear testimony; to bear witness; to prove; to testify 2. evidence; proof; testimony 3. a certificate; a card 4. a symptom
【證明 or 證實】to prove; to testify
【證明書】a certificate; a voucher
【證道】(to give) a testimonial
【證婚人】a witness at a wedding
【證件】papers supporting a claim; documentary proof; credentials
【證據】testimony; evidence; witness; proof
【證券】securities (bills, bonds, etc.); stocks and bonds
【證書】a certificate; a diploma; credentials
【證人】a witness
【證詞】testimony given at a court of law
【證物】physical evidence; an exhibit

譎 3774
ㄐㄩㄝˊ jué
1. to cheat; to deceive; to swindle 2. wily; artful; crafty; cunning; tricky
【譎詭】unpredictable; constantly changing

識 3775
ㄕˋ shì
1. to know; to recognize; to discern 2. an opinion; a view 3. knowledge
【識別】①to discern; to distinguish ② identification
【識別證】an I.D. card
【識破】to see through
【識途老馬】an old horse which knows the way—an experienced person
【識貨】to appreciate; able to evaluate wares correctly
【識趣】to have tact; tactful
【識相】to know one's own limitations
【識字】able to read; literate

譚 3776
ㄊㄢˊ tán
1. same as 談—to talk 2. a Chinese family name

譜 3777
ㄆㄨˇ pǔ
1. a register; a table; a list 2. (music) a score 3. to compose (a song) 4. a general idea; a rough picture 5. a manual; a guide

【譜曲】to compose a song

十三畫

議 3778 ㄧˋ yì

1. to discuss; to argue; to debate; to negotiate; to talk over 2. an opinion; a view 3. to criticize; to comment; criticism; comment 4. argumentative writing; argumentation; an essay; a treatise

【議定】to arrive at a decision after discussion or negotiation
【議定書】a protocol
【議題】a topic for discussion; a subject of debate
【議論】① argument; debate ② to discuss; to talk ③ comments
【議論文】argumentative writing
【議和】to negotiate peace
【議會】a parliament; an assembly; a council
【議價】① to negotiate over the price ② the negotiated price
【議長】the speaker, president, or chairman of an assembly, parliament, etc.
【議程】agenda
【議案】a bill; a proposal
【議員】a councilor; a parliamentarian
【議院】a parliament; a legislature

警 3779 ㄐㄧㄥˇ jǐng

1. to guard; to keep watch 2. to warn; to alert 3. an alarm 4. quick; alert; agile 5. the police

【警報】an alert; an alarm; a warning
【警報器】a siren
【警報信號】a warning signal
【警探】a police detective
【警惕】① to be wary; to be alert; to be watchful ② a warning
【警鈴】a warning bell; an alarm bell
【警告】①to warn; to caution; to admonish ②a warning
【警官】a police officer
【警官學校】a police academy
【警戒】① to be on the alert ② to warn and admonish
【警句 or 警語】an epigram
【警覺】vigilant; alert; watchful
【警犬】a police dog
【警察派出所】a police substation; a station house
【警察局】county (or city) police headquarters
【警察學校】a police school; a police academy
【警車】a squad car; a police car
【警衛】① to guard ② a guard
【警員 or 警察】a policeman; a cop

譬 3780 ㄆㄧˋ pì

1. to liken; to compare 2. a simile; an example 3. to tell 4. to understand

【譬如 or 譬若】for instance; for example; suppose
【譬喻】a simile or metaphor

譯 3781 ㄧˋ yì

to translate; translation

【譯本】a translation
【譯碼器】a decoder; a decipher
【譯名】a translated name
【譯者】a translator
【譯文】translated texts

十四畫

護 3782 ㄏㄨˋ hù

1. to protect; to guard; to defend; to shield 2. to take sides; to be partial to

【護理】①to act for a senior official ②nursing
【護花使者】a protector of women
【護駕】to guard (or escort) the emperor
【護照】a passport
【護士】a nurse
【護身符】① an amulet ② anything which one uses as a protective shield
【護衛or護送】to guard; to escort; to convoy

譴 3783 ㄑㄧㄢˇ qiǎn

1. to reproach; to reprimand; to upbraid 2. punishment

【譴責】to reprimand; to reproach

譽 3784 ㄩˋ yù

1. fame; honor; glory 2. to eulogize; to praise

【譽滿全球】world-famous

十五畫

讀 3785 1. ㄉㄨˊ dú

1. to read 2. to attend school; to go to school, college, etc. 3. to

〔言部〕

study 「course, etc.)
【讀本】a reader (for a language
【讀卡機】(computers) a card reader

〔言部〕

【讀者】the reader
【讀者文摘】*The Reader's Digest*
【讀書】① to read books ② to study
【讀音】pronunciation (of a word)
【讀物】reading matter; reading

讀 3785
2. ㄉㄡˋ dòu
pauses in a sentence

十六畫

變 3786 ㄅㄧㄢˋ biàn
1. to change; to alter; to become different 2. to turn into; to become 3. extraordinary; uncommon 4. an accident; misfortune; tragedy; upheaval; disturbance 5. changeable 「ing
【變本加厲】to get worse; worsen-
【變賣】to sell (possessions) to meet an immediate financial need
【變電所】a power substation
【變動】①(said of organizations, arrangements, etc.) to change; to reorganize ② alteration ③ variation
【變態】①(zoology) metamorphosis ②abnormality 「stances
【變通】to adapt oneself to circum-
【變革】(said of an institution, etc.) to change or reform
【變更】to change (plans, methods, etc.); to alter; to modify
【變故】an accident; mishap; misfortune
【變卦】to change one's mind
【變化】① to transform; to transmute ② to change ③ changeable
【變化多端】changeable
【變換】①to convert (foreign money, etc.) ② to change; to vary; to switch
【變幻】to change; to metamorphose
【變幻莫測】to metamorphose in an unpredictable way 「price
【變價出售】to sell at the current
【變局】a critical situation; a crisis
【變遷】evolution; change; vicissi-
【變心】to jilt a lover 「tudes
【變形】to transfigure; to transform
【變性】①to change sex by surgical means ② denaturation
【變質】① to change in quality or objectives ② to deteriorate; to go bad ③ to degenerate
【變成】to become; to change into
【變色龍】a chameleon
【變速】to change in speed; gearshift 「style, appearance, etc.
【變樣】to change in patterns,

十七畫

讒 3787 ㄔㄢˊ chán
to misrepresent; to slander; to calumniate; to defame
【讒害 or 讒陷】to incriminate by false charges 「talk
【讒言】malicious, or slanderous

讓 3788 ㄖㄤˋ ràng
1. to give way; to make a concession; to back down; to yield; to give ground 2. to allow; to let; to permit 3. to turn over; to transfer; to surrender; to cede 4. by 5. to step aside; to make way; to let by
【讓步】to give way; to yield
【讓渡】to turn over; to transfer
【讓路】to get out of the way
【讓開】to make way; to step aside
【讓棗推梨】to show brotherly love
【讓座】to yield a seat
【讓位】① to yield the throne; to abdicate the throne ② to yield to

讖 3789 ㄔㄣˋ chèn
1. a prophecy; an omen 2. books about omens

十九畫

讚 3790 ㄗㄢˋ zàn
to commend; to eulogize; to praise; to applaud; to laud
【讚佩】to esteem; to admire
【讚美】to praise; to eulogize; eulogy; laud; praise
【讚歎】to sing the praises of
【讚許】to speak favorably of
【讚賞】to praise; to appreciate
【讚揚】to glorify; to exalt; to uphold; commendation; glorification

谷部
ㄍㄨˇ gu

谷 3791
ㄍㄨˇ gǔ
1. a valley; a waterway between two mountains; a ravine 2. a hollow; a pit 3. a dilemma; a difficult situation; a predicament
【谷底】the bottom of a valley

十畫

豁 3792
1. ㄏㄨㄛ huō
1. a crack; a break; a breach 2. to crack; to break open; to split 3. to give up; to sacrifice; to risk one's life for
【豁出去】to forge ahead in disregard of the consequence

豁 3792
2. ㄏㄨㄛˋ huò
1. to open up; clear 2. to exempt from (duties, etc.)
【豁免】to exempt from (taxes, military service, etc.); immunity
【豁達】①open and clear ②open-minded

谿 3793
ㄒㄧ xī
1. a valley; a gorge 2. a stream; a creek; a brook 亦作「溪」
【谿谷】a valley
【谿壑】a ravine

豆部
ㄉㄡˋ dòu

豆 3794
ㄉㄡˋ dòu
1. beans and peas collectively 2. a vessel of wood for containing flesh, sauces, etc. at sacrifices and feasts
【豆腐】bean curd; tofu
【豆腐乳】soybean cheese
【豆蔻年華 or 荳蔻年華】(said of girls) in their teens
【豆漿】soybean milk
【豆沙】mashed beans
【豆子】beans or peas

三畫

豈 3795
ㄑㄧˇ qǐ
an interrogative particle implying a conflicting or dissenting view or answer—how; what
【豈能】How can...?
【豈敢】(a term implying humbleness or sarcasm) How dare I...? 或 would not dare...
【豈只】not only that...(but)
【豈有此理】What kind of reasoning is that? 或 How absurd!

八畫

豌 3796
ㄨㄢ wān
as in 豌豆—peas; garden peas

豎 3797
ㄕㄨˋ shù
1. to erect; to set up; to stand 2. upright; perpendicular; vertical 3. a young servant 4. petty officers in the palace 5. a downward, perpendicular stroke in calligraphy
【豎笛】a clarinet
【豎立】to erect
【豎起大拇指】thumbs up
【豎琴】the harp

十一畫

豐 3798
ㄈㄥ fēng
1. abundant; luxuriant; copious; fruitful; plentiful; plenty; thick; big 2. a crop; a harvest
【豐沛】copious or plentiful (rainfall, etc.)
【豐滿】① rich; affluence; plentiful ② (said of a woman's figure) plump; buxom ③ full-fledged
【豐富】① abundant ② to enrich
【豐收】a rich harvest; a bumper crop
【豐盛】luxuriant; sumptuous
【豐饒】plentiful; abundant; fertile
【豐衣足食】well-fed and well-clad
【豐腴】plump; buxom and fair
【豐裕】abundance; plentiful; high (pay, etc.)

二十一畫

〔豕・豸部〕

豔 3799 (艷) ㄧㄢˋ yàn

1. plump; voluptuous 2. beautiful and captivating (literary writings, etc.) 3. gorgeous; colorful; gaudy 4. anything pertaining to love, as a love story, love song, etc.; amorous 5. a beauty 6. radiant 7. to admire or envy

【豔麗】radiantly beautiful; magnificent; charming

【豔陽天】bright sunny skies

【豔遇】an encounter with a beautiful woman

豕 部 ㄕˇ shǐ

五畫

象 3800 ㄒㄧㄤˋ xiàng

1. an elephant 2. a portrait; an image snapshot 3. a phenomenon; the outward appearance or expression of anything—especially weather, heavenly bodies, etc.; shape; an image 4. ivory

【象棋】Chinese chess

【象徵】① to symbolize ② a symbol

【象牙】ivory; elephant tusks

【象牙木】ivorywood

【象牙塔】the ivory tower

七畫

豪 3801 ㄏㄠˊ háo

1. a person outstanding in intelligence or talent; a heroic person 2. a leader; a ringleader 3. a proclivity to the use of force, bullying ways, etc. 4. tiny; fine hair 亦作「毫」

【豪邁】straightforward and carefree

【豪門】a rich and powerful family

【豪放】vigorous and unrestrained

【豪華】luxurious; swanky; plush

【豪傑】a man of outstanding intelligence and courage

【豪爽】bold and generous; chivalrous

【豪雨】a downpour; to rain cats and dogs

【豪語】big talk

九畫

豫 3802 ㄩˋ yù

1. comfort; to be at ease 2. same as 預—to get ready; beforehand 3. to travel; to make a trip 4. to cheat; to lie 5. to hesitate 6. short for Honan (河南) 7. happy; delighted; pleased

豬 3803 ㄓㄨ zhū

1. a pig; a hog 2. a pigheaded person

【豬排】a pork chop

【豬肝】pig's liver

【豬圈】a pigsty; a pigpen; a hogpen

【豬肉】pork

【豬鬃】hog's bristles

【豬油】lard

豸 部 ㄓˋ zhì

三畫

豹 3804 ㄅㄠˋ bào

a leopard; a panther

豺 3805 ㄔㄞˊ chái

1. *Canis hodophilax*, a ravenous beast, akin to the wolf 2. cruel; wickedly cunning

【豺狼當道】(figuratively) wicked persons in power

五畫

貂 3806 ㄉㄧㄠ diāo

the sable; the marten; the mink

【貂皮】sable skin or fur; mink

【貂皮大衣】a mink (coat)

七畫

貌 3807 ㄇㄠˋ mào

1. a facial appearance; features 2. a general appearance; a manner; form; bearing 3. to appear or pretend to be like 4. a cere-

monious manner

【貌美】(said of a woman) beautiful

【貌合神離】to appear united outwardly but divided at heart

【貌似】to look like

九畫

貓 3808 (猫) ㄇㄠ māo

the cat

【貓頭鷹】the owl

【貓哭老鼠一假慈悲】to shed crocodile tears

【貓熊】(animal) a panda

貝部 ㄅㄟ bèi

貝 3809 ㄅㄟˋ bèi

1. shells; cowries (used in ancient China as currency) 2. valuable; precious; treasure 3. (physics) bel 4. a Chinese family name

【貝殼】seashells; shells

二畫

負 3810 ㄈㄨˋ fù

1. defeat(ed); beaten; to lose; to fail 2. to bear; to sustain; to shoulder 3. to take refuge in 4. to be proud and complacent 5. to owe 6. negative; minus 7. to turn one's back on; ungrateful 8. to let (someone) down; to disappoint

【負擔】①a burden; a load ②to support (a family, etc.) or pay the expenses ③liability

【負荷】①to bear or sustain ②the load (of electricity, etc.)

【負號】the negative sign(—)

【負荊(請罪)】to offer a modest apology; to apologize

【負氣】sullen; morose; ill-humored

【負心】ungrateful; heartless

【負債】to be in debt; to owe; to incur debts

【負傷】to be wounded; to sustain injuries

【負數】a negative number

【負責 or 負責任】to be responsible

【負約】to break a promise, contract, etc.

貞 3811 ㄓㄣ zhēn (又讀 ㄓㄥ zhēng)

1. chastity of a woman 2. pure; virtuous 3. to be incorruptible; to be correctly firm 4. devotion; dedication 5. to divine; to inquire by divination

【貞潔】chaste and pure; virtuous

【貞節】①tenacity to hold on to one's virtuous way or integrity ②(said of a woman) chastity; purity; virtue

【貞操】①purity and chastity in one's conduct ②a woman's chastity or virginity

三畫

貢 3812 ㄍㄨㄥˋ gòng

1. the tribute from a vassal state; to offer tribute 2. to recommend (a person to an office, etc.); to submit 3. (in ancient China) land tax 4. to contribute; to offer

【貢品】items offered as tribute

【貢獻】to offer or contribute (oneself to the national cause, etc.)

財 3813 ㄘㄞˊ cái

wealth; riches; money

【財寶】money and jewels; valuables

【財迷心竅】to have one's head turned by greed

【財富】wealth or fortune; riches

【財團】a consortium

【財團法人】a juridical person

【財經】finance and economy

【財政】finance; financial administration

【財政部】Ministry of Finance

【財主】a capitalist; a millionaire

【財產 or 財物】property; belongings

【財務】finance; financial affairs

【財源 or 財力】financial resources

四畫

貧 3814 ㄆㄧㄣˊ pín

1. poverty; poor; destitute; impoverished 2. deficiency; defi-

〔貝部〕

cient; lack 3. garrulous
【貧病交迫or貧病交加】to be beset by poverty and illness
【貧民】poor people; a pauper
【貧民窟】a slum area; a shanty-town
【貧乏】wanting; destitute; insufficient
【貧苦】poor; destitute; poverty-stricken
【貧困】impoverished; in straitened circumstances; poor
【貧瘠】(said of land) poor and barren
【貧窮】penury; poor; needy; destitution; poverty; impoverishment
【貧血】anaemia; anaemic
【貧嘴】talkative; garrulous

貨 3815
ㄏㄨㄛˋ huò

1. commodities; goods; products; freight; cargo 2. money; currency; property 3. to bribe; bribery 4. to sell 5. used as a term of reviling with an abusive suffix
【貨幣】currency; money
【貨品 or 貨物】commodities; goods
【貨單】a manifest; an invoice
【貨輪】cargo tanker; cargo vessel
【貨櫃】a container 亦作「貨箱」
【貨款】payment for goods
【貨機】an air freighter
【貨眞價實】(a commercial slogan) goods of high quality sold at reasonable prices
【貨車】a freight car; a lorry; a cargo truck
【貨船】a freighter; a cargo boat
【貨艙】the hold of a freighter; the cargo bay (of a plane)
【貨色】kinds, material or quality of goods; stock in trade; stuff
【貨運】transportation service

販 3816
ㄈㄢˋ fàn

1. to buy and sell; to deal in; to trade in 2. to carry about for sale; to peddle 3. a seller of goods; a peddler; a monger
【販賣】to deal in; to sell; to peddle
【販賣部】a commissary (in barracks, schools, etc.); a store
【販夫走卒】people of the lower class
【販毒】to deal in narcotics

貪 3817
ㄊㄢ tān

1. to desire for more than one's rightful share 2. to hope or wish for; to probe or search for
【貪得無饜】never satisfied with what one has got
【貪圖】to hanker after; to covet
【貪官污吏】corrupt officials
【貪求】to desire or long for (usually more than one's rightful share)
【貪心or貪婪】avarice; cupidity; greed
【貪吃 or 貪嘴】gluttonous; piggish
【貪生怕死】cowardly; cowardice
【貪贓】to take bribes; to practice graft
【貪污】corruption; graft
【貪玩】to be fond of playing or fooling around

貫 3818
ㄍㄨㄢˋ guàn

1. a thread for stringing holed copper coins; to string on a thread 2. a string of 1,000 holed copper coins 3. to see through; throughout; to pass through; to pierce through; thorough 4. to be linked together; to follow in a continuous line 5. to hit the target 6. one's native place
【貫通】① to have a thorough understanding ② to link up
【貫徹始終】to remain consistent from the start to the very end
【貫穿】① to run through ② to penetrate or pierce through ③ to understand thoroughly

責 3819
ㄗㄜˊ zé

1. one's duty, responsibility, obligation, etc. 2. to demand; to be strict with 3. to punish; punishment 4. to upbraid; to censure; to reprimand; to blame
【責備】to upbraid; to reprimand; to reproach
【責罵】to upbraid; to blame; to scold
【責罰】to punish; a penalty
【責打】to punish by beating
【責難】①(ㄗㄜˊ ㄋㄢˊ) to urge someone to a difficult task; to hold high expectations for another person ②(ㄗㄜˊ ㄋㄢˋ) to upbraid; to censure
【責怪】to blame
【責任】① duty; responsibility; an obligation ② responsibility for a fault; blame
【責任保險】liability insurance
【責無旁貸】There's no shirking the

responsibility.
【責問】 to blame and demand an explanation

五畫

貯 3820
ㄓㄨˇ zhǔ
to store up; to hoard; to save up; to deposit
【貯蓄】 to store up; to hoard
【貯水池】 a pond for storing water; a reservoir
【貯藏】 ① to store up; to hoard ② (mineral) deposits
【貯藏室】 a storage room
【貯存】 to store up; to stockpile; to deposit

貳 3821
ㄦˋ èr
1. (in ancient China) a deputy; to serve as a deputy 2. to suspect; to doubt; to distrust 3. changeable 4. an elaborate form of "two" (used in writing checks, etc. to prevent forgery) 5. to repeat 6. doubleness 7. a Chinese family name
【貳心】 a rebellious mind
【貳志】 disloyalty

貴 3822
ㄍㄨㄟˋ guì
1. high-placed; high-ranking; honorable; distinguished 2. expensive; costly; high-priced 3. to esteem; to treat with respect 4. to treasure; to value highly; to prize 5. valuable; precious 6. a polite expression referring to another person—you or your 7. a Chinese family name 8. short for Kweichow Province (貴州省)
【貴賓】 distinguished guests
【貴賓室】 a VIP room; a VIP lounge
【貴婦】 a noblewoman
【貴幹】 What can I do for you? 或 May I help you?
【貴庚】 How old are you?
【貴國】 your country
【貴客】 the guest of honor
【貴姓】 May I know your distinguished name?
【貴重】 precious; expensive; rare; valuable; highly treasured
【貴人】 a distinguished, high-ranking person
【貴族】 the nobility; an aristocrat

貶 3823
ㄅㄧㄢˇ biǎn
1. to reduce or lower (prices, etc.); to devalue 2. to degrade; to reduce; to demote 3. to disparage; to condemn; to censure 4. to dismiss; to send away
【貶低】 to belittle; to depreciate; to play down
【貶值】 to devalue or debase (especially referring to a currency); devaluation; depreciation
【貶謫】 to demote and exile an official; to relegate
【貶抑】 to debase; to devalue; to belittle; to depreciate

買 3824
ㄇㄞˇ mǎi
1. to buy; to purchase 2. to win over (usually with a promise of favors in return)
【買賣】 ①(ㄇㄞˇ ㄇㄞˋ) to buy and sell ②(ㄇㄞˇ ·ㄇㄞ) a line of business; trade
【買方 or 買主】 the buyer
【買通】 to offer bribes to facilitate one's operations; to buy off
【買空賣空】 to speculate (on the stock, etc. markets)
【買進 or 買入】 to buy
【買醉】 to buy drinks

貸 3825
ㄉㄞˋ dài
1. to loan; to lend or borrow; a loan 2. the credit side in bookkeeping 3. to pardon; to be lenient 4. to shift (responsibility); to shirk
【貸款】 a loan (of money)

費 3826
ㄈㄟˋ fèi
1. expenditure; expenses; fees; dues; charges 2. to waste; to use more than is needed; wasteful; consuming too much 3. to consume; to use; to spend; to cost; to expend 4. a Chinese family name
【費力】 ① to need or use great effort ② difficult (tasks)
【費工(夫)】 to take a lot of time or work
【費解】 difficult to understand
【費盡心機】 to exhaust all mental efforts
【費心 or 費神】 ① requiring mental exertion ② Many thanks (for doing this for me).
【費時】 to take, need or waste a lot

of time; time-consuming
【費事】requiring a lot of trouble to accomplish; difficult
【費用】expenditure; expenses; costs

〔貝部〕

貼 3827
ㄊㄧㄝ tiē
1. to paste; to stick; to glue 2. to keep close to; to nestle closely to 3. to make up the deficiency; to subsidize; subsidies; an allowance 4. proper; appropriate; comfortable 5. attached to
【貼補】to make up a deficiency; to supplement
【貼近】nearby; close to; to press close to; to nestle up against
【貼切】proper or appropriate; apt
【貼現】(banking) discount
【貼心】intimate; close
【貼身】① personal servants ② closely attached, as children, undergarments, concubines, etc.

貽 3828
ㄧˊ yí
1. to give to; to present to 2. to hand down; to transmit; to pass on to; to bequeath; to leave behind
【貽笑大方】to become a laughing-stock
【貽誤】to cause hindrance or delay; to bungle

賀 3829
ㄏㄜˋ hè
1. to congratulate; to send a present in congratulation 2. a Chinese family name
【賀電】a congratulatory cable or telegram
【賀年 or 賀歲】to offer congratulations on New Year's Day
【賀禮】a congratulatory present
【賀喜】to congratulate; to felicitate
【賀詞】greetings; congratulations
【賀爾蒙】hormones 亦作「荷爾蒙」

貿 3830
ㄇㄠˋ mào
1. to trade; to barter 2. mixed 3. rashly
【貿然】rashly; blindly
【貿易】trade; to trade
【貿易公司】a trading company or firm
【貿易商】a trader

六畫

賃 3831
ㄌㄧㄣˋ lìn
1. to rent; to hire 2. a hireling
【賃租】to rent
【賃屋】to rent a house

賂 3832
ㄌㄨˋ lù
1. to send a gift 2. to bribe

賄 3833
ㄏㄨㄟˋ huì
(又讀 ㄏㄨㄟˇ huǐ)
1. to bribe; bribery 2. money; wealth
【賄賂】to bribe; bribery
【賄選】to try to win in an election by means of bribery

資 3834
ㄗ zī
1. money; wealth; property; means; capital 2. expenses; fees; charges 3. natural endowments or gifts; one's disposition 4. to avail of 5. to aid or help; to assist; to subsidize; to support 6. to supply; to provide 7. one's qualifications, position, or record of service 8. to trust to
【資本家】a capitalist
【資方】the management (of a shop, factory, etc.); capital
【資歷】qualifications and experiences (of an applicant, etc.); professional background
【資料】data
【資格】qualifications, requirements, or seniority of a person
【資金 or 資本】funds; capital
【資遣】to dismiss (employees) with severance pay
【資訊】information
【資質 or 資稟】one's natural gifts or endowments
【資助】to help another with money
【資產】① property; real estate ② (accounting) assets
【資深】senior; seniority
【資優生】a student with a high IQ
【資源】resources; natural resources

賈 3835
1. ㄐㄧㄚˇ jiǎ
a Chinese family name

賈 3835
2. ㄍㄨˇ gǔ
1. a merchant; a businessman 2. to buy; to trade

賊 3836
ㄗㄟˊ zéi (讀音 ㄗㄜˊ zé)
1. a thief; a burglar; a robber; a bandit 2. rebels; traitors 3. to

harm 4. to kill 5. pests on the farm 6. a term of reviling 7. clever; cunning; crafty
【賊頭賊腦】acting stealthily; thief-like
【賊寇】rebels; bandits
【賊害】to cause harm or injury to another
【賊性難改】The habitual criminal is incorrigible.
【賊船】a pirate ship; a ship owned by bandits or rebels
【賊營】the camp of rebels, bandits, etc.

七畫

賑 3837
ㄓㄣˋ zhèn
1. to relieve or give aid to the distressed; to support 2. rich; wealthy; prosperous
【賑濟 or 賑贍】to relieve or give aid to the distressed; to provide relief for
【賑災】to relieve the afflicted area; to relieve victims of a natural disaster

賒 3838
ㄕㄜ shē
1. to buy or sell on credit 2. distant; faraway 3. slow; slowly 4. to put off or postpone 5. luxurious or extravagant
【賒貸】credit
【賒欠】to buy on credit
【賒賬】to buy on account or credit

賓 3839
(賔) ㄅㄧㄣ bīn
1. a guest; a visitor 2. to treat as a guest 3. to obey; to follow instructions; to submit 4. a Chinese family name
【賓館】a guesthouse
【賓客】guests and visitors
【賓至如歸】Guests flock to the place like returning home.—to feel at home in a place
【賓主盡歡】Both the guests and the host are having a great time.

八畫

賙 3840
ㄓㄡ zhōu
to give; to aid; to relieve
【賙濟】to relieve the needy

賜 3841
ㄙ sì (語音 ㄘ cì)
1. to bestow or confer on an inferior; to grant 2. favors; benefits 3. to order; to appoint
【賜覆】Please reply.
【賜教】(a polite expression) your instructions
【賜予or賜與】to bestow or confer upon

賞 3842
ㄕㄤˇ shǎng
1. to reward; to award; to bestow; to grant; to give to an inferior 2. a reward; an award 3. to appreciate; to enjoy; to admire 4. (a polite expression) to be given the honor of...
【賞光】(a polite expression) to honor me with your gracious presence or company
【賞金】reward money; a bonus
【賞錢】tips (for waiters, servants, etc.)
【賞心悅目】to flatter the heart and please the eye—beautiful and restful
【賞識】to appreciate the virtues in a person or thing
【賞賜】to bestow money or presents on an inferior or junior
【賞玩】to enjoy or appreciate the sight of; to delight in
【賞月】to enjoy moonlight

賠 3843
ㄆㄟˊ péi
1. to compensate or indemnify; to make up for a loss due to one's fault; to pay for 2. to offer (an apology) 3. to lose money
【賠本】to lose money in business
【賠不是or賠禮or賠罪】to apologize
【賠款】an indemnity; a compensation; reparations
【賠還】to repay
【賠錢】① to make a pecuniary compensation ② to lose money in business
【賠償】compensation; indemnity; to recompense; to make amends for

賢 3844
ㄒㄧㄢˊ xián
1. capable; able; versatile; talented 2. good; worthy; virtuous 3. to admire; to praise; to esteem 4. a term of respectful address to another
【賢明】capable and virtuous
【賢內助】a good wife
【賢良】virtuous; the virtuous

【賢惠 or 賢慧】(usually said of women) virtuous and intelligent
【賢妻良母】a dutiful wife and loving mother
【賢淑】(usually said of women) virtuous and understanding
【賢人】a person of virtue and talents

〔貝部〕

賣 3845 ㄇㄞˋ mài
1. to sell 2. to betray; to harm another in order to benefit oneself 3. to show off; to flaunt
【賣命】①to work oneself to the bone for somebody ②to die (unworthily) for
【賣方 or 賣主】the seller
【賣力 or 賣力氣】①to work as a laborer ②to work hard willingly
【賣弄】to flaunt; to show off
【賣國賊】a traitor
【賣價】the selling price
【賣勁】to exert all one's strength
【賣唱】to live on singing
【賣座】①(said of a theater, etc.) to draw large audiences ②(said of a restaurant, etc.) to attract large numbers of customers
【賣完 or 賣光】sold out

賤 3846 ㄐㄧㄢˋ jiàn
1. cheap; inexpensive; low cost 2. lowly; humble; inferior in position 3. low-down; base; ignoble; despicable 4. to slight; to look down on 5. my, a self-derogatory expression
【賤貨】①(a term of revile) a tramp ②worthless goods
【賤價】a low price; low-priced
【賤人】a slut or tramp

賦 3847 ㄈㄨˋ fù
1. a tax; revenue 2. troops; the army; military levies 3. to bestow; to give 4. natural endowments or gifts 5. to spread; to diffuse 6. to compose or sing (especially poems) 7. one of the Chinese literary forms akin to poetry
【賦稅】farm tax and excise tax
【賦予 or 賦與】to give; to endow

質 3848 1. ㄓˊ zhí
1. matters; substances; elements 2. one's disposition or temperament; qualities 3. simple; plain 4. to question 5. to confront
【質朴or質樸】simple and unadorned
【質地】①quality of something ②one's disposition or endowments ③material of piece goods
【質料】quality; raw materials
【質量】①(physics) mass ②quality
【質詢】to interpellate; interpellation
【質疑】to question; to query
【質問】①to interrogate ②to raise questions in order to resolve one's doubt

質 3848 2. ㄓˋ zhì
1. to pawn 2. a pledge; a hostage
【質押】to mortgage

賬 3849 (帳) ㄓㄤˋ zhàng
1. as in 賬目—accounts 2. debts 3. credits; loans; bills
【賬簿】accounts; account books
【賬房】①a cashier's office ②a cashier; a teller
【賬單】bills; invoices

九畫

賭 3850 ㄉㄨˇ dǔ
1. to gamble; to bet; to wager 2. to compete 3. to swear
【賭博】to gamble; gambling
【賭本】money to gamble with
【賭徒】a gambler
【賭鬼】a congenital gambler
【賭氣】to do something out of spite (or in a rage)
【賭債 or 賭賬】a gambling debt
【賭注】stakes
【賭場】a gambling joint; a gambling den or house

賴 3851 ㄌㄞˋ lài
1. to rely on; to depend on 2. to accuse without grounds or evidence; to put the blame on somebody else 3. to repudiate (a debt); to disavow; to deny something which one has said or done 4. to postpone or procrastinate intentionally 5. no good; poor; bad 6. lazy 7. a Chinese family name

【賴皮】①a person without any sense of shame; a rogue ② shameless
【賴賬】①to repudiate accounts ② to go back on one's word

十畫

賺 3852 ㄓㄨㄢˋ zhuàn
1. to earn; to make money; to gain 2. to cheat; to deceive
【賺錢】to earn money; to make a profit

購 3853 ㄍㄡˋ gòu
as in 購置—to buy; to purchase
【購買】to buy
【購買力】purchasing power
【購物】to go shopping

賽 3854 ㄙㄞˋ sài
1. to compete; to contest; to rival; to contend for superiority 2. a race; a tournament; a match; a game 3. to surpass 4. a Chinese family name
【賽跑】to run a race on foot; a foot race
【賽馬】a horse race
【賽馬場】a race course (or ground)
【賽車】a car race; to race cars

十一畫

贅 3855 ㄓㄨㄟˋ zhuì
1. useless; superfluous; redundant 2. repetition; to repeat; repetitious 3. to follow around, as children 4. to be burdensome 5. to pawn things for money 6. to meet; to congregate 7. a son-in-law who takes the place of a son in his wife's parental family which is lacking for an heir
【贅瘤】a wen; an excrescence
【贅述】a repetitious or superfluous statement
【贅言】verbosity

十二畫

贋 3856 (贗) ㄧㄢˋ yàn
a counterfeit; a sham; a fake; bogus; spurious; forged
【贋品】a counterfeit; an imitation; a phony; a sham; a fake; a forgery

贈 3857 ㄗㄥˋ zèng
to send (gifts); to confer or bestow (titles); to give
【贈品】a gift; a present 「a grant
【贈款】to present money as a gift;
【贈送or贈與】to present; to give; to donate
【贈言】words of advice
【贈閱】(said of publications) given free of charge

贊 3858 ㄗㄢˋ zàn
1. to assist; to aid; to help; to support; to back 2. to praise; to commend; to exalt; to glorify; to extol; to eulogize
【贊不絕口】to praise profusely; to heap praises on...
【贊美】to praise; to extol; to exalt
【贊歎】to exclaim in praise
【贊同】to consent to; to approve of; to agree
【贊許】to approve of 「support
【贊助】to sponsor; to patronize;
【贊助人】a patron; a sponsor
【贊成】to agree to; to be in favor of 「extol; to admire
【贊賞】to commend; to praise; to
【贊揚】to exalt; to glorify; to extol; to praise

十三畫

贍 3859 ㄕㄢˋ shàn
1. to provide; to supply 2. adequate; abundance; plenty
【贍養】to provide with means of support; to support
【贍養費】alimony

贏 3860 ㄧㄥˊ yíng
1. to win; to beat 2. gains; 「profits
【贏得】to win (honor, a privilege, etc.)
【贏家】the winner

十四畫

贓 3861 ㄗㄤ zāng
1. bribes; to bribe 2. loot; booty; stolen goods; plunder; spoils
【贓款】money acquired illicitly
【贓物】plunder; booty; loot; spoils

〔赤·走部〕

十五畫

贖 3862 ㄕㄨˊ shú
1. to redeem; to ransom 2. to atone for; to expiate
【贖款 or 贖金 or 贖價】a ransom
【贖回】to recover by paying money; to redeem; to ransom
【贖罪】① to atone for a sin; to expiate a sin ② to buy freedom from punishment ③ (Christianity) redemption

十七畫

贛 3863 ㄍㄢˋ gàn
1. an alternative name of Kiangsi Province 2. a river in Kiangsi Province 3. a county in Kiangsi Province

赤部 ㄔˋ chì

赤 3864 ㄔˋ chì
1. red 2. bare; naked 3. sincere; loyal; single-hearted
【赤膊 or 赤背】with the upper half of the body bared; naked to the waist
【赤貧】extreme poverty
【赤道】① the equator ② (astronomy) the celestial equator
【赤膽忠心】utter devotion
【赤裸裸】① stark-naked; naked ② unadorned; frank; plain
【赤化】to communize
【赤脚】① bare feet ② barefooted
【赤誠】sincerity; loyal; upright
【赤手 or 赤手空拳】① bare hands ② barehanded
【赤子之心】(literally) a child's heart—man's natural kindness
【赤字】a deficit

四畫

赦 3865 ㄕㄜˋ shè
an amnesty to pardon; to excuse; to forgive;
【赦免】to pardon (an offender)

五畫

赧 3866 ㄋㄢˇ nǎn
to turn red from shame or embarrassment; to blush
【赧愧】to blush; to be ashamed

七畫

赫 3867 ㄏㄜˋ hè
1. bright; glowing 2. brilliant; glorious 3. angry; indignant 4. a Chinese family name
【赫赫有名】illustrious; far-famed

走部 ㄗㄡˇ zǒu

走 3868 ㄗㄡˇ zǒu
1. to walk; to go on foot 2. to run; to go swiftly 3. to go; to travel 4. to leave; to go away; to depart 5. to let out or lose (unintentionally); to leak out 6. to visit
【走避】to run away from; to shun; to evade;
【走遍】to travel all over (an area)
【走不開】not able to leave
【走馬看花】to examine a thing hurriedly
【走訪】① to interview; to have an interview with ② to visit
【走道】① a pavement; a sidewalk ② a path; a footpath ③ an aisle
【走動】① to take a walk; to go for a stroll ② to have intercourse; to visit
【走投無路】to have no one to turn to
【走漏】(said of secrets, plots, etc.) to leak
【走廊】a corridor; a hall; a veranda
【走路】to walk; to go on foot
【走狗】a lackey; a tool
【走開】Beat it! 或 Get out of the way!
【走火】① (said of firearms) to go off accidentally ② (electricity) a short circuit
【走向】① the run; the trend ② (geology) strike ③ to move toward; to head for; to be on the

way to
【走著瞧】to wait and see
【走失】(said of persons, animals, etc.) to get lost; to be missing
【走私】to smuggle
【走散】①to walk away in different directions ②to get separated from other travelers
【走樣】①to get out of shape; to lose shape; to deviate from the original ②to be different from what is expected or intended
【走味兒】to turn stale; to lose flavor
【走運】to be in luck; to have good luck

二畫

赳 3869 ㄐㄧㄡˇ jiǔ
(又讀 ㄐㄧㄡ jiū)
valiant; gallant

赴 3870 ㄈㄨˋ fù
to go to; to proceed to
【赴湯蹈火】to go through fire and water; to defy all difficulties and dangers
【赴會】to go to a meeting
【赴任】to proceed to one's new post
【赴宴】to attend a banquet
【赴約】to leave for an engagement

三畫

起 3871 ㄑㄧˇ qǐ
1. to begin; to start 2. to rise; to get up; to stand up; to go up 3. to happen; to take place 4. to unfold; to uncover 5. to build; to establish 6. a numerary adjunct for incidents
【起泡】①to get blisters ②to form bubbles
【起碼】at least
【起飛】to take off; a takeoff
【起伏】①to undulate; undulation ②ups and downs; the rise and fall
【起點】a starting point
【起動】to start (a machine, etc.)
【起頭】①the origin; the beginning ②at first; in the beginning
【起跳】(sports) to take off
【起來】①(ㄑㄧˇ ㄌㄞˊ) ⓐto stand up; to sit up; to rise ⓑto get up ②(·ㄑㄧ ·ㄌㄞ) an adverbial phrase used after a verb denoting that an action is taking place
【起立】to stand up
【起落】rising and falling
【起火】①to catch fire; to be on fire ②to lose one's temper ③to cook meals
【起鬨or起閧】to create disturbances
【起勁】(said of actions, performances, etc.) showing much zeal; eager; energetic; vigorous; with gusto
【起居】one's everyday life at home
【起訖】the beginning and the end
【起先or起初】at first; in the beginning
【起程】to start on a journey; to set out
【起牀】to get out of bed; to get up
【起身】①to set out; to leave; to get off ②to get up
【起子】①(dialect) baking powder; leaven ②(dialect) a screwdriver ③a bottle opener
【起草】to prepare a draft; to draft
【起死回生】to revive the dead; to come back to life
【起色】①a sign of improvement ②a sign of recovery
【起訴】(said of a prosecutor) to file a formal indictment
【起疑】to begin to suspect; to become suspicious
【起意】to conceive a design; to have an idea (of doing something)
【起義】to start an uprising (in a righteous revolution); to revolt
【起眼】to attract attention
【起因】a cause
【起源】the origin; the source; the beginning

五畫

趁 3872 (趂) ㄔㄣˋ chèn
1. to take advantage of; to avail oneself of 2. while
【趁火打劫】(literally) to plunder a house when it is on fire—to try to profit from another's misfortune; to fish in troubled waters
【趁勢】to take advantage of the prevailing circumstances
【趁熱】①while it is still hot ②to act before it is too late
【趁熱打鐵】to strike while the iron

is hot
【趁人之危】to take advantage of others' perilous states
【趁早】as early as possible

〔走部〕

超 3873 ㄔㄠ chāo
1. to jump over; to leap over 2. to be more than; to exceed 3. to be better than; to excel; to surpass 4. to rise above; to transcend 5. to overtake
【超凡入聖】to transcend worldliness and attain holiness
【超等 or 超級】of a special grade; of a special class
【超脫】to transcend worldliness; to detach oneself from
【超齡】to be over the specified age
【超過】① to exceed; to be more than ② to excel; to surpass; to outweigh
【超級】super
【超級明星】a superstar
【超級市場】a supermarket
【超前】①(electricity) lead ② to overtake
【超群】head and shoulders above all others; preeminent; surpassing
【超支】to overspend; to overdraw
【超重】① an overload ② excess; overweight
【超車】to overtake a car
【超出】to exceed; to surpass; to overtake
【超人】a superman
【超載】overloading; to overload
【超速】speeding
【超額】to exceed a quota or target amount
【超音波】supersonic waves
【超越】① to excel; to surpass ② to fly across; to jump over

越 3874 ㄩㄝˋ yuè
1. to go beyond; to transgress 2. to skip; to climb over; to cross over; to go across 3. even more; the more 4. name of an ancient state 5. a Chinese family name
【越南】Vietnam
【越來越…】more and more; increasingly more
【越雷池一步】to transgress the bounds
【越過】① to exceed; to overstep ② to go across; to cross
【越軌】to go beyond what is proper
【越界】to go beyond the boundary
【越權】to act without authorization
【越野賽跑】a cross-country race
【越獄】to break jail; a jailbreak

七畫

趙 3875 ㄓㄠˋ zhào
1. name of an ancient feudal state 2. a Chinese family name

趕 3876 ㄍㄢˇ gǎn
1. to pursue; to catch up with; to overtake; to keep up with 2. to drive; to expel 3. to hurry; to rush; to hasten 4. to try to catch; to make a dash for; to rush for
【趕不及】unable to manage to be on time
【趕不上】① unable to catch up with ② inferior to ③ to be too late for (the train, etc.) ④ to miss; unable to chance upon
【趕忙】with haste; hurriedly
【趕明兒】some other day; later
【趕路】to walk hurriedly; to travel in haste
【趕開】to drive away
【趕快 or 趕緊】to make haste; quickly; at once; to hurry
【趕集】to go to market 亦作「趕墟」
【趕盡殺絕】to injure and oppress to the extreme
【趕車】① to drive a cart or carriage ② to catch a bus or train
【趕場】(said of actors) after finishing a performance, to hurry to another place for a new one
【趕時髦】to follow the fashion; to try to be in the swim
【趕上】① to catch up with; to overtake; to keep pace with ② to be in time for ③ to chance upon

八畫

趣 3877 ㄑㄩˋ qù
interest; fun; interesting; funny
【趣事】an amusing incident; an interesting episode
【趣味】fun; interest; taste
【趣聞】an amusing report; interesting news

趟 3878 ㄊㄤˋ tàng
an auxiliary noun for verbs meaning "to walk," "to journey," etc.

十畫

趨 3879
ㄑㄩ qū
1. to go quickly; to hasten; to hurry 2. to be inclined; to tend; to follow
【趨利】to go after material gain
【趨向】①a tendency; a trend ②to tend to; to incline to
【趨之若鶩】to go after in a swarm
【趨勢】①a trend; a tendency ②to go after men of power
【趨炎附勢】to hang on men of influence

足 部
ㄗㄨˊ zú

足 3880
ㄗㄨˊ zú
1. the foot; the leg 2. the base (of an object) 3. sufficient; full; enough; adequate
【足不出戶】to refrain from stepping outside the house ⌈ample
【足夠】enough; sufficient; full;
【足迹】①whereabouts ②footprints; footmarks; tracks
【足見】it serves to show
【足金】pure gold
【足球】football; soccer
【足球隊】a football team ⌈game
【足球賽】a football game; a soccer
【足智多謀】wise and resourceful
【足足】full; no less than; as much as ⌈certain age
【足歲】to have actually reached a
【足以】sufficient to; enough to

二畫

趴 3881
ㄆㄚ pā
1. to prostrate oneself; to lie face downwards 2. to bend over
【趴下】①to prostrate oneself; to lie face downwards ②to fall flat on the ground ⌈prostrate
【趴著】lying flat on the ground;

四畫

趾 3882
ㄓˇ zhǐ ⌈tracks
1. a toe 2. a foot 3. footprints;
【趾高氣揚】(literally) to walk in a vain, swaggering manner—elated
【趾甲】a toenail ⌊and proud

五畫

跋 3883
ㄅㄚˊ bá
1. to travel 2. a postscript 3. to trample ⌈of authority
【跋扈】to be rampant in defiance
【跋涉】to trudge; to trek; to wade

跆 3884
ㄊㄞˊ tái
1. to trample 2. 參看「跆拳道」
【跆拳道】taekwondo; tae kwon do

跌 3885
ㄉㄧㄝˊ dié ⌈3. a fall
1. to fall; to drop 2. to stamp
【跌倒】to stumble and fall; to fall down ⌈stagger forward
【跌跌撞撞】to walk unsteadily; to
【跌停板】(stock trading) to fall to the lowest point allowed for a single trading day; to hit the rock bottom
【跌落】to go down; to fall; to drop
【跌價】to cut a price; a price drop
【跌跤】①to have a fall; to stumble and fall; a fall ②to make a mis-
⌊take

跑 3886
ㄆㄠˇ pǎo
1. to run 2. to run away; to flee
【跑步】to run; on the double
【跑道】①a track ②a runway
【跑堂】a waiter
【跑腿】to run errands
【跑壘】(baseball) base running
【跑路】to travel on foot ⌈role
【跑龍套】to play an insignificant
【跑鞋】spiked shoes (of a sprinter)
【跑車】a racer; a sports car

跛 3887
ㄅㄛˇ bǒ
lame; crippled: 跛子 a cripple

距 3888
ㄐㄩˋ jù ⌈—distance
1. a bird's spur 2. as in 距離

六畫

〔足部〕

跨 3889 ㄎㄨㄚˋ kuà

1. to take a stride; to stride 2. to sit astride on; to straddle; to ride 3. to cut across; to go beyond; to extend across

【跨年度】to go beyond the year
【跨國公司】a multinational corporation
【跨海】to cross the sea; to sail across the ocean
【跨越】to stride over (a ditch, etc.)

跟 3890 ㄍㄣ gēn

1. the heel 2. to follow 3. to attend upon 4. and

【跟班】an attendant (especially of an official)
【跟不上】unable to keep pace with; unable to catch up with
【跟定】to decide to follow (a leader) for good
【跟進】to follow suit
【跟前】①(ㄍㄣ ㄑㄧㄢˊ) the front, side, or presence (of a person) ②(ㄍㄣ ·ㄑㄧㄢ) used with reference to children in the presence of their parents
【跟蹤】to keep track of; to tail
【跟隨】①to go closely behind; to follow ②a retainer; an attendant

跡 3891 (迹) ㄐㄧ jī

traces; tracks; relics; a print

跪 3892 ㄍㄨㄟˋ guì

to kneel

【跪拜】to kowtow
【跪倒】to go on one's knees; to kneel down; to prostrate oneself; to grovel
【跪下】to kneel down
【跪謝】to express thanks on one's knees

路 3893 ㄌㄨˋ lù

1. a way; a road; a path 2. a sort; a kind; a gang 3. a way; means 4. directions; courses 5. province (an administrative division during the Sung Dynasty) 6. a Chinese family name

【路標】a road sign; a signpost
【路旁】the roadside
【路面】a road surface
【路燈】a streetlamp
【路段】a section of a highway or railway
【路途】way; a road
【路過】to pass by or through (a place)
【路口】an entrance to a road or street; a street intersection; a street crossing
【路基】a road base
【路肩】the shoulder of the road
【路徑】a way; a road; a route
【路線】a route; a road; a course
【路障】a roadblock
【路程】a journey; traveling distance
【路上】on the way; along the way; en route
【路人】①a wayfarer ②a stranger

跳 3894 ㄊㄧㄠˋ tiào

1. to jump; to leap; to bounce; to spring 2. to throb; to pulsate; to beat 3. to skip (over); to make omissions

【跳板】①a gangplank ②a diving board; a springboard ③a steppingstone
【跳票】a bounced check; a check that bounced
【跳動】to throb; to pulsate; to beat
【跳欄】(sports) hurdle race; the hurdles
【跳高】(sports) high jump (in track and field)
【跳過】to jump over or across; to succeed in jumping over or across
【跳級】(education) to skip a grade
【跳腳】to stamp one's foot
【跳棋】Chinese checkers
【跳繩】rope jumping
【跳水】to dive; to jump into the water; to dive from a diving board (or a springboard)
【跳蚤】a flea
【跳槽】to abandon one occupation in favor of another; to get new employment
【跳傘】to parachute
【跳舞】to dance; dancing
【跳躍】to jump; to leap; to hop
【跳遠】(sports) the broad jump; the long jump

跤 3895 ㄐㄧㄠ jiāo

a stumble; a fall

八畫

踐 3896 ㄐㄧㄢ jiàn

1. to tread upon; to trample 2. to fulfill; to carry out; to perform 3. to ascend; to occupy
【踐踏】① to trample; to tread on ② to abuse

踏 3897
ㄊㄚˋ tà
1. to step upon; to tread upon; to trample 2. to go to the spot (to make an investigation or survey)
【踏板】① a footboard; a footrest; a footstool ② a pedal; a treadle
【踏脚石】 a steppingstone
【踏青】 to go hiking on a spring day; a spring outing
【踏實】 (said of actions, etc.) practical; realistic

踟 3898
ㄔˊ chí
to hesitate
【踟蹰 or 踟躇】 ① linked together ②to hesitate ③a comb ④to be in perplexity

踢 3899
ㄊㄧ tī
1. to kick 2. to play (football)
【踢皮球】 ① to kick a ball ② to shirk (responsibility, etc.)
【踢踺舞】 tap dance
【踢開】 ① to kick open (a door) ② to kick (something) out of the way
【踢毽子】 the game of repeatedly bouncing a shuttlecock off a foot
【踢正步】 to march in goose steps

踩 3900
(跴) ㄘㄞˇ cǎi
to tread upon; to trample; to step upon
【踩高蹺】 to walk on stilts

九畫

踰 3901
ㄩˊ yú
1. same as 逾—to pass over; to cross; to go beyond; to transgress; to exceed 2. excessive; overly
【踰矩】to transgress the bounds of correctness
【踰越】 to go beyond; to transgress

踱 3902
ㄉㄨㄛˋ duò
as in 踱步—to stroll; to walk slowly

踵 3903
ㄓㄨㄥˇ zhǒng
1. the heel 2. to follow 3. to call personally at; to go personally to; to call in person
【踵至】 to arrive just behind

蹂 3904
ㄖㄡˊ róu
1. to tread upon; to trample 2. to tread out grain
【蹂躪】 ①to trample ②to devastate; rapacious acts

蹄 3905
(蹏) ㄊㄧˊ tí
1. (zoology) a hoof 2. the feet of beasts
【蹄膀】 (dialect) the uppermost part of legs of pork

十畫

蹈 3906
ㄉㄠˇ dǎo
1. to tread; to step; to stamp one's foot 2. to follow; to pursue

蹉 3907
ㄘㄨㄛ cuō
a failure; a miss
【蹉跎】 ① to slip and fall ② to miss a chance; to waste time

蹊 3908
ㄒㄧ xī
1. a path; a footpath 2. to trample; to tread
【蹊蹺】 extraordinary; strange; queer

十一畫

蹣 3909
ㄇㄢˊ mán
1. to jump over 2. to limp
【蹣跚】 limping; to walk haltingly; to hobble

蹙 3910
(蹴) ㄘㄨˋ cù
1. to contract; to draw together 2. urgent; imminent 3. sad; sorrowful; discomposed
【蹙眉】 to knit the brows; to frown

蹤 3911
(踪) ㄗㄨㄥ zōng
1. a footprint; a track; traces; a vestige 2. to follow the tracks of; to keep track of; to trail
【蹤跡】 ①a track; traces; a vestige ② to keep track; to follow up clues
【蹤影】 traces; a vestige

蹦 3912
ㄅㄥˋ bèng
jump; to leap to skip; to caper; to trip; to
【蹦蹦跳跳】 skipping; capering; tripping; romping; frolicsome

〔足部〕

〔身部〕

蹧 3913
ㄗㄠ zāo
as in 蹧蹋—to spoil; to ruin

十二畫

蹲 3914
ㄉㄨㄣ dūn
(讀音 ㄘㄨㄣˊ cún)
1. to squat; to crouch 2. to stay

蹩 3915
(蹩) ㄅㄧㄝˊ bié
to limp
【蹩脚】①lame ②inferior in quality; poor ③ dejected

蹺 3916
ㄑㄧㄠ qiāo
1. same as 蹻—to raise one's feet 2. on tiptoe 3. stilts
【蹺班】to play hooky
【蹺辮子】to die
【蹺課】(slang) to avoid attending classes
【蹺家】(slang) to run away from home
【蹺蹺板】a seesaw; a teeterboard

十三畫

躁 3917
ㄗㄠˋ zào
1. irritable; hot-tempered 2. uneasy 3. rashness
【躁急】impatient; uneasy

十四畫

躊 3918
ㄔㄡˊ chóu
1. hesitant 2. complacent; confident
【躊躇】①to hesitate; to waver; to falter; to vacillate ②confident; complacent

躍 3919
ㄩㄝˋ yuè
(語音 ㄧㄠˋ yào)
to jump; to leap; to bound; to spring
【躍然紙上】(said of things portrayed in literature or paintings) full of life; vivid
【躍躍欲試】impatient to have a try; eager to do something

十五畫

躑 3920
ㄓˊ zhí
to falter; to hesitate
【躑躅】① to falter; to hesitate; to loiter around ②(botany) an azalea

十八畫

躡 3921
ㄋㄧㄝˋ niè
1. to tread on; to step over 2. to follow; to pursue 3. to walk lightly; to tiptoe
【躡手躡脚】walking with light steps; walking stealthily

身部
ㄕㄣ shēn

身 3922
ㄕㄣ shēn
1. a body; a trunk 2. one's own person; oneself 3. a child in the womb 4. in person; personally
【身敗名裂】to lose both one's fortune and honor
【身不由主】unable to act according to one's own will; involuntarily
【身份證】a citizenship card; an identity card; an ID card
【身段】① physique; a figure ② postures (of a dancer, etc.)
【身體】① the body ② health
【身體力行】to carry out by actual efforts
【身體檢查】a physical examination; a physical checkup
【身臨其境】to experience personally; to be personally on the scene
【身高】stature; height
【身後】after one's death
【身懷六甲】to be pregnant
【身家調查】the investigation of one's family background
【身家淸白】of respectable descent or parentage
【身價】one's social position or prestige
【身價百倍】to receive a tremendous boost in one's social position or prestige
【身教】to teach by personal example
【身心健康】sound in body and mind; physically and mentally healthy
【身世】experiences in one's lifetime
【身手】agility; dexterity; artistic

skill「have something) with one
【身上】① on one's body ② (to}
【身在福中不知福】Living in happiness, one often fails to appreciate what happiness really means.
【身材】physique; physical build; figure
【身外之物】(literally) things that are not part of one's body — money; material wealth

三畫

躬 3923
ㄍㄨㄥ gōng
1. the body; the person 2. in person; personally 3. to bend (the body)

四畫

躭 3924
(耽) ㄉㄢ dān
to delay (unintentionally)
【躭擱】to delay (unintentionally); to fail to complete in time
【躭心 or 躭憂】to be worried; to be apprehensive
【躭誤】① to mismanage (a thing) by an improper delay ② to delay

六畫

躲 3925
ㄉㄨㄛˇ duǒ
1. to escape; to shun; to avoid 2. to hide
【躲避】to dodge; to ward off; to「shun」
【躲避球】dodge ball (a kind of ball game played by children)
【躲躲閃閃】① moving carefully so as to avoid danger ② bashful; timid; shy
【躲債】to run away from one's creditor; to avoid a creditor
【躲藏】to hide oneself; to hide

八畫

躺 3926
ㄊㄤˇ tǎng
to be in a lying position; to lie down
【躺椅】a couch; a deck chair; a「divan」

十一畫

軀 3927
ㄑㄩ qū
1. the body; the trunk 2. a child「in the womb」
【軀幹】①(anatomy) the trunk ② the body; the physical build

〔車部〕

車部
ㄐㄩ jū

車 3928
1. ㄐㄩ jū
name of a chessman in a kind of Chinese chess known as 象棋

車 3928
2. ㄐㄩ jū
(語音 ㄔㄜ chē)
1. a vehicle 2. a wheeled machine 3. to carry in a cart 4. to shape (things) on a lathe; to lathe; to turn 5. to lift water by a waterwheel
【車牌】the license plate (on a「vehicle)」
【車票】a train or bus ticket
【車馬費】transportation allowances
【車門】doors of a vehicle
【車費 or 車錢】a fare
【車夫】a cabman; a chauffeur; a driver; a rickshaw man; a carter
【車道】roads or lanes for vehicular traffic
【車燈】the headlight of an automobile or a motorcycle or bicycle
【車輛】vehicles; rolling stock
【車輪】wheels of a vehicle
【車輪戰】to fight an enemy by turns in order to wear him down
【車庫】a garage; a vehicle barn
【車行】① a vehicle dealer's shop ② a taxi company
【車禍】a traffic accident
【車廂】cars (of a train); railway carriages; compartments
【車站】① a railway station ② a bus station; a bus stop; a bus terminal
【車掌】a bus conductress or con-「ductor」
【車水馬龍】(literally) Carts flow like a stream and horses move like a dragon.—Traffic is heavy.
【車速】the speed of a motor vehicle

一畫

〔車部〕

軋 3929
1. ㄧㄚˋ yà
to crush; to grind

軋 3929
2. ㄍㄚˊ gá
1. (in the Wu dialect) to crowd 2. (in the Wu dialect) to make friends 3. (in the Wu dialect) to check
【軋頭寸】(informal) to scramble for cash to meet a payment

二畫

軌 3930
ㄍㄨㄟˇ guǐ
1. the space between the right and the left wheels of a vehicle 2. a rut; a track; a path 3. an orbit 4. a rule; a regulation 5. to follow; to obey
【軌道】① a railway track ② an orbit ③ laws and conventions ④ a course; a track
【軌跡】① (mathematics) a locus ② (astronomy) an orbit

軍 3931
ㄐㄩㄣ jūn
1. the military; forces; of national defense 2. corps (as a military unit) 3. an armed service
【軍備】armaments; arms
【軍部】the war ministry; the defense department
【軍民】soldiers and civilians
【軍閥】the militarist; the warlord
【軍法】military law
【軍費】a defense budget; military expenses
【軍方】the military authorities
【軍服】(military) uniform
【軍隊】troops; the armed forces
【軍團】① an army (a unit consisting of a number of corps) ② any large unit of troops; a legion
【軍禮】military rites; a military salute
【軍力】military strength (or power)
【軍令如山】Military orders cannot be disobeyed or revoked.
【軍律or軍紀】military laws; military discipline
【軍歌】a war song; a martial chant
【軍港】a naval harbor; a naval port
【軍國主義】militarism
【軍官】(military) an officer
【軍火】arms; munitions
【軍火庫】an arsenal
【軍機】① a military secret ② a military aircraft
【軍階】(military) a rank; a grade
【軍界】the military circles; the military
【軍艦】a war vessel; a warship; a man-of-war
【軍警】the military and the police
【軍眷】a soldier's dependants
【軍情】a military (or war) situation
【軍校】a military school
【軍餉】pay and allowances for soldiers; military payroll
【軍訓】military training
【軍職】a military (as opposed to civilian) office or post; a military appointment
【軍政】① a military government ② the administration of the armed forces
【軍中無戲言】(literally) There are no jokes in the armed forces.—A military pledge or order must be carried out.
【軍種】branches of the armed forces; the armed services
【軍事】military affairs
【軍事地區】a military area; a military scope; a military district
【軍事基地】a military base
【軍事演習】military maneuvers; military exercises; war games (or exercises)
【軍人】a soldier; a serviceman
【軍醫】(military) a surgeon; a medic
【軍營】a military camp
【軍樂隊】a military band
【軍援】military aid
【軍用】for military use; military

三畫

軒 3932
ㄒㄩㄢ xuān
1. a carriage formerly used by high officials 2. the high front of a chariot or carriage 3. a balcony; a porch 4. a window 5. open; wide 6. high; lofty 7. smiling; laughing; delighted 8. a studio; a room
【軒輊】difference in height, rank, excellence, etc.
【軒然大波】(literally) towering waves—great repercussions

四畫

軟 3933 (輭) ㄖㄨㄢˇ ruǎn

1. soft; pliable; tender 2. gentle; soft; mild 3. weak; cowardly 4. poor in quality, ability, etc. 5. easily moved or influenced

【軟片】(photographic) film

【軟綿綿】① soft ② (said of songs) sentimental ③ weak

【軟木塞兒】a cork stopper; a cork

【軟糖】a fondant; fudge

【軟體】software

【軟膏】ointment

【軟禁】to put under house arrest; to confine informally

【軟弱】weak; feeble; flabby

【軟硬不喫 or 軟硬不吃】to yield to neither the carrot nor the stick

【軟硬兼施】to use both hard and soft tactics

五畫

軫 3934 ㄓㄣˇ zhěn

the wooden bumper at the rear of a cart

【軫念】to remember with deep emotion

軸 3935 ㄓㄡˊ zhóu (讀音 ㄓㄨˊ zhú)

1. an axis; a pivot; an axle 2. (said of mounted paintings or calligraphic works) a scroll

【軸心】an axis

軼 3936 ㄧˋ yì

1. to excel; to surpass 2. to be scattered; to go loose

【軼事】an anecdote (not included in history)

【軼聞】an anecdote

六畫

較 3937 ㄐㄧㄠˋ jiào (又讀 ㄐㄧㄠˇ jiǎo)

1. to compare 2. in a greater or lesser degree; more or less; earlier or later 3. clear; conspicuous; obvious; marked 4. to compete; to dispute 5. fairly; quite; relatively

【較量】to compare (strength, etc.) in a contest

【較勁兒】① to have a trial of strength ② to get worse; to become worse

載 3938 1. ㄗㄞˋ zài

1. (said of vehicles, vessels, etc.) to carry (loads); to load 2. to record; to publish 3. to fill

【載歌載舞】to sing and dance at the same time

【載重】① to carry heavy loads; heavily loaded ② carrying capacity

【載運】to transport; to carry

載 3938 2. ㄗㄞˇ zǎi

a year

七畫

輓 3939 ㄨㄢˇ wǎn

1. to draw or pull (a cart) 2. to mourn 3. late 亦作「晚」

【輓聯】funeral scrolls

【輓歌】a funeral hymn; a dirge; an elegy

輔 3940 ㄈㄨˇ fǔ

1. human cheeks 2. protective bars on both sides of a cart or carriage 3. to assist; to help; to complement

【輔弼】① to assist ② a prime minister

【輔導】① to assist and guide ② guidance

【輔助】to assist

輕 3941 ㄑㄧㄥ qīng

1. light 2. simple; easy; facile 3. mild; gentle; soft; tender; lightly 4. mean; base; lowly; unimportant 5. frivolous; flippant; fickle; rash; reckless 6. to slight; to neglect; to ignore

【輕薄】① frivolous; flippant ② disrespectful; irreverent ③ to insult

【輕便】handy; convenient; light; portable

【輕飄飄】very light; lightly

【輕蔑】to despise; to disdain; to contemn; to slight

【輕描淡寫】to describe in a light, moderate tone

【輕浮】flippant; frivolous; playful

【輕佻】frivolous; flippant; capricious

【輕工業】light industry

【輕快】① agile; brisk; spry; nimble;

〔車部〕

〔車部〕

sprightly ② lighthearted ③ lively
【輕騎】① a light cavalryman; light cavalry ② a sprightly horse
【輕舉妄動】to act rashly and blindly; to do something foolish
【輕巧】①light and efficient; handy ②dexterous(ly)
【輕取】to beat easily; to win an easy victory
【輕信】credulous; to believe lightly
【輕裝】light and simple luggage
【輕重】① weight; light and heavy ② degree of seriousness; of relative importance ③ propriety
【輕視or輕看】to make light of; to slight
【輕傷】a slight injury; a minor wound
【輕生】to commit suicide
【輕率】① to make light of; to neglect; to slight; to ignore ② careless
【輕爽】relaxed; easy; comfortable
【輕柔】soft; gentle
【輕鬆】① to lighten; to relax ② easy; comfortable
【輕而易舉】easy to accomplish
【輕易】① easy; facile; effortless ② reckless; rash
【輕音樂】light music
【輕盈】(said of a woman) nimble and shapely
【輕微】light; slight; little

八畫

輜 3942 ㄗ zī
1. a curtained carriage 2. a wagon for supplies
【輜重】①luggage②military supplies

輛 3943 ㄌㄧㄤˋ liàng
a numeraty adjunct for vehicles

輝 3944 ㄏㄨㄟ huī
brightness; splendor; light; luster; luminosity; brilliance
【輝煌】magnificent; splendid; glorious; brilliant
【輝映】to emit and reflect light

輟 3945 ㄔㄨㄛˋ chuò
to stop; to halt; to suspend; to cease
【輟學】to drop out of school

輩 3946 ㄅㄟˋ bèi
1. rank; a grade 2. a generation
【輩分】seniority (among relatives); difference in seniority

輪 3947 ㄌㄨㄣˊ lún
1. a wheel 2. to recur; to alternate 3. majestic; stately 4. to take turns; by turns; in relays
【輪暴】to gang-rape; gang rape
【輪班】to go on duty by rotation; to take turns; in relays; in rotation
【輪番】to assume duties in turn
【輪胎】the tire (of a wheel)
【輪流】to take turns; by turns
【輪廓】an outline; a silhouette
【輪迴】① to recur successively; to move in a cycle ② transmigration (of the soul); metempsychosis
【輪休】to rest by turns; to take a day off by turns
【輪值】to go on duty in turn; to take turns
【輪唱】① (singing) to troll ② to chant Buddhist prayers ③ a canon (a form of musical composition)
【輪船】a steamship; a steamer
【輪椅】a wheelchair

九畫

輯 3948 ㄐㄧˊ jí
1. friendly 2. to collect; to compile; to gather

輸 3949 ㄕㄨ shū
1. to transport; to convey; to haul 2. to hand in; to contribute; to donate; to submit 3. to be beaten; to lose (a game, contest, etc.)
【輸不起】①to display ill humor after losing a game, etc.; to lack sportsmanship ②cannot afford to lose
【輸家】the loser
【輸錢】to lose money in gambling
【輸血】① (medicine) blood transfusion ② to give aid and support; to give somebody a shot in the arm
【輸出】① export (of goods); to export ②(computers) output
【輸入】① import (of goods); to import ②(computers) input
【輸送】to transport; to convey
【輸贏】losses and gains (in gam-

bling, etc.); defeat or victory (in a game, etc.)

3950 輻 ㄈㄨˊ fú
spokes (of a wheel)
【輻射】 to radiate; radiation
【輻射線】 radiant rays

十畫

3951 輾 1. ㄓㄢˇ zhǎn
to turn over; to roll over
【輾轉】 ①to roll about; to toss ② to take a roundabout course; to pass through many places
【輾轉反側】 to toss about in bed

3951 輾 2. ㄋㄧㄢˇ niǎn
same as 碾—to grind; to run over
【輾斃】 to be run over by a vehicle and got killed

3952 輿 ㄩˊ yú
1. a carriage; a vehicle 2. a sedan chair 3. the land; the earth 4. all; general 5. to carry; to transport
【輿論】 public opinion
【輿論界】 the media; press circles
【輿情】 public sentiment; public feeling

3953 轄 ㄒㄧㄚˊ xiá
1. a linchpin 2. to govern; to administer; administration; to manage 3. the noise of wheels
【轄區】 an area under the jurisdiction (of a magistrate, etc.); magistracy

十一畫

3954 轉 1. ㄓㄨㄢˇ zhuǎn
1. to turn 2. to take a turn; to shift; to change 3. to transport; to convey; to transfer 4. indirect; roundabout 5. to roll 6. to migrate; to move
【轉播】 to relay a broadcast or telecast
【轉播站】 a relay station
【轉敗爲勝】 to turn a defeat into a victory; to turn the tables (on someone)
【轉變】 ①to undergo changes; to change ②a change or shift (of attitude, thinking, etc.)
【轉賣】 to resell
【轉達】 to transmit through another person or office; to convey
【轉動】 ①to turn; to revolve; to rotate ②to budge; to move
【轉念】 to change one's mind; to have second thoughts
【轉捩點】 a turning point
【轉告】 to pass on (words); to communicate; to transmit
【轉口】 transit
【轉化】 ①to change; to transform ②to react chemically
【轉換】 transition; to change; to switch
【轉機】 a turning point (usually from bad to good); a favorable turn
【轉嫁】 ①(said of a woman) to remarry ②to transfer (a tax burden upon consumers, etc.)
【轉交】 to send or deliver through or in care of another person
【轉向】 (said of wind) to change directions
【轉學】 to transfer to another school
【轉賬】 to transfer accounts (in banking
【轉車】 to change trains or buses; to transfer to another train or bus
【轉世】 (said of the soul) to transmigrate into another body
【轉手】 ① to fall into another's hands; to change hands ② a very brief period of time
【轉守爲攻】 to change from the defensive to the offensive
【轉身】 to turn the body; to turn round
【轉讓】 to transfer (ownership, title, etc.)
【轉送】 to pass on; to transmit on
【轉移】 to change in position or direction; to divert; to shift; to turn; to transfer
【轉業】 to change one's trade; to change one's career
【轉眼】 a very brief period of time; in the twinkling of an eye; an instant
【轉危爲安】 ① to become safe; to avert a danger; to turn the corner ② (said of a gravely ill patient) out of danger
【轉彎】 to take a turn; to turn in another direction
【轉彎抹角】 ①to go along a zigzag course ②to talk in a roundabout

〔車部〕

way; to beat around the bush; to mince
【轉運】①to transport; to convey; to forward ②to be in a constant cyclic motion ③to have a turn of luck (for the better)

〔辛部〕

轉 3954
2. ㄓㄨㄢˋ zhuàn
to turn round and round; to rotate; to revolve; to gyrate
【轉向】①to lose one's bearings; to lose one's way ②a change in one's philosophy, beliefs, etc.
【轉椅】a swivel chair

十二畫

轎 3955
ㄐㄧㄠˋ jiào
a chair; a sedan chair; a palanquin or a palanquin
【轎車】a sedan (a kind of automobile)
【轎子】a chair; a sedan chair

十四畫

轟 3956
ㄏㄨㄥ hōng
1. noise of a number of vehicles 2. noise; an uproar 3. grand; magnificent 4. to bombard; to blast
【轟動】①to cause an uproar; to create a sensation ②to excite (the public)
【轟轟烈烈】in a grand fashion; on a grand and spectacular scale
【轟炸】to bomb (from an airplane)

十五畫

轡 3957
ㄆㄟˋ pèi
reins; a bridle

辛部
ㄒㄧㄣ xīn

辛 3958
ㄒㄧㄣ xīn
1. the eighth of the Ten Celestial Stems 2. bitter; acrid 3. hard; toilsome; laborious
【辛辣】pungent; hot; bitter; acrid and peppery
【辛苦】①laborious; toilsome ②to work hard; to go through hardships
【辛亥革命】the Revolution of 1911 (the year of 辛亥), which led to the overthrow of the Ching Dynasty
【辛勤】hardworking; industrious; diligent

五畫

辜 3959
ㄍㄨ gū
1. sin; crime; guilt 2. to be negligent in an obligation or expectation; to fail 3. a Chinese family name
【辜負】to fail to live up to (another's expectation, etc.)

六畫

辟 3960
(避) ㄅㄧˋ bì
1. a monarch 2. to summon; to call 3. to govern; to take the law (to people) 4. to avoid; to escape
【辟邪】to ward off evils

七畫

辣 3961
ㄌㄚˋ là
1. pungent; piquant; hot 2. (said of smell or taste) to burn; to bite 3. vicious; ruthless
【辣椒】capsicum

九畫

辦 3962
ㄅㄢˋ bàn
1. to manage; to handle; to transact; to deal with; to attend to 2. to try and punish 3. to purchase
【辦不到】unable to accomplish or manage; impossible to accomplish
【辦法】means; schemes; ways; resources
【辦妥】to complete (procedures); to finish doing something properly
【辦理】to handle; to manage
【辦公】to attend to business; to do office work
【辦公室】an office
【辦喜事】to host a party on a joyous occasion (especially a wed-

ding)
【辦事】to handle business; to manage an affair
【辦案】to handle a (legal or business) case

辦 3963
ㄅㄧㄢˋ biàn
1. to distinguish 2. to identify; to recognize
【辨別】to distinguish between; to see the difference between
【辨明是非】to distinguish right from wrong
【辨識or辨認】to recognize; to recognition; to identify

十二畫

辭 3964
ㄘˊ cí
1. language; words; a phrase; an expression 2. to decline; to refuse 3. to leave; to part from; to depart 4. to resign
【辭別】to bid farewell; to say goodbye; to take one's leave; to make one's adieus
【辭典】a dictionary; a lexicon; a thesaurus
【辭退】①to remove from office ② to resign from office
【辭令】diction appropriate to the occasion
【辭海】a collection of words
【辭彙】vocabulary
【辭謝】to decline with thanks; to ask to be excused
【辭行】to take leave of; to say goodbye to
【辭職】to resign from one's post; resignation
【辭章 or 詞章】① literary compositions; poetry and prose ② the art of writing; rhetoric
【辭呈】a formal notice of resignation; a resignation
【辭世】to depart from the world; to die; to pass away
【辭藻】expressions in literary compositions
【辭源】the origin of a phrase or expression

十三畫

辮 3965
ㄅㄧㄢˋ biàn
1. to plait; to braid 2. a queue; a pigtail; a braid
【辮子】① a queue; a pigtail; a braid; a plait ② a mistake or defect that may be exploited by an opponent

十四畫

辯 3966
ㄅㄧㄢˋ biàn
1. to debate; to argue; to dispute 2. to use specious arguments
【辯論】to debate; a debate
【辯護】① to speak in defense of; to defend verbally; to defend ② (law) to plead; to defend; defense
【辯護人】defense counsel; an advocate
【辯解】to provide an explanation; to try to defend oneself

辰部 ㄔㄣˊ chén

辰 3967
ㄔㄣˊ chén
1. the fifth of the Twelve Terrestrial Branches (地支) 2. 7:00-9:00 in the morning; early morning 3. a time 4. fortune; luck 5. a heavenly body—the sun, the moon and stars

三畫

辱 3968
ㄖㄨˋ rù (又讀 ㄖㄨˇ rǔ)
1. disgrace 2. to disgrace; to insult; to dishonor 3. to condescend; to deign 4. undeservingly

六畫

農 3969
ㄋㄨㄥˊ nóng
1. agriculture; farming 2. to farm 3. a farmer; a peasant
【農民】farmers; peasants; the farming population
【農夫or農人】a husbandman; a farmer
【農婦】a farm woman
【農田or農地】agricultural fields; farmland
【農曆】the lunar calendar
【農會】a farmers' association (or cooperative)
【農家】a farming family
【農具】farm tools; agricultural implements
【農學】science of agriculture

【農產物】farm products; agricultural products
【農場】a farm
【農時】the seasons for farming—spring for plowing, summer for weeding, and autumn for reaping
【農事】farming; agricultural operations
【農舍】a farmhouse
【農作物】farm products; crops
【農村】farm village
【農業】agriculture; farming
【農藥】pesticide; agricultural chemicals

辵 部
ㄔㄨㄛˋ chuò

三畫

迂 3970 ㄩ yū

1. impractical; unrealistic; stale; old-fashioned; trite 2. roundabout; indirect; circuitous; winding 3. to make a detour 4. absurd; preposterous

【迂腐】stale; hackneyed; pedantic
【迂迴】① twisty; circuitous (road) ② (military) detouring tactics; flanking tactics

迄 3971 ㄑㄧˋ qì

up to; down to; so far; till

【迄今】up to now; until now; so far; to this day

迅 3972 ㄒㄩㄣˋ xùn

swift; rapid; sudden

【迅雷不及掩耳】as swift as a sudden clap of thunder which leaves no time for covering the ears; out of the blue
【迅速or迅捷】by leaps and bounds; quick; swift; rapid

四畫

迎 3973 ㄧㄥˊ yíng

to receive; to greet; to meet; to welcome

【迎面】right against one's face in the opposite direction
【迎風】① facing the wind; against the wind ② down the wind; with the wind
【迎風招展】to flutter in the wind
【迎頭痛擊】to make a frontal attack
【迎頭趕上】to try hard to catch up
【迎合】①to cater to ②to make an appointment to meet each other in the future
【迎接】to receive; to greet; to welcome
【迎親or迎娶】to go to meet one's bride at her home before escorting her back to one's own home for the wedding
【迎新】① to see the New Year in ② to welcome new arrivals
【迎新送舊】to usher in the new and send off the old
【迎刃而解】(said of a difficult problem) to be solved neatly

近 3974 ㄐㄧㄣˋ jìn

1. near or close (in space) 2. near or close (in time); immediate; recent 3. near or close (in abstract relation); intimate 4. to approach; to approximate

【近代】modern times; recent times
【近代史】modern history
【近年】in recent years
【近來 or 近日】recently; lately
【近鄰】a close neighbor
【近路】a shortcut
【近況】a recent situation; how things stand
【近海】near the sea; coastal; offshore
【近郊】suburbs; outskirts
【近期】in the near future
【近親】close relatives
【近朱者赤，近墨者黑】Good companions have good influence while bad ones have bad influence.
【近視】nearsightedness; myopia
【近水樓臺先得月】A waterfront pavilion gets the moonlight first.—the advantage of being in a favorable position
【近在咫尺】very near as if just a few feet away
【近在眼前】very near as if located right before one's eyes; right under one's nose
【近因】an immediate cause

返 3975 ㄈㄢˇ fǎn

1. to go back; to come back; to return 2. to send back; to give back

【返老還童】to regain youth; to rejuvenate oneself
【返國】to return from abroad
【返航】to return to a base or port
【返校】to return to school

迕 3976
ㄨˇ wǔ
1. to meet 2. to oppose; to disobey
【迕逆】① to go against one's superiors ② delinquent in filial piety

五畫

迢 3977
ㄊㄧㄠˊ tiáo
far; distant; remote
【迢迢】faraway; far and remote

迥 3978
(逈) ㄐㄩㄥˇ jiǒng
1. faraway 2. widely different
【迥然不同】not in the least alike; diametrically different

迪 3979
(廸) ㄉㄧˊ dí
1. to advance; to progress 2. to enlighten; to teach
【迪斯可】disco

迫 3980
(廹) ㄆㄛˋ pò
1. to press; to force; to compel 2. pressing; urgent; imminent 3. distressed; pressed
【迫不得已】to have no alternative (but to)
【迫不及待】too impatient to wait
【迫害】to persecute; to oppress cruelly
【迫降】a forced landing; a distress landing
【迫使】to force or compel (one to do a thing)
【迫在眉睫】① extremely urgent and near ② imminent
【迫於】to have no other alternative because of...

述 3981
ㄕㄨˋ shù
1. to give an account of; to explain; to expound 2. to follow (precedents); to carry forward
【述職】to report in person the performance of one's official duties

六畫

迴 3982
(廻) ㄏㄨㄟˊ huí
1. to turn; to rotate; to revolve 2. to zigzag; to wind 3. same as 回—to return
【迴避】① to avoid meeting (another person) ② (law) to withdraw; withdrawal ③ to decline an offer, or resign from a job, in order to avoid likely suspicion of favoritism
【迴廊】a winding corridor
【迴旋】to turn round and round; to circle
【迴轉】to turn round
【迴腸盪氣】(said of music, poetry, etc.) to deeply affect one's emotions; very touching
【迴紋針】a paper clip

迷 3983
ㄇㄧˊ mí
1. indistinct; vague; dim 2. to enchant; to be crazy about; to charm; to fascinate 3. a fiend; a fan
【迷湯】flatteries; honey words
【迷途】① to go astray; to get lost ② a wrong path
【迷途知返】able to return to the proper path after going astray; able to correct one's own mistake
【迷你】mini
【迷你裙】a miniskirt
【迷路】to go astray; to get lost
【迷宮】a labyrinth; a maze
【迷糊 or 迷迷糊糊】① vague; dim; indistinct ② unconscious; half awake and half asleep ③ dazzled ④ muddleheaded
【迷惑】① to misguide; to delude; to confuse; to mislead ② confused; puzzled; bewildered
【迷幻藥】a hallucinogenic
【迷信】to believe blindly; superstition
【迷失】to get lost; to lose (one's way, etc.)
【迷人】charming; fascinating; enchanting
【迷藏】hide-and-seek
【迷罔 or 迷惘】bemused

迹 3984
(跡) ㄐㄧ jī
footprints; traces; tracks
【迹象】signs; marks; indications

追 3985
ㄓㄨㄟ zhuī
1. to chase; to pursue; to follow; to trace 2. to drive; to expel 3. to demand insistently; to dun for

4. to try to recover (stolen goods, etc.)

【追本溯源】 to trace to the very source of something

【追捕】to pursue and apprehend; to chase

【追到】 to catch up with

【追悼】to commemorate (the dead)

【追念】to remember with nostalgia or gratitude

【追趕】 to pursue; to chase; to try to catch up with

【追根問底 or 追根究底】 to raise one question after another (in order to reach the bottom of a matter)

【追回】①to recover (what has been taken away illicitly) ②to catch up with someone on the way and make him come back

【追擊】to chase and attack; to give chase

【追加】 to make an addition (to a document, etc.)

【追究】①to try insistently to find out (the ultimate cause, etc.) ②to investigate (a fault, offense, etc.) and punish (the guilty)

【追求】①to seek; to pursue; to go after ②to court (a woman); courtship

【追尋】 to seek; to pursue

【追逐】 to chase; to pursue

【追查】 to investigate; to trace (by observing marks, tracks, bits of evidence, etc.)

【追蹤】①to follow the examples of the predecessors ②to trace; to trail

【追溯】 to trace the origin of; to trace back

【追隨】 to follow

【追憶】 to call to memory; to remember; to look back

【追問】 to question insistently

退 3986 ㄊㄨㄟˋ tuì

1. to retreat; to withdraw; to recede; to regress; to retrogress 2. to recoil; to shrink 3. to bow out; to retire 4. to send back; to give back; to return

【退避】 to withdraw and avoid

【退避三舍】 (literally) to retreat ninety *li* (里)—to retreat as far as possible in the face of a strong adversary or contestant

【退步】①to fall off; to regress; to retrogress; to fall backwards; to suffer a relapse ②to retreat

【退票】①(said of theaters, music halls, etc.) to refund; to return the ticket and get the money back ②(said of checks) to be dishonored; to bounce

【退敵】 to repel the enemy

【退路】①a retreat ②something to fall back on

【退款】 to reimburse

【退後】 to fall backward; to move backward

【退化】 to degenerate; to atrophy

【退貨】 to return goods already purchased

【退回】①to return (a gift, defective merchandise, etc.); to send back ②to retreat; to turn back

【退還】 to return (a gift, defective merchandise, etc.)

【退換】 to return (merchandise) in exchange for another; to exchange a purchase

【退婚 or 退親】to break off a marital engagement

【退卻】①to retreat ②to decline

【退席】to withdraw (from the presence of others)

【退休】 to retire from active life

【退休金】 a retiring allowance; a pension

【退學】 to withdraw from a school; to drop out of a school

【退潮】 (said of the tide) to ebb

【退場】 to leave the stage; an exit

【退出】 to withdraw or retreat (from a city or position)

【退燒or退熱】 to reduce or remove fever

【退縮】 to shrink; to recoil; to flinch

【退而求其次】 to seek what is less attractive than one's original objective

【退伍】 to retire or to be discharged from military service

【退伍軍人】 a retired soldier; veterans

送 3987 ㄙㄨㄥˋ sòng

1. to send; to dispatch; to deliver; to convey 2. to present; to give 3. to see someone off; to send off; to wish Godspeed to

【送報生】 a newsboy

【送別 or 送行】 to see someone off; to give a send-off; to wish Godspeed to

【送達】 ①to deliver to; to dispatch

to; to send to ②(law) to serve (a writ on a person)

【送禮】to give presents; to send gifts

【送故迎新 or 送舊迎新】①to bid farewell to those departing and greet the arrival of new comers ②to send off the old year and usher in the new year

【送客】①to escort a visitor on his way out ②to speed a parting guest

【送貨】to deliver goods

【送回or送還】to send back; to return

【送信】to carry letters; to deliver letters

【送終】to prepare for the burial of one's parents

【送葬】to attend a funeral; to take part in a funeral procession

【送死】①to prepare for the burial of one's parents ②to bring death upon oneself

逃 3988 ㄊㄠˊ táo

1. to run away; to flee; to fly; to abscond; to escape 2. to dodge; to evade; to avoid; to shirk

【逃避】to run away from; to shirk; to evade; to dodge

【逃兵】a deserter; a fugitive soldier

【逃跑 or 逃走】to run away; to flee; to escape

【逃命】to flee for one's life

【逃犯】a fugitive from the law; a jailbreaker; a wanted criminal

【逃脫】to escape from; to free oneself from; to succeed in escaping from

【逃難】to seek refuge from calamities

【逃家】to run away from home

【逃學】to play truant; to cut class; to truant

【逃債】to run away from the creditor

【逃生】to flee for one's life

【逃稅】to avoid tax payment; tax evasion

【逃亡】to run away; to escape; to flee

逅 3989 ㄏㄡˋ hòu (又讀 ㄍㄡˋ gòu)

to meet unexpectedly; to come across; to run into

逆 3990 ㄋㄧˋ nì

1. to meet; to welcome 2. to oppose; to go against 3. beforehand; in advance 4. inverse; converse; adverse

【逆風】①a head wind ②against the wind

【逆來順受】to accept adversity philosophically; to be resigned to one's fate

【逆境】adverse circumstances; adversity

【逆向】in the opposite direction

【逆差】(commerce) an adverse balance of trade; a deficit

【逆水行舟】a boat going against the stream

七畫

逍 3991 ㄒㄧㄠ xiāo

1. to wander in a leisurely manner; to saunter; to loiter 2. free and unfettered; to be leisurely and carefree

【逍遙】to loiter about; to saunter about

【逍遙法外】to remain out of the law's reach; to get off scot-free

逝 3992 ㄕˋ shì

1. to pass; to be gone; to depart 2. to pass on; to die

【逝世】to pass away; to die

透 3993 ㄊㄡˋ tòu

1. to pass through; to penetrate 2. to let out or through 3. thorough; quite; complete 4. to appear; to show

【透明】transparent

【透風】①to let the wind through ②to divulge a secret; to let out a secret

【透露】(said of something) to come to light; to divulge; to reveal; to let out

【透過】①to pass through; to penetrate ②through the intermediary of

【透光】①diaphaneity ②to let the light pass through

【透鏡】lenses

【透氣】①to let air through ②to give vent to a pent-up feeling of discontent ③to relax from strain

【透支】to overdraw; to spend more than the budgeted fund

【透視】①to see through; to penetrate ②to observe what is behind a solid covering (by X-ray, etc.) ③to gain a perspective of; perspective

〔辵部〕

逐 3994 ㄓㄨˊ zhú

1. to chase; to pursue; to follow 2. to drive off; to banish; to exile; to expel 3. little by little; gradually

【逐步】step by step; to proceed orderly

【逐年】year by year; year after year

【逐利】to pursue material gains

【逐客令】an announcement to a visitor that he is unwelcome

【逐漸】little by little; gradually; by degrees

【逐字】word by word; word for word

逕 3995 ㄐㄧㄥˋ jìng

1. a path 2. direct

【逕庭】very unlike; quite different; poles apart

途 3996 ㄊㄨˊ tú

as in 途徑—a way; a road

【途中】on the way; en route

逗 3997 ㄉㄡˋ dòu

1. to stay; to linger; to remain; to pause 2. to stir; to rouse; to tickle 3. funny 4. a slight pause in reading

【逗點 or 逗號】a comma(，)

【逗弄】to make fun of; to sport with

【逗留】to stay; to stop over; to linger

【逗趣】to amuse; to entertain (with jokes, etc.)

【逗人喜愛】(said of a child) to arouse the affection of adults

這 3998 1. ㄓㄜˋ zhè

1. this (a pronoun) 2. this (a demonstrative adjective); such

【這邊】①this side; here ②this side; our side

【這步田地】(to) such a pass; (to) such a deplorable situation

【這麼】so; thus; (in) this way; like this: 大家都這麼說。So they say.

【這麼一來】as a result of that; as a result; in this way; consequently

【這裏】here; this place; where we are

【這還了得】How dare! 或 How can such a thing be tolerated!

【這會兒】now; at the moment

【這山望着那山高】(figuratively) One is never satisfied with one's own present circumstance, position, etc.

【這次】this time; present; current

這 3998 2. ㄓㄟˋ zhèi

this or that (an emphatic demonstrative adjective)

【這邊兒】over here; on this side

【這個】this one

通 3999 ㄊㄨㄥ tōng

1. to go, move, or flow unobstructed 2. to communicate; to interchange 3. to lead to; to reach 4. to understand thoroughly; to be versed in 5. to let through; through 6. smooth; fluent 7. open; passable 8. all; general; overall; throughout 9. thorough 10. common; popular 11. (said of a sentence) well-constructed; containing no fallacy

【通報】to notify

【通病】common ills; common deficiencies; common faults

【通風】①to let the wind through; ventilation ②to let out news or secrets

【通達】① to understand clearly ② unobstructed ③ (said of a road) to lead to

【通道】a passage; a way

【通敵】to collaborate with the enemy secretly

【通通】wholly; altogether

【通力合作】to make a concerted effort; to join forces with

【通路】a thoroughfare; a passageway; a route

【通告】① to notify ② a public notice; an announcement

【通過】① to pass through ② (said of a motion or bill) to be passed ③ (said of a nomination or appointment) to be confirmed or approved

【通航】air or sea navigation

【通話】to communicate by telephone or radio

【通貨膨脹】(economics) inflation

【通婚】to marry (said of members of two families, tribes, etc.); to intermarry

【通姦】adultery; illicit intercourse

【通氣】① sympathetic to each

other ② breathing freely ③ not airtight
【通緝犯】a criminal wanted by the law
【通情達理】sensible; reasonable
【通宵】all night; the whole night
【通宵達旦】all night long; till daybreak
【通曉】to be familiar with; to understand
【通信】in correspondence with
【通行】① to travel through (a road, etc.) ② common practice
【通行證】a safe-conduct; a pass
【通學】to commute
【通訊】correspondence; communication
【通訊錄】an address book
【通知】to inform; to notify; a notification
【通知單】a notification
【通車】(said of roads, etc.) to be open (to vehicular traffic)
【通常】normally; usually; generally
【通暢】①(said of writings) smooth; easy to read; highly readable ② passing freely or smoothly
【通稱】a popular name; popularly (or generally) known as...
【通商】to have commercial intercourse; to trade
【通順】(said of writings) fluent; smooth
【通融】① departure from principles for convenience; compromise; to accommodate; to compromise ② to accommodate somebody with a short-term loan
【通才】an all-round talent; a versatile scholar
【通俗】popular; common
【通郵】postal communication
【通運】to transport; to ship
【通用】①(said of words or characters) interchangeable ② in common use ③ practicable; usable ④ (said of currency) in circulation

逛 4000
ㄍㄨㄤˋ guàng
to stroll; to roam; to ramble; to wander about
【逛街】to stroll down the street; to go window-shopping

逞 4001
ㄔㄥˇ chěng
1. to indulge in (pleasures, etc.) 2. to use up; to exhaust 3. to display; to show off 4. fast; speedy 5. to presume on; presumptuous
【逞能】to display or show off one's ability, feat, etc.; boastful
【逞強】to parade one's superiority; to bully; to throw one's weight around

速 4002
ㄙㄨˋ sù
1. quick; speed; speedy; prompt 2. to invite
【速讀】speed-reading
【速度】① velocity; speed ② (music) a tempo
【速記】speedwriting; shorthand
【速戰速決】a blitzkrieg strategy
【速成】to attain goals within a short time
【速食】fast food
【速食麵】instant noodles
【速食店】a fast food restaurant
【速賜康】pentazocine

造 4003
ㄗㄠˋ zào
1. to create; to make 2. to manufacture; to produce 3. to make up; to invent 4. to build 5. to arrive at; to reach 6. (law) a party concerned in the suit 7. an era; a period 8. to institute
【造反】to rebel; to rise up against; revolt; uprising
【造福人羣】to do good deeds to benefit mankind
【造孽】to do evil things
【造化】①(ㄗㄠˋ ㄏㄨㄚˋ) Heaven; Mother Nature; the Creator ②(ㄗㄠˋ ·ㄏㄨㄚ) one's luck or fortune
【造化弄人】to be a sport of fate
【造就】① to educate; to bring up ② one's achievement or accomplishment
【造句】to make a sentence
【造型】① modeling; mold-making ② a model; a mold ③ (machinery) molding
【造成】① to complete; to build up; to compose ② to result in
【造船】to build a ship
【造船廠】a shipbuilding yard; a dockyard
【造字】to coin words
【造作】① to make ② affectations
【造詣】① one's scholastic attainment, depth or profundity ② to call on; to visit
【造謠】to start a rumor
【造謠生事】to spread rumors to cause trouble
【造物主】the Creator

〔辵部〕

逢 4004 ㄈㄥˊ féng

1. to meet; to come across 2. to happen; to fall in with 3. to talk or act in order to please (a superior, etc.)

【逢年過節】on New Year's Day or other festivals

【逢凶化吉】to turn bad luck into good fortune

【逢場作戲】to participate in pleasure-seeking as a social activity without being a slave to it

【逢迎】①to receive (guests, visitors, etc.) ②to ingratiate; to flatter

連 4005 ㄌㄧㄢˊ lián

1. to connect; to join; to unite 2. in succession 3. a company (of soldiers) 4. together with 5. even; and; including 6. a Chinese family name

【連忙】promptly; quickly; immediately; at once

【連綿不絕】in endless succession; continuously

【連帶】joint (responsibility, obligation, etc.)

【連天】①to stab deep into the sky ②incessantly; continuously ③to shake the sky ④for several days in a row ⑤ to merge with the sky

【連同】together with; in addition to; along with

【連累】to involve; to get someone into trouble

【連理】① trees whose branches interlock or join together ②a couple very much in love

【連連】① continuously; unceasingly; again and again ②one after another

【連絡】liaison; to make contact with

【連貫】①to link up; to piece together; to hang together ② coherent

【連環圖畫】comics; a comic strip

【連接】①continuously ②to adjoin

【連繫】to keep in contact; contact

【連心】the meeting of minds; bosom (friends)

【連續】successive; continuous; incessantly

【連續劇】(television) a soap opera; a drama series

【連戰皆捷】to win one victory after another

【連長】a company commander

【連珠炮】①a rapid-fire gun ② continuous firing; drumfire

【連串】to string together; a string (of events, etc.); a series of

【連手】①to take concerted action ②(gambling) to gang up on cheating

【連署】to sign jointly; joint signatures

【連日】for consecutive days

【連任】to continue in one's office for another term; to be reappointed or reelected

【連載】to publish serially in a newspaper or magazine

【連鎖店】a chain store

【連夜】all through the night

八畫

迸 4006 (迸) ㄅㄥˋ bèng

1. to scatter; to explode 2. to crack

【迸裂】to crack; to split; to dash out

逮 4007 1. ㄉㄞˋ dài

1. to reach; to come up to 2. to hunt; to chase and make arrest

【逮捕】to make arrest

逮 4007 2. ㄉㄞˇ dǎi

to capture; to catch

【逮住】to catch (a thief, a ball, etc.)

週 4008 ㄓㄡ zhōu

1. a week; a period 2. a cycle; a revolution; to revolve

【週末】a weekend

【週密】careful; thorough

【週到】(often said of service, etc.) thoughtful; considerate

【週年】a full year; an anniversary

【週年紀念】commemoration of an anniversary

【週刊】a weekly periodical; a weekly

【週會】a weekly meeting

【週期】a period; a cycle

【週全】①complete and perfect ② to help; assistance

【週轉】① circulating or revolving (funds) ②to have enough to meet the need

【週歲】a full year (especially said of a child's age)

【週而復始】to repeat the cycle all over again

進 4009 ㄐㄧㄣˋ jìn

1. to go ahead; to move forward; to proceed; to advance 2. to improve; improvement; progress 3. to recommend; to introduce 4. to offer (advice, presents, etc.) 5. a generation 6. income 7. rooms in a house divided by a courtyard; a courtyard 8. to enter 9. to eat; to take; to have

【進步】 to improve; to progress; improvement; progress; progressive

【進度】 (said of work) degree of progress

【進退】 ① to advance or retreat ② to stay or quit a job ③ to employ or fire a person ④ a sense of propriety

【進退兩難】 difficult either to proceed or retreat; in a dilemma

【進來】 Come in. 或 to enter

【進攻】 to attack; attack; offensive

【進口】 ① to import; importation ② an intake (for liquid or gaseous matters)

【進化】 to evolve; evolution

【進取】 ① to be aggressive, as in jockeying for position, etc. ② to forge ahead with effort; to advance

【進修】 to advance in study; to engage in advanced studies

【進行】 ① to advance; to march forward ② to proceed (with one's business, plan, etc.); to carry on

【進展】 progress; headway

【進場】 to get into an examination room, a sports arena, etc.

【進出】 ① to get in and out; incoming and outgoing ② (business) a turnover

【進出口】 ① imports and exports ② exits and entrances

【進食】 to eat; to take food

【進水】 (said of a house) to get flooded; water flowing in

【進入】 to enter; to get in; to reach

【進一步】 to take one step ahead; to move further ahead

【進言】 to offer advice

逶 4010 ㄨㄟ wēi

winding; curved; tortuous (road, way)

【逶迤】 ① to wind; winding (river, road, etc.) ② long; distant

逸 4011 ㄧˋ yì

1. to flee; to escape; to run away 2. to go beyond; to exceed 3. to rusticate; to live in retirement 4. ease; leisure 5. to let loose; to let go 6. a fault; an error; a mistake 7. quick; rapid 8. lost 9. superior; outstanding

【逸樂】 enjoyment of an easy life

【逸趣橫生】 replete with humor or refined interest

【逸事 or 軼事】 an anecdote; an episode

九畫

逾 4012 ㄩˊ yú

1. to exceed; to pass over; more than 2. to transgress 3. added

【逾矩】 to transgress what is right

【逾期】 to exceed a time limit

【逾越】 ① to pass over; to scale (a wall, etc.) ② to do what one is not supposed to do

逼 4013 ㄅㄧ bī (又讀 ㄅㄧˋ bì)

1. to press; to compel; to pressure; to force; to coerce 2. to close in; to draw near 3. to importune; to harass; to annoy 4. narrow; strait

【逼不得已】 to be compelled or forced to; can't help but

【逼迫】 to compel; to force

【逼供】 to force a confession

【逼近】 to draw near; to press

【逼債】 to press for payment of debts

【逼眞】 (said of acting, performances, etc.) lifelike; almost real

【逼視】 to stare at sternly

【逼上梁山】 to be forced to do something, especially to break the law

【逼人太甚】 to push someone too hard

【逼問】 to question closely

遁 4014 ㄉㄨㄣˋ dùn

1. to run away; to escape 2. to conceal oneself; to retire

【遁形】 to become invisible; to vanish

【遁世】 to live incognito

【遁走】 to flee; to take to one's heels

【遁辭】 an excuse; a pretext

4015
遂 ㄙㄨㄟˋ suì
(又讀 ㄙㄨㄟˊ suí)
1. to have one's will; to satisfy; to fulfill 2. successful; to succeed 3. to proceed to; to reach 4. then; consequently; thereupon 5. to flee

【遂心】to have one's will; to satisfy

〔辵部〕

4016
遇 ㄩˋ yù
1. to meet; to run into; to come across; to encounter 2. to treat; treatment 3. opportunity; luck 4. meeting of minds; to win confidence (of a superior, king, etc.) 5. to rival; to match with

【遇到】to run into; to meet with; to encounter
【遇難】①to get killed in an accident ②to be murdered by enemy troops, rebels, etc.
【遇害】to be murdered or assassinated
【遇見】to meet with; to run into; to come across; to bump into
【遇人不淑】to have married a bad husband
【遇刺】to be attacked by an assassin

4017
遊 ㄧㄡˊ yóu
1. to travel; to go to a distance 2. to roam; to saunter 3. to befriend; to make friends 4. freely wield (a sword), move (one's eyes), stretch (one's sight), etc.

【遊伴】a travel companion
【遊牧】to move about to search for pasture; to rove around as a nomad
【遊牧民族】a nomadic people or tribe
【遊蕩】to fool around; to act like a bum or vagrant
【遊艇】a yacht
【遊樂】to make merry; entertainment
【遊樂場】an amusement park
【遊覽】①to visit; to tour; sightseeing ②to read extensively
【遊覽車】a bus or train for tourists or sightseers
【遊客】a traveler; a tourist
【遊記】a travelogue (in writing); a writing about one's travels
【遊戲】to play; play
【遊行】① to parade; a parade ②to demonstrate (in protest)
【遊學】to study abroad; to pursue advanced study far away from home
【遊手好閒】to be a lazy good-for-nothing; to lead a parasitic life
【遊山玩水】to travel high and low and enjoy the sights of mountains and rivers
【遊說】to travel around and try to talk people into accepting one's views; to lobby; to canvass
【遊刃有餘】to handle a difficult task with great ease
【遊子】a traveler; a wanderer
【遊玩】to play; to recreate

4018
運 ㄩㄣˋ yùn
1. to move; to revolve 2. to transport; to ship 3. to utilize; to make use of 4. one's luck or fortune

【運費】a freight charge; freight
【運動】① sports; physical exercises ② motion; movement ③ a social movement; a campaign; a drive ④ to lobby
【運動會】an athletic meet; a sports meeting; games
【運動場】a playground; a stadium; a gymnasium; a sports arena
【運動員】① an athlete; a sportsman ② a lobbyist
【運河】① a canal ② the Grand Canal in China
【運貨】to transport goods
【運氣】①(ㄩㄣˋ ㄑㄧˋ) (Chinese pugilism) dynamic tension of muscles ②(ㄩㄣˋ ·ㄑㄧ) luck or fortune
【運銷】to ship (goods) for sales; shipping and marketing
【運行】to move in an orbit, as a planet or satellite
【運轉】① to revolve; revolution ② to work; to operate; to run
【運輸】transportation; to transport
【運算】(mathematics) an operation
【運送】to convey; to transport; to deliver; to ship
【運用】to employ; to make use of; to exercise

4019
遍 ㄅㄧㄢˋ biàn
(語音 ㄆㄧㄢˋ piàn)
1. a time 2. throughout; everywhere

【遍布】all over; everywhere
【遍地】everywhere; throughout the land
【遍體鱗傷】with wounds all over the body

4020
過 ㄍㄨㄛˋ guò
(又讀 ㄍㄨㄛ guō)

1. to pass; to pass through or by; to ford 2. across; past; through; over 3. to spend or pass (time) 4. after; past 5. to go beyond the ordinary or proper limits; to surpass 6. too much; excessive 7. a mistake; a demerit 8. a particle indicating the past perfect tense 9. contagious 10. to visit 11. to transfer 12. to die; death 13. to arrive; to get to

【過半】more than half
【過磅】to weigh
【過不去】①unable to get through ②to feel sorry for ③intentionally to make it difficult for somebody
【過門不入】to act beyond the call of duty
【過分】to go beyond the normal or proper limits; to overdo
【過得去】①not too bad; so-so; fair ② not to embarrass another ③ to be at peace with oneself ④ passable; able to get through
【過度】①to go beyond the normal limits; to overdo ②excessive
【過渡時期】a period or stage of transition; a transitional stage or period
【過多】too many or much; excessive
【過冬】to pass the winter; to winter
【過頭】to go beyond the norm or the set goal; to overdo
【過年】①to pass the New Year ② next year
【過來人】a person who has had the experience of something in question
【過來】Come here. 或 Come on.
【過量】an overdose; to go beyond the limits
【過路】to pass by; in transit
【過濾】to filter; to filtrate
【過關】①to go through a checkpoint ②to pass a critical test ③ to come up to the standard
【過客】a traveler; a passerby
【過河拆橋】(literally) to destroy the bridge after one has crossed the river—very ungrateful
【過戶】to transfer the ownership (of bonds, stocks, or property) from one person to another
【過活】to make a living
【過火】to go beyond the proper limits; to overdo; to go too far
【過繼】①(said of an heirless person) to adopt a son of one's brother or relative as one's own ②to have one's own child adopted by a male relative as his heir
【過節】①to pass (or celebrate) a festival ②a grudge
【過江之鯽】as numerous as a large school of fish migrating in a river
【過獎】① to overpraise; to flatter ② (a polite expression) I don't deserve your praise.
【過境】to pass through; in transit
【過期】to have passed the deadline; (said of permits, etc.) to have passed the date of expiration; overdue
【過去】① in the past; formerly; once ②to go over ③to pass; to pass by ④to die; to pass away
【過程】(in) the process; (in) the course (of)
【過失】errors committed unintentionally; faults
【過時不候】The deadline (appointed time, or specified date) will not be extended.
【過世】to pass away; to die; dead
【過生日】to celebrate a birthday
【過剩】a surplus
【過日子】①to practice economy ② to live
【過錯】mistakes; faults
【過意不去】①very much obliged; unable to express one's thanks adequately ②to feel sorry
【過夜】①to pass the night; to overnight ②to spend a whole night with a prostitute (as distinct from "short-time quickies")
【過猶不及】Too much is as bad as not enough.
【過眼煙雲】(literally) ephemeral
【過癮】①to do something to one's heart's content ②to satisfy the urge of an addiction
【過問】①to make inquiry about; to ask about ②to interfere with ③to care
【過往】①comings and goings ② social contacts

【辵部】

〔辵部〕

遏 4021 ㄜˋ è

1. to curb; to stop; to restrain; to prevent 2. to cause one's own extinction; to extinguish; to ruin

【遏止】 to check; to hold back; to stop

遑 4022 ㄏㄨㄤˊ huáng

1. hurry; to hurry 2. disturbed anxious 3. leisurely 4. not to

【遑論其他】 not to mention the others; let alone the other points

遐 4023 ㄒㄧㄚˊ xiá

1. distant; far 2. a long time 3. advanced in years 4. to die down; to vanish 5. to abandon; to cast off 6. Why not? 或 How? 或 What?

【遐想】 wild and fanciful thoughts

遒 4024 ㄑㄧㄡˊ qiú

1. strong; powerful; vigorous 2. to come to an end; to close 3. to gather; to concentrate

道 4025 ㄉㄠˋ dào

1. a road; a path; a street 2. the "way"(in the metaphysical sense) 3. a way; a method 4. Taoism; a Taoist 5. to say; to speak 6. an administrative district in old China 7. a theory; a doctrine 8. to govern; to lead 9. to think; to suppose 10. a skill; an art; a craft

【道不同不相爲謀】 People adhering to different principles will not map their plan together.

【道貌岸然】 ① to maintain a serene look or dignified appearance ② to pretend to be a moralist

【道德】 morality; morals

【道聽塗說】 groundless talk; rumor; hearsay

【道統】 orthodoxy of teachings or precepts

【道理】 ① the right way; the proper way ② reason; rationality

【道路】 a road

【道高一尺, 魔高一丈】 The force of evil always manages to beat the force of law.

【道賀】 to congratulate

【道家】 the Taoist school

【道教】 (religion) Taoism

【道具】 stage properties

【道歉】 to make an apology; to apologize

【道謝】 to thank; to express thanks

【道學】 ① the emphasis on rationality in learning as advocated by the Sung scholars ② the teachings of Taoism

【道士】 a Taoist priest

【道義】 morals; morality; a sense of righteousness; honor

達 4026 ㄉㄚˊ dá

1. intelligent; smart; understanding; reasonable 2. prominent; successful 3. to reach; to arrive at 4. to inform; to tell 5. open-minded

【達到】 to reach (a decision or conclusion); to achieve or attain (a goal, etc.)

【達賴喇嘛】 Dalai Lama, the ruler and chief monk of Tibet

【達觀】 a kind of wisdom which enables a person to be oblivious of emotions and adversity

【達官貴人】 prominent officials and eminent personages

【達成】 to succeed in (a mission, etc.); to accomplish; to reach (an agreement)

違 4027 ㄨㄟˊ wéi

1. to go against; to defy; to disobey; to disregard 2. to be separated 3. to avoid 4. evil; fault

【違背】 to defy; to disobey; to disregard; to be contrary to

【違法】 to be against the law; to be unlawful; to violate the law; to be illegal

【違反】 to contradict; to disregard (the rules, etc.)

【違規】 to be against regulations

【違抗】 to defy and oppose; to disobey

【違禁】 to defy a prohibition

【違警】 to break a police regulation

【違憲】 unconstitutional; violation of the Constitution

【違心之論】 insincere utterances, comments, etc.

【違章建築 or 違建】 buildings erected without a license or against the provisions of the building code; illegal construction

【違約】 a breach of contract; to break a contract or agreement

【違約金】 a forfeit or penalty

十畫

遜 4028 ㄒㄩㄣˋ xùn
(又讀 ㄙㄨㄣˋ sùn)
1. respectful and compliant; obedient 2. to resign; resigning; to surrender; to abdicate; yielding 3. humble; modest 4. not as good as; inferior to
【遜讓】to surrender (a position) to another; to yield
【遜色】inferior to; not as good as
【遜位】to abdicate; abdication

遙 4029 ㄧㄠˊ yáo
distant; far; remote
【遙控】remote control; telecontrol
【遙遙領先】to be far ahead
【遙遙無期】in the indefinite future
【遙望】to take a distant look
【遙遠】far and remote

遛 4030 ㄌㄧㄡˋ liù
to stroll; to walk slowly; to roam
【遛達】to take a walk; to stroll as an exercise

遞 4031 ㄉㄧˋ dì
1. to forward; to transmit; to hand or pass over to 2. to substitute; to alternate
【遞補】to fill a vacancy
【遞交】to hand over; to deliver
【遞減】to decrease progressively
【遞上】to forward; to present
【遞增】to increase progressively
【遞送】to deliver (a letter, etc.)

遠 4032 1. ㄩㄢˇ yuǎn
1. far; distant; remote 2. deep; profound 3. to keep at a distance
【遠方】a distant place; remote places
【遠房】related through remote ancestry; distantly related
【遠大】very promising (person, etc.); (to look) far ahead
【遠道】faraway; distant; afar
【遠離】① to depart for a distant place② to keep away at a great distance
【遠離塵囂】far from the madding crowd
【遠交近攻】to make friends with distant countries and attack the neighboring ones
【遠見】foresight; a farsighted view; prescience
【遠近】① far and near ② remote or close (relatives, etc.) ③ distance
【遠景】① a vista; a distant view; a long-range perspective ② (movies) a long shot
【遠親不如近鄰】Distant relatives are not as helpful as close neighbors.
【遠行】to travel to a distant place; a journey to a distant place
【遠征】to do battle in a distant land; an expedition
【遠處】distant; located far away; distant places
【遠視】① farsightedness (as a physical defect); hypermetropia ② to look from a distance
【遠涉重洋】to cross many seas—to go abroad
【遠水不救近火】Water from afar cannot quench a nearby fire.
【遠走高飛】to go (or flee) far away
【遠足】an excursion; an outing
【遠洋】① an ocean ② of the open sea beyond the littoral zone; oceanic

遠 4032 2. ㄩㄢˋ yuàn
to keep at a distance; to keep away from; to avoid; to shun
【遠小人】to keep away from mean persons

遣 4033 ㄑㄧㄢˇ qiǎn
1. to dispatch; to send 2. to kill (time); to forget (one's sorrow); to divert 3. to banish 4. to release
【遣返】to send back; to send home
【遣詞造句】the choice of words and building of sentences
【遣散】to disband
【遣送】to send away; to deport

十一畫

遭 4034 ㄗㄠ zāo
1. to meet with; to incur; to be victimized; to suffer 2. times of binding or turning around, as with a rope 3. a time; a turn
【遭逢】① to meet with ② vicissitudes in one's life
【遭難】to meet with difficulty, mis-

〔辵部〕

fortune, or death
【遭受】 to incur (losses, etc.); to be subjected to
【遭殃】to meet with misfortune or disaster
【遭遇】 ① to meet with; to encounter ② vicissitudes in one's life

遨 4035
ㄠˊ áo
to travel for pleasure; to ramble
【遨遊】 to ramble; to travel

適 4036
ㄕˋ shì
1. to go; to arrive at; to reach 2. just right; exactly; appropriate; fit; just 3. comfortable; at ease with oneself 4. (said of a girl) to marry 5. to follow; to be faithful to 6. only 7. by chance; accidentally 8. just now
【適得其反】 to get exactly the opposite
【適當】 proper; appropriate; fit
【適度】 appropriate; within limits
【適可而止】 to stop at the right moment or point
【適合】 suitable or suitable for; to fit
【適者生存】 the survival of the fittest
【適中】proper; adequate; appropriate
【適時】 at the right time
【適宜】 fit; suitable; proper
【適應】 to adapt; adaptation (to environment, etc.)
【適用】 fit or suitable for use

遮 4037
ㄓㄜ zhē
1. to hide; to cover; to screen; to shade; to shield; to conceal; to shut out 2. to intercept; to block
【遮蔽】 to cover; to screen
【遮擋】 to fend
【遮蓋】 to cover; to cover up
【遮羞】 to hush up a scandal
【遮住】 to obstruct; to block; to cover
【遮醜】 to hide one's shame
【遮掩】 ① to hide; to cover up; to conceal ② to cover; to envelop
【遮蔭】 to shade
【遮陽】 to protect from the sunlight

遯 4038
ㄉㄨㄣˋ dùn
1. to escape; to run off 2. to cheat

十二畫

遲 4039
ㄔˊ chí
1. late 2. slow; dilatory; tardy 3. to delay 4. (said of a person) dull; stupid 5. a Chinese family name
【遲到】 to come or arrive late
【遲鈍】 stupid; awkward; clumsy
【遲緩】 slow; tardy; tardiness
【遲早】 sooner or later
【遲疑】 to hesitate; hesitancy

遴 4040
ㄌㄧㄣˊ lín
to choose or select carefully
【遴選】 to choose or pick (a person); to select

遵 4041
ㄗㄨㄣ zūn
1. to follow 2. to observe (rules, regulations, etc.); to abide by (laws, etc.)
【遵命】 to obey orders; to observe instructions
【遵奉】 to observe; to obey
【遵循】① to follow; to accord with; to obey; to go by ② to hesitate
【遵旨】 to follow imperial orders or decrees
【遵照】 to follow; to observe; to accord with; to obey
【遵守】 to observe; to abide by; to keep (a promise)
【遵從】 to follow; to comply with; to obey (orders, etc.)

遶 4042
ㄖㄠˋ rào
to surround

遷 4043
ㄑㄧㄢ qiān
1. to move; to remove 2. to change 3. (said of officials, etc.) to get transferred 4. to be banished
【遷調】 to get transferred to another post
【遷都】 to move the national capital
【遷怒】 ① to blame a person for one's own blunder, failure, etc. ② to shift or transfer one's anger from one person to another
【遷就】 to compromise
【遷居】 to move into a new residence
【遷徙】 to move; to remove
【遷善】 to reform one's ways
【遷移】 to move (to a new address)

選 4044
ㄒㄩㄢˇ xuǎn

1. to select; to choose; choice 2. to elect; elections
【選拔】 to select
【選美】 a beauty contest
【選民】 the eligible voters among the citizenry; constituency
【選定】 to decide on a selection
【選讀】 ① to take an elective course in a college ② selected readings
【選購】 to select and make purchase
【選課】 to take courses in a college
【選舉】 to elect; to vote; elections
【選舉權】 the right to vote
【選舉人】 a voter
【選賢與能】 to pick the good and select the capable for public posts
【選出】 to pick out; to select; to elect
【選手】 a member of a sports team or delegation representing a school, an area or a country; a contestant
【選擇】 a choice; to choose
【選擇題】 a multiple-choice question
【選用】 to select and appoint to a post

遺 4045
1. ㄧˊ yí
1. to lose; lost 2. things lost 3. to miss; an omission due to negligence 4. to forget 5. to leave over 6. remnants; leftovers 7. to abandon; to desert 8. anything left behind by the deceased; to bequeath; to hand down; a legacy 9. to urinate 10. short for nocturnal emission
【遺命】 the injunctions of a dead person
【遺體】 ① the remains (of a deceased person); the corpse ② one's body (handed down by one's parents)
【遺老】 ① ministers of the preceding emperor (father of the current emperor) ② ministers of the preceding dynasty ③ old, experienced men in the country
【遺漏】 to omit or miss; an omission; an oversight
【遺留】 to leave behind either intentionally or unintentionally
【遺落】 ① to lose; lost ② carefree; indifferent to what's happening around
【遺孤】 orphans
【遺骸】 one's remains; one's corpse
【遺憾 or 遺恨】 to regret; regret; to feel sorry; regrettable
【遺跡】 relics; vestiges; traces
【遺教】 ① exhortation of a dying person ② teachings of a dead person
【遺棄】 ①(law) to desert, or to fail to support one's legal dependents ② to cast away; to abandon
【遺像】 the portrait of a dead person
【遺址】 the old site of some building or a city which no longer exists
【遺志】 the ideal or wish not carried out before one's death
【遺囑】 ① the will of a dead person ② instructions of a dying person
【遺著】 a posthumous book
【遺臭萬年】 a bad reputation that will be long remembered
【遺產】 ① property left behind by a deceased person ② a legacy
【遺傳】 to inherit; hereditary; heredity
【遺失】 to lose; lost
【遺書】 ① letters written by a suicide ② ancient books scattered or lost ③manuscripts published posthumously
【遺孀】 a widow
【遺容】 ① the portrait of a dead person ② remains (of the deceased)
【遺族】 survivors of a deceased person's family
【遺言】 instructions, words, etc. of a dying person; a will
【遺物】things left behind by a dead person
【遺忘】 to forget; to neglect

遺 4045
2. ㄨㄟˋ wèi
1. to send or present as a gift 2. to be left to; to be laid upon

遼 4046
ㄌㄧㄠˊ liáo
1. distant; far 2. the Liao River in Manchuria 3. the Liao Dynasty (916-1125) founded by the Kitan Tartars in the greater part of northern China
【遼闊 or 遼廓】 vast; distant

十三畫

避 4047
ㄅㄧˋ bì
1. to avoid; to shun; to evade; to hide 2. to prevent; to keep away;

to repel
【避不見面】to avoid meeting some-one
【避不作答】to parry a question
【避免】to avoid; to forestall
【避難】to escape a calamity; to avoid disaster; to take refuge
【避雷針】a needle gap arrester
【避開】to get out of the way
【避諱】①(an old Chinese custom) to avoid mentioning the emperor or one's ancestors by name or using any character of it in writing except the family name ②to evade
【避邪】to avoid evil spirits or in-fluences
【避嫌】to avoid suspicion
【避重就輕】①to take the easier way out; to choose the easier of the two alternatives ②to dwell on the minor points but avoid touching the core of a matter
【避暑】to run away from summer heat
【避姙or避孕】to avoid pregnancy; contraception

遽 4048
ㄐㄩˋ jù
1. suddenly; abruptly; hastily; hurriedly 2. scared; frightened; agitated; agitation 3. a stage-coach

邀 4049
ㄧㄠ yāo
1. to invite; to ask; to request 2. to intercept 3. (now rarely) to weigh or measure
【邀功】to take credit for the deeds achieved by someone else
【邀請】to invite; invitation
【邀宴】①to invite to a feast ②an invitation to a luncheon or dinner party
【邀約】①an engagement; an invitation ②to invite; to make an appointment

邁 4050
ㄇㄞˋ mài
1. to surpass or exceed 2. to stride; to step 3. to go on a long journey 4. old (age) 5. to pass
【邁進】to forge ahead
【邁向】to march toward

邂 4051
ㄒㄧㄝˋ xiè
to meet without a prior engagement; to meet by chance
【邂逅】to meet by chance; to meet accidentally; to meet (a relative, friend, etc.) unexpectedly

還 4052
1. ㄏㄨㄢˊ huán
1. to return; to come back; return 2. to repay; to pay back; to restore
【還報】to repay; repayment
【還禮】①to return a salute ②to send a present in return
【還擊】① to fight back; to return fire ② (fencing) a riposte
【還清】to settle an account; all paid—as an account or debt
【還鄉】to return to one's home-town
【還債】to repay a debt
【還手】to strike back; to retaliate
【還原】①to return to normal or original status ②(chemistry) reduction
【還願】to fulfill a vow—to thank god for answering one's prayers

還 4052
2. ㄏㄞˊ hái
1. yet; still 2. passably; fairly; quite 3. also 4. even 5. at the same time 6. or 7. had better
【還好】① passable; so-so; not bad ② fortunately
【還是】① still; nevertheless ② again ③ had better ④ or (showing doubt)
【還在】① still here ② still (working, gambling, etc.)
【還早】still early
【還有】① There are still some left. ② furthermore; in addition

十四畫

邈 4053
ㄇㄧㄠˇ miǎo
1. distant; remote 2. same as 藐—to slight; to look down upon
【邈視】to despise; to look down upon

十五畫

邊 4054
ㄅㄧㄢ biān
1. an edge; the end of something; a verge; a margin 2. a side 3. a hem; a decorative border 4. the border of a nation's territory; a boundary 5. limits; bounds 6. nearby; near to
【邊防】border defense; frontier defense

〔辵部〕

【邊幅】① the appearance of a person; attire ② the margin (of a piece of cloth, etc.)
【邊際】①a boundary ②(Buddhism) the extremity of things ③ the substance of one's speech or writing
【邊界】the national boundary
【邊疆】a borderland; a frontier
【邊疆民族】tribes living on the borderland
【邊境】the national boundary or border; the frontier
【邊陲】a border; a borderland; a frontier
【邊塞】strategic positions along the border; a border pass
【邊緣】the edge; the verge

十九畫

邏 4055 ㄌㄨㄛˊ luó
to patrol; to inspect
【邏輯】logic

邑部 ㄧˋ yì

邑 4056 ㄧˋ yì
1. a town 2. a political district in ancient China 3. a county 4. a state 5. a capital city 6. same as 悒—sad or melancholy

四畫

那 4057 1. ㄋㄚˋ nà
1. that; those 2. then; in that case
【那麼】① so; that; in that way ② then; such being the case ③ about; or so
【那裏】that place; there; over there
【那個】① that one ② embarrassing ③ funny ④too much, too far, too hot, etc.
【那些】those

那 4057 2. ㄋㄟˋ nèi
combined form of 那一 (that+one), often used to indicate emphasis or contempt
【那邊】that way or side; over there; there (often emphasizing "not here")

那 4057 3. (哪) ㄋㄚˇ nǎ
an interrogative particle—Who? Which? What? Where?
【那怕】① what to be afraid of ② even if
【那裏】① Where? ② a negative particle—how can ③ You're being too modest, polite, etc.
【那個】① Which one? 或Which? ② Who?

那 4057 4. ㄋㄟˇ něi
an interrogative particle—which+one
【那邊or那邊兒】which way or direction
【那年】what year; which year

邦 4058 ㄅㄤ bāng
1. a state; a country; a nation 2. a manor given to a nobleman by the emperor in feudal China
【邦聯】a confederation
【邦國】a nation; a country; a state
【邦交】international relations

邪 4059 ㄒㄧㄝˊ xié
1. evil; depraved; wicked; mean; vicious 2. pertaining to sorcery or demonism; abnormal
【邪不勝正】The evil will not triumph over the virtuous.
【邪門歪道】crooked ways; dishonest practices
【邪教】paganism; heathendom
【邪說】heresy; perverted views
【邪惡】evil and wicked; debauchery

五畫

邵 4060 ㄕㄠˋ shào
1. advanced, as age 2. a Chinese family name

邱 4061 ㄑㄧㄡ qiū
1. same as 丘—a hill 2. name of a county in Shantung Province 3. a Chinese family name

邸 4062 ㄉㄧˇ dǐ
1. the residence of a prince or the nobility; the residence of a high official 2. princes and noblemen 3. (now rarely) a screen 4. the bottom of something 5. a

Chinese family name
【邸第】residences of lords and the nobility

六畫

〔邑部〕

郁 4063
ㄩˋ yù
1. adorned; colorfully ornamented; beautiful; refined 2. a Chinese family name
【郁烈】permeated with strong aroma

郊 4064
ㄐㄧㄠ jiāo
1. suburbs of a city 2. a ceremony for offering sacrifices to Heaven and Earth
【郊區】suburban districts; suburbs; outskirts; a suburban area
【郊遊】an outing; an excursion
【郊外】suburbs

七畫

郝 4065
ㄏㄠˇ hǎo
(讀音 ㄏㄜˋ hè)
1. name of an ancient place in today's Shensi Province 2. a Chinese family name

郎 4066
(郎) ㄌㄤˊ láng
1. an official rank in ancient times 2. a man 3. the husband; the beau 4. the master (as opposite to servants) 5. a Chinese family name
【郎君】① a term of address for a man ② your son (a polite expression) ③ the husband
【郎中】① an official rank in ancient China ② a physician ③ a card shark
【郎才女貌】a perfect match between a man and a woman

郡 4067
ㄐㄩㄣˋ jùn
a political division in ancient China; a county
【郡縣】prefectures and counties; administrative districts smaller than a province
【郡主】a princess
【郡守】the magistrate of a prefecture

八畫

部 4068
ㄅㄨˋ bù
1. a department; a section; a division; a class; a sort 2. a cabinet ministry 3. a volume; a complete work, novel, writing, etc. 4. to lead; to head
【部門】a class; a section; a department
【部隊】troops; a military unit
【部落】a tribe
【部下 or 部屬】subordinates
【部長】① a cabinet minister ② (in U.S.) the Secretary (of the army, the navy, the air force, the Defense Department, the Agriculture Department, etc.)
【部首】radicals of Chinese characters
【部署】to make preparations or arrangements

郭 4069
ㄍㄨㄛ guō
1. as in 城郭 —a town 2. the outer wall of a city 3. the outer part of anything 4. a Chinese family name

郵 4070
ㄧㄡˊ yóu
1. a post office 2. postal 3. to deliver mails, letters, etc. 4. a wayside station where couriers on government service change horses 5. a hut; a lodge in the field
【郵包】a postal parcel
【郵票】postal stamps
【郵費 or 郵資】postal charges
【郵遞】to send by mail; to deliver through postal service; mail service
【郵遞區號】zip code
【郵購】① mail order ② to buy by mail order
【郵寄】to send by mail; to mail
【郵簡】an air letter
【郵件】mail matter; postal items; the post; mail
【郵局】a post office
【郵箱】a postbox; a mailbox; a letter box 亦作「郵筒」
【郵政信箱】a post-office box (P.O.B.)
【郵政支局】a (postal) suboffice
【郵政儲金】savings deposits in a department of the post office
【郵差】a mailman; a postman
【郵戳兒】a postmark; a postal dater
【郵務 or 郵政】postal administra-

tion; postal service; postal affairs

九畫

都 4071
1. ㄉㄨ dū
1. a large town; a city; a metropolis 2. the capital of a nation; to make a city the national capital 3. beautiful; elegant; fine
【都會 or 都市】 a big city; a metropolis
【都市化】 to urbanize; urbanization

都 4071
2. ㄉㄡ dōu
1. all; altogether 2. even 3. already

十畫

鄉 4072
ㄒㄧㄤ xiāng
1. a village; the country, as contrasted with a city or town 2. rural 3. a small administrative unit comprising several villages 4. one's native place or birthplace; one's village
【鄉巴佬】 a country bumpkin; a hillbilly; an unsophisticated villager
【鄉民】 villagers; countryflok
【鄉土】 ① one's native place ② local geography and history
【鄉里】 ① the village where one resides or grew up ② people from the same hometown
【鄉公所】 a public office in charge of the administration of a group of villages
【鄉間】 in the countryside; in the rural area
【鄉親】 ① people hailing from the same area ② local people; villagers
【鄉下】 countryside; a rural area
【鄉下人 or 鄉民】 villagers; rustics; countryfolk; the country people
【鄉鎮】 a small town which is essentially a rural village
【鄉愁 or 鄉思】 homesickness; nostalgia
【鄉村】 a village; a country; a rural area
【鄉村音樂】 country music
【鄉野】 rural; pastoral
【鄉音】 one's native accent; a local accent
【鄉愿】 a hypocrite or an impostor in the countryside

鄒 4073
ㄗㄡ zōu
1. name of a state in the Epoch of Warring States 2. a Chinese family name

十一畫

鄙 4074
ㄅㄧˇ bǐ (又讀 ㄅㄧˋ bì)
1. mean; base; lowly; despicable 2. superficial; shallow 3. remote 4. to despise; to scorn
【鄙陋】 ① mean; base ② shallow
【鄙視 or 鄙夷】 to despise; to disdain; to slight; to look down upon; to scorn
【鄙人】 ① I (self-depreciatory); your humble servant ② a hillbilly
【鄙俗】 vulgar; philistine

十二畫

鄧 4075
ㄉㄥˋ dèng
1. a Chinese family name 2. name of an ancient state in what is today's Honan

鄭 4076
ㄓㄥˋ zhèng
1. solemn; formal; serious 2. a Chinese family name 3. name of an ancient state in what is today's Honan
【鄭重】 ①cautious; careful ②solemn; serious
【鄭重其事】 ①to treat it with seriousness ②very careful or cautious

鄰 4077
(隣) ㄌㄧㄣˊ lín
1. neighboring; adjoining; contiguous 2. neighborhood; a community 3. a neighbor 4. a basic community unit which consists of a number of families in the same neighborhood
【鄰邦】 a neighboring state or country
【鄰里】 neighborhood; a community
【鄰國】 a neighboring country
【鄰近】 ① located nearby; located in the vicinity ② neighborhood
【鄰居】 neighbors; people next-door

酉部
ㄧㄡˇ you

酉部

酉 4078 ㄧㄡˇ yǒu

1. the tenth of the Twelve Terrestrial Branches 2. 5:00-7:00 p.m.

二畫

酋 4079 ㄑㄧㄡˊ qiú

1. the chief of a clan or tribe; a chieftain 2. to end

【酋長】① a chieftain; the chief of a tribe ② a sheik(h); an emir

三畫

酌 4080 ㄓㄨㄛˊ zhuó

1. to drink 2. to pour (wine) 3. to weigh and consider

【酌量】 to weigh and consider

【酌酒】 to pour wine

配 4081 ㄆㄟˋ pèi

1. to join in marriage 2. to mate 3. to pair; to match 4. to fit; to suit; to be a match for; to match; to equal 5. to dispense (medicines); to prepare (according to a demand) 6. to exile 7. a spouse; a partner 8. subordinate; supplementary; supporting; attached 9. to deserve; to be worthy of

【配備】①an outfit; equipment ②to provide; to fit out

【配方】 to dispense prescriptions

【配對】 to pair; to be a pair

【配合】 to be in tune with; to be adapted to

【配給】 ① to distribute in rations; to allocate ② allocation

【配件】 accessories

【配角】 ① to appear with another leading player; to costar ② a supporting role; a minor role

【配製】 to prepare or concoct according to a recipe or prescription

【配種】 (animal husbandry) breeding

【配色】 to blend (or match) colors

【配偶】 a spouse; a mate

【配藥】 to dispense medicines; to fill a prescription

【配音】 (movies) to dub; dubbing; to synchronize; synchronization

【配樂】 to dub in background music; incidental music

酒 4082 ㄐㄧㄡˇ jiǔ

alcoholic drinks (brewed or distilled); wine; liquor; spirits

【酒吧】 a bar (for alcoholic drinks)

【酒杯】 winecups

【酒保】 a bartender; a waiter

【酒瓶】 a bottle for alcoholic drinks

【酒鋪 or 酒店】 a tavern; a saloon

【酒逢知己千杯少】 One can drink far more than usual with a bosom friend.

【酒德or酒品】 decorum in drinking

【酒桶】 a wine barrel or cask

【酒量】 one's capacity for drinking

【酒鬼】 ① a drunkard; a sot ② a toper; a wine bibber

【酒館or酒樓】 a tavern; a pub; a saloon; a bar

【酒客】 a drinker

【酒酣耳熱】 The enlivening effect of alcohol is just at its height.

【酒壺】 a wine pot or jar

【酒家】 ①a tavern; a bar; a wineshop ② the Chinese version of the geisha house in Japan; a girlie restaurant

【酒家女or酒女】a barmaid; a bargirl

【酒窖】 a wine cellar

【酒精】 alcohol

【酒廠】a brewery; a winery; a distillery

【酒肉朋友】 friends in one's revels (not in one's need); fair-weather friends

【酒醉】 drunk; intoxicated; tipsy

【酒醉飯飽】 having drunk and eaten to one's heart's content

【酒色之徒】 a libertine; a debauchee

【酒色財氣】 wine, women, wealth, and power—four main temptations to a man

【酒友】 a bottle companion

【酒宴 or 酒席】 a feast; a banquet

【酒癮】 addiction to alcohol

【酒窩兒】 dimples on one's cheeks

四畫

酗 4083 ㄒㄩˋ xù

to lose one's temper when drunk

【酗酒】 to indulge in excessive drinking

五畫

酣 4084
ㄏㄢ hān
1. to enjoy intoxicants; to drink wine 2. to one's heart's content; as much as one wants; without inhibition
【酣眠 or 酣睡】to sleep soundly
【酣醉】deeply intoxicated by alcoholic beverages
【酣飲】to drink as much as one can; to drink like a fish

酥 4085
ㄙㄨ sū
1. brittle; fragile 2. crunchy; crisp 3. lustrous
【酥餅】a kind of crisp biscuit; shortcake
【酥麻】frail and numb
【酥糖】crunchy candy; sugar cakes
【酥胸】the soft and smooth skin of a woman's bosom
【酥軟】lacking strength; feeble

六畫

酩 4086
ㄇㄧㄥˇ mǐng
(又讀 ㄇㄧㄥˊ míng)
as in 酩酊—drunk; intoxicated; inebriety; inebriate; tipsy

酪 4087
ㄌㄠˋ lào
(讀音 ㄌㄨㄛˋ luò)
1. alcoholic drinks 2. animal milk 3. as in 酪餅—cheese 4. fruit jam 5. junket 6. thick fruit juice; fruit jelly

酬 4088
ㄔㄡˊ chóu
1. to toast; to offer or present a cup of spirits 2. to reward; to requite; to reciprocate; reward 3. to fulfill; to realize
【酬勞】to reward services
【酬金】a cash reward; a bounty
【酬謝】to thank or reward (with money or gifts)

七畫

酵 4089
ㄒㄧㄠˋ xiào
as in 酵母—yeast; leaven
【酵母菌】a yeast fungus
【酵素】an enzyme

酷 4090
ㄎㄨˋ kù
1. (said of intoxicants) strong 2. (said of fragrance) very stimulating 3. cruel; brutal; harsh 4. exceedingly
【酷寒】severe cold
【酷刑】to torture; torture
【酷熱】torturing heat; extremely hot
【酷似】to resemble very closely
【酷愛】to be very fond of (a thing)

酸 4091
ㄙㄨㄢ suān
1. sour; acid; tart 2. stale; spoiled 3. sad; grieved; sorrowful 4. aching; a tingle; an ache 5. jealous; envious 6. stingy 7. (chemistry) acid
【酸葡萄】something scorned because it cannot be had
【酸梅】sour plums
【酸疼 or 酸痛】(said of muscles) to ache from overexertion
【酸甜苦辣】sour, sweet, bitter, and hot—the sweets and bitters (of life)
【酸牛奶】yoghurt; sour milk
【酸辣湯】a kind of soup seasoned with vinegar and pepper
【酸味】acid; a sour taste

八畫

醃 4092
ㄧㄢ yān
to pickle; to salt
【醃肉】salted pork; salted meat
【醃菜】pickled vegetables

醇 4093
ㄔㄨㄣˊ chún
1. rich wine; strong wine 2. pure; unadulterated 3. gentle; gracious 4. ethyl alcohol
【醇美】pure and fair
【醇朴】gentle and honest

醉 4094
ㄗㄨㄟˋ zuì
1. drunk; intoxicated 2. infatuated; charmed
【醉鬼】a drunkard; a drunken person
【醉心】infatuated with (a pursuit)
【醉醺醺】inebriated; sottish; drunk
【醉生夢死】to live a befuddled life
【醉翁之意不在酒】to be secretly interested in something while

pretending to show interest in another

醋 4095 ㄘㄨˋ cù
vinegar
【醋罈子】 a jealous person, especially a woman
【醋勁兒】 jealousy

〔釆部〕

九畫

醒 4096 ㄒㄧㄥˇ xǐng
1. to recover from (drunkenness, a stupor, etc.) 2. to awake; to wake up; to be roused 3. to be clear or cool in mind
【醒目】 ① to catch the eye; to attract attention; eye-catching; refreshing ② awake; not asleep
【醒酒】 to sober up from drunkenness
【醒悟】 to awake (from errors, illusions, etc.)

十畫

醜 4097 ㄔㄡˇ chǒu
1. ugly; homely 2. abominable; vile; bad 3. shameful; infamous
【醜態】 scandalous behavior; a disgraceful manner
【醜陋】 ugly; bad-looking
【醜化】 to smear; to uglify; to defame
【醜惡】 ugly; repulsive; hideous
【醜聞 or 醜事】 scandal

醞 4098 ㄩㄣˋ yùn
1. to brew; to ferment 2. to deliberate on; deliberation 3. wine
【醞釀】 ① to brew (wine or liquor) ② (said of a storm, disturbance, etc.) to begin to form; to brew

十一畫

醫 4099 ㄧ yī
1. to cure or treat (diseases) 2. a doctor; a physician; a surgeon 3. medical science; medical service
【醫德】 medical ethics
【醫科】 the department of medicine (at a university)
【醫界】 the medical circles; the medical world
【醫學】 medical science
【醫學院】 a college of medicine
【醫治】 to cure (a disease); medical treatment; to doctor
【醫生 or 醫師】 a doctor; a physician; a surgeon
【醫術】 medical skill; the art of healing
【醫藥費】 a hospital bill; a doctor's fee; medical expenses
【醫院】 a hospital

醬 4100 ㄐㄧㄤˋ jiàng
1. soybean sauce; soy 2. food in the form of paste; jam
【醬瓜】 cucumbers, etc. pickled in soybean sauce
【醬菜】 cabbages, etc. pickled in soybean sauce
【醬油】 soybean sauce; soy; soy sauce

十四畫

醺 4101 ㄒㄩㄣ xūn
as in 醺醺—drunk; intoxicated; tipsy

十七畫

釀 4102 ㄋㄧㄤˋ niàng
1. to brew; to ferment 2. to take shape or form slowly 3. wine
【釀酒】 to brew wine
【釀成】 to bring about slowly; to lead slowly to; to breed; to form gradually
【釀造】 to brew

十八畫

釁 4103 ㄒㄧㄣˋ xìn
1. to anoint (drums, bells, etc.) with blood in worship 2. to anoint (the body) 3. a rift (between people)
【釁端】 the cause of a fight

釆部
ㄅㄧㄢˋ biàn

一畫

采 4104 ㄘㄞˇ cǎi
1. to gather; to collect 2. to

pick; to select 3. bright colors

五畫

釉 4105
ㄧㄡˋ yòu

glaze

【釉藥】substance used to produce glaze for pottery; glaze

十三畫

釋 4106
ㄕˋ shì

1. to explain; to interpret 2. to set free 3. to relieve 4. to disperse; to dispel 5. of Buddha or Buddhism

【釋迦牟尼】Sakyamuni

【釋然】① at ease; relaxed ② having all the misunderstandings cleared up

【釋義】expatiation; interpretation

里部
ㄌㄧˇ ㄅㄨˋ

里 4107
ㄌㄧˇ lǐ

1. a neighborhood, or community, of 25 families (in ancient times); a neighborhood 2. *li* (a unit of linear measure about one third of a mile)

【里巷】streets

【里巷之談】idle talk in the street; gossip

【里長】the head of a subdivision of the district, or borough, in a city or county

【里程】① mileage ② the course of development; course

【里程碑】a milestone; a milepost

二畫

重 4108
1. ㄓㄨㄥˋ zhòng

1. heavy; weighty; much 2. to weigh; weight 3. difficult 4. serious; grave 5. severe 6. important; significant 7. to value; to emphasize

【重病】a serious illness

【重犯】an important criminal; a criminal who is guilty of a serious crime

【重大】①important; of great consequence; significant ② serious; grave

【重擔】a heavy burden (or responsibility)

【重點】the point or center of emphasis

【重讀】to stress

【重頭戲】①a play involving much singing and action ② a role involving much singing and action

【重聽】weak in hearing; hard of hearing

【重力】gravity

【重量】weight

【重工業】heavy industry

【重金禮聘】to employ with good pay

【重金屬】heavy metals

【重心】the center of gravity

【重刑】severe punishment

【重鎮】① key positions (in military operations); an important city ② a key figure

【重酬】a substantial reward; a handsome reward

【重創】①(ㄓㄨㄥˋ ㄔㄨㄤ) a serious wound ②(ㄓㄨㄥˋ ㄔㄨㄤˋ) to inflict a severe blow on (the enemy)

【重視】to pay much attention to; to consider important

【重傷】a serious injury

【重賞】to reward generously

【重賞之下，必有勇夫】Generous rewards rouse one to heroism.

【重任】an important mission; an important office or post

【重義氣】particular about loyalty to friends

【重要】important; significant; vital

【重音】(phonetics) accent; stress

【重於泰山】(literally) heavier than Mount Tai—very weighty; very important

【重用】to give (someone) an important assignment

重 4108
2. ㄔㄨㄥˊ chóng

1. to pile one upon another 2. to repeat; to duplicate 3. layers 4. double; manifold 5. numerous

【重返】to go back; to return

【重犯】to repeat (an error or offense)

【重逢】to meet again; to have a reunion

【重複】① to repeat; repetition ② to duplicate

【重蹈覆轍】to follow the same old disastrous road; to fall into the same trap
【重疊】to pile one upon another; to superimpose
【重來】to do a thing over again; to repeat from the start; to return
【重建】to rebuild; to reconstruct
【重見天日】to see daylight again—to regain freedom; to be liberated or emancipated
【重起爐灶】to begin all over again
【重修舊好】to renew friendly relations; to patch up; to reconcile
【重新】anew; afresh
【重整旗鼓】to rearm; to make preparations for a comeback
【重施故技】to play the same old trick
【重申】to reaffirm; to reiterate; to restate
【重操舊業】to return to one's old trade
【重遊】to revisit
【重演】to repeat the performance of; to repeat
【重洋】the ocean
【重圍】a many-layered siege; a tight encirclement
【重溫舊夢】to revive an old dream; to reproduce the good old days

四畫

野 4109 ㄧㄝˇ yě
1. the countryside; fields; the wilderness 2. the people (as opposed to the government) 3. wild; uncultured; undomesticated; coarse; barbarous; rude
【野馬】a wild horse; a mustang
【野蠻】①barbarous; savage; uncivilized ②unreasonable; rude; brutal
【野地】① the countryside ② the wilderness
【野兔】a hare
【野牛】a wild ox; a bison; a buffalo
【野老】an aged rustic; an old peasant
【野合】illicit copulation or connection
【野孩子】an urchin; a street urchin
【野花】①a wild flower ②a harlot
【野火】① will-o'-the-wisp ② prairie fire; bushfire; wildfire ③ farm fire (for clearing the field)
【野鷄】①a pheasant ②a streetwalker ③unlicensed taxicabs
【野心】① ambition; careerism ② greediness
【野心勃勃】full of ambition
【野性】jungle instincts; ungovernableness; untamedness; unruliness
【野戰】(military) field operations
【野豬】a boar
【野史】unofficial history
【野獸】a wild beast; a brute
【野生】wild; undomesticated
【野生動物】undomesticated animals
【野人】① a rustic ② a barbarian; a savage
【野人獻曝 or 野人獻日】(literally) a rustic offering sunshine—a trivial contribution
【野草】a weed
【野餐】a picnic; a barbecue
【野營】outdoor camping
【野外】the outdoors; the open

五畫

量 4110 1. ㄌㄧㄤˊ liáng
to measure
【量杯】a graduated cylinder; a measuring glass or cup
【量度】to measure; to estimate

量 4110 2. ㄌㄧㄤˋ liàng
1.quantity 2.capacity 3.to estimate
【量力而爲】to estimate one's resources or strength before acting
【量入爲出】to regulate one's expenses according to one's income
【量詞】a classifier (as 個、隻、次)

十一畫

釐 4111 ㄌㄧˊ lí
1. a unit of linear measure equal to one thousandth of the Chinese foot 2. a unit of weight equal to one thousandth of the tael 3. to administer; to arrange; to manage; 4. to revise; to reform; to correct 5. same as 嫠—a widow
【釐米】centimeter
【釐定】to formulate (rules, etc.)

金部
ㄐㄧㄣ jīn

金 4112
ㄐㄧㄣ jin
1. gold 2. metal 3. wealth; money 4. weapons; arms 5. excellent; precious; fine 6. golden 7. durable 8. a Chinese family name
【金榜題名】 to emerge successful from a competitive examination
【金鎊】 pound sterling
【金幣】 gold coins
【金碧輝煌】 (said of a building) resplendent; gorgeous; grand; splendid; magnificent
【金牌】 a gold medal
【金木水火土】 metal, wood, water, fire and earth—the five elements in ancient Chinese philosophy and fortunetelling
【金髮女郎】 a blond(e)
【金童玉女】 young boys and girls attending upon an immortal
【金蘭】 sworn brotherhood; harmonious friendship
【金縷衣】 a gold-threaded robe
【金剛】 ① hard metal ② a Buddhist god sometimes identified with Indra
【金剛經】 *The Diamond Sutra*
【金剛石】 diamond
【金龜壻 or 金龜婿】 a fine (or a rich) son-in-law
【金龜子】 a tumblebug
【金光黨】 swindlers; racketeers
【金光閃閃】 glittering; glistening
【金科玉律】 the golden rule; an immutable law
【金庫】 coffers; a treasury
【金塊】 gold bullion; a gold ingot
【金礦】 a gold mine
【金婚】 a golden wedding; the 50th wedding anniversary
【金黃色】 bright yellow; golden
【金匠】 a goldsmith
【金器】 a gold vessel
【金錢】 money; cash; riches; wealth
【金錢豹】 a spotted leopard
【金錢萬能】 Money is almighty.
【金像獎】 an Oscar (award)
【金星】 (astronomy) Venus
【金枝玉葉】 a term referring to the members of the royal family
【金釵】 a gold hairpin
【金蟬脫殼】 to escape by a cunning maneuver
【金石】 ① metal and stone—a symbol of durability ② gold and precious stones ③ weapons; arms ④ bronze and stone inscriptions
【金石爲開】 Sincerity can make metal and stone crack.
【金屬】 metals
【金融】 finance; banking; a monetary situation
【金融卡】 a fiscard
【金字塔】 a pyramid
【金字招牌】 (literally) a signboard with gilded inscriptions—a good reputation; high prestige
【金子】 gold
【金絲雀】 a canary bird; a canary
【金額】 the amount of money
【金銀財寶】 treasures; wealth
【金屋藏嬌】 to build a magnificent house for a beloved woman (especially a concubine or mistress)
【金文】 ancient inscriptions on bronze
【金魚】 goldfish
【金玉滿堂】 to have one's house filled with riches
【金玉良言】 a wise saying; good counsel
【金玉其外, 敗絮其中】 a rotten interior beneath a fine exterior

二畫

釘 4113
1. ㄉㄧㄥ dīng
1. nails (for fastening things) 2. to look steadily
【釘鞋】 boots with nailed soles (for wet weather); track shoes
【釘梢】 to tail; to shadow; to trail

釘 4113
2. ㄉㄧㄥˋ dìng
to fasten (with nails, etc.)
【釘書機】 a stapler

釜 4114
ㄈㄨˇ fǔ
1. a cauldron; a kettle 2. an ancient unit of capacity
【釜底抽薪】 to remove the ultimate cause of trouble

針 4115
(鍼) ㄓㄣ zhēn
1. a needle; a pin; a probe 2. a stitch
【針砭】 ① acupuncture ② remonstrance with equal harshness
【針鋒相對】 to oppose each other
【針對】 ① to aim directly at; to

focus on ② in accordance with
【針灸】acupuncture and moxibustion; acupuncture and cauterization
【針線】① a needle and thread ② needlework 「knitting
【針織品】knit goods; knitwear;

〔金部〕

三畫

釣 4116 ㄉㄧㄠˋ diào
1. to fish (with a hook and line); to angle 2. to lure; to tempt
【釣名 or 釣譽】to angle for fame; to seek publicity
【釣鉤】a fishhook
【釣竿】a fishing rod; a fishing pole
【釣線】a fishing twine; a fishing line
【釣餌】a bait
【釣具】fishing gear; fishing tackle
【釣魚】to fish; to angle

釦 4117 ㄎㄡˋ kòu
buttons (on garments)

四畫

鈔 4118 ㄔㄠ chāo
("鈔票"又讀 ㄔㄠˋ chào)
1. to copy; to transcribe 2. as in 鈔票—bank notes; paper money

鈍 4119 ㄉㄨㄣˋ dùn
blunt; dull; obtuse
【鈍角】an obtuse angle

鈕 4120 ㄋㄧㄡˇ niǔ
buttons: 鈕孔 a buttonhole

鈞 4121 ㄐㄩㄣ jūn
1. a unit of weight (equal to 30 catties) in former times 2. (in addressing a superior in a letter) you; your
【鈞安】May you enjoy peace. —a form of complimentary close in a letter to a superior

鈣 4122 ㄍㄞˋ gài
calcium: 鈣片 a calcium tablet 鈣質 calcium content

五畫

鈴 4123 ㄌㄧㄥˊ líng
bells: 鈴聲 the tinkle of bells (jingling)

鉀 4124 ㄐㄧㄚˇ jiǎ
potassium

鉅 4125 ㄐㄩˋ jù
1. great 亦作「巨」 2. steel
【鉅款】a large sum of money
【鉅子】a great man; a tycoon; a magnate

鉗 4126 ㄑㄧㄢˊ qián
1. pincers; forceps; tweezers; tongs; pliers 2. chains put around a prisoner's neck 3. to hold with tongs, etc.
【鉗制 or 箝制】to keep under control with force; to tie down or pin down
【鉗子】① tweezers; pincers; forceps; tongs ② a convict; a prisoner ③ earrings

鉛 4127 ㄑㄧㄢ qiān
lead (a metal)
【鉛筆】a pencil; a lead pencil
【鉛礦】lead ore
【鉛華】cosmetics; face powder
【鉛球】a shot (thrown in the shot put)
【鉛字】lead type (in printing)

鉢 4128 (鉢、盔) ㄅㄛ bō
1. an earthenware basin or bowl 2. a Buddhist priest's rice bowl

鉤 4129 (鈎) ㄍㄡ gōu
1. a hook 2. to hook 3. to probe; to investigate 4. to entice; to lure
【鉤毛衣】to crochet a wool sweater
【鉤肩搭背】to hold each other's arms while walking side by side
【鉤心鬥角】to strain the wits of each other (in a contest, etc.); to engage in a battle of wits
【鉤爪】talons
【鉤針】a crochet hook; a crochet needle
【鉤子】a hook

鈾 4130 ㄧㄡˊ yóu
uranium

鈷 4131 ㄍㄨ gū

cobalt

六畫

銀 4132
ㄧㄣˊ yín
1. silver 2. money; wealth 3. silvery
【銀幣】a silver coin; silver
【銀牌】a silver medal
【銀樓】a jeweler's shop
【銀礦】① silver ore ② silver mine
【銀河】the Milky Way; the Galaxy
【銀行】a bank
【銀貨兩清】completion of a business transaction with goods delivered and payment made
【銀婚】a silver wedding; the 25th wedding anniversary
【銀器】silverware
【銀元 or 銀圓】silver dollar

鉸 4133
ㄐㄧㄠˇ jiǎo
1. scissors; shears 2. hinges 3. to shear
【鉸鏈】hinges

銅 4134
ㄊㄨㄥˊ tóng
copper; bronze; brass
【銅板or銅幣or銅錢】copper coins
【銅牌】a bronze medal
【銅鑼】a copper gong
【銅礦】① copper ore ② copper mine
【銅器】bronze utensils
【銅牆鐵壁】impregnable like walls of brass and iron
【銅像】a bronze image; a bronze statue

銓 4135
ㄑㄩㄢˊ quán
1. to weigh 2. to evaluate qualifications in selecting officials
【銓敍】to select and appoint officials
【銓敍部】Ministry of Personnel
【銓選】to select (officials) after evaluating qualifications

銖 4136
ㄓㄨ zhū
1. an ancient unit of weight; the ancient coinage of Han 2. blunt; dull

銘 4137
ㄇㄧㄥˊ míng
1. to engrave; to inscribe; to imprint 2. inscriptions
【銘記在心】to imprint on one's mind
【銘謝】to show gratefulness

銜 4138
ㄒㄧㄢˊ xián
1. a bit (in a horse's mouth) 2. the title (of an official) 3. to hold in the mouth 4. to harbor; to cherish 5. to follow (orders)
【銜接】to adjoin; to lie next to; to connect; to dovetail

銬 4139
ㄎㄠˋ kào
manacles; handcuffs

七畫

銳 4140
ㄖㄨㄟˋ ruì
1. sharp; acute; keen 2. quick-witted; intelligent; clever 3. energetic; vigorous
【銳不可當】too sharp to resist; too powerful to stop
【銳利】sharp; pointed
【銳角】an acute angle
【銳減】to decline sharply; to drop markedly
【銳氣】dash; mettle; vigor; virility; aggressiveness

銷 4141
ㄒㄧㄠ xiāo
1. to melt 2. to be marketed; to be circulated; to sell 3. to vanish; to dispel; to cancel 亦作「消」 4. pig iron; crude iron
【銷路】a sale; a market
【銷毀】to destroy
【銷魂】enraptured; transported; carried away
【銷假】to begin work anew after a leave of absence or vacation
【銷售量】sales volume
【銷聲匿跡】to vanish without leaving any trace behind; to go into hiding

鋁 4142
ㄌㄩˇ lǚ
alumin(i)um: 鋁箔 alumin(i)um foil

鋃 4143
ㄌㄤˊ láng
1. chains for prisoners 2. the tolling of a bell
【鋃鐺入獄】to be shackled and imprisoned; to be jailed

鋅 4144
ㄒㄧㄣ xīn
zinc: 鋅版 zincotype; zincograph

鋌 4145
ㄊㄧㄥˇ tǐng
to rush

〔金部〕

〔金部〕

【鋌而走險】to be forced to break the law; to risk danger in desperation

鋒 4146
ㄈㄥ fēng
1. sharp point 2. the vanguard
【鋒芒】①sharp point (as of a lance, etc.) ②dash; mettle; vigor
【鋒芒畢露】to show one's intelligence, ability, etc. to the full extent
【鋒利】① sharp-pointed; sharp ② vigorous; energetic; keen; incisive

鋤 4147
ㄔㄨˊ chú
1. a hoe 2. to hoe
【鋤奸】to wipe out the wicked elements

銼 4148
ㄘㄨㄛˋ cuò
1. a kind of widemouthed cauldron used in ancient China 2. a file 3. to make smooth with a file; to file
【銼刀】a file (a steel tool)

鋪 4149
1. ㄆㄨ pū
to lay in order; to spread; to arrange; to pave
【鋪路】to surface a road; to pave a road
【鋪蓋】bedding
【鋪敍】to state in detail
【鋪張】① to arrange; to lay in order ② to make an ostentatious or vain show; to be pompous
【鋪陳】① to state in detail; to elaborate ②to arrange for display
【鋪牀】to make the bed
【鋪設】to lay in order; to arrange

鋪 4149
2. (舖) ㄆㄨˋ pù
a store; a shop; a grocery
【鋪面】the shop front; the facade of a store
【鋪位】a bunk

銲 4150
(釬) ㄏㄢˋ hàn
to solder; to weld
【銲接】to join with solder; to weld; to solder

銹 4151
(鏽) ㄒㄧㄡˋ xiù
rust: 銹斑 rust stains

八畫

鋸 4152
ㄐㄩˋ jù
1. a saw 2. to saw; to cut with a saw: 鋸開 to saw asunder 3. to amputate
【鋸齒】teeth of a saw
【鋸子】a saw

鋼 4153
ㄍㄤ gāng
steel: 鋼板 a steel plate
【鋼筆】a fountain pen
【鋼鐵】steel; steel and iron
【鋼盔】a steel helmet; a helmet
【鋼筋】steel bars; steel rods; wire mesh
【鋼筋水泥】reinforced concrete
【鋼琴】a piano
【鋼絲】steel wire

錄 4154
ㄌㄨˋ lù
1. to take down; to copy; to record 2. to accept (applicants) 3. a record
【錄放影機】a videocassette recorder
【錄取】to accept
【錄音】① to record ② recording
【錄音帶】a recording tape
【錄音機】a tape recorder; a recorder
【錄影帶】a videotape
【錄用】to accept for employment

錐 4155
ㄓㄨㄟ zhuī
1. an awl 2. to pierce; to bore; to drill; to make a hole 3. conical
【錐形】a taper; a cone
【錐處囊中】Real talent will be discovered.

錘 4156
ㄔㄨㄟˊ chuí
1. a weight on a steelyard 2. an ancient unit of weight 3. a kind of ancient weapon 4. to hammer; to pound 5. a hammer
【錘鍊】①to forge (metal); to temper ②to polish

錙 4157
ㄗ zī
an ancient unit of weight (said to equal 8 taels)
【錙銖必較】to be particular even about a trifling amount

錚 4158
ㄓㄥ zhēng
1. a clang of metal 2. gongs
【錚錚】①a clang of metal ②righteous; incorruptible; upright

錠 4159
ㄉㄧㄥˋ dìng
1. a kind of ancient utensil 2.

ingots of gold or silver 3. a spindle 4. a (medical) tablet: 錠劑 medicine in tablet form

錢 4160 ㄑㄧㄢˊ qián

1. money; cash 2. a unit of weight (equal to 1/10th of a tael) 3. a Chinese family name

【錢包】a wallet; a purse
【錢幣】① coin ② currency; money
【錢櫃】a cash box
【錢莊 or 錢鋪】a banking house (in former times)
【錢財】wealth; riches
【錢財身外物】Money is not an inherent part of the human being.

錦 4161 ㄐㄧㄣˇ jǐn

1. brocade; tapestry 2. brilliant and beautiful 3. glorious

【錦標】①a championship (in a tournament) ②a trophy; a cup
【錦緞】brocade
【錦囊妙計】a clever scheme yet to be revealed
【錦旗】an embroidered flag; a pennant
【錦繡河山】land of splendor—one's fatherland
【錦繡前程】a glorious or promising future; a bright or rosy future
【錦上添花】to give someone or something additional splendor; to cap it all
【錦衣玉食】to lead a luxurious life; to live in luxury

錫 4162 ㄒㄧ xī

1. tin 2. to bestow...on; to confer... on

【錫礦】① tin ore ② tin mine
【錫紙or錫箔】tinfoil; tinfoil (or silver) paper

錮 4163 ㄍㄨˋ gù

1. to run metal into cracks 2. to confine; to keep in custody; to imprison 3. sturdy; secure

【錮疾】a chronic complaint, disease or ailment

錯 4164 ㄘㄨㄛˋ cuò

1. wrong; mistaken; erroneous 2. a mistake; an error 3. untidy; uneven; irregular; intricate 4. a grindstone

【錯別字】characters wrongly written or mispronounced
【錯亂】disorderly; confused; abnormal deranged
【錯過】to let (a chance) slip by; to miss
【錯怪】to blame unjustly or wrongly
【錯開】to stagger
【錯覺】a false impression; hallucination; illusion
【錯認】to misidentify
【錯字】misspelling; a misprint
【錯綜複雜】very complicated; intricate
【錯誤】① an error; a mistake; a fault ② erroneous; wrong
【錯誤百出】full of mistakes; riddled with errors

錳 4165 ㄇㄥˇ měng

manganese

錶 4166 ㄅㄧㄠˇ biǎo

a watch; a timepiece

【錶帶】a watchband

九畫

鍊 4167 ㄌㄧㄢˋ liàn

1. to smelt; to refine; to forge; to temper 2. to polish 3. a chain

【鍊丹】to make pills of wonder; to practice alchemy
【鍊鋼】to refine steel
【鍊子】a chain

錨 4168 ㄇㄠˊ máo

1. to anchor 2. an anchor: 拋錨 to cast (or drop) anchor 起錨 to weigh anchor

鍋 4169 ㄍㄨㄛ guō

a cooking pot; a pan; a boiler; a caldron

【鍋巴】burnt rice that sticks to the bottom and sides of the cooking pot
【鍋貼兒】lightly fried dumpling
【鍋爐】a boiler (especially of a steam engine)
【鍋蓋】the cover of a cooking pot; a pot cover

鍍 4170 ㄉㄨˋ dù

to plate; to gilt: 鍍金to plate with gold

鍘 4171 ㄓㄚˊ zhá

1. a long knife hinged at one end for cutting hay; a fodder chopper 2. to cut up with a hay cutter

〔金部〕

鍛 4172
(煅) ㄉㄨㄢˋ duàn
1. to smelt; to refine 2. to forge (iron, etc.)
【鍛鍊】①to forge (metal); to temper ②to train (oneself)

鍥 4173
ㄑㄧㄝˋ qiè
to carve
【鍥而不舍】to carve without rest —to make steady efforts

鍰 4174
ㄏㄨㄢˊ huán
1. an ancient unit of weight 2. money; cash: 罰鍰 to fine or to be fined cash

鍵 4175
ㄐㄧㄢˋ jiàn
key (to a door or on a musical instrument, etc.)
【鍵盤】a keyboard (on a piano, typewriter, etc.)

鍼 4176
ㄓㄣ zhēn
a needle; a pin; a probe 亦作「針」

鍾 4177
ㄓㄨㄥ zhōng
1. a kind of wine container 2. to concentrate; to accumulate 3. a Chinese family name
【鍾情】to fall in love
【鍾愛】to cherish; to dote on; to love deeply (especially children)

鎂 4178
ㄇㄟˇ měi
magnesium
【鎂光燈】a magnesium light

十畫

鎖 4179
(鏁) ㄙㄨㄛˇ suǒ
1. a lock 2. fetters; chains 3. to lock 4. to confine 5. to lockstitch
【鎖鏈】chains
【鎖匠】a locksmith

鎊 4180
ㄅㄤˋ bàng
pound sterling

鎔 4181
(熔) ㄖㄨㄥˊ róng
1. to melt; to smelt; to fuse 2. a mold 3. a kind of spear
【鎔爐】a smelting furnace; a cupola
【鎔化 or 鎔解】to melt; to fuse
【鎔鑄】to cast (metal)

鎗 4182
(槍) ㄑㄧㄤ qiāng
firearms; guns; pistols; rifles
【鎗靶】the target for shooting
【鎗斃 or 鎗決】execution by a firing squad; execution by shooting
【鎗彈】bullets
【鎗林彈雨】heavy gunfire; a hail of bullets
【鎗桿】rifles; firearms
【鎗口】the muzzle of a gun
【鎗戰】gun battle
【鎗手】①a gunman ②a substitute writer in an examination

鎚 4183
ㄔㄨㄟˊ chuí
1. to hammer 2. a hammer 3. an ancient weapon

鎧 4184
ㄎㄞˇ kǎi
armor; a coat of mail
【鎧甲】armor

鎮 4185
ㄓㄣˋ zhèn
1. to subdue; to suppress; to quell; to put down 2. to cool with water or ice 3. weight 4. whole 5. a town; a township 6. a garrison post
【鎮暴】riot control
【鎮定 or 鎮靜】calm; cool self-composed;
【鎮痛劑】an anodyne; a painkiller
【鎮公所】a town hall; a town house
【鎮靜劑】a sedative; a tranquilizer
【鎮壓】to suppress; to put down; suppression

鎳 4186
ㄋㄧㄝˋ niè
nickel: 鎳幣 nickel coins

鎢 4187
ㄨˋ wù
wolfram; tungsten: 鎢絲 a tungsten filament

十一畫

鎩 4188
ㄕㄚ shā
1. a lance 2. to shed (feathers)
【鎩羽】①having shed feathers ②discouraged; crestfallen; disheartened; defeated

鏈 4189
ㄌㄧㄢˋ liàn
a chain
【鏈球】(sports) ①a hammer ②hammer throw

鏖 4190
ㄠ́ áo
to fight hard
【鏖戰】to engage in hard fighting

鏗 4191
ㄎㄥ kēng
1. the clang of metal; clatter 2. the twang of a string
【鏗鏘】① a tinkle; a clang ② (figuratively) sonorous and forceful

鏘 4192
ㄑㄧㄤ qiāng
a tinkle; a clang

鏟 4193
ㄔㄢˇ chǎn
1. a shovel; a scoop 2. to shovel; to scoop
【鏟除】to eliminate; to uproot

鏡 4194
ㄐㄧㄥˋ jìng
1. a mirror 2. lenses; spectacles; glasses 3. to mirror 4. to take warning (from a past failure)
【鏡片】a lens
【鏡頭】① the lens of a camera ② a scene captured by the camera
【鏡框】a picture frame
【鏡花水月】things appealing but unreal

鏢 4195
ㄅㄧㄠ biāo
1. a dart; a dartlike weapon 2. an escort; a guard; a bodyguard
【鏢客】(in former times) hired escorts for traveling merchants, etc.
【鏢鎗】a javelin

鏤 4196
ㄌㄡˋ lòu
to engrave; to carve
【鏤空】to hollow out; hollowed-out
【鏤花】ornamental engraving

十二畫

鐘 4197
ㄓㄨㄥ zhōng
1. a bell (which tolls as distinct from that which jingles) 2. a clock 3. a Chinese family name
【鐘擺】a pendulum
【鐘錶 or 鐘表】timepieces; clocks and watches
【鐘錶店】a watchmaker's shop
【鐘點費】remuneration paid by the hour
【鐘頭】an hour
【鐘樓】a bell tower; a belfry
【鐘聲】the toll of a bell
【鐘乳石】a stalactite

鐃 4198
ㄋㄠˊ náo
1. a kind of bell used in the army in ancient times 2. cymbals

鐐 4199
ㄌㄧㄠˊ liáo
(又讀 ㄌㄧㄠˋ liào)
shackles; fetters; manacles

十三畫

鐲 4200
ㄓㄨㄛˊ zhuó
1. a kind of bell used in the army in ancient times 2. a bracelet; an armlet

鐫 4201
ㄐㄩㄢ juān
1. as in 鐫刻—to carve; to engrave 2. (said of an official) to be demoted

鐮 4202
ㄌㄧㄢˊ lián
as in 鐮刀—a sickle

鐵 4203
ㄊㄧㄝˇ tiě
1. iron 2. firm; indisputable; unyielding (like iron) 3. cruel; merciless; unfeeling 4. arms; weapons
【鐵板】①an iron plate; sheet iron ②a kind of percussion instrument
【鐵棒】an iron club
【鐵餅】a discus
【鐵皮】iron sheet
【鐵馬】① strong cavalry ② (colloquial) a bicycle ③ armored horses
【鐵門】① a metal security door ② name of a county in Honan
【鐵面無私】inflexibly just and fair
【鐵飯碗】a very secure job
【鐵釘】iron nails
【鐵定】definitely; ironclad; unalterable; not subject to change
【鐵塔】an iron or steel tower
【鐵鏈】an iron chain
【鐵路 or 鐵道】a railroad; a railway
【鐵軌】iron rails (of a railway)
【鐵觀音】a variety of oolong tea
【鐵公雞】a stingy person
【鐵礦】① iron ore ② an iron mine
【鐵甲】steel armor
【鐵匠】an ironsmith; a blacksmith

〔金部〕

【鐵器】 ironware
【鐵靑】 livid; bluish black
【鐵銹】 rust
【鐵證如山】 irrefutable, decisive evidence
【鐵杵磨針】 Steady efforts can work miracles.
【鐵鎚】 an iron hammer; a hammer
【鐵窗】 ①a window with metal gratings ②a prison
【鐵石心腸】 a cold heart; an unfeeling heart; iron-hearted; hard-hearted
【鐵沙掌】 a Chinese version of karate
【鐵樹開花】 something that very rarely happens
【鐵人】 ①an iron man ②a man of great physical strength
【鐵絲 or 鐵線】 iron wire
【鐵絲網】 ① wire netting; wire meshes ②barbed-wire entanglements
【鐵腕】 iron hand; iron fist

鐸 4204
ㄉㄨㄛˊ duó
1. a large bell 2. a Chinese family name

鐺 4205
ㄉㄤ dāng
1. the sound of striking a gong
2. shackles

十四畫

鑄 4206
ㄓㄨˋ zhù
1. to melt or cast metal; to coin; to mint 2. to make or commit (blunders, etc.) 3. to educate and influence (a person) 4. a Chinese family name
【鑄像】 to erect a metal statue
【鑄成大錯】 to commit a serious mistake; to make a gross error

鑑 4207
ㄐㄧㄢˋ jiàn
1. a mirror 2. to mirror; to reflect 3. to study or examine; to scrutinize 4. an example serving as a rule or warning
【鑑別】 to distinguish (the genuine from an imitation); to judge or identify; to discriminate
【鑑定】 to examine and determine; to judge; to make an appraisal
【鑑賞】 to examine and appreciate
【鑑往知來】 to foresee the future by reviewing the past

鑒 4208
(鑑) ㄐㄧㄢˋ jiàn
to examine, etc.

十五畫

鑛 4209
(礦) ㄎㄨㄤˋ kuàng
a mine or mineral

十六畫

鑫 4210
ㄒㄧㄣ xīn
a word of no definite meaning, used only in names, with a connotation of prosperity or good profit

十七畫

鑰 4211
ㄧㄠˋ yào
(讀音 ㄩㄝˋ yuè)
1. as in 鑰匙—a key 2. a lock

鑲 4212
ㄒㄧㄤ xiāng
1. to fill in (a tooth, etc.); to mount; to inlay; to set (jewels, etc.) 2. to edge; to border; to hem
【鑲邊】 to edge or hem
【鑲牙】 to fill in an artificial tooth; to crown a tooth

十八畫

鑷 4213
ㄋㄧㄝ niē
1. tweezers; pincers; forceps 2. to pull out; to nip
【鑷子】 a pair of tweezers

十九畫

鑼 4214
ㄌㄨㄛˊ luó
a gong
【鑼鼓喧天】 noisy celebration of a festival or carnival

鑽 4215
1. ㄗㄨㄢ zuān
1. to pierce; to drill; to bore; to dig through; to penetrate 2. to go through; to make one's way into 3. to gain (profit, a position, etc.) through special favor, contact, relations, etc. 4. to study intensively; to dig into; to

bury oneself in
【鑽牛角尖】to get oneself into a dead-end alley through sheer stubbornness
【鑽研】to study or scrutinize thoroughly
【鑽營】to seek advantage for oneself by all means

鑽 4215
2. ㄗㄨㄢˇ zuǎn
(又讀ㄗㄨㄢ zuān)
to bore or pierce a hole
【鑽孔】to make a hole; to perforate

鑽 4215
3. ㄗㄨㄢˋ zuàn
1. a gimlet; an awl or auger; a borer; a drill 2. a diamond; a jewel
【鑽戒】a diamond ring
【鑽石】a diamond

鑾 4216
ㄌㄨㄢˊ luán
1. bells around the neck of a horse 2. the imperial carriage

二十畫

鑿 4217
ㄗㄨㄛˋ zuò
(語音ㄗㄠˊ záo)
1. to chisel or dig; to bore or pierce through 2. a chisel 3. real; true; actual; indisputable; authentic; conclusive 4. to make a forced interpretation of text
【鑿壁偷光】very studious
【鑿洞】to bore or drill a hole

長部
ㄔㄤˊ cháng

長 4218
1. ㄔㄤˊ cháng
1. long; length 2. a forte; strong points 3. to be good at; to excel
【長袍】a long gown; a robe
【長跑】a long-distance foot race
【長篇大論】a harangue or tirade; a lengthy comment; a ponderous talk; a long speech
【長篇小說】a novel
【長方形】a rectangle; an oblong
【長櫈】a bench
【長度】length
【長短】①long or short ②length ③mishaps or accidents which may endanger one's life ④good or bad; malicious criticism
【長短不齊】not uniform in length
【長歎】to sigh deeply
【長途】a long distance; a long journey
【長途電話】a long-distance call
【長年】yearlong; all the year round
【長年累月】year in, year out; over the years
【長廊】a roofed corridor or passage; a gallery
【長龍】a long line; a long queue
【長工】a regular laborer on a farm; a farm hand; a long-term hired hand
【長褲】a pair of trousers
【長話短說】to make a long story short
【長久】permanent; a very long time
【長江】the Yangtze River
【長頸鹿】a giraffe
【長期】①a long time ②long-term; long-range; long-standing
【長驅直入】to march in without opposition
【長袖善舞】to be resourceful, especially in a dishonest way
【長吁短歎】to sigh incessantly; to sigh and groan
【長治久安】a lengthy peaceful reign
【長征】an expedition (usually military); to take a long journey to a distant place
【長城】①the Great Wall ②someone who can be trusted
【長處】merits; good points; advantages
【長時間】a long time
【長舌】to be fond of gossip; long-tongued; loquacious
【長壽or長命】longevity; a long life
【長生不老】(especially in Taoism) immortality
【長生果】peanuts
【長足進步】marked progress; to come a long way
【長存】to exist forever; to last forever
【長音】a long vowel
【長遠】for a long time; long-range; long-term
【長遠之計】a long-range plan (for the future)

長 4218
2. ㄓㄤˇ zhǎng
1. senior; old 2. the eldest 3. a head; a chief; a leader; a commander; a chairman 4. to grow 5. to increase; to advance 6. to look; to appear; to become

〔長部〕

【長輩】the senior generation; the older member of a family; an elder

【長大】to grow up; to attain manhood; to mature

【長得】to look (beautiful, etc.)

【長女】the eldest daughter

【長老】①seniors or oldsters ②a presbyter ③reverent address for a monk

【長老會】the Presbyterian Church

【長瘤】to have a tumor

【長官】one's superior in office, etc.; (a polite expression) officers or officials; a commanding officer

【長見識】to increase one's knowledge or to gain experience

【長進】to make progress

【長相兒】one's looks or appearances

【長者】a senior; an elder; a person of virtue

【長上】elders and superiors

【長子 or 長男】the eldest son

【長孫】①the eldest of one's grandsons ②a Chinese compound surname

【長幼】young and old; seniority among family members

長 4218
3. ㄓㄤˇ zhǎng

a surplus; a remainder

【長物】property; belongings

門部
ㄇㄣˊ mén

門 4219
ㄇㄣˊ mén

1. a door; a gateway 2. a clan; a family 3. a sect; a school 4. a class; a category 5. the key; the turning point 6. a piece of (artillery); a (cannon) 7. gatekeeping 8. a Chinese family name

【門把】a doorknob; a door handle

【門牌】a doorplate

【門派】a sect

【門票】an admission ticket; an entrance ticket

【門楣】①a beam over a doorway ②family standing

【門面】①the front of a store ②the outward appearance; a facade

【門房】①a gatekeeper; a janitor; a doorman ②a gatehouse

【門縫】crevices or cracks in the door

【門當戶對】families of equal standing; well matched

【門第】family standing or reputation; family status

【門庭若市】①(said of a store, etc.) doing booming business ②(said of a household) swarmed with visitors; much visited

【門徒】one's students, pupils, followers, or disciples

【門簾or門帘】a door curtain or screen

【門鈴】the doorbell

【門路】①one's means of approach, contacts, connections, etc. ②a key or tip to a beginner in the pursuit of a certain skill; a knack

【門可羅雀】(said of a store, fallen family, etc.) where visitors are few and far between; deserted

【門口】a gate; a doorway; an entrance

【門戶】①a family ②a strategic position ③a sect; a bloc ④a door

【門戶開放】an open-door policy

【門戶之見】prejudiced or biased views of a particular sect, bloc, gang, etc.

【門禁】a checkpoint at the gate

【門禁森嚴】The gate is strictly guarded.

【門下 or 門生】pupils or disciples

【門診】to treat patients at the OPD; the outpatient service

【門齒 or 門牙】front teeth; incisors

【門市】to sell by retail; to sell over the counter

【門市部】a retail department; a sales department

【門閂 or 門栓】a latch; a door bolt

一畫

閂 4220
ㄕㄨㄢ shuān

1. to fasten with a bolt or latch 2. the latch of a door

二畫

閃 4221
ㄕㄢˇ shǎn

1. to flash; a flash, as of lightning; a very brief glimpse 2. to

dodge; to evade; to avoid 3. to twist, strain or sprain (one's back, etc.) 4. to cast away; to leave behind

【閃避】 to dodge quickly

【閃電】 ① to lighten ② lightning ③ with lightning speed

【閃動】 to move fast; to shine off and on

【閃光】 ① sparks; a flash ② to flash; to sparkle

【閃光燈】 a flashlight; a blinker

【閃開】 to dodge quickly; to avoid (a hit, collision, etc.)

【閃失】 ① errors or mistakes ② an accident

【閃身】 ① to dodge ② sideways

【閃爍】 ① to twinkle; twinkling; to scintillate ② vague; evasive

【閃爍其詞】 to speak evasively

【閃腰】 to strain a muscle on the waist

【閃耀】 to glint; to twinkle; to sparkle

三畫

閉 4222 ㄅㄧˋ bì

1. to close; to shut 2. (said of a conference, etc.) to conclude; to end 3. to block up; to stop; to obstruct 4. to restrain

【閉門羹】 to treat someone to a closed door; to close the door on

【閉門造車】 to do something impractical, useless, or out of one's pure imagination

【閉門思過】 to reflect on one's faults or misdeeds in private

【閉幕】 (said of shows, meetings, etc.) to close or conclude

【閉路電視】 closed-circuit television

【閉關自守】 to adopt a policy of exclusion or isolation

【閉塞】 ① to block up; to obstruct ② backward ③ hard to get to

四畫

開 4223 ㄎㄞ kāi

1. to open 2. to drive 3. to begin; to start 4. to reveal; to disclose 5. to state; to explain 6. to found; to expand 7. to eliminate 8. to divide into 9. to write down; to list 10. to undo; to unfold; to wind off 11. a carat 12. to run (a shop or business)

【開辦】 to start or open (a shop, school, business, etc.)

【開砲】 ① (said of a fieldpiece, battery, or artillery) to open fire ② to launch a verbal attack

【開盤】 (said of a market) the opening quotation

【開闢】 to open up or develop (a new market, farm plot, etc.); to start

【開票】 ① to count ballots or votes ② to make out an invoice

【開麥拉】 ① a camera ② (a movie director's command) Camera!

【開門見山】 to talk or write right to the point

【開明】 enlightened; open-minded

【開幕】 ① to raise the curtain ② to open; to begin a meeting

【開發】 to develop; development (of natural resources, industry, etc.)

【開飯】 to prepare food for a meal

【開放】 ① to open (to trade, traffic, etc.); to be open ② to liberalize or hand over a government monopoly to private operations ③ to lift a ban ④ to come into bloom

【開刀】 ① to operate on (a patient); an operation 亦作「手術」 ② to punish ③ to behead

【開導】 to educate and enlighten

【開倒車】 ① to back a car, train, etc. ② to be old-fashioned or anachronistic; to turn back the clock; to retrograde

【開燈】 to turn on the light

【開端】 the beginning or start

【開天闢地】 ① to open or develop ② creation of the world

【開天窗】 ① to open up a skylight ② open space in a newspaper

【開庭】 to start a court trial; to hold a court session

【開拓】 to open up, enlarge or expand (new frontiers, territory, etc.)

【開通】 ① modern-minded; enlightened ② to do away with all obstructions

【開朗】 ① to clear up, as weather ② open and clear ③ broad-minded and outspoken

【開路】 to pioneer; to cut the way, as in a jungle

(門部)

【開路先鋒】a pioneer; a trailblazer; to blaze a trail
【開關】① a switch or similar device to put on or shut off an electric current, etc. ② to open and close
【開工】to go into operation; to start work; to begin a building project
【開口】to open one's mouth; to speak
【開墾】to open up wasteland for farming
【開闊】① spacious; open; wide ② broad-minded
【開快車】①(said of a car, etc.) to speed; speeding ② to hasten up with one's work
【開航】① to open up for navigation ② to set sail
【開戶】to open a bank account
【開花】① to flower; to blossom ② (said of shells) to burst
【開化】civilized
【開火】to open fire; to engage in battle
【開懷】joyful; jubilant; happy
【開會】to hold a meeting; to attend a meeting or conference
【開價】to ask for a price; to quote; the price quoted
【開戒】to break one's resolution
【開獎】to draw the winning numbers of a lottery
【開講】to begin a speech or lecture; to begin telling a story
【開卷有益】Reading is always beneficial.
【開啓】to open
【開竅】to open one's eyes to
【開槍】to shoot; to fire
【開銷 or 開消】① expenses; (an) expenditure ② to pay expenses
【開心】① happy; to have a grand time ② to play a joke on; to amuse oneself at somebody's expense
【開心果】a pistachio
【開學】The school starts.
【開支】expenses; (an) expenditure
【開支票】to write a check
【開展】to expand; to spread out; to develop
【開戰】to declare war; to do battle
【開張】① to open a shop; to start doing a business ② to expand, spread out or develop
【開車】to drive a car
【開場】the beginning of a show or anything
【開場白】a prologue; a speech that opens a show or a meeting
【開誠布公】to wear one's heart on one's sleeve
【開除】to dismiss; to fire
【開船】to set sail; to weigh anchor
【開創】to found (a nation, big business, etc.); to start
【開始】to begin; to commence; to start
【開市】to start trading; to open the market
【開釋】to release (a prisoner, etc.); to set free
【開設】to establish; to set up
【開山祖師】the founder of a religion or a sect of religion
【開水】boiled water
【開鑿】to dig (a well, canal, etc.); to drill
【開罪】to offend another with what one says, writes or does
【開採】to excavate; to mine
【開恩】to have mercy on; to grant special favor to
【開業】to start doing business; to start practicing (law, medicine, etc.)
【開夜車】to burn the midnight oil; to sit up late at night
【開眼界】to expand one's experience and horizon
【開外】upwards of; over or more than
【開胃】① appetizing; to whet or stimulate one's appetite ② to make fun of; to tease
【開玩笑】to play a joke; to joke
【開往】①(said of a train, ship, etc.) to leave for; to be bound for ② (said of troops, etc.) to move; to set out
【開源節流】to open more sources of income and cut down expenses

間 4224

1. ㄐㄧㄢ jiān

1. between two things; the space between; among 2. a numerical adjunct for rooms 3. within a definite time or space

間 4224

2.(閒) ㄐㄧㄢˋ jiàn

1. a crevice; a leak; space in between 2. to divide; a division of a house; to separate 3. to put a space between; to drive a wedge between; to part friends 4. to change; to substitute 5. to block up 6. (said of illness) to get a little better 7. occasionally

【間不容髮】① very close; imminent ② precarious

【間諜】a spy; a secret agent
【間斷】suspended; interrupted
【間隔】① separated; spaced at intervals ② distance; intervals
【間接】indirect; vicariously
【間歇】①intermittent; sporadic ② short intervals or stops; a pause

閏 4225
ㄖㄨㄣˋ rùn
1. with surplus or leftover 2. usurped; deputy or substitute 3. extra, inserted between others, as a day, or a month; to intercalate
【閏年】a leap year; an intercalary year
【閏月】an intercalary moon or month

閑 4226
ㄒㄧㄢˊ xián
1. a fence; a bar; a barrier 2. to defend 3. big 4. familiar with; accustomed to 5. same as 閒—leisure 6. laws or regulations 7. a stable
【閑磕牙】leisure talks or conversation about nothing in particular
【閑靜】peaceful and calm in mind —without desires
【閑習】to be well versed in or familiar with
【閑暇 or 閒暇】leisure; spare time
【閑書 or 閒書】books for killing time, as novels, etc.

閒 4227
ㄒㄧㄢˊ xián
1. quiet; tranquil; calm; placid 2. leisure; spare time
【閒蕩】to saunter; to stroll; to loaf
【閒談】idle talk; to chat
【閒聊】①to chat; to gossip ②a gossip; a chat
【閒逛】to saunter; to stroll
【閒工夫】leisure; spare time
【閒話】① random or idle talk; gossip; complaint ② to talk casually about; to chat about
【閒居】to lead an idle, leisure, or quiet life
【閒情逸致】a peaceful and comfortable mood
【閒置】to leave unused; to let something lie idle; to set aside
【閒事】matters not of one's concern; others' business; matters one has nothing to do with
【閒適】quiet and comfortable
【閒人】① idlers; persons with nothing to do ② persons not concerned
【閒雜】without fixed duties
【閒言閒語】sarcastic remarks or complaints; gossips

五畫

閘 4228
ㄓㄚˊ zhá
1. a floodgate; a lock; a sluice 2. a brake 3. a switch or similar devices
【閘門】a floodgate

六畫

閣 4229
ㄍㄜˊ gé
1. a room; a chamber; a pavilion 2. an attic 3. a cabinet 4. a boudoir
【閣樓】an attic; a garret
【閣揆】the premier; the prime minister
【閣下】Your Excellency; you (a polite expression)
【閣員】cabinet ministers; members of the cabinet

閤 4230
(闔) ㄏㄜˊ hé
1. to close (doors) 2. whole; all
【閤第 or 閤府】your whole family

閥 4231
ㄈㄚˊ fá
1. a threshold; a doorsill 2. an influential person, family, or clique; a bloc 3. a valve

閨 4232
ㄍㄨㄟ guī
1. a small door 2. the women's apartment 3. feminine
【閨房】a boudoir
【閨女】a maiden; an unmarried girl
【閨秀】a well-educated girl brought up in a good family

閩 4233
ㄇㄧㄣˇ mǐn
(又讀 ㄇㄧㄣˊ mín)
1. another name for Fukien Province 2. name of a river and an ancient tribe in today's Fukien Province
【閩南語(話)】the southern Fukien dialect

七畫

〔門部〕

閭 4234
ㄌㄩˊ lǘ
1. a community of 25 families in ancient China 2. the gate of a village 3. to meet; to gather together
【閭里 or 閭巷】 alleys or lanes—① one's neighbors; one's neighborhood ② one's native village

閱 4235
ㄩㄝˋ yuè
1. to read; to go over (examination papers) 2. to review; to inspect; to examine; to observe 3. to experience 4. to pass
【閱報】 to read newspapers
【閱兵】 to inspect or review troops
【閱讀 or 閱覽】 to read
【閱覽室】 a reading room
【閱歷】 ① to see, hear, or do for oneself ② experience; background
【閱卷】 to grade examination papers

八畫

閻 4236
ㄧㄢˊ yán
1. a village gate; the gate of a lane 2. a Chinese family name
【閻羅王 or 閻王】 ① the Ruler of Hades; the King of Hell ② a tyrant; one who is feared by all others

閹 4237
ㄧㄢ yān
1. to castrate 2. a eunuch
【閹割】 to castrate
【閹人】 a castrated person; a eunuch

九畫

闃 4238
ㄑㄩˋ qù
quiet; without people around
【闃寂】 still; quiet

闇 4239
ㄢˋ àn
1. to shut the door 2. dark; obscure; obscurity 3. evening; night 4. lunar or solar eclipses 5. stupid and dull
【闇然】 obscure; concealed

闈 4240
ㄨㄟˊ wéi
1. the side doors of a palace 2. the living quarters of the queen and the imperial concubines 3. ladies' living quarters; private quarters 4. (formerly) a hall where the civil service examination took place

闊 4241
ㄎㄨㄛˋ kuò
1. broad; wide; width 2. separated; widely apart 3. rich; loaded; wealthy; extravagant
【闊別】 separated for a long time
【闊步】 to walk with big strides; to stride
【闊老 or 闊佬】 a rich man
【闊氣】 extravagant in spending; lavish
【闊綽】 extravagant; throwing money around; lavish

闌 4242
ㄌㄢˊ lán
1. a door curtain or screen 2. a fence 3. to block up; to cut off 4. the end of (a year, etc.); late (in the night, etc.) 5. weakened; withered
【闌干】 ① a fence; banisters; a balustrade; railings ② the eye sockets ③ a crisscross
【闌珊】 withered; declining; waning
【闌尾】 the appendix 亦作「盲腸」

闆 4243
ㄅㄢˇ bǎn
the boss; the owner

十畫

闔 4244
ㄏㄜˊ hé
1. a leaf of a door 2. to shut or close 3. all; the whole 4. Why? 或 Why not?
【闔府】 your whole family
【闔府平安】 Hope your whole family is doing well.
【闔第光臨】 Please come with your whole family.
【闔家】 the whole family

闕 4245
1. ㄑㄩㄝˋ què
1. a watchtower outside the palace gate in ancient China 2. a palace

闕 4245
2. ㄑㄩㄝ quē
1. faults; errors; mistakes; defects 2. to lack; deficient
【闕失】 a mistake; an error
【闕如】 lacking; wanting; deficient

闖 4246
ㄔㄨㄤˇ chuǎng

1. to rush in all of a sudden; to intrude into 2. to be trained by experience; to hew out one's way 3. to cause (a disaster, etc.)

【闖關】to run a blockade; to try to break into a guarded point
【闖禍】to cause a disaster
【闖紅燈】to run through a red light
【闖江湖】to roam about to make a living

十一畫

關 4247
ㄍㄨㄢ guān

1. to shut; to close 2. a frontier pass or checkpoint 3. the bar across the door 4. a customs house; a customs barrier 5. a key point; a turning point 6. related; relationship; to involve; to concern 7. to negotiate; to go between 8. to draw (money, or pay) 9. a Chinese family name

【關閉】① to close ② to close down; to shut down (a store, etc.)
【關門】① to close the door ② to close a shop ③ to close its door —to go bankrupt
【關門大吉】to close down for good
【關防】① the seal of a government agency ② a military position at a strategic point on the border
【關島】Guam
【關聯】related; involved; connection
【關卡】a customs station or barrier
【關懷 or 關心】to be concerned about; to show concern; concern
【關節】① joints in the human body ② to bribe; a bribe ③ illegal transactions between the examiner and the examinee ④ key links; crucial links
【關鍵】a key (to a problem); an important turning point
【關禁閉】(military) to be put in a dark cell as a form of punishment
【關係】① relation; connection; ties ② to matter
【關照】① to notify; to inform ② to take care of; to look after
【關說】to lobby illegally, usually by pedaling one's influence
【關稅】customs duty
【關愛】to express solicitude for the well-being of someone
【關於】concerning; with regard to

十二畫

闡 4248
ㄔㄢˇ chǎn

1. to make clear; to elucidate; to expound 2. evident; clear

【闡明】to elucidate; to clarify
【闡發】to expound and promote
【闡釋】to explain; to expound
【闡述】to expound; to elaborate

十三畫

闢 4249
ㄆㄧˋ pì

1. to open up; to develop 2. to rid; to do away with 3. to refute

【闢地】to open up land for cultivation
【闢邪】to refute heresy
【闢謠】to refute rumors; to clarify rumored reports

阜部
ㄈㄨˋ fù

阜 4250
ㄈㄨˋ fù

1. a mound; a small hill 2. the continent; the mainland 3. flourishing; abundant; numerous

三畫

阡 4251
ㄑㄧㄢ qiān

1. paths on farms; a footpath between fields, running north and south 2. the path leading to a grave

【阡陌】paths on farmland
【阡陌縱橫】crisscross paths on farmland

四畫

阨 4252
ㄜˋ è

1. a strategic position 2. a precarious position 3. to block up or obstruct 4. destitute; difficulty; poverty-stricken

〔阜部〕

阮 4253 ㄖㄨㄢˇ ruǎn

1. name of an ancient state in today's Kansu Province 2. an ancient musical instrument 3. a Chinese family name

【阮囊羞澀】short of cash; poor

阱 4254 ㄐㄧㄥˇ jǐng

a trap; a snare

防 4255 ㄈㄤˊ fáng

1. to defend; defense 2. to prepare for; to take precautions; to prevent

【防備】to get ready or prepared (for an incident, etc.); to guard against

【防不勝防】There's no way of preventing it.

【防範】to be alert against; to take precautions; to guard against

【防風林】a windbreak

【防腐劑】antiseptic; preservative

【防盜】prevention of burglary; to guard against burglary

【防彈】bulletproof; to protect against bullets

【防毒】anti-poison; gas defense

【防毒面具】a gas mask; a protective mask

【防癆】tuberculosis prevention; TB control

【防空】air defense; antiaircraft

【防空洞】an air-raid or bomb shelter

【防火】to guard against fire hazards; fireproof

【防患未然】to take precautions against a calamity

【防洪】flood control

【防線】a line of defense

【防止】to prevent; to guard against; to prohibit

【防治】prevention and treatment (of diseases)

【防震】shock-resistant; quakeproof

【防蟲】pest control; pest prevention

【防守or防衛or防禦】to defend; to guard

【防身】to guard personal safety; self-protection

【防身術】the science (or art) of self-defense

【防水】① waterproof; watertight ② to guard against flood; anti-flood

五畫

阻 4256 ㄗㄨˇ zǔ

1. to prevent; to stop; to prohibit 2. to separate; separated 3. to hinder; to obstruct; to impede; to blockade 4. difficulty; to suffer 5. to rely on 6. a strategic pass

【阻擋】to stop; to be in the way

【阻力】the force of resistance

【阻隔】① to be separated; to be isolated ② to cut off

【阻止】to stop or prevent; to prohibit or proscribe; to block

【阻塞】① to block up; to clog; to obstruct ② a jam; a block

【阻礙】an obstacle or hindrance; to obstruct; obstruction; to impede

阿 4257 1. ㄜ ē

1. to favor; to toady; to assent; to pander to; to play up to 2. to rely on 3. a riverbank 4. the corner or edge 5. a pillar 6. slender and beautiful 7. to discharge (night soil, urine, etc.)

【阿彌陀佛】Amitabha, the Buddha of infinite qualities

【阿諛】to flatter

阿 4257 2. ㄚˋ à (又讀 ㄚ ā)

1. an initial particle; a prefix to a name or a term of address 2. a word often used in transliterations

【阿們】Amen

【阿富汗】Afghanistan

【阿拉】(Mohammedan) Allah

【阿拉伯】① Arabia ② Arab

【阿拉伯數字】Arabic numerals

【阿里山】Mt. Ali, Taiwan

【阿根廷】Argentina; the Argentine

【阿司匹靈 or 阿斯匹靈】aspirin

【阿姨】① an aunt ② a stepmother

陀 4258 ㄊㄨㄛˊ tuó

craggy; rugged terrain

【陀螺】a top

附 4259 ㄈㄨˋ fù

1. to rely on; to be dependent on; to attach to; to adhere to 2. to enclose; to send along with; to append 3. near or close to 4. to add to; to increase 5. (said of an evil spirit) to be possessed by

【附帶】① supplementary ② to

attach ③ in passing
【附圖】an attached map or drawing; a figure
【附錄】an appendix or annex
【附款】appendant provisions in a legal document
【附和】to agree without conviction
【附會】to twist in making an explanation
【附加】①to add to ②supplementary
【附件】an enclosure; an accessory; an attachment (of a letter, etc.)
【附近】around; nearby; the vicinity
【附註】remarks; notes
【附著】to adhere to; to stick together
【附上】enclosed herewith
【附屬】accessory; subordinate; to affiliate with; to be attached to
【附議】to second a motion; to support a proposal

六畫

陋 4260
ㄌㄡˋ lòu
1. narrow and small 2. ugly 3. vile; low; mean; humble 4. ignorant; crude; simple-minded 5. poor (performances, knowledge, etc.); inferior; superficial; shallow 6. stingy; tight-fisted
【陋規】bad practices
【陋習】bad habits; corrupt practices
【陋巷】a narrow, dirty alley; slums
【陋室】a crude abode; a humble room
【陋俗】vile customs; vulgar customs

陌 4261
ㄇㄛˋ mò
paths in the rice field
【陌生】unfamiliar; strange; inexperienced
【陌生人】a stranger

降 4262
1. ㄐㄧㄤˋ jiàng
1. to descend 2. to lower 3. to condescend; to deign 4. to drop; to decline 5. to surrender
【降臨】① to come down; to fall ② to condescend (to visit)
【降落】① to land; landing; descent; to descend ② to drop; to rain down
【降落傘】a parachute
【降格】to lower the scale, standard, standing or status
【降級】to degrade; to downgrade; to demote
【降旗】to lower the flag
【降世】to come down to the world
【降生】to be born into the world
【降溫】① to lower the temperature (as in a workshop) ②to drop in temperature
【降雨量】rainfall

降 4262
2. ㄒㄧㄤˊ xiáng
1. to surrender; to submit to 2. to conquer
【降服】① to surrender and give allegiance to the new master ② to bring to terms; to subdue
【降龍伏虎】to overcome powerful adversaries
【降旗】the white flag signifying surrender

限 4263
ㄒㄧㄢˋ xiàn
1. a boundary; a line 2. a doorsill or threshold 3. limits; restriction; to limit or restrict 4. to specify; to fix
【限定】to limit
【限度】limits; limitation; degree
【限量】limits; limitation
【限價】price control; a price fixed under a government specified ceiling
【限期】① a time limit; a deadline ② within a definite time
【限制】limitations; to restrict
【限時】to fix or set the time; to set a time limit or deadline
【限時專送】prompt delivery
【限額】a quota

七畫

陛 4264
ㄅㄧˋ bì
wide and high steps in the palace; the steps to the throne
【陛下】Your Majesty; His or Her Majesty

陟 4265
ㄓˋ zhì
1. to mount; to ascend 2. to advance; to elevate; to promote

陡 4266
ㄉㄡˇ dǒu
1. suddenly; abruptly 2. steep; precipitous
【陡坡】a steep slope
【陡峭】steep; precipitous

院 4267
ㄩㄢˋ yuàn

1. a courtyard; a yard 2. a designation for certain government offices and public places 3. short for the Executive Yuan, Legislative Yuan, Examination Yuan, Judicial Yuan, or Control Yuan

【院轄市】 a special municipality

【院長】 the dean of a college or court of law; the director of a hospital, museum, etc.

【院子 or 院兒】 a yard; a courtyard

陣 4268 ㄓㄣˋ zhèn

1. a column or row of troops; the army; the rank and file 2. to battle; to go to war 3. anything that occurs in a certain duration or spell of time

【陣地】 a (military) position

【陣痛】 labor pangs

【陣前】 on the battlefield

【陣線】 line of battle

【陣勢】 order of battle; battle array

【陣容】 ① the appearance of 2 military deployment; the layout of troops ② the lineup of a cabinet ③ the cast of a movie

【陣營】 a camp; an encampment

【陣亡】 to be killed in action

【陣雨】 occasional drizzle; showers

除 4269 ㄔㄨˊ chú

1. (mathematics) to divide; division 2. to remove; to rid of; to wipe out 3. to be appointed to an official rank or office 4. to subtract; to deduct 5. except; besides; unless 6. to change or turn, as a new year

【除暴安良】 to get rid of lawless elements and protect the good

【除名】 to dismiss; to strike one's name off the list; to expel

【除法】 (mathematics) division

【除非】 unless

【除掉】 to remove; to get rid of

【除害】 to get rid of evils, bad habits, practices, etc.

【除號】 the sign of division "÷"

【除舊布新】 to remove the old and introduce the new; to replace the old with the new

【除去】 to remove; to except

【除夕】 Lunar New Year's Eve

【除濕機】 a dehumidifier

【除數】 a divisor

【除此之外】 besides this (or these); in addition

【除草】 to weed (in farming); to mow grass or cut weeds

【除外】 except; to except

陝 4270 ㄕㄢˇ shǎn

short for Shensi Province

八畫

陪 4271 ㄆㄟˊ péi

1. to accompany; to keep company 2. same as 賠—to make up for; to compensate 3. to assist

【陪伴】 to keep company; to accompany

【陪客】 ①(ㄆㄟˊ·ㄎㄜ) guests invited to keep the guest of honor company ②(ㄆㄟˊ ㄎㄜˋ) ⓐ to receive guests; to keep guests company ⓑ (said of girls in gay establishments) to attend on patrons

【陪嫁】 the dowry given to a daughter on her marriage

【陪酒】 (said of a bar girl, etc.) to accompany a patron in drinking

【陪笑】 to put up a smiling face in order to please or placate someone

【陪襯】 to serve as a background in order to bring out the subject with greater brilliance; to serve as a prop

【陪審】 ① to act (or serve) as an assessor (in a law case) ② to serve on a jury

【陪葬】 to bury (a person or things) along with the deceased

【陪罪】 to ask forgiveness; to apologize

陰 4272 1. ㄧㄣ yīn

1. negative (as opposite to positive, as electricity) 2. feminine; female 3. cloudy; dark 4. shady 5. secret 6. the back side 7. the north side of a mountain 8. the south side of a stream 9. reproductive organs of both sexes 10. Hades; hell 11. cunning and crafty 12. time 13. a Chinese family name

【陰平】 (Chinese phonetics) the first tone

【陰霾】 haze; thin mist

【陰謀】 a plot; a secret scheme; a

conspiracy
【陰謀詭計】schemes and intrigues; dark schemes and tricks
【陰府or陰曹地府】Hades; the nether world
【陰德】one's unpublicized good deeds
【陰天】a cloudy day
【陰冷】①(said of weather) gloomy and cold; raw ②(said of a person's look) somber; glum
【陰曆】the lunar calendar
【陰涼】shady and cool
【陰溝】① a covered drain; a sewer ② the vagina
【陰乾】to be placed in the shade to dry; to dry in the shade
【陰魂不散】The soul (or spirit) refuses to leave.
【陰極】the cathode; the negative pole
【陰間】Hades; the shades; the underworld
【陰險】cunning; crafty; deceitful; sinister
【陰性】① negative ② female
【陰沈】① gloomy (sky) ② quiet and designing (persons)
【陰錯陽差】due to all sorts of accidental mishaps
【陰森森】gloomy; weird; ominous
【陰暗】dim; dark; gloomy; overcast
【陰陰沈沈】gloomy; dusky; dreary
【陰陽】*yin* (shade) and *yang* (light)
【陰陽怪氣】① to act or speak in an odd or queer manner ② eccentric; queer
【陰影】shades; shadows
【陰雨】cloudy and rainy; overcast and rainy

陰 4272
2. (蔭) ㄧㄣˋ yìn
shaded by trees

陳 4273
1. ㄔㄣˊ chén
1. a Chinese family name 2. to arrange; to display; to spread out 3. to tell, state, or narrate; to explain 4. old; stale; preserved for a long time 5. name of a dynasty (557-589) 6. to make public
【陳皮梅】sugar preserved prunes
【陳腐】old or hackneyed (expressions, etc.); stale (food or fruit)
【陳年】of many years' standing
【陳年老酒】alcoholic drinks that have been preserved for a long time; aged wine
【陳列】to arrange and display; to set out; to exhibit
【陳列品】articles on display; exhibits
【陳糧】old grain
【陳規】out-of-date conventions
【陳貨】old goods; goods from old stock
【陳迹】relics; vestiges; things of the past; an old trace
【陳酒】old wine
【陳舊】old; worn-out; outmoded; obsolete; shabby
【陳腔濫調】hackneyed expressions; clichés; corny statements
【陳情】to give a full statement or account of a situation, etc.
【陳陳相因】to copy or follow precedents, old practices, etc.; writing without new ideas
【陳屍】to exhibit or expose a corpse
【陳設】to display; to decorate; to exhibit; to set out; to furnish
【陳述】to tell; to narrate; to state

陳 4273
2. (陣) ㄓㄣˋ zhèn
tactical deployment of troops

陵 4274
ㄌㄧㄥˊ líng
1. a high mound 2. the tomb of an emperor; a mausoleum 3. to offend; to insult; to outrage 4. to usurp 5. to climb; to scale
【陵墓】a tomb; a grave; a mausoleum
【陵寢】the tomb of an emperor or king; a mausoleum
【陵夷】to deteriorate; to decay

陶 4275
ㄊㄠˊ táo
1. to make pottery or earthenware; pottery or earthenware 2. happy; joyful 3. to move and influence a person 4. a Chinese family name
【陶器】pottery; earthenware
【陶鑄】to educate and mold persons of talent
【陶醉】to be intoxicated (with success, etc.); very happy; highly gratified
【陶瓷】pottery and porcelain
【陶冶】① to mold (pottery) and smelt (metals) ② to cultivate or shape (taste, character, etc.)
【陶冶性情】to shape or cleanse one's spirit

陷 4276
ㄒㄧㄢˋ xiàn

〔阜部〕

1. to sink; to fall; to submerge; to stick; to bog 2. to frame (up); to harm another with trumped-up charges 3. to entrap; to beguile 4. to crush (the enemy position); to fall; to capture (a city, etc.) 5. a defect; a deficiency 「drowned
【陷溺】to sink; to submerge; to be
【陷落】① to sink; to submerge ② (said of a city, position, etc.) to be lost to the enemy
【陷害】to frame; to snare; to harm another with a trumped-up charge, slander, etc. 「trap
【陷阱】a trap; a snare; a booby
【陷入絕境】to get into extreme 「difficulty

陸 4277 ㄌㄨˋ lù
1. land; the shore; a continent 2. by way of land; land transportation 3. an elaborate form of 六 (six) used in documents or checks to prevent forgery 4. a Chinese family name
【陸地】land
【陸路】by land; a highway or railway; by way of land
【陸海空】land, sea and air
【陸軍】the army; the land force
【陸橋】① an overpass 亦作「天橋」 ② a land bridge
【陸續】continuous; one by one; one after another 「Corps
【陸戰隊】the marines; the Marine

九畫

陽 4278 ㄧㄤˊ yáng
1. positive (electricity, etc.) 2. male; masculine 3. the sun; solar; sunlight 4. the north of a stream 5. the south of a hill 6. bright; brilliant 7. the male genitals 8. pertaining to this world, as opposed to Hades
【陽平】(Chinese phonetics) the second tone
【陽明山】Yangmingshan
【陽奉陰違】to observe rules or obey orders ostensibly; to pretend to obey
【陽臺】① a veranda or balcony ② a trysting place; a tryst
【陽曆】the solar calendar; the Gregorian calendar
【陽剛】tough, strong, positive, stern, etc. in character
【陽光】sunshine; sunlight; sunbeams 「living
【陽間 or 陽世】the world of the
【陽性】① positive (electricity, etc.) ② the male sex; masculinity
【陽宅】a human habitation; a house; the residence of the living
【陽春】springtime 「any dressing
【陽春麪】cooked noodles without
【陽壽】one's predestined life span
【陽傘】a parasol; an umbrella

隄 4279 (堤) ㄊㄧˊ tí (又讀 ㄉㄧ dī)
as in 隄防 or 隄岸—a dike, levee 「or embankment

隅 4280 ㄩˊ yú
1. a corner; a nook 2. an angle 3. an out-of-the-way place; a 「recess

隆 4281 ㄌㄨㄥˊ lóng
1. prosperous; flourishing; brisk (business, etc.); booming 2. lofty; eminent; glorious 3. abundant; ample; generous 4. the rumble (of thunder, vehicles, artillery fire, etc.)
【隆冬】(in) the depth of winter; winter at its coldest
【隆隆】① flourishing; booming ② (said of sound) roaring, booming or rumbling 「bulge
【隆起】to rise up; to swell up; to
【隆情厚誼】great kindness, hospitality and friendship 「emn
【隆重】impressive, grand and sol-

隋 4282 ㄙㄨㄟˊ suí
name of a dynasty (581-618)

隊 4283 ㄉㄨㄟˋ duì 「the troops
1. a group; a team; a batch 2.
【隊旗】the flag of a team; the team
【隊形】formation 「pennant
【隊長】the team leader; the captain of a sports team; the commanding officer of a small military unit 「② a line of (people)
【隊伍】①troops in ranks and files
【隊員】members of a team or 「group

階 4284 ㄐㄧㄝ jiē
1. a way leading to the main

hall 2. a flight of steps or stairs 3. a grade or a rank 4. to rely on

【階段】 a stage or phase

【階梯】 ① a flight of stairs or steps ② (figuratively) a way, ladder or step leading to success

【階級】 a rank; a class (of people)

【階下囚】 a prisoner; a captive

【階層】 subdivisions within a class of people; a class of people

十畫

隔 4285 ㄍㄜˊ gé

1. to separate; to divide; to partition 2. blocked; to obstruct; to be veiled 3. at a distance from; at an interval of

【隔壁】 next door

【隔斷 or 隔絕】 blocked or obstructed; to separate; to cut off

【隔年】 in the following year; in the year following

【隔離】 to separate; to isolate; to segregate; to quarantine

【隔開】 to separate; to set apart; to partition

【隔閡】 no meeting of minds; a mental barrier

【隔間】 a partition

【隔牆有耳】 It's difficult to keep a secret.

【隔靴搔癢】 not to the point; having no effect; to attempt an ineffective solution

【隔日】 ① the next day or the day after next ② every other day

【隔熱】 (construction) heat insulation

【隔岸觀火】 to be indifferent; to show no concern

【隔夜】 after a night; last night

【隔音】 soundproof

隕 4286 ㄩㄣˇ yǔn

1. to fall 2. to die

【隕落】 ① to fall from the sky or outer space ② to pass away; to die

【隕石】 a meteorite

隘 4287 ㄞˋ ài

1. a strategic pass 2. narrow 3. urgent 4. destitute

【隘口】 a (mountain) pass

隙 4288 (隟) ㄒㄧˋ xì

1. a crack; a fissure; a crevice 2. a grudge; a dislike; a dispute; a quarrel; a complaint 3. spare time; leisure 4. an opportunity; a loophole 5. an important passageway or corridor

【隙罅】 a crack, crevice, or fissure

十一畫

際 4289 ㄐㄧˋ jì

1. (to occur) at the time or on the occasion of 2. a border or boundary; an edge 3. by the side of; beside 4. in the middle; between; among 5. opportunity; fortune or luck

【際會】 ① to meet; to encounter ② a happenstance

【際遇】 ① opportunity; chance ② what one has experienced in one's life

障 4290 ㄓㄤˋ zhàng

1. to separate; to screen; a barrier; a screen 2. a dike; an embankment 3. to defend; to guard; to shield 4. to guarantee 5. to hinder; to obstruct

【障蔽】 to screen; to obstruct

【障礙】 ① obstacles; barriers; obstructions ② a malfunction; a handicap

【障眼法】 ① legerdemain ② a cover-up; camouflage

十三畫

隨 4291 ㄙㄨㄟˊ suí

1. to follow; to trace; to come after 2. to listen to; to submit to; to comply with 3. to let (it go, it be, etc.) 4. to accompany 5. to resemble; to look like

【隨波逐流】 ① to follow the currents in sailing ② to speak and behave as others do without views of his own

【隨筆】 to write as one's thought rambles; literary rambles

【隨便】 ① as you like; as you see fit; as you please ② casual; careless

【隨帶】 to carry about; to take along

【隨地吐痰】 to spit freely at any place

【隨同】 to follow or accompany; together with

【隨口】 to slip out of one's tongue without much thought

【隨和】easygoing; amiable
【隨後】immediately afterward; right off; in no time at all; right after

〔阜部〕

【隨機應變】to adapt oneself quickly to the changing circumstances
【隨叫隨到】to arrive as soon as it is ordered by telephone call; to be on call at any hour
【隨心所欲】to do anything one's heart dictates
【隨行】to follow or accompany someone on a trip「in pace with」
【隨着】along with; in the wake of;
【隨時】at all times; anytime
【隨時隨地】at all times and places; anytime and anyplace; wherever and whenever「ately」
【隨手】at hand; readily; immedi-
【隨身】to carry something with one; to take something with one; to carry about
【隨身聽】a walkman「tendants」
【隨從】an entourage; aides; at-
【隨俗】to act according to the prevailing customs or practices
【隨意】according to your wish; as you like it; as you please
【隨遇而安】to feel at ease under all circumstances

隧 4292 ㄙㄨㄟˋ suì

1. an underground passage; a tunnel: 隧道 a tunnel 2. (in ancient China) a tower on the wall to watch signal fires

險 4293 ㄒㄧㄢˇ xiǎn

1. dangerous; danger 2. obstructed; difficult 3. a strategic pass 4. mean and crafty; cunning; sinister 5. nearly; almost
【險灘】a dangerous shoal; rapids
【險境】a dangerous situation
【險峻】(said of terrain) of highly strategic significance; (said of hills, etc.) precipitous
【險象環生】dangers lurking on all sides; to be beset with danger
【險詐】treacherous; treachery
【險勝】to win by a narrow margin
【險遭不測】to escape death by a hair's breadth
【險遭毒手】to have a narrow escape from assassination, murder, etc.
【險阻】hazardous; precarious (situations, etc.); difficult (terrain)
【險惡】① dangerous; perilous; ominous; precarious ② devious; diabolic
【險要】(said of a place) strategic and capable of being easily defended

十四畫

隱 4294 ㄧㄣˇ yǐn

1. hidden; concealed; secret; mysterious 2. dark; obscure; not evident or obvious 3. to retire; to reject public life; to live like a hermit 4. painful; grievous 5. a riddle 6. destitute; poor 7. to examine and study 8. a low wall
【隱瞞】to hide the truth; to cover up「secret」
【隱秘】① to conceal; to hide ② a
【隱遁 or 隱居】to retire from public life; to live in reclusion
【隱退】to retire; retirement
【隱諱】① taboo (on the parent's or emperor's personal name) ② to avoid mentioning; to cover up
【隱疾】① ailments beneath one's garment ② ailments one wants to keep to oneself, as syphilis, impotence, etc.
【隱情】secrets; things which cannot be revealed to others
【隱形眼鏡】contact lenses
【隱性】(genetics) recessive
【隱姓埋名】to live incognito
【隱士】a retired scholar; a recluse
【隱藏】to hide; to conceal
【隱私】one's secrets; private matters one wants to hide
【隱私權】privacy
【隱惡揚善】to cover up another's bad deeds and praise his virtues
【隱逸】a recluse; a retired person
【隱憂】hidden or latent worries
【隱隱作痛】to feel dull pain
【隱喻】a metaphor「ous; abstruse」
【隱約】indistinct; obscure; ambigu-

隰 4295 ㄒㄧˊ xí「opened farmland」

1. low, marshy land 2. newly

十六畫

隴 4296 ㄌㄨㄥˇ lǒng
1.another name of Kansu (甘肅) Province 2.a mound 亦作「壟」 3.prosperous
【隴畝】a rural community; the farm

隶 部 ㄉㄞˋ dài

九畫

隸 4297 ㄌㄧˋ lì
1. to be subordinate to; inferior; to belong or attach to 2. slaves; servants; underlings 3. a type of Chinese calligraphy
【隸屬】to be attached to

隹 部 ㄓㄨㄟ zhuī

隹 4298 ㄓㄨㄟ zhuī
a general name of short-tailed birds, such as pigeons

二畫

隻 4299 ㄓ zhī
1. a numerary adjunct for a hen, pigeon, bird, ox, goat, hand, foot, etc. 2. single; alone; one of a pair 3. odd (number)
【隻身】alone; all by oneself
【隻言片語】a few words

三畫

雀 4300 ㄑㄩㄝˋ què (語音 ㄑㄧㄠˇ qiǎo)
1.a general name of small birds, as sparrows, chickadees, etc. 2. freckled
【雀斑】freckles
【雀屏中選】to be selected as someone's son-in-law
【雀戰】to play a game of mah-jong
【雀巢鳩佔】to usurp other's position, property, etc.
【雀躍】to jump up with joy; greatly excited with joy

四畫

雄 4301 ㄒㄩㄥˊ xióng
1. male; masculine; virile 2. a person or state having great power and influence 3. heroic; brave; strong; ambitious 4. to win; to triumph; victory 5. to scold others with insulting words
【雄霸一方】to hold a part of the country and to exercise undisputed authority
【雄辯】a forceful presentation of one's points in a debate; eloquence
【雄風】an awe-inspiring air; a gallant and stately manner
【雄厚】ample; plentiful; rich; abundant
【雄渾】powerful; grand; grandiose
【雄赳赳】imposing; looking brave and resolute; valiantly
【雄健】powerful; vigorous; strapping
【雄心】ambition; great expectations
【雄壯】virile; powerful; strong; majestic
【雄師】crack troops; a powerful army
【雄姿】a dashing look; a manly form
【雄才大略】(said of a ruler) extremely capable
【雄偉】grandeur; majestic; stately

雁 4302 (鴈) ㄧㄢˋ yàn
the wild goose
【雁行】①to walk like flying wild geese, one after another ②brothers
【雁足傳書】to bring a message

雅 4303 ㄧㄚˇ yǎ
1. refined; polished; sophisticated; not common or vulgar 2. elegant; graceful 3. usually; often; frequently; much 4. name of an ancient musical instrument 5. friendship; acquaintance 6. (now rarely) a wine vessel
【雅痞】Yuppie or Yuppy (a young, ambitious, and well-educated city-dweller who has a professional career and an affluent life-

style)
【雅美族】the Yamis, an aborigine tribe on Orchid Island
【雅量】① broad-mindedness; generous; magnanimity ② a great capacity for drinking
【雅觀】graceful and elegant in appearance
【雅興】enthusiasm in refined pursuits
【雅致】① refined tastes; refinement ② fine; delicate; elegant; tasteful
【雅事】refined activities of the intelligentsia
【雅賊】a thief who steals only books and works of art
【雅座】a nicely fixed chamber or room in a restaurant for customers who desire privacy
【雅俗】the refined and the vulgar; the sophisticated and the simple-minded
【雅俗共賞】to appeal to both the sophisticated and the simple-minded
【雅言】① things one often talks about ② well-intentioned criticism; honest advice

集 4304 ㄐㄧˊ jí
1. to assemble; to collect; to gather together; to concentrate 2. a collection of works by one or more authors; to compile; to edit 3. achievements 4. a fair; a periodical market
【集大成】a theory, etc. representing a generalization of many views or ideas; eclectic
【集體】collective
【集團】a bloc; a faction; a clique
【集團結婚】a mass wedding
【集合】to assemble; to gather together; to muster
【集會】a meeting; a conference; an assemblage; an assembly
【集結】to concentrate (troops)
【集錦】a collection of homogeneous passages from various literary pieces
【集權】centralization of authority; concentration of power
【集訓】to train many people at the same place and same time
【集中】① to concentrate; to center; to centralize ② to gather
【集中營】a concentration camp
【集思廣益】to canvass various opinions and benefit from them
【集郵】philately; stamp collection

雇 4305 ㄍㄨˋ gù
to employ or hire
【雇工】① a hired laborer ② to hire a laborer
【雇主】the employer
【雇員】an auxiliary employee of very low rank in a government office

五畫

雍 4306 ㄩㄥ yōng
1. harmonious; harmony; peaceful; union 2. to block up; to obstruct
【雍容】a majestic, stately or imposing appearance
【雍容華貴】(said of a woman) graceful and poised; regal
【雍容自得】in the peace of mind

雉 4307 ㄓˋ zhì
1. a pheasant 2. a unit of volume measure in ancient China (about 30' square by 10')

雌 4308 ㄘ cī
1. female; feminine; womanlike; soft (voice, etc.) 2. weak; retiring 3. to scold 4. to expose or show (the teeth) 亦作「齜」
【雌黃】① orpiment (As_2S_3) ② to make changes in writing ③ to criticize without grounds; to malign
【雌性】female
【雌雄】① the female and the male ② the victor and the loser
【雌雄莫辨】unable to distinguish the sex identity
【雌蕊】a pistil

雋 4309 1. ㄐㄩㄣˋ jùn
1. good-looking 2. outstanding; talented; extraordinary
【雋拔】outstandingly talented

雋 4309 2. ㄐㄩㄢˋ juàn
1. fat meat 2. meaningful
【雋永】very interesting or intriguing; meaningful

八畫

雕 4310
ㄉㄧㄠ diāo

1. to engrave; to carve or cut, as in sculpture 2. an eagle; a hawk 3. to exhaust; to weaken

【雕梁畫棟】carved beams and painted rafters—a richly ornamented building
【雕刻】① sculpture ② to engrave
【雕像】① a sculptured statue ② portrayal of a person
【雕琢】① to cut and polish (gems) ② to polish a piece of writing; to write in an ornate style
【雕蟲小技】a petty skill or craft; a skill which has no significant value
【雕塑】① sculpture ② to cut wood or clay for a statue or idol

九畫

雖 4311
ㄙㄨㄟ suī
(又讀 ㄙㄨㄟˊ suí)

1. although; even though; even if; supposing 2. to push away; to dismiss 3. only 4. (now rarely) a lizard-like reptile

【雖敗猶榮】to feel proud even in defeat
【雖然】even though; although; in spite of; even if

十畫

雙 4312
ㄕㄨㄤ shuāng

1. a pair; a brace; a couple; persons or things that come in pairs 2. two; both; even (as distinct from odd)

【雙倍】double; twofold; twice the amount or number
【雙胞胎】twins
【雙邊會談】bilateral talks
【雙面】two-sided; double-faced; reversible; double-edged
【雙方】both parties or sides
【雙打】to play in doubles (as tennis); doubles
【雙料】articles, products built with added strength, durability, etc. by using better and more raw materials
【雙關】ambiguous; subject to two different interpretations
【雙關語】a double entendre; a pun
【雙管齊下】① to do two things simultaneously in order to attain an objective; a double-barreled move ② ambiguous; subject to two different interpretations
【雙號】an even number
【雙親】one's parents
【雙喜臨門】to have simultaneously two happy events in a family
【雙下巴】a double chin
【雙餉】double pay for soldiers
【雙向溝通】two-way communication
【雙重】double; dual; twofold
【雙十節】the "Double Tenth", October 10
【雙殺】(baseball) double play
【雙手】the two hands; both hands
【雙手萬能】With two hands, one can work miracles.
【雙生】twin; twins
【雙雙對對】in pairs and couples
【雙人房】a double room; a twin room
【雙人牀】a double bed
【雙層】double layers; double decks
【雙宿雙飛】to live like man and wife; to sleep and move together
【雙氧水】hydrogen peroxide

雛 4313
ㄔㄨˊ chú

1. a chick 2. a very young bird —a fledgling 3. a small kid or toddler

【雛鳥】a very young bird—a fledgling
【雛妓】a very young prostitute
【雛形】a miniature form; a scaled-down model of anything

雜 4314
ㄗㄚˊ zá

1. to mix; to blend; mixed; blended 2. miscellaneous 3. motley; medley 4. petty and numerous

【雜牌】a less known and inferior brand
【雜費】miscellaneous expenses; sundry charges
【雜念】distracting thoughts
【雜糧】miscellaneous grain crops, as oat, millet, etc. (as opposed to rice and wheat which are staple foods)
【雜亂】confused and disorderly; to be jumbled
【雜亂無章】motley; disorderly
【雜貨】groceries; sundry goods
【雜貨店】a sundry store; a grocery
【雜燴】a dish of mixed food items
【雜記】a miscellany; miscellaneous

〔隹部〕

notes; random notes; jottings
【雜交】①(biology) to hybridize; to cross ②hybridization; cross-breed; a cross; interbreeding ③promiscuity
【雜七雜八】a motley; a jumble of various things; odds and ends
【雜質】impurities 「journal
【雜誌】a magazine; a periodical; a
【雜種】①a mixed breed; a hybrid ②(in ancient China) a foreign race or tribe ③a bastard; son of a bitch 「or variety show
【雜耍】juggler's feats; a vaudeville
【雜草】weeds 「iegated
【雜色】motley; parti-colored; var-
【雜音】noises; (recording) humming or other unwanted sounds
【雜務】chores; miscellaneous duties
【雜物】miscellaneous articles or objects; odds and ends
【雜文】essays

雞 4315
(鷄) ㄐㄧ jī
a chicken; a hen; a cock; a fowl
【雞皮疙瘩】goose pimples; goose flesh
【雞皮鶴髮】(said of the aged) with shriveled skin and hoary-headed
【雞毛撣子】a chicken-feather duster
【雞毛蒜皮】petty or trifling things
【雞鳴狗盜】small tricks; various kinds of talent or skill useful in
【雞蛋】a hen's egg 「emergency
【雞蛋碰石頭】like an egg hitting a rock—to attack someone much stronger than oneself
【雞蛋裏挑骨頭】to look for a flaw where there is none; to find fault on purpose; to nitpick
【雞蛋糕】sponge cake
【雞啼】the crowing of cocks
【雞腿】drumsticks; chicken's legs
【雞冠】the cockscomb
【雞口牛後】It's better to be the boss of a small group than the top lieutenant in a large organization. 「pandemonium
【雞犬不寧】great disturbance; a
【雞犬相聞】to live nearby or in the neighborhood
【雞犬升天】the rise of a powerful person's underlings
【雞肉】chicken (as food)
【雞尾酒】cocktail

十一畫

離 4316
ㄌㄧˊ lí
1. to leave; to depart; to separate; separation 2. to defy; to go against 3. distant from; apart from 4. to run into; to meet with 5. (said of light) bright
【離別】to say good-bye; to leave; to separate
【離譜】too far away from what is normal or acceptable
【離題】to depart from the topic
【離開】to separate from; to leave; to depart; to keep away from
【離婚】to divorce; a divorce
【離家】to leave home; to be away from home; to depart from home
【離間】to drive a wedge between; to alienate (allies, etc.); to sow discord 「thodox teachings
【離經叛道】to rebel against or-
【離境】to leave a country or place
【離奇】odd; fantastic; strange
【離棄】to abandon; to desert
【離去】to leave; to go away; to depart 「and live alone
【離羣索居】to leave one's friends
【離席】to leave or withdraw a dinner party, conference, etc.
【離鄉背井】to travel to a distant land; to stay far away from home
【離職】① to leave or resign from one's office ② to retire from one's office
【離愁】parting sorrow or grief; sadness at separation
【離散】separated and scattered; dispersed
【離異】to separate; to divorce

難 4317
1. ㄋㄢˊ nán
1. difficult; not easy; hard 2. unable; not in a position to 3. unpleasant; not good 「able
【難免】can hardly avoid; inescap-
【難分難捨】(said of a couple in love) very reluctant to separate
【難得】① rare; hard to get; hard to come by ② fortunate; lucky ③ rarely; seldom
【難倒】to confound; to daunt
【難道】Is it possible...? 或Do you

really mean to say...?
【難度】degree of difficulty; difficulty
【難懂】hard to understand
【難逃法網】It's hard to escape the dragnet of law. 或 Crime does not pay.
【難題】a hard nut to crack; a tough problem; a puzzle
【難聽】① unpleasant to hear; to grate on the ear ② offensive; coarse ③ scandalous
【難耐】unable to endure; unbearable
【難能可貴】rare and commendable
【難過】① to feel uneasy; to feel bad; to feel sorry ② hard to endure or bear; uncomfortable ③ difficult; hard
【難怪】① cannot hold responsible for ② no wonder that; it's understandable that
【難關】an impasse; an obstacle or obstruction difficult to overcome; a difficult situation; a crisis
【難堪】① to embarrass; embarrassment ② intolerable; unbearable
【難看】① bad-looking; not pleasant to the eye; ugly; offensive; repulsive ② embarrassing; awkward
【難解難分】①difficult to separate ②to be locked together (in a struggle)
【難講】hard to say; difficult to predict
【難吃】unbearable to palate; unpalatable; tasting bad
【難纏】hard to deal with
【難產】①(medicine) difficult labor; dystocia ②hard to come into being or materialize
【難處】①(ㄋㄢ ㄔㄨˇ)hard to get along with ②(ㄋㄢ ˙ㄔㄨ) difficult points; problems
【難事】a difficult task; something not easy to manage; a difficult matter
【難受】① to feel bad; to feel sorry ② unbearable; intolerable ③ to suffer pain; to feel unwell
【難說】① hard to say or predict ② difficult to speak out ③ not easy to express with words
【難色】an expression of reluctance
【難以】difficult; hard to
【難以相信】incredible; difficult to believe; hard to believe
【難以相處】hard to get along with
【難以形容】indescribable; beyond description
【難以爲繼】hard to carry on; difficult to continue
【難言之隱】secrets or problems one doesn't want to reveal
【難爲情】to feel ashamed, uneasy or embarrassed; bashful
【難忘】difficult to forget; unforgettable

難 4317
2. ㄋㄢˋ nàn

1. disaster; calamity; misfortune 2. to rebuke; to reprove; to reprimand 3. to discountenance
【難民】refugees
【難兄難弟】fellow sufferers

雨 部
ㄩˇ yǔ

雨 4318
ㄩˇ yǔ

rain; rainy: 雨天 a rainy day
【雨棚】a rainshed
【雨帽】a rain hat; a rain cap
【雨滴 or 雨點兒】raindrops
【雨量】(meteorology) the amount of rainfall or precipitation; rainfall
【雨露】favors and kindness; benevolence
【雨過天青】(literally) When the rain is over, the sky clears up. —When the incident (or confusion) is over, everything goes back to normal.
【雨後春筍】to mushroom like bamboo shoots after rain
【雨季】the rainy season; the monsoon
【雨具】things for wet weather
【雨鞋】rainshoes; galoshes
【雨水】① rain water ② one of 24 climatic periods in the solar calendar, which falls on February 19 or 20
【雨傘】an umbrella
【雨衣】a raincoat

三畫

雪 4319
1. ㄒㄩㄝˇ xuě

1. snow 2. to clean; to wash or wipe away
【雪片】① snowflakes ② to come in like an avalanche
【雪地冰天】a land of snow and ice
【雪堆】a snowbank; a snowdrift

【雪泥鴻爪】(literally) talon marks on the snow — traces of past events
【雪花】snowflakes
【雪茄】cigars
【雪景】a landscape of snow; a snow scene
【雪橇】a sled; a toboggan; a sledge
【雪球】a snowball
【雪中送炭】to give timely assistance; to send things which are in urgent need, as food for hungry refugees
【雪上加霜】disasters coming one after another in succession

〔雨部〕

4319
雪 2. ㄒㄩㄝˋ xuè
(又讀 ㄒㄩㄝˇ xuě)
1. snow-white; snowy 2. to avenge; to wipe out grievances
【雪白】snow-white; snowy
【雪亮】bright as snow; shiny
【雪恨】to avenge one's grudge; to avenge wrongs done to one
【雪恥】to wipe out a shame; to avenge an insult or humiliation

四畫

4320
雯 ㄨㄣˊ wén
the coloring on the clouds

4321
雲 ㄩㄣˊ yún
1. clouds 2. a cloud of; a large number of 3. short for Yunnan Province
【雲鬢】the hairdo of a beautiful woman—like floating clouds
【雲梯】a scaling ladder
【雲吞】Chinese ravioli
【雲南】Yunnan Province
【雲量】cloud cover; cloud amount; cloudiness
【雲開見日】(literally) When the clouds part, one sees the sun.—a turn of fortune for the better
【雲海】a sea of clouds
【雲集】to congregate; to gather; to flock together
【雲氣】thin, floating clouds
【雲雀】a skylark; a meadowlark
【雲霞】① clouds ② one who is unmoved by monetary gains or high positions; a person of high virtue
【雲霄】the sky—very high
【雲霄飛車】a roller coaster
【雲消霧散】(literally) clouds dissipating and fog melting away —The troubles are over.
【雲彩】clouds illuminated by the rising or setting sun
【雲層】layers of clouds
【雲遊】to travel without a destination; to wander about
【雲煙】clouds and smog
【雲霧】clouds and fog—obscure places
【雲雨】① grace and favor ② sexual intercourse; making love

五畫

4322
零 ㄌㄧㄥˊ líng
1. zero; nil; nought 2. a fraction; fractional; remainder 3. to flow down 4. a light rain; drizzle
【零賣】① retail sales ② to sell by the piece or in small quantities
【零分】① (grading examination papers) zero; no marks ② (sports) scoreless
【零丁孤苦】solitary; lonely
【零度】zero; nought degrees
【零頭】oddments
【零零碎碎】fragmented; piecemeal
【零落 or 零零落落】① desolate and scattered; dilapidated; run-down ② withered and fallen
【零亂】disorderly; in confusion; in-disorder
【零工】① odd jobs; short-term hired labor ②an odd-job man; a casual laborer
【零件】component parts; spare parts
【零錢】small change; petty cash; odd change
【零星】① fragmented; fractional; not as a whole ② scattered
【零食or零嘴】snacks; refreshments
【零售】retail sales; to sell by retail
【零售商】a retailer
【零散】scattered
【零碎】fragments; fragmentary; fractions
【零用】① (said of money) for everyday expenses of a nondescript nature ② pocket money
【零用錢】pocket money

4323
雷 ㄌㄟˊ léi
1. thunder 2. a mine (an explosive)
【雷鳴】① roars of thunder; thun-

derpeal ② very loud sounds; thunderous
【雷達】 a radar
【雷電】 lightning and thunder
【雷電交加】 It's thundering and lightening.
【雷霆萬鈞】 overwhelming or overpowering (power, strength, etc.)
【雷同】 similar; identical; exactly the same
【雷厲風行】 to enforce a law or rule with speed and great determination
【雷公】 the thunder god
【雷陣雨】 a thundershower
【雷射】 a laser
【雷射唱片】 a compact disc (CD)
【雷聲】 a thunderclap; thunder
【雷聲大，雨點小】 to talk a great deal about something with little or no follow-up action
【雷雨】 a thunderstorm

電 4324 ㄉㄧㄢˋ diàn

1. electricity; power 2. short for cable or telegram
【電波】 electric waves
【電報】 a cable; a telegram; a wire
【電表】 ① any meter for measuring electricity, such as an ammeter or a voltmeter ② a kilowatt-hour meter
【電冰箱】 a refrigerator; an ice box
【電費】 a power rate; a power bill
【電燈】 electric lights or lamps
【電燈泡】 ① an electric bulb ② (colloquial) an unwanted third party who accompanies a courting pair
【電鍍】 electroplate
【電動】 powered by electricity
【電動玩具】 ① a battery-powered toy ② a video game; a TV game; a computer game
【電臺】 a radio station
【電毯】 an electric blanket
【電燙】 to wave or curl hair by electricity
【電梯】 an electric lift; an elevator
【電筒】 a flashlight
【電腦】 a computer; an electronic computer
【電腦程式】 a computer program
【電鈕】 a button that controls electric currents
【電纜】 a cable (usually submarine)
【電力】 electric power
【電力公司】 a power company
【電流】 an electric current
【電聯車】 an electric multiple unit railcar
【電鈴】 an electric bell; a buzzer
【電爐】 an electric stove; a hot plate
【電路】 an electric circuit
【電鍋】 an electric rice cooker
【電光】 electric light; a flash of lightning
【電光石火】 anything that vanishes in a flash
【電工】 an electrician
【電賀】 to congratulate by cable
【電銲】 electric welding; electric soldering
【電話】 telephone; phone
【電話簿】 a telephone directory; a telephone book
【電話答錄機】 an answerphone
【電話亭】 a telephone booth
【電話號碼】 a telephone number
【電話機】 a telephone set
【電機】 electrical machinery
【電機系】 the department of electrical engineering in a college
【電擊】 an electric shock; struck by lightning
【電氣】 electric
【電氣用品or電器】 electric appliances
【電線】 electric wires
【電線走火】 a short circuit
【電信】 telecommunications
【電信局】 a telephone and telegraph office
【電池】 an electric battery; a dry cell
【電車】 a tramcar; a streetcar; a trolley car
【電廠】 a power plant
【電唱機】 a record player; an electric phonograph
【電視】 television; TV
【電視臺】 a television station
【電視機】 a TV set
【電視節目】 a TV program
【電視劇】 a teleplay
【電視遊樂器】 a video game
【電視影片】 a telefilm
【電扇 or 電風扇】 an electric fan
【電子】 an electron
【電子計算機】 an electronic computer
【電子琴】 an electronic organ
【電磁】 electromagnetism
【電磁爐】 an induction cooker
【電椅】 the electric chair
【電壓】 voltage
【電影】 movies; motion pictures

【電影明星】 a movie star
【電影院】 a movie theater; a cinema
【電源】 the source of electricity
【電熨斗】 an electric iron

〔雨部〕

六畫

需 4325 ㄒㄩ xū
1. to need; to require; to demand 2. expenses; provisions; needs; necessaries 3. hesitation; delay
【需求】 to need; to require; needs; demands or requirements
【需要】 to need or require; needs

七畫

震 4326 ㄓㄣˋ zhèn
1. to shake; to tremble, as an earthquake 2. to excite; to shock 3. terrified; scared 4. (now rarely) thunder; a thunderclap 5. the 4th of the Eight Diagrams
【震動】 ① to vibrate; to shake; to move ② to be shocked or shaken
【震怒】 greatly infuriated; wrath; rage
【震古鑠今】unprecedented; peerless
【震撼】 to shake; shaken
【震驚】 greatly surprised
【震懾】 to awe; to frighten
【震耳欲聾】 deafening; earsplitting

霄 4327 ㄒㄧㄠ xiāo
1. the sky 2. night 3. to exhaust; to dissolve 4. clouds or mist
【霄壤】 heaven and earth

霉 4328 ㄇㄟˊ méi
1. musty; moldy; mildewed 2. mildew; mold
【霉菌】 mold; mildew
【霉氣】 ① a moldy smell; musty ② bad luck or fortune

八畫

霍 4329 ㄏㄨㄛˋ huò
very rapidly; in a flash; suddenly
【霍亂】 cholera

霏 4330 ㄈㄟ fēi
the falling of snow and rain

霑 4331 ㄓㄢ zhān
1. soaked; to become wet or damp; to moisten 2. to receive (benefits, etc.)
【霑染】 ① to get affected by a communicable disease ② to gain a small advantage

霓 4332 ㄋㄧˊ ní
a rainbow; a colored cloud: 霓虹燈 the neon light

霖 4333 ㄌㄧㄣˊ lín
a copious rain falling continuously; a continuous heavy rain
【霖雨】 ① a pouring rain ② graces; favors; benevolence

九畫

霜 4334 ㄕㄨㄤ shuāng
1. frost; hoarfrost 2. white and powdery—like hoarfrost 3. coolness; indifference; grave 4. virtuous; pure and clean
【霜鬢】 hoary hair on the temples
【霜害】damage to farm crops caused by frost; frostbite; frost injury
【霜淇淋】 soft ice cream
【霜雪】① frost and snow ② snow-white

霞 4335 ㄒㄧㄚˊ xiá
colored, low-hanging clouds; rosy clouds
【霞光】rays of morning or evening sunlight

十一畫

霧 4336 ㄨˋ wù
fog; mist; vapor
【霧裏看花】 (literally) to look at flowers in a fog—failing eyesight of the aged
【霧氣】 fog or mist

十二畫

露 4337 1. ㄌㄨˋ lù
1. dew 2. uncovered; exposed; to show; to reveal; to betray 3. a cold, soothing and aromatic drink; beverages distilled from flowers, fruit or leaves

頁部
ㄧㄝˋ yè

頁 4373
ㄧㄝˋ yè 「(of paper, etc.)
a page (in books, etc.); a sheet
【頁碼 or 頁次】 the page number

二畫

頂 4374
ㄉㄧㄥˇ dǐng
1. the top of anything 2. the crown of the head 3. topmost; extremely; very 4. to carry (a weight) on one's head; to push the head against; to wear on the head 5. to gore; to butt 6. to push up; to prop up 7. to cope with; to stand up to 8. to substitute 9. to equal; to be equivalent to 10. to offend intentionally; to retort; to turn down 11. used as a unit 「pinnacle
【頂峰】 the peak; the summit; the
【頂點】 the pinnacle; the topmost
【頂多】 at (the) most; at best
【頂端】 the top; the peak; the apex
【頂頭上司】 the immediate boss
【頂替】 ① to assume someone's name with the intent to cheat ② to represent someone; to take someone's place 「domitable
【頂天立地】 independent and in-
【頂呱呱】 topmost; the top; the best; excellent; first-rate
【頂好】 the best; the first; the topmost; good; excellent; wonderful
【頂尖】 the peak; the highest point; the top; the best
【頂住】 to support with the head
【頂撞】 to talk back; to offend or dispute with words; to contradict
【頂嘴】 ① to quarrel ② to argue with a superior or an elder
【頂罪】 to act as a fall guy

頃 4375
ㄑㄧㄥˇ qǐng
1. a moment; an instant; just; just now 2. a hundred *mu* (畝) —10,000 square meters 3. to lean toward one side; to incline
【頃刻】 in a short moment

三畫

項 4376
ㄒㄧㄤˋ xiàng
1. the back of the neck; the nape 2. the back of a cap or crown 3. an item; an article; a matter; a kind; a class 4. funds; a sum of money 5. (mathematics) a term 「agreement, etc.)
【項目】 an item; an article (in an
【項鍊】 a necklace

順 4377
ㄕㄨㄣˋ shùn
1. to follow; to submit to; obedient 2. in the same direction as 3. agreeable; favorable; comfortable 4. to arrange; to put in order 5. convenient; smooth 6. to take the opportunity to
【順便】 at one's convenience; without taking extra trouble
【順風】 ① to move with the wind ② good luck ③a favorable wind; a tail wind
【順風轉舵】 to trim one's sails; to take one's cue from changing conditions
【順道】 ①to obey good reasons ② to do something on the way to a place, which requires no additional travel 「smooth
【順當】 without a hitch; easy and
【順理成章】 as a matter of course
【順利】 (going) smoothly; having no trouble; easy (going); encountering no difficulties 「way
【順路】 in passing; while on the
【順口】 ①to speak without much thought; to slip out of one's tongue ②easy to speak, read or sing ③to suit one's taste
【順口溜】 doggerel; a jingle
【順境】 in easy circumstances; in favorable circumstances
【順其自然】 to let nature take its course; in accordance with its natural tendency
【順心】 satisfactorily; gratifying
【順序】 according to right order
【順差】 favorable balance; surplus
【順暢】 smooth; unhindered
【順勢】 to take advantage of an opportunity (as provided by an opponent's reckless move)

【順手】① smooth (operation); easy (going) ② to do something without extra trouble ③ handy; conveniently

【順手牽羊】to steal something in passing; to pick up something on the sly

【順水推舟】to approve something that is sure to succeed

【順水人情】to do someone a favor without causing oneself any trouble

【順從】① to obey; obedient ② (psychology) submission

【順遂】without a hitch or obstruction; very smooth or easy going; in satisfactory circumstances

【順耳】pleasant to the ear

【順延】to postpone

【順眼】to please the eye; pleasant to the eye

【順應】to adjust

【順應潮流】to conform to modern trends

須 4378 ㄒㄩ xū

1. to have to; must; to need 2. necessary; proper 3. probably 4. a beard 5. a moment; a while 6. to wait for 7. to stop at 8. a Chinese family name

【須知】① to have to know; should know ② that which is essential to know—common knowledge; to note

【須臾】in an instant; a short while

四畫

頌 4379 ㄙㄨㄥˋ sòng

1. to praise; to acclaim; to extol; to eulogize; to laud 2. a hymn to something; a composition in praise of some achievements, etc.; an ode; a eulogy; a paean; an accolade 3. a section in *The Book of Poetry* (詩經)

【頌聲載道】praises all along the way—popular support

【頌揚】to praise; to acclaim; to eulogize

預 4380 (豫) ㄩˋ yù

1. beforehand; previously; in advance 2. to prepare; to make ready; reserve (funds, troops, etc.) 3. to take part in

【預備】to prepare; to get ready beforehand; preparatory

【預報】a forecast; an advance notice

【預謀】to scheme or plan beforehand

【預防】to prevent beforehand; to nip in the bud; to prepare against

【預定】① to reserve (seats, rooms, etc.) ② to set (a date, etc.); to be scheduled

【預料】to predict; to surmise; to anticipate; to expect

【預留】to put aside for later use; to keep something in reserve

【預告】to inform or notify beforehand; advance notice; to herald

【預感】① a premonition; a presentiment ② to have a premonition

【預計】to estimate; to surmise; estimates; to calculate in advance

【預期】to expect; to estimate; to anticipate

【預習】① (said of students) to prepare lessons before class ② to rehearse or drill; a rehearsal or drill

【預先】beforehand; in advance

【預支】to draw (salary) in advance

【預知】to know beforehand or in advance; a foreknowledge

【預兆】an omen; premonition; a presage; a sign; a harbinger

【預祝】to congratulate (victory or success) beforehand

【預測】to predict; to make a forecast

【預賽】a preliminary competition

【預算】an estimate; a budget; to calculate in advance

【預言】① prophecy; a prediction; a forecast ② to predict; to foretell

【預言家】a prophet; a fortuneteller

【預演】a preview; a rehearsal

【預約】a preliminary agreement; to make an appointment

頑 4381 ㄨㄢˊ wán

1. stupid; dull; ignorant 2. obstinate; stubborn 3. recalcitrant; unruly; defiant 4. to play 5. naughty or impish

【頑皮】naughty or impish (children)

【頑童】naughty or unruly children; an urchin

【頑劣】good-for-nothing; stubborn and stupid

【頑固】① stubborn; obstinate; headstrong ② ultraconservative

【頑抗】 to resist stubbornly; stubborn resistance
【頑強】 stubborn; obstinacy; tenacious
【頑石點頭】 (said of statements or teachings) so persuasive and moving that even the rocks nod in agreement

頒 4382 ㄅㄢ bān

1. to bestow on; to grant; to confer on 2. to proclaim; to make public; to promulgate 3. to distribute; to send out
【頒布】 to proclaim or promulgate
【頒發】 to bestow; to award or distribute (prizes, etc.)
【頒獎】 to hand out an award or prize

頓 4383 ㄉㄨㄣˋ dùn

1. to stop or halt; to pause 2. to kowtow 3. to stamp (the foot) 4. to arrange; to put in order 5. a time; a turn 6. immediately; promptly 7. to be tired; to fall apart 8. to be broken
【頓號】 a punctuation mark "、" indicating a very brief pause in reading
【頓首】 to make a ceremonious nod
【頓足】 to stamp one's foot
【頓挫】 ① to encounter failure; to receive a setback ② (said of musical notes) rising and falling
【頓悟】 to realize suddenly; to come to a sudden realization

五畫

領 4384 ㄌㄧㄥˇ lǐng

1. the neck 2. the collar; the neckband 3. a piece of clothing 4. to lead; to head; to guide 5. to receive; to get 6. to understand 7. (now rarely) to manage; to operate
【領班】 the leader of a team; a headman; a foreman
【領兵】 ① to lead troops ② a military officer
【領帶】 ① a necktie ② to lead
【領帶夾】 a tie clip
【領導】 ①to lead; leadership ②a guide
【領導有方】 to lead correctly; wise leadership
【領隊】 ①the leader of a group or team ②to lead a group
【領土 or 領地】 territory
【領路】 to lead the way
【領略】 to understand; to taste; to experience; to appreciate
【領口】 the collar of a garment; the neckband
【領款】 to receive funds; to draw money
【領空】 territorial air; an aerial domain
【領海】 territorial waters or seas
【領會】 to understand; to appreciate
【領結】 the loop of a necktie; a bow tie
【領教】 ① to be taught; to get instruction ②(a polite expression) to have received your reply
【領巾】 a scarf
【領獎】 to receive an award or prize
【領情】 to appreciate favors given; to feel grateful to somebody
【領取】 to get; to receive
【領袖】 a leader; the leading figure
【領先】 ①to lead; to walk ahead ② the lead; the first place or position
【領銜】 ①the first to sign in a list of signatures ②to be the first on a name list ③to play the lead in a film
【領薪水】 to receive pay; to get salary
【領事】 (diplomacy) a consul
【領受】 to receive
【領賞】 to receive a reward
【領子】 the collar or neck of a garment
【領罪】 to admit guilt; to plead guilty
【領養】 to adopt (a child)
【領悟】 to understand; to comprehend
【領域】 ①the territory of a nation ② a realm; a domain; a sphere; a field

頗 4385 ㄆㄛˇ pǒ

1. somewhat 2. quite; very; fairly; considerably; rather
【頗表同情】 rather sympathetic
【頗知一二】 (literally) to know it rather well
【頗爲滿意】 rather or much satisfied

七畫

頤 4386 ㄧˊ yí

1. the cheeks 2. to nourish; to

〔頁部〕

rear; to take care of oneself

【頤指氣使】to order about; to be extremely bossy

【頤養】to nourish; to keep fit; to take care of oneself; to recuperate

頭 4387 1. ㄊㄡˊ tóu

1. the head 2. the top; the first; first; the beginning 3. the chief; the boss; the leader; the head (of a group) 4. the two ends (of anything); a side; an aspect 5. a head (of cattle, etc.) 6. an auxiliary, as a suffix

【頭版】①the front page (of a newspaper) ②the first edition

【頭部 or 頭顱】the head

【頭破血流】with one's head broken and bleeding

【頭皮】the scalp

【頭皮屑】dandruff

【頭目】a chief; a leader; a ringleader; a chieftain

【頭髮】hair on the head

【頭等】first class; the best quality

【頭等艙】a first-class cabin

【頭頂】①the top of one's head ②to wear or support with one's head

【頭胎 or 頭生兒】the firstborn

【頭套】an actor's headgear

【頭頭是道】logically (arranged and narrated); systematically and orderly (stated)

【頭痛 or 頭疼】a headache

【頭痛醫頭，脚痛醫脚】to treat only where the pain is—not to find the source of a disease

【頭腦】①brains; mind ②main threads; clues ③the chief or boss

【頭腦不淸】muddle-headed; mixed-up

【頭路】①a clue; a main thread ②one's occupation; one's job ③access

【頭盔】a helmet

【頭號新聞 or 頭條新聞】the leading story in a paper; headline news

【頭昏】dizzy; giddy

【頭昏腦脹】to feel dizzy and have a headache

【頭昏眼花】dizzy

【頭家】the operator of a gambling joint

【頭巾】a turban; a kerchief

【頭獎】the first prize

【頭角】①a lead or clue ②looks of a promising youth; brilliance (of a young person); talent

【頭銜】the official title of a person

【頭緒】①(said of a complicated affair) leads or clues; main clues ②ways or means ③sequence; systematical

【頭重脚輕】top-heavy

【頭子】①the best; the winner ②the leader (of bandits, rebels, etc.)

【頭寸】cash; money supply

【頭一回】for the first time

【頭尾】head and tail—beginning and end

【頭暈】dizzy; giddy; dizziness

頭 4387 2. ·ㄊㄡ tou

1. a suffix indicating positions or directions 2. as a suffix to certain verbs to indicate the worthiness

頰 4388 ㄐㄧㄚˊ jiá

the cheeks

【頰骨】the cheekbone

頷 4389 ㄏㄢˋ hàn

1. the chin; the jaws 2. a slight nod of the head

【頷首】to nod the head—a sign of approval

【頷首之交】a nodding acquaintance

頸 4390 ㄐㄧㄥˇ jǐng

the neck; the throat

頹 4391 ㄊㄨㄟˊ tuí

1. to crumble; to collapse; disintegrated; ruined; dilapidated 2. weakened; withered; emaciated; declining; decadent 3. bald 4. to descend; to cascade down 5. a Chinese family name

【頹廢】①ruined; weakened; decadent ②low-spirited; depressed

【頹風】depraved or decadent customs; moral degeneracy

【頹勢】a declining tendency

【頹喪】beaten; ruined; discouraged

頻 4392 ㄆㄧㄣˊ pín

1. incessant; successive; continuous; frequently or repeatedly 2. urgent; precarious 3. same as 顰—to knit the brows 4. frequency

【頻頻】incessantly; repeatedly; continuously

【頻繁】frequent; incessant; busy

【頻道】(television) a channel
【頻年】years in a row; year after year
【頻率】frequency

八畫

顆 4393 ㄎㄜ kē
a drop or droplet; a grain; a pill; a numerary adjunct for (bombs, bullets, etc.): 顆粒 a grain; a drop; a bead

九畫

額 4394 ㄜˊ é
1. the forehead 2. a fixed number, amount, value, etc.; a quota 3. a horizontal tablet
【額頭】the forehead
【額角】the temples
【額手稱慶】to be overjoyed
【額外】extra
【額外收入】extra income

題 4395 ㄊㄧˊ tí
1. the forehead 2. a sign; a signal 3. a subject; the title of a composition or speech 4. commentaries; notes 5. to sign; to write; to inscribe 6. the end; the top 7. the ornamental woodwork under the eaves of public buildings
【題名】to name a work; to entitle
【題目】① the subject or title of a composition or speech; a theme or heading ② a question or problem
【題解】① explanatory notes on the title or background of a book ② keys to exercises or problems
【題詩】to write verses on something
【題字】to write on something; an inscription; an autograph
【題材】material constituting the main theme of an article, composition, etc.

顎 4396 ㄜˋ è
1. the jowl; jaws 2. high-cheekboned 3. reverence
【顎骨】the jawbones; maxillary bones

顏 4397 ㄧㄢˊ yán
1. face (physically); countenance; features 2. reputation 3. dyes; colors 4. a Chinese family name
【顏面】① honor ② countenance; face
【顏料】dyestuffs; pigments
【顏色】① color; hue; pigment ② countenance; facial expression ③ a lesson
【顏色自若】to be composed with the face unchanged

十畫

願 4398 ㄩㄢˋ yuàn
1. to be willing; to be desirous of; to hope; to wish 2. anything one wishes or desires; an ambition or aspiration 3. a vow 4. to think
【願天下有情人皆成眷屬】May all lovers unite in marriage!
【願意】① to be willing ② to like; to want ③ to approve of
【願望】one's wish or aspiration; what one's heart desires

顛 4399 ㄉㄧㄢ diān
1. the top; the highest spot; the head 2. to fall; to topple; to upset 3. to jolt; to bump 4. upside down 5. mad; lunatic
【顛簸】to shake; to joggle or jolt; to bump; to toss
【顛沛流離】suffering hardships and deprivations; to lead a vagrant life
【顛撲不破】irrefutable; absolutely right
【顛覆】to topple; to subvert
【顛倒】① upside down; to reverse ② mentally deranged; infatuated
【顛倒是非】to confuse justice and injustice; to distort truth; to twist facts
【顛三倒四】① in total disorder; all in confusion ② lunatic; insane

類 4400 ㄌㄟˋ lèi
1. a species; a kind; a class; a race; a group; a category 2. similar; alike 3. (now rarely) good; virtue 4. a kind of wildcat 5. (now rarely) biased; prejudiced
【類比】(logic) analogy
【類別】classification; categorization
【類推】to reason by analogy; to draw analogies

〔頁部〕

【類型】a type; a category
【類似】to resemble; similar to; like

十二畫

〔頁部〕

顧 4401 ㄍㄨˋ gù

1. to look at; to gaze 2. to turn the head around and look 3. to attend to; to mind; to care for; to concern oneself about; to regard; to look after 4. to visit; to call on 5. however; but; nevertheless 6. indeed; really

【顧不得】unable to take care of; to have to disregard
【顧盼生姿】to look around charmingly
【顧面子】①to care for one's face or reputation ②to value friendship; unwilling to embarrass others
【顧名思義】(literally) as a term suggests—self-explanatory
【顧念】①to care for; to be worried about ②to think of with affection
【顧慮】to show concern about; misgivings; concern; scruple
【顧客】customers; patrons; clients
【顧及】to care about; to attend to
【顧忌】misgivings; scruple; fear
【顧前不顧後】to act with no regard for the consequences
【顧全】to have consideration for and take care to preserve
【顧全大局】in the interest of the whole; for the sake of the country, organization, etc.
【顧主】a customer; a patron; a client; clientele
【顧左右而言他】to fudge a question
【顧此失彼】to take care of one thing and miss the other
【顧影自憐】self-glorification; narcissism; to look at one's shadow and lament one's lot
【顧問】an advisor; a consultant; a counsellor

十三畫

顫 4402 ㄔㄢˋ chàn (又讀 ㄓㄢˋ zhàn)

to tremble; to shake; to shiver; to quiver; to vibrate

【顫抖】to quiver; to shiver; to shake; to tremble
【顫動】to shake; to tremble

十四畫

顯 4403 ㄒㄧㄢˇ xiǎn

1. evident; manifest; clear 2. high-positioned; eminent; prominent 3. well-known; renowned; famed; reputed 4. to expose; to make known; to display; to show; to manifest 5. a prefix referring to one's forebears

【顯明】evident; clear; remarkable
【顯達】to attain high office; to achieve prominence in officialdom
【顯得】to look; to seem; to appear
【顯靈】omens, etc. given by the soul of a dead person; a divine manifestation
【顯露】to appear; to show; to unveil; to manifest
【顯露頭角】to show one's promise
【顯貴】bigwigs; eminent personages
【顯赫】outstanding; illustrious; renowned; powerful; mighty; prominent
【顯花植物】a flowering plant
【顯宦】a ranking or high official
【顯現】to appear; to reveal
【顯性基因】a dominant gene
【顯著】evident; clear; notable; eyecatching; marked; remarkable
【顯出】to appear; to show
【顯示】to indicate; to show; to reveal
【顯身手】to show one's talent or skill
【顯然】evident; clearly visible; obvious
【顯而易見】evidently; apparently
【顯要】bigwigs; notables; VIPs (very important persons)
【顯眼】conspicuous; striking; eyecatching
【顯揚】to cite; to commend; to praise
【顯微鏡】a microscope

十六畫

顱 4404 ㄌㄨˊ lú

1. the skull 2. the head 3. the forehead

【顱骨】the skull; the parietal bone

風部
ㄈㄥ fēng

風 4405
ㄈㄥ fēng

1. wind; a breeze; gust; a gale 2. education; influence 3. a fad; customs; practices; fashion; fashionable 4. a scene 5. a style; a manner; deportment; taste 6. fame; reputation 7. rumor 8. ailments supposedly caused by wind and dampness

【風波】disputes; quarrels; disturbances
【風暴】a storm; a windstorm
【風平浪靜】a calm and unruffled sea
【風馬牛不相及】things entirely not related; irrelevant
【風貌】①style and features ②a view; a scene
【風靡一時】to become a fad or vogue of the time; to become fashionable for a time
【風帆】a sailboat
【風範】①appearance; an air; a manner ②a model; a paragon
【風風雨雨】①storms ②rumors being rife; gossips going the rounds
【風度】a manner; poise; bearing
【風度翩翩】graceful bearing
【風頭】①a situation ②the way the wind blows ③popularity, distinction or prominence
【風調雨順】favorable weather (for raising crops); a timely wind and rain
【風土人情】local customs and practice
【風浪】①wind and waves at sea ②a storm
【風力】wind power; the force of the wind
【風流】①an elegant style; a refined taste ②to have a weakness for women
【風流事】a romance; a romantic episode
【風流倜儻】charming; casual and elegant bearing; dashing
【風涼】cool
【風涼話】irresponsible and satiric remarks
【風鈴】aeolian bells
【風格】a style
【風骨】①incorruptibility; moral fortitude ②the vigor of style
【風光】①scenery ②elegant style or taste ③glory; good reputation
【風和日麗】the bright sunshine and gentle breezes; warm and sunny weather
【風寒】a cold; flu; a chill
【風花雪月】all ingredients for a gay life; love affairs
【風華】elegance and talent; grace
【風華絕代】unsurpassed elegance and intellectual brilliance
【風化】①customs and cultural influence; decency ②(chemistry) efflorescence ③erosion by the elements
【風化區】a district of loose women
【風紀】discipline; general moral standards
【風景】scenery; a landscape
【風景畫】a landscape
【風景區】scenic spots
【風起雲湧】like rising winds and surging clouds—popular support; an enthusiastic response
【風氣】①customs; a general mood; common practices; traditions ②air; manner; bearing
【風琴】(a musical instrument) an organ
【風情】①romantic feelings ②flirtatious expressions ③fine taste; refined feelings
【風趣】interesting; funny; humorous; witty; wit
【風險】risk; danger
【風向】the direction of wind
【風行】to become fashionable
【風箏】a kite
【風燭殘年】old age; in the closing years of one's life
【風馳電掣】to whip along as fast as wind and lightning
【風車】①a windmill ②a kind of toy wheel which turns by the power of wind ③a winnower
【風潮】①directions of wind and tide ②disturbance; upheaval ③a storm
【風塵】①confusion of the world ②hardships of traveling around ③the world of prostitution
【風塵僕僕】dust-covered and tired from traveling; to be travel-worn and weary
【風塵女郎】a prostitute; a call girl
【風吹草動】disquiet; slight disturbance; slight commotion

【風濕】 rheumatism
【風沙】 a sandy wind; a sandstorm
【風扇】 ① a fan ② an electric fan
【風尚】 fashion; a custom; a vogue; a fad; taste of the time
【風聲】 news; rumor; information
【風聲鶴唳】 to sense danger everywhere
【風水】 fengshui—the direction and surroundings of a house or tomb, supposed to have an influence on the fortune of a family and their offsprings; a geomantic omen
【風霜】 ① wind and frost—hardships; suffering ② severe; severity ③ time-honored
【風姿】 looks; graceful bearing
【風餐露宿】 the hardships of traveling or fieldwork
【風騷】 ① seductive; coquettish ② refinement in literary works
【風俗】 customs; accepted practices
【風俗習慣】 customs and habits
【風速】 wind velocity (or speed)
【風衣】 a thin, usually waterproof, overcoat for warding off wind and rain
【風雅】 ① matters pertaining to writing of poems or other literary works; refinement ② graceful; tasteful
【風味】 ① the bearing and taste of a person ② elegance ③ the taste and style of food
【風聞】 rumored; according to unconfirmed reports; to get wind of
【風雨】 wind and rain; the elements —trials and hardships
【風雨同舟】 to be in the same boat
【風雨無阻】 to take place on schedule regardless of weather changes
【風月】 ① matters concerning love ② easy and random
【風雲】 ① wind and clouds ② unpredictable changes ③ imposing; high-positioned; high and exalted
【風雲變色】 drastic change of a political situation; catastrophic
【風雲人物】 a famed personage; a heroic figure; a man of the hour
【風韻】 charms; poise and bearing
【風韻猶存】 (said of a middle-aged woman) to look still attractive

五畫

颯 4406 ㄙㄚˋ sà
1. the sound of wind; rustling 2. weakened; failing; declining

颱 4407 ㄊㄞˊ tái
as in 颱風—a typhoon; a hurricane

六畫

颳 4408 ㄍㄨㄚ guā
wind blowing; to blow: 颳風 blowing wind

八畫

颶 4409 ㄐㄩˋ jù
as in 颶風—a hurricane; a gale; strong gusts at sea; a cyclone

十一畫

飄 4410 ㄆㄧㄠ piāo
1. to blow (in the air); to waft; to move with the wind 2. a cyclone; a whirling wind 3. to float; to drift
【飄泊】 to drift about—with no fixed lodging place
【飄飄欲仙】 light, airy, comfortable, and complacent
【飄蕩 or 漂蕩】 to drift along without fixed lodging; to float
【飄流】 ① to drift; to float ② to knock about; to wander aimlessly
【飄零】 ① (said of leaves and plants) falling and withering ② to drift about alone; wandering; homeless
【飄落】 to fall down slowly in the air
【飄忽】 ① to float in the air hither and thither ② to have no fixed address ③ light and speedy
【飄忽不定】 to drift from place to place
【飄雪】 snowflakes falling
【飄洒】 to float; to drift
【飄散】 dispersed and flying about
【飄逸】 elegant; high, stately and graceful
【飄搖】 ①to dance and toss about in the wind ②precarious; unsteady
【飄洋】 to take a sea voyage
【飄揚】 to be blown about in the wind; to flutter

十二畫

飆 4411
(颷) ㄅㄧㄠ biāo
violent winds; gales
【飆車】to speed a car or a motorcycle

飛 部
ㄈㄟ fēi

飛 4412
ㄈㄟ fēi
1. to fly; to flit 2. quickly; rapidly 3. high, as a bridge 4. to hang in the air; in the air
【飛奔】to run very fast; to fly
【飛盤】a Frisbee
【飛毛腿】a fast runner; fleet-footed
【飛刀】① to wield the knife ② a flying knife
【飛彈】①a stray bullet or shell ②a missile
【飛碟】a flying saucer; an unidentified flying object (UFO)
【飛騰】① to fly high (as one's fortune) ② to soar (as prices)
【飛來橫禍】sudden, unexpected calamity or misfortune
【飛快】① with lightning speed; at full speed; fast ② extremely sharp
【飛黃騰達】to make rapid advances in one's career
【飛機】an airplane; a plane
【飛機場】an airport; an airfield; an airdrome
【飛禽走獸】birds and beasts
【飛翔】to fly; to glide in the air; to hover in the air
【飛行】① to fly, as a plane ② flight; flying
【飛行員】the pilot of a plane
【飛漲】(said of prices) to soar rapidly; to skyrocket
【飛砂走石】sand and stones flying all about—a very strong wind
【飛昇】to ascend; to soar
【飛走】①birds and beasts ②to fly away
【飛蛾撲火】to flirt with death; to dig one's own grave
【飛簷走壁】to fly on eaves and walk on walls—acrobatic feats
【飛揚】to rise up and flutter, as a flag; to float in the air, as music; to fly about, as dust
【飛揚跋扈】unruly and haughty
【飛舞】①to dance in the wind ② to flutter
【飛吻】to throw someone a kiss
【飛躍】by leaps and bounds; advancing rapidly

食 部
ㄕˊ shí

食 4413
ㄕˊ shí
1. to eat 2. food; meal 3. livelihood; living 4. (an old usage) salary; pay 5. same as 蝕—eclipse
【食不知味】to eat food but without knowing its taste—deep anxiety, grief, etc.
【食品】foods; food items; foodstuffs
【食品防腐劑】food disinfectant
【食品店】a store for selling food items; a food store; a confectionary
【食譜】a cookbook; a collection of recipes
【食道】①the ways of eating; table manners ②the route for transporting foodstuffs ③the gullet; the esophagus
【食堂】a mess hall; the restaurant
【食糧】foodstuffs; food grain; provisions
【食量】the quantity of food one consumes; appetite
【食古不化】to read a lot of classics without digestion; to be pedantic
【食客】dependent advisors under a leader in ancient times, especially during the Epoch of Warring States
【食具】a table service (such as bowls, etc.)
【食指浩繁】many mouths to feed
【食宿】board and lodging; bed and board
【食鹽】kitchen salt; table salt
【食言而肥】to grow fat by eating one's words—to break a promise
【食物】eatables; provisions; foodstuffs
【食物鏈】a food chain
【食物過敏】food allergy
【食物中毒】food poisoning
【食慾】appetite
【食慾不振】a poor appetite; lack of appetite
【食用】① edible ② living expenses

〔食部〕

二畫

飢 4414 ㄐㄧ jī
hungry; hunger; starving; famine
【飢不擇食】When one is hungry, one is not particular about what he is going to eat.
【飢民】starved people; famished people
【飢渴】hungry and thirsty
【飢寒交迫】to suffer from hunger and cold
【飢荒or飢饉】famine
【飢腸轆轆】to feel very hungry
【飢餓】hunger; hungry; starvation

四畫

飩 4415 ㄊㄨㄣˊ tún
as in 餛飩—stuffed dumplings

飪 4416 (餁) ㄖㄣˋ rèn
to cook

飭 4417 ㄔˋ chì
1. severe 2. reverent; respectful; careful 3. to manage; to make ready; to keep in order 4. to order; to instruct or direct
【飭令】to order; to instruct or direct

飲 4418 1. ㄧㄣˇ yǐn
1. to drink 2. drinks 3. to swallow (insult, anger, etc.) 4. to be hit (by a bullet, an arrow, etc.)
【飲料】beverages; drinks
【飲恨】① to swallow grievances ② to be defeated in a competition
【飲酒】to drink wine or liquor
【飲泣】to weep in deep sorrow
【飲茶】①(in Kwang-tung) to drink tea along with refreshments ②to drink tea
【飲食】① to drink and eat ② drink and food
【飲食店】a small restaurant; an eatery
【飲食衛生】dietetic hygiene
【飲水】① drinking water ② to drink water
【飲水機】a drinking fountain; a water fountain
【飲水思源】grateful for favors received; not to forget one's origin

飲 4418 2. ㄧㄣˋ yìn
to make animals drink: 飲馬to water a horse

飯 4419 ㄈㄢˋ fàn
1. cooked rice; cooked grain for food 2. a meal 3. to feed 4. a profession; a means of living
【飯票】① a food coupon ②(slang) a husband
【飯店】① a restaurant ② a hotel
【飯廳】a dining room; a mess hall
【飯桶】① a tub for storing cooked rice ② a good-for-nothing; a stupid or clumsy fellow
【飯來張口】to live an easy life, with everything provided
【飯量】an appetite; capacity for eating
【飯鍋】a pot for cooking rice
【飯盒】a lunch box; a rice container
【飯局】a luncheon or dinner party
【飯前酒】aperitif
【飯桌】a dining table
【飯菜】① dishes to go with rice ② a meal; a repast; food
【飯碗】① a rice bowl ②(slang) one's job

五畫

飼 4420 ㄙˋ sì
to feed; to raise (domesticated animals)
【飼料】animal feed; fodder; forage
【飼養】to raise; to breed

飽 4421 ㄅㄠˇ bǎo
1. to eat to the full; surfeited 2. satisfied 3. full; plump 4. fully; to the full
【飽滿】well-stacked (figures, etc.); full; plump
【飽和】saturation; saturated
【飽經風霜】to have experienced the hardships of life
【飽經世故】well-experienced in the ways of the world
【飽學之士】a learned scholar; an erudite person
【飽食終日】well-fed all day (without doing anything worthwhile)
【飽受】to suffer (insult, grievances, etc.) to the fullest extent
【飽入私囊】to embezzle public funds

飾 4422 ㄕˋ shì

1. to ornament; to decorate; to polish (writing) 2. ornamentation; decorations 3. to excuse oneself on a pretext, etc.; to fake 4. clothing and dresses 5. to whitewash; to deceive; to cover up 6. to play the role of; to act the part of

【飾非 or 飾過】to hide and gloss over one's faults or mistakes

【飾物】adornments; decorations

六畫

餃 4423
ㄐㄧㄠˇ jiǎo
stuffed dumplings; ravioli

餉 4424
ㄒㄧㄤˇ xiǎng
1. pay, provisions, rations, etc. for the military or the police 2. to entertain with food; to feast; to present food as a gift

養 4425
1. ㄧㄤˇ yǎng
1. to grow; to raise; to breed; to rear; to bring up 2. to support or keep (a family, etc.) 3. to give birth to 4. to nourish; to cultivate (one's mind, etc.) 5. to educate 6. to nurse (a wound or illness) 7. oxygen 亦作「氧」

【養兵】to maintain and train soldiers (in preparation for war)

【養兵千日, 用在一朝】(literally) to maintain an army for a thousand days to use it for a moment

【養病】①to convalesce; to recuperate ②convalescence; recuperation

【養母】a foster mother

【養分】the amount of nutritious substance in a given food item; nutrition

【養父】a foster father

【養女】an adopted daughter; a foster daughter

【養老】①(said of persons) to retire and enjoy the fruit of one's work in the past ②to provide for the aged

【養老金】an old age pension

【養老院】a home for destitute old people

【養料】nutrition; nutritious value

【養虎遺患】To keep a tiger is to invite calamity.—Appeasement brings disaster.

【養活】① to support or keep (a family or somebody) ②to rear; to bring up

【養家or養家活口】to support one's family

【養精蓄銳】to nourish and discipline one's stamina; to nurse one's strength (in preparation for a challenging task ahead)

【養殖】to breed (aquatics)

【養成】to discipline and train; to cultivate (good habits, etc.)

【養神】to have mental relaxation; to give one's mental faculty a rest

【養傷】to nurse one's injuries or wounds

【養生】to preserve one's health; to keep in good condition

【養生之道】a regimen; the formula of healthy living

【養生送死】to support one's parents when they are alive and to look after their funeral arrangement upon their death (which is the duty of a son)

【養子】①a foster or an adopted son ②to bring up children

【養尊處優】to live in luxury (or clover)

【養兒防老】to raise sons as insurance against the insecurity of old age

【養育】to rear; to raise and educate

養 4425
2. ㄧㄤˋ yàng
to support one's parents

餌 4426
ㄦˇ ěr
1. to bait; to entice; bait 2. cakes 3. food 4. to eat

餅 4427
(餠) ㄅㄧㄥˇ bǐng
1. cakes; biscuits; pastry 2. anything round and flat, as a disc

七畫

餐 4428
(湌) ㄘㄢ cān
1. a meal 2. to eat 3. food

【餐風宿露】hardships of traveling in old times

【餐廳】a restaurant; a dining hall; a mess hall

【餐巾】a napkin

【餐具】a dinner set; tableware; a dinnerservice

【餐券】a meal coupon; a meal ticket

〔食部〕

【餐車】a diner; a dining car
【餐飲業】restaurants, bars, coffee houses and tearooms

餒 4429
ㄋㄟˇ něi
1. to starve; hungry 2. decay or decomposition of fish 3. lacking in confidence, courage, etc.; disheartened; dispirited

餓 4430
ㄜˋ è
1. hungry; hunger 2. greedy; covetous 3. to starve
【餓鬼】① a person who is always hungry ② a person who eats piggishly
【餓壞了】to be starving
【餓死】to be starved to death

餘 4431
ㄩˊ yú
1. remaining; the remnant or remainder; the rest 2. a surplus; an overplus; an excess 3. a balance 4. a complement of a number or figure; odd 5. after
【餘波蕩漾】The effect (of a major event) is still being felt.
【餘黨】remnants of an outlawed faction or disbanded gang
【餘地】a spare space; an alternative; elbowroom; leeway
【餘孽】remnants of rebel groups, secret societies, etc.
【餘年】the remaining years of one's life
【餘力】strength or energy to spare
【餘糧】surplus grain
【餘款】remaining funds; a favorable balance; surplus funds
【餘暉 or 餘輝】twilight at sunset
【餘悸】a lingering shock or fear
【餘暇】spare time; leisure
【餘興】① an entertainment program arranged for a gathering ② a lingering interest
【餘震】aftershocks in the wake of a strong earthguake
【餘生】① the remaining years of one's life; old age ② a survival (after a disaster)
【餘數】① the balance ② (mathematics) the complement of a number ③ the residue; the remainder
【餘額】① a surplus amount; a balance ② vacancies to be filled
【餘音繞樑】The thrilling voice keeps reverberating in the air after the vocalist has stopped singing.
【餘威】the influence or power of someone that remains after his death
【餘味】pleasant memories; an aftertaste

八畫

餚 4432
ㄧㄠˊ yáo
dishes and foods

餛 4433
ㄏㄨㄣˊ hún
as in 餛飩—stuffed dumplings with delicate flour wrapping; ravioli

餞 4434
ㄐㄧㄢˋ jiàn
1. a farewell dinner or luncheon 2. to send off; to convoy 3. to present as a gift 4. preserves; jam
【餞別or餞行】to entertain a parting friend with a feast

餡 4435
ㄒㄧㄢˋ xiàn
anything serving as stuffing for dumplings, etc.
【餡兒】stuffing

館 4436
(舘) ㄍㄨㄢˇ guǎn
1. a house; a guesthouse; a hotel 2. to stay or lodge 3. an official residence 4. an embassy; a legation; a consulate 5. a place for cultural activities 6. premises 7. a school (in former times) 8. a suffix for a library, teahouse, restaurant, etc.
【館長】a superintendent; a curator; the head of a library or an institute, etc.
【館子】① a restaurant ② a theater

九畫

餬 4437
ㄏㄨˊ hú
1. congee; porridge; gruel 2. paste
【餬口】just to make ends meet; to make a bare living

餵 4438
(餧) ㄨㄟˋ wèi
to feed; to raise
【餵奶】to feed a baby with milk; to breast-feed
【餵養】to raise; to rear; to keep

十畫

饅 4439 ㄙㄡ sōu

1. decayed; rotten; stale 2. foul; lousy

【餿主意】a lousy idea

餾 4440 ㄌㄧㄡˋ liù

1. to steam 2. distilled (water)

十一畫

饅 4441 ㄇㄢˊ mán

steamed buns; steamed bread; stuffed or unstuffed dumplings

【饅頭】steamed dumplings

饉 4442 ㄐㄧㄣˇ jǐn

as in 饑饉—famine; hunger

十二畫

饋 4443 (餽) ㄎㄨㄟˋ kuì

1. to offer food to a superior 2. to send someone a present; to present as a gift

【饋贈】to present (a gift); to make a present of something

饌 4444 ㄓㄨㄢˋ zhuàn

1. to prepare food 2. food and drink; dainties 3. to eat and drink

【饌具】food vessels

饑 4445 ㄐㄧ jī

1. a year of famine 2. hunger; hungry

【饑寒交迫】to suffer from both the cold and hunger

【饑饉 or 饑荒】starvation; famine

饒 4446 ㄖㄠˊ ráo

1. abundant; plentiful; full of; fertile 2. to give something extra as a gift; to let somebody have something into the bargain 3. to forgive; to spare; to have mercy; to let somebody off 4. lenient; liberal 5. (now rarely) even though; in spite of the fact that; whatever

【饒富】abundant; plentiful

【饒命】to spare a life

【饒舌】loquacious; talkative; garrulous

【饒恕】to forgive; to pardon

十三畫

饗 4447 ㄒㄧㄤˇ xiǎng

1. to dine and wine guests; to give a big party or a banquet 2. a sacrificial ceremony

【饗宴】a feast

饔 4448 ㄩㄥ yōng

1. cooked food 2. breakfast 3. slaughtered animals

【饔飧不繼】discontinuation of supper after breakfast — poverty-stricken

饕 4449 ㄊㄠ tāo

1. name of a legendary ferocious animal 2. a fierce person 3. a greedy and gluttonous person

【饕餮】gluttons; greedy persons

十四畫

饜 4450 ㄧㄢˋ yàn

1. full-stomached; sufficient; surfeited; satiated 2. to partake plentifully of

【饜足】surfeited; satiated

十七畫

饞 4451 ㄔㄢˊ chán

piggish; gluttonous; greedy

【饞涎欲滴】(said of mouth) to water; to drool over; to covet

【饞嘴】gluttonous

首 部 ㄕㄡˇ shou

首 4452 ㄕㄡˇ shǒu

1. the head 2. the king; the emperor; the chief; the leader 3. the first; the beginning 4. a (poem, song, etc.)

【首府】the capital city

【首當其衝】the first to bear the brunt of

【首都】the (national) capital

〔香・馬部〕

【首推】 to consider (a person) first
【首腦(人物)】 the chief; the boss; the key member; the mastermind
【首領】 ① the leader; the chief ② head and neck
【首肯】 to nod one's head in approval; to approve
【首揆 or 首相】 the prime minister; the premier
【首級】 the human head
【首屆】 the first (conference, assembly, etc.)
【首屈一指】 the foremost; second to none; the best
【首席】 the highest-ranking or highestpositioned; the senior
【首先】 the very first; at first; first of all
【首長】 the chief; the leading cadre
【首創】 to found; to start; to initiate
【首飾】 jewelry; ornaments; trinkets
【首任】 the first to be appointed to an office
【首如飛蓬】 disheveled hair
【首次】 the first time
【首要】 of the first importance; first of all; chief
【首要條件】 a prerequisite; the number one condition
【首映】 the premiere (of a movie)
【首尾】 ① the head and the tail; the beginning and the end ② from beginning to end
【首尾相應】 head and tail (or beginning and end) corresponding with each other
【首位】 ①the place of honor ②the first place

香部
ㄒㄧㄤ xiāng

香 4453 ㄒㄧㄤ xiāng
1. sweet-smelling; fragrant; aromatic; balmy 2. tasty; delicious 3. fair; beautiful 4. spice; balm; incense
【香檳 or 香賓】 champagne
【香噴噴的】 smelling very good; sweet-smelling
【香片】 jasmine tea
【香袋 or 香囊】 a sachet
【香甜】 ① sweet; delicious ② (to sleep) soundly
【香料】 spice; balm
【香爐】 a thurible; a censer
【香港】 Hong Kong, or Hongkong
【香港脚】 athlete's foot
【香菇】 a kind of edible mushroom grown on wooden logs
【香瓜】 a muskmelon; a cantaloupe
【香閨】 a lady's chamber
【香客】 visitors to temples; pilgrims
【香花】 fragrant flowers
【香火】 ①incense burned and candles lighted in honor of a deity, an ancestor, etc. ②an oath; a vow
【香灰】 ashes of incense
【香蕉】 a banana
【香蕉油】 banana oil
【香精】 essence
【香氣】 a sweet smell; a pleasant odor; fragrance
【香消玉殞】 (literally) The fragrance is gone and the jade is fallen.—The beauty is dead.
【香燭】 incense and candles—materials for the altar
【香腸】 sausage
【香水】 perfume; scent
【香肉】 (euphemism) dog meat
【香皂】 perfumed soap; toilet soap
【香草】 ① vanilla ② a fragrant herb
【香油】 ① perfumed oil; aromatic oil ② sesame oil
【香煙】 ① cigarettes ② continuity of the family line ③ smoke of burning incense
【香味】 spicy taste; aromatic flavor

九畫

馥 4454 ㄈㄨˋ fù
fragrance; aroma: 馥郁 powerfully fragrant

十一畫

馨 4455 ㄒㄧㄣ xīn
(又讀 ㄒㄧㄥ xīng)
fragrance or aroma (especially that which comes from afar)

馬部
ㄇㄚˇ mǎ

馬 4456 ㄇㄚˇ mǎ

a horse: 馬匹 horses; horseflesh
【馬背】horseback
【馬錶】a pocket watch; a stop-watch
【馬鞭子】a horsewhip
【馬不停蹄】to do something without stop or a single halt
【馬棚 or 馬房 or 馬廐】a stable
【馬屁精】a flatterer; a toady
【馬馬虎虎or馬虎】① careless; perfunctory; sloppy; slovenly ② not very good; so-so
【馬夫】a groom
【馬達】a motor
【馬到成功】to be accomplished quickly and easily; with immediate success
【馬蹄】① hoofs of a horse ② a horseshoe
【馬蹄形】the shape of a hoof; U-shaped
【馬桶】a chamber pot; a close-stool
【馬拉松】① marathon ② Marathon
【馬來西亞】Malaysia; Malaysian
【馬力】horsepower
【馬鈴薯】a potato
【馬路】a street; a highway; a road
【馬路如虎口】The street is as dangerous as a tiger.— Beware of traffic accidents.
【馬褂】the ceremonial jacket of a mandarin
【馬克】a Deutsche mark; an ostmark
【馬後砲】①belated action ②I-told-you-so remarks
【馬球】polo
【馬戲】a circus show; a circus
【馬戲團】a circus troupe; a circus
【馬靴】jackboots; riding boots
【馬齒徒增】having accomplished nothing despite one's advanced age
【馬車】a carriage; a coach; a landau
【馬首是瞻】to follow someone; to look on someone as an example
【馬上】① on horseback ② right away; at once; immediately; without delay
【馬術】horsemanship
【馬祖】the Matsu Islands
【馬鞍子】a saddle
【馬爾地夫】the Maldive Islands

二畫

馭 4457 ㄩˋ yù
1.to drive 2.to govern; to rule; to control 3. a driver

馮 4458 ㄈㄥˊ féng
a Chinese family name
【馮婦】as in 重作馮婦—a role one has played before

三畫

馱 4459 ㄊㄨㄛˊ tuó
to carry (a load) on the back
【馱畜】a pack animal

馳 4460 ㄔˊ chí
1. to go swiftly; to fleet; to rush; to speed 2. to exert; to exercise 3. to spread; to propagate
【馳名】① to spread one's fame ② renowned
【馳名中外】renowned at home and abroad
【馳騁】① to rush about on horseback ② to play an active part in

馴 4461 ㄒㄩㄣˊ xún
(又讀 ㄒㄩㄣˋ xùn)
1. tame 2. mild; well-bred; obedient; docile 3. gradual 4. to tame; to put under control; to break (an animal)
【馴服】to tame; to subdue; to break in; subdued; obedient
【馴良】docile; obedient; tractable; gentle
【馴鹿】a reindeer
【馴和or馴善】gentle; mild; good-natured
【馴養】to raise (animals); to domesticate (animals); to tame

四畫

駁 4462 ㄅㄛˊ bó
1. variegated; parti-colored 2. mixed; impure; jumbled 3. to rebut; to dispute; to refute; to disprove 4. to transport; to ship; to load and unload
【駁倒】to defeat in a debate
【駁回】to reject; to turn down; to overrule (an appeal, request, etc.)
【駁斥】①to refute; to rebut; to disprove ②to reject (an appeal)
【駁雜】mixed; impure
【駁色】variegated; parti-colored

〔馬部〕

五畫

駐 4463 ㄓㄨˋ zhù

1. to halt 2. to remain temporarily; to station (troops, diplomatic representatives, etc.)

【駐兵】to station troops
【駐防】to garrison (a place)
【駐軍】①to station troops ②an occupation force ③a garrison; garrison troops
【駐紮 or 駐屯】(said of troops) to be stationed at
【駐守】to station troops at a place for defense purpose
【駐顏】to preserve a youthful complexion
【駐顏有術】to possess the secret of preserving a youthful complexion

駑 4464 ㄋㄨˊ nú

1. an old, worn-out horse; a jade; a hack 2. incompetent; stupid; good-for-nothing

【駑馬】a hack; a jade; an old, worn-out horse
【駑鈍】incompetent; incapable

駒 4465 ㄐㄩ jū

1. a young and fleet-footed horse; a foal; a colt 2. (figuratively) the sun

駕 4466 ㄐㄧㄚˋ jià

1. to ride; to drive; to pilot 2. to excel; to surpass 3. to yoke; to put the horses to the carriage 4. vehicles 5. an honorific epithet 6. to control; to reign or rule 7. the emperor

【駕崩】(said of the emperor) to pass away
【駕臨】to give (our humble place) the honor of your visit
【駕機】to pilot a plane
【駕輕就熟】to do a task with ease
【駕駛】①to drive (automobiles); to pilot (aircraft); to steer (boats) ②a driver
【駕駛執照】a driver's license
【駕駛員】a driver; a pilot
【駕馭】①to drive (horse-drawn vehicles) ②to control; to tame

駙 4467 ㄈㄨˋ fù

1. extra horses harnessed by the side of the team 2. swift

【駙馬】① an ancient official title ② imperial son-in-law

駛 4468 ㄕˇ shǐ

1. (said of vehicles) to run; (said of vessels) to sail 2. fast; fleeting

駝 4469 ㄊㄨㄛˊ tuó

1. a camel 2. hunchbacked 3. to carry on the back 4. to pay

【駝背】hunchbacked; humpbacked
【駝鳥】an ostrich

駟 4470 ㄙˋ sì

1. a team of four horses 2. horses 3. four 4. name of a star

【駟馬難追】Even with a team of four horses, it is difficult to overtake carelessly uttered words.

六畫

駭 4471 ㄏㄞˋ hài

1. to terrify; to frighten; to startle; to scare; to amaze; to surprise 2. to marvel; to wonder

【駭怕】scared; frightened
【駭人聽聞】(said of crimes, atrocities, etc.) frightening; bloodcurdling; shocking (news)

駱 4472 ㄌㄨㄛˋ luò

1. a white horse (or steed) with black mane 2. a camel

【駱駝隊】a camel train; a caravan of camels

七畫

騁 4473 ㄔㄥˇ chěng

1. to go swiftly; to speed 2. to exert; to unfold; to develop 3. to give free play to; to lend wings to

【騁目】to look as far as the eyes can see
【騁能】to give full display to one's abilities

駿 4474 ㄐㄩㄣˋ jùn

1. a fine horse; a swift horse 2. great; large 3. swift; speedy 4. rigorous; stringent 亦作「峻」 5. outstanding

【駿馬】a fine horse
【駿逸】distinguished; outstanding

八畫

4475
騎 ㄑㄧˊ qí
(名詞讀音 ㄐㄧˋ jì)
to ride (a horse, etc.); to sit astride on
【騎兵】cavalry; mounted troops
【騎馬找馬】to hold a temporary position while seeking a better job
【騎樓】an arcade (a covered avenue)
【騎虎難下】in a position from which there is no easy retreat; unable to stop or quit
【騎師】a jockey
【騎士】①a knight ②a horseback rider
【騎術】equitation; horsemanship

4476
駢 (駢) ㄆㄧㄢˊ pián
1. a pair of horses 2. to stand, lie, or go side by side
【駢體文】a euphuistically antithetic style of writing
【駢肩】shoulders by shoulders—crowded

九畫

4477
騖 ㄨˋ wù
1. to rush; to speed 2. unrestrained; uninhibited
【騖遠】impractically ambitious; overambitious

4478
騙 ㄆㄧㄢˋ piàn
1. to cheat; to defraud; to swindle; to deceive 2. to get by fraud
【騙局】a fraud; a swindle; a trick; a chicanery; a deception; a hoax
【騙取】to obtain by fraud; to cheat
【騙術】a trick; a ruse; a stratagem
【騙子】a swindler; a cheat; a confidence man; a racketeer; an impostor

十畫

4479
騰 ㄊㄥˊ téng
1. to prance; to rear; to leap; to jump 2. to go up; to rise; to fly; to soar 3. to turn over; to surrender; to transfer
【騰達】to prosper; to thrive
【騰空】to fly in the sky; to soar
【騰雲駕霧】①to sail clouds and ride mist (as immortals do) ② fast; quick

4480
騷 ㄙㄠ sāo
1. to disturb; to agitate 2. to worry; to feel concerned 3. ill-smelling; stinking 4. (colloquial) amorous; erotic
【騷動】disturbance; upheaval; unrest
【騷亂】disturbance; tumult; agitation
【騷客 or 騷人墨客】a poet; a bard
【騷擾】to disturb; to harass; to agitate

十一畫

4481
騾 ㄌㄨㄛˊ luó
a mule
【騾子】① a mule ② a stubborn person

4482
驀 ㄇㄛˋ mò
1. sudden; abrupt 2. to mount the horse
【驀地or驀然】suddenly; all of a sudden

4483
驃 ㄆㄧㄠˋ piào
1. a horse with a yellowish white color 2. valiant 3. galloping
【驃騎】an ancient title of general rank

4484
驅 ㄑㄩ qū
1. to go before others 2. to drive; to urge 3. to expel 4. to command
【驅迫】to force; to be driven; to compel
【驅遣】① to send away (a person so as to get rid of him) ② to order (a person) about
【驅邪】to expel evil; to keep evil spirits away
【驅逐 or 驅除】to drive out; to get rid of; to expel; to eliminate
【驅使】to order (a person) about
【驅策】① to urge; to spur ② to order (a person) about
【驅散】to disperse by force; to scatter; to dispel

十二畫

4485
驕 ㄐㄧㄠ jiāo
1. untamed; intractable; disobedient 2. proud; haughty; arrogant;

overbearing 3. severe; harsh; intense
【驕態】proud bearing; haughty manner; an overbearing attitude
【驕誇】to boast; to brag
【驕矜】puffed up; conceited; self-important; proud; haughty
【驕氣】overbearing airs; arrogance
【驕者必敗】Pride goes before a fall.
【驕奢淫佚】pride, luxury, dissolute and self-indulgence
【驕縱】disregardful of all authority; proud and unruly
【驕傲】proud; haughty; disdainful
【驕陽】the intense sunshine; the hot sunshine

(馬部)

驍 4486
ㄒㄧㄠ xiāo
1. having courage and agility; brave; valiant 2. a fine horse
【驍雄】capable and ambitious

十三畫

驗 4487
(騐) ㄧㄢˋ yàn
1. to test; to examine; to analyze 2. to produce an effect 3. to verify; to prove
【驗明】to ascertain by a test or examination
【驗明正身】to make a positive identification of a criminal before execution
【驗尿】a urine test; a urinalysis
【驗光】optometry
【驗血】a blood test
【驗證】to test and verify
【驗屍】a postmortem examination; an autopsy
【驗收】to accept (goods, buildings, etc.) after ascertaining that the quality or quantity meets requirements
【驗傷】to examine an injury by competent authorities of law
【驗算】to check computations

驚 4488
ㄐㄧㄥ jīng
1. to startle; to surprise; to amaze; to astound; to alarm; to flabbergast; to dumbfound; to terrify; to frighten 2. afraid; frightened; scared; fearful; terrified 3. to marvel; to be surprised; to be amazed
【驚怕or驚恐or驚懼】scared; fearful; afraid
【驚動】① to astonish; to startle; to stir up; to alarm ② to bother; to disturb
【驚濤駭浪】(said of the sea) churning; furious; choppy; mountainous waves
【驚歎】to marvel; to exclaim
【驚歎號】an exclamation mark; an exclamation point
【驚天地，泣鬼神】to startle the universe and move the gods
【驚天動地】to startle even the universe; world-shaking; earthshaking
【驚弓之鳥】a person seized with fear because of some frightening experience encountered in the past
【驚駭】frightened; terrified
【驚魂未定】not yet become calm or normal from a fright
【驚慌】to lose one's head from terror; to be frightened and confused
【驚惶失措】to lose one's head from fear; terrified and not knowing what to do; to panic
【驚鴻一瞥】to have a fleeting glimpse of a beauty
【驚悸】quickened heartbeat due to fear
【驚叫】to cry in fear; to scream
【驚懼】scared; afraid; fearful
【驚奇】to be surprised; to marvel
【驚喜】pleasantly surprised
【驚嚇】to frighten; to scare; to alarm suddenly
【驚險】breathtaking; alarmingly dangerous; thrilling
【驚心動魄】heart-shaking; horrified; soul-stirring
【驚醒】to cause to wake up with a startle
【驚世駭俗】to astound the world with an extraordinary idea, etc.
【驚擾】to disturb
【驚人】surprising; astounding; astonishing; startling; amazing; sensational
【驚愕】to be astonished
【驚異or驚訝or驚奇】to marvel; to be surprised; to be amazed

驛 4489
ㄧˋ yì
a station where couriers rested in former times; a courier station
【驛馬車】a stagecoach
【驛站】a courier station

十四畫

驟 4490
ㄗㄡˋ zòu
1. to gallop 2. swift; sudden 3. frequent
【驟降】 a rapid fall (of snow)
【驟至】 to arrive suddenly
【驟然】 suddenly

十六畫

驢 4491
ㄌㄩˊ lǘ
an ass; a donkey
【驢脣不對馬嘴】 incongruous; irrelevant

驥 4492
ㄐㄧˋ jì
1. a very fast horse 2. a man of outstanding ability; a great man

十九畫

驪 4493
ㄌㄧˊ lí
1. a black horse 2. to drive a carriage drawn by two horses
【驪歌】 a song of farewell

骨部 ㄍㄨˇ gǔ

骨 4494
1. ㄍㄨˇ gǔ
1. a bone 2. a framework; a frame; a skeleton
【骨董】 curios; antique objects
【骨骼 or 骨格】 a frame of the body; a skeleton
【骨幹】 ① (anatomy) a diaphysis ② the backbone; a mainstay
【骨科】 osteopathy
【骨科醫生】 an osteopath
【骨灰】 bone ashes
【骨架 or 骨子】 a frame; a framework; a skeleton
【骨節 or 骨關節】 joints (of bones)
【骨氣】 fortitude; backbone; pluck
【骨折】 a bone fracture
【骨瘦如柴】 thin and emaciated; very skinny
【骨肉】 one's own flesh and blood—blood relations
【骨髓】 marrow
【骨癌】 cancer in the bone

骨 4494
2. ㄍㄨˊ gú
a bone (in some colloquial phrases)
【骨頭】 ① bone ② a contemptible person ③strong character; fortitude; guts
【骨碌】 rolling; to turn round and round

四畫

骰 4495
ㄕㄞˇ shǎi
1. dice 2. to dice

骯 4496
ㄤ āng
dirty; filthy; foul: 沼池中的水是骯髒的。The water in the swamp is foul.

五畫

骷 4497
ㄎㄨ kū
as in 骷髏—a human skeleton

六畫

骸 4498
ㄏㄞˊ hái
1. the shinbone 2. a skeleton

骼 4499
ㄍㄜˊ gé
a bone; a skeleton

十三畫

髒 4500
ㄗㄤ zāng
dirty; filthy
【髒話】 on obscene word; a swear-word; a profane word
【髒兮兮的】 very much soiled; very dirty

髓 4501
ㄙㄨㄟˇ suǐ
marrow; pith; essence

體 4502
ㄊㄧˇ tǐ
1. the body 2. shape; form 3. an entity; a unit 4. a style; a fashion; a system 5. substance; essence 6. theory (as opposed to practice)
【體魄】 the human body as the source of strength
【體面】 ① honor; dignity; face ② appearing good; looking elegant

骨部

〔高部〕

【體罰】corporal punishment
【體大思精】(said of a book) extensive in scope and penetrating in thought
【體態】①outward form; an exterior look ②a manner, deportment, or a carriage
【體貼】kind; considerate; thoughtful
【體統】①a system; an organized whole ②propriety in conduct
【體能or體力】stamina; physical agility
【體念】to be understanding
【體例】general form
【體諒】to be understanding or sympathetic toward; to be considerate of
【體格】physique
【體格檢查or體檢】a physical examination
【體會】to understand through something beyond the intellect
【體積】volume (of a solid)
【體系】a system; orderliness
【體型】an external physical appearance; (physical) build
【體恤】to be considerate of and sympathize with
【體質】a bodily constitution; a physical make-up
【體制】a system of rules; a system
【體重】body weight
【體察】① to examine or investigate with intensive personal attention ②to be understanding or sympathetic toward
【體認】to perceive intuitively
【體裁】a form or a style (of writing)
【體操】gymnastics; calisthenics
【體操選手】a gymnast
【體驗】to experience firsthand; firsthand experience
【體無完膚】injured all over the body (often used figuratively for damage inflicted by verbal attacks)
【體味】to appreciate; to savor
【體溫】body temperature
【體溫計】a clinical thermometer
【體育】①physical education ②athletics
【體育記者】a sportswriter
【體育館】a gymnasium
【體育場】a stadium; a play ground
【體育用品】sports goods; sports requisites

高 部
ㄍㄠ gāo

高 4503
ㄍㄠ gāo

1. high; tall 2. of a high level or degree; above the average 3. lofty
【高不可攀】too high to be reached
【高不成低不就】unable to find a mate or employment because the object available is either beyond one's reach or below one's minimum expectations
【高攀】① to climb high ② to cultivate friendship with the socially elevated
【高朋滿座】All the seats are occupied by distinguished guests.
【高帽(子)】flattery; soft soap
【高明】①clever; wise; superior ② an expert; a master; a qualified person
【高飛球】(baseball) fly
【高飛犧牲打】(baseball) sacrifice fly
【高峯】the peak; the summit; the climax
【高風亮節】noble character and incorruptible principle
【高大】tall and big; colossal
【高蛋白】high protein
【高等】high or advanced (in the grade)
【高等教育】higher education
【高低】① height ② a sense of propriety; discretion ③ (dialect) on any account; simply ④ (dialect) at last; after all ⑤relative superiority or inferiority
【高低不平】uneven; rugged; irregular
【高地】high ground; uplands
【高調】①a high-pitched note ② high-sounding (but impractical) assertions
【高度】①an altitude; a height; an elevation ②highly; great
【高擡貴手】(literally) Raise your noble hands.—Please be merciful.
【高談闊論】to talk freely; to talk in a lively atmosphere
【高堂】①a hall with a high ceiling ② parents
【高樓大厦】skyscrapers;tall buildings
【高麗參】ginseng

【高利貸】 usury
【高粱】 kaoliang; sorghum; kafir
【高粱酒】 kaoliang wine
【高齡】 advanced age; great age; old age
【高論】 an outstanding statement; original remarks
【高歌】 to sing aloud
【高高在上】(literally) situated high above—(figuratively) lofty; aloof
【高跟鞋】 high-heeled shoes
【高崗】the peak or summit; a high mountain
【高貴】 noble; exalted
【高官厚祿】 a high position and a good salary
【高亢】 proud and indomitable
【高空】 high altitude; upper air
【高呼】 to shout; to call out aloud
【高級】 ① a high grade; a high class; superior ② advanced (courses)
【高級中學or高中】 a senior middle (or high) school
【高價】a high price; an exorbitant price
【高架橋】 a viaduct
【高就】 opportunity for a high or higher position, a good or better employment, etc.
【高見】 your esteemed opinion or advice
【高攀】 ① to raise high; to uplift ② to become a hermit
【高強or高超】 surpassing; superior; outstanding
【高下】 superiority and inferiority
【高興】 glad; elated; delighted
【高血壓】 high blood pressure; hypertension
【高雄】 Kaohsiung
【高瞻遠矚】 farseeing; provident; farsighted
【高枕無憂】to sleep in peace; to be free from worries
【高漲】 to rise
【高潮】 ① a high tide ② a climax
【高傳眞】 high fidelity (Hi-Fi)
【高射砲】an antiaircraft machine; an ack-ack
【高燒】 a high fever
【高手】 a master; an expert
【高壽】 ① advanced age; old age; great age ② your age
【高山症】 mountain sickness; altitude sickness
【高山景行】 to admire great virtue
【高山族】 the aborigines of Taiwan
【高山仰止】 (figuratively) A man of virtue is so great that one looks up to him awfully.
【高深】 recondite; abstruse; profound; advanced; lofty
【高尙】 ① noble; exalted ② high-class; refined; respectable
【高陞】 to get a promotion; to be promoted
【高人一等】 a cut above other people
【高足】 (an honorific term) your capable student; your brilliant disciple
【高祖】 ① one's ancestor ② one's great-greatgrandfather ③ the founder of a dynasty
【高才生】 a bright and excellent student
【高速】 high speed
【高速公路】 a freeway; a motorway; an expressway
【高聳】 to tower; to rise high
【高傲】proud; overbearing; haughty
【高昂】(said of prices, morale, etc.) rising high
【高爾夫球】 golf
【高爾夫球場】 a golf course; a golf links
【高雅】 elegant; noble and graceful
【高音】 ① treble ② a soprano
【高音喇叭】 a tweeter
【高位】 a high position
【高溫】 a high temperature
【高原】 highlands; plateaus

髟 部
ㄅㄧㄠ biāo

四畫

髦 4504
ㄇㄠˊ máo
1. a children's hair style with front hair covering the forehead
2. the mane 3. a man of talent

五畫

髮 4505
ㄈㄚˇ fǎ
1. hair (covering human heads)
2. a hairbreadth; a hair's breadth
【髮髻】 hair tied in a knot
【髮夾】 a hairpin; a bobby pin
【髮膠】 hair spray; fixture for hair
【髮妻】 one's first wife
【髮型】 a hair style; a hairdo; a coiffure
【髮指】 so angry that the hair rises; to boil with anger

【髮油】hair oil; pomade

髯 4506 (髯) ㄖㄢˊ rán
1. whiskers 2. a heavily bearded man

髭 4507 ㄗ zī
moustaches: 髭鬚 moustaches and beards

六畫

髻 4508 ㄐㄧˋ jì
a coiffure with a topknot

八畫

鬆 4509 ㄙㄨㄥ sōng
1. loose; lax; slack 2. to relax 3. to loosen 4. soft; light
【鬆動】① to become less crowded ② not hard up; well-off ③ to become relaxed or flexible
【鬆口氣】to relax for a while; to get a breathing spell
【鬆開】to loosen
【鬆緊帶】an elastic string, band, etc.
【鬆懈】to relax efforts, attention, etc.
【鬆弛】① relaxed; flabby ② lax; slack
【鬆手】to let go the hands; to relax the hold
【鬆輭】loose and soft
【鬆散】incompact; loosely arranged

鬈 4510 ㄑㄩㄢˊ quán
1. fine hair 2. curled hair
【鬈髮】crimps
【鬈曲】to crinkle; to curl

九畫

鬍 4511 ㄏㄨˊ hú
as in 鬍鬚—beard

十二畫

鬚 4512 ㄒㄩ xū
1. beard; whiskers 2. whiskers (of a cat, etc.) 3. an awn
【鬚眉】① beard and eyebrows ② men

十四畫

鬢 4513 ㄅㄧㄣˋ bìn
as in 鬢髮—hair on the temples
【鬢角】temples (beside the ears)

鬥部 ㄉㄡˋ dòu

鬥 4514 ㄉㄡˋ dòu
same as 鬬—to struggle

五畫

鬧 4515 ㄋㄠˋ nào
1. to disturb; to agitate; to trouble 2. to have or experience (disasters, sickness, etc.) 3. noisy; uproarious; stormy; clamorous
【鬧彆扭】to act peevishly; to show resentment; to be dissatisfied
【鬧翻】to fall out with somebody
【鬧翻天】to raise a hell of a noise; to raise a rumpus
【鬧肚子】to have loose bowels
【鬧鬼】① haunted ② to play tricks behind somebody's back
【鬧轟轟】① arousing intense excitement; sensational ② noisy; uproarious; clamorous
【鬧饑荒】to have a famine
【鬧酒】to start a drinking bout; to engage in a drunken brawl
【鬧劇】a farce
【鬧情緒】to be in a bad mood; to be in low spirits
【鬧笑話】to arouse ridicule; to make oneself a laughingstock
【鬧新房】rough horseplay at a wedding
【鬧著玩兒】to raise hell just for fun or joke
【鬧鐘】an alarm clock
【鬧事】to cause trouble or uproar
【鬧市】a busy shopping district

八畫

鬩 4516 ㄒㄧˋ xì
to quarrel; to conflict
【鬩牆】to quarrel within the family; an intramural fight

十四畫

鬭 4517
(鬥、鬦) ㄉㄡˋ dòu
to struggle; to fight; to contend; to conflict; to vie; to compete; quarrelsomeness
【鬭牛】 a bullfight
【鬭弄】 ① to seduce; to flirt with ② to play jokes on; to make fun of
【鬭狠】 to compete in ferocities
【鬭雞】 a cockfight; cockfighting
【鬭雞眼】 crossed eyes; convergent strabismus
【鬭蟋蟀】 a cricketfight
【鬭志】 the determination to compete or fight; pugnacious spirit
【鬭智不鬭力】 to fight a battle of wits, not of limbs
【鬭爭】 struggle; conflict; strife
【鬭嘴 or 鬭口】 to quarrel; to wrangle
【鬭毆】 to have a fight; to brawl

鬯 部
ㄔㄤˋ chàng

十九畫

鬱 4518
ㄩˋ yù
1. a tulip 2. a plum (*Prunus japonica*) 3. held in check; pent-up; stagnant 4. luxuriant; lush
【鬱悶】 to have pent-up emotions or thoughts
【鬱積】 pent-up (feelings); to smolder
【鬱金香】 a tulip
【鬱鬱寡歡】 to mope; to feel low; one's spirits droop

鬲 部
ㄌㄧˋ lì

鬲 4519
ㄌㄧˋ lì
a kind of caldron

十二畫

鬻 4520
ㄩˋ yù
1. to sell 2. to bring up 3. young; childish
【鬻文】 to write for pay

鬼 部
ㄍㄨㄟˇ guǐ

鬼 4521
ㄍㄨㄟˇ guǐ
1. spirits; ghosts; demons; devils 2. cunning; crafty; wily; deceitful 3. sinister; evil; a dirty trick, work, etc.
【鬼門關】 the gate to the land of ghosts; the gate of hell
【鬼迷心竅】 to be possessed
【鬼斧神工】 prodigious workmanship
【鬼點子】 wicked ideas; tricks
【鬼胎】 an evil plot; a dark scheme
【鬼臉】 a grimace
【鬼怪or鬼魅】 monsters; goblins; bogies
【鬼鬼祟祟】 stealthy; sneaky; furtive
【鬼哭神號】 to give dreary cries and screams
【鬼話】 false words; lies; nonsense
【鬼話連篇】 to tell a whole series of lies
【鬼畫符】 ① a very poor work of calligraphy ② a hypocritical talk
【鬼火】 a jack-o'-lantern; a will-o'-the-wisp
【鬼魂】 ghosts; spirits of the dead
【鬼混】 to spend days in an idle, slovenly way
【鬼主意】 a crafty idea; a dark scheme
【鬼使神差】 to do something inexplicably as if manipulated by supernatural beings
【鬼神】 ghosts and deities; spirits and gods; spiritual beings
【鬼才】 a genius in an unorthodox way

四畫

魁 4522
ㄎㄨㄟˊ kuí
1. the chief; the head; the leader 2. tall; big; great
【魁梧】 tall and robust; husky

魂 4523
ㄏㄨㄣˊ hún

as in 魂魄—a soul; a spirit
【魂不附體】frightened out of one's wits
【魂飛魄散】① frightened out of one's senses; frightened out of one's wits ② as good as dead

五畫

魄 4524
1. ㄆㄛˋ pò
1. (Taoism) vigor; animation; life 2. form; shape; body 3. the dark part of the moon
【魄力】guts; decisiveness; the ability to make major decisions promptly

魄 4524
2. ㄊㄨㄛˋ tuò
as in 落魄 —dispirited; out of luck

魅 4525
ㄇㄟˋ mèi
1. a mischievous spirit; a goblin; an elf 2. to charm; to mislead
【魅力】glamor; sexiness; attractiveness; spell; charm; charisma
【魅惑】to bedevil; to bewitch

八畫

魍 4526
ㄨㄤˇ wǎng
as in 魍魎—a kind of monster

魏 4527
ㄨㄟˋ wèi
1. lofty; stately; magnificent 2. a Chinese family name

十一畫

魑 4528
ㄔ chī
a mountain demon resembling a tiger
【魑魅魍魎】all sorts of monsters and goblins

魔 4529
ㄇㄛˊ mó
a wizard; a witch; a demon; a devil
【魔法or魔術】witchcraft; wizardry; sorcery; magic
【魔力】magic power; wizardly ability; charm; spell
【魔鬼】devils; demons; evil spirits
【魔掌】devil's clutches; evil hands
【魔爪】devil's talons
【魔術方塊】a magic square
【魔術家】a magician
【魔王】the Devil; Satan; Prince of Darkness

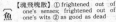

魚部
ㄩˊ yú

魚 4530
ㄩˊ yú
fish: 魚雷 a torpedo 魚鉤 a fish-hook
【魚米之鄉】land of agriculture and fishery; land of plenty
【魚苗 or 魚秧】fry (of fish)
【魚目混珠】(literally) to pass fish eyes as pearls—① to masquerade ② to offer something bogus
【魚販】a fishmonger
【魚肚白】silver-gray (like the belly of a fish) —gray dawn
【魚塘 or 魚池】a fishpond
【魚類】fishes; Pisces
【魚鱗】scales (of fish)
【魚卵】roe; spawn
【魚竿】a fishing rod; a fish pole
【魚肝油】cod-liver oil
【魚缸】a fish globe
【魚貫】in a column; in procession
【魚蝦】fish and shrimps
【魚腥味】a fishy smell
【魚翅】shark's fins
【魚叉】a harpoon; a gaff; a fish spear
【魚市】a fish market
【魚肉】① fish and meat ② victims of oppression ③ to oppress; to bully
【魚肉鄉民】to oppress the people
【魚子醬】caviar
【魚鬆】dried fish floss
【魚餌】fish bait
【魚鹽之利】gain from marine resources
【魚尾紋】crow's-feet
【魚丸】a fish ball
【魚塭】a fish farm
【魚網】a fishnet; a fishing net
【魚與熊掌】unable to make up one's mind as to which of two desirable things to choose

四畫

魷 4531
ㄧㄡˊ yóu
a cuttlefish

魯 4532 ㄌㄨˇ lǔ
1. stupid; dull 2. vulgar 3. name of an ancient kingdom in what is today's Shantung; an alternative name of Shantung 4. a Chinese family name
【魯莽】① rude; disrespectful; uncivil; ill-mannered; discourteous ② rash; careless
【魯鈍】dull; slow-witted

五畫

鮑 4533 ㄅㄠˋ bào
1. an abalone 2. salted fish 3. a Chinese family name
【鮑魚】① an abalone ② salted fish
【鮑魚之肆】a market for salted fish—an objectionable environment

六畫

鮪 4534 ㄨㄟˇ wěi
a tuna: 鮪釣 a tuna liner

鮭 4535 ㄍㄨㄟ guī
a salmon

鮮 4536 1. ㄒㄧㄢ xiān
1. fresh; new 2. delicious; tasty 3. bright; attractive
【鮮美】fresh and delicious
【鮮明】① sharp; distinct ② bright-colored
【鮮嫩】fresh and tender
【鮮花】fresh flowers
【鮮紅】bright red
【鮮血】fresh blood; blood
【鮮血淋漓】drenched with blood
【鮮豔 or 鮮豔奪目】bright-colored; resplendent; attractively

鮮 4536 2. ㄒㄧㄢˇ xiǎn
rare; few; seldom
【鮮有】seldom to have; rare

七畫

鯁 4537 ㄍㄥˇ gěng
1. a fishbone stuck in the throat 2. honest; straightforward
【鯁直】honest; straightforward; outspoken

鯉 4538 ㄌㄧˇ lǐ
1. a carp 2. letters; epistles
【鯉魚】a common carp
【鯉魚跳龍門】to succeed in the civil service examination in former times

鯊 4539 ㄕㄚ shā
a shark

八畫

鯨 4540 ㄐㄧㄥ jīng
a whale
【鯨吞蠶食】aggression by engulfing and nibbling processes
【鯨油】whale oil

九畫

鯽 4541 ㄐㄧˋ jì
a gold carp

鰓 4542 ㄙㄞ sāi
gills (of fish)

十畫

鰥 4543 ㄍㄨㄢ guān
1. a kind of huge predatory fish 2. a widower 3. a bachelor
【鰥夫】① a widower ② a bachelor
【鰥寡孤獨】those who have no wives, husbands, parents or children

鰭 4544 ㄑㄧˊ qí
fins

十一畫

鰻 4545 ㄇㄢˊ mán
an eel

鱈 4546 ㄒㄩㄝˇ xuě
a cod

鰲 4547 (鼇) ㄠˊ áo
a sea-tortoise
【鰲頭】the top successful candidate in the civil service examination in former times

〔鳥部〕

十二畫

鱗 4548 ㄌㄧㄣˊ lín
scales (of fish etc.)
【鱗片】① scales (of fish, etc.) ② a bud scale
【鱗甲】hard scales (of crocodiles, etc.)
【鱗爪】(literally) scales and claws—minutiae; trifles

十六畫

鱸 4549 ㄌㄨˊ lú
a perch; a bass: 鱸魚 the sea bass

鱷 4550 ㄜˋ è
a crocodile; an alligator

鳥部 ㄋㄧㄠˇ niao

鳥 4551 ㄋㄧㄠˇ niǎo
a bird: 鳥蛋 bird's eggs 鳥籠 a birdcage
【鳥瞰】①to have a bird's-eye view ② an aerial view; a bird's-eye view
【鳥盡弓藏】to discharge a worthy official in times of peace
【鳥之將死，其鳴也悲】A man's last words are sincere.
【鳥爪】① bird's talons ② fine, delicate human finger tips
【鳥巢 or 鳥窩】a bird's nest
【鳥獸】birds and beasts
【鳥獸散】to disperse in confusion like birds or beasts
【鳥爲食亡，人爲財死】Birds die in pursuit of food, and human beings die in pursuit of wealth.
【鳥語花香】birds singing and flowers radiating fragrance—the joyous scene in spring
【鳥園】an aviary

二畫

鳩 4552 ㄐㄧㄡ jiū
1.a pigeon; a dove 2.to collect; to assemble
【鳩占鵲巢】enjoying the fruits of others' without having worked hard; to usurp what is another's

三畫

鳳 4553 ㄈㄥˋ fèng
Feng—a male phoenix
【鳳毛麟角】rare treasures or talents; something extremely rare
【鳳梨】a pineapple
【鳳冠霞帔】the headgear and dress of a lady or bride in former times
【鳳凰】Feng-huang — phoenixes (鳳 being male and凰being female)
【鳳凰于飛】a couple of phoenixes on the wing—happy marriage
【鳳仙花】a balsam; a garden balsam

鳴 4554 ㄇㄧㄥˊ míng
1. (said of birds) to sing; to chirp; to warble; (said of cocks) to crow 2. the notes of birds 3. to make sounds; to sound
【鳴放】the airing of views (through posters, meetings or other media)
【鳴笛】to blow a whistle; to signal with a siren
【鳴鼓而攻】to attack while beating the drum
【鳴金收兵】to beat the gong to call back the troops
【鳴槍】to fire rifles into the air
【鳴謝】to express gratitude
【鳴鐘】to strike or toll a bell
【鳴寃】to complain of unfairness; to air grievances

鳶 4555 ㄩㄢ yuān
1.a kite; a hawk 2.a kite (a toy)
【鳶飛魚躍】kites flying and fishes jumping—natural freedom of things in the universe

四畫

鴆 4556 ㄓㄣˋ zhèn
1. a kind of venomous bird 2. poisoned wine
【鴆毒】① poison; venom ② to slander; to harm by devious means

鴇 4557 ㄅㄠˇ bǎo
1. *Otis dybowskii*, a bird resembling the wild goose 2.a prosti-

tute 3. a procuress
【鴇母】 a procuress

鴉 4558
ㄧㄚ yā
a crow; a raven
【鴉片】 opium
【鴉雀無聲】 so quiet that not a single voice can be heard

五畫

鴕 4559
ㄊㄨㄛˊ tuó
as in 鴕鳥—an ostrich

鴛 4560
ㄩㄢ yuān
the male mandarin duck
【鴛鴦】 mandarin ducks, which always live in pairs—a symbol of lovers
【鴛鴦蝴蝶派】 literature characterized by shallow love stories

鴟 4561
ㄔ chī
1. a kite 2. an owl 3. wine-cups
【鴟鴞】 an owl

鴦 4562
ㄧㄤ yāng
the female mandarin duck

鴨 4563
ㄧㄚ yā
a duck
【鴨蛋】 ① a duck's egg ② (slang) 「scoreless; zero」
【鴨蛋臉兒】 an oval face (regarded as an ideal shape for a woman's face)
【鴨舌帽】 a cap with a visor
【鴨子】 a duck

六畫

鴿 4564
ㄍㄜ gē
a pigeon; a dove
【鴿棚 or 鴿籠】 a pigeon house
【鴿子】 a pigeon
【鴿子傳書】 transmission of messages by homing pigeons

鴻 4565
ㄏㄨㄥˊ hóng
1. a wild swan; a wild goose 2. great; huge; large
【鴻毛】 swan's down—something very light or insignificant
【鴻福齊天】 One's vast happiness is as high as the heaven.
【鴻圖】 ① a great plan; a great enterprise; a great undertaking ② a great domain
【鴻鵠之志】 great ambition
【鴻爪】 traces that one leaves behind 「by wild swans」
【鴻雁傳書】 to deliver messages

七畫

鵑 4566
ㄐㄩㄢ juān
as in 杜鵑—① the cuckoo ② 「an azalea」

鵝 4567
(鵞、䳘) ㄜˊ é
a goose; a gander
【鵝毛】 goose feathers 「oval face」
【鵝蛋臉兒】 an egg-shaped face; an
【鵝鑾鼻】 name of the southernmost cape of Taiwan
【鵝卵石】 pebbles

鵠 4568
1. ㄏㄨˊ hú
1. a swan 2. standing quietly; standing erect
【鵠面鳩形】 emaciated from hunger
【鵠立】 to stand on the lookout

鵠 4568
2. ㄍㄨˇ gǔ
a target
【鵠的】 the target; the bull's-eye

八畫

鵬 4569
ㄆㄥˊ péng
Peng, a fabulous bird supposed to be the greatest of all kinds, comparable to the roc
【鵬圖】 great ambition
【鵬程萬里】 (literally) a journey of 10,000 miles faced by the roc—of great promise

鵰 4570
ㄉㄧㄠ diāo
a bird of prey; a vulture 亦作「鷲」

鵲 4571
ㄑㄩㄝˋ què
(又讀 ㄑㄧㄠˇ qiǎo)
a magpie
【鵲報(喜)】 the magpie's lucky chirp—a good omen

鶉 4572
ㄔㄨㄣˊ chún

〔鳥部〕

a quail
【鶉衣百結】coarse clothes with many patches

十畫

〔鹵部〕

鶴 4573 ㄏㄜˋ hè
(語音 ㄏㄠˊ háo)
a crane
【鶴髮童顏】a hoary head with a youthful face
【鶴立】to expect (or await) eagerly
【鶴立雞羣】(literally) a crane standing among chickens—far surpassing the others; to stand head and shoulders over others
【鶴唳】the cries of cranes

鶯 4574 ㄧㄥ yīng
a greenfinch; a Chinese oriole
【鶯啼燕語】Orioles sing and swallows chatter. (a phrase descriptive of a fine spring day)
【鶯鶯燕燕】a crowd of women chattering together pleasantly

鶼 4575 ㄐㄧㄢ jiān
a fabulous bird having only one wing so that a pair must unite in order to fly
【鶼鰈】birds and fishes that move in pairs—a devoted couple

鷂 4576 ㄧㄠˋ yào
a hawk; a sparrow hawk
【鷂子】① a sparrow hawk ② a kite (a toy)
【鷂子翻身】a hawk's turn (a fast bodily motion in Chinese pugilism)

鷄 4577 (雞) ㄐㄧ jī
fowls

十一畫

鷗 4578 ㄡ ōu
a gull
【鷗鷺忘機】(said of a hermit) so much in harmony with nature that the water birds are not frightened away by his presence

十二畫

鷥 4579 ㄙ sī
an egret

鷸 4580 ㄩˋ yù
a snipe
【鷸蚌相爭】a quarrel which benefits only a third party

鷺 4581 ㄌㄨˋ lù
Egretta garzetta, an egret
【鷺鷥】an egret

十三畫

鷹 4582 ㄧㄥ yīng
a hawk; an eagle; a falcon
【鷹鉤鼻子】an aquiline nose
【鷹架】a scaffold
【鷹犬】① falcons and dogs used in hunting ② hired ruffians; rapacious underlings

十七畫

鸚 4583 ㄧㄥ yīng
as in 鸚鵡—a parrot
【鸚鵡學舌】to parrot another's statement, theory, etc.

十九畫

鸞 4584 ㄌㄨㄢˊ luán
1. a *luan* (a fabulous bird related to the phoenix) 2. the bells at horses' bits
【鸞鳳】① a married couple ② a *luan* (a fabulous bird) and a phoenix—(figuratively) good beings ③ handsome; gallant
【鸞鳳和鳴】harmony in marriage

鹵部 ㄌㄨˇ lǔ

鹵 4585 ㄌㄨˇ lǔ
1. alkaline or saline soil 2. natural salt 3. rude; unrefined 亦作「魯」 4. to capture; to seize 亦作「擄」
【鹵莽】rude; rash; foolhardy
【鹵味】① pot-stewed fowl, meat, etc. served cold ② a salty taste;

saltiness

九畫

鹹 4586
ㄒㄧㄢˊ xián
saltish; salty; briny; salted
【鹹蛋】 salted eggs
【鹹海】 Lake Aral
【鹹湖 or 鹹水湖】 salt lakes
【鹹水】 saline water; salt water
【鹹肉】 salted meat
【鹹菜】 pickled vegetables; pickles
【鹹味】 a salty taste; saltiness
【鹹魚】 salted fish

十三畫

鹼 4587
(鹻) ㄐㄧㄢˇ jiǎn
lye; alkali
【鹼性】 alkalinity

十四畫

鹽 4588
ㄧㄢˊ yán
common salt; salt
【鹽巴】 (dialect) salt; common salt
【鹽田】 a salt garden; a salt pond
【鹽礦】 a salt mine
【鹽井】 a salt well
【鹽水】 salt solution; salt water; brine
【鹽酸】 hydrochloric acid
【鹽味】 a salty taste; saltiness

鹿部
ㄌㄨˋ lù

鹿 4589
ㄌㄨˋ lù
a deer; a stag; a doe
【鹿皮】 deerskin
【鹿角】 antlers
【鹿茸】 young antlers (regarded as a very valuable medicine)
【鹿死誰手】 (literally) Who is to kill the deer?—Who will win?

五畫

麈 4590
ㄓㄨˇ zhǔ
1. a kind of deer 2. to whisk; to dust
【麈尾】 a duster

六畫

麋 4591
ㄇㄧˊ mí
Alces machlis, a kind of deer
【麋鹿】 ① (animal) the elk and the deer ② (figuratively) a rude person

八畫

麒 4592
ㄑㄧˊ qí
the male of a fabulous animal resembling the deer
【麒麟】 Chi-lin, a fabulous animal resembling the deer said to appear only in time of peace and prosperity

麓 4593
ㄌㄨˋ lù
the foot of a hill or mountain

麗 4594
ㄌㄧˋ lì
1. beautiful; elegant; fine; magnificent 2. to hang 3. same as 儷—dual; double
【麗質】 beauty (especially feminine)
【麗人】 a beauty; a belle; a beautiful woman 亦作「美人」

十畫

麝 4595
ㄕㄜˋ shè
a musk deer
【麝香】 musk

十一畫

麞 4596
ㄓㄤ zhāng
Moschus chinloo, a deer-like animal
【麞頭鼠目】 a roe's head and a mouse's eyes—a mean physiognomy

十二畫

麟 4597
ㄌㄧㄣˊ lín
the female of a fabulous animal resembling the deer
【麟角 or 麟角鳳毛】 rare things
【麟兒】 a fine son

〈鹿部〉

麥部
ㄇㄛˋ mò

4598
麥 ㄇㄞˋ mài
(讀音 ㄇㄛˋ mò)
1. wheat; barley; oats 2. a Chinese family name
【麥餅】wheaten cake
【麥片】oatmeal
【麥苗】young wheat, barley, etc.
【麥粉】flour
【麥麩】wheat bran
【麥田】wheatland; a wheat field
【麥浪】the wavy motion of wheat, etc., in the field when winds blow
【麥克風】a microphone
【麥加】Mecca, Saudi Arabia
【麥酒】beer 亦作「啤酒」
【麥子】wheat; barley
【麥穗】ears of wheat, etc.
【麥芽】malt
【麥芽糖】malt sugar; maltose

四畫

4599
麪 (麵) ㄇㄧㄢˋ miàn
1. flour 2. dough 3. noodles
【麪包】bread
【麪包店】a bakery
【麪包屑】crumbs of bread
【麪包師】a baker
【麪包樹】a breadfruit tree
【麪粉】flour
【麪條】noodles; spaghetti; vermicelli
【麪糰】dough
【麪筋】gluten of flour
【麪茶】porridge made by mixing roasted flour in boiling water
【麪食】wheaten foods; pastry

六畫

4600
麯 (麴) ㄑㄩˊ qú
a ferment for brewing

九畫

4601
麵 (麪) ㄇㄧㄢˋ miàn
1. flour 2. noodles

麻部
ㄇㄚˊ má

4602
麻 ㄇㄚˊ má
1. hemp; jute; ramie; sisal; flax 2. sesame 3. numb; torpid 4. a tingle; to tingle 5. pockmarked 6. rough 7. pitted; spotty
【麻痺】paralysis; palsy; numbness
【麻布】linen; gunny; hempen fabrics
【麻面 or 麻臉】a pockmarked face
【麻木】paralyzed; numbed; palsied
【麻木不仁】numbed; paralyzed; unsympathetic; unfeeling
【麻煩】① troublesome ② trouble ③ to bother
【麻袋】a jute bag; a hemp bag
【麻花】a fried dough twist
【麻醬】sesame paste
【麻將牌】mah-jong pieces
【麻雀】① a sparrow ② mah-jong
【麻雀雖小，五臟俱全】small but complete
【麻疹】(medicine) measles
【麻繩】hemp cordage; hemp rope
【麻子】① a pockmarked person ② pockmarks
【麻醉】① to anesthetize ② to dope; to drug
【麻醉劑 or 麻藥】① an anesthetic ② narcotics; drugs; dopes
【麻油】sesame oil

三畫

4603
麼 1. ㄇㄛˊ mó
1. a special particle found in dramatic dialogues 2. tiny

4603
麼 2. (麼、嗎) ·ㄇㄚ ma
a final interrogative particle

4603
麼 3. ㄇㄚˊ má
a particle used in the phrase「幹麼」(why)

4603
麼 4. ·ㄇㄜ me
a particle used in the interrogative phrase「甚麼」(what)

四畫

麾 4604
ㄏㄨㄟ huī
1. a flag; a banner; a standard 2. to command; to lead
【麾軍】 to lead an army
【麾下】 ① under a general's command ② sir (in addressing a general)

黃部
ㄏㄨㄤˊ huáng

黃 4605
ㄏㄨㄤˊ huáng
1. yellow 2. a Chinese family name
【黃包車】 a ricksha(w)
【黃袍】 ① high-ranking Buddhist monks (marked by their yellow robes) ② the imperial robe
【黃麻】 jute
【黃梅調】 a popular folk melody originated from 黃梅 (revived by Hong Kong film makers)
【黃毛丫頭】 a fledgling little girl
【黃髮垂髫】 the aged and the young
【黃蜂】 wasps
【黃道吉日】 a lucky day
【黃豆】 soybean
【黃膽病 or 黃疸】 jaundice; icterus
【黃帝】 Huang Ti, or the Yellow Emperor, a legendary ruler
【黃湯】 wine
【黃土】 loess
【黃銅】 brass
【黃牛】 ① a common Chinese ox ② a scalper of tickets, etc. ③ (slang) to fail to appear on an appointment
【黃牛票】 scalped tickets
【黃老】 ① Huang Ti (黃帝) and Lao-tzu (老子) ② Taoism
【黃鸝(鳥)】 the oriole
【黃曆】 (colloquial) an almanac
【黃臉婆】 the yellow-faced woman—my wife
【黃瓜】 a cucumber
【黃河】 the Yellow River
【黃河流域】 the Yellow River Valley
【黃河水澄清】 the clearing of the Yellow River—an impossibility
【黃海】 the Yellow Sea
【黃花閨女】 a virgin
【黃昏】 dusk
【黃金】 gold
【黃金時代】 the golden age
【黃泉】 Hades
【黃種人】 the yellow race; the Mongolian race
【黃澄澄】 glistening yellow; golden
【黃鼠狼】 a weasel 亦作「鼬」
【黃熱病】 yellow fever
【黃色】 ① yellow ② decadent; obscene; pornographic
【黃色小說】 a sex novel; a pornographic novel and periodicals
【黃色書刊】 pornographic books and periodicals
【黃鶯】 an oriole
【黃魚】 a yellow croaker

黍部
ㄕㄨˇ shǔ

黍 4606
ㄕㄨˇ shǔ
as in 黍稷—a variety of millet

三畫

黎 4607
ㄌㄧˊ lí
1. many; numerous 2. black; dark 3. a Chinese family name
【黎巴嫩】 Lebanon
【黎明】 dawn; daybreak

五畫

黏 4608
ㄋㄧㄢˊ nián
1. to stick 2. sticky; glutinous; gluey; adhesive; clammy; viscid
【黏膜】 the mucous membrane
【黏度】 (chemistry) viscosity
【黏貼】 to glue; to paste; to stick
【黏土】 clay
【黏力】 adhesive power; viscosity
【黏性】 viscosity
【黏住】 to stick; to adhere
【黏液】 viscous liquid; mucus

黑部
ㄏㄜˋ hè

〔黑部〕

黑 4609 ㄏㄟ hēi
(讀音 ㄏㄜˋ hè)
1. black; dark 2. evil; sinister; gloomy
【黑白】black and white—right and wrong, good and bad, etc.
【黑白分明】① right and wrong clearly distinguished ② the sharp contrast between black and white
【黑斑】dark spots; black specks
【黑板】a blackboard
【黑板擦】an eraser; a wiper
【黑啤酒】dark beer; stout
【黑幫】a reactionary gang
【黑名單】a blacklist
【黑道人物】a gangster; an underworld figure
【黑店】an inn that kills and robs lodgers
【黑洞】(astronomy) a black hole
【黑體字】boldface type
【黑奴】Negro slaves
【黑盒子】a cockpit voice recorder
【黑海】the Black Sea
【黑漆漆】pitch-dark; very dark
【黑心肝】an ungrateful person
【黑猩猩】a chimpanzee
【黑種 or 黑種人】the black race
【黑市】a black market
【黑社會】underworld society; the underworld; gangsterdom
【黑手】a vicious backstage manipulator
【黑手黨】the Black Hand; the Mafia
【黑人】a Negro; a black
【黑死病】the Black Death
【黑色】black
【黑暗】darkness; dark
【黑壓壓】extremely crowded; a dense or dark mass of
【黑夜】a dark night; night
【黑煙】① black smoke ② opium

四畫

黔 4610 ㄑㄧㄢˊ qián
1. black 2. Kweichow (an alternative name)
【黔黎】the common people
【黔驢技窮】the Kweichow donkey at the end of its resourcefulness—a person who has exposed his limited ability

默 4611 ㄇㄛˋ mò
1. speechless; silent 2. quiet; still
【默不作聲】to keep silence; to keep quiet; to refuse to speak
【默默】① quietly; silently ② secretly; in one's heart
【默默無言】wordless; speechless; silent; in silence
【默默無聞】obscure; unknown to the public
【默念】① to repeat (a passage, etc.) silently inside the mind ② to ponder or think
【默記】silently remember
【默劇】pantomime 亦作「啞劇」
【默契】a tacit understanding; an implicit agreement; a secret agreement
【默寫or默書】to write from memory
【默許】tacit permission
【默想】to meditate; to contemplate
【默認】tacit consent, confession or approval
【默哀】to stand in silent tribute

五畫

點 4612 ㄉㄧㄢˇ diǎn
1. a dot; a spot; a speck 2. a point 3. a drop; a small amount; a little 4. snacks; refreshments 5. hours 6. to dot; to mark 7. to instruct; to teach 8. to check; to examine; to investigate; to review 9. to light; to ignite 10. to select; to pick out 11. to nod (the head) 12. to touch; to point at
【點播】(agriculture) dibble seeding; dibbling
【點破】to unravel (a mystery, etc.); to point out
【點名】① to call the roll; to make a roll call ② to mention somebody by name
【點名簿or點名册】a roll (of names)
【點到爲止】to go through the motions
【點燈】to light lamps
【點滴】① drops; small amounts; a bit ② (medicine) an intravenous drip
【點頭】to nod
【點鐵成金】to make a poor writing into a literary masterpiece by skillful retouching

【點化】 to enlighten; to point out the correct path
【點火】 to light a fire
【點清】 to count accurately
【點心】 snacks; refreshments
【點醒】 to point out someone's errors and make him realize them
【點穴】 ① (Chinese boxing) to attack a vital point ② to select the site of a grave through geomancy, etc.
【點綴】 to provide decorative accessories; to embellish
【點鐘】 hours; o'clock
【點唱】 (said of a music audience, etc.) to select one's desired numbers or songs for the performers to sing or play
【點收】 to check and accept (articles that are delivered or handed over)
【點燃】 to light; to kindle; to ignite
【點字】 Braille
【點子】 ①a dot; a spot; a speck ② a little; a bit ③a key point ④ ideas
【點菜】 to order favorite dishes at a restaurant
【點眼藥】 to apply eye lotion

黛 4613 ㄉㄞˋ dài
1. a bluish-black material used by ancient women to blacken their eyebrows 2. a beauty

黜 4614 ㄔㄨˋ chù
1. to reject; to dispel 2. to dismiss; to degrade; to demote
【黜免】 to dismiss from office; to remove from office
【黜退】 to dismiss; to send away

黝 4615 ㄧㄡˇ yǒu
bluish black
【黝黑】 (said of a complexion) dark; swarthy

六畫

黠 4616 ㄒㄧㄚˊ xiá
1. smart; clever; shrewd 2. crafty; cunning; artful; wily
【黠慧】 clever; smart; shrewd

八畫

黥 4617 ㄑㄧㄥˊ qíng
ancient punishment of tattooing the face; branding
【黥面 or 黥首】 ancient punishment of tattooing the face

黧 4618 ㄌㄧˊ lí
dark yellow; sallow
【黧黑】 (said of a complexion) dark

黨 4619 ㄉㄤˇ dǎng
1. a party; a faction; a clique; a gang; an association 2. relatives 3. a community of 500 families (in ancient times) 4. to take sides; to associate; to be a partizan 5. as in 鄉黨—village
【黨部】 the headquarters of a political party
【黨派】 factions; parties; cliques
【黨同伐異】 to unite with those who agree and fight those who differ
【黨齡】 party standing
【黨綱】 the platform of a political party
【黨國】 the party and the nation
【黨國元老】 an elder statesman of the party and the nation
【黨魁】 a party boss; a party chieftain
【黨徽】 the emblem of a political party
【黨籍】 a party affiliation
【黨紀】 party discipline
【黨旗】 the flag of a political party
【黨章】 the constitution of a political party
【黨爭】 a factional fight; a partisan war
【黨政】 the party and the government administration
【黨證】 a membership card of a political party
【黨務】 party affairs
【黨外】 outside the party
【黨羽】 adherents or followers (especially of a condemned leader)
【黨員】 a party member; a partisan

九畫

黯 4620 ㄢˋ àn
1. very dark; pitch-dark 2. miserable; dismal
【黯然消魂】 deeply affected (as by the sorrow of parting)
【黯然失色】 to appear very dull or

poor in comparison; to be outshone; to be eclipsed
【黯然神傷】to feel dejected (or depressed)

十一畫

黴 4621 ㄇㄟˊ méi
1. mold; mildew; must 2. germs; bacteria 3. fungi 4. dirty; dingy
【黴菌】① fungi; mold fungi ② germs; bacteria

十五畫

黷 4622 ㄉㄨˊ dú
1. to tarnish 2. to be rash about 3. to corrupt
【黷武】to use military might rashly

黹 部 ㄓˇ zhǐ

黹 4623 ㄓˇ zhǐ
embroidery; needlework

黽 部 ㄇㄧㄣˇ mǐn

黽 4624 ㄇㄧㄣˇ mǐn
to strive; to endeavor
【黽勉】to strive; to endeavor; to exert oneself

十一畫

鼇 4625 ㄠˊ áo
a huge sea turtle
【鼇頭 or 鰲頭】the top successful candidate in a civil service examination under the former system

十二畫

鼈 4626 (鱉) ㄅㄧㄝ biē
Trionyx sinenis, a kind of fresh-water turtle 亦作「甲魚」

鼎 部 ㄉㄧㄥˇ dǐng

鼎 4627 ㄉㄧㄥˇ dǐng
1. a huge tripod of bronze with two ears; a heavy three-legged caldron or sacrificial vessel 2. vigorous; thriving; flourishing 3. involving three parts or things; triangular
【鼎沸】tumultuous; boiling; hubbub; noisy and confused
【鼎鼎大名】renowned; famous; illustrious; celebrated; a great reputation
【鼎力】① great strength; herculean strength ② your kind effort
【鼎立】(said of rival groups, etc.) to develop a triangular balance of power
【鼎盛】in a period of great prosperity; prosperous; thriving; vigorous; flourishing
【鼎足而三】divided into three rival groups; developing into a triangular balance of power

鼓 部 ㄍㄨˇ gǔ

鼓 4628 ㄍㄨˇ gǔ
1. drums 2. to drum; to beat a drum 3. to vibrate; to quiver 4. to rouse; to stir up; to instigate
【鼓膜】the eardrum
【鼓動】to instigate; to rouse; to incite; to stir up; to excite
【鼓勵】to encourage; to hearten
【鼓號樂隊】a drum and bugle band
【鼓惑】to instigate; to induce to go astray
【鼓起勇氣】to pluck up courage
【鼓掌】to clap the hands; to give applause
【鼓吹】①(ㄍㄨˇ ㄔㄨㄟ) to advocate; to uphold; to promote; to propagate ②(ㄍㄨˇ ㄔㄨㄟˋ) a kind of ancient court music

【鼓槌】 a drumstick
【鼓舌如簧】 to wag one's tongue (for honeyed words, malicious gossip, etc.)
【鼓手】 a drum player; a drummer
【鼓聲】 drumbeats
【鼓譟 or 鼓噪】 to raise an uproar; to be uproarious
【鼓舞】 ① to rouse; to inspire; to stir up; to excite; to spur on ② to dance for joy; to rejoice
【鼓舞士氣】 to enhance troop morale; to cheer up troops

鼠 部
ㄕㄨ shu

鼠 4629 ㄕㄨˇ shǔ
a mouse; a rat
【鼠輩】 a mean fellow
【鼠目寸光】 shortsighted; lacking foresight
【鼠蹊】 the groin
【鼠竄】 to run away like frightened rats
【鼠牙雀角】 (figuratively) to carry on a lawsuit; to litigate

五畫

鼬 4630 ㄧㄡˋ yòu
a weasel
【鼬鼠】 a weasel

七畫

鼯 4631 ㄨˊ wú
a flying squirrel
【鼯鼠】 a flying squirrel
【鼯鼠技窮】 at one's wit's end

鼻 部
ㄅㄧˊ bí

鼻 4632 ㄅㄧˊ bí
1. a nose 2. before any others; first
【鼻竇炎】 sinusitis
【鼻涕】 nasal mucus or drips; snivel
【鼻孔】 nostrils
【鼻青臉腫】 a bloody nose and a swollen face—bruised in the face
【鼻腔】 the nasal cavity
【鼻息】 the breath
【鼻血】 nosebleed; nasal hemorrhage
【鼻子】 a nose
【鼻祖】 a founder; an originator
【鼻塞】 to have a stuffy nose; nasal congestion
【鼻煙壺】 a snuff bottle
【鼻炎】 nasal catarrh
【鼻癌】 nasopharyngeal cancer
【鼻音】 (phonetics) nasal sounds; nasals

三畫

鼾 4633 ㄏㄢ hān
to snore
【鼾聲】 sound of snoring
【鼾聲如雷】 to snore terribly
【鼾睡】 a heavy sleep with snoring

齊 部
ㄑㄧˊ qí

齊 4634 ㄑㄧˊ qí
1. equal; uniform; to be on a level 2. name of an ancient feudal state 3. name of a dynasty 4. to set in order 5. a Chinese family name
【齊備】 everything ready; everything complete
【齊步】 in step; uniform steps
【齊眉】 respect between husband and wife
【齊名】 equally well-known; equal in fame
【齊頭並進】 to go ahead together; to march together
【齊年】 of the same age
【齊集】 all assembled
【齊家】 to govern one's family
【齊驅】 to advance abreast—to be equal in ability
【齊全】 everything complete; nothing missing; all in readiness
【齊心】 of one mind
【齊聲】 in unison; with one voice
【齊人之福】 to have more than one wife; to have a concubine
【齊一】 uniform; equal

〔齒部〕

三畫

齋 4635 (斋) ㄓㄞ zhāi
1. pious; respectful; chaste; pure 2. to abstain from meat; to fast 3. to purify oneself 4. to provide Buddhist monks with meals 5. a room for study; a study; a school 6. a vegetarian meal
【齋飯】a vegetarian meal for a Buddhist monk
【齋堂】a dining room in a Buddhist temple
【齋戒】to abstain from meat, wine, etc. (when offering sacrifices to gods); to fast
【齋戒沐浴】to purify oneself by observing abstinent rules and bathing
【齋舍】① a room for fasting ② a study; a school
【齋僧】to provide Buddhist monks with meals

七畫

齎 4636 (賫、賷) ㄐㄧ jī
1. to present; to offer 2. to harbor; to have in one's mind; to entertain
【齎志】to cherish unfulfilled ambitions

齒部 ㄔˇ chǐ

齒 4637 ㄔˇ chǐ
1. teeth 2. age 3. to speak of; to mention 4. a toothlike part of anything
【齒髮】one's tooth and hair—one's age
【齒輪】a cogwheel; a gear wheel; a gear
【齒垢】tartar (on the teeth)
【齒科】dentistry
【齒寒】(said of either of two interdependent beings) to suffer due to failure of the other
【齒如編貝】very beautiful teeth
【齒牙餘論】to praise others
【齒齦】gums (of the teeth)
【齒亡舌存】The strong is more likely to fall than the weak.

五畫

齟 4638 ㄐㄩˇ jǔ
irregular teeth
【齟齬】① irregular teeth ② to have discord; to disagree

齠 4639 ㄊㄧㄠˊ tiáo
to shed the milk teeth
【齠年】the age of shedding the milk teeth—childhood

齡 4640 ㄌㄧㄥˊ líng
age; years

齣 4641 ㄔㄨ chū
1. a chapter (of old-style novels) 2. a numerary adjunct for plays

齜 4642 ㄗ zī
1. to open the mouth and show the teeth 2. uneven teeth
【齜牙】to open the mouth and show the teeth

六畫

齦 4643 ㄧㄣˊ yín
gums (of the teeth)

齧 4644 (嚙、囓) ㄋㄧㄝˋ niè
to gnaw; to bite
【齧噬】to bite; to gnaw
【齧合】①to clench the teeth ② (said of gears) to mesh; to engage

七畫

齪 4645 ㄔㄨㄛˋ chuò
as in 齷齪—① narrow; small ② dirty

齬 4646 ㄩˇ yǔ
as in 齟齬—① uneven teeth ② to disagree; to have discord

九畫

齷 4647 ㄨㄛˋ wò
【齷齪】① narrow; small ② dirty

齲 4648 ㄑㄩˇ qǔ

tooth decay
【齲齒】a decayed tooth; a carious tooth

龍 部
ㄌㄨㄥˊ lóng

龍 4649
ㄌㄨㄥˊ lóng
1. a dragon 2. of the emperor; imperial 3. a huge extinct reptile 4. a Chinese family name
【龍袍】an imperial robe
【龍蟠虎踞】like a dragon that coils and a tiger that crouches — impressive terrain
【龍門】fame; success; glory
【龍飛鳳舞】vivid and vigorous flourishes in calligraphy
【龍鳳】① fine offspring; excellent children ② men of wisdom ③ a noble look ④ man and woman ⑤ dragon and phoenix
【龍鳳呈祥】prosperity brought by the dragon and the phoenix—in extremely good fortune
【龍套】① a kind of costume in Chinese opera ② a character in such a costume in Chinese opera —a role that requires neither acting nor singing ③ a very insignificant role
【龍頭】① a faucet; a tap; a cock ② the top successful candidate in the imperial examination under the former civil service examination system ③ the leader of a sect, secret society, etc.
【龍潭虎穴】places of extreme danger
【龍騰虎躍】dragons rising and tigers leaping — a scene of bustling activity
【龍肝鳳髓】rare delicacies
【龍井茶】a kind of green tea produced at Hangchow, Chekiang
【龍捲風】a tornado; a cyclone; a twister
【龍蝦】a lobster
【龍行虎步】the dignified manner of an emperor
【龍舟 or 龍船】a dragon-shaped racing boat
【龍舟競渡】a dragon-boat race
【龍爭虎鬥】a fierce battle between giants
【龍蛇混雜】the wise and the unwise huddled together
【龍山寺】Lung Shan Temple, an old temple in Taipei, Taiwan
【龍生龍，鳳生鳳】Like father, like son.
【龍顏】the noble face of the emperor
【龍眼】longan
【龍王】the sea god

六畫

龔 4650
ㄍㄨㄥ gōng
1. reverential 亦作「恭」 2. a Chinese family name

龕 4651
ㄎㄢ kān
a niche for an idol

龜 部
ㄍㄨㄟ guī

龜 4652
1. ㄍㄨㄟ guī
a tortoise; a turtle
【龜甲】tortoiseshell
【龜兆】① marks on seared tortoiseshell used for divination in ancient times ② omens
【龜筮】divination

龜 4652
2. ㄐㄩㄣ jūn
chapped; cracked
【龜裂】chapped; cracked

龠 部
ㄩㄝ yuè

龠 4653
ㄩㄝ yuè
1. a kind of flute 2. a kind of measuring vessel

九畫

龥 4654
(籲) ㄩˋ yù
to call for; to make an appeal for
【龥天賜福】to implore Heaven for a blessing

〔龍・龜・龠部〕

國語注音符號索引

編　法：本索引係照單字讀音，按國語注音符號順序編列，其讀音相同者，再按部首順序。單字後註明單字編號。

用　法：遇有僅知讀音不熟悉字形之單字，可按國語注音符號，查出索引中單字，再根據單字編號，查出書內單字及這一單字爲首所組成的詞語。

MANDARIN PHONETIC SYMBOL INDEX

In this index the characters are arranged according to their respective MPS transcriptions. Characters with the same pronunciation are arranged according to their respective radicals. The figure to the right of each character is its identification number under which the character can be found in the body of the dictionary.

If the dictionary user knows the pronunciation of the character he is looking for but is unfamiliar with its strokes, he can find it in the index according to its MPS transcription. Using the identification number as a guide, he can locate in the dictionary the character and the entries beneath it.

單字	字號
ㄅ	
ㄅㄚ	
八	267
叭	467
吧	514
巴	1073
扒	1418
疤	2610
笆	2923
芭	3351
ㄅㄚˊ	
八	267
拔	1463
跋	3883
ㄅㄚˇ	
把	1436
靶	4354
ㄅㄚˋ	
壩	774
把	1436
灞	2333
爸	2419
罷	3140
耙	3181
霸	4339
˙ㄅㄚ	
吧	514
罷	3140
ㄅㄛ	
剝	345
撥	1591
播	1598
波	2119
玻	2505
番	2594
般	3329
菠	3406
鉢	4128
缽 (鉢)	4128
盋 (鉢)	4128
ㄅㄛˊ	
伯	103
勃	372
博	423
帛	1084
搏	1558
柏	1834
泊	2111
浡	2146
渤	2207
白	2669
百	2670
箔	2944
脖	3250
膊	3277
舶	3331
蔔	3466
薄	3478
駁	4462
ㄅㄛˇ	
跛	3887
ㄅㄛˋ	
北	399
播	1598
薄	3478
˙ㄅㄛ	
蔔	3466
ㄅㄞ	
掰	1536
ㄅㄞˊ	
白	2669
ㄅㄞˇ	
伯	103
擺	1633
柏	1834
百	2670
ㄅㄞˋ	
拜	1471
敗	1659
稗	2866
ㄅㄟ	
卑	418
埤	727
悲	1305
揹	1555
杯	1810
盃	2690
碑	2783
背	3227
ㄅㄟˇ	
北	399
ㄅㄟˋ	
倍	168
備	206
悖	1281
憊	1365
焙	2363
背	3227
臂	3291
蓓	3453
被	3603
褙	3628
貝	3809
輩	3946
ㄅㄠ	
剝	345
包	393
炮	2347
炰 (炮)	2347
胞	3231
苞	3363
褒	3635
ㄅㄠˊ	
薄	3478
ㄅㄠˇ	
保	156
堡	734
寶	982
寳 (寶)	982
褓	3627
飽	4421
鴇	4557
ㄅㄠˋ	
報	733
抱	1444
暴	1754
瀑	2320
爆	2409
豹	3804
鮑	4533
ㄅㄢ	
扳	1428
搬	1570
斑	1676
班	2508
般	3329
頒	4382
ㄅㄢˇ	
板	1815
版	2427
闆	4243
ㄅㄢˋ	
伴	106
半	416
扮	1425
拌	1457
瓣	2555
絆	3044
辦	3962
ㄅㄣ	
奔	806
犇 (奔)	806
ㄅㄣˇ	
畚	811
本	1793
畚	2585
ㄅㄣˋ	
奔	806
犇 (奔)	806
笨	2928
ㄅㄤ	
傍	202
幫	1101
帮 (幫)	1101
梆	1884
邦	4058
ㄅㄤˇ	
榜	1929
綁	3056
膀	3275
ㄅㄤˋ	
傍	202
旁	1692
棒	1892
磅	2799
膀	3275
蚌	3520
謗	3761
鎊	4180
ㄅㄥ	
崩	1045
繃	3102
綳 (繃)	3102
ㄅㄥˊ	
甭	2573
ㄅㄥˇ	
繃	3102
綳 (繃)	3102
ㄅㄥˋ	
榜	1929
蹦	3912
迸	4006
进 (迸)	4006
ㄅㄧ	
逼	4013
ㄅㄧˊ	
鼻	4632
ㄅㄧˇ	
匕	397
妣	835
彼	1186
比	2044
筆	2931
鄙	4074
ㄅㄧˋ	
壁	763
婢	879
幣	1100
庇	1114
弊	1153
必	1219
拂	1451
敝	1660
斃	1672
比	2044
泌	2113
璧	2546
畢	2592
碧	2790
祕	2822
秘 (祕)	2822
臂	3291
蔽	3468
裨	3617
辟	3960
逼	4013
避	4047
鄙	4074
閉	4222
陛	4264
ㄅㄧㄝ	
憋	1364
鼈	4626
鱉 (鼈)	4626
ㄅㄧㄝˊ	
別	323
蹩	3915
ㄅㄧㄝˇ	
癟	2656
瘪 (癟)	2656
ㄅㄧㄝˋ	
彆	1171
ㄅㄧㄠ	
彪	1180
杓	1802
標	1948
鏢	4195
飆	4411
飇 (飆)	4411
ㄅㄧㄠˇ	
婊	883
表	3592
裱	3618
錶	4166
ㄅㄧㄢ	
編	3082
蝙	3545
邊	4054

鞭	4360
ㄅㄧㄢˇ	
匾	409
扁	1411
蝙	3545
褊	3625
貶	3823
ㄅㄧㄢˋ	
便	145
弁	1150
徧	1206
辮	3114
變	3786
辨	3963
辯	3965
辦	3966
遍	4019
ㄅㄧㄣ	
儐	236
彬	1179
斌	1674
檳	1977
濱	2315
瀕	2324
繽	3116
賓	3839
賔	3839
(賓)	
ㄅㄧㄣˋ	
儐	236
擯	1625
殯	2029
鬢	4513
ㄅㄧㄥ	
兵	272
冰	290
ㄅㄧㄥˇ	
丙	15
屏	1016
柄	1833
炳	2349
秉	2847
稟	2862
餅	4427
餠	4427
(餅)	
ㄅㄧㄥˋ	
並	18
併	163
倂	163
(併)	
弁	1105
摒	1578
柄	1833
病	2617
ㄅㄨˊ	
不	8
ㄅㄨˇ	
卜	424
哺	562
捕	1499
補	3613
ㄅㄨˋ	
不	8
佈	114
埠	726
布	1077
怖	1239
步	2005
簿	2974
部	4068
ㄆ	
單字	字號
ㄆㄚ	
趴	3881
ㄆㄚˊ	
扒	1418
爬	2414
琶	2523
耙	3181
ㄆㄚˋ	
帕	1080
怕	1240
˙ㄆㄚ	
琶	2523
ㄆㄛ	
坡	708
波	2119
潑	2280
ㄆㄛˊ	
婆	873
ㄆㄛˇ	
叵	474
頗	4385
ㄆㄛˋ	
拍	1459
朴	1796
泊	2111
珀	2506
破	2773
迫	3980
廹	3980
(迫)	
魄	4524
ㄆㄞ	
拍	1459
ㄆㄞˊ	
徘	1201
排	1518
牌	2428
ㄆㄞˋ	
派	2142
湃	2214
ㄆㄟ	
披	1446
胚	3230
ㄆㄟˊ	
培	724
裴	3620
賠	3843
陪	4271
ㄆㄟˋ	
佩	126
沛	2098
珮	2509
轡	3957
配	4081
ㄆㄠ	
抛	1456
拋	1456
(抛)	
泡	2121
ㄆㄠˊ	
刨	324
咆	530
庖	1117
炮	2347
袍	3601
ㄆㄠˇ	
跑	3886
ㄆㄠˋ	
泡	2121
炮	2347
疱	2620
皰	2683
砲	2775
礮	2815
ㄆㄡˇ	
剖	342
ㄆㄢ	
攀	1636
潘	2282
番	2594
ㄆㄢˊ	
槃	1933
盤	2702
磐	2803
胖	3229
蟠	3564
ㄆㄢˋ	
判	322
叛	455
拌	1457
拚	1468
畔	2584
盼	2711
ㄆㄣ	
噴	660
ㄆㄣˊ	
盆	2688
ㄆㄤ	
乓	26
滂	2245
磅	2799
ㄆㄤˊ	
傍	202
龐	1145
彷	1184
徬	1210
旁	1692
旁	1692
(旁)	
膀	3275
螃	3553
ㄆㄤˋ	
胖	3229
ㄆㄥ	
怦	1242
抨	1445
澎	2294
烹	2361
砰	2771
ㄆㄥˊ	
彭	1181
朋	1781
棚	1897
澎	2294
硼	2781
篷	2964
膨	3283
蓬	3456
鵬	4569
ㄆㄥˇ	
捧	1504
ㄆㄥˋ	
碰	2786
掽	2786
(碰)	
ㄆㄧ	
丕	12
劈	356
匹	408
批	1429
披	1446
砒	2768
紕	3026
被	3603
霹	4338
ㄆㄧˊ	
啤	582
埤	727
枇	1814
毗	2045
琵	2522
疲	2613
皮	2682
罷	3140
脾	3261
ㄆㄧˇ	
仳	90
劈	356
匹	408
否	494
疋	2603
痞	2632
癖	2654
ㄆㄧˋ	
僻	228
屁	1007
譬	3780
闢	4249
ㄆㄧㄝ	
撇	1592
瞥	2750
ㄆㄧㄝˇ	
撇	1592
ㄆㄧㄠ	
漂	2261
飄	4410
ㄆㄧㄠˊ	
嫖	895
瓢	2554
ㄆㄧㄠˇ	
漂	2261
縹	3098
ㄆㄧㄠˋ	
剽	353
漂	2261
票	2830
驃	4483
ㄆㄧㄢ	
偏	190
扁	1411
片	2426
篇	2957
翩	3165
ㄆㄧㄢˊ	
便	145
胼	3253

胼 3253
(胼)
駢 4476

ㄆㄧㄢ
偏 1206
片 2426
遍 4019
騙 4478

ㄆㄧㄣ
姘 876
姸 876
(姸)
拼 1521
拚 1521
(拼)

ㄆㄧㄣˊ
貧 3814
頻 4392

ㄆㄧㄣˇ
品 547

ㄆㄧㄣˋ
牝 2431
聘 3194

ㄆㄧㄥ
乒 33
娉 864

ㄆㄧㄥˊ
坪 714
屏 1016
平 1103
憑 1363
瓶 2558
甁 2558
(瓶)
秤 2854
萍 3417
蘋 3505
評 3692

ㄆㄨ
仆 72
扑 1417
撲 1601
鋪 4149

ㄆㄨˊ
僕 218
匍 395
朴 1796
樸 1952
璞 2545
脯 3249
菩 3421
葡 3431
蒲 3445

ㄆㄨˇ
圃 687
埔 723
普 1735
浦 2149
溥 2237
譜 3777

ㄆㄨˋ
暴 1754
曝 1763
瀑 2320
舖 3321
鋪 4149

ㄇ

單字	字號

ㄇㄚ
媽 891

ㄇㄚˊ
痲 2635
麻 4602
麼 4603

ㄇㄚˇ
嗎 619
瑪 2539
碼 2796
螞 3555
馬 4456

ㄇㄚˋ
罵 3139

˙ㄇㄚ
嗎 619
麼 4603
麽 4603
(麼)

ㄇㄛ
摸 1582

ㄇㄛˊ
摩 1583
摹 1584
模 1950
磨 2804
糢 3008
膜 3279
魔 4529
麼 4603

ㄇㄛˇ
抹 1448

ㄇㄛˋ
墨 759
寞 969
抹 1448
末 1792
歿 2014
殁 2014
(歿)
沒 2094
沫 2099
漠 2267
磨 2804
脈 3244
衇 3244
(脈)
脉 3244
(脈)
膜 3279
茉 3372
莫 3396
陌 4261
驀 4482
麥 4598
默 4611

˙ㄇㄜ
麼 4603

ㄇㄞˊ
埋 719

ㄇㄞˇ
買 3824

ㄇㄞˋ
脈 3244
衇 3244
(脈)
脉 3244
(脈)
賣 3845
邁 4050
麥 4598

ㄇㄟˊ
媒 886
枚 1823
梅 1873
楣 1919
沒 2094
湄 2218
煤 2371
玫 2497
眉 2715
莓 3390
霉 4328
黴 4621

ㄇㄟˇ
每 2042
浼 2156
美 3145
鎂 4178

ㄇㄟˋ
妹 839
媚 887
寐 966
昧 1721
瑁 2526
眛 2717
謎 3757
魅 4525

ㄇㄠ
摸 1582
貓 3808
猫 3808
(貓)

ㄇㄠˊ
毛 2046
矛 2755
茅 3371
錨 4168
髦 4504

ㄇㄠˇ
卯 428

ㄇㄠˋ
冒 281
帽 1094
茂 3368
貌 3807
貿 3830

ㄇㄡˊ
牟 2432
眸 2722
謀 3753

ㄇㄡˇ
某 1835
牡 2433

ㄇㄡˋ
茂 3368

ㄇㄢˊ
埋 719
漫 2272
瞞 2743
蠻 3579
蹣 3909
饅 4441
鰻 4545

ㄇㄢˇ
滿 2259

ㄇㄢˋ
慢 1339
曼 1774
漫 2272
蔓 3460
謾 3766

ㄇㄣ
悶 1303
燜 2399

ㄇㄣˊ
們 170
捫 1505
門 4219

ㄇㄣˋ
悶 1303
燜 2399

˙ㄇㄣ
們 170

ㄇㄤˊ
忙 1225
氓 2054
盲 2708
芒 3346
茫 3376

ㄇㄤˇ
莽 3398
莾 3398
(莽)
蟒 3563

ㄇㄥ
矇 2752

ㄇㄥˊ
懵 1381
懜 1381
(懵)
朦 1789
檬 1973
氓 2054
濛 2306
盟 2699
矇 2752
萌 3416
蒙 3443

ㄇㄥˇ
懵 1381
猛 2468
錳 4165

ㄇㄥˋ
夢 789
孟 920

ㄇㄧ
咪 537

ㄇㄧˊ
彌 1172
瀰 2328
獼 2490
糜 3003
謎 3757
迷 3983
靡 4349
麋 4591

ㄇㄧˇ
弭 1166
米 2984
靡 4349

ㄇㄧˋ

符	2929
縛	3091
芙	3347
輻	3950
ㄈㄨˇ	
俯	160
府	1120
撫	1597
斧	1684
父	2418
甫	2571
脯	3249
腐	3257
腑	3258
輔	3940
釜	4114
ㄈㄨˋ	
仆	72
付	81
傅	201
副	346
咐	534
婦	880
富	965
復	1208
服	1782
父	2418
腹	3270
複	3624
覆	3648
訃	3668
負	3810
賦	3847
赴	3870
阜	4250
附	4259
馥	4454
駙	4467
ㄉ	
單字	字號
ㄉㄚ	
搭	1567
答	2938
ㄉㄚˊ	
打	1419
答	2938
達	4026
ㄉㄚˇ	
打	1419
ㄉㄚˋ	
大	792
ㄉㄜˊ	
得	1200
德	1215
˙ㄉㄜ	
得	1200
的	2673
ㄉㄞ	
呆	512
待	1191
獃	2478
ㄉㄞˇ	
歹	2012
逮	4007
ㄉㄞˋ	
代	84
大	792
帶	1090
待	1191
怠	1253
戴	1405
殆	2016
玳	2502
袋	3600
貸	3825
逮	4007
黛	4613
ㄉㄟˇ	
得	1200
ㄉㄠ	
刀	309
叨	458
ㄉㄠˇ	
倒	171
導	993
島	1035
搗	1563
擣	1623
禱	2840
ㄉㄠˋ	
倒	171
到	328
導	993
悼	1293
盜	2697
稻	2874
蹈	3906
道	4025
ㄉㄡ	
兜	261
都	4071
ㄉㄡˇ	
抖	1439
斗	1677
陡	4266
ㄉㄡˋ	
痘	2627
荳	3400
讀	3785
豆	3794
逗	3997
鬥	4514
鬭	4517
ㄉㄢ	
丹	24
單	613
擔	1611
担(擔)	1611
殫	2026
耽	3187
躭	3924
ㄉㄢˇ	
撢	1604
撣(撢)	1604
膽	3287
胆(膽)	3287
ㄉㄢˋ	
但	112
彈	1170
擔	1611
旦	1702
氮	2062
淡	2182
澹	2300
石	2764
萏	3420
蛋	3527
誕	3715
ㄉㄤ	
噹	659
璫	2549
當	2598
鐺	4205
ㄉㄤˇ	
擋	1613
檔	1969
當	2598
黨	4619
ㄉㄤˋ	
擋	1613
檔	1969
當	2598
盪	2705
蕩	3476
ㄉㄥ	
燈	2391
登	2666
ㄉㄥˇ	
等	2933
ㄉㄥˋ	
凳	303
櫈(凳)	303
澄	2292
凳	2668
櫈(凳)	2668
瞪	2747
鄧	4075
ㄉㄧ	
低	116
提	1541
氐	2052
滴	2256
隄	4279
堤(隄)	4279
ㄉㄧˊ	
嫡	896
敵	1667
滌	2253
狄	2454
的	2673
笛	2927
荻	3386
迪	3979
廸(迪)	3979
ㄉㄧˇ	
底	1116
抵	1447
氐	2052
牴	2439
砥	2769
詆	3687
邸	4062
ㄉㄧˋ	
地	699
帝	1086
弟	1163
的	2673
第	2930
締	3080
蒂	3439
遞	4031
ㄉㄧㄝ	
爹	2420
ㄉㄧㄝˊ	
喋	600
疊	2602
叠(疊)	2602
碟	2793
蝶	3551
諜	3741
跌	3885
ㄉㄧㄠ	
凋	294
刁	310
叼	459
碉	2785
貂	3806
雕	4310
鵰	4570
ㄉㄧㄠˋ	
弔	1159
吊(弔)	1159
掉	1517
調	3730
釣	4116
ㄉㄧㄡ	
丟	17
ㄉㄧㄢ	
巔	1058
滇	2248
癲	2663
顛	4399
ㄉㄧㄢˇ	
典	275
碘	2787
點	4612
ㄉㄧㄢˋ	
佃	111
墊	755
奠	813
店	1118
惦	1300
殿	2036
澱	2298
玷	2501
甸	2579
電	4324
ㄉㄧㄥ	
丁	2
叮	468
玎	2495
町	2580
疔	2606
盯	2707
釘	4113
ㄉㄧㄥˇ	
頂	4374
鼎	4627
ㄉㄧㄥˋ	
定	945
訂	3667
釘	4113
錠	4159
ㄉㄨ	
督	2734
都	4071
ㄉㄨˊ	

毒	2043
瀆	2318
犢	2448
獨	2483
讀	3785
黷	4622

ㄉㄨˇ

堵	738
睹	2736
篤	2961
肚	3213
覩	3655
賭	3850

ㄉㄨˋ

妒	830
妬 (妒)	830
度	1121
杜	1806
渡	2204
肚	3213
蠹	3578
蠧 (蠹)	3578
鍍	4170

ㄉㄨㄛ

哆	549
多	785

ㄉㄨㄛˊ

多	785
奪	816
鐸	4204

ㄉㄨㄛˇ

朶	1798
朵 (朶)	1798
躲	3925

ㄉㄨㄛˋ

剁	330
咄	529
墮	761
度	1121
惰	1308
舵	3330
踱	3902

ㄉㄨㄟ

堆	732

ㄉㄨㄟˋ

兌	257
對	992
敦	1664
隊	4283

ㄉㄨㄢ

端	2919

ㄉㄨㄢˇ

短	2761

ㄉㄨㄢˋ

斷	1688
段	2031
緞	3078
鍛	4172
煅 (鍛)	4172

ㄉㄨㄣ

墩	760
敦	1664
燉	2394
蹲	3914

ㄉㄨㄣˋ

噸	657
沌	2089
燉	2394
盾	2713
遁	4014
遯	4038
鈍	4119
頓	4383

ㄉㄨㄥ

冬	289
咚	524
東	1812

ㄉㄨㄥˇ

懂	1372
董	3432

ㄉㄨㄥˋ

凍	296
動	377
恫	1264
棟	1896
洞	2133
胴	3238

ㄊ

單字	字號

ㄊㄚ

他	79
塌	740
她	823
它	933
牠	2434

ㄊㄚˇ

塔	743

ㄊㄚˋ

拓	1462
榻	1930
沓	2097
獺	2488
踏	3897

ㄊㄜ

牠	2434

ㄊㄜˋ

特	2440

ㄊㄞ

胎	3228
苔	3360

ㄊㄞˊ

台	470
擡	1621
抬 (擡)	1621
枱	1848
檯	1976
臺	3307
苔	3360
跆	3884
颱	4407

ㄊㄞˋ

太	794
態	1336
汰	2081
泰	2128

ㄊㄠ

叨	458
掏	1515
滔	2251
濤	2310
韜	4366
饕	4449

ㄊㄠˊ

桃	1864
淘	2179
濤	2310
萄	3413
逃	3988
陶	4275

ㄊㄠˇ

討	3669

ㄊㄠˋ

套	810

ㄊㄡ

偷	198

ㄊㄡˊ

投	1437
頭	4387

ㄊㄡˋ

透	3993

˙ㄊㄡ

頭	4387

ㄊㄢ

坍	704
探	1526
攤	1642
灘	2332
癱	2664
貪	3817

ㄊㄢˊ

壇	766
彈	1170
曇	1756
檀	1966
潭	2287
痰	2633
罈	3128
覃	3647
談	3733
譚	3776

ㄊㄢˇ

坦	710
忐	1222
毯	2048
袒	3602

ㄊㄢˋ

探	1526
歎	1997
嘆 (歎)	1997
炭	2351
碳	2792

ㄊㄤ

湯	2228

ㄊㄤˊ

唐	569
堂	730
塘	745
搪	1571
棠	1898
糖	3002
膛	3282
螳	3558

ㄊㄤˇ

倘	174
淌	2174
躺	3926

ㄊㄤˋ

燙	2398
趟	3878

ㄊㄥˊ

疼	2615
籐	2978
藤	3496
謄	3758
騰	4479

ㄊㄧ

剔	341
梯	1880
踢	3899

ㄊㄧˊ

啼	592
提	1541
蹄	3905
隄	4279
堤 (隄)	4279
題	4395

ㄊㄧˇ

體	4502

ㄊㄧˋ

倜	177
剃	336
嚏	664
屜	1017
屉 (屜)	1017
弟	1163
悌	1277
惕	1298
替	1776
涕	2164

ㄊㄧㄝ

帖	1081
貼	3827

ㄊㄧㄝˇ

帖	1081
鐵	4203

ㄊㄧㄠ

挑	1482

ㄊㄧㄠˊ

條	1877
調	3730
迢	3977
齠	4639

ㄊㄧㄠˇ

挑	1482
窕	2894

ㄊㄧㄠˋ

眺	2724
跳	3894

ㄊㄧㄢ

天	793
添	2197

ㄊㄧㄢˊ

塡	747
恬	1265
滇	2248
甜	2564
田	2574
畋	2583

ㄊㄧㄢˇ

忝	1237
殄	2017
舔	3320

ㄊㄧㄥ	
廳	1146
汀	2067
聽	3202
ㄊㄧㄥˊ	
亭	66
停	193
婷	885
庭	1124
廷	1148
ㄊㄧㄥˇ	
挺	1493
町	2580
艇	3333
鋌	4145
ㄊㄧㄥˋ	
聽	3202
ㄊㄨ	
禿	2844
秃	2844
(禿)	
ㄊㄨˊ	
凸	305
圖	694
塗	744
屠	1018
徒	1199
突	2890
荼	3387
途	3996
ㄊㄨˇ	
吐	486
土	696
ㄊㄨˋ	
兔	260
兎	260
(兔)	
吐	486
ㄊㄨㄛ	
它	933
托	1423
拖	1465
拕	1465
(拖)	
牠	2434
脫	3248
託	3674
ㄊㄨㄛˊ	
陀	4258
馱	4459
駝	4469
鮀	4559
ㄊㄨㄛˇ	
妥	836
橢	1963
ㄊㄨㄛˋ	
唾	576
拓	1462
魄	4524
ㄊㄨㄟ	
推	1529
ㄊㄨㄟˊ	
頹	4391
ㄊㄨㄟˇ	
腿	3274
ㄊㄨㄟˋ	
蛻	3533
退	3986
ㄊㄨㄢ	
湍	2221
ㄊㄨㄢˊ	
團	695
ㄊㄨㄣ	
呑	491
ㄊㄨㄣˊ	
囤	681
屯	1023
臀	3290
飩	4415
ㄊㄨㄣˋ	
褪	3630
ㄊㄨㄥ	
恫	1264
痌	2622
通	3999
ㄊㄨㄥˊ	
僮	224
同	482
桐	1868
瞳	2746
童	2915
筒	2936
銅	4134
ㄊㄨㄥˇ	
桶	1871
筒	2936
統	3052
ㄊㄨㄥˋ	
慟	1341
痛	2626
ㄋ	
單字	字號
ㄋㄚˊ	
南	422
拿	1486
挐	1486
(拿)	
ㄋㄚˇ	
哪	570
那	4057
ㄋㄚˋ	
吶	501
娜	869
納	3022
那	4057
˙ㄋㄚ	
哪	570
˙ㄋㄜ	
呢	515
ㄋㄞˇ	
乃	27
奶	821
ㄋㄞˋ	
奈	804
耐	3179
ㄋㄟˇ	
那	4057
餒	4429
ㄋㄟˋ	
內	264
那	4057
ㄋㄠˊ	
撓	1593
鐃	4198
ㄋㄠˇ	
惱	1309
瑙	2530
腦	3264
ㄋㄠˋ	
淖	2175
鬧	4515
ㄋㄢˊ	
南	422
喃	595
男	2578
難	4317
ㄋㄢˇ	
赧	3866
ㄋㄢˋ	
難	4317
ㄋㄣˋ	
嫩	899
ㄋㄤˊ	
囊	674
ㄋㄤˇ	
曩	1765
ㄋㄥˊ	
能	3240
ㄋㄥˋ	
濘	2305
ㄋㄧˊ	
呢	515
尼	1003
泥	2122
霓	4332
ㄋㄧˇ	
你	105
擬	1624
ㄋㄧˋ	
匿	410
暱	1755
昵	1755
(暱)	
泥	2122
溺	2242
膩	3284
逆	3990
ㄋㄧㄝ	
捏	1502
揑	1502
(捏)	
捻	1509
ㄋㄧㄝˋ	
乜	37
孽	931
孼	931
(孽)	
涅	2158
湼	2158
(涅)	
蘖	3502
糵	3502
(蘖)	
躡	3921
鎳	4186
鑷	4213
齧	4644
嚙	4644
(齧)	
囓	4644
(齧)	
ㄋㄧㄠˇ	
嬝	906
嫋	906
(嬝)	
裊	3607
鳥	4551
ㄋㄧㄠˋ	
尿	1005
溺	2242
ㄋㄧㄡ	
妞	832
ㄋㄧㄡˊ	
牛	2430
ㄋㄧㄡˇ	
忸	1231
扭	1424
紐	3023
鈕	4120
ㄋㄧㄡˋ	
拗	1464
謬	3768
ㄋㄧㄢˊ	
年	1104
拈	1453
粘	2988
黏	4608
ㄋㄧㄢˇ	
捻	1509
撚	1594
攆	1635
碾	2795
輾	3951
ㄋㄧㄢˋ	
唸	589
念	1234
ㄋㄧㄣˊ	
您	1287
ㄋㄧㄤˊ	
娘	867
孃	867
(娘)	
ㄋㄧㄤˋ	
釀	4102
ㄋㄧㄥˊ	
凝	298
嚀	662
寧	971
擰	1629
檸	1972
獰	2485
ㄋㄧㄥˇ	
擰	1629
ㄋㄧㄥˋ	
佞	125
濘	2305

ㄋㄨˊ
奴 820
駑 4464

ㄋㄨˇ
努 366

ㄋㄨˋ
怒 1251

ㄋㄨㄛˊ
娜 869
挪 1489

ㄋㄨㄛˇ
娜 869

ㄋㄨㄛˋ
懦 1377
糯 3011
穤(糯) 3011
稬(糯) 3011
諾 3752

ㄋㄨㄢˇ
暖 1749

ㄋㄨㄥˊ
儂 230
濃 2303
穠 2882
膿 3286
農 3969

ㄋㄨㄥˋ
弄 1151

ㄋㄩˇ
女 819

ㄋㄩˋ
忸 1231

ㄋㄩㄝˋ
瘧 2643
虐 3511
謔 3756

ㄌ

單字	字號

ㄌㄚ
喇 597
拉 1455

ㄌㄚˊ
剌 339
拉 1455

ㄌㄚˇ
喇 597

ㄌㄚˋ
剌 339
瘌 2642
腊 3262
臘 3298
蠟 3573
辣 3961

˙ㄌㄚ
啦 585

˙ㄌㄛ
咯 540

ㄌㄜˋ
勒 376
垃 713
捋 1495
樂 1942
肋 3209

˙ㄌㄜ
了 45

ㄌㄞˊ
來 132
萊 3414

ㄌㄞˋ
癩 2660
賴 3851

ㄌㄟ
勒 376

ㄌㄟˊ
擂 1606
累 3037
纍 3121
羸 3155
雷 4323

ㄌㄟˇ
儡 242
壘 770
磊 2801
累 3037
蕾 3479

ㄌㄟˋ
擂 1606
淚 2180
泪(淚) 2180
累 3037
肋 3209
類 4400

ㄌㄠ
撈 1588

ㄌㄠˊ
勞 381
嘮 641
撈 1588
牢 2435
癆 2653

ㄌㄠˇ
佬 139
姥 853
潦 2285
老 3174

ㄌㄠˋ
勞 381
潦 2285
烙 2359
絡 3048
落 3427
酪 4087

ㄌㄡ
摟 1577

ㄌㄡˊ
嘍 635
樓 1947

ㄌㄡˇ
摟 1577
簍 2966

ㄌㄡˋ
漏 2263
鏤 4196
陋 4260
露 4337

˙ㄌㄡ
嘍 635

ㄌㄢˊ
婪 881
嵐 1047
攔 1637
欄 1981
瀾 2329
籃 2975
藍 3491
蘭 3507
襤 3641
闌 4242

ㄌㄢˇ
懶 1380
攬 1645
擥(攬) 1645
欖 1984
纜 3124
覽 3659

ㄌㄢˋ
濫 2312
瀾 2329
爛 2412
纜 3124

ㄌㄤˊ
廊 1133
榔 1924
浪 2151
狼 2463
琅 2514
郎 4066
鋃 4143

ㄌㄤˇ
朗 1785

ㄌㄤˋ
浪 2151

ㄌㄥˊ
楞 1915
稜 2865

ㄌㄥˇ
冷 292

ㄌㄥˋ
愣 1313
楞 1915

ㄌㄧ
哩 558

ㄌㄧˊ
棃 1887
梨(棃) 1887
犂 2442
犁(犂) 2442
犛 2447
狸 2464
璃 2543
籬 2981
罹 3141
蠡 3574
釐 4111
離 4316
驪 4493
黎 4607
黧 4618

ㄌㄧˇ
俚 155
哩 558
李 1799
浬 2150
理 2513
禮 2839
裏 3609
裡(裏) 3609
里 4107
鯉 4538

ㄌㄧˋ
例 134
俐 151
儷 245
利 325
力 361
勵 387
厲 444
吏 488
唳 575
曆 1758
栗 1852
歷 2010
涖 2165
瀝 2326
痢 2629
礫 2812
礪 2813
立 2910
笠 2926
粒 2987
荔 3375
莉 3397
蒞 3455
隸 4297
鬲 4519
麗 4594

˙ㄌㄧ
裏 3609

ㄌㄧㄚˇ
倆 164

ㄌㄧㄝˊ
咧 535

ㄌㄧㄝˇ
咧 535

ㄌㄧㄝˋ
列 319
劣 364
烈 2354
獵 2486
裂 3606

ㄌㄧㄠ
撩 1599

ㄌㄧㄠˊ
僚 219
嘹 648
寥 974
撩 1599
潦 2285
獠 2482
療 2651
繚 3105
聊 3191
遼 4046
鐐 4199

ㄌㄧㄠˇ
了 45

燎	2393
瞭	2748
ㄌㄧㄠˋ	
廖	1135
料	1678
燎	2393
瞭	2748
鐐	4199
ㄌㄧㄡ	
溜	2234
ㄌㄧㄡˊ	
劉	357
榴	1931
流	2143
瀏	2323
琉	2510
留	2588
畱(留)	2588
瘤	2648
癅(瘤)	2648
硫	2777
磂(硫)	2777
ㄌㄧㄡˇ	
柳	1839
ㄌㄧㄡˋ	
六	269
溜	2234
遛	4030
餾	4440
ㄌㄧㄢˊ	
帘	1082
廉	1132
怜	1248
憐	1357
漣	2268
簾	2973
聯	3197
蓮	3457
連	4005
鐮	4202
ㄌㄧㄢˇ	
臉	3294
ㄌㄧㄢˋ	
戀	1387
斂	1671
歛	1999
殮	2028
煉	2369
練	3086
鍊	4167
鏈	4189
ㄌㄧㄣˊ	
嶙	1052
林	1820
淋	2178
琳	2524
磷	2807
臨	3302
遴	4040
鄰	4077
霖	4333
鱗	4548
麟	4597
ㄌㄧㄣˇ	
凜	297
凛	2304
ㄌㄧㄣˋ	
吝	490
淋	2178
賃	3831
ㄌㄧㄤˊ	
梁	1872
涼	2171
粱	2994
糧	3010
良	3338
量	4110
ㄌㄧㄤˇ	
倆	164
兩	266
ㄌㄧㄤˋ	
亮	67
晾	1742
諒	3736
輛	3943
量	4110
ㄌㄧㄥ	
拎	1460
ㄌㄧㄥˊ	
令	85
伶	107
凌	295
囹	684
怜	1248
泠	2117
淩	2184
玲	2500
綾	3070
羚	3147
聆	3190
菱	3422
鈴	4123
陵	4274
零	4322
靈	4342
齡	4640
ㄌㄧㄥˇ	
嶺	1054
領	4384
ㄌㄧㄥˋ	
令	85
另	462
ㄌㄨˊ	
廬	1144
爐	2411
盧	2704
蘆	3501
顱	4404
鱸	4549
ㄌㄨˇ	
擄	1607
櫓	1978
艪(櫓)	1978
滷	2277
虜	3515
魯	4532
鹵	4585
ㄌㄨˋ	
六	269
勠	385
戮	1402
碌	2782
祿	2832
綠	3061
賂	3832
路	3893
錄	4154
陸	4277
露	4337
鷺	4581
鹿	4589
麓	4593
ㄌㄨㄛ	
囉	673
捋	1495
ㄌㄨㄛˊ	
囉	673
籮	2982
羅	3142
蘿	3509
螺	3559
邏	4055
鑼	4214
騾	4481
ㄌㄨㄛˇ	
擄	1607
虜	3515
裸	3616
ㄌㄨㄛˋ	
咯	540
洛	2134
烙	2359
絡	3048
落	3427
酪	4087
駱	4472
ㄌㄨㄢˊ	
鑾	4216
鸞	4584
ㄌㄨㄢˇ	
卵	431
ㄌㄨㄢˋ	
亂	44
ㄌㄨㄣ	
掄	1514
ㄌㄨㄣˊ	
倫	183
圇	689
掄	1514
淪	2185
論	3737
輪	3947
ㄌㄨㄣˋ	
論	3737
ㄌㄨㄥˊ	
窿	2905
籠	2979
聾	3203
隆	4281
龍	4649
ㄌㄨㄥˇ	
壟	771
籠	2979
隴	4296
ㄌㄨㄥˋ	
弄	1151
ㄌㄩˊ	
閭	4234
驢	4491
ㄌㄩˇ	
侶	142
呂	511
屢	1019
履	1021
捋	1495
旅	1693
縷	3097
褸	3634
鋁	4142
ㄌㄩˋ	
律	1195
慮	1355
氯	2061
濾	2319
率	2492
綠	3061
ㄌㄩㄝˋ	
掠	1523
略	2591
畧(略)	2591
ㄌㄩㄢˊ	
攣	932
ㄍ	
單字	字號
ㄍㄚ	
咖	533
ㄍㄚˊ	
軋	3929
ㄍㄜ	
割	349
咯	540
哥	555
戈	1388
擱	1627
歌	1996
疙	2607
胳	3246
鴿	4564
ㄍㄜˊ	
咯	540
嗝	624
格	1857
葛	3430
蛤	3531
閣	4229
隔	4285
革	4352
骼	4499
ㄍㄜˋ	
個	166
各	479
箇	2950
ㄍㄞ	
該	3706
ㄍㄞˇ	
改	1648
ㄍㄞˋ	
丐	9
概	1940
槩(概)	1940
溉	2264
蓋	3451
盖(蓋)	3451
鈣	4122
ㄍㄟˇ	
給	3050

ㄍㄠ	
皋	2677
皐(皋)	2677
睪	2735
睾(睪)	2735
篙	2962
糕	3001
羔	3146
膏	3276
高	4503
ㄍㄠˇ	
搞	1574
攪	1643
槁	1934
槀(槁)	1934
稿	2871
稾(稿)	2871
ㄍㄠˋ	
告	508
膏	3276
誥	3722
ㄍㄡ	
勾	391
句	461
枸	1831
溝	2233
鉤	4129
ㄍㄡˇ	
枸	1831
狗	2456
苟	3373
ㄍㄡˋ	
勾	391
垢	716
夠	788
够(夠)	788
媾	892
搆	1557
構	1935
詬	3701
購	3853
遘	3989
ㄍㄢ	
乾	43
乹(乾)	43
尲	1000
干	1102
柑	1838
甘	2562
竿	2922
肝	3215
ㄍㄢˇ	
感	1327
擀	1616
敢	1662
桿	1886
橄	1955
稈	2860
趕	3876
ㄍㄢˋ	
幹	1107
贛	3863
ㄍㄣ	
根	1856
跟	3890
ㄍㄣˇ	
艮	3337
ㄍㄣˋ	
亙	54
艮	3337
ㄍㄤ	
剛	343
岡	1028
崗	1042
綱	3064
繮	3110
缸	3125
肛	3214
鋼	4153
ㄍㄤˇ	
岡	1028
崗	1042
港	2210
ㄍㄤˋ	
槓	1938
虹	3519
ㄍㄥ	
庚	1119
更	1770
羹	3154
耕	3182
ㄍㄥˇ	
哽	564
埂	721
梗	1876
耿	3188
鯁	4537
ㄍㄥˋ	
亙	54
更	1770
ㄍㄨ	
估	104
呱	519
咕	522
姑	847
孤	922
沽	2105
菇	3408
辜	3959
鈷	4131
ㄍㄨˊ	
骨	4494
ㄍㄨˇ	
古	460
汩	2080
穀	2870
股	3216
臌	3296
蠱	3576
谷	3791
賈	3835
骨	4494
鵠	4568
鼓	4628
ㄍㄨˋ	
估	104
僱	225
固	685
故	1652
痼	2636
錮	4163
雇	4305
顧	4401
ㄍㄨㄚ	
刮	326
括	1475
瓜	2553
聒	3192
蝸	3552
颳	4408
ㄍㄨㄚˇ	
寡	972
ㄍㄨㄚˋ	
卦	427
掛	1524
挂(掛)	1524
罣	3133
褂	3623
ㄍㄨㄛ	
渦	2209
過	4020
郭	4069
鍋	4169
ㄍㄨㄛˊ	
國	688
摑	1576
ㄍㄨㄛˇ	
果	1822
菓	3424
裹	3621
ㄍㄨㄛˋ	
過	4020
ㄍㄨㄞ	
乖	34
ㄍㄨㄞˇ	
拐	1458
枴	1826
柺(枴)	1826
枴(枴)	1826
ㄍㄨㄞˋ	
怪	1246
ㄍㄨㄟ	
傀	200
圭	698
歸	2011
瑰	2538
瓌	2552
皈	2676
規	3652
閨	4232
鮭	4535
龜	4652
ㄍㄨㄟˇ	
癸	2665
詭	3702
軌	3930
鬼	4521
ㄍㄨㄟˋ	
劊	358
會	1778
桂	1863
檜	1970
櫃	1975
貴	3822
跪	3892
ㄍㄨㄢ	
倌	167
冠	284
官	943
棺	1902
矜	2756
觀	3660
關	4247
鰥	4543
ㄍㄨㄢˇ	
管	2948
舘	3322
館	4436
ㄍㄨㄢˋ	
冠	284
慣	1340
灌	2330
盥	2703
罐	3130
貫	3818
ㄍㄨㄣˇ	
滾	2258
滚(滾)	2258
ㄍㄨㄣˋ	
棍	1891
ㄍㄨㄤ	
光	255
胱	3237
ㄍㄨㄤˇ	
廣	1143
ㄍㄨㄤˋ	
逛	4000
ㄍㄨㄥ	
供	137
公	268
功	362
宮	952
工	1064
弓	1157
恭	1273
攻	1649
紅	3018
躬	3923
龔	4650
ㄍㄨㄥˇ	
拱	1476
汞	2077
鞏	4357
ㄍㄨㄥˋ	
供	137
共	271
貢	3812

ㄎ

單字	字號
ㄎㄚ	
咖	533
ㄎㄚˇ	
卡	426
咳	542
ㄎㄚˋ	
喀	593
ㄎㄜ	
刻	334
柯	1842
棵	1903
瞌	2742
磕	2800

科 2849
窠 2899
苛 3362
蝌 3546
顆 4393

ㄎㄜˊ

咳 542
殼 2034
㱿(殼) 2034
殻(殼) 2034

ㄎㄜˇ

可 469
坷 711
渴 2213

ㄎㄜˋ

克 256
刻 334
剋 338
可 469
嗑 628
客 948
恪 1263
溘 2231
課 3726

ㄎㄞ

揩 1549
開 4223

ㄎㄞˇ

凱 302
嘅 632
嘅(嘅) 632
慨 1342
楷 1921
鎧 4184

ㄎㄞˋ

慨 1342

ㄎㄠˇ

拷 1484
烤 2357
考 3175
攷(考) 3175

ㄎㄠˋ

犒 2446
銬 4139
靠 4348

ㄎㄡˇ

口 457

ㄎㄡˋ

叩 463
寇 964
扣 1421
蔻 3458
釦 4117

ㄎㄢ

刊 315
勘 378
堪 735
戡 1400
看 2716
龕 4651

ㄎㄢˇ

侃 131
坎 705
檻 1974
砍 2767

ㄎㄢˋ

勘 378
看 2716

ㄎㄣˇ

啃 587
墾 764
懇 1376
肯 3221
肎(肯) 3221
肻(肯) 3221

ㄎㄤ

康 1127
慷 1343
糠 3007

ㄎㄤˊ

扛 1422

ㄎㄤˇ

慷 1343

ㄎㄤˋ

亢 59
伉 95
抗 1438
炕 2342

ㄎㄥ

傾 214
坑 707
鏗 4191

ㄎㄥˇ

肯 3221
肎(肯) 3221
肻(肯) 3221

ㄎㄨ

哭 559
枯 1825
窟 2898
骷 4497

ㄎㄨˇ

苦 3365

ㄎㄨˋ

庫 1123
袴 3604
絝(袴) 3604
褲 3632
酷 4090

ㄎㄨㄚ

夸 800
誇 3711

ㄎㄨㄚˇ

垮 718

ㄎㄨㄚˋ

胯 3235
跨 3889

ㄎㄨㄛˋ

廓 1136
括 1475
擴 1632
闊 4241

ㄎㄨㄞˇ

蒯 3309

ㄎㄨㄞˋ

儈 233
劊 358
塊 739
快 1229
會 1778
檜 1970
筷 2941
膾 3288

ㄎㄨㄟ

盔 2695
窺 2904
虧 3517

ㄎㄨㄟˊ

暌 1750
睽 2737
葵 3435
魁 4522

ㄎㄨㄟˇ

傀 200

ㄎㄨㄟˋ

匱 407
喟 608
愧 1329
媿(愧) 1329
憒 1361
潰 2291
饋 4443

ㄎㄨㄢ

寬 979

ㄎㄨㄢˇ

款 1990
欵(款) 1990

ㄎㄨㄣ

坤 709
昆 1710
琨 2516

ㄎㄨㄣˇ

捆 1494
綑 3059

ㄎㄨㄣˋ

困 680
睏 2727

ㄎㄨㄤ

匡 403
框 1866
筐 2935

ㄎㄨㄤˊ

狂 2453

ㄎㄨㄤˋ

曠 1762
框 1866
況 2108
况(況) 2108
礦 2814
鑛 4209

ㄎㄨㄥ

空 2888

ㄎㄨㄥˇ

孔 914
恐 1267

ㄎㄨㄥˋ

控 1527
空 2888

ㄏ

單字 字號

ㄏㄚ

哈 551

ㄏㄚˊ

蛤 3531

ㄏㄚˇ

哈 551

ㄏㄜ

呵 521
喝 606
訶 3684

ㄏㄜˊ

何 121
劾 370
合 476
和 532
曷 1771
核 1854
河 2103
涸 2170
盍 2692
盒 2694
禾 2843
荷 3385
褐 3626
覈 3649
閤 4230
闔 4244

ㄏㄜˋ

和 532
喝 606
嚇 663
荷 3385
賀 3829
赫 3867
郝 4065
鶴 4573
黑 4609

ㄏㄞˊ

孩 923
還 4052
骸 4498

ㄏㄞˇ

海 2154

ㄏㄞˋ

亥 61
咳 542
害 954
駭 4471

ㄏㄟ

嘿 651
黑 4609

ㄏㄠˊ

嗥 647
嚎 661
壕 769
毫 2047
濠 2308
號 3516
蠔 3572
豪 3801
鶴 4573

ㄏㄠˇ

好 824

郝	4065
ㄏㄠˋ	
好	824
昊	1712
浩	2148
澔	2170
皓	2679
耗	3184
號	3516
ㄏㄡˊ	
侯	141
喉	598
猴	2474
ㄏㄡˇ	
吼	505
ㄏㄡˋ	
候	175
厚	439
后	485
後	1196
逅	3989
ㄏㄢ	
憨	1367
酣	4084
鼾	4633
ㄏㄢˊ	
函	308
含	496
寒	967
汗	2072
涵	2169
韓	4365
ㄏㄢˇ	
喊	599
罕	3132
ㄏㄢˋ	
悍	1279
憾	1371
捍	1498
撼	1605
旱	1707
汗	2072
漢	2271
瀚	2325
翰	3167
菡	3419
銲	4150
釬	4150
(銲)	
頷	4389
ㄏㄣˊ	
痕	2624
ㄏㄣˇ	
很	1193
狠	2460
ㄏㄣˋ	
恨	1261
ㄏㄤˊ	
杭	1809
沆	2088
航	3328
行	3581
ㄏㄤˋ	
沆	2088
ㄏㄥ	
亨	63
哼	563
ㄏㄥˊ	
恆	1257
恒	1257
(恆)	
橫	1965
衡	3589
ㄏㄥˋ	
橫	1965
ㄏㄨ	
乎	31
呼	526
忽	1235
戲	1404
ㄏㄨˊ	
囫	683
壺	780
弧	1165
湖	2224
狐	2457
瑚	2534
糊	2997
胡	3232
葫	3433
蝴	3550
餬	4437
鬍	4511
鵠	4568
ㄏㄨˇ	
唬	588
滸	2257
琥	2518
虎	3510
ㄏㄨˋ	
互	51
怙	1241
戶	1407
戽	1408
護	3782
ㄏㄨㄚ	
嘩	639
花	3352
ㄏㄨㄚˊ	
划	318
劃	354
嘩	639
滑	2250
猾	2477
華	3407
譁	3772
ㄏㄨㄚˋ	
劃	354
化	398
樺	1954
畫	2595
華	3407
話	3705
ㄏㄨㄛ	
豁	3792
ㄏㄨㄛˊ	
活	2141
ㄏㄨㄛˇ	
伙	102
夥	791
火	2335
ㄏㄨㄛˋ	
和	532
壑	768
惑	1304
或	1396
獲	2484
禍	2834
穫	2884
豁	3792
貨	3815
霍	4329
ㄏㄨㄞˊ	
徊	1194
懷	1379
淮	2188
ㄏㄨㄞˋ	
壞	772
ㄏㄨㄟ	
徽	1217
恢	1260
揮	1551
暉	1745
灰	2336
詼	3709
輝	3944
麾	4604
ㄏㄨㄟˊ	
回	678
徊	1194
洄	2129
蛔	3529
迴	3982
廻	3982
(迴)	
ㄏㄨㄟˇ	
悔	1278
會	1778
毀	2037
燬	2404
誨	3724
賄	3833
ㄏㄨㄟˋ	
匯	406
卉	417
卉	417
(卉)	
喙	603
彗	1174
彙	1175
惠	1306
慧	1349
晦	1733
會	1778
燴	2406
穢	2881
繪	3109
蕙	3472
薈	3481
誨	3724
諱	3747
賄	3833
ㄏㄨㄢ	
歡	2001
ㄏㄨㄢˊ	
寰	980
環	2547
還	4052
鍰	4174
ㄏㄨㄢˇ	
浣	2147
緩	3083
ㄏㄨㄢˋ	
喚	604
宦	951
幻	1109
患	1285
換	1546
渙	2200
煥	2372
ㄏㄨㄣ	
婚	878
昏	1715
葷	3436
ㄏㄨㄣˊ	
混	2193
渾	2217
餛	4433
魂	4523
ㄏㄨㄣˇ	
混	2193
ㄏㄨㄣˋ	
混	2193
渾	2217
溷	2241
諢	3743
ㄏㄨㄤ	
慌	1334
荒	3383
ㄏㄨㄤˊ	
凰	301
徨	1207
惶	1310
潢	2283
皇	2675
磺	2808
簧	2969
蝗	3548
遑	4022
黃	4605
ㄏㄨㄤˇ	
幌	1096
恍	1259
晃	1728
謊	3759
ㄏㄨㄤˋ	
晃	1728
ㄏㄨㄥ	
哄	548
烘	2356
轟	3956
ㄏㄨㄥˊ	
宏	941
弘	1161
泓	2114
洪	2137
紅	3018
虹	3519
鴻	4565
ㄏㄨㄥˇ	
哄	548
ㄏㄨㄥˋ	
汞	2077
ㄐ	
單字	字號
ㄐㄧ	
乩	41
几	299
唧	607
喞	607

訖 3673
迄 3971

ㄑㄧㄚ

掐 1516

ㄑㄧㄚˊ

卡 426

ㄑㄧㄚˇ

卡 426

ㄑㄧㄚˋ

恰 1266
洽 2140

ㄑㄧㄝ

切 313

ㄑㄧㄝˊ

茄 3370

ㄑㄧㄝˇ

且 11

ㄑㄧㄝˋ

切 313
契 808
妾 841
怯 1245
愜 1318
慊 1333
挈 1487
竊 2909
鍥 4173

ㄑㄧㄠ

撬 1600
敲 1666
橇 1958
蹺 3916

ㄑㄧㄠˊ

僑 217
喬 612
憔 1359
樵 1953
橋 1959
瞧 2749
翹 3170

ㄑㄧㄠˇ

巧 1066
悄 1275
愀 1315
雀 4300
鵲 4571

ㄑㄧㄠˋ

俏 150
峭 1033
撬 1600
殼 2034
㱿(殼) 2034
壳(殼) 2034
竅 2907
翹 3170
鞘 4358

ㄑㄧㄡ

丘 14
秋 2848
秌(秋) 2848
蚯 3523
邱 4061
鞦 4361

ㄑㄧㄡˊ

囚 676
求 2068
泅 2112
球 2512
裘 3612
遒 4024
酋 4079

ㄑㄧㄡˇ

糗 3000

ㄑㄧㄢ

仟 83
千 413
嵌 1046
愆 1323
慳 1344
搴 1573
牽 2441
簽 2972
籤 2980
籖(籤) 2980
謙 3762
遷 4043
鉛 4127
阡 4251
韆 4362

ㄑㄧㄢˊ

乾 43
前 340
掮 1532
潛 2281
箝 2947
虔 3512
鉗 4126
錢 4160
黔 4610

ㄑㄧㄢˇ

淺 2195
繾 3118
譴 3783
遣 4033

ㄑㄧㄢˋ

倩 182
塹 751
慊 1333
欠 1985
歉 1995

ㄑㄧㄣ

侵 143
嶔 1053
欽 1991
衾 3596
親 3656

ㄑㄧㄣˊ

勤 384
擒 1614
琴 2521
禽 2842
秦 2851
芹 3355
衾 3596

ㄑㄧㄣˇ

寢 973

ㄑㄧㄣˋ

沁 2085

ㄑㄧㄤ

嗆 616
搶 1568
槍 1937
腔 3259
鎗 4182
鏘 4192

ㄑㄧㄤˊ

強 1169
强(強) 1169
彊(強) 1169
戕 1397
牆 2425
墻(牆) 2425
薔 3483

ㄑㄧㄤˇ

強 1169
强(強) 1169
彊(強) 1169
搶 1568
襁 3636
襁(襁) 3636

ㄑㄧㄤˋ

嗆 616

ㄑㄧㄥ

傾 214
卿 437
氫 2060
清 2194
蜻 3543
輕 3941
青 4343

ㄑㄧㄥˊ

情 1296
擎 1619
晴 1739
黥 4617

ㄑㄧㄥˇ

請 3734
頃 4375

ㄑㄧㄥˋ

慶 1356
罄 3127
親 3656

ㄑㄩ

區 411
屈 1010
嶇 1049
曲 1768
泃 2096
祛 2824
趨 3879
軀 3927
驅 4484

ㄑㄩˊ

劬 368
渠 2206
衢 3590
麴 4600

ㄑㄩˇ

取 453
娶 875
曲 1768
齲 4648

ㄑㄩˋ

去 445
漆 2262
趣 3877
闃 4238

ㄑㄩㄝ

缺 3126
闕 4245

ㄑㄩㄝˊ

瘸 2650

ㄑㄩㄝˋ

卻 435
却(卻) 435
怯 1245
恪 1263
榷 1939
殼 2034
㱿(殼) 2034
壳(殼) 2034
確 2794
闋 4245
雀 4300
鵲 4571

ㄑㄩㄢ

圈 690

ㄑㄩㄢˊ

全 265
卷 432
拳 1485
權 1983
泉 2127
痊 2623
蜷 3542
詮 3703
銓 4135
鬈 4510

ㄑㄩㄢˇ

犬 2450

ㄑㄩㄢˋ

券 327
勸 388

ㄑㄩㄣˊ

羣 3149
群(羣) 3149
裙 3608

ㄑㄩㄥ

穹 2887

ㄑㄩㄥˊ

瓊 2551
穹 2887
窮 2902

ㄒ

單字 字號

ㄒㄧ

兮 270
吸 502
唏 568
嘻 649
奚 812
嬉 900
希 1079
悉 1284
攜 1640
携(攜) 1640
擕(攜) 1640
擕(攜) 1640

晰 1737
皙 1738
曦 1764
析 1818
栖 1850
棲 1901
欷 1989
淅 2172
溪 2239
熙 2379
熹 2396
熺 2396
(熹)
犀 2443
犧 2449
畦 2589
禧 2837
稀 2858
羲 3152
膝 3280
蜥 3538
蟋 3561
西 3645
谿 3793
蹊 3908

ㄒㄧˊ
媳 890
席 1088
息 1272
惜 1301
昔 1717
檄 1967
熄 2382
習 3160
腊 3262
蓆 3449
襲 3644
錫 4162
隰 4295

ㄒㄧˇ
喜 605
徙 1203
洗 2132
璽 2550
禧 2837

ㄒㄧˋ
係 146
夕 783
戲 1404
戯 1404
(戲)
汐 2071
系 3012
細 3038
繫 3112
隙 4288
隟 4288
(隙)
鬩 4516

ㄒㄧㄚ
瞎 2740
蝦 3549

ㄒㄧㄚˊ
俠 157
匣 404
峽 1037
挾 1497
暇 1744
洽 2140
狎 2455
狹 2465
瑕 2529
轄 3953
遐 4023
霞 4335
黠 4616

ㄒㄧㄚˋ
下 7
嚇 663
夏 782
廈 1131
暇 1744

ㄒㄧㄝ
些 55
歇 1993
蠍 3571

ㄒㄧㄝˊ
偕 191
協 421
挾 1497
擷 1631
攜 1640
擕 1640
(攜)
携 1640
(攜)
攜 1640
(攜)
斜 1679
脅 3243
諧 3744
邪 4059
鞋 4356

ㄒㄧㄝˇ
寫 978
血 3580

ㄒㄧㄝˋ
卸 433
屑 1015
懈 1373
械 1881
楔 1914
榭 1926
泄 2110
洩 2136
瀉 2321
蟹 3567
蠏 3567
(蟹)
褻 3638
褺 3638
(褻)
謝 3764
邂 4051

ㄒㄧㄠ
削 337
哮 560
囂 671
宵 956
枵 1827
梟 1878
消 2160
瀟 2327
簫 2970
蕭 3475
逍 3991
銷 4141
霄 4327
驍 4486

ㄒㄧㄠˊ
學 929

ㄒㄧㄠˇ
小 994
曉 1759

ㄒㄧㄠˋ
傚 207
哮 560
嘯 642
孝 919
效 1653
効 1653
(效)
校 1855
笑 2924
肖 3211
酵 4089

ㄒㄧㄡ
休 101
修 159
羞 3148

ㄒㄧㄡˇ
宿 960
朽 1797

ㄒㄧㄡˋ
嗅 615
宿 960
秀 2845
繡 3107
綉 3107
(繡)
臭 3304
袖 3599
銹 4151

ㄒㄧㄢ
仙 82
先 254
孅 910
掀 1511
纖 3123
鮮 4536

ㄒㄧㄢˊ
咸 543
啣 584
嫌 894
嫺 901
嫻 901
(嫺)
弦 1164
涎 2162
絃 3041
賢 3844
銜 4138
閑 4226
閒 4227
鹹 4586

ㄒㄧㄢˇ
洒 2131
洗 2132
癬 2662
蘚 3506
險 4293
顯 4403
鮮 4536

ㄒㄧㄢˋ
憲 1368
獻 2489
現 2511
綫 3074
線 3077
縣 3089
羨 3150
腺 3271
限 4263
陷 4276
餡 4435

ㄒㄧㄣ
心 1218
新 1687
欣 1987
歆 1994
莘 3392
薪 3486
辛 3958
鋅 4144
鑫 4210
韽 4369
馨 4455

ㄒㄧㄣˊ
尋 991

ㄒㄧㄣˋ
信 158
釁 4103

ㄒㄧㄤ
廂 1130
湘 2225
相 2710
箱 2951
襄 3637
鄉 4072
鑲 4212
香 4453

ㄒㄧㄤˊ
祥 2829
翔 3161
詳 3707
降 4262

ㄒㄧㄤˇ
享 64
想 1319
響 4372
餉 4424
饗 4447

ㄒㄧㄤˋ
像 216
向 487
嚮 665
巷 1074
橡 1962
相 2710
象 3800
項 4376

ㄒㄧㄥ
惺 1314
星 1718
猩 2473
腥 3263
興 3313
馨 4455

ㄒㄧㄥˊ
刑 317
型 717
形 1176
形 1176
(形)
行 3581

ㄒㄧㄥˇ
惺 1314
擤 1628
省 2714
醒 4096

ㄒㄧㄥˋ
倖 173
姓 848
幸 1106
性 1244
悻 1291

單字	字號
杏	1801
興	3313
行	3581
ㄒㄩ	
吁	477
嘘	640
墟	756
戌	1390
虛	3514
需	4325
須	4378
鬚	4512
ㄒㄩˊ	
徐	1197
ㄒㄩˇ	
栩	1851
煦	2377
許	3682
ㄒㄩˋ	
卹	434
壻	778
婿	778
(壻)	
序	1115
恤	1262
敍	1654
敘	1654
(敍)	
叙	1654
(敍)	
旭	1706
畜	2586
絮	3054
緒	3075
續	3119
蓄	3448
酗	4083
ㄒㄩㄝ	
噱	656
薛	3484
靴	4353
ㄒㄩㄝˊ	
學	929
ㄒㄩㄝˇ	
雪	4319
鱈	4546
ㄒㄩㄝˋ	
削	337
穴	2885
血	3580
雪	4319
ㄒㄩㄢ	
喧	609
宣	949
暄	1743
瑄	2528
萱	3426
諠	3742
軒	3932
ㄒㄩㄢˊ	
懸	1382
旋	1694
漩	2270
玄	2491
璇	2542
縣	3089
ㄒㄩㄢˇ	
癬	2662
選	4044
ㄒㄩㄢˋ	
旋	1694
渲	2211
漩	2270
炫	2345
眩	2719
絢	3049
衒	3583
ㄒㄩㄣ	
勳	386
熏	2381
燻	2381
(熏)	
薰	3489
醺	4101
ㄒㄩㄣˊ	
尋	991
巡	1062
廵	1062
(巡)	
徇	1192
循	1209
旬	1705
荀	3380
詢	3697
馴	4461
ㄒㄩㄣˋ	
徇	1192
殉	2020
汛	2076
訊	3670
訓	3671
迅	3972
遜	4028
馴	4461
ㄒㄩㄥ	
兄	250
兇	253
凶	304
匈	394
洶	2139
胸	3239
胷	3239
(胸)	
ㄒㄩㄥˊ	
熊	2380
雄	4301
ㄓ	
單字	字號
ㄓ	
之	29
指	1481
支	1646
枝	1821
梔	1875
巵	1875
(梔)	
氏	2051
汁	2066
知	2759
祗	2819
織	3103
肢	3217
脂	3241
芝	3348
蜘	3539
隻	4299
ㄓˊ	
值	180
執	728
姪	856
指	1481
擲	1630
植	1904
殖	2022
直	2709
職	3201
蟄	3560
質	3848
躑	3920
ㄓˇ	
只	464
咫	538
址	702
徵	1213
指	1481
旨	1703
止	2002
沚	2095
砥	2769
祇	2819
紙	3028
趾	3882
黹	4623
ㄓˋ	
制	331
幟	1099
志	1223
摯	1585
智	1741
桎	1867
治	2106
滯	2254
炙	2343
畤	2590
痔	2625
痣	2630
知	2759
秩	2855
稚	2864
穉	2864
(稚)	
窒	2893
緻	3087
置	3136
至	3305
致	3306
致	3306
(致)	
製	3622
誌	3713
質	3848
陟	4265
雉	4307
ㄓㄚ	
扎	1416
查	1845
渣	2205
ㄓㄚˊ	
扎	1416
札	1794
炸	2350
箚	2949
紮	3035
紥	3035
(紮)	
鍘	4171
閘	4228
ㄓㄚˇ	
眨	2720
ㄓㄚˋ	
乍	30
咋	531
搾	1560
柵	1847
榨	1928
炸	2350
蚱	3524
詐	3690
ㄓㄜ	
折	1440
螫	3557
遮	4037
ㄓㄜˊ	
哲	561
懾	1385
折	1440
摘	1575
摺	1581
蟄	3560
褶	3633
謫	3767
ㄓㄜˇ	
者	3177
ㄓㄜˋ	
宅	935
浙	2144
蔗	3461
這	3998
˙ㄓㄜ	
著	3429
ㄓㄞ	
摘	1575
齋	4635
斋	4635
(齋)	
ㄓㄞˊ	
宅	935
擇	1612
ㄓㄞˇ	
窄	2892
ㄓㄞˋ	
債	212
寨	976
ㄓㄟˋ	
這	3998
ㄓㄠ	
招	1470
昭	1723
朝	1787
著	3429
ㄓㄠˊ	
著	3429
ㄓㄠˇ	
找	1430
沼	2104
爪	2413
ㄓㄠˋ	
兆	252
召	466
照	2378
罩	3134
肇	3207
詔	3691
趙	3875
ㄓㄡ	
周	516
州	1061
洲	2138
粥	2990
舟	3326
賙	3840
週	4008
ㄓㄡˊ	

妯	838
軸	3935
ㄓㄡˇ	
帚	1083
肘	3212
ㄓㄡˋ	
胄	282
咒	517
宙	944
晝	1731
皺	2684
紂	3015
縐	3090
胄	3226
ㄓㄢ	
占	425
毯	2050
毡	2050
(氈)	
氊	2050
(氈)	
沾	2107
瞻	2751
詹	3708
霑	4331
ㄓㄢˇ	
展	1014
嶄	1051
斬	1685
盞	2698
輾	3951
ㄓㄢˋ	
佔	120
占	425
戰	1403
暫	1753
棧	1895
湛	2226
站	2911
蘸	3508
顫	4402
ㄓㄣ	
偵	196
振	1491
斟	1680
椹	1909
榛	1925
珍	2504
甄	2559
眞	2721
真	2721
(眞)	
砧	2770
箴	2954
診	3685
貞	3811
針	4115
鍼	4176
ㄓㄣˇ	
枕	1819
疹	2614
縝	3092
診	3685
軫	3934
ㄓㄣˋ	
振	1491
朕	1784
枕	1819
賑	3837
鎮	4185
陣	4268
陳	4273
震	4326
鴆	4556
ㄓㄤ	
張	1168
彰	1182
樟	1945
獐	2481
璋	2544
章	2914
蟑	3562
麞	4596
ㄓㄤˇ	
掌	1534
漲	2275
長	4218
ㄓㄤˋ	
丈	4
仗	80
嶂	1050
帳	1089
幛	1098
杖	1805
漲	2275
瘴	2649
脹	3252
賬	3849
長	4218
障	4290
ㄓㄥ	
丁	2
崢	1044
征	1188
徵	1213
怔	1247
掙	1522
正	2003
烝	2355
爭	2415
猙	2467
癥	2659
睜	2730
箏	2943
蒸	3446
諍	3735
貞	3811
錚	4158
ㄓㄥˇ	
拯	1474
整	1670
ㄓㄥˋ	
幀	1095
掙	1522
政	1651
正	2003
症	2618
証	3695
證	3773
鄭	4076
ㄓㄨ	
侏	136
朱	1795
株	1853
珠	2507
硃	2776
蛛	3530
誅	3710
諸	3750
豬	3803
銖	4136
ㄓㄨˊ	
燭	2407
竹	2921
築	2959
軸	3935
逐	3994
ㄓㄨˇ	
主	25
囑	675
屬	1022
堵	2201
煮	2374
煑	2374
(煮)	
矚	2754
貯	3820
麈	4590
ㄓㄨˋ	
佇	113
住	117
助	365
柱	1843
注	2124
祝	2825
竚	2912
箸	2953
粥	2990
著	3429
蛀	3525
註	3686
鑄	4206
駐	4463
ㄓㄨㄚ	
抓	1435
ㄓㄨㄚˇ	
爪	2413
ㄓㄨㄛ	
捉	1496
桌	1860
ㄓㄨㄛˊ	
卓	420
啄	578
拙	1466
擢	1622
濁	2302
濯	2313
灼	2338
琢	2515
茁	3367
著	3429
酌	4080
鐲	4200
ㄓㄨㄟ	
椎	1905
追	3985
錐	4155
隹	4298
ㄓㄨㄟˋ	
墜	757
綴	3066
贅	3855
ㄓㄨㄢ	
專	987
甎	2560
塼	2560
(甎)	
磚	2806
ㄓㄨㄢˇ	
囀	670
轉	3954
ㄓㄨㄢˋ	
傳	211
撰	1602
篆	2958
賺	3852
轉	3954
饌	4444
ㄓㄨㄣ	
諄	3732
ㄓㄨㄣˇ	
准	293
準	2235
ㄓㄨㄤ	
妝	834
庄	1113
樁	1944
粧	2992
莊	3388
裝	3614
ㄓㄨㄤˋ	
僮	224
壯	777
撞	1596
狀	2452
ㄓㄨㄥ	
中	20
忪	1232
忠	1233
盅	2687
終	3042
衷	3595
鍾	4177
鐘	4197
ㄓㄨㄥˇ	
冢	287
塚	741
種	2868
腫	3265
踵	3903
ㄓㄨㄥˋ	
中	20
仲	89
眾	2725
種	2868
重	4108
ㄔ	
單字	字號
ㄔ	
吃	478
喫	478
(吃)	
嗤	626
痴	2639
癡	2657
魑	4528
鴟	4561
ㄔˊ	
匙	400
尺	1002
弛	1162
持	1479
池	2073
治	2106
踟	3898
遲	4039
馳	4460
ㄔˇ	
侈	133
呎	513
尺	1002
恥	1274
耻	3189
褫	3631
齒	4637

猶	2472
由	2575
遊	4017
郵	4070
鈾	4130
魷	4531
ㄧㄡˇ	
友	450
有	1780
莠	3394
酉	4078
黝	4615
ㄧㄡˋ	
佑	119
又	447
右	473
囿	686
幼	1110
有	1780
柚	1840
祐	2821
莠	3394
誘	3716
釉	4105
鼬	4630
ㄧㄢ	
咽	544
奄	802
嫣	897
殷	2032
淹	2196
烟	2358
焉	2362
煙	2370
燕	2397
胭	3234
腌	3255
菸	3411
醃	4092
閹	4237
ㄧㄢˊ	
嚴	667
妍	857
姸 (妍)	857
岩	1032
巖	1059
延	1147
檐	1968
沿	2109
炎	2340
焰	2368
燄 (焰)	2368
癌	2652
研	2778
硏 (研)	2778
筵	2940
簷	2971
言	3665
閻	4236
顏	4397
鹽	4588
ㄧㄢˇ	
偃	185
儼	246
奄	802
掩	1531
演	2265
眼	2723
衍	3582
ㄧㄢˋ	
厭	443
咽	544
唁	565
嚥	666
宴	955
彥	1177
晏	1725
沿	2109
焰	2368
燄 (焰)	2368
燕	2397
硯	2780
艷	3341
諺	3751
豔	3799
贗	3856
雁	4302
饜	4450
驗	4487
ㄧㄣ	
因	679
姻	859
慇	1337
殷	2032
氤	2058
湮	2227
陰	4272
音	4368
ㄧㄣˊ	
吟	492
垠	715
夤	790
寅	963
淫	2189
銀	4132
齦	4643
ㄧㄣˇ	
引	1158
癮	2661
隱	4294
飲	4418
ㄧㄣˋ	
印	429
廕	1137
胤	3233
蔭	3467
陰	4272
飲	4418
ㄧㄤ	
央	798
殃	2018
泱	2125
秧	2853
鴦	4562
ㄧㄤˊ	
佯	127
揚	1544
楊	1913
洋	2130
瘍	2640
羊	3144
陽	4278
ㄧㄤˇ	
仰	88
氧	2059
癢	2658
痒 (癢)	2658
養	4425
ㄧㄤˋ	
怏	1238
恙	1269
樣	1951
養	4425
ㄧㄥ	
嬰	907
應	1375
櫻	1982
瑛	2531
罌	3129
膺	3289
英	3366
鶯	4574
鷹	4582
鸚	4583
ㄧㄥˊ	
嬴	905
楹	1922
熒	2385
營	2400
瑩	2535
盈	2689
縈	3088
螢	3556
蠅	3570
贏	3860
迎	3973
ㄧㄥˇ	
影	1183
景	1736
穎	2877
頴 (穎)	2877
ㄧㄥˋ	
應	1375
映	1719
硬	2779
ㄨ	
單字	字號
ㄨ	
嗚	622
屋	1011
巫	1068
於	1690
汚	2078
汙 (汚)	2078
污 (汚)	2078
烏	2353
誣	3720
ㄨˊ	
吳	499
吾	507
巫	1068
无	1699
梧	1870
毋	2040
無	2366
蕪	3477
蜈	3537
誣	3720
鼯	4631
ㄨˇ	
五	52
伍	97
侮	140
午	415
娬	884
嫵 (娬)	884
忤	1228
摀	1572
武	2007
舞	3325
ㄨˋ	
兀	247
務	379
勿	392
塢	748
悟	1282
惡	1307
戊	1389
晤	1732
物	2437
誤	3721
迕	3976
鎢	4187
霧	4336
鶩	4477
ㄨㄚ	
呱	519
哇	550
挖	1483
窪	2901
蛙	3528
ㄨㄚˊ	
娃	862
ㄨㄚˇ	
瓦	2556
ㄨㄚˋ	
瓦	2556
襪	3642
˙ㄨㄚ	
哇	550
ㄨㄛ	
倭	184
渦	2209
窩	2900
ㄨㄛˇ	
我	1395
ㄨㄛˋ	
喔	601
握	1547
斡	1681
沃	2086
渥	2208
臥	3301
齷	4647
ㄨㄞ	
歪	2008
ㄨㄞˋ	
外	784
ㄨㄟ	
倭	184
偎	189
委	849
威	861
微	1212
萎	3418
逶	4010
ㄨㄟˊ	
危	430
唯	573
圍	691
巍	1057
帷	1091
微	1212
惟	1302
桅	1865
為	2352
爲	2416
維	3063
薇	3480

違	4027
闈	4240
韋	4363
ㄨㄟˇ	
偉	187
僞	220
唯	573
委	849
娓	863
尾	1004
猥	2471
瑋	2527
緯	3085
鮪	4534
ㄨㄟˋ	
位	115
僞	220
味	520
喂	594
尉	989
慰	1350
未	1791
為	2352
爲	2416
畏	2582
胃	3225
蔚	3462
衛	3588
謂	3755
遺	4045
餵	4438
魏	4527
ㄨㄢ	
剜	344
彎	1173
灣	2334
蜿	3544
豌	3796
ㄨㄢˊ	
丸	23
完	940
玩	2498
紈	3019
頑	4381
ㄨㄢˇ	
娩	872
婉	877
宛	946
挽	1492
晚	1730
浣	2147
琬	2520
皖	2680
碗	2789
椀	2789
(碗)	
莞	3393
輓	3939
ㄨㄢˋ	
惋	1297
曼	1774
玩	2498
翫	3166
腕	3260
萬	3425
万	3425
(萬)	
ㄨㄣ	
溫	2229
温	2229
(溫)	
瘟	2644
ㄨㄣˊ	
文	1673
紋	3021
聞	3196
蚊	3521
雯	4320
ㄨㄣˇ	
刎	316
吻	504
穩	2883
ㄨㄣˋ	
問	580
文	1673
紊	3032
聞	3196
ㄨㄤ	
汪	2082
ㄨㄤˊ	
亡	58
忘	1224
王	2494
ㄨㄤˇ	
往	1187
惘	1299
枉	1817
網	3065
罔	3131
魍	4526
ㄨㄤˋ	
妄	827
往	1187
忘	1224
旺	1708
望	1786
王	2494
ㄨㄥ	
嗡	627
翁	3157
ㄨㄥˇ	
蓊	3454
ㄨㄥˋ	
甕	2561
ㄩ	
單字	字號
ㄩ	
淤	2183
瘀	2637
紆	3016
迂	3970
ㄩˊ	
予	46
于	49
余	122
娛	868
愉	1317
愚	1326
於	1690
榆	1916
歟	2000
渝	2202
漁	2260
瑜	2532
盂	2686
腴	3268
與	3312
諛	3740
踰	3901
輿	3952
逾	4012
隅	4280
餘	4431
魚	4530
ㄩˇ	
予	46
宇	936
嶼	1055
禹	2841
羽	3156
與	3312
語	3718
雨	4318
齬	4646
ㄩˋ	
喩	610
域	725
寓	968
御	1205
愈	1324
慾	1352
拗	1464
欲	1988
汩	2080
浴	2152
熨	2389
燠	2402
獄	2479
玉	2493
癒	2655
禦	2836
籲	2983
育	3222
與	3312
芋	3344
裕	3611
語	3718
諭	3739
譽	3784
豫	3802
遇	4016
郁	4063
預	4380
馭	4457
鬱	4518
鬻	4520
鷸	4580
籲	4654
ㄩㄝ	
曰	1767
約	3017
ㄩㄝˋ	
岳	1030
嶽	1056
悅	1276
月	1779
樂	1942
粵	2991
耀	3173
葯	3440
藥	3497
越	3874
躍	3919
鑰	4211
閱	4235
龠	4653
ㄩㄢ	
冤	285
寃	285
(冤)	
淵	2191
鳶	4555
鴛	4560
ㄩㄢˊ	
元	249
原	440
員	554
園	692
圓	693
援	1553
源	2230
猿	2475
猨	2475
(猿)	
緣	3081
袁	3597
ㄩㄢˇ	
遠	4032
ㄩㄢˋ	
怨	1255
苑	3358
遠	4032
院	4267
願	4398
ㄩㄣ	
暈	1746
ㄩㄣˊ	
云	50
匀	390
耘	3183
芸	3354
雲	4321
ㄩㄣˇ	
允	248
殞	2024
碩	2802
隕	4286
ㄩㄣˋ	
孕	915
慍	1331
暈	1746
熨	2389
蘊	3504
藴	3504
(蘊)	
運	4018
醞	4098
韻	4371
ㄩㄥ	
傭	209
壅	765
庸	1128
慵	1345
擁	1608
臃	3292
雍	4306
饔	4448
ㄩㄥˊ	
傭	209
庸	1128
慵	1345
ㄩㄥˇ	
俑	152
勇	374
壅	765
擁	1608
永	2064
泳	2126
涌	2166
湧	2223
甬	2572
臃	3292
蛹	3532
詠	3688
咏	3688
(詠)	
ㄩㄥˋ	
用	2569

聯合國華語注音符號索引

編　法：本索引係照單字讀音，按聯合國華語注音符號順序編列。其讀音相同者，再按部首順序。單字後註明單字編號。

用　法：遇有僅知讀音不熟悉字形之單字，可按聯合國華語注音查出索引中單字，再根據單字編號，查出書內單字及這一單字爲首所組成的詞語。

U. N. MANDARIN PHONETIC SYMBOL INDEX

In this index the characters are arranged according to the alphabetical order of U. N. MPS. Characters with the same pronunciation are arranged according to their respective radicals. The figure to the right of each character is its identification number under which the character can be found in the body of the dictionary.

If the dictionary user knows the pronunciation of the character he is looking for but is unfamiliar with its strokes, he can find it in the index according to the alphabetical order of U.N.MPS. Using the identification number as a guide, he can locate in the dictionary the character and the entries beneath it.

單字	字號
A	
ā	
啊	581
腌	3255
阿	4257
à	
阿	4257
a	
啊	581
āi	
哀	546
哎	553
唉	567
埃	722
挨	1488
ái	
呆	512
挨	1488
捱	1507
獃	2478
癌	2652
皚	2681
ǎi	
嗳	658
矮	2762
藹	3499
靄	4341
ài	
嗳	658
嬡	904
愛	1328
曖	1760
碍	2788
礙	2811
艾	3343
隘	4287
ān	
安	938
庵	1125
諳	3748
鞍	4355
àn	
岸	1031
按	1480
暗	1748
案	1859
闇	4239
黯	4620
āng	
腌	3255
骯	4496
áng	
昂	1709
àng	
盎	2693
āo	
凹	306
熬	2387
áo	
嗷	629
嗸	629
(嗷)	
熬	2387
獒	2480
翱	3172
遨	4035
鏖	4190
鰲	4547
鼇	4625
ǎo	
拗	1464
襖	3640
ào	
傲	210
奧	815
懊	1374
拗	1464
澳	2299
燠	2402
B	
bā	
八	267
叭	467
吧	514
巴	1073
扒	1418
疤	2610
笆	2923
芭	3351
bá	
八	267
拔	1463
跋	3883
bǎ	
把	1436
靶	4354
bà	
壩	774
把	1436
灞	2333
爸	2419
罷	3140
耙	3181
霸	4339
ba	
吧	514
罷	3140
bāi	
掰	1536
bái	
白	2669
bǎi	
伯	103
擺	1633
柏	1834
百	2670
bài	
拜	1471
敗	1659
稗	2866
bān	
扳	1428
搬	1570
斑	1676
班	2508
般	3329
頒	4382
bǎn	
板	1815
版	2427
闆	4243
bàn	
伴	106
半	416
扮	1425
拌	1457
瓣	2555
絆	3044
辦	3962
bāng	
傍	202
幫	1101
帮	1101
(幫)	
梆	1884
邦	4058
bǎng	
榜	1929
綁	3056
膀	3275
bàng	
傍	202
旁	1692
棒	1892
磅	2799
膀	3275
蚌	3520
謗	3761
鎊	4180
bāo	
剝	345
包	393
炮	2347
炰	2347
(炮)	
胞	3231
苞	3363
褒	3635
báo	
薄	3478
bǎo	
保	156
堡	734
寶	982
寳	982
(寶)	
褓	3627
飽	4421
鴇	4557
bào	
報	733
抱	1444
暴	1754
瀑	2320
爆	2409
豹	3804
鮑	4533
bēi	
卑	418
埤	727
悲	1305
揹	1555
杯	1810
盃	2690
碑	2783
背	3227
běi	
北	399
bèi	
倍	168
備	206
悖	1281
憊	1365
焙	2363
背	3227
臂	3291
蓓	3453
被	3603
褙	3628
貝	3809
輩	3946
bēn	
奔	806
犇	806
(奔)	
běn	
畚	811
本	1793
畚	2585
bèn	
奔	806
犇	806
(奔)	
笨	2928
bēng	
崩	1045
繃	3102
綳	3102
(繃)	
béng	
甭	2573
běng	
繃	3102
綳	3102
(繃)	
bèng	
榜	1929
蹦	3912
迸	4006
迸	4006
(迸)	
bī	
逼	4013
bí	
鼻	4632
bǐ	
匕	397
妣	835
彼	1186
比	2044
筆	2931
鄙	4074
bì	
壁	763
婢	879
幣	1100
庇	1114
弊	1153
必	1219
拂	1451
敝	1660
斃	1672
比	2044
泌	2113
璧	2546
畢	2592
碧	2790
祕	2822
秘	2822
(祕)	
臂	3291